ddon • Naomi Feil • Kenneth F. Ferraro • J

egener • Gerda G. Fillenbaum • David B. Finkelstein • Marjori

ner • Marquis D. Foreman • Barry Fortner • Shawna Freshwa

edland • Brant E. Fries • James F. Fries • Christine L. Fry • Timot

Fulmer • Ari Gafni • Danielle D. Gagne • Dolores Gallagher-Thor

elfand • Louis E. Gelwicks • Linda K. George • Scott Miyake Ge

arrusso • Lou Glasse • Norval D. Glenn • Charles J. Golden • Ju

anet D. Griffith • Jessie Gruman • Juan J. Guiamét • Elizabeth

ongMao Guo • Jack M. Guralnik • Barry J. Gurland • Lisa P. Gw

Hagestad • Franz Halberg • Stephen W. Harkins • Calvin B. Har

rrington • Alan A. Hartley • Lynn Hasher • Betty Havens • Robe

Catherine Hawes • Robert P. Heaney • Susan C. Hedrick • Marth

anz Hefti • Margaret L. Heidrick • Jon Hendricks • John C. Hen

Hess • Nancy Hikoyeda • Brian F. Hofland • Carol C. Hogue

lden • Elma L. Holder • Darlene V. Howard • William J. Hoy

dson • Kathryn Hyer • Bradley T. Hyman • Margaret B. Ingraha

gram • James S. Jackson • S. Michal Jazwinski • Nancy S. Jeck

hnson • Elizabeth Joyce • F. Thomas Juster • Marja K. Jylhä • I

a Kahana • Fran E. Kaiser • Richard A. Kalish • Robert L. Kar

ne • George A. Kaplan • Marshall B. Kapp • Robert J. Kastenba

szniak • Donald H. Kausler • John R. Kelly • Joseph W. Kemnitz

Susan Kemper • Robert D. Kennedy • Gary M. Kenyon • Me

uglas C. Kimmel • Thomas B. L. Kirkwood • Anne J. Kisor • F

rman R. Klinman • Leon W. Klud • Alan Kluger • William E. K

ight • Harold G. Koenig • Nathan Kogan • Martin Kohli • Mary G

THE ENCYCLOPEDIA OF AGING

A Comprehensive Resource in Gerontology and Geriatrics

Third Edition

THE ENCYCLOPEDIA OF AGING

A Comprehensive Resource in Gerontology and Geriatrics

Third Edition

GEORGE L. MADDOX, PhD

EDITOR-IN-CHIEF

Robert C. Atchley, PhD, **J. Grimley Evans,** MD,
Robert B. Hudson, PhD, **Rosalie A. Kane,** DSW,
Edward J. Masoro, PhD, **Mathy D. Mezey,** RN, EdD, FAAN,
Leonard W. Poon, PhD, and **Ilene C. Siegler,** PhD

ASSOCIATE EDITORS

Sheri W. Sussman
MANAGING EDITOR

 SPRINGER PUBLISHING COMPANY • NEW YORK

Copyright © 2001 by Springer Publishing Company, Inc.

Springer Publishing Company, Inc.
536 Broadway
New York, NY 10012-3955

Cover design by Susan Hauley
Acquisitions Editor: Sheri W. Sussman
Production Editor: Helen Song/Elizabeth Keech

01 02 03 04 05 / 5 4 3 2 1

Library of Congress Cataloging-in-Publication Data

The encyclopedia of aging: a comprehensive resource in gerontology and geriatrics / George L. Maddox, editor-in-chief.—3rd ed.
    p. cm.
  Includes bibliographical references and index.
  ISBN 0-8261-4842-5 (set)
  1. Gerontology—Encyclopedias. 2. Aged—Encyclopedias. I. Maddox, George L. II. Title.
  HQ1061 .E53 2001
  305.26'03—dc21
                                            00-049663
                                          CIP

Printed in the United States of America by Maple-Vail Book Manufacturing Group

CONTENTS

*To Ursula Springer, who encouraged the development
of gerontology's first encyclopedia, and
to the scholars and scientists who
made three editions possible.*

THE EDITORS

George L. Maddox, PhD, Professor Emeritus of Medical Sociology, directs the Long Term Care Resources Program of the Duke University Center for the Study of Aging and Human Development. He has served as Director of the Duke center (1972–1982) and the Chair of the University Council on Aging and Human Development (1982–1992). His research continues to focus on factors that affect the capacity for functioning independently in later life and on the comparative study of the organization and financing of care of older adults. Dr. Maddox has served as President of the Gerontological Society of America, as Secretary General of the International Association of Gerontology, and as a Founding Member of the National Advisory Committee, National Institute of Aging/National Institutes of Health. He has been honored with the Sandoz International Prize for Longitudinal Research on Aging, the Kleemeier Research Award, the Distinguished Mentorship Award and the Career Contribution Award of the Gerontological Society of America, the Distinguished Contribution Aging Award of the American Sociological Association, and the Tibbits Award for the Advancement of Gerontology in Higher Education. He has published widely in scientific journals on social aspects of adult development and aging. His books have addressed a variety of topics in human development including social and economic predictors of aging well, alcohol use in adolescence and adulthood, the diversity of older populations, and long-term care policy. Dr. Maddox is currently Editor of *Contemporary Gerontology: A Journal of Reviews and Critical Discourse.*

Robert Atchley, PhD, is Professor and Chair of the Department of Gerontology at Naropa University in Boulder, Colorado. His gerontology interests include adult development, spiritual development, long-term care, public policy, work and retirement, health change and disability, and family issues. Dr. Atchley was President of the 10,000-member American Society on Aging from 1988 to 1990 and has also served in numerous leadership positions in the Gerontological Society of America and the Association for Gerontology in Higher Education. He was the founding editor of the journal, *Contemporary Gerontology.* From 1974 to 1998, he was Director of the Scripps Gerontology Center at Miami University in Oxford, Ohio. He has authored over 100 articles and book chapters in the social gerontology literature, as well as more than a dozen books and research monographs, including *Understanding American Society* (1970), *The Sociology of Retirement* (1976), *Aging: Continuity and Change* (1987), *Continuity and Adaptation in Aging: Creating Positive Experiences* (1999), and nine editions of his introductory gerontology text, *Social Forces and Aging* (2000). He has received more than a dozen awards for his scholarship, teaching, and professional service in the field of aging.

John Grimley Evans, MD, FRCP, FFPHM, FMedSci, is Professor of Clinical Geratology at the University of Oxford and Consultant Physician in Geriatric and General (Internal) Medicine to the Oxford Hospitals. His research interests lie in the clinical medicine of later life and in epidemiological approaches to the design and evaluation of health services for older people. He was Vice President of the Royal College of Physicians (1993–1995), and also a member of the Medical Research Council and Chairman of its Health Services and Public Health Research Board (1989–1994). He is currently a member of the Central Research and Development Committee of the National Health Service Executive and of the National Screening Committee. He served as Editor of *Age and Ageing* (1988–1995), and is Senior Editor of the *Oxford Textbook of Geriatric Medicine*.

Robert B. Hudson, PhD, is Professor of Social Welfare Policy, Boston University School of Social Work. His research interests are in the policies and politics of aging, the place of the old in contemporary welfare states, and the design and implementation of social policy. His work in these areas has appeared in *International Social Security Review*, *Milbank Quarterly*, *Social Service Review*, and *Journal of Health Politics, Policy and Law*, among other publications. He currently serves as Editor of *Public Policy and Aging Report*, the quarterly publication of the National Academy on an Aging Society. Dr. Hudson is also the editor of *The Future of Age-Based Public Policy*, and serves on the editorial boards of *The Gerontologist*, *Generations*, and *Journal of Aging and Social Policy*. He has been a recipient of the Donald P. Kent Award from the Gerontological Society of America and the Arthur S. Flemming Award from the National Association of State Units on Aging. Dr. Hudson is a Fellow of the Gerontological Society of America and an elected member of the National Academy on Social Insurance, where he also serves as Chair of the John A. Heinz Dissertation Award Committee.

Rosalie A. Kane, DSW, is a Professor of Public Health at the University of Minnesota where she is also on the graduate faculty of the School of Social Work and the Center for Biomedical Ethics. She directs the University of Minnesota National Long-Term Care Resource Center, which was established originally by the Administration on Aging. Her research revolves around long-term care for elderly people and other populations needing long-term care; topics of her research include quality assurance, nursing homes, home care, case management, assisted living, family care, and values and ethics on long-term care. She is past Editor-in-Chief of *The Gerontologist* (1988–1992) and of *Health and Social Work* (1979–1982). She has served on three Institute of Medicine Committees, and was on the Medical and Scientific Advisory Board of the Alzheimer's Association as well as the Veteran's Administration National Advisory Council on Geriatrics and Gerontology. She is a Senior Fellow for the Brookdale Foundation's National Fellowship in Geriatrics and Gerontology. She is a prolific writer and contributor to scholarly journals. With Robert L. Kane she has collaborated on seven books, including most recently, *Long-Term Care: Principles, Programs and Policies* (1987), *The Heart of Long-Term Care* (also with Richard C. Ladd) (1998), and *Assessing Older People: Measurement Meaning and Practical Applications* (2000). With Joan D. Penrod, she edited *Family Caregiving in an Aging Society: Policy Perspectives* (1995). With Arthur Caplan, she has written *Everyday Ethics: Resolving Dilemmas in Nursing Home Life* (1990) and *Ethical Conflicts in the Management of Home Care: The Case Manager's Dilemma* (1993). Since June 1998, she has been directing a national study to measure and improve quality of life in nursing homes.

Edward J. Masoro, PhD, received both his PhD in physiology and AB from the University of California at Berkeley. He chaired the Department of Physiology at the University of Texas Health Science Center at San Antonio (UTHSCSA) from 1973 to 1991 and is currently Professor Emeritus of physiology. He was the founding director of the Aging Research and Education Center at UTHSCSA. He has served as President of the Gerontological Society of America, Chair of the Board of Scientific Counselors of the National Institute on Aging, Editor of the *Journal of Gerontology: Biological Sciences*, and President of the Association of Chairmen of Departments of Physiology. His research in biological gerontology has focused on the anti-aging action of caloric restriction in rodent models, for which he received the Allied-Signal Achievement Award in Aging, the Robert W. Kleemeier Award, the Irving Wright Award of Distinction, and the Glenn Foundation Award.

Mathy D. Mezey, EdD, RN, FAAN, received her undergraduate and graduate degrees from Columbia University. She worked as a public health nurse and on medical and surgical units at Jacobi Hospital, as well as at the acute care facility of the New York City Health and Hospitals Corporation. Dr. Mezey taught at Lehman College of the City University of New York. For 10 years she was a professor at the University of Pennsylvania School of Nursing, where she directed the geriatric nurse practitioner program and was Director of the Robert Wood Johnson Foundation Teaching Nursing Home Program. Since 1991 she has been the Independence Foundation Professor of Nursing Education at New York University. Her current research and writing focus is on ethical decision-making about life-sustaining treatment. Dr. Mezey is exploring decision-making by spouses of patients with Alzheimer's disease and preparing guidelines to assist in decisions related to the transfer of patients between nursing homes and hospitals. In September, 1996, Dr. Mezey assumed the position of Director of the John A. Hartford Foundation Institute for the Advancement of Geriatric Nursing Practice. Dr. Mezey has authored five books and has over 50 publications that focus on nursing care of the elderly and bioethical issues that affect decisions at the end of life. She is Series Editor for the Springer Series on Geriatric Nursing. Dr. Mezey was a member of the Ethics Group of Hillary Rodham Clinton's Health Care Reform Task Force. She is a Trustee Emeritus of Columbia University, a Fellow in the Gerontological Society of America, and sits on the board of the Visiting Nurse Service of New York and the American Federation of Aging Research (AFAR).

Leonard W. Poon, PhD, is Professor of Psychology, Director of the Gerontology Center, and Chair, Faculty of Gerontology, at the University of Georgia. After receiving his BS degree in Engineering in 1966 from San Jose State University in California, he practiced as a systems engineer at Lockheed Missiles and Space Corporation (1966–1969). Dr. Poon then received his MA and PhD degrees in 1972 in Experimental Psychology from the University of Denver, and did his post-doctoral fellowship in Gerontology, Psychophysiology, and Neuropsychology at the Center for the Study of Aging and Human Development at the Duke University Medical Center (1972–1974). Prior to assuming his current positions at the University of Georgia in 1985, he worked as Director of the Mental Performance and Aging Laboratory at the Veterans Administration Medical Research Service, and as Assistant Professor of Psychiatry, Harvard Medical School, and Massachusetts General Hospital, Boston. A Fellow of the American Psychological Association, American Psychological Society, Association of Gerontology in Higher Education, and the Gerontological Society of America, Dr. Poon was President of the Division on Aging and Human Development of the American Psychological Association (1983–1984). He is past Vice President of the Gerontological Society of America and Chair of the Society's Behavioral and Social Science section (1992–1993). Dr. Poon has authored over 130 journal papers, chapters, and books.

Ilene C. Siegler, PhD, MPH, is Professor in Medical Psychology in the Department of Psychiatry and Behavioral Sciences, and Professor of Psychology: Social and Health Sciences at Duke University, and Adjunct Professor of Epidemiology in the School of Public Health at the University of North Carolina at Chapel Hill. She is Director of the UNC Alumni Heart Study and conducts research at the Duke University Behavioral Medicine Research Center. Her major research interests are understanding developmental health psychology, that is, the role of aging and health in adult development and the role of personality and behavioral risk factors in chronic disease. She has written over 168 publications and is currently a member of the National Advisory Council on Aging of the National Institute of Aging, an associate editor of *Health Psychology* and past President of Division 20 (Adult Development and Aging) of the American Psychological Association.

INTERNATIONAL ADVISORY BOARD

FOREWORD
TO THE THIRD EDITION

The Encyclopedia of Aging has lived up to expectations. Over the last 15 years it has become the authoritative, comprehensive, multidisciplinary, and readable introduction to gerontology and geriatrics that we set out to create. Teachers have encouraged their students to use it for both broad explorations and the pursuit of very specific topics. The bibliography of the second edition was one of the most comprehensive and up-to-date multidisciplinary resources in the field of aging. The bibliography for the third edition, which appears at the end of Volume II, while it will include some of the classic older references, will constitute a current comprehensive overview of the literature in gerontology and geriatrics since 1995. And the third edition represents the further involvement of international colleagues and coverage of issues and research outside the United States.

For years now, when students, colleagues, friends and general inquirers have asked me about a variety of topics in aging, my initial response has always been, "Have you checked *The Encyclopedia of Aging*?" It has proven to be a useful strategy for a beginning or even an advanced exploration. I recommend the *Encyclopedia* because I find it useful myself.

The important questions about aging individuals, populations, and societies are not reducible to any single discipline as gerontologists and geriatricians know well. Consequently, the eight Associate Editors who represent key disciplines in the field of aging were essential in selecting the topics to be covered and the experts to cover them. While not all scientific issues can be explained easily in plain English, the Editors have made an effort to achieve a volume that can be read by most educated laypersons. Achieving this in the domains of biological and biomedical sciences is a special challenge. My debt to the Associate Editors is large and is gratefully acknowledged here.

The comprehensive index that is found in both volumes, and the extensive cross-referencing within the text provide readers with information about the authors of entries, links between entries, and particular issues in-depth within various entries and will help readers get maximum benefit from this volume. Sheri W. Sussman, Managing Editor of the volume, and her assistant Susanna Fry have given particular attention to making this third edition readable and useful. Sheri Sussman's competence as an editor is exceeded only by her persistent good humor and optimism.

In my office at Duke University, personal assistant Peggy Smith kept the lines of communication open with Springer Publishing in New York, and the manuscripts moving on schedule. In the home office, Evelyn Godbold Maddox was a very effective trouble manager, always with a sense of humor.

Dr. Ursula Springer, who originally proposed and supported the encyclopedia project, has remained a staunch supporter, colleague, and friend. We are all in her debt.

GEORGE L. MADDOX, PHD
Editor-in-Chief

PUBLISHER'S NOTE

The ever-growing quest for knowledge about aging—what to expect, what to explore, what to avoid—inspired this third edition of our *Encyclopedia of Aging*. The complex nature of the subject and of the sciences engaged in its exploration justified and inspired the encyclopedic medium. In fact, this pioneering publication has developed into a resounding success. The present third edition of *The Encyclopedia of Aging* stands on the shoulders of its predecessors. The first edition, published in 1987, was the pioneer. It had a printing of 10,000 copies, of which a book club purchased 4,000, and was translated into Japanese by the University of Waseda Press.

In the second edition we updated the content and added certain features, some requested by readers: mainly more international elements, and more on medical and nursing materials. We complied since we realized that a larger number of users came from the healthcare fields than we originally envisioned. This edition was translated into French by the publishing section of Serdi.

The third edition required the addition of much material from the social and health sciences, thus expanding the number of articles needed. It was time for a two-volume edition, the one you see here. The multidisciplinary nature of "aging" is flourishing (even if "cross-pollination" remains modest). Biology, physiology, genetics, medicine, psychology, sociology, economics, technology, architecture, political science—all provide research and information on aging. We have tried to capture the basic elements of that knowledge in this new edition.

For the "applied" sciences, the ever-expanding health and social services, we have created a separate medium, the *Encyclopedia of Elder Care*. It is, in its own right, nearly 800 pages in volume and offers the latest information on nursing care, medical care, social work, nursing, assisted living, rehabilitation services, etc. Obviously, these fields are growing so fast that a solid basis of knowledge as offered in this new *Encyclopedia of Elder Care* will provide much useful information.

There is only a small amount of overlap of articles in the two encyclopedias, primarily in the health service topics. But the new two-volume *Encyclopedia of Aging* (3rd edition) is a rich source—and the only one—of the most comprehensive collection of scientific knowledge on aging.

URSULA SPRINGER, PhD
Publisher

CONTRIBUTORS

W. Andrew Achenbaum, PhD
College of Humanities, Fine Arts,
*   and Communication*
University of Houston
Houston, Texas

Rebecca G. Adams, PhD
Department of Sociology
University of North Carolina at
*   Greensboro*
Greensboro, North Carolina

Judd M. Aiken, PhD
Department of Animal Health and
*   Biomedical Sciences*
University of Wisconsin, Madison
Madison, Wisconsin

Marilyn Albert, PhD
Gerontology Research Unit
Harvard Medical School
Charlestown, Massachusetts

James E. Allen, PhD
School of Public Health
University of North Carolina at
*   Chapel Hill*
Chapel Hill, North Carolina

Robert G. Allen, PhD
Lankenau Institute for Medical
*   Research*
Wynnewood, Pennsylvania

Susan Allen, PhD
Center for Gerontology and Health
*   Care Research*
Brown University
Providence, Rhode Island

Elaine J. Amella, PhD, RN
College of Nursing
Medical University of South
*   Carolina*
Charleston, South Carolina

Norman B. Anderson, PhD
Department of Psychiatry
Harvard University
Cambridge, Massachusetts

W. Banks Anderson, Jr., MD
Department of Ophthalmology
Duke University Eye Center
Durham, North Carolina

Gary R. Andrews, MB, FRACP
Centre for Ageing Studies
Flinders University
Bedford Park, Australia

Robert A. Applebaum, PhD
Scripps Foundation Gerontology
*   Center*
Miami University
Oxford, Ohio

Robert Arking, PhD
Department of Biological Sciences
Wayne State University
Detroit, Michigan

Robert C. Atchley, PhD
Chair, Department of Gerontology
The Naropa Institute
Boulder, Colorado

Alejandro R. Ayala, MD
National Institute of Health
Bethesda, Maryland

Kurt W. Back, PhD (deceased)
Department of Sociology
Duke University
Durham, North Carolina

Beverly A. Baldwin, PhD
**   (deceased)**
School of Nursing
University of Maryland at
*   Baltimore*
Baltimore, Maryland

Jennifer L. Balfour, PhD, MPH
Epidemiology, Demography and
*   Biometry Program*
National Institute on Aging
Bethesda, Maryland

Arthur K. Balin, MD, PhD,
**   FACP**
Medical Director
The Sally Balin Medical Center for
*   Dermatology and Cosmetic*
*   Surgery*
Media, Pennsylvania

Margret M. Baltes, PhD
**   (deceased)**
Department of Gerontopsychiatry
Free University Berlin
Berlin, Germany

Paul B. Baltes, PhD
Max Planck Institute for Human
*   Development and Education*
Berlin, Germany

George J. Banziger, PhD
Department of Psychology
Marietta College
Marietta, Ohio

John C. Barefoot, PhD
Department of Psychiatry
Duke University Medical Center
Durham, North Carolina

Kristen Lawton Barry, PhD
Department of Psychiatry
University of Michigan
Ann Arbor, Michigan

Uriel Barzel, MD
Department of Medicine
Albert Einstein College of
Medicine
Bronx, New York

Nir Barzilai, MD
Divisions of Geriatrics and
Endocrinology, and
The Diabetes Research and
Training Center
Albert Einstein College of
Medicine
Bronx, New York

Michael T. Bayliss, BSc, PhD
Department of Connective Tissue
Biochemistry
Royal Veterinary College
London, England

John W. Baynes, PhD
Department of Chemistry and
Biochemistry
University of South Carolina
Columbia, South Carolina

Ann Benbow, PhD
SPRY Foundation
Washington, DC

Vern L. Bengtson, PhD
Ethel Percy Andrus Gerontology
Center
University of Southern California
Los Angeles, California

Edit Beregi, MD
International Association of
Gerontology
Budapest, Hungary

K. Berg, PhD
Center for Gerontology and Health
Care Research
Brown University
Providence, Rhode Island

Manfred Bergener, MD, PhD
Medical Director
Johannes Seniorendienste
Klinik Betriebs GmbH
Bonn, Germany

Nancy Bergstrom, RN, PhD,
FAAN
Graduate Nursing Program
University of Nebraska Medical
Center
Omaha, Nebraska

Helen A. Bertrand, PhD
Department of Physiology
The University of Texas Health
Science Center at San Antonio
San Antonio, Texas

David E. Biegel, MSW, PhD
Mandel School of Applied Social
Sciences
Case Western Reserve University
Cleveland, Ohio

Robert H. Binstock, PhD
Department of Epidemiology and
Biostatistics
Case Western Reserve University
Cleveland, Ohio

Dan G. Blazer, MD, PhD
Department of Psychiatry
Duke University Medical Center
Durham, North Carolina

Frederic C. Blow, PhD
Department of Psychiatry
University of Michigan
Ann Arbor, Michigan

James A. Blumenthal, PhD
Department of Psychiatry
Duke University Medical Center
Durham, North Carolina

Marvin O. Boluyt, PhD
Laboratory of Molecular
Kinesiology
University of Michigan
Ann Arbor, Michigan

Enid A. Borden, MA
Executive Director
Meals on Wheels Association of
America
Alexandria, Virginia

Edgar F. Borgatta, PhD
Institute on Aging
University of Washington
Seattle, Washington

Elizabeth A. Bosman, PhD
Department of Psychology
University of Toronto
Toronto, Ontario, Canada

Raymond Bossé, PhD
Normative Aging Study
VA Outpatient Clinic
Bedford, Massachusetts

Hayden B. Bosworth, PhD
Senior Health Scientist
Duke University Medical Center
Durham, North Carolina

Meg Bourbonniere, MS, RN
School of Nursing
University of Pennsylvania
Philadelphia, Pennsylvania

Kevin Brabazon, MPA
President
New York State Intergenerational
Network
New York, New York

James D. D. Bradley, MA
Center for Psychological Services
Nova Southeastern University
Fort Lauderdale, Florida

Kevin Bradley, MA, MRCP,
FRCR
Oxford Project to Investigate
Memory and Ageing
Oxford, England

John C. S. Breitner, MD, MPH
Department of Mental Hygiene
Johns Hopkins University
Baltimore, Maryland

Harold Brody, MD, PhD
Department of Anatomy
State University of New York
School of Medicine
Buffalo, New York

Susan V. Brooks, PhD
Department of Physiology and
Biomedical Engineering
University of Michigan
Ann Arbor, Michigan

Scott C. Brown, PhD
The Center for Applied Cognitive
Research on Aging
University of Michigan
Ann Arbor, Michigan

W. Ted Brown, MD, PhD
Department of Human Genetics
New York State Institute for Basic
Research in Developmental
Disabilities
Staten Island, New York

Winifred Brownell, PhD
College of Arts and Sciences
University of Rhode Island
Kingston, Rhode Island

Hans J. Bruns, MD
College of Medicine
State University of New York
Syracuse, New York

Entela Bua, MD
Department of Animal Health and
Biomedical Sciences
University of Wisconsin, Madison
Madison, Wisconsin

Christopher J. Bulpitt, MD,
FRCP, FFPM
Department of Geriatric Medicine
Hammersmith Hospital
London, England

Elisabeth O. Burgess, PhD
Department of Sociology
Georgia State University
Atlanta, Georgia

Ewald W. Busse, MD
Department of Psychiatry
Duke University School of
Medicine
Durham, North Carolina

Robert N. Butler, MD
President and CEO
International Longevity Center
USA, Ltd.
New York, New York

Leonard D. Cain, PhD
Department of Sociology
Portland State University
Portland, Oregon

Richard T. Campbell, PhD
Department of Sociology
University of Illinois at Chicago
Chicago, Illinois

Laura Carstensen, PhD
Department of Psychology
Stanford University
Stanford, California

Gregory D. Cartee, PhD
Department of Kinesiology
University of Wisconsin, Madison
Madison, Wisconsin

Jane A. Cases, MD
Division of Endocrinology and
The Diabetes Research and
Training Center
Albert Einstein College of
Medicine
Bronx, New York

John Cerella, PhD
Department of Psychology
Brandeis University
Waltham, Massachusetts

Neil Charness, PhD
Department of Psychology
Florida State University
Tallahassee, Florida

Yung-Ping Chen, PhD
Gerontology Institute
University of Massachusetts
Boston, Massachusetts

David A. Chiriboga, PhD
Clinical Gerontology Program
University of Texas Medical
Branch at Galveston
Galveston, Texas

Petrina Chong
Director of Communications
Center for the Advancement of
Health
Washington, DC

Helena Chui, MD
Department of Neurological
Sciences
University of Southern California
Downey, California

Victor G. Cicirelli, PhD
Department of Psychological
Sciences
Purdue University
West Lafayette, Indiana

Giovanni Cizza, MD, PhD
National Institute of Health
Bethesda, Maryland

Robert L. Clark, PhD
Department of Business
Management
North Carolina State University
Raleigh, North Carolina

Elizabeth C. Clipp, PhD
GRECC Associate Director for
Research
Duke University Medical Center
Durham, North Carolina

Thomas L. Coffman, PhD
Department of Psychology
Virginia Polytechnic Institute and
State University
Blacksburg, Virginia

Harvey Jay Cohen, MD
Center for the Study of Aging and
Human Development
Duke University Medical Center
Durham, North Carolina

Kenneth J. Collins, MD, DPhil, FRCP
Senior Clinical Lecturer
University College and Middlesex Hospitals
London, England

Fofi Constantinidou, PhD
Department of Psychology
Miami University
Oxford, Ohio

Fay Lomax Cook, PhD
School of Education and Social Policy
Northwestern University
Evanston, Illinois

Susan G. Cooley, PhD
Chief, Geriatric Research and Evaluation
U.S. Department of Veterans Affairs
West Palm Beach, Florida

Teresa M. Cooney, PhD
Department of Individual and Family Studies
University of Delaware
Newark, Delaware

Constance Saltz Corley, PhD, LCSW
School of Social Work
University of Maryland
Baltimore, Maryland

Germaine Cornélissen, PhD
Halberg Chronobiology Center
University of Minnesota
Minneapolis, Minnesota

Joan C. Cornoni-Huntley, PhD, MPH
School of Medicine
Duke University
Chapel Hill, North Carolina

John F. Corso, PhD
Department of Psychology
State University of New York
Cortland, New York

Joseph F. Coughlin, PhD
M.I.T. Age Lab
Massachusetts Institute of Technology
Cambridge, Massachusetts

Raymond T. Coward, PhD
Institute for Health Policy Research
University of Florida
Gainesville, Florida

Vincent J. Cristofalo, PhD
Lankenau Institute for Medical Research
Wynnewood, Pennsylvania

William H. Crown, PhD
Vice President
The Medstat Group
Cambridge, Massachusetts

Stephen Crystal, PhD
Institute for Health, Health Care Policy, and Aging Research
New Brunswick, New Jersey

Neal E. Cutler, PhD
Boettner Institute of Financial Gerontology
Widener University
Chester, Pennsylvania

Stephen J. Cutler, PhD
Departments of Sociology and Gerontology
University of Vermont
Burlington, Vermont

Bleddyn Davies, AcSS, DPhil
Personal Social Services Research Unit
University of Kent and Manchester
Canterbury, Kent, England

Elizabeth M. Dax, MD, PhD
National Institute on Aging and Johns Hopkins School of Medicine
Baltimore, Maryland

Horace B. Deets
Executive Director
American Association of Retired Persons
Washington, DC

Gordon H. DeFriese, PhD
Department of Social Medicine
University of North Carolina at Chapel Hill
Chapel Hill, North Carolina

Edmund F. Dejowski, JD, PhD
Office of Management Planning
Human Resources Administration
New York, New York

Judith K. DeJoy, PhD
Department of Community Education Programs
University of Georgia
Athens, Georgia

Marie-Claude Delisle, PhD
Department of Neurology and Neurosurgery
McGill University
Verdun, Quebec, Canada

Nancy W. Denney, PhD
Department of Psychology
University of Wisconsin, Madison
Madison, Wisconsin

Helen Dennis, MA
Andrus Gerontology Center
University of Southern California
Redondo Beach, California

Samantha Devaraju-Backhaus, MA
Center for Psychological Studies
Nova Southeastern University
Fort Lauderdale, Florida

Rose Ann DiMaria, PhD, RN, CNSN
School of Nursing
West Virginia University
Charleston, West Virginia

Ann Donahue, MA
Department of Sociology
University of Vermont
Burlington, Vermont

Elizabeth B. Douglass, MA
Executive Director
Association for Gerontology in Higher Education
Washington, DC

Michael Duffy, PhD
Department of Educational Psychology
Texas A and M University
College Station, Texas

Carl Eisdorfer, MD, PhD
Department of Psychiatry
University of Miami
Miami, Florida

Frederick R. Eisele, PhD
Department of Health Planning and Administration
Pennsylvania State University
University Park, Pennsylvania

David J. Ekerdt, PhD
Center on Aging
University of Kansas Medical Center
Lawrence, Kansas

Dariush Elahi, PhD
Director, Geriatric Research Laboratory
Massachusetts General Hospital
Boston, Massachusetts

Glen H. Elder, Jr., PhD
Department of Sociology
University of North Carolina
Chapel Hill, North Carolina

J. Charles Eldridge, PhD
Department of Physiology and Pharmacology
Wake Forest University School of Medicine
Winston-Salem, North Carolina

Bernard T. Engel, PhD
School of Medicine
Johns Hopkins University
Raleigh, North Carolina

Joan T. Erber, PhD
Department of Psychology
Florida International University
Miami, Florida

Patricia Espe-Pfeifer, MA
Center for Psychological Services
Nova Southeastern University
Fort Lauderdale, Florida

Carroll L. Estes, PhD
Institute for Health and Aging
University of California
San Francisco, California

J. Grimley Evans, MD
Division of Clinical Geratology
University of Oxford
Oxford, England

Lois K. Evans, DNSc, RN, FAAN
School of Nursing
University of Pennsylvania
Philadelphia, Pennsylvania

Monsignor Charles J. Fahey, LLD, MSW
Third Age Center
Fordham University
Bronx, New York

John Faulkner, PhD
Department of Physiology and Biomedical Engineering
University of Michigan
Ann Arbor, Michigan

Jeffrey S. Feddon, MA
Department of Psychology
Florida State University
Tallahassee, Florida

Naomi Feil, MSW
Executive Director
Validation Training Institute, Inc.
Cleveland, Ohio

Kenneth F. Ferraro, PhD
Department of Sociology
Purdue University
West Lafayette, Indiana

Steven H. Ferris, PhD
Aging and Dementia Research Center
New York University School of Medicine
New York, New York

Janice Jackson Fiegener
National Association of Area Agencies on Aging
Washington, DC

Gerda G. Fillenbaum, PhD
Center for the Study of Aging and Human Development
Duke University Medical Center
Durham, North Carolina

David B. Finkelstein, PhD
Pathobiology Program Director
National Institute on Aging
Bethesda, Maryland

Marjorie Fiske, PhD (deceased)
Human Development and Aging Program
University of California, San Francisco
San Francisco, California

Anne Foner, PhD
Department of Sociology
Rutgers University
New Brunswick, New Jersey

Marquis D. Foreman, PhD, RN, FAAN
College of Nursing
University of Illinois at Chicago
Chicago, Illinois

Barry Fortner, PhD
Rush-Presbyterian-St. Luke's Medical Center
Chicago, Illinois

Shawna Freshwater, PhD
Center for Psychological Services
Nova Southeastern University
Fort Lauderdale, Florida

Robert B. Friedland, PhD
Director
National Academy on Aging
Washington, DC

Brant E. Fries, PhD
Institute of Gerontology
University of Michigan
Ann Arbor, Michigan

James F. Fries, MD
Department of Medicine
Stanford University School of Medicine
Stanford, California

Christine L. Fry, PhD
Department of Anthropology
Loyola University
Chicago, Illinois

Timothy Fuller
National Gray Panthers
New York, New York

Terry T. Fulmer, RN, PhD,
FAAN
Division of Nursing
New York University
New York, New York

Ari Gafni, PhD
Institute of Gerontology
University of Michigan
Ann Arbor, Michigan

Danielle D. Gagne, BA
Department of Psychology
University of New Hampshire
Durham, New Hampshire

Dolores Gallagher-Thompson,
PhD, ABPP
Department of Psychiatry
Stanford University School of
Medicine
Palo Alto, California

Donald Gelfand, PhD
Department of Sociology
Wayne State University
Detroit, Michigan

Louis E. Gelwicks
Gerontological Planning
Association
Santa Monica, California

Linda K. George, PhD
Center for the Study of Aging and
Human Development
Duke University
Durham, North Carolina

Scott Miyake Geron, PhD
Faculty of Medicine, Dentistry, and
Nursing
University of Manchester
Manchester, England

Roseann Giarrusso, PhD
Ethel Percy Andrus Gerontology
Center
University of Southern California
Los Angeles, California

Lou Glasse, MSW
President Emerita
Older Women's League
Poughkeepsie, New York

Norval D. Glenn, PhD
Department of Sociology
University of Texas at Austin
Austin, Texas

Charles J. Golden, PhD
Center for Psychological Services
Nova Southeastern University
Fort Lauderdale, Florida

Judith G. Gonyea, PhD
School of Social Work
Boston University
Boston, Massachusetts

Janet D. Griffith, PhD
Research Triangle Institute
Research Triangle Park,
North Carolina

Jessie Gruman, PhD
Executive Director
Center for the Advancement of
Health
Washington, DC

Juan J. Guiamét, PhD
Instituto de Fisiología Vegetal
Universidad Nacional de La Plata
La Plata, Argentina

Elizabeth C. D. Gullette, PhD
Department of Psychiatry and
Behavioral Sciences
Duke University Medical Center
Durham, North Carolina

ZhongMao Guo, PhD
Department of Physiology
University of Texas Health Science
Center at San Antonio
San Antonio, Texas

Jack M. Guralnik, MD, PhD
Epidemiology, Demography and
Biometry Program
National Institute on Aging
Bethesda, Maryland

Barry J. Gurland, MD
Center for Geriatrics and
Gerontology
Columbia University
New York, New York

Lisa P. Gwyther, MSW
Director, Family Support Program
Duke Center for Aging
Durham, North Carolina

Gunhild O. Hagestad, PhD
College of Human Development
Pennsylvania State University
University Park, Pennsylvania

Franz Halberg, MD
Director, Halberg Chronobiology
Center
University of Minnesota
Minneapolis, Minnesota

Stephen W. Harkins, PhD
Department of Gerontology
Medical College of Virginia
Richmond, Virginia

Calvin B. Harley, PhD
Chief Scientific Officer
Geron Corporation
Menlo Park, California

Charles R. Harrington, PhD
Department of Mental Health
University of Aberdeen
Aberdeen, Scotland

Alan A. Hartley, PhD
Department of Psychology
Scripps College
Claremont, California

Lynn Hasher, PhD
Department of Psychology
University of Toronto
Toronto, Ontario, Canada

Betty Havens, DLitt
Department of Medicine
University of Manitoba
Winnipeg, Manitoba, Canada

Robert J. Havighurst, PhD
Department of Education
University of Chicago
Chicago, Illinois

Catherine Hawes, PhD
Health Science Center
School of Rural Public Health
Texas A and M University
College Station, Texas

Robert P. Heaney, MD
John A. Creighton University
*   Professor*
Creighton University
Omaha, Nebraska

Susan C. Hedrick, PhD
School of Public Health and
*   Community Medicine*
University of Washington
Seattle, Washington

Martha Lou Hefley, MD
Straub Geriatric Health Services
Straub Hospital Clinic
Honolulu, Hawaii

Franz Hefti, PhD
Vice President
Merck Sharp & Dohme
Essex, England

Margaret L. Heidrick, PhD
College of Medicine
University of Nebraska
Omaha, Nebraska

Jon Hendricks, PhD
University Honors College
Oregon State University
Corvallis, Oregon

John C. Henretta, PhD
Department of Sociology
University of Florida
Gainesville, Florida

Thomas M. Hess, PhD
Department of Psychology
North Carolina State University
Raleigh, North Carolina

Nancy Hikoyeda, MPH
Stanford Geriatric Education
*   Center*
University of California, Los
*   Angeles*
San Jose, California

Brian F. Hofland, PhD
The Retirement Research
*   Foundation*
Chicago, Illinois

Carol C. Hogue, PhD, RN
School of Nursing
University of North Carolina at
*   Chapel Hill*
Chapel Hill, North Carolina

Karen C. A. Holden, PhD
Department of Public Affairs and
*   Consumer Science*
University of Wisconsin, Madison
Madison, Wisconsin

Elma L. Holder
National Citizens' Coalition for
*   Nursing Home Reform*
Washington, DC

Darlene V. Howard, PhD
Department of Psychology
Georgetown University
Washington, DC

William J. Hoyer, PhD
Department of Psychology
Syracuse University
Syracuse, New York

Robert B. Hudson, PhD
School of Social Work
Boston University
Boston, Massachusetts

Kathryn Hyer, DrPA
Department of Geriatrics
University of South Florida
Tampa, Florida

Bradley T. Hyman, PhD
Department of Neurology Research
Massachusetts General Hospital
Boston, Massachusetts

Margaret B. Ingraham, MA
Director of Policy and Legislation
Meals on Wheels Association of
*   America*
Alexandria, Virginia

Donald K. Ingram, PhD
Gerontology Research Center
National Institute on Aging
Baltimore, Maryland

James S. Jackson, PhD
African American Mental Health
*   Research Center*
University of Michigan
Ann Arbor, Michigan

S. Michal Jazwinski, PhD
Department of Biochemistry and
*   Molecular Biology*
Louisiana State University Health
*   Science Center*
New Orleans, Louisiana

Nancy S. Jecker, PhD
Department of Medical History
*   and Ethics*
University of Washington
Seattle, Washington

Thomas E. Johnson, PhD
Institute for Behavioral Genetics
University of Colorado at Boulder
Boulder, Colorado

Elizabeth Joyce, MA
Silver Spring, Maryland

F. Thomas Juster, PhD
Institute for Social Research
University of Michigan
Ann Arbor, Michigan

Marja K. Jylhä, MD, PhD
School of Public Health
University of Tampere
Tampere, Finland

Boaz Kahana, PhD
Department of Psychology
Case Western Reserve University
Cleveland, Ohio

Eva Kahana, PhD
Department of Sociology
Case Western Reserve University
Cleveland, Ohio

Fran E. Kaiser, MD
Department of Medicine
St. Louis University School of
*   Medicine*
St. Louis, Missouri

Richard A. Kalish, PhD
(deceased)
Antioch University
Yellow Springs, Ohio

Robert L. Kane, MD
School of Public Health
University of Minnesota
Minneapolis, Minnesota

Rosalie A. Kane, DSW
National Long-Term Care
*   Resource Center*
University of Minnesota
Minneapolis, Minnesota

George A. Kaplan, PhD
Department of Epidemiology
University of Michigan
Ann Arbor, Michigan

Marshall B. Kapp, JD, MPH
Office of Geriatric Medicine and
*   Gerontology*
Wright State University School of
*   Medicine*
Dayton, Ohio

Robert J. Kastenbaum, PhD
Department of Communication
Arizona State University
Tempe, Arizona

Alfred W. Kaszniak, PhD
Department of Psychiatry
University of Arizona
Tucson, Arizona

Donald H. Kausler, PhD
Department of Psychology
University of Missouri, Columbia
Columbia, Missouri

John R. Kelly, PhD
University of Illinois at Urbana-
*   Champaign*
Champaign, Illinois

Joseph W. Kemnitz, PhD
Wisconsin Regional Primate
*   Research Center*
University of Wisconsin, Madison
Madison, Wisconsin

Peter Kemper, PhD
Center for Studying Health System
*   Change*
Washington, DC

Susan Kemper, PhD
Department of Psychology
The University of Kansas
Lawrence, Kansas

Robert D. Kennedy, MD, ChB
Albert Einstein College of
*   Medicine*
Beth Abraham Hospital
Bronx, New York

Gary M. Kenyon, PhD
Gerontology Program
St. Thomas University
Fredericton, New Brunswick,
*   Canada*

Meeryoung Kim, MSSW
School of Social Work
University of Wisconsin, Madison
Madison, Wisconsin

Douglas C. Kimmel, PhD
Department of Psychology
City College of the City University
*   of New York*
New York, New York

Thomas B. L. Kirkwood, PhD
Institute for the Health of the
*   Elderly*
University of Newcastle
Newcastle, England

Anne J. Kisor, PhD
School of Social Work
Virginia Commonwealth University
Richmond, Virginia

Paul Kleyman
Aging Today
American Society on Aging
San Francisco, California

Norman R. Klinman, MD, PhD
Department of Immunology
The Scripps Research Institute
La Jolla, California

Leon W. Klud, PhD
Congressional Joint Committee on
*   Taxation*
Washington, DC

Alan Kluger, PhD
Aging and Dementia Research
*   Center*
New York University School of
*   Medicine*
New York, New York

William E. Klunk, MD, PhD
Laboratory of Neurophysics
University of Pittsburgh Medical
*   Center*
Pittsburgh, Pennsylvania

Bob G. Knight, PhD
Department of Gerontology and
*   Psychology*
University of Southern California
Los Angeles, California

Harold G. Koenig, MD
Department of Psychiatry
Duke University Medical Center
Durham, North Carolina

Nathan Kogan, PhD
New School for Social Research
New York, New York

Martin Kohli, Prof.
Department of Sociology
Free University Berlin
Berlin, Germany

Mary Grace Kovar, DPH
National Opinion Research Center
Washington, DC

B. Josea Kramer, PhD
Department of Veterans Affairs
Geriatric Research, Education and
Clinical Center
Sepulveda, California

Iseli K. Krauss, EdD
Department of Psychology
Clarion University of Pennsylvania
Clarion, Pennsylvania

John A. Krout, PhD
Gerontology Institute
Ithaca College
Ithaca, New York

Margaret E. Kuhn
National Gray Panthers
Philadelphia, Pennsylvania

Margie E. Lachman, PhD
Department of Psychology
Brandeis University
Waltham, Massachusetts

Edward G. Lakatta, MD
Laboratory of Cardiovascular
Science
Gerontology Research Center
National Institute on Aging
National Institute of Health
Baltimore, Maryland

Martin Lakin, PhD
Department of Psychology
Duke University
Durham, North Carolina

Stanford I. Lamberg, MD
Department of Dermatology
Johns Hopkins Medical Institutions
Baltimore, Maryland

Felissa R. Lashley, RN, PhD,
ACRN, FAAN
School of Nursing
Southern Illinois University
Edwardsville, Illinois

M. Powell Lawton, PhD
Philadelphia Geriatric Center
Philadelphia, Pennsylvania

Barry D. Lebowitz, PhD
National Institute of Mental Health
Bethesda, Maryland

Makau P. Lee, MD, PhD
Department of Medicine
University of Mississippi Medical
Center
Jackson, Mississippi

Ursula Lehr, Prof. Dr. Dr. h.c.
Deutsches Zentrum für
Alternsforschung
Heidelberg, Germany

Sonne Lemke, PhD
Center for Health Care Evaluation
Stanford University Medical Center
Palo Alto, California

Jeffrey S. Levin, PhD
Department of Family and
Community Medicine
Eastern Virginia Medical School
Norfolk, Virginia

Sue E. Levkoff, ScD, MSW
Department of Psychiatry
Harvard Medical School
Boston, Massachusetts

Phoebe S. Liebig, PhD
Ethel Percy Andrus Gerontology
Center
University of Southern California
Los Angeles, California

Robert D. Lindeman, MD
Department of Medicine
University of New Mexico School
of Medicine
Albuquerque, New Mexico

Jeri A. Logemann, PhD
Department of Communication
Sciences and Disorders
Northwestern University
Evanston, Illinois

Charles F. Longino, Jr., PhD
Department of Sociology
Wake Forest University
Winston-Salem, North Carolina

Helena Z. Lopata, PhD
Department of Sociology
Loyola University
Chicago, Illinois

Jonathan D. Lowenson, PhD
Department of Chemistry and
Biochemistry
University of California
Los Angeles, California

Cindy Lustig, MA
Department of Psychology
Duke University
Durham, North Carolina

J. Beth Mabry, PhD
Ethel Percy Andrus Gerontology
Center
University of Southern California
Los Angeles, California

David M. Macfayden, MD, MSc,
FRCP, FFCM
Global Program for Health of the
Elderly
World Health Organization
Copenhagen, Denmark

George L. Maddox, PhD
Long Term Care Resources
Program
Duke University Center for the
Study of Aging
Durham, North Carolina

Kevin J. Mahoney, PhD
Graduate School of Social Work
Boston College
Lexington, Massachusetts

Mary L. Mahrou, MA
Center for Psychological Services
Nova Southeastern University
Fort Lauderdale, Florida

James Malone-Lee, MD, FRCP
Department of Geriatric Medicine
University College London Medical
School
London, England

Ronald J. Manheimer, PhD
North Carolina Center for Creative
Retirement
University of North Carolina at
Asheville
Asheville, North Carolina

Kenneth G. Manton, PhD
Center for Demographic Studies
Duke University
Durham, North Carolina

Jennifer A. Margrett, PhD
National Institute of Mental Health
Pennsylvania State University
University Park, Pennsylvania

Kyriakos S. Markides, PhD
Department of Psychiatry
University of Texas Medical
Branch
Galveston, Texas

Lori N. Marks, PhD
Center on Aging
University of Maryland
Kensington, Maryland

Elizabeth W. Markson, PhD
Gerontology Center
Boston University
Boston, Massachusetts

Gail R. Marsh, PhD
Department of Medical Psychology
Duke University
Durham, North Carolina

Lynn M. Martire, PhD
Department of Psychiatry and
University Center for Social and
Urban Research
University of Pittsburgh
Pittsburgh, Pennsylvania

Edward J. Masoro, PhD
Department of Physiology
University of Texas Health Science
Center
San Antonio, Texas

Roger J. M. McCarter, PhD
Department of Physiology
University of Texas
San Antonio, Texas

Richard J. McClure, PhD
Laboratory of Neurophysics
University of Pittsburgh
Pittsburgh, Pennsylvania

Anna M. McCormick, PhD
Biology of Aging Program
National Institute on Aging
Bethesda, Maryland

Robert R. McCrae, PhD
Gerontology Research Center
National Institute on Aging
Baltimore, Maryland

Zhores A. Medvedev, PhD
National Institute for Medical
Research
London, England

Diane Meier, MD
Director, The Lilian and Benjamin
Hertzberg Palliative Care
Institute
Department of Geriatrics and
Adult Development
Mount Sinai School of Medicine
New York, New York

Mathy D. Mezey, RN, EdD,
FAAN
Division of Nursing
New York University
New York, New York

Meredith Minkler, DrPH
School of Public Health
University of California at
Berkeley
Berkeley, California

Ethel L. Mitty, EdD, RN
Division of Nursing
New York University
New York, New York

Charles V. Mobbs, PhD
Mount Sinai School of Medicine
New York, New York

Abraham Monk, PhD
School of Social Work
Columbia University
New York, New York

Rhonda J.V. Montgomery, PhD
Gerontology Center
The University of Kansas
Lawrence, Kansas

Harry R. Moody, PhD
Brookdale Center on Aging of
Hunter College
The City University of New York
New York, New York

James T. Moore, MD
Halifax Psychiatry Center
Daytona Beach, Florida

Rudolf H. Moos, PhD
Center for Health Care Evaluation
Stanford University Medical Center
Palo Alto, California

Vincent Mor, PhD
Center for Gerontology and
Health Care
Brown University School of
Medicine
Providence, Rhode Island

Russell E. Morgan, Jr., DrPh
President
SPRY Foundation
Washington, DC

John E. Morley, MB, BCh
Department of Gerontology
St. Louis University Health
Sciences Center
St. Louis, Missouri

Eric M. Morrell, PhD
Behavioral-Physiology Clinic
Rogue Valley Medical Arts Center
Medford, Oregon

Roger W. Morrell, PhD
The Practical Memory Institute
Silver Spring, Maryland

John N. Morris, PhD
Institute for Research and Training
Hebrew Rehabilitation Center for
Aged
Roslindale, Massachusetts

Malcolm H. Morrison, PhD
Department of Sociology
George Washington University
Washington, DC

Graham Mulley, DM, FRCP
Department of Geriatric Medicine
St. James University Hospital
Leeds, England

Norbert Mundorf, PhD
Department of Speech
  Communication
University of Rhode Island
Kingston, Rhode Island

George C. Myers, PhD
(deceased)
Center for Demographic Studies
  and Department of Sociology
Duke University Medical Center
Durham, North Carolina

Robert J. Myers, LLD
National Commission on Social
  Security Reform
Washington, DC

Ganesh C. Natarajan, MD
Boston University Medical Center
Boston, Massachusetts

Karl M. Neher, DrPhil
Max Planck Institute for Human
  Development and Education
Berlin, Germany

Robert A. Neimeyer, PhD
Department of Psychology
University of Memphis
Memphis, Tennessee

Charles A. Nelson, BA
Creative Action, Inc.
Akron, Ohio

John R. Nesselroade, PhD
College of Human Development
Pennsylvania State University
University Park, Pennsylvania

Julie K. Netzer, PhD
Institute for Health Policy
  Research
University of Florida
Gainesville, Florida

Bernice L. Neugarten, PhD, DSc
School of Education
Northwestern University
Evanston, Illinois

Robert Newcomer, PhD
Department of Social and
  Behavioral Sciences
University of California
San Francisco, California

Linda S. Noelker, PhD
Margaret Blenkner Research
  Center
The Benjamin Rose Institute
Cleveland, Ohio

Larry D. Noodén, PhD
Department of Biology
University of Michigan
Ann Arbor, Michigan

Reinhard Nuthmann, PhD
Max Planck Institute for Human
  Development and Education
Berlin, Germany

Corinne N. Nydegger, PhD
Medical Anthropology Program
University of California
San Francisco, California

Anthony O'Brien, MD, MSc,
  FRCP, FFPM
Department of Geriatric Medicine
Hammersmith Hospital
London, England

Dawn D. Ogawa, BA
Institute for Health and Aging
University of California
San Francisco, California

Morris A. Okun, PhD
Department of Educational
  Psychology
Arizona State University
Tempe, Arizona

Angela M. O'Rand, PhD
Department of Sociology
Duke University
Durham, North Carolina

William E. Oriol, BA
Silver Spring, Maryland

Michael O'Rourke, MD, DSc
Medical Professorial Unit and
  Clinic
St. Vincent's Hospital
University of New South Wales
Sydney, Australia

Marcia Ory, PhD, MDH
Department of Behavioral
  Medicine and Public Health
National Institute on Aging
Bethesda, Maryland

Nancy J. Osgood, PhD
Department of Gerontology and
  Sociology
Virginia Commonwealth University
Richmond, Virginia

Erdman B. Palmore, PhD
Departments of Psychiatry and
  Sociology
Duke University Medical Center
Durham, North Carolina

Kanagasabai Panchalingam, PhD
Laboratory of Neurophysics
University of Pittsburgh Medical
  Center
Pittsburgh, Pennsylvania

Denise C. Park, PhD
The Center for Applied Cognitive
  Research on Aging
University of Michigan
Ann Arbor, Michigan

Tonya M. Parrott, PhD
Department of Sociology
Quinnipiac College
Cheshire, Connecticut

Nancy L. Pedersen, PhD
Department of Medical
  Epidemiology
Karolinska Institute
Stockholm, Sweden

Lawrence C. Perlmuter, PhD
Department of Psychology
University of Health Sciences
North Chicago, Illinois

Marion Perlmutter, PhD
Department of Psychology
University of Michigan
Ann Arbor, Michigan

Dan Perry
Alliance for Aging Research
Washington, DC

David A. Peterson, PhD
Leonard Davis School of
*   Gerontology*
University of Southern California
Los Angeles, California

James Peterson, PhD, DD
** (deceased)**
Leonard Davis School of
*   Gerontology and Emeriti Center*
University of Southern California
Los Angeles, California

Caroline Petit-Turcotte, MSc
McGill Center for Studies in Aging
Douglas Hospital Research Center
Verdun, Quebec, Canada

Jay W. Pettegrew, MD
Laboratory of Neurophysics
University of Pittsburgh Medical
*   Center*
Pittsburgh, Pennsylvania

John P. Phelan, PhD
The Biological Laboratories
Harvard University
Cambridge, Massachusetts

Charles D. Phillips, PhD, MPH
Department of Health Policy and
*   Management*
School of Rural Public Health
Texas A and M University Health
*   Science Center*
College Station, Texas

Russell I. Pierce, MD, MPH
Honolulu, Hawaii

Robert J. Pignolo, MD, PhD
Division of Geriatric Medicine
University of Pennsylvania
Philadelphia, Pennsylvania

Brenda L. Plassman, PhD
Department of Psychiatry
Duke University Medical Center
Durham, North Carolina

Judes Poirier, PhD
Department of Neurology and
*   Neurosurgery*
McGill University
Verdun, Quebec, Canada

Leonard W. Poon, PhD
Gerontology Center
The University of Georgia
Athens, Georgia

Joyce A. Post, MSLS
Philadelphia Geriatric Center
Philadelphia, Pennsylvania

Lidia Pousada, MD, FACP
Division of Geriatrics and
*   Gerontology*
New York Medical College
New Rochelle, New York

Patricia Prinz, PhD
School of Medicine
University of Washington
Seattle, Washington

Thomas R. Prohaska, PhD
School of Public Health
University of Illinois at Chicago
Chicago, Illinois

Jon Pynoos, PhD
Ethel Percy Andrus Gerontology
*   Center*
University of Southern California
Los Angeles, California

Sara H. Qualls, PhD
Department of Psychology
University of Colorado
Colorado Springs, Colorado

Joan L. Quinn, MS
Anthem Blue Cross-Blue Shield of
*   Connecticut*
North Haven, Connecticut

Mary Joy Quinn, RN, MA
San Francisco Superior Court
San Francisco, California

Dan Quirk
Executive Director
National Association of State Units
*   on Aging*
Washington, DC

William Rakowski, PhD
The Memorial Hospital
Pawtucket, Rhode Island

Gloria Ramsey, RN, BSN, JD
Division of Nursing
New York University
New York, New York

G. William Rebeck, PhD
Neurology Service
Massachusetts General Hospital
Boston, Massachusetts

Barry Reisberg, MD
Department of Psychiatry, Aging
*   and Dementia Research Center*
New York University School of
*   Medicine*
New York, New York

Russel J. Reiter, PhD
Department of Cellular and
*   Structural Biology*
University Texas Health Science
*   Center*
San Antonio, Texas

S. Maggie Reitz, PhD, OTR/L,
** FAOTA**
Department of Occupational
*   Therapy*
Towson University
Columbia, Maryland

Arlan Richardson, PhD
Department of Physiology
Geriatric Research, Education, and
*   Clinical Center*
University of Texas Health Science
*   Center of San Antonio*
San Antonio, Texas

Matilda White Riley, DSc
Bowdoin College
Brunswick, Maine

Patricia A. Riley
*National Academy for State Health
    Policy*
Portland, Maine

Sara Rix, PhD
*American Association of Retired
    Persons*
Public Policy Institute
Washington, DC

Jay Roberts, PhD
Department of Pharmacology
Medical College of Pennsylvania
Philadelphia, Pennsylvania

Gia S. Robinson, BA
*Ethel Percy Andrus Gerontology
    Center*
University of Southern California
Los Angeles, California

Judith Rodin, PhD
President
University of Pennsylvania
Philadelphia, Pennsylvania

James C. Romeis, PhD
School of Public Health
St. Louis University
St. Louis, Missouri

Debra J. Rose, PhD
Department of Gerontology
California State University
Fullerton, California

Miriam Rose, MEd
Myers Research Institute
*Menorah Park Center for Senior
    Living*
Beachwood, Ohio

Edwin Rosenberg, PhD
*Department of Sociology and
    Social Work*
Appalachian State University
Boone, North Carolina

Carolyn Rosenthal, PhD
Centre for Gerontology Studies
Department of Sociology
McMaster University
Hamilton, Ontario, Canada

Allen D. Roses, MD
*Department of Medicine and
    Neurobiology*
Duke University Medical Center
Durham, North Carolina

John W. Rowe, MD
Mount Sinai School of Medicine
Mount Sinai Medical Center
New York, New York

**Laurence Z. Rubenstein, MD,
MPH**
Department of Geriatric Medicine
*University of California School of
    Medicine*
Sepulveda, California

David C. Rubin, PhD
Department of Psychology
Duke University Medical Center
Durham, North Carolina

Alice S. Ryan, PhD
*Baltimore Veterans Affairs Medical
    Center*
*University of Maryland School of
    Medicine*
Baltimore, Maryland

Janet S. Sainer, MSW
The Brookdale Foundation Group
New York, New York

Judith A. Salerno, MD, MS
*Geriatrics and Extended Care
    Strategic Healthcare Group*
Department of Veterans Affairs
Washington, DC

Timothy A. Salthouse, PhD
School of Psychology
Georgia Institute of Technology
Atlanta, Georgia

Paul Saucier, MA
*Edmund S. Muskie School of
    Public Service*
University of Southern Maine
Portland, Maine

Ann M. Saunders, PhD
*Department of Medicine and
    Neurobiology*
Duke University Medical Center
Durham, North Carolina

K. Warner Schaie, PhD
*Department of Human
    Development and Family
    Studies*
Pennsylvania State University
University Park, Pennsylvania

Malvin Schechter, MS
*Department of Geriatrics and
    Adult Development*
Mount Sinai School of Medicine
New York, New York

Susan S. Schiffman, PhD
Department of Psychiatry
Duke University Medical School
Durham, North Carolina

Nancy K. Schlossberg, EdD
*College of Education, Counseling
    and Personnel*
University of Maryland
College Park, Maryland

Maria Schmeeckle, MA
*Ethel Percy Andrus Gerontology
    Center*
University of Southern California
Los Angeles, California

Robert L. Schneider, DSW, PhD
School of Social Work
Virginia Commonwealth University
Richmond, Virginia

Richard Schulz, PhD
*Department of Psychiatry and
    University Center for Urban
    Research*
University of Pittsburgh
Pittsburgh, Pennsylvania

Carol A. Schutz
Gerontological Society of America
Washington, DC

Arthur G. Schwartz, PhD
Fels Institute
*Temple University School of
    Medicine*
Philadelphia, Pennsylvania

Susan R. Sherman, PhD
School of Social Welfare
University at Albany
Albany, New York

Nathan W. Shock, PhD
National Institute on Aging
Francis Scott Key Medical Center
Baltimore, Maryland

Tarek M. Shuman, EdD
United Nations World Assembly on Aging
New York, New York

Eugenia L. Siegler, MD
Department of Geriatric Medicine
University of Pennsylvania School of Medicine
Philadelphia, Pennsylvania

Merril Silverstein, PhD
Ethel Percy Andrus Gerontology Center
University of Southern California
Los Angeles, California

Lori Simon-Rusinowitz, PhD
Center on Aging
University of Maryland
Kensington, Maryland

Dean Keith Simonton, PhD
Department of Psychology
University of California
Davis, California

Alan J. Sinclair, MSc, MD,
FRCP (Lond), FRCP (Edin)
Department of Geriatric Medicine
University of Birmingham
Birmingham, England

Marilyn McKean Skaff, PhD
Center for Social and Behavioral Sciences
University of California
San Francisco, California

Celette Sugg Skinner, PhD
Cancer Prevention, Detection and Control Program
Duke University Medical Center
Durham, North Carolina

Stanley L. Slater, MD
National Institute on Aging
National Institutes of Health
Bethesda, Maryland

Anderson D. Smith, PhD
School of Psychology
Georgia Institute of Technology
Atlanta, Georgia

Jacqui Smith, PhD
Max Planck Institute for Human Development and Education
Berlin, Germany

Matthew J. Smith, PhD
Department of Physiology
University of Kentucky
Lexington, Kentucky

Roger Smith, MD PhD
Nuffield Orthopaedic Centre
Oxford, England

Michael A. Smyer, PhD
Graduate School of Arts and Sciences
Boston College
Chestnut Hill, Massachusetts

David Snyder, PhD
Department of Pharmacology
Medical College of Pennsylvania
Philadelphia, Pennsylvania

Jay H. Sokolovsky, PhD
Department of Anthropology
University of South Florida
St. Petersburg, Florida

William E. Sonntag, PhD
Department of Physiology and Pharmacology
Wake Forest University School of Medicine
Winston-Salem, North Carolina

Rainier Patrick C. Soriano, MD
Department of Geriatrics
Mount Sinai Medical Center
New York, New York

Marta Sotomayor, PhD
National Hispanic Council on Aging
Washington, DC

Elaine Souder, PhD, RN
College of Nursing
University of Arkansas for Medical Sciences
Little Rock, Arkansas

Liduïn E.M. Souren, RN, MSN
Aging and Dementia Research Center
New York University School of Medicine
New York, New York

David W. Sparrow, DSc
Department of Medicine
Boston University School of Medicine
Brookline, Massachusetts

Avron Spiro, III, PhD
Boston VA Medical Center and Outpatient Clinics
Bedford, Massachusetts

Ron Stall, PhD, MPH
Center for AIDS Prevention Studies
University of California
San Francisco, California

Bernard D. Starr, PhD
Gerontology Program
Marymount Manhattan College
New York, New York

Ursula M. Staudinger, PhD
Institute of Psychology
Dresden University of Technology
Dresden, Germany

Anthony A. Sterns, MA
Creative Action, Inc.
Akron, Ohio

Harvey L. Sterns, PhD
Department of Psychology
The University of Akron
Akron, Ohio

Ronni S. Sterns, PhD
Institute for Life-Span Development and Gerontology
The University of Akron
Akron, Ohio

Elizabeth A. L. Stine-Morrow, PhD
Department of Psychology
University of New Hampshire
Durham, New Hampshire

Leroy Stone, PhD
University of Montreal and
    Statistics Canada
Ottawa, Ontario, Canada

John R. Stradling, MD, FRCP
Oxford Centre for Respiratory
    Medicine
University of Oxford
Oxford, England

Gordon F. Streib, PhD
Department of Sociology
University of Florida
Gainesville, Florida

Neville E. Strumpf, PhD, RN,
    FAAN
School of Nursing
University of Pennsylvania
Philadelphia, Pennsylvania

Robert J. Sullivan, Jr., MD,
    MPH
Department of Medicine
Duke University Medical Center
Durham, North Carolina

Eileen M. Sullivan-Marx, PhD,
    RN, FAAN
School of Nursing
University of Pennsylvania
Philadelphia, Pennsylvania

Richard M. Suzman, PhD
Department of Behavioral and
    Social Research
National Institute on Aging
Bethesda, Maryland

Alvar Svanborg, MD, PhD
Department of Medicine
University of Illinois
Chicago, Illinois

Jeanette C. Takamura, MSW,
    PhD
United States Department of
    Health and Human Services
Washington, DC

Larry W. Thompson, PhD
Pacific Graduate School of
    Psychology
Los Altos, California

Esther C. Thrasher, PAC
Department of Dermatology
Francis Scott Key Hospital
Baltimore, Maryland

Daniel Thursz, ACSW
The National Council on the
    Aging, Inc.
Bethesda, Maryland

Rein Tideiksaar, PhD
Falls and Immobility Program
Southwest Medical Associates
Las Vegas, Nevada

Sheldon S. Tobin, PhD
School of Social Welfare/State
    University at Albany
Nelson A. Rockefeller College of
    Public Affairs and Policy
Albany, New York

Catherine J. Tompkins, PhD
Association for Gerontology in
    Higher Education
Fairfax, Virginia

Edgar A. Tonna, PhD, FRMS
Institute for Dental Research
New York University Dental Center
New York, New York

Fernando M. Torres-Gil, PhD
School of Public Policy
University of California
Los Angeles, California

Michael Tuffiash, BA
Department of Psychology
Florida State University
Tallahassee, Florida

R. Alexander Vachon, PhD
Legislative Assistant
Office of Senator Bob Dole
Washington, DC

Joan F. Van Nostrand, DPA
National Center for Health
    Statistics
Centers for Disease Control and
    Prevention
Potomac, Maryland

James W. Vaupel, PhD
Center for Health and Social
    Policy
Max Planck Institute for
    Demographic Research
Rostock, Germany

Lois M. Verbrugge, MPH
Institute of Gerontology
University of Michigan
Ann Arbor, Michigan

Jan Vijg, PhD
Basic Research Laboratory
Cancer and Therapy Research
    Center
San Antonio, Texas

Charalambos Vlachopoulos, MD
Medical Professorial Unit and
    Clinic/St. Vincent's Hospital
University of New South Wales
Sydney, Australia

Marnie Waldman, BA
Assisted Living Federation of
    America
Fairfax, Virginia

Christi A. Walter, PhD
The University of Texas Health
    Science Center
San Antonio, Texas

Jonathan Wanagat, BS
Department of Animal Health and
    Biomedical Sciences
University of Wisconsin, Madison
Madison, Wisconsin

Eugenia Wang, PhD
Bloomfield Centre for Research in
    Aging
Sir Mortimer B. Davis Jewish
    General Hospital
Montreal, Quebec, Canada

Walter F. Ward, PhD
University of Texas Health Science Center at San Antonio
San Antonio, Texas

Huber R. Warner, PhD
Biochemistry and Metabolism Branch
National Institute on Aging
Bethesda, Maryland

Gregg A. Warshaw, MD
Department of Family Medicine
University of Cincinnati Medical Center
Cincinnati, Ohio

Tracy A. Weitz, MPA
Institute for Health and Aging
University of California
San Francisco, California

Patricia Flynn Weitzman, PhD
Department of Social Medicine
Harvard Medical School
Boston, Massachusetts

Susan Krauss Whitbourne, PhD
Department of Psychology
University of Massachusetts at Amherst
Amherst, Massachusetts

Heidi K. White, MD
Duke University Medical Center
Durham, North Carolina

Monika White, PhD
Center for Healthy Aging
Santa Monica, California

Carol J. Whitlach, PhD
Margaret Blenkner Research Center
The Benjamin Rose Institute
Cleveland, Ohio

Frank J. Whittington, PhD
Department of Sociology
Georgia State University
Atlanta, Georgia

Joshua M. Wiener, PhD
The Urban Institute
Washington, DC

Kathleen H. Wilber, PhD
University of Southern California
Los Angeles, California

Brent C. Williams, MD
Department of Internal Medicine
University of Michigan Medical Center
Ann Arbor, Michigan

Sherry L. Willis, PhD
Department of Human Development
Pennsylvania State University
University Park, Pennsylvania

Arthur Wingfield, PhD
Department of Psychology
Brandeis University
Waltham, Massachusetts

Phyllis M. Wise, PhD
Department of Physiology
University of Kentucky
Lexington, Kentucky

Douglas A. Wolf, PhD
Center for Policy Research
Syracuse University
Syracuse, New York

Rosalie S. Wolf, PhD
Institute on Aging
The Medical Center of Central Massachusetts
Worcester, Massachusetts

F. Eugene Yates, MD
Department of Medicine/Gerontology
University of California
Los Angeles, California

Gwen Yeo, PhD
Stanford Geriatric Education Center
Stanford University School of Medicine
Palo Alto, California

Diane L. Zablotsky, PhD
Department of Sociology
University of North Carolina
Charlotte, North Carolina

Heying J. Zhan, PhD
Department of Sociology
Georgia State University
Atlanta, Georgia

LIST OF ENTRIES

Italics indicates that this subject is covered under a different title.

THE ENCYCLOPEDIA OF AGING

A Comprehensive Resource in Gerontology and Geriatrics

Third Edition

A

ABILITIES

Systematic exploration of the domain of intellectual development began in the 1930s with the study of children and young adults and eventually produced several taxonomies of abilities intended to identify the "building blocks of the mind." The most prominent taxonomies of abilities are those associated with Thurstone, Guilford, and Cattell.

Thurstone empirically identified 10 major dimensions by factoring a battery of 60 mental ability tests. Of these the first five factors have been most frequently explored in work with adults. The most important abilities include Verbal Meaning, Spatial Orientation, Inductive Reasoning, Number and Word Fluency. Adult age changes occur at different rates for these abilities. For example, only late-life decline is found for verbal meaning, while decline on number skill begins in late midlife (Schaie, 1996). Abilities also display differential cohort patterns. There has been a substantial increase in level over successive generations for reasoning and a smaller increase for spatial orientation and verbal ability, while there has been a decline for number ability (Willis, 1989).

Guilford (1967), in a more theoretical analysis, proposed a structure-of-intellect model that includes the three major dimensions of (1) operations (evaluation, convergent production, divergent production, memory, and cognition), (2) products (units, classes, relations, systems, transformations, and implications), and (3) content (figural, symbolic, semantic, and behavioral). This system yields a total of 120 possible ability components, only a limited number of which were fully operationalized.

Cattell, whose early work in the ability realm was concerned with the development of culture-fair measures, identified two major higher order dimensions that resulted from the factor analysis of primary mental ability measures. These are the constructs of *fluid ability*, involved in the solution of novel problems, and *crystallized ability*, involving knowledge acquired in the course of the social-ization process of a given culture. Observable ability measures may be more or less pure measures of these higher-order abilities or may involve both components as well as the additional higher-order components of short-term acquisition retrieval, long-term storage-retrieval, and speed or fluency (cf. Horn, 1982). The Cattell-Horn ability model has been of particular interest to researchers on aging because cross-sectional data suggest early adult decline for the fluid abilities but maintenance or modest increments for the crystallized abilities into advanced age. Tests suitable for ability measurement in adults are described in Schaie (1985) and in Ekstrom, French, Harman, and Derman (1976).

K. WARNER SCHAIE

See also
    Competence
    Expertise
    Intelligence
    Problem Solving

ABSTRACT THINKING

Young children understand the relation between objects and events in a functional manner, such that the first object is seen to go with or to operate on the second object. Complementarity criteria are an integral component of their thinking. Older children and young adults, by contrast, tend to use similarity criteria. In old age, however, the use of complementarity criteria has been found to increase once again (Reese & Rodeheaver, 1985). The reversal to complementarity in old age is thought to be caused by environmental factors rather than being attributable to changes in competence. Young children as well as the elderly are rarely required to state their thoughts in a specifically prescribed way, and complementary categorization therefore seems more natural, since such categorization groups occur naturally in time and space. Older adults do not necessarily lose the ability to use more abstract criteria but are often more willing to indulge in an alternative mode that offers greater imaginary scope. Complementarity as an aspect of thinking has been found to be more prevalent in nonprofessional than in professional men or women over the age range from 25 to 69, with neither age nor gender differences being significant (Denney, 1974). Luria observed the same phenomena in a study in Central Asia where uneducated peasants were more likely to engage in concrete thinking, and educated collective farm members were more prone to use abstract thought.

The subject of abstract thinking and aging also has been investigated in the context of the crystallized-fluid ability model. Convergent fluid abilities that involve abstract thinking have shown average decline somewhat earlier than was found for the more concrete information–based crystallized abilities. Paradoxically, abstract thinking may become more important as old age is reached because many lifelong experiences must be reappraised, and even overlearned everyday behaviors that previously could be performed in a routine and concrete manner may now require a modicum of abstract thought to provide a novel response given changed circumstances (Schaie & Willis, 1999; Willis & Schaie, 1993).

The contention that the increased incidence of concrete thought in the elderly may be due to experiential rather than neurological factors is further supported by positive results of training studies that involved persons who had not earlier used abstract classification principles (Denney, 1974) or who had declined in their performance on abstract ability measures (Schaie & Willis, 1986; Willis & Schaie, 1994).

K. WARNER SCHAIE

See also
  Abilities
  Cognitive Processes
  Metamemory
  Problem Solving

ABUSE
See
  Crime (Against and by the Elderly)
  Elder Abuse and Neglect

ACCIDENTS
See
  Falls
  Injury

ACID-BASE BALANCE

Hydrogen ion (H^+) is a highly reactive cation. For that reason it is essential that the concentration of H^+ in the body fluids be tightly regulated. In healthy people the H^+ concentration of the blood plasma ranges from 36 to 43 nanomoles per liter (pH 7.45–7.35). H^+ is produced by acids and consumed by bases; thus, the regulation of the H^+ concentration is called acid-base balance.

The body is continuously producing acids and bases. The production of carbon dioxide, which is a major end product of metabolism, is equivalent to producing carbonic acid. Although large quantities of carbon dioxide are produced each day, they are eliminated from the body by the lungs through alveolar ventilation as quickly as they are produced. The important point is that the nervous system controls alveolar ventilation so that the concentration of carbon dioxide in the blood plasma is maintained at the level needed for the maintenance of an appropriate H^+ concentration in the body fluids. The body also produces fixed acids (i.e., acids not eliminated by the lungs) and produces bases. If fixed acid production is in excess of base production, the kidneys excrete the excess H^+ in the urine. It is also the case that if base production is in excess of the fixed acid production, the kidneys excrete the excess base in the urine. Although the finely regulated pulmonary and renal functions can sometimes transiently fail to do the job, no immediate problem occurs because the body is rich in chemical buffers that serve to blunt rapid change in H^+ concentration.

Do these exquisite systems for the control of H^+ concentration continue to function effectively at advanced ages? It has long been held that healthy elderly living in usual unchallenged conditions have no problem in maintaining normal acid-base balance (Lye, 1998). However, a careful meta-analysis of published data on acid-base balance and age has challenged this long-held view (Frassetto & Sebastian, 1996). This analysis indicates that a significant rise in steady-state blood H^+ concentration occurs with increasing adult age. Moreover, assessment of the concentration of blood carbon dioxide concentration revealed a decrease with age, and this would be expected because of the increase in alveolar ventilation by the respiratory system in response to a rising blood H^+ concentration. On the basis of these findings, plus the meta-analysis assessment that plasma bicarbonate concentration decreases with age, it is likely that the age-associated deterioration of kidney function is responsible for the increasing H^+ concentration. Of course, to be certain of the gerontological validity of the findings of this meta-analysis requires data from a well-designed longitudinal study. The results of such a study have yet to be reported. However, if the conclusions from this meta-analysis are valid, an age-associated progressive increase of this magnitude in the near steady-state H^+ concentration could have negative consequences in regard to bone loss, muscle mass loss, and kidney function.

In contrast to uncertainty of the effect of age on unchallenged, near steady-state acid-base balance, the evidence is clear that healthy elderly people respond less well than the young to an acid-base challenge. In an early study, young and old were challenged by a load of ammonium chloride (Adler, Lindeman, Yiengst, Beard, & Shock, 1968). The body metabolizes ammonium chloride to hydrochloric acid. In that early study, it was found that increased blood levels of H^+ and decreased levels of bicarbonate ion persisted much longer in old than in young individuals. Altered kidney function appears to be the main reason for this difference between young and old. Indeed during the first 8 hours following ammonium chloride administration, a much greater percentage of the acid load is excreted in the urine by the young than by the old (Lubran, 1995). There is also evidence that the elderly cope less effectively with increased acid loads caused by exercise. This decrease in the ability of the kidney to excrete H^+ predisposes the elderly to the development of and delayed recovery from metabolic acidosis (Lindeman, 1995). Whether the respiratory change in alveolar ventilation is as effective in the elderly in compensating for changes in blood H^+ concentration is subject to debate; not all studies have found the response of the respiratory system to chemical stimuli to be blunted with increasing age (Rubin, Tack, & Cherniack, 1982).

Of course, the elderly have many age-associated diseases that predispose them to acid-base disorders (e.g., chronic obstructive pulmonary disease and chronic renal disease). Thus, acid-base disorders are commonly encountered in geriatric medicine.

EDWARD J. MASORO

See also
   Kidney and Urinary System
   Respiratory System

ACTIVE LIFE EXPECTANCY

Life expectancy is the average length of life that a particular group may expect to live. For example, at the beginning of the 1990s, the estimated average life expectancy at birth for white males was 72.7 years and for white females, 79.2 years; by contrast, average life expectancy at birth for black males was 64.8 years and for black females 73.5 years. These estimates are computed by knowing the age-specific death rates for a group and applying these death rates to the group for each successive age period. It is possible to estimate the average remaining life for a group at any point in time. For example, for the population of the United States at the beginning of the 1990s, the average remaining life expectancy of persons 65 years old was 17.2 years; for those 75 years old, 10.9 years; for those 85 and older, 6.2 years.

Information on age-specific death rates is essential to understanding changes in the age distribution of the population. Many general demographic studies have indicated that the population of the United States—in fact, of all societies—is aging; that is, life expectancy is increasing and more persons are living to older ages. Since health and other problems are associated with older ages, the trend of increasing numbers and proportions of older persons has been of interest not only to demographers and other social scientists but also to policy makers and social planners. Particularly if extending the period of old age means extending the period that the average person will be *dependent* on others and require care, policy makers and social planners become concerned with what the changes mean in terms of economic and other resources required.

Thus, an important question centers on whether dependency increases as life expectancy increases, and this question is focused particularly on the active life expectancy at older ages, i.e., the nondependent period.

Fries and Crapo (1981) advanced a major theoretical formulation that bears on the period of dependency as life expectancy increases. They note that longevity, or the upper limit of life, is not likely to change materially in the foreseeable future. As persons live longer because disease, disorders, and disabilities are reduced or delayed, the problems can only happen in a shorter and shorter period of remaining life. The conclusion then follows that the period of dependency is shortened or compressed as life expectancy is extended. There have been many critiques of this theory and the facts on which the theory presumably rests (Grundy, 1984; Review Symposium, 1982; Schneider & Brody, 1983). Actual studies that bear on the issue require unique data, so the theory cannot be fully tested easily. Among the criticisms, however, a frequently recurring theme is that we are keeping alive longer people who have chronic disabilities. We have remarkable life support systems available. Some persons may be kept alive who may have a high level of dependency and for whom prognosis of recovery of function is small. Katz and his associates (1983) published a study that bears directly on the theory. For example, active life expectancy for women in their study was longer than for men, but the women had longer life expectancy also, and it turned out that the percentage of active life expectancy for men was higher for all age groups. Other aspects of the study were not consistent with the theory.

Active life expectancy as a concept involves information critical to understanding the amount of resources that will be required to maintain an aging population. Many issues are involved in considering active life expectancy, including ethical and moral considerations that define the level of medical and long-term care that is to be provided and the circumstances under which life is to be prolonged. For a general discussion and review of evidence, see Manton and Soldo (1985).

In the 1990s there has been a more general acceptance of the notion that most of the communicable diseases that at one time quickly killed the aged are largely controllable, and thus the vast majority of people will die of degenerative diseases and systemic failures associated with aging. Of the degenerative diseases, heart attacks and strokes frequently lead to a quick death, but most others can involve a prolonged period of disability. Similarly, bodily organ and systemic failures usually are progressive and extended over long periods, so that the notion that one is on a genetic time clock that stops ticking all at once simply does not correspond to reality as it is encountered. This has led to an expectation that a large proportion of the aging population may involve long periods of dependency, and a secondary alternative has become more prominent in the practical consideration about how this can be managed, namely, the notion that older persons should have a more direct part in determining how long and under what circumstances their lives should continue in a dependent status, particularly when factors of quality of life are at issue. The issues of quality of life involve not merely pain, mobility, and the ability to carry out normal functions, but also transition to conditions of mental deterioration, coma, or other vegetative states.

For a discussion of the origins of the construct *active life expectancy*, its early use in Canadian research, and the connection of the construct to *disability-free life expectancy* and *quality-adjusted life expectancy*, see Maddox (1994).

EDGAR F. BORGATTA

See also
Demography
Life Expectancy
Multidimensional Functional Assessment

ACTIVITIES

Activities are what people do. They may be special or routine, strenuous or relaxing, solitary or social. Some are commonplace and ordinary, such as walking the dog before breakfast or watching the television news before going to bed. Others are extraordinary, such as a once-in-a-lifetime trip to Australia or a family celebration of a 25th wedding anniversary. As a consequence, no article or study can encompass all the activities that older people do—in even a week, much less a year or a lifetime. There are, however, several generalizations that offer a framework for understanding what later-life adults do and something of what those activities mean.

The first generalization is that older people go on doing most of the same activities they have done in earlier life periods. There are, in fact, no "activities of the old," stereotypes notwithstanding. The continuities of the later life course far outweigh discontinuities, at least until major traumas force drastic changes or significant decrements seriously reduce abilities and resources. The general rule, then, is simple: Older people continue most of the activities that contributed to their lives previously. This is especially true for those "core" activities that are accessible, usually in or near the residence, and that form an integral part of the ongoing round of daily life: informal interaction and conversation, media use, reading, walking, and playing with routine tasks and procedures. In fact, home-based activities may actually increase for adults over 64 years of age (Iso-ahola, Jackson, & Dunn, 1994).

Most later-life adults seek a balance of activities (Kelly, 1987). The balance includes activities that are demanding and demonstrate skill and those that are restful and relaxing, those that involve communication with other people and those that offer withdrawal and disengagement, those that take regular time slots during the day and week and those that punctuate periods with some change or novelty. That balance changes through the life course as work, family, community, and leisure roles shift in salience and as resources and responsibilities change.

Activities and Aging

Each person builds a repertoire of skills, interests, associations, values, and commitments through life's journey. There is, therefore, no time when that history is abandoned or when we become different persons. Rather, our identities and the ways in which we have coped with life tend to demonstrate considerable continuity with those of the past (Atchley, 1993). It is hardly surprising, then, that activity patterns and investments also tend to display considerable continuity. Further, we do not at some magical or critical moment define ourselves as different people because of chronological age.

Rather, our self-definitions are more "ageless" than age-defined (Kaufman, 1993).

There are, then, no age-designated activities that move prominently to the fore as men and women pass the age of 65, retire, or are widowed. One reason is that older adults, like younger ones, do so many different things that they continue, at a somewhat slower rate, to engage in a process of adding, subtracting, and substituting activities (Iso-ahola, Jackson, & Dunn, 1994). The demographics of population aging, however, are one factor in the increased participation in two outdoor activities, walking and golf. Clearly, those formerly labeled as "old" by passing the age of 65 do not suddenly cease or transform their activities. Rather, most are now called the "active old" or the "young old" and have become the targets of high levels of recreation and travel marketing.

Development of Activity Study

In 1961 a landmark collection edited by Robert Kleemeier, *Aging and Leisure*, drew attention to the significance of activity in the lives of middle-aged and older adults. Several chapters were based on the Kansas City study in which a variety of activities were found to be articulated with changing roles and orientations. The multidimensional meanings of the activities were embedded in community and family contexts. Activities, even those designated as leisure, were not segmented and separate from the ongoing flows of life meanings, attachments, and commitments. Rather, they tended to be integrated with the social roles of that life course period including intimate relationships, organizational histories, gender roles, personality development, and economic and cultural resources.

At the same time, Cumming and Henry (1961) proposed the hypothesis that growing old inevitably involves a natural process of "disengagement" that is indexed by decreases in activities. In response, others argued that activity changes were adaptive but that engagement remains significant in aging and that decrements are selective rather than inevitable. This is consistent with the later Houston study in which lower rates of participation varied according to the type of activity as well as life circumstances (Gordon, Gaitz, & Scott, 1976.) A more recent study found that overall activity level was significantly lower with age, especially for those age 75 and above, but that social and family activities, as well as some cultural and organizational activities, did not follow that pattern of loss. Rather, the marked declines were concentrated in travel, exercise and sport, and other outdoor or physically demanding activity.

Perhaps the pattern that best encompasses both declines and continuities is that called "selective optimization with compensation" (Baltes & Baltes, 1990). Older persons are seen as active agents who strategize and negotiate with their own abilities and resources to maintain as much continuity of satisfaction and meaning as possible (Atchley, 1993). Activities are vehicles of meaning, self-investment, and salient relationships that are central to who we are at any age or set of conditions. There may, indeed, be some contraction and constriction of activity range in later life, but there is also a possibility of innovation and replacement rather than simple decline and loss.

Significance of Activities

There is now a broad consensus that remaining active is a major factor in later-life satisfaction and health (Kelly, 1993). In a longitudinal study, for those with viable health and income, activities outside the home have been found to be the main factor distinguishing high levels of later life satisfaction for both men and women (Palmore, 1979). Although it is difficult to ascribe causation, such engagement has been consistently found to be an essential element of an overall lifestyle that is relatively high in quality. Simply having financial and health resources is not enough unless they are employed in activity that is personally and socially involving.

For those moving into a final phase of "frailty," a gradual or traumatic loss of health and physical or mental ability also includes a constriction of activities, especially those that are strenuous physically or require full mobility. In that period, however, activities that maintain social integration and exercise developed skills continue to be important. Factors in sustaining activity are access, transportation, communicative skills, and an atmosphere of inclusion. For residential care institutions, activities that challenge abilities and give a sense of worth

and community are especially critical (Voelkl, 1993).

Community-dwelling older adults, however, are not found to be sitting around waiting for "senior" or "golden age" programs. Only 15% of respondents aged 65 and older in a massive national survey had visited a senior center even once in the previous year and less than 10% participated at all regularly (Cutler & Danigelis, 1993). Rather, older adults usually find their lives more or less filled by ongoing relationships, activities, and responsibilities. They commonly report being "too busy" to take on new activities. Even in retirement, the other roles and relationships of their lives tend to expand to fill and reconstruct the schedule formerly dominated by employment. Their continuing activity settings tend to be age-integrated rather than age-designated and age-segregated.

All activities, however, are not alike. Filling time is not a major problem for the active old. "Ordinary" life is not empty, but there are possibilities for extraordinary levels of satisfaction and meaning in later life. Several studies suggest what those activities are likely to be. First, they express lifelong values and give a sense of worth (Kaufman, 1993). Second, they involve regular associations with other people who are valued, especially family and friends. And, third, they involve a consistent commitment to activities that utilize skills and challenge abilities (Mannell, 1993). Such activities yield two significant outcomes: a sense of competence in the face of challenge and a community of those engaged in the common activity.

Several research approaches have identified such factors in an engaged later life. Both life course role shifts and stressful events can have significant impacts on activity engagement. In a community study, particular types of activity were correlated with high levels of life satisfaction: travel and cultural activities for those aged 40 to 64, social and travel for those 65 to 74, and family and home-based activity for those 75 and older (Kelly, 1987). Of course, such activities are usually associated with higher levels of resources. A recent study identified the kinds of activity associated with higher levels of satisfaction as those requiring high levels of involvement, commitment, and skill (Mannell, 1993). These "high investment" activities, sometimes termed "serious leisure," exercise skills developed over years of engagement and usually involve communities of common action and identification.

The picture suggests that being entertained or consuming experiences provided by others, however well meaning, does not fill fundamental needs at any age. Certainly, at any age people need some periods of disengagement from demand. However, they also need activity that challenges and yields communities of common action. Later-life adults still need activity that allows them to identify themselves as persons of worth and ability who are significantly related to others. Such engagement may be found in ongoing sets of relationships and responsibilities or may be found in special commitments to challenging activities. Such activities, especially when they continue long-term involvement, become contexts of action and community.

Summary of Later-Life Activity

In summary, the activities of older adults demonstrate the following characteristics:

1. Most older persons are not sitting around with nothing to do. Their routines of ordinary activity usually fill the day and evening.
2. Those most satisfied with their lives are most often engaged in regular activities outside the home that provide challenge and in relationships with friends and family.
3. Such activity does not, for the most part, occur in age-segregated settings.
4. Significant activities usually continue to be those proven satisfying in earlier life, although the active old do still select, replace, and even start activities. Continuity is demonstrated in identities, established competencies, self-images, values, and relationships.
5. As a consequence, activities most likely to attract older adults build on familiarity, established abilities and identities, communities of action and interaction, and histories of satisfaction. Programs attract primarily by their quality rather than by age designation.
6. Conversely, activity programs that require older persons to redefine themselves as old or in any way incompetent or inferior are unlikely to be attractive. The "ageless self"

tends to retain values and self-definitions of ability that are not redefined by age alone.

Both personal and social histories are significant in the development of activity interests and ability. As cohorts have entered later life with higher levels of education and greater financial resources, their range of activities has increased. As coming cohorts of women and minorities will have experienced fuller opportunities, their interests, resources, and abilities will expand their activity possibilities in later life. For all, however, their particular history of associations, life chances, circumstances, and crucial events differentiated by gender, race, ethnicity, sexual orientation, and social class construct a life in which activities are integrated throughout the life course.

Guidelines for Professionals

Again, there seems to be no limit to the kinds of activities that older persons, even in long-term care facilities, may find satisfying. There are, however, guidelines for those who provide activity programs and resources from activity research. The first, clearly, is to build on continuities, on histories of part engagement and even commitment. The second is to avoid labeling or contexts that require older persons to redefine themselves as "old" and incompetent. The third is to foster community, communication, and personal relationships as part of the context of activity. The fourth is to provide and promote activities that yield a sense of ability appropriate to the individual or group rather than just entertainment. And the fifth is to support empowerment in which people who were formerly able and valued can have a sense of efficacy and competence. Finally, administrators should not view activity providers as peripheral to the central mission of the organization. Activity, defined inclusively, is central to the still-developing lives of older adults.

JOHN R. KELLY

See also
Activity Theory
Exercise
Leisure

ACTIVITIES OF DAILY LIVING

The term *activities of daily living* (ADL) has been used to refer to a range of common activities whose performance is required for personal self-maintenance and independent community residence. The theoretical model proposed by Katz (1983) suggests that three areas should be examined: mobility; instrumental ADL (IADL), which is concerned with complex activities needed for independent living; and basic personal care tasks (BADL). Several excellent reviews, which also reproduce the ADL measures used in assessment of the elderly and in rehabilitation, are available (e.g., McDowell & Newell, 1996; Salek, 1998; Tamburini, 1998). These reviews also focus on alternative conceptualizations of ADL assessments and approaches to measurement.

Standardized ADL assessments have increased in use, acceptance, and importance over the past 40 years. Current measures date back to the Katz Index of Independence in Activities of Daily Living (Katz et al., 1959) and to the Barthel Index (Mahoney & Barthel, 1965). Both were developed in rehabilitation settings to measure tasks basic to personal self-care. They include comparable items: feeding, continence, transferring, use of toilet, dressing, bathing, and, for the Barthel, mobility.

These scales have since diverged. Various modifications of the Barthel have been developed, permitting increasingly specific focus on the type of rehabilitative intervention required and the impact of that intervention. Experience with this and related assessments used in rehabilitation have culminated in the Functional Independence Measure (FIM; Linacre, Heinemann, Wright, Granger, & Hamilton, 1994). In addition to the self-care activities mentioned above, the FIM also includes inquiry into locomotion (ability to use stairs, travel, or go distances), communication (comprehension and expression), and social cognition (i.e., memory and cognitive performance). The FIM consists of 18 items, each scored on a carefully described 7-point scale (1 = complete dependence, 7 = complete independence), typically by a specially trained rehabilitation provider. The FIM provides the basis for reimbursement and enjoys extensive use in rehabilitation settings.

The Katz scale has been used increasingly to determine eligibility for long-term care. Because the majority of elderly can perform the Katz items, this scale does not discriminate well among the older community-resident population. Further, the items are concerned with basic personal self-maintenance tasks and do not address more complex activities required to remain a functioning member of society.

It is to this area that Lawton and Brody (1969) have made a significant contribution by the introduction of their measures of IADL. Initially gender-specific, these measures were modified by the Older Americans Research and Services (OARS) project to reduce gender bias and combined into a single seven-item measure on which each item is assessed on a 3-point scale. The items of this scale include, in increasing order of difficulty, taking own medications, using the telephone, handling everyday finances, preparing meals, shopping, traveling, and doing housework. Comparable items have been included in major surveys of the elderly.

Because, on average, ability to perform IADL tasks is lost before loss of ability to perform BADL tasks, the question has arisen as to whether IADL and BADL items constitute a hierarchical scale or whether these activities of daily living are multidimensional. Evidence for both exists.

Factor analyses indicate that the Katz items typically fall on one factor, whereas instrumental ADL items fall on one or two other factors (Fillenbaum, 1985; Stump, Clark, Johnson, & Wolinsky, 1997; Thomas, Rockwood, & McDowell, 1998). Within each factor, the items have sometimes been found to constitute a hierarchical measure, but this is not invariable; in fact a multiplicity of hierarchies have been identified for the Katz items (Lazaridis, Rudberg, Furner, & Cassel, 1994).

The three main groups into which the ADL items fall have been variously called basic ADL or basic self-care, household ADLs or intermediate self-care, and advanced ADLs or complex self-management. The last is recognized as having a substantial cognitive component. Although there is considerable overlap across studies in the items included in each of these groups, the precise items presented reflect the data set from which information was drawn. The study of Thomas, Rockwood, and McDowell (1998), based on data from the Canadian Study of Health and Aging, which used the OARS ADL scale (see "OARS Multidimensional Functional Assessment Questionnaire"), sorts the items as follows:

Basic self-care: toileting, dressing, eating, transferring, grooming

Intermediate self-care: bathing, walking, housework, meal preparation, shopping, walking outside

Complex self-management: handling money, phone use, self-medicating

To complement these activities by providing information on mobility, measures such as the abbreviated three-item Rosow-Breslau (Rosow & Breslau, 1969) or inquiry into upper- and lower-limb functioning may be added.

Some investigators have determined that commonly used ADL measures are multidimensional, and others have identified sets of BADL and IADL items that constitute a hierarchical scale (Spector & Fleishman, 1998; Suurmeijer, Doeglas, Moum, Braincon, Krol, Sanderman, et al., 1994). Spector and Fleishman (1998), in particular, have used a set of items that overlap considerably with those of Thomas, Rockwood, and McDowell (1998)—the only differences are the absence of grooming and the inclusion of help with incontinence, doing laundry, and specification that housework is light—yet they have come to a different conclusion regarding multidimensionality. Possibly alternative statistical procedures and different samples of elders (nationally representative vs. disabled) help to explain the discrepant findings.

In addition to ADL scales that have been developed for general use, there are scales specific to certain health conditions, such as arthritis, dementia, multiple sclerosis, and stroke (e.g., Duncan, 1994; Loewenstein, Amigo, Duara, Guterman, Hurwitz, Berkowitz, et al., 1989; Mahurin, DeBettignies, & Pirozzolo, 1991; Pfeffer, Kurosaki, Harrah, Chance, & Filos, 1982; Slater & Raun, 1984; Spitz & Fries, 1987).

ADL assessments vary in a number of ways, resulting in estimates of prevalence of disability that can differ by up to 60% (Wiener, Hanley, Clark, & van Nostrand, 1990), creating substantial difficulty in estimating service needs and associated costs. They differ with respect to the number of categories used to assess adequacy of performance. These may range from the very general (e.g., can

do unaided vs. other) to 3-point categories, which seem to be the easiest to use (i.e., can do unaided, needs help, can't do), or they can be more specific. The categories may distinguish among the types of help used (e.g., a device, a person), with mechanical devices recognized as providing greater independence than human help. The level of specificity of performance may vary. Information on pain is sometimes included. Assessment may be made by the person being assessed, a family member, or a service provider. Information from the three is not equivalent (Dorevitch, Cossar, Bailey, Bisset, Lewis, Wise, et al., 1992). Assessment may be based on observation of actual performance, but often it is not. In the latter case, when the assessed person is not permitted or does not have access to facilities needed to perform the activity (e.g., where unattended bathing is not allowed, where there are no cooking facilities), assessment may reflect hopeful expectation. The advantages of performance-based assessments may, however, have been overestimated (Myers, Holiday, Harvey, & Hutchinson, 1993). Some scales are sex-specific. Environmental factors that might affect performance are rarely considered.

ADL measurement is central to any assessment of level of personal independent functioning. Information on ADL capacity has been used more extensively and for a greater variety of purposes than has information from any other type of assessment. It has been used to indicate individual social, mental, and physical functioning, as well as for diagnosis; to determine service requirement and impact; to guide service inception and cessation; to estimate the level of qualification needed in a provider; to assess need for structural environmental support; to justify residential location; to provide a basis for personnel employment decisions; to determine service change and provide arguments for reimbursement; to calculate active and disabled life expectancy; and to estimate categorical eligibility for specific services (e.g., attendant allowances). Accurate assessment of ADL is probably one of the most valuable of measures.

GERDA G. FILLENBAUM

See also

Cash Payments for Care
Comprehensive Assessment

ACTIVITY THEORY

In the gerontology of the early 1960s, activity theory and disengagement theory became opposing grand metaphors for successful aging. In the case of activity theory, the archetype image portrayed an old person who had managed to maintain vigor and social involvement despite the vagaries of aging. For disengagement theory, the archetype image was of an old person who had voluntarily and gracefully disengaged from the hustle and bustle of midlife to a more serene and satisfying contemplation of life from a distance. These dualistic images of two very different paths of aging have been a part of Western civilization for a very long time.

Robert Havighurst and his colleagues at the University of Chicago (Havighurst, 1963; Havighurst, Neugarten, & Tobin, 1963) were the early spokespersons for activity theory. Havighurst laid no claim to have invented activity theory; he simply put in writing what many practitioners of the day assumed: that keeping active was the best way to enjoy a satisfying old age. According to this view,

except for the inevitable changes in biology and health, older people are the same as middle-aged people, with essentially the same psychological and social needs. In this view, the decreased social involvement that characterizes old age results from the withdrawal by society from the aging person; and the decrease in interaction proceeds against the desires of most aging men and women. The older person who ages optimally is the person who stays active and who manages to resist the shrinking of his [or her] social world. [She or] he maintains the activities of middle age as long as possible, and then finds substitutes for those activities he [or she] is forced to relinquish—substitutes for work when [she or] he is forced to retire; substitutes for friends or loved ones whom he [or she] loses by death. (Havighurst, Neugarten, & Tobin, 1963, p. 419)

In contrast to activity theory, disengagement theory (Cumming & Henry, 1961) held that successful aging involved growing old gracefully by gradually replacing the equilibrium system of social relations typical of midlife with a new equilibrium more appropriate to the interests of people approaching the end of life. This new equilibrium was presumed to involve a lower overall volume of social relations and less psychological investment in the social affairs of the larger community.

Rosow (1963) picked up this theme of equilibrium in his rendition of activity theory, but his position was that the best course of action was to maintain the equilibrium of middle age. He argued that Americans do not want to grow old and that, by inference, their "basic premise in viewing old age is that the best life is the life that changes least" (Rosow, 1963, p. 216). He went on to argue that a "good adjustment" to old age involves maximum stability and minimum change in life pattern between late middle age and old age.

Activity theory assumed that activity produced successful aging through the relationship between activity and life satisfaction or subjective well-being. It was presumed that activity level was the cause and life satisfaction the effect.

Major Concepts of Activity Theory

Activity theory is built around four major concepts: activity, equilibrium, adaptation to role loss, and life satisfaction. Each of these very general concepts is open to a variety of interpretations, which has led to no small amount of confusion.

Activity. At its simplest, activity is any form of doing. But in Havighurst's original formulation of activity theory, activity was not just a *level* of doing but also a *pattern* of activity that formed the person's lifestyle. Activity theory predicted that maintaining both level and pattern of activities from middle age into old age would lead to the highest level of life satisfaction in old age.

Equilibrium. Activity theory makes the functionalist assumption that activity patterns arise to meet needs and that the needs of older people are no different from the needs of middle-aged people; therefore, whatever equilibrium the person has achieved in middle age should be maintained into old age. Significant assaults to this midlife equilibrium are best resisted, and lost activities or roles should be replaced. Simply dropping out would not meet functional needs and would therefore be expected to lead to lowered life satisfaction.

Adaptation to Role Loss.   Role loss was assumed to be a common experience for aging individuals because of the withdrawal of society from the aging person. Activity theory predicted that the most successful way to adapt to role loss was to find a substitute role to satisfy needs. The original formulation assumed that role substitutes should be roughly equivalent to the roles lost, so retirement would lead to a search for job substitutes, for example. Later, the concept of substitution was broadened by Maddox (1963) to include alternative activities of any kind.

Life Satisfaction.   How do we know when a person has aged successfully? Both activity theorists and disengagement theorists agreed on one thing. Life satisfaction was the best criterion for measuring social and psychological adjustment. Havighurst and colleagues' (1963) concept of life satisfaction was made up of five components: zest and enthusiasm, resolution and fortitude, a feeling of accomplishment, self-esteem, and optimism. This construct addressed the level of subjective well-being experienced by an individual, not his or her evaluation of specific objective circumstances. The Life Satisfaction Index B (Havighurst, 1963) was constructed to measure these attributes, and it has been most often used as the dependent variable in formal tests of activity theory.

Evolution of Activity Theory

In its original form, activity theory was a homeostatic, equilibrium theory of the relation between activity patterns and life satisfaction. However, the theoretical ties between activity theory and functional equilibrium theory were largely ignored, although they were made explicit by Rosow (1963).

Lemon, Bengtson, and Peterson (1972) reformulated activity theory into an interactionist theory. By *interactionist*, they meant both symbolic interaction in the form of a relation between self and role and the use of reflected appraisals to bolster the self, as well as social interaction in the form

of role supports going from others to the aging individual. Thus, for Lemon et al., the motivation for maintaining activity was not the meeting of functional needs but the need to maintain a socially supported self-structure that was assumed to lead to optimal life satisfaction.

Lemon, Bengtson, and Peterson (1972) developed a formal propositional theory that attempted to explain why high activity levels could be expected to produce high life satisfaction and declines in activity could be expected to result in lower life satisfaction. Their theory was based on a series of assumptions about the relationships among role loss, role supports (feedback from others about role performance), self-esteem, and life satisfaction. This reformulation of activity theory was essentially a domino theory, in which role loss was presumed to lead to less role support and lower activity, which were presumed to lead to lower self-esteem, which in turn was presumed to cause lower life satisfaction. On the other hand, maintaining high activity levels by substituting for lost roles would maintain activity level and role support, which would maintain self-esteem and thereby maintain life satisfaction. Further, they classified activities into informal, formal, and solitary and hypothesized that all three types would be associated with life satisfaction, but informal activity was expected to show the strongest association because of its greater likelihood of providing role support, followed by formal activity; and solitary activity was expected to show the lowest association with life satisfaction because of its presumed lack of role support. Unfortunately, their test of the theory provided little support for this reformulation. The only significant association they found between activity and life satisfaction occurred for informal activities among married women.

Longino and Kart (1982) retested Lemon, Bengtson, and Peterson's (1972) hypotheses and reported more support for the hypothesized relationships between types of activities and life satisfaction. They also suggested several additional hypotheses to be included in the interactionist activity theory:

• Formal activity damages self-concept and lowers morale. This hypothesis was based on the notion that service use is the most common type of formal activity in an older population and that service use results in negative role support.

- Lower life satisfaction leads to increased formal activity. Here they argued that the causal direction of activity theory may be wrong. Elders with low morale tend to be targeted by formal service providers; therefore, low life satisfaction causes formal activity, not the reverse.

- Formal activity is a variable context, and its effects on life satisfaction depend on the extent to which it offers opportunities for supportive human relationships.

- Role supports may not be substitutable. If confidants are lost, they may not be replaceable.

- Frequency of activity is as important as the type of activity. They found that *any* level of informal activity resulted in life satisfaction near the sample mean, whereas an *absence* of informal activity resulted in a significant deficit in life satisfaction compared to the sample mean.

Part of the difficulty with the interactionist version of activity theory may have been its simplistic assumptions about the relation of self and roles. Research evidence on the relationship between self and role in later life suggests that the linkage is neither as direct nor as simple as the interactionist formulations of activity theory indicate. For example, Markus and Herzog's (1991) review of the literature on aging and the self conceptualized the self as a dynamic, complex structure made up of past, current, and future images of the self arising from specific antecedents. Self-schema are used to organize and interpret experience, regulate affect, and motivate behavior. Life satisfaction is presumed to be one of the consequences of these self processes. In this formulation all roles are not equally important to the self, only those that are part of the set of core self schema that persists over time. Likewise, the place of specific activities in the core self could be expected to be a significant intervening variable in the relations among activity patterns, activity change, the self, and life satisfaction. Recent research on activity has addressed some of these concerns.

Larson, Zuzanek, and Mannell (1985) and Mannell (1993), for example, looked at the meaning of specific activities for the individual as a significant intervening variable in the relationship between activity and life satisfaction. Larson et al. reported that the retired adults in their study voluntarily spent almost half their waking hours alone, but being alone was not a negative experience for the majority of them. When they were alone, they were engaged in activities that required concentration and challenge. Mannell probed this issue further and found that the link between specific activities and life satisfaction was the culmination of a complex string of contingencies. First, activities had to be available that had a high potential for attracting individual investment of time and energy. Second, activities had to be freely chosen, not obligatory, and accompanied by a sense of commitment. Third, activities had to produce the experience of *flow*, life experience transported to a higher level of quality by activities that focus attention, match challenges to capabilities, reduce self-consciousness, and increase feelings of control. *If* these contingent conditions were met, *then* we could expect activities to bolster life satisfaction.

Important Unaddressed Issues

Does activity theory apply equally to men and women as they age? To what reference point in the past should patterns of activity and life satisfaction in old age be compared? When does old age begin chronologically? Does activity influence some of the components of life satisfaction more than others? Does activity influence life satisfaction, or is it the other way around? Is activity level correlated with life satisfaction consistently?

Gender differences are very obvious in the findings of research on aging and activities. The number and types of activities and the frequency of participation in an array of activities have all been found to differ substantially by gender, with activity patterns of older men showing a stronger relation to life satisfaction than the activity patterns of older women. However, there has been no attempt to integrate these findings into activity theory, to explain *why* activities are more important to the life satisfaction of older men than to older women.

Activity theory might be further refined by looking at specific components of subjective well-being. It is likely that self-esteem is not the only mental construct that is influenced by the experiences gained from a person's activities. Lawton (1983) mapped a number of dimensions of subjective well-being that could profitably be used in research on activity theory.

Finally, activity level is not always correlated with life satisfaction. Indeed, in a meta-analysis of 10 predictors of subjective well-being among elders, Okun, Stock, Haring, and Witter (1984) found that activity level was only modestly related to life satisfaction when the effect of health was controlled. Health was by far the strongest predictor of life satisfaction. Research on activity theory should be sure to control the effects of health and life stage before coming to conclusions about the influence of activity level on life satisfaction.

Directions for Activity Theory

Current research using activity theory falls into two categories: research aimed at comparing activity theory with other theories as descriptions of typical patterns related to aging; and research aimed at testing and extending the social psychological components of activity theory to better specify the causal relationships between activity and life satisfaction.

Researchers who focus primarily on activities tend to describe activity patterns and then compare their descriptions to the ideal descriptions presented in the homeostatic, functional version of activity theory. Because there is usually a good bit of change in the frequency of specific activities over time in later adulthood, the equilibrium hypothesis of activity theory is usually rejected.

However, researchers who focus primarily on life satisfaction are increasingly looking at the social psychological relation between specific activities and life satisfaction. These researchers have met with increasing success in identifying specific conditions under which activity is strongly related to life satisfaction. But as the list of specifications grows, the power of activity theory as a general theory of aging is diminished.

Despite the many difficulties with activity theory, its ties to the cultural conception of successful aging have made gerontologists reluctant to abandon it. Some of each new generation of gerontologists are attracted to the basic ideas contained in activity theory. Instead of rejecting the theory out of hand, it is used as an ideal standard against which to compare actual activity patterns. For those more interested in activity theory as theory, the focus has shifted to understanding the conditions under which the kernel of truth contained in the cultural conception could be expected occur in its more obvious forms.

ROBERT C. ATCHLEY

See also
    Disengagement
    Kansas City Studies of Adult Life

ADAPTATION

Perhaps no issue has so completely engaged the intellectual curiosity of aging researchers than well-being, as broadly defined. This sustaining interest is pursued under a variety of terms, including well-being, successful aging, quality of life, and adaptation. A large and ever growing research base addresses the epidemiology of well-being and the factors that facilitate or impede quality of life in old age.

Traditionally, the term *adaptation* was used to denote an overall evaluation of life quality or personal well-being. Most commonly, adaptation was viewed as individuals' subjective evaluations of the quality of their lives and operationalized via measures of life satisfaction, happiness, morale, and similar concepts. Less common, but far from rare, were studies that defined adaptation in more objective terms, focusing on parameters such as health and functional status. And a few studies operationalized adaptation in terms of multidimensional measures that included both objective and subjective indicators.

This broad, overarching use of the term *adaptation* has become less common in the past decade. Increasingly, subjective well-being and quality of life have become the constructs used to denote the overall status of persons of all ages but especially older adults. Adaptation is now used in a narrower sense and is most often addressed in two types of gerontological research: (a) studies of role transitions, especially role losses; and (b) efforts to understand the fit (or lack thereof) of older adults to their residential environments.

Adapting to Role Transitions

During the 1980s, understanding the effects of role transitions on individual well-being was a major theme of gerontological research (e.g., Elwell & Maltbie-Crannell, 1981; George, 1980). Based on the social stress perspective and expectations that late life is characterized by multiple role losses, this research initially hypothesized that role transitions in general and role losses in particular would be associated with lower levels of adaptation or well-being. Empirical findings quickly refuted this simplistic hypothesis; role transitions were typically not harbingers of decrements in well-being. Investigators then turned to the more appropriate issue of identifying the circumstances under which role transitions did and did not lead to declines in well-being. Three factors account for the differential consequences of role transitions. First, the character of the role transition is related to its threat to adaptation. Decrements in adaptation are most likely when the transition is involuntary and perceived as detrimental. Second, temporal issues are critical in assessing the consequences of role transitions. Declines in adaptation are most likely as initial responses to transitions; in the longer term, adaptation typically returns to pretransition levels. Third and most important, the adaptive consequences of role transitions largely depend on the social, economic, and personal resources available. Given sufficient resources, long-term decrements in adaptation are unlikely.

It was also during the 1980s that a different meaning of the term *adaptation* began to appear in the stress literature, as an adjunct to social psychological perspectives on coping (e.g., Lazarus & DeLongis, 1983). Research in this tradition focused on the ways that specific coping strategies or combinations of strategies were associated with adaptation to stress, resulting in better or worse health and well-being. In general, successful adaptation is associated with the use of active, problem-focused coping strategies, keeping one's emotions in manageable limits, and using cognitive strategies to reappraise the stressor as less threatening.

One of the confusing aspects of the literature on adaptation is that the term is used to describe both a *state* and a *process*. Thus, for most investigators, adaptation was used to refer to a level or state of well-being (and was measured on a continuum of low to high). Some researchers, however, used adaptation to refer to the overall processes in which individuals confront stressors or challenges and respond to them, with varying outcomes. In general, adaptation as a state was the focus of studies of role transitions. The coping literature was less clear-cut, and adaptation was used in both ways.

Studies of role transitions and their effects on the health and well-being of older adults remain a focus of gerontological research, although the volume of studies has decreased. Studies of widowhood, other bereavements, and retirement remain the focus of much of this research. Interest in the potential adaptive challenges of role *gain* in later life has emerged as well. Two role gains that have received substantial attention are (a) taking on caregiving responsibilities for an impaired older adult (e.g., Skaff & Pearlin, 1992) and (b) becoming surrogate parents for one's grandchildren (e.g., Szinovacz, DeViney, & Atkinson, 1999). Not surprisingly, these nonnormative, demanding roles are much more likely to lead to declines in well-being than more normative and/or predictable role transitions such as retirement.

Adaptation and Person-Environment Fit

Investigations of the effects of residential environments on the health and well-being of older adults has a long but intermittent history in social gerontology. Carp (1976), one of the pioneers in this area, referred to this research focus as environmental psychology. Her work and that of others in the 1970s and 1980s focused on the degree of "fit" between persons and their environments, taking into account the needs and capacities of individuals and the resources and demands of their environments. The theoretical importance and implications of person-environment fit were articulated by Lawton and Nahemow (1973). The person-environment fit perspective proved to be useful not only for assessing how well older individuals were faring in their environments but also for evaluating the effects of relocation to "enriched" environments (e.g., Moos, 1976; Moos & Lemke, 1994). Not surprisingly, when older persons moved to environments that met their needs, compensating for deficits in capacity, well-being improved. Throughout this research base, the term *adaptation* is used to refer to the fit between individuals and their environments.

Issues of environmental adaptation continue to be the focus of theory, basic understandings of the capacities of older adults, and the design and staffing of residential environments for older adults. Identification of the subjective functions of residential environments has been an important part of the history of this field. Carp (1976) first proposed that the two primary functions of residential environments are the provision of security and autonomy; that is, residents should have as much control as possible within the bounds of safety. Moos and Lemke (1994) provide the most sophisticated methods to date of assessing these environmental characteristics via their concept of *social climate*. Their research suggests that the well-being of older adults is maximized in environments in which autonomy, choice, and involvement are promoted to the extent possible—and this is as true for nursing home residents as it is for older adults living independently in the community. In this research literature, adaptation is a condition in which there is a "match" between the capacities of the individual and the physical and social climate of the residential environment.

Another useful variant of the person-environment fit perspective is the work of Paul Baltes and Margaret Baltes (Baltes, 1996; Baltes & Baltes, 1990). Their work focuses on frail and disabled older adults and the extent to which their environments can promote or protect against dependency. On the one hand, their work suggests that caregivers of the impaired elderly tend to promote dependency rather than sustain maximal independence; and the major route to excess dependency is via "messages" from caregivers that one is globally incompetent, rather than having deficits in selected areas. On the other hand, evaluations of carefully designed interventions demonstrate that it is possible for caregivers to meet the needs of impaired older adults while promoting as much independence as possible—a strategy that the Balteses term "selective optimization with compensation."

The Future of Adaptation

Conceptual precision is one hallmark of an established scientific domain. Thus, it is time to cease using the term *adaptation* as a synonym for subjective well-being or quality of life. Using the term in studies of role transitions and/or coping also has proved to have little advantage. Those research efforts have failed to generate a consensual and specific definition of adaptation. A strong case can be made, however, for restricting the term *adaptation* to the study of person-environment fit.

By linking it to person-environment fit, adaptation acquires a distinctive focus on the consequences of context, which differentiates it from concepts such as well-being and quality of life. Linking adaptation to person-environment fit also provides a temporal focus for future research. Understanding the joint effects of personal capacities and environmental characteristics on adaptation at a single point in time is important, providing a measure of current status. Taking a longitudinal view, changes in personal capacities can be related to individuals' decisions to change, modify, or remain in specific environments, and the effects of those decisions on adaptation can be determined. Thus, forging a distinctive conceptual identity for adaptation has the potential to reinvigorate the concept and apply it in research that can contribute to knowledge about the ways to optimize functioning and well-being in later life.

LINDA K. GEORGE

See also
   Coping
   Functional Age
   Life Events
   Social Stress and Life Events
   Stress and Stressors

ADAPTIVE CAPACITY

A major characteristic of living things is the ability to adapt to environmental changes. For example, upon perceiving a threat, mammals will incur an immediate activation of the sympathetic nervous system, which will stimulate heart and breathing rate in preparation for increased metabolic demands of fighting or fleeing. If the metabolic demand is actually activated (e.g., by running), heart and breathing rate will be further activated as long as the metabolic demand from the muscles continues. However, there are limits to the extent to which organisms can adapt. For example, each individual can sustain a maximum metabolic demand only at peak performance (such as during a sprint). In humans the maximum sustainable metabolic demand, constrained by a number of factors but especially by cardiovascular capacity, is often measured by the rate of oxygen consumed at maximum short-term effort on a treadmill (a parameter called VO_{2max}). Thus VO_{2max} constitutes a major indicator of the capacity of the cardiovascular system to adapt to short-term metabolic stress; thus VO_{2max} may be considered to reflect short-term adaptive capacity for metabolic demand. It is has been amply demonstrated that in healthy humans VO_{2max} decreases steadily during aging, about 9% per decade (Rosen, Sorkin, Goldberg, Hagberg, & Katzel, 1998).

On the other hand, short-term adaptive capacity can be modified by chronic stimulation, a phenomenon that may be termed long-term adaptive capacity. For example, repetitive aerobic exercise (e.g., endurance training at 70% VO_{2max} for 30 minutes three times per week for 12 weeks) enhances VO_{2max}, apparently by inducing remodeling of the cardiovascular system. The enhancement of VO_{2max} by chronic training appears to occur about as often in healthy elderly men as in younger men, and elderly master athletes exhibit higher VO_{2max} than do healthy elderly nontrained humans. Nevertheless, VO_{2max} decreases about as fast in athletes who are in training as in age-matched controls (although trained athletes continue to exhibit higher VO_{2max} than do nontrained healthy controls as they age). Furthermore, since the effect of age on VO_{2max} is substantially greater than the training effect on VO_{2max}, even though training can enhance VO_{2max} about as well in elderly as in younger individuals, this effect of training cannot completely reverse or prevent the reduction in VO_{2max} during aging (Trappe, Costill, Vukovich, Jones, & Melham, 1996).

Short-term and long-term adaptive capacity occur in response to many perturbations, including changes in temperature, altitude, diet, and many other environmental factors. In general, short-term adaptive capacity decreases with age. For example, a cold environment causes many physiological responses, including shivering and enhanced heat production, which allow maintenance of normal body temperature; these adaptations to cold are enhanced after chronic exposure to low temperature. As with VO_{2max} (and possibly related to this parameter), the ability to adapt to a cold environment is impaired with age (Anderson, Meneilly, & Mekjavic, 1996). However, chronic exposure to cold enhances adaptation to cold about as well in older as in younger individuals. Nevertheless, as with VO_{2max}, because the effect of age on cold tolerance is greater than the effect of chronic exposure to cold, chronic exposure to cold cannot fully reverse the effects of age on cold tolerance. This pattern of greater impairments of short-term than of long-term adaptive capacity is common for many responses to environmental perturbations.

An important but largely unresolved question is the physiological significance of adaptive capacity during aging under circumstances in which environmental fluctuations are minimal, as in the case of most human populations. The fact that the elderly are more likely to die of hyperthermia or hypothermia clearly indicates that in extreme circumstances impairments in short-term adaptive capacity can have profound effects. On the other hand, the vast majority of deaths during aging, either in human populations or in the laboratory, occur without major fluctuations in the environment. Nevertheless, VO_{2max} is closely related to cardiovascular health, suggesting that long-term adaptive capacity, which is less impaired during aging than short-term adaptive capacity, could play an important role in mediating effects of lifestyle on health and mortality during aging (Bortz & Bortz, 1996). Since long-term adaptive capacity is relatively intact during aging, and especially since short-term adaptive capacity seems to be intrinsically reduced during aging, training and other lifestyle changes may be at least as valuable in the elderly as in the young. Consistent with this principle, elderly individuals who maintain a lifelong engagement with intellectual stimulation exhibit fewer cognitive impairments than do nonengaged controls. While a training effect on age-related cognitive deficits has not yet been rigorously demonstrated, this question obviously is of great practical interest.

Adaptive capacity may reflect a fundamental process of aging. For example, long-lived lines of fruit flies and nematodes not only live longer but even when young are more resistant to the effects of numerous environmental stresses than are shorter-lived strains (Lin, Seroude, & Benzer, 1998). Thus, genetic influences on longevity also influence short-term adaptive capacity, suggesting that adaptive capacity may play an important role in age-related mortality even in benign environments.

CHARLES V. MOBBS

See also
    Adaptation
    Behavior Modification
    Biofeedback

ADHERENCE

When a physician prescribes a medication for a patient, an implied contract is made between the two—one requiring specific behaviors by both doctor and patient. The doctor must prescribe the correct drug in the proper dose, provide the patient with adequate instructions for its use and warnings about possible adverse effects, and monitor the patient's use of the drug to ensure a therapeutic outcome. The patient is expected to purchase the medication, take it as directed, and report to the physician any untoward side effects—in other words, to adhere to the doctor's instructions. For elderly patients, adherence may be particularly difficult, given their greater risk of adverse effects from medication.

Types of Nonadherence

Nonadherence (or noncompliance, as it is still sometimes called) can be classified as overuse, underuse, erratic use, and contraindicated (or inappropriate) use. Patients who overuse drugs either take more types of drugs than necessary, take more than the prescribed amount of one drug, or take a "prn" (i.e., take as needed) drug when it is not actually needed. Underuse includes the failure to have the prescription filled ("initial noncompliance"), the premature discontinuation of the drug, and the consistent failure to take as much of the drug as the doctor ordered. Erratic use means that the patient generally fails to follow instructions. This type includes missed doses (underuse), double doses

(overuse), and drug confusion, which is taking the wrong drug by mistake or taking doses at the wrong time, by the wrong route of administration, or with the wrong liquid. Contraindicated drug use occurs when the patient takes a drug that is inappropriate either because it is unnecessary or potentially harmful. This can occur when the older patient self-medicates incorrectly or when the physician prescribes the wrong drug—one that is ineffective, produces a harmful or unwanted side effect, or interacts negatively with other medications being taken, food, or alcohol. Obviously, these four types of nonadherence are not mutually exclusive, and the older patient may engage in more than one at a time.

Most researchers agree that the failure to take medications (underuse) is by far the most common type of nonadherence, generally comprising over half of all reported instances (e.g., Gurwitz, Glynn, Monane, Everitt, Gilden, Smith, et al., 1993). Although underuse can have serious consequences for a person for whom the medication is necessary for control of a dangerous condition, it is probably the safest form of misuse for those who take psychotropic medications and many of those on multiple drug regimens. This behavior has been termed intelligent noncompliance.

Shimp and Ascione (1988) have differentiated between unintentional nonadherence, when the patient merely forgets a dose or gets confused about how or when to take it, and intentional nonadherence, which occurs when the patient deliberately alters the dose or the timing or chooses not take it at all. Evidence suggests that intentional nonadherence may be more common with up to 30% of prescriptions never even filled by the patient. A majority of older patients state that they would discontinue taking a drug that they felt was not working and self-medicators will stop using a drug or use less because they do not like the drug, the dosage, the side effects, or the cost, or they get better results by taking it their way.

Extent of Nonadherence

It is extremely difficult to estimate how often physicians do not live up to their responsibilities under the doctor-patient contract; the consensus is that the failure rate is quite high (Simonson, 1994). We have somewhat better data on the patient's side of the bargain. Nonadherence is, of course, a problem in patients of all ages. Early researchers suggested that nonadherence is particularly likely among elderly persons, because it is known to correlate highly with several factors common to old age, including chronic illness, multiple prescription drugs, social isolation, and mental confusion. Later reviews of adherence studies, however (e.g., Simonson, 1984), concluded that no clear evidence exists of any relationship between age and adherence. Simonson (1984) reports that researchers have estimated that nonadherence by the elderly ranges from 2% to 95%. Most studies place the proportion of older people who admit some nonadherence in taking prescription drugs at around 40%–60% (Botelho & Dudrak, 1992), although many instances probably are not therapeutically significant.

Nevertheless, Ascione (1994) argues that nonadherence in an older person is likely to have much more serious consequences than in a younger individual because of the elder's greater likelihood of serious illness and comorbidity. The results of nonadherence in older persons include failure to recover, aggravation of the condition, hospitalization, and the addition of medications to treat the supposed intractable symptoms. So far, few investigators have attended to sex or race differences in adherence, though some findings suggest that they may exist (Bazargan, Barbre, & Hamm, 1993; Kail, 1992).

Causes of Nonadherence

Many factors can contribute to nonadherence among older persons. Simonson (1984) has organized them into three main groups: those related to the patient, to therapy, and to the health professional. Patient-related causes include failure to understand the importance of therapy; misunderstanding the doctor's instructions; self-medication; not feeling well; physical disabilities, including sensory losses; and lack of supervision. Factors associated with the therapy itself include the number of drugs prescribed, the frequency of doses, difficult dosage forms, adverse drug reactions, and the expense of medications. Health professionals, including physicians, nurses, and pharmacists, also

can precipitate nonadherence in their elderly patients by failing to establish a good relationship with the patient, expressing doubt about the drug's efficacy, and being unwilling to spend time educating patients. Using a different organization scheme, Ascione (1994) lists the contributing factors as (1) complexity of the drug regimen; (2) the patient's poor drug knowledge; (3) the patient's physical limitations (especially sensory losses); (4) poor communication between professional and patient; and (5) psychosocial characteristics of the patient, such as health beliefs and social isolation.

Some researchers (e.g., Morrell, Park, Kidder, & Martin, 1997) have suggested poor cognitive function, especially memory problems and the inability to understand complex medical instructions, as a possible cause of nonadherence in older people. Research so far seems to show that both memory and visual perception can affect adherence, at least among the oldest-old, and that various memory aids can improve adherence (Morrow, Hier, Menard, & Leirer, 1998). On the other hand, nonadherence is patient-initiated and represents a majority of older people's attempt to control their own therapy. Thus, it seems likely that cognitive deficits are a significant cause of nonadherence for older persons who suffer such losses but may have little or no effect on the vast majority of elders.

Older people are at risk of nonadherence due to many factors outside their control, including their own health status, the number and types of drugs they are prescribed, the failure of therapeutic instructions, health care organization costs, and social isolation. In fact, nonadherence can create significant problems for elderly persons (Ascione, 1994), but many writers (e.g., Simonson, 1994) agree that, compared with the inability of health care professionals to prescribe and administer drugs properly and to monitor their use by older patients, nonadherence is relatively less troublesome.

Reducing Noncompliance

Ascione (1994) aptly summarizes what little is known about reducing nonadherence among older persons: "What appears most successful is a comprehensive approach that assesses the individual needs of the patient, uses multiple strategies . . . , and incorporates a medication monitoring system to give continual feedback to the patient." He groups the strategies developed so far as dissemination of drug information, simplification of the administration process, and teaching medication management skills.

FRANK J. WHITTINGTON

See also
Doctor-Patient Relationships

ADIPOSE TISSUE
See
Biology of Fat in Aging, The
Body Composition
Obesity

ADRENAL CORTEX
See
Sodium Balance and Osmolarity Regulation

ADULT DAY CARE

Adult day care has been defined as follows: "Adult day services are community-based group programs designed to meet the needs of functionally and/or cognitively impaired adults through an individual plan of care. These structured, comprehensive programs provide a variety of health, social, and other related services in a protective setting during any part of a day, but less than 24-hour care" (National Adult Day Services Association, 1999). Centers vary greatly in the services provided, most including therapeutic activities, meals, and personal care and others providing or arranging for nursing care, social services, rehabilitation therapies, counseling, and transportation. Adult day care regulations differ widely across states and funding sources. The National Adult Day Services Association (NADSA), a unit of the National Council on Aging, has developed "Standards and Guidelines" (1997) designed to assist states that license these programs. The Commission on Accreditation of Rehabilitation Facilities (CARF) conducts voluntary accreditation

at the request of the programs. Adult day centers are not reimbursed by Medicare, and funding sources vary from state to state, including private pay, philanthropic support, Medicaid, other state programs, and private long-term care insurance.

The most recent national survey was conducted by NADSA in 1997. They sent questionnaires to 4,000 programs that appeared to be adult day centers, receiving unduplicated responses from 1,699 centers that are now entered into the NADSA directory, with 1,653 reported to be adult day services centers. The characteristics of these centers as reported in this survey are as follows: 90% are nonprofit; most are affiliated with another service agency; the average number of enrollees is 39, of daily attendees, 22; and the average daily rate is $43.

NADSA serves as an important resource for programs, providing the "Standards and Guidelines," training manuals and videos, a staff certification process, national conferences, a website and newsletter, and a nation advocacy role (NADSA, The National Council on Aging, Inc., 409 Third Street SW, Suite 200, Washington, DC 20024. *www.ncoa.org/nadsa).*

Another resource is Partners in Caregiving: The Adult Day Services Program. This program is conducted by the Wake Forest University School of Medicine and funded by the Robert Wood Johnson Foundation. This program is designed to provide technical assistance on a national level to improve adult day care programs' financial viability and quality of care through such programs as mobile adult day services colleges, a teaching day center, a hotline, a website, and a newsletter. (Partners in Caregiving, Wake Forest University School of Medicine, Medical Center Boulevard, Winston-Salem, NC 27157-1087.)

Evaluations of Program Effectiveness

There have been a number of nonrandomized evaluations of outcomes for caregivers associated with adult day care programs, which have found mixed results (Henry & Capitman, 1995; Strain, Chappell, & Blandford, 1988; Zarit, Stephens, Townsend, & Greene, 1998). Problems in the design of these studies threaten the validity of the findings and limit their generalizability to other settings and patient populations. Six studies assessing the effects of adult day care on a wide range of both patient and caregiver outcomes using more rigorous, randomized designs have been reported. Two of these studies (Tucker, Davison, & Ogle, 1984; Weissert, Wan, Livieratos, & Katz, 1980) found some positive effects on health status; four studies (Cummings, Kerner, Arones, & Steinbock, 1985; Eagle, Guyatt, Patterson, Turpie, Sackett, & Singer, 1991; Engedal, 1989; Hedrick, Rothman, Chapko, Ehreth, Diehr, Inui, et al., 1993) found no such effects. Of the five studies that measured effects on the costs of care, one (Engedal, 1989) found that patients with dementia served in an adult day care program in Norway had reduced costs of care, a study of day hospital care demonstrated equal costs (Cummings et al., 1985), and three studies found that patients using adult day care services had increased overall costs of care (Hedrick et al., 1993; Tucker et al., 1984; Weissert et al., 1980).

In the most recent systematic review, Forster, Young, and Langhorne (1999) reviewed 12 controlled trials of day hospital care, defined as "an outpatient facility where older patients attend for a full or near full day and receive multidisciplinary rehabilitation in a health care setting." This review included many of the studies described above and some additional international studies, primarily focused on centers providing rehabilitation of patients with strokes. It did not include studies without adequate designs, studies of social day care programs, or day hospitals exclusively for patients with dementia or psychiatric or other single conditions. It was found that overall there were no significant differences between day hospital and alternative care programs in any outcome studied, including death, disability, and use of resources. Of the eight trials reporting costs, six reported that day hospital care was more expensive, and two reported that the costs were similar.

The largest and most comprehensive study was an evaluation of the effectiveness of adult day health care at eight Department of Veterans Affairs Medical Centers (Hedrick, Rothman, Chapko, Ehreth, Diehr, Inui, et al., 1993). Patients at enrollment met criteria based on characteristics of patients at risk for nursing home placement and were served in VA medical centers or on contract in the community. The study compared patients assigned to receive adult day health care to those receiving usual care on multiple outcomes, including patients' physical and psychosocial health status; the informal caregiver's physical and psychosocial health status; patient and caregiver satisfaction with care; patient utilization of health care; and the costs of services, including nursing homes, hospitals, outpatient care, out-of-pocket costs, and caregiver time costs. One year after enrollment, adult day health care patients and their caregivers had the same health status outcomes but significantly higher health care costs than those assigned to usual care.

Options for program revision in light of the results of these and other studies of community-based long-term care include (1) targeting adult day health care to those types of patients who may be most likely to benefit, (2) further exploration of innovative models for enhancing individualized care in a group setting, and (3) reducing the costs of services through increasing enrollment, reducing staffing costs, decreasing length of stay, and increasing substitution of adult day health care for other services (Capitman, 1993; Hedrick, Chapko, Ehreth, Rothman, Kelly, & Inui, 1993; Weissert & Hedrick, 1994, 1999).

SUSAN C. HEDRICK

See also
　　Home and Community-Based Care
　　Home Health Care
　　Nursing Homes

ADULT DEVELOPMENT

A classic perspective on development, one appropriate to all points of the life course, was expressed by Werner (1967): "Wherever development occurs it proceeds from a state of relative globality and lack of differentiation to a state of increasing differentiation, articulation, and hierarchical integration" (p. 126). This perspective suggests that both direction and an end point are implicit to the concept.

The research of child specialists such as Piaget, Loevinger, and Kohlberg, insofar as it charts changes in the early years of life, reveals the progressive unfolding of characteristics central to Werner's supposition. When attention turns to studies of adults, on the other hand, evidence for universal and systematic change becomes far less convincing. Some researchers, indeed, have suggested that because change in adulthood and aging often does not proceed in systematic fashion, there is no such thing as adult development.

Evidence to support the lack of developmental progression during the adult years comes primarily from the fact that few if any studies have demonstrated the kind of invariance and progression suggested by any of the stage theories of adulthood. Evidence for consistencies and development is generally found when the focus of attention lies in particular social and personal attributes of individuals (e.g., Atchley, 1999). For example, personal attributes such as the self-concept demonstrate highly significant correlations over periods of 10 or more years (e.g., McCrae, Costa, Ostendorf, Angleitner, Hrebickova, Avia, et al., 2000).

Models of Development

Nearly all studies of adult development have addressed, either directly or indirectly, the question of whether people show evidence of systematic progression over time. One school of thought emphasizes the stability of personal characteristics such as personality. As William James (1950) once stated, by the age of 30 an individual's personality "has set like plaster and will never soften again" (p. 121). On the opposing side are those who suggest that the pace and fragmentation of modern life is a destabilizing force.

Research evidence for or against stability is inconclusive, even though the results consistently point in the direction of greater stability. In part the lack of definite answers is due to the length of time required to provide evidence of stability. There also are few studies that cover the period extending from childhood or adolescence to later life, the same instruments are rarely used across studies, and social scientists sometimes resort to highly inferential strategies to impute stability or change.

Another reason for the continuing lack of closure in stability research may be that we have simply been asking the wrong questions. It is probably not a matter of whether there is any evidence *for* stability, because there usually is. At issue is how much stability exists across personal characteristics and what circumstances promote or hinder stability.

Perhaps more important, what is the significance of being stable or demonstrating change?

Templates of Development

As a means of addressing questions of stability and change, it is helpful to consider the ways in which various types of developmental theories evaluate evidence for or against stability in personal functioning. From a historical perspective, studies of development in middle and later life have generally followed one of three underlying models of development. As outlined by Gergen (1982), the most widely used of these models emphasizes stability in development. According to the classic psychoanalytic perspective, as presented by Freud, for example, the trajectory of personal development becomes relatively fixed by the age of 5 or 6 years. Those who employ a stability model tend to view change after the early years as a reflection of continued development of established characteristics, as measurement error, or as arising from factors such as dementia or mental illness.

At present, there is a resurgence of interest in the stability of personality and behavior over the adult life course. Given the extensive evidence that has accrued in support of stability, it is not surprising that the past 10 years has seen a renewed interest in what used to be called "trait" psychology.

A somewhat different orientation can be found in Gergen's (1982) second model, which emphasizes not stability but an orderly pattern of change. Theories following this model view development as a progression of orderly and perhaps invariant changes over time. This is another way of saying that they often are stage theories, one of the most popular ways of conceptualizing development. A more promising variant is to seek regularities or "lawfulness" in behavior by considering variability in social and personal behavior across multiple situations as well as over time (e.g., Lang, Featherman, & Nesselroade, 1997).

There is, finally, a more recently developed model that emphasizes the role of chance in our lives. Labeled the Random Change model, its central thesis is that human beings run out of genetic programming by late adolescence. Thereafter, the role of chance factors, such as exposure to major stress conditions or transitions, becomes more important as a shaper of personality. Support for this model can be found in longitudinal studies that have included stress conditions (e.g., Holahan, Moos, & Holahan, 1999). From the mainstream of psychological research, the research of Mischel and Shoda (1999) also emphasizes the importance of the situational context in determining levels of stability in personal attributes. And although no well-formulated theories of personality have yet been developed that follow this model, several researchers are taking active steps (e.g., Elder, 1999).

Although the three templates or models of change presented above are not inherently contradictory to each other, they are often treated that way by their adherents. That is, they are often treated as if only one model could hold true, so evidence against the favored model is often dismissed or reinterpreted. Encouragingly, theorists are now beginning to integrate the concepts integral to the templates (e.g., Gubrium & Holstein, 1999, Settersten, 1999).

Adult Development: Progression or Diversion?

One disquieting aspect of research on adult development is that very little of it seems to support the theories that have been proposed. The lack of evidence to support stage theories of personality development during adulthood is just one example.

What the evidence does suggest is that the personal and social characteristics associated with purported stages of development exist and often represent fundamental aspects of human existence. Take, for example, Erikson's (1982) portrayal of ego integrity as the last stage in his epigenetic sequence. One individual may become immersed in issues related to self-acceptance quite early in life, perhaps as a result of an "off-schedule" confrontation with death or following religious conversion. Another may have achieved ego integrity in a "timely" fashion, only to find his or her entire worldview shifted as a result of dramatically changed life circumstances. The situational context, in short, may exert a strong influence not only on the stability but also on the unfolding of this attribute.

The lack of research support for stage theories, it should be emphasized, does not necessarily mean that such theories should be ignored. One area for

future research involves a melding of the three underlying models of development, those involving stability, orderly change and random change. Studies of what some call developmental contextualism, which bring into place the person and the context, are an exciting step in this direction.

DAVID A. CHIRIBOGA

See also
Developmental Tasks
Life Course
Life Events

ADULT EDUCATION

Education of older people is primarily an offshoot of the adult education movement—a movement as old as the nation itself, with roots in the social, cultural, and political concerns of the time. Educational programs for older persons today reflect this history and heritage, involving a wide variety of formats and purposes.

This instruction includes heterogeneity of sponsors, program types, audiences, and content. No central system supports or monitors these activities, so idiosyncratic patterns have developed around the preferences of administrators and the needs of local communities. This has frequently made the programs responsive to the wishes of the constituent clientele but has neither facilitated development of program categories nor provided much assistance in generating program models that can be replicated in other sites and with other sponsors.

One of the earliest comprehensive surveys of educational programs for older people (Donahue, 1955) indicated wide availability of instructional offerings by the mid-1950s; it suggested that older people were not the primary audience but were included in programs designed originally for other age groups. Later, these programs were modified to make them more appealing and more specifically oriented toward older people.

The 1960s involved the inclusion of programs in a greater number of agencies and institutions. The 1961 White House Conference on Aging gave an impetus to this growth by increasing the visibility and emphasizing the growing social concern for older persons. Instructional efforts for older people took on a social service orientation (Moody, 1976), emphasizing the crisis of adjustment to retirement and the need for outside assistance to overcome the trauma of role change. Program rationales emphasized the needs of older people and the responsibility of social institutions to meet these needs through service programs.

A shift from a social service orientation can be noted in the background paper to the 1971 White House Conference on Aging. In it, McClusky (1971) accurately reflected the new orientation when he emphasized the positive nature of education and the potential of every person, regardless of age.

A major development beginning in the 1970s was the rapid growth of residential education for older persons. Through the Elderhostel program, weeklong courses of instruction, field visits, and entertainment were provided by colleges and universities across the nation. The response to this offering has proved that a combination of stimulating atmosphere, congenial company, and varied activities is both desired and appreciated by older people.

Another example of a program designed for the well-educated senior can be seen in the Institutes for Retired Professionals. These programs draw retired teachers, professionals, and community leaders into study programs that are administered and taught by older persons.

The 1981 White House Conference on Aging emphasized a theme that is rapidly growing in the United States—self-help. In relating this theme of older people and education, the emphasis has been placed on the development of instructional programs that will result in increased problem-solving abilities, especially those that can be used in the workplace or in volunteer roles.

The federal government has encouraged employers, state governments, and community organizations to offer instruction that will assist older persons in holding or gaining contributive roles in the community. A number of job placement programs, many using the name Second Careers, are being created in major cities, and instruction in job search skills, self-concept, and specific content is growing.

Technological developments are increasingly being used for instruction of older learners. Net-works of computer users (e.g., E-mail distribution lists, list servers), videotapes on exercise or skills development, local access television programming, extensive information on CD-ROM and the World Wide Web, two-way video workshops, and televised classes are all available to adults desiring to learn or to pursue a degree but who are not able or interested in traveling to a campus to attend lecture classes.

Educational programs for older people in the United States have developed to such a point that we can now begin to gain some perspective on their growth and to identify several implications for the future. Three will be mentioned. First, there now seems to be general acceptance that we are living in a learning society, in which persons of every age will be required to continue to expand their knowledge and skills in order to survive and prosper. Community colleges, public schools, universities, libraries, museums, recreation centers, clubs, senior centers, department stores, and corporations are offering instruction in a broad and rapidly growing variety of topics (Peterson, 1983).

Second, there is now general acceptance that a multipurpose rationale for the conduct of educational programs for older people exists. No longer do the purpose statements of instructional programs deal only with the difficulties and crises of old age; now they frequently emphasize the ability that persons have to grow and develop throughout their lives. Older persons are seen as individuals with potential who can contribute and serve as well as cope and survive. This change in orientation has led to many more programs on self-actualization and growth. Liberal studies, psychological growth, and broadening experience are becoming a greater part of the programs, and lifelong planning is replacing adjustment to retirement.

Finally, as the enrollment of older persons increases, institutions that have simply encouraged older people to participate in their regular programs are beginning to develop special offerings exclusively for them. As this occurs, recognition of the need to accommodate the unique characteristics of older people has developed. It is now apparent that they will often not accept the bureaucratic procedures of admission, advisement, and registration that younger students have tolerated. They need adaptations that will make these administrative processes more streamlined and abbreviated. Likewise, they expect educational content and method to be developed to suit their interests and preferences. As institutions begin to understand these needs, major modifications of the usual administrative and instructional procedures will be demanded.

The growth of the number of older students is leading to increased interest in their learning abilities and classroom performance. Researchers and academics are quantitatively and qualitatively examining various issues related to both participation and outcomes of adult learning. For example, gender and cultural issues (Guy, 1999; Williamson, 2000) and method of instruction (Spigner-Littles & Anderson, 1999) are variables being examined. The continuing development of knowledge about the older person as a learner will be helpful not only in the educational institutions but in a variety of community settings where assistance to older people is provided and where their talents are needed for the good of the community (such as serving members of other generations and taking leadership positions in community organizations). Older learners tend to be highly motivated, organized, and determined.

Elderhostel is a major national and international resource in adult education. For more information on the Elderhostel program, visit their website: *www.Elderhostel.org.*

DAVID A. PETERSON
UPDATED BY CATHERINE J. TOMPKINS

See also
Institutes for Learning in Retirement

ADULT FOSTER CARE

Although definitions differ across jurisdictions, Adult foster care (AFC), or adult family care, typically refers to a *community-based residence* that houses no more than about six nonrelated individuals (typically one to three) with a private family or individual for supportive care. AFC generally provides 24-hour supervision, housekeeping, meals, personal care, sociability, and transportation. The care can range from minimal assistance with daily living tasks to skilled nursing care. AFC can be distinguished from group homes or hostels, which are generally staffed by professionals or

paraprofessionals and attempt to be more therapeutic. Typically, AFC has been more supportive and better supervised than unlicensed board and care homes. AFC also differs from assisted living, shared housing, and community residence programs. AFC has been used for the frail or cognitively impaired elderly and for persons with mental retardation, mental illness, or alcoholism. Specific programs have targeted Alzheimer's disease patients, persons with HIV/AIDS, and the homeless. Even among persons with mental illness or mental retardation, AFC populations tend to be older.

History and Current Trends

Although AFC has been designated specifically for the elderly only relatively recently, the practice of taking unrelated dependent adults into one's home has occurred for centuries in Europe (Sherman & Newman, 1988). AFC has dual origins in almshouses for the poor elderly and in community care for the mentally ill. Early development of AFC in this country may be traced to the influence of the English Poor Laws in the colonies: unrelated families provided food, shelter, and care to aged and helpless poor and were reimbursed from public funds. Development continued with public foster family care programs for mentally ill adults in the nineteenth century, boardinghouses in the late 19th and early 20th centuries, boardinghomes for the elderly in the 1930s and 1940s, foster family care for adults with mental retardation in the 1930s, proprietary rest homes during the Depression, the deinstitutionalization movement, and Title XX services in 1975.

AARP has published a survey study of 26 states with AFC programming, demonstrating variations across states in size, percentage of elderly, sponsorship, and supervision. The most recent development is growth of nonprofit agency (including hospitals), corporate, or partnership ownership of AFC, though the majority of homes are still family owned and operated (Folkemer, Jensen, Lipson, Stauffer, & Fox-Grage, 1996). Debate continues as to the benefits of each model.

Sponsorship and Management

AFC programs may be supervised and sponsored by public agencies such as state or local (regional, district, county) departments of social services, aging, health, mental health, mental retardation/ developmental disabilities, the Department of Veterans Affairs (VA), or hospitals and other voluntary agencies or institutions. A single program may be supervised by different agencies for licensure, placement, and ongoing supervision. Service provision by outside providers, such as day care (Folkemer, Jensen, Lipson, Stauffer, & Fox-Grage, 1996), continues to supplement the owner's provision, and programs have recognized the need for respite services for the provider. AFC is paid for through Supplemental Security Income (SSI), and state supplements to SSI, Medicaid waivers, other public funds, or private resources, such as Social Security, VA, and other pensions.

Care Providers

Foster care providers are frequently recruited informally through other providers, friends, kin, church and other informal organizations, as well as newspapers, television, and radio public service announcements. At present there is a shortage of providers in several states (Folkemer, Jensen, Lipson, Stauffer, & Fox-Grage, 1996). Providers tend to be in their 50s, with somewhat more than half married. Some providers have had previous health care experience.

Training

Care providers should be trained both before placement and during service. Training can be offered to groups of providers and to individual providers during home visits. Frequent topics include legal issues, budgeting and management, home safety, accident prevention, emergency care, personal hygiene, nutrition, medication, exercise, and use of community resources. Various levels of training can be provided for different levels of resident impairment.

Placement and Case Management

Placement involves *matching resident and provider preferences* as to age, gender, race, religion and religiosity, rural/urban location, sociocultural inter-

ests, presence of children in the home, and special needs of residents. Reinardy and Kane (1999) found that foster care residents perceived a greater sense of personal control in their decision to move than did nursing home (NH) residents. Case management may be provided by a multidisciplinary team, including physician, nurse, nurse practitioner, social worker, recreation therapist, and rehabilitation counselor (Tobin, 1999). The case manager must balance protection of the resident with an avoidance of overregulation that would detract from the qualities of a family. Folkemer, Jensen, Lipson, Stauffer, and Fox-Grage (1996) recommend more development of outcome-based assessment.

Strengths and Weaknesses

Although there has been less research on AFC than on other options in long-term care, several strengths have been demonstrated. First is its informality, sociability, and spontaneity. Sherman and Newman (1988) found that *familism* (affection, social interaction, minimal social distance, and ritual) characterized about two-thirds of the homes they studied, and familism was more frequently reported between provider and resident than among residents themselves (Skruch & Sherman, 1995). AFC offers family and a meaningful role for the care provider, who otherwise might be living alone.

A second strength of AFC is integration with the community and in particular with providers' networks of kin, friends, and neighbors. *Community acceptance* has been shown to be high because the provider is part of the community and private homes are less obtrusive than are institutions. Residents' level of community participation was found to be related to that of the provider. AFC residents are more likely than those in other settings to go outside the residence for community activities and resources.

Third, AFC provides a balance between support and independence for the frail elderly, offering the flexibility of increasing challenge as the resident improves or increasing support as the resident declines. This permits long-term stays, with many residents remaining until death, thus avoiding or delaying the more costly option of nursing facilities.

Resident outcome research presents conflicting findings. Stark, Kane, Kane, and Finch (1995) found greater decline in physical functioning when

AFC residents were compared to NH residents but suggested that the AFC resident might be willing to balance autonomy and freedom to take risks in a homelike environment against greater physical functioning.

With regard to weaknesses, some have suggested that it is more difficult to monitor these small homes, dispersed in the community, although there appear to have been far fewer abuses than in other community alternatives. To recruit the necessary complement of providers, it may be necessary to increase reimbursement, particularly for difficult clients. Because these homes cannot offer the same level of formal or organized activities that an institution can, there is a need to access and depend on community resources for extrafamilial social integration. Finally, questions have been raised about the staff/resident ratio and the lack of professionalism of the caregivers.

Conclusion

Concomitant with the growing numbers of frail elderly, there has been an increasing interest in AFC to delay or avoid institutionalization. Since the 1994 edition of the *Encyclopedia of Aging* we have witnessed the growth of the National Adult Family Care Organization, which has an annual meeting and is working toward national standards for adult foster family care. AFC is particularly useful for persons without family members to provide care or for those whose family members themselves are infirm, in the work force, or geographically distant. It is thought to be cost-effective and to offer social and health benefits. With the *flexibility* inherent in the model and with optimal placement, training, and support, AFC offers opportunities for a wide range of older adults.

Susan R. Sherman

See also
Home and Community-Based Care

ADULT PROTECTIVE SERVICES

Early Years

The need of older persons for adult protective services (APS) was first articulated as a social problem

in 1953 by the American Public Welfare Association and reaffirmed by Congress in the enactment of the 1962 Public Welfare Amendments to the Social Security Act. According to a handbook released by the U.S. Department of Health, Education, and Welfare (Lehmann, 1967), persons in need of protective services were "those who because of physical or mental limitations are unable to act in their own behalf; are seriously limited in the management of their affairs; are neglected or exploited; or, are living in unsafe or hazardous conditions" (p. 12). Three years later, the act was again amended to authorize payments to "others" acting on behalf of those incapable of managing their own affairs.

Throughout this period and until 1972, a series of federally funded demonstration projects, under both private and public auspices, was conducted to determine the nature, need, organization, clientele, and effectiveness of protective services. In a review of the project findings, Anetzberger (1994) noted several themes common to the projects:

- potential use of legal authority and the importance of accessing a wide array of services;
- emphasis on safety over client autonomy in intervention;
- identification of "protective clients" as those adults whose deteriorated mental or physical capacity made them unable to protect themselves or their interests; and
- need for clear lines of authority, generous and flexible funding, multidisciplinary diagnosis, specific client-oriented service goals, and a social worker in the leadership position.

Although these projects furnished information for the first time on many aspects of protective service delivery, serious questions about program effectiveness were raised (Hornby, 1982). The Benjamin Rose Institute found that the intervention in their cases neither prevented deterioration nor improved the mental and physical competence of clients but did increase the likelihood of institutionalization and the possible risk of death (Blenkner, Bloom, & Nielson, 1971).

Despite the findings, proponents for expansion of the protective service programs were successful in obtaining the passage of Title XX of the Social Security Act in 1974, which mandated and funded protective services for all adults 18 years and older without regard for income. By 1977 most states were providing APS under Title XX, either through their departments of public welfare (human services) or under contract to other public and private agencies. Only a few, however, had passed specific APS legislation. Gradually, the program came under criticism because of its questionable effectiveness, high cost of providing the service, potential for infringement of civil rights, and stigma of public welfare, and further development came to a halt (Anetzberger, 1994).

Elder Abuse

Within a few years, the fate of APS changed. Testimony about "parent battering" at a 1978 congressional subcommittee hearing on family violence and subsequent reports and investigations alerted the nation and the media to the "new" problem of *elder abuse*. Because cases of abused elders were already being handled by APS and covered under APS laws, it was not necessary to create a new system to serve them. Reconceptualizing the problem from "adults in need of protective services" to "victims of elder abuse, neglect, and exploitation" gave new life to the APS movement. Most states responded by amending their APS laws or passing new statutes, incorporating a *mandatory reporting* provision as was done with child abuse.

Service Delivery

If a state program operates under an APS statute, it is generally limited to "incapacitated" or "vulnerable" adults, leaving other agencies, such as the police, legal services, and the criminal justice system, to handle situations involving more competent and physically able persons. Conversely, programs authorized under elder abuse legislation usually apply to any older individual who is at risk of abuse, neglect, or exploitation. Some states restrict their cases to persons living in their own homes; others include group and institutional settings as well.

The state systems also vary in their administrative structures. Although most programs are state-administered (e.g., Texas and Tennessee), some are county-operated with state supervision or coordina-

tion (e.g., California, South Carolina, and Wisconsin). Most APS programs are placed within the state's department of human services, which may include both aging and adult services. In 27 states, the state unit on aging has assumed responsibility for the protection of adults 60 years and older.

When a call is made to APS, it is screened for potential seriousness. If mistreatment is suspected or the safety of an individual is threatened, an investigation is conducted by a caseworker. Should the situation be an emergency, the investigation must be done within a few hours. On the basis of a comprehensive assessment that includes physical, psychological, social, environmental, and financial components, a care plan is developed and, if agreeable to the individuals involved, the services are provided.

In most states once the abuse or neglect situation has been addressed, the case is turned over to other community agencies for ongoing case management and services delivery if needed. Most funds supporting these activities in the states still come from the federal government under Title XX of the Social Security Act, now the Social Service Block Grant program. However, the states with the more highly developed programs use additional state appropriations or county tax dollars.

Reported Cases

Because of the great variability in state laws regarding definitions and eligibility criteria, national incidence statistics cannot be directly obtained from state reporting data. The National Center on Elder Abuse estimated the number of elder abuse reports received by APS to be 293,000 in 1996, of which 62.4% were substantiated (Tatara & Kusmeskus, 1997). Of the latter group, 31.7% was "self-neglect" and 25.4% was "abuse by others." (The remaining 4% was not categorized.)

In 1998 the National Center on Elder Abuse released the results of a national elder abuse incidence study utilizing a "sentinel" approach (NCEA, 1998). In 20 randomly selected counties information on new cases was obtained from the local APS agency and a specifically trained group of individuals (termed sentinels) drawn from agencies that ordinarily serve older people, such as hospitals and clinics, law enforcement agencies, senior citizen programs, and banking institutions. The study estimated that 551,011 persons aged 60 and over experienced abuse, neglect, and/or self-neglect in domestic settings nationwide in 1996. Of this total, 70,942 were reported to and substantiated by APS agencies; the remaining 378,982 were not reported to APS but were identified by the sentinels. For every case reported to APS, five cases were not reported.

Rights and Responsibility

Even though APS has gained greater visibility and credibility in the past decade, it is still a controversial area of service. The emphasis on individual safety over client autonomy, which was evident a quarter of a century ago, is no longer the rule. Today, the client's right to *self-determination* is paramount. When a competent, abused, neglected, or exploited person refuses services, the APS worker has to withdraw from the case, often to the dismay of friends, neighbors, and other professionals who believe the health and property of the person to be in danger. If a case involves an incompetent individual, court action may be required, often resulting in the client's losing all rights.

New Directions

The 1990s was a period marked by the realignment of APS programs in state human services departments; refinement of APS due process statutes; proliferation of APS curricula for workers, law enforcement personnel, and bank employees; participation of APS in community-wide coalitions; and formation of the National Association of Adult Protective Services Administrators. On the agenda for the new century will be the development of best practice standards for casework intervention; identification and application of successful models of cooperative community approaches; establishment of basic ethical principles for APS workers; and creation of a culturally competent workforce. Underlying all these activities is the commitment to preserve the dignity and security of the older client.

ROSALIE S. WOLF

See also
    Elder Abuse and Neglect
    Guardianship/Conservatorship

Legal Services
Proxy Decision Making

ADVANCE DIRECTIVES IN HEALTH CARE
See
    Living Wills and Durable Power of Attorney
    Proxy Decision Making

ADVANCED GLYCATION END-PRODUCTS

As we age, the long-lived proteins in our body become gradually browner, more fluorescent, more highly cross-linked and less soluble. These changes are most apparent in the lens of the eye, which becomes visibly yellow and brown with age, interfering with the transparency of the lens and color vision. Similar changes occur in collagen, the major structural protein of the body, found in skin and tendons and in the basement membranes of the kidneys, arteries, and other tissues. The gradual browning and cross-linking of arterial collagen is associated with the age-dependent decrease in elasticity and compliance of the arterial wall. These age-related changes in tissue proteins are thought to result, in part, from nonenzymatic reactions between proteins and reducing sugars in extracellular fluids. In 1984, Anthony Cerami and colleagues introduced the term *advanced glycation end-product* (AGE) to describe the class of products irreversibly formed by chemical reactions between sugars and proteins. The term *AGE* is a play on words—AGEs accumulate with age. They are involved in the chemical aging of tissue proteins and contribute to the age-dependent chemical modification and cross-linking of tissue proteins.

The chemistry of "AGEing" reactions in vivo is similar to that of Maillard, or browning, reactions that occur during the cooking of foods and enhance their color, taste, and aroma. One of the first steps in this reaction is the condensation of a reducing sugar with an amino group in protein, yielding a Schiff base (imine) adduct, which then undergoes an Amadori rearrangement to form a ketoamine adduct to the protein (Figure 1). This process of addition of a sugar to a protein is known as nonenzy-

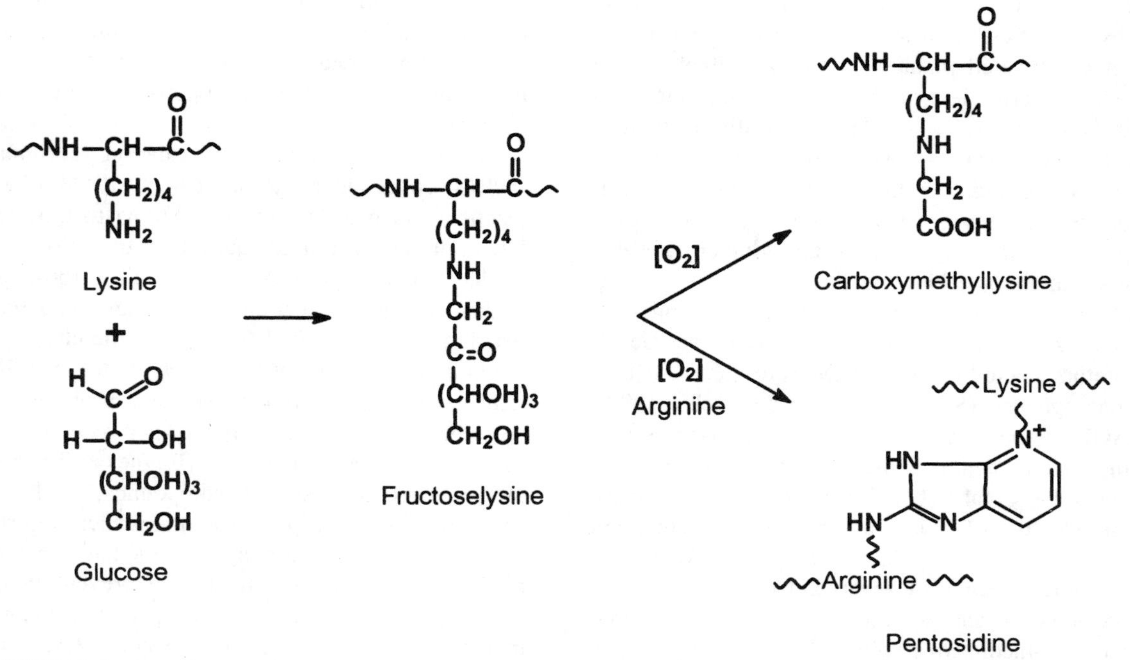

FIGURE 1 Reaction of lysine with glucose to form the Amadori compound, fructoselysine, the primary glucose adduct on glycated proteins. Fructoselysine is oxidized to form AGEs, for example, by oxidative cleavage to form carboxymethyllysine or by oxidative reaction with arginine to form pentosidine.

matic glycosylation, or glycation, of protein. The Amadori product is not brown or fluorescent, nor is it a protein cross-link. It is a reversible modification of protein but is a precursor of irreversible chemical modifications and cross-links known as AGEs.

The Maillard reaction first attracted the interest of biomedical scientists in the mid-1970s, when a modified form of hemoglobin, isolated from normal human blood, was shown to contain glucose as an Amadori adduct. During the 120-day life span of the red cell, less than 10% of human hemoglobin is converted to this glycated form, now known as HbA_{1c}. However, the steady-state concentration of HbA_{1c} is increased in the blood of diabetic patients and correlates strongly with their mean blood glucose concentration during the previous 1-month period. Measurements of HbA_{1c} or glycated hemoglobin are now widely used for monitoring long-term blood glucose concentrations in diabetes.

Glycation is now recognized as a common chemical modification of body proteins, occurring mostly at the ε-amino group of lysine residues. The

glycation of proteins in vivo suggested that the later, browning stages of the Maillard reaction also take place in the body, leading to the formation of AGEs. Indeed, several structurally characterized AGEs are now known to accumulate with age in long-lived proteins, such as lens crystallins and tissue collagens (Baynes & Thorpe, 1999); these same compounds are found in cooked foods, pretzels, and toasted bread. They include lysine modifications such as N^ε-carboxymethyllysine, N^ε-carboxyethyllysine, and pyrraline; and fluorescent cross-links such as pentosidine, crosslines, and vesperlysines. Most of these AGEs increase in lens proteins with age and, because of chronic hyperglycemia, are found at higher concentrations in collagen and other proteins from patients with diabetes. Increased age-corrected levels of AGEs in tissue collagens are associated with the development of retinal, renal, neurological, and vascular complications of diabetes (Paul & Bailey, 1996). AGEs are also detectable at high concentration in protein deposits in the brains of patients with Alzheimer's disease, in atherosclerotic plaque, and in amyloid plaque of patients with hemodialysis-associated amyloidosis (Thorpe & Baynes, 1996). In these diseases, AGEs appear to be formed adventitiously on precipitated plaque proteins and may have a role in recruitment of macrophages, causing local inflammation and tissue damage. AGEs on collagen and plaque proteins may also chelate metal ions, catalyzing oxidative stress, and may react with soluble proteins, contributing to deposition of plasma protein in the vascular wall and glomerular basement membrane in diabetes.

AGE proteins are recognized by scavenger receptors on macrophages and by AGE-specific receptors, including RAGE (receptor for AGE) on macrophages (Sano, Nagai, & Horiuchi, 1999). AGE receptors and RAGE are also found on endothelial and neural cells, myocytes, and lymphocytes. The uptake of AGE proteins by macrophages and endothelial cells is associated with generation of oxygen radicals and release of cytokines that promote collagen turnover and biosynthesis, cell proliferation, and tissue remodeling, suggesting that receptor-mediated binding of AGEs may trigger the revitalization of tissues (Bierhaus, Hofmann, Ziegler, & Nawroth, 1998).

The meaning of the term *AGE* has evolved over time, referring initially to yellow-brown, fluorescent chromophores that accumulated irreversibly in proteins exposed to glucose and mediated the cross-linking of proteins in vivo. The term is now used to refer globally to a range of carbohydrate-derived products formed during advanced stages of the Maillard reaction. AGE products now encompass compounds that are not fluorescent, nor are they necessarily cross-links, nor do they necessarily accumulate with age, nor are they necessarily end products or always glucose-derived. AGE proteins also react with and form cross-links with other proteins, so they are not necessarily end products of the Maillard reaction. AGEs have also been detected in phospholipids and in DNA, so they are not necessarily found only in protein. AGEs may also be formed from a variety of carbohydrates other than blood sugar (glucose), including ascorbate, fructose, sugar phosphates, and even simpler molecules, such as methylglyoxal. Ascorbate is present at high concentrations in the lens and may be a major precursor of AGEs in lens proteins. Products similar to AGEs, known as advanced lipoxidation end products (ALEs), are also formed during oxidation

of lipids in tissues. Although AGEs are detectable in tissue proteins throughout the body by chemical analysis and immunological methods, the majority of the brown and fluorescent products, cross-links, and other AGEs on proteins are still uncharacterized.

Oxygen and catalysts of oxidation reactions, such as copper and iron ions, accelerate the Maillard reaction, and most AGEs that are known to accumulate in protein with age require both glycation and oxidation reactions, or partially oxidized forms of sugars, for their formation. Oxygen and oxidative reactions are considered fixatives of the chemical modification of proteins by carbohydrates, and the term *glycoxidation* product has been proposed to describe the subclass of AGEs formed by both glycation and oxidation reactions (Baynes & Thorpe, 1999). Antioxidants and compounds, such as aminoguanidine and pyridoxamine, which trap reactive sugars and dicarbonyl intermediates in formation of AGEs, are effective in preventing or retarding the development of complications in animal models of diabetes and are being tested in clinical trials. Although the relationship between AGEs and aging is still associative, caloric restriction results in life-span extension in rodents and inhibits the accumulation of AGEs in tissue collagens, probably because of a combination of decreases in blood glucose, protein glycation, and oxidative stress. Studies on the effects of caloric restriction on AGE formation and life span in primates are in progress. Future research will continue to focus on the structure and mechanism of formation of AGEs, especially on the application of pharmacological approaches to inhibit AGE formation.

JOHN W. BAYNES

See also
Carbohydrate Metabolism
Diabetes Mellitus

AFFECT AND MOOD
See

AFRICAN AMERICAN ELDERLY

In the first and second editions of this volume it was indicated that social gerontological research on the Black elderly was undergoing a period of growth and transition. During the past 5 years even more substantial progress has been made, and research and scholarly literature has again expanded at a rapid rate (Miles, 1999). Although recent research continues to focus on "racial" comparisons, especially Black-White contrasts, more within-group studies and analyses are being done, with greater attention to the variability within the Black aged as a heterogenous population group (Markides, Liang, & Jackson, 1990). Demographic projections make clear that the fastest growth among all elderly groups will be within racial and ethnic minority populations, including Blacks (Friedland & Summer, 1999; Miles, 1999; Siegel, 1999). Earlier research focused on comparisons of the Black and White aged populations, documenting the relative disadvantaged social and economic position of Blacks. More recent research has taken J. J. Jackson's (1985) suggestion for more systematic, empirical research on the nature of the aging experience within the Black population as a legitimate and important area of investigation in social gerontology (Jackson, Lockery, & Juster, 1997). Recent social gerontological research on the Black aged has seen the use of more representative samples and the application of methodologically sophisticated data collection and analytic methods (e.g., Smith & Kington, 1997b).

In prior volumes the areas of socioeconomic status, health status, family and social support, psychological well-being, and work and retirement were highlighted. Similar categories are now used, and progress over the intervening 5 years is noted in each.

Socioeconomic Status

The Black aged continue to lag behind Whites in social and economic statuses (Chen, 1999; Siegel, 1999). Indicators of income, education, and health status document the deprived position of Blacks relative to Whites. For those who argued that this was a cohort effect, the lingering poor relative position of Blacks refutes this; new cohorts of the Black

elderly are not faring significantly better than prior ones. Previously, I had noted the continuing disadvantage of middle-aged and younger Blacks, relative to Whites, in housing, income, occupation, health, and education. Recent reports (e.g., Chen, 1999; Smith & Kington, 1997b) on the circumstances of Blacks across the entire life course continue to show the presence of relatively poorer circumstances, especially wealth (Conley, 1999–2000), suggesting that new cohorts of elderly Blacks will continue to experience relative disadvantage in comparison to other groups (Farley, 1996).

Again, I hasten to add that even though approximately a third of the Black elderly continue to live below the poverty level, today's Black elderly are better fed, better housed, and in better health than in earlier eras (Manton & Stallard, 1997b; Richardson, 1996). Most of this improvement is attributable to government assistance programs, still the prime support of African Americans in older age groups (Chen, 1999). Unfortunately, a larger proportion of Blacks, because of histories of poor occupational opportunities, lack of wealth, and private retirements funds, are heavily dependent on these government programs (Jackson, 1996). It is still unclear whether future cohorts of older Blacks will enjoy what may be the relative luxury of today's elderly. Recent diminution of federal programs; a change in the economy, favoring job creation in high technological and specialized education–intensive sectors of the economy (computers and communications); and simultaneous growth in low-paying service positions (e.g., fast food restaurants) provide little room for today's Black adult and middle-aged cohorts, many of whom lacked basic educational opportunities during their formative years (Farley, 1996). It is now predictable that future cohorts of older Blacks will not be as well off as their White counterparts, and it is still unlikely that they will be as well off as today's cohort of Black elders, many of whom have worked in union-intensive industries (Smith & Kington, 1997b; Williams & Collins, 1995).

Health Morbidity and Mortality

At nearly every point from birth to death African Americans have higher morbidity and mortality than do Whites (Richardson, 1996; Smith & Kington, 1997a). It is also well documented that there is an increased longevity among Blacks who live to approximately the age of 84 or so. Many have suggested a possible selection bias, indicating the survival of particularly robust and hardy individuals, or differential rates of aging within the Black and White populations (e.g., Manton & Stallard, 1997). Others have claimed that this supposed crossover is only an artifact of faulty reporting and exaggerated age claims. The effect has been firmly established, although there remains no widely accepted explanation (Elo & Preston, 1997). The racial mortality crossover appears to be a real phenomenon (Seigel, 1999); one that may involve some type of "survival of the fit."

Recent research on the oldest-old (Smith & Kington, 1997b) continues to document the heterogeneity of the social and psychological health of very old Blacks. This type of data provides strong support for a thesis that views the mortality crossover as involving the survival of hardier old Blacks, not a methodological artifact. Similarly, work by Manton and Stallard (1997) show some evidence for greater functional health, in comparison to Whites, among older elderly Blacks, though the effect seems highly dependent on educational status.

Other recent research points to differences between Blacks and Whites in the nature of self-reported health. Early in the decade, Gibson (1991) found that the largest differences were in the validity of the subjective interpretations of health state. These findings challenge traditional thinking and research regarding possible race differences in health. At this point, whether there are differences in the structure of health, the processes of health, or the influence of service use on experienced health problems remain open questions (Smith & Kington, 1997a). What is clear is that changing health policies may have increasing negative effects on the ability of Black elderly to receive adequate health care in the new century (Mebane, Oman, Kroonen, & Goldstein, 1999; Wallace & Villa, 1999).

Family and Social Support

Historically, research on the Black family and social support networks has been based predominantly on anecdotal data. Two myths have dominated this area. The first is a view of older Blacks as cared for by loving extended family members and fictive kin. The other is a view of the impoverished lonely older Black abandoned by a disorganized and incompetent family system. National and other large social surveys indicate a reality somewhere in between (Connell & Gibson, 1997; Dilworth-Anderson & Burton, 1999; Silverstein & Waite, 1993). These recent research findings document the existence of extended family forms but also demonstrate that much of the assistance is reciprocal, that the Black aged often provide help to younger family members and neighbors (Connell & Gibson, 1997; Dilworth-Anderson & Burton, 1999). The importance of community institutions like the church as sources of physical and emotional support to older Blacks also has been documented recently (Taylor, Hardison, & Chatters, 1996; Taylor, Ellison, Chatters, Levin, & Lincoln, 2000). Other work points to the considerable obstacles faced by African Americans in providing services to demented and mentally ill relatives (Biegel, Johnson, & Shafran, 1997).

Psychological Well-Being

Research on psychological well-being has shown an increasing sophistication over the past 4 years (Adams & Jackson, 2000). Structural factors, like income and education, tend to show small but positive relationships to well-being. Adams & Jackson's (2000) recent work suggests that psychological well-being may be strongly tied to family and health satisfactions. Some recent evidence also suggests that younger cohorts of Blacks may be less satisfied than older cohorts at comparable periods in the life span (Adams, 1997). This is in sharp contrast to Whites, who have shown the opposite pattern. This lowered satisfaction and happiness in younger Blacks may be related to rising expectations and structural constraints that are likely to persist into old age (Adams, 1997; Jackson, 1996).

Work and Retirement

It was noted in the last volume that little empirical research had been devoted to the study of work and retirement in the Black aged. This is changing (e.g., Jackson, Lockery, & Juster, 1997). Some earlier work had speculated that the entire retirement process, viewed within a life span context, may be very different for Blacks (Jackson, 1996). Because Blacks often have long histories of dead-end jobs with poor benefits and bleak expectations, the advantages of retirement are lessened. Thus, inadequate income, poor housing, and uncertain futures may face older Blacks at retirement age (Chen, 1999). Faced with limited retirement resources, many older Blacks may continue to work past customary retirement ages out of desperation. Some research indicates that these individuals are physically, psychologically, and socially worse off than their retired Black counterparts. As suggested earlier, even the relatively poor but stable government retirement support that Blacks may receive (if they are fortunate enough to qualify) may, in contrast, be better than sporadic and poor jobs in the regular labor market (Chen, 1999; Jackson, 1996). Thus, retirement may provide a small but secure government income, leading to increased psychological and social well-being (Jackson, 1996).

In sum, today, in contrast to 5 years ago, more research on the social gerontology of the Black aged is being included within the general investigation of ethnicity and cultural factors in aging (Martin & Soldo, 1997; Miles, 1999). The existence of large national datasets and more powerful analytical techniques are increasing the quality and quantity of research on African American aging in all areas (Smith & Kington, 1997a). National longitudinal data collection efforts, like the Health and Retirement Survey, are improving the available data on the aging experience of African Americans (Smith & Willis, 1999). Although better data are always needed, especially those based on longitudinal and cross-sequential designs, the improvement in a relatively few short years has been impressive (Miles, 1999). Similarly, the approach to research on the Black elderly has also seen a greater recognition of the heterogeneity among elderly Blacks (Miles, 1999). Research is now more focused on the role of culture, socioeconomic status, and gender as important markers of potential process differences within and among aging groups of color, especially African Americans.

It can no longer be said that ethnogerontology is hampered in the study of the Black aged by the lack of an extensive history of empirical research on within-group variation, at least not to the same extent as a decade ago. Recent research is reversing this historical trend, and generalizable high-quality findings are emerging concerning health, socioeconomic status, social support, family patterns, well-being, work, and retirement for Blacks (Miles, 1999).

JAMES S. JACKSON

See also
   Ethnicity
   Minorities and Aging
   Minority Populations: Recruitment and Retention in Aging Research

AGE AND EXPERTISE

Age and expertise are two powerful predictors of human performance. Recent experimental investigations have focused on the pattern of their joint effects to try to understand the following paradox. Age is negatively associated with performance on laboratory tasks that tap basic human abilities, even in experienced practitioners (e.g., memory for music notation: Meinz & Salthouse, 1998); yet age bears no relationship to measures of job performance (e.g., Salthouse & Maurer, 1996). Acquired skill in the form of superior knowledge or information processing efficiency is thought to be a compensatory factor that can account for such findings.

Expertise is often assessed by self-report of years of experience or via peer evaluations. Years of experience can be a poor predictor of skill because one may accumulate considerable experience without achieving more than basic competence. Peer evaluations are not ideal indicators because peers may have personal biases toward or lack information about potential experts. A more rigorous technique for assessing expertise is the measurement of typical real-world performance under controlled laboratory conditions. Such studies find that it takes about 10 years of *deliberate* practice—practice aimed at improving performance—to reach international levels of performance (Ericsson & Lehmann, 1996).

Life Span Trends in Expertise

Popular belief holds that skill in a given domain will increase early in life and decrease later in life. By and large, this belief seems to hold up under scientific analyses. In a broad analysis of life-span productivity by prominent figures in many different domains, Lehman (1953) observed a curvilinear function between age and performance. The function is usually characterized by a sharp rise in performance in young adulthood, with a peak in the decade of the 30s, followed by gradual decline thereafter. Despite the ubiquity of this function, there are two underlying trends worth considering. First, peak performance in physically demanding domains tends to occur earlier in life than peak performance in more intellectual domains. In athletics, peak performance tends to occur in the 20s (Stones & Kozma, 1995), whereas in intellectual domains, such as chess, it tends to occur in the 30s or 40s (Charness, Krampe, & Mayr, 1996). Second, elite performers tend to maintain excellent performance for longer periods than do mediocre or poor performers. According to Simonton (1997), the ability of elite artists and scientists to maintain exceptional performance with age is not entirely due to consistent success but rather to consistent productivity. In both science and sports, individuals who were seemingly past their prime have occasionally broken world records or won world championships but not without several previous attempts. Thus, although it seems natural that expert performance should decline due to physiological and psychological aging processes, the occurrence of high-level performance and achievements by older experts requires the consideration of more detailed explanatory mechanisms.

Maintenance, Remediation, and Compensation

It appears that experts can partially circumvent general age-related declines in physical and psychological capacities by deliberately engaging in counteractive measures. One counteractive measure, maintenance practice, involves extensive task-relevant practice to sustain performance. For example, despite declines in general psychomotor speed, Krampe and Ericsson (1996) found small age-related declines in speeded music-related performance (tapping task) among older expert pianists. Relative to the older experts, older amateur pianists exhibited significantly slower performance in both tasks. Both cumulative and current levels of practice related positively to performance. Similarly, Tsang and Shaner (1998) reported that age-related declines among pilots in flight simulator tasks appear to be somewhat attenuated by experience. In particular, when older active pilots were asked to perform two aviation-relevant tasks at the same time, their performance was comparable to middle-aged and younger pilots. However, when the same individuals were asked to perform two general tasks, older active pilots performed substantially worse than their younger colleagues did. In both of the above cases, current task-relevant practice appeared to be critical for maintaining expert performance, but the positive effects of maintenance practice were restricted to the domain of expertise.

Whereas maintenance entails positive effects from continued use, remediation involves training to reverse the negative effects of disuse. Retraining for older workers has become increasingly popular in the past decade. However, there is limited empirical evidence to support the effectiveness of such training. Furthermore, attempts to remediate broader skills, such as spatial ability, have had only modest success, presumably because the interventions were not specific or lengthy enough to accrue the advantages provided by domain-specific knowledge (Tsang & Shaner, 1998). Given the recent increases in the proportion of older employees in the work force, there is clearly a need for more research on this topic.

Compensation generally refers to circumventing a potential decline in performance through substitution of skills or goals. A good example of skill substitution can be found in a study of transcription typists. Salthouse (1984) showed that older transcription typists compensated for age-related slowing in component processes (e.g., translating visual symbols to keystrokes) by adopting extended "eye-hand" spans. By looking further ahead from the currently typed character, older typists were able to compensate for declines in speed by preparing keystrokes earlier. In a demonstration of compensation via goal modification, Stones and Kozma (1995) found that older race walkers finished better in long-distance events than in short-distance events during the 1993 world championships. The investigators argued that the larger proportion of older race walkers finishing well in the long-distance events reflected their choice to focus on endurance, which is easier to sustain with age than speed. This explanation could be generalized to other athletes, who may change their event or sport with age in order to remain competitive.

Conclusion

A review of observational and experimental studies of realistic expert performance reveals mixed findings. Although there is a general tendency for performance to decline with age, critical skills in some domains may be sustained through practice. When experts cannot postpone age-related declines in skill, they may compensate or adapt in other ways. However, the nature and potency of these compensatory mechanisms are not thoroughly understood and will undoubtedly spur further investigations.

NEIL CHARNESS
JEFFREY S. FEDDON
MICHAEL TUFFIASH

This work was supported by grants from the National Institute on Aging (5R01-AG13969) to the first author.

See also
Abilities

AGE CONFLICTS

Age conflicts are pervasive in all societies. Antagonisms between younger and older people may be muted, but often they erupt into open clashes of varying intensity, ranging from verbal arguments to violent actions. Age conflicts typically are confined to particular institutional spheres, like the family, the workplace, or religious associations. Occasionally, they become society-wide, spilling over into many areas of social life.

Like other forms of social conflict, age conflicts characteristically involve struggles over values or over scarce resources. Age disagreements over values often stem from differences in the social, politi-

cal, and economic context of the periods in which successive cohorts grow up and grow older. For example, political attitudes about war and peace generally differ among those who enter young adulthood during wartime and those who enter during peacetime, just as attitudes about family life differ among those starting families during a severe depression and those who do so in good times. New economic, social, or political trends are particularly likely to influence the young who have not had time to become committed to established patterns, whereas older adults sometimes cling to the values to which they were socialized earlier. The result is that young and old often have opposing views about many matters: lifestyles, cultural tastes, and political and world views (Riley, Foner, & Riley, 1999).

Age inequalities are another source of age conflicts (A. Foner, 1974). In modern societies the young and the old are most likely to be disadvantaged, whereas people in the middle years tend to have greater access to material benefits, power, and prestige. Struggles occur when the disadvantaged make claims for more power or other social goods while the more advantaged seek to protect their privileges. In American society parents often resist adolescents' claims for more autonomy; in agricultural societies fathers have rebuffed sons' pressures to cede land; established political leaders often fend off the demands of "young turks"; and in the United States there has been debate about *generational equity*, spurred by extensive government supports for older people and complaints by some in middle age about the tax burden they bear in supporting public pensions for the old (Schulz, 1999). When resentments over age inequalities are accompanied by *value differences*, the potential for age conflicts is heightened (A. Foner, 1974).

Nevertheless, a number of factors operate to check sharp age conflicts at both interpersonal and societal levels:

1. The *legitimation of age inequalities* on the basis of relative needs or contributions serves to weaken the motivation to initiate hostile actions.
2. People of working age often accept the economic burden of providing public support for the old as it reduces the need for private support of elders in their family.

3. Government programs for the old benefit the young and middle-aged indirectly by permitting the old to provide gifts and loans to younger family members.
4. Ties of affection or feelings of obligation, as in many family relationships, often counterbalance anger.
5. Physical and social separation of age groups outside the family limit opportunities to interact and thus forestall incidents that otherwise might trigger clashes (Bengtson & Harootyan, 1994; A. Foner, 1974; N. Foner, 1984).

In modern societies, with their multiple institutions and forms of social differentiation, several other factors help account for the relative infrequency of *society-wide age cleavages* specifically. If age conflicts do emerge in given institutions, they are unlikely to culminate in a single line of age cleavage because the issues and timing vary from one institution to another. Furthermore, class, gender, race, and ethnic divisions within an age stratum act to undermine solidarity within the stratum and reduce the salience of age identities; thus, the group's ability and motivation to engage in struggles with other age groups is weakened (see entries on "Social Stratification" and "Age Stratification").

To be sure, society-wide age conflicts have erupted on occasion; they have generally been initiated by the young, in good times and over moral issues, suggesting that *conflict-reducing mechanisms* are least effective under this combination of conditions. Nevertheless, certain circumstances might engender age conflicts over material issues in the future. Older people might well resist reductions in publicly supported programs for the old, while the middle-aged rebel against increases in the tax burden they bear in maintaining these government programs. Whether it is such material issues or moral issues that spark age conflicts, the outcome is likely to be a change in the distribution of privileges or power.

ANNE FONER

See also
Age Stratification
Cohorts

Intergenerational Relationships
Intergenerational Stake Hypotheses

AGE DISCRIMINATION
See
Ageism
Equal Employment Opportunity Commission
United States Commission on Civil Rights

AGE GRADING AND GROUPING

Age grading is the division of a population into broad age groupings, such as childhood, adulthood, and old age. Age grading is used along with gender to broadly define the family, work, and community roles thought to be appropriate to members of each age-sex group. Age grading requires people to undergo role transitions as they age and move from one age-sex grouping to the next. Often there are formal ceremonies (rites of passage), such as puberty rites or induction into the council of elders, that mark these transitions.

As societies increase in complexity, separate age grades within childhood tend to proliferate, mainly in response to the age-graded structure of formal education (Chudacoff, 1989). Also, in complex societies the level of agreement about the exact boundaries of age-sex groupings may vary (Settersten, 1999). For example, in the United States, men and women are generally treated as adults at age 18, but there is much less agreement about the age at which a person enters or leaves middle age. As societies age, age grades may proliferate within the older population in response to increased diversity in perceived interests, orientations, and service needs. Thus, some analysts speak of the young-old (age 65 to 74), the middle-old (age 75 to 84), and the old-old (age 85 and over) as having very different needs and resources.

As the proportion of an age group that diverges from the age norms for various roles and life transitions increases, the nature of age groupings becomes more ambiguous. For example, as retirement ages have continued to drop and a large proportion of people retire prior to age 60, the link between retirement and an age grouping called old age becomes more and more tenuous.

It is important to remember that age grading and grouping, as part of a society's culture, are arbitrary conventions, often carried over from many years in the past; they vary to suit the needs of a wide array of different types of societies and therefore range from very simple to very complex systems of age grading and grouping.

The subject of age grading and grouping has not been a high priority in gerontology research, and studies are sparse. Much of the discussion of the life course, age grading, age grouping, and life stages is based on studies done many years ago or on assumptions about the current situation, not on rigorous current research (Keith, Fry, Glascock, Ikels, Dickerson-Putnam, Harpending, et al., 1994). Gerontologists must be particularly careful to avoid reifying the categories they use for research convenience into cultural icons. The language gerontologists use to describe age grading and grouping and the age categories used in research are often very different from the cultural conceptions in use in society at large (Green, 1993).

ROBERT C. ATCHLEY

See also
   Age Stratification
   Cohorts
   Social Stratification

AGE IDENTIFICATION

Age identification is a component of self-concept reflecting personal interpretation of the aging process and mediating behavior and patterns of interaction. A basic proposition of the concept as used in gerontology is that it encompasses personal assessments of one's relative position in an age-graded system, as well as enduring roles and social relationships. Social circumstances are relevant, as they shape one's sense of self and thereby one's behavior (Stryker, 1991). The foundation of age identity lies with cultural values, age norms, and personal competencies in successive and salient realms of involvement. Boundary conditions, social networks, and such transient factors as health or emo-

tional distress contribute, insofar as they facilitate or constrain expressions of competence, control, and management of age identity, as well as self–other comparisons in the construction of the autobiographical self (Herzog & Markus, 1999).

Operationalization of this widely used concept often occurs by means of adjective checklists, semantic differentials, and self-selected descriptions of personal age. Multivariate analyses suggest that age identity is composed of a number of subfeatures (Kastenbaum, Derbin, Sabatini, & Arrt, 1972). Among these are somatic, cognitive, and affective dimensions, as well as the demographic, socioeconomic, and social-psychological (Herzog & Markus, 1999). This last measurement is usually elicited in response to some variation of the query "Would you describe yourself as young, middle-aged, or old?" Occasionally, a comparative slant is put to the question: "Compared with others your age, would you say you are younger, about the same, or older?" The reasoning behind both concept and testing builds on the broad stream of symbolic interactionist literature, especially labeling and identity theories, with their attention to negotiated and dynamic aspects of self-concept. Age identity embodies more than just recognition of chronological age. In large measure, personal assessments, regardless of age, reflect a complex set of socioeconomic or lifestyle factors, perceived age norms and age-appropriate behavior, social and anticipated timetables, health and physical limitations, and interaction patterns in both formal and informal networks. For example, presence of children, marital status, life satisfaction, or sense of purpose are as integral to age identification as is biological status and physical health (Logan, Ward, & Spitze, 1992). Although age identification is a fluid concept, marked by constancy as well as change over time, it provides a reference point for individuals seeking confirmation of their self-concept. Whether or not there is a stable or core "self" that serves as a basis around which age transitions occur is the subject of debate, but investigators agree that appropriate age identities promote adaptation to changing circumstances. Researchers agree, however, that sequential age identities reflect changing priorities in factors upon which self-concepts are erected (Breytspraak, 1984).

Although age identification is usually thought to be a enveloping attitude, prompting people to think of themselves in broad, age-defined categories, it may also be that particular substantive dimensions of selfhood result in differential age identities. Stryker (in press) notes that there may be as many self-concepts as there are salient role relationships. In either instance, age identification carries with it both content information about appropriate modes of behavior and organization strategies necessary for personal integration as behavioral changes occur or are expected. Because it reflects social roles and status, age identification also may suggest distinct gender-based differences wherein certain behavior or expectations are characteristic of women and of men (Harris, 1994; Herzog & Markus, 1999). The importance of temporally linked aspects of self-identity have broad-ranging implications for behavior in middle and later life, cutting across a number of realms, from occupational choices to sense of well-being.

JON HENDRICKS

See also
Images of Aging in the Media
Self-Concept

AGEISM

Ageism is defined as a process of systematic stereotyping and discrimination against people because they are old, just as racism and sexism accomplish this for skin color and gender. Older people are categorized as senile, rigid in thought and manner, and old-fashioned in morality and skills. In medicine, terms like "crock" and "vegetable" have been commonly used. Ageism allows the younger generation to see older people as different from themselves; thus, they suddenly cease to identify with their elders as human beings. This behavior serves to reduce their own sense of fear and dread of aging. Stereotyping and myths surrounding old age are explained in part by a lack of knowledge and insufficient contact with a wide variety of older people. But another factor comes into play—a deep and profound dread of growing old. Ageism is a broader concept than gerontophobia, which refers to a rarer, "unreasonable fear and/or irrational hatred of older people, whereas ageism is a much more comprehen-

sive and useful concept" (Palmore, 1972). This concept and term was introduced in 1968 (Butler, 1969).

The underlying psychological mechanism of ageism makes it possible for individuals to avoid dealing with the reality of aging, at least for a time. It also becomes possible to ignore the social and economic plight of some older persons. Ageism is manifested in a wide range of phenomena (on both individual and institutional levels), stereotypes and myths, outright disdain and dislike, or simply subtle avoidance of contact; discriminatory practices in housing, employment, and services of all kinds; epithets, cartoons, and jokes. At times, ageism becomes an expedient method by which society promotes viewpoints about the aged in order to relieve itself from the responsibility toward them, and at other times ageism serves a highly personal objective, protecting younger (usually middle-aged individuals, often at high emotional cost), from thinking about things they fear (aging, illness, and death).

Ageism, like all prejudices, influences the behavior of its victims (Hausdorff, Levy, & Wei, 1999). The elderly tend to adopt negative definitions about themselves and to perpetuate the various stereotypes directed against them, thereby reinforcing societal beliefs. The elderly in a sense "collaborate" with the enemy, with stereotypes. Margaret Thaler Singer observed similarities between the Rorschach test findings in members of a sample of healthy aged volunteers in the face of aging and of a sample of American prisoners of war who collaborated with their captors in Korea.

Some older people refuse to identify with the elderly and may dress and behave inappropriately in frantic attempts to appear young. Others may underestimate or deny their age.

Ageism can apply to stages of life other than old age. Older persons have many prejudices against the young and the attractiveness and vigor of youth. Angry and ambivalent feelings may flow, too, between the old and the middle-aged. The middle-aged often bear many of the pressures of both young and old, and they experience anger toward both groups.

Since the introduction of the concept of ageism, there have been some gains on the part of the elderly. The Age Discrimination and Employment Act of 1967, amended in 1978, ended mandatory retirement in the federal government and advanced it to age 70 in the private sector.

Some of the myths of age include a lack of productivity, disengagement, inflexibility, senility, and loss of sexuality (Bytheway, 1995; Stone & Stone, 1997). There have been some advances in, and more attention to, the productive capabilities of older people, and a better understanding that older persons have desires, capabilities, and satisfaction with regard to sexual activities. The "write-off" of older persons as "senile" because of memory problems, for example, is being replaced by an understanding of the profound and most common forms of what is popularly referred to as senility, namely, Alzheimer's disease. Senility is no longer seen as inevitable with age. Rather, it is understood to be a disease or group of diseases. When means of effectively treating dementia are available, ageism also will decline.

Reminiscence or life review has helped focus attention on what can be learned from listening to the lives of the old. Indeed, the memoir has become, in the minds of some, the signature genre of our age. By the 1990s old age was in the process of being redefined as a more robust and contributory stage of life. Unfortunately, the underlying dread, fear of, and distaste for age remains.

ROBERT N. BUTLER

See also
Age Segregation
Attitudes

AGE NORMS

Regularities are observed in the timing of occurrences of events in people's lives. These regularities may be due to the timing of biological events in relation to aging or to social rules and norms, but they are not necessarily due to either except in the most general sense. For instance, the peak of physical strength in early adulthood will look like a natural justification for concentrating compulsory military service in a narrow age range and even set an upper limit (35 years in the United States) for voluntary enlistment; but reserve systems in different countries require this service through a much

larger proportion of the life span, and some potentially physically demanding activities, like the Peace Corps, set no age limits. Such socially defined age norms often become seen as natural necessities, not needing any formal definition and justification. Social norms can, however, be inferred from small dispersions of behavior and peculiar forms of the distribution functions or in consequences of deviation from these norms. One could infer deviations from norms if people feel constrained to explain this deviant behavior. For an early discussion of age norms, see Neugarten, Moore, and Lowe (1965).

Social age norms represent, in part, belief in endogenic stages of development and, in part, needs and organization of the society. Society is organized in such a way that certain functions and roles must be filled, and the requisite skills to fill these roles must be acquired previously. Norms are thus determined jointly by individual development and by social concerns. The former has both descriptive and normative aspects: in determining a sequence from statistical regularities one moves almost without knowing it to claiming at what point of development a person should be at a certain age, that person becoming precocious or retarded when deviations occur. Social concerns add to these prescriptions, assigning rights and duties according to age.

Thus, age norms are often seen as necessary consequences of biological or psychological development. For instance, children are weaker than adults and sexually immature, and the childbearing time of women is limited. However, this argument is often used to explain current arrangements, which may look necessary but on closer inspection become dependent on social arrangements.

The concept of life stage is intended to integrate a number of psychological, emotional, and social developments and connote a large degree of associated social norms. In most discussions of life stages, the early stages, perhaps up to midlife, are more clearly established than the later ones. This is comprehensible because the norms of childhood and youth refer to the acquisition of skill and abilities, and the norms of old age refer to the expected relinquishment of some capacities. The earlier stages reflect biological conditions: infants are not able to assume many of the adult roles and responsibilities. The tasks of an infant are quite universal; childhood and adolescence also have quite common problems. Experiences during adulthood, however, can be so disparate that the tasks of later life become dependent as much on life experiences as on general principles, at least until physical decline imposes a certain uniformity.

A popular arrangement of life stages, with explicit or implicit age norms, that has remained influential is that of Erikson (1959). He identified eight stages of life, each with its characteristic conflict and normative developmental task to be achieved, with the respective crises and strengths to be achieved: (1) infancy, with the crisis of terror versus basic mistrust; engendering hope; (2) early childhood, autonomy versus shame and doubt; will; (3) play age, initiative versus guilt; purpose; (4) school age, industry versus inferiority; competence; (5) adolescence, identity versus identity confusion; fidelity; (6) young adulthood, intimacy versus isolation; love; (7) adulthood, generativity versus stagnation; care; (8) old age, integrity versus despair and disgust; wisdom. The stages are related only implicitly to ages, and ages are not defined by specific numbers. The early stages are treated in much more detail than the later ones: postadolescence, for instance, includes about three quarters of the life span but only three of the eight stages. The ages of interest to the gerontologist are virtually limited to the last stage, with some overlap with the previous stage. Although Erikson's work was concerned mainly with adolescents and young adults, not with later stages, the contrast of the detailed division of earlier life and the broad strokes of later ages may actually represent the declining importance of intrinsic norms in later life, but it also represents the distribution of interest of scholars of human development. This bias has been partially corrected in recent years by the work of Erikson himself and others (Erikson, 1982; Kotre, 1984).

Thus, norms are more clearly specified and more tightly enforced in the young than in the old. Developmental norms derived from informal observations or in some societies from formal testing become social norms for classifying individuals as advanced, normal, or retarded for their age. Certain duties and privileges may be prescribed at certain ages. Informally, parents, peers, and others watch closely the passage to actions appropriate to a given age. However, the contrasting interests of the individual and society militate against a formal enforcement of age norms, especially in later ages (Neugarten, 1979).

Norms based on purely chronological age compete with those based on other determinants. Prominent here are the relationships to social institutions, particularly the family, where positions are determined by a sequence of relationships that are partly dependent on age. Ascending kinship members are generally older and descending, younger; normative roles, privileges, and duties are partly determined by the implied age difference. An analogous process can be seen in occupational and public institutions. Thus, one can speak of different kinds of time—chronological, family, and industrial time (Hareven, 1991, 1994). Age norms refer primarily to chronological time, and this time can be of varying importance in different societies.

Within the past two centuries the place of chronological age has shifted. In comparison with the 19th century (and most other periods) it has assumed surpassing importance, corresponding to a general quantifying trend. Exact dating and documentation of age and date of birth are seen as natural, to the despair of census takers in foreign cultures. Special norms for one's place in the birth order—for instance, in leaving the parental household—have lost their importance, and attention to them is seen as disturbing the natural precedence of chronological age for these decisions. Thus, norms are given for persons 65 years old or older, not for the first-born son or last-born daughter in the family. This corresponds to a generally egalitarian norm within the society, namely, to treat people independently of personal characteristics—except for age.

The reliance on the sequence of numbers corresponds to the general linear arrangement of modernistic culture; in arranging the life course in modern society the normative sequence demanded a period of learning, followed by a period of functioning (in occupation or family), and finally a period of retirement, abandoning these roles. Some suggestions have been made that these linear arrangements do not fit current society; that increase of leisure, lifelong learning, and occupational productivity into later ages is becoming a new norm, and that governmental programs should further this development. This weakening of age would also correspond to the general trend of postmodernist ideals (Riley & Riley, 1994).

KURT W. BACK

See also
   Life Course
   Life Cycle
   Retirement
   Social Roles

AGE SEGREGATION

Two principles can be conveniently identified in the study of human associations: similarity and functional dependence. This division becomes useful in considering the importance of age in this regard. Age is a quality that individuals often use in choosing associates, but age difference in aging may link people through mutual dependence; the old may need the young and vice versa. However, the two principles are contradictory: integration by similarity, such as same age, results in segregation between different age groups. Cultural values and social structures will determine the balance of these two trends.

Situational constraints and cultural preferences will lead to processes that promote age segregation and integration. The family and the household are the principal institutions that preserve age integration. The household can contain individuals of widely different ages who are brought together by social rules and who are linked by complementary needs and obligations as well as by dyadic emotional ties. The aged may be more likely to stay in a household, being part of a group of different ages, or prefer associations with persons of similar age and experience.

The dominance of households consisting of nuclear families has directed popular attention to age segregation. This condition has developed in part because of demographic conditions, especially migration. The European–North American tradition kept the basic family unit relatively small and found various ways of providing for the remaining household members (Laslett, 1972). These provisions included retirement homes for the aged, outside assis-

tance for those who could not maintain themselves, and at-home services in existing households. One important stimulus was the tradition of migration in European society—mainly westward—which was spearheaded by colonizing by small nuclear families; this is usually the part of the family that is able to establish a new residence far away (Borkenau, 1981).

These migration patterns have both large-scale and small-scale consequences. New, pioneering areas will attract the younger population; older, stagnating areas have the remaining older residents, leading to regional segregation. This would lead to nuclear, age-homogeneous households, but this trend is partly counteracted by the increase in the proportion of old people because of declining mortality and fertility. This larger group of older survivors forms a base for age-homogeneous living groups and households. These conditions will influence household composition, including integration and segregation by age, regardless of the family norms. By contrast, the region between West Africa and Southeast Asia is characterized by general territorial stability and multifamily households. Here, relations between the generations are rigorously established, leading to contact between age groups but also to unequal power relations, generally to the detriment of wives brought into the household and of small children (Caldwell, 1990).

Norms toward nuclear families are complemented by increased emphasis by the aged on contacts with people of similar current concerns and experiences, that is, convoylike associations. Migration of the aged as individuals (or couples) will be toward areas that have attractions for them in climate and facilities, thus complementing the region with a high concentration of the aged because of outflow of young family. Other areas, such as the Sunbelt, exhibit this concentration because of the immigration of the aged. The result of this migration is the creation of some segregated enclaves and also considerable demographic regional differences in age distribution.

The ideals of age segregation and integration, although moderated by demographic conditions, influence the general perception of the situation in the society and policies advocated to deal with them. The general values in the society on the issues of segregation come into play here; the contemporary ambivalence on this issue in general is also reflected in the public discussion on relations between age groups. As in relations between races, sexes, and ethnic groups, we find in the present society strong norms in favor of integration, as well as those promoting group identity (including association with persons having the same identification).

In the field of aging these two points of view are represented by such programs as surrogate grandparenting on the one side and the furthering of retirement communities on the other. Arguments can be made for the advantages of either policy: Each age group can contribute to the welfare of the other; the young give support and a certain rejuvenation to the aged, whereas the old provide direct support and a feeling of continuity and tradition, especially within the family. Against this must be weighed the degree of exploitation: exploitation of the younger by the older group can be seen in the extended family, and examples of reverse exploitation and "elder abuse" have been documented in the current society. The segregation of a group that shares common problems, amenable to solution by mutual help, and does not have to defer to the need of another group offers great advantages, which may outweigh the lack of continuity and abrupt changes that often accompany age segregation (Hochschild, 1973; Rosow, 1974; Streib, 1978, 1990).

To arrive at a general judgment of the value of trends toward (and away from) age segregation is difficult. Individual developmental needs are influenced by general social expectations; the needs of social well-being must be weighed against individual life satisfaction. Thus, the balance in the society between a familylike ideal as against supportive age-homogeneous communities will influence the evaluation of any arrangement, even the interpretation of any specific effects that may be found. A new understanding may be coming from the concept of a group of individuals who help and protect a person (Antonucci & Akiyama, 1993; Kahn & Antonucci, 1980; Plath, 1980). Although originally consisting principally of family members, it typically evolves into a group selected by friendship and common experiences; it becomes homogeneous in age but still can integrate the individual into other sectors of the society. The persistence of convoys has been shown to be related to well-being of the aged (Antonucci & Akiyama, 1991); convoys cannot be created through gerontological programs but are functions of the experiences of the whole life course and of the society in which it unfolds.

KURT W. BACK

See also
  Family
  Housing
  Intergenerational Relationships
  Retirement Communities

AGE STATUS

Among the criteria in every society's maintenance and modification of its social system are the variously defined ages of its members and their aging (Cain, 1964). The ubiquity and the importance of age status systems have been recognized increasingly during the past half-century. Linton (1942) identified seven universal age/sex statuses: infant, male and female child, male and female adult, and male and female elder.

Neugarten and Moore (1968) established that age status systems emerge in all societies "in which duties, rights, and rewards are differentially distributed to age groups which themselves have been socially defined" (p. 5). Elder (1975) highlighted the complexity of the age factor:

> Age distinctions are expressed in normative expectations, privileges, and rewards. As socially recognized divisions of the life course, whether generalized across society or restricted to institutional domains, age grades are defined by norms that . . . specify appropriate behavior, roles, and schedules. (pp. 167–168)

There have been challenges to the assertion of ubiquity of age status systems. Keith (1990), after affirming wide variations in cultural responses to the life course, reported that there are some small-scale communities that do not exhibit use of age-related norms or roles, although terms such as *child* or *old person* may be employed. Keith adds that efforts by researchers in some small communities have failed to elicit any genuine names for any age-related stages of the life course.

There is evidence of diminished relevance of age awareness in some postliterate "experimental" or "partial" societies. Kibbutzim in pre-Israel Palestine sought, in their early stages, to declare age differences to be irrelevant (Talmon, 1972). Total institutions, including prisons, convents, and military units, may invite their members to "go on ice," to cast aside concern for age-related factors (San Giovanni, 1978). Chudacoff (1989) suggests a diminished role for age awareness in Western societies before industrialization. His evidence indicated that before 1850 institutions in America "were not structured according to age-defined divisions, and [America's] cultural norms did not strongly prescribe age-related behavior" (p. 10). In sharp contrast, a decade or more before Chudacoff, historians Fischer (1977), Achenbaum (1978), and Haber (1983) provided abundant evidence and interpretation that from the early colonial period in America there was a distinctive, often evolving status for the elderly. Henceforward, our position is that age status and associated life course patterns are of significance in all societies, especially those that are bureaucratized.

Cole (1992) has located the origins of the modern life course and its age statuses in America "in the search for religious and social order in early modern Northern Europe (from the late fifteenth to the seventeenth century)" (p. 4). Sennett (1998) presents a much shorter time frame:

> The "long-term" order [i.e., the age-status institution, especially bureaucratically developed and protected career patterns] at which the new regime [i.e., "late modernity"] takes aim . . . was short-lived. Nineteenth-century capitalism lurched from disaster to disaster. . . . [A]fter World War II this disorder was brought somewhat under control. (p. 23)

In proposing that age status be viewed as an institution, note that normative responses, especially in bureaucratized societies, provide direction and pace to the life courses of individuals and to the history of successive birth cohorts. Kohli (1986) and Kohli and Rein (1991) employ "life course institution" to identify these age-related phenomena. We dare to suggest that age-status institutions, linked to life course patterns, be given emphasis comparable to that provided political, economic, religious, educational, and marriage/family institutions.

It must be emphasized that age seldom stands alone. Gender, social class, race and ethnicity, region, and religion, among other variables, force modifications on any standardized age-status system. Vagaries of history and demographic shifts produce cohort effects that place strains on an age-related normative order.

Advancing age status as the appropriate concept to encompass the vast array of age-related issues that confront societies needs explication. The concept "age differentiation" (Elder, 1975; Fry, 1980) conveys a similar meaning but does not incorporate the concept of role or the exercise of status. Another alternative, age stratification, was introduced in the early 1970s (Riley, Johnson, & Foner, 1972). A critique (Cain, 1987) proposed that age stratificationists "have failed to provide the basis for theoretical tools to move beyond declarations of conflict and tensions (between those of different ages) into issues of justice and equity" (p. 288). Riley (1994) subsequently abandoned "age stratification," suggesting that it is "overly static, failing . . . to reflect the dynamic aspects of both lives and structures" (p. 436). Her substitute concept is the "aging and society paradigm."

A major problem is that both *age* and *status* have multiple meanings. Currently, chronological age (i.e., counting forward from birth) is accepted as definitive for many purposes. However, "functional age," based on capacity to perform roles often associated loosely with chronological age, appears in many guises. These means of determining age and thereby age status are rooted in individual attributes, as culturally defined. Another determination of age may be identified as "social age," which is based on relationships with certain others. Examples include seniority and grandparenthood.

The concept of status has had two distinct meanings. One is associated with a hierarchy of esteem; the focus is on inequality among those of different ages. Age stratification, cited above, conveyed "vertical" inequality among those of varying ages. A second meaning, advocated here, focuses on differentiation, with emphasis on a "horizontal" progression through the life course. A horizontal approach to age status invites consideration by a society of issues of equity/inequity among the statuses, whereas a vertical approach perforce focuses on equality/inequality issues and thus presumes, possibly promotes, conflict among various age categories (Cain, 1987). Cole (1989) and Somerville (1989) have explored issues of intergenerational justice and equity. An age-status approach does not discount the possibility of a filiocentric or a gerontocratic society.

The following age-generated needs appear to contribute to the establishment of age-status institutions by every society:

1.   The persistent aging of its members, both as individuals and as cohort collectivities. Responses typically include socialization processes, which equip members to occupy successive age statuses, and rites of passage, which herald shifts to new age statuses (Van Gennep, 1909). Patterns of death influence the responses, dramatically as a result of war or epidemics or similar factors.

2.   Variations among individuals and, on occasion, cohorts in moving through life-course stages or successive age statuses "on time" (Neugarten & Lowe, 1965). The normatively ordered system may be strained by those who enter college early or late, bear children early or late, or retire early or late. On occasion, cohorts or segments thereof have been called upon to age prematurely or to be held in abeyance. Wars, economic depressions, and other catastrophes may lead to "off time" adaptations. With abolition of mandatory retirement, with the average age of college students moving toward 30, with women at 60 bearing children, the on time/off time distinction has become blurred.

3.   Variations in the pace of physical aging and social maturation among members, factors that may put a strain on the system and a steady cohort flow.

4.   The prospect that members may be called upon to move through the life course at an asynchronous pace; that is, members may be called upon to be an adult breadwinner before having adult suffrage privileges or to retire when family responsibilities to children remain.

Thus, as a society responds to the types of challenges outlined above, the institutionalization of an age-status system proceeds. Adaptation and revision appear to be pervasive, at least in bureaucratized societies. Note also that age-status institutions may have two distinguishable forms: one based on the idealized expectations for the occupants of the various statuses and another based on the actual results of adaptations to historically conditioned realities.

Some recent theorists, including Giddens (1991), Sennett (1998), and Wallulis (1998) in reference to both career and family patterns, have announced a deinstitutionalization of age status and the life course in the emergent "late modern" period.

Giddens (1991) admits that "the life course is [still] seen as a series of 'passages,' . . . but they are not [now] institutionalized, or accompanied by formalised rites" (p. 79). For Giddens, "self-actualization" has replaced an institutionally charted life course. But there is no attention given to the prospect of a rapidly expanding population of the elderly, whose ability to survive the risks of self-actualization may be both limited and undesired. Furthermore, Giddens is oblivious to the continuing significance of legal age, of statutes and regulations that continue to provide proscriptions and protections that both restrict and permit self-actualization.

Sennett (1998) detects a trend similar to that noted by Giddens but questions whether the loss of traditional age-status institutions, specifically regarding career patterns, will corrode the formation of "character" and thus diminish society. His concluding words are quite personal, as he critiques the "rulers of the flexible realm":

> The new masters have rejected careers in the old English sense of the word, as pathways along which people can travel; . . . [T]his regime might . . . lose its current hold over the imaginations and sentiments of those down below. . . . [I]f change occurs it happens . . . between persons speaking out of inner need. . . . What political programs follow from these inner needs, I simply don't know. But I do know a regime which provides human beings no deep reasons to care about one another cannot long preserve its legitimacy. (pp. 147–148)

Wallulis (1998) also deals with the recent expansion of emphasis on individualism and independence and its promotion of insecurity among ordinary citizens regarding both jobs and family. He proposes political action to overcome the "destandardization" of career (p. 178).

These studies do indeed reveal transitions that expose the inadequacies of an only recently developed age-status institution. Called for is the invention of a new institution that can incorporate independence and individuality but also can provide meaning, security, and hope for the general citizenry.

Among the oversights of scholars of age, especially gerontologists, one of the most difficult to fathom has been the inattention given to aging and the law. Although the major gerontological associations remain deeply involved in monitoring legislative and judicial activities and although the status of the elderly, as well as that of other age categories, is determined to a considerable extent by laws, research and scholarship have been minimal. Effective use of the concept of age status, especially by gerontologists, awaits a concerted effort to understand the dramatic role of law in defining the rights, obligations, and privileges of those in various age categories in society. A case in point is the emergence, in widely varying contexts, of a subtle shift from chronological age to counting backward from projected death, that is, turning to years remaining to be lived rather than years already lived to determine eligibility for old-age status.

LEONARD D. CAIN

See also
  Social Stratification

AGE STEREOTYPE

An age stereotype is a simplified, undifferentiated portrayal of an age group that is often erroneous, unrepresentative of reality, and resistant to modification. Although the word *stereotype* was first used in the technology of duplicate printing, where a metal plate (i.e., the stereotype) was cast into a mold, the American journalist Walter Lippmann introduced its usage for both scholarly and popular audiences in his 1922 book *Public Opinion*. Lippmann argues that seeing things freshly and in detail is exhausting and so people see a trait that marks a type and "fill in the rest of the picture by means of the stereotypes we carry about in our heads" (p. 89). Age stereotypes have to do with people "filling in the picture" of a person or group of people after knowing only one characteristic—age.

Most research on age stereotypes has focused on how people view the elderly rather than on how they view younger age groups.

Political scientist Robert Binstock (1983, 1994) makes a frequently cited argument that, since the 1960s and 1970s Americans have reversed their "compassionate stereotype" of the elderly as poor, frail, and dependent to a new stereotype of the elderly as prosperous, active, and politically powerful. Neither image is accurate, notes Binstock. However, to date, no longitudinal research on age stereotypes using nationally representative samples of the public allows for the testing of Binstock's hypothesis.

Researchers define stereotypes as sets of traits attributed to social groups and try to learn what these traits are. The work of Palmore (1999) and Hummert, Garstka, Shaner, and Strahm (1994) show that people often hold multiple stereotypes of the elderly rather than a single negative or positive stereotype. Palmore (1999) identifies nine negative stereotypes about the elderly (the belief that most aged are sick, impotent, ugly, senile, mentally ill, useless, isolated, poor, and depressed) and eight positive stereotypes (the image of most elderly as kind, wise, dependable, affluent, politically powerful, free, happy, and hopeful of eternal youth). Hummert and colleagues (1994) identify 69 descriptive traits that they reduce to four negative (severely impaired, shrew/curmudgeon, recluse, despondent) and three positive stereotypes (perfect grandparent, John Wayne conservative, golden ager).

The mass media, an important institution for socialization in the United States, often receive the blame for disseminating stereotypes. According to work done in the early 1980s, the elderly appeared with only one-fifth their actual prevalence in the U.S. population among prime-time television characters (Kubey, 1980). Further, when they *were* portrayed, they were depicted as in poorer health, less good at doing things, more financially dependent, less sexually active, and more narrow-minded than they actually are in life (Gerbner, Gross, Signorielli, & Morgan, 1980). More recently, some researchers (e.g., Bell, 1992) present evidence to show that this negative portrayal has changed and that television now presents a stereotype of healthy, active elderly persons—a stereotype that is just as exaggerated as the old one, according to Bell. An important question for researchers and one on which there is some disagreement is the extent to which media portrayals affect knowledge and attitudes about older adults (e.g., contrast Gerbner et al., 1980, with Passuth and Cook, 1985).

The reason that stereotypes are considered cause for concern is that a link is assumed to exist between systematic stereotyping on the basis of age and discrimination against people over 65. Little research has explored this linkage. What research there is shows high support for social programs that assist older people and even a willingness to pay higher taxes if programs for the elderly were threatened with cuts (Cook, 1979; Cook & Barrett, 1992). Exploring the possible links between stereotyping and discrimination is a ripe area for further research, particularly examining the ways in which linkages—to the extent they exist—are complexly determined, exist in some domains (for example, employment) but not others, and are stronger toward some elderly groups than others as measured by such factors as functional capacity or work status or appearance or frailty.

In trying to understand and measure stereotypes, the problem with which gerontologists grapple is how to probe stereotypes about the elderly when, in fact, "the elderly" are such a heterogeneous group. Whereas researchers continue to measure attitudes and media portrayals about the elderly as if "the elderly" or "older persons" or "people over 65" were homogeneous and represent some unitary construct, the most powerful fact on which all gerontologists agree is that the elderly are heterogeneous on nearly all the attributes ever measured. Researchers may continue to find the existence of stereotypes if they continue to pose questions about "the elderly." It may be that the more specific the questions, the less stereotyping may be found. For example, Schonfield (1982) showed that misbeliefs about older persons' inflexibility, loneliness, and religiosity diminished markedly when respondents were instructed to indicate which statements were representative of at least 80% of the elderly. More recently, Kite (1996) found that negative stereotyping of the elderly is reduced when contextual information about the elderly was provided, particularly information about their work-related roles.

FAY LOMAX COOK

See also
Consumer Issues: The Mature Market

AGE STRATIFICATION

Age stratification—now called the aging and society paradigm—is a multifaceted conceptual framework for studying and interpreting age phenomena in social life. First formulated in Riley, Johnson, and Foner (1972) and updated in Riley (1994), the paradigm is a heuristic tool for assessing and codifying the massive outpourings of social science research on age. Its unique feature is its dual emphasis on age as a component of both human lives and social structures. Its approach is dynamic, focusing on the two "dynamisms" of changing lives and changing structures, conceived as interdependent but distinct sets of processes. At any given time, these processes produce "age strata" (or layers) of people who differ in age and who confront structures differentially appropriate for particular ages. The paradigm, as a parsimonious set of broad concepts and postulated relationships, draws on two lines of social research and theory (referenced in Riley, 1994): aging over the life course (e.g., by Thomas, Znaniecki, Neugarten, Clausen, Elder, Schaie, Baltes, and Dannefer), and the place of age in social structures (e.g., by Sorokin, Parsons, Eisenstadt, Mannheim, Ryder, and Cain).

Continuing Development of the Paradigm

The paradigm has been used over the decades for working back and forth between theory and data and has undergone continual clarification, specification, revision, and terminological redefinition; and it is destined for further development in the future. As one major revision, the change of name from "age stratification" to "aging and society" was designed to convey the dynamic emphases on both human lives and social structures and also to avoid widespread confusion with class stratification. To be sure, stratification based on age shares certain generic properties with class stratification systems, including socially structured inequalities that foster potentials for within-stratum solidarity and between-strata conflict (see Foner, 1974). Nevertheless, age-based stratification has certain distinguishing characteristics. Unlike social mobility, whereby only some members cross class boundaries, the mobility of aging and cohort succession is inevitable and involves everyone. Moreover, primordial differences based on age and gender may well antedate even the earliest history of social thought about stratification.

This paradigm, together with its variants, has been used in many ways (Riley, Foner, & Riley, 1999). Depending on the objectives of particular studies, the paradigm has made room for emphases on people and groups at all levels (ranging from micro through meso to macro) for subjective and objective views; and for cross-disciplinary, cross-national, and cross-temporal perspectives. The paradigm has informed teaching and research in diverse disciplines, professional practice, and public policy and (during the decade of the 1980s) the Behavioral and Social Research Program at the National Institute on Aging. These uses can be illustrated through examples of work by many scholars in the two main areas of concern: human lives and social structures.

Research on Lives

A great deal of attention has been paid to one half of the paradigm: what is often called the "life course approach" (cf. Dannefer & Uhlenberg, 1999). It is a universal principle that people grow up, grow old, die, and replace each other in an endless succession of cohorts as long as the society endures. In part, individuals are active agents of their own changes: As individuals who are growing older, they change in diverse ways—biologically, psychologically, and socially. In part also, because society and its institutions continually change, the overall patterns of people's lives cannot be the same from one cohort to the next. Numerous contemporary cohort differences have been identified. For example, on the average, members of cohorts now old differ from those who grew old in the past with respect to educational level, family history, work history, diet and exercise, standard of living, number of years in retirement, and—perhaps most significant of all—the number of years they can expect to survive.

Such cohort differences affect the meaning of lives. Studies show, for example, how people start their lives in one historical period, when the age strata and people's cognitive maps of those strata are organized in a particular way; and as people in a cohort age, society and its social structures are continually being revised and reorganized. Thus, people who were young earlier in this century learned the dominant societal age patterns and norms of that period: most attended school for no more than 6 or 7 years—adequate education for the jobs then held by their fathers—and most developed images of old age from the characteristics of their few surviving grandparents. But now that those people have grown old, the society is different from that of their grandparents. Similarly, the young today confront an occupational ladder being transformed by microtechnology, and they see struggles over the current institutionalization of retirement as an entitlement. Moreover, in the future none of these young people will themselves be old in the same society in which they began. They will grow older in institutional structures that are changing. Hence, there is an intrinsic pressure for readjustments between what they expect and need, and the shifting exigencies of firms, families, communities, and other social structures.

Research on Structures

These and many other types of research on lives demonstrate that the shapes of these lives are affected, not exclusively by biology as earlier believed but also by the surrounding social structures. Experiments that make particular interventions in social structures have demonstrated dramatic enhancement of people's health, effective functioning, and quality of life—whatever their biological predispositions. Hence, more research is currently needed on the structural side of the paradigm: on how age-related structures change and can be changed.

Age is relevant to social structures both directly and indirectly. Directly, chronological age (or some surrogate for age) is often built into structures as criteria for entering or leaving particular roles, defining performance expectations, allocating resources, or designating rewards and punishments. Indirectly, many social changes, without specifying age, have consequences for people that differ by age: according to stages of the life course, cohort membership, or the age strata to which people belong at a particular period of study. For example, structural changes associated with industrialization produced age barriers that have long restricted the participation of older people (as well as children) in the economy and of middle-aged people in education or leisure pursuits. As a consequence, lives could be deprived at particular ages of full opportunities, not only for income and power but also for affection, respect, self-esteem, or new adventure.

Despite the importance of age as an aspect of structures and structural change, however, it has not attracted a full share of research attention. Especially in recent times, there is a tendency toward "life course reductionism," in which structures, if noted at all, are treated as contextual characteristics of people, not studied as research units in their own right or recognized as subject to change processes of their own. Yet wider implementation of this half of the paradigm is essential if likely future changes are to be anticipated or if alternative outcomes of clinical or policy interventions are to be assessed in advance.

Contributions of the Paradigm

Whatever the shortcomings of the aging and society paradigm, several themes and premises derived from it are gradually being formulated for use as working principles. For example, principles referring to each of the two dynamisms or the interplay between them include the lifelong, multifaceted, and mutable character of the processes of aging and cohort succession; the varying changes or stabilities in the social structures that influence and are influenced by people's lives; and the relevance of old age for all ages. Methodologically, the paradigm has stimulated further development and use of longitudinal and cohort analyses and has raised still unanswered research questions about the interplay between lives and structures. It has identified several common types of fallacies or misinterpretation of findings, such as the "life-course fallacy" (misinterpreting age differences as if they were caused by aging) and the "fallacy of cohort centrism" (assuming falsely that all cohorts are precisely like our own). Pinpointing these fallacies has helped to correct erroneous beliefs about biological determinism—the presumed inevitability and universality of deterioration because of growing old.

Implementation of the paradigm in the work of many scholars has led to a range of useful concepts.

These include "disordered cohort flow" and "cohort norm formation" as the sizes or attitudes and behaviors in incoming cohorts produce structural changes (Riley, 1978); "asynchrony," as the differences in timing between the two dynamisms cause strains in both people and structures; "structural lag," a serious contemporary problem, as increasing numbers and capacities of older people outstrip the 20th-century age constraints on work, education, and leisure (see the entry on Structural Lag); and the ideal type of an "age-integrated society" as removal of such age constraints could open these domains to people of every age.

Future Agenda

However useful or provocative of debate the evolving aging and society paradigm may have been in the past, the ultimate test will depend on its continuing development in the future. Within the various plans for future research on age, several gaps in the paradigm have been identified. Given the current tendency toward life-course reductionism, many of these gaps relate to the dynamism of changing structures (an area to which the National Institute on Aging's Program on Age and Structural Change has been directing attention). Several remaining questions will illustrate some of these gaps: How is gender built into the interplay between changing lives and changing structures? How are cross-temporal and cross-cultural differences built into this interplay? How is social change brought about by extrinsic factors (such as policy interventions) interacting with intrinsic pressures from people's changing lives? How can lives and structures be studied simultaneously as particular individuals move through particular structures?

Whatever the future may bring, the aging and society paradigm (as it is now called) has already gone far. Despite mistakes and false starts, it provides a broad heuristic framework for formulating fundamental principles about age and aging, clarifying potential misinterpretations of data, integrating miscellaneous findings into a cumulative body of knowledge, specifying significant research objectives, and emphasizing the policy implications of the realization that both individual lives and societal structures are not immutable but subject to change.

MATILDA WHITE RILEY

See also

  Age Conflicts
  Cohorts
  Longitudinal Research
  Social Stratification

AGING NETWORK

Few of the elements now considered part of the "aging network" existed in the early 1960s. Nursing homes and convalescent centers provided care for seriously impaired older persons, and the Social Security Administration provided beneficiaries with their monthly checks. On the federal level, research about aging was implemented primarily through different programs at the National Institutes of Health, particularly the National Institute of Child and Human Development.

As was true in many areas of social welfare, rapid change began in the 1960s. In the field of aging, the landmark Medicare and Medicaid legislation and the Older Americans Act (OAA) were enacted in 1965. Besides providing health coverage for most older Americans, the Medicare program was an impetus for the growth of nursing homes. However, it was the OAA that fostered the growth of an aging network and what some authors have termed the "aging enterprise" (Estes, 1979). The aging network has been defined as "the system of public and semipublic organizations responsible for implementing the Older Americans Act" (Montgomery, 1987). Senior centers, meals programs, social service agencies, home care agencies, and case management programs are usually included under the aging network rubric.

Under the OAA, a federal agency, the Administration on Aging (AoA), was for the first time authorized to coordinate services for the elderly. Funded by Congressional appropriations, AoA in turn funded State Units on Aging, which planned and monitored aging programs. Rather than having one organization that attempted to develop pro-

grams for older people throughout the state, each state had local organizations, the Area Agency on Aging (AAA), that planned and coordinated locally oriented programs. The AAA was not expected to operate programs but rather to serve as a planning, coordinating and monitoring organization. Funds allocated to the AAA by the State Unit on Aging were in turn allocated to organizations that actually ran the programs. Although the number of AAAs in each state was relatively small during the late 1960s and early 1970s, smaller political divisions in localities began to demand their own AAAs. An example is the AAA of Central Maryland, which represented a few counties; by the end of the 1970s, each of these counties had developed its own AAA.

Whether this level of local control was necessary is not clear, but the number of AAAs had grown to approximately 670 by 1993. In addition to the organizations related to the AoA, the aging network also includes volunteer programs, such as Foster Grandparents, that are authorized under the OAA and administered by ACTION, the federal volunteer agency. Although not usually considered part of the aging network, organizations such as the American Association of Retired Persons (AARP), the National Council on the Aging, the National Council of Senior Citizens (NCSC), the American Health Care Association (which represents the proprietary nursing home industry), the American Association of Homes and Services for the Aging (which represents the nonprofit nursing home industry), and the American Society on Aging have important roles in the development of policies and programs for older Americans.

Organizations that have large memberships of older persons, such as the AARP and the NCSC, play an important role in the daily activities of many older people through their local chapters. In addition, the Gerontological Society of America and the American Geriatrics Society represent the academic and research disciplines concerned with the processes of aging. These and other national organizations concerned with aging programs and policies now meet monthly to coordinate their efforts at the national level.

The continued amending of the OAA since 1965 has produced not only a growth in the types of programs offered to older persons but a proliferation of organizations and individuals involved with these efforts. Churches and synagogues offer congregate meals, recreation departments at the county levels operate programs for older persons, and adult day care centers offer daylong programs for "frail elderly" under a variety of profit and nonprofit auspices. Within large senior centers, a variety of professionals offer art therapy, music therapy, dance therapy, or more basic rehabilitative services, such as physical and occupational therapy. The growth of interest in aging can be found in the formation of geriatric interest sections within organizations such as the American Occupational Therapy Association and the American Physical Therapy Association.

A major component of the OAA is the effort to develop employment for workers over the age of 55. These Title V job slots are administered through the Department of Labor, eight national contractors, and the individual states. The eight national contractors include minority aging organizations such as the National Caucus on Black Aged, the National Association for Hispanic Elderly, and the National Indian Council on Aging. These and other minority aging organizations have become important elements of the nongovernmental aging network.

Finally, case management has become and will continue to be an important component of the aging network in many states. Both public and private case managers will be increasingly vital links between the older person and service delivery organizations, especially for older persons and their families who need intensive assistance. AAAs have become increasingly active in promoting case management, particularly through partnerships with large corporations interested in developing "elder care" initiatives for their employees. For further information, refer to Gelfand (1999).

DONALD E. GELFAND

See also
Federal Council on the Aging
Older Americans Act
Organizations in Aging

AIDS/HIV IN OLDER ADULTS

At the end of 1998, about 33.4 million people were living with HIV/AIDS, and about 13.9 million had died since the recognition of the epidemic (UNAIDS/WHO, 1998). Infection with human immunodeficiency virus (HIV) eventually progresses to HIV disease and acquired immunodeficiency syndrome (AIDS). AIDS can be thought of as one end of the spectrum of HIV-related conditions that may include acute infection, an asymptomatic period, and eventually certain opportunistic infections, neoplasias, and other conditions. The Centers for Disease Control and Prevention (CDC) have a detailed surveillance definition and classification system for AIDS based on documentation of HIV infection, degrees of laboratory evidence of immunosuppression using $CD4^+$ lymphocyte counts, and specified symptoms and AIDS indicator conditions (CDC, 1992). The major result of HIV infection is both quantitative and qualitative immune impairment that largely affects the T-helper lymphocytes (T4, $CD4^+$ cells), but macrophages, monocytes, glial cells, fibroblasts, and antigen-presenting dendritic cells can also become infected. This results in increased susceptibility to opportunistic infections (OIs) and neoplasms. Major conditions resulting from OIs in the HIV-infected person include *Pneumocystis carinii* pneumonia (PCP); encephalitis due to *Toxoplasma gondii*; severe diarrhea and gastrointestinal problems due to *Cryptosporidium* spp., *Isospora belli*, and others; meningitis from *Cryptococcus neoformans*; candidiasis of the oral cavity, esophagus, and in women, the vagina; tuberculosis; herpes simplex virus lesions; retinitis due to cytomegalovirus; and disseminated infections due to cytomegalovirus, *Mycobacterium avium* complex, and others. Major neoplasms include Kaposi's sarcoma and non-Hodgkin's lymphomas (Cohen, Sande, & Volberding, 1999; Lashley, 2000; Sande & Volberding, 1999). HIV also has direct effects on certain cells and tissues, particularly in the central nervous system (Kolson, Lavi, & Gonzalez-Scarano, 1998). The nervous system may be affected, even asymptomatically, in all persons with HIV disease; effects such as AIDS dementia complex (ADC), vacuolar myopathy, and peripheral neuropathy are common. Medical treatment has been directed (1) against HIV itself through the use of combinations of antiretroviral drugs, including nonnucleoside reverse transcriptase inhibitors, nucleoside reverse transcriptase inhibitors, and protease inhibitors; (2) at immune system enhancement; and (3) at preventing and treating specific opportunistic infections and conditions. The latter includes nonpharmacological measures and the use of pharmacological and biological agents, including vaccines. Integral to the treatment has been the monitoring of viral load and CD4+ cell counts as well as clinical status. Details of treatment and prophylaxis may be found in CDC (1998), Cohen, Sande, and Volberding (1999), Durham and Lashley (2000), Sande and Volberding (1999), and CDC (1999b). Treatment in the older adult parallels that of other adult age groups, with the necessary adaptations in dosage and/or regimens resulting from the physiological and psychosocial consequences of aging, the presence of non-HIV-related coexisting chronic illness, and consideration of interactions with drugs used to treat these.

Transmission of HIV

The major documented transmission modes for HIV are those in which persons are exposed to HIV-containing blood or body fluid (1) through intimate homosexual or heterosexual contact; (2) through parenteral or blood-borne exposure via transfusions, needlesticks, injection drug use, or similar means; and (3) vertically from an infected mother to her infant in the prenatal, perinatal, or immediate postnatal period. Other factors influence the acquisition of HIV. Among these are risky behaviors that increase the likelihood of HIV acquisition, such as unprotected sexual encounters, sex with high-risk partners, engaging in risky sexual acts such as receptive anal intercourse, and sharing apparatus to inject drugs. All of the modes of HIV transmission (except perinatal) that apply to the other age groups also apply to those who acquire HIV when they are elderly. Currently, sexual transmission is the leading mode of HIV acquisition in older adults (Bender, 1997).

Exposure Categories

The CDC classifies U.S. cases of AIDS by the major exposure categories in a hierarchical manner. These categories for all adults and their approximate percentages are as follows: men who have sex with men (48%); injection drug use (26%); men who have sex with men and inject drugs (6%);

hemophilia/coagulation disorder (1%); heterosexual contact (10%); receipt of blood transfusion, blood components, or tissue (1.2%); and risk not reported or identified (8.3%) (CDC, 1999a). In the past, blood transfusion and/or tissue transplantation has been an important mode of acquisition of HIV in those over 55 years of age, at one time even accounting for the majority of cases in those 65 years of age and older (Ship, Wolff, & Selik, 1991). Because of protective mechanisms now in place to screen the blood supply, this acquisition mode has already decreased and is expected to decrease further in the future. On the other hand, AIDS cases due to heterosexual transmission have increased in those 65 years of age and older.

AIDS Cases in Older Adults

The term "invisible" has been used to describe many groups affected by the AIDS epidemic, including women, children, and the elderly. However, it does seem as though little attention has been paid to both the present and future aspects of HIV in the older adult. The CDC, in its standard statistical reporting of AIDS cases, gives data by 5-year intervals until age 65 years, after which they lump together the cases in the age group of 65 years and older. In 1999, approximately 10% of cumulatively reported U.S. adult AIDS cases occurred in adults 50 years of age and older, about 3% occurred in those who were 60 years of age and older, and about 1.4% occurred in those who were 65 years of age and older (CDC, 1999a). Among persons with AIDS who are 50 and 65 years of age and older, respectively, the ratio of men to women is about 7:1 and 4:1 (CDC, 1999a; Woolery, 1997). These percentages have remained relatively constant since reporting began.

The statistics described above report the age at the time of *diagnosis* of AIDS. It is expected that an increased absolute number of cases of both HIV infection and AIDS will eventually be seen in the older population, as well as a greater relative proportion due to the decrease in perinatal transmission. Some reasons for this include the following: (1) HIV-infected persons may progress to symptomatic states and AIDS over a long period of time, due in part to early and increasingly effective therapy; thus, persons who were infected in the middle-aged group will move into the elderly age category; (2) persons in older age groups may continue to receive blood transfusions and tissue/organ transplantation at higher rates than other age groups, so a certain number of cases (although relatively few and decreasing) will continue to arise from this source; (3) older persons, may engage in risky sexual behaviors, such as not using condoms for sexual encounters, for many reasons, including lack of concern about birth control, lack of awareness about HIV risks, and difficulty with manipulation due to conditions such as arthritis, thus becoming more vulnerable to infection with HIV and/or other sexually transmitted diseases; (4) the life expectancy for persons in the United States continues to increase, and older people enjoy better health and mobility, allowing them to pursue risky behaviors and activities; and (5) age-related changes in immune function and in protective mechanical barriers, such as drying of vaginal mucosa in women, make the elderly more susceptible to acquisition of HIV infection when they are exposed.

Sex, Drugs, and the Elderly

Since the majority of cases of HIV transmission involve sexual contact, and/or drug abuse, these are a major focus of general AIDS prevention, assessment, and educational efforts. Society still subscribes to many false beliefs and negative views of sexuality in the older adult. Often, the elderly are seen as relatively asexual or as secure in a monogamous relationship. Little has been described in the literature about sexual practices in the elderly, including risky behavior, multiple and/or same sex sexual partners, and so on. Leary (1998) found that nearly half of those over 60 years of age engaged in sex at least once a month. Health care workers may not ask about sexual activity as part of the health history in the older person. Most studies of sexuality among the elderly have concentrated on sexual dysfunction as opposed to sexual activity. Older persons may also believe they should hide their sexual activity—heterosexual, homosexual, or both. They may not readily volunteer or discuss risk factors or exposures. They may fear the reaction of friends or family if they acknowledge experiencing sexual relationships, especially if those relationships are outside their usual partnership or mar-

riage. Decades ago, sex-related activities were not openly discussed or displayed. "Gray" and "gay" were seen as antithetical terms, and men who had sex with other men were accustomed to being closeted to avoid discrimination. However, it is estimated that at least 1 million male homosexuals are over age 65 years (Ship, Wolff, & Selik, 1991). This may be an underestimate and may not consider cultural definitions of sexuality or occasional same sex experiences.

Sexual transmission of HIV occurs proportionately frequently in the older population. More than 50% of all reported AIDS cases in those aged 60 and over are classified in some exposure category pertaining to sexual transmission. However, only about 11% of all cases in the category "men who have sex with men" occur in those 50 years of age and older, and 13% of those in the "heterosexual contact" exposure category are 50 years or older (CDC, 1997). Probable heterosexual transmission of HIV was reported in a woman of 89 years (Rosenzweig & Fillit, 1992). Sexual relationships outside monogamous ones may be becoming increasingly common in the elderly. Some examples include (1) older men whose long-term partner has died may now have sexual contact with several other partners who may be younger, increasing the risk of exposure to HIV; (2) elderly women may seek sexual fulfillment with younger men in a nonmonogamous relationship; and (3) elderly men (married or not) may pay for sexual relationships with prostitutes (male or female) or seek available sexual companionship, which, particularly in longterm care settings, may be with a male. All of these individuals may now be at risk for HIV infection but be reluctant to disclose this behavior unless the health care provider asks specific questions regarding sexual behavior. Primary care providers may not discuss topics related to HIV risk as frequently with older patients as with younger ones and may fail to recommend HIV testing or consider HIV in the differential diagnosis (CDC, 1998).

A sentinel study examined risk factors and behaviors in a large national sample of adults over 50 years of age. The prevalence of a known risk factor for HIV infection, such as being a transfusion recipient, having multiple sexual partners, or having a partner with known risk for HIV infection, was 10%. Very few of these respondents used condoms during sex or had had HIV testing, particularly in comparison with a younger sample (Stall & Catania, 1994). In another study, few persons over 50 years of age (11%) had discussed AIDS with their physician (Gerbert, Maguire, & Coates, 1990).

While sexuality in the older adult is a topic that is often avoided in discussion, so is drug abuse. Few studies have addressed injection drug use for nonprescribed or nonmedical purposes in the elderly. Yet medical conditions that cause pain and discomfort might cause older adults to seek drugs, as might social conditions or other reasons. Furthermore, drug users who began such use at younger ages may continue this habit into old age. Thus, health care workers also need to consider drug use when assessing risk for HIV exposure in the older person, although currently AIDS attributed to this exposure category is infrequent in the elderly.

Clinical Aspects of HIV/AIDS and Survival in the Elderly

AIDS may mimic other conditions in the elderly, and it can be difficult to recognize HIV infection in this group (CDC, 1998). It can present with vague and nonspecific signs and symptoms, such as weight loss and wasting; aches and pains; fever; cough; and/or cognitive impairment and confusion. Symptoms in the elderly may present against a background of multiple other actual or potential illnesses and medication side effects and interactions. Cases of HIV infection in the elderly have been described in which ADC was the presenting and/or sole feature. The symptoms of ADC can include forgetfulness, slow thought processes, personality changes, depression, loss of concentration, apathy, and other features. Many of these are similar to problems seen in the elderly from other causes, including the dementia seen in Alzheimer's disease and in extrapyramidal disorders (Kernutt, Price, Judd, & Burrows, 1993), as well as delirium. Because HIV infection can persist for years, with few manifestations, some persons acquiring it later in life may live their life span without showing major recognizable symptoms. Thus, clinicians must be ready to consider a differential diagnosis of HIV disease in the older adult regardless of gender.

Persons 50 years and older with AIDS were more likely to be reported with an OI than were younger patients (CDC, 1998). Once AIDS-associated opportunistic infections are acquired by older persons, they may be clinically worse or have higher fatality rates. Other debilitating conditions of aging may complicate those due to HIV infection, compounding and/or accelerating disease progression and decreasing functional capabilities. Changed social networks and other conditions make the indirect consequences of AIDS significant for the older person.

Although some persons who have been known to be HIV-infected for 20 years or more and who seem to have nonprogressive disease are still living, the ultimate outcome of HIV infection is considered to be death; and yearly overall mortality rates remain high, although treatment with protease inhibitors and HAART (highly active antiretroviral therapy) have increased life spans. HIV has been found to progress more rapidly in older people than in younger ones, and increased age was found to be one of the factors shortening survival in those already HIV-infected (Rezza, 1998).

FELISSA R. LASHLEY

See also
AIDS: The Epidemiological and Social Context

AIDS: THE EPIDEMIOLOGICAL AND SOCIAL CONTEXT

Although AIDS is typically thought of as a disease of the young, the presence of older Americans in the HIV/AIDS epidemic has been clearly demonstrated throughout the epidemic. It is now possible to move beyond speculation to describe and discuss the impact of AIDS on mature Americans. The Centers for Disease Control and Prevention (CDC) has reported that by the end of June 1999, 75,266 Americans aged 50 and older were diagnosed with AIDS. This represents slightly more than 10% of all diagnosed cases in those aged 13 and older, a stable trend throughout the epidemic. The 9,657 cases of AIDS among those aged 65 and older is greater than the 6,672 pediatric cases diagnosed over the same period (CDC, 1999). Between 1991 and 1996, newly diagnosed cases of AIDS rose twice as fast among those aged 50 and older than among those aged 13–49; and when comparing actual chronological age rather than age at diagnosis, nearly 15% of the AIDS caseload is composed of the older group (Ory & Mack, 1998).

Although the number of AIDS cases among Americans aged 50 and over is substantially greater than the pediatric caseload, the social and scientific attention paid to older Americans with AIDS is much less. Thus, despite the enormous size of the AIDS epidemic among older Americans (greater than the number of American casualties during the Vietnam War), we do not yet have sufficient data with which to identify the most effective means of preventing AIDS among the older age group.

Of those aged 50 and over who are diagnosed with AIDS, 86% are men, 47% are White, 36% are African American, and 16% are Hispanic, although racial breakdown is somewhat different between genders: half of all mature men with AIDS are White, 33% are African American, and 16% are Hispanic. Among women in the same age group, 28% are White, 51% are African American, and 20% are Hispanic (CDC, 1999). Since 1989 the proportion of older women of color among those with AIDS has increased. The most frequent mode of HIV infection reported by people aged 50 and over is sexual transmission. Data from 1986 to 1996 illustrate that there has been a decrease in transmission among men having sex with men but an increase in heterosexual transmission. Furthermore, the proportion of those infected through injection drug use has increased, but those who got HIV through a blood transfusion has decreased to only 6%. It is also noteworthy that older people with AIDS are twice as likely as younger groups to have an unidentified transmission route, and the percentage of those with an undetermined exposure category has increased as age increases (Ory & Mack, 1998).

The factors that keep older individuals at risk for HIV infection and a poor prognosis after being diagnosed with AIDS are both social and physiological. Older individuals have not been targeted for educational and intervention programs. Cross-sectional data indicate that older Americans have less HIV/AIDS-related knowledge and have a minimal perception of risk for contracting HIV. Because symptoms of AIDS are often similar to those of age-related diseases (e.g., wasting, dementia, night sweats), older people have been misdiagnosed. If physicians do not suspect HIV infection in older

people, they are more likely to proceed along the undiagnosed disease trajectory, and consequently miss the opportunity for early intervention and treatment.

Among older individuals with a risk factor, those aged 50 and older were much less likely to use condoms or be tested for HIV infection, compared to their younger counterparts (Stall & Catania, 1994). Age-related physical risk factors include decreased immune system function, inadequate caloric intake and vitamin and mineral deficiency, age-related thinning of vaginal and anal mucosa, comorbidity, and intolerance to medication regimens (Zelenetz & Epstein, 1998).

There have been some investigations of the social characteristics of older persons with HIV infection and AIDS. Among women with AIDS, those aged 50 have different social resources and sexual activities from younger women. They are less likely to be married or living with a partner and less likely to engage in sexual activity after receiving their diagnosis. Eighty-six percent of the women aged 50 and older never used condoms before receiving their diagnosis (compared to 67% of the younger women), and older women were significantly more likely to receive their HIV test while hospitalized (Schable, Chu, & Diaz, 1996). Mature adults with HIV/AIDS have been found to be financially vulnerable, with African Americans at even greater risk than their White counterparts for living below the poverty level (Speer, Kennedy, Watson, Meah, Nichols, & Watson, 1999).

The single largest risk category of AIDS cases among older Americans is that of men who have sex with men (MSM). A recent analysis of a household-based sample of MSM in Chicago, Los Angeles, New York, and San Francisco showed that celibacy increased with age in this population, so about one third of MSM past the age of 60 were celibate in the past year. Nonetheless, nearly half of the MSM in the sample were in steady partnerships, and the number of male sex partners reported by men in the sample did not substantially decline with age. Sexual contact with women was comparatively rare among both older and younger men, and high-risk sex with women was rare (less than 5% in the past year) across the life course of MSM. The prevalence of high-risk sexual practices with other men also declined with age (Stall, 1999).

In the second decade of investigation of AIDS, it has become clear that the approach to addressing the needs and concerns of older Americans and HIV/AIDS must incorporate two groups: those who are becoming infected in middle and later life and those who are aging with their HIV infection or AIDS. As mortality rates decrease, the prevalence of infection among older adults will continue to increase. Consequently, there remains a need to differentiate the progression of HIV disease from the experience of typical age-related changes. Similarly, the influence of comorbidity experienced by adults with HIV/AIDS requires further investigation (Ory, Zablotsky, & Crystal, 1998).

Older people have been identified in many areas of the HIV/AIDS epidemic: engaging in risk-related behaviors, living with HIV/AIDS, providing care to persons with AIDS (or their survivors) in both formal and informal settings, and volunteering in community-based AIDS organizations. Undoubtedly, there needs to be increased education directed both at older individuals and the health providers who care for them.

DIANE L. ZABLOTSKY
RON STALL

See also
AIDS/HIV in Older Adults

ALAMEDA COUNTY STUDY

The Alameda County Study is a prospective, population-based study of people aged 16 to 94, who, in 1965, were residents of Alameda County (Berkman & Breslow, 1983; Hochstim, 1970; Kaplan, 1992a). The California Department of Health Services Human Population Laboratory has conducted the study since 1965, when an initial cohort of 6,928 persons was interviewed. Reinterviews were conducted in 1974, 1983, and 1994. The Alameda County Study is one of a number of community-based epidemiologic studies that were begun in the late 1950s and early 1960s, following the earlier successes of the Framingham Study in identifying risk factors for disease. They represented a move from clinic-based studies to studies of populations in the community. A risk factor for a disease is

any factor to which an individual is exposed that increases the risk of the individual developing that disease. These factors include any aspects of behavior or lifestyle, environmental conditions, or any other factors that are causally related to the disease. The Alameda County Study differs from many of the other studies started in the same period in several important ways. It was not designed to focus on a specific disease or organ system but rather was an attempt to study risk factors for health, including the physical, psychological, and social dimensions. To accomplish this, considerable effort was devoted to the design of a comprehensive questionnaire measuring aspects of physical, social, psychological, behavioral, economic, and other domains of functioning. Also, the Alameda County Study was unique for its time in that it had no upper-age restrictions on participation; the oldest respondent was 94 years of age.

Well over 140 publications have been based on data collected from the Alameda County Study cohort; these publications have been referred to more than 6,000 times in the scientific literature. They cover a broad range of areas of research, with a focus on behavioral, social, psychological, and socioeconomic aspects of health and disease. Several articles relate specifically to primary and secondary prevention in the elderly, both with respect to longevity and to functional status. For example, behavioral and social factors were found to be strongly associated with 19-year risk of death, even in those who were older than 70 years of age at baseline (Kaplan, Seeman, Cohen, Knudsen, & Guralnik, 1987; Seeman, Kaplan, Knudsen, Cohen, & Guralnik, 1987). The increased risk associated with many of these risk factors did not decline substantially with increasing age. Behavioral, social, psychological, and socioeconomic factors were also found to be associated with changes in depression and perceived health status (Yen & Kaplan, 1999), in physical functioning (Kaplan, 1992b; Kaplan, Wilson, Kauhanen, Cohen, Wu, Salonen, et al., 1993; Strawbridge, Kaplan, Camacho, & Cohen, 1992), healthy aging (Guralnik & Kaplan, 1989), and functional status, among those aged 80 or older (Camacho, Strawbridge, Cohen, & Kaplan, 1993). Current analyses focus on 29-year predictors of health and functioning and the determinants of active life expectancy. With its large population-based origin, breadth of domains of measurement, repeated waves of data collection, and almost three decades of follow-up, the Alameda County Study cohort represents an important data source for understanding health and aging. Data from the Alameda County Study are currently being archived in the National Archive of Computerized Data on Aging.

GEORGE A. KAPLAN

See also
Longitudinal Data Sets in Aging

ALCOHOLISM

Background

Alcohol use disorders are important public health problems in older adults. There is emerging evidence that problem drinking affects a larger proportion of older adults than previously thought (Adams, Barry, & Fleming, 1996). In the United States, an estimated 2.5 million older adults have problems related to alcohol, and 21 percent of hospitalized people over age 40 have a diagnosis of alcoholism. Related hospital costs are as high as $60 billion per year (Schonfeld & Dupree, 1995).

In 1990, those over the age of 65 comprised 13% of the U.S. population; by the year 2030, older adults will account for 22% of the population. The projected population explosion, coupled with the changes in attitudes toward alcohol and drug use from the current elderly cohort to the next cohort (baby boom generation), has serious implications both for the number of alcohol-related problems likely to occur among the elderly and the subsequent costs involved in responding to them. In fact, the health costs of untreated alcoholism have been well described but may be even greater among the elderly, who are already at increased risk for many health problems (Adams, Barry, & Fleming, 1996). These include greater risk for harmful drug interactions, injury, depression, memory problems, liver disease, cardiovascular disease, cognitive changes, and sleep problems. Treatment for alcohol abuse and dependence are important for economic as well as humane reasons because underrecognition may result in the ineffective use of health care resources without treatment for the underlying cause. Less intense brief alcohol interventions have demonstrated positive results with older adults (Fleming, Manwell, Barry, Adams, & Johnson, 2000).

In considering problems related to alcohol use in older adults, it is important to include a range of drinkers rather than including only those who meet criteria for alcohol abuse or dependence. Drinking can be medically hazardous for this group even if the frequency and amount of consumption do not warrant a formal diagnosis of alcohol abuse or dependence (Blow, 1998). Some experts use the model of at-risk, heavy, and problem drinking in place of DSM-IV criteria for older adults because it allows more flexibility in characterizing problems related to alcohol use in older adulthood. *At-risk use* is a pattern of alcohol use that, although not currently causing problems, may bring adverse consequences to the drinker or others (e.g., driving after drinking at social gatherings) (Barry, 1999). *Heavy or problem* alcohol use is associated with a number of adverse health effects in this population. These include greater risk for harmful drug interactions, injury, depression, memory problems, liver disease, cardiovascular disease, cognitive changes, and sleep problems (Gambert & Katsoyannis, 1995).

Prevalence

Prevalence estimates for older at-risk and problem drinking using community surveys have ranged from 1% to 15% (Adams, Barry, & Fleming, 1996). Among adults over 60 in a large primary care study, 15% of the men and 12% of the women regularly drank in excess of the limits recommended by the National Institute of Alcoholism and Alcohol Abuse. Rates vary widely, depending on the definition of at-risk and problem drinking and the methodology used to obtain samples.

The elderly seen in medical settings have consistently higher rates of alcohol-related problems (Dufour & Fuller, 1995) than those in the general population. Among clinical populations, however, estimates of alcohol abuse/dependence are substantially higher because problem drinkers of all ages are more likely to present in health care settings. Among elderly patients seeking treatment in hospitals, primary care clinics, and nursing homes for medical or psychiatric problems, rates of concurrent alcoholism have been reported to be between 15% and 58% (Adams, Barry, & Fleming, 1996). Rates for alcohol-related hospitalizations among older patients are similar to those for heart attacks.

The lifetime prevalence of alcohol dependence among randomly selected hospitalized medical patients has been reported as 20.4% for those aged 60–69, declining to 13.7% among patients aged 70–79 and to 0% for those aged 80+ years (Gambert & Katsoyannis, 1995). The prevalence of alcohol dependence, defined as those patients currently drinking and meeting dependence criteria, was somewhat lower for all patients, with 10.4% for those 60–69, 6.8% for those 70–79, and 0% over age 80. Although the rates of alcohol dependence are generally shown to decline with age, in one study of hospital discharge data, the 65-and-older group consistently had the highest proportion (approximately 60%) of alcohol-related diagnoses that were not primary diagnoses. The prevalence rates are often underestimates of the problem because of the tendency to underestimate alcohol problems in older adults (Blow, 1998).

Drinking Guidelines

Guidelines now recommend no more than one drink a day for men and women over 65. More than three drinks per occasion, two or more times in a month, is considered binge drinking in this age group. These guidelines are consistent with empirical evidence for health functioning and risk-free drinking among older adults. There have been studies addressing the benefits of alcohol use, and the recommendations are consistent with the current evidence on the positive health effects of drinking weighed against negative consequences (Blow, 1998). It is important to note that, because of concomitant medical conditions (e.g., diabetes, hypertension) or potential adverse interactions with medications, some older adults should be advised to abstain. What might be considered light or moderate drinking for individuals in their 30s may have multiple negative health effects in an older person. Therefore, clinicians who treat older patients should assess alcohol use levels and be aware of health implications of their patients' alcohol use.

Screening

Alcohol screening can be done as part of routine mental and physical health care and updated annually, before the older adult begins taking any new medications or in response to problems that may be alcohol- or medication-related. Screening questions can be asked by verbal interview, by paper-and-pencil questionnaire, or by computerized questionnaire. All three methods have equivalent reliability and validity. Any positive responses can lead to further questions about consequences. There are few alcohol screening instruments developed specifically for or tested with older adults. The Michigan Alcoholism Screening Test—Geriatric Version (MAST-G) developed by Dr. Blow and colleagues was designed for use with this population and screens for alcohol problems and consequences. In addition, alcohol consumption questions have been tested and used in large trials with this population (Fleming, Manwell, Barry, Adams, & Johnson, 2000). Screening for alcohol consumption and problems in a systematic way will increase the likelihood that appropriate advice and interventions will be given to older adult at-risk and problem drinkers.

Spectrum of Problem Drinking and Treatment Approaches

Several reports have suggested that, based on age at onset, three relatively distinct patterns of older problem drinking exist: (1) the early-onset pattern consists of lifelong problem drinkers who have managed despite the odds to survive into old age; (2) late-onset problem drinkers are those whose problems with alcohol began late in life, often as a response to the life changes and stressors common to the older adult; (3) finally, those experiencing episodic periods of alcohol abuse over the years are often referred to as having an intermittent pattern of problem drinking (Blow, 1998). It has been estimated that two-thirds of elderly alcoholics have the early-onset pattern, and approximately one-third have the late-onset patterns. Age of onset has been associated with severity of other alcohol-related problems that may influence outcomes, such as social consequences, other drug use, legal problems, and medical complications. The relationship of age of onset of drinking problems to treatment outcome has not been widely studied, although among a group of older problem drinkers not in treatment, late-onset individuals were more likely to be remitted at 1-year follow-up than were those with the early-onset pattern.

The spectrum of alcohol interventions for older adults ranges from prevention/education for persons who are abstinent or low-risk drinkers to minimal advice or brief structured interventions for at-risk or problem drinkers and formalized alcoholism treatment for drinkers who meet criteria for abuse and/or dependence (Barry, 1999; Blow, 1998). Formalized treatment is generally used with persons who meet criteria for alcohol abuse or dependence and cannot discontinue drinking with a brief intervention protocol. Although a small number of elder-specific formal treatment programs for substance abuse have been developed, the research on programs designed to address the unique issues facing older persons with alcohol problems (stigma, physical health problems, emotional losses, retirement) is limited.

Conclusion

In the past decade it has been demonstrated that at-risk drinking and alcohol use disorders have significant and costly consequences for older adults. Innovative strategies such as elder-specific brief alcohol interventions and elder-specific substance use treatment have been developed but are not widespread. To implement alcohol prevention, intervention, and treatment strategies in clinical settings will require the development of systematized protocols that provide easy service delivery. The need to implement effective strategies with a variety of older drinkers who are at risk for more serious health, social, and emotional problems, is high, both from a public health and from a clinical perspective. With changes in the health care system to managed models of health care, the time is right to move forward into a comprehensive system of alcohol interventions with older adults, considered a fast-growing and vulnerable segment of the population.

FREDERIC C. BLOW
KRISTEN LAWTON BARRY

See also

Alcohol Use
Drug Interactions

Drug Reactions
Medication Misuse and Abuse
Substance Abuse Programs

ALCOHOL USE

Beverage alcohol (ethanol) has complex physiological and psychological effects on those who drink it, as well as a complex social history. Its use is ancient and almost universal, particularly in the development of Western civilization. Ancients often described alcohol as "the water of life"; they attributed magical significance to its effects in religious and social ceremonies and marked life-course transitions from birth to death with drinking behavior. Consuming alcohol in religious communion services and in convivial social toasts, such as "to your health," are well-known cultural celebrations. Alcohol as a beverage appears in a remarkable variety of tastes, smells, and colors. It is consumed in a variety of settings, often with elaborate attention to the aesthetics of presentation. In sum, beverage alcohol in Western societies has a long history and has become a domesticated drug whose addictive potential tends to be understated (Roueche, 1960).

Beverage alcohol has a darker side. It can be misused as well as used to produce intoxication, and for a persistently and significantly large minority of drinkers it results in addictive behavior, clinically recognized as alcoholism. The ambivalence toward beverage alcohol is dramatically illustrated by national prohibition of beverage alcohol in the United States (1917–1933), a country in which a large majority of adults historically have drunk alcohol and in which an estimated 5% of adult drinkers persistently exhibit serious problems associated with their drinking.

Interest in how drinking and abuse of alcohol relate to aging is relatively recent. Scholars who know the relevant scientific literature note that, in the first two decades of the major journal in the field, *The Quarterly Journal of Studies on Alcohol* (1940–1960), only one article referred to aging, old age, or gerontology. In this journal's third decade (1960–1969), 13 articles referenced aging; only after 1970 did references to age and aging become common. By 1980 a comprehensive bibliography on aging and alcohol use listed 1,200 articles, over half of which had been published in the previous decade (Barnes, Abel, & Ernst, 1980). Also in that year, a monograph on alcohol and old age was published (Mishra & Kastenbaum, 1980). Increased interest in the drinking behavior of older adults in the 1980s, particularly abuse of alcohol, appeared to have two sources. One was the assumption that loss of status through retirement and the stresses of growing older would, particularly among men, increase the risk of abusive use of alcohol as an expression of frustration. A second source appears to have been the concern of social welfare agencies and administrators of long-term care facilities; they reported that the everyday problems of some older adults were in fact sometimes exacerbated by intoxication and apparent alcoholism.

Adequate evidence for characterizing the relationship between drinking behavior and aging, however, has continued to be somewhat sparse. Systematic comparisons of drinking behavior and alcohol abuse between societies are not available. But here, in general, is what the growing body of evidence indicates about drinking among older adults in the United States (Maddox, Robins, & Rosenberg, 1985; Midanik & Clark, 1994; Mishra & Kastenbaum, 1980):

1. A substantial majority of adults in the United States are not abstinent. A minority of males (perhaps 20%) at any point are abstinent or are ex-drinkers, and a larger minority of females are abstinent. A minority of males who drink and a smaller minority of females exhibit significant personal and social problems with their drinking. The usual estimate of alcoholism or serious problems with drinking among adults is 5%.

2. Among adults who drink, both the frequency and the quantity of alcohol consumed tend to decrease with age. Available cross-sectional evidence tends to be flawed as the basis for concluding that there is an age-related decrease in consumption; the same outcome could be explained by the different drinking patterns of earlier and later cohorts of adults. However, changing patterns of sociability with age, age-related health problems, and the complicated interaction of alcohol with prescribed medication appear to have a moderating effect on drinking behavior in later life.

3. Earlier assumptions that abusive drinking in adulthood ensured an early death appear to be wrong. Adults with a lifetime history of abusive drinking are observed in long-term care institutions.

The assumption that "late-onset alcoholism" (i.e., an adult with no history of abuse who develops problems late in life) is common but is not supported by evidence. Problems with drinking in later life appear typically to be a continuation of drinking patterns established in the adult years.

4. When abusive drinking or alcoholism is observed in later life, therapeutic intervention is at least as effective with older adults as with adults generally. Trend analysis of drug use (Johnson, 1996) and research on alcohol use among community-dwelling older adults (LaKhani, 1997) continue to reinforce these conclusions.

Although recognition of possible cohort differences requires one to be cautious in making broad generalizations about future patterns of drinking behavior among older adults, no current evidence has established an increased risk of abusive drinking in later life. Evidence continues to suggest that social factors associated with aging tend to moderate drinking behavior.

GEORGE L. MADDOX

See also
Alcoholism
Substance Abuse Programs

ALLIANCE FOR AGING RESEARCH

The Alliance for Aging Research is an independent nonprofit organization that promotes a broad research agenda in human aging. By spurring greater private-sector as well as governmental, academic, and public support for aging research and training, the nonprofit alliance has become the nation's leading citizen advocacy organization for science to ensure greater health and independence for older Americans. The organization urges translating new insights from research into better prevention of disease and improved patient care. The alliance conducts a variety of mass media educational campaigns aimed at both health professionals and the general public.

The founding of the alliance in 1986 was encouraged by a bipartisan study group of Congress acting unofficially with some of the nation's leading science and health policy leaders from the private sector. The alliance today is guided by a bipartisan Congressional Advisory Board and a Science Advisory Board, and is governed by a board of directors composed of executives from major U.S. corporations and foundations and from private philanthropy.

The Alliance for Aging Research is funded by grants from foundations, corporations, membership organizations, and individual donors. Activities fall into four major categories: (1) promotion of aging research; (2) public and professional education in healthy aging; (3) advocacy for geriatric medical education and training; and (4) monitoring public policy to advance the health and independence of aging Americans.

Promotion of Aging Research

The alliance unites public officials, policy experts, business leaders, the philanthropic community, and the public to work for a greater national investment in aging research. These coalitions can be informal and short-term or more formal and long-standing, such as the alliance-sponsored Task Force for Aging Research Funding. This coalition of over 70 national health, aging, veterans, and religious organizations issues an annual report to Congress highlighting recent research advances and pressing for appropriate public sponsorship of governmental and academic research. The Alliance for Aging Research was one of three nonfederal bodies represented on the Congressionally mandated Task Force on Aging Research. The task force report covers research issues ranging from basic biology to mental health, health services delivery, and women's health, and recommends to the secretary of the U.S. Department of Health and Human Services the types of aging research that should be conducted by the federal government, projects that should be given funding priority, and the amount of funds that should be appropriated for such research.

The alliance manages and promotes private funding for high-benefit projects such as the Allied Signal Award for Research on Aging. This $200,000 prize is given each year to an outstanding project in aging research. The Allied Signal Award provides direction and stimulates research projects that may significantly improve the health of Americans as they age.

The alliance's efforts have made aging research one of the fastest-growing priorities for medical research today. Since the organization was created, federal support for aging research has more than tripled, and private research and development in aging is at an all-time high.

Public Information

The alliance interprets and disseminates reliable information on new treatments for chronic conditions that threaten the independence of older people and on health promotion for people as they age. In recent years, the alliance has conducted nationwide campaigns to inform health professionals and the public about symptoms and treatment of incontinence, cataract, congestive heart failure, breast and prostate cancer, and the relationship of optimal nutrition to disease prevention. The alliance targets information on such topics as older women's health, nutrition, physical frailty, older veterans, long-term care options, and aging with a disability in its efforts to help seniors remain independent as possible as long as possible, avoiding costly hospitalizations and long-term nursing home stays.

The alliance also conducts and releases studies and surveys examining important medical, behavioral, and social issues associated with aging, including a widely quoted annual survey of older Americans' attitudes toward health and fitness, plus frequent studies of their views on health and retirement. Reports on the social and economic implications of added years of health in an aging society, such as *Meeting the Medical Needs of the Senior Boom: The National Shortage of Geriatricians,* highlight steps America can take today to prepare for the "graying" of the baby boom generation.

Other alliance publications have examined promising areas of aging research and forecasts of future breakthroughs (*Aging Research on the Threshold of Discovery*) and the inadequacy of current national investments in research to find preventions and cures for many of the disabling conditions associated with growing older (*The Research Gap: The Need for Boosting Research to Achieve Independence for Older Americans*). The alliance has also issued a series of monographs: *Investing in Older Women's Health, Improving Health with An-*

tioxidants, A Blueprint for a Healthier Older America, and other topics.

Advocacy for Geriatric Education and Training

Though they treat increasing numbers of older patients, most U.S. doctors do not receive formal training in geriatrics while in medical school. Physicians in the United States can expect to spend at least 50% of their time caring for older patients, yet only 13 of the nation's 126 medical schools require course work in the medical care of the elderly.

The alliance is taking a leadership role in promoting professional training in geriatrics, gerontology, and aging research. Another new venture is a landmark project to produce instructional materials for home care aides caring for the elderly. Although they do not provide medical services to their clients, home care aides do perform essential custodial services such as bathing, dressing, toileting, and transferring, that help seniors remain in their own homes.

In 1994 a special donor campaign by friends of the Alliance for Aging Research helped launch the Paul Beeson Physician Faculty Scholars in Aging Program, a $14.3 million initiative jointly sponsored with the John A. Hartford Foundation and The Commonwealth Fund of New York. The program supports 10 junior faculty each year, at least through 1998, to be future leaders in academic geriatrics in U.S. medical schools. This cadre of promising teachers and researchers will in turn train their students in aging research, thus helping to mainstream geriatrics into all primary care and specialty medical education.

An Influential Voice for the Health of Older Americans and Aging Americans

The alliance works with policymakers in the nation's capital and across the country to focus greater attention on the health of older Americans and on the need for breakthroughs in research to improve the quality of life for future generations.

Among the new initiatives undertaken by the alliance is the founding of a national coalition to work for patients' rights and patient education, a subject thought by many to be more critical than ever, given the growing reliance on managed care. In the coming years the Alliance for Aging Research will commit itself to seeking a larger role and responsibility by adding a grassroots dimension in its membership component so that a new national constituency is created for promoting and supporting aging research and healthy aging.

DAN PERRY

See also
Organizations in Aging

ALZHEIMER'S ASSOCIATION

Alzheimer's disease, the most common form of dementia, is a progressive degenerative disease of the brain. An estimated 4 million Americans have Alzheimer's disease, and an estimated 19 million family members consider themselves caregivers for persons with Alzheimer's disease. Alzheimer's disease care takes a unique physical, emotional, and financial toll on families (Ory, Hoffman, Yee, Tennstedt, & Schulz, 1999), and recent research even links increased risk of mortality associated with spousal care strain in Alzheimer's disease (Schulz & Beach, 1999).

The Alzheimer's Association is the only national voluntary health organization dedicated to research for the causes, cures, treatment, and prevention of Alzheimer's disease and to providing education and support services to affected individuals and their families. The national Alzheimer's Association, headquartered in Chicago, with a public policy office in Washington, DC, operates through a network of more than 200 local and area chapters. Chapters sponsor support groups, publish newsletters, run volunteer telephone help lines, and provide education and support to patients, families, and health and social service professionals caring for persons with Alzheimer's disease.

Funding biomedical research both through association funds and at the National Institutes of Health is at the top of the association's federal agenda. Since 1990 the association has been successful in boosting federal research funding from $146 million to about $450 million, and the association itself has funded more than $76 million in research grants since 1982.

The association's vision is to create a world without Alzheimer's disease while optimizing quality of life for individuals and their families. The organization has moved over time from a sole focus on family support to a broader focus on individuals with Alzheimer's disease. There is now good evidence of a long latent or preclinical phase of Alzheimer's disease before symptoms develop and new evidence that persons with mild cognitive impairment are at high risk of converting to Alzheimer's disease in 3 years. With earlier diagnosis, more persons are diagnosed at a point of insight, and their families are looking for support programs that focus on the patient as well as the family.

A primary goal of the Alzheimer's Association is to mobilize worldwide resources, set priorities, and fund select projects for biomedical, social, and behavioral research. In 2000 the Alzheimer's Association led and directed the World Alzheimer Congress, a first world congress joining an international Alzheimer's Research conference with the annual meeting of Alzheimer's Disease International, the international federation of 50 countries' Alzheimer's Societies.

Other goals of the association are to promote, develop, and disseminate education programs and guidelines for health and social service professions; to increase public awareness and concern for the impact of Alzheimer's disease on individuals and families in a diverse society; and to expand access to services, information, and optimal care techniques. Current programs focus on personalized knowledge services through toll-free lines, the World Wide Web, and publications and care coordination services on the local level.

Perhaps the greatest success of this voluntary organization has been its public policy coalitions and extensive federal, state, and local advocacy networks that promote legislation responsive to the needs of individuals with Alzheimer's disease and their families. An annual public policy conference provides opportunities for family advocates from the entire country to discuss with elected representatives a national program to conquer Alzheimer's disease. A state policy clearinghouse tracks long-term care and other legislation, at the state and local level, that affects Alzheimer's disease families.

The Chicago office of the national Alzheimer's Association houses the Green-Field Library, publishes research and practice updates for physicians and consumers, coordinates Memory Walks as a national fundraising and awareness program, and hosts an annual education conference for care professionals. A national toll-free hotline and website link families and professionals to local and area chapters and support groups (800-272-3900; *www.alz.org*).

LISA P. GWYTHER

See also
Alzheimer's Disease: Clinical
Alzheimer's Disease: Genetic Factors
Alzheimer's Disease: Special Care Units
Organizations in Aging

ALZHEIMER'S DISEASE: CLINICAL

Alzheimer's disease (AD) is the most common form of dementia among persons over 50 years of age. It is a progressive disorder that is characterized by the insidious onset of cognitive difficulties.

It is generally accepted that the early stage of AD is marked by a memory deficit. Patients have increasing difficulty in learning new information and retaining it over a delay. For example, patients typically forget recent events and become more repetitive. The speed at which information is lost over time is particularly marked in AD patients.

There is recent evidence to suggest that difficulty with executive function, particularly abilities related to cognitive flexibility and the concurrent manipulation of information, is the next major area of cognitive difficulty to develop early in the course of AD. Patients typically experience difficulty with everyday tasks that require concurrent manipulation of information, even when the components of the task are very well learned (e.g., preparing meals, paying bills, balancing a checkbook).

Subsequently, language and spatial difficulties emerge. Patients have increasing difficulty in finding the words they need to express themselves and may have trouble finding their way around a familiar environment.

Behavioral changes also occur in AD. Early in the disease, patients are frequently described as apathetic and less interested in the things around them. Some patients are more irritable in the early stages of AD. As the disease progresses, many patients develop psychiatric symptoms. It is not uncommon for moderate or severely impaired patients to develop delusions or hallucinations. Agitation can also occur.

Early in the course of disease, patients with AD typically have a neurological exam that is within normal limits. A subset of patients develop extrapyramidal signs (e.g., reduced facial movement, increased rigidity, and posture and gait abnormalities). When these neurological changes develop, they are usually associated with a more rapid rate of decline (Stern, Albert, Brandt, Jacobs, Tang, Marder, et al., 1994).

Ultimately, patients are unable to manage basic activities of daily living and require total care. The course of disease, from onset to death, is highly variable, averaging 10–12 years.

For additional information, see Terry, Katzman, and Bick (1994) and Kawas (1999).

MARILYN ALBERT

See also
Alzheimer's Association
Alzheimer's Disease: Genetic Factors
Alzheimer's Disease: Special Care Units

ALZHEIMER'S DISEASE: GENETIC FACTORS

Molecular genetic strategies for mapping diseases on the human genome started to become reality in the early 1980s. Alzheimer's disease (AD) was not considered a genetic disease at the time because most cases appeared to arise sporadically. However, there were several large families in which AD was segregated as an apparent autosomal dominant trait, with an earlier age of onset compared to common sporadic cases. The collection of AD families for use in linkage analyses, using the emerging molecular genetic markers, became a priority in many laboratories. The rationale was that if the underlying genetic defect could be identified in these families, there would be immediate insight into the pathogenesis of the common forms of AD as well.

The first linkage for four families with autosomal dominant, early-onset AD was to chromosome 21 (St. George-Hyslop, Tanzi, Polinsky, Haines, Nee, Watkins, et al., 1987). Because the *amyloid precursor protein* (APP) locus is also located on chromosome 21, there was immediate enthusiasm to conclude that the gene responsible for coding the peptide deposited in the amyloid plaques of AD brains was the chromosome 21 AD locus (Goldgaber, Lerman, McBride, Saffiotti, & Gajdusek, 1987; Tanzi, Gusella, Watkins, Bruns, St. George-Hyslop, Van Keuren, et al., 1987). Two research groups that were studying other collections of AD families published contradictory results. Schellenberg, Bird, Wijsman, Moore, Boehnke, Bryant, et al. (1988) reported that the genetic locus for a collection of autosomal dominant, early-onset families could be excluded from this region of chromosome 21, and Pericak-Vance, Yamaoka, Haynes, Speer, Haines, Gaskell, et al. (1988) reported that a chromosome 21 locus was excluded for a group of 30 late-onset AD families. Other groups reported isolated families that appeared to be linked to chromosome 21. There was considerable controversy in the field.

In 1991, Pericak-Vance and colleagues reported that there was a linkage between a region of chromosome 19 and late-onset familial AD (Pericak-Vance, Bebout, Gaskell, Yamaoka, Hung, Alberts, et al., 1991). These studies incorporated new methods of statistical analyses that were not dependent on mode of inheritance. It has since been stated that virtually no other research group believed these data (Lander & Schork, 1994). Other research groups continued to examine the APP gene in early-onset families and continued screening the human genome for more robust and reproducible regions of linkage.

Also in 1991, Goate and collaborators reported a mutation in the APP gene in two families with early-onset AD that had shown suggestive linkage to chromosome 21 (Goate, Chartier-Harlin, Mullan, Brown, Crawford, Fidani, et al., 1991). Additional APP mutations were demonstrated within a short period of time, but it was also shown that these were very rare mutations, occurring in only 20 or so families in the world (Chartier-Harlin, Crawford, Hamandi, Mullan, Goate, Hardy, et al., 1991). By identifying these families, it became very obvious that early-onset AD was heterogeneous, with an APP locus in those families that had evidenced chromosome 21 linkage and a different locus in other early-onset families.

In July 1992 a series of new genetic markers was developed from a region of chromosome 14 that had previously been somewhat bare of highly polymorphic probes. Within months two groups, virtually simultaneously, had very strong linkage data indicating a chromosome 14 locus in many large early-onset families (Schellenberg, Bird, Wijsman, Orr, Anderson, Nemens, et al., 1988; St. George-Hyslop, Haines, Rogaev, Mortilla, Vaula, Pericak-Vance, et al., 1992). It was clear at the end of 1992 that the majority of early-onset, autosomal dominant AD families were linked to a locus on the long arm of chromosome 14.

In October 1992, at a meeting of the Alzheimer's Disease Research Center Directors, Roses reported an association between a variant of the chromosome 19 apolipoprotein E gene, known as APOE4, and late-onset familial and sporadic AD. These data were subsequently published in March 1993 (Stritt-matter, Saunders, Schmechel, Pericak-Vance, En-ghild, Salvesen, et al., 1993) and quickly followed by the publication of a large autopsy-confirmed series of sporadic AD cases and the demonstration that the age of onset of AD was related to the dosage of APOE4 inherited (Corder, Saunders, Strittmatter, Schmechel, Gaskell, Small, et al., 1993; Saunders, Strittmatter, Schmechel, St. George-Hyslop, Pericak-Vance, Joo, et al., 1993). The genetic association of APOE4 has been con-firmed in series of AD patients throughout the world; however, its association in African Ameri-cans and Hispanics remains controversial (Farrer, Cupples, Haines, Hyman, Kukull, Mayeux, et al., 1997). Corder and colleagues further demonstrated that APOE2, another less common allele, decreased the risk of disease and increased the age of onset (Corder, Saunders, Risch, Strittmatter, Schmechel, Gaskell, et al., 1994). The APOE4 allele is also associated with earlier-onset sporadic AD cases and early-onset familial AD in pedigrees without APP or presenilin 1 (PS1) mutations (Chartier-Harlin, Parfitt, Legrain, Perez-Tur, Brousseau, Evans, et al., 1994; Okuizumi, Onodera, Tanaka, Kobayashi, Tsuji, Takahashi, et al., 1994; van Duijn, de Knijff, Cruts, Wehnert, Havekes, Hofman, et al., 1994). Interestingly, APOE genotypes also appear to mod-ify the age of onset in patients with APP mutations

(Nacmias, Latorraca, Piersanti, Forleo, Piacentini, Bracco, et al., 1995; St. George-Hyslop, McLach-lan, Tsuda, Rogaev, Karlinsky, Lippa, et al., 1994). A similar interaction may exist within families with presenilin 2 (PS2) mutations (Nochlin, Bird, Ne-mens, Ball, & Sumi, 1998).

In 1995, Sherrington and collaborators reported on five different missense mutations in a chromo-some 14 gene now known as PS1 that cosegregated with early-onset AD in the chromosome 14–linked families (Sherrington, Rogaev, Liang, Rogaeva, Levesque, Ikeda, et al., 1995). Although mutations in PS1 account for less than 2% of all AD cases, it is the causative gene for the majority of early-onset, familial cases of AD with an autosomal dom-inant inheritance, and at least 49 different mutations in the gene have been reported (Dermaut, Cruts, Slooter, Van Gestel, De Jonghe, Vanderstichele, et al., 1999). Very quickly after the identification of PS1, two research groups independently found a homologous gene on chromosome 1, now known as PS2, that is mutated in a very rare form of early-onset, autosomal dominant AD composed of seven families with a Volga-German founder (Levy-Lehad, Wasco, Poorkaj, Romano, Oshima, Pet-tingell, et al., 1995; Rogaev, Sherrington, Rogaeva, Levesque, Ikeda, Liang, et al., 1995).

In 1997, linkage to a second late-onset form of familial AD was identified on chromosome 12 (Pericak-Vance, Bass, Yamaoka, Gaskell, Scott, Terwedow, et al., 1997) and confirmed in 1998 (Rogaeva, Premkumar, Song, Sorbi, Brindle, Pater-son, et al., 1998). The finding was of particular interest because low density lipoprotein receptor-related protein 1 (LRP1), a neuronal receptor for apo E, and alpha-2-macroglobulin, another LRP1 ligand that can mediate the clearance of amyloid β-peptide, are located within the broad linkage region. The genetic relevance of either of these loci to chromosome 12–linked AD has been examined by multiple laboratories but remains controversial (Blacker, Wilcox, Laird, Rodes, Horvath, Go, et al., 1998; Lendon, Talbot, Craddock, Han, Wragg, Morris, et al., 1997; Rogaeva, Premkumar, Grub-ber, Serneels, Scott, Kawarai, et al., 1999; Scott, Yamaoka, Bass, Gaskell, Conneally, Small, et al., 1998).

Table 1 illustrates the current status of the genet-ics of the ADs. It is apparent that there is locus heterogeneity, with at least four known loci: APP, PS1, PS2, and APOE. Genome-wide scans indicate

TABLE 1   Genetic Classification of the Alzheimer Diseases

Type	Chromosome	Gene	Prevalence
AD1: Early-onset familial, autosomal dominant inheritance	21q21	APP	< 20 families
AD2: Late-onset familial and sporadic, APOE4-associated	19q13	APOE	50%–60%
AD3: Early-onset familial, autosomal dominant inheritance	14q24	PS1	< 2%
AD4: Early-onset familial, autosomal dominant inheritance	1q42	PS2	Volga-German founder, very rare
AD5: Late-onset familial (and sporadic?)	12p11–q13	Unknown	10%–30%
AD+: Other forms of AD			

that there are at least a few more loci associated with late-onset AD (Pericak-Vance, Bass, Yamaoka, Gaskell, Scott, Terwedow, 1997; Rogaeva, 1998; Kehoe, Wavrant-De Vrieze, Crook, Wu, Holmans, Fenton, et al., 1999). During the past several years there has been a flurry of reports on new susceptibility genes for the disease, including butylcholinesterase, bleomycin, cytochrome c oxidase, interleukin-1, and the very low density lipoprotein receptor. To date, none of these associations has been widely confirmed and accepted. Current updates on these and other loci possibly associated with AD can be found on the National Center for Biotechnology Information's website for the Online Mendelian Inheritance in Man (OMIM) database (*www.ncbi.nlm.nih.gov/Omim/*; keyword search: Alzheimer's disease).

Hypotheses for the pathogeneses of AD are being tested, with considerable difference of opinion on the seminal pathways affected that lead to the phenotype. There is strong support for the central role of amyloid in the causation of AD. Alternative viewpoints include central roles for APOE and tau. Tau, the primary component of neurofibrillary tangles, has long been considered integrally involved in the pathogenesis of AD by a minority of researchers. Interest in tau and AD soared recently when mutations in tau were shown to cause frontotemporal lobe dementia (Hutton, Lendon, Rizzu, Baker, Froelich, Houlden, et al., 1998).

From a genetic overview, there are several important points that are generally accepted.

1. There are several genetic etiologies for autosomal dominant, early-onset AD. It is unknown whether the mode of pathogenesis is the same or quite distinct.

2. There are APOE allele-dependent processes that affect the risk and age of onset of familial and sporadic late-onset AD.

3. The discovery of genetic loci did not provide instant insight into the modes of pathogeneses of the ADs but did provide relevant starting points for determining disease processes. The coming years will see connections made between the relevant genetic factors and the mechanisms of disease expression.

ALLEN D. ROSES
ANN M. SAUNDERS

See also
  Alzheimer's Association
  Alzheimer's Disease: Clinical
  Alzheimer's Disease: Special Care Units
  Apolipoprotein E

ALZHEIMER'S DISEASE: SPECIAL CARE UNITS

Alzheimer's disease units in nursing facilities developed in the late 1970s and early 1980s in response to concerns expressed by families, advocates, and providers about the quality and adequacy of dementia long-term care. By 1996, 22% of nursing facilities in the United States had some form of specialized dementia care unit. Although innovations in special care units (SCUs) originated in the nonprofit sector, the majority of SCUs are part of for-profit chains.

Current estimates suggest that 50%–75% of skilled nursing facility residents have dementia. Of those, about 10% are residents of SCUs at any one time. National data in 1998 indicate that persons admitted to nursing facility SCUs are more likely to be younger males who are admitted from home earlier in the course of their dementia when they are still independently mobile. Nursing facility SCU residents are also more likely to be private-pay, have a clinical diagnosis of Alzheimer's disease, and have fewer other physical limitations.

Nursing facilities that have older SCUs are often forced to develop late-stage, palliative or hospice model units for residents aging in units designed, programmed, and staffed for social-model, less intensive nursing care.

Case for Special Care Units

Nursing homes develop SCUs for a variety of reasons: to improve quality of care and quality of life for both cognitively impaired and frail intact residents, to respond to deficiencies identified in the traditional medical-model nursing home, to market to or attract private customers, or to circumvent moratoriums on nursing home bed construction with waivers for specialized unmet service needs.

The trend toward offering specialized care, although initially positive in intent, may too often simply segregate memory-impaired residents but fail to provide for their special needs. The "special" in the term SCU remains elusive after more than 20 years of innovation and experimentation. There is increasing professional consensus that SCUs are most appropriately used to develop and characterize dementia care models that can be adapted to all levels of residential and institutional care.

What Is "Special"?

Approaches to special care include a special philosophy of care; staff specification, selection, and training; activity programming for the cognitively impaired; specialized personal care strategies; segregated and modified physical and social environments; and admission and discharge policies and procedures profiling which residents are appro-

priate or likely to benefit from SCU care. However, in 1995, less than 44% of the SCUs provided all the above minimum features. Unfortunately, many facilities simply market a secured area of the facility as special, leaving consumers unable to evaluate relative cost-benefit ratio for a family member.

The Alzheimer's Association endorsed state legislative trends requiring full disclosure by facilities of their advertised special services. Further, the association's *Key Elements of Dementia Care* (1997) and *Residential Care: A Guide for Choosing a New Home* (1998) are examples of provider and consumer educational materials to address this unmet need for materials to define special care. Successful units are described as ones that assess residents frequently and comprehensively, reduce physical restraints, minimize medications, balance risk taking and safety, and support and reward staff.

A 1997 consensus on a core philosophy of special care included promoting safety and security, enhancing connections to others, mitigating disruptive emotional and physical behaviors, supporting cognitive function, maximizing independent function, and regulating stimulation.

Models of Special Care

There are four primary models of specialized dementia care. The curative model is based on treating all related medical conditions, often referred to as "excess disabilities." The rehabilitative or habilitation model focuses on maintaining or enhancing function through specialized programming and personal care strategies. Environmental models adapt or modify the physical and human environment to achieve an elusive "optimal" amount of stimulation and retreat toward the goal of ideal fit between environmental demand and the diverse but diminishing capacities of residents with progressive dementias. Finally, palliative models provide a safe, comfortable environment with limited active medical treatment. Quality of life and attention to enriched spiritual and emotional resources are focused on achieving "quality of dying" as well.

All the above models emphasize person-centered care in which the setting and staff adapt to the residents rather than the reverse. Activity programming is planned for facilitating pleasure in the moment, providing sensory stimulation and social interaction, drawing out apathetic residents and calming agitated residents with a balance of stimulation and rest. Music, exercise, reminiscence, traditional work, social and religious rituals, and expressive arts predominate.

Trends in Growth

The new growth in SCUs and specialized facilities has moved to the burgeoning and largely unregulated private assisted living industry. Assisted living facilities are marketing themselves as a preferred residential option for people diagnosed earlier in the course of their dementia. Families are seeking and choosing these residential settings when affordable and available.

Current estimates suggest that 30%–50% of residents of assisted living facilities have a dementia. Large assisted living corporations and some nursing home special care wings market Alzheimer's disease units with euphemistic names like "Spring Garden" to address potential labeling stigma. Increasingly, these facilities have been forced to move from a housing with amenities industry to a health care or personal nursing care model.

Unfortunately, studies suggest frequent discrepancies between marketing materials that promise more service in assisted living as a resident's needs increase and practices that force people to move when dependency actually does increase and functional impairments necessitate more supervision and care.

In 1998, 18% of assisted living facilities had SCUs with an average occupancy rate of 87%, equal to the occupancy rate of nursing home SCUs. Some assisted living facilities are entirely dementia-specific. The average length of stay in assisted living SCUs was 26 months. The average SCU resident in assisted living is an 82-year-old White female with at least three impairments in activities of daily living. This prototypical assisted living SCU resident had an average income of $26,138 and resources of $165,000; 86% of residents paid for assisted living services with no help from outside sources (Wright, 1999). In contrast, in 1997, 64% of persons over 75 had annual incomes below $15,000, whereas the price of assisted living was $17,000 to $22,000 per year. Most private assisted living is not affordable for low- and moderate-income elderly. Studies the same year documented that two thirds of persons over 65 cannot afford private long-term care insurance, which is not even available once one has a need for SCU residential care. Until there is state or federal support for nonnursing home care, SCUs in assisted living facilities will serve a minority of those in need.

Despite the growth in SCUs in residential and nursing home settings, most people with dementia are still cared for at home or in the general nursing home population. Research to date has failed to definitely answer the question of whether or not SCUs offer measurable quality-of-life or quality-of-care benefits over traditional integrated care settings.

Problems Identified

The marketing of SCUs has focused on physical design, despite the fact that most units are minimally retrofitted—the most common, and frequently the only change being the addition of a security system that limits egress without use of physical restraints. In 1997, however, one SCU that advertised "restraint-free" care was observed to have 16% of residents physically restrained on one given day (Zimmerman, Sloane, Gruber-Baldini, Calkins, Leon, Magaziner, et al., 1997). Providers were originally encouraged to create small, secure, dignified, and stable personalized environments. Unfortunately, the industry trade journals assert that a cost-effective unit must have a minimum of 30 beds (Wright, 1999).

The ideal model was expected to provide predictable familiarity, stable routines, and flexible stimulation without overload in "homelike" living units that were safe but enriched with redundant cues like signs, pictures, familiar items, and reminders. Experts urged the reduction of noise, glare, and traffic with small units, fewer residents, and a higher ratio of selected and deployed nonrotating staff to enhance resident recognition, family trust, and skills in guiding residents through steps in personal care. The focus was on discrete perimeters that facilitate unobstructed safe movements under staff surveillance between private areas and group, dining, and outdoor spaces.

Complaints continue to highlight the quality and appropriateness of self-designated SCUs. These complaints cluster around staff ratios, training, knowledge, consistency, and deployment; inappropriate use of restraints; lack of orientation cues; unusable wandering spaces; and lack of specialized approaches to personal care tasks like eating and bathing.

Research Comparing SCUs and Traditional Units

Studies comparing SCU and traditional care remain inconclusive. For example, aspects of the environment that have been studied include safety (controlled exits or constant monitoring), orientation cues to rooms and bathrooms, personal objects for continuity with the past, minimization of adverse stimuli like noise, and availability of engaging tactile or visual stimuli (Buckwalter & Mentes, 1997). One study of enhanced visual, auditory, and olfactory stimuli to create a home environment and an outdoor nature setting resulted in increased preferential use of the enhanced settings by residents and families and a trend toward less agitation, trespassing, and exit seeking by residents, but the effect size was limited. It appears that an ideal environment must engage but not overwhelm.

Another large national study (Phillips, Sloane, Hawes, Koch, Jan, Spry, et al., 1997) of SCU outcomes found no differences in the speed of decline in functions like locomotion, transferring, toileting, eating, dressing, or weight loss for residents in SCUs relative to traditional units. SCUs have been found to have less frequent rotation of staff, more nurse's aides per resident, and more dementia-specific training, although the magnitude of the training differences from traditional unit staff training is negligible.

Outcome studies often identify more benefits of specialized care in terms of reduced staff turnover and increased satisfaction of staff and families. Some studies hint at benefits for cognitively intact residents who are not exposed to behavioral manifestations of the residents with dementia, but again the effect is difficult to quantify.

Although it is assumed that SCUs are special environments, some studies suggest that one fourth of SCUs have no programmatic, architectural, cueing, or staffing modifications. Despite the focus on adapting environments to reduce behavioral disrup-

tions, studies show no positive or negative effect of SCUs on the frequency of aggressive behaviors (Leon & Ory, 1999). In fact, some studies indicate that reduced physical aggression among SCU residents is primarily attributable to increased use of psychotropic medication and decreased use of physical restraints. Even the addition of highly marketed wandering areas or parks in many new SCUs failed to document use of these areas. Significant safety issues associated with the design of such outdoor areas deserve further study.

Some studies have looked at the effects of family education on SCU resident outcomes. A family visit education program demonstrated the feasibility of training family members to communicate and interact more effectively with nursing home residents with dementia. These enhanced family visits had a modest beneficial effect on the residents but not on the staff's management of problem behaviors.

Finally, studies document that SCU placement explains very little variance in service costs relative to traditional unit care despite generally higher private-pay charges for SCU-level care.

Challenges Remain

The major challenges to providers of specialized Alzheimer's disease care are staffing issues and responding to the diverse needs of people who "dement" in place in residential settings. The shortage of trained, quality direct care providers threatens the growth of SCUs as it does for the entire long-term care industry. With population aging, an anticipated relative decline in the number of women between 22 and 44 years old, who provide the bulk of physically and emotionally demanding dementia care, will put the entire industry in jeopardy.

Conclusion

Dementia is increasing in prevalence among residents of all residential, nursing facility, and assisted living settings. The value of specialized settings is uncertain, in part because persons with dementia have varying responses to environmental and programmatic interventions (Dyer, 1996). Research studies suggest that SCUs represent a continuum rather than a single tangible intervention. Inherent contradictions in philosophies of special care complicate the picture as much as variations in the size and target population preclude a single approach. Further, practice does not necessarily reflect philosophy. Cost, access, and a relative lack of positive outcome data will further limit SCU development (Gladwell, 1997).

LISA P. GWYTHER

See also
Alzheimer's Association
Alzheimer's Disease: Clinical
Alzheimer's Disease: Genetic Factors

AMBULATORY CARE

The spectrum of elderly ambulatory care encompasses everything from walk-in clinics to capitated case management and can comprise symptom-oriented diagnosis and interventions and comprehensive geriatric evaluation. Ambulatory care is a necessary component of a comprehensive care delivery model, as is the home visit for selected patients.

The increasing reliance on ambulatory care and other community-based alternatives, such as various configurations of home care, has promoted a dramatic increase in the provision of ambulatory services for the elderly. This is further enhanced by the adoption of managed care as a major mechanism for ensuring primary health care and controlling (one hopes) health care costs. In such programs, the emphasis should be on care, not cost management, as the overall outcome. To be successful, this will require the development of interactive networks of care organizations at community, district, and regional levels (Lee, 1994).

Ambulatory care is increasingly a component of expanding for-profit and not-for-profit managed care organizations. Such programs are now being implemented in several countries with a varied mix of provider-purchaser arrangements. An informative comparison of differing dimensions of such systems in New Zealand, Australia, Finland, the United Kingdom, and the United States can be found in an article by Mason and Morgan (1994). The authors point out that only in Finland has any

formal evaluation of the effect of these new methods of care delivery on health been instituted.

The emphasis on primary ambulatory care as a major element of managed care progress could have a major impact on the renaissance of community-based medical practice and is already having a profound impact on medical school training in the United States. At present, older people over 65 have, on average, eight visits to doctors each year, most of them in ambulatory practice, compared to six for middle-aged people. This further increases to 11 per year over the age of 75. Reasons are the increasing level of functional dependence with age and the prevalence of chronic disease. Of the young elderly (i.e., those aged 65–70 years), 20% are functionally dependent, compared with 66% aged 85 and over.

Health maintenance organizations (HMOs) have until recently not been significant players in the geriatric care scene. However, a major shift in emphasis now appears under way. Increasingly, major HMOs are actively recruiting elderly subjects, providing those enrolled with services ranging from a loose mix of managed care with varied options to a more comprehensive all-risk care situation, again using case managers. The focus on ambulatory primary care in these developments again underlines the requirement to provide primary care practitioners who are adequately skilled in geriatric practice. These requirements can only increase as federal and state mandates in the United States increasingly promote managed care and HMOs seek to recruit an expanding population base of the elderly. HMOs are now increasingly providing comprehensive primary care at all levels, including acute as well as ambulatory care, or contracting with agencies which have developed a continuity of primary care at varied levels, from ambulatory to nursing home care. However, ambulatory care, whether practiced by allopathic physicians or health care extenders, often in rural areas, renders a major community component of the medical management of the majority of those enrolled in HMOs.

An emerging concern relates to the quality of care delivered by HMOs, and this is relevant where elderly populations with multiple impairments are recruited. As yet there has been little outcome research on the efficacy of HMO practice compared with non-HMO care delivery, but the little so far available suggests that care practice is comparable between both care models. A randomized study of the effects of capitation on the health and functional status of the elderly in Hennepin County, Minnesota, showed no harmful effects on the capitated subjects over 1 year of follow-up, in respect of management of diabetes and hypertension, activities of daily living, and mortality. The capitated group had a reduced likelihood of hospitalization, reduced lengthy hospital stay, and fewer outpatient and emergency room visits than the fee-for-service group (Lurie, Christianson, Finch, & Moscovice, 1994). A comparison of anticoagulant management for atrial fibrillation in clinical trials and in HMO practice showed that annual rates of stroke and major bleeding rates were not significantly different between the two groups despite greater prevalence of comorbidities in the HMO patients (Gottlieb & Salem-Schatz, 1994). Nevertheless, it has been suggested that a gatekeeper system (HMOs) may pose questions of undertreatment if physicians or gatekeepers are not well prepared for their task.

Most ambulatory care visits involve primary care practitioners. The ratio of primary care physicians to population has been shown to be the only consistent predictor of age-specific mortality rates (Farmer, Stokes, Fiser, & Papini, 1991). This increase in effective primary care is also associated with a decrease in costs. Care expenditure among the U.S. elderly with Medicare insurance is lower in areas of the country with high ratios of primary care physicians to population (Welch, Miller, Welch, Fisher, & Wennberg, 1993). Using international data from 11 Western industrial nations from the mid-1980s, a study on levels of health as measured by 14 health indicators, expenditure for care, medication use, and satisfaction with health services, showed that the primary (consisting largely of ambulatory) care orientation of a national health system is associated with lower costs, higher satisfaction level of the population served, better health levels, and lower medication use. The "best"-ranked countries were those in which supply is regulated according to perceived need for resources, and those in the "worst"-ranked group have market health systems. Outcome using these indicators ranks the Netherlands and Denmark as most satisfactory and the United States as least satisfactory (Starfield, 1994). As the greatest health care users proportionately for population, the influence of the elderly on these assessments is noteworthy.

Controversy exists in the United States regarding the role of geriatric medicine as a primary care of subspecialty discipline, in contrast to the European system, where geriatrics is generally regarded as a specialty discipline. There, most primary care family practitioners have had required training in geriatric medicine, especially in Scandinavia, the Netherlands, and the United Kingdom. In the United States, surveyed certified family practice candidates for the specialty-certifying examination in geriatrics indicated that primary care represented 90% of their workload rendered to older persons, compared with 78% for internal medicine-trained geriatricians and 66% for internists with no expressed interest in geriatric medicine (Reuben, Wanziger, Bradley, & Beck, 1994).

Most medical ambulatory care for the elderly in the United States is conducted by internists or subspecialists without any formal training in geriatric medicine. New educational guidelines for resident training are attempting to improve this situation in the future, but population projections indicate a continuing major deficit for several decades of geriatric medicine trained practitioners. Thus, the ambulatory care of the elderly is often provided by doctors with little formal training in the care of the elderly. This is particularly relevant to preventive medicine and functional assessment. Increasingly, geriatric ambulatory experience is required in accredited internal medicine and family practice training programs. Training in geriatric ambulatory experience is required in accredited internal medicine and family practice training programs. Training in geriatric ambulatory care occurred in less than 50% of family practice and internal medicine training programs surveyed by Reuben and colleagues (Reuben, Fink, Vivell, Hirsch, & Bedi, 1990).

Geriatric ambulatory care is practiced by a range of health care professionals other than those qualified in allopathic medicine. In several U.S. states, certified nurse practitioners or physicians' assistants are major providers of ambulatory care for the elderly and other populations, especially in areas of physician shortage. The legislation surrounding employment of such physician extenders is state-specific, with a wide variety of care-specific abilities permitted. Increasingly, due to anticipated demographic changes, ambulatory practices at primary care and tertiary care sites or institutions have been developed and encouraged.

Outcome research in ambulatory care usually focuses on outpatient geriatric assessment. In this population, suggested medical and environmental interventions are common (Eagle, Guyatt, Patterson, Turpie, Sackett, & Singer, 1991). Predictors of mortality in elderly outpatients include impaired instrumental activities of daily living, then increasing comorbidity (Keller & Potter, 1994). There is little literature regarding the specific needs, diagnoses, and outcomes of elderly seeking ambulatory care. Some studies do report the outcome of outpatient ambulatory geriatric evaluation and management. Several indicate that targeted outpatient geriatric evaluation is associated with reduced mortality, reduced use of emergency rooms, and reduced use or delay in admission to nursing homes (Boult, Boult, Murphy, Ebbitt, Luptak, & Kane, 1994).

Such groups can be defined in the community, the emergency room, or as inpatients. In one example, elderly inpatients admitted from the emergency department to a medical service were screened for candidates at risk of hospitalization and also suitable for outpatient management. When two groups of these subjects, one receiving usual ambulatory care from clinic doctors in a general medical clinic and the other from a geriatric assessment team after discharge, were compared at the end of 1 year, outcome measurements demonstrated that the patients followed by the team had less impairment in functional activity, and higher self-rated health (Rubin, Sizemore, Loftis, & Loret de Mola, 1993). Ambulatory geriatric evaluation has also indicated that such patients would frequently benefit from a change in their home situation, such as improved or increased home support services, including day care or other interventions. Associated risk factors with this need for change are dementia, visual deficits, lower educational level, increased number of medical diagnoses, and functional impairment (Altkorn, Ramsdell, Jackson, & Renvall, 1991).

Success of geriatric ambulatory evaluation requires patient compliance with the total evaluation and suggested interventions and monitoring. Assessing these beliefs concerning perceived risks and benefits can predict level of compliance (Reuben, Posey, Hays, & Lim, 1994). There is no firm consensus on the value of instruments as predictors of uptake of community or institutional resources for frail ambulatory elderly unless targeted for specific groups. Ambulatory care as a preventive measure to forestall institutionalization or limit resource use

succeeds only with monitoring of interventions and follow-up by the assessing team. New or rediscovered strategies in ambulatory care are now in evaluation in some countries, such as capitated case management with the elderly in the United States, where the provider assumes all health-related fiscal risks but controls care use through an ambulatory care model employing primary-care–trained doctors and case managers. Where used, telephone care as a substitute for face-to-face office visits has led to a decrease of medical visits (Wasson, Gaudette, Wheley, Sauvigie, Baribeau, & Welch, 1992). Similarly, European studies using health visitors (public health nurses) and district nurses (visiting nurses) have found similar outcomes (Hendriksen, Lund, & Strømgård, 1984).

Advancing age and cognitive decline adversely influence the knowledge ambulatory clinic patients have about their current therapy (Burns, Austin, & Bax, 1990). The risk of drug interactions causing side effects and hospital admissions rises with the number of medications taken, as does the use of multiple doctors with inadequate communication. Monitoring of both prescribed and over-the-counter medications is an essential component of elderly ambulatory care (Murai & Matsumoto, 1993). Screening of ambulatory elderly clinic patients' drug interactions reveals a high prevalence of both potential and actual adverse drug reactions leading to hospitalization in some. Associated risk factors include frailty from multiple pathology, potentially harmful drugs, drugs requiring therapeutic monitoring, and geriatric clinic attendance (Schneider, Mion, & Frengley, 1992).

ROBERT D. KENNEDY

See also
  Adult Day Care
  Continuum of Care
  Self-Care

AMERICAN ASSOCIATION OF HOMES AND SERVICES FOR THE AGING

The American Association of Homes and Services for the Aging (AAHSA), located in Washington, DC, represents approximately 5000 not-for-profit nursing homes, continuing-care retirement communities, senior housing facilities, and assisted-living and community services organizations. Approximately 1 million older persons of all income levels, creeds, and races are served by member organizations of AAHSA. Formerly, this organization was known as the American Association of Homes for the Aging (AAHA); the formal name change in 1994 reflects the shift in focus to other parts of the continuum of care and the organization's interest in developing other models of residential care in addition to the nursing home.

Representing member organizations' interests to Congress and federal agencies is a primary focus. To constantly improve quality of care, AAHSA offers a Certification Program for Retirement Housing Professionals, provides accreditation for continuing-care retirement communities through the Continuing Care Accreditation Commission, sponsors conferences and programs through the AAHSA Professional Development Institute, and sponsors publications for the long-term care and retirement housing fields.

In recent years AAHSA has offered group purchasing and insurance programs to its members. It has also established the AAHSA Development Corporation, an AAHSA subsidiary that makes capital more readily available to members, as well as assisting in the development process associated with capital improvements.

The AAHSA mission is to advance the interests of its members through leadership, advocacy, networking education, and other services. Its vision is a comprehensive system of care and services that recognizes the dignity of all persons and enhances the quality of life for older adults and others with special needs. AAHSA also sponsors a job mart and provides career information.

AAHSA was established in 1961 by a group of 99 persons, meeting at Arden House, who were motivated by a felt need to critically examine services to the elderly and provide leadership to not-for-profit organizations seeking to provide quality care to current and future generations of elderly persons.

The website address is: *www.aahsa.org.*

JAMES E. ALLEN

See also

Assisted Living: A New Model of Supportive Housing with Long-Term Care Services

Home and Community-Based Care
Housing
Organizations in Aging
Nursing Homes

AMERICAN ASSOCIATION OF RETIRED PERSONS (AARP)

AARP is a nonprofit membership organization of persons 50 and older dedicated to addressing their needs and interests. AARP seeks, through education, advocacy, and service, to enhance the quality of life for all by promoting independence, dignity, and purpose.

Founded in 1958 by retired California educator Dr. Ethel Percy Andrus, AARP (formerly known as the American Association of Retired Persons) today represents more than 33 million members, making it the nation's largest organization devoted to meeting the needs of the rapidly growing 50+ population.

AARP's vision is to excel as a dynamic presence in every community, shaping and enriching the experience of aging for each member and for society. To make this vision real and to better understand the needs and interests of its members and potential members, AARP addresses a common theme that resonates across all age groups of its diverse membership: the search for services and products that contribute to "quality of life." AARP recognizes that this phrase means different things to different people. For some it is coping with the matters of day-to-day living. For others, it is getting involved in personally rewarding activities. And for yet others, it is making the most of their leisure time.

Regardless of where members are on life's continuum, they will find AARP to be their foremost source of new and innovative ways to plan and enjoy life after 50. To fulfill this promise, AARP focuses its efforts and resources in four areas: (1) health and long-term care, (2) economic security and work, (3) life transitions and independent living, and (4) personal enrichment. AARP members, as well as long experience in successful aging, have told us that these areas are central to members' quality of life as they grow older.

AARP's business is serving people—working full-time, working part-time, or retired; married, widowed, or single; urban, suburban, or rural; taking care of children, taking care of parents, or both. In short, AARP helps millions of Americans with widely varying lives age successfully.

AARP has made lives better for its members and for all generations by living the motto that Dr. Andrus gave the association at its founding more than four decades ago: "To Serve, Not to Be Served." The association serves its members and society primarily in four ways: (1) by providing quality information and education, (2) through legislative and consumer advocacy at both the national and state levels, (3) by providing services and opportunities for involvement in their communities, and (4) by making available a wide range of services to AARP members.

AARP's bimonthly magazine, *Modern Maturity*, is the largest in circulation in the country, each issue reaching approximately 22 million households. The monthly newspaper, the *AARP Bulletin* (which also reaches 22 million households), keeps members up to date on the issues that affect their lives both in Washington and in the states. The association's website, *AARP Webplace*, is one of the most popular on the Web for the 50+ population, offering visitors valuable information, a sense of community and connectedness, and the opportunity to interact with others. AARP's *Prime Time Radio* and *Mature Focus Radio* programs offer listeners a wide array of guests and opinions on current topics of interest to the 50+ population. And *Maturity Broadcast News*, a program of video news releases (VNRs) is the largest such program in the country, allowing AARP to reach millions of Americans with news on issues important to them.

For the past two years (1997–1998), *Fortune* magazine has named AARP the nation's most powerful lobbying organization. This is quite an accomplishment given the fact that AARP is a nonprofit, nonpartisan organization that does not have a political action committee (PAC), does not contribute money to candidates or political parties, does not endorse or oppose political candidates or parties, and is engaged in so many other activities. Members choose to be involved in the issues that affect them and their families. Whether the issue is Social Security, Medicare, Medicaid, consumer protections in managed care, pension protection and reform, age discrimination, long-term care, work and retirement, or transportation, AARP volunteers make

their voices heard on Capitol Hill and in state capitals throughout the country.

AARP members are not only letting their views be known at the federal and state levels, but they are active advocates on consumer issues as well. AARP volunteers are active in fighting consumer fraud (including telemarketing, sweepstakes, and mail fraud), advocating the rights of grandparents, and advocating on behalf of midlife and older Americans on issues ranging from utility and telephone deregulation to standards for manufactured housing.

AARP volunteers are the heart and soul of the association. The members of its board of directors and its national officers are all unpaid volunteers, as are the regional volunteer directors, state presidents, and thousands of legislative and program volunteers and chapter leaders. In addition to the advocacy efforts mentioned above, they are involved in a number of innovative community service and education programs, including tax preparation assistance, driver training and reeducation, grief and loss counseling, and independent living programs. Through their involvement in national, state, and local affairs, AARP volunteers are shaping the experience of aging for members and for society.

Dr. Andrus was a pioneer in establishing group health insurance for older Americans. She recognized then, as AARP does today, that making such services available to—and affordable for—older Americans is essential to maintaining the quality of life for all people as they get older. Today, AARP offers a wide range of services to enhance the quality of life for people as they get older. These include the AARP Pharmacy Service, from Retired Persons, Inc.; AARP Health Care Options, from United HealthCare and MetLife Insurance; the AARP Investment Program, from Scudder; the AARP Auto & Homeowners Insurance Program, from The Hartford; the AARP Life Insurance Program, from New York Life; the AARP Mobile Home Insurance Program, from Foremost; the AARP Credit Card Program, from Bank One/First USA; and the AARP Legal Services Network.

In 1999, AARP created a taxable subsidiary, AARP Services, Inc., to direct and manage the association's member services. In addition to managing those services listed above, AARP Services, Inc., also manages AARP's Purchase Privilege Program, which provides hotel, motel, and other travel discounts to AARP members, and is responsible for developing new products and services to enhance the quality of life for its members in the areas of health and wellness, economic security and work, life transitions and independent living, and personal enrichment.

AARP also works to enhance the lives of people as they get older by expanding an understanding of aging through the AARP Andrus Foundation. The mission of the AARP Andrus Foundation is to enhance the lives of older persons through aging research, educational initiatives, and public information programs that emphasize financial security and living with chronic health conditions. In its 30 years of grantmaking, the AARP Andrus Foundation has supported over 630 projects with grants, totaling approximately $35 million.

America is aging. In fact, more years have been added to the average life expectancy in this century than in all of history combined. AARP is helping to shape and enrich that experience of aging through all of its programs, services, and products. Yet we are reminded, by the United Nations declaration of 1999 as the International Year of Older Persons, that aging is not just an American phenomenon, it is occurring worldwide. As an active participant in the UN's activities surrounding the International Year of Older Persons and through its work as part of Coalition 99, AARP has helped spread the message that, like every other stage of life, the journey through middle and old age may be filled with life's ups and downs, but it is also filled with the same opportunities, excitement, and vitality as life itself. Older people represent a tremendous resource that no government and no society can afford to waste.

AARP recognizes that aging is synonymous with living. At different points along life's continuum we find that what matters most is not age but experiences along the way. AARP's founder, Dr. Ethel Percy Andrus once observed, "The stereotype of old age—increasingly costly and troublesome—is contradicted by the host of happy and productive older people participating and serving beyond the call of duty. Second only to the desire to live is the natural yearning to be wanted and needed, to feel that one's contribution to life is essential."

AARP and its members are committed to helping people plan and live long, healthy, and engaging lives, as useful citizens and to bring new vitality to our aging society.

HORACE B. DEETS

See also
Foundations
Organizations in Aging

AMERICAN COLLEGE OF HEALTH CARE ADMINISTRATORS

The American College of Health Care Administrators (ACHCA), located in the Washington, DC, area, is the professional organization for nursing home administrators. Membership consists of more than 6,000 licensed long-term care administrators who are engaged in the administration of facilities or in activities designed to improve the quality of nursing home administration.

Founded in 1962, its staff administers a $2 million-plus annual budget that supports a number of publications and member services. Publications are *The Journal of Long Term Care Administration*, *Long Term Care Administrator* (a newsletter), and *College Notes* (also a newsletter). The primary member services are LTC On-Line (an information service specializing in long-term care and administration); professional certification (for members); a variety of educational publications, seminars, and conferences; Job Bank USA; and an insurance program.

The primary activities of the organization are to (1) represent the interests of long-term care administrators to Congress and the federal agencies, and (2) provide professional education and development for its membership.

The website address is: *www.achca.org*.

JAMES E. ALLEN

See also
Organizations in Aging

AMERICAN COLLEGE OF HEALTHCARE EXECUTIVES

The American College of Healthcare Executives (ACHE), founded in 1933 and headquartered in

Chicago, has a membership of over 28,000. At the heart of its current mission statement is the goal of enhancing the quality of health care through helping leaders in hospitals, managed care, and additional health care settings create and manage change. The vision of the ACHE is to be the leader in providing knowledge, skills, and values that assist health care executive leaders in improving the health status of society.

The ACHE offers an extensive education program for its members, with approximately 12,000 of its 28,000+ members participating annually. Approximately 4,000 attend the association's annual meeting, the weeklong Congress on Administration. As part of its education effort, ACHE offers a credentialing program that includes Certified Healthcare Executive (CHE) and Fellow of the American College of Healthcare Executives (FACHE). All members must meet a continuing education requirement and be recertified periodically.

Publications are a major service to the membership. ACHE publishes the journal *Hospital and Health Services Administration* and a bimonthly magazine, *Healthcare Executive*. Also, over 120 books are published by ACHE.

The association requires members to subscribe to a code of ethics it has developed, encourages members to be part of the public policy-making process, aids members in career development, and, through a monthly employment newsletter, *Career Mart*, provides information about positions in the field.

The website address is: *www.ache.org*.

JAMES E. ALLEN

See also
Organizations in Aging

AMERICAN FEDERATION FOR AGING RESEARCH

The American Federation for Aging Research (AFAR), founded in 1980, is a national voluntary organization dedicated to raising and distributing funds in support of biomedical research on the aging process and on age-related diseases and disorders. It conducts an annual grant program in which research proposals, chosen in a peer-review process, are selected for awards of up to $25,000. AFAR grants are especially targeted to encourage creative research by younger investigators and those newly interested in the field of aging.

Grantees chosen from universities, medical schools, and research laboratories across the country have explored questions such as the biological process of aging, the influence of heredity in aging, the effect of exercise and diet on aging, the effect of aging on the immunological defenses against disease, and the relationship of aging to the functioning of the brain, heart, liver, and other organs.

Another AFAR objective is to encourage the training of younger scientists and physicians in geriatric medicine. To that end, it offers scholarships to medical students to enable them to work, under appropriate supervision, in leading geriatric clinical or research facilities and thus gain an understanding of the needs and opportunities of geriatric medicine.

AFAR convenes annual scientific meetings in cooperation with the American Geriatrics Society, which provides a forum for the exchange of information and ideas among scientists and physicians. From time to time, AFAR holds specialized seminars and symposiums and it publishes a quarterly newsletter. It presents the AFAR Award of Distinction annually to an individual who has made an exceptional contribution to aging research. Recipients include Nathan W. Shock, Ph.D., Leonard Hayflick, Ph.D., Robert N. Butler, M.D., and Reubin Andres, M.D.

AFAR is governed by a Board of Directors of physicians, scientists, and laymen. An Executive Committee serves as a central forum of policy discussion. The National Scientific Advisory Council and the Research Committee, each comprised of leading scientists, are responsible for evaluating grant proposals.

CARL EISDORFER

See also
Organizations in Aging

AMERICAN GERIATRICS SOCIETY

Founded in 1942, the American Geriatrics Society (AGS) is the leading clinical society devoted to the care of older adults. Its 6,000 members include primary care physicians, geriatricians, geropsychiatrists, nurse practitioners, social workers, physician assistants, physical therapists, pharmacists, and others who are dedicated to improving the health, independence, and quality of life of all older people. Among its members are the leaders in academic geriatric medicine from medical schools around the country.

The AGS promotes high-quality, comprehensive, and accessible care for America's older population, including those who are chronically ill and disabled. The organization provides leadership to health care professionals, policy makers, and the public by developing, implementing, and advocating programs in patient care, research, professional and public education, and public policy.

Today the major programs and publications of the AGS include the following:

- The AGS/AFAR annual scientific meeting, the premier forum for the latest information on clinical geriatrics, research on aging, and innovative models in health care delivery as well as teaching in geriatrics
- *The Journal of the American Geriatrics Society*, rated number 1 in the ISI Science Citation Index for geriatrics and gerontology publications
- *The Geriatrics Review Syllabus: A Core Curriculum in Geriatric Medicine*, now in its fourth edition
- *Geriatrics at Your Fingertips*, a comprehensive, pocket-size clinical reference
- *AGS Newsletter* and AGS website (*www.americangeriatrics.org*)
- *The American Geriatrics Society's Complete Guide to Aging and Health*
- Policy position statements and clinical practice guidelines
- Special projects in professional education/outreach, funded by foundations and industry sponsors
- The Geriatrics Recognition Award, to recognize physicians and nurses who are committed to advancing their continuing education in geriatrics
- The AGS awards program, which includes the AGS Edward Henderson Award State-of-the-Art Lecture, AGS Clinician of the Year, AGS/Merck New Investigator Award, Pfizer/AGS Postdoctoral Fellowship Awards, Dennis W. Jahnigen

Memorial Award, the Nascher/Manning Award, the Otsuka/AGS Clinical Investigation Award, the Edward Henderson Student Award, and the AGS Student Research Award

The AGS is a leading provider of continuing education and clinical information resources on the health needs of older persons. In addition to its annual meeting (which drew some 2,000 attendees in 1999), the AGS publishes the *Geriatrics Review Syllabus (GRS)*, the groundbreaking self-assessment, continuing education program for primary care providers and premier source of clinically relevant information in geriatric medicine. In late 1998 the AGS released the first edition of *Geriatrics at Your Fingertips*, a comprehensive, pocket-size reference to clinical geriatrics that provides up-to-date, practical information on the evaluation and management of diseases and disorders most common to elderly people. Updated annually, *Geriatrics at Your Fingertips* was released in its second edition in March 2000.

The AGS has a successful track record in developing statements and guidelines that benefit the health of the geriatric population. The "AGS Clinical Practice Guidelines: The Management of Chronic Pain in Older Persons," published in the May 1998 issue of the *Journal of the American Geriatrics Society*, is a recent example of the process that the society uses to alert the clinical community, policy makers, and the public to its recommendations. Currently, AGS committees have guidelines or statements on the following topics slated for development: falls screening and prevention, management of type II diabetes, breast cancer screening, and ambulatory senior care services.

The AGS has long championed efforts to expand the national work force of clinicians with the knowledge, skills, and attitude to care for our aging population. Since the early 1990s, with funding from the John A. Hartford Foundation of New York City, the AGS has worked effectively to increase geriatrics expertise among subspecialists in internal medicine, practicing primary care physicians, and non-primary care specialists.

As a result of these and other initiatives, the AGS has developed an impressive network of liaisons with the nation's leading primary care and specialty organizations, including: the American College of Physicians, American Academy of Family Physicians, American Urological Association, American College of Obstetricians and Gynecologists, American Academy of Neurology, American Academy of Ophthalmology, American Academy of Otolaryngology, American Academy of Physical Medicine and Rehabilitation, American Society of Anesthesiologists, American Academy of Orthopedic Surgeons, Association of Program Directors in Surgery, Society for Academic Emergency Medicine, American Society of Clinical Oncologists, Council of Geriatric Cardiology, Foundation for Anesthesia Education and Research, and Society for Thoracic Surgeons.

In 1999 the AGS reached beyond its traditional role as a professional medical society and launched the Foundation for Health in Aging (FHA). The FHA aims to build a bridge between the research and practice of geriatrics health care professionals and the public and to advocate on behalf of older adults and their special needs: wellness and preventive care, self-responsibility and independence, and connections to the family and community.

The FHA (*www.healthinaging.org*) will focus on public education, clinical research and public policy, championing initiatives that:

- advance the principles and practice of geriatric medicine;
- educate policy makers and the public on the health care needs and concerns of older adults;
- support aging research to reduce disability and frailty and improve quality of life and health outcomes;
- encourage older adults to be effective advocates for their own health care;
- help family members and other caregivers take better care of their older loved ones and themselves.

HARVEY JAY COHEN

See also
 Gerontological Society of America
 Organizations in Aging

AMERICAN HEALTH CARE ASSOCIATION

The American Health Care Association (AHCA) is a federation of 50 state health organizations repre-

senting nearly 12,000 nonprofit and for-profit assisted living, nursing facility, and subacute care providers that care for more than 1 million elderly and disabled individuals nationally. The AHCA is the primary trade association of for-profit long-term care providers (approximately 90% of its members), but it also has a substantial number of not-for-profit providers who are members as well.

The AHCA was established in 1949 to promote standards for professionals in long-term health care delivery and quality care for residents. The AHCA requires that nursing facility members of AHCA affiliates and their administrators be licensed by their state governments.

The AHCA is located in Washington, DC, and keeps a strong presence before Congress and the federal agencies through representing the interests of its membership in proposed legislation and rule making by federal agencies such as the Health Care Financing Administration (HCFA), which administers Medicare and Medicaid. The AHCA was instrumental, for example, in achieving legislation that ameliorated the impacts imposed on long-term care facilities by the 1998 prospective payment system financial burdens.

Professional and Trade Associations in the Long-Term Care Field

By the early 1990s expenditures on long-term care exceeded $50 billion each year, second in extent only to hospital expenditures. Professional and trade associations in the field activity represent the concerns of the industry before Congress and the federal and state legislatures and agencies. Two major professional organizations serve as trade associations: the AHCA, representing mostly the for-profit U.S. long-term care industry, and the American Association of Homes and Services for the Aging (AAHSA), representing primarily the nonprofit sector. In addition, a 6,000-member association, the American College of Health Care Administrators (ACHCA), represents health care administrators serving the long-term care industry.

The association also provides extensive information and educational assistance to its members. Its publications include *Provider*, a monthly magazine covering a variety of legislative and regulatory initiatives and subjects such as health care management, facility administration, and products and services; and AHCA *Notes*, a monthly newsletter focusing on regulatory and legislative developments in long-term care policy. Extensive continuing education offerings are provided through its affiliates and its annual meetings. A broad array of educational materials is also published by the AHCA.

The association serves a major source of information and training for its members concerning the rapid changes that have occurred in the industry in recent years, such as the Nursing Home Reform Act and the prospective payment system.

The website address is: *www.ahca.org.*

JAMES E. ALLEN

See also
Organizations in Aging

AMERICAN INDIAN AGED

Native American is not the term preferred by most elders. Instead, they usually identify themselves by their tribal affiliation or use the referent term *American Indian.* Conceptually, "elder" refers to a social and/or physical status, not to chronological age. The role of an elder is imbued with positive value and social functions, unlike such roles in mainstream society. Rather than living in retirement and isolation, elders are generally expected to be more engaged in the community by maintaining and transmitting cultural values. Understanding the status of current elders requires a life-course perspective to appreciate their experiences in this century and the association of life-cycle stages at comparatively younger ages (John, 1999).

The diversity of over 500 American Indian nations, tribes, bands, and Alaskan Native villages cannot be overstated. Today about 150 indigenous languages continue to be spoken. Just as there is no one American Indian language, there is no single cultural tradition. This great cultural and regional diversity is evident in the variation among American Indians in health behaviors, health status, and the rates of morbidity and mortality. That diversity is further cross-cut by residence in sovereign reservation communities or in U.S. towns and cities. The Indian Health Service (IHS) provides universal health care on reservations of federally recognized tribes but delegates that responsibility to states for American Indians living off-reservation. Although the IHS maintains a comprehensive health database for about 40% of the population, there is no systematic source of information on urban American Indian health problems. The sparse information on urban American Indians is derived from a few isolated, cross-sectional surveys.

IHS data show that the leading two causes of death for older American Indians are the same as for the general population: diseases of the heart and malignant neoplasms (U.S. Department of Health and Human Services [USDHHS], 1996). As is true of Americans as a whole, the most common cancer sites related to mortality are trachea, bronchus, and lung. Mortality and morbidity rates vary across geographic/sociocultural groupings, including cancer frequencies and site (Bleed, Risser, Sperry, Hellhake, & Helgerson, 1992; Lanier, Bulkow, & Ireland, 1989). Likewise, age-adjusted mortality rates from diseases of the heart vary from 75 per 100,000 in the Albuquerque, New Mexico, area to 298 per 100,000 in the Aberdeen, South Dakota, area; the U.S. age-adjusted rate is 166 per 100,000 (USDHHS, 1993). These differences have variously been ascribed to cultural differences in health behaviors that affect risk factors, socioeconomic status, environmental and other exposures, changes in diet, technology and subsistence patterns, and the demographics of small populations.

The 1990 U.S. census reported that only 22% of the total American Indian population now lives on reservations or trust lands, whereas more than half (59%) of the total American Indian population lives in our nation's cities and towns. Similarly, about half (52%) of American Indians over age 65 live in our nation's cities and towns; the remaining half (48%) live in rural areas. These elders represent a mere 6% of the rural-reservation and 5% of the urban American Indian populations. Despite these relatively small proportions, the number of elders over age 60 has increased a dramatic 52% between 1980 and 1990. Elders (60+ years) are concentrated in 10 states, with more than half of this older cohort living in Oklahoma, California, Arizona, New Mexico, and North Carolina.

In some ways the migration of American Indians to industrialized areas from rural reservations mirrored the post–World War II demographic transformation of America to a nation of city-dwellers. However, the American Indian migration differed significantly. Their resettlement was facilitated by federal relocation programs that supported a policy to terminate the special relationship between the tribes and the federal government. The West Coast economy and environment attracted many American Indians during this period, and today the largest and most heterogeneous concentrations of urban American Indians are found in California. For instance, a survey of 350 elders living in Los Angeles in 1987–1989 found that 93 tribal affiliations were represented (Los Angeles County, 1989). Because urban American Indians do not benefit from special federal or tribal health and supportive services, urban elders can be expected, in ever increasing numbers, to turn to local providers for health care and for community-based long-term care services.

Overall, urban American Indians and Alaskan Natives of all ages experience poorer health and functional status across nearly all measures, compared to the general U.S. population or their reservation counterparts (Grossman, Krieger, Sugarman, & Foquera, 1994). Elders living in Los Angeles reported higher prevalence of problems with eyesight, hypertension, diabetes, asthma, stroke, speech pathologies, liver disease, cancer, and amputations. Self-reported health status is a good marker of morbidity and mortality. The number of elders evaluating their own health as fair (33%) or poor (14%) is disturbingly high at about twice the expected rates. In addition, older urban women had significantly more health risks than men did and reported higher frequencies of hypertension, heart disease, impairments of activities of daily living, and social isolation (Kramer, 1992, 1999).

A number of risk factors are greater for American Indians than for other populations. The 1990 U.S. census continues to indicate the social, economic, and health disparities between the American Indian, Eskimo, and Aleut elders and other U.S. populations. American Indians have the lowest median age (26.2 years) of the census race groups, have the highest percentage of people living below the poverty line (30.9%), the smallest percentage of adults living to age 65 (5.4% of the total population), and a higher proportion of disabled older adults than do Whites, Hispanics, or Asian/Pacific Islanders. In addition, American Indians have the poorest 5-year cancer survival rate. The national 1992 Health and Retirement Survey found that older American Indians reported higher proportions of chronic lung disease, heart disease, and arthritis than other census groups, as well as greater frequency and intensity of pain; they were seen most frequently by doctors in the past year. The rates of chronic disease are rising among American Indian and Alaskan Natives (Kramer, 1997).

Even at middle age, American Indians may report physical, emotional, and social impairments that are more typically found in older U.S. cohorts. In a landmark national study, the National Indian Council on Aging (1981) found that, by age 45, reservation elders had the characteristics of other older Americans aged 65 years. By age 55, urban elders also reported these characteristics. Lowered age eligibility for supportive services is made available on reservations only through Title VI of the Older Americans Act. Targeting Title III Older Americans Act programs to urban elders is difficult because the elders are dispersed throughout metropolitan areas, with typically less than a dozen American Indian elders per metropolitan zip code. Furthermore, resources are limited because these elders generally represent less than 1% of the older population in a Planning and Service Area (Kramer, 1991). As if to underscore that point, the Senate Committee on Aging report on American Indian elders is titled "The Forgotten People." The document omits any reference to urban elders who are not only forgotten but statistically invisible.

At the close of the 20th century, our society often continues to express a systematic and racist bias that, at best, reduces American Indians to stereotypical caricatures. No other ethnic group is depicted as friendly, furry animal creatures on holiday (e.g., Thanksgiving) greeting cards, nor is any other ethnic group considered an appropriate costume for Halloween. In a country whose constitution guarantees religious freedom, no other group's religion has been banned by acts of Congress, nor the right to belief, if not practice, restored as the 1974 Indian Freedom of Religion Act. Having experienced the effects of racism and prejudice, many elders have been reluctant to access formal non-Indian service systems or do not feel that they will be treated fairly (National Indian Council on Aging, 1982).

To date, relatively little research has documented aging among American Indian populations.

The existing research indicates that this extremely diverse ethnic group may benefit from services targeted to local/regional needs and, on the average, may be in need of health and supportive services at younger ages than other older Americans. Collaborative involvement of American Indian organizations in the design, implementation, and evaluation of interventions should be a primary consideration in applied research on American Indian aging.

B. JOSEA KRAMER

See also
Ethnicity
Minorities and Aging
Minority Populations: Recruitment and Retention in Aging Research

AMERICAN SOCIETY ON AGING

The American Society on Aging (ASA) is a network of nearly 10,000 professionals in aging-related fields. ASA's members comprise the largest multidisciplinary national professional organization working with and on behalf of older people.

The membership includes representatives of the public and private sectors: service providers, researchers, educators, advocates, health-allied social service and long-term care professionals, students and the retired, policy makers and planners, administrators and managers, business executives, professionals in private practice, aging network staff, and clergy and lay leaders.

Founded in 1954 as the Western Gerontological Society, the ASA has been a resource for both professionals and lay persons interested in the field. Its documents state that it seeks to foster a sense of community among professionals working with and on behalf of the aging; provide quality professional education and training; promote research and disseminate knowledge; facilitate innovative approaches to service delivery; promote a public image of aging that respects the wisdom, dignity, experience, and independence of aging people; influence social and public policies and structures by facilitating debate on new and developing issues; enhance and increase the involvement of ethnic, racial, and other minorities in the field of aging

and in the leadership and governance of ASA; and collaborate with other organizations to enhance the well-being of older people and their families.

Access to state-of-the-art information is considered an important benefit of membership in ASA. Through its publications, training programs, conferences, special projects, and membership affinity groups, ASA is committed to keeping its members well informed.

ASA is a leading provider of state-of-the-art training and education in aging. Its ASA Learning Center provides many resources and programs for the field. Among regular offerings are:

- the Summer Series on Aging, a week of intensives on a variety of subjects, offered in such places as San Francisco, Los Angeles, Chicago, Washington, DC, and Atlanta;
- a 2-day Fall Conference focusing on a major critical issue, covering practice, research, and policy perspectives;
- regional seminars, 1-day programs on topics of immediate concern to practitioners, offered throughout the year in many locations; and
- public forums that address pressing issues of concern and help to build ongoing local and national coalitions to work for solutions.

ASA's annual meeting is a major event on the yearly calendar of thousands of providers, academics, policy makers, administrators, and researchers in the field of aging.

ASA's publications offer updates, analysis, and criticism. The journal *Generations* has a national reputation as one of the most authoritative and informative quarterly journals in the field of aging. *Aging Today*, a bimonthly newspaper, provides continuous national coverage of developments in public policy, innovative practice, and research. *Inside ASA*, a semiannual newsletter available to members only, links members with one another, with ASA's leadership and staff, and with the ongoing programs of the organization. In addition, ASA publishes a series of monographs and books, Critical Debates in an Aging Society, and other specialized publications. The organization has a series of special-interest affinity groups: Lifetime Education and Renewal Network; Managed Care and Aging Network; the Forum on Religion, Spirituality and Aging; Healthcare and Aging Network; Lesbian and Gay Aging Issues Network; Multicultural Aging Network; Mental Health and Aging Network; Business Forum on Aging; and the Network on Environments, Services and Technologies for Maximizing Independence.

ASA is headquartered in San Francisco. Organizational policy is directed by a diverse 30-person board. The staff is headed by Gloria Cavanaugh, a longtime leader in the field of aging.

CHARLES J. FAHEY

See also
Organizations in Aging

AMERICANS WITH DISABILITIES ACT

The Americans With Disabilities Act (ADA) of 1990 (P.L. 101-336) is a civil rights law to promote equal opportunity and greater participation by people with disabilities in employment, services offered by state and local governments and private businesses, and telecommunications. ADA prohibits discrimination on the basis of disability, with protections like those provided under civil rights laws for race, sex, national origin, and religion. However, unlike other civil rights laws, ADA requires various proactive measures to ensure access.

History and Theory of Disability Rights Laws

Two historically unprecedented trends of the past 25 years underpin ADA: the development of federal disability rights law and the empowerment of people with disabilities.

The Architectural Barriers Act of 1968 (P.L. 90-480) is the first modern federal disability rights law. Introduced in January 1967 by Senator E. L. Bartlett, its purpose was "[t]o ensure that public buildings financed with federal funds are so designed and constructed as to be accessible to the physically handicapped" (Public Law 90-480). After hearings and amendments, it was signed into law in August 1968 (Katzmann, 1986).

The act was drafted by Bartlett aide Hugh Gallagher. His story not only illustrates a personal struggle with exclusion and accessibility but exemplifies other stories that later convinced Congress of the need for ADA.

In 1952, while in college, Gallagher developed polio and subsequently required use of a wheelchair. In 1963, he went to work for Senator Bartlett. On many occasions he wanted to visit public buildings in Washington, DC, but most were inaccessible. For example, to enter the National Gallery of Art he needed a small ramp to climb the two-step, 10-inch curb at the museum's entrance on Constitution Avenue.

Gallagher wrote to the National Gallery, asking for a ramp, and was told that one would "destroy the architectural integrity of the building" (H. Gallagher, personal communication, April 3, 1992). Gallagher thought his request was simple and reasonable, and that the National Gallery, as a national museum, was the property of all Americans, not just those who could walk into it. Gallagher eventually got his wish when Senator Bartlett prevailed on the National Gallery's Trustees to install a ramp—which turned out to be nearly invisible.

To solve this access problem generally, Gallagher drafted a bill with Senate Legislative Counsel, one that was "short and simple and that would put in a civil rights context," a mandate that "buildings constructed wholly or in part with federal funds be available to all citizens" (H. Gallagher, personal communication, July 27, 1992).

Although modest—only a page long and with no enforcement provision, the act departed fundamentally from existing laws for the disabled. Previous legislation involved social welfare measures (e.g., providing cash assistance or job training). The Barriers Act was a civil rights law, to promote integration and pointing to constitutional claims of equal protection and due process. It was also the first law built on the theory that disability is not simply a function of an individual's impairment, but an interaction between impairment and environment. Environments—physical and otherwise—can disable or enable a person with a disability. As a corollary, the act was the first disability law that did not require an individual to identify himself as disabled to benefit. Lastly, it expressed new national aspirations for disability policy.

The second disability rights law was Title V of the Rehabilitation Act of 1973 (P.L. 93-112), in particular section 504. Section 504 is a broad guarantee that "No otherwise qualified handicapped individual . . . shall be excluded from the participation in, be denied the benefits of, or be subjected to discrimination under any activity or program receiving Federal financial assistance. . . . " Section 504 was drafted by Senate aides using language from other civil rights laws (Scotch, 1984).

A second trend in the push for disability rights was the birth of the "independent living movement" in the late 1960s—a movement by and for people with disabilities. For example, Ed Roberts, an early leader, also had had polio and required use of a ventilator and wheelchair. In the mid-1960s he entered the University of California at Berkeley over the objections of school officials and later helped found the first "independent living center" in Berkeley in 1972. Today, a nationwide network of such centers provides peer support, advocacy, and services. This movement also reflected the increasing prevalence and complexity of disability—following the success of medical science in keeping people alive from once-fatal conditions but with lifelong disability (Vachon, 1987). For a history of this movement, see Shapiro (1993).

Although these two trends began independently, they married with great force in the mid-1970s when the Carter administration delayed publishing federal regulations to implement section 504. This led to nationwide demonstrations by disabled persons, including sit-ins at federal office buildings, and was perhaps the single most important event in coalescing a "disability community" nationwide and fostering its political education (Bowe, 1986; Scotch, 1984).

Other federal disability rights laws have been enacted subsequently. For a summary, see U.S. Department of Education (1992).

ADA was first proposed by a Reagan-appointed National Council on Disability in a 1986 report entitled, "Toward Independence." Created in 1979, the National Council is an independent federal agency charged with advising the president and Congress on disability policy. The first ADA bill was introduced in Congress in April 1988 but died when the session ended. A substantially revised bill, modeled on section 504 and other civil rights laws, was introduced in May 1989, passed over-whelmingly in 1990 with broad bipartisan support, and was signed into law by President Bush on July 26, 1990. Bush had spoken out forcefully on disability rights issues as vice-president (Shapiro, 1993).

Specific Provisions of ADA

Preamble. The opening sections describe congressional findings and purposes, including the historical segregation and exclusion experienced by people with disabilities and the nation's disability policy goals, and define disability.

Title I—Employment. Employers may not discriminate against an individual with a disability in hiring, promotion, or other employment benefits if that person is otherwise qualified for a job. Employers must provide "reasonable accommodations" to assist an individual with a disability to meet job requirements, such as job restructuring and adaptive equipment, except where accommodations would be an "undue hardship." Title I only applies to employers with more than 15 employees and is enforced by the Equal Employment Opportunity Commission and private lawsuit.

Title II—Public Services. Title II applies to state and local governments, and has two major subtitles. Subtitle A prohibits discrimination against individuals with disabilities, and requires government facilities and services to be accessible. Subtitle B applies to public transportation—requiring accessible buses, paratransit, or comparable transportation services for individuals who cannot use fixed route bus services, and accessible train cars, bus, and train stations. Title II is enforced by the U.S. Departments of Justice and Transportation, and private lawsuit.

Title III—Public Accommodations and Services Operated by Private Entities. Private entities, such as restaurants, hotels, and retail stores, may not discriminate and must provide auxiliary aids and services to individuals with vision or hearing impairments and other disabilities, unless an undue burden. Physical barriers in existing facilities must be removed, if "readily achievable." If not, other means of providing services must be provided, again if readily achievable. All new construction and alterations must be accessible. Title III is enforced by the U.S. Department of Justice and private lawsuit.

Title IV—Telecommunications. Companies offering telephone services to the general public must offer relay services to individuals who use telecommunications devices for the deaf (TDDs). Title IV is enforced by the Federal Communications Commission.

The Americans With Disabilities Act and Older Americans

Given both the relationship between aging and disability and the aging of the U.S. population, the benefits of ADA can be expected to be especially significant for older Americans and for the nation at large. Although only experience will prove the value of ADA (Vachon, 1992), possible benefits include increased employment, access to public transit, and access to a greater number of restaurants, stores, and service establishments; and greater opportunities to enjoy films, sporting events, and other performances at accessible theatres and stadiums—especially through audio amplification technologies, closed captioning, and wheelchair-accessible seating.

For Further Information

Useful texts on ADA include Gostin and Beyer (1993) and West (1991). For a detailed explanation of ADA regulations, see U.S. Equal Employment Opportunity Commission and U.S. Department of Justice (1991). For inquiries about ADA, contact the U.S. Department of Justice, Civil Rights Division, Coordination and Review Section, P.O. Box 66118, Washington, DC 20035-6118; (202) 514-0301 and (202) 514-0381 (TDD).

R. ALEXANDER VACHON

See also
Disability

ANIMAL AND PLANT AGING MODELS
See
Diet Restriction
Models for the Study of Aging: Flies
Models for the Study of Aging: Nematodes
Models for the Study of Aging: Rodents
Models for the Study of Aging: Transgenic Mice/Genetically Engineered Animals
Models for the Study of Aging: Yeast and Other Fungi

ANIMAL ASSISTED THERAPY
See
Pets

ANTIBODIES
See
Autoimmunity
Immune System
Immunizations

ANXIETY

Anxiety is an affect characterized by tension and apprehension; when directed at a specific object (such as death or AIDS), it is commonly called fear. Psychologists use the term *anxiety* to refer both to a temporary or acute state and to a chronic trait or predisposition to experience that state; individuals with trait anxiety are nervous, fearful, and worry-prone.

Older men and women face a number of potential threats—declining health, economic insecurity, bereavement—that might be expected to increase their general level of anxiety and that sometimes do so acutely. For example, Jacobs, Hansen, Kasl, Ostfeld, Berkman, and Kim (1990) have shown that anxiety disorders are relatively common among widows and widowers in the 6-month period following bereavement. But older people as a group do not show high levels of trait anxiety. In fact, measures of trait anxiety decline from age 20 to 30 and remain relatively stable thereafter (Costa & McCrae, 1994). Human beings, including the elderly, have an extraordinary capacity to adapt to life circumstances, and quickly return to their own characteristic levels of psychological functioning after a threat or loss (McCrae & Costa, 1988a).

The individual's level of trait anxiety is an enduring aspect of his or her personality. Longitudinal studies have shown stability coefficients ranging from .67 to .82 for self-reports and spouse ratings of anxiety over a 6-year interval (Costa & McCrae, 1988). Further, trait anxiety is known to be closely related to other variables (like trait depression and anger) that together define a broad dimension of personality known as neuroticism or negative affectivity. Measures of this domain have shown substantial stability over intervals of as long as 30 years (Costa & McCrae, 1997). Neuroticism-related traits are also known to be substantially heritable (Riemann, Angleitner, & Strelau, 1997), so the stability of anxiety may reflect in part its enduring genetic basis.

The implication of these findings is that anxiety at any period in the life span is more likely to reflect enduring features of the individual than either age or life circumstances. For example, most older people do not have a marked fear of death; those who do are likely to have had a lifelong history of general anxiety (Kastenbaum & Costa, 1977).

Anxiety is a major feature in a class of psychiatric conditions that include panic disorder, social phobia, and obsessive-compulsive disorder. These disorders occur at all ages and are often continuous or recurring across the life span; they show little change in prevalence after age 25 (Regier, Farmer, Rae, Myers, Kramer, Robins, et al., 1993). The stability of anxiety disorders is probably attributable in part to the stability of underlying trait anxiety.

High levels of acute anxiety can adversely affect cognitive performance, and poorer cognitive performance by older subjects is sometimes attributed to their higher levels of test anxiety. But younger subjects also experience performance anxiety, and it has become clear that differences in anxiety alone are unlikely to explain age differences in learning and memory (Salthouse, 1989). However, those older men and women who are prone to anxiety may benefit from relaxation techniques in memory training (Yesavage, Sheikh, Tanke, & Hill, 1988).

ROBERT R. MCCRAE

See also
Coping
Mental Health
Mental Health and Illness
Stress and Stressors

APHASIA

Aphasia is the object of study of many disciplines, including neurology, speech-language pathology, psychology, and linguistics. It is defined as a reduction in the ability to interpret and formulate meaningful language secondary to cerebral damage (Benson & Ardila, 1996). Aphasia can affect all language modalities, such as reading, writing, speaking, and understanding.

Normal Aging and Language Abilities

Aphasia should be differentiated from the changes observed in language abilities during normal aging. In the area of lexical retrieval, cross-sectional and longitudinal studies have reported differences in the retrieval of proper names, nouns, verbs, and referents to a definition. These changes seem to become noticeable in the 70s and climax in the 80s. Nicholas, Connor, Obler, and Albert (1998) reported that the decline in 80-year-olds was 2.5 standard deviations (SD) for noun retrieval and 3.5 SD for verb retrieval, compared to 30-year-olds. One explanation for this decline might be inaccessibility of the phonological code, as older adults seem to benefit from phonemic cueing. This may be the reason for the tip-of-the-tongue phenomenon that increases as a function of age.

Another language area that is affected by age is language comprehension. This change may be due to a combination of auditory/hearing deficits, decreased speed of processing, reduction in handling complex grammar, and mild difficulty in word meaning (Benson & Ardila, 1996). Older adults may experience difficulty in their ability to comprehend complex sentences, such as ones with embedded and relative clauses. In addition to comprehension, there is difficulty in producing syntactically complex sentences, and the trend increases with age (Nicholas, Connor, Obler, & Albert, 1998). One plausible explanation may be that older adults experience a decrement in syntactic processing abilities (Kemper, cited in Nicholas et al., 1998). In contrast, in aphasia there is also a decline in syntactic knowledge.

Research on discourse function in the elderly is inconclusive and does not support changes as a function of aging. Part of the difficulty lies in methodological issues in investigating discourse, such as levels of interest of the research participant regarding a given topic.

What is the underlying mechanism that causes changes in syntactic processing and also affects word retrieval abilities? Research has pointed out that a decrease in the working memory capacity associated with aging may affect language functions. In our lab (Constantinidou & Baker, 1999) we found significant changes in the working memory mechanisms (such as in the ability to learn and recall nouns) with older adults (50–77) compared to younger cohorts (20–45). Whereas current research supports a decline in working memory in older adults, future research should determine the exact relationship of such findings to precise language functions.

Changes in language functions also have been attributed to slowness in cognitive processing. Cognitive processing can be affected by the number of steps required for the task completion and by the finite time required for task completion. Older adults perform significantly more slowly on tasks that require shifting between two mental categories, such as the Trail Making Test (Constantinidou & Baker, 1999).

The aforementioned changes in language and cognition can be attributed to neuroanatomical and neurochemical changes in the brain that occur with aging. These include alterations in cell size, loss of myelin sheath, and the presence of neurofibrillary tangles (see "Hemispheric Specialization"). Consequently, the connectivity of the system can be hampered, causing word-finding and comprehension problems (Nicholas, Connor, Obler, & Albert, 1998).

The cognitive and neurobiological changes associated with normal aging occur gradually and allow the system to adapt. Healthy older individuals maintain the language effectiveness, and many continue to be intellectually productive into their 80s and 90s. In contrast, aphasia (which is a result of organic brain pathology) often results in a functional communication handicap and hampers quality of life.

Symptoms of Aphasia

Because aphasia can affect all language modalities, such as reading, writing, speaking, and understanding, there is great variability in the symptoms and degree of severity among patients. Some of the symptoms of aphasia include slow, effortful speech; paraphasias; difficulty with comprehension of spoken or written language; word-finding difficulties; jargon; echolalic speech; and writing problems.

Various classifications of aphasia have been generated in the past two centuries in an effort to separate the types of aphasia based on the clusters of symptoms. Variations of *aphasia syndromes* have been presented in the recent years; however; they all seem to follow the patterns of the original classification systems. Benson and Ardila (1996) proposed a classification system of aphasia in relationship with the rolandic fissure and seem to provide more precise neuroanatomical descriptions of lesion location.

The prerolandic syndromes are nonfluent types of aphasia characterized by limited output, grammatical errors, and articulatory struggle. These include the following: Broca, transcortical motor, and mixed transcortical (or isolation syndrome) types. The postrolandic types are fluent aphasias with increased verbal output, limited comprehension abilities, paraphasias, and empty language. Postrolandic types include Wernicke, transcortical sensory, conduction, and anomic aphasias.

Causes

Neuropathologies that compromise the left (or language-dominant) hemisphere of the brain can result in aphasia. These neuropathologies include cerebral vascular accidents (CVA), or stroke, brain injury, Alzheimer's disease (AD), multiinfarct dementia, tumors, and infections (such as HIV infection, AIDS, and herpes simplex encephalitis). Of the above etiologies, CVA is the leading neuropathology and is also the most common neuropathology in the older population, followed by AD.

The anatomical location of the lesion is the critical factor in aphasia symptomatology, not the etiology of the brain damage. However, certain neuropathologies affect several parts of the brain in addition to the language areas and can cause additional neurobehavioral problems. Furthermore, the medical etiology of aphasia is particularly important, as each of the above neuropathologies has a separate course, thus influencing recovery from aphasia.

Aphasia and Aging

There seems to be an interaction between type of aphasia and age. Specifically, Broca's aphasia tends to be more prevalent with younger patients, whereas Wernicke's aphasia is more common with older patients (Eslinger & Damasio, as cited in Nicholas, Connor, Obler, & Albert, 1998; Obler, Albert, Goodglass, & Benson, as cited in Nicholas et al., 1998). Initially, there was an attempt to provide a neuroanatomical explanation for this age-related pattern, suggesting that anterior lesions occur more frequently in younger patients compared to posterior lesions in older patients. However, it appears that age interacts with stroke survival, and the aforementioned patterns are due to selection bias rather than the effects of age on lesion location. Older patients may not survive large, nonfluent-aphasia lesions, and the increase in frequency of Wernicke's aphasia in the elderly could be due to lower mortality rates (Coppens, as cited in Nicholas et al., 1998).

Diagnosis

Neurodiagnostic, medical, and linguistic assessments are needed to diagnose aphasia precisely and to make prognostic statements for recovery. Neurodiagnostic tests, such as computerized tomography (CT) and magnetic resonance imaging (MRI) findings are the traditional measures used in emergency rooms and hospitals to diagnose a brain pathology that could cause aphasia. Although both of these tools will provide information about the anatomical integrity of the structures, the MRI is able to identify small lesions within minutes of onset. Furthermore, MRI provides higher resolution, and the development of the technology has resulted in earlier diagnosis of white-matter disease. On the other hand, the CT technology continues to be fast, very convenient, and portable, and it can be used with patients with pacemakers or other metallic implants. Positron emission tomography (PET) and functional MRI can provide physiological as well as anatomical information. However, these measures are not readily available to all patients.

Recovery From Aphasia

Aphasia is most prevalent in the older adult population, and therefore most outcome studies include older subjects. When it is the result of a stable lesion, such as a CVA or a brain injury (rather than a degenerative disease like AD), the most dramatic recovery is accomplished during the first few months after brain damage. The behavioral recovery is the result of spontaneous recovery exhibited by the central nervous system. *Spontaneous recovery* can be seen as a reduction in the size of lesion, as evidenced by CT or MRI scan, or as an increase in glucose metabolism in the affected areas during PET studies (Goldenberg & Spatt, 1994).

Although spontaneous or early recovery lasts only 5–6 months following an ischemic type of lesion, late recovery has been documented for years following the onset of aphasia. Several factors contribute to the rate and success of recovery, such as size and location of the lesion. Smaller anterior lesions have a better recovery rate than do larger lesions in the temporobasal area (Goldenberg & Spatt, 1994). In addition, patient age, premorbid intelligence, educational level, support systems, and intensity and quality of rehabilitation also contribute to recovery.

In a meta-analysis of 21 (Robey, 1994) and 55 (Robey, 1998) aphasia efficacy studies, Robey reported that the *treatment effect* of speech-language therapy beginning in the acute stage of recovery is nearly twice as large (1.83 times greater) as the effect of spontaneous recovery alone, with a moderate–large effect. Treatment in the postacute phase results in a small effect size, but it is 1.68 times greater for treated versus untreated individuals. In the chronic stages the average effect size is small for treated individuals, but it is greater, by a factor of 12, than for untreated patients. It is clear, on the basis of the information above, that therapy is beneficial to patients with aphasia during all stages of recovery.

FOFI CONSTANTINIDOU

See also
    Central Nervous System: Motor Functions
    Communication: Processes and Issues

Communication Disorders
Stroke

APNEA

See

Respiratory System
Sleep Disorders
Sleep Disorders: Apnea

APOLIPOPROTEIN E

Apolipoprotein E (ApoE) is one of the proteins that helps transport cholesterol and other lipids through the bloodstream. ApoE binds to the surface of lipid particles and interacts with receptors on cells, directing lipid uptake into cells that need lipid and cholesterol. It has been studied for many years by scientists interested in arteriosclerosis and heart disease because of its role in cholesterol transport. ApoE can be inherited in several different forms. The major types are designated ApoE2, ApoE3, and ApoE4. These differ from each other by single amino acid changes. Depending on which of these types of ApoE one inherits, the cholesterol-carrying abilities of the protein vary slightly. Inheritance of ApoE4 is associated with increased low-density lipoprotein (LDL) cholesterol and a 1.5–2.0-fold increased risk of coronary heart disease (Wilson, Myers, Larson, Ordovas, Wolf, & Schaefer, 1994).

Recently, ApoE's role in the brain, where it may contribute to lipid metabolism and neuronal regeneration after injury, has received attention (Mahley, 1988). In a surprising discovery in 1993, Roses and colleagues at Duke University found that inheritance of the ApoE4 type is associated with a very high incidence of developing Alzheimer's disease (Strittmatter, Saunders, Schmechel, Pericak-Vance, Enghild, Salvesen, et al., 1993). The term *allele frequency* describes the percentage of total genes that are of a certain type. In the general population the allele frequencies are ApoE2, 0.10; ApoE3, 0.76; ApoE4, 0.14. In Alzheimer's disease, the ApoE4 allele frequency nearly triples to about 0.36 (Rebeck, Reiter, Strickland, & Hyman, 1993; Strittmatter et al., 1993). The overrepresentation of ApoE4 implies that inheritance of ApoE4 is a risk factor for Alzheimer's disease. In addition, some data now suggest that inheritance of the ApoE2 allele makes one less likely than average to develop Alzheimer's disease (Corder, Saunders, Risch, Strittmatter, Gaskel, Rimmler, et al., 1994; West, Rebeck, & Hyman, 1994).

These data also suggest that there is an influence of ApoE genotype on age of onset of dementia, with ApoE4 associated with a relatively younger average age of onset and ApoE2 with a later age of onset, compared to ApoE3 (Corder, Saunders, Strittmatter, Schmechel, Gaskell, Small, et al., 1993). However, it is important to note that some individuals inherit ApoE4 and live in good health to old age (90+) (Rebeck, Perls, West, Sodhi, Lipsitz, & Hyman, 1994).

These new observations about the inheritance of a risk factor for Alzheimer's disease have spawned intensive research to understand how ApoE4 could predispose individuals to developing Alzheimer's disease, and it is hoped that they will provide new insight into the causes of this illness. A review by St. George-Hyslop (1999) helps place ApoE in the overall context of the genetics of Alzheimer's disease. Two additional reviews (Finch & Sapolsky, 1999; Martin, 1999) illustrate the status and prospects of research on ApoE for research on aging.

BRADLEY T. HYMAN
G. WILLIAM REBECK

See also

Alzheimer's Disease: Genetic Factors
Atherosclerosis
Cerebrovascular Disease
Lipoproteins, Serum

APOPTOSIS

Cells, like organisms, are in general mortal, and their life span in host tissues is usually defined genetically. For some cells, such as neurons, this life span equals that of the organism; for others, such as the intestinal epithelium and hemopoietic systems, the cellular life span is only as long as their functional operation lasts. The mortality of a cell, then, is crucial to the total count of cell numbers in a given tissue. Too much will result in the loss of functional units, detrimental to the host system's optimal functionality, such as neurodegeneration-associated neuronal cell loss; and too little will create excess baggage for the system to support, such as the neoplastic growth found in cancer. To achieve the proper number of healthy cells for any given tissue, nature provides an exquisitely controlled genetic mechanism, called apoptosis, or programmed cell death, a process that, when activated, commits cells to undergo suicide (Ashkenazi & Dixit, 1998; Deveraux & Reed, 1999; Li, Nijhawan, Budhardio, Srinivasula, Ahmad, Alnemri, et al., 1997; Wang, 1997; White, 1996; Widmann, Gibson, & Johnson, 1998). This self-elimination is directed by the orchestration of hundreds of genes' function, and it is seen in many physiological events when an excess number of cells is produced or when cells are damaged via infection, toxin, oxidative damage, or UV-irradiation.

In general, most genes associated with apoptosis are classified into pro-apoptotic, or pro-survival, defined as to whether their action promotes or prevents death. Large families of genes have been discovered in the last few years whose members function in either the pro-life or pro-death camps of genetic function. Most noted of these are the families of CASPASE and Bcl-2 classes. The CASPASE genes uniformly act pro-apoptotically; their action is, in general, via proteolysis, mainly by cleaving other substrate proteins into fragments, thereby annulling their crucial function in the cells. This proteolytic activity is the culprit that performs the final act of death by severing vital cellular proteins into pieces. These protein victims include actin, vimentin, DNA repair enzymes, and RNA synthetic machinery members; the list of candidate CASPASE substrates increases as new proteins are identified daily in this category. The Bcl-2 family, on the other hand, initially acts as a pro-survival factor; the best-known member is the original Bcl-2 gene. Interestingly enough, not all members of this family are "good guys" for survival; many of them behave molecularly in the opposite fashion (i.e., they promote death). This change to the opposite function is due to the fact that the protective mode of the Bcl-2 family is composed of unique molecular domains. Some members of the Bcl-2 family can bind to their sisters' survival functional domains and therefore disable the sister's protective function. In other cases, genetic mutations occur and change the functional domain from protective to killing mode. In all, the balance between the pro- and anti-apoptotic molecular forces is always in action at many checkpoints when an apoptotic event is activated, allowing the cell ample opportunity to change its mind on the road to self-inflicted death.

The genetic script dictating the regulation of apoptotic death was initially thought of as a duet-playing party of good guys versus bad guys. Since then, astounding discoveries show that there are many checkpoints within the cellular milieu to map out the apoptotic path. Individual checkpoints are identified by major players such as the CASPASE or Bcl-2 family genes; however, the completion of their function may involve dozens of other proteins, serving to help or block their action. Therefore, the clusters at each checkpoint serve largely as gatekeepers, to determine whether a signal to die ever passes through that particular checkpoint. Who are these helpers, and how do they function as the facilitators of apoptotic death? The answer is that, although any protein can play this role, they are mainly the members of the intertwining signal transduction pathways, and they act at the transcriptional, translational, and posttranslational modification steps to facilitate the passing or blocking of the signals through the checkpoints.

To a nonbiologist, these signal transduction pathways may make it seem that life is composed of dismantled telephone wires, with no clue as to how a cell can ever maintain its operation through this chaos. Nevertheless, there is method in this madness; in general, this method follows a simple rule, starting with the signal generators (usually at the plasma membrane), with hundreds of receptors as the antennae to receive stimuli from the extracellular environment. Once the signal is received, it generates a cascade of multiple reactions, in parallel and/or serially, eventually targeting the nucleus, mitochondria, or other cytoplasmic organelles as the final point. The final executive decision is then the sum of the many balanced biochemical actions to dictate whether the cell lives or dies. A complete picture of how this complex system works is possible only when we are able to know all the players' identities and their roles in this genetic symphonic dance.

As described above, apoptosis is mostly seen during development, as the way to get rid of extra cells that are not needed in the formation of a given organ. This molecular sculpturing act is essential to the production of a new organism, to make its tissue pattern fit the designated function. For example, in the central nervous system (CNS), far more neurons than ultimately required are produced during development, but only those that can successfully generate a neuronal network survive; the rest of them are deleted by the cellular suicidal program of apoptosis. As CNS neurons possess no regenerative ability, the strategy is not to have apoptosis occur postdevelopmentally. The loss of any of them is a permanent loss to the organism. In contrast, for breast ductal epithelium, the cells lining the milk-producing ducts follow a precise menopausal cue to dispose of themselves in postmenopausal women. Intestinal epithelial cells are yet another example; each traverses a villus from the crypt to the tip in 8 days, and afterward die, via apoptosis, and the cell corpse is shed into the intestinal lumen. Therefore, strategies for the operation of *apoptosis signals* in different tissues are vastly different and unique to the functional and developmental path for each tissue.

Obviously, to maintain a successful aging process is to have neurons stay alive and healthy as long as possible by blocking the apoptotic process from ever happening and to have the breast ductal epithelial cells all gotten rid of by promoting apoptotic death, so that no cells will be left as the seed hotbed for cancer development in postmenopausal women. How can these programs ever be maintained for as long as an organism's life? For humans, this need may require a duration as long as 100 years in centenarians. The answers lie in the area of genetic and environmental elements, that is, the nature and nurture factors that influence individuals' lives. Age-dependent defects in maintaining the balance of apoptosis between tissues are contributed to by heritable traits working together with our environment in terms of oxidative stress, UV exposure, and so on.

The etiology of many age-dependent diseases is thought to be related to the cells' inability to maintain some intended program, either pro- or anti-apoptosis. Every tissue precisely regulates the critical cell mass needed for its specific function. The number of cells contributing to the composition of this critical mass is in general determined by the cell proliferation program. This number is largely determined during prenatal development for those tissues composed of permanently growth-arrested cells, such as neurons and cardiomyocytes; therefore, loss of such cells via excess apoptotic activity precipitates cardiovascular and neurological disorders. On the other hand, if the critical number of cells exceeds the tissue's needs because of too little apoptotic activity, this scenario creates an environment of too many cells or retaining cells that are no longer needed, a prelude to hyperplasia and eventually neoplastic growth. Thus, too little apoptosis causes cancer-related problems, and too much apoptosis in certain tissues creates neurodegenerative disorders such as Alzheimer's disease; both are perils of the elderly.

The obvious connection to use drug- or gene-directed therapeutic treatment has been thought to be the next frontier of science to combat the old-age plague, largely by reducing or increasing apoptotic activity in tissues where too much or too little is observed. This simple logic is, however, complicated by the fact that the orchestration of the apoptotic process in a cell requires several dozen checkpoints, each controlled by yet other dozens of molecular players. The art of fine-tuning the molecular symphony to its optimal functional output in producing suicidal death or not doing so is a learned skill contributed to by both inherited traits and environmental influences. Moreover, the ultimate question remains: Wherever the pro- or anti-apoptotic phenotype is, why does it take a lifetime to develop, with time of onset differing among individuals? For some, this onset of abnormal apoptosis occurs at middle age; for others in the late 80s; and for yet others it never occurs. This fact speaks loudly of an individual genetic signature for apoptosis regulation. With the advent of high-throughput biochip technology, this genetic signature for individuals is within our grasp, and we look forward to the days when a gene profile for an individual's apoptosis regulation is the guideline for prognostic and diagnostic tools against age-dependent diseases. With this hope, we anticipate that age-dependent debility can be reduced via apoptosis regulation by therapeutic treatment, and then we can all aspire to a life such as that of the world's oldest individual, Madame Calmette, who died at the age of 122 in fairly good health.

EUGENIA WANG

The author would like to thank Mr. Alan N. Bloch for critical review and editing of this manuscript. This work was supported by grants from the National Institute on Aging of the National Institutes of Health (RO1 AG09278) and from the Defense Advance Research Project Agency of the USA to Eugenia Wang.

See also
Senescence and Transformation

ARCHITECTURE

Architecture specifically designed for older adults has served as a catalyst in the past 40 years in the effort to enhance the quality as well as the quantity of life for the aging person.

Architects, possibly more than any other professionals, have been responsible for bringing together a multitude of disciplines and professions to address the problems associated with living to an advanced age. The individual's declining abilities to respond appropriately to his/her environment requires architecture that will contribute to, rather than detract from, the individual's maximum physical, mental, and emotional functioning.

The initial focus on designing better buildings for the elderly came in the late 1940s and early 1950s in response to the construction of a small but increasing number of facilities such as homes for the aging and nursing homes. Architects were soon to go beyond the boundary of their drawing boards to address the social and health needs of the elderly. They were required to create new building forms, including housing for the elderly, congregate living facilities, personal care units, senior centers, retirement communities, life-care communities, and continuing-care retirement communities.

The impetus behind this creative effort came in the early 1960s and shaped the field of housing for the elderly for the next two decades. Major governmental agencies, including the Federal Housing Administration, Public Housing Administration, Administration on Aging, Farmers Home Administration, and later the Department of Housing and Urban Development were among those that initiated programs, standards, and financing mechanisms for a wide variety of services and facilities for the elderly to which architecture and architects responded.

Private agencies and organizations such as the National Council on Aging and the American Association of Retired Persons supported research, training, and demonstration projects toward improving the design of environments for the elderly. The Gerontological Society of America established the Aging and Environments project directed by Thomas Byerts, AIA.

Early publications by architects having a major influence in the field were *Buildings for the Elderly* (Musson & Heusinkveld, 1963) and *Planning Housing Environments for the Elderly* (Gelwicks & Newcomer, 1974). The latter encouraged a multidisciplinary approach emphasizing the programming of housing to incorporate the psychosocial components of care. The purpose was to produce an environmental match between the resident and the architecture.

The research of psychologists and sociologists exerted an important influence on many architects. M. Powell Lawton, research psychologist at the Philadelphia Geriatric Center and Leon Pastalan, sociologist at the University of Michigan, engaged in many collaborative works with architects, and their research on the effect of physical environment on the behavior, life satisfaction, and health of older persons provided an important behavioral basis for design. Lawton's book, *Environment and Aging* (1980), addressed key interdisciplinary issues for architects.

Architectural schools committed to the generalist educational approach became increasingly aware of the role of buildings for the elderly as a useful medium to challenge students in the solving of interrelated physical, social, and psychological design problems. Major federal funding for such programs as the graduate program in environmental design for the elderly at the Andrus Gerontology Center, University of Southern California, encouraged many schools of architecture to develop courses and programs in the design of facilities for the elderly. The Andrus Center established the Environmental Studies Laboratory, directed by Victor Regnier, and has since 1976 offered a dual degree in gerontology and urban planning.

A major impact on architecture and architects has come from three distinguished women: Ollie Randall, Wilma Donahue, and Marie McGuire Thompson. Randall, a social worker and pioneer in the field of aging, encouraged and assisted many architects. In 1966 she shared her podium in Vienna with the first architect to present a paper at the

International Congress of Gerontology. Her initiatives led to the founding of both the National Council on Aging and the American Association of Homes for the Aging.

Donahue, a sociologist at the University of Michigan, developed interdisciplinary programs involving both architecture and sociology and was instrumental in the development of a variety of housing projects for the elderly.

In 1961 Marie McGuire Thompson, Executive Director of the Housing Authority in San Antonio, Texas, which had just completed the first federally financed public housing high-rise building for the elderly, Victoria Plaza, addressed the first White House Conference on Aging as the keynote speaker. Her long and distinguished career includes her appointment as U.S. Commissioner of Public Housing. In that post she established regional programs for architects to promote better design in housing for low-income elderly persons.

The 1980s brought new interest and new players in the development of housing for older adults. These developments were triggered by the slump in the home building and multifamily housing market, a significant increase in the numbers of older people (as well as their retirement incomes), and health care legislation including changes in Medicare and Medicaid reimbursement. The latter changes encouraged hospitals to develop multiple levels of care and facilities to meet the needs of a rapidly expanding older population.

Developers and major national corporations, including hotel chains and hospitals, are currently developing housing linked to a continuum of care. Architects, desiring to serve these clients, in turn are expanding their services to include planning and programming for the elderly. Planning firms specialize in the planning, programming, and marketing of facilities and services for the elderly.

To attract the elderly market many health care providers offer a full continuum of care ranging from acute to home care. Within the continuum, the development of congregate housing and continuing-care retirement communities has become an important option. The architectural design of each element of the continuum and their interrelationship plays an essential role in the older person's ability to negotiate the health care environment.

The current market is a new generation, which for the first time in history is composed of two generations of elderly. This population has an entirely new set of lifetime experiences and preferences. The future success of architecture for older adults will be determined by the professional response to the demands as well as the needs of the consumer.

Discussion of both design and policy issues of particular relevance for architects interested in the special requirements of frail and disabled adult populations are found in the American Institute for Architects Foundations (1985) and in Regnier and Pynoos (1987).

LOUIS E. GELWICKS

See also
Housing

ARTHRITIS

Arthritis (inflammation of a joint) is a disease category known as rheumatic disease that includes more than 100 different conditions, varying in symptomatology and probable cause. The etiology of most is yet unknown. Most forms of arthritis are chronic and endure for many years exhibiting inflammation consisting of swelling, redness, warmth, and pain of joints. Rheumatoid arthritis and osteoarthritis (often a noninflammatory condition) are the two most common forms seen in the aged.

Rheumatoid arthritis is not considered a disease of old age, and in 70% of cases the disease makes its appearance between the ages of 25 and 54 years (Calkins, 1992). It affects 75% more women than men. Severe crippling can result from inflammation of the synovial membrane, periosteum, and tendon sheath of a joint. This disease can involve numerous organs and systems of the body, but appears most frequently in joints, e.g., fingers, wrists, elbows, knees, hips, and ankles. Persistent bilateral pain, swelling of joints, and morning stiffness are common symptoms. Treatment must be initiated early to prevent joint damage (Calkins & Reinhard, 2000).

Osteoarthritis (also known as degenerative joint disease, hypertrophic arthritis, arthrosis, and osteoarthrosis) is the most common disease of movable joints. This disease is often a milder condition than rheumatoid arthritis, exhibiting no symptoms initially; occasionally there is pain and joint stiffness, and sometimes considerable pain and disability occur. Sixteen million Americans exhibit symptoms severe enough to require treatment. Women are more prone than men to osteoarthritis at the end of finger joints and at the base of the thumb. Forty million adults in the United States exhibit positive radiographs of hands and feet (Radin & Bruce Martin, 1984). The incidence and severity of osteoarthritis increase with age, although some believe it is not an invariable result of aging. Although wear-and-tear injuries of the internal surface are probable causes of some cases, trauma, heredity, disorders of the endocrine or immunobiological systems, disordered mineral metabolism, overweight, and aging are believed to represent the etiology of other cases. Mechanical insults and aging are the two principal etiologic factors commonly evoked.

Some form of degenerative joint disease is almost always present in older persons (80% in persons more than 55 years old and 100% in those 70 years and over), but it can occur at any age, especially after joint injury (Kelly, Harris, Ruddy, & Sledge, 1981). Most often involved are the weight-bearing joints (Sokoloff, 1969), e.g., knees, hips, and spine, although fingers, wrists, and even the temporomandibular joints are involved. Hands, wrists, and elbows are most commonly affected (Riddle, 1979). Primary and secondary forms of the disease are recognized. Although in the primary form there may be no history of previous abnormality of, or trauma to, an affected joint, the secondary form is a consequence of abnormality or damage. Damage may arise from direct injury to a joint, as in the rupture of a knee cartilage, or indirectly, for example, through misalignment after a fracture of a limb bone. Minor forms of congenital abnormality are thought to underlie a proportion of cases of osteoarthritis of the hip. It may well be that intrinsic degeneration of articular tissue underlies the development of the disease from whatever cause and that the varying symptomatology is due to susceptibility, time, and severity. Sokoloff (1984) has suggested that osteoarthritis may be due to an aberration of the repair processes of cartilage.

Normally, the ends of bones meet in diarthroses (synovial, movable joints) and are covered by smooth, rubbery cartilage that allows joint motion. In osteoarthritis the cartilage frays and becomes softened and thin, losing its elasticity. It can be completely worn away so that the exposed bone ends rub against each other (eburnation). This mechanical stimulation results in aberrant bone production at the ends of bones, producing spurs (osteophytes). Where osteoarthritis affects the spine, bone spurs may pinch nerves creating pain distant from the joint. Muscles become irritated and strained, producing more pain.

Osteoarthritis can be diagnosed by examination and X-rays, while laboratory blood tests are used to exclude other types of arthritis. The treatment of the symptoms of the disease is generally effective, but not corrective. While a number of analgesics are used to relieve minor pain, intra-articular injections of cortisone derivatives temporarily relieve more severe pain and allow resumption of motion. Joint surgery, especially for hips and knees, is most effective in patients with uncontrolled pain and limited motion (Davidson & Wordsworth, 2000).

EDGAR A. TONNA
Updated by
J. GRIMLEY EVANS

See also
  Connective Tissues
  Disability
  Mobility
  Musculoskeletal System

ARTS
See
  Humanities and the Arts

ASIAN AND PACIFIC ISLANDER AMERICAN ELDERS

Older Americans from Asian and Pacific Island backgrounds are the most rapidly growing of the four federally recognized ethnic minority categories. In the 1990 census, nearly half a million (454,458) people 65 and older identified themselves as Asian or Pacific Islander, an increase of 114% over 1980's 212,000, although both are widely acknowledged to be undercounts; by 1995 they were estimated to number over 665,000. In 1990 they were 1.5% of all U.S. elders and are projected to be 8% by 2050. Almost two thirds of Asian/Pacific Islanders (A/PI) elders in the United States live in California and Hawaii (Young & Gu, 1995). There are more than 30 national backgrounds represented among the A/PI elders, the largest of which are listed in Table 1, along with selected demographic characteristics.

Vast heterogeneity exists both between and within elders of each A/PI ethnic group, including time in the United States, acculturation level, income, education, rural/urban background, and religion. Although the term "Asian" is limited in its usefulness, A/PI elders are often lumped together in national statistics or excluded from analyses altogether because of their relatively small numbers. Compared with other racial/ethnic categories, cumulatively, A/PI elders have been found to be less likely to live alone or in institutions (related perhaps to the traditions of filial piety in many Asian populations) and have longer life expectancy, although,

again, there is considerable variation between and within the ethnic groups.

Data on most groups are very limited, and almost no literature exists on Asian Indian elders in the United States. Some known characteristics of the larger groups are summarized below.

Chinese American Elders

The largest group of A/PI elders is extremely diverse within itself. They may be second- or third-generation American-born or immigrants from Mainland China, Hong Kong, Taiwan, or Vietnam. The first known Chinese immigrants to the United States were males in the 1850s who came to "Gold Mountain" (California). They were exposed to sometimes violent anti-Chinese sentiment, resulting in the Chinese Exclusion Act of 1882, making immigration of laborers illegal until 1943. Many families were separated for decades until the laws changed, which allowed over 9,000 wives to immigrate after World War II (Kitano & Daniels, 1988).

TABLE 1   Asian/Pacific Islander Elders 65 and Over, 1990: Selected Characteristics

Ethnic Identification	Number 65+	% of A/PI 65+	% Foreign-born	% in Poverty	% With Education < 9 Yrs.	Bachelor's +	% Linguistically Isolated
Asian/Pacific Islander American	454,458	100%	69.7%	11.5%	39.0%	12.9%	30%
Chinese	133,977	29.5%	83.5%	14.7%	43.3%	15.3%	46%
Japanese	105,932	23.3%	17.2%	5.0%	23.0%	9.8%	19%
Filipino	104,206	22.9%	94.6%	7.9%	43.2%	15.7%	17%
Korean	35,247	7.8%	91.7%	20.4%	41.8%	10.6%	53%
Asian Indian	23,004	5.1%	82.6%	8.3%	39.4%	20.8%	12%
Vietnamese	18,084	4.0%	97.4%	18.2%	55.7%	4.8%	46%
Cambodian	3,724	0.8%	97.8%	29.5%	79.6%	1.5%	54%
Laotian	3,697	0.8%	97.8%	27.6%	77.3%	2.3%	48%
Hmong	2,535	0.6%	96.1%	46.7%	92.4%	0.8%	59%
Thai	1,416	0.3%	97.2%	12.0%	44.3%	6.7%	31%
Other Asian	7,901	1.7%					
Native Hawaiian	10,233	2.3%	1.8%	10.8%	32.0%	4.7%	3%
Samoan	2,047	0.5%	38.3%	16.4%	35.5%	5.3%	11%
Guamanian	1,523	0.3%	16.1%	13.1%	47.3%	6.5%	10%
Other Pacific Islander	930	0.2%					

Source: Young & Gu, 1995.

Elders of Chinese ancestry continue to come to the United States in large numbers, especially from Taiwan and Hong Kong, in most cases as "followers of children."

Some Chinese American elders have done well economically, but the poverty rate exceeds that for older Americans in general. Many older immigrants do not receive pension income, and some are not eligible for Medicare.

Mortality rates for older cohorts of Chinese Americans are about two thirds that of older Whites and higher for foreign-born than for American-born. Health risks are similar to those of other U.S. elders, with the following exceptions: higher rates of liver, esophageal, and pancreatic cancers and three times higher suicide rate for older Chinese women. Preliminary data also indicate higher risk for diabetes and multiinfarct dementia but lower risks for Alzheimer's disease. Heart disease and colorectal cancer appear to be less common in the countries of origin but increase with acculturation. Although many Chinese American elders accept Western biomedical health beliefs, many also accept aspects of classical Chinese health beliefs, such as the balance theory of health (yin/yang) and the importance of Chi (McBride, Morioka-Douglas, & Yeo, 1996).

Japanese American Elders

Four historical periods for Japanese Americans have been identified: (1) *immigration* (1890–1924) of young male laborers and women; (2) *prewar* (1924–1941) era of growing hostility and anti-Japanese discrimination; (3) *wartime evacuation* (1941–1945) and internment of all people of Japanese descent from the West Coast to relocation centers; and (4) *postwar* (1945–present). The current older cohort includes *issei* (early immigrant pioneers); *nisei* (American-born children of issei); older *sansei* (nisei offspring); *kibei* (niseis sent to Japan to study when young); and *shin-issei* (post-1965 immigrants) (Kitano & Daniels, 1988).

Although generational, geographic, and socioeconomic variations are common, as a whole, Japanese Americans are the most acculturated and assimilated Asian subgroup. Although Japanese American elders are at lower risk for heart disease, they have been found to be at higher risk for diabe-

tes, multiinfarct dementia, stomach cancer, and suicide; males are at higher risk for esophageal and pancreatic cancers and females for osteoporosis (McBride, Morioka-Douglas, & Yeo, 1996). To provide culturally competent care several Japanese American communities have developed ethnic-specific skilled nursing and assisted living facilities (Yeo & Hikoyeda, 1992).

Filipino American Elders

Large numbers of men from the Philippines were recruited to work in Hawaii and California from 1910 to 1930. As the U.S. economy worsened in the 1930s, severe discrimination and legal restrictions intensified, culminating in the Tydings-McDuffie Act of 1934 setting an annual quota of 50 Filipino immigrants. During World War II the U.S. Navy recruited residents of the Philippines with promises of U.S. citizenship; after the war, veterans and family members of U.S. residents immigrated in large numbers. After quotas were relaxed in 1965 and continuing through the 1990s, there has been a dramatic increase in immigration of elders from the Philippines, many times following adult children who have come as health care professionals. In 1990 the U.S. Immigration Act amendments allowed naturalization of Filipino veterans of World War II who had not been given U.S. citizenship as promised. By 1994 over 2,000 older veterans had been resettled in California, swelling the already large numbers of single older Filipino men living alone or in male rooming houses (Yeo, Hikoyeda, McBride, Chin, Edmonds, & Hendrix, 1998).

Mortality rates are roughly half that of their White counterparts and higher for foreign-born (Liu & Yu, 1985). High rates of diabetes, hypertension, and gout have been found in Filipino elders (McBride, Morioka-Douglas, & Yeo, 1996).

Korean American Elders

Waves of Korean migration to the United States include (1) *recruited migration* (1903–1905) of farmworkers and families to Hawaii; (2) *restricted migration* (1905–1924) of picture brides, students, and political exiles; (3) *dependent* (1952–1964) immigrants, including war brides and war orphans;

and (4) *new waves of settlers* (1965–present), over 20,000 annually, many well-educated, urban professionals and their extended families (Yamato, Chin, Ng, & Franks, 1993).

Traditional Korean American characteristics include: A high regard for filial piety, clearly divided family roles, family collectivity and interdependence overriding individualism, and importance of a good education (Chin, 1993). Christian churches are social and educational centers providing group ties, identity, and acceptance. Many own businesses unrelated to their professional training because of cultural/language barriers.

Korean Americans tend to underutilize health care and tend to seek care during later disease stages. The following conditions are reported to be higher among Korean Americans: depression, diabetes, esophageal and stomach cancers, liver cancer and cirrhosis in males, and cervical cancer in females. Hypertension appears to be lower (Zane, Takeuchi, & Young, 1994).

Asian Indian American Elders

The minimal literature that exists on elders who have immigrated from India describes a very heterogeneous population. Some came as farmers from Punjab in the early 1900s and endured considerable discrimination, and a more highly educated group has come since 1965. Many call themselves Indo-Americans or South Asians.

Familism is still strong in Asian Indian communities in the United States, as is respect for elders. The traditional health beliefs and practices in India were founded on Ayurvedic medicine, which emphasizes balance of the basic five elements and their analogues in the body (McBride, Morioka-Douglas, & Yeo, 1996).

Southeast Asian American Elders

Since 1975 nearly 2 million refugees have fled Vietnam, Cambodia, and Laos due to wars, politics, and famine; about half have settled in the United States in two migration waves (Yamato, Chin, Ng, & Franks, 1993). The first (1975–1977) followed the fall of Saigon, when 130,000 Vietnamese and Cambodians escaped by helicopters, sea lifts,

or self-evacuation. This more advantaged cohort included military personnel, civil servants, teachers, farmers, fishermen, and American employees (Kitano & Daniels, 1988). The second wave (post-1979) of Vietnamese, Cambodian, Hmong, and Laotian refugees were poor, rural, and illiterate; they survived harrowing escapes and refugee camps. Both waves included older adults who came with families, although individuals aged 65 and over make up only 2%–3% of the population.

The Hmong were forced to flee their Laotian tribal homelands because of mass exterminations. Hmong communities are characterized by clans as the basic family/political units and sources of identity, problem solving, and mutual aid; large, male-dominated families; and strong spiritual influences on health beliefs and behaviors. No written language existed until 1953, and there was little exposure to formal education or Western culture prior to their forced migration (Fadiman, 1998).

Over 1 million Cambodians were exterminated during the rule of the Khmer Rouge. Those who survived spent many years in refugee camps before immigrating to the United States. Elders' most frequent chronic complaint is headache, many times with dizziness, which they frequently attribute to "thinking too much" (about the trauma and the lost loved ones) (Handelman & Yeo, 1996).

Mental health problems are common among Southeast Asian refugees, who suffer from survival guilt, relocation depression, and posttraumatic stress disorder. Studies reveal that they suffer from hepatitis B, liver disorders, tuberculosis, thalassemia trait, and malnutrition more than other U.S. elders do. They also encounter: language/cultural barriers, high poverty rates, disrupted families, intergenerational conflict, loss of identity, and racial discrimination (Kagawa-Singer, Hikoyeda, & Tanjasiri, 1997; McBride, Morioka-Douglas, & Yeo, 1996; Zane, Takeuchi, & Young, 1994).

GWEN YEO
NANCY HIKOYEDA

See also
Ethnicity
Minorities and Aging
Minority Populations: Recruitment and Retention in Aging Research

ASSESSMENT

See

    Community Needs Assessment
    Comprehensive Assessment
    Geriatric Assessment Units
    Long-Term Care Assessment
    Minimum Data Set
    Multidimensional Functional Assessment
    OARS Multidimensional Functional Assessment Questionnaire
    Psychological Assessment

ASSISTED LIVING: A NEW MODEL OF SUPPORTIVE HOUSING WITH LONG-TERM CARE SERVICES

Although families continue to be the major source of long-term care, various types of residential long-term care settings have emerged to supplement their efforts. A variety of factors have contributed to an increased demand for residential facilities that offer supportive services for the frail elderly. First, the population of older persons is growing rapidly, with estimates that the number of elderly needing long-term care will double to 14 million over the next two decades. Second, most elderly have a strong preference for remaining in their own homes and, when long-term care is needed for receiving it outside a nursing home. Finally, policies in many states constrain access to nursing home care. The result has been continued expansion of in-home and community-based services, including a variety of supportive housing options (Harrington & DuNah, 1994). The option currently attracting the most attention is assisted living.

Other than nursing homes, the most common form of residential setting offering supportive long-term care services are entities generically referred to as board and care homes (Hawes, Mor, Wildfire, Lux, Green, Iannacchione, et al., 1995). Such facilities are known by more than 30 different names, such as shelter care homes, adult congregate living facilities, adult care homes, personal care homes, domiciliary care homes, and residential care homes for the elderly (Hawes et al., 1995). Most states also have begun to include assisted living facilities (ALFs) in their board and care stock. As of the early 1990s, there were an estimated 40,000 board

and care facilities, licensed and unlicensed, with an estimated 750,000 beds nationwide (Hawes et al., 1995; Hawes, Wildfire, & Lux, 1993). (Many states did not require licensure for ALFs in the early 1990s, particularly if they were apartment-style ALFs. Thus, they were included in the estimated count of unlicensed residential care facilities.)

Since the early 1990s, the most rapidly expanding form of senior housing has been ALFs (American Seniors Housing, 1998; ALFA, 1998; Citro & Hermanson, 1999). Indeed, one-third of facilities that call themselves assisted living have been in business for 5 or fewer years, and 60% have been in operation for 10 or fewer years (Hawes, Rose, & Phillips, 1999).

Assisted living has largely been viewed as a market phenomenon, a response to both consumer demand and the availability of private investment. The availability of funds for construction and renovation through private investment, including lenders and the stock market, has also been a major impetus for the industry's growth, attracted by their view of demographics and the resulting effect on demand and also by the high rates of return shown by some assisted living companies (American Seniors Housing, 1998; Conway, MacPherson, & Sfiroudis, 1997). However, part of this growth can also be attributed to increased state involvement.

The first licensure regulation specifically directed toward assisted living was in Oregon in 1989. By 1992 fewer than 10 states had such regulations in place. However, by 1998 most states had expanded their definition of residential care to include a specific licensure category known as "assisted living" or simply incorporated these facilities into their traditional concept of residential care. Further, more than half the states provided some type of Medicaid funding for services in ALFs by 1998 (Mollica, 1998).

Despite this phenomenal growth in both public and private support for assisted living, no consensus emerged on the appropriate regulatory model for assisted living during the past decade. Models have varied from state policies that sought to create assisted living as a unique long-term care arrangement, with distinctive environmental features (e.g., requiring apartments with kitchens) to those that basically allowed the same types of shared rooms and limited services as typically found in board and care homes. In addition, states differed on whether the features that ought to be subject to regulation should include the housing component or should be limited to only the service component, in effect treating assisted living as a kind of home health service (Mollica, 1998). This variability in public policy has been matched by diversity among providers, who differ in size, ownership, auspices, target population, physical environment, and services (Hawes, Rose, & Phillips, 1999; Manard & Cameron, 1997). Thus, both public and private policies caused different models to emerge around the country, leading to a lack of uniformity in terms of the environment, services, and other policies.

Despite this lack of consensus about an appropriate regulatory model and the diversity that one finds in the industry that calls itself assisted living, there is surprising consensus about the "philosophy" of assisted living. In the view of many observers, assisted living represents a promising new model of long-term care, one that blurs the invidious distinction between nursing homes and community-based care and reduces the chasm between receiving long-term care in one's own home and in an "institution." ALFs are thought to provide (or be capable of providing) a range of services that makes them a viable but less institutional alternative to nursing homes (Kane & Wilson, 1993). This premise is rooted in the philosophical principles underlying the conceptual model of assisted living.

The key elements or philosophical tenets of assisted living derive from the premise that the goal of assisted living is to meet consumers' needs and preferences, preserve independence and dignity, and allow residents to age in place in a homelike environment. As defined by the Assisted Living Quality Coalition (1998) (the coalition is a group representing the Alzheimer's Association, AARP, the American Association of Homes and Services for the Aging, the Assisted Living Federation of America, the American Seniors Housing Association, and the American Health Care Association/ National Center for Assisted Living), an assisted living setting is:

A congregate residential setting that provides or coordinates personal services, 24-hour supervision and assistance (scheduled and unscheduled), activities, and health related services; designed to minimize the need to move; designed to accommodate individual residents' changing needs and preferences; designed to maximize residents' dignity, autonomy, privacy, independence, and safety; and designed to encourage family and community involvement.

Key elements of the philosophy of assisted living have typically been operationalized as an environment with single-occupancy units, shared only by choice, that contain specific areas for sleeping, living, and preparing food, as well as private baths. The philosophy also emphasizes flexible service arrangements that facilitate aging-in-place, support self-care in the performance of ADLs and instrumental activities of daily living (IADLs, such as medications, meals, and transportation), and assume responsibility for management of care across all domains (ALFA, 1998; Hodlewsky, 1998; Wilson, 1996).

Despite agreement on the philosophical underpinnings of assisted living, there is no consensus about which facilities are and which are not assisted living. As the National Center on Assisted Living observed, "Assisted living . . . is known by dozens of different terms throughout the country. . . . The multitude of names for assisted living reflects the diversity of services offered in the cloudy nexus between retirement housing and skilled nursing care" (Hodlewsky, 1998). As a result, there are widely divergent perceptions about the total number of ALFs, with estimates that range from 10,000 to 40,000 facilities that provide services to between 350,000 and 1,000,000 residents (ALFA, 1998; Citro & Hermanson, 1999). Probably the best estimate comes from a study funded by the U.S. Department of Health and Human Services (DHHS). This study surveyed a national probability sample of facilities and arrived at an estimate of the number of ALFs nationwide that met a generally agreed on definition of assisted living. (The study was done for the DHHS Office of the Assistant Secretary for Planning and Evaluation [ASPE] and excluded small homes [2–10 beds] that are mostly adult care homes or other types of board and care facilities. It included only those places that served the elderly and called themselves assisted living or were facilities that provided 24-hour oversight, at least two meals a day, housekeeping, and assistance with at least two of the following: medications, bathing, dressing.) This study found that at the beginning of 1998, there were an estimated 11,500 ALFs with a total of just over 600,000 beds, housing more than one-half million residents. The average size was 53 beds; 67% of the ALFs had 11–50 beds; 21% had 51–100 beds; and 12% had more than 100 beds. Facility occupancy averaged 84% (Hawes, Rose, & Phillips, 1999).

Although the DHHS study was restricted to places that called themselves assisted living or that provided a specified range of services, the study still found tremendous variation among the ALFs. Fewer than half the resident units (43%) were apartments; most accommodations (57%) were bedrooms. The vast majority (73%) were private, but a sizable proportion of accommodations (27%) were shared by two or more unrelated individuals. Moreover, more than one-third (35%) of the resident accommodations had a shared bathroom (Hawes, Rose, & Phillips, 1999). Thus, the majority of ALFs offered considerably more privacy than do nursing homes or traditional board and care homes. This is particularly important, given the overwhelming preference of older persons for private accommodations (Jenkens, 1997; Kane et al., 1998). At the same time, a significant number of ALFs did not conform to what many view as a key element of the philosophy underlying assisted living.

Assisted living facilities also differed in the services they offered and the way in which they were provided. Nearly all facilities provided or arranged for 24-hour staff, three meals a day, and housekeeping. More than 90% of the ALF administrators also reported that the facility provided medication reminders and assistance with bathing and dressing; 88% of the ALFs provided or arranged for central storage of drugs or assistance with administration of medications. However, they differed with respect to care or monitoring by a licensed nurse. About half (52%) of the facilities provided some care or monitoring by a licensed nurse (RN or LPN) with their own staff. One-quarter (25%) arranged for nursing care with an outside agency. However, one in five ALF administrators (21%) reported that the facility did not arrange for or provide any care or monitoring by a licensed nurse (Hawes, Rose, & Phillips, 1999).

Admission and retention policies varied among ALFs, as well. Most ALFs reported a willingness to admit and retain residents with moderate physical limitations, such as using a wheelchair (71%) or needing help with locomotion (62%). But fewer than half the ALFs were willing to retain a resident who needed assistance with transfers (i.e., in or out of bed, a chair or wheelchair). More than half (55%) of the ALFs would not definitely retain a resident with moderate to severe cognitive impairment, and 76% would not retain residents with behavioral symptoms (e.g., wandering). Seventy-two percent of the ALFs would not retain a resident who needed nursing care for more than 14 days (Hawes, Rose, & Phillips, 1999).

As a result of these policies, the degree to which ALFs match the service-related philosophical tenets of assisted living is an open question. For example, the ability of ALFs to meet health-related needs of residents is unknown, in part because of facility policies (e.g., staffing, retention criteria, or discharge policies) and in part because of potential constraints imposed by state licensure regulations. Similarly, the ability of residents to age in place was limited in some facilities by policies that would lead to discharge of residents whose physical or cognitive limitations progressed beyond a certain point. This was likely to be a particularly troublesome problem for residents with conditions like Alzheimer's disease, which are associated with progressive cognitive impairment and often with behavioral manifestations. Further, these policies on retention and nursing care also meant that the majority of ALFs did not serve the same population as that currently found in the typical nursing home.

Assisted living has been greeted by the public and policymakers with largely uncritical enthusiasm, in large measure because of the allure of its philosophy, consumers' preference for privacy and aging-in-place, and the general desire to avoid nursing home placement (Jenkens, 1997; Kane et al., 1998). However, recent research has raised some serious questions about the role of ALFs in meeting the long-term care needs of older persons. Three issues are of particular import.

First, there is tremendous variation among places calling themselves assisted living and the degree to which they embody the key philosophical principles of assisted living. Some ALFs were found to be in line with consumer preferences on privacy and to provide or arrange for an array of services that should enable many residents to age in place. For other facilities, the phrase "assisted living" appears to be more useful as a marketing tool than as a description of the actual nature of their operation.

Second, assisted living is fairly costly, relative to the income of most older persons. With an average annual cost in early 1998, for basic services, of more than $21,000 plus ancillary charges, assisted living was largely unaffordable for moderate- and low-income elderly unless they disposed of their assets and used them to supplement their income and pay for care.

Third, some concerns have been raised about both quality and consumer protection issues (U.S. General Accounting Office, 1999). In particular, consumers faced difficulty in determining whether assisted living would meet their needs and in deciding which facility to select because of the variation among places that called themselves assisted living facilities. Moreover, lack of clarity about retention and discharge criteria made it difficult for consumers and families to determine how long a resident could stay in a particular ALF and the conditions under which he or she would be expected to leave.

To date, assisted living offers a compelling philosophy, one that has the potential to inform and transform much of residential long-term care, including nursing homes. It certainly resonates with the elderly and their families, trapped between their difficulties in remaining at home and their horror at the idea of living in an "institution." At the same time, the current supply of facilities does not uniformly reflect that philosophy. Thus, it is difficult to understand the real-world role of ALFs in meeting the long-term care needs of the frail elderly. Moreover, it is a question that will become more crucial as the number of facilities expands and the resident acuity levels increase.

CATHERINE HAWES
CHARLES D. PHILLIPS
MIRIAM ROSE

See also

Continuing Care Retirement Community
Home and Community-Based Care
Nursing Homes

ASSISTED LIVING FEDERATION OF AMERICA

The Assisted Living Federation of America (ALFA) was formed in 1990 through the pioneering efforts of several assisted living providers. Over the decade, ALFA has helped the assisted living industry, which started as a "cottage industry," to grow to nearly 40,000 residences with over 6,500 members. ALFA is the largest trade group representing the assisted living industry. Industry members include a range of senior housing with a strong focus on consumer flexibility and care options.

ALFA defines an assisted living residence as a special combination of personalized supportive services and health care that is provided in a home-like setting and is designed to meet the needs, both scheduled and unscheduled, of older adults and others who require help with activities of daily living. Part of ALFA's mission is dedicated to improving the quality of life for those consumers who choose assisted living residences as their home.

The industry is currently regulated at the state level, and definitions of assisted living vary by state. ALFA has 34 state affiliates, representing 37 states, who educate legislators, regulators, the media, and consumers on the assisted living philosophy of care and represent providers on a number of regulatory issues that may impact residents' rights, independence, quality of care, costs, and quality of life.

State affiliates work closely with ALFA University, ALFA's training arm, to provide training opportunities that meet and exceed regulatory requirements. Typical training for administrators includes fire safety, medication management, Occupational Safety and Health Administration (OSHA) requirements, CPR, Alzheimer's/dementia training, residents rights, care skills, and sensitivity training. ALFA University currently offers marketing certificate programs and has submitted its complete curriculum to the National Association of Board of Examiners of Long-Term Care Administrators (NAB) for continuing education unit (CEU) credits.

ALFA also offers a number of training opportunities and certification programs on the national level. ALFA University publicizes award-winning workbooks and videos that ALFA members can purchase at a discount to train employees in the areas of development, leadership skills, Alzheimer's/dementia care, medication management, orientation, human resource issues, and marketing. The university recently released two consumer education videos to help residents and their families make a smooth transition into assisted living.

ALFA's spring and fall conferences offer additional education, including CEU credits for administrators and special panels, roundtables, and networking opportunities led by industry experts. ALFA also provides the industry with unique conferences and summits in the areas of nursing, legislation and regulations, marketing, and operations.

Over the past 10 years the association has used a "strength in numbers" approach to educate consumers and impact legislation by forming coalitions with other groups representing consumer organizations, elder groups, the long-term care insurance industry, managed care, real estate, hospitality, health care, and Alzheimer's/dementia.

ALFA is a leader on the Assisted Living Quality Coalition (ALQC), a group of six consumer and trade groups including the Alzheimer's Association, AARP, American Association of Homes and Services for the Aging, the American Health Care Association, and the American Senior Housing Association. In 1998 the coalition released *Assisted Living Quality Initiative: Building a Structure That Promotes Quality*, the first official document providing national proactive guidance on quality issues to providers, states, consumers, and third-party payers as they continue to understand, develop, and regulate assisted living. A newly released version of the *National Assisted Living Resident Satisfaction Study* was launched at the spring conference, April 2–4, 2000.

In 1999, ALFA endorsed the Commission on Accreditation of Rehabilitation Facilities (CARF) in their development of a new independent, voluntary accreditation program for assisted living communities that provides guidance on quality standards and further protects consumers in choosing a quality assisted living residence in their community. The assisted living accreditation program was to be in effect by midyear 2000.

ALFA also formed several internal subgroups in 1999 that members can join to foster networking and problem solving and to voice the needs of a diverse industry, including the Human Resources Executive Council, Nurses Council, Senior Living Continuum Council, CEO Forum, and Marketing Forum. Additionally, ALFA members can join several action teams that focus on program development, public relations, quality and ethics, legislative/regulatory issues, public policy, and research.

To provide support and leadership, ALFA also has an executive board and board of directors.

When members join ALFA, they receive a number of key publications: a national membership directory; ALFA's award-winning magazine, *Assisted Living Today*; ALFA's monthly 12-page association newsletter, the *Advisor*; ALFA's quarterly *Member Update* newsletter; and the electronic newsletter, *Briefings on Assisted Living Weekly*, which contains the latest news briefs on the industry. Members also receive discounts on various products, services, and publications.

To help members save on operational costs, ALFA's Member Savings Program offers the opportunity to purchase at a discount business products and services such as insurance programs, computer software, emergency response systems, paper products, first aid/medical supplies, and payroll and basic forms. This program was initiated to meet the needs of ALFA's small-provider members, who did not have the benefit of an in-house purchasing agent nor the volume to participate in bulk-purchasing options. This program has expanded in scope to meet the diverse needs and benefits of all members. The Member Savings Program identifies companies that produce goods and services needed by members and negotiates national contracts for the best group purchase discount.

To meet public demand for the latest demographic trends and hard data on the industry, ALFA has produced several publications. Every year, ALFA publishes *An Overview of the Assisted Living Industry*, which is packed with charts, graphs, and survey results on finance, regulations, and design. In 2000, ALFA released its first *National Assisted Living Residential Satisfaction Study*, a comprehensive report of satisfaction surveys completed by more than 12,000 residents family and employees from 170 independent living, assisted living, and nursing care communities in the United States.

To help educate consumers, ALFA also publishes the award-winning *Assisted Living Consumer Guide & Checklist*, a comprehensive 15-page educational brochure that consumers can take with them when they visit an assisted living residence. The checklist covers atmosphere and features, services, contracts, costs, activities, and questions to help consumers find the right assisted living residence to fit their needs. This brochure is free to consumers.

Other free resources ALFA provides the public include industry fact sheets, a sample Consumer Information Statement (a disclosure form for assisted living communities) and a sample *Resident Agreement.* Many members and consumers have turned to ALFA's award-winning website at *www.alfa.org,* which offers information and free resources on the industry and provides members with exclusive and timely information via a Members-Only page.

To help consumers find an appropriate assisted living residence in their area, ALFA partnered and linked with CareGuide, an on-line consumer referral database, which consumers can search by criteria and location. In addition to on-line resources, ALFA also has a full time consumer-referral manager to answer consumers' many questions on assisted living.

In 2000, ALFA continues to work proactively with its state affiliates to ensure that assisted living is recognized in state regulations as a viable care alternative and will continue to provide flexibility and choice for consumers. ALFA also will continue supporting state and federal initiatives for long-term care insurance, reverse mortgages, tax breaks, and other programs that help consumers afford long-term care and retain control over their choices.

MARNIE WALDMAN

See also
    Assisted Living: A New Model of Supportive
    Housing with Long-Term Care Services

ASSISTED SUICIDE
See
    Euthanasia
    Physician-Assisted Suicide

ASSOCIATION FOR GERONTOLOGY IN HIGHER EDUCATION

The Association for Gerontology in Higher Education (AGHE) was established in 1974 as a membership organization of colleges and universities that provides research, education, training, and service programs in the field of aging. Its basic goal is to provide an organizational network to assist faculty and administrators in developing and improving the quality of gerontology and geriatric programs in institutions of higher education.

The current membership of AGHE consists of over 300 institutions throughout the United States, Canada, and abroad. Members range from small 2-year colleges to large research universities as well as aging organizations outside higher education. The gerontology programs within AGHE member schools range from developing programs, offering only a few courses, to the major centers for aging in the United States, offering numerous credentials in gerontology and geriatrics and conducting multidisciplinary aging research. Although most members are colleges and universities, organizations other than institutions of higher education that have an interest in gerontological education, research, and training may join the association as nonvoting organizational affiliates. Individuals not affiliated with a member organization who are interested in maintaining contact with the AGHE's activities and services may, for a modest fee, be added to the association's mailing list.

The AGHE carries out its purposes through the following services and programs:

Meetings. Through annual meetings, workshops, and seminars information and ideas are shared on curriculum and program development and evaluation, faculty training, and other issues of gerontological education.

Publications. AGHE publications, such as the *AGHExchange* newsletter, the *Directory of Educational Programs in Gerontology and Geriatrics, Gerontology Program Development and Evaluation,* and *Standards and Guidelines for Gerontology Programs,* provide vehicles for sharing information about educational developments and opportunities, practical assistance, innovative programs, and research related to gerontological education.

Programs and Services. The central office in Washington, DC, serves as a clearinghouse for information about gerontology programs in higher education for students, faculty, and other interested persons. The Brief Bibliography Series (with over

30 titles) points faculty to the best quality instructional materials in various topical areas of gerontology education. A Consultation Service assists institutions in locating consultants who can provide individualized guidance on gerontology program development and evaluation. The *Database on Gerontology in Higher Education* is a computerized listing of over 1,000 gerontology and geriatrics programs in the United States. A newly established Program of Merit is an initiative establishing the AGHE as the organizational body that evaluates and recognizes educational programs at all levels (i.e., certificate/specialization, minor, undergraduate and graduate degrees) following national standards and guidelines. The AGHE administers scholarships and fellowships funded by the AARP Andrus Foundation for graduate and, most recently, undergraduate students.

Advocacy.   A major service of the association is that of monitoring and advocating the interests of gerontology and geriatrics education and training among national leaders and government officials and in the private sector. In addition, the AGHE promotes the interests of research and education among the gerontological service community and the interests of gerontology among the higher education community.

Research.   The association regularly undertakes analyses, such as the project cosponsored with the Andrus Gerontology Center at the University of Southern California, "Core Principles and Outcomes of Gerontology, Geriatrics and Aging Studies Instruction." These analyses are designed to provide assistance in improving the character and quality of academic programs in gerontology.

The AGHE, an educational unit of the Gerontological Society of America, is a nonprofit organization, and the resources for carrying out its activities are derived from members' annual dues, conference registration revenues, sales of publications, and grants and contracts. For further information, please visit the AGHE website: *www.aoa.dhhs.gov/aoa/dir/64.html.*

ELIZABETH B. DOUGLASS
UPDATED BY
CATHERINE J. TOMPKINS

See also
    Gerontological Society of America
    Organizations in Aging

ATHEROSCLEROSIS

Atherosclerosis is characterized by abnormal fatty deposits in and fibrosis of the inner lining of the arteries and is the most common cause of ischemia in the peripheral and central nervous system (*Merriam-Webster's Medical Dictionary*, 1995; Phillips & Mate-Kole, 1997). Ischemia is common in the United States and is accelerated by such factors as hypertension, aging, diet, smoking, diabetes, and blood lipid abnormalities.

An atheroma consists of plaque material that accumulates on the inside of arterial walls, thickening and hardening the walls of the artery and narrowing the space through which blood can flow. Atheromas tend to occur more frequently at certain sites in the brain, such as the internal carotids at their origin in the neck, the horizontal stem of the middle cerebral arteries, the posterior cerebral arteries as they wrap around the midbrain, the anterior cerebral arteries as they curve over the corpus callosum, and the vertebral and basilar arteries (Adams, Victor, & Ropper, 1997).

With time, the atheromatous plaque will grow, progressively narrowing the artery, obstructing the flow of blood, and hindering the diffusion of nutrients from the blood to the deeper tissues of the artery wall (Snyder & Nussbaum, 1998). The plaque can become ulcerated, exposing subendothelial collagen to the blood. Platelets in the blood accumulate with collagen on the ulcerated plaque, causing further narrowing of the artery and deterioration of the elastic fibers. Although atheromatosis can have its onset in childhood and adolescence, only in the middle and late years is it likely to have clinical effects (Adams, Victor, & Ropper, 1997). As such, atherosclerosis is considered to be a disease that is progressive in nature.

Restriction or blockage of blood flow will occur slowly over time. Restriction of blood flow can cause personality change or cognitive deficits characteristic of the area of the brain that is served by the blocked artery. However, reduction of blood flow does not always lead to symptoms. Arteries can be fully restricted without symptoms as long as adequate collateral circulation from another artery is available. In fact, if the artery narrows slowly, the brain will automatically attempt to develop additional circulation to perfuse affected areas. In such cases, even total blockage may be symptomless. Simple narrowing of the artery can be compensated for by higher rates of blood flow, although the latter will cause increases in blood pressure. A rise in blood pressure can lead to the problems associated with hypertension, which worsens atherosclerosis.

In general, the presence of plaques cannot be associated with any specific neurological or neuro-psychological deficits due to the above factors. Such techniques as measurement of regional cerebral blood flow can be used to see if the blood supply is adequate to each part of the brain. If it is, then symptoms are unlikely. Serious blockage of the arteries can be corrected by neurosurgical techniques that "clean out" the plaques and reopen the narrowed vessels. New techniques in this area include experimental use of lasers to produce arteries that are free of plaques.

In cases where there is not adequate collateral circulation, the client will have ischemic attacks ("strokes") as blood flow is cut off or reduced to a specific area of the brain. Such attacks may result in either transient losses (transient ischemic attack [TIA]) or permanent symptoms such as paralysis, loss of vision or hearing, loss of sense of touch, problems in the expression or understanding of language, frontal lobe dysfunction, or loss of spatial skills. Because of the seriousness of such attacks, preventive measures such as changes in diet, lowering of blood pressure, low-dose aspirin or other anticoagulant drugs to reduce clotting in the blood, and other noninvasive techniques are often recommended to at-risk individuals. In some cases, more invasive surgical techniques to reduce plaque buildup in arteries may be necessary.

CHARLES J. GOLDEN
PATRICIA ESPE-PFEIFER

See also
Blood
Cardiovascular System: Overview
Cardiovascular System: The Heart
Cardiovascular System: Vascular

ATTENTION

The mental landscape is a blooming, bustling confusion of sensory inputs, thoughts, and memories. We would be paralyzed by this confusion if we did not have some way to select out of it the information that is of importance to us, that is relevant to our actions, and that allows us to pursue our train of thought and behavior. Attention is the name given to those processes that allow us to carry out that selection. The central question here is whether advancing age is accompanied by changes in attention.

Casual observation suggests the answer to this question is yes. Older adults are more likely than younger adults to report that their mind has wandered from what they are reading and that they have to go back and reread, that they start doing one thing around the house and are unintentionally distracted into doing something else, that they forget why they went from one part of the house to another, or that they cannot locate what they want on a supermarket shelf even when it is there. There are many situations in which lapses of attention can have serious consequences. For example, older adults have more accidents per mile driven and are more likely to commit driving violations caused by inattention to relevant information.

Despite these findings, a review of empirical research will show that age-related differences in the basic processes of attention are far smaller and less uniform than might be expected. Several comprehensive reviews of this area have recently appeared (for a recent review, see McDowd & Shaw, 1999). As a result the present review will not list extensive citations for generally accepted conclusions, highlighting, instead, studies that are quite recent or that contradict or qualify those conclusions.

Attention has been thought of by some, following William James (1890), as a spotlight illuminating first one then another part of the mental landscape. Others have thought of attention as a distribution of processing resources with attended information receiving more resources than unattended information. These theories are largely isomorphic, and either can provide a useful metaphor for thinking about attention and how it might change with advancing age. For a recent review of theories of attention, see LaBerge (1999).

Externally Initiated Reallocation of Attention

In many cases shifts in the spotlight or reallocation of resources are in response to external events, as, for example, when a flashing taillight warns a driver that the car ahead is about to turn or when a road sign warns of "Trucks Entering from Left."

The flashing taillight can be said to capture attention. There is no evidence that attention is more easily captured in older adults or that they have more difficulty resisting attention capture. Movements of attention are usually accompanied by eye movements. Interestingly, older adults appear more likely than younger adults to make reflexive eye movements to a stimulus that appears suddenly, especially when they are consciously aware that the stimulus may occur (Kramer, Hahn, Irwin, & Theeuwes, 1999).

The effect of advance warnings about imminent events, such as road signs, has been studied in the laboratory by providing advance cues about upcoming information. The benefits of a correct cue and the costs of an incorrect cue have generally been found to be equivalent for younger and older adults, even though older adults are, overall, slower to respond. This is true both for cues that appear at the location where the information will appear (called exogenous cues) and for those that appear elsewhere but instruct the person where it will be (called endogenous cues). The ability to spread attention over a wider area or to narrow it down also appears similar in older and younger persons. Some have found that the speed with which attention can be shifted or reallocated is unaffected by age, but others have found that the speed is slower in older adults, particularly when the cue is difficult to decode or when distracting information is present (see McDowd & Shaw, 1999). Older adults are not always more susceptible to distraction. When the important information (the target) is in a known location and the distracting information is in other locations, older adults are no more distractible than younger adults. It is when the target location is unknown or unpredictable or when the target and distracting information are part of the same stimulus that older adults are disadvantaged (e.g., Little & Hartley, 2000).

Internally Initiated Reallocation of Attention

Shifts or reallocation of attention can also be internally generated, particularly when we are searching for something, searching either our minds or the visual environment. The goal, the target we are looking for, may be provided to us, but the process by which we seek out candidates, examine them, and evaluate them is internally controlled. Older adults almost always take longer to locate the goal than do younger adults, and the difference increases strikingly as the number of distracting, non-goal items increases. The exception is the case in which the goal is distinguished by a single feature, as when we are searching for the sole red-backed book among a shelf of blue-backed books. It is also the case that extensive practice can, in some situations, erase the age differences. Why the age differences in search occur is a question of both practical and theoretical importance, but it is unanswered. It may be that older adults have difficulty in disengaging from a distractor once they have attended to it. It may be that they search inefficiently, returning to items they have already. Or it may be that search is less well guided and that younger adults select for examination locations where the target is more likely to be.

Selecting a nontarget for examination has consequences that extend in time. If an item that has been rejected as not a target becomes the target on the next trial, the time to identify the item is slower than if it had not been previously rejected. This is called identity suppression or negative priming. Similarly, a location that has been checked and rejected is responded to more slowly if the target appears there subsequently. This is called location suppression or location negative priming. A number of studies have reported that identity suppression is found in younger adults but not in older adults, leading to the hypothesis that inhibitory functioning is impaired in older adults (e.g., May, Kane, & Hasher, 1995). Others have found equivalent identity suppression in younger and older adults (e.g., Little & Hartley, in press), so even the impairment in identity suppression does not occur under all conditions. Similarly, there is disagreement in the results of studies of location suppression. Some find no age differences, whereas others find reduced location suppression in older adults in some situations but not in other situations. Suppression may function to keep thoughts on track and avoid distraction, and it has been hypothesized that impaired suppression in older adults could account for their greater distractibility. The results to date are not consistent with any such straightforward conclusion.

If attention has been directed to a location and if nothing appears at that location within about 800 ms or if attention is then deliberately redirected, an event at the original location is likely to be either missed or responded to more slowly. This is called the inhibition of return of attention. Hartley and Kieley (1995) found that this attentional inhibition was equivalent in younger and older adults.

Attending to More Than One Task

People are often called on to carry out more than one line of mental processing and action. This is true both in the laboratory (where it is called the dual task situation) and in real life, as when we drive and carry on a conversation. Whether we carry out the two tasks at the same time or we switch rapidly from one to another, it is clear that we require attention to the coordination of the two tasks that goes beyond the attention devoted to each of the tasks itself. Older adults are widely believed to be more challenged by handling two tasks at once than are younger adults, even when the demands of each task alone are carefully equated. Recent experiments have carefully controlled when the information about the second task arrives relative to the start of the first (e.g., Hartley & Little, 1999). In these studies, age differences have been quite circumscribed. Older adults have more difficulty than do younger adults in managing two tasks that require similar motor responses (e.g., movements of the left and right hand). Age differences are largely removed if the responses are different (e.g., speaking and moving a hand). There is also some evidence that older adults require somewhat longer to begin working on a second task when the response mapping rules for that task are complex.

Generalizations and Explanations

In summary, the basic processes of allocating attention to relevant information, selecting that information, and filtering out surrounding information are little affected by age. In contrast, there are limited changes in managing more than one task at the same time and substantial and reliable changes with

age in searching through a number of possibilities for a target. A number of explanations have been offered for these facts. One is that cognitive processing resources decline with advancing age. This explanation has the disadvantages that it can be tautological if not carefully applied and that it is not readily falsifiable. Another explanation is that inhibitory functioning is impaired in old age. This explanation is simply inconsistent with the available evidence. Some argue that a generalized change, such as slowing of central cognitive processes, could account for the results, although others have argued that this account, too, is inconsistent with available evidence.

A promising explanation derives from recent advances in the neurosciences and neuropsychology: Age differences will be substantial in attentional functions critically dependent on the integrity of the frontal lobes; attentional functions dependent on posterior cortical and midbrain areas will be relatively well preserved in old age. This explanation has been termed the frontal lobe hypothesis (West, 1996). It accounts well for the data and is consistent with the evidence for reductions in cerebral blood flow and for tissue loss in old age. Raz, Briggs, Marks, and Acker (1999) found that the volume of prefrontal cortex in vivo is predictive of cognitive performance in older adults. Reuter-Lorenz and colleagues (Reuter-Lorenz, Jonides, Smith, Hartley, Miller, Marshuetz, et al., 2000) have demonstrated hyperactivation of prefrontal cortex in older adults during cognitive tasks, activation that is more diffuse and less selective than in younger adults. Future research will determine the value of the frontal lobe hypothesis as an explanation for the patterns of age-related sparing and impairment of function.

ALAN A. HARTLEY

See also
Cognitive Processes
Processing Resources

ATTITUDES

The Nature of Attitudes

Attitudes should be distinguished from such related concepts as beliefs, stereotypes, and knowledge

(Atchley, 2000a). *Attitudes* refers to the evaluation of an object, to a favorable or unfavorable disposition toward the object, or more simply, to a like or dislike. Beliefs or knowledge, in contrast, are cognitive responses to an object rather than evaluations. Stereotypes are composites of beliefs, and the term is often reserved for perceptions that are factually incorrect. It is particularly important to make these distinctions if research on attitudes about the aged is not to be misleading. For instance, responding in the affirmative when asked whether older persons are politically conservative may represent the expression of a belief or knowledge about the aged, not an evaluation. As has been noted (e.g., Palmore, 1982), research presumably designed to yield information on attitudes about aging or the aged has frequently confounded attitudes and knowledge, making it difficult to separate negative attitudes from factual perceptions of characteristics or conditions.

Attitudes About the Aged and Aging

Attitudes about older persons and about old age as a stage of the life course can be examined from several perspectives and in a variety of ways. Historians have shown how societal attitudes change over time (Achenbaum, 1996), and anthropologists have noted that there is considerable variation between and within societies at any given time (Fry, 1996). Individual-level studies in the United States, using different methodological approaches, suggest that negative attitudes about aging and the elderly are widespread, although positive evaluations along some dimensions are also in evidence (Slotterback & Saarnio, 1996). One study (Newman, Faux, & Larimer, 1997), for example, found that children's perceptions of the elderly and attitudes toward the aging process were largely positive. The depiction of older persons on television has been mixed: how the aged are depicted differs with the type of programming. Atchley (2000a) suggests that images range from fairly positive on continuing series and on public affairs and talk shows to fairly negative on news programs, with commercials occupying an intermediate position.

In general, attitudes about older persons and old age vary by time, place, and source. Negative attitudes exist but not to the exclusion of more positive

and balanced evaluations. However, existing research has been plagued by a number of problems, and promising new approaches have been suggested. A useful summary of previous studies and their limitations, along with new research directions, may be found in Visser and Krosnick (1998).

Attitudes of Older Persons

Research on older persons has also focused on their attitudes about a variety of social, political, and economic issues. Most studies have been concerned with describing age differences, although some have examined age and cohort changes. Many of the specific substantive issues that have been addressed have an underlying "liberal-conservative" dimension, and a good deal of work has sought implicitly, if not explicitly, to answer two related questions: (1) are the elderly more conservative than younger persons, and (2) do persons become more conservative or attitudinally rigid as they grow older. Following Glenn (1974), conservatism is viewed here as opposition to social change, a high valuation of social order, an emphasis on authority and obedience, and the adoption of a restrictive rather than permissive stance toward human behavior.

Are Older Persons More Conservative? Many studies have sought to determine whether the attitudes of older persons are more conservative than those of younger persons. Campbell and Strate (1981), in perhaps the most comprehensive analysis, compared the responses of persons aged 65+ years with those of persons aged 30–64 years on 40 issues asked at least twice in the 14 American National Election Studies conducted between 1952 and 1980. Of the 40 issues examined, they found the attitudes of older persons to be more conservative than younger persons on 22 and more liberal on only 5. By specific area, older persons expressed more conservative opinions on "law and order" and on social and lifestyle issues. They were more conservative on foreign affairs issues, although Campbell and Strate suggest this may reflect an isolationist stance. More conservative responses were seen for racial issues that might touch the lives of older persons directly (e.g., open housing), but on more remote racial issues (e.g., the civil rights movement) or on those that affect young people (e.g., school integration), the differences were not substantial. Self-interest did override more general orientations and result in more liberal attitudes about domestic policies when the issue was of direct benefit to the elderly (e.g., government support of health care); otherwise, their responses were more conservative. However, more recent studies (Day, 1990; DiMaggio, Evans, & Bryson, 1996) have found that between-group differences in social attitudes have declined in a number of areas in recent years and that age differences produce less variation than do factors such as race, ethnicity, gender, and socioeconomic status.

Do Persons Become More Conservative as They Grow Older? If it is true that older persons have often held more conservative attitudes, is it because they became more conservative with age, as widely held stereotypes would suggest? Or did these age differences result from cohort effects? Fortunately, a number of studies are available that consistently demonstrate that aging is not necessarily or inevitably accompanied by a shift to more conservative sociopolitical attitudes.

Studies that have examined changes in attitudinal support for civil liberties have found that all cohorts had become more liberal between 1954 and the early 1970s, although the magnitude of change was greater for the younger than for the older cohorts. Similar patterns of change in the direction of less traditional attitudes, coupled with intercohort variation in the rate of change, have been seen on reported approval of the admission of Communist China to the United Nations and on willingness to vote for a Jew or a Catholic for president, on willingness to vote for a woman for president, and on gender role attitudes.

These findings led some to propose an aging-stability hypothesis that posits attitude change within all cohorts during times of growing liberalism in public opinion but with a lesser propensity for change among the older cohorts. However, other studies raise doubts about the universality of the aging-stability model as a description of attitude change. An analysis of cohort changes in attitudes about legalized abortion found that reported support increased at approximately the same rate for all cohorts. An examination of tolerance of school desegregation found increasing forbearance within each cohort and the persistence of constant between-cohort differences. Other attitudes about race

relations also showed change in a liberal direction, at the same rate for all cohorts. In one attitudinal domain characterized by pronounced conservative shifts in public opinion—law and order—all cohorts shared equally in the trend toward more conservative attitudes (for more detailed summaries of these studies, see Cutler, 2000, and Danigelis & Cutler, 1991).

Taken together, these and other studies (e.g., Tyler & Schuller, 1991) support the idea that aging is associated with neither attitudinal inflexibility nor increasingly conservative attitudes. In fact, Visser and Krosnick (1998) suggest that, on the contrary, greater susceptibility to attitude change is found among younger and older adults than among those in middle adulthood. The social and cultural forces influencing attitudes and attitude change, whether in a liberal or conservative direction, appear to affect older as well as younger persons—in some cases to the same extent (i.e., attitudes about abortion, race relations, law and order), in others to different degrees. That older persons have often been found in cross-sectional studies to *be* more conservative does not mean they have *become* more conservative. Rather, these age differences seem to stem from enduring cohort effects associated with earlier socialization.

STEPHEN J. CUTLER
ANN DONAHUE

See also
　Ageism
　Cohorts

AUDITORY PERCEPTION
See
　Central and Peripheral Nervous Systems Morphology
　Hearing

AUSTRALIAN LONGITUDINAL STUDY OF AGEING

The Australian Longitudinal Study of Ageing (ALSA) is a cross-disciplinary prospective study of adults aged 70 years and over that began in Adelaide, Australia, in 1992. It is a population-based biopsychosocial and behavioral study of 2,087 older adults residing in the community and in residential care. The study is being conducted by the Centre for Ageing Studies of Flinders University of South Australia. The Center for Demographic Studies, Duke University, Durham, North Carolina (USA) has collaborated in the study, and partial funding was obtained for the first four rounds from the National Institute of Aging.

The general purpose of this research is to gain further understanding of how social, biomedical, and environmental factors are associated with age-related changes in the health and well-being of persons aged 70 years and older. Emphasis is given to the effects of social and economic factors on morbidity, disability, acute and long-term care service use, mortality, and "successful" aging. The aim is to analyze the complex relationships between individual and social factors and changes in health status, health care needs, and service utilization dimensions.

The sample for the Australian study was randomly generated from within the Adelaide Statistical Division, using the State Electoral Database as the sampling frame. The sample was stratified by gender and the age groups 70–74, 75–79, 80–84, and 85 and over. Both community- and institutional-dwelling individuals were included in the list of specified persons. An additional component was that spouses aged 65 and over of specified persons also were invited to participate, as were other household members aged 70 years and over.

The baseline data collection for ALSA began in September 1992 and was completed in March 1993. Components of this wave included a comprehensive personal interview, conducted via computer-assisted personal interview (CAPI); a home-based assessment of physiological functions; self-completed questionnaires; and additional clinical studies. Personal interviews were carried out at this first wave for 2,087 participants, including 566 couples (i.e., persons 70 years of age and over and their spouses, if 65 or older). Clinical assessments were obtained for 1,620 of the participants.

After an interval of 1 year from the initial interview, respondents were recontacted by telephone. These interviews lasted an average of 15 minutes and included questions regarding changes in domi-cile, current health and functional status, new morbid conditions, changes in medication, major life events, general life satisfaction, and changes in economic circumstances. In Wave 2, 1,779 participants were reinterviewed.

The third wave of the study began in September 1994. This phase was a complete reassessment: face-to-face interviews, clinical assessments, self-completed questionnaires, and other clinical and laboratory studies were again carried out. CAPI was used in administration of the personal interview, which made it possible to preload selected prior information, thereby avoiding repetition of information divulged by the respondent in Wave 1. A separate, shorter proxy instrument was developed and used in this third wave, which proved very successful in maintaining a high participation rate. A total of 1,679 interviews were carried out in Wave 3, and 1,423 clinical assessments were conducted.

Data collection for the fourth wave began in November 1995 and was completed by the end of February 1996. Wave 4 is a short telephone interview similar to Wave 2. A total of 1,504 interviews were completed. A fifth wave of telephone interviews was conducted during February 1998, resulting in 1,171 completed interviews.

In addition to the primary data collection from respondents, ancillary data collection has been ongoing since the initiation of the study. Data has been collected from secondary providers, including Domiciliary Care and Rehabilitation Services, Meals on Wheels, and the Royal District Nursing Society. Lists of ALSA participants are compared biannually with the agencies' lists to determine the prevalence and incidence of receipt of services from these organizations.

Another source of information has been the collection of data from the participants' general practitioners. Each respondent's personal and medical practitioner gives a rating of overall health status, history of services received, and current services provided. Current morbidity, medication use, and referrals to specialists also are recorded.

Extensive analyses utilizing the longitudinal data have been carried out in both Australia and the United States and will continue, with active groups of collaborators analyzing data relating to ADL/IADL performance, cognitive function, comorbidity, cardiovascular disease and risk factors, dental health, diet and nutrition, diabetes, exercise and physical activity, family relationships and support, formal service use, hearing function, injuries and falls, mortality, sensory function, social activities, social interactions between couples, "successful" aging, and other parameters.

Data from ALSA has been progressively archived with the Interuniversity Consortium for Political and Social Research (ICPSR). Data is available for further analysis from ICPSR or, for specific purposes, on application to Gary R. Andrews at the Centre for Ageing Studies, Flinders University, Science Park, Bedford Park SA 5042 Australia. A sixth wave of data collection involving comprehensive face-to-face reinterviews, clinical assessments, and laboratory studies commenced in September 2000.

For further study, please refer to the following general and illustrative publications: Andrews, Cheok, and Carr (1989); Casson, Giles, and Newland (1996); Clark and Bond (1995); Dolinis, Harrison, and Andrews (1997); Finucane, Giles, Withers, Silagy, Sedgwick, Hamdorf, et al., (1997); Gilbert, Luszcz, and Owen (1993); Mawby, Clark, Kalucy, Hobbin, and Andrews (1996); Ranzijn and Luszcz (1994); van Doorn and Kasl (1998).

GARY R. ANDREWS

See also
Longitudinal Studies of Aging

AUTOBIOGRAPHICAL MEMORY

Autobiographical memory is a topic of study rather than a strictly defined concept. Partly because research is expanding rapidly, variation in the usage of the term exists. Nonetheless, autobiographical memory almost always refers to memories containing images or considerable detail and accompanied by the belief that the events recalled were personally experienced. Because autobiographical memory is the study of memory for a lifetime, it inherently involves a life-span approach. For instance, in most autobiographical memory studies, memories of events from one age are recalled by subjects of a different age. Differences in encoding, retention, and retrieval at various stages of development therefore enter in ways that they need not in laboratory studies of memory.

Early research on autobiographical memory was undertaken most notably by Galton and by Freud. Work stemming from these two traditions along with life-span developmental, cognitive, and neuropsychological approaches are responsible for the major contributions.

Before the turn of the century, Galton cued himself with objects and words in order to obtain an inventory of all his memories. Crovitz and Schiffman (1974) adapted this task by requiring subjects to produce only datable events. They found a distribution of memories over the life span that is of the same form as that obtained in laboratory recall, indicating that autobiographical memory has the same retention curve as other types of memory. In subjects over 40, this finding breaks down. For instance, 20- and 70-year-olds show similar retention functions for the most recent 20 years of their lives. The 70-year-olds, however, do not continue with a monotonically decreasing function for the earliest 50 years of their lives. Rather, they show an increase in autobiographical memories for events from when they were approximately 15 to 25 years old; that is, they show *reminiscence*. Subjects of all ages demonstrate *childhood amnesia*, a sharp drop in the number of autobiographical memories from their early years.

Autobiographical memory is very sensitive to insult, and thus its loss is a symptom in many forms of memory deficits. Whether this is because of some special mechanism or just because much of autobiographical memory is for events that occurred only once and therefore were less well learned is not clear. Nonetheless, the loss of autobiographical memory can be a major problem in patients who have Alzheimer's disease, closed head injury, frontal lobe damage, and Korsakoff's syndrome, or who have recently undergone electroconvulsive therapy. The type of loss varies with the diagnosis. For instance, patients with frontal lobe damage are more likely to produce memories for implausible, nonoccurring events, and Korsakoff's syndrome patients are likely to show periods of retrograde amnesia that are much longer than those of other patients.

Edited books containing both tutorial and empirical chapters providing references to a wide range of research include Conway, M. A., Rubin, D. C.,

Spinnler, H., & Wagenaar, W. A. *Theoretical perspectives on autobiographical memory* (Dordrecht: Kluver, 1992); Rubin, D. C. (Ed.), *Autobiographical memory* (New York: Cambridge University Press, 1986); Rubin, D. C. (Ed.), *Remembering our past: Studies in autobiographical memory* (New York: Cambridge University Press, 1996). A general review can be found in Conway, M. A., *Autobiographical memory: An introduction* (Milton Keynes: Open University Press, 1990).

DAVID C. RUBIN

See also
    Biography

AUTOIMMUNITY

The term *autoimmunity* refers to the development of immune responses by an individual to self-constituents (constituents of that individual's own body) to which the immune system should not react. Immune reactions are mediated by effector cells such as B-lymphocytes, which differentiate into antibody-secreting plasma cells, by T-lymphocytes, which produce lymphokines and mediate cellular immunity, and by monocytes and tissue macrophages. These effector cells are regulated by an intricate network of control mechanisms that include specific receptors on lymphocyte surface membranes, secreted antibody and lymphokines, and specialized subpopulations of T-lymphocytes that modulate and regulate the effector cells. Autoimmunity is the result of abnormal or excessive activity on the part of immune effector cells. Autoimmune responses can include the production of autoantibodies by B-lymphocytes and infiltration or destruction of self-tissue by lymphocytes and macrophages. Evidence indicates that potentially autoreactive lymphocytes are present in the normal individual and sensitive assays usually reveal low levels of autoantibody in healthy individuals. In the healthy individual, however, the autoreactive lymphocytes are generally held in check by the control mechanisms, and development of autoimmune responses appears to be the result of a breakdown or deterioration of the control mechanisms (Hausman & Weksler, 1985).

Autoimmune Diseases

There are a number of diseases that clearly have autoimmune reactions as a component, and the term *autoimmune disease* is used for such diseases in which specific and relevant autoimmune responses (organ specific or systemic) can be demonstrated. Such diseases include: systemic lupus erythematosus, rheumatoid arthritis, scleroderma, Sjögren's syndrome, autoimmune thyroid disease, Addison's disease, insulin-dependent diabetes, pernicious anemia, chronic active hepatitis, multiple sclerosis, autoimmune hemolytic anemia, and myasthenia gravis. For some of these diseases the circumstantial evidence linking the development of autoimmune responses and the symptoms of the disease is so strong that a cause-and-effect relationship is evident, whereas in other diseases the relationship is less clear (Rose & MacKay, 1985).

Autoantibodies and Aging

The level of autoantibodies increases with age, and it is quite common to find older people whose sera test positive for autoantibodies, but who show no signs of any corresponding clinical disease.

Autoimmune Diseases and Aging

Although experimental animals and humans develop autoantibodies with age, autoimmune diseases do not increase in frequency. The most conspicuous autoimmune conditions are probably thyrotoxicosis, systemic lupus, myasthenia gravis, and autoimmune hemolytic anemias, none of which is commonly associated with old age. Thus, autoimmune diseases do not appear to be diseases characteristic of old age but are more likely due to a genetic predisposition to the autoimmune disease. There is evidence that diseases that are either generally accepted as autoimmune in character or have some other immunopathological quality show significant correlations with a given histocompatibility antigen. The major histocompatibility complex (MHC) (H-2 region in mice and the HLA gene cluster in the human) regulates immune responsiveness and the age-related rate of maturation and decline to different immunogenic stimuli. There is a correlation of many autoimmune conditions with a particular HLA group indicating an important genetic component, in the absence of which the disease cannot appear. The relevant antigens are HLA-8, W-27, and HLA-7. It is obvious that any genetic factor is only part of the etiology; environmental influences and accumulating genetic errors in lymphocyte lines must also be considered.

The most characteristic feature of autoimmunity in old age, then, is its common occurrence, but generally inconspicuous character. Genetic errors, involving both germ-line and somatic genomes, which interfere with the self-monitoring function of the immune system, are thought to be the principal cause of autoimmune disease. For a general discussion of issues, see Walford, Weindruch, Gottesman, and Tam (1981).

Recently, the theory has been advanced that atherosclerosis is an autoimmune disease (Wick & Xu, 1999). If this theory is correct, autoimmunity may play a major role in human aging because atherosclerosis is a common occurrence, progresses in severity with age, and is a major player in coronary heart disease and stroke.

MARGARET L. HEIDRICK

See also
Immune System

AUTONOMIC NERVOUS SYSTEM
See
Central and Peripheral Nervous Systems Morphology

AUTONOMY AND AGING

Autonomy is a central value of American society. For the past 20 years the autonomy of patients has dominated biomedical ethics and has been a central force in changing general codes of patients' rights and a variety of health care practices.

Autonomy literally means "self-rule," deriving from the Greek *autos* (self) and *nomos* (rule or law or governance), and was originally used to refer to self-governance in Greek city-states. Today autonomy is a concept with many definitions. Collopy (1988) defined autonomy "as a cluster of notions including self-determination, freedom, independence, liberty of choice, and action. In its most general terms, autonomy signifies control of decision making and other activity by the individual. It refers to human agency free of outside intervention and interference" (p. 10).

Lidz, Fischer, and Arnold (1992) developed a three-pronged definition of autonomy. Autonomy as free action means that an action is voluntary, intentional, and free from coercion. Autonomy as effective deliberation involves decision-making based on comprehension of the situation, the various alternative courses of action, and the consequences of the action chosen. Autonomy as consistency emphasizes that autonomous decisions and actions are those that are authentic or consistent with an individual's life history, commitments, values, habits, and life plans. These three dimensions of autonomy, as outlined by Lidz and his colleagues, are ideals that many or most people do not achieve in everyday life. They should be thought of as a continuum rather than an either/or phenomenon.

Autonomy is a major issue in aging because older adults are often treated by others in very paternalistic ways. This is particularly true for older adults with physical or cognitive disabilities. In both residential and home care settings, the autonomy of older persons is sometimes seriously and unduly restricted.

Findings from a series of studies (Hofland, 1990) examining autonomy issues in long-term care indicated that home care clients and nursing home residents value autonomy highly and want more control over everyday aspects of their lives and care, including their personal space, home or room, and day-to-day lifestyle. In nursing homes other persons control basic features of everyday life, such as what to wear and eat, when to get up and go to bed, and who one's roommate is. In guardianship proceedings due process rights may be routinely violated. The older proposed ward is frequently absent from the hearing and is often ambiguously represented. A physician's report heavily influences a determination of incompetency and is often completed by a physician unskilled in geriatric and cognitive assessment. In home care, options frequently are severely restricted and inappropriate, with a paternalistic agency deciding the particulars of care.

Some attention has recently been given to providing correctives to this situation, in which the autonomy of older adults receiving long-term services is seriously compromised and often not even recognized. In the nursing home setting, for example, Gamroth, Semradek, and Tornquist (1995) have offered a number of strategies.

It is important to remember, however, that autonomy for older adults is not a supreme value that trumps all other values. Some ethicists, gerontologists, health care professionals, and long-term care professionals see autonomy as a value that has begun to shake health and long-term care from the grip of heavy paternalism. Others view autonomy as a value gone amok, with too heavy an emphasis on narrow individualism. The danger is an "ethic of strangers," in which care providers and care receivers cannot trust each other and inescapably engage in adversarial relationships. These issues have come into sharp relief in end-of-life decision making. The use of advance directives (living wills, durable powers of attorneys for health care) and increased attention to physician-assisted suicide and euthanasia have called into question the relationship of care providers, patients, and their families and the balance between autonomy and community.

The challenge for an aging society is to respect the autonomy of older individuals in large and small ways while at the same time creating a caring community in which older persons with impairments can live and die within an ethic of intimacy that recognizes the human need for affiliation and tenderness.

BRIAN F. HOFLAND

See also
Competence
Guardianship/Conservatorship
Living Wills and Durable Power of Attorney

B

BABY BOOMERS AND THEIR FUTURE

In the academic imagination as well as in public perception, particularly in the United States, the idea of the baby boom generation has had pervasive influence on thinking about the present and future of aging. This cohort, usually considered to include those born between 1946 and 1964, has been called the "most over-defined group of our time" (Helen O'Connor, cited in Bouvier & DeVita, 1991), serving as fodder for sweeping generalizations of all sorts despite its manifest diversity. Such overgeneralizations have led some demographers to question the utility of the whole concept of a distinct baby boom generation and the emphasis given to it in the United States. Clearly, however, the cohort born in the years following World War II has faced, at each stage of its life history, economic and social circumstances distinct from those faced by their predecessors and successors at similar ages.

One important strand in debates over baby boomers emerged by the early 1960s; it concerns the extent to which this cohort's large size, relative to preceding and succeeding cohorts, would be critical in shaping its destiny (Easterlin, 1962). This argument was presented in extended form by Easterlin (1987), who argued that large cohorts such as the baby boom generation would face labor surpluses and hence encounter more competition for jobs, command lower wages, face more economic uncertainty, and in consequence delay or forgo marriage and family commitments. Such a view would imply discouraging prospects for baby boomers' own retirement prospects, a concern augmented by evidence of wage stagnation during the 1970s and 1980s (Levy & Murnane, 1992). Some researchers, indeed, concluded that baby boomers seemed to be doing less well economically than did their parents' cohort at similar ages (Levy & Michel, 1991). Other researchers, however, have found otherwise. In an early study, Russell (1982) concluded that the baby boomers' economic prospects were at least comparable to those of previous generations. By the 1990s, with the oldest baby boomers well into their working lives, the Congressional Budget Office (1993) estimated that at ages 35–44 leading-edge boomers had an 82% advantage over their parents' generation in median household income adjusted for household size. Similarly, Crystal and Johnson (1998), using data from the National Longitudinal Surveys, found that at ages 40 to 44, women in the 1949–1953 birth cohort experienced 51% improvement in mean family income, adjusted for family size, compared with the cohort of women born in 1923–1927. These improvements in size-adjusted family income were largely achieved through changes in family economic behavior—a shift toward two-earner families and smaller family sizes—rather than through improvements in earnings rates.

Of course, these comparisons of averages mask enormous heterogeneity among baby boomers. Indeed, an important question concerns the impact of the process of cumulative advantage and disadvantage (Crystal & Shea, 1990; Crystal & Waehrer, 1996) on the economic prospects of baby boomers. Will this cohort, whose careers have unfolded in an era of increasing income gaps between those with high education and skills and those without, experience very high income inequality in their later years? Crystal and Johnson (1998) found that the Gini coefficient of inequality among leading-edge baby boomers in their early 40s was comparable to that among earlier cohorts, but what will happen as this group nears retirement age is not yet known.

As with any simplifying scheme applied to complex realities, the notion of a distinct baby boom generation is to some extent a figment of the imagination. Americans born in the two decades following World War II are an extraordinarily diverse group. Demography is not necessarily destiny, and

cohort size alone is only one of the large number of economic, demographic, political, technological, and other circumstances that make each cohort's historical experience unique. Nevertheless, its pervasive use suggests that the idea of a distinct "baby boom generation" has been a compelling one.

STEPHEN CRYSTAL

See also
Cohorts
Demography

BALTIMORE LONGITUDINAL STUDY OF AGING

The Baltimore Longitudinal Study of Aging (BLSA) (Shock, Greulich, Costa, Andres, Lakatta, Arenberg, et al., 1984), initiated in 1958, was designed to characterize aging with respect to a number of physiological and psychological variables in normal, healthy men living independently in the community.

Subjects for the study are volunteers recruited primarily from the area surrounding Washington, DC. They are primarily scientists, teachers, and other professionals who were recruited to the study by a friend who was already participating. Criteria for admission to the study are: (1) introduction by a participant or a staff member of the Gerontology Research Center, (2) ability to provide own transportation to the Gerontology Research Center located at the Baltimore City Hospitals in Baltimore, and (3) willingness to make a commitment to return for visits at annual or biannual intervals for the remainder of their lives. This method of self-recruitment has yielded an active, healthy, community-residing population that has a higher educational level than average, an adequate income, an interest in science, and a personal dedication to the study.

The original population was restricted to men because of limited facilities for housing subjects overnight. When resources were expanded in January 1978, women were added to the study group. As of May 20, 1985, 1,243 men have been examined once. Of this group, 598 are active participants, some of whom have been tested as often as 21 times; 296 dropped out of the study and 349 died.

As of May 1985, 413 women have been tested at least once; 335 are currently active participants, 65 have dropped out, and 13 have died.

Subjects come to the laboratory every 18 to 24 months for a period of 2 1/2 days, during which they participate in an extensive series of physiological, biochemical, clinical, and psychological tests. Specific tests are repeated at regular intervals ranging from 2 to 7 years. Ages of subjects at entry into the study range from 18 to 96 years. One subject, aged 60 when first tested, has been seen 21 times.

At each visit each subject is carefully examined to identify the presence of disease. Subjects who show clinical evidence of disease are not excluded from the study, but observations made on them are excluded from analyses of age changes in the variables involved. Thus, the study focuses on the progressive changes that take place with the passage of time in individual subjects. Repetition of clinical evaluations at 1- or 2-year intervals makes it possible to time the appearance of disease in normal subjects as they age and to trace the effects of disease.

In addition to anthropometric measurements, estimates of body composition (fat and water content and bone density) are made. Tests of the performance of the heart, kidneys, lungs, muscles, endocrines, and other organs are included. Tests of neuromuscular function and exercise performance as well as perception (sight, hearing) are carried out. Rates of recovery from physiological displacements (oxygen uptake, heart rate, blood pressure) induced by standardized exercises are measured. Specially designed tests provide measures of cognitive functions such as learning, logical problem solving, concept problem solving, memory, and reaction times. Tests of personality, methods of responding to psychological stress, and methods of coping with life situations are also identified by paper-and-pencil tests and structured interviews.

Preliminary findings indicate the potential power of longitudinal observations in identifying age changes. It is possible to calculate the regression on age for individual subjects with respect to specific variables if an adequate number of observations have been made. In most instances, at least five observation points are needed to give a reliable estimate of the regression on age, and in some instances as many as 15 or 20 observations may be required.

Most physiological functions show, on the average, a gradual decrement over the entire adult life span. Figure 1, based on cross-sectional observations in which different individuals were measured at each age, shows the average change in kidney function (standard creatinine clearance, ml/min/1.73M²) with advancing age. Although the standard error of the mean values as indicated by the vertical lines at each point is small because of the large number in the study, individual differences are large. Tests of many other physiological function, such as heart, lung, muscle, and nerve function, show similar average changes with age, although functions differ widely in the rates of change with age (Shock, 1985).

However, longitudinal observations (repeated measurements on the same subject as he/she ages) show that individual subjects may reveal quite different pathways of aging. Figure 2 shows aging paths followed by kidney function in four individual subjects (Lindeman, Tobin, & Shock, 1985). Individuals differ greatly in terms of the rate of fall in kidney function with age as well as the age at which the decline in function begins. Although many subjects, such as Subject 101 shown in Figure 2, follow

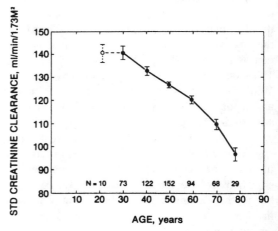

FIGURE 1 Average values for standard creatinine clearance (ml/min/1.73 M²) in normal males by age decades. The number of subjects in each age group is indicated above the abscissa. Vertical lines at each point indicate ±1 standard error of the mean, cross-sectional analysis. (*From* Shock, Greulich, Costa, Andres, Lakatta, Arenberg, et al., 1984.)

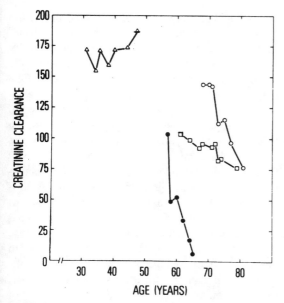

FIGURE 2   Age changes in kidney function (creatinine clearance) in four subjects—longitudinal observation. Age regression: △—△, Subject 199, +1.0006 ml/min/yr; ☐—71, Subject 101, 1.425 ml/min/yr; ○—○, Subject 554, 6.179 ml/min/yr; ●—●, Subject 123, 11.233 ml/min/yr. (*From* Lindeman, Tobin, & Shock, 1985.)

an aging pattern similar to that predicted from the average curve, others such as Subjects 554 and 123 show much greater rates of decline with age. In contrast, a young man (Subject 199) showed an increase in creatinine clearance (age regression, +1.006 ml/min/yr between the ages of 30 and 50).

Correlations between age changes in different physiological and psychological performances are relatively low, so there is little evidence for the existence of a single "aging process" that controls the rate of aging in a number of different functions.

Complex tasks such as maximum breathing capacity or physical exercise, which require the integrated performance of a number of organ systems (lungs, heart, muscles, nervous system, etc.), show greater age decrements than simple tasks such as muscle strength, which can be performed without complicated interactions among different organs. Thus it is apparent that many age changes are the result of the breakdown of physiological and psychological control mechanisms.

The BLSA has the longest record of serial data collection in existence (since 1958). Furthermore,

the study is still continuing. It has served to illustrate the power of longitudinal data in the study of aging.

Although a single longitudinal study confounds the effects of aging with the effects of cultural changes, two or more longitudinal samples tested simultaneously permit the isolation of the effects of age. Identification of interrelationships between age changes in different variables in the same person requires longitudinal data. The longitudinal method remains the "gold standard" for the study of age changes.

NATHAN W. SHOCK

See also
    Longitudinal Data Sets in Aging
    Longitudinal Studies: Europe
    Longitudinal Studies of Aging

BEDSORES
See
    Pressure Ulcers

BEHAVIORAL MEDICINE

Behavioral medicine emerged in the later 1970s as a field whose development signified the growing recognition that many of the risk factors for serious illness and premature death involved lifestyle and were behavioral in nature. Moreover, the development of increasingly sophisticated techniques for organic and surgical intervention in scientific medicine had been associated with spectacular success in the treatment of certain conditions but at the price of ignoring less salient interrelationships between behavior and disease as well as the patient's desire to be perceived as a whole person rather than as an assemblage of organs and tissues. Behavioral medicine was in part a reaction to this trend.

The broadest definition of the field (Schwartz & Weiss, 1978) holds that behavioral medicine is the integration of behavioral and biomedical knowledge and techniques relevant to health and illness. As it is more narrowly defined (Pomerleau & Brady, 1979), behavioral medicine is viewed as the application of behavior modification therapies to medical disorders and problems in health care and the conduct of research contributing to the functional analysis and understanding of behavior relevant to physical health. As Surwit, Williams, and Shapiro (1982) pointed out, a feature of behavioral approaches is that they work backward from demonstrated pathophysiology to the identification of relevant behavioral interventions. Furthermore, the behavioral model focuses on operationally definable constructs in which treatment involves modification of physiology or alteration of behaviors related to disease; unlike its psychosomatic predecessor, the demonstration that particular psychosocial variables are causally related to the course of the disease is no longer a precondition for intervention. Thus, by taking pathophysiology as its beginning point, behavioral medicine applies to all medical disorders, not just to those defined as psychological or psychophysiological in nature (Surwit, Feinglos, & Scovern, 1983).

During the early 1980s work in behavioral medicine has been shifting from descriptive and correlational studies of situational and behavioral factors in disease and health to multivariate functional analyses that incorporate behavioral, physiological, biochemical, and hormonal responses as well as subjective and social variables (see Pomerleau & Rodin, 1986). This trend holds much promise for the study of aging, in particular, because the health problems of the aged are not only chronic, but multiple in nature, with physical, psychological, and social factors all playing mutually influential roles in determining a person's condition. Behavioral medicine is a field working toward greater knowledge about these interactions between biobehavioral mechanisms and pathophysiological processes. As such, it may provide the scientific basis for more effective, rational approaches to prevention and management, especially since the use of psychological procedures in the management of medical problems and the burgeoning interest in understanding health-promoting and health-damaging behaviors are of great significance in the study of aging.

Behavioral medicine could also be influenced by the investigation of aging since, in its early development, the field has been dramatically affected by the need to modify health-related behaviors in a clinically useful way and by the desirability of developing a research tradition that is compatible with the biomedical model. Insistence on well-defined treatment procedures and on accountability and controlled clinic trials will continue to provide the basis for improved therapeutic efficacy. Furthermore, behavioral medicine appears to have established itself firmly within the health care system. Therefore, prevention and treatment options for the elderly will be expanded by developments in the area of behavioral medicine and may move away from a medical model to a broader self-management model. A recent joint task force of the American Medical and Nursing Associations that addressed the improvement of health care of the aged chronically ill concluded that a sense of purpose and control over one's life is integral to the health of the aged, thereby noting the significance of self-control in health and health care in older people. Both preventive interventions and the treatment of multiple chronic ailments require rather substantial changes of lifestyle, and behavioral medicine techniques are the strategies of choice for increasing self-management potential.

A national organization, the Association of Behavioral Medicine Research, currently holds annual meetings and publishes a research journal.

JUDITH RODIN

BEHAVIOR MODIFICATION

Historically, behavior modification has been tied to classical theories of learning, particularly *behaviorism* (B. F. Skinner). Central to behaviorism in its varied forms are general learning principles that describe and explain human behavior. The objective is always to specify the conditions that increase or decrease the probability of particular responses, their likely antecedents, and consequences. In general, then, behaviorism provides behavior modification with a theoretical paradigm, emphasizing antecedent-consequent relationships to describe, explain, and modify person-environment interactions. It also procures methodological strategies (Baer, 1973)—an experimental one analyzing for reversibility of behavior problems, a sequential observational one identifying the behavioral stream outlining person-environment interaction patterns, and an ecological intervention strategy attempting to modify person-environment interactional systems. When applied as convergent operations, these strategies allow a comprehensive understanding of behavior problems as Baltes (1988, 1995) has demonstrated with her work on dependency in the elderly.

The impact of behaviorism and behavior modification for the description, explanation, and modification of aging processes has been discussed by several authors (Baltes, 1992; Baltes & Barton, 1979; Carstensen, 1988). First, aging processes are not considered biologically determined but influenced by a triad of factors, such as social, psychological, and biological conditions. Second, the notion of modifiability and reversibility of aging processes is in line with life-span developmental perspectives toward aging emphasizing plasticity (reversibility) and growth in aging.

Thus, the behavioral paradigm, stressing the interrelationship between person and environment and the importance of environmental conditions, assures compensation and qualification of the role of biological determinants in aging processes and highlights the need for designing age-friendly environments. The study of aging processes within the behavioral framework has been termed behavioral gerontology (Carstensen, 1988).

Behavioral gerontology (Baltes, 1992; Carstensen, 1988) with its emphasis on psychological aging as modifiable, reversible, and context dependent began with single-subject experimental work demonstrating the powerful influence of social and physical environments on the behavior of nursing home residents. It was this early work that helped disconfirm the irreversibility of aging decline. Problem behaviors addressed were, for instance, social isolation, passivity or inactivity, dependence in everyday life, and incontinence. The primary goal of behavioral interventions is to enhance and prolong independent living in old age. In the meantime, the breadth of problems and level of intervention (from simple problems and single persons to more complex problems and groups or systems) has been enlarged (Carstensen & Edelstein, 1987; Wisocki, 1991). Interest has focused on psychological and physical health problems, such as depression, paranoia, anxiety, pain, and malnutrition; cognitive and sensory losses, such as problems with memory, hearing, vigilance, and communication; and drug and medication abuse.

Specific strategies used to bring about change in problem behaviors are cognitive training programs to improve memory and problem-solving performances, cognitive therapy to change depression, biofeedback to enhance brain functioning or prevent incontinence, imaging to control pain, exercise and relaxation to alleviate hypertension, or enhancement of feelings of personal control to ensure self-esteem and well-being.

Empirical evidence overwhelmingly confirms that old people respond well to behavior change programs. This confirms the environmental docility hypothesis (Lawton, 1982) stressing the notion that environmental conditions play a much larger role when biological and psychological vulnerability is increased—which is definitely true for old age—than vice versa. Despite this evidence for positive treatment outcomes, reality indicates that elderly people get much less effective treatment than younger people, and that, if treated, they often receive a medical diagnosis and medical drug treatment rather than psychological, behavioral treatment. Possible reasons reside with the elderly (i.e., reluctance to see psychotherapists), in the environment (i.e., psychotherapists are not keen on treating elderly clients), as well as with the situation (i.e., assessment difficulties resulting from multidimensionality of problems of the elderly, such as multimorbidity).

In sum, from an applied research standpoint, the behavioral paradigm has had a major impact on the design of prosthetic devices for the elderly, both in institutions and in the community (Parmelee & Lawton, 1990). From a basic research standpoint, the behavioral study of plasticity and its limits might assist in identifying what aging could be rather than what it happens to be under one particular set of events that happen to exist at one point in time.

MARGRET M. BALTES

See also
Coronary-Prone Behavior

BEREAVEMENT

Bereavement is one of the major life stressors that an older individual can experience, whether it be death of his or her spouse, adult child, grandchild, or other close family member (e.g., sibling) or friend. Considerable research has shown that significant loss, particularly of a spouse or other individual with whom a close, long-term relationship existed, often results in both physical and psychological problems that can take years to abate (if at all) (Gallagher-Thompson & Thompson, 1996). Since most existing empirical research has been conducted with the spousally bereaved, data reviewed here will focus on those individuals.

The annual incidence of spousal loss through death has been estimated to be 1.6% for elderly men, compared to 3.0% for elderly women. About 800,000 persons in the United States become newly widowed each year, with most of these deaths being in the over-65 age group. Some of the more significant yet also common problems documented in a variety of studies include major depression (about one third of widows and widowers are clinically depressed a month after losing their spouse, about one fourth at 6 months after the death, and about 15% a year later) (Zisook, 1994); increased risk for suicide, particularly for men (see Conwell's 1994 review); and increased mortality, particularly for men (Stroebe & Stroebe, 1993). In addition, several studies have found increased complaints of physical health problems, along with some actual decrements in health (Stroebe & Stroebe, 1987), with greater complaints generally reported by bereaved older women and more actual health changes reported by bereaved older men. Other studies examined the pattern of change in symptoms of grief over time (i.e., seeing or hearing the deceased, feeling his or her presence, being unable to sort through and dispose of belongings, etc.) and have found that grief symptoms do not completely abate even over a 30-month interval, despite improvement in other symptoms (Thompson, Gallagher-Thompson, Futterman, Gilewski, & Peterson, 1991). This suggests that long-term grief may be the norm rather than the exception for older individuals who have lost a spouse. At the same time, it is important not to pathologize what it is viewed by many as a normal life transition with which they will cope effectively, as they have done in the past with other significant life events (Parkes, 1993). The distinction between normal and abnormal, or complicated, grief can be difficult to make; sources such as Worden (1991) can be helpful in that regard.

Researchers also have studied risk factors that are likely to increase the probability of a difficult bereavement process. These include: male gender, inadequate social support network, an unexpected or traumatic mode of death, the survivor's own poor health, conflicted versus a prior satisfactory relationship with the deceased, and significant depressive symptoms at 2 months post-loss (reviewed in Gallagher-Thompson & Thompson, 1996). Individuals with a number of these risk factors simultaneously should be considered candidates for psychotherapeutic and/or pharmacological interventions so that they can receive support in transition through the normal phases of grieving and come to terms with their loss without developing significantly more distress.

A wide variety of interventions have been used with older adults to assist them in coping with grief, depression, and related symptoms (Parkes, 1993; Worden, 1991). For uncomplicated or relatively normal grief, facilitation can be through a self-help program such as the Widow to Widow program, or participation in church- or community-sponsored groups that encourage expression of feelings and increase awareness that one is not alone in grief. Other programs exist that are designed for those with more complicated grief reactions, such as major depression that is superimposed on grief. These include: use of antidepressant medication in combination with interpersonal psychotherapy (Reynolds, Miller, Pasternak, Frank, Perel, Cornes, et al., 1999) and the use of individual and/or group psychotherapy to help resolve other associated features of abnormal or pathological grief (such as delayed, exaggerated, or masked grief reactions; see Worden, 1991). In addition, recent publications have described the use of other kinds of interventions, such as family therapy and cognitive-behavioral therapy, to assist the older individual in accomplishing what Worden (1991) has described as the tasks of mourning. The latter include accepting the reality of the loss, experiencing the pain of grief, adjustment to an environment without the deceased, and reinvesting emotional energies into new relationships or other opportunities. For example, in cognitive-behavioral therapy, the individual is helped to challenge common cognitive distortions (e.g., "I can't be happy with this person gone") and is encouraged to develop adaptive behavior patterns needed to resume aspects of normal life. These might include learning to socialize without one's spouse and reviving former interests or hobbies that may have been set aside for years (particularly if the spouse was also a primary caregiver, as in the case of Alzheimer's disease or another form of dementia) (see Hill, Lund, & Packard, 1996).

Finally, the study of grief and its impact on older adults would not be complete without reference to unique ethnic and cultural differences in both the experience and expression of grief. For example, among Americans in the dominant culture, grief is often experienced as significant dysphoria, whereas among many Asian cultures (including recent Asian immigrants) grief is somaticized or expressed through the medium of the body, which experiences physical pain, weakness, and other kinds of discomfort (Rosenblatt, 1993). In contrast, many Mexican Americans celebrate the Day of the Dead in early November, in which ancestors are remembered and prayed to, because in that culture death is viewed as part of daily life. Given these significant cultural differences in the meanings ascribed to loss and in how one is expected to respond, the evaluation and treatment of grief reactions among different ethnic and cultural groups can be quite complex and is worthy of increased research attention in the new millennium.

DOLORES GALLAGHER-THOMPSON

See also

Behavior Modification
Death
Depression
Loss
Psychotherapy
Widowhood

BERLIN AGING STUDY

The Berlin Aging Study (BASE) is a multi- and interdisciplinary study of a heterogeneous (representative) sample of old and very old persons from the former city of West Berlin, Germany (Baltes, Mayer, Helmchen, & Steinhagen-Thiessen, 1999; cf. Mayer & Baltes, 1996; Baltes, 1987). The study was initiated in 1989 by the Academy of Sciences and Technology in Berlin and its study group on aging and societal development. From 1994 until 1998, BASE was sponsored by the Berlin-Brandenburg Academy of Sciences. The study is directed by a steering committee consisting of P. B. Baltes, psychology, H. Helmchen, psychiatry, K. U. Mayer, sociology, and E. Steinhagen-Thiessen, internal medicine and geriatrics. The institutions involved are the Free University Berlin, the Humboldt University of Berlin, and the Max Planck Institute for Human Development.

Features of BASE

Distinctive features of BASE are (1) local representativeness and heterogeneity of the subjects, using a stratified random sample selected from an obligatory city register; (2) a focus on the age range from 70 to 100 years and above; (3) a broad-based, in-depth multidisciplinary assessment battery; and (4) the collection of a reference data set from the elderly population of a large city. The core sample consists of 516 subjects equally stratified by age and sex so that the very old and males are oversampled. Since 1993 this BASE core sample has been examined longitudinally at three additional measurement occasions.

Research Units, Prototypical Questions, and Theoretical Orientations

Four research units—internal medicine and geriatrics, psychiatry, psychology, and sociology and social policy—cooperated closely in BASE, encompassing more than 40 scientists from biochemistry, physiology, internal medicine, dentistry, radiology, psychiatry, neuropsychology, psychology, sociology, and economics. The cooperation was guided by three prototypical questions, which refer to (1) the prediction of age differences from life-history data, (2) the degree and direction of differences within the domains identified by each discipline, and (3) interdisciplinary relationships between age differences and defined levels of functioning. Furthermore, the research units adopted four common theoretical orientations of gerontological research: (1) differential aging, (2) continuity versus discontinuity of aging, (3) range and limits of plasticity and reserve capacity, and (4) aging as a systemic and interdisciplinary phenomenon. The research questions of the BASE longitudinal study focused on (1) recording aging processes, (2) assessing temporal stability and change of individual trajectories, and (3) testing causal hypotheses on determinants of aging and mortality. The research questions and theoretical orientations formed a framework for the research units' objectives, hypotheses, and instruments as well as discipline-specific and interdisciplinary data analyses.

Levels and Intensity of Assessment

BASE was designed to allow several levels of participation at each measurement occasion differentiated by the amount of contact and intensity of assessment, ranging from a short initial contact and completion of a one-session Intake Assessment to participation in the study's Intensive Protocol, with data collection addressing the research questions of the four units (Baltes, Mayer, Helmchen, & Steinhagen-Thiessen, 1999). The *initial contact* contained a subset of questions from the Intake Assessment providing first basic information. In addition, using rating scales and a questionnaire, observations on the study participants' general appearance, health status, and residential situation were collected. The *one-session multidisciplinary Intake Assessment* contained measures of physical, psychiatric, psychological, social, and economic functioning. At each measurement occasion, it yielded a first set of comprehensive data, comparable in time and effort to a typical survey of older people. The *Intensive Protocol* varied in length and was conducted on three occasions, at Time 1, Time 3, and Time 4. At Time 1 the Intensive Protocol consisted of the Intake Assessment and 13 additional sessions, with each of the four research units primarily responsible for three or four sessions. At Time 3 and Time 4 the number of sessions was reduced to six, involving the multidisciplinary Intake Assessment and five further sessions of data collection on the longitudinal research questions of the four BASE units. At Time 2 only the one-session Intake Assessment was carried out (interim follow-up examination).

Methods and Major Constructs of Assessment

Methods ranged widely from biomedical analyses through psychological tests to interviews and social survey methodologies. The main topics and constructs developed by the Sociology and Social Policy Unit (Mayer, Maas, & Wagner, 1999) concentrated on life course antecedents and generational experiences, later phases of the family life course, social resources and social participation, economic conditions, and the provision of care. Life history accounts and information on current life conditions were collected with a comprehensive questionnaire.

The Psychology Unit (Smith & Baltes, 1999) covered three areas of individual psychological functioning: intelligence and cognition, self and personality, social functioning and social networks. The constructs investigated in these areas were guided by life-span developmental theory (Baltes, 1987) and concepts of successful aging (Baltes & Baltes, 1990). Methods ranged from a computerized battery of standard measures from intelligence tests, standard personality tests, and open-ended responses about the self, to a structured interview about social life and support networks.

The central foci of the Psychiatry Unit (Helmchen, Baltes, Geiselmann, Kanowski, Linden, Reischies, et al., 1999) were psychiatric morbidity, especially depression and dementia but also *subdiagnostic morbidity*; life history antecedents and current correlates of psychiatric morbidity and comorbidity; neuropsychological functioning; and coping with psychiatric morbidity. This included the examination of everyday competence and daily activity profiles by means of a retrospective "Yesterday Interview" (Baltes, Maas, Wilms, Borchelt, & Little, 1999). The methods applied included a standardized psychiatric interview and various psychiatric scales, information from subjects' physicians, and questionnaires dealing with subjects' health complaints, subjective conceptions of illness, drug consumption and use of medical assistance. Consensus conferences also were conducted with the Internal Medicine and Geriatrics Unit to specify or modify psychiatric and somatic diagnoses.

Finally, the Internal Medicine and Geriatrics Unit (Steinhagen-Thiessen & Borchelt, 1999) concentrated on aspects of objective and subjective health, functional capacity, risk profiles, multimorbidity, and medical treatment. Data collection involved a standardized medical anamnesis, a full-body, noninvasive examination, information from subjects' physicians, the collection of blood samples for an extensive set of biochemical analyses, a dental examination, color-coded ultrasound and computer tomography examinations to study blood flow patterns and bone structure. In addition, blood samples were saved for future analyses.

Data Collection

Data collection at Time 1 (main study) involving the 14-session Intensive Protocol began in 1990 and ended in 1993. The interim follow-up examination at Time 2 was carried out in 1993–1994. Data collections at Time 3 and Time 4, involving the reduced six-session Intensive Protocol, were conducted in 1995–1996 and 1997–1998. All sessions were organized by the central project coordination, lasted 1–2 hours, and were conducted by highly trained research assistants and medical personnel, including internists, psychiatrists, dentists, and radiologists. Most sessions took place at the participants' residences.

In addition, information on the mortality of the original BASE parent sample has been regularly obtained from the Berlin city register twice a year since 1992.

Samples in BASE

The verified parent sample at Time 1 (1990–1993) consisted of 1,908 persons. The initial contact could be realized with 1,219 (64%). The Intake Assessment was completed by 928 persons (49%). Out of this group, 516 (27%) participated in the full 14-session Intensive Protocol. In this final core sample, women and men of six age/cohort groups (70–74, 75–79, 80–84, 85–89, 90–94, 95+ years, born between 1885 and 1922) were equally represented with 43 in each cell defined by age/cohort and gender. This cross-sectional design was selected to provide comparable statistical power for analyses of age and gender.

At Time 2 (1993–1994), 431 members of the original core sample of 516 had survived. Of these, 361 (84%) completed the Intake Assessment. At Time 3 (1995–1996), the initial sample for the reduced six-session Intensive Protocol consisted of 313 survivors. Of these, 244 (78%) took part in a repeat of the Intake Assessment, and 206 (66%) completed all six sessions of the reduced Intensive Protocol. At Time 4 (1997–1998), 239 members of the initial core sample were still alive. Of these, 164 (69%) participated in the Intake Assessment, and 132 (55%) completed the entire reduced Intensive Protocol.

Generalizability (Selectivity) of Findings

As is true for most intense multidisciplinary assessments, the BASE sample is affected by selective sampling and selective dropout. Because generalizability and heterogeneity were key objectives of the BASE main study, problems of sampling bias and selectivity were analyzed intensively, examining the various losses from the total parent sample to the verified parent sample and first contacts with the subjects, as well as losses at the various assessment stages. For these analyses, demographic data, information on the mortality within the total sample provided by the Berlin city register, and observational and other data collected during all stages of assessment were used. The analyses (Lindenberger, Gilberg, Little, Nuthmann, Pötter, & Baltes, 1999) showed that the Intensive Protocol sample (core sample) remained representative of the parent population despite some small positive selection effects (all below half of a standard deviation). In particular, there was no indication that correlation patterns and variances differed among the participation levels.

In-depth selectivity analyses are also planned for the BASE longitudinal study. In these analyses the amount of selectivity effects due to mortality and to other reasons for dropout will be considered separately.

Results and Access to the Data

The major cross-sectional findings of the BASE main study, interdisciplinary as well as discipline-specific, were published in a comprehensive mono-graph (Mayer & Baltes, 1996; Baltes & Mayer, 1999). Furthermore, more than 260 journal articles and book chapters on BASE results were published between 1991 and 1999. A package of journal articles on longitudinal findings of BASE, involving the first three measurement occasions, was published in 1999 (Baltes & Mayer, 1999). After the main research questions have been answered, the BASE data set also will be opened for analyses by external scientists.

KARL M. NEHER
REINHARD NUTHMANN

See also
Longitudinal Studies of Aging
Longitudinal Studies: Europe

BIOFEEDBACK

Biofeedback is an intervention technique used for a number of disorders, including hypertension (Buby, Elfner, & May, 1990), muscle contraction and vascular headache (Blanchard, Appelbaum, Radnitz, Morrill, Michultka, Kirsch, et al., 1990; Cott, Parkinson, Fabich, Bedard, & Marlin, 1992), chronic pain (Roberts, Sternbach, & Polich, 1993), incontinence (Houston, 1993), Raynaud's disease (Surwit, 1982), diabetes (Rice & Schindler, 1992), insomnia (Sittenfeld, 1977), alcoholism (Denney & Baugh, 1992), tinnitus (Landis & Landis, 1992), chemotherapy nausea (Burish & Jenkins, 1992), and general anxiety (Townsend, House, & Addario, 1975). The procedure is based on the premise that voluntary control of autonomic and neuromuscular functions can be facilitated by electronic amplification of physiological signals presented to the individual through an auditory or visual medium. The individual utilizes this continuous feedback to modify the response incrementally in the desired direction through a series of increasingly stringent criterion levels. It is generally assumed, though not universally accepted, that the successful result is due to the reinforcing effect of the feedback itself, which continuously "updates" the patient as to the physiological changes produced.

Major advantages of biofeedback include economy, a reduced reliance on pharmacological agents, and good outcome with certain conditions that resist medical management (e.g., muscle contraction headache). Not surprisingly, much attention has been given to biofeedback (for a review, see Andrasik, Coleman, & Epstein, 1982), although little attention has been devoted to its applicability for the elderly. This is unfortunate because the elderly might be especially appropriate for nonpharmacological intervention. They use more medications than do younger patients, and in addition are more vulnerable to the side effects ("Drugs and the Elderly," 1977; Hunt, 1976). Biofeedback could reduce the risks and costs associated with long-term medication regimens. Additionally, biofeedback entails the learning of a skill used to control one's own condition. Based on the importance of control in aging, one could predict that such an intervention would be especially desirable (Cautela & Mansfield, 1977).

Perhaps the primary concern would be the elderly person's ability to increase his or her awareness and control of visceral and neuromuscular functions. Research shows rather clearly that the elderly acquire conditioned and other learned responses less readily than do younger subjects (Schonfield, 1980). However, the confounding influences of motivation, arousal, and attitude (Ross, 1968) are also clear. Regardless, based on present evidence, advanced age is not a contraindication for biofeedback, although it should be emphasized that the elderly in particular should receive biofeedback in the context of a larger treatment package (Gaarder, 1978). Perhaps the major suggestion to increase its efficacy with the elderly would be to employ strategies such as a slower-paced rate of training, simplicity of instructions, a nonthreatening environment, and continued encouragement (Schonfield, 1980). Such individual considerations are well suited to the typical biofeedback training paradigm.

One application of biofeedback showing particular promise for the elderly is neuromuscular reeducation for central nervous system deficits such as stroke (Intiso, Santilli, Grasso, Rossi, & Caruso, 1994) or more nonspecific autonomic dysregulation

(Chiarioni, Scattolini, Bonfante, & Vantini, 1993). The encouraging results of neuromuscular reeducation can give new hope to patients often frustrated by the loss of ordinary abilities such as facial or limb movement (Ross, Nedzelski, & McLean, 1991; Sunderland, Tinson, Bradley, Fletcher, Langton, Hewer, et al., 1992) and bowel or bladder control (Burgio & Engel, 1990; Wald, 1990).

There are some factors that contraindicate or limit biofeedback applications in general. A history of psychosis or dissociative processes merits caution because such symptoms can be precipitated when the individual is sensitized to internal states during the various biofeedback procedures. Severe depression or dementia—conditions common in aging—will also handicap a biofeedback effort through the disruption of attentional processes and motivation.

In conclusion, biofeedback for the elderly holds promise based on its limited side effects, cost effectiveness, and encouraging results with certain previously discouraging, age-relevant disorders. However, the recommendation is not an unqualified one. Clinicians should be attuned to any relevant precautions and should modify the training to accommodate the limitations of the elderly.

ERIC M. MORRELL

See also
Behavioral Medicine

BIOGRAPHY

The term *biography*, as it is employed in the field of aging, has at least three related meanings (Birren, Kenyon, Ruth, Schroots, & Svensson, 1996; Kenyon, Clark, & de Vries, 2001). First, it refers to the use of narratives, life histories, autobiographies, and life stories as sources of data in research. Second, biography refers to several forms of intervention in aging, such as life review, reminiscence, and guided autobiography. Third, biography refers to the life story of a person, expressed in either written or verbal form and told to oneself or another. It is important to note that literary forms of biography are also effective sources of knowledge of

aging in these three areas (Cole, Kastenbaum, & Ray, 1999).

In research, biographical approaches provide an excellent medium for investigating both the idiosyncratic and shared aspects of human aging over the life span. For example, personal recollections of developmental tasks, turning points, stresses, and individual coping strategies can be analyzed. These sources of information facilitate insight into how a life *has been* lived, how it *is* lived, and how it *can be* lived. By employing biographical approaches it is also possible to describe how cultures, subcultures, or family patterns are reflected in individual lives, and how particular people adapt to or expand the possibilities and limits set by the historical period in which they live.

A particular research strength of biographical materials is that they provide data on both individual and societal levels. They give glimpses of the historical periods of the society that the narrator has lived through—that is, shared experiences such as wars and difficult economic times, as well as significant leaps forward in the development of a culture as evidenced in such things as the welfare state. Life stories thus can also be viewed as individual interpretations of cultural conditions of earlier times.

There are important aspects of biography in the field of aging that require further theoretical discussion as well as empirical inquiry (Kenyon, Ruth, & Mader, 1999; Kenyon, Clark, & de Vries, 2001). For example, there is the question as to whom stories are told and why. A narrative may be produced out of special concerns, such as to provide an authorized career biography, act as a research subject, enhance change in therapy, or lend consolation in spiritual counseling. The *storyteller* will present himself or herself in a specific way and different parts of his or her life story will emerge as a function of the intended audience. The reasons for telling the story, as well as the medium, partly form the message. Such issues as these also give rise to methodological concerns that are actively debated both from technical and philosophy of science perspectives.

Studies exploring the reality within stories are also receiving increased attention in research (Gubrium & Holstein, 1997, 1998; Kenyon & Randall, 1997). Questions concerning the presumed reader of the text, the relation between storyteller and society, culturally rooted expressions in life stories, and the role of memory in biography are considered fruitful topics of investigation. Nevertheless, the most important issue remains that of concentrating on the *subjective meaning* that is communicated concerning central issues and decisive situations in life, within the context of the larger story we live in, which co-authors our biography (Kenyon & Randall, 1997).

Biographical forms of intervention are increasingly being considered crucial to the field of aging, both in the context of assessment and diagnosis, in such areas as competence and community care, and in the context of therapy modalities such as life review, reminiscence, and narrative therapy. The understanding of *dementia stories* is also a growing area of interest, with the goal of providing a better quality of life for both clients and caregivers (Gubrium, 1993; Kenyon, Clark, & de Vries, 2001).

In addition to the foregoing, there are biographical forms of intervention that serve to enhance personal meaning and quality of life from a learning, in contrast to a therapeutic, perspective. Guided autobiography would be an example of this approach. Important *ethical issues* arise in connection with the distinction between therapy and learning, as they do in the area of aging and biography as a whole (Josselson, 1996).

The discussion of biography and aging from the point of view of a personal life story is significant because meaning is expressed through metaphors, which are the raw materials out of which one constructs one's narratives, life story, and autobiography. In other words, "the story of my life" is made up of images and perceptions, characters and plots, that are significantly figurative and creative in nature, rather than imprints of factual events. Consequently, the relationship between personal meanings of aging and biography is fundamental in that not only do people express or communicate meaning through stories of various kinds, but storytelling also is basic to the organization of experience.

From the viewpoint of "narrative gerontology" (Kenyon, Clark, & de Vries, 2001), human beings are always constructing stories that reflect an intersection of genetic predispositions, past experience (intrapersonal and interpersonal and sociocultural), and personal choice. Further, biographies contain cognitive, affective, and motivational components. Our thoughts, feelings, and actions are influenced by the stories we tell ourselves about ourselves and the world. Storytelling (and story listening) is an ontological phenomenon in that not only do we *have* a life story but we *are* stories. Finally, our biographies may constitute a key to the further understanding of *wisdom*, including the "ordinary wisdom" in each of our lives (Randall & Kenyon, 2000).

GARY M. KENYON

See also
   Life Review
   Life Review: Reminiscence

BIOLOGICAL RHYTHMS
See
   Chronobiology: Rhythms, Clocks, Aging, and
   Other Trends

BIOLOGY OF FAT IN AGING, THE

Aging is associated with increases in body weight and total body fatness—most importantly, increase in intra-abdominal fat (i.e., visceral adiposity is observed in humans and animal models). This increase in visceral adiposity with age is independent of body mass index. Increase in fat and visceral adiposity is associated with decrease in the ability of insulin to stimulate glucose-uptake into skeletal muscle. The development of such an insulin-resistant state with aging is demonstrated by increases in fasting and postprandial insulin levels, impaired glucose tolerance, and higher risk for developing type II diabetes mellitus with aging. Furthermore, the development of visceral adiposity and insulin resistance with aging also determines the risks for developing diseases such as dyslipidemia, hypertension, and atherosclerosis, as well as early death. Recent findings have demonstrated that fat is not an inert tissue but rather a very active endocrine tissue, and variety of fat-derived peptides have been demonstrated to exert multisystemic actions.

Fat as an Active Endocrine Tissue

An increasing number of fat-derived peptides have been identified and investigated. These include leptin, tumor necrosis factor-α (TNF-α), plasmino-gen activator inhibitor-1 (PAI-1), angiotensinogen (AT), adipoQ or Acrp30, and complement factors (B, C3, D).

The discovery of the 16kd peptide called leptin best exemplifies the cross-talk between fat, brain, and peripheral tissues. Plasma leptin level increases directly with increased total fat mass in animals and humans. Leptin is secreted from fat, circulates in the plasma, and acts through a receptor in the hypothalamus. This interaction results in powerful suppression of appetite and increase in energy expenditure in animals. These actions are important in maintaining body weight and thus preventing obesity. Moreover, leptin also has peripheral actions, especially in the regulation of fat distribution and the modulation of insulin action. Despite its novel action to prevent obesity, aging is characterized by increased body weight and fat mass, which in the presence of increasing leptin levels signifies a failure in its action. This state is partly due to human eating behavior in which meals are taken regularly regardless of the plasma leptin level, the degree of appetite, or the degree of obesity and accumulation of visceral fat.

TNF-α, previously known as lymphotoxin and cachectin, is a cytokine that is also secreted from fat. Its levels are directly correlated with fat mass and directly involved in the development of insulin resistance in obesity. Increased local secretion of TNF-α from fat embedded in myocytes may have a role on impairing the insulin signaling pathway and inducing insulin resistance.

PAI-1 is also secreted from fat and is increased with obesity; however, the extent of the contribution of fat to plasma levels has not been determined. Increased PAI-1 level is associated with decreased fibrinolytic activity in the blood; thus it is a risk factor for acute coronary events.

All the renin-angiotensin system is expressed in fat. AT, the precursor of the potent pressor agent angiotensin, is expressed and secreted from fat tissue most dramatically. It is increased with obesity and may have a potential role in inducing hypertension in the insulin-resistant patient.

AdipoQ or Acrp30 binds preferentially to muscle and is regulated acutely and chronically by insulin, signifying a potential role in glucose metabolism or metabolic functions of the muscle.

Lastly, complement factors (B, C3, D) are secreted for fat and may have a role in controlling immune responses.

Deleterious Effects of Visceral Adiposity in Aging

The overwhelming deleterious effects on health of visceral adiposity in aging were demonstrated by using an epidemiological tool to assess visceral fat, called the waist-to-hip ratio. An increase in waist-to-hip ratio was an independent risk factor for the development of diabetes mellitus, stroke, and coronary artery disease, and mortality. Recent studies done on aging rodent models further supported the cause-and-effect relationship between increased visceral fat and insulin action. For example, caloric restriction reversed the age-related increases in plasma insulin, glucose, and glycosylated hemoglobin to youthful levels. In fact, it restored liver and muscle insulin sensitivity to youthful levels independent of age. Furthermore, surgical extraction of visceral fat in rats has dramatically reversed the defects in insulin action. These findings support fat accretion as a risk factor of insulin resistance independent of age. Interestingly, leptin administration specifically decreases visceral fat, suggesting a role of the leptin system in the failure to regulate body fat distribution.

Conclusion

Aging is often associated with weight gain and almost always with visceral adiposity that is detrimental to human health, leading to early mortality. The age-related processes may be due to the interplay of the different fat-derived peptides. Thus, prevention of visceral adiposity is key in preventing age-related diseases such as type II diabetes mellitus, dyslipidemia, coronary artery disease, and hypertension. Moreover, understanding fat tissue biology may be helpful in finding therapy to prevent these age-related processes.

JANE A. CASES
NIR BARZILAI

See also
  Body Composition
  Obesity

BIOMARKER OF AGING

Although the term *biomarker of aging* has generated extensive use in the gerontological literature, no consensus has emerged regarding a clear definition of the concept and standards for its application to research questions. In its simplest application the term refers to any biological parameter that is correlated with the chronological age of an organism; however, this concept has little use other than descriptive. In its more complex application, a biomarker of aging is a biological parameter intended as a quantitative measure of the rate of aging in an organism that represents a more accurate index than the chronological age of the organism can provide. In this latter form, the standards and procedures for defining and validating a biomarker of aging have generated considerable debate within gerontology.

The more complex application of a biomarker of aging emerged from the research demand to assess the effectiveness of interventions that purport to alter the rate of aging. If two individuals are of the same chronological age but have experienced an *intervention* that might affect the rate of aging, how can this difference be detected? In 1982, Reff and Schneider published a monograph entitled *Biological Markers of Aging,* as the report of a workshop in which investigators were challenged to consider how interventions might be assessed by using biomarkers of aging representing a variety of physiological systems. This approach was considered further in a meeting report by Regelson and Sinex published in 1983 and referenced as *Intervention in the Aging Process.* A special issue of the journal *Experimental Aging Research,* titled "The Measurement of Biological Age," edited by Ludwig and Masoro also was published in 1983 and offered the view of many investigators on this topic.

It was not until 1988, however, that a formal definition of biomarker of aging was offered by Baker and Sprott in a special edition of the journal *Experimental Gerontology,* that emerged from a workshop held in 1987 during which participants discussed current strategies of research on biomarkers of aging (Sprott & Baker, 1988). The definition offered was as follows: "a biological parameter of an organism that either alone or in some multivariate composite will, in the absence of disease, better predict functional capacity at some later age than will chronological age" (p. 223). Although the concept had not been formally defined previously, specific criteria of a biomarker of aging had been offered by Reff and Schneider (1982) as follows: (1) nonlethal, (2) highly reproducible, (3) displays significant alterations during relatively short time periods, (4) critical to effective maintenance of health and prevention of disease. To this set of criteria, Baker and Sprott (1988) offered the following additions: (5) reflects a measurable parameter that can be predicted at a later age, (6) reflects some basic biological process of aging and metabolism, (7) should have high reproducibility in cross-species comparisons.

Ingram (1983, 1988) and McClearn (1988) attempted to clarify the criteria offered above and offer a strategy for developing a biomarker of aging in its more complex application. The structure of this strategy had been used for developing psychological tests. The major challenge is how to determine the *reliability* and *validity* of a biomarker of aging. Reliability relates to criterion 2 above. Are the data obtained in an assay reproducible? Reliability refers to how much of the variability in a parameter can be attributed to genuine *individual differences* versus measurement error. Several statistical procedures exist for addressing this question, such as estimation of test-retest correlations. Over a longer period of time, the term, *stability* of individual differences emerges in considering reliability issues, but this concept also addresses the ability of the biomarker to be predictive and thus also begins to relate to the concept of validity. Validity refers to demonstrating the utility of a biomarker. Predictive validity relates to criterion 5 above. Can a measure at one age predict future performance in this measure or represent future status in some other measure or set of measures? Inherent in the definition of Baker and Sprott (1988) presented above, there is an emphasis on functional capacity at a later age. Several criteria related to this predictive ability can be considered, such as life span or the age of onset of specific age-related diseases. If functional capacity is the primary predictive criterion, then the ability to withstand a specific stressor could be considered. Construct validity relates to criteria 4, 6, and particularly 7 above. How well does a biomarker of aging reflect the underlying construct, or definition of aging? Strong support for construct validity of a biomarker of aging would be provided if the biomarker could differentiate between groups with established differences in the rate of aging and/or life span.

This latter approach was central to efforts initiated by the National Institute on Aging to identify biomarkers of aging in rodent models (Baker & Sprott, 1988; Sprott, 1999). The validation process involved comparing a candidate biomarker in rodent populations on control and experimental diets. Specifically, on the experimental diet, rodents underwent *calorie restriction* (CR) compared to ad libitum feeding for the controls. This is a well-established intervention that produces marked differences in the rate of aging evidences as reduced mortality rates and the incidence of age-related pathology. Thus, if the candidate biomarker of aging showed a slower rate of change in the CR group compared to controls, such demonstration would support the construct validity of the biomarker. Clearly, the parameter would reflect "effective maintenance of health and prevention of disease" (criterion 4) as well as "reflects some basic biological process of aging and metabolism" (criterion 6).

As an example of this strategy for biomarker development, Miller (1997) examined age-related changes in subsets of T cells of mice to identify immunological biomarkers of aging. The proportion of cells known as CD-4 memory T cells increased with age as measured cross-sectionally and longitudinally, and the change in this parameter was slowed in mice undergoing CR. As an additional demonstration of the validity of this biomarker of aging, Miller, Chrisp, and Galecki (1997) also demonstrated that this parameter measured at 18 months of age was predictive of individual life span in the mice.

Although this strategy would apply to validating biomarkers of aging in short-lived species, it is difficult to apply to longer-lived species, such as humans, in which populations that differ in the rate of aging are much more difficult to discern and life span data require decades to accumulate. To this end, Nakamura, Lane, Roth, Cutler, and Ingram (1994) and Nakamura, Lane, Roth, and Ingram (1998) addressed the issues of reliability and validity that can be applied to studies of long-lived species, such as nonhuman primates. They offered the following criteria of a biomarker of aging that are more statistically oriented than those proposed by Baker and Sprott (1988): (1) significant cross-sectional correlation with age, (2) significant longitudinal change with age consistent with the cross-sectional correlation, (3) significant stability of individual differences, and (4) rate of age-related change proportional to differences in life span among related species. Criterion 3 relates to reliability in the short term and predictive validity in the long term. Criterion 4 is an extension of criterion 7 offered by Baker and Sprott. Examples of this approach are represented in papers by Lane, Ingram, Ball, and Roth (1997) and Sell and colleagues (Sell, Lane, Johnson, Masoro, Mock, Reiser, et al., 1996). The age-related change in serum dihydroepiandrosterone, an adrenal steroid, in the former paper and in pentosidine, an advanced glycation end product measurable in skin samples, in the latter were examined across different species. The logic here is that if a biomarker of aging is a valid reflection of the rate of aging, then the rate of change across different species should be proportional to differences in species life span. Thus, for example, the rate of change in a candidate biomarker of aging in chimpanzees should be twice that of humans (60 vs. 120 years maximum life span); in rhesus monkeys three times that of humans (40 vs. 120 years maximum life span). Although this strategy of cross-species comparison has been applied in efforts to identify genetic determinants of longevity (Cutler, 1982), this method of validation for identifying biomarkers of aging has been used sparingly, but it clearly appeals to construct validity.

Short, Williams, and Bowden (1997) offered an example of an alternative method for validating biomarkers of aging in a long-lived species. Specifically, they attempted to correlate the rate of aging in several biological parameters measured in monkeys to antioxidant status in monkeys. This approach would relate to criteria 4 and 6 offered by Baker and Sprott.

As the number of interventions that purport to retard the rate of aging increases, the demand for identifying biomarkers of aging will likely increase. Progress in this regard will emerge as a consensus is built to determine the definition and methods for establishing the reliability and validity of biomarkers of aging.

DONALD K. INGRAM

See also
Normative Aging Study
Successful Aging

BLOOD

Blood is composed of two major components: formed elements (cells) and the fluid phase (plasma) in which the former are suspended. The former include red blood cells (erythrocytes), white blood cells (leukocytes), and platelets (thrombocytes) (Beutler, Lichtman, Coller, & Kipps, 1995). Plasma is an aqueous solution of electrolytes, nutrients, and lipids plus a large variety of proteins. These components transport substances that are of vital importance to the maintenance of normal homeostasis to tissues and cells of the body and transport waste substances away from the tissues and cells to points of excretion. The blood is an extremely complex structure and the array of functions performed by it equally so.

Functions

Respiration. This vital function involves the transport of oxygen from the lungs to all living cells. Of equal importance is the removal of the waste product of cellular metabolism, carbon dioxide, from the cells to the lungs where it is expired. This function is performed mainly by hemoglobin contained within the red blood cells.

Nutrition. All nutrients required by cells are transported by the blood including minerals, salts, amino acids (the building blocks for proteins), carbohydrates (glucose), fats, and vitamins. These are mainly transported in the plasma, frequently bound to specific transport proteins.

Excretion. Waste products as well as some toxic substances are carried by the blood to the major excretory organs, which include the liver and kidneys as well as the lungs. These products include water, electrolytes, nitrogen-containing compounds, certain drugs, and breakdown products of hemoglobin (bilirubin).

Defense. A major function of the blood involves the body's defense against foreign substances (bacteria, viruses, etc.). Both cells and plasma contribute to defense, with the phagocytic leukocytes, particularly granulocytes and monocytes, acting directly to kill invaders. Lymphocytes also act directly, as well as participating in the production of antibodies that circulate as part of the plasma protein component, and assist in the destruction of such invading organisms.

Vascular Integrity. The blood helps maintain the vascular tree intact and protects against destruction from trauma. This function, called hemostasis, is accomplished by an interaction of the platelets and the protein-clotting factors to form a blood clot to seal such destructions.

Components of the Blood and Changes With Age

Plasma. This consists predominantly of water (>90%), and the major soluble substances are the proteins. Salts, glucose, amino acids, vitamins, hormones, and waste products are the other constituents. Most proteins (including albumin, the one with the highest concentration) are produced in the liver. Immunoglobulins (antibodies) are produced by lymphocyte-derived cells in many organs including the bone marrow, lymph nodes, and spleen. The general composition of the plasma does not change dramatically with age. There are small decreases in the serum albumin concentration, perhaps related to chronic disease, and subtle alterations in the concentration of the types of antibody molecules. The most striking of these is the emergence of an aberrant immunoglobulin protein, in up to tenfold normal concentration, in as many as 10% to 15% of normal people older than the age of 70 (Cohen, 1999). These proteins are known as monoclonal immunoglobulins because of their derivation from a single clone of lymphocyte-derived cells, the plasma cells. Another age-related change occurring in the blood—in part, related to the plasma—is a change in the erythrocyte sedimentation rate (ESR). This phenomenon, which measures the rate of sedimentation of red blood cells in the plasma, is an indirect measure of the viscosity of the plasma. Both the ESR and the plasma viscosity increase somewhat with age. This is brought about by several different plasma proteins but appears to be related more to an increase in the number of infectious and inflammatory diseases with age rather than the aging process itself.

Cells

The more prominent changes in the blood with age and disease involve the cells (Cohen & Crawford, 1992). All blood cells are produced in the bone marrow from a common stem cell. With advancing age, the cell production in bone marrow decreases by approximately one third; however, renewal of peripheral blood cells remains normal except in circumstances of excess stress. There appears to be some reduction in bone marrow stem cell reserve for both red and white blood cells, with the decrease in the latter perhaps the partial cause of the somewhat decreased response to infection in the elderly. With normal aging, there appears to be an only slight decrease in the number of red blood cells and the level of the main red blood cell protein hemoglobin, which is the major oxygen-carrying molecule. The leukocyte count in peripheral blood in the elderly tends to decrease only slightly but may be less readily mobilized under stress. The ability of the phagocytic leukocytes (granulocytes and monocytes) to kill bacteria appears unchanged. The platelet count appears to remain normal throughout the life span in normal aging individuals.

Most of the changes seen in the blood cells with age are related to the increased prevalence of a number of age-related diseases. Anemia, or a decrease in red cells and hemoglobin, is the most frequently encountered hematologic problem in the elderly (Gautier, Crawford, & Cohen, 1998). This is a sign of several potential underlying, primary diseases. In general, anemia can result from either an underproduction of red blood cells or their overdestruction. The former is most frequently seen. Anemia frequently results in characteristic changes in the appearance of the red blood cells. One type, in which the red cells become much smaller than normal (microcytic), includes the common anemia produced by iron deficiency. Iron deficiency is generally the result of blood loss, often from the gastrointestinal tract, and much more rarely from dietary deficiency. Treatment of this condition with iron replacement may be easily accomplished, but the initial cause of the deficiency must be actively sought. Another microcytic form of anemia is the anemia of chronic disease. This is a secondary form of anemia in which iron appears to be trapped in storage sites within the body and not made available

to the developing erythrocytes. In this case, treatment with iron is not indicated, but rather, when possible, resolution of the illness in question (e.g., infection and inflammation) is necessary.

A second major group of anemias is those in which the red blood cells are larger than normal, or macrocytic. These are most frequently produced by deficiency of either vitamin B_{12} or of folic acid. Folic acid deficiency is common in the elderly and is usually a result of dietary insufficiency. Vitamin B_{12} insufficiency is frequently caused by an intrinsic failure to absorb the vitamin, because of the lack of certain transport proteins in the stomach, which leads to pernicious anemia. Though dietary deficiency of vitamin B_{12} can occur, it is relatively infrequent. A somewhat decreased blood level of vitamin B_{12} with advancing age appears to occur. Both of these vitamins are critical in the formation of the DNA (basic genetic material) of the cell, which is necessary for cell proliferation. Once diagnosed, these anemias can be easily treated by replacement of the appropriate vitamin.

Increased destruction of red blood cells occurs less frequently and is referred to as hemolytic anemia. Most often, this is due to the production of an antibody by the body, directed against certain membrane components of the red blood cell, which then induces destruction of these cells. This is called autoimmune hemolytic anemia. The process of autoantibody production appears to increase rather strikingly with age, although red blood cell destruction still remains relatively infrequent.

Overproduction of red blood cells may occur, but this is usually accompanied by overproduction of the white blood cells or platelets as well. Such disorders constitute the myeloproliferative disorders, which also occur with increasing frequency in the elderly (Gautier & Cohen, 1997). In polycythemia rubra vera all three cell lines proliferate. This results in high red blood cell count (and hemoglobin levels), high white blood cell counts, and high platelet counts. In chronic granulocytic leukemia, there is dramatic overproduction of granulocytes and platelets because of an uncontrolled hyperactivity of the bone marrow. This disease requires treatment with chemotherapeutic agents. After a period of a few years of relatively easy control, it frequently becomes uncontrollable and changes into a more acute form of the disease similar to acute granulocytic leukemia, and usually results in death. Acute granulocytic (or myeloblastic) leukemia is a dramatic disease with a rapid clinical course and short survival. More than half of all patients with acute granulocytic leukemia are over the age of 60. In this disorder, there is an overproduction and accumulation of the most primitive form of the granulocyte, called the myeloblast. These cells invade and occupy the major portion of the bone marrow, and, by overcrowding and failing to differentiate to more mature forms, prevent the production of the normal cellular elements. Thus, reductions in granulocytes, platelets, and red blood cells result. These primitive myeloblasts may also break loose from the bone marrow and circulate in the blood peripherally in large numbers, although in the elderly they are frequently confined to the bone marrow, making the diagnosis somewhat more difficult. In younger individuals, treatment for this disease involves extremely aggressive chemotherapy. Because the elderly appear to be less able to tolerate this initial aggressive treatment (and even with treatment, which may be toxic, survival is short), alternative treatment approaches have been suggested.

Specific disorders of the thrombocyte also occur in the elderly, with thrombocytopenia (decreased platelets) being the most common. This may be due to a myeloproliferative disorder, as described earlier, or may be caused by antibodies to the thrombocytes, in a manner similar to that described previously for red cells. A frequent problem in the elderly is thrombocytopenia produced by drugs. This may result from immune reactions or from suppression of the bone marrow.

Drugs in general may play an important role in causing blood disorders in the elderly. Many drugs have side effects that produce either immunologic reactions or direct suppression of the bone marrow, resulting in decreases in all the cellular elements as in pancytopenia or decreases in individual components as in aplastic anemia (decreased red blood cells), granulocytopenia, and thrombocytopenia. With the generally increased numbers of drugs used by elderly individuals, this etiology must be strongly considered when these phenomena are noted.

HARVEY J. COHEN

See also

Atherosclerosis

Cardiovascular System: Overview

Cardiovascular System: The Heart

Cardiovascular System: Vascular

Lipoproteins, Serum

BOARD AND CARE HOMES

A variety of terms are used to label licensed board and care homes. Most common in state regulation and statute are *board and care* and *residential care facilities* (RCFs). Other labels include *adult congregate living, adult foster care, community care, assisted living, domiciliary care, personal care, sheltered care, supervised care.* Terms like *boarding homes, congregate care,* and *group homes* often refer to unlicensed facilities. More than 800,000 aged and disabled adults lived in state-licensed board and care homes in the United States in 1997 (Harrington, Swan, Wellin, Clemeña, Carrillo, Griffin, et al., 1999). This is a 60% increase from 1990.

Both RCFs and boarding home services usually include cleaning the residents' room, laundering linens, and providing meals. In addition, RCFs (i.e., licensed facilities) are often responsible for helping with transportation and shopping; supervising the taking of medication; assisting in obtaining medical and social services; and on a more limited basis, assisting with dressing, grooming, eating, bathing, and transporting. Some RCFs, either through the terms of their license or waivers in regulations, can provide assistance for those with special needs, such as being nonambulatory or using oxygen or assistive devices, or those with relatively severe cognitive impairments. Hospice care is also available on a limited basis in a few states. The provision of these higher levels of care is commonly becoming known as assisted living (Mollica, 1998).

Almost half the residents of RCFs for the elderly and adults are estimated to have measurable depression or to be receiving psychotropic medications (Spore, Mor, Larrat, Hiris, & Hawes, 1996), more than a third have at least two limitations in activities of daily living, and up to a third have moderate to severe levels of cognitive impairment (Spector, Reschovsky, & Cohen, 1996).

A common theme in discussions of residential care is whether this level of care can reduce or replace time as a nursing home resident. At least one study estimates that as many as 35% of nursing home residents could be appropriately served in other levels of care, such as adult foster care and assisted living settings (Spector, Reschovsky, & Cohen, 1996). Other studies suggest much more modest shifts from nursing homes (e.g., Newcomer, Preston, & Roderick, 1995; Swan & Newcomer, 2000).

Preadmission screening and community-based-care programs (as nursing home alternatives) illustrate policies and programs that may be affecting the caseload and resident mix of RCFs. Other examples include policies that affect the cost of operations of either nursing homes or RCFs (e.g., changes in staff-to-client ratios and building codes). Reimbursement rates for services or levels of care also may influence bed availability. How far and how fast any expansion of RCF care capability should be taken is an issue without clear resolution. Historically, the federal role in RCF financing and regulation has been generally limited to SSI payments, the financing of state ombudsmen, and the provision of mortgage insurance. The government's role has begun to broaden as RCF services become more clearly linked to Medicaid and other elements in the long-term care continuum (Mollica, 1998).

ROBERT NEWCOMER

See also
   Adult Day Care
   Ambulatory Care
   Assisted Living: A New Model of Supportive
      Housing with Long-Term Care Services

BODY COMPOSITION

One might expect that studies of body composition would include the volume and chemical composition of body fluids and the size and composition of organs. However, although many of these subjects have been studied individually, body composition as a whole has not been assessed in such a detailed fashion. Rather, when investigating body composition, physiologists have concentrated on measuring height and weight (body mass), as well as components of body mass. The model most used to determine components of body mass has been the classic two-compartment model, in which body mass is divided into fat mass and fat-free mass (often called lean body mass). To estimate the size of these two compartments, measurements of body density or total body water or total body potassium are most commonly used (Holloszy & Kohrt, 1995). Because each of these yields data on fat mass and fat-free mass that are based on different assumptions, each yields somewhat different numerical values. In recent years, improvements in the technology of neutron activation analysis and dual-energy x-ray radiography have led to the development of multicompartment models. The components of a six-compartment model (Heymsfield & Waki, 1991) are fat, water, protein, osseous mineral (mineral content of bone), extraosseous mineral, and carbohydrate. The first component is the same as the fat component of the two-compartment model; the combined last five components are similar to the fat-free mass, or lean body mass, of the two-compartment model.

Height and Weight

Height decreases with age, starting at age 20 in women and age 25 in men (Spirduso, 1995). Over an 11-year period, the height of men in the 55–64 age range decreased on average one-half inch; that of women in the same age range decreased by one inch. The loss in height is primarily due to compression of the cartilaginous disks between the vertebrae and to vertebral bone loss.

Based on both cross-sectional and longitudinal studies, body weight increases in men and women up to age 55. In cross-sectional studies, body weight was found to decrease after age 55. However, longitudinal studies show that it continues to increase until age 65, after which it decreases, probably accelerating with advancing age (Carmelli, McElroy, & Rosenman, 1991). The difference between the cross-sectional and longitudinal studies is probably due to a birth-cohort effect.

Fat-Free Mass and Its Components

Based on cross-sectional studies, it appears that fat-free mass (lean body mass) is relatively stable in men and women until about age 40 (Holloszy & Kohrt, 1995). Between ages 40 and 60, fat-free mass declines with age, a decrease of about 3% per decade in men and 4% per decade in women; the decline between ages 60 and 80 is about 6% per decade for men and 10% per decade for women. However, these values are based on cross-sectional studies and thus may be an overestimate due to birth-cohort effects.

In a cross-sectional study on nonhuman primates, fat-free mass was also found to decrease with advancing age (Hudson, Baum, Frye, Roecker, & Kemnitz, 1996). However, in a longitudinal study on rats, there was no decrease in fat-free mass until just before death (Yu, Masoro, Murata, Bertrand, & Lynd, 1982).

Whereas total body water decreases in humans with increasing adult age, there is debate as to whether this decrease relates primarily to a change in intracellular or extracellular water (Steen, 1988). The decrease in total body water is proportional to the decrease in fat-free mass.

Osseous mineral decreases with age in both men and women (Snead, Birge, & Kohrt, 1993). In men the decrease is proportional to the decrease in fat-free mass, but in postmenopausal women the decrease is greater than the decrease in fat-free mass.

Fat Mass

In humans, body fat content increases until late middle age (Kohrt, Malley, Dolsky, & Holloszy, 1992). For example, sedentary men in their 20s have a fat content of about 17%, compared to 29% for sedentary men in their 60s. Although endurance-trained men have a lower fat content than do sedentary men, they also show an age-associated increase in body fat; endurance-trained men in their 20s have a fat content of about 10%, compared to 17% for comparably trained men in their 60s. A similar pattern has been shown in women. Sedentary women in their 20s have a fat content of about 24%, compared to 38% for sedentary women in their 60s. Endurance-trained women in their 20s have a fat content of about 17%, compared to 25% for endurance-trained women in their 50s. However, at ages older than the 60s, the body fat content of both men and women decreases (Kannel, Gordon, & Castelli, 1979).

Rhesus monkeys also exhibit an increasing fat content through middle age, followed by a decrease in old age (Hudson, Baum, Frye, Roecker, & Kemnitz, 1996). In rats, too, body fat increases until middle age and declines in late life (Bertrand, Lynd,

Masoro, & Yu, 1980). It seems likely that this pattern of change in fat content with age is common to most mammals.

The increase in body fat with age occurs preferentially in the abdominal region in humans (Shimokata, Tobin, Muller, Elahi, Coon, & Andres, 1989). Men have a progressive increase in abdominal fat with increasing adult age, but such an increase does not occur in women until they are postmenopausal. (Young women have a preferential distribution of fat in the buttocks and thighs.) Studies using magnetic resonance imaging or dual-energy absorptiometry indicate that the age-associated increase in abdominal fat is primarily visceral rather than subcutaneous (Ley, Lees, & Stevenson, 1992). Habitual exercise decreases the age-associated redistribution of body fat (Kohrt, Malley, Dolsky, & Holloszy, 1992). Increased levels of abdominal visceral fat heighten the risk of coronary heart disease (Williams, Jones, Bell, Davies, & Bourne, 1997), stroke (Walker, Rimm, Ascherio, Kawachi, Stampfer, & Willett, 1996), hypertension (Selby, Friedman, & Quesenberry, 1989), and diabetes mellitus (Ohlson, Larsson, Svardsudd, Welin, Eriksson, Wilhelmsen, et al., 1985).

EDWARD J. MASORO

See also
    Bone
    Biology of Fat in Aging, The
    Obesity
    Sodium Balance and Osmolality Regulation

BONE
See
    Calcium Metabolism
    Osteomalacia
    Osteoporosis
    Parathyroid Hormone, Calcitonin and 1,25 Dihydroxyvitamin D

BRAIN IMAGING
See
    Central and Peripheral Nervous Systems Morphology
    Medical Imaging

BRAIN MEMBRANE AND ENERGY METABOLISM: MAGNETIC RESONANCE SPECTROSCOPY ANALYSES

In the brain, aging can be characterized as a gradual decline in the ability to maintain normal membrane function. In brain, plasma membranes appear to be the most vulnerable to normal aging of the various cellular organelles (Bosman, Bartholomeus, & de Grip, 1991). The brain is exquisitely dependent on a constant supply of energy for the survival of neurons. The critical energy dependency of the brain is predominantly due to the synaptic discharge of the neurons and the accompanying synaptic processes such as 5'-adenosine triphosphate (ATP)–dependent ion pumping. Magnetic resonance spectroscopy (MRS) is an excellent physical technique to measure levels of metabolites that reflect membrane and high-energy metabolism in brain. Changes in membrane and high-energy metabolism with aging provide molecular insights into brain aging and help to distinguish aging effects from those of degenerative diseases, such as Alzheimer's disease (AD).

Magnetic Resonance Spectroscopy

In order for a molecule to be detected by MRS, it must have an element with an intrinsic nuclear spin (uneven number of protons and neutrons in the nucleus). The nuclear spin produces a magnetic moment that is responsive to a magnetic field. To obtain an MRS spectrum, a radiofrequency pulse characteristic for the nuclei of interest is applied for a few microseconds while the sample is in a strong, uniform magnetic field. The movement of the nuclear dipoles results in a small electrical signal that is recorded by a spectrometer and mathematically processed to produce a conventional MRS spectrum (Figure 1a). The chemical environment of nuclei significantly affects MRS spectral patterns, predominantly through covalent bonds, which facilitates identification of metabolites; ^{1}H and ^{31}P are the nuclei most commonly utilized for biological applications.

MRS techniques are adaptable for studying brain tissues from a variety of sources, such as autopsy tissue, freeze-clamped brain tissue that is frozen

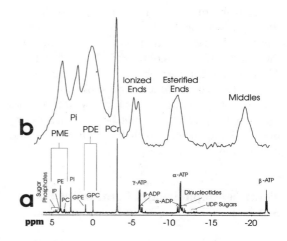

FIGURE 1   Comparison of (**a**) ^{31}P MRS in vitro spectrum of perchloric acid extract of freeze-clamped rat brain tissue at a magnetic field strength of 11.7 Tesla and (**b**) ^{31}P MRS in vivo spectrum of human brain (dorsal prefrontal cortex) at a magnetic field strength of 1.5 Tesla. In the in vivo spectrum, ionized ends = γATP and βADP, the esterified ends = αATP and αADP, and middles = βATP. PME, phosphomonoesters; Pi, orthophosphate; PDE, phosphodiesters; PCr, phosphocreatine; IP, phosphoinositol; PE, phosphoethanolamine; PC, phosphocholine; GPE, glycerophosphoethanolamine; GPC, glycerophosphocholine; ATP, 5'-adenosine triphosphate; ADP, 5'-adenosine diphosphate; and UDP, uridine diphosphate. (*From* McClure, R. J., et al. Magnetic resonance spectroscopy applications for the neurosciences. *NEUROPROTOCOLS: A Companion to Methods in Neurosciences* 5:81–90, 1994, Academic Press, Inc., with permission.)

with liquid nitrogen at the time of harvesting, and intact living brain. Autopsy tissue is an important source of brain tissue for measuring membrane metabolite levels found to be stable after death; however, high-energy metabolites such as ATP and phosphocreatine (PCr) are not stable in autopsy tissue. Freeze-clamping brain tissue of animals minimizes the loss of labile high-energy metabolites. High-resolution in vitro ^{31}P MRS (Figure 1a) analyses of either water-soluble or lipid extracts of brain tissue provide measurements of the concentration of membrane phospholipids and individual phosphomonoesters (PME) and phosphodiesters (PDE), acknowledged precursors and catabolites, respectively, of membrane phospholipids. In vivo ^{31}P MRS is a noninvasive technique that provides measurements of both high-energy metabolites and PME and PDE classes of phospholipid metabolites. The in vivo spectra are obtained at lower resolution (Figure 1b) because of technical limitations, which results in the loss of detailed information for the individual PME and PDE metabolites. Brief examples of the application of MRS to membrane and high-energy metabolism follow.

Neurodevelopment and Aging of the Fischer 344 Rat

A number of ^{31}P MRS studies have been conducted in the Fischer 344 rat from newborn (12 hours of age) to aged (24 months of age) (Pettegrew, Panchalingam, Withers, McKeag, & Strychor, 1990). Water-soluble perchloric acid (PCA) extracts of freeze-clamped rat brains were analyzed by ^{31}P MRS. These studies demonstrate a marked influence on high-energy phosphate and membrane phospholipid metabolism during brain development and, to a lesser degree, aging. Concentrations of PME, phospholipid membrane precursors, are high in the newborn rat brain and rapidly decrease to their adult levels. The high PME levels in the developing brain probably reflect the active synthesis of membranes associated with the development of neuritic processes. In contrast, levels of PDE, phospholipid membrane catabolites, are very low in the newborn rat and then rapidly rise to their adult levels. The PME/PDE ratio, an estimate of membrane phospholipid turnover, is high in the newborn period (PME/PDE > 1500), rapidly decreases by 3 months of age (PME/PDE ≈ 1–2), and then remains relatively constant to 12 months of age. After 12 months of age the PME/PDE ratio decreases slightly (PME/PDE < 1), suggesting that membrane phospholipid breakdown is slightly greater than membrane phospholipid synthesis during the aging process.

The PCr/inorganic orthophosphate (Pi) ratio, a measure of brain energy metabolism, is low in the newborn rat until 5 days of age, then rapidly increases up to 3 months of age. The PCr/Pi ratio remains relatively constant until 12 months of age, then slowly increases to 24 months of age. This may indicate either that the aging brain synthesizes

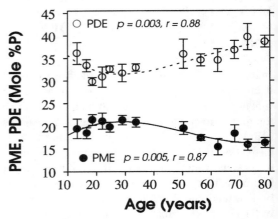

FIGURE 2   Mole % PME and PDE levels determined by ^{31}P in vivo MRS of the dorsal prefrontal cortex brain region of 62 human subjects of various ages. The open circles are PDE values; the closed circles are PME values. The data were group-averaged by age, with 3 to 8 samples per age region; the error bars show the standard error of the mean of the averaged points. (*From* McClure, R. J., et al. [31]P magnetic resonance spectroscopy study of brain metabolism in schizophrenia. In *Search for the Causes of Schizophrenia*, vol. 3, H. Hafner and W. F. Gattaz (Eds.), 228–251, 1995, Springer Verlag, with permission.)

PCr at an increased rate or that the aging brain utilizes PCr at a decreased rate.

^{31}P MRS of Aging Human Brain

In vivo ^{31}P MRS was performed on the prefrontal cortex of 62 normal volunteers, aged 12 to 81 years, in our laboratory (Panchalingam, Pettegrew, Strychor, & Tretta, 1990). All subjects had normal medical and neurological examinations. The in vivo ^{31}P MRS study demonstrated a decrease in the levels of PME with age and an increase in the levels of PDE (Figure 2). These findings probably reflect the loss of neuritic processes with normal aging. The changes in phospholipid metabolite levels are similar to the in vitro ^{31}P MRS results in aging rats (Pettegrew, Panchalingam, Withers, McKeag, & Strychor, 1990) discussed in the preceding section. There were no age-related changes detected in the in vivo levels of the high-energy metabolites PCr,

Pi, or ATP (Panchalingam, Pettegrew, Strychor, & Tretta, 1990).

Alzheimer's Disease

Many ^{31}P MRS studies have demonstrated alterations in membrane phospholipid metabolite levels in AD (reviewed in Pettegrew, Klunk, Panchalingam, McClure, & Stanley, 1997). Other studies have revealed alterations in the enzymes involved in phospholipid metabolism (Kanfer, Pettegrew, Moossy, & McCartney, 1993). The changes in phospholipid metabolite levels correlate with neuropathological hallmarks of the disease (Pettegrew, Moossy, Withers, McKeag, & Panchalingam, 1988) and measures of cognitive decline (Pettegrew, Panchalingam, Klunk, McClure, & Muenz, 1994). Glycerophosphocholine (GPC), a PDE phospholipid metabolite that is elevated in normal aging and more markedly in AD, enhances β-amyloid aggregation over fourfold (Klunk, Xu, McClure, Panchalingam, Stanley, & Pettegrew, 1997), providing a possible explanation for the significant influence of aging on the incidence of AD. A presumed clinically normal individual who later developed dementia showed alteration in these same membrane metabolite levels 4 years prior to the onset of any cognitive changes (Pettegrew, Klunk, Kanal, Panchalingam, & McClure, 1995). The changes in membranes also provide a plausible explanation for changes in other markers of AD such as deposition of Aβ peptide and possible predictors of the disease such as apolipoprotein E genotype (Pettegrew, Klunk, Panchalingam, McClure, & Stanley, 1997).

In a study in our laboratory (Pettegrew, Panchalingam, Klunk, McClure, & Muenz, 1994), the in vivo ^{31}P MRS spectra from 12 probable AD subjects (5 males, 7 females) and 21 control subjects (11 males, 10 females) 63 years of age or older were examined. Mattis test scores, a neuropsychological measure of clinical severity of AD, were used to classify the AD patients as mild (>120) or moderate (60–119). The results of this study demonstrate that PME levels of the mildly demented group are increased, compared to the moderately demented group. Also, PME levels correlate negatively with the clinical rating Mattis score. Taken together, these results indicate that the milder the dementia, the greater the PME levels. This suggests that alterations in membrane phospholipid metabolism could be an early "molecular trigger" in AD, perhaps resulting in alterations to mitochondrial membranes as well as the plasma membrane.

Levels of PCr were decreased in the mildly demented AD subjects and increase as the dementia worsened. The data indicate that both of the immediate precursors of ATP (PCR and 5'-adenosine diphosphate) are diminished early in AD. This decrease in energy availability and reserve may lead directly to neuronal dysfunction and possibly place neurons at more risk of neurotoxic insult from glutamate (Henneberry, 1989).

Conclusion

MRS provides useful information about the status of high-energy and phospholipid metabolism from observations of their characteristic metabolites. MRS is useful for studying AD brain both in vivo and in vitro. MRS findings in AD support the suggestion that derangement of both the membrane structure and the metabolism of characteristic membrane lipids exists, which would contribute to deranged cellular functions. MRS techniques are uniquely suited to assess these molecular changes.

RICHARD J. MCCLURE
KANAGASABAI PANCHALINGAM
WILLIAM E. KLUNK
JAY W. PETTEGREW

This work was supported in part by NIA grants AG08371, AG08974, AG50133, AG9017.

See also
Energy and Bioenergetics
Membranes

C

CALCIUM METABOLISM

Calcium and Life

Calcium is the fifth most abundant element in the earth's crust, where life evolved. A unique relationship exists between this key mineral and the molecules of life. Proteins, which constitute both the structural elements and the catalytic machinery of all cells, are essentially limp, floppy molecules. Their three-dimensional structure and functional activities depend upon binding metal ions that effectively stabilize and activate them. While several metals serve this role for specific proteins, the ionic radius of the calcium atom is just right for binding to the folds of the peptide backbone of proteins; hence, calcium functions as a principal activator of most cell functions (Heaney, 1999).

To regulate that activation, resting cells must maintain very low levels of calcium in their internal water (the cytosol), typically less than $10^{-3} \times$ the concentration outside the cell. Then, when a cell action is called for (e.g., a muscle fiber is signaled to contract), calcium channels in the cell membrane open, calcium pours into the cytosol from the extracellular fluid, the contractile machinery is activated, and the cell contracts. Then calcium is promptly pumped back out, and the cell rests again. This description oversimplifies a much more complex process, but it captures its essential elements: (1) the role of calcium in activating virtually every cell function and (2) the way cells regulate this activation.

Multicellular organisms use calcium in two additional ways. Calcium is maintained at relatively high concentrations in the blood and extracellular fluids, where it is needed to facilitate such functions as blood coagulation and intercellular communication. Calcium is also the principal cation of the mineral of bones and teeth, tissues that serve mechanical functions essential to higher organisms.

Integration of the Calcium Control System

The three roles of calcium in animals—the intracellular, the extracellular, and the skeletal—are beauti-

fully integrated in ways that are still being explored. The best-understood aspect of the control system involves the regulation of ionized calcium level in the blood and extracellular fluid (ECF [Ca^{++}]), which in all vertebrates is maintained at about 1.25 mmol/L. This is accomplished in mammals by the concerted action of three hormones, parathyroid hormone (PTH), calcitonin, and calcitriol (the most active form of vitamin D). The PTH prevents ECF [Ca^{++}] from falling by (1) activating bone resorption, thus releasing calcium into the circulation; (2) raising the calcium excretory threshold at the kidney; and (3) stimulating conversion of vitamin D to calcitriol, thereby increasing extraction of calcium from ingested food. Calcitonin, working in the other direction, prevents ECF [Ca^{++}] from rising by suppressing bone resorption. In all these interactions the skeleton serves as a large, portable reserve of calcium, a reservoir to be drawn upon in time of need and, within limits, a place to store a calcium surplus in times of plenty.

Calcium Metabolism and Chronic Disease

The principal disorders involving the regulation of ECF [Ca^{++}], particularly prominent at the end of life, are over- or underactivity of the parathyroid glands and depletion of the skeletal calcium reserves. These result in hyperparathyroidism, hypoparathyroidism, and osteoporosis, respectively. Hyper- and hypoparathyroidism are relatively uncommon and generally not preventable.

Depletion of the Reserve. Osteoporosis is the most common of all bone diseases in the industrialized nations, and it contributes to virtually all late-life fractures. Osteoporosis has many causes (Heaney, 1997), but one of these is low calcium intake, particularly later in life when ability to utilize dietary calcium generally wanes. Calcium deficiency osteoporosis can be prevented by ensuring a high calcium intake, lifelong but particularly at two critical life stages—during adolescence, when most bone is being amassed under the impetus of growth, and after age 65, when body capacity to adapt to a low calcium intake decreases (thereby unmasking preexisting dietary inadequacies). More than 150 studies have been reported on this topic in the past 15 years (Heaney, 2000). Essentially all the investigator-controlled studies of augmented calcium intake showed greater bone gain during growth or reduced bone loss and fractures in the elderly. Additionally, more than 80% of the observational studies relating calcium intake to bone status have found higher bone mass and/or reduced bone loss with age in those consuming high-calcium diets. These findings have led to substantial upward revisions in recommended calcium intakes for most ages, but especially for the elderly (Food and Nutrition Board, 1997).

These revised recommendations move closer to but still are substantially below the calcium intakes of hunter-gatherer humans and high primates. The abundance of calcium in the biosphere and the essential link of calcium with life are reflected in high calcium contents in many plant tissues (which, of course, constitute the ultimate food of animals). The diets of all agriculture-based societies, by contrast, exhibit low calcium densities, mainly because they are based in seed foods (cereal grains and legumes), which today provide more than 60% of the caloric intake of the world's population but which were virtually absent from the paleolithic diet to which our physiologies adapted over the millennia of evolution.

The Luminal Function of Diet Calcium. A second group of disorders is based on the functionality of unabsorbed calcium in the gut lumen. Our bodies are adapted to prevent calcium intoxication rather than to deal with chronic scarcity; hence, gut absorption of calcium is very poor, with net absorption averaging about 10% at recommended intakes. The unabsorbed calcium forms complexes with (and hence detoxifies) certain other food residues, mainly oxalic acid and unabsorbed bile and fatty acids. Oxalate is an important contributor to kidney stone risk, and by preventing its absorption from the intestinal lumen, high-calcium diets reduce the risk of developing kidney stones (Curhan, Willett, Rimm, & Stampfer, 1993). Similarly, by forming salts with unabsorbed fatty acids and bile acids, calcium neutralizes their irritant effect on the colon mucosa. In individuals with a propensity for colon cancer, high-calcium diets effectively remove these substances from the colon contents and stop

their calcium-promoting action (Holt, Atillasoy, Gilman, Guss, Moss, Newmark, et al., 1998; Baron, Beach, Mandel, van Stolk, Haile, Sandler, et al., 1999).

Dietary Calcium and Cellular Calcium Dysregulation. A final group of disorders arises because of unusual sensitivity to the body's normal reaction to low calcium intakes. When absorbed dietary calcium is insufficient to sustain ECF [Ca^{++}], PTH secretion rises and, as noted above, stimulates synthesis of calcitriol from vitamin D, which thereby directly improves intestinal calcium absorption. In addition to this action, calcitriol also opens, slightly, the calcium channels in cells throughout the body, allowing calcium to move more readily into their cytosol. The cells work to pump it back out, but in certain individuals with limited capacity, cytosolic [Ca^{++}] rises, leading to partial cellular activation. This appears to be the mechanism by which low calcium intakes contribute to hypertension (Appel, Moore, Obarzanek, Vollmer, Svetkey, Sacks, et al., 1997). In this case it is the arteriolar smooth muscle cell that is activated, maintaining a higher than appropriate level of arteriolar contractile tension. Recently, similar effects have been observed in human fat cells, which, when exposed to high levels of calcitriol, exhibit elevated cytosolic [Ca^{++}] and switch cell activity from lipolysis to lipogenesis (Zemel, Shi, Zemel, & DiRienzo, 2000). This latter effect, for which there is now an impressive array of ancillary evidence, is probably behind the otherwise puzzling observation that risk of obesity is inversely related to dietary calcium intake. Other disorders linked to low calcium intake and possibly explained by the same basic mechanism, include two problems of the reproductive years, premenstrual syndrome (Thys-Jacobs, Starkey, Bernstein, & Tian, 1998) and polycystic ovary syndrome (Thys-Jacobs, Donovan, Papadopoulos, Sarrel, & Bilezikian, 1999).

In this third group of disorders, tissues with limited ability to counter the tendency of calcium ions to enter the cell express one or more of their characteristic actions, but in this case inappropriately. Such disorders may be likened to favism, a hemolytic anemia occurring in individuals of Mediterranean ancestry who have a defective gene for a key energy-producing enzyme (glucose-6-phosphate dehydrogenase). When such individuals consume fava beans (or are given certain drugs such as antimalarials), which interfere with energy metabolism in red blood cells, cell access to energy drops and the cells die, releasing their hemoglobin into the blood stream. It takes an inherent susceptibility (G-6-PD deficiency) plus a trigger (fava beans) for the anemia to manifest itself. Similarly, in these calcium-related disorders, it takes a combination of at least two (and perhaps three) factors for the disease to express itself (e.g., an inherent sensitivity, triggered by low calcium intake). Thus, not all persons with low calcium intakes will be obese or develop hypertension or suffer PMS. All these disorders are, of course, multifactorial, and low calcium intakes explain only a part of each problem. Nevertheless, removing the trigger prevents the expression of the disorder in the subsets of the population with the requisite susceptibilities.

Race and the Calcium Requirement.   There are important racial differences in how these interactions express themselves. Thus, Blacks have a bony apparatus relatively resistant to PTH (Aloia, Mikhail, Pagan, Arunachalan, Yeh, & Flaster, 1998). Hence, they are able to build and maintain a skeleton on lower calcium intakes than Whites or Asians can. But, for the same low calcium intakes, they necessarily have higher PTH and calcitriol levels than do Whites. This may well be the explanation for both the low risk of osteoporosis and the high risk of hypertension in Blacks, as well as for the blood pressure reduction produced by milk in Blacks. Currently, the functional indicator for determination of the human calcium requirement is skeletal health. This is probably the wrong indicator for Blacks, in whom the calcium requirement for cardiovascular health is higher than for skeletal health.

The primitive human diet, for persons of contemporary body size, would have provided 2000–3000 mg/day of calcium. Intakes today (1200–1800 mg) probably provide most or all of the benefits of the aboriginal diet. Intakes lower than 1200 mg will almost certainly increase individual risk of a bewildering variety of seemingly unrelated diseases, as well as the population burden and cost of those disorders.

ROBERT P. HEANEY

See also

Osteoporosis

Parathyroid Hormone, Calcitonin, and 1,25 Dihydroxyvitamin D

CANADIAN RESEARCH ON AGING: RECENT STUDIES

Canadian research on aging covers many aspects of individual, cohort, and population aging. Canadian research centers and groups focusing on aspects of aging are based primarily at universities and teaching hospitals but also include two governmental centers of aging-related data and research. Acclaimed data-and-research initiatives in this field are the longitudinal Aging in Manitoba Study and the Canadian Study on Health and Aging.

In addition to the data sources just cited, a wide variety of other sources are used to support research on aging in Canada. These include the censuses of Canada, General Social Survey, Health and Activity Limitation Survey, Survey on Ageing and Independence, Survey of Old Age Security and Canadian Pension Plan Retirement Recipients, and the National Population Health Survey. Furthermore, there are small-scale surveys mounted in local areas or among special populations by university-based researchers, notably the recent survey of Chinese elderly in British Columbia, involving centers on aging at the University of Victoria and at Simon Fraser University.

This article will focus on studies that treat aspects of persons and populations and thus will omit those dealing with characteristics of caring systems or procedures targeted largely at the elderly. Among the fields of aging research that are of concern here, at least four recurrent fields of concentration are prominent in recent research on aging in Canada. These may be characterized as individual aging, demography of aging, living arrangements (including institutionalization), and elders' informal networks and supports. Each of these topics will be the subject of brief commentary below.

Several additional themes in Canadian research merit further discussion; however, space limitation precludes more than their identification. These themes include elder care (Keating, Fast, Frederick, Cranswick, & Perrier, 1999), self-care among older adults, elder abuse (Aronson, Thornwell, & Williams, 1995), determinants of healthy aging (Chappell, 1998), older workers, leisure (Pedlar, Dupuis, & Gilbert, 1996), retirement (McDonald, 1996), volunteering among the elderly, consumer expenditures and behavior (Zimmer & Chappell, 1996), and patterns of service utilization.

Individual Aging

Disease processes and functional deficits highly correlated with progress through advanced ages are a major focus of Canadian studies on aspects of individual aging. Studies of dementia and of needs of families who care for a demented member are especially notable (see, e.g., Tuokko, MacCourt, & Heath, 1999). Researchers at the medical faculties of Dalhousie University and the University of Manitoba have collected data in seven major clinical dementia centers across Canada and are analyzing risk factors associated with vascular cognitive impairment and related issues in diagnosis.

Tracking trends over time in the nature and degree of changes in ADL (activities of daily living) function, IADL (instrumental activities of daily living) function, and aspects of frailty has been a focus of recent research at Simon Fraser University. Based on Waves I and II of the Canadian Study of Health and Aging, the work includes tests of the predictive power of self-reported health status with regard to frailty, institutionalization, and death over a 5-year period. Researchers at the centers on aging at the University of Manitoba and the University of Victoria collaborated in a longitudinal study of chronic illness and disability in later life. The study focused on the effects on disability of chronic conditions, use of resources, and personal and social factors.

Several studies have addressed issues in the area of changing muscle strength and function with aging (see, e.g., Winegard, Hicks, & Vandervoot, 1996). Others have analyzed memory change with aging (Hultsch, Hertzog, Dixon, & Small, 1998).

Demography of Aging in Canada

Since the early 1970s there have been several Canadian studies in the demography of aging. Most of these rather global analyses of aspects of aging have come out of Statistics Canada, Québec Bureau of Statistics, and Département de demographie at l'Université de Montréal. Notable among the most recent studies are cohort-oriented analyses (e.g., Denton & Spencer, 1999).

Population Aging and Attributes of the Older Population. Profiles of the changing size and composition of the senior population, geographic distribution and mobility, and living arrangements are commonly found in the Canadian demographic studies (Moore, Rosenberg, & McGuinness, 1997). Interrelationships among socioeconomic characteristics of the elderly population are recurrently a concern of these studies (see, e.g., Hurtubise, Légaré, & Carrière, 1997).

In 1996, Canada's older population constituted 12.2% of the total population (3.53 million aged 65 or more). Persons aged 75 comprised 5.1% (1.47 million). Women predominate in the 75 and older age group, and many are widows and live alone. Over one-third of these women live below the low-income cut-off as defined by Statistics Canada. After the age of 80, the prevalence and severity of disability increases rapidly with aging, and the need for support is significantly affected (Moore, Rosenberg, & McGuinness, 1997).

Life Expectancy. Several Canadian studies address issues involving life expectancy and associated gender differences. Increased attention is being focused on length of life free of moderate or severe disability. Notable in this focus is concern with socioeconomic factors in disability-free and handicap-free life expectancies. It has been found that, at the age of 65, women can expect to live another 19 years and men another 15 years. However, the gender gap is much narrower for disability-free life expectancy. Disability-free life expectancy for those 65 years and older is 9 years for women and 8 years for men (Wilkins, Rochon, & Lafontaine, 1995).

Implications of Population Aging. A feature of recent analyses of aspects of Canadian population aging is the significant number of papers that raise cautions concerning the tendency of media and public policy officials to attribute various economic, social, and health care system problems to the aging of the population (Gee & McDaniel, 1992). These studies acknowledge that population aging is a factor in the range of processes discussed; but generally they contend that too much focus is being placed on aging when much more influential factors are evident and worthy of analysis and policy concern (Denton, Fretz, & Spencer, 2000; Gee & Gutman, 2000).

Living Arrangements and Institutionalization of the Elderly

Studies on living arrangements, including aspects of residence in institutions, have had a prominent place in the profile of Canadian studies since the 1970s. Several studies have analyzed factors that help to predict institutionalization. Recent studies focus on ways of anticipating how the evolution of sociodemographic characteristics of tomorrow's elderly will affect the demand for institutional facilities in the future (Carrière & Pelletier, 1995). Other studies have highlighted the substantial increase in people living alone after age 65 in Canada, attributing this in large part to the improvement of the economic situation of older persons (Légaré, Martel, Stone, & Denis, 1998).

Several studies have dealt with patterns of family care provided to residents of institutions. How families participate in the care of members who are institutionalized, and the consequences of this caring activity have been addressed in Rosenthal, Sulman, and Marshall (1992) and in Gladstone (1995).

Elders' Informal Networks and Supports

Work on the informal support networks of older persons has helped establish a picture of the relative roles played by various family members in providing support to older persons (McDaniel & McKinnon, 1993). As well, Canadian researchers have been exploring the experiences of childless older persons and the influence of both marital and parent status on informal support in later life (Wu & Pollard, 1998). Canadian research also has made a major contribution to the understanding of sibling ties in later life, a relatively unexplored but potentially significant tie in older age (Campbell, Connidis, & Davies, 1999). Research is also under way on the relationships between informal and formal care in the community setting (Penning, 1995).

Several Canadian studies have dealt with intergenerational relations, focusing on adult children and their parents, as well as support issues arising from co-residence of older persons with their children (Penning, 1998). The experiences of middle-aged women, especially issues associated with the playing of multiple roles by those involved in parent care, have been a focus of analysis in the 1990s

(Rosenthal, Martin-Matthews, & Matthews, 1996). The impact of family composition on the pattern of flow of supports to older parents also has been examined (Connidis, Rosenthal, & McMullin, 1996). Parent-child exchanges of supports have been examined in the context of social policy issues pertaining to intergenerational equity (Stone, Rosenthal, & Connidis, 1998).

LEROY STONE

See also
  International Perspectives
  Longitudinal Studies: Europe

CANCER

Cancer is characterized by an increase in the number of abnormal cells derived from a given normal tissue, invasion of adjacent tissues by these abnormal cells, and in the case of metastatic disease, lymphatic or blood-borne spread of malignant cells to regional lymph nodes and distant sites. An interplay between genetic and environmental factors is involved in the development of cancer. A large body of evidence indicates stable mutations of the cellular DNA must occur before a cell becomes malignant. These mutations can arise from exposure to environmental chemical carcinogens, endogenous or exogenous oxidants, ionizing radiation, or UV light. In the absence of a perfectly efficient DNA repair system, such DNA lesions or mutations become fixed in the cellular genome and accumulate with time (Ames, 1989).

In many human cancers the incidence rises exponentially with age. Cumulative cancer risk increases with the fourth power of age in both short-lived species such as rats and mice (~30% have cancer by the end of the 2–3-year life span) and long-lived species such as humans (~30% have cancer by the end of an 85-year life span) (Ames, 1989; Henderson, Ross, & Pike, 1993). These data strongly suggest that multiple cumulative events are required for the development of cancer. In fact, cancers that are found with increased frequency in older adults such as lung, colon, breast, and prostate cancer have been shown to require multiple mutagenic events. This multistep process of carcinogenesis begins with preneoplastic changes which may under certain conditions progress to malignant cancers. Studies of colorectal cancer by Vogelstein et al. have demonstrated this multistep process at the molecular level. The development of colorectal tumors requires the progression from normal mucosa to late-stage adenomas, and finally to carcinoma. During neoplastic progression of colon cancer, colonic mucosal cells accumulate a series of genetic alterations/mutations, including activation of the ras oncogenes as well as the inactivation of the p53 tumor suppressor gene (Sidransky, 1996).

Reduction of total calories consumed per day (30%–40% reduction) has been shown to have dramatic effects on aging and cancer in several experimental animal models. Caloric restriction (CR) retards the rate of aging, delays the appearance of age-related pathologies, including cancer, and extends the life span of several animal species (McCay, Crowell, & Maynard, 1994; Thurman, Bucci, Hart, & Turturro, 1994; Weindruch & Walford, 1988). Considerable evidence indicates that CR markedly retards spontaneous tumor formation in rodents (summarized by Weindruch, Waldford, Fligiel, & Guthrie, 1986). CR decreases tumor incidence and increases p53 gene expression in breast tumors in the cancer-prone MMTV/v-Ha-*ras* transgenic mouse (Fernandes, Chandrasekar, Troyer, Venkatraman, & Good, 1995). In addition, CR has recently been shown to delay spontaneous tumorigenesis in mice carrying a mull mutation of the p53 tumor suppressor gene (Hursting, Perkins, & Phang, 1994). However, the mechanism(s) of tumor suppression by CR are poorly understood: It is not known if a single common mechanism or multiple mechanisms are involved in tumor suppression and life span extension by CR in rodents. Studies are currently under way in nonhuman primates to determine if CR has similar effects on aging, age-related diseases, and life span (Roth, Ingram, & Lane, 1999). The effects of CR on human aging processes and age-related diseases are not known.

Normally, cells that develop abnormalities are detected and removed from tissues by the process of apoptosis (*q.v.*). In contrast with the process of necrosis (the form of cell death that follows, for example, lack of oxygen), apoptosis does not provoke inflammatory responses from the surrounding tissue. Normal cells are already primed to undergo apoptosis but are inhibited from doing so by messages exchanged with other cells. If some abnormality in a cell disrupts its capacity to participate properly in this exchange of messages, the apoptotic mechanism will be triggered. It is possible that ability to evade this complex process of "mutual policing" in tissues is an important element in the survival of potentially cancerous cells.

It has been known for many years that normal cells in culture can undergo only a limited number of cell divisions, the so-called Hayflick limit (Hayflick, 1965). Human fetal cells can divide about 50 times but cells from older subjects have a capacity for fewer divisions than cells from younger individuals. Cancer cells can continue to divide indefinitely. The means whereby normal cells can "count" how many division they have undergone has been obscure but is now thought to rest with the telomere (*q.v.*).

Telomeres are specialized structures at the ends of chromosomes that function in chromosome protection and replication (Blackburn, 1991). In vertebrates, telomeres consist of hundreds to thousands of tandem repeats of the DNA sequence TTAGGG and associated proteins (Blackburn, 1991; Moyzis, Buckingham, Cram, Dani, Deaven, Jones, et al., 1988). In all normal somatic cells examined to date, chromosomes lose about 50–200 nucleotides of telomeric sequence per cell division (Allsopp, Vaziri, Patterson, Goldstein, Younglai, Futcher, et al., 1992; Harley, Futcher, & Greider, 1990; Vaziri, Schachter, Uchida, Wei, Zhu, Effros, et al., 1993). Telomere shortening has been proposed as the mitotic clock by which cells count their divisions (Harley, 1991), and a significantly short telomere may signal replicative senescence in normal somatic cells (Allsopp et al., 1992; Vaziri, Schachter, Uchida, Wei, Zhu, Effros, 1993; Martin, 1994). Telomeres are believed to shorten because most normal somatic cells lack the enzyme telomerase, a specialized enzyme needed to synthesize new telomeric repeats (Marx, 1994). In most human cancer cells studied to date, the cellular production of the telomerase enzyme is somehow reactivated, an event that may contribute to the cells' ability to divide continuously or become immortal (Counter, Avilion, LaFeuvre, Stewart, Greider, Harley, et al., 1992; Kim, Piatyszek, Prowse, Harley, West, Ho, 1995). A survey of telomerase activity in a wide variety of human cells and tissues revealed the presence of telomerase in 98 of 100 cultured immortal cell lines, 90 of 101 primary tumors, and adult germ line tissues. Telomerase was undetectable in 22 normal somatic cells cultures and in 50 normal or benign tissue samples. It has now been shown that introducing telomerase into normal human cells will, as predicted, extend their capacity to divide (Bodnar, Ouelette, Frolkis, Holt, Chiu, Morin, et al., 1998).

It has been suggested that in long-lived species such as humans, lack of telomerase in somatic cells evolved as a means of reducing the probability of cancer. This seems unlikely since the Hayflick limit is set at a level more than sufficient to support fatal malignancies. Furthermore, because cancer is, in general, a disease of later life, selection pressure against it would have been weak during our evolution (Medawar, 1952). It is more likely that the lack of infinite capacity for replication of somatic cells, as distinct from germ cells, evolved simply as a means of not wasting energy and resources in attempts to prolong the existence of bodies that inevitably have limited life spans (Kirkwood & Rose, 1991).

During the past decade, molecular biology has made enormous contributions to our understanding of the regulation of normal cell proliferation and the genetic and molecular bases of cancer and aging. Disturbances in the regulatory pathways controlling normal cell division have been shown to be involved in the uncontrolled proliferation that is characteristic of cancer cells and the loss of replicative potential seen in senescent cells. Two new classes of "cancer genes" were identified: oncogenes, which stimulated cell proliferation and the development of cancer, and tumor suppressor genes that inhibited cell proliferation and the development of neoplastic cells. The transforming genes identified in RNA tumor viruses (oncogenes) were shown to be homologous with genes in normal human DNA (proto-oncogenes). Furthermore, the activation and/or altered expression of these proto-oncogenes were shown to be responsible for the expression of the cancer phenotype. The protein products tumor suppressor genes have been found to prevent the emergence of the malignant phenotype. These tumor suppressor proteins were shown to be components of cellular growth inhibitory pathways, which negatively regulate or inhibit cell proliferation. Mutated versions of tumor suppressor genes (antioncogenes) lose their capacity to inhibit cell pro-

liferation, resulting in a disturbance in the critical balance between positive and negative regulators of cell division. In such instances, this crucial homeostatic balance is tipped in favor of uncontrolled proliferation.

ANNA M. MCCORMICK
HUBER R. WARNER
DAVID B. FINKELSTEIN

See also
  Cancer Control and Aging
  Cell Aging In Vitro
  Cell Aging Relationship Between In Vitro and
    In Vivo Models
  Mitochondrial DNA Normalities
  Senescence and Transformation

CANCER CONTROL AND AGING

Cancer control has been defined as a sequence of research from hypothesis testing to large-scale demonstration. Primary prevention is the most desirable goal of cancer control; secondary prevention (of morbidity and mortality associated with cancer) is also a major focus.

Prevention and Early Detection

For many years, older adults were not regarded as an appropriate target for cancer control and were excluded from prevention and control trials, much as they were from therapeutic trials. Now older adults have been identified as a special target group for cancer control efforts by such organizations as the National Cancer Institute (NCI), National Institute on Aging (NIA), and the American Cancer Society (ACS). This is appropriate because incidence of all major cancers (except testicular) is significantly higher among older than middle-aged or younger adults (Hansen, 1998). For example, more than half of all breast cancers are diagnosed in women older than 65 (Kimmick & Muss, 1997); incidence of colorectal cancer rises after the age of 50 and doubles with each successive decade (Cohen, 1996). However, due to limited inclusion in research trials, we know little about effectiveness of prevention and research among older adults; what we do know is based largely on extrapolation from studies of middle-aged cohorts.

Lifestyle Changes.   Conclusive data about reduction in cancer risks due to lifestyle changes among older adults is also lacking. However, behaviors that may lower cancer risk—eating more fruits and vegetables and less fat, exercising, and limiting alcohol (Tominaga, 1999)—also have other health benefits and thus may generally be encouraged among older adults. Further, participation in clinical trials to assess risk-reduction benefits of such behaviors also may be encouraged among older adults.

Smoking Cessation.   Tobacco use has been strongly linked to a variety of cancers and accounts for "some 20–30% of all sites of cancer" (Tominaga, 1999). Although we encourage smokers to quit long before they reach older ages, it is never too late to stop smoking. Cessation benefits take longer to achieve for lung cancer than for heart disease or stroke, but there are nevertheless compelling reasons to encourage cessation among older smokers. For example, cessation for a decade can result in 30%–50% reduction in lung cancer mortality (Cinciripini, Hecht, Henningfield, Manley, & Kramer, 1997). A number of programs targeted to older adults have achieved favorable quit rates (Rimer, Orleans, Cristinzio, Telepchak, & Keintz, 1994).

Chemoprevention.   The use of chemicals to prevent disease is a relatively new area in cancer control. Due to lack of conclusive data, chemoprevention recommendations are not straightforward among any age group. Unlike lifestyle changes that have across-the-board benefits, chemoprevention agents may raise one risk while lowering another. For example, the drug tamoxifen (Fisher, Constantino, Wickerham, Redmond, Kavanah, Cornin, et al., 1998), may reduce breast cancer risk while increasing risk of endometrial cancer. Moreover, tamoxifen use may have side effects and may prohibit simultaneous use with other potentially beneficial drugs, such as hormone replacement therapy. In the United States, women are considered candidates for tamoxifen use for primary prevention if their breast cancer risk equals that of a 60-year-old woman. Thus, more and more older women will likely consider tamoxifen use in coming years. How to assist their decisions about whether to use such chemoprevention agents is an important new area of cancer control research.

Cancer Screening Tests.   Prostate cancer screening is controversial because it has not been shown to reduce mortality, but for breast, cervical, and colorectal cancer, there is compelling evidence for the benefit of early diagnosis achieved through screening. For older men and women, yearly digital rectal exams and fecal occult blood tests are recommended yearly, with sigmoidoscopy every 5 years. Older women are advised by the NCI and ACS to get regular mammograms and Pap smears, but decisions about periodic screening past age 75 are left to individual women and their physicians. Comorbidities must be factored into all screening decisions. In the absence of solid data concerning screening benefits for older adults, clinical judgment and informed decision making must prevail. Advice from the 1992 Forum on Breast Cancer Screening, that women should continue to be screened well into their 70s if they are otherwise healthy (Costanza, 1992), may be prudent for other screening modalities.

Despite the fact that cancer risk increases with age, adults over 65 are less likely to be screened. Explanations are multifactorial. There is some evidence that older adults are less likely to understand cancer risks and benefits of screening (Skinner, Arfken, & Sykes, 1998). Also, their physicians may be less likely to recommend screening, because of lack of data supporting efficacy of screening or because many older adults have chronic or acute medical problems on which their providers focus to the exclusion of screening. Cost may become less of a barrier to screening in coming years; Medicare has already begun to cover mammography costs for enrolled women.

Family Issues in Cancer Control

We are now beginning to recognize the familial nature of cancer risk. In coming years it may become increasingly important for older adults with cancer to consider the roles of both nature and nurture in their family members' cancer risk.

Family History and Genetics.   Family history is a major contributor to cancer risk. A number of genetic mutations that greatly increase cancer risk have been identified (Futreal, Liu, Shattuck-Eidens, Cochran, Harshman, Tavtigian, et al., 1994; Wooster, Neuhausen, Mangion, Quirk, Ford, Collins, et al., 1994; Kinzler & Vogelstein, 1998), and genetic testing has become commercially available. In some ways, cancer genetics is a more salient issue for younger adults because cancers arising from inherited predispositions are often associated with early-age onset. However, older adults may have important information, either in their memories or in their genes, that applies to younger family members' cancer risks. Because an entire profile of cancer within extended families is important for estimating individuals' cancer risks, documentation of specific cancer diagnoses and ages of onset is quite important. Information from older relatives may be especially crucial in constructing an accurate family pedigree. Additionally, older adults who have survived an early cancer diagnosis may be the most appropriate family members for cancer genetic testing, and test results will have implications for younger family members.

Family Behaviors.   Behavioral factors related to cancer risk (e.g., diet, physical activity, smoking) also can be familial issues. Behaviors detrimental to one generation can be taught or modeled for the next, as when high-fat meals are routinely served or active and passive smoking (Hackshaw, 1998) are an integral part of home life. Older adults may play an important role in encouraging family members to reduce their own cancer risk by making lifestyle changes.

CELETTE SUGG SKINNER

See also
   Cancer

CARBOHYDRATE METABOLISM

Aging is associated with altered regulation of carbohydrate metabolism. The most significant clinical manifestation of altered carbohydrate metabolism, the syndrome of diabetes mellitus, is a growing health problem among the elderly. Diabetes in the elderly is most commonly associated with a stable elevation of blood glucose levels both after an overnight fast and following ingestion of a meal. This condition is often termed noninsulin dependent diabetes mellitus (NIDDM), but the American Diabetes Association has recently recommended that this terminology be replaced with type 2 diabetes (American Diabetes Association, 1999). The elevation of blood glucose levels with type 2 diabetes is not immediately life-threatening and does not usually require insulin therapy. However, type 2 diabetes is associated with a number of long-term complications, including accelerated atherosclerosis, kidney failure, nerve damage, and disturbances in vision.

The problem of overt diabetes represents only the tip of the iceberg of the abnormality of glucose and insulin dynamics in the elderly. Many studies have demonstrated that aging is associated with a more subtle abnormality characterized by a delay in the return of blood glucose to basal values following glucose ingestion (Davidson, 1979). Insulin resistance refers to a condition in which a given amount of insulin elicits a subnormal biological effect. Most older people with type 2 diabetes are insulin resistant, and even many older people who are not diabetic are insulin resistant. Independent of glucose tolerance status (i.e., the ability to lower glycemia after an oral glucose load), insulin resistance has been implicated as a risk factor in the development of atherosclerosis (Howard, O'Leary, Zaccaro, Haffner, Rewers, Hamman, et al., 1996).

Pathophysiology of Glucose Regulation in Aging

Skeletal muscle, liver, and adipose tissue are important insulin-sensitive tissues for regulating blood glucose concentration. Even in the absence of diabetes, each of these tissues may become insulin resistant in older people (Muller, Elahi, Tobin, & Andrew, 1996). Skeletal muscle is quantitatively the most important tissue for insulin-stimulated glucose disposal. The rate of glucose transport into the muscle cell is a critical, rate-controlling step for skeletal muscle glucose metabolism (Holman & Kasuga, 1997).

At the cellular level, insulin's binding to the insulin receptor leads to activation of the receptor's tyrosine kinase, which in turn phosphorylates several intracellular proteins, including the insulin receptor substrate (IRS) proteins (Holman & Kasuga, 1997). The tyrosine phosphorylated IRS proteins (in skeletal muscle, IRS-1 and IRS-2 are expressed) bind to downstream signaling proteins, including phosphatidylinositol-3-kinase (PI3-kinase). This enzyme is crucial for insulin-stimulated translocation of intracellular GLUT4 glucose transporter proteins to the cell surface and thereby increasing the glucose transport rate.

Skeletal muscle levels of GLUT4 are not greatly influenced by advancing age during adulthood (Houmard, Weidner, Dolan, Leggett-Frazier, Gavigan, Hickey, et al., 1995). This finding suggests that, rather than low GLUT4 abundance, the insulin resistance is attributable to a reduced ability of insulin to cause the GLUT4 glucose transporter to move from the cell interior to the cell surface, where it can facilitate glucose uptake. The precise molecular reason for the putative reduction in GLUT4 translocation is unknown.

Studies with experimental animals have clearly demonstrated an age-related impairment of function of the pancreatic B cells that secrete insulin (Reaven & Reaven, 1981). In elderly humans insulin levels during oral glucose tolerance tests tend to be relatively normal (Davidson, 1979), although interpretation of such responses is difficult because of the higher glucose levels during the test in the elderly. When this is taken into account, it appears that impaired B-cell adaptation to insulin resistance also plays a role in the age-related deterioration of glucose tolerance (Chen, Bergman, Pacini, & Porte, 1985). Circulating insulin concentration is determined by both insulin secretion and insulin clearance. Some, but not all, studies have indicated that, in addition to abnormal insulin secretion, insulin clearance rate is attenuated in older people (Muller, Elahi, Tobin, & Andres, 1996).

A number of potential mechanisms could be contributing to the age-related impairment of B-cell function or tissue insensitivity to insulin. Morphological studies of pancreatic islets suggest the presence of age-related B-cell damage (Reaven & Reaven, 1981). Reduced carbohydrate in the diet, which has been reported in some studies of dietary patterns of the elderly, also can result in diminished insulin secretion or carbohydrate intolerance.

Role of Lifestyle in Age-related Changes in Glucoregulation and Insulin Action

Lifestyle plays a pivotal role in age-related insulin resistance. Increased adiposity in elderly subjects

appears to be a critical factor, because there is a close association between adiposity and insulin resistance. Chronic physical inactivity is associated with elevated abdominal fat stores and insulin resistance (Holloszy & Kohrt, 1995). In young and old people, regular exercise training can improve insulin sensitivity. This benefit is the result of several adaptations, including reduced fat mass and increased skeletal muscle GLUT4 protein levels. Independent of these chronic adaptations, a single bout of vigorous exercise can lead to enhanced insulin sensitivity for as long as a day after the activity (Holloszy & Kohrt, 1995). Many insulin-resistant older people can benefit from physical activity–induced improvements in insulin action. However, exercise is not usually effective in restoring glucose tolerance when there is a profound deficit in pancreatic B-cell function.

Reduced calorie intake can lead to improved insulin sensitivity and glucose homeostasis. Calorie restriction leads to weight loss, especially visceral fat loss, and this effect is likely important for improved insulin action (Holloszy & Kohrt, 1995). Studies with rats indicate that the diet-induced improvement in insulin action is attributable, at least in large part, to enhanced glucose transport in skeletal muscle because of greater translocation of GLUT4 in response to insulin (Dean, Brozinick, Cushman, & Cartee, 1998).

Despite the known benefits of altered lifestyle on body composition and insulin sensitivity, the recent trend for increased prevalence of obesity in many societies suggests that age-related glucose intolerance and insulin resistance will continue to be important health problems.

GREGORY D. CARTEE

See also
Diabetes Mellitus

CARBOHYDRATES
See
Carbohydrate Metabolism

CARDIOVASCULAR SYSTEM: OVERVIEW

The cardiovascular system includes all of the blood vessels throughout the body and the heart, which provides the force necessary to move blood through the system. The effects of aging on this system are often confused with diseases and the effects of inactivity or deconditioning. Diseases of the cardiovascular system are the leading cause of death throughout the nation: it is estimated that 40% of individuals over the age of 65 die of heart disease. Fifteen percent of deaths in the aged are attributed to strokes. Both represent malfunctions within the cardiovascular system. Intense effort is focused on understanding cardiovascular diseases in an attempt to control illness and to preserve functioning of individuals until late in life.

Components of the Cardiovascular System

Arteries are relatively thick-walled tubes that carry blood away from the heart. A branching network of vessels carries blood to tissues throughout the body, where the arteries terminate in extremely small vessels called capillaries. The capillaries are microscopic in size, barely large enough for the passage of one blood cell at a time. Their walls are extremely thin, permitting transfer of nutrients and waste products between the blood within the capillary and surrounding tissues. The capillaries eventually join together and terminate in larger vessels called veins, which collect the blood and return it to the heart. Veins are relatively thin-walled, compared with arteries, but still contain muscle cells within their walls that permit contraction and expansion of the vessel size. As will be seen later, this contributes to the ability of the body to adjust the system capacity according to need. The purpose of the circulation system is to permit the collection of nutrients from ingested food and body stores and transport them to tissues in need of sustenance. By-products of the energy production process are carried away by the blood and discarded through the lungs and kidneys. Body temperature is preserved through heat retention or radiation by diverting blood to surface areas of extremities where heat is lost or by retaining blood circulation within the body core, thus preserving heat.

The heart provides blood movement. This organ represents two pumps in one package. Each pump has two chambers: an atrium and a ventricle, each of which contributes to pump performance. The right side of the heart receives blood returning from body tissues and forwards it to the lungs at a low pressure. In the lungs, oxygen is received and carbon dioxide eliminated. Blood returns from the lungs to the left side of the heart, where it is sent throughout the body at a relatively high pressure. Hormones secreted into the bloodstream are moved to target organs, where they induce various reactions. Nutrients from the intestine are transported to the liver for processing and then to body stores or tissues for metabolism. Wastes are moved to the kidneys and discarded in urine. Heat generated in this process is dissipated through the passage of warm blood through skin in the extremities where radiation or sweat evaporation provides needed cooling. All this is accomplished involuntarily.

Regulation of this remarkable system is exceedingly complex. Constant adjustments are being made to compensate for changes in workload, alterations in position, changing thermal demands, shifts in emotions, dietary intake, or trauma. The result of regulation is a precisely metered flow to vital organs in response to their need. Sensors detect changes in flow, pressure, temperature, metabolic components, and fluid composition, which are then balanced through system adjustments. Variations in heart rate and muscle tone in artery and vein walls and variable fluid reabsorption and excretion of blood components permit a careful balance of the system in the face of repeated environmental challenges. Even in the face of extreme conditions, a remarkable degree of balance is achieved.

Normal Aging

With the passage of time, elastin within the arterial walls changes somewhat. It becomes less resilient and somewhat elongated. Calcium deposition may occur where none was previously evident. The result is a loss of elasticity and slight elongation of arteries, resulting in tortuosity. Heart valves become less flexible. Some circulation shifts occur in blood flow as tissues decline in function. Kidney flow is substantially reduced. However, flow to the head and heart remain virtually constant throughout life. A rise in blood pressure occurs in part due to loss of arterial elasticity, with resultant failure to absorb the peak pressure generated by each heartbeat. Instead, the pulse is transmitted throughout the system as a rapid, high-pressure wave.

Heart changes with age are modest. A slight increase in the size of the heart muscle is attributed partly to higher arterial pressures. Loss of valve flexibility causes blood turbulence, with subsequent creation of murmurs. The maximum heart rate declines with age, yielding loss of some reserve. This is compensated for in part by a dilation of the heart with exercise, allowing more blood to enter the heart and a higher percentage of blood ejection per beat, resulting in little loss of performance throughout life. In the absence of disease, cardiovascular performance is capable of remaining excellent throughout life.

Cardiovascular Diseases

Atherosclerosis is the major problem affecting the cardiovascular system. Atheromatous plaques, which progressively restrict flow, develop within the interior lining of arteries. The plaques are composed of inflammatory cells, muscle cells, fat, and calcium. Initially evident as small streaks of yellow discoloration within arterial walls, seen in early life, the problem progresses until large areas of arterial wall are covered with thickened plaques in later years.

The cause of atherosclerosis is not fully understood. Age and genetic background are important. Males are more prone to the disease than females. Smoking substantially escalates atheromatous change, as does uncontrolled hypertension. Persons suffering from blood lipid abnormalities, diabetes, and obesity are known to suffer increased disease frequency. Personality factors (Type A) also have been thought to be associated with accelerated atheromatous degeneration. (See "Coronary-Prone Behavior.")

Vessel narrowing effectively reduces flow capacity. Initially, no effect is evident because the flow rate may still equal peak demand. Later, in stress situations, flow will be inadequate, and symptoms will develop. Late in the disease, symptoms will be evident at rest. Common clinical syndromes associated with atherosclerosis include leg pain when walking, the result of inadequate nutrient flow to leg muscles. Surgery can sometimes reopen narrowed vessels. On occasion, vessel replacement with grafts taken from elsewhere in the body or the use of synthetic materials may be necessary. When heart vessels are narrowed, chest pain (angina pectoris) may occur on exertion. Brief episodes of thinking problems, paralysis, or sensory disorders may be evident when brain circulation is compromised. When blood clots form at the site of narrowing, complete block of the artery can occur. Occasionally, small clots will form on the surface of plaques and break free to drift downstream (emboli). As the arterial system narrows, these clots will lodge and block circulation. A toe may suddenly turn blue. Occasionally, a foot or leg may be deprived of circulation by such events. When blockage occurs in arteries supplying the heart, a heart attack (myocardial infarction) will occur. Blockage in brain circulation results in a stroke (cerebral infarction). Medications can sometimes reestablish flow. Often there is no alternative but to await spontaneous recovery or development of alternative circulation routes around the blocked artery.

Aneurysms represent a weakness within arterial walls, with subsequent bulging. Aging, hypertension, and a small number of inherited diseases have been found associated with this condition. As a result of such events, the artery wall becomes stretched beyond its usual dimensions and is subject to rupture, commonly resulting in death. In its mildest form, no treatment is necessary. If life-threatening enlargement occurs, surgical replacement of the vessel, using a synthetic graft, is possible.

Venous diseases are fairly common among elderly persons. Varicosities are caused by nonfunctioning valves that normally direct blood flow back toward the heart. Genetic causes are usually suspected as the underlying problem. In many situations, varicose veins present purely cosmetic difficulties, and no treatment is required. If moderate or severely tortuous veins are present, skin deterioration and ulcer formation can occur. Elastic support stockings are extremely helpful in promoting normal blood return to the heart. Sometimes surgical removal of veins is helpful.

Phlebitis, or thrombophlebitis, is a term used to describe the formation of clots within veins, which subsequently become inflamed. Causes include coagulation disorders within the circulating blood system, local trauma, or inactivity. Failure to move extremities for prolonged periods results in sluggish blood flow and can promote clotting. Veins involved in clotting may become tender and firm to the touch, making diagnosis easy. Sometimes veins deep within the legs, arms, or pelvis will become clotted. Symptoms tend to be nonspecific such as swelling of an extremity or mild fever. The diagnosis can be established with contrast venography or color Doppler sonography. Prevention involves regular physical activity to promote normal circulation and avoiding long episodes of sitting in a chair or lying without motion. Elastic support hose will improve venous return and minimize chances of coagulation. Individuals placed at bedrest may require anticoagulants to reduce the chance of phlebitis formation.

Pulmonary emboli can occur when deep venous thrombosis (DVT) subsequently breaks free and drifts back to the lung (embolization) after passing through the right side of the heart. Small clots cause little problem, as ample reserve circulation exists to bypass blocked lung vessels. If large numbers of clots break free or a single large clot enters the lung circulation, life-threatening blockage can result. The body is capable of dissolving clots and reestablishing circulation, provided serious flow disruption does not occur. Diagnosis of this condition can be exceedingly difficult because symptoms are vague and nonspecific. Anticoagulants are sometimes effective in reducing clot formation and subsequent embolization during the healing process.

Heart valves can be damaged by a variety of mechanisms resulting in heart murmurs, which are due to turbulent blood flow across a valve. Flow can be blocked by failure of the valve to open properly. Valve leakage with blood backflow is possible when leaflets fail to seal properly. Valve replacement may be required to reestablish normal flow patterns through the heart. Valve damage also can occur when bacteria lodge on their surface, resulting in local destruction and valve dysfunction (bacterial endocarditis). Bacteria cast into the bloodstream from valve infections can spread throughout the body and present a host of confusing symptoms for the diagnostician. This condition requires intensive antibiotic therapy, and often replacement with a synthetic valve is necessary. For this reason anyone with a heart murmur should be considered for antibiotic therapy during diagnostic and surgical procedures associated with transient bacteria in the bloodstream, such as dental procedures and colonoscopy. Individuals with synthetic valves are at particular risk for developing bacterial endocarditis.

Angina pectoris occurs when arterial narrowing prevents satisfactory flow to heart muscle. The patient experiences chest pain or pressure, which spreads to the arms or jaw, commonly on the left side. Symptoms may be more vague in older adults, such as extreme fatigue or shortness of breath. Exercise aggravates the pain, and rest relieves it. Medications that limit cardiac response to exercise or alter blood circulation throughout the body can relieve symptoms. No muscle damage occurs, and each symptom episode is usually short-lived.

Myocardial infarction, commonly know as heart attack, is a more serious manifestation of arterial narrowing that results in heart muscle death when an atherosclerotic plaque ruptures and a clot forms. At the time of muscle injury, some individuals may be totally unaware that a problem exists. Diabetics are particularly susceptible to such silent events, owing to changes in their nervous system. Some individuals may suspect they are suffering "heartburn." Many elderly persons will manifest confusion, stomach upset, or weakness as their only symptoms. When severe, crushing, and prolonged chest pain occurs, associated with nausea, myocardial infarction is extremely likely. An electrocardiogram and measurement of enzymes within the bloodstream can provide definitive evidence of muscle damage. Treatment may involve thrombolytic agents to dissolve the clot or even emergent revascularization with balloon angioplasty and stent placement or coronary artery bypass graft surgery. Early mobilization rather than bedrest is now advocated following myocardial infarction. This does not interfere with healing and helps to prevent orthostaic symptoms, thromboembolic complications and musculoskeletal deconditioning. An outpatient cardiac rehabilitation program is generally recommended. Repeated infarction results in replacement of heart muscle with fibrous tissue and subsequent severe performance limitations.

Congestive heart failure is a syndrome characterized by cough, shortness of breath, and poor exercise tolerance. Sluggish flow through the lungs leads to fluid accumulation, with a characteristic cough and change in breath sounds heard through a stethoscope. Fluid may accumulate in feet and legs, giving a swollen, bloated appearance. Occasionally, fluid accumulation can progress to include the torso and body organs. Poor exercise tolerance is an inevitable result of decreased pumping ability of heart muscle. There are many causes of congestive heart failure. Atherosclerotic heart disease and myocardial infarction can damage the heart muscle, leading to dilation of the heart and decreased pumping ability. Untreated hypertension can lead to a thickening of the heart muscle, which compromises the ability of the heart to fill with blood, again limiting the pumping ability. It is estimated that 30% of individuals aged 90 have suffered deposits of a material called amyloid within heart muscle, which reduced performance substantially. Such deposits are especially common in the presence of chronic diseases such as rheumatoid arthritis. Viral illness also can seriously deteriorate heart muscle performance. Heart muscle disease of all types reduces pump performance, causing symptoms of congestive heart failure. Another common cause of congestive heart failure is a particular arrhythmia called atrial fibrillation, during which the pumping ability of the atria is lost and the heart functions with contraction of only the ventricles. Treatment of congestive heart failure includes fluid elimination by means of diuretics. Blood pressure and arterial resistance may be altered with a variety of new medications that have yielded outstanding symptom control. In the most serious cases of congestive heart failure, heart transplantation may be necessary.

Arrhythmia (irregular heartbeat) is an exceedingly common problem in elderly persons. The normal smooth sequential spread of electric activity throughout the heart chambers activating muscle contraction is interrupted. Absence of initiation of the beat, blockage of normal spread, and premature initiation in remote heart areas represent the most common malfunctions encountered. Failure to initiate the heartbeat within the normal sites found in the atrium can be compensated for by initiation of the heartbeat elsewhere within the system albeit at a reduced rate. Insertion of artificial pacemakers can often return the heart to its former level of performance. Blockage of normal beats as electric transmission occurs through the muscle can likewise be offset by artificial pacemakers, activating muscle beyond the block. Of much greater concern is initiation of rapid, uncoordinated beats or sudden absence of heartbeat, which commonly occurs at the moment of myocardial infarction. For this reason,

persons are placed on electronic monitoring equipment in coronary care units for a period of 2 or 3 days following a heart attack. Stability of heart rate over a period of 48 hours is associated with relatively few complications, and monitoring can be discontinued.

Orthostasis represents a loss of our ability to quickly adjust blood pressure to changes in position. Most individuals have experienced episodes of lightheadedness when quickly arising from a reclining or sitting position. The elderly are particularly affected by this condition, as arterial flexibility and changes in the nervous system reduce their ability to quickly raise blood pressure in response to position changes. Avoiding diuretics and the use of support hose can reduce symptoms in some individuals. Others are obliged to change position extremely slowly to avoid losing consciousness.

Syncope (fainting) is the result of a transient blood pressure loss. A frightening appearance is presented to the onlooker when an individual suddenly falls to the ground unconscious. The countenance is extremely pale, and blood pressure and pulse may be unobtainable. Usually spontaneous recovery begins immediately upon falling to the ground, and within a short period the person regains consciousness and improves in appearance. An evaluation is usually necessary to determine a cause, such as cardiac arrhythmia, blood loss, acute illness, stroke, or seizure. Frequently, no specific cause can be found, and it is attributed to orthostasis or nervous system dysfunction of unknown origin. At the first sign of dizziness, one should sit or recline to avoid total loss of consciousness. Regular meals and frequent position changes are thought to reduce the occurrence of this relatively common problem.

Shock is a term used to describe loss of blood pressure due to serious vessel damage. Unlike syncope, which is transient and benign, shock is life-threatening. Blood loss is a common cause of this condition. In the elderly, bleeding from an intestinal ulcer, diverticulitis, or angiodysplasia within the gait may be contributing factors. Anticoagulation can contribute to blood loss that may initially be hidden within body cavities, making diagnosis difficult. Immediate blood replacement is essential to bring blood pressure back to normal. Serious infections can cause loss of blood pressure due to the effects of bacterial toxin on capillary walls.

Fluid loss correlates with a dramatic drop in circulating blood volume and subsequent pressure reduction. Intensive antibiotic therapy coupled with fluid replacement is essential. Shock invariably requires intensive care, which is often delivered in specialized hospital units with automated monitoring equipment.

Hypertension is a particularly widespread problem in older persons. Although diastolic blood pressure levels off after age 60, the degeneration of elastin results in gradually increasing systolic blood pressure throughout later life. Elevated pressures increase the risk for stroke, atherosclerotic heart disease, heart failure, kidney disease, aortic disection, aortic aneurysm rupture, and retinal damage with loss of vision. Thus, maintenance of pressures below a level of 140–160/90 is desirable, with avoidance of orthostatic hypotension and maintenance of renal function. Weight loss, reduction of dietary salt intake, and modest exercise may lower blood pressure and avoid the need for medication. Diuretics are commonly employed to reduce vascular volume. Numerous agents are available to alter arterial and venous muscle tone, with subsequent pressure reduction. Flexibility and caution are required when approaching hypertension therapy in the elderly because of potential side effects of the medications.

Deconditioning of the cardiovascular system is thought to be a prevalent condition among the elderly. Loss of heart muscle strength and vessel responsiveness to central nervous system control are believed to result from inactivity. Data to support such a theory have begun to emerge from studies of astronauts experiencing prolonged weightlessness in space. Exercise protocols are now routine for space flights and have reversed the terrible debilitation documented in early exploration efforts. Exercise programs tailored to the needs of the elderly may prevent deterioration in muscle strength and cardiovascular performance among the elderly as well. This is currently an area of intense research.

Diagnosis

Numerous diagnostic methods are involved in determining cardiovascular diseases. Most important among them are a careful history and physical examination with measurement of blood pressure and heart rate and with auscultation of cardiac sounds, using the stethoscope. Electric activity of the heart can be documented by means of the electrocardiogram. Additional information is obtained when electric activity is checked during an exercise stress test such as a treadmill or bicycle ergometer evaluation. X-rays can determine abnormal cardiac configuration, and sound waves can be bounced from interior chambers to assess architectural variations. Radioactive material injected within the bloodstream permits painless assessment of heart performance at rest and exercise. Dye injected within the heart by means of a catheter passed through the arterial system can determine valve damage, cardiac chamber abnormalities, and cardiac circulation difficulties. Additional cardiac assessment tools are under development, which will further our understanding of performance of this critical system.

Health Promotion and Disease Prevention

A number of steps are possible to encourage optimal performance of the cardiovascular system. Smoking should be avoided because it promotes atherosclerosis and is associated with myocardial infarction. Blood pressure regulation in hypertension also will retard atheroma formation and reduce the occurrence of strokes. Careful regulation of sugar levels in diabetes is valuable in retarding cardiovascular problems. For those with elevated blood cholesterol level and in particular elevated LDL cholesterol level, a diet low in fat can help reduce the risk of cardiovascular disease. Regular exercise of even moderate intensity, such as walking performed five to six times per week, has been proposed as important for maintenance of cardiovascular system performance. Maintenance of an ideal weight by control of sugar and fat intake may promote health through its effects on blood pressure and cholesterol blood level. Taken together, such elements comprise a "healthy lifestyle" promoting cardiovascular health.

For additional research and its clinical implications, see the following references: Cassel, Cohen, Larson, Meier, Resnick, Rubenstein, et al. (1997);

Friesinger (1999); Hazzard, Blass, Ettinger, Halter, & Ouslander (1999).

ROBERT J. SULLIVAN, JR.
UPDATED BY HEIDI K. WHITE

See also

Blood
Cardiovascular System: The Heart
Cardiovascular System: Vascular
Framingham Studies of Heart Disease

CARDIOVASCULAR SYSTEM: THE HEART

Heart Structure and Function at Rest

Changes in Heart Size and Shape With Advancing Age in Humans. Studies of volunteer subjects without cardiovascular disease indicate that the left ventricular (LV) wall thickness increases progressively with age in both sexes. At rest, the LV cavity size at end-diastole and end-systole increases moderately with age in healthy, normotensive, sedentary men but does not vary with age in women. The age-associated increase in left ventricular wall thickness with aging is caused mostly by an increase in the average size of cardiac myocytes (muscle cells). An increase in the amount and a change in the physical properties of collagen (a protein that holds the myocytes together) also occurs within the myocardium with aging. However, the cardiac muscle-to-collagen ratio in the older heart either remains constant or increases.

There is an increase in elastic and collagenous tissue in all parts of the heart's conduction system with advancing age. Fat accumulates around the sinoatrial (SA) node, sometimes producing a partial or complete separation of the node from the atrial musculature. Beginning by age 60 there is a pronounced decrease in the number of pacemaker cells in the SA node, and by age 75 less than 10% of the pacemaker cell number found in the young adult remains. A variable degree of calcification of the left side of the cardiac skeleton, which includes the aortic and mitral annuli, the central fibrous body,

and the summit of the interventricular septum, occurs with aging. Because of their proximity to these structures, the atrioventricular (AV) node, AV bundle, bifurcation, and proximal left and right bundle branches may be affected by this process.

Age-Associated Changes in Heart Function in Humans at Rest. Supine, basal heart rate does not differ among younger and older individuals. In the sitting position, however, the heart rate decreases slightly with age in both men and women. The respiratory variation of the resting heart rate becomes diminished with advancing age, as does the spontaneous variation in heart rate. The decreased variation in heart rate is thought to be influenced by age-associated changes in both the parasympathetic and sympathetic nervous systems. A modest prolongation of the PR interval of the electrocardiogram occurs with aging in healthy individuals, and is localized to the proximal PR segment, probably reflecting delay within the atrioventricular junction. An increase in the number of premature beats occurs in healthy older men and women compared to their younger counterparts.

The peak rate at which the LV fills with blood during early diastole is reduced by 50% with aging between the ages of 20 and 80 years. The time

TABLE 1   Seated Rest: Changes in Cardiac Output Regulation Between 20 and 80 Years of Age in Healthy Humans

Cardiac index	No change
Heart rate	↓ (10%)
Stroke volume	↑ (10%)
Preload	
EDV[a]	↑ (12%)
Early filling	↓
Late filling	↑
Afterload	
Compliance	↓
Reflected waves	↑
Inertance	↑
PVR	↔
Contractility	No change
Ejection fraction	No change
LV mass	↑

[a]Females differ from males—see text.

course of isovolumic myocardial relaxation becomes prolonged by 40% with adult aging in both men and women. While the reduced early filling rate with aging may be due, in part, to age-associated alterations in LV wall structure or passive properties, it is likely that reduced early filling also reflects, in part, the age-associated prolonged relaxation phase of cardiac muscle contraction. Asynchrony of relengthening among ventricular segments also increases with aging and contributes to the reduction in filling rate. The age-associated reduction in early filling rate does not result in a reduced end diastolic volume in healthy older individuals, because greater filling occurs later in diastole, particularly during the atrial contraction. The enhanced atrial contribution to ventricular filling with advancing age is associated with left atrial enlargement, and a more forceful atrial contraction, which is the basis of an audible fourth heart sound in most healthy older individuals.

The *contractility*, or strength of heart muscle contraction, independent of mechanical loading, is not reduced at rest with age in either healthy men or women. The LV *ejection fraction* (EF) is also not altered with aging in healthy men or women at rest. The *stroke volume index* (SVI; amount of blood pumped per beat/body surface area) is increased in males, due to a slight increase in the LV end-diastolic volume. Thus, in healthy older men, the *cardiac index* (CI; amount of blood pumped per minute/body surface area) is not reduced, because the stroke volume index is increased, due to end-diastolic dilatation. In contrast to men, CI in the sitting position at rest is slightly decreased in older versus younger healthy women, as neither the resting *end-diastolic volume index* (EDVI) nor SVI increases with age to compensate for the modest reduction in heart rate. These gender differences appear, in part, to be due to differences in body composition and thus in demand for blood flow in men and women. Specifically, the apparent gender difference in CI, in part, may be an artifact of normalization of cardiac output to body surface area, as the proportion of body fat increases with age in women to a greater extent than in men, and is not accounted for in the indexed value.

Reserve Capacity of the Heart

Seated Upright Dynamic Exercise Response in Humans.
The peak work rate and oxygen consumption of healthy, sedentary men and women during upright, seated cycle ergometry, declines by approximately 50% with advancing age between 20 and 90 years, and is attributable to approximate declines of 30% in cardiac output and 20% in the ability of the skeletal muscles to extract oxygen from the blood. The age-associated decrease in peak cardiac output is due entirely to a reduction in heart rate, as the stroke volume index does not decline with age in either men or women. However, the manner in which stroke volume is achieved during exercise varies dramatically with aging. The EDVI increases during vigorous exercise in older but not younger men and women. But, because the end-systolic volume (ESV) in older persons fails to become reduced to the same extent as in their younger counterparts, the percentage of the total blood ejected per beat (EF) decreases, and the SV is not greater in older versus younger persons. In other words, although the Frank-Starling mechanism (a unique property of the heart that results in a stronger heartbeat when more blood is present in the heart at the beginning of a contraction) is utilized in older persons during exercise, its effectiveness is reduced due to failure of the LV in older persons to empty to the extent to which it does in younger ones. Thus, the older heart, while contracting from a larger preload (amount of blood in the ventricle at end-diastole) at all levels of exercise than the younger heart, does not deliver a stroke volume that exceeds that of the younger heart.

The deficiency in the ability of the old heart to "squeeze down" and reduce LV end-systolic volume during exercise in healthy older individuals likely results from increased stiffness of the arteries, from decreased contractility of the heart muscle, and from a decline in the response of the heart to the sympathetic nervous system (β-adrenergic responsiveness).

Acute β-Adrenergic Modulation of Cardiovascular Performance in Humans.
During exercise, excitement, or stress, the sympathetic nervous system becomes activated and releases norepinephrine and epinephrine (commonly referred to as adrenaline). Norepinephrine and epinephrine act in the heart by binding to β-adrenergic receptors and increase both the heart rate and the strength of contraction. The effects of norepinephrine and epinephrine can be abolished by drugs that block their

TABLE 2 Exhaustive Upright Exercise: Changes in Aerobic Capacity and Cardiac Regulation Between 20 and 80 Years in Healthy Men and Women

Oxygen consumption	↓ (50%)
(A-V)O$_2$	↓ (25%)
Cardiac index	↓ (25%)
Heart rate	↓ (25%)
Stroke volume	No change
Preload	
EDV	↑ (30%)
Afterload	↑
Vascular (PVR)	↑ (30%)
Cardiac (ESV)	↑ (275%)
Cardiac (EDV)	↑ (30%)
Contractility	↓ (60%)
Ejection fraction	↓ (15%)
Plasma catecholamines	↑
Cardiac and vascular responses to β-adrenergic stimulation	↓

receptors (β-adrenergic blockade). The exercise hemodynamic profile of elderly individuals is strikingly similar to that of younger subjects who exercise during β-adrenergic blockade. The age-associated differences in the relationship between the LV stroke volume and end-diastolic volume, in the LV early diastolic filling rate and in heart rate during exercise, are abolished when this exercise is performed during β-adrenergic blockade. In contrast, the maximum heart rate that can be elicited by external electric pacing, which is far in excess of that elicited by drugs that activate the β-adrenergic receptors, is not altered with advancing age. Thus, one of the most prominent changes in the cardiovascular response to exercise stress that occurs with aging in healthy individuals is a reduction in the ability of norepinephrine and epinephrine to activate the β-adrenergic system of the heart, thereby limiting the maximum heart rate and strength of contraction in the aging heart.

Resting sympathetic nervous activity increases progressively with aging. Plasma levels of epinephrine and norepinephrine increase with age, due to enhanced spillover into the circulation and to reduced clearance. The increased spillover does not occur from all body organs but is increased within the heart and is thought to be due, in part at least, to a reduced reuptake by the nerve endings following release. The net result is likely an enhanced postsynaptic receptor occupancy by neurotransmitter, leading to β-adrenergic receptor desensitization. Deficits in β-adrenergic signaling with aging are attributable, in large part, to changes in enzymes and proteins that relay the signals from the β-adrenergic receptor to the molecules inside the heart muscle cell that control the rate and force of contraction.

Research on aging and cardiovascular functioning is illustrated by Fleg, O'Connor, Gerstenblith, Becker, Clulow, Schulman, et al. (1995), Lakatta (1993), and White, Roden, Minobe, Khan, Larrabee, Wollmering, et al. (1994).

MARVIN O. BOLUYT
EDWARD G. LAKATTA

See also
Cardiovascular System: Overview
Cardiovascular System: Vascular

CARDIOVASCULAR SYSTEM: VASCULAR

Arteries are not just conduits delivering nutrients to the organs; they have an additional important task: to convert the intermittent power generation of the heart into a continuous flow vital for the metabolic exchanges at cellular level. The principal design of the cardiovascular system and modifications through evolution are responsible for the optimal coupling of the heart and the arteries. The heart and the arteries are closely interrelated, with the function of the latter affecting the performance of the former to a great extent. The cardiovascular system undergoes progressive changes with advancing age. It is important to acknowledge that changes in the heart are largely secondary to significant changes in the vasculature. It is of equal importance to acknowledge that the aging changes of the vasculature are underestimated by conventional blood pressure recordings.

Structural Changes

Structural changes are the basis for the functional changes observed with aging. There is no distinct

TABLE 1   Arterial Changes With Age

Structural changes
  Large arteries
    Microscopic
      The media is mainly affected
      Disorganization of elastic fibers and elastic
        lamellae
      Thinning and fragmentation of elastin fibers
      Increased collagen, deposition of calcium
    Macroscopic
      Arteries dilate and become tortuous
      Reduction in capillary density
      Increase of media thickness-to-lumen ratio

Functional changes
  Increased stiffness (increased pulse wave velocity)
  Reflected wave arrives early
  Ventricular-vascular "detuning"
  Pressure waveform: late systolic peak/exponential
    decay of diastolic wave
  Reduced amplification in the periphery
  For trends of pressures (see Figure 3)
  Impaired endothelial function

Theoretical model
  Fatigue and fracture of elastin fibers due to cyclic stress
  Transfer of stress to the stiffer collagen fibers
  Central arteries affected more due to greater pulsation
    (greater stretch)

transitional age point from "young" type to "elderly" type of structure of the arterial wall. Rather, the changes follow a progressive course, and some are evident from early adulthood (see Table 1).

Large Arteries. The media, the load-bearing layer of the arterial wall, is the focus of marked structural alterations. The initially orderly arrangement of elastin fibers and lamellae become disorganized, and elastin fibers undergo thinning, splitting, fraying, and fragmentation. There is also an increase in collagen and in ground substance and often deposition of calcium and gradual loss of smooth muscle cells. Moreover, there is evidence of functional changes in the structural elements of the arterial wall. Cystic medial degeneration and medionecrosis, or extensive medial calcification, represent extremes of these processes. These changes are mostly marked in the "elastic-type" arteries, like the aorta, rather than in the "muscular-type" arteries, like the brachial artery. In addition, the intima undergoes changes (hyperplasia) as well,

yet to a lesser extent compared to the media. The arteries also undergo macroscopic morphological changes by dilating and becoming tortuous (Nichols & O'Rourke, 1998; O'Rourke, 1982).

Small Arteries. Capillary density decreases in association with cellular apoptosis and organ atrophy, and the media thickness-to-lumen ratio is increased.

Functional Changes

Stiffness. The first seeds of scientific understanding for the importance of arterial elasticity for cardiac metabolism and function were found in the works of C. S. Roy in 1880, followed by the pioneering investigations of Frank in 1920 and Bramwell and Hill in 1922. With increasing age, the arteries progressively stiffen, and the velocity at which the pulse wave travels within them increases. This effect of aging is independent of and stronger than any other factor that has an unfavorable effect in arterial elasticity, such as hypertension. Aging affects almost exclusively the aorta and central, predominantly elastic arteries. In contrast, there is little or no consistent change in the stiffness of the femoral, radial, or brachial arteries (Figure 1; Avolio, Fa-Quan, Wei-Qiang, Yao-Fei, Zhen-Dong, Lian-Fen, et al., 1985). Pulse wave velocity can be measured by dividing the delay of the foot (upstroke) of the wave between central and peripheral arteries into the distance between recording sites. Typical values for young humans in the ascending aorta are 5 m/s, rising up to 10–12 m/s for an elderly person. Pulse wave for the brachial artery of a young person is approximately 8 m/s but increases little with advancing age. The importance of the alterations in arterial stiffness with aging is stressed by the emergence of aortic elastic properties as significant predictors of cardiovascular risk (Blacher, Asmar, Djane, London, & Safar, 1999).

Compliance of the small vessels also is affected as a result of the structural changes that they undergo.

Ventricular-Vascular Interaction. The effect of aging on ventricular-vascular interaction is best appreciated in studies of vascular impedance. In simple terms, vascular impedance is the opposition to flow presented by the arterial system and is expressed as a ratio of pressure to flow. An efficient

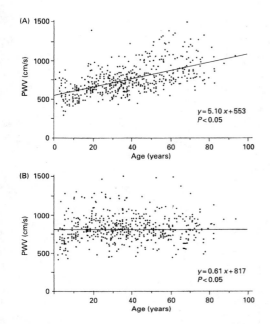

FIGURE 1   Relationship between aortic (A) and arm (B) pulse wave velocity (PWV) with age in the rural southern Chinese community of Guanzhou. Note that whereas pulse wave velocity increases with age in the aorta, it remains practically constant in the upper limb arteries. (*From* Avolio, Fa-Quan, Wei-Qiang, Yao-Fei, Zhen-Dong, Lian-Fen, et al., 1985.)

cardiovascular coupling is characterized by a combination of maximal flow and low pressure values (low values of impedance) and vice versa. With aging there is a progressive "detuning" of ventricular-vascular coupling, and impedance curves are shifted toward higher values. Thus, lower values of flow are achieved at the same pressure levels, or generation of higher pressures is required to achieve desired values of flow. This has important implications for cardiac hypertrophy, a significant predictor of cardiovascular morbidity and mortality, and on the deterioration in cardiac performance. Although the changes of cardiovascular performance are minor at rest, exercise performance is gradually decreased, beginning with competitive performance in the third decade, followed by social and recreational performance in subsequent decades, and ending with different degrees of dysfunction in probably all elderly subjects (Nichols & O'Rouke, 1998; O'Rouke, 1982).

Flow and Pressure Waves.   The pressure waveform recorded at any site of the arterial tree is the sum of a forward waveform and a backward-traveling one, which is the "echo" of the incident wave reflected at peripheral sites. Wave reflection is an important determinant of *left ventricular load* and *coronary blood flow*. A reflected wave occurring at systole increases systolic pressure and thereby increases ventricular load. In contrast, return of the reflected wave during diastole is highly desirable since augmentation of pressure during diastole aids coronary perfusion (Nichols & O'Rourke, 1998).

The changes in arterial pressure waveform with aging were first described by Mahomed in 1872. In younger subjects the first systolic peak in the pressure wave of the *ascending aorta* is not followed by a later systolic pressure rise; instead, a prominent diastolic pressure wave is apparent. With progressing age, a late systolic peak appears, and the diastolic wave disappears. Thus, in older subjects the pressure wave rises from an early systolic shoulder to a later systolic peak, with no secondary diastolic wave following the incisura and a fall in pressure during diastole, which has a nearly exponential form. Intermediate types of waveforms are seen in in-between ages (Figure 2). These changes are responsible for the increase in pulse pressure and in systolic pressure, resulting in "isolated systolic hypertension," an increasingly important cause of morbidity and mortality in contemporary societies (Nichols & O'Rourke, 1998; Vlachopoulos & O'Rourke, 2000). Changes in pulse wave contour can be explained by timing of wave reflection. As pulse wave velocity in the aorta increases with age, the pulse travels down the arterial tree and returns faster after being reflected at the periphery. Thus, the reflected pressure wave merges with the incident wave at an earlier point of the cardiac

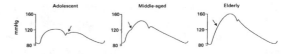

FIGURE 2   Pressure waves recorded in the ascending aorta. In adolescents, the reflected pressure wave (beginning at the arrow) occurs in diastole, and a diastolic pressure wave is apparent. With advancing age the reflected wave arrives earlier, occurs in systole and a late systolic peak appears, whereas the diastolic wave has a nearly exponential form. (*From* Nichols & O'Rourke, 1998.)

cycle, augmenting the pressure waveform at systole rather than diastole. For aging changes in the pulse waveforms of peripheral arteries, which are also explained on this basis, see Kelly, Hayward, Avolio, and O'Rourke (1989), and Vlachopoulos and O'Rourke (2000).

Changes in flow waves with aging are relatively small: a small decrease in peak velocity in the aorta and a progressive change in contour of the ascending aortic flow wave. In late systole the descending part of the wave is convex to the right in young age. With aging, this convexity gradually disappears; then the descending part of the wave becomes concave to the right.

Effect on Amplification of the Pressure Waveform—Pressure Trends with Age. Figure 3 shows trends of systolic, diastolic, and pulse pressure of both central and peripheral arteries with age (Nichols & O'Rourke, 1998; Franklin, Gustin, Wong, Larson, Weber, Kannel, et al., 1997). Mean pressure also increases progressively and this can occur despite an unchanged or slightly reduced cardiac output, because of an increase in peripheral resistance that results from the alterations in small blood vessels.

The arterial pulse increases in amplitude toward the periphery (due to an increase in systolic pressure; diastolic pressure is practically the same), and in adolescents and young adults the peripheral (brachial, radial, femoral) arterial pulse can be even 50% higher than that in the ascending aorta. However, the changes in the contour of pressure waveforms with age are associated with decreased amplification of the pulse between central and peripheral arteries. Thus, in elderly subjects central and peripheral waveforms are virtually identical. Thus, sphygmomanometrically determined pressure in younger ages exaggerates aortic systolic pressure, but in late adulthood the pressure values are nearly equal (Figure 3). This has important epidemiological implications. Indeed, it explains why brachial *diastolic* pressure is a better predictor for cardiovascular risk in young ages (when sphygmomanometrically determined brachial systolic pressure overestimates aortic systolic pressure) and why *systolic* and *pulse* pressure become better predictors in older ages (when brachial systolic pressure reflects more accurately aortic systolic pressure). Moreover, conventional sphygmomanometry underestimates the trend of aging changes from the third to the fifth decade by registering a relative plateau in systolic pressure in contrast to the continuous increase in

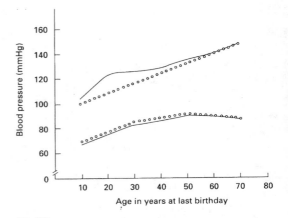

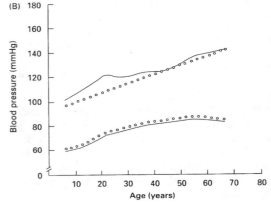

FIGURE 3   Change in arterial blood pressure with age in (A) the United States (U.S. National Health Survey, 1977) and (B) Australian National Heart Foundation, (1989) populations. Solid lines represent published data of sphygmomanometrically determined blood pressure in the brachial artery; dotted lines indicate predicted pressures in the ascending aorta, based on known differences in brachial pressure amplification with age. (*From* Nichols & O'Rourke, 1998.)

pulse wave velocity reflecting the progressive increase in stiffness of central arteries (Figures 1 and 3).

Endothelial Function.   Aging has been associated with progressive endothelial impairment, which appears to occur earlier in men than in women.

Theoretical Model

All the degenerative changes in the arterial media with aging can be explained according to a theoretical model that incorporates engineering principles applied to materials with physical characteristics similar to those of the elastin fibers. Accordingly, the cyclic stress applied to the elastin fibers over the years has an accumulating fatiguing effect that, when it reaches the critical breakage point of the material, results in fracture of these fibers. Consequently, the arterial wall is weakened and stretches so that the stress is transferred to the collagen fibers; these fibers, however, are less compliant, leading to the increased stiffness of the vessel. The degeneration is greater in the central arteries due to the larger stretch per heartbeat: central arteries pulsate approximately 10% with each heartbeat, in contrast to a less than 5% pulsation of peripheral muscular arteries (Nichols & O'Rourke, 1998; O'Rourke, 1982).

Time is associated with never-ending changes of all material substances, and aging of living organisms is an inevitable process interwoven with this component of our nature. The progressive changes that the arterial system undergoes with age have a significant impact on cardiac performance and constitute important predictors of cardiovascular morbidity and mortality.

CHARALAMBOS VLACHOPOULOS
MICHAEL O'ROURKE

See also
Cardiovascular System: Overview
Cardiovascular System: The Heart

CAREGIVER BURDEN

The provision of assistance and support by one family member to another is a regular and usual part of family interactions and is, in fact, a normative and pervasive activity. Thus, caregiving due to chronic illness and disability represents something that, in principle, is not very different from traditional tasks and activities rendered to family members. The difference, however, is that caregiving in chronic illness often represents an increment in care that goes beyond the bounds of normal or usual care. Caregiving in chronic illness involves a significant expenditure of time and energy over extended periods of time, involves tasks that may be unpleasant and uncomfortable, is likely to be nonsymmetrical, and is often a role that had not been anticipated

(Biegel, Sales, & Schulz, 1991). The prevalence of caregiving in the United States is high. A recent national survey of caregivers reported that there were 22.4 million households that met broad criteria for the presence of a caregiver in the past 12 months (Ory, Hoffman, Yee, Tennestedt, & Schulz, 1999).

Family members provide extensive amounts of care to elderly persons who become dependent due to chronic physical and mental illnesses. In fact, the family is the primary source of care for dependent elders living in the community. Although caregiving can have positive aspects for the caregiver (Beach, Schulz, Yee, & Jackson, 2000; Walker, Pratt, & Eddy, 1995), many caregivers experience burden and significant symptoms of depression as well (Alspaugh, Stephens, Townsend, Zarit, & Greene, 1999).

Stages of Research Development About Caregiver Burden

Research on the effects of caregiving on the caregiver has gone through several stages of development. The first caregiver research studies tended to be action and advocacy oriented, with emphasis on the description of the roles, needs, and burdens of family caregivers, many times in the words of the caregivers themselves. Most of these early studies did not utilize any theoretical frameworks. Nevertheless, they served an important role in helping to focus attention on the nature of the problems—the needs of family caregivers. These first studies were followed by attempts to develop better conceptualizations and quantitative measures of the concept of burden itself. Various burden scales were developed, and burden was correlated with a variety of caregiver and care recipient demographic and socioeconomic characteristics and also with such caregiver variables as personality, coping style, and social support. Studies began to use various theoretical frameworks to guide the analysis. However, this wave of studies tended to be cross-sectional in design and to utilize small samples.

Later studies, based primarily on stress/coping theoretical frameworks, used more sophisticated longitudinal designs, variable measurements, and multivariate analytic techniques. Most recently, caregiver research has begun to shift the focus of caregiver outcomes from caregiver stress or burden to the "harder" outcomes of caregiver morbidity, both psychiatric and physical, and caregiver mortality (Schulz & Beach, 1999). Part of this shift has included a focus on the search for mediating mechanisms, both physical and psychosocial, that affect caregiver morbidity and mortality outcomes. A separate stream of caregiving research has focused on testing the degree to which interventions for caregivers can help address the deleterious effects of caregiving—caregiver burden as well as physical and mental health outcomes for caregivers.

Conceptualization and Measurement of Caregiver Burden

The caregiving literature contains little consensus as to the conceptualization and measurement of caregiver burden, with definitions of burden ranging from examinations of care-recipient behaviors to caregiver tasks and general caregiver well-being (Vitaliano, Young, & Russo, 1991). In fact, the definition of what constitutes caregiving and the caregiving experience varies widely among studies (Malone, Beach, & Zarit, 1991). It is generally agreed that caregiver burden contains both objective and subjective dimensions. Objective burden can be defined as the time and effort required for one person to attend to the needs of another. Thus, it might include the amount of time spent in caregiving, the type of caregiving services provided, and financial resources expended on behalf of the dependent elder (Biegel, Sales, & Schulz, 1991). Subjective burden refers to perceived beliefs and feelings of the caregiver about the performance of caregiver tasks and assumptions of the caregiver role. Subjective burden is more varied than objective burden, and studies have included such elements as the extent to which caregiving causes strain with regard to work, finances, and emotional and physical status (Cantor, 1983); assessment of caregiver-related feelings about health, well-being, family relationships and social life (Zarit, Reever, & Bach-Peterson, 1980); emotional impact of caregiving (Horowitz & Schindelman, 1983); and emotional distress associated with caregiving (Gilleard, Belford, Gilleard, Whittick, & Gledhill, 1984). Some researchers have suggested that specific burdens are linked to specific types of impairment (Poulshock & Deimling, 1984).

Effects of Caregiving

Significant problems of family caregivers identified by researchers include coping with increased needs of the dependent family member caused by physical and/or mental illnesses; coping with disruptive behaviors, especially those associated with cognitive disorders or mental illness, such as dementia; restrictions on social and leisure activities; infringement of privacy; disruption of household and work routines; conflicting multiple role demands; lack of support and assistance from other family members; disruption of family roles and relationships; and lack of sufficient assistance from human service agencies and agency professionals (Coen, Swanwick, O'Boyle, & Coakley, 1997).

Many families report that caregiving is an emotional, physical, and, at times, financial burden. This burden may be a major factor in the decision to institutionalize an elderly parent (McFall & Miller, 1992; Townsend, 1990). Data indicate that almost one-third of caregivers do not receive any assistance in their caregiving functions from other informal or formal providers and that family caregivers are more likely to have lower income and lower self-reported health than the population at large (Stone, Cafferata, & Sangl, 1987).

When one examines the relationship between a range of caregiver and care-recipient demographic, socioeconomic, and illness characteristics to caregiver burden, the results across studies are consistent for some variables and inconsistent for others. Generally, findings concerning the role of objective stressors, illness-related variables, are more consistent than are findings concerning contextual variables such as caregiver demographic and socioeconomic characteristics and social support.

Concerning objective stressors, one consistent finding across illnesses that vary considerably in symptomatology, pattern of onset, and trajectory is that the more severe the illness, the greater the burden on caregivers (Biegel, Sales, & Schulz, 1991). Additionally, in illnesses with a sudden onset or sudden diagnosis, such as stroke, cancer, or heart attacks, caregiver stress is highest at the acute stage of the illness. There is also a strong relationship between care-recipient behaviors and caregiver burden. Care-recipient behaviors that are known to be especially burdensome include incontinence, severe functional impairments, hallucinations, suspiciousness, agitation, wandering, catastrophic emotional reactions, disruptiveness at night, behaviors dangerous to the patient, and the need for constant supervision (Pearlin, Mullan, Semple, & Skaff, 1990). Because many of these characteristics are common among dementia patients, it is believed that caregiving for an elderly person with dementia is more difficult than providing care to an elderly person with physical rather than mental limitations (Ory, Hoffman, Yee, Tennstedt, & Schulz, 1999).

Although the fact that the literature shows a moderate relationship between the level of patient disability and psychological distress of the caregiver, there is considerable variability in caregiver outcomes. Such outcomes are thought to be mediated and/or moderated by a variety of factors, including economic and social support resources available to the caregiver, the quality of the relationship between caregiver and care recipient, and a host of individual difference factors, such as gender, personality attributes (optimism, self-esteem, self-mastery), and coping strategies used (Bookwala & Schulz, 1998; Kendig & Brooke, 1997; Lawrence, Tennstedt, & Assman, 1998; Schulz, O'Brien, Bookwala, & Fleissner, 1995; Townsend & Franks, 1997; Williamson, Shaffer, & Schulz, 1998; Yates, Tennstedt, & Chang, 1999). Researchers have further extended basic stress-coping models to include examination of secondary stressors, such as the number and variety of the caregivers' other roles and role conflict engendered by caregiving demands (Pearlin, Aneshensel, & LeBlanc, 1997), and have applied many additional theoretical perspectives borrowed from social and clinical psychology, sociology, and the health and biological sciences to help understand specific aspects of the caregiving situation.

A number of studies indicate that female caregivers show higher levels of caregiver burden than do males (Miller & Cafasso, 1992). Studies show that spouse caregivers have higher burden levels than do nonspouse caregivers, but this finding may be confounded with age. Malone, Beach, and Zarit (1991) believe that some of the inconsistencies in the effects of caregiver characteristics on caregiver burden are due to our failure to disentangle caregiver gender, age, and relationship, which can interact to cause confounding effects. This complexity is compounded if we add ethnic identity as another factor to this mix. For example, data indicate that

African American caregivers do not have the same levels of stress and depression as do White caregivers and that African American and Hispanic caregivers are more likely to provide more challenging personal care and experience greater financial hardship than do Asians or Whites (Calderon & Tennstedt, 1998; Connell & Gibson, 1997; Haley, Roth, Coleton, Ford, West, Collins, et al., 1996; National Alliance for Caregiving and the American Association of Retired Persons, 1997).

It also has been noted, however, that caregiving can have positive aspects for the caregiver as well. Adult children who are caregivers to elderly parents report that they find caregiving gratifying because they can "pay back" the care that the parent provided to them when they were young. Similarly, spouses who view caregiving as a reciprocation of past affection report caregiving to be more gratifying. In addition, caregivers report that being a caregiver helps them gain inner strength or learn new skills (Archer & MacLean, 1993).

Interventions to Address Caregiver Burden

A variety of intervention programs have been developed for caregivers; these are designed to reduce the burden that caregivers often experience and provide supportive assistance to enable families to continue their caregiving roles. The services can be categorized into several types. Support groups—either professionally or peer-led—are designed to provide caregivers with emotional support, informational support, and enhancement of coping skills. Educational interventions emphasize the provision by professionals of information and/or skills, usually in a group format, to family caregivers to enable them to meet their needs. Clinical interventions are direct service interventions that include counseling/therapy, respite care, behavioral/cognitive stimulation, hospice care, day care, and general psychosocial interventions.

Although anecdotal reports of early intervention efforts were generally positive, the first critical reviews of the literature were considerably more sobering (Biegel & Schulz, 1999). Toseland and Rossiter's (1989) review of 29 studies concluded that although caregivers evaluated interventions positively there was "no clear link . . . between participants' satisfaction (with group interventions) and other important outcomes for caregivers such as improving coping skills, preventing psychological disturbances, increasing caregiver support systems, or improving caregivers' ability to care for themselves" (p. 438). Similarly, "time-limited psychoeducational interventions have modest therapeutic benefits as measured by global ratings of well-being, mood, stress, psychological status, and caregiving burden" (p. 481). Focusing exclusively on interventions aimed at alleviating caregiver distress, Knight, Lutszky, and Macofsky-Urban (1993) concluded that individual psychosocial interventions and respite programs are moderately effective; psychosocial interventions with groups are less effective. Zarit and Teri (1992), in describing the available intervention literature as the "first generation" of studies, point out that interpretation of this preliminary work should be tempered by the fact that expectations for particular intervention outcomes and the malleability of caregivers have been overly optimistic and that some intervention effects may be underestimated because of methodological limitations of the studies.

Bourgeois, Schulz, and Burgio's (1996) review of the caregiving interventions literature was organized around six broad categories: support groups, individual and/or family counseling, case management, respite and day care services, skills training, and various combinations of these strategies. Detailed assessments of the complex literature in each of these areas are contained in the original review. However, a number of general conclusions can be derived from their analysis of the literature. First, the complexity and rigor of intervention studies continues to improve with an increasing emphasis on randomized designs. Second, the literature on the whole supports the conclusion that more is better. Multicomponent interventions that blanket caregivers with a diversity of services and supports in hopes that a combination of components will have a greater impact on a caregiver's unique needs tend to generate larger effects than narrowly focused interventions. Similarly, single-component interventions with higher intensity (frequency and duration) also have a greater positive impact on the caregiver than that of similar interventions with lower intensity. Third, achieving generalization of effects beyond the specific target of an intervention has been difficult. Thus, for example, a skills training intervention may effectively enhance a caregiver's ability to manage the patient but may not necessarily reduce his or her sense of subjective burden.

On the basis of their review, Bourgeois, Schulz, and Burgio (1996) conclude that future intervention research should address three recurrent themes. First, caregiver characteristics must be considered more systematically in tailoring interventions to individual needs. Without a thorough knowledge and understanding of individual caregivers and their unique personal and psychological histories and circumstances, interventions can only continue to be designed for the "average" caregiver, with average results. Second, "fidelity" of treatments should be examined, with treatments being described, measured, and monitored to ensure that caregivers are receiving the treatment as prescribed and to permit replication of treatment effects with similar groups. Without a complete understanding of what comprises an efficacious treatment and how subject characteristics interact with treatment factors, caregivers and professionals may waste their time in efforts that yield only mediocre outcomes. Finally, the desired outcomes of interventions must be more clearly articulated: What constitutes a reasonable outcome for a given intervention and how might it vary for different caregivers, patients, families, and professionals?

DAVID E. BIEGEL

See also
Caregivers of Chronically Ill Elderly
Informal Caregiving
Support Groups

CAREGIVERS OF CHRONICALLY ILL ELDERLY

According to results from the 1996 survey of 1,500 U.S. households, conducted by the National Alliance for Caregiving (NAC) (1997) and the American Association of Retired Persons (AARP), there currently are more than 25 million households providing informal (in-home) care to a disabled adult. Approximately three-fourths of self-identified caregivers are women (the majority being wives, followed by daughters or daughters-in-law). Estimates vary somewhat, but about one-fourth of caregivers nationally are over the age of 65, the majority being middle-aged (i.e., over age 35). Taken together, family members provide close to 80% of all home care to disabled adults, whose conditions vary greatly and can include those with severe vision and hearing problems, those with greater functional impairment (as associated with advanced heart disease, cancer, or stroke), and those with significant cognitive impairment (as is typical in Alzheimer's disease or related forms of dementia).

Several review papers have described the negative effects of caregiving in terms of its impact on a variety of psychological and physiological variables. Schulz, O'Brien, Bookwala, and Fleissner (1995) reviewed close to 50 empirical studies and found that virtually all reported elevated levels of depressive symptoms among caregivers; some also showed high rates of depressive disorders in caregivers compared to matched noncaregiving individuals. In contrast, they found that fewer actual negative effects on physical health status could be documented, although self-reports of poor health and use of psychotropic medications were higher among caregivers than noncaregivers. Other reviews (Dunkin & Anderson-Hanley, 1998; Gallagher-Thompson, Coon, Rivera, Powers, & Zeiss, 1998) discuss additional factors, such as gender differences, relationship between duration of caregiving and perceived burden, and the role of social support, all of which can mediate the negative effects of caregiving on physical and mental health outcomes.

Although it is true that the amount and kind of care vary greatly according to the nature of the disability, it is generally accepted that those caring for a demented family member will have a harder job, overall, than those caring for persons who are physically impaired but cognitively intact. Recently, this observation was confirmed by Ory, Hoffman, Yee, Tennstedt, and Schultz (1999) in their more detailed analysis of data from the NAC/AARP survey. They found that dementia caregivers spent significantly more hours per week providing care than nondementia caregivers (17 vs. 12). They also reported greater impact in terms of employment complications, caregiver strain, mental and physical health problems, disruption of leisure time and activities, and family conflict. These differential impacts remained even after controlling for sociodemographic factors, suggesting the need to tailor

programs and services to the unique challenges of dementia caregivers. Yet despite the many negative impacts that caregivers reported in this survey, some noted positive benefits as well, such as receiving personal satisfaction from doing their job well and feeling appreciated by the care receiver. The study of positive impacts of family caregiving is relatively new but surely will be a focus of future research, as more and more families take on long-term responsibilities for frail and/or demented relatives.

Given the significant stress experienced by many family caregivers (irrespective of the diagnosis of their loved one), a great deal of attention has been focused on developing and evaluating interventions of various kinds to reduce this distress. Several reviews of this literature have been published in the past decade, including work by Zarit and Teri (1991), Knight, Lutzsky, and Macofsky-Urban (1993), Bourgeois, Schulz, and Burgio (1996), and Gatz, Fiske, Fox, Kaskie, Kasl-Godley, McCallum, et al. (1998), the latter two being the most comprehensive. Zarit and Teri (1991) pointed to various methodological shortcomings in studies done prior to that time, and Knight et al. (1993) conducted a meta-analysis of existing studies to determine effect sizes. They concluded that individual psychosocial interventions and organized overnight or day respite programs were moderately effective in reducing caregiver distress, whereas group-based interventions tended to be less effective. Bourgeois et al. (1996) discussed not only the results obtained from their review of 66 published intervention studies but also several factors affecting intervention outcomes, such as measurement of program implementation to determine if the strength and integrity of the intervention were preserved in the actual study. They found that most studies did not monitor program implementation variables; yet this may be an important factor to account for the less-than-consistent pattern of results obtained from these studies. Some interventions have been found to be clearly effective, however, for certain outcomes. For example, a family-oriented program that included individual and family counseling along with support group participation and as-needed phone consultation was effective in delaying time to nursing home placement in a sample of over 200 spouse caregivers of dementia patients (Mittelman, Ferris, Shulman, Steinberg, & Levin, 1996). Studies that used psychoeducational interventions (various skills such as mood monitoring, challenging negative thoughts, and increasing participation in everyday pleasant activities) have also demonstrated effectiveness in terms of significant improvement in clinical depression among those most distressed at the outset (Gallagher-Thompson, Lovett, Rose, McKibbin, Coon, Futterman, et al., 2000; see also Gallagher-Thompson, Coon, Rivera, Powers, & Zeiss, 1998, for more details on other effective interventions).

Recently, increased attention has been paid to the influence of ethnicity and culture on caregivers' perceived stress and coping; reviews by Aranda and Knight (1997) and Connell and Gibson (1997) confirmed the importance of these variables. For example, compared to White caregivers, non-Whites were less likely to be spouses and more likely to be adult children. Non-Whites reported lower levels of distress (particularly African Americans), endorsed more strongly held beliefs about filial support, and were likely to use prayer and religion as coping mechanisms. The study of how ethnicity and related variables affect responsiveness to interventions to reduce caregivers' distress is only beginning. A large multisite study that enrolled high proportions of African American and Hispanic/Latino caregivers (as well as White/Euro-Americans) is currently in process. Called the REACH project (Resources for Enhancing Alzheimer's Caregiver Health), its results will become available early in the new century. A description of the interventions used in REACH can be found in Gallagher-Thompson, Arean, Menendez, Takagi, Haley, Arguelles, et al. (2000).

In sum, the fields of caregiving research and service delivery have expanded significantly in the past decade and no doubt will continue in the new millennium as increasing numbers of older persons live longer and require long-term care from their family members.

DOLORES GALLAGHER-THOMPSON

See also
Caregiver Burden
Informal Caregiving

Respite Care
Support Groups

CAREGIVING (INFORMAL)
See
Caregiver Burden
Caregivers of Chronically Ill Elderly
Informal Caregiving
Support Groups

CASE MANAGEMENT

Case management is a function directed at locating and coordinating care from a variety of resources in response to identified need. Client goals include maximizing independence, providing choices, and enhancing functioning. The case manager assumes responsibility for identifying needs, planning and arranging service delivery, and monitoring service provision and outcomes. Primarily a process that links individuals and families with needed services, case management has some specific characteristics:

- It is individualized to the unique needs of each client.
- It is based on a holistic orientation that views all aspects of the individual, situation, and environment.
- It seeks to enhance client self-care and self-determination by involving the client in problem solving and decision making and focusing on client values and preferences.
- It is aimed at providing continuity of appropriate care.
- It utilizes a wide range of services from a variety of sources.
- It is implemented through coordinating an existing set of services and resources from both formal and informal systems.

Evolution of Case Management

The principal function of case management—that of obtaining essential resources on behalf of clients in collaboration with both formal and informal sources—is rooted in social casework, public health and community nursing, child and family services, and related services. Every discipline can and does lay claim to contributing toward what is now case management (White & Gundrum, 2000). Although aspects of these disciplines remain an integral part of case management, the dimension of managing and monitoring many types of care, systems, service delivery, interagency agreements, cost containment, provider efficiency, and quality add complexity and a greater level of formalization to more traditional methods.

The emergence of community-based long-term care research and demonstration projects under Medicaid waivers in the early 1970s and 1980s stimulated case management development, particularly in community-based and in-home programs serving dependent populations such as the frail elderly. Over time the case management function has become more systematic. This is most apparent in client-related tasks, relationships with providers, development of professional training for case managers, more clearly defined target groups, and stated requirements for case management in funded research, demonstration, and ongoing programs.

The popularity and success of case management are evidenced by its proliferation in all types of settings, as it is performed by professionals from most human service disciplines. Other growth indicators include its utilization in a broad range of service arenas performing many functions and activities, including the following:

- Telephone screening, assessment, and consultation;
- Information and referral services;
- Elder care services for corporations and businesses;
- Long-term care insurance assessments and care management;
- Private practice care management;
- Acute care facility and medical case management;
- Home health and custodial management;
- Physician office linkages to community services;
- Guardianship/conservatorship and fiscal management;

- Community-based programs and senior center services; and
- State, local, and national referral and insurance service networks.

Case Management Process

The case management process generally includes the set of tasks and activities shown in Figure 1.

After intake, client status is assessed to determine needs, and a plan of care is developed to address them. Assessment instruments vary from program to program but most commonly include health and functional, cognitive, and psychosocial elements that assist in determining the appropriate level of care needed and the supports available for the individual client. A social work, health care, or other professional with good interviewing skills usually conducts assessment. In some settings, members of a multidisciplinary team, including population (e.g., elderly) or service (e.g., physical therapy) specialists do the assessment. Family members, other informal sources, physicians, attorneys, and current or past service providers may be contacted for verification or additional information.

The care plan is implemented by locating, arranging, or coordinating the delivery of services from available sources. In a community setting, for example, the case manager may obtain such services as home chores, bathing and personal care, laundry, shopping, day care, and transportation. In cases where a family is a caregiver for a homebound person, arrangements may be made for periodic

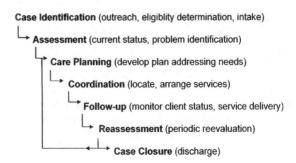

Case Identification (outreach, eligiblity determination, intake)
↳ **Assessment** (current status, problem identification)
  ↳ **Care Planning** (develop plan addressing needs)
    ↳ **Coordination** (locate, arrange services)
      ↳ **Follow-up** (monitor client status, service delivery)
        ↳ **Reassessment** (periodic reevaluation)
          ↳ **Case Closure** (discharge)

FIGURE 1   Case management process.

respite services. Often case managers assist families who are making placement or relocation decisions.

Service provision is monitored to assure continuity, quality, and appropriateness; clients are monitored for response to care and for changes in status. Regular contact with the client, the clients' national support sources, and providers establishes a channel of communication to ensure early intervention if problems arise. In addition to this ongoing interaction, a periodic reassessment is conducted to evaluate whether the clients' situation is better or worse and whether the client needs more, fewer, or different services. Follow-up activities provide the opportunity to monitor client status and service delivery and respond to changes or problems. This is essential for continuity and to assist clients to maintain or improve their situation. Finally, discharge from case management takes place under a variety of circumstances: the client situation stabilizes, the client no longer requires the service, or the client no longer wishes to receive the service. Clients also can fall out of eligibility by virtue of changes in income, place of residence, or condition.

Although the process is depicted as linear, it is not unusual for clients to avail themselves of only a part of it. For instance, there may be a request for just an assessment and suggestions for services, or a family may ask for monitoring of services already in place. This is particularly true for private practice and fee-for-services case management, where clients are not required to meet eligibility criteria nor to follow a prescribed schedule.

The conduct of the specific tasks varies considerably among programs. For example, some programs provide only short-term case management (normally defined as 3 months or less), whereas others continue service as long as needed. Some acquire clients from a host agency or an affiliate organization that may perform the case finding or assessment tasks. Some programs limit coordination to those services that can be delivered directly, whereas others develop contractual relationships and agreements with a variety of providers. Regardless of how, by whom, or where the activities are actually carried out, the case management process itself remains relatively intact.

Case Management Program Models

Case management models are usually described by a variety of program elements. Many elements dis-

tinguish case management programs from one another. Among them are the level of responsibility for client care and the degree of authority to purchase and allocate resources. The complexity of case management functions is directly related to the presence or absence of these characteristics. Examples of other variables that affect case management models are shown in Table 1.

The purpose of case management programs is related to its goals and, most commonly, to its funding source, which typically defines the target population. For example, if the purpose of a program is to provide alternatives to nursing home placement, the focus will be on individuals eligible for nursing home care. In such programs the goals would likely be to maintain the individuals in the community at a lower cost than that of the nursing home. Eligibility for case management can be based on age, income, geographic location, and functional, cognitive, or physical status, as in publicly funded programs, or simply be based on an ability to pay for services as in the fee-for-service model.

Staffing depends largely on funding, the type of intervention needed or offered, the function that the case manager performs, and the type of client served. Case managers with psychosocial skills usually staff community-based and mental health programs, whereas nurses or other health care case managers work with those who need skilled care. In some programs, case management teams offering

TABLE 1   Selected Case Management Program Variables

Variable	Examples
Purpose	Nursing home alternative, service access
Target	Frail, high cost, ability to pay
Funding	Grants, contracts, fees
Function	Broker, provider
Staffing	Social worker, nurse, gerontologist
Caseload	Mandated, mix/intensity
Duration	Short term, long term
Setting	Community, acute care, managed care
Authority	Admission, planning, purchase
Outcomes	Cost savings, client satisfaction
Tools	Information systems, care pathways

both health and psychosocial perspectives are utilized. Programs also differ by the size of their caseloads and the duration of case management service variables often mandated by funders. Other variations include the level of authority to admit clients into programs; care planning and how services are acquired; the anticipated outcomes to be achieved, ranging from dollar savings to client satisfaction; and what types of tools are utilized to facilitate information flow and tracking of cases and costs. To date, no one case management program or model has emerged to suit all situations.

Continuing Challenges in Case Management

In spite of increasing numbers and types of case management programs and practices, several issues remain unresolved. One is the ongoing practice of payers to reimburse solely for medically related case management services. Another is the proliferation of case management credentialing organizations with little consensus between them on content, purpose, or even terminology (Rosen, Bodie-Gross, Young, Smolenski, & Howe, 2000). The continuing effort to "professionalize" case management through credentialing activities and formulation of standards (Geron & Chassler, 1994) has significant implications for future education and training needs. A related and important issue is the critical need to understand and deal with the ethical issues case managers face, whether these issues are associated with costs of care (Mullahy, 1999), home care (Kane & Caplan, 1993), or client preferences and values (Degenholtz, Kane, & Kivick, 1997).

A growing ethnic diversity in the aging population presents several challenges for case managers, including methods for enhancing culturally sensitive practice, learning about differences in target groups and increasing consumer input (Trejo, 1999). Work on case management standards has progressed (Bulger & Feldmeier, 1998) but has evolved discipline by discipline rather than across professional identities. Other issues needing further clarification and resolution include:

• Strengthening service systems to counter resource limitations;

• Improving targeting methods to assure appropriate client populations;
• Clarifying the goals of case management vis-à-vis the host agency or payer;
• Determining the best staffing qualifications and mix;
• Determining the most appropriate and feasible caseload size and mix;
• Strategizing cooperative agreements with service providers;
• Integrating medical and nonmedical services and care;
• Determining intake, service provision, and monitoring and reporting methods among multiple providers;
• Defining case management outcome measures;
• Improving information systems to facilitate communication, management, and clinical tasks; and
• Determining pricing and reimbursement mechanisms for all case management services.

Case management has proved to be particularly successful with vulnerable and dependent populations such as the frail elderly and the disabled. It has provided a means for assisting clients to maintain an optimal level of independence in the midst of a fragmented, duplicative, and confusing "nonsystem." It also has facilitated interorganizational linkages, collaborative planning, and community-wide awareness of system gaps for needy populations.

There is both public and private support for the basic concepts underlying case management. Increasing numbers of autonomous agencies are participating in developing a continuum of care through networking and systems-building activities. Technological advances are being utilized to assist case managers in tracking the most effective and efficient services and enhancing productive decision making. The future of case management programs may rest on their ability to fit into existing structures, to mold their function to suit current policies and programs, to operate at varying levels of complexity, and to further refine their purpose. As care increasingly moves from acute and institutional facilities to home and community settings, the principles of collaboration and coordination inherent to case management are essential to the success of future service systems. Yet, as Austin observes (Austin & McClelland, 1996), case management by itself does not create the changes needed in the service systems. It also requires policy and financial support as systems undergo reform. With such support case management can continue to serve important facilitation and linking functions through management of care and resources.

MONIKA WHITE

See also

> Case Mix in Long-Term Care
> Comprehensive Assessment
> On Lok and PACE Replications
> Resource Utilization Groups

CASE MIX IN LONG-TERM CARE

Case mix describes the blend of different types of patients, residents, or clients in an institutional setting or other care program. However, the term currently is used almost exclusively to denote the link between types of patients and the cost of their care. Thus, a case-mix system can measure how heavy care costs are for the patients in a nursing home, a unit of a nursing home, or a home care program. With an accurate measure of case mix, it is possible to design systems for paying higher rates for patients whose care cost more, for example, by states paying nursing homes under the Medicaid system. We discuss this and other applications of case mix later. Good case-mix systems should jointly provide a good explanation of the differences between patients in the cost of their care, should be clinically sensible, and should provide appropriate incentives (or at least avoid inappropriate disincentives) to provide good care (Fries, 1990).

In determining case mix, where the focus is on patient-specific costs of care, currently accepted approaches use only the characteristics of individual patients and ignore facility characteristics, such as location, staffing, and financing. When the concepts of case mix were first applied in acute care facilities, the goal was to explain the total cost of a hospital stay, which is proxied well by length of stay. For example, the diagnosis-related groups (DRG) system, the first and most widely applied case-mix classification system for acute hospitals, uses variables such as primary diagnosis and the performance of a surgical procedure in defining several hundred case-mix groups representing hospital episodes of care (Fetter et al., 1981).

In nursing homes very different systems have evolved. No system has been successful in predicting length of stay, so case-mix systems have focused on per diem resource use. The costs that vary most between residents are those for staff time—nurses and aides. Other costs have been found to be either strongly correlated with these, uncorrelated with the type of resident (such as utility or capital costs), or inconsequential. Further, characteristics of residents are related to cost differences, so case mix is based on resident assessments. Measures of resident function, such as activities of daily living (ADLs), are the most influential in explaining cost, whereas age or the presence of chronic disease diagnoses play more minor roles. The most prevalent case-mix measurement system in nursing homes is the resource utilization groups (RUGs). The current version, RUG-III, defines 44 distinct types of residents and provides the relative cost of caring for an average resident of each type (the Case-Mix Index) (Fries, Schneider, Foley, Gavazzi, Burke, & Cornelius, 1994).

There are some similarities as well between the acute and long-term care case-mix systems. Both are based on a system of patient groups, with a case-mix index for each group, representing the relative cost of caring for these patients.

Case-mix systems are available for other settings, such as rehabilitation care (Stineman, Escarce, Goin, Hamilton, Granger, & Williams, 1994); in home care (Phillips, Brown, Schore, Klein, Schochet, Hill, et al., 1992), ambulatory care, and mental health, the systems are less advanced. A current issue is whether the basis of the system should be the cost for an episode of care (such as DRGs) or for a single day (such as RUGs).

Case-mix measurement is often confused with case-mix payment. The derivation of the case-mix system is primarily a scientific issue. A case-mix payment system will incorporate case mix to acknowledge differences in a facility's patient population. By paying more for more costly patients, it removes the incentive in a flat-rate system to admit and retain the least costly patients. A case-mix payment system also must incorporate all costs, including those unrelated to patient characteristics, and recognize only selected facility characteristics that may be associated with cost differences. Choosing which facility characteristics will affect payment is primarily a political issue, as is the overall financing level. Other issues that must be addressed include the frequency at which changes in the patient are recognized, the types of costs that are adjusted for case mix, and incentives for improving a patient's condition.

In the United States, case-mix payment is used for both acute care hospitals (employing DRGs) and nursing homes (using RUG-III). Recent laws have mandated implementation of such systems as well for home care, rehabilitation care, ambulatory care, and mental health.

Although payment is the most prevalent use of case-mix measurement, it is also employed in applications that range from the management of facilities, such as understanding staffing loads, to policy research, such as the identification of trends in long-term care.

BRANT E. FRIES
BRENT C. WILLIAMS

See also
Case Management
Channeling Demonstration
Home Health Care
On Lok and PACE Replications
Resource Utilization Groups

CASH PAYMENTS FOR CARE

Cash payments for care refers to various financing mechanisms that provide a cash benefit to consumers or their representatives, thus allowing them to address their particular needs and preferences for personal assistance services (PAS). Depending on program rules, consumers may have complete latitude on how the cash is spent or they may have to use cash allowances only for PAS and other types of services (i.e., assistive devices, home modifications, transportation) needed to maintain their independence. Personal assistance services encompass a range of human and technological assistance provided to persons with disabilities who need help with certain types of activities, such as activities of daily living (ADLs), including bathing, dressing,

toileting, transferring, and eating, and instrumental activities of daily living (IADLs), including housekeeping, cooking, shopping, laundry, and managing money and medication.

Although cash payment programs are not new, there has been growing interest as policy makers have sought new ways to control long-term services costs while maintaining or increasing consumer satisfaction. When a program design emphasizes minimal restrictions on uses of a cash benefit, cash payments may be considered an ultimate form of consumer direction.

Consumer-directed services, which emanated from the disability rights and independent living movements, promote maximum consumer choice and control (DeJong, Batavia, & McKnew, 1992). The language of the disability movement—referring to "consumers" rather than "patients"—reflects the movement's empowerment goals. The aging community began to adopt consumer-direction principles more recently, with the development of a coalition between the aging and younger disabilities communities (Ansello & Eustis, 1992; Kapp, 1996; Simon-Rusinowitz & Hofland, 1993).

Traditional Home Care Payment Methods

To understand cash payments for care, it is helpful to describe basic methods for financing PAS in this country. Public or private third-party payers can use any of three PAS financing methods: (1) cash benefits (payments to qualified clients or their representatives); (2) vendor payments (a case-manager determines the types or amounts of covered services and arranges for and pays authorized PAS providers to deliver these services); and (3) vouchers (clients use funds for authorized purchases).

Most existing public programs that finance PAS in the United States follow a vendor-payment model. The program purchases services for consumers from authorized vendors (i.e., service providers or equipment suppliers). In some programs, the list of covered services and authorized vendors is restricted. Other programs may have a broader range of covered services, adding adult day care, transportation, home modifications, and assistive devices. Clients may sometimes hire independent providers not employed by home health agencies to be in-home aides.

In recent years, many state program officials have adopted the concerns of disability rights advocates who want PAS programs that promote consumer choice and avoid program rules that may foster dependency in the name of consumer protection. In addition, most Medicaid PAS programs require case managers (registered nurses or social workers) to assess clients and monitor care plans. Case management can be expensive, and researchers and administrators question whether it is always necessary. A consumer-directed cash payment program is likely to decrease case management and other administrative functions, possibly resulting in decreased program costs.

Although this article focuses primarily on programs in the United States, cash payment programs are available in many other countries (Tilly, 1999). Cameron and Firman (1995) reported that most Western industrialized countries provide some sort of long-term care allowance for persons with disabilities. Freedman and Kemper (1996) studied home- and community-based service programs in nine foreign countries and identified disability allowances in Austria and Germany as well as an individualized cash benefit in the Netherlands.

In this country there has been increased interest in "cash and counseling," a consumer-directed cash payment demonstration that offers a cash allowance and information services to persons with disabilities. This program is currently under study in a national demonstration and evaluation conducted in three state Medicaid programs (Arkansas, New Jersey, and Florida). The cash-and-counseling design can be considered a modified pure cash benefit. The accountability required by publicly funded programs imposes some restrictions on uses of the cash. The cash option, which is basically the cash equivalent of the care plan the consumer would have been receiving under the traditional agency-delivery system, can *only* be used to meet PAS needs. Consumers develop "cash plans," but they can be very creative in proposing how they intend to meet their individual needs.

The Cash and Counseling Demonstration and Evaluation: An Overview

The Cash and Counseling Demonstration and Evaluation (CCDE), an ongoing policy-driven study funded by the U.S. Department of Health and Human Services and the Robert Wood Johnson Foundation, is evaluating the impact of cash payments for services. The University of Maryland Center on Aging (UMCA) serves as the national program office. The evaluation compares the cash option with traditional agency-delivered services. The three demonstration states are offering the cash option to elders (over 65 years old) and adults with disabilities (ages 18–64). Children with developmental disabilities are also included in Florida.

The method for administering the cash option varies somewhat across the demonstration states. However, in general, persons eligible for participation include those who are currently receiving Medicaid personal care (or in Florida, Home and Community-Based Services waiver services), are age 18 or older, require assistance with ADLs, and are interested and willing to participate. Using the cash benefit, consumers choose who provides their services as well as when and how the services are provided. For example, consumers may hire a friend or relative who knows their preferences to help them on evenings or weekends when agency services may be unavailable. Counseling and bookkeeping services are offered to help consumers manage the cash allowance and required fiscal tasks. Persons who need help making decisions about their daily personal assistance may have a representative.

Background work for this national demonstration began in October 1995, and implementation began in December 1998, when Arkansas enrolled the first cash-option consumers. New Jersey began enrollment in November 1999, and Florida began enrolling consumers in early 2000. The evaluation, conducted by Mathematica Policy Research, randomly assigns consumers interested in the cash option to treatment and control groups. This comprehensive evaluation focuses on consumers' service utilization and preferences, quality of care, and service costs, as well as issues related to paid and informal workers.

Issues to Consider

When implementing cash payment programs, policy makers and program managers need to consider numerous issues. This discussion will address several key decisions they must make in designing cash payment programs: defining policy objectives, choosing whether to offer a cash payment as an only option versus one option among others, deciding whether to offer support services, and addressing fraud and abuse concerns.

Defining Policy Goals. Policy makers should be clear about the policy objectives they want to achieve with a cash payment program. At times, policy makers may be interested in many, possibly conflicting, policy goals. They may, for example, see cash payment programs as a vehicle to enhance the quality of life for persons with disabilities (and their families) by offering more consumer choice. However, policy makers may be primarily concerned about controlling public spending. The priority would most likely result in a program that restricts program eligibility (to avoid exploding demand and a "woodwork effect") and uses of the cash payment. Yet even when policy makers are clear about their policy goals, there is little guidance available regarding the best program design to achieve specific goals. Freedman and Kemper (1996) identify this area as one ripe for future research.

Key Cash Payment Program Design Choices. When considering types of cash payment programs to offer, program designers will need to consider two key program choices. Will they offer only a cash payment program, without giving consumers the choice of traditional services, as in Austria? Or will they provide a choice of a cash payment program and traditional services, as in the CCDE? Will they offer a cash benefit alone, without support services for those consumers needing help in managing the cash benefit, as is typical in the German program? Or will they make available support services, such as those in the CCDE, to teach consumers how to manage their services and possibly conduct the fiscal tasks for those consumers who choose not to do so? Each program choice will reflect a philosophy and program goal.

When considering whether to offer a cash payment as the only option, it is important to consider consumers' preferences for traditional versus consumer-directed services. Background research conducted for the CCDE by the UMCA indicated strong interest in a consumer-directed cash option;

however, a sizable number of consumers would want to maintain their traditional services. Across the demonstration states, interest in a cash option among consumers answering for themselves ranged from 29%–59%; interest among representatives answering for consumers ranged from 39%–49% (Simon-Rusinowitz, Mahoney, Desmond, Shoop, Squillace, & Fay, 1998). In addition, survey respondents also thought it was important to be able to back out of the cash option and return to traditional services if they so desired. This information provides support for offering a cash option as one choice among others. In either case, policy makers have to decide whether the benefit level will be set by formula or based on an individualized assessment.

Offering Support Services. When considering whether to offer support services along with a cash option, several design choices must be addressed. What type of support services should be offered? Should support services be offered on a voluntary or a mandatory basis? The decision whether to offer support services also has implications for program costs. Background research for the CCDE and initial program experience indicate a strong desire for support services and can provide guidance regarding some choices for types of services. The telephone surveys indicated that those consumers who were interested in the cash option wanted help or training with the following tasks, in order of preference: payroll and taxes (77%–84%), deciding how much to pay a worker (76%–86%), doing a worker background check (73%–82%), finding emergency backup workers (65%–82%), finding a personal care worker (51%–67%), interviewing a worker (51%–67%), and firing a worker (44%–67%). Consumer representatives reported similar interest in help with these tasks.

Future findings from the CCDE will provide guidance about the costs and design of counseling services, as well as questions related to mandatory versus voluntary participation in such services. All three states are offering support services and will learn precise costs for this option.

Fraud and Abuse Concerns. Finally, especially in programs that restrict the use of funds, concern about potential fraud and abuse in cash payment programs receives much attention from policy makers and program administrators. Experience from the CCDE may be instructive, as this project has needed to address such concerns in each demonstration state's program design, including the possibility that consumers and/or their families might abuse the cash benefit or be exploited by others (Doty, 1997). Misuse of the cash benefit includes the possibility that consumers might not pay taxes on their workers. Background research for the CCDE indicated that these possibilities are limited (Simon-Rusinowitz, Mahoney, Desmond, Shoop, Squillace, & Fay, 1997, 1998). As explained earlier, a majority of consumers and representatives interested in the cash option said they would want help or training with payroll and taxes (77%–84% and 71%–78%, respectively). More precisely, most clients are likely to elect to have the payrolling and tax withholding for their workers done for them by accounting professionals. This would greatly reduce the amount of cash that consumers receive and manage (Doty, 1997). In fact, in Arkansas's first year of program experience the vast majority of consumers have chosen a bookkeeping service to conduct their fiscal tasks. There have been no reported cases of fraud and abuse to date.

To prevent consumer exploitation by others (and subsequent suffering of ill effects), the CCDE allows and encourages the use of surrogate decision makers to represent consumers who are unable to make all decisions independently. The use of representatives may be especially comforting for those concerned about frail elders who may not be able to conduct all employer tasks independently. To date, there has only been one case of consumer self-neglect in Arkansas, and that problem was addressed with the use of a representative.

Conclusion

Cash payments for care, a financing mechanism that provides a cash benefit to consumers and/or their representatives, is not new in this country or abroad. However, policy makers have become increasingly interested in this payment method, as it has the potential to contain program costs and maintain or increase consumer satisfaction by enhancing consumer autonomy. There is much to learn about the impact of a cash payment program's design on outcomes (such as enhanced consumer choice) and cost. A national demonstration and

evaluation of one type of cash payment program, Cash and Counseling, is currently under way in three state Medicaid programs. This research will shed light on design issues, as well as consumer interest in and satisfaction with this cash option.

KEVIN J. MAHONEY
LORI SIMON-RUSINOWITZ
LORI N. MARKS

See also
   Activities of Daily Living
   Personal Care/Personal Assistant Services
   Medicaid
   Self-Care

CAUTIOUSNESS

Cautiousness in the elderly has been a topic of concern to aging researchers for more than 30 years (see Botwinick, 1984). Studies of slow or delayed response to stimuli vary in the extent to which cautiousness is examined implicitly or explicitly. In the former case some cognitive process, such as perception, learning, or memory, is purportedly under study, but the pattern of the findings lends itself to a cautiousness interpretation. In the latter case cautiousness itself is under examination, and measures are designed specifically to assess it. It should be noted that the two traditions of cautiousness research have proceeded along fairly independent paths for a long time; recent efforts to link them will be discussed.

Cautiousness in the Context of Cognitive Functioning

Speed-Accuracy Trade-Offs. This tradition of research can be traced to Welford's (1951) studies of psychomotor slowing in the elderly. Though such slowing often enhanced accuracy of performance, Welford (1958) chose to interpret such outcomes as a reflection of biopsychological processes. In other words, the slower speed of the elderly was not considered a volitional cautious strategy intended to increase accuracy. Indeed, elderly relative to younger individuals were sometimes slower and *less* accurate.

The foregoing findings are in some respect analogous to more recent work on reflection impulsivity in the elderly (see Kogan, 1982). Research on reflection-impulsivity involves the use of perceptual matching procedures in which respondents are required to select one of a set of highly similar variants that is identical to a standard. Speed and accuracy on that type of task are inversely related: *reflectives* are slow and accurate; *impulsives* are fast and inaccurate. Three independent studies (Coyne, Whitbourne, & Glenwick, 1978; Denney & List, 1979; Kleinman & Brodzinsky, 1978) failed to find evidence that elderly individuals are slow-accurate reflectives. Where the elderly do cautiously sacrifice speed for accuracy, the strategy does not yield a positive outcome. Even though motivated to be accurate, elderly subjects appear to have problems with selective attention that make for inefficiency when scanning the standard and comparison stimuli for matching features.

Errors of Omission. In a variety of cognitive tasks in which the elderly respondent has the option of venturing an answer when less than completely certain, or withholding a response entirely, the latter option is generally chosen. It is this kind of responding in the face of uncertainty that distinguishes the elderly individual from younger cohorts, and that has given rise to the conclusion that the elderly are cautious. The preference of the elderly for making errors of omission rather than commission has been demonstrated in a number of contexts, e.g., paired-associate learning (Korchin & Basowitz, 1957), serial learning (Eisdorfer, Axelrod, & Wilkie, 1963), and perceptual integration (Basowitz & Korchin, 1957). These results do not imply that the elderly possess less ability or knowledge than the young in the foregoing tasks. Indeed, when older and younger subjects were matched on ability in a tachistoscopic word-recognition task, the former nevertheless were more inclined toward the omission error when the procedure permitted such cautious behavior to occur (Silverman, 1963). Further, older respondents can be induced to forgo the omission error through differential monetary rewards and costs (Birkhill & Schaie, 1975; Leech & Witte, 1971; but see Erber, Feely, and Botwinick (1980) and Erber and Botwinick (1983) for more mixed results in this regard.

Cautiousness in Explicit Decision-making Tasks

Initial Studies. Wallach and Kogan (1961) constructed a Choice-Dilemmas Questionnaire (CDQ) containing 12 lifelike situations in which the respondent advises a protagonist as to the level of risk to assume in the choice between a more desirable, risky alternative and a less desirable, cautious alternative. Administration of the CDQ to elderly and young adults yielded a significant age difference favoring more caution in the former, particularly for those items entailing financial risks. This relationship between age and caution was also obtained by Vroom and Pahl (1971), who used a large sample of business managers ranging in age from 22 to 58. Botwinick (1966) further confirmed the foregoing relationship with a set of CDQ-type items in which the protagonists were elderly individuals facing decisions typical for their age. In a subsequent study Botwinick (1969) noted that the most extreme alternative on the CDQ involved a reluctance to choose rather than extreme caution as such. When that alternative was removed, the distribution of responses was comparable for young and old. It thus appears that elderly individuals may be more reluctant than younger persons to make a decisional commitment rather than being more cautious as such (see also Okun, Stock, & Ceurvorst, 1980). This phenomenon is analogous to the age difference in the preference for omission errors.

More Recent Developments. Okun and DiVesta (1976) devised a Vocabulary Risk Task (VRT) providing payoffs proportional to difficulty level such that all alternative vocabulary items were of equal expected value. Older adults were observed to be more cautious (i.e., chose less difficult, lower-payoff problems) and had lower levels of aspiration than did younger individuals. When the VRT was pitted against the CDQ in an effort to predict cautiousness in a verbal learning task (omission error preference), both tasks predicted equally well, though uncorrelated with each other (Okun, Siegler, & George, 1978). Controlling for level of cautiousness removed the association between age and omission errors, thus supporting the view that the foregoing association is at least partially attributable to a dispositional cautious style.

In the work discussed above, alternative choices were of equal expected value. When expected value was made to increase directly or inversely with risk (making it more and less rational, respectively, to choose the riskier alternative), age differences were essentially eliminated (Okun & Elias, 1977). Thus, age differences in cautious behavior emerge only when rationality considerations are absent.

An alternative approach to the study of cautious behavior is offered by Chaubey (1974), who argues that old age is accompanied by a decline in achievement motivation, and therefore, according to the theory of Atkinson and Feather (1966), older adults should seek to avoid moderate risks. The hypothesis was confirmed in an Indian sample and subsequently replicated by Okun and Siegler (1976) in an American sample. Regrettably, though both studies maintain that the elderly *avoid* intermediate risks, no indication is given as to whether they conform to the predicted bimodal pattern of selecting *both* low and high risks.

The generality or convergent validity of risk-caution measures in the elderly remains an understudied topic. Limited generality has been observed in the research of Wallach and Kogan (1961) and of Okun, Stock, and Ceurvorst (1980), but no one has undertaken the kind of large-scale study of the generality of cautiousness that Kogan and Wallach (1964) carried out on samples of college students. On the basis of the sparse evidence currently available, however, it is reasonable to conclude that cautiousness in the elderly is a multivariate rather than a unitary construct.

NATHAN KOGAN

See also
Learned Helplessness
Personality
Reaction Time

CELL AGING IN VITRO

Limited Proliferative Capacity of Normal Human Cells

Early studies by Carrel and coworkers suggested that individual cells, when separated from the or-

ganism were potentially immortal, in the same way that bacteria and most protozoa are considered immortal. However, subsequent studies conducted in a number of laboratories, especially those of Hayflick at the Wistar Institute in Philadelphia, established that normal human diploid cells replicate only a finite number of times. After explanation, there is an initial phase of rapid proliferation, during which cell cultures can be subcultivated frequently. This initial phase is followed by one of declining proliferative capacity, which ultimately culminates in a total loss of mitotic activity. During this later phase the cells change in size and morphology, become granular, and accumulate debris. The inability of cell cultures to proliferate indefinitely cannot be ascribed to various technical difficulties, such as inadequate nutrition, pH variation, toxic metabolic products, and microcontaminants or to depletion by serial dilution of some essential metabolite. Hayflick and Moorhead (1961) concluded that the limited-life-span phenomenon could be programmed and/or that genetic damage may be accumulated, and they interpreted their observation as a cellular expression of aging.

A limited proliferative life span has been described for a variety of cell types, including fibroblasts, glial cells, keratinocytes, vascular smooth muscle cells, lens cells, endothelial cells (Mueller, Rosen, & Levine, 1980), and lymphocytes. These observations on limited proliferative life span also have been noted for cells from other mammalian species. Although the proliferative capacity differs between various types of cells, for any given cell type the proliferative capacity tends to be relatively constant.

Dynamics of Cell Aging In Vitro

In general, the evidence appears very strong that the loss of proliferative capacity in human diploid cell populations is a well-regulated phenomenon, during which substantial heterogeneity develops in the population, and that changes include both an increased generation time and failure of an increasing fraction of the population to replicate at all. Cristofalo (1972) suggested that cellular aging may follow a differentiation lineage model. Similarly, Martin, Sprague, Norwood, and Pendergrass (1974) postulated that the finite life span may represent a differentiation of cell types and that the process of diploid cell growth may have an in vivo counterpart in hyperplastic processes. Chronological time appears to be significantly less important than division events in determining in vitro life span (for a discussion, see Cristofalo & Pignolo, 1993).

Changes in Cell Morphology and Contact

The steady loss of replicative potential is accompanied by a greater heterogeneity of cell sizes, as well as a shift to much larger cell sizes. Characteristic morphological alterations accompany the changes in cell size seen with senescence in culture. An increase in nuclear size, in nucleolar size, and in the number of multinucleated cells parallels the increase in cell size seen in slowly replicating or nonreplicating cultures. Prominent Golgi apparati, evacuated endoplasmic reticula, increased numbers of cytoplasmic microfilaments, vacuolated cytoplasm, and large lysosomal bodies have been observed in senescent human fibroblasts (for discussion, see Cristofalo & Pignolo, 1993).

Late-passage cultures display a reduced harvest density and a lowered saturation density at the plateau phase of growth. At the end of their life span in vitro, substantial cell death occurs; however, a stable population emerges that can exist in a viable, nonproliferative state for many months (Pignolo, Rotenberg, & Cristofalo, 1994). This stable population is capable of maintaining only an extremely low saturation density, equivalent to less than 5% of that reached by early-passage cultures. The observed decrease in saturation densities probably reflects an increased sensitivity to intercellular contact, rather than increased numbers of larger cells (Pignolo et al., 1994). Changes at the level of extracellular matrix (ECM), specific secretory proteins not connected with the ECM, and membrane-associated molecules occur in late-passage cells, but it is unclear whether they account for alterations in the nature of cell contact among these cells (for a detailed review, see Cristofalo & Pignolo, 1993).

Changes in Macromolecular Content, Synthesis, and Cell Cycle Progression

In general, as cells approach the end of their proliferative life span in vitro, the synthesis rate of macro-molecules decreases, whereas the cellular content of macromolecules, except DNA, increases. These observations are reminiscent of the phenomenon of unbalanced growth in bacteria described more than 40 years ago by Cohen and Barner. In senescent cells, it appears that DNA synthesis becomes uncoupled from other macromolecular syntheses, and there is a general dysregulation of coordinated processes (for review, see Cristofalo & Pignolo, 1993).

Cells tend remain essentially diploid (two of each chromosome) until the very near the end of their life span in vitro, when they exhibit structural chromosomal changes and increasing levels of tetraploidy (four of each chromosome) and polyploidy (more than two of each chromosome). DNA, RNA, and protein synthetic rates decrease in late population-doubling level cultures and may be related to the altered chromatin template activity in senescent cells.

Continuously dividing cells pass through several stages that can be identified both morphologically and biochemically. From the end of mitosis to the beginning of the synthesis, or S phase, there is a time interval known as gap-1 (G_1). A similar gap phase is observed between the end of S phase and the beginning of mitosis (G_2). Removal of growth factors from young cells causes growth arrest in a so-called G_0 phase. In terms of the genes that are being expressed and the biochemical pathways that are active, G_0 is very different from either G_1 or G_2. Much evidence supports the view that senescent cells are blocked in late G_1 near the G_1/S boundary in the cell cycle, rather than in G_0. Both young and senescent cells appear to respond to fresh growth factors (mitogens) by carrying out some of the same cell cycle processes in roughly the same time frame. However, the ability to complete the mitogen-initiated cascade of signal transduction pathways and synthesize DNA is lost in senescent cells (see Cristofalo, Volker, Francis, & Tresini, 1998).

Response of Senescent Cells to Growth Signals

Human diploid cells, at or near the beginning of their in vitro replicative life span, vigorously respond to serum or a defined combination of growth factors (mitogens) by initiating DNA synthesis and mitosis. As these cells approach the end of their proliferative potential in culture, they become increasingly refractory to mitogenic signals. The basis for this loss of responsiveness cannot be attributed to any dramatic reductions in the number of cell surface growth-factor receptors or to the affinities with which these receptors bind ligands. Intrinsic changes at the level of the growth-factor receptors, however, have been delineated (for reviews, see Cristofalo & Pignolo, 1993; Cristofalo, Volker, Francis, & Tresini, 1998).

Cells respond to mitogens through the intracellular actions of secondary events, including phospholipid turner, phosphorylation cascades, and calcium mobilization. Alterations in postreceptor transduction pathways have been documented for each of these pathways. Repression of *c-fos* transcription (a gene involved in the transcription of other genes) provides evidence for an early block in one or more pathways potentially required for DNA synthesis. However, expression of the same late-acting, cell-cycle-regulated genes, including cyclins and cyclin-associated gene products, is also diminished in senescent cells. Interestingly, in skin fibroblast cultures derived from individuals with Werner's syndrome (a disease of premature aging), *c-fos* expression in response to serum is equal in young and senescent cultures (see Cristofalo, Volker, Francis, & Tresini, 1998).

Arrest State of Senescent Cells

The hallmark of senescence in culture is the inability of cells to replicate their DNA. The formal possibility exists, then, that replicative enzymes themselves and/or replication-associated processes, such as control of DNA hierarchical structural orders, are reduced or altered. Although these findings might suggest changes in the DNA synthetic machinery of senescent cells, the observation that simian virus 40 (SV40) can initiate an additional round of semiconservative DNA synthesis in old cells indicates, at least superficially, that this machinery is still capable of functioning (Cristofalo, Volker, Francis, & Tresini, 1998).

Senescent cells reach an irreversibly arrested condition that is distinct from either the G_0 phase that young cells achieve or any other definable state within the cell cycle. When cultured under conditions that would define the quiescent state in early-passage cells, the pattern of gene expression exhibited by senescent cells is different from that of a functional G_0 state. Furthermore, examination of chromatin condensation in senescent cells, using a fluorescent dye, revealed patterns consistent with arrest in late G_1. Taken together, the evidence suggests that growth arrest in senescent cells probably occurs in a physiologic state fundamentally distinct from that of the G_0, quiescent state (Pignolo, Martin, Horton, Kalbach, & Cristofalo, 1998). The fact that late-passage cells can express some of the gene characteristics of the G_1/S boundary suggests an abortive attempt to initiate DNA synthesis and arrest in a unique state.

An important biomarker that is linked to the cessation of mitotic activity associated with cellular senescence is the progressive loss of chromosomal telomeric repeats (Levy, Allsopp, Futcher, Greider, & Harley, 1992). Telomeres protect chromosomes from degradation, rearrangements, end-to-end fusions, and chromosome loss (Feng, Funk, Wang, Weinrich, Avilion, Chiu, et al., 1995). The telomeres of human chromosomes are composed of several kilobases of simple repeats (TTAGGG)n. During replication, DNA polymerases synthesize DNA in a 5' to 3' direction; they also require an RNA primer for initiation. The terminal RNA primer required for DNA replication cannot be replaced with DNA, which results in a loss of telomeric sequences with each mitotic cycle of normal cells (Feng et al., 1995; Levy et al., 1992). The observation that telomere shortening correlates with senescence leads to the hypothesis that, with the shortening of telomeres, there is an associated loss of genetic information at or near the ends of chromosomes that is responsible for replicative decline. It also provides an attractive model for the way in which cells might "count" divisions. This hypothesis further suggests that there is a loss of telomerase activity in normal human fibroblasts that is preserved or restored in cells that have obtained an immortalized phenotype. Wright and Shay (1992) have proposed that senescence could be regulated by essential genes near the ends of chromosomes, not as the result of a physical loss of genetic material at these regions (although this also would occur) but by the activation or inactivation of telomeric sequences by changes in adjacent local chromatin condensation.

Genetic Basis for Cellular Aging

The replicative life span of cells in vitro is directly related to the species' maximal life span potential. Furthermore, skin fibroblasts from pairs of monozygotic twins showed no significant difference in replicative life span within each pair but did show such differences among pairs. These observations appear to support the existence of a genetically regulated mechanism that at least partially controls the rate of aging. It is also noteworthy that in heterokaryons formed by the fusion of early- and late-passage cells, the nonproliferative senescent phenotype is dominant over the early-passage, proliferative phenotype and over immortalization. Exceptions to this dominant effect were found in immortalized variants having high levels of DNA polymerase alpha (DNA pol α) or those transformed by DNA tumor viruses. There are numerous reports documenting the presence of inhibitor(s) of DNA synthesis in senescent cells, although the nature of these inhibitor(s) is poorly understood, and whether any of them plays a causal role in senescence is unclear (for review, see Cristofalo & Pignolo, 1993). The idea that senescent cells actively make an inhibitor of DNA synthesis, however, is supported further by the observation that poly A+ RNA derived from senescent fibroblasts, when microinjected into proliferation-competent cells, can inhibit their entry into DNA synthesis (Lumpkin, McClung, Pereira-Smith, & Smith, 1986).

Some of the most compelling evidence in support of a genetic component for cellular senescence has been the finding that introduction of particular chromosomes into immortalized cells causes them to acquire a senescent, or at least a nongrowing, phenotype. Evidence that the cessation of proliferation may be a programmed phenomenon has been provided by studies that characterized the apparently reversible escape from cellular senescence using SV40 large T antigen as a mediator of this transition. This evidence suggests that senescence confers at least two distinct mortality states. The search for chromosomes carrying senescence-inducing genes has relied on the cytogenetic comparison of hybrids between immortal and normal human diploid fibroblasts for the loss of specific chromosomes and the concomitant potential for unlimited division. Thus far, these studies have implicated human chromosomes 1 and 5 as putative sites for senescence-related genes, although it is not clear that the presence of these chromosomes induces a state of growth arrest that is identical to senescence as it normally occurs.

Genetic influences over the process of cellular senescence would necessarily be reflected in reproducible changes in gene expression. The list of molecular markers of senescence in culture has dramatically increased as the result of examining genes isolated from selective libraries and monoclonal antibody pools. The number of genes isolated by these methods remarkably includes those involved with the extra-cellular matrix (ECM), secretory proteins involved in growth factor–mediated function, differentiation and shock proteins, inhibitors of DNA synthesis, and genes of unknown function (Cristofalo, Volker, Francis, & Tresini, 1998). Currently, it is unclear whether differentially expressed genes are regulators of the process of senescence or downstream effects of a higher-order change, which then results in a new but dysfunctional phenotype. For a comprehensive review of cell aging in vitro, including reference material prior to 1980, see Cristofalo and Pignolo (1993).

VINCENT J. CRISTOFALO
ROBERT J. PIGNOLO
ROBERT G. ALLEN

See also
Cell Aging Relationship Between In Vitro and In Vivo Models
Senescence and Transformation
Telomere Senescence Theory

CELL AGING RELATIONSHIP BETWEEN IN VITRO AND IN VIVO MODELS

Interactive Components of Organismal Aging

Senescent changes in the organism involve different kinds of cells and tissues and thus may have multiple mechanisms for their occurrence. For example, aging in fixed postmitotic cells, such as neurons, may proceed by a different set of mechanisms than those driving aging in proliferating tissues such as skin, the lining of the gut, or the blood-forming elements. Matrix macromolecules, such as collagen and elastin, are also altered by aging, but with their own unique parameters of senescent degeneration, because the molecules are directly affected by environmental factors and by changes in the cells that produce them. The interactions of different types of cells and biological components also may change with time, potentially exerting profound effects at the level of the organism.

Decline of Replicative Capacity In Vivo

In general, proliferating cells in vivo exhibit an initially high rate of cell doubling (during developmental phases), followed by a gradual but sustained decline in proliferation rate. With the notable exception of cells of the stomach lining, there is an age-associated decline in mitotic activity and proliferation rates in a wide variety of human and rodent tissues in vivo. However, many studies of cell proliferation in vivo fall short of elucidating the relative contribution of intrinsic versus extrinsic factors (such as alterations in the extracellular matrix) to this decline. Thus, evaluation of various biochemical and morphological parameters of functional capacity that accompany the decline in proliferative capacity in vitro may be of considerable importance to our understanding of the mechanisms of senescence and of the control of cell proliferation in vivo. A group of studies bearing on this point involves the serial transplantation of normal somatic tissues to new, young, inbred hosts each time the recipient approaches old age. In general, normal cells serially transplanted to inbred hosts seem to show a decline in proliferative capacity and probably cannot survive indefinitely (for review, see Cristofalo & Pignolo, 1993). Also, mouse epidermis from old donors retains an increased susceptibility to carcinogens, whether transplanted into young or old recipients.

Decreased antibody production by spleen cells (but not bone marrow cells) from old mice transplanted into young irradiate recipients suggests that senescence of immune-reactive cells in mice may be related to a change undergone by these cells when they migrate from bone marrow to spleen. The proliferative capacity of spleen cells derived from old animals and transplanted into young irradiate hosts is reported to be reduced; however, the trauma of transplantation cannot be ruled out as a contributing factor to this proliferative decline.

Cell Culture as a Model for Aging In Vivo

The suggestion that aging changes in vivo are reflected in various properties of tissue cultures has a long history. For example, it has been known since the early 1900s that age-associated changes that occur in plasma can inhibit cell growth in vitro. In addition, the time elapsing prior to cell migration from explanted tissue fragments increases with increasing age. Both are examples of the expression in vitro of aging in vivo.

In vitro studies on aging have used two kinds of cell cultures. The predominant one has been fetal- or neonatal-derived cultures that show aging changes when serially subcultured; some of these alterations parallel aging changes in vivo. The other, related paradigm is that of cells derived from donors of different ages and studied after only one or a few subcultivations. In either case, attempts to relate changes in these individual cells to changes occurring in organisms as they age forms one basis of the use of the in vitro model for studies of in vivo aging.

Supporting the usefulness of this model, several laboratories, using different types of normal human cells maintained in culture, have presented evidence for a negative correlation between donor age and proliferative life span in vitro (for review, see Cristofalo, Allen, Pignolo, Martin, & Beck, 1998b). The existence of such a relationship clearly suggests that aging in situ, which is a function of donor age, modulates proliferative life span. Hence, the physiological effects of aging in vivo must be reflected by the life span of cells maintained in vitro. Furthermore, the colony-forming capacity of individual cells has also been reported to decline as a function of donor age. A relationship between growth potential and maximal life span of the donor has been reported for several other species. This also appears to support the view that an inverse relationship exists between donor age and proliferative capacity in vitro (for review, see Cristofalo et al., 1998b).

Unfortunately, few studies actually accessed the health status of the donors from whom the cell lines were established. In fact, many of the cell lines used in studies of donor age effects on proliferative capacity were established from cadavers. It is known that cultures established from donors with diabetes exhibit significantly shorter proliferative life spans in culture, and it seems probable that other diseases can also affect in vitro proliferative capacity. A study of 124 cell lines established from 116 donors who participated in the Baltimore Longitudinal Study of Aging (BLSA) and 8 samples of fetal skin revealed no relationship between donor age and proliferative life span in vitro (Cristofalo, Allen, Pignolo, Martin, & Beck, 1998b). In this study, all of the donors were medically evaluated and determined to be "healthy" by the criteria of the BLSA. None had diabetes when the cell lines were established. To evaluate the effects of age on in vitro life span within individuals, multiple cell lines established from the same individuals at time intervals spanning as long as 15 years were compared. Surprisingly, this longitudinal study also revealed no relationship between donor age and proliferative capacity in five individuals. In fact, the proliferative potentials of cultures established when donors were older were frequently greater than observed in lines established at younger donor ages (Cristofalo et al., 1998b).

As noted above, the colony-forming capacity of individual cells also was reported to decline with donor age. However, this assay is strongly influenced by variations in growth rates. Both the initial growth rates and the labeling indices of the fetal fibroblast lines are higher than those observed in adults, which indicates that cell lines established from fetal skin divided more frequently initially, even though the replicative life span of these cell lines did not exceed that observed in the postnatal cell lines. It would seem equally relevant that the labeling indices and initial growth rates of large groups of lines established from adults do not vary significantly with respect to age, although considerable heterogeneity in growth rates can be observed within groups of lines established from adults. In view of differences in initial growth rates and intraclonal variations in the proliferative potential of single cells, it seems probable that the clone size distribution method of estimating proliferative life span and an actual determination of replicative life span measure different things (Cristofalo, Allen, Pignolo, Martin, & Beck, 1998b).

Although these observations fail to support a direct relationship between donor age and proliferative life span in vitro, they do not exclude the possibility that a phenomenon comparable to proliferative senescence occurs in vivo. We recently found that EPC-1, a protein that declines with proliferative aging, is present in a mosaic pattern in skin sections. Furthermore, the average length of chromosome terminal regions (telomeres), which decreases progressively with increasing numbers of mitoses (Levy, Allsopp, Futcher, Greider, & Harley, 1992), exhibits large variations in multiple subclones established from one individual (Allsopp & Harley, 1995). These observations suggest that loss of proliferative potential, in vivo, occurs in a mosaic pattern and that both long- and short-lived cells may lie in close proximity in tissues. When cells are placed in a culture environment, the majority of the population is derived from the cells in vivo that retain the greatest growth capacity. Hence, the selection during the procedure to establish cultures probably obscures differences in proliferative capacity that exist in vivo.

Genetic Disorders and Cellular Aging In Vivo

Goldstein, Moerman, Soeldner, Gleason, and Barnett (1978) and Martin (1978) showed that cells from patients with Hutchinson-Gilford syndrome or Werner's syndrome, both diseases associated with progeroid syndromes, have a reduced proliferative capacity, compared with control cells from normal donors of the same ages. Interestingly, fibroblast cultures established from individuals with Hutchinson-Gilford progeria syndrome exhibit shorter telomeres and a lower proliferative capacity than do cells from normal individuals; however, the rate of telomere shortening per cell division appears to be similar in progeria fibroblasts and normal cells (Allsopp, Vaziri, Patterson, Goldstein, Younglai, Futcher, et al., 1992). Progeroid syndromes are generally defined by the premature appearance of characteristics of senescence. None of them can be considered an exact phenocopy of normal human aging. Thus, Martin (1978) has suggested that they be referred to as "segmental" progeroid syndromes that approximate certain aspects of the aging process. Other workers have reported decreased mitotic activity, DNA synthesis, and cloning efficiency for cells from these persons. In addition, cells derived from diabetic individuals have a reduced ability to grow and survive in culture, as reflected in a reduced plating efficiency, although these studies are complicated by other factors. Cultures established from patients with Werner's syndrome and from individuals with Down's syndrome also have been reported to exhibit decreased proliferative potential, albeit, results with the replication of Down's syndrome cells are more variable and remain controversial.

Biomarkers of Cellular Aging In Vitro and In Vivo

In addition to the loss of division potential associated with aging in vitro and in vivo, as described above, many other significant alterations that occur with senescence in vitro also occur with cellular senescence in vivo. These changes include but are not limited to increased chromosome number (ploidy), increased cell size, decreased response to growth signals, the decreased expression of genes potentially involved in growth control, the increased expression of genes that help shape the extracellular matrix, and various changes in cell morphology (for review, see Cristofalo & Pignolo, 1993, Cristofalo, Volker, Francis, & Tresini, 1998a). In addition, a correlation between replicative capacity and initial telomere length of cells derived from donors between the ages of 0 and 93 years has been reported (Allsopp, Vaziri, Patterson, Goldstein, Younglai, & Futcher, 1992, also see "Cell Aging In Vitro").

One potentially universal marker of aging was reported by Dimri, Lee, Basile, Acosta, Scott, Roskelley, et al. (1995), who observed increases in cytochemically detectable β-galactosidase activity (SA β-gal) at pH 6.0, both in cell cultures and in tissue sections obtained from old donors. They also observed that immortal cells exhibited no SA β-gal staining under identical culture conditions (Dimri et al., 1995). Additionally, they interpreted their results as providing a link between replicative senescence and aging in vivo. Their observation appeared to be supported by Pendergrass, Lane, Bodkin, Hansen, Ingram, Roth, et al. (1999) who reported that SA β-gal positive staining increased as a function of age in rhesus monkeys. However, these observations remain controversial. SA β-gal positive cells have been observed in quiescent cultures of Swiss 3T3 as well as some types of human cancer cells that were chemically stimulated to differentiate, neither of which can be classified as senescent. Furthermore, biochemical analysis has been used to demonstrate β-gal activity in a number of different tumor lines at both pH 6.0 and pH 4.5. We also examined this phenomenon recently and observed that SA β-gal positive staining was present in subconfluent senescent WI-38 fibroblasts but was essentially absent from subconfluent early-passage cells, which supported the conclusion of Dimri and colleagues (1995). Conversely, we were unable to detect any correlation with donor age, either in tissue sections or in skin fibroblast cultures established from donors of different ages. The source of these discrepancies cannot be entirely elucidated; however, it is clear that this type of staining cannot be used as a marker for all types of aging under all conditions.

The possibility exists that these relationships are indirect and that the cell culture system is simply a model to study the regulation of cell proliferation, which, in turn, shows age-associated changes. Even then, however, it remains an important model for aging in vivo because the two principal age-associated diseases, cancer and atherosclerosis, represent failures in the regulation of cell proliferation. Overall, it is clear that characteristic aging changes in vivo are expressed in cell culture. Detailed analysis of these changes in vivo shows that they have the same apparent trajectory as aging in vitro and appear tightly coupled to the capacity for cell proliferation. For a comprehensive review of cell aging in vivo, including reference material prior to 1980, see Cristofalo and Pignolo (1993).

VINCENT J. CRISTOFALO
ROBERT J. PIGNOLO
ROBERT G. ALLEN

See also
Cytogerontology
Telomere Senescence Theory

CELL MORPHOLOGY

See

CELL TRANSFORMATION

See

CENTENARIANS

Belle Boone Beard, a lifelong centenarian researcher, said that "ninety years is old, but 100 is news." Centenarians capture the attention, curiosity, and imagination of almost everyone, from the lay person to the media to researchers who are interested in longevity and survival of the human species.

Centenarians have become the fastest growing segment of most industrialized countries, with about 1 centenarian in a population of 5,000 to 10,000 people. In the past 20 years, a number of studies have investigated the "secrets" of centenarians—studies from Denmark, France, Germany, Hungary, Japan, Sweden, and the United States. Most of the extant studies are descriptive, summarizing characteristics of centenarians. Other studies attempted to isolate unique characteristics of centenarians that may be different from younger cohorts who were most likely not to survive to be centenarians (Poon, Clayton, Martin, Johnson, Courtenay, Sweaney, et al., 1992). However, little is known about factors that contribute to extreme longevity and predictors of survival to extreme old age. How much can genetic predisposition, the environment, and coping styles account for extreme longevity? Is surviving to 100 or beyond different from surviving to 70 or 80 years? Are centenarians inherently different from the average adult? What similarities

and differences are there among the long-lived across different cultures? These are important research questions for the next generation of centenarian research.

Perhaps one important finding from centenarian studies is that differences among centenarians are large (Hagberg, Alfredson, Poon, & Homma, in press). The functional capacity of centenarians can range from those who are still in the work force to those who are bedridden. In a test of learning of new word pairs, for example, some centenarians can learn 15 pairs of words in the first trial (surpassing most college students). However, most centenarians are found to be significantly poorer in mental and physical capacity than younger cohorts. In his studies of German centenarians, Franke (1977, 1985) found that about 20%–30% of the centenarians are functioning well in everyday life, 50% have some dementia of varying severity, and 20%–30% are bedridden and severely demented.

Some Selected Findings

The following are characteristics of cognitively intact and community-dwelling centenarians, compared to those who are 80 and 60 years old, in the Georgia Centenarian Study (Poon, Clayton, Martin, Johnson, Courtenay, Sweaney, et al., 1992).

Health and Health Habits. Centenarians tended to practice health habits that were found to prolong life. That is, few smoked, were obese, or consumed excessive alcohol. They remained active throughout life and ate breakfast on a regular basis. Compared to cohorts in their 60s and 80s, centenarians tended not to have any more illnesses, prescription medications, visits to a physician, or nights in a hospital over a 6-month period. Further, centenarians tended to escape contracting chronic diseases during their lifetime (Nickols-Richardson, Johnson, Poon, & Martin, 1996).

Dietary Habits. The intake of most nutrients were similar among 60-, 80-, and 100-year-old community-dwelling groups with a few exceptions: (1) centenarians consumed about 20%–30% more carotenoids and vitamin A from foods; (2) centenarians consumed breakfast more regularly and avoided weight-loss diets and large fluctuations in body weight; and (3) centenarians tended to consume more whole milk and less 2% milk and yogurt and were less likely to avoid dietary cholesterol (Williams, Johnson, Poon, & Martin, 1995).

Cognition and Intelligence. In a comparison of cognitively intact centenarians with younger cohorts, centenarians showed poorer performances in most cognitive functions except for everyday problem-solving tasks (Holtsberg, Poon, Noble, & Martin, 1995; Poon, Martin, Clayton, Messner, & Noble, 1992). The magnitudes of age differences were smaller in crystallized intelligence than in fluid intelligence. Education was shown to have a profound positive effect that mitigated the level of performance differences between subjects, especially centenarians. It is interesting to note that when centenarians used their everyday experiences in problem solving, their performances were found to be similar to the younger cohorts. Cognition accounted for about 20% of the variance in instrumental activities of daily living (IADL) for all subjects. When functional and mental health, as well as social and economic resources, were included in the regression equation, the amount of IADL variance that could be predicted increased to 37%. These findings show that cognition, health, and resources are all important predictors of everyday functions.

Personality and Coping Styles. Centenarians were more dominant, suspicious, practical, and relaxed than those in their 60s and 80s. Centenarians were less likely to use active behavioral coping but were more likely to use cognitive coping behaviors, compared to octogenarians. They were more likely to acknowledge problems than those in other age groups, and they were less likely to seek social support as a coping strategy for their problems (Martin, Poon, Kim, & Johnson, 1996).

Support Systems. Community-dwelling centenarians reported fewer potential visitors. They were less likely to talk on the telephone or have a spouse as a primary caregiver but more likely to have their children as caregivers and to receive help with food and meal preparation from family and friends (Martin, Poon, Kim, & Johnson, 1996). However, they were just as likely as those in their 60s and 80s to have someone help them if they were sick or disabled, to have a confidante, and to have daily visitors.

Mental Health. Compared to younger community-dwelling cohorts, centenarians tended to report more somatic but not emotional symptoms. Although centenarians were found to have a higher level of depression, no clinical depression was found among the sample of community-dwelling centenarians. African American centenarians had significantly higher levels of depression and poorer self-perceived health than did their White counterparts. However, when education and income were taken into account, differences in self-perceived health were eliminated and differences in mental health decreased but remained significant (Kim, Bramlett, Wright, & Poon, 1998). This was found for all three age groups. This finding shows that concomitant measures such as education, socioeconomic background, and mental health are very important and could influence survivorship and quality of life of the oldest old.

LEONARD W. POON

See also
Life Expectancy
Life Span
Longevity: Societal Impact
Long-Lived Human Populations

CENTER FOR THE ADVANCEMENT OF HEALTH

The Center for the Advancement of Health, a nonprofit organization based in Washington, DC, promotes recognition of the profound and pervasive influence of psychosocial, behavioral, economic, and environmental factors on human health and illness.

The center advances this expanded view of health through a multifaceted program designed (a) to strengthen the capacity of the biobehavioral research community to conduct high-quality research, (b) to communicate the research findings to decision makers and the public, and (c) to translate and integrate the research findings into health policy and practice.

The Center for the Advancement of Health was established in 1992 by the John D. and Catherine T. MacArthur Foundation and the Nathan Cummings Foundation, which continue to support its core activities. Funding for specific projects is provided by the Robert Wood Johnson Foundation, the Burroughs Wellcome Fund, the American Cancer Society, and others. At a time of growing public awareness about the role of behavior in preventing and managing illness among the elderly, the center has undertaken several initiatives aimed at addressing behavioral health issues within the context of aging populations.

In 1999 the center jointly convened, along with the Health Care Financing Administration (HCFA) and the National Institute on Aging (NIA), a series of three meetings to explore what is known about health-related behavior in older persons and the role of health care in shaping and supporting positive engagement of patients in disease prevention and management. The purpose of the meetings was to bring together researchers, clinicians, practitioners, and insurance payers to discuss how to address systematically and effectively the behavioral and psychosocial concerns that significantly affect the health of older persons. Three reports, all available from the center, emerged from these meetings: *How Managed Care Can Help Older Persons Live Well With Chronic Conditions, Interventions to Improve Adherence to Medical Regimens in the Elderly,* and *Imagining a Behavioral Insurance Benefit for Older Persons.*

The center continues to highlight topics particularly germane to elderly populations in its *Facts of Life,* issue briefings for health reporters. Each monthly issue offers an in-depth look at current issues in biobehavioral research. Recent topics have included elderly use of preventive services, the health of caregivers, coping with arthritis, and how lifestyle choices can improve the health of seniors.

One of the center's early projects was coordinating the dissemination and promotion of *Successful Aging* by John W. Rowe, MD, and Robert L. Kahn, PhD. *Successful Aging* emerged as a result of the MacArthur Foundation Study of Aging in America. The results of the study focused on how to maintain optimum physical and mental strength throughout later life.

In addition to activities geared specifically toward addressing the behavioral health issues surrounding aging populations, the center engages in several core activities and projects that promote the expanded view of health within all populations. A few of them are mentioned below.

To strengthen the capacity of biobehavioral research, the center coordinates and sponsors the Health and Behavior Alliance, a group of 26 professional research societies working together to increase the priority of and resources devoted to health behavior research. Current activities of the alliance focus on training health behavior researchers, increasing health-related behavioral and social science research funding at the National Institutes of Health and other public and private agencies, and addressing national policy issues relating to the support and dissemination of health and behavior research.

The Center for the Advancement of Health staffs the alliance and publishes the triweekly electronic newsletter *HABIT (Health and Behavior Information Transfer).* Each issue contains news, updates on funding and policy issues, opportunities to take action, and listings of funding, conferences, calls for submissions, and information sources.

The center publishes *Journal Highlights,* summaries of the most relevant behavioral health research findings in peer-reviewed journals, to help researchers, clinicians, and other health professionals stay informed of related findings outside their chosen specialties.

To communicate the research findings to decision makers and the public, the Center for the Advancement of Health offers a news service to reporters that issues monthly news releases on the most exciting discoveries published in top peer-reviewed research journals, to foster media coverage of the progress of biobehavioral science. The center serves as a referral service to link qualified experts and researchers with journalists and writers who are researching topics that deal with the expanded view of health care (see the organization's website: *www.cfah.org*).

To translate and integrate research findings into health policy and practice, the center has undertaken several recent activities, including the Changing Health Behavior in Managed Care initiative. Funded by the Robert Wood Johnson Foundation, the initiative assessed the availability, access, and integration of health behavior change strategies in managed care in 1999. The center conducted a survey of HMO medical directors in five states and the District of Columbia, interviewed 55 public and private health care purchasers, and critically reviewed the scientific literature on behavior change interventions in clinical settings.

Despite a solid knowledge base, many individuals and organizations connected with traditional medical and public health systems remain either uninformed about the expanded view of health or, in some areas, resistant to its integration into standard medical and public health practice.

The major health problems of our time will not be solved unless biomedical and behavioral science is fully integrated into health research, policy, and practice. The Center for the Advancement of Health is committed to increasing the amount of high-quality research on these topics and to translating its findings into effective health care practice and policy.

JESSIE GRUMAN
PETRINA CHONG

See also
Health Beliefs
Organizations in Aging

CENTRAL AND PERIPHERAL NERVOUS SYSTEMS MORPHOLOGY

The nervous system may be divided into the central nervous system (CNS)—the brain and spinal cord—and the peripheral nervous system (PNS), the receptors and effectors of the body, the peripheral ganglia, and the nerve processes connecting these structures with the CNS. Given the complexity of the human nervous system, an appreciation of normal structure and function is necessary so that the reader may understand the changes that may occur with increasing age. The first section of this review will, therefore, concentrate on the anatomical parts of the brain (brain stem, cerebellum, and cerebral hemispheres) before continuing with changes that describe the relationship with aging.

The CNS occupies the cavity of the skull lying above the foramen magnum, where it continues caudally into the vertebral canal as the spinal cord. The brain may be subdivided into the brain stem, the cerebellum, and the telencephalon. The brain stem is most caudal, extending from the spinal cord to the anterior end of the third ventricle at the lamina terminalis. It makes up about 4.5% of total brain weight and is subdivided into four main subdivisions: medulla oblongata, pons, midbrain, and diencephalon. Dorsal to and overriding the medulla and pons is the cerebellum, about 10.5% of total brain weight, and the remaining telencephalon forms about 85% of total brain weight. It is composed of the cerebral cortex and cortical white matter, the basal ganglia with its component major nuclear groups, the caudate nucleus, the lentiform nucleus, the amygdaloid complex and claustrum, and the basal forebrain, which, although poorly demarcated and understood, contains nuclei and fiber connections that associate it with the limbic and olfactory systems.

The Brain Stem

The most caudal portion of the brain, which is continuous with the spinal cord at the foramen magnum, is the medulla oblongata. This also constitutes the lowest part of the brain stem, a name applied to the central area of the brain appearing identical to a stalk from which two structures grow: the cerebral hemispheres, and the cerebellum. Fiber systems that originate from the spinal cord, the cerebral hemisphere, or the cerebellum may ascend or descend the CNS by passing through the brain stem. The brain stem is the location of groups of cells related to the cranial nerves, which receive and project information between structures in the head (eye and ear) and the CNS. It also plays a major role in the control of automatic activity in thoracic and abdominal viscera.

Diencephalon

The diencephalon is the most rostral portion of the brain stem, and the structures contained within it have an appearance and organization different from the remainder of the brain stem. In part, it is composed of several collections of neurons with intervening white matter, including the thalamus and hypothalamus. The thalamus is a major relay and processing center concerned with communicating sensory information to and from the cerebral cortex. Although the hypothalamus occupies about only 0.5% of the volume of the human brain, "it plays a major role in the regulation of the release of hormones from the pituitary gland, maintenance of body temperature, and the organization of goal seeking behaviors such as feeding, drinking, mating and aggression, and behavioral adjustments to changes in the internal and external environment" (Carpenter & Sutin, 1983, p. 552). The basal ganglia, also located in the diencephalon, include groups of cells whose normal activity is involved in the initiation and control of motor activity. Among these groups of cells are those that form the substantia nigra, a structure that is implicated in Parkinson's disease and is more specifically located in the midbrain.

Cerebellum

On the dorsal surface of the brain stem positioned over the surface of the medulla and pons is the cerebellum. This structure is related anatomically and physiologically to the brain stem by bundles of fibers that are the means by which information may be communicated with the spinal cord and the more rostral levels of the brain stem and secondarily with the cerebral cortex. The cerebellum is involved in the control of posture, eye movements, and auditory and vestibular functions; patients with cerebellar dysfunction experience unsteadiness of gait and inability to estimate the range of voluntary movement, resulting in overshooting the mark, as in attempting to grasp an object. Such an individual may also exhibit difficulty in performing rapid movements and may have slurred speech and a tremor that is exaggerated as the target is approached. *Dizziness* in the elderly may have its focus in the brain stem or the cerebellum but equally at fault may be diseases of the cerebral cortex or the influence of systemic disease on function in the inner ear or the CNS. Whatever the source, dizziness occurs in many elderly persons. Although 30% of the elderly have experienced dizziness, Luxon (1984) indicates that by 80 years of age, 66% of

women and 33% of men have had episodes of dizziness, and Koch and Smith (1985) report dizziness as the most common complaint in patients older than 75 years. Faced with secondary factors affecting normal age changes, dizziness is paramount among the complaints from the older age group. Parker (1994) has reported that the syndrome of multiple sensory deficits seen more frequently but not exclusively among the elderly is a common cause of dizziness and impairment of balance.

Cerebral Hemispheres

Situated over the diencephalon are the cerebral hemispheres, each of which may be divided into lobes: the frontal, parietal, temporal, and occipital. The surface of each lobe is folded into convolutions, or gyri, separated from each other by grooves or sulci. If one were to cut across a gyrus with a knife, one would find that the surface is composed of nerve cells arranged in layers parallel to the surface of the gyrus. Thus, the cerebral cortex may be 1.5 mm to 4.5 mm in thickness and for the entire cortex comprises an area of approximately 2.5 sq ft, most of it hidden within the sulci. It has been estimated that the cerebral cortex contains between 10 and 12 billion nerve cells. The center of each gyrus (the white matter) is composed of nerve processes either entering or leaving that particular gyrus. Although the functions of each lobe may be distinct, a most remarkable aspect of the central nervous system is the degree of integration occurring between these areas.

Frontal Lobe. This is the most anterior lobe of the hemisphere. It extends posteriorly for approximately one half the length of the brain. A large portion of the frontal lobe is concerned with the control of movement of the limbs and trunk of the body, head, and eyes. A region of the left inferior frontal gyrus is known as Broca's area and (in most individuals) is associated with expression or motor mechanisms of speech. The most anterior (frontal) part of the frontal lobe (the prefrontal cortex) controls certain aspects of personality, judgment, and foresight and is involved in permitting an evaluation of the consequences of one's actions.

Parietal Lobe. This lobe is located between the frontal and occipital lobes. Within it is Wernicke's area, a region associated with receptive or comprehensive speech, and in the most anterior position in this lobe is the primary somesthetic area, which receives somesthetic information from the opposite half of the body (Burt, 1993).

Temporal Lobe. Hearing and olfaction are two major systems whose conscious level is related to the temporal lobe, which lies laterally in the skull, deep in the temple region of the head. In addition to these activities, the temporal lobe contains within its deeper region structures that are prominent in the limbic system. These are the amygdaloid nucleus and the hippocampus, intimately related to learning and memory.

Occipital Lobe. This lobe is located most posteriorly in the brain and occupies an area in the back of the skull. Its primary function is to serve as the conscious level for the visual system.

General Considerations of Aging in the Brain

Brain. Consideration of aging and its relationship to the brain requires recognition, if not acceptance, of the concept that the aging process is best understood as a stage in development, albeit an end stage. In the normal aging process, therefore, it should be expected that time and use may alter the functioning of the organism. It is a concern with these changes and their effect on behavior and the physiology of the nervous system that directs attention to this area. The prospect that alterations in behavior and cognitive function may interfere with a person's ability to carry out what have been normal life processes has been emphasized in recent years in relation to the increase in human life expectancy. A better appreciation of this process may have an impact on medical care and social relationships in the elderly population. Humans age in different ways. Examination of a randomly selected group of elderly persons will reveal that although some individuals may show very slight deterioration in motor, sensory, or cognitive ability, others will have a marked loss in memory and in the ability to relate to others and to the environment. This latter group has increased in step with the increase in life expectancy, resulting in increased costs for

care and a concern as to whether this is an ultimate problem that most older persons will face in the future.

The CNS consists of a complex series of structures containing numerous types of cells, with basic functions of communication and elaboration of information brought to it by stimuli in the environment, in addition to the maintenance of a normal metabolism and milieu. The basic cell types are neurons, or nerve cells and neuroglia cells. These will be considered in relation to aging. Other factors that may have an influence on aging in the CNS relate to brain weight and the size of the ventricular system.

Brain Weight. The brain at birth weighs approximately 375 g, whereas in the adult the weight of the brain is about 1,400 g in the male and 1,250 g in the adult female.

Age-related changes in brain weight have been investigated well back into the 19th century. This was probably related to the practice of weighing the brain as a normal part of the standard autopsy. These studies showed a decrease in brain weight, that peaked in the third decade (20–30 years of age). An article by Dekaban and Sadowsky (1978) reviewed their own as well as six other large series of brain studies and found that a peak occurred in male subjects at about 20 years of age and at 17 in female subjects. These continue to be generally acceptable as a period when maximum brain weight is achieved. Brain weight then decreases at a rough average of 100 g per brain or 2 g per decade for both sexes and 7%–11% by the 10th decade (Miller, Alston, & Corsellis, 1980). These authors also reported an increasing ratio between gray and white matter, suggesting that the predominant loss was in the white matter, a fact that has been supported by careful imaging studies. This confirms the fact that gyral atrophy affecting both gray and white matter occurs in aging rather than in cortical atrophy alone. This usually affects the convexities of the frontal lobes, the parasagittal region, and the temporal and parietal lobes. It should be noted that these same regions are involved in Alzheimer's disease. The base of the brain and the occipital lobe are generally spared.

Because specimens are examined at one point (cross-sectional series) rather than in a longitudinal fashion, differences between younger and older individuals may relate more to overall larger body size (and consequently larger brain size) in the younger generation than to an actual loss in brain weight in the elderly. Although a great deal of attention has been given to the question of brain weight changes, the results may not be true changes unless the subject's body size is also considered. This has not been done up to this time. Other considerations are the time elapsed between death and weighing of the brain, as well as the cause of death. Both factors may result in brain shrinkage and a consequent lower weight, especially in the older person. Conversely, the number of studies performed on diverse populations (and even under different conditions) indicates that a decrease in brain weight is a true concomitant of aging in the human.

Ventricular System

Within the substance of each hemisphere, a system of spaces or ventricles exists. These are continuous with each other, finally communicating with the subarachnoid space that surrounds the brain and spinal cord. The ventricles and subarachnoid spaces contain a colorless fluid (cerebrospinal fluid) that is produced by the filtration and secretory actions of blood vessels contained within the ventricles. The largest of the ventricles are found within each hemisphere. When enlargement of the ventricles occurs, it does so at the expense of neighboring white and gray matter, interfering with the normal activity of nerve cells and their processes.

Although there have been conflicting statements in the literature regarding changes in ventricular size, the bulk of the studies support the concept that ventricular enlargement does occur and is related to increasing age. This has been confirmed by imaging studies, most recently in 79 healthy male subjects below the age of 87 years, in which the fluid volume remained stable until age 60 and then increased dramatically, a finding in agreement with five other studies (Stafford, Albert, Naeser, Sandor, & Garvey, 1988). It has also been stated by Massman, Bigler, Cullum, and Naugle (1986) that although ventricular enlargement and gyral atrophy often appear in the same specimen, the processes are independent of each other. It should be possible to examine this question of ventricular change in a series of living subjects, correlating imaging findings with behavioral and other functional examinations in the living person, which may provide a final answer to this question.

Spinal Cord

Relatively little is known about age changes in the spinal cord. This may be related to the difficulty in obtaining suitable specimens. The anterior horn cells provide motor fibers to peripheral nerves, and these large-sized nerve cells demonstrate age-related degenerative changes during the fifth decade of life. Lipofuscin deposition begins at about 40 years of age and, as indicated in the "Lipofuscin" entry, the entire cytoplasm is often filled with this material by age 60. A loss of Nissl material, which leads to reduced protein synthesis, is also observed; however, as occurs in brain stem nuclei, the relation between Nissl loss and cell death is not clear. Tomlinson and Irving (1977), however, counted anterior horn cells in lumbosacral spinal cord segments of subjects 13–95 years old and found no changes in neuronal number until age 60, after which there was a continuing decrease of one third until the 91–95 age.

Cells of the CNS

The two major groups of cells in the CNS are the neuroglia and neurons, or nerve cells. The neuroglia are found in gray and white matter, whereas neurons are present in only gray matter.

Neuroglia. Little attention has been given to changes of neuroglia with age. These cells are difficult to identify in a tissue section, and their functional relationships have not been completely understood. There are several neuroglial (glial) types.

Oligodendrocytes are responsible for the production of the myelin covering of nerve fibers in the CNS. These cells show no change with increasing age.

Astrocytes have traditionally been considered to provide the basic support or matrix for the CNS. More important, they are involved in providing an ionic homeostatic environment in the CNS, and they aid in the metabolism of several neurotransmitters. Although lipofuscin is found in astrocytes with increasing age, it appears in different parts of the brain at different ages.

To determine changes in the number of astrocytes in aging human cerebral cortex, Hansen, Armstrong, and Terry (1987) examined the cortices of 25 dementia-free persons, using immunolabeling of fibrous astrocytes. They found that although changes in cell numbers could not be correlated with increasing age, there was a significant linear increase in the older specimens when they were divided into those younger than age 70 and those older.

Microglia are the smallest of the neuroglial cells. They appear to have developed from blood cells (monocytes). Functionally, they are considered to be the phagocytes of the CNS. Microglia have been examined more thoroughly than any other glial cell. With increasing age, large amounts of lipofuscin are found in these cells, lending support to a concept that the microglial cell ingests the material from neighboring abnormal brain tissue. The lipofuscin may, conversely, be a product of microglial metabolism, just as it may have a similar relationship in the neuron (see "Lipofuscin").

Sturrock (1983) emphasizes the few studies of changes in glial numbers with increasing age. A finding similar to that in neurons indicates a regional difference in changes in glial numbers. Microglia increase to the largest extent among neuroglial cells, but this may be related to a response to neuronal loss or other pathology. An increase in the number of astrocytes appears to be related to neuronal death or metabolic changes that occur in aging brain. The question of changes in the number of astrocytes, however, is unsettled, although proliferation of processes of existing astrocytes has been noted in animals and humans. In this way, changes in glial cell activity or in numbers may be a mechanism adopted by the nervous system to compensate for the loss of neurons. Although previously ignored, the relationship of neuroglial cells to CNS metabolism and activity should encourage further aging studies.

The Neuron.   The neuron is the major functional unit of the CNS. It is composed of a cell body containing the nucleus and a number of processes or nerve fibers, including the dendrites, which bring information from other cells to the cell body, and a single axon that communicates this information

to other neurons in the specific pathway. The point of contact for transmission of information between neurons occurs at the synapse.

Neuron population studies in the aging CNS emphasize the unique character of the nervous system. It is clear that there is a specificity for cell loss in certain brain areas and not in others (e.g., between 13 and 85 years in the human, there is a neuronal loss of 52% in the subiculum of the hippocampal area and 31% in the hilus of the dentate gyrus, whereas none of the remaining hippocampal structures shows significant change in cell numbers [West, 1993]), that certain species demonstrate cell loss whereas others do not, and that the age at which cell loss occurs varies from one brain region to another. In the human cerebral cortex, significant decreases in the numbers of neurons have been reported in the superior frontal gyrus, superior temporal gyrus, precentral gyrus (most posterior portion of the frontal lobe), and occipital cortex, whereas no changes were evident in the inferior temporal gyrus or the postcentral gyrus (most anterior part of the parietal lobe). Decreases are of a linear nature, continuing from 20 years of age. The cell types involved also appear to have a specificity in that smaller size neurons (Golgi type II neurons)—the association cells that play a role in the integration of nervous system activity—are affected to a greater degree than those of large size. Because smaller cells are considered to develop later than larger cells, there may be a time sequence resulting in the greater loss of younger cortical cells.

In contrast to earlier changes in cell numbers, which have been reported since the 1950s, the use of newer technology has made possible more specific and repeatable examination of the cerebral cortex. A series of nonbiased cell counts by Pakkenberg, Evans, Møller, Braendgaard, and Gündersen in 1989 did not demonstrate a cell loss with increasing age; therefore, it appears from these studies that with a changing technology, the argument regarding age-related neuronal losses is still unsettled.

In the cerebellar cortex, the decrease in Purkinje cells in the vermis was statistically significant (Sjöbeck, Dahlen, & Englund, 1999).

There is a distinct difference between aging effects in brain stem nuclei and those in the cerebral cortex. Of the many brain stem structures that have been examined, only two demonstrate a significant reduction in cell number. The cells in these structures (locus ceruleus and substantia nigra) are characterized by their content of melanin and their elaboration of two major neurotransmitters, norepinephrine and dopamine, respectively.

In addition to the decrease in the number of neurons, another significant change occurs in the dendrites of neurons in the normal aging process. The axon of a neuron communicates with the next order of neurons in a particular pathway (sensory or motor) through synaptic endings or spines on the dendrites. If the dendritic branches or spines should decrease in number, though the cell body is relatively normal, the effect could be disastrous for the continuing ability of that neuron to maintain its normal communication with other nerve cells. There is abundant evidence that this is precisely what occurs, at least when one considers the morphological integrity of the nerve cell (Scheibel & Scheibel, 1975). Whether the physiological activity is altered is not presently known, although this would be a natural conclusion. Evidence indicates that although the dendritic changes occur in some cells in normal aging, there is a simultaneous increase and thickening of these branches in other cortical neurons, suggesting an attempt to compensate for the degenerative neuronal changes (Buell & Coleman, 1981; Coleman & Buell, 1985: Coleman & Flood, 1987). Of significance is the absence of such growth in the cortical neurons of Alzheimer's disease subjects, suggesting a differing potential for neuronal repair between normal aging individuals and those with this form of dementia. Increased longevity is unfortunately associated with increasing illness and susceptibility to deterioration in several of the body's systems. None is more challenging and provocative for study than the effect on the structure and function of the CNS. Neuronal loss and dendritic change may have the ultimate effect of interfering with normal activity. It is this fear that is uppermost in the minds of older individuals. The changes that occur must be understood if we are to be able to deal with the effect of normal changes in the CNS and with its disease states.

The Peripheral Nerves. Sensory stimulation, such as stroking of the skin, is transmitted from a receptor (nerve ending in skin) to the CNS by way of a peripheral nerve. This nerve also carries the response to the stimulus from the CNS to an effector organ, which in this case may be a muscle. Nerve fibers that communicate between the CNS and the body are collected in bundles, forming spinal nerves when related to the spinal cord and cranial nerves when connected with the brain. The connection between the spinal nerve and the spinal cord is by roots or nerve fibers oriented to the dorsal and ventral aspects of the cord. The dorsal root contains sensory fibers from somatic and visceral structures and is a means by which sensory information passes from the spinal nerve into the CNS. The ventral root contains motor fibers that transmit information from the CNS into the peripheral nerve to be distributed to muscles and visceral organs. The peripheral nerve, therefore, contains a mixture of sensory and motor fibers that are difficult to distinguish from each other.

Although the presence or amount of myelin around nerve fibers may vary, each nerve fiber is enclosed by a neurilemmal sheath, from which myelin may develop and which itself originates as the plasma membrane of a neurilemmal cell. Surrounding the nerve fiber and its neurilemmal sheath are a series of connective tissue coverings. The first of these is the endoneurium, which is a delicate membrane surrounding each nerve fiber. A group of nerve fibers are collected together into bundles, or fascicles, by connective tissue (perineurium), and groups of fascicles are combined into the peripheral nerve by an encircling thick layer of connective tissue called the epineurium.

In animal studies of aging, some features are recognized as being related to increasing age. Whether quantitative changes occur in peripheral nerves is controversial and may depend on the specific nerve studied. Although in the rat a decrease in the number of fibers has been reported (Krinke, 1983), a stability in the population of myelinated fibers (Sharma, Bajada, & Thomas, 1980) has also been maintained. A prominent feature of changes in the peripheral nervous system in the aging rat is the development of spontaneous, demyelinating changes in the roots, manifested by myelin balloon formation, infoldings and reduplication, and axonal atrophy. The ventral root is frequently more affected than the dorsal root, and lesions may extend distally into spinal nerves or centrally into the spinal cord (Braund, McGuire, & Lincoln, 1982). Among the common changes occurring in human nerve fibers are a progressive reduction in the number and density of myelinated fibers directly related to fiber size. This is accompanied by thickening of the perineurial, epineurial, and endoneurial sheaths. As a reflection of generalized atherosclerotic change, blood vessels of peripheral nerves may be involved. A complex relationship between Wallerian degeneration and axonal regeneration also occurs after 60 years of age, although these changes are not as common as are the demyelinating lesions (Vital, Vital, Rigal, Decamps, Emeriau, & Galley, 1990).

Among age changes seen in the spinal roots are mild fibrosis, endothelial hyperplasia, and vascular thickening. With these degenerative changes affecting ventral roots to a greater extent than dorsal roots, the elderly patient will have difficulty in motor activity to a greater extent than sensory impairment and a greater involvement of the lower extremities, because the lumbosacral roots are more involved than the cervicothoracic roots. Atrophy of root myelinated fibers also may be found, with a significant reduction occurring by 50–60 years of age (Mittal & Logmani, 1987). Still, in the interests of developmental anatomy, it should be emphasized that the most dramatic reduction in myelinated fiber density occurs between birth and 2 years of life (from 20,000 to 4,000–7,000 myelinated fibers per mm^2) (Jacobs & Love, 1985).

There are conflicting findings regarding changes in anterior horn cells that contribute motor fibers in peripheral nerves. Lipofuscin deposition begins at about 40 years of age and, as is the case in the brain stem nucleus of the inferior olive, 75%–95% of the cell volume may be occupied by this pigment by the age of 80 years. This accumulation of lipofuscin pigment probably does not have a relation to cell death (see "Lipofuscin"). Nevertheless, computer-assisted analysis of anterior horn cells in the L3, L4, and L5 segments of the spinal cord have demonstrated a loss of 175 to 260 cells per decade (Kawamura, O'Brien, Okazaki, & Dyck, 1977), a fact that may relate to the decline in myelinated fibers in peripheral nerves.

Just as changes have been reported in anterior horn cells, spinal roots, and peripheral nerves, age-related changes also have been noted at the neuromuscular junction beginning during the third decade. Meissner's tactile corpuscles, which are related to reception of light touch stimuli, are reduced by 80% in the elderly. Pacinian pressure corpuscles also become smaller in size. Sensory nerve conduction studies illustrate abnormalities, becoming obvious between 30 and 50 years of age, with a decrease in the amplitude of the action potential. Sensory and motor nerve velocities also are decreased, indicating in the latter case a loss of motor units after 60 years of age.

Indications of peripheral neuropathy in older persons have been reported in otherwise intact individuals. Complaints of tingling, numbness, diffuse weakness, decreased deep tendon reflexes, the loss of ankle reflexes, and poor balance, together with increased sensory thresholds to the usual sensory stimuli, are commonly reported by patients without other neurological complaints. These may be related to some of the factors discussed in this section. For a general discussion of degenerative disorders of the peripheral nerve see Aisen (1994).

Autonomic Nervous System

The reader is advised to obtain a basic understanding of the anatomy, physiology, and chemical importance of the autonomic nervous system by referring to chapters on the subject in a standard neuroanatomy textbook by authors such as de Groot and Chusid, 1988, and Afifi and Bergman, 1986.

Basically, the response to stress is under the control of the autonomic nervous system. This may influence activities of internal organ systems such as the heart, kidney, endocrine glands, gastrointestinal system, and urinary system, which receive information from the brain or spinal cord, and transmit these signals to end organs in the body. The end structure that receives input from the central nervous system may then be stimulated to either increase or decrease its activity, resulting in an increase or decrease in its output, so the organ (e.g., the heart) may show slowing or quickening of its action.

The response to stress is the critical difference or hallmark of aging; in comparison with the younger individual, it is not the resting level of performance but how the organ (or organism) adapts to external stress that determines the effect of aging (Kane, Ouslander, & Abrass, 1999). This decreased response to stress can be seen in the performance of other endocrine systems or the cardiovascular system. The older person may have a normal resting pulse and cardiac output but not be able to achieve an adequate increase in either with exercise. It is essential, therefore, that the examiner be aware of the range of responses, or lack thereof, of a specific organ when stressed in order to understand the range of responses that are possible.

For further study on nervous systems see Brody and Vijayashankar (1977); Burt (1993); Costran, Kumar, and Robbins (1994); Kato, Maruyama, Naoi, Hashizuma, and Osawa (1998); Mann (1988); Monagle and Brody (1974); Rogers, Silver, Shoemaker, and Bloom (1980); Sohal (1981); Strehler, Mark, Midvan, and Gee (1959).

HAROLD BRODY

See also
Neurotrophic Factors and Aging

CENTRAL NERVOUS SYSTEM: COGNITIVE FUNCTIONS
See

CENTRAL NERVOUS SYSTEM: MOTOR FUNCTIONS

Morphological and functional changes occurring within the central nervous system (CNS) with advancing age appear to have the most profound and observable impact on motor function. When older adults are compared to younger adults across a variety of different motor tasks, significant differences are evident in the speed with which older adults initiate and execute movements, particularly when the number of response choices available and the complexity of the movement to be performed increases. Qualitative differences in the strategy used to accomplish the goal of the movement are also evident in some cases.

Despite the many age-associated structural and functional changes occurring within the central and peripheral nervous systems, not all changes occurring within specific regions, in and of themselves, necessarily result in observable and/or adverse effects on motor function. That is because optimal motor function is achieved through the interaction of multiple systems both within and external to the CNS. When multiple systems exceed a threshold of minimum function, however, their synergistic combination will almost certainly produce significant motor dysfunction. At a behavioral level, these cumulative system changes occurring in the aging nervous system appear to manifest themselves in a reduced ability to perform a variety of complex movements that require speed and accuracy, balance, strength, and/or coordination.

Morphological and Neurochemical Changes

Age-related morphological changes within the CNS include a decrease in brain weight, gyral thickness, myelin sheaths, and the total number of large, myelinated nerve fibers. An increase in the overall size of the ventricles is also evident with age. A 40% reduction in the number of neurons, dendritic spines, and dendrites also has been documented in the frontal cortex of deceased 80- and 90-year-olds when compared to younger adults. These changes may have important implications for motor function because of the important role played by the frontal cortex in the development of goal-directed action plans. Age-related losses of Purkinje cells in the cerebellum, known to play an important role in the planning and execution phases of movement, also have been reported. Neurochemical changes have been demonstrated within the aging CNS, the most notable being a 50% decrease in the dopamine content of the human neostriatum in 80-year-olds (Katzman & Terry, 1992). Also, a selective reduction in the activity of the dopaminergic, noradrenergic, and cholinergic systems has been reported. Although the relationship between changes in specific regions of the brain and motor function is difficult to quantify, the cumulative effects of these changes in multiple regions of the CNS, known to be active contributors to the planning and control of movements (i.e., basal ganglia, cerebellum, and motor cortex), will adversely affect motor function.

Sensory System Changes

Vision.   Age-related changes in the peripheral and central components of the visual, somatosensory, and/or vestibular systems can be expected to affect motor function because of the interdependency that exists between the processing of incoming sensory information, the selection of an appropriate motor response, and its subsequent control. Central processing of visual, somatosensory, and vestibular information provides an internal representation of the body's position in space, movement, and the spatial layout of the environment. This internal representation is then used to guide the ensuing motor response.

Common age-related changes in visual function include reduced acuity, depth perception, and contrast sensitivity, as well as a narrowing of the visual field, particularly in the peripheral region, and altered perception of true vertical and horizontal. The presence of cataracts and presbyopia (due to diminishing lens accommodation) also affects visual function. Collectively, these changes can be expected to adversely affect the older adult's ability to accurately perceive and/or anticipate changes in normal surface conditions and the presence of hazards in the environment. As a result, the ability to avoid obstacles, negotiate curbs and stairs, and efficiently ambulate in conditions of low or changing light will be adversely affected. Decrements within the visual system, particularly within the peripheral visual field, have been associated with increased risk for falls among older adults.

Somatosensation.   Age-related changes within the somatosensory system have been shown to have a direct impact on postural stability and the ability to restore upright control following a loss of balance. A two- to tenfold increase in vibration threshold, indicating reduced cutaneous receptor sensitivity, has been documented among older adults. Age-related changes in muscle spindle activity primarily

and joint receptor activity to a lesser degree also are believed to influence postural control. These proprioceptors provide the CNS with information relative to absolute and dynamic changes in joint angle and therefore contribute to optimal motor function. Reduced cutaneous receptor sensitivity is thought to be a primary contributing factor to the decreases observed in hand dexterity with age. The time required to manipulate small objects (e.g., cards, pens, etc.) has been shown to increase by 25% to 40% of initial speed by age 70. Fine motor activities, such as fastening buttons, handwriting, tying shoelaces, and eating become more difficult to perform as a result of declining hand dexterity.

Vestibular.   A gradually decreasing density of labyrinthine hair-cell receptors, beginning at age 30, and a significant reduction in vestibular receptor ganglion cells, beginning around age 55–60 years, constitute the primary age-related anatomical changes occurring within the vestibular system. A moderate reduction in the gain of the vestibular-occular reflex (VOR) also has been noted with age. The primary roles of this system are to maintain balance when the other systems are not available, stabilize vision during head motions, and provide an internal orientation reference that is critical in the resolution of conflict that arises between the sensory systems in complex visual environments (e.g., crowded malls, freeway traffic, etc.). Although a direct relationship between vestibular function and motor control in older adults has not been established, there is some evidence to suggest that older adults may not be able to stabilize the head as well as younger adults can when the body is perturbed. Postural sway among older adults also increases markedly when the orientation of the vestibular apparatus is altered (i.e., head tilted backward with eyes closed).

The contribution of each of the sensory systems to upright postural control has been quantified by using dynamic posturography. Results comparing healthy older adults with younger adults indicate that, whereas sway amplitude increases only moderately when one sensory system is no longer available, when two systems are compromised, sway amplitude increases markedly, leading to a loss of balance in many cases. These results suggest that older adults require more sensory feedback for the control of bodily orientation in space, compared to younger adults. The need for more sensory feedback is also evident when older adults are asked to perform goal-directed aiming movements requiring a speed and accuracy component. Although older adults exhibit similar speeds to younger adults during the initial ballistic phase of the movement, movement speed slows significantly as the target is approached, indicating a deficit in sensorimotor processing.

Sensorimotor Processing

Changes in sensorimotor processing as a function of age have been well documented. Chronometric measures (i.e., simple and choice reaction time, movement time, and response time) used to quantify the time required to plan and execute actions have revealed that the most significant age-related declines are in the action-planning phase (i.e., time to process incoming sensory information and formulate an appropriate motor response (Spirduso, 1995). Electromyographic (EMG) studies have further revealed significant age-related differences in the temporal sequencing of muscle activation patterns in response to unexpected perturbations. Unlike the stereotypical and symmetrical responses of their younger counterparts, apparently healthy older adults exhibit considerably more variable activation patterns and a reduced ability to inhibit inappropriate responses (Stelmach, Phillips, DiFabio, & Teasdale, 1989). Inappropriate postural responses are most evident when the functional base of support is reduced, the support surface is compliant or unstable, or visual input is altered (Alexander, 1994). The control of these more automatic types of postural responses is thought to originate at a cortical level (e.g., supplementary motor cortex), whereas the actual generation of limb movements is believed to be controlled at the level of the spinal cord.

Practice Effects on Motor Function

On a positive note, studies conducted with healthy older adults have demonstrated moderate to large improvements in motor function as a result of practice. With repeated exposure to changing task demands and/or environmental constraints, significant improvements in multiple dimensions of bal-

ance have been documented (Wolfson, Whipple, Derby, Judge, King, Amerman, et al., 1996).

Not only does practice have a positive effect on motor function in healthy older adults, but it has also demonstrated moderate to large improvements in sensory and motor function in frailer or posturally unstable older adults (Rose & Clark, 2000). These improvements in motor function suggest that the CNS remains capable of adaptation, even with advancing age.

DEBRA J. ROSE

See also
  Mobility
  Neurotransmitters in the Aging Brain
  Parkinson's Disease
  Reaction Time

CENTRAL NERVOUS SYSTEM: SENSORY FUNCTIONS
See
  Central and Peripheral Nervous Systems Morphology
  Hearing
  Pain
  Taste and Smell
  Vision and Visual Perception

CEREBROVASCULAR DISEASE

Stroke refers to the sudden onset of neurological deficit due to cerebrovascular disease. In the United States an estimated 500,000–700,000 strokes occur each year (American Heart Association, 1998; Broderick, Brott, Kothari, Miller, Khoury, Pancioli, et al., 1998). Stroke is the leading cause of serious long-term disability, the second ranking cause of dementia, and the third most frequent cause of death. During the past three decades, improved recognition and treatment have led to decreased mortality following acute stroke. However, the number of stroke survivors living with a chronic disability has increased. Furthermore, the total number of new strokes continues to grow, due to the progressive "graying" of the population and the increase in the incidence of stroke as a function of age.

Pathophysiology

The cerebrovascular system comprises a network of arteries, capillaries, and veins that transport essential substrates to the brain and clear metabolic waste products. The brain, unlike other organs in the human body, depends minute by minute on the cerebrovasculature to deliver a continuous supply of oxygen and glucose for energy metabolism. When blood flow is completely disrupted, neurons become dysfunctional within 6–9 seconds and start to die within 30–60 minutes. A variety of conditions may lead to disruption of blood flow, including:

1. occlusion of the artery lumen by a blood clot that develops as a local thrombus or embolizes from the heart or carotid artery;
2. rupture of the vessel wall, causing bleeding or hemorrhage;
3. a sudden drop in blood pressure (e.g., due to cardiac arrest or acute blood loss); and
4. severe narrowing of multiple blood vessels (e.g, due to atherosclerosis or arteriolosclerosis).

The term *ischemia* refers to conditions where blood flow is not sufficient to support normal cell function. In the United States, approximately 75% of strokes are due to ischemia, and 25% result from hemorrhage.

Within a certain range of mean arterial blood pressures (e.g., 60–150 mmHg), autoregulatory mechanisms in the brain maintain a constant level of cerebral blood flow. Outside this range, cerebral perfusion goes up and down directly with blood pressure. When perfusion pressure decreases throughout the brain, the arterial end zones and border zones are the first to suffer. An end zone is the last area to receive blood from a single artery; a border zone is the last area to receive blood from two or more arteries.

There is a critical window of ischemia, known as the penumbra (i.e., shadow), where oxygen and glucose delivery is too low to maintain electrical function but still sufficient to maintain vital membrane pumps and ion gradients (Hossman, 1994). If blood flow is returned quickly, neuron function may be completely restored. The clinical manifestation of this temporary, reversible neurological dysfunction is a transient ischemic attack (TIA). If blood flow is not promptly restored, irreversible membrane failure and cell death occurs. Tissue necrosis may range from incomplete and selective loss of neurons (incomplete infarction) to cystic necrosis of all tissue elements, including neurons, glia, and endothelial cells (complete infarction) (Garcia, Lassen, Weiller, Sperling, & Nakagawara, 1996). The sudden appearance of permanent neurological deficit is recognized clinically as a stroke. Sometimes, however, complete and incomplete infarction of the brain may not produce obvious clinical symptoms (i.e., silent stroke). The goal of thrombolytic therapy (clot busters) is to restore blood flow to neurons lingering in the penumbra, or shadow, of death.

Structural and Functional Changes in the Cerebrovascular System

Normal aging is associated with several changes in blood vessels. The subintimal layer of arteries thickens as a result of migration and proliferation of smooth muscle cells, increased deposition of collagen, fragmentation of elastin, and accumulation of lipids (Cooper, Cooke, & Dzau, 1994). Increased tortuosity of cerebral arteries is observed, beginning in the fourth decade (Akima, Nonaka, Kagesawa, & Tanaka, 1986). Responses to various chemical vasodilators diminish with age. This combination of structural and biochemical changes leads to increased wall stiffness and resistance to blood flow and may decrease autoregulatory capacity. Progressive stiffening of the blood vessel wall is markedly accelerated by atherosclerosis, arteriolosclerosis, and amyloid angiopathy.

Atherosclerosis refers to the thickening and hardening of the walls of larger arteries (e.g., carotid, vertebral-basilar, major cerebral, and coronary arteries). Numerous risk factors predispose to atherosclerosis, including age, male gender, family history, hyperlipidemia, hypertension, hyperglycemia, smoking, and obesity (Sacco et al., 1997). High levels of low-density lipoprotein (LDL) cholesterol and low levels of high-density lipoprotein (HDL) cholesterol are major modifiable risk factors. The atherosclerotic process begins in the subendothelial layer and progresses through several stages. At first, a fatty streak made of foamy macrophages appears in the luminal wall. Later, a palpable fibrous nodule develops from elastin and extracellular lipid. Finally, a complicated plaque forms, harboring variable degrees of calcification, necrosis, thrombosis, and ulceration. Internal fragments from a complicated plaque may embolize and occlude distal branches of the arterial tree, causing TIA or stroke. Alternatively, progressive narrowing of the vessel lumen may lead to decreased flow and incomplete infarction in arterial border zones. Finally, the arterial wall may become progressively weakened, leading to fusiform aneurysmal dilatation and hemorrhage.

Arteriolosclerosis refers to structural changes that affect small parenchymal arteries and arterioles. Hypertension and diabetes mellitus are major risk factors. The media of arterioles thicken due to hypertrophy of smooth muscle cells and deposition of collagen, elastin, and proteoglycans. Arteriolosclerosis may lead to either infarction or hemorrhage. Occlusion of small arteries produces small infarcts (less than 1.5 cm in diameter) known as lacunes. Widespread arteriolosclerosis may lead to ischemia and incomplete infarction in the periventricular and deep white matter, the end zones of the deep penetrating (so-called medullary) arteries. The formation of miliary saccular aneuryms (Charcot-Bouchard aneurysms) in weakened blood vessel walls may result in hemorrhage. Both infarction and hemorrhage associated with arteriolosclerosis tend to occur in the basal ganglia, thalamus, pons, cerebellum, and deep cerebral white matter.

Cerebral amyloid angiopathy refers to the deposition of amyloid proteins in the blood vessel wall (Vinters & Duckwiler, 1992). Beta-A4 type amyloid is deposited in normal aging, in Alzheimer's disease, and in the Dutch form of hereditary cerebral amyloidosis with hemorrhage (HCAWH). Cerebral amyloid angiopathy may lead to microaneurysms and subsequent hemorrhage, usually in the major lobes of the cerebral hemispheres. Amyloid angiopathy may also cause microinfarcts in the cerebral cortex and incomplete infarction in the deep white matter. Unfortunately, it is difficult to diagnosis the sporadic forms of cerebral amyloid angiopathy in the absence of biopsy or autopsy tissue.

Saccular, or berry, aneurysms are the leading cause of subarachnoid hemorrhage in young and middle-aged adults but may present throughout the life span (Sahs, Perret, Locksley, & Nichioka, 1969). These aneurysms develop at arterial branch points, usually clustered at or near the circle of Willis at the base of the brain. Congenital arteriovenous malformations account for approximately 5% of intracerebral hemorrhages and present mainly in younger age groups.

Cardiovascular disease is a major cause of stroke in the elderly. The prevalence of atrial fibrillation increases exponentially with age (6% over age 65 years) and increases the risk of stroke 12–16-fold (Sacco, Benjamin, Broderick, Dyken, Easton, Feinberg, et al., 1997). Diminished cardiac stroke volume, antihypertensive medications, acute blood loss, and dehydration are other causes of hypotension and stroke among elderly persons.

Clinical Syndromes

The clinical syndromes associated with stroke reflect the functional anatomy of the injured brain. The anterior circulation of the brain arises from paired internal carotid arteries, which bifurcate intracranially to form the anterior and middle cerebral arteries. The middle cerebral artery (MCA) supplies the largest area of the brain, and strokes occur most commonly in this distribution. An MCA stroke is associated with contralateral hemiparesis (with predominant arm weakness), hemisensory anesthesia, and blindness in the contralateral visual field (homonymous hemianopia). In addition, impairment of language (spoken, auditory, and written), known as aphasia, is observed with left-hemisphere MCA strokes. Neglect, on the other hand, appears with right-hemisphere MCA strokes. Strokes in the anterior cerebral artery (ACA) distribution cause hemiparesis (with predominant leg weakness). Bilateral ACA strokes may produce akinetic mutism, characterized by loss of initiation of both movement and speech.

The posterior cerebral circulation comprises paired vertebral arteries that join to form the basilar artery in the brain stem and then two posterior cerebral arteries that supply the inferior-medial temporal and occipital lobes. Strokes in the distribution of the vertebral and basilar arteries may affect movement and sensation of all four limbs, as well as cranial nerve and cerebellar function. Occlusion of one posterior cerebral artery causes homonymous hemianopia; bilateral posterior cerebral artery (PCA) occlusion causes cortical blindness.

The border zones between the distal branches of the three major cerebral arteries (anterior, middle, and posterior) are particularly vulnerable to systemic drops in perfusion pressure that accompany cardiac arrest or acute blood loss. Border-zone infarction is associated with cortical blindness, transcortical sensory aphasia, loss of proprioception, and quadriparesis with predominant shoulder weakness.

Medium- and small-size arteries and arterioles penetrate the brain substance in parallel arrays and terminate in the deep white matter surrounding the ventricles. Occlusion of these arteries gives rise to lacunar infarcts, extrapyramidal signs, and cognitive impairment. Widespread arteriolosclerosis or systemic hypotension causes ischemia in the end zones of the periventricular and deep white matter. Incomplete infarction of the deep white matter is associated with mental slowing; slow, unsteady, and shuffling gait; and urinary incontinence, known as Binswanger's syndrome.

Treatment

Treatment can be directed to every phase related to stroke. The best treatment, of course, is preventive. The identification and treatment of risk factors, such as hypertension, diabetes, hyperlipidemia, atrial fibrillation, and smoking, can significantly reduce the long-term chances of stroke. Treatment modalities may include changes in lifestyle or medications.

- A 6 mmHg reduction of systolic or diastolic blood pressure in persons with hypertension reduces the risk of initial stroke by 40% (for review, see Collins & MacMahon, 1994; Laird & Studenski, 1999).
- A 25% reduction in LDL cholesterol, using hydroxymethylgluaryl coenzyme A reductase inhibitors (statin), reduces the risk of stroke by 19% to 31% (for review, see Streja, 2000).
- The relative risk (RR) of subsequent stroke in persons with TIA or minor stroke is reduced by antiplatelet medications: 17% by aspirin and 25% by ticlopidine (for review, see Cohen, 2000).
- In patients with symptomatic high-grade carotid artery stenosis (70%–99%), the RR of subsequent stroke in patients surgically treated with carotid endarterectomy is reduced by 51%, compared to those treated with best medical therapy (Barnett, Taylor, Eliasziw, Fox, Ferguson, Haynes, et al., 1998).
- Anticoagulation with warfarin (coumadin) reduces the risk of stroke associated with atrial fibrillation by 68% (Atrial Fibrillation Investigators, 1994).

Prompt administration of thrombolytic therapy during the first 3 hours following acute ischemic stroke can lyse the blood clot, restore blood flow, and minimize the extent of infarction (National Institute of Neurological Disorders and Stroke rt-PA Stroke Study Group, 1995). In the immediate aftermath of a completed stroke, treatment is directed toward controlling secondary brain complications, such as increased pressure due to brain swelling and hemorrhage, systemic hypotension, or vasospasm. Surgery is indicated to clip the base of a ruptured berry aneurysm and, at times, to control increased intracranial pressure. At present there is no proven means to promote regeneration of damaged neurons. Nonetheless, rehabilitation therapy optimizes function by limiting unnecessary complications, fostering remaining abilities, and developing compensatory and alternative functional strategies.

HELENA CHUI

See also
    Apolipoprotein E
    Stroke
    Vascular Dementia: Multi-Infarct Dementia

CHANNELING DEMONSTRATION

The National Long-Term Care Demonstration, known as the Channeling Demonstration, was the largest of a series of social experiments that tested the effects of providing publicly financed home and community-based care to persons at risk of nursing home placement. (For reviews of these experiments, see Kane & Kane, 1987; Kemper, Applebaum, & Harrigan, 1987; Weissert, Cready, & Pawelak, 1988). Many believed that public long-term care financing, which is limited primarily to nursing home care under the Medicaid program, was so biased toward care in nursing homes rather than at home that it led to inefficiently high use of nursing home care and hence unnecessarily high long-term care costs. By paying for home and community-based care, it was argued, less costly care at home would be substituted for care in nursing homes, thereby reducing long-term care costs overall.

Channeling Interventions

The demonstration, conducted between 1982 and 1985, tested the effects of expanding public provision of home care in 10 diverse communities in the United States. The target population was elderly persons at high risk of nursing home placement. In addition to age, applicants had to meet eligibility criteria that included moderate to severe disability, unmet need, and noninstitutional residence (unless certified by a physician as able to be discharged home). Consistent with these criteria, the applicants eligible for Channeling turned out to be old and frail. The average age was 79 years, and most had multiple functional limitations. Indeed, 19% were so seriously disabled that they needed help with all five of the activities of daily living (ADL): bathing, dressing, toileting, transferring, and eating. The sample was poor—average monthly income was just under $530. An estimated 5% of the elderly population met the Channeling eligibility criteria. The demonstration served between 4.5% and 31.9% of the eligible population in the experimental communities. Thus, the experiment was not (and was not intended to be) a systemwide intervention.

Two Channeling interventions were tested, each in five communities. Both interventions provided case management (which was defined as needs assessment, care planning, service coordination, monitoring, and client advocacy). This case management was more comprehensive and was provided over a longer period than that offered by existing organizations such as home health agencies and hospital discharge planners. Channeling was imple-

mented through case management agencies that were separate units of existing nonprofit or government agencies.

The two interventions differed with respect to the extent of funding for home- and community-based services. The basic intervention had very limited financing for additional home care. The financial intervention substantially expanded coverage of these services, regardless of eligibility under existing categorical programs. Case managers could authorize payment for the full range of home- and community-based services, including personal care (e.g., help with bathing, toileting, or eating) and supportive services (e.g., help with housecleaning, meal preparation, or shopping), as well as traditional home health care (nursing, therapy, and home health aide care) and community services (e.g., transportation, home-delivered meals, and adult day care).

Although the financial intervention substantially expanded public coverage of home care, expenditures were subject to limits on individual and average expenditures and, for high income participants, cost sharing. Individual expenditures were limited to 85% of nursing home costs, and average expenditures for the caseload as a whole were limited to 60% of nursing home costs. Neither limit turned out to be constraining. Participants with income more than twice the eligibility level for Supplemental Security Income were required to share in the cost of services. Because the participants were generally poor and because certain services were exempted, only 5% of participants turned out to be subject to cost sharing. Thus, the financial intervention was direct provision of home care subject to a case manager's authorization and cost limits, not an unconstrained entitlement to subsidized home care.

Evaluation

The experiment was evaluated using a randomized experimental design. After an eligibility screening interview, eligible applicants within each community were randomly assigned to a treatment or control group. An in-person follow-up interview was administered 6, 12, and, for half the sample, 18 months after randomization. The follow-up interviews obtained extensive information on service use and costs, indicators of quality of life, living arrangements, and hours of care received from formal and informal caregivers. In addition, Medicare and Medicaid claims files and death records provided information on service use and death. Separate follow-up interviews were administered to primary informal caregivers of a subsample of disabled elderly persons. (The evaluation data were made available for public use; see Wooldridge, Carcagno, Kemper, Dunston, & Holden, 1987.)

Evaluation of the experiment by Kemper, Brown, Carcagno, Applebaum, Christianson, and Corson (1988) found that Channeling benefited clients and their informal caregivers in several ways: it increased the amount of home and community-based care received, reduced reported unmet needs, increased confidence in receipt of care and satisfaction with arrangements for it, and increased overall life satisfaction of both the participants and their primary informal caregivers. However, Channeling failed to limit services to persons at high risk of nursing home placement—a year after randomization over 80% of survivors remained in the community. Because of the inability to target successfully, the cost of the additional home care—provided in most cases to participants who would not have entered nursing homes even without expanded home care—was not offset by reductions in nursing home cost. Hence, contrary to the original intent, total costs increased. The evaluation also found that declines in informal care were generally small and not statistically significant, despite substantial increase in the use of paid home care.

Although the evaluation used a rigorous randomized design, the findings are nonetheless subject to limitations. Inherent in such a social experiment is uncertainty about the extent to which the results can be generalized beyond the population served, the follow-up period, and the communities where the demonstration took place. In addition, Channeling did not test the effect of a comprehensive care through strict limits on nursing home admissions and bed supply combined with increased coverage of home care. Nor did the experiment evaluate case-managed home care compared with its total absence. Rather, the experiment rigorously tested the effect of adding case-managed home care to an existing service system that already provided some home- and community-based services.

Implications

Concern about the bias toward nursing homes in the Medicaid program and lack of coverage of third-party coverage of home and community-based care remains two decades after the start of the community care demonstrations. However, the nature of the debate about long-term care financing has shifted as a result of the evaluations of Channeling and the other demonstrations. Incremental expansion of coverage of home and community-based care beyond what already exists should no longer be justified on the basis of its ability to reduce costs by substituting care at home for care in nursing homes. Instead, it must be justified on the basis of its ability to reduce unmet needs of people living at home and to improve the quality of life of persons with disabilities and the family members who care for them.

Peter Kemper

See also
 Case Management
 Case Mix in Long-Term Care
 Home and Community-Based Care

CHRONOBIOLOGY: RHYTHMS, CLOCKS, CHAOS, AGING, AND OTHER TRENDS

Chronobiology (n): a computer-aided science, particularly important for the elderly, quantifying, mapping, and investigating mechanisms of biological time structure(s), chronome(s), consisting of rhythms, organizing chaos, and underlying trends, with age and/or with any other manifestation of life, such as change in disease risk and/or actual injury and illness (Cornélissen & Halberg, 1994; Halberg, Cornélissen, Halberg, Fink, Chen, Otsuka, et al., 1998; Halberg, 1969).

Rhythm means a "measure," denoting a recurring quantitatively or qualitatively patterned change of a biological or natural physical variable. Often, not invariably, the rhythm can be seen with the naked eye, wherever it occurs. The site of a rhythm may be biological (e.g., sleep/wake behavioral rhythm, with the alternation of closed vs. open eyes), or it may be geographic, such as the alternation of snow and rain and other features of summer and winter or other hot/cold and/or light/dark rhythms (e.g., of day and night). There are other, more subtle rhythms in natural environmental and/or organismic factors, related perhaps to some nonphotic as well as photic solar and galactic drivers, with about 10-yearly and about 21-yearly rhythms. The heartbeat shows different ways to define any rhythm in us or around us: it is seen with the unaided eye once the chest is opened; it is palpated and plotted as the radial pulse; it can also be visualized in a plot as a function of time of the heart's action potentials, such as R-R intervals, all time-macroscopically in an electrocardiogram. When resampled (e.g., at 4 Hz), the action potentials can be coded for a time-microscopic computer analysis in order to quantify the characteristics of a chaotic and/or rhythmic time structure or chronome.

The prefix *circa-*, meaning about, here used as an uncertainty to be measured in inferential statistical terms, is applied to biological rhythms in several ways, which are best validated as mathematical endpoints. "About," then, stands for the fact that we are dealing, in the case of biological rhythms, with approximations that invariably have some margin of error. The rhythms of life, like those of physical nature such as the weather or the broader climate, all involve recurrences of about the same phenomena, but they are not the recurrence of identical events at identical intervals in identical sequences. In the similarity as opposed to identity lies a world of inferential statistics. The intervals between the recurrence of similar events differ greatly in the spectrum of rhythms encountered in any one variable. The intervals may stem from the firing of brain cells, being contributed by action potentials, such as those recorded in an electroencephalogram in fractions of a second; they may be in the region of a second or so in the electrocardiogram. They may also involve 10.5- and 21-year cycles in the human heart rate or the urinary excretion of hormonal metabolites (17-ketosteroids). Certain intervals or the periods they represent, such as a day, a week, a month, a year, or a decade, correspond to about (the fifth circa) but not precisely to the length of (nearly) matching environmental cycles. These circa-periodicities persist when organisms (1) are kept under ordinary conditions but deprived by surgery or genetics of the major transducer of the dominant synchronizing environmental cycle, such as the eyes, (2) are isolated under conditions rendered as constant as possible on earth with respect to environmental light, temperature, and the absence of societal interactions, and/or (3) are able to self-select the given regimen (e.g., of lighting and/or eating) or (4) are constrained to periodic rest-activity regimens exceeding the range of synchronizability of the circadian system, whether these are, for example, 21- or 28-hour days of activity and rest in bright or dim light or whether one administers (as treatment for schizophrenia) regressive electric shocks at 12-hour intervals until the subject is disoriented in space and time. Under all these conditions, the organism can show about 24-hour or circadian or other circa-periods, described as free-running when they differ with statistical significance from those found under synchronization with their environmental near (circa) match, such as a day, a half-week, a week, a month, a half-year, a year, or even a decade.

The foregoing fifth use of *circa* includes the indirect demonstration of desynchronized, if not free-running, periods as the genetic basis of rhythms that characterize and constitute the mechanisms of life, such as the heartbeat, respiration, and practically every biological variable examined thus far. Operationally, in an original study of 18 sham-operated mice, the period synchronized by a regimen of 12 hours of light alternating with 12 hours of darkness was estimated as 23.99 hours with a standard deviation of 0.0175 hours, standard error of 0.004 hours, and a coefficient of variation of 0.073%. The corresponding slightly, yet clearly, different nonoverlapping values for 14 blinded mice were 23.49 hours, 0.1231 hours (*SD*), 0.033 (*SE*), and CV of 0.524% (Halberg, 1969). Behind these superficially tight summary statistics lies a great deal of variability from one fraction of a second to the next in the brain and from hour to hour and day to day in metabolism, once we turn to the study of everyday physiology. Hence, the first four circas qualify rhythms as inferential statistical phenomena and render methods of biometry indispensable for a complete quantification of rhythms (Halberg, 1969).

When beat-to-beat electrocardiographic records are analyzed, an entire spectrum of rhythms with widely differing periods (τ) may be found, including an about 1-second and an about 10-year period, among others. In any given variable one or the other component may be missing: an about-yearly component, prominent in the blood pressure, may not be found in the heart rate of the same person. Time series can also be made of indices of variability, such as standard deviations, or of intermediate computations (imputations), such as endpoints of rhythms or deterministic chaos, for variables such as heart rate and blood pressure. For instance, an endpoint of chaos is the correlation dimension that in its turn undergoes rhythms and underlies trends, as do characteristics of rhythms such as the amplitude, acrophase, and mean.

Rhythms—parts of time structures, chronomes—complement cells in spatial structures. Like genes in genomes, some biological rhythms in chronomes may not be seen by the unaided eye in an original record such as that of telemetered body core temperature, in mice with bilateral suprachiasmatic nuclear (SCN) lesions. The circadian (about 24-hour) temperature rhythm, however, becomes apparent by stacking data, a method for time macroscopy (i.e., they are seen even without quantification by computer analyses). Circadian rhythms—not only in core temperature but also in alcohol drinking, cell division in the cornea, and DNA labeling throughout the gastrointestinal tract, as well as in serum corticosterone sampled every 4 hours for 24 hours—persist, usually with a reduced amplitude and advanced phase, quantified by time microscopy, with cosine fitting, while the about 24-hour rhythms of motor activity and water drinking cannot be detected. Likewise, the loss of the outer part of the adrenal gland, its cortex, entails the loss of the circadian rhythm in the count of blood eosinophils and in pinnal epidermal cell division but not of the circadian rhythm in serum iron. Different rhythms behave differently when tested by a remove-and-replace approach. A master clock illusion could have been laid to rest when a rhythm persisted after removal of the brain above the pons, a need that became even more obvious when "clocks galore" were found not only in peripheral parts of fruit flies but in single cells. Doubts about the merits of replacing the concept of a cell by that of a clock led to the formulation of time structures, chronomes, an empirical approach analyzing the components of variation in time series. In essence, the concept of a "clock" has to be broadened to

incorporate the important "circas," conveying much variability and also a critical integration feature for within-organism and external "adaptation"— summarized as "coordination" of the dynamics of life itself in the everyday range of chronomes in and around us.

Too much "regularity" can be a warning of an elevated disease risk. For instance, once a reduced heart rate variability sinks below a threshold, so that the heartbeat approaches the regularity of a metronome's beat, the risk of coronary artery disease, stroke, and nephropathy is high. Such a disease risk syndrome also occurs when blood pressure swings too much each day along the scale of 24 hours (Halberg, Cornélissen, Halberg, Fink, Chen, Otsuka, et al., 1998). Recognizing such conditions requires inferential statistical tools for the objective quantification of rhythms, chaos, and trends. Thereby, one acquires a time-microscopic test of a hypothesis about the presence of a rhythm or of deterministic chaos or of a trend. Whether or not the null hypothesis (e.g., no-rhythm or zero-amplitude) is rejected, one can proceed to estimate parameters with their confidence intervals. One can use the endpoints thus obtained as an intermediate result for further summaries (e.g., by quality-control procedures, such as cumulative sums).

The midline-estimating statistic of rhythm (MESOR) is usually more accurate and/or more precise than the arithmetic mean; the derivation of added parameters, the amplitude and acrophase, as a measure of the extent and timing of change, can be informative when the best mean value is not, for example, when the circadian amplitudes of circulating aldosterone and melatonin decrease with aging from adulthood to senescence without a change in average concentration. An elevated circadian amplitude of urinary melatonin can give a warning of a high risk of breast cancer. The assessment of endpoints from both rhythms and deterministic chaos differentiates coronary artery disease from health, for example, by the assessment of a 24-hour and a 12-hour component in a series of 4-hourly correlation dimensions covering 24 hours. A multifrequency patterning is critical in immuno(chrono)therapy. When equal daily doses of an intended immunomodulator, lentinan, are given "as usual," the tumor is made to grow faster and the life span is shortened. An administration of the same total weekly dose with an about 7-day pattern, gradually increasing and then decreasing doses, contributes to reversing the stimulation of a malignancy into an inhibition and the shortening into a prolongation of the life span (Cornélissen & Halberg, 1994).

Curve-fitting also helps recognize, by an unduly elevated circadian amplitude of blood pressure, the highest risk of stroke among those tested, higher than the risk of a high blood pressure or advanced age, although the overall average pressure may be acceptable (Halberg, Cornélissen, Halberg, Fink, Chen, Otsuka, et al., 1998). The study of biological rhythms developed into the topic of a discipline in its own right, chronobiology, over the documentation of biological clocks and calendars, still specialized areas of research, on biological time measurement per se. These areas should but as yet mostly do not focus with inferential statistical approaches on periods and phases, but even when they eventually do, it will be useful also to consider amplitudes and MESORs, which can be computed concurrently.

As prominent circadian rhythmicity was found at different levels of organization, several series of experiments were carried out under rigorous standardized laboratory conditions that investigated the effect of a single physical stimulus, such as the exposure to noise. Outcomes were as different as no response, convulsion, and even death, as a function of the circadian stage at which the organism was exposed to noise. Whether the stimulus was audiogenic or consisted of the exposure to an endotoxin, to drugs such as ouabain, or to whole-body irradiation, predictable changes were found as a function of the circadian stage at which the stimulus was applied, albeit with differences in timing (Halberg, 1969). Remove-and-replace experiments established the roles of the adrenal cortex and the central nervous system, each for the maintenance of some but not all rhythms yet both contributing to circadian amplitude and phase relations.

Chronomes and Aging

Time structure or chronome characteristics (i.e., those of rhythm, chaos, and trend at different levels of organization) provide scholars of aging with opportunities for both a better basic science of aging

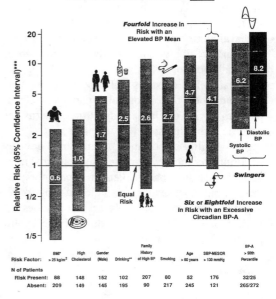

AMONG RISK FACTORS, AN EXCESSIVE CIRCADIAN BLOOD PRESSURE (BP) AMPLITUDE (A) *RAISES* THE RISK OF *ISCHEMIC STROKE MOST*

* BMI (Body Mass Index) correlates positively with BP-MESOR.
** Drinking increases BP-A.
*** Relative Risk (RR) is risk of patients with risk factor (e.g., smoking or excessive BP-A) present relative to risk of patients with risk factor absent (whose RR = 1) computed as a ratio of incidences.

CC 11/94

FIGURE 1   In a 6-year prospective study involving 297 patients, the incidence of cerebral ischemic events (top) and nephropathy (bottom) was statistically significantly larger in those patients who had an excessive vs. those who had an acceptable circadian amplitude of blood pressure, i.e., blood pressure overswinging or CHAT (*circadian hyper-amplitude-tension*) (20–25% vs. <5%). This result was extended by a meta-analysis of data using the proxy outcome of a left ventricular mass index (LVMI) on over 1,000 patients. With either index, event or LVMI, the relation of the circadian blood pressure amplitude to disease risk was nonlinear (not shown). A threshold had to be exceeded before the relative risk increased (not shown).

and progress in disease prevention, diagnosis, and treatment, based on the combination of several new technologies. These are:

• the availability of portable, personal, long-term ambulatory monitors of biological variables. Blood pressure, the electrocardiogram and electroencephalogram, motor activity, core temperature, and gastric acidity are cases in point. These and other variables undergo changes that recur spontaneously and as responses;

- the availability of database systems to acquire, edit, and archive volumes of data obtained from personal monitors;
- the availability of statistical procedures to analyze and model the biological dynamics and from them to devise optimal dosage time patterns for specific individuals;
- the availability of portable, programmed devices to administer therapy (e.g., by physiological rate-adjusted cardiac pacemakers, defibrillators, or drug pumps that respond in a closed loop to the diagnostic information analyzed as one goes);
- a chronobiological understanding of the health effect of time structures that quantify aging and health positively, inside the range of usual variation.

Thus, effects of aging on the circadian and extracircadian amplitudes are detected that otherwise go unrecognized, such as a change from circadian to extracircadian variance with age in heart rate and blood pressure. Rhythms and their broader discipline, chronobiology, constitute an objective, useful, and often indispensable way of approaching any problem in biology broadly and particularly in aging. Rhythmic changes in many variables (e.g., those recurring each day) can be greater in extent than those occurring over many decades and are thus powerful confounders of aging research if ignored. Alternatively, changes in chronome characteristics, if evaluated, are sometimes extremely useful sources of information occurring in the absence of changes in mean values, indicating, by a decrease in circadian amplitude of circulating melatonin and aldosterone, a participation in aging of potentially important critical central pineal and peripheral adrenocortical mechanisms. Temperature telemetry on the rodent demonstrates an advance in circadian acrophase and/or a decrease in circadian amplitude with aging that corresponds to the effect of SCN. The detection by 7-day monitoring of disease risk syndromes, such as an excessive blood pressure variability (circadian hyper-amplitude-tension, CHAT) or a decrease below a threshold of circadian heart rate variability are disease risk syndromes

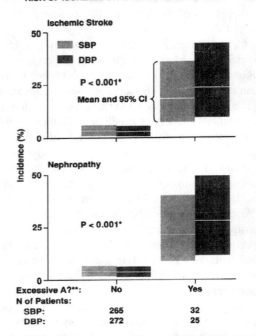

FIGURE 2   In the 6-year study summarized in Figure 1, the relative risk of ischemic stroke associated with blood pressure overswinging, CHAT, was higher than that of any other condition investigated. Diastolic CHAT had a risk of 720%, blood pressure elevation a risk of 310%, old age a risk of 370%, alcohol or tobacco use a risk of 150%, and positive family history of vascular disease a risk of 160%.

that detect a risk elevation greater than an increase in the average of blood pressure and/or old age, the use of alcohol or tobacco, or a positive family history of vascular disease. Other changes within the currently neglected normal range can also be anticipated to be diagnostically useful and to prompt timed treatment that has already doubled 2-year disease-free survival time from the historically and methodologically interesting treatment of large perioral cancers by treating at the time of peak tumor temperature rather than at other times or as usual.

For the supplementary text, consult *Introduction to Chronobiology* and the *New SIRMCE Confederation Resolution* (Brussels, March 17–18, 1995) on our website: *http://revilla.mac.cie.uva.es/chrono*.

FRANZ HALBERG
GERMAINE CORNÉLISSEN

See also
  Melatonin

CLINICAL EEG: COGNITIVE CHANGES

The clinical electroencephalogram (EEG) can be useful in the evaluation of cognitive dysfunction in older adults (Holschneider & Leuchter, 2000; Hutton, 1980; Sim, 1979), provided that its limitations are recognized and caution exercised in its interpretation. One important factor to be considered in its interpretation is that of normal age-related changes. Cross-sectional comparisons of older adult age groups have shown the mean EEG alpha frequency (synchronous EEG oscillations in the 8 to 12 cps range) to change from approximately 10 cps (Hz) in middle age to 9.5 Hz at age 70, 9 Hz at age 80, and 8.5 Hz after age 90 (Drechsler, 1978; Hughes & Cayaffa, 1977). Similar slowing of the alpha frequency with age has been demonstrated in longitudinal studies (e.g., Wang & Busse, 1969). Although Wechsler Adult Intelligence Scale (WAIS) performance IQ has been related to slowed alpha frequency in older persons with vascular disease (e.g., Obrist, 1975), healthy community volunteers have not shown this relationship (see review by Marsh & Thompson, 1977). In general, the specific cause of age-related alpha frequency slowing and its cognitive correlates among healthy elderly remain controversial.

Focal EEG abnormalities, i.e., typically episodic high-voltage waves in theta (5 to 7 Hz) to delta ($\leq$ 4 Hz) frequency range and predominantly over the temporal areas of the brain (maximal on the left side), have been repeatedly observed in 17% to 59% of apparently healthy elderly people (Holschneider & Leuchter, 2000). The origin and significance of this focal abnormality is unclear. Among elderly persons living in the community, it is unre-

lated to either WAIS Full Scale IQ scores or WAIS Verbal-Performance IQ discrepancy, although some relationship to decline in Verbal IQ scores over a 3 1/2 year period has been reported (Wang, Obrist, & Busse, 1970).

More diffuse distribution of theta activity, observed in only 7% of a sample of apparently healthy elderly subjects (Wang & Busse, 1969), or theta activity slowing into the delta range, is typically indicative of disease. Diffuse EEG slowing has been found to be more common in elderly subjects with decompensated heart disease and lung disease and has been found to be associated with lower intelligence test scores (Thaler, 1956; Wang & Busse, 1974). Vascular, toxic (including drug effects), metabolic, and infectious disorders, with either direct or indirect effects on the brain, can produce diffuse EEG slowing, epochs of bilateral delta activity appearing during drowsiness, and/or minor sharp- and slow-wave activity over the anterior and middle temporal regions (see review by Keller, Largen, Burch, & Maulsby, 1985). In the absence of such disorders, diffuse EEG slowing is observed most frequently in primary degenerative dementia in older age (Muller & Schwartz, 1978). The degree of EEG slowing in such patients has been shown to be correlated with the degree of cognitive impairment documented by various psychometric instruments (Johannesson, Hagberg, Gustafson, & Ingvar, 1979; Kaszniak, Garron, Fox, Bergen, & Huckman, 1979).

Despite these documented relationships, diagnostic utility of the EEG is limited by the fact that patients early in the course of primary degenerative dementia may show normal or only mildly abnormal clinical EEGs (Sim, 1979). The EEG appears to have even less diagnostic utility in assessing patients with multi-infarct dementia. Muller and Schwartz (1978) found that brain infarcts may produce no EEG abnormalities if they are small and/or remote from the cortical surface. Johannesson, Hagberg, Gustafson, and Ingvar (1979) found the EEG to be normal or only slightly abnormal in their 24 patients with dementia secondary to cerebrovascular lesions. Computer spectral analysis of the EEG (with its attendant improvement in sensitivity and accuracy over clinical evaluation of EEG slowing) may improve diagnostic accuracy and show stronger relationships with cognitive functioning

(Albert, Naeser, Duffy, & McAnulty, 1986; Holschneider & Leuchter, 2000; Nuwer, 1997).

Quantitative EEG analysis has been shown to be more sensitive than clinical (i.e., visual) EEG assessment in the detection of moderate dementia, although specificity appears to be comparable with either approach (Brenner, Reynolds, & Ulrich, 1998). EEG abnormalities in persons with depression, although not specific for concomitant dementia, may identify risk for future intellectual and functional decline (Liston, 1979). Quantitative EEG appears to be more sensitive than clinical EEG in discriminating persons with depression from those with dementia (for review, see Pollock & Schneider, 1990).

ALFRED W. KASZNIAK

See also
Cognitive Processes
Sleep Disorders

CLINICAL MEMORY ASSESSMENT

The primary goal of clinical memory assessment of an older individual is to ascertain whether a perceived memory problem is transient, situation-specific, health-related, and/or a sign that should be an issue for concern or treatment (see Poon, Gurland, Eisdorfer, Crook, Thompson, Kaszniak, et al., 1986, for a review of theoretical, clinical, and practical issues). Memory loss is one of two major concerns frequently articulated by older adults (Lowenthal, Berkman, & Brissette, 1967). The other major concern is the loss of energy. Professionals and service providers who work closely with older adults often are confronted with memory complaints, and these professionals have to make a decision on whether a referral is needed for a formal memory assessment.

It is noted that memory complaints are frequently associated with transient depression and that complaints may be abated when the transient depression is successfully treated (Thompson, 1986). From this perspective, memory complaints may not be entirely due to a person's alleged inability to remember but to a host of other factors, such as anxiety, depression, health-related problems such as drug interaction or vitamin B_{12} deficiency, which are treatable and reversible. One of the central questions faced by the assessing clinician is whether the memory ability of the older adult is within normal range, affected by situational or transient factors, or caused by a pathology such as Alzheimer's disease. The most difficult assessment for a clinician is to differentiate normal aging from the beginning stage of dementia (Poon, 1989, 1997). The difficulty associated with early detection is due to (1) the large number of factors that could cause transient or progressive memory failure or memory complaint and (2) the large range of memory performances that is considered normal. It is clear that memory deficiency at the moderate to severe stages is significantly easier to detect and diagnose. Several studies on the rate of misdiagnosis in the 1980s (e.g., Gurland & Toner, 1983) showed misdiagnosis can range from under 10% to over 50%. Misdiagnoses were not restricted to nonspecialists but also were made by neurologists, psychiatrists, psychologists, and internists (Gurland & Cross, 1986). The misdiagnosis rate has improved significantly in the past decade; however, detecting of early memory dysfunction is still a difficult task for most clinicians. It is interesting to note that a clinician can take a conservative approach by examining the patient over time, as dementia of the Alzheimer's type is progressive in that memory functions do deteriorate over time.

Memory and aging research has been the most prolific area of investigation into psychological aspects of gerontology in the past 30 years. However, there are three common sources of confusion in the use of laboratory findings for clinical memory assessment and in the selection of appropriate tests. One, there are many underdeveloped tests in the market in which sensitivity and specificity for older adults have not been defined. Many of the tests are not designed to validate the everyday memory complaints of the older individual. Two, most memory laboratory paradigms were designed to understand age-related differences, not to isolate and predict memory deficits. These paradigms may not be suitable for the assessment of the absence or presence and the severity of a dysfunction or a process. Three, generalization of experimental findings is often not established, so clinical application is premature without further testing.

Clinical memory diagnosis cannot be accomplished by any one memory test or memory battery, as differential diagnosis is an interdisciplinary challenge to experimental and clinical psychologists, neuropsychologists, psychiatrists, neurologists, geriatricians, and general practitioners. From this perspective, there is no one standardized battery that is being endorsed by any one group of clinicians. At present, there is a potpourri of available tests, some standardized and age-normed and others not, that purport to examine strengths and weaknesses in the memory system. However, most of these memory tests do not assess the potential concomitant and peripheral factors, and clinicians must include these tests when appropriate.

Memory tests can be divided into five general subtypes (see Crook, 1986, for a review). Each subtype satisfies specific goals for memory assessment. One set of tests examines memory complaints and assists the clinician in defining the origin and circumstance of the complaint. Another evaluates presenting signs and symptoms. A further set is designed to evaluate longitudinal change or treatment effects, such as a drug trial. Yet another type is designed to evaluate neuropsychological status that could be descriptive of the memory problem. Finally, some memory tests are derivatives of laboratory studies to isolate information-processing abilities and psychometric intelligence. The choice of tests depends on the hypotheses and questions posed by the clinician and the reasons for the memory assessment.

In conclusion, clinical memory assessment of older adults is a hypothesis-testing process involving:

1. an understanding of theoretical processes underlying the memory problem and the known interactions between the process under examination and a number of concomitant conditions;
2. an understanding of the immediate concerns of the patient, family members, and treatment personnel;
3. a clear objective for the evaluation; and
4. cooperation from the patient and/or the family to test and confirm hypotheses about the dysfunction.

LEONARD W. POON

See also
Memory and Memory Theory

CLINICAL MEMORY TESTING: EXTERNAL VALIDATORS

Selection of appropriate instruments for the clinical assessment of memory in older individuals is dependent upon knowledge of the validity of such instruments. In judging the validity of any assessment instrument, one must ask both what the test measures and how well it does so (Anastasi, 1982). Questions concerning what an assessment instrument measures fall under the domains of "content" and "construct" validity, whereas questions regarding how well an instrument measures what it is presumed to measure is the domain of criterion-related or external validation procedures. It is these latter procedures, in which performance on a measure is assessed against some independent measure, with which this discussion is concerned. A more extended treatment of issues in external validation of memory assessment instruments can be found in Kaszniak and Davis (1986).

Issues in External Validation

In externally validating a memory assessment instrument, the first issue faced concerns the choice of the criterion measure to be employed. The external criterion must be justified on the basis of a theoretical rationale relating the memory assessment instrument to the criterion. Preferably, such a theoretical rationale will rest on prior empirical information linking the particular construct that the memory assessment instrument is attempting to operationalize (e.g., episodic memory or semantic memory) with the criterion measure.

The second issue concerns the availability of empirical information on the reliability and validity of the external criterion itself. If the criterion cannot be measured reliably (in terms of either test-retest, scorer, or internal consistency reliability), error variance will be high, and any relationship between the memory assessment instrument and the criterion will be necessarily attenuated (Anastasi, 1982, pp. 102–130). Even if the criterion can be reliably measured, it may not be validly related to the phenomenon it attempts to operationalize. This lack of validity may be due to systematic contributions of technical artifacts, as well as the influence of other intervening variables. Such problems in validity of the criterion are particularly prevalent when neurobiologic measures are employed as external criteria because techniques available for noninvasive study of humans may be several steps removed from the neurobiologic phenomenon of interest (e.g., radiographic imaging of anatomic structure, rather than tissue examination of the anatomy itself; plasma or cerebrospinal fluid measures of centrally active neurotransmitter activity; statistical averages of bioelectric phenomena).

Once an external criterion has been rationally selected and its own reliability and validity determined, one can begin to examine its relationship to the particular memory measure. A variety of problems must be dealt with at this stage. One of the most serious problems relates to issues in sampling. If subjects selected for study (e.g., patients with Korsakoff's syndrome or dementia of the Alzheimer's type) are not reasonably representative of the full range of severity of the illness (e.g., either all are very mildly impaired or all very severely impaired), that truncation of range will affect the magnitude of any relationship that can be observed between the memory test and the external criterion (e.g., anatomic, physiologic, or neurochemical measures). Similarly, if the memory assessment instrument samples only a limited range of variability in the construct it is designed to operationalize (i.e., task difficulty is either very high or very low), the potential magnitude of the observed relationship between the external criterion and the assessment instrument will be limited. Finally, logistic problems may be encountered in validational studies, which limit the generality of any conclusions that can be drawn. For example, although a sample of patients may be representative of the full range of illness severity, those most severely impaired may be unable or unwilling to cooperate sufficiently with procedures required for measurement of either the memory construct or the external criterion. Validational studies that employ longitudinal change within a particular patient group (e.g., those with dementia of the Alzheimer's type) as the external criterion (Wilson & Kaszniak, 1986) are notoriously plagued by selective attrition owing

to failure to cooperate with repeat assessments, disappearance, or death (Schaie, 1977).

Only after the above issues are given due consideration can one address the question of whether the magnitude of the relationship between the memory test and the external criterion supports the instrument's validity. Confidence in answering that question is directly dependent upon the issues discussed above. All of these issues impact on the ultimate question of implications for clinical application of the memory assessment instrument. Thus, research may reveal that a particular memory test is validly related to clinical diagnosis (an external criterion, provided that the memory test results do not play a role in determining that diagnosis) for a particular disorder (e.g., dementia of the Alzheimer's type), but does not validly reflect expected differences in longitudinal change between such patients and age-matched healthy controls (Wilson & Kaszniak, 1986). The lack of validity, as judged against the longitudinal change criterion, may be secondary to issues in sampling (e.g., either the initial severity of illness or the difficulty of the memory test results in a truncation of measurement range and consequent "basement" effects at repeat assessment). Such observation would imply that the particular memory assessment instrument in question is likely more appropriate for purposes of initial clinical diagnosis than for clinical applications in which change over time must be assessed.

External Validators

Validation studies of clinical memory assessment instruments for the examination of older adults have generally employed one of three major classes of external validators: clinical diagnosis, longitudinal change within particular diagnostic groups, and various neurobiologic measures. Although the rationale for selection of external criteria falling within those categories may appear obvious, it is worthy of some brief discussion.

Memory disorder is a pervasive symptom of a wide variety of central nervous system diseases (Butters, 1979; Russell, 1981; Squire & Butters, 1984; Squire & Cohen, 1984; Squire & Shimamura, 1996). Although many of these diseases can and do occur within the older adult population, memory assessment instrument validation studies have focused primarily on those most prevalent diseases: dementia of the Alzheimer's type, multi-infarct dementia, and disorders associated with relatively focal cerebral damage, such as that seen with space-occupying lesions (e.g., tumors), cerebrovascular infarct, and some toxic/nutritional diseases (e.g., Korsakoff's syndrome). The prevalence of some of those diseases, such as dementia of the Alzheimer's type (Mortimer, Schuman, & French, 1981), difficulties in making accurate clinical diagnoses (e.g., Ron, Toone, Garralda, & Lishman, 1979), and the consequences of misdiagnosing a potentially reversible disorder resulting from a progressive, untreatable disease (Cummings, Benson, & LoVerme, 1980) all point to the importance of clinical diagnosis as an external validator. Results of a number of recent studies employing clinical diagnosis of different dementing illnesses as external criteria (see review by Kaszniak, 1996) have provided encouraging support for the diagnostic validity of various memory assessment instruments.

Current diagnostic criteria for dementia of the Alzheimer's type (McKhann, Drachman, Folstein, Katzman, Price, & Stadlan, 1984), as well as for other dementing illness, emphasize the progressive nature of memory and other cognitive impairment. Hence, valid measures of memory impairment in such dementias would be expected to reflect such deterioration in longitudinal study. Much effort (for review, see Bondi, Salmon, & Kaszniak, 1996) is, therefore, being focused on sensitivity of memory assessment instruments to longitudinal change in dementia. Thus far, the results of such studies provide some support for the validity of their respective memory assessment instruments against criteria of longitudinal change. However, the studies also indicate specific limits to such validity, dependent upon memory task difficulty, type of memory processes assessed, and severity of dementia at the time patients enter the study (Kaszniak & Davis, 1986).

Owing in large part to the impressive reliability and validity of various modern neurobiologic measures, several recent studies have employed such measures as external validators for memory assessment instruments. Computerized tomographic (CT) scanning and magnetic resonance imaging (for review, see Bigler, 1997; Coffey, 2000) have been frequently employed, given their sensitivity to various structural brain lesions and ability to visualize ventricular spaces and brain tissue density. Techno-logical advances in obtaining electrophysiologic measures of interest, such as computer-assisted analysis of electroencephalographic frequency or sensory evoked potentials, have resulted in increasing application of such measures as validation criteria. Similarly, considerable enthusiasm has been generated by positron emission tomography, allowing imaging of intracranial regional blood flow and metabolism, functional magnetic resonance imaging, and single photon emission computed tomography (for review, see George, McConnell, Lorberbaum, Greenshields, Bohning, & Mintzer, 2000).

Advances in understanding basic memory-brain relationships, improvement in the psychometric construction of memory assessment instruments, and a growing body of external validity evidence have made clinical memory testing a critical component of any comprehensive neuropsychological examination of older adults.

ALFRED W. KASZNIAK

CLINICAL MEMORY TESTING: INSTRUMENT REVIEW

The assessment of memory is an extremely important function in the psychological evaluation of the elderly, but actual assessment presents a number of problems. In the case of many memory instruments, there are no generally accepted norms for individuals over the age of 65. This limitation has shown some level of improvement in recent times, with investigative efforts extending normative data to include people over 65 (i.e., WMS-III; Weschler, 1997). However, even when normative data are available for the elderly, such data rarely include corrections for educational level or intelligence, two factors that may have a profound impact on test results. Another major problem is the difficulty in separating memory loss that occurs normally in aging from losses due to some pathological process, especially in the early stages of the disorder when the diagnosis is most in doubt (Poon, Crook, Davis, Eisdorfer, Gurland, Kaszniak, et al., 1986).

Clinical memory tests may be divided into several classifications. First, one can test whether they are measures of *long-term, immediate, delayed*, or *working* memory. Most of the tests now available are measures of working, immediate, or delayed memory. Delayed tests include those that measure memory with interference or with a time delay. Interference occurs when the patient is asked to do another task (such as counting) before being asked to recall the previously presented material. Thus, one can be asked to remember three words, then be asked several unrelated questions, and finally, be asked to recall the three words. In lieu of interference, one can be asked to recall something simply after a delay of time, which can be as short as several seconds or as long as a day or more.

Long-term memory involves the recall of events that happened in the past. This can include orientation questions (where do you live?) or questions of facts (who was the president before Bill Clinton?). Long-term memory is generally found to be intact except in the cases of substantial dementia or in cases where the material was never learned in the first place. The latter circumstance must be differentiated from true long-term memory deficit.

Memory tests are also classified on the basis of the kind of material that is measured. The gross classifications divide tests into verbal and nonverbal. These can be refined along such dimensions as whether material is meaningful or nonsense, related or unrelated, and simple or complex. Tests also may be classified as to whether they require recognition, free recall, controlled recall (recall in a specific order or manner), or multitrial learning (in which there are multiple presentations of the material). Depending on the individual's specific deficits, there will be distinct variations in test performance according to which of these types of memory tests are employed. Clients may do well on one test and poorly on another. Only clients with the most severe disorders are likely to do poorly on all the memory tests.

Most memory tests available are tests of one specific combination of the traits described above. Most of these are used only when one wishes to assess that specific function. Although hundreds of such tests exist in one form or another, many are poorly standardized and many are unpublished. These are available through such sources as Lezak (1995) or Spreen and Strauss (1998).

Among the tests of single functions, one of the most often used is the Benton Visual Retention Test (Benton, 1963). This test consists of a series of 10 drawings with one or more geometric figures. The most popular administrations of the test involve immediate recall or copying, along with a delayed recall form. The normative data included in the original manual cover an age range from 18 to 69. However, new normative data sets have recently been published with the release of the new manual (Silvan, 1992), which gives a more detailed normative data set extending to age 80. Although this new normative data set has been broadened to include a large portion of the elderly population, the revised manual still fails to correct for IQ and education.

The failure to correct for educational level has been moderated by researchers over the past few years. Youngjohn and colleagues (Youngjohn, Larrabee, & Crook, 1993) have produced a normative data sample that accounts for education and extends to the age of 84, providing the examiner with a more useful data set to which a client's performance can be compared. These authors have also produced a regression equation in which an examiner can use a client's age and level of education to obtain an expected score, which can be compared to the actual performance in order to assess for a deficiency in nonverbal immediate memory. Attempts to provide corrections for intelligence have improved over the past decade. However, such attempts remain limited to younger populations (ages 18–30; Randall, Dickson, & Plasay, 1988). With such improvements in the normative data over the past decade, this test has become a much more valuable tool in assessing nonverbal immediate memory dysfunction in older adults.

Another popular test is the Rey Auditory Verbal Learning Test (Rey, 1964). This test examines immediate recall memory for a list words, as well as a person's ability to learn over repeated trials. It also examines memory with interference. The original normative data is of limited utility as it is based on a Swiss population; however, multiple researchers have created more useful normative data for this test. Most of these data sets range from early childhood to age 84. Ivnik and colleagues (Ivnik, Malec, Tangalos, Petersen, Kokmen, & Kurland, 1992) have recently created a normative data set based on Americans ranging in age from 56 to 97, allowing this test to be a useful measure of verbal recall and learning across the vast majority of older

Americans. Other individual tests examine such factors as memory for sentences, faces, stories, paragraphs, numbers, paired associates, complex figures, tactile impressions, sounds, and other specific material in a variety of short and delayed term paradigms.

More popular than individual tests have been the memory test batteries. The most popular of these has been the Wechsler Memory Scales (Wechsler, 1945). The newly released third edition (WMS-III; Wechsler, 1997) of this battery includes subtests measuring: orientation, attention, sequencing, recognition of verbal material, and immediate memory for stories, faces, pictures, and verbal paired associates. Several of these subtests are also normed for a 30-minute delayed trial to assess delayed memory functions. This battery yields overall immediate and general memory indices that assess overall immediate and delayed memory functioning, in addition to a number of more specific indices that allow for the examination of verbal and nonverbal memory functioning across both immediate and delayed conditions. There is also an index that assesses attention/concentration (i.e., working memory).

One major advantage of this battery over earlier forms is the large normative data set that allows for assessment of individuals ranging in age from 16–84. Also, normative data are available for each individual subtest, which allows for subtests to be used in isolation. One problem with the latest version is that the normative data set fails to account for a person's level of education or intelligence. However, this test is a useful measure of general memory functioning, although parts of it are likely too difficult for impaired elderly clients.

The Dementia Rating Scale (Mattis, 1988) is a relatively new battery that was created for the purpose of assessing the presence of degenerative conditions that affect memory functions. This gives a relatively brief screening of orientation and verbal and nonverbal immediate memory. This measure also has subtests that assess motor functioning, as well as cognitive functions such as abstraction and visual-spatial skills. The brief administration of this measure and the normative data gathered across both normal and demented populations make this instrument useful in assessing memory functions in those suspected of having a degenerative condition.

The Randt Memory Test (Randt & Brown, 1983) is a measure of memory with the potential for great clinical utility, as it allows for an evaluation of both short- and long-term memory (up to 24 hours). Each subtest yields specific normed scores that can be compared across areas. Overall scores may be generated, as well as separate scores for immediate and delayed memory ability. Use of this battery with the aged requires interpretive caution; however, it has great utility, as it allows for a much longer delay in assessing delayed memory ability.

All memory batteries suffer from the fact that they do not cover all areas. Thus, no single battery or individual test is appropriate for the examination of all memory problems. In choosing which tests to give a specific patient, it is important to recognize that the best tests may differ from person to person. One may begin with a "standard" battery of tests, but such batteries must be supplemented as necessary in appreciation of the referral question and the patient's presenting appearance. In addition, expect for the WMS-III, all the major instruments in use have been around for a long time and fail to reflect advances in the field of memory. This may indicate that there is a need for substantial reevaluation and restructuring of such tests during the next decade. For a comprehensive review of instruments for clinical memory testing, see Spreen and Strauss (1998) or Lezak (1995). For a comprehensive review of memory testing solely in the elderly, please see Poon, Crook, Davis, Eisdorfer, Gurland, and Kaszniak (1986).

CHARLES J. GOLDEN
JAMES D. D. BRADLEY

See also
Clinical Memory Testing: External Validators
Memory and Memory Theory

CLINICAL PSYCHOLOGY

Although there have been clinical psychologists who have worked with older adults since at least the 1920s (e.g., the Martin Method), the growth of *clinical psychology* with older adults has taken place primarily in the past 30 years or so (see Knight, Kelly, & Gatz, 1992). Behaviorally oriented psychologists worked with older adults in institutional settings and provided an important counterpoint to the commonly shared view that problems of aging were physiological, inevitable, and nonmodifiable. These early pioneers in clinical psychology with older adults often remarked on the scarcity of colleagues in the field and raised questions about the existence of the field as a separate entity.

Their efforts paid off, however. The years since the 1960s have seen an expansion of training programs in clinical psychology and aging at both the university campus and the internship and postdoctoral levels. In 1993 a separate subsection for *clinical geropsychology* was formed within the Division of Clinical Psychology of the American Psychological Association. In 1998 clinical geropsychology was officially recognized as a competency area by the American Psychological Association. These developments represent important formal recognition of the subspecialty of clinical geropsychology. As is true for clinical psychology in general, clinical geropsychology is concerned with research, training, and practice in the areas of assessment and individual differences, psychopathology in later life, and interventions with older adults.

Since 1980 there has been considerable improvement in psychological tests that can be used for older adults. Recent revisions of tests for adult populations now typically include norms for people up to age 89 or so (e.g., the Wechsler Adult Intelligence Scale–III, the Wechsler Memory Scale–III, and the Minnesota Multiphasic Personality Inventory–2). The field of neuropsychology for older adults has been especially active, given the concern with distinguishing the dementing illnesses from other psychological disorders (see Nussbaum, 1997).

The study of psychopathology in later life is important both as a guide to assessment and treatment (Qualls & Smyer, 1998; Zarit & Zarit, 1998) and as an important topic in its own right. The past decade has seen important research advances in understanding the causes of depression in later life; in whether age trends for depressive symptoms show a curvilinear pattern over the entire life span, with the highest scores among younger adults and those over age 75; and in examining possible cohort differences in rates of depression. Important research advances have also been undertaken in de-

termining genetic and environmental markers for Alzheimer's disease (Holmes, 1997; Lopera, Ardilla, Martinez, Madrigal, Arango-Viana, Lemere, et al., 1997) and in treating this type of dementia (Zarit & Zarit, 1998). The next decade will likely see an increased interest in anxiety disorders, schizophrenia, substance abuse, and comorbid disorders (depression, anxiety, medical illnesses) among older adults.

With regard to *psychotherapy* and behavior change with older adults, clinical psychologists have played a major role in designing, adapting, and evaluating interventions for older adults. The 1980s and 1990s have seen a veritable explosion of writing in this area (e.g., Knight, 1996; Zarit & Zarit, 1998). Clinical psychologists also have been active in evaluating the effectiveness of interventions with older adults; a meta-analysis of these studies by Scogin and McElreath (1994) concluded that psychosocial interventions with older adults are highly effective, with a level of effectiveness similar to that found with younger adults. These interventions included cognitive, behavioral, psychodynamic, and reminiscence therapies. A review of empirically validated psychological treatments for older adults by Gatz and colleagues (Gatz, Fiske, Fox, Kaskie, Kasl-Godley, McCallum, et al., 1998) found behavioral and environmental treatments for behavior problems in dementia to be well established, and several treatments were probably efficacious: cognitive, behavioral, and brief psychodynamic therapy for depression; life review for depressive symptoms or restricted independence; cognitive behavioral treatment of sleep disorders; support groups for caregivers, using a psychoeducational model; and memory and cognitive retraining with dementia patients. There have also been increasing reports of the effective use of psychological interventions with frail elderly in nursing homes, as well as consultation with staff and with the family members of nursing home residents.

Clinical geropsychologists work in a wide variety of settings, including academic and research institutes; inpatient and outpatient mental health settings of all kinds, such as private practice, hospital, and other medical settings; and nursing homes. As noted at both of the conferences on training psychologists to work with older adults ("Older Boulder" in 1981 and "Older Boulder II" in 1992), this work necessarily involves collaboration with other health and social service disciplines. Clinical geropsychology is a young and growing field that seeks applied science solutions to the problems faced by older adults.

BOB G. KNIGHT
GIA S. ROBINSON

See also
    Behavior Modification
    Psychotherapy
    Social Work

COGNITIVE PROCESSES

Internal mental processes control behavior. Although mental, or cognitive, processes cannot be observed directly, they are necessary components of an adequate description of behavior. Cognitive processes are intervening variables that come between the array of stimuli in the environment and the responses or behaviors that can be directly observed. Cognitive processes are inferred through a careful analysis of human behavior.

Cognitive psychologists studying aging have devoted a great deal of effort to understand the cognitive processes of older adults and how they may be different from those of younger adults. In fact, a majority of all the psychological research published in the *Journal of Gerontology* over the past 25 years has dealt with cognitive aging. The interest in cognitive aging has generated several very good integrated research reference books (Blanchard-Fields & Hess, 1996; Craik & Salthouse, 1999; Kausler, 1994; Park & Schwarz, 2000). These sources provide good summaries of the research findings in cognitive aging.

There are several approaches to the study of cognitive processes. The information-processing paradigm has been adopted by many psychologists to organize the complex array of mental abilities assumed to comprise cognition. We perceive, remember, reason, make decisions, solve problems, and form complex mental representations of world knowledge. We have developed elaborate symbolic systems to represent the knowledge we gain from our experiences, and these natural language and imagery systems provide the format for cognitive representations.

In addition to the information-processing approach to cognition, there are two other approaches: the psychometric approach and the contextual approach. Some psychologists are more interested in individual differences than in normative principles of cognition, and the "psychometric" approach represents this method of analysis. Psychological tests are developed to measure differences in cognitive processes among individuals. In early psychometric research, the definition of cognition using this approach was empirical. Subtests that measure some particular cognitive ability are assumed to be important measures only if they contribute empirically to detecting individual differences among people. If variance among individuals is not accounted for by a particular subtest, it is not included in a battery used to measure individual differences in cognition.

A third approach attempts to combine the individual difference (psychometric) and the normative (information-processing) approaches. This "contextual" view of cognition assumes that individual differences, information-processing abilities, and the context of the cognitive performance are all important in understanding cognition. Because cognitive processes are used in a specific context, the everyday social context and the individual traits of the subject interact in dynamic ways. Therefore, both are important in understanding complex behavior.

Psychometric Approach

The psychometric approach to cognition has concentrated primarily on measuring intelligence, the cognitive abilities and capacities contributing to intelligent behavior. Early research using intelligence tests found large "deficits" as a function of aging (Wechsler, 1958). Cross-sectional studies comparing cognitive measures across different age groups often found dramatic declines in performance across the life span. These declines, however, were found by Schaie and his colleagues to be overestimated (see Schaie, 1996). Using cross-sequential designs (a combination of longitudinal and cross-sectional strategies), Schaie found that much of the decline was due to the different birth cohorts and not due to age per se. Even with these sequential designs, however, substantial declines in cognitive measures were found after age 60. Another result of more careful analysis of psychometric measures of cognitive functioning is that different subtests in intelligence batteries show differential age effects. Vocabulary, for example, declines little with age, whereas the ability to substitute digits for symbols declines a great deal.

To account for the differential declines of different abilities, Horn (1982) distinguishes between crystallized and fluid intelligence. Fluid intelligence declines across the adult age span because it represents the efficiency of cognitive functioning. Crystallized intelligence is assumed to remain fairly stable or even increase through the adult age span because it represents the accumulation of world knowledge (e.g., the products of past fluid activities) (Salthouse, 1999).

Information-Processing Approach

Rather than designing tests to account for individual variation, information-processing tests typically measure some hypothesized component of the information-processing system (e.g., working memory, encoding into semantic memory). There has been a concentration on memory as the focus of cognitive operations. For this reason, much of the information-processing research on cognitive processes has examined memory functioning. In general, the research has demonstrated that age-related memory differences are selective and that not all memory changes with age (Smith, 1996; Zacks, Hasher, & Li, 1999). Laboratory information-processing research on aging and memory generally shows that adult age differences are small or nonexistent when the tasks are designed to provide support of learning and remembering with little self-initiated processing required to perform the task. Age differences emerge, however, when the processing requirements of the task increase. In fact, recent modeling studies have shown that much of the age-related variance in cognitive performance (such as on memory tasks) can be accounted for by simple cognitive mechanisms such as perceptual speed (Salthouse, 1997) or working memory (Park, Smith, Lautenschlager, Earles, Frieske, Zwahr, et al., 1996). These mechanisms are assumed to represent measures of cognitive resources. In one sense,

these modeling studies showing the moderating effects of cognitive mechanisms on cognitive processes represent a blending of individual difference research (psychometric) and theory-driven information-processing research.

Contextual Approach

The contextual approach assumes that four classes of variables must be considered simultaneously to understand the cognitive processing of different aged adults (Smith, 1980). These classes are the tasks used in the evaluation or measurement of cognition (e.g., criterial tasks), the individual characteristics of the subjects (e.g., age, cognitive ability, and health), the cognitive strategies and self-efficacy beliefs of the subjects (e.g., expectations and mode of processing), and the materials used in the task (e.g., familiarity and meaningfulness of the stimuli). In other words, there are many influences that determine cognitive performance, and all of them must be considered. Another characteristic of the contextual approach is an emphasis on functional or practical behavior. Because cognition is seen as adaptive to different contexts, there is a greater emphasis on studying the context in which cognition takes place (Hess & Pullen, 1996).

When using a contextual approach to cognitive processes, some psychologists have attempted to identify qualitative differences between the cognitive processes of different adult age groups. It is assumed that these qualitative differences in cognitive processes among adult age groups reflect adaptive responses of the different age groups to their changing contexts and the cognitive requirements necessary to deal with those contexts. For example, Labouvie-Vief (1992) reviews research on changes in the ways in which adults of different ages interpret narrative text passages. In general, the research shows that older adults' interpretations are more interpretive and subjective, suggesting a unique mature adult style of symbolic processing, qualitatively different from that of younger adults.

Often, the goal of contextual research, especially that research dealing with everyday cognition, is to show that the deficits in older adults, so characteristic of psychometric and experimental approaches to cognition, do not reflect the true underlying relationship between aging and cognitive processes. Early researchers viewed the poorer performance of older adults on cognitive tasks as contrived and not reflective of the everyday memory requirements of older adults. In other words, the tasks used to measure cognition in older adults were not seen as ecologically valid (see Poon, Rubin, & Wilson [1989], for a discussion of these issues). More recently, however, it has become clear that age differences are found on ecologically valid, everyday cognitive tasks (Smith, 1996). So rather than assuming that age deficits are artifacts of the tasks used, most contextually oriented cognitive aging researchers now concentrate on individual differences in how these deficits become manifest in everyday life. For example, Baltes and Baltes (1990) view "successful" cognitive aging not as the absence of cognitive deficits but rather as adaptation to such changes through the processes of selection (emphasizing those cognitive abilities that show minimum change) and optimization (continued improvement through practice and training) and compensation (accomplishing the cognitive task in different ways). Clearly, such an approach emphasizes the adaptive nature of cognition. To achieve a better understanding of the cognitive processes of older adults, we need better research procedures that are sensitive to the everyday cognitive operations required for daily living, procedures that are better able to separate cognitive performance from cognitive competence, and theories of adult cognition that are sensitive to these issues.

ANDERSON D. SMITH

See also
  Abilities
  Learning
  Longitudinal Research
  Memory and Memory Theory

COGNITIVE THERAPY

Cognitive therapy is a term that refers to an approach to the treatment of common psychological problems of later life, such as depression and anxiety disorders, that was developed from the cognitive theory of psychopathology formulated by Beck and associates. According to this theoretical perspective, depression (and other types of emotional dysregulation and distress) arise from the "negative cognitive triad," or negative views about oneself, one's experiences, and the future, which are held despite challenging or even disconfirming evidence to the contrary (Beck, 1995). Part of why persistent negative views are maintained and cannot be changed without formal treatment involves faulty information processing, or the distortion of information that results when certain cognitive errors or inaccurate thinking processes are present. Certain specific unhelpful thinking patterns tend to be present in affective disorders, which in turn both generate and maintain distress. Several that are common in older depressed individuals include overgeneralization (or assuming that because one negative thing happened, such as serious relationship difficulties, things will never be repaired with that person), mind reading (or jumping to conclusions about what others think about you, based not on data they are giving but on your own internal judgment), and the "what if's" (what if my spouse did not have dementia, how different our lives would be) (Dick, Gallagher-Thompson, & Thompson, 1996). According to cognitive theory, these persistent negative thinking patterns tend to be self-reinforcing, so that a "downward spiral" occurs: cognitive distortions lead to depressed mood and inefficient behaviors, which in turn lead to more disparaging views of oneself, one's experiences, and the future, and that in turn maintains continued depression.

A therapeutic approach based on these views was developed; it uses a variety of methods to help distressed individuals to challenge their unhelpful thinking patterns and to learn to develop more adaptive ways to perceive and respond to whatever the situation or self-appraisal may be. Such methods include learning to identify one's own unhelpful thinking patterns and in what particular situations they emerge, then learning to challenge them by examining the evidence (or more systematically checking out the data on which the negative conclusions were drawn); doing a "cost-benefit analysis" of maintaining specific negative views (or evaluating their pros and cons), and trying to see the situation from a different perspective (how would someone else in a similar situation respond?) (Dick, Gallagher-Thompson, & Thompson, 1996).

Modifications of the basic approach are needed when applying it to older adults, for a variety of reasons. Suggested modifications and case examples are described in sources such as Coon, Rider, Gallagher-Thompson, and Thompson (1999) and Zeiss and Breckenridge (1997) and are briefly presented here. First, older adults may be less flexible in their thinking and may have had years of viewing things negatively, so they often require more time in treatment to understand the basic conceptual model and to work with it sufficiently so that their thoughts, feelings, and behaviors actually change. Second, older adults may have memory and concentration problems that can make this approach difficult. To address that issue, it is recommended that information be presented slowly, multimodally (i.e., not only talking about the situation and one's responses but also writing it down if possible and reviewing it in the auditory mode as well, for example, by audiotaping therapy sessions and reviewing them outside treatment), and with the use of memory aids (such as a therapy notebook in which to keep relevant material). Third, older adults who are depressed and/or anxious often also have behavioral deficits in addition to their cognitive distortions, so the key features of behavioral therapy must be incorporated into treatment in addition to the more standard cognitive methods (Thompson, Powers, Coon, Takagi, McKibbin, & Gallagher-Thompson, 2000). These include activity scheduling, learning to identify and increase potentially pleasant everyday activities, and learning ways to relax in stressful situations (such as caregiving for a demented relative). Thus, most clinicians and researchers in the field of geropsychology refer to their work as cognitive-behavioral therapy (CBT).

CBT is one of the most systematically researched treatment approaches for late-life depression, and, overall, results have been very positive. They are reviewed in Gatz, Fiske, Fox, Kaskie, Kasl-Godley, McCallum, et al. (1998). These authors conclude that CBT for late-life depression meets current standards in the field for being considered "probably efficacious" as an empirically validated approach because several studies have documented its effectiveness, randomized controlled clinical trials have been used to test the approach, and treatment manuals exist to encourage replication across a wide variety of practice settings.

For the most part, CBT has been done in a one-to-one format (individual therapy). However, several studies and numerous published case reports suggest its usefulness when done in a group format as well. The basic approach has been modified for depressed and distressed family caregivers of dementia victims (Gallagher-Thompson, Lovett, Rose, McKibbin, Coon, Futterman, et al., 2000) and has been applied to other ethnic and cultural groups, such as older Hispanics/Latinos (Gallagher-Thompson, Leary, Ossinalde, Romero, Wald, & Fernandez-Gamarra, 1997). It also has been used effectively to treat sleep disorders, substance abuse, and depression in early-stage dementia patients (see Gatz, Fiske, Fox, Kaskie, Kasl-Godley, McCallum, et al., 1998, for detailed references and discussion of these findings).

In sum, CBT seems to be appealing to a wide variety of older adults as a treatment modality because it emphasizes learning cognitive and behavioral skills with which to cope, and as such it increases both self-efficacy and the sense of self-control over difficult problems and situations. It can be used effectively to treat many of the common psychological problems of later life.

DOLORES GALLAGHER-THOMPSON

See also
Depression
Group Psychotherapy
Psychotherapy
Social Work

COHORT ANALYSIS

A cohort analysis is any study in which any kind of cohort is an independent variable or in which the population studied is defined by cohort boundaries. A cohort, in turn, consists of individuals (persons or other units of analysis) who experienced some significant event within a given period of time. The period may be long, such as a decade, or short, such as a year or month, and the event may be birth, marriage, joining an organization, receipt of an educational credential, and so forth. For instance, persons born in the 1950s are a cohort, as are 1960 high school graduates, or persons first elected to the U.S. Senate in 1998. The units of analysis are usually human individuals, but they may be marriages, organizations, or even inanimate objects, such as automobiles. Cohorts are labeled according to the event that defines them, so there are birth cohorts (sometimes incorrectly called age cohorts), marriage cohorts, and so forth. The word *cohort* without a modifier usually refers to a birth cohort (Glenn, 1977).

The most common use of cohort analysis is to estimate the effects of aging on the units of analysis, and the term *cohort analysis* is sometimes restricted to studies designed to estimate age effects and separate them from the effects of cohort membership and period of time. Such research requires data from several cohorts and several points in time, usually from a series of cross-sectional surveys, so that change within cohorts can be traced and different cohorts can be compared at the same age levels.

A common misconception is that cohort analysis can definitively separate age, cohort, and period effects. It cannot do so, but a theoretically guided cohort analysis combined with evidence from other sources can support strong, though tentative, conclusions about the effects (Fienberg & Mason, 1985; Glenn, 1977).

No analysis can definitively separate the effects of age, cohort, and period because each variable is a linear function of the other two. For instance, a person's age can be calculated from his/her date of birth and the current date, and date of birth can be calculated from the person's age at a particular date. Stated differently, the multiple correlation of any two of the variables with the third one is unity, and thus there is extreme collinearity that makes a straightforward simultaneous estimation of the effects of the three variables impossible. This conundrum, known as the identification problem, afflicts all research designed to estimate the difference between two variables when each of those variables may also affect the dependent variable.

The linear dependence of each variable on the other two means that the linear effects of the variables are confounded in such a way that no statistical analysis can accurately separate them. An infinite number of combinations of age, cohort, and period effects can account for linear variation in cohort data, and the selection of the combination that reflects reality depends on theory and "side information," that is, information from outside the data at hand.

The inherent ambiguity of linear variation of the values of a dependent variable in cohort data is illustrated by the hypothetical data in Table 1. The data may reflect only age effects, or they may reflect a combination of offsetting cohort and period effects, or they could reflect an infinite number of combinations of age, cohort, and period effects. One might be tempted to conclude that a one-variable explanation of such data would always be the most plausible one, but sometimes a more complex explanation makes sense. This is the case with reported job satisfaction, which, in the data from several surveys conducted in the United States in the 1950s, 1960s, and 1970s, bore an approximately linear positive relationship with age from young adulthood through late middle age while remaining at about the same level in each age category. There are reasons to think there is typically a positive age effect on job satisfaction, as persons try various jobs until they find one that suits them better than their earlier ones. However, during the time covered by the data, each succeeding cohort of persons who reached adulthood became more demanding in what they expected of their work and thus, one would think, less inclined to be satisfied with their jobs. This trend in itself should have led to a decline in job satisfaction, at least among young adults. However, there was a concurrent increase in wages and salaries and an improvement in the average conditions of work. Thus, a combination of cohort and period effects apparently kept the level of job satisfaction approximately constant while creating or contributing to the positive relationship of job satisfaction to age.

Most proposed statistical solutions to the identification problem in cohort analysis depend on a recoding or transformation of one or more of the three interrelated variables to break their linear dependence on one another. For instance, simply using different-size intervals for one of the variables will allow a regression or similar analysis to estimate the effects of all three variables. However, the recoding does not change the linear dependence in the real world, and thus it is a mechanical, artificial solution to the identification problem that may provide grossly inaccurate estimates.

The strongest causal evidence from cohort data is for nonlinear effects. For instance, a nonlinear pattern of variation by age that cuts across different birth cohorts and periods is rather clear evidence for age effects, unless it is at the older ages (in the case of human individuals) and could plausibly result from differential mortality. An example is a nonlinear increase (first steep and then gradual) in voter turnout in the United States in all cohorts that have aged in recent years from young adulthood to middle age.

There were numerous cohort studies in the 1970s and 1980s that used political variables, such as party identification, as dependent variables. These studies brought about reconsideration of the belief that aging leads to conservatism and cast light on the extent to which attitudes and values tend to stabilize as people grow older. More recently, cohort studies have been used to address such issues as the course of marital success and failure in aging marriage cohorts (Glenn, 1998) and whether or not an intercohort increase in years of school completed in the United States has led to a corresponding in the United States has led to a corresponding increase in vocabulary (Alwin, 1991; Alwin & McCammon, 1999; Wilson & Gove, 1999).

TABLE 1   Pattern of Data Showing Pure Linear Age Effects, Offsetting Cohort and Period Effects, or a Combination of Age Effects and Offsetting Cohort and Period Effects

Age	Year				
	1950	1960	1970	1980	1990
20–29	50	50	50	50	50
30–39	55	55	55	55	55
40–49	60	60	60	60	60
50–59	65	65	65	65	65
60–69	70	70	70	70	70

Numbers in the cells are hypothetical values of a dependent variable.
Alternative explanations:
1. Each 10 years of aging produces a 5-point increase in the dependent variable.
2. There is a 5-point per 10 years positive period effect on the dependent variable and a 5-point per 10 years negative cohort effect.
3. There is some combination of age and offsetting period and cohort effects on the dependent variable. An infinite number of combinations of such effects could produce the pattern of variation in the dependent variable shown in the table.

Cohort analyses are likely to become more common as continuing data collection projects, such as the General Social Surveys and the National Election Studies in the United States and similar projects in other countries, provide an increasing amount of data appropriate for such research.

NORVAL D. GLENN

See also
Baby Boomers and Their Future
Cohorts

COHORTS

Cohort is a demographic concept long used in actuarial studies. It refers to an aggregate of individuals that retains its identity through time, by analogy to the military cohort that retains its identity despite progressive depletions on the battlefield. Cohorts are established by year of birth; when grouped, 5- or 10-year intervals are traditional.

Cohorts have been followed over time to determine survivorship for actuarial tables, morbidity rates for epidemiological studies, fertility rates, and so on. These studies illustrate the impact of social history on the life chances of successive cohorts. For example, widespread public health measures early in the 20th century dramatically lowered the risk of infectious disease in subsequent cohorts; the reduction of infant and life span; and with the drop in maternal mortality, women's life expectancy rose to equal, then surpass, that of men. The impact of historical crises is also clear: high mortality in certain cohorts during war and lower fertility during severe economic crises. Thus the cohort is an index to major life environments and experiences, and it links the life course to history.

Similar Constructs

Cohort is similar to two other constructs: generation and age set. During the period between the World Wars, Mannheim (1952) and others popularized the term *generation* to characterize the changing social contexts of successive, sharply differentiated cohorts. During its long and varied usage, generation has developed numerous meanings, only one of which is the same as cohort (see Bengtson, Cutler, Mangen, & Marshall, 1985, for an excellent discussion of generations). Except for generations within descent lines, the term *cohort* is less ambiguous and is now generally preferred.

Age sets occur in that relatively small number of societies that have developed systems of compulsory age grading through which all males pass (women's systems are infrequent and simplified) and move from grade to grade as a group (Stewart, 1977). Age sets are groups of interacting individuals who are age peers, whereas cohorts are aggregates assigned to a common classification by date of birth. For this reason, age sets cannot be simply equated with cohorts, but they may be considered to be a limiting case of cohort membership.

Cohort Succession

As cohorts move through time together, they age and die; new cohorts are born and grow up to replace them. This orderly succession, or flow, of cohorts provides continuity and stability to a society: allocated roles and age-graded positions are emptied as new individuals are ready to fill them. (An extensive discussion of this process is presented in Chapter 12 of Riley, Johnson, & Foner, 1972.) However, misfits can occur due to abrupt differences in size or composition of adjacent cohorts or to social changes altering the availability of positions. When cohort flow is disordered, adjustments are made that "may occasion temporary or relatively lasting social change" (Waring, 1975, p. 238). Thus, social change can both cause, and result from, cohort differences.

Intercohort Differentiation

Cohorts are differentiated from one another in many ways, such as the mix of races and natal languages, frequency of various-size families, and so forth. For example, the size of cohorts fluctuates and permanently affects members' life chances in areas such as education, job opportunities, and retirement pressure.

Cohort differentiation also results from the uneven impact of major historical events or movements. Wars affect adjacent cohorts differently; depressions delay employment and marriage for the young and reduce fertility for the next older cohort; revolutions drastically alter the social environments and values of adjacent cohorts. Insofar as such events also interact with distinctive characteristics of the cohorts (e.g., size or education), cohorts are further differentiated.

Though less well documented, cohort members share more than life chances based on structural characteristics of their cohort. Because individuals grow up in the context of their particular cohort and experience its history in common, presumably they have had a common socialization and share many attitudes, values, and beliefs. In an influential article, Ryder (1965) emphasized this social meaning of cohort by defining it in experiential, rather than actuarial, terms: "the aggregate of individuals (within some population definition) who experienced the same event within the same time interval" (p. 845).

The importance of cohort membership in understanding the life course (Riegel, 1972), coupled with renewed interest in intergenerational relations and social change in the 1960s, encouraged attempts to detail specific cohort histories (e.g., Easterlin, 1980; Elder, 1974; Hareven, 1978). The thrust of this work is to pinpoint the various ways in which unique historical contexts exert a common influence on members of affected cohorts and the ways those influences interact with major life stages and events. Changes in the social meanings of aging are gradually being delineated by this sociohistorical research.

Age/Cohort Confounds

In gerontology, attention has been focused on the cohort largely in terms of its confounding with age: at any given time, persons of different ages are simultaneously members of different birth cohorts. Thus, age has a double meaning, one of which includes the life experience of the cohort. In order to determine the effects of age per se, the exogenous influence of cohort membership must be assessed.

Early recognition of the misleading results of analyses by age alone led to the development of cohort analysis techniques. For example, Frost (1939) questioned the apparent "aging" of mortality from tuberculosis (TB) (shifting from young adulthood to the 60s). Recasting these data into cohort-specific tables, he demonstrated that TB mortality rates had been lowered for all cohorts, but that the age pattern of mortality remained unchanged. At any one time (i.e., in cross-sectional analyses), the data simply reflected the higher overall rates for older cohorts. The apparent aging of TB mortality was an artifact of methods that ignored cohort differences.

Gerontological attention was devoted to this problem primarily in regard to intelligence testing. Intelligence test scores are strongly influenced by amount of education, which has risen dramatically since the turn of the century. It is now clear that, as with TB mortality, cross-sectional results showing severe decrements with age also were artifacts of the age/cohort confound.

Life span researchers are faced with a third confounded variable: the impact of the social environment at the time of study (the period or time of measurement effect) is a major influence in many problems. It affects all cohorts (sometimes in similar, sometimes in dissimilar, ways) and obscures age and cohort effects. These methodological problems have received a great deal of attention, and the classic exposition is Schaie's (1965) model. In brief, at any time of data collection, an individual is simultaneously a particular age, a member of a particular cohort, and responding in the context of a particular point in history. When all three influences are indexed by units of time, a triple confound results; for only one span of time is involved, regardless of how it is measured. "It is as if we used a triangular ruler, each side in a different metric: the faces show different intervals [birth intervals, age, and time of measurement] but, since the length is the same, the correlation between faces is perfect. Any two sides yield the third" (Nydegger, 1981, p. 7).

Schaie (1965) proposed a method to disentangle these influences by means of multiple analyses using both longitudinal and cross-sectional data (a version of the time-lag method). The technique is generally referred to by the name of one of the three recommended solutions: the cross-sequential

method. Recent discussions have pointed out serious flaws in the interpretation of such studies. Currently, there is general agreement that statistical solutions alone are insufficient. "Side information" (Glenn, 1977), such as substantive knowledge or hypothesis about each of the three sources, must enter into analytic decisions. (A succinct overview of the statistical solutions and model assumptions can be found in Maddox and Campbell, 1985 and an extensive discussion in Glenn, 1977.) Ryder (1965) and others have maintained that the best solution lies in finding indices other than time units. However, if those are substantially correlated with any time unit, confounding is unavoidable.

Reformulations and reanalyses are now under way in many topical areas to try to assess cohort effects more accurately. However, results to date do not lead to a simple conclusion. For example, Bengtson, Cutler, Mangen, and Marshall (1985) describe three studies on differing aspects of political attitudes that posited cohort, period, and age effects, respectively; each was supported. Nevertheless, research on topics as diverse as intelligence and voting behavior suggests that both cohort and period effects may be more likely to prove significant than will age effects. Only when age is directly implicated (as in support for government medical aid or Social Security programs) have age effects been strongly supported.

Within-Cohort Variability

Cohort characteristics and historical events do not affect all members of a cohort in the same way. "The attractive simplicity of birth cohort membership . . . cannot conceal the ways in which this identification is cross-cut and attenuated by differentiation with respect to education, occupation, marital status, parity status, and so forth" (Ryder, 1965, p. 847). Heterogeneity within cohorts produces complex interactions that reduce or even mask cohort effects.

Specification of sources of intracohort variability is essential for refined cohort analysis, and attention to this issue is growing. In addition to demographic characteristics, variability arises from differences in event exposure. Bengtson, Cutler, Mangen, and Marshall (1985) refer to "touch" versus "saturation" of events, and long-term consequences of different degrees of exposure to the depression of the 1930s have been traced by Elder (1974). Additional sources of differential effects can be found in choices of life pathways (Uhlenberg, 1969) and in the timing of life stages. For example, timing of parenthood determines the social context of child rearing (Nydegger, 1986), and timing of job entry influences layoff vulnerability and retirement options.

Conceptual Problems

The methodological problems of cohort analysis have taken precedence over the conceptual problems posed by the concept. However, Rosow (1978) among others has called attention to the difficulties of determining cohort boundaries. Traditionally, cohorts have been defined arbitrarily by convenient and equal interval birthdates. But if these intervals do not match experiential watersheds, they obscure meaningful effects. One solution is to use unequal-interval cohorts defined by significant events (Ryder, 1965). However, the theoretical criteria necessary to distinguish those events that define distinctive experiential cohorts have not been developed.

The lasting effects of cohort membership have been attributed to the enduring structuring of life chances (e.g., job opportunities) and to socialization to the unique sociohistorical cohort niche (Riley, Johnson, & Foner, 1972). The first is being detailed for various time periods, but cohort socialization has received no empirical attention. In what ways does cohort socialization differ from family or other socialization?

As Ryder (1965) noted, variation in schedules among roles poses a distinctive kind of cohort heterogeneity problem. Those who are off-time occupationally, for example, share job rank and experience job contingencies in common with members of an adjacent cohort rather than with members of their own. Across roles, they are members of different cohorts. The notion of a role cohort is one way of conceptualizing multiple cohort membership caused by schedule variations. It has proved useful in pinpointing the importance of the parent role cohort in intergenerational conflict (Nydegger, 1986).

Although cohort is less precise than it appears on the surface and its meaning is not well specified,

it remains the one index of those common life experiences that distinguish aggregates of age peers as they succeed one another through time. Most scholars agree with Ryder (1965) that, "As a minimum, the cohort is a structural category with the same kind of utility as a variable like social class" (p. 847).

CORINNE N. NYDEGGER

See also
  Cohort Analysis
  Demography
  Generations
  Longitudinal Research

COLLAGEN

Collagen constitutes 25%–30% of total body protein, and it consists of five types found in varying connective tissues (Kohn, 1971). Type I collagen is the most prevalent. It is a fibrous macromolecular that is extruded by fibrogenic cells as the basic molecule tropocollagen. Following biosynthesis of the basic structure, it undergoes numerous covalent changes and cross-linking, including side-to-side aggregation and possibly end-to-end polymerization. Robins, Shimolomaki, and Bailey (1973) reported that chemically reducible cross-links decrease with maturation and are virtually absent in aged tissues. Tissue distribution may also differ, as in bone and dentin collagen (Kuboki & Mechanic, 1982). The general metabolic turnover of collagen is slower than most other proteins of the body. Collagen undergoes little degradation and replacement; consequently, it has a prolonged exposure to various substances over time so that its aldehyde side groups can react with many substances and with themselves.

In young or growing tissue, an appreciable amount of collagen is extractable with neutral salt solution. The fraction represents tropocollagen and poorly cross-linked aggregates. With maturation, less collagen is extractable. In older individuals, only traces are soluble. The insoluble fraction, present throughout life, is a candidate for age changes. With cessation of growth, almost all collagen is in the form of mature insoluble fibrils and remains constant in amount, exhibiting very little turnover in the absence of severe tissue stress or inflammation. Old collagen becomes less susceptible to digestion by collagenase and less easily gelatinized.

With increasing time the initial loose meshwork of fibers becomes more closely organized. The fibers thicken in cross section, become more homogeneous and deeply stained, and exhibit a wavy arrangement. Few cells are associated with collagen. After 60 years of age, the fibers become thinner and more elongated and stretched, losing their wavy appearance (Klein & Rajan, 1984). Electron-microscopic data show that fiber diameter size and uniformity and effects of age on fiber size vary with each tissue. In young to old human tissues, collagen fiber diameters range from 15–150 nm for bone, 30–170 nm for tendon, and 20–100 nm for cartilage, and they remain unchanged (25–30 nm) throughout life for the cornea (Klein & Rajan, 1984).

No significant difference in water content is reported between young and old collagen; however, developing bone has $\approx 60\%$ water, whereas old cortical bone contains $\approx 10\%$ water. Studies have been limited in this regard, and the data may be misleading for numerous reasons.

The osmotic swelling of collagen serves to determine the degree of stable cross-linking that restricts the amount of swelling possible. Swelling data for human tendon collagen shows an increase in the time required for swelling as a function of age. Between 30 and 50 years, a significant decline is noted in swelling ability, which continues throughout life but at a slower rate (Kohn & Rollerson, 1959).

When collagen fibers are heated to 60°C or immersed in KI solution, they contract and exhibit elastic properties. This process is thought to depend on the melting of crystalline zones in collagen and rupture of hydrogen bonds. The force of contraction appears to be dependent on the amount of stable cross-links. Verzár (1956), studying rat tail tendon, found that the force needed to inhibit thermal contraction increases with age.

All of the age-related changes that occur in collagen can be reproduced by treatment with a tanning agent, or cross-linker (e.g., formaldehyde). It has therefore been postulated by some investigators that collagen aging is a tanning process, a physical-chemical maturation process dependent on concentration, time, and temperature. The process can be reproduced in vitro by long periods of incubation of collagen without enzymes or other agents. However, recent studies of nitrile-induced collagen defects suggest that an amine oxidase may be required in vivo. If cross-linking is dependent only on time and temperature, it is difficult to determine why it takes humans 70 years to cross-link their collagen to an equivalent seen in an old rat of 22 1/2 years. Certainly, smaller animals with shorter life spans have a higher metabolic rate than do larger, longer-lived animals. The metabolic rate may be a factor, yet no requirement for this has yet been shown.

EDGAR A. TONNA

See also
Connective Tissues

COMMUNICATION DISORDERS

The term *communication disorders* (CD) encompasses a variety of disorders affecting *hearing*, *language*, *cognition*, *speech*, and *voice*. One in six Americans (or 42 million people) in the United States has some type of communication impairment (Bello, 1995).

Audiologists and speech-language pathologists are specialists in communication disorders. Audiologists specialize in the prevention, identification, diagnosis, and treatment of hearing and balance disorders. Speech-language pathologists specialize in the prevention, identification, diagnosis, and treatment of speech, language, cognitive, voice, and swallowing problems. The American Speech-Language-Hearing Association (ASHA) is the national organization that serves the interests of the communication disorders specialists and also the consumers. For information, consumers may use the toll-free hotline (1-800-498-2017) or website (*www.asha.org*).

Hearing and Auditory Comprehension

The ability to hear is a combination of physical, mechanical, and electrochemical processes. Sound waves are created by displacement of air molecules.

They travel from the outer (or external) ear canal and set the tympanic membrane (in the ear canal) into vibration. The vibration in turn creates mechanical forces that set the ossicular chain in the middle ear into motion. That mechanical energy in the middle ear eventually transforms into electrochemical energy in the inner ear, and the message is transferred to the central nervous system for further processing. Disruption in any of the points of energy transfer can result in hearing difficulties. The *hearing loss* that is a result of outer or middle ear problems is called conductive hearing loss; inner ear problems result in sensorineural hearing loss.

In normal aging, auditory comprehension is hampered by conductive and/or sensorineural changes affecting the peripheral auditory mechanism. For instance, cerumen production increases with age, and impacted cerumen in the outer ear can significantly hamper the transfer of energy to the middle ear. Cerumen management is therefore indicated in patients with a history of that condition in order to prevent a conductive hearing loss.

Older adults are more prone to falls than younger adults because of a decrease in postural reflexes, osteoporosis, and/or vestibular dysfunction. If the patient demonstrates a sudden hearing loss after a fall, then he/she needs to be evaluated to determine whether the fall caused the middle ear bones to dislocate. Furthermore, vestibular testing by the audiologist is often indicated in patients with complaints of dizziness and balance problems in order to identify the cause of the balance disorder.

Presbycusis (or *presbyacusis*) is the term used to indicate changes in hearing threshold due to the aging process. This sensorineural hearing loss initially affects high-frequency sounds, but eventually it extends to affect lower frequencies as well. Higgins and Nash (1987) projected that by 2000, 46% of persons over 65 will have a hearing impairment. That figure was projected to increase to 59% by 2050 (as cited in Schein, 1989). Consequently, a large number of adults over 65 have a hearing loss in at least one ear.

The above peripheral changes in hearing are often compounded with central nervous system changes in auditory processing. Aging causes increased latency times during auditory brain-stem responses. Thus, the central nervous system may require more time to process auditory information.

Consequently, the aforementioned changes can interfere with the older individual's ability to receive information clearly and at a rapid rate. The individual may find group conversations unpleasant or difficult to follow. She/he may misinterpret information, resulting in communication breakdown. Although hearing aids are extremely helpful in amplifying information and have become sophisticated in increasing signal/noise ratio, the hearing-impaired older adult has to make considerable adjustments to maintain social/communicative levels of functioning.

Language and Cognition

The older adult may experience some difficulties in language, such as auditory comprehension and word-finding problems during speech. However, these changes occur gradually and allow for adaptation. In the case of pathology such as cerebrovascular accident (CVA), brain injury, or degenerative disease (such as Alzheimer's), language, speech, voice, and cognition can be affected.

Damage in the left hemisphere of the brain typically causes aphasia, whereas damage to the right hemisphere causes more cognitive than linguistic deficits, such as difficulties in attention, memory, affect, prosody, and others. Degenerative disease can cause a combination of linguistic, cognitive, and motor problems.

Dementia refers to global deterioration of intellectual functions that affect more than one cognitive area, such as memory and language. Dementia can have a sudden onset or a gradual onset over a period of weeks, months, or years.

Infections common in older adults, such as urinary tract infections, and metabolic changes such as abrupt sugar level changes in adults with diabetes mellitus can result in dementia with sudden onset. Hormonal changes, such as thyroid problems, also may result in gradual alteration of cognitive functions. Once the infection and the metabolic and hormonal imbalances are treated, the cognitive functions are restored.

Degenerative diseases such as Alzheimer's disease (AD), multi-infarct disease, Parkinson's disease, Huntington's disease, and Pick's disease result in nonreversible dementia types. Dementia associated with AD and multi-infarct dementia account for over 70% of dementias. Initial symptoms include word-finding problems (e.g., tip-of-the-tongue phenomena) and memory difficulties (e.g., forgetting an appointment). Eventually, the person becomes cognitively impaired with significant judgment, physical, and communication problems that render him or her unable to maintain an independent lifestyle. The use of medication such as Aricept® (donepezil HCl) during the early and middle stages of the disease has been helpful alleviating the memory deficits in patients with AD. Cognitive treatment during the early stages is also important to help the patient and family implement memory strategies and environmental changes to enhance communication and maximize the patient's level of functioning.

Depression is fairly common in older adults and could be a result of neurochemical changes, organic disease, and environmental stressors. As many as 10% of older adults living in the community are affected by symptoms of depression, and as many as 3% of people over 65 are thought to have major clinical depression. That figure rises to 35% for older people with one or more medical conditions (National Institute of Mental Health, 1995; Jefferson & Greist, 1996). Clinical depression can resemble dementia (hence the term *pseudodementia*) and may result in changes in concentration and memory as well as in alterations of other mental functions, thus hampering communication. The decline in cognitive performance is due to lack of motivation and lack of energy to engage in purposeful cognitive communication activities. Given the high incidence of depression in older adults, mental health screenings and referrals for further evaluation should be part of the older adult's preventive care for early identification and treatment of the disease.

Speech

Older adults with neurological problems also can suffer speech difficulties such as apraxia and dysarthrias. Apraxia of speech is a sensorimotor speech disorder resulting from damage to the cortex, and it affects the sequencing of speech movements. Dysarthrias are a cluster of motor speech disorders caused by damage to the central and/or peripheral nervous system. They can result in problems in

phonation (tremor and pitch breaks), articulation (slurred speech), hypernasality, prosody (monotone), and respiration (soft, breathy voice).

Treatment of motor speech disorders will differ depending on the degree of involvement and the nature of the disease that produced the disorder. In severe cases, augmentative communication devices are also used to help the patient establish rapport with the environment. Drill work, breathing exercises, and the use of compensatory strategies are incorporated to maximize progress.

Voice

The human voice is probably one of the most distinguished individual characteristics. The voice quality, resonance, pitch and intonation, range, and depth all combine to create a person's voice. Consequently, voice can be affected by pathology and also by vocal abuse and misuse. Besides pathology and vocal abuse, certain changes occur in the vocal mechanism as a result of the aging process.

The laryngeal mechanism becomes stiffer due to ossification of the cartilage and decreases in the collagenous fibers of the intrinsic laryngeal muscles. Furthermore, there seems to be a direct relationship between physiological fitness and the older individual's voice. Decreased physiological fitness contributes to a decrease in lung competence, which in turn results in producing fewer words per breath. The need to renew a breath more often results in a slower speaking rate, particularly in older adults over 80 (Boone & McFarlane, 1994).

Physiological fitness may also be partially responsible for problems with vocal fold vibration (such as glottal-fry), inefficient voice projection, and laryngeal noise. Chronic gastroesophageal reflux disorders (GERD) can contribute to changes in voice quality by causing irritation in the vocal folds, frequent coughing, and hoarseness. Laryngeal cancer often requires partial or total removal of the larynx (laryngectomy), and the patient has to learn alternative techniques, such as the use of esophageal speech and/or an electric larynx.

With increasing age, the fundamental frequency (e.g., the perceived overall pitch of an individual's voice) in males and females decreases slightly up to age 50. After that there seems to be an age-by-gender interaction. In females the fundamental frequency continues to decrease slightly after the fifth decade. In contrast, the pitch of the male voice rises slightly after age 50 (Boone & MacFarlane, 1994). Such changes can be partially attributed to hormonal changes and hormonal differences between males and females.

A Note on Drugs

Older adults may take multiple prescription and nonprescription medications for the management of chronic and acute conditions. Often these multiple medications can cause drug interactions that are exacerbated in older adults due to changes in body mass, liver function, and drug metabolism. For instance, antianxiety drugs can cause sleepiness, slowness, and concentration difficulties. Furthermore, certain antibiotics (such as gentamicin, amikacin, and kanamycin in the aminoglycoside family) used to treat serious systemic infections are ototoxic with varying degree of vestibular and cochlear involvement. Therefore, the patient should be under audiological monitoring during treatment with these drugs.

An older adult may be faced with a variety of mental, physical, and emotional challenges that could interfere with effective communication. It is important to identify those challenges and work with the individual to assist him/her in implementing the necessary strategies for independence and improved quality of life.

FOFI CONSTANTINIDOU

See also
   Aphasia
   Hearing

COMMUNICATION: PROCESSES AND ISSUES

Effective communication contributes much to life satisfaction at all ages. It is through effective communication that rewarding interpersonal relationships are developed and maintained, cooperative projects accomplished, and needs and wishes expressed.

What, then, is effective communication? The basic model of human communication includes a message, a sender, a receiver, a modality through which message transmission occurs, and processes of encoding and decoding the message for comprehension. Often communication is an interactive process (e.g., as friends converse, each functions as sender-receiver). Effective communication can be defined as the accurate transmission of a message from sender to receiver. An act of communication can be more or less effective. For example, part of the message may be lost or distorted or accurate conveyance of the message may have required more time, money, or effort than necessary.

Specialists in communication studies have started to contribute useful information on older adults, and observations have also been made by other disciplines. It should be noted, however, that we are still in the early days of systematic research into the elderly adults as communicators.

Face-to-Face Communication in the Later Adult Years

Face-to-face communication has long been integral to daily life for most people. A mutually satisfying episode of interpersonal communication is contingent on several factors. These include the following:

• *Opportunity for the interaction to occur.* Whatever factors limit mobility and access to a broad range of possible interactants will also limit communicational episodes. Furthermore, contextual factors, such as noisy surroundings or lack of privacy, will also reduce the frequency, duration, and depth of face-to-face interactions. Residents of congregate care facilities and elders who are isolated in their homes are likely to have fewer opportunities for spontaneous and voluntary communicational interactions.

• *Willingness of two or more people to participate in the interaction.* Older adults may be excluded not only from social conversations but also from functional interactions (e.g., the salesperson addressing remarks to the accompanying adult daughter rather than to the woman who is actually shopping for clothes). Older adults may themselves be resistant to interactions, as when approached by people who are perceived as untrustworthy or intrusive. It has been confirmed that younger and older adults tend to hold mutually negative expectations of communicational interactions with each other (Fox & Giles, 1993).

- *Establishment of a common frame of reference and modus operandi.* Effective communication involves not only agreement on subject matter but also on the rules that should govern the exchange. Interactions may become distorted or fall apart if the participants operate on different implicit sets of rules. For example, generational differences may show up in such implicit rules as (1) younger people should not speak unless spoken to; (2) adults should not be addressed on a first-name basis unless a personal relationship has been well established; and (3) women are supposed to listen while men argue their points and make their decisions. Tannen's (1990) findings regarding gender differences in discourse could have useful applications to avoiding misunderstandings in intergenerational contacts. Gender differences in socialization were even greater when today's elders were young. There may also be a divergence in implied rules of communication when interacting with a person of an ethnic or racial background different from one's own. Two elders who have lived most of their lives within their respective cultural enclaves may make each other uncomfortable because they adhere to different rules. "This person is unfriendly, never gives me a smile" may be reciprocated by "This person does not respect me, and I always show my respect with a serious expression." Age, gender, and ethnic/racial differences in implicit rules of communication can operate simultaneously to interfere with potentially effective and rewarding interactions.

- *Acceptable and unacceptable topics.* This is also a rule-governed aspect of communication but deserves separate attention because it is a frequent source of difficulty. People who are now in their middle adult years often report that neither sex nor death could be openly discussed in the home. A woman just shy of her 90th birthday observed that her mother had 11 children, "but she never was *pregnant*, and, of course, she and Papa never did you-know-what." Politics, religion, and money are other topics traditionally limited to private discussions among a few people. Some health conditions have also been considered too

delicate or appalling to discuss. Some elderly adults welcome the more open communication milieu that exists today; others remain true to their upbringing.

- *Elderly men and women may enter communicational situations in a submissive or one-down status.* The loss of occupational role and status tends to undercut the older person's power in some situations. Society's emphasis on youth and discrimination against age can pressure elderly adults into accepting submissive roles, a reversal of the traditional adult-child power relationship. The elder who resists this role may thereby become embroiled in conflict. It is important to recognize the power relationship within which elders are expected to communicate. Problems in effective communication may reflect not the older person's knowledge and abilities but the implicit dominance-submissiveness rules. This problem can be intensified when the context of communication already has a built-in role/power inequity (e.g., the physician as an authority figure that a "lowly" patient might hesitate to question).

Communication Predicament of Aging

This useful concept refers to a frequently occurring situation in which elderly adults themselves may contribute to ineffective and unsatisfying communicational interactions.

> As a consequence of lower expectations for performance, older people often experience *the communication predicament of aging.* By this term, we refer to the situation in which undesirable discrepancies occur between the actual communicative competence of an elderly person and the negative perception of his/her competence. The focus of attention has typically been upon the impact of the negative perceptions held by individuals in other age groups, but . . . to the extent that older people share societal expectations that old age is a time of disengagement, dependence, and sharply declining abilities, these expectations would tend to be self-fulfilling. (Ryan, Giles, Bartolucci, & Henwood, 1986)

Patronization and *overaccommodation* have been identified as key factors in the communication predicament of aging. Elderly adults tend to be recipients not only of infantilizing speech but also of infantilizing intonations (Ryan, Bourhis, & Knops, 1991). Institutionalized elders are especially distressed by the sing-song baby talk intonation that is commonly used with them (Whitbourne, Culgin, & Cassidy, 1995). Consequently, they often feel that they are not being respected and taken seriously.

When an elder responds to patronizing communications by withdrawal, regression, or anger, the speaker is likely to take these behaviors as confirmation that one needs to "make allowances" for older adults rather than expect them to hold their own. Younger adults tend not only to patronize elders but also to overaccommodate to their real or assumed communicational limitations. Speaking very loudly and slowly, for example, may be an inappropriate way of conversing with an elderly person who simply needs the other person to speak clearly and to be free from distracting background noise. Similarly, a younger adult may overaccommodate to the supposed cognitive limitations of an elder by simplifying and abridging messages that actually need to be understood in their full complexity. Elders tend to contribute to this process by being somewhat underaccommodating, that is, they make less effort to attune themselves to the other person (Coupland, Henwood, Coupland, & Giles, 1990).

Sending, Receiving, and Processing Messages

Age-related changes in sensory, motor, and cognitive functions neither exercise a uniform nor an independent effect on communication competence. The individual's characteristic pattern of communication remains a major determinant. A person who has always avoided self-disclosure situations, meeting new people, and speaking on the telephone will not respond to age-related changes in the same way as a person with the opposite tendencies. The current situation will also have a strong influence on communication competence (e.g., living among strangers in an institution or with people who have known them since way back when).

The interaction between preexisting characteristics of the person and age-related changes can be seen readily in both speech and hearing. The larynx tends to become a less effective sound generator with advancing age. Reduction in the elasticity and strength of the laryngeal musculature reduces vocal intensity and has several other effects (e.g., "vocal jitter and shimmy") that contribute to the stereotype of the aging voice (Ringel & Chodzko-Zajko, 1990). Nevertheless, there are individual differences in voice effectiveness among older adults. Actors, singers, and others who have developed a high level of voice control usually continue to speak effectively. People who have lacked confidence in their ability to communicate orally or whose lifestyle has resulted in pathological deterioration of the speech mechanisms may show a significant decline in communicational competence. Furthermore, overall health status also seems to be related to maintaining one's speech abilities at a high level.

The distinction between hearing and listening also illustrates the broad spectrum of age-related changes in communication. It is common to experience hearing loss (presbycusis) with advancing age. Speech intelligibility becomes an increasing problem. Not quite catching all the words he or she is hearing, an elderly person may resort to guesswork to fill in the gaps. Given the same level of hearing impairment, one person may withdraw from situations in which speech intelligibility is a problem, while another person finds various ways to compensate (e.g., hearing aid, reducing the environmental noise level, or asking others to repeat what they have said). Furthermore, the individual's listening skills may be crucial in the maintenance of competence communication. Some people move into their later adult years without having developed either the motivation or the strategies for listening effectively (Arnold, 1993). When a reduction in the ability to detect speech sounds is added to the habitual inattention, such individuals may intensify their communication predicament. Recently established programs that encourage and assist elders to improve their listening skills deserve close attention (Strom, 1993).

Information processing is a major component of the communication process. The sender evaluates, selects, and shapes information into the form required for an effective message. The receiver detects and interprets the message, enriching it with the appropriate semantic context. An effective message can be as minimal as a wink of the eye and a slight nod of the head ("Let's go someplace where we can be alone together"). It can be as subtle as slipping a word with specialized associations into an otherwise public discussion: Only insiders will know what is really meant. It can be as complex as a configuration of verbal and nonverbal communication in which the speaker is actually warning the listener by gesture, expression, and intonation not to believe what is being said. Impaired attention, concentration, memory, judgment, abstract thinking, or ability to integrate verbal and nonverbal messages are state-of-the-organism barriers to effective communication. All that is learned about cognitive changes with age has bearing on communication processes in the later adult years.

Competent communication in the later adult years is especially important for maintaining mutually supportive relationships and looking after one's own interests in discussing health and financial issues. A newly proposed communication enhancement model (Ryan, Meredith, MacLean, & Orange, 1995) may be pointing the way toward a future in which intergenerational communication is more effective and enjoyable for all persons involved.

ROBERT KASTENBAUM

See also
Aphasia
Language Comprehension
Language Production

COMMUNICATION TECHNOLOGIES AND OLDER ADULTS

Communication technologies offer a promising future for older adults. The ability to manage information technologies is a critical condition for professional and perhaps even private success in the Information Age (Mundorf, Brownell, & Bryant, 1997). In examining issues associated with older adults and the media, the fact that new communication technologies can help older adults avoid isolation and helplessness is generally overlooked. During the 1990s, it was found that information technologies, personal computers, and the Internet can be used by older adults as a supplement to face-to-face encounters. Some older adults use them to overcome environmental and physical barriers

while allowing them to fulfill interpersonal needs. Recent experiences with the Internet have shown that older adults who learn to use computers are simultaneously developing practical and conversational skills with which the younger generations are familiar, enhancing possibilities for intergenerational relationships.

Technological progress has brought about a number of communication tools for older adults. Some communication networks, such as SeniorNet, were designed specifically with older adults in mind. They have been successful among those adults with the appropriate skills and motivation. Also, older adults have shown considerable interest in computer courses at community colleges. Current hardware and software developments promise to make computer-based technologies even more user-friendly and suitable for needs of elders. Voice recognition and touch-screen technologies are particularly suited to facilitate appropriate interactions. There is currently a widespread introduction of multimedia to the home (Dholakia, Dholakia, & Mundorf, 1996; Mundorf & Westin, 1996). Although children are the prime motivators at this point, home access to all age groups is increasing.

As schools and libraries nationwide have expanded the use of computer technologies and the Internet as tools in education and information access, more families are going on-line. Grandchildren have stimulated intergenerational use of the Internet to coordinate reunions, vacations, weddings, graduations, and other family-oriented occasions. In the past, some of these events have taken many phone calls and letters to plan or resolve conflicts that can now be handled in a few messages on-line. Although some family members without computer technology may become isolated, the Internet has offered many grandparents an almost immediate look at a new grandchild, via a photograph scanned into an E-mail message, and regular, efficient, and low-cost access to family dialogues. Individuals who might have felt isolated from a generation that may not write thank-you notes can now interact frequently and even instant-message family members for more immediacy. Others forward messages to family members and friends on their electronic recipient lists of amusing, inspiring, and alarming issues of concern that they want other family members to read. Some have used the Internet to send electronic greeting cards complete with sound effects, songs, and colorful graphics of flowers.

Older adults have also begun to take advantage of E-commerce. Those with serious mobility problems, people isolated by bad weather, and individuals unable to drive or locate transportation can find what they need thanks to the Internet and even purchase items on-line. Various search engines and website links make locating products much easier than it was a few years ago. Specialty items that might never have been carried by a local retailer are readily available at affordable prices via the Internet. Some older adults have enjoyed bidding for items through auctions, purchasing stock, managing their money and investments, and submitting their tax returns via the Internet.

Despite positive examples, older adults have exhibited some reluctance to accept change, and new communication technologies typically generate dramatic changes in how we interact with one or more other people. Technology adoption tends to be inversely related to age and positively related to income and education. In particular, the aging of the baby-boom generation is expected to contribute to greater technology acceptance among older demographics. There is still some reluctance among many older adults to do banking or purchase anything on-line when they can still interact with people or trust that their financial information is safe from hackers. Older adults are not a homogeneous group. Certain types of technologies have considerable appeal to particular segments. Independent living, safety, and communication with family and friends have high priority.

Communication needs are addressed by the Internet, even though keyboard skills can be a problem for those who are inexperienced, have had a stroke or other health problem that limits mobility, or suffer from arthritis. In addition, videoconferencing technology is becoming more affordable. Several field trials have successfully installed ISDN-based videophones in elderly households. This technology avoids the keyboard as a bottleneck; but cost and especially limited penetration of videoconferencing technology in private households currently limit it. Internet-based videoconferencing presumably will lead to widespread availability within a few years.

The "smart house" uses technology to increase comfort, health, and safety in a living environment by integrating communication and control systems to maximize independence and functioning of older adults. Such "intelligent homes" can reduce the risk of injuries from falls, burns, poison gases, crime, and fires. Given the needs and concerns of older adults, types of technology that enhance feelings of security would be more likely to gain acceptance.

Smart-house technology typically is developed for high-end or special-needs homes, and some of these technologies filter down into existing mid-level homes. Smart-house features are often built into stand-alone appliances. A key problem is rewiring and networking existing homes, which can be prohibitively expensive. However, such features lend themselves to newly constructed or remodeled independent living facilities.

Another key issue is concern about the added complexity that the invasion of the home by the computer will bring for older persons. Some authors call for a small, self-sufficient "information appliance" that can interface with other household appliances without the need for central programming or computer expertise.

A particularly promising development for older adults is telemedicine. Remote access to health care is particularly critical in cases of limited mobility. Other benefits of telemedicine include access to specialists and quality care for patients in remote rural areas. The Internet again helps the older user obtain information and access to people and health professionals in a way that has never been possible before. Interactive computer-based education appears to have a very positive effect on mental stimulation, competencies, skills, and feelings of autonomy in long-term care residents.

Telemedicine utilizes a range of technologies, from low-tech telephone to high-tech videoconferencing and data transmittal. Even though the focus of discussion has been on the high-tech aspects, such as remote surgery, even low-tech interventions have great potential, especially in medication compliance and prevention. For instance, transmission of glucose levels from patients to physicians lead to significant decreases for diabetic patients; similar findings are reported for diet education programs and treatment compliance (Huffman, 1998). Incentives for the use of telemedicine are greater in areas where access to physicians and specialists is limited and in cases of routine transactions that do not necessarily require the physical presence of the patient.

A number of researchers have been developing Internet-based health promotion programs. One leading example is a stage-based smoking cessation system utilizing James Prochaska's Transtheoretical Model (Prochaska, 1997). This model permits targeting people at different stages of readiness to change risky behaviors. An expert system collects data, including the stage of change, temptations for risky behavior, and suitable processes of change. The system then produces an individualized report, which gives the subject appropriate feedback and recommendations. The model combines the public health approach, which is designed to reach a large number of people at low per person cost, and the individualized clinical approach, in which small numbers of individuals are treated at fairly high cost (Velicer & Prochaska, 1999). Currently, the expert system is being linked to a website, which will permit thousands of users to access it at low incremental cost. Such an approach has the potential to improve health behavior independent of the user's location. The system also permits greater convenience and privacy and empowers the patient, as it can be used at home or at work. In the future, such a system may be connected with "virtual support groups" that might give elderly users support from their peers.

Adoption of telemedicine has tremendous potential, but realizing it requires considerable training and a shift in attitudes by providers and users of these services. Telemedicine has the potential to improve health services to the home, enhance consumer knowledge, and significantly improve the effectiveness and reach of health promotion campaigns.

Older adults will adopt technologies when advantages are offered and communicated. Older adults who are most likely to adopt new communication technologies include those with higher income, those living in multiunit dwellings, and those who use print media.

Older consumers tend to be more reluctant to use emerging technologies than are their younger counterparts. This tendency is somewhat confounded by gender effects, as men, across age groups, tend to feel more comfortable with most technologies than do women. Many age differences are apparently the result of societal misconceptions.

Mundorf, Dholakia, Dholakia, and Westin (1996) explored age differences in an intercultural context with Americans and Germans. Overall, they found that younger respondents tended to be more familiar with technology than are older groups, and men are generally more oriented toward technology than are women, with the exception of telephone technology, where their orientations are comparable. They also found that college-age adults are much more familiar with computers than are older adults. In their sample of German citizens, older and younger adults had comparable levels of familiarity with technologies, and older German males displayed a more positive attitude toward technology than did their college-age counterparts. Americans, regardless of age, are generally more familiar with new technologies than are German adults. The gender differences may disappear with the aging of the baby-boom generation.

Communication technologies offer important advantages for older adults. Although familiarity, acceptance, and adoption of new communication technologies may not be as high among older as in younger adults today, they will increase as older adults have a chance to learn more about the potential for these technologies to improve the quality of their lives. Efforts should be directed toward providing training and access to communication technologies for older adults so that discretionary income and education do not limit their opportunities.

NORBERT MUNDORF
WINIFRED BROWNELL

See also
    Health Information Through Telecommunication
    Internet and E-mail Resources

COMMUNITY CARE: RESEARCH ON OUTCOMES
See
    Home and Community Care
    Outcomes of Community Service: Evidence from the United States and the United Kingdom

COMMUNITY NEEDS ASSESSMENT

Assessing the individual needs of older persons and developing community resource profiles was an important activity during the 1970s and early 1980s. These activities became much less influential, as witnessed by the decreased number of relevant citations in AgeLine, during the 1980s. However, needs assessments have enjoyed a relative rediscovery in the early 1990s because of their use in resource allocation decisions (Lagergren, 1994; Young, 1993). The increased number of AgeLine citations documented this reestablished importance. During the latter half of the 1990s the devolution of resource allocation decisions to smaller, more local geographic units, generally tied to health reforms, has firmly entrenched both *individual needs assessments* and *community resource profiles* among the administrative planners in these new districts, areas, or other planning units. This has resulted in community needs assessments being used more broadly, in terms of age groups, rather than being dominated by the needs of older persons. At the same time, however, the number of AgeLine citations has markedly increased, and the studies cited tend to be based either on smaller geographic units or on more specialized subpopulations. One relatively recent title within a health reform context sums up the former group: *Introduction of Needs-Based Allocation of Resources to Saskatchewan District Health Boards for 1994–95* (Saskatchewan Health, 1994). The burgeoning citations relative to mental health or developmental disabilities needs and the needs of Hispanic Americans are examples of the latter category.

Issues in Community Needs Assessment

Like the field of gerontology, the technology of individual assessment has become multidimensional and multidisciplinary. However, several major issues continue to plague designers and users of this technology. These issues include lack of unanimity about the definition of needs and lack of specificity about the difference between individual needs assessment and community resource profiles. There is a continuing lack of agreement on the dimensions and, hence, the disciplines to be involved in these assessments. Finally, lack of clarity about the appropriate uses for or applications of assessments and profiles continues, despite the increased use of these techniques. In a recent literature review by Billings and Cowley (1995), these issues are ably summarized. The authors indicate that much of the history of community needs assessments derives from epidemiology, from sociology, and more recently, from health economics. This is certainly true of community profiles; however, they have neglected the importance of developmental psychology in individual needs assessments. They have made an important contribution to this literature by calling particular attention to the reliability and validity of the data and data sources to be used in community needs assessments.

One of the difficulties encountered in searching for consensus on the *definition of needs* is that needs means different things to different people. Dill's (1993) article places the definitional issue in a systems context. However, much of the work on individual needs assessment within gerontology has been derived from the tradition of developmental psychology. Tobin (1965) synthesized the major elements of this approach. Within this tradition the tautology of equating needs with service use is avoided. That is, if the services of community resources are used, then one can argue that need no longer exists. Simultaneously, this approach recognizes explicitly that use can occur only within the context of community resources.

The conceptualization of community resource profiles is less well developed. The unit of analysis for community resource profiles must be the community or similar geographic area. It is inappropriate to infer the needs of a community from either the characteristics of its resources or the use of resources within the community. It is equally inappropriate to infer the community resource profile as the aggregation of the individual needs of older residents in that community. In other words, resources exist at the aggregate community level, whereas needs exist at an individual level. Use is, at best, a proxy for the relationship between these two concepts. However, to substitute measures of use for either individual needs assessments or community resource profiles means ignoring both individual and structural dimensions of use.

Typically, the dimensions of individual needs assessment include physical health status or functioning, mental health status or functioning, basic activities and instrumental activities of daily living (ADLs and IADLs). Psychosocial functioning (e.g., general well-being, morale, social networks, loneliness); cultural needs (racial, ethnic, or religious); housing (or shelter) needs; household maintenance capability; and economic functioning or status are also generally included. To complete the dimensions of individual needs, one should include the *availability* and *accessibility* of services from both formal resources and informal support networks. Although community resource profiles include these same dimensions, they are structured to indicate the degree to which community resources are capable of responding to the needs of individuals. Given the range of dimensions, it is difficult to identify any human service–related profession or discipline that would not be involved appropriately in a comprehensive needs assessment or community resource profile.

A final area of confusion stems from incomplete specification of the goals of needs assessments and resource profiles. For example, assessments may be used to expand our knowledge about the aging process, to determine whether needs are hierarchical, to form the basis of planning processes, or to allocate or redistribute human and fiscal resources. It is therefore essential to specify adequately the goals of each needs assessment and community resource profile activity to determine the most appropriate methodology, measurement technique, and means of data collection. It is not only possible but desirable for any given needs assessment or community profile to use more than one methodology in order to be comprehensive and satisfy all the goals specified. The steps in the iterative process of needs analysis, according to McKillip (1987) include identifying users and uses, describing both the target population and the service environment, identifying needs through describing both problems and solutions, evaluating the primacy of needs, and communicating the results.

Seven Methodological Approaches

Within the field of gerontology, individual needs assessments and community resource profiles have typically employed seven different methodologies or approaches. Warheit, Bell, and Schwab (1974) have provided the most concise summary of these methods to date. All of the current assessment, screening, and data collection tools and techniques have been derived from one of these methods or approaches, or a combination of two or more. The advantages of using more than one approach to individual needs assessments and community resource profiles are underscored by noting that the examples given below for the methodological approaches identify the same authors for more than one approach.

The seven approaches, and relevant examples, are:

1. epidemiological (Reese, 1998);
2. social statistics or social indicators (Gesler, DeFriese, & Rabiner, 1998);
3. town hall or community forum (Gesler, DeFriese, & Rabiner, 1998);
4. key informants (Lee-Han, Dwyer & Johnson, 1996);
5. consumer method (Shi, Samuels, Brown, & Martin, 1996);
6. economic method (Shapiro, 1986);
7. survey method (Shi, Samuels, Brown, & Martin, 1996).

All of these methods have been employed to measure or assess the needs of older individuals and to construct community resource profiles. Each method has its own strengths and weaknesses. Each is appropriate in specific circumstances. No one method is, nor should be expected to be, appropriate in all situations. A review of research instruments available to gerontologists in assessing needs and developing community profiles has been reported by this author elsewhere (Havens, 1984).

BETTY HAVENS

See also
　　Comprehensive Assessment
　　Multidimensional Functional Assessment

COMMUNITY PSYCHOLOGY

Community psychology is a philosophy or set of principles that governs both research and practice

(Dejowski, 1987). Although its intellectual roots can be traced to the work of Kurt Lewin and others (Sarason, 1974), a major impetus for community psychology came from the Joint Commission on Mental Illness and Health (1961), with its call for innovative approaches to mental health treatment and subsequent legislation establishing community mental health centers. During the next 30 years, however, community psychology expanded its substantive scope to include mental health, physical health, and social interventions (Seidman, 1983), with broader targets than an individual's mental health (e.g., community structures that can serve as protective factors). At the same time, a variety of theoretical paradigms emerged within community psychology, including those emphasizing ecological epistemology, developmental perspectives, organizational psychology, social empowerment, behavioral approaches, systems theory, and prevention.

Community Psychology and Aging

Konnert, Gatz, and Hertzsprung (1999) and Smyer (1995) provide comprehensive reviews of preventive research on older adults. Following Mrazek and Haggerty's (1994) scheme, they differentiate preventive research into three approaches: indicated, selective, and universal preventive measures. Indicated prevention focuses on high-risk individuals who show some signs or biological markers of a mental disorder but who do not meet full diagnostic criteria for a disorder. Selective preventive intervention targets those who are at risk for a disorder but who show no signs of one. Universal preventive interventions target all individuals regardless of relative risk for a disorder.

Within the indicated domain, Konnert, Gatz, and Hertzsprung (1999) highlighted efforts designed to prevent or forestall institutionalization. Konnert and her colleagues noted that these efforts have had two disappointing results: little reduction in rates of institutionalization (perhaps because of targeting those with a low risk of entry) and little cost savings.

Selective prevention efforts often target individuals at risk because of a particular life stress, for example, widowhood or physical illness. In addition to focusing on the at-risk individual, many studies have focused on interventions with caregivers to avoid excess disability (e.g., Zarit, Pearlin, & Schaie, 1993).

Universal interventions have included two emphases: building neighborhood networks of mutual assistance and supporting the empowerment of older adults by using their talents as peer counselors, advocates, and volunteers.

Future Directions

Despite recent developments in community psychology and aging, several challenges remain. Much of the research literature does not reflect the diversity of the aging community and the potential impact of that diversity on the need for and efficacy of preventive interventions. In addition, previous research has focused primarily on public sector efforts, with little attention to the role of community psychology and prevention efforts within a private-sector, managed care context (e.g., Edmunds, Frank, Hogan, McCarty, Robinson-Beale, & Weisner, 1997).

Gatz (1995) has suggested four broader goals for a community psychology of aging: improving the health of older adults (both physical and mental health); providing financial security for older adults; improving the functional independence of older adults so that they have a shorter period of dependence and, in some cases, of institutionalization; and assisting older adults in achieving a sense of meaning or "vital involvement" in later life. To achieve these goals, community psychologists and gerontologists will have to identify the optimal combination of interventions, risk factors, and protective mechanisms that allows older adults to adapt in the midst of all challenges of later life. In short, we will have to answer a simple question: Under which conditions, for which individuals, will which interventions have the desired outcomes?

MICHAEL A. SMYER

See also
Environmental Psychology

COMPETENCE

Although originating in the health and clinical domains, the study of competence has broadened to include legal and social-psychological competence. Indeed, behavioral competence in adulthood has been studied from multiple perspectives, including functional competence, everyday cognitive competence, and legal competence. Functional competence has typically been concerned with the individual's ability to care for himself or herself and to engage in activities required for independent living (Fillenbaum, 1985; Lawton & Brody, 1969). Study of everyday cognitive competence is concerned with the application of cognitive abilities and skills to the solution of problems experienced in daily life (Poon, Rubin, & Wilson, 1989; Willis, 1996a). Legal competence has focused largely on judgments regarding the adult's capacity or incapacity to care for himself or herself or to manage his or her property and the assignment of guardian or conservator responsibilities (Kapp, 1992; Smyer, Kapp, & Schaie, 1995; Smyer, Schaie, & Kapp, 1996).

As diverse disciplines have studied competence, not only has the definition and approach varied, but the assessment of competence has differed as well. Assessment of functional and everyday competence has typically relied on self- or proxy ratings of performance. More recently, researchers have begun to develop "objective" measures of competence that are based on the actual or observed performance of the elderly (Willis, 1996b). Increasingly, the strengths and limitations of various approaches have been acknowledged and the feasibility of a single functional assessment tool questioned (Mezey, Rauckhorst, & Stokes, 1993; Ward, Jagger, & Harper, 1998). In the legal domain, which relies solely on professional judgment to assess competence, competence is not considered an "all-or-nothing" proposition (Grisso & Appelbaum, 1998; Kapp & Mossman, 1996). It is argued that assessment of competence should be domain-specific (e.g., financial management, medication usage) and dynamic (i.e., sensitive to change), allowing for review of competence and, when appropriate, withdrawal of guardianship.

The various approaches to the study of functional competence do share important commonalities in the conception of the phenomena that contribute to a more complete understanding of competence in old age (Willis, 1996a). First, competence as defined in each perspective represents the potential or capability of the individual to perform a task, not the actual daily behavior of the individual. It is important to differentiate between competence and the behaviors the adult regularly performs in daily life. For example, functional assessment has traditionally addressed the question "*Can* the individual perform an activity?" rather than "*Does* the individual perform the activity on a regular basis?" Similarly, in legal judgments the focus recently has been on whether the individual is capable of making sound financial decisions, not whether the individual behaves in a manner considered financially astute by others (Altman, Parmelee, & Smyer, 1992).

Second, each approach is concerned with the capacity to carry out significant real-world activities required for independent living. The focus is not on academic tasks but rather on tasks considered important in daily life (Park, 1992; Puckett & Reese, 1993). The question arises, then: What are considered the critical activities for functioning in the real world? A criterion is needed against which to judge the importance or criticality of the innumerable activities of daily life. Capacity to live independently within the community has been the criterion used most frequently in work on functional and legal competence (Grisso, 1986). Both approaches to competence have emphasized two broad activity domains associated with independent living: the ability to care for oneself (e.g., bathing, eating, toileting) and the ability to manage one's affairs. Within the study of functional competence, care of oneself is represented by the activities of daily living (ADLs) and management of one's affairs by the instrumental activities of daily living (IADLs). Regarding legal competence, the Uniform Probate Code (1989, 1997; Uniform Acts: ABA Codes, 1999) distinguishes between legal proceedings regarding care of the person (guardianship) and those related to property (conservatorship). In the social sciences there has been a distinction between obligatory and committed activities (i.e., activities similar to ADLs and IADLs) and discretionary activities (i.e., activities not necessary for independent living, such as leisure activities) (Baltes, Maas, Wilms, Borchelt, & Little, 1999; Verbrugge, Gruber-Baldini, & Fozard, 1996). In research on everyday cognition, the focus has been on salient tasks of daily living that are high in cognitive demands (e.g., medication compliance and financial or medical decision making).

Third, each approach gives special attention to cognitive abilities and skills in the conceptualization and assessment of competence (Fillenbaum, 1985; Salthouse, 1990). Legal judgments involve a specification of the cause of the incompetence or incapacity. Cognitive deficiencies, either pathological or resulting from sociocultural factors, are most commonly cited for incompetence and the need for a guardian or conservator (Anderer, 1990). In research on functional competence, cognition has been viewed as one of the major contributors to adequate functioning, along with physical health and social support (Kane, 1993). Brief global measures of cognition have been most frequently used in assessments related to functional and legal competence; however, the need for measures to assess cognition within the context of IADL (e.g., memory demands of medical compliance or executive functioning involved in medical treatment decision making) has been noted in both the functional and legal competence literatures (Grisso, 1986; Loewenstein, Amigo, Duara, Guterman, Hurwitz, Berkowitz, et al., 1989). The cognitive demands of everyday activities are a major focus of applied cognitive aging research. In our own research we have found that solving problems related to IADL-type activities (e.g., comprehending a prescription drug label or decision making regarding financial transactions) involves multiple primary mental abilities, including abstract reasoning, verbal ability, and memory; significant variance in everyday problem solving can be accounted for by performance on these mental abilities (Schaie, 1996; Willis, 1996b). In addition, research has shown that to minimize energy expenditure and reduce anxiety, many elderly seek quick resolutions to cognitively demanding problems in daily life. They rely heavily on prior experience and previously acquired problem-solving strategies and are less likely to consider newly acquired information (Leventhal, Leventhal, Schaefer, & Easterling, 1993; Meyer, Russo, & Talbot, 1995).

Finally, each perspective recognizes that competence and perception of competence does not reside solely in the individual. Rather, the context (e.g., unique characteristics of the individual and setting, expectations and biases of involved professionals) must be considered (Castellucii, 1998). The individual's level of competence represents the congruence between the individual's knowledge and skills and the demands of the environment (Lawton, 1987; Lawton & Parmelee, 1990). Functional impairment does not necessarily lead to disability (Jette & Branch, 1985), and disability occurs only when the individual acknowledges that the impairment has consequences for his or her daily life (Warshaw & Murphy, 1995). In an environment that is both physically and socially supportive, even an individual with some deficiencies may function adequately. Conversely, a well-functioning individual may have difficulty in a resource-deprived environment.

SHERRY L. WILLIS
JENNIFER A. MARGRETT

See also
  Abilities
  Intelligence
  Legal Services
  Problem Solving
  Proxy Decision Making

COMPREHENSIVE ASSESSMENT

A comprehensive, multidimensional functional assessment is a systematic procedure for describing the functional abilities, general situation, and unmet needs of an older person and gaining insights into how abilities might be enhanced or needs met. Such assessments are used by care coordinators (sometimes called case managers) to determine eligibility for various services and/or to tailor care plans to the particular needs of a given older person. They are typically done in a home visit. Over the past few decades, systematic comprehensive assessment protocols have proliferated (Gallo, Reichel, & Anderson, 1995; Kane & Kane, 1981, 2000; Rubenstein, Weiland, & Bernabei, 1995).

What Is Distinctive About Comprehensive, Multidimensional Functional Assessments?

Assessment is a process of information gathering, diagnosis, and evaluation common to most human service professions. But the assessments discussed here are distinctive because of their comprehensiveness of detail, their multidimensionality (i.e., their coverage of physical, psychological, social, environmental, and other dimensions), their reliance on standard question-and-answer or observational formats, and their emphasis on depicting objective functioning or behavior. A multidimensional assessment instrument may be designed to reflect the concerns and interests of a wide range of professionals. For example, pharmacists may have assisted with questions on the use of medications; physical therapists, on questions about range of motion. Typically, the assessment protocol is administered by a single assessor, such as a social worker or a registered nurse. Some multidimensional assessments, in contrast, are administered by multidisciplinary teams (working sequentially or simultaneously). At the other extreme, some are effectively administered by well-trained paraprofessionals.

The typical comprehensive assessment takes, on average, an hour to administer and relies heavily on a questionnaire format. In other variations, professionals make observations (e.g., about the older person's functioning or home environment). Some approaches go beyond this to include a demonstration by the older person of some of the physical or cognitive abilities in question.

The assessments are functional in the sense that they emphasize what the older person is able to do and ordinarily does. A person's capabilities are the product of physical and cognitive abilities, psychological states, and social circumstances. But the end result is a set of functional abilities or behaviors that can be measured. Functioning has conventionally been divided into the ability to perform activities of daily living (ADL) and the ability to perform instrumental activities of daily living (IADL). As developed by Katz, Ford, Moskowitz, Jackson, and Jaffe (1963), ADL activities refer to basic self-care, such as eating, using the toilet, getting in and out of bed, dressing, and bathing. Urinary continence (though strictly speaking a physiological function) is often measured as an ADL, as is ability to walk. IADL, on the other hand, refers to a more varied and complex set of activities related to independent living. Items sometimes appearing on IADL scales include cooking, cleaning, doing laundry, driving a car, shopping, using the telephone, taking medica-

tions, managing money, and doing heavy household and yard work. Dozens of scales have been developed to measure both ADL and IADL, and these in turn have been incorporated into multidimensional measures.

Components

Although assessment instruments vary in detail, they usually address similar dimensions. In addition to the direct measurement of ADL and IADL functions described above, the assessment typically includes physical functioning, cognitive functioning, emotional functioning, and social functioning.

Physical functioning can be measured by some combination of the following: diagnoses, symptoms, reported health, days in bed during a specified period, use of hospital or physicians during a specified period, and reported pain and discomfort. Often the assessor systematically reviews the prescribed and over-the-counter drugs that the older person uses. The cognitive assessment involves at least a brief screening questionnaire to determine whether the subject is oriented for time, place, and person and is intact in recent and distant memory. Failure to achieve an adequate score on such a cognitive screening test might be a signal to obtain the rest of the information from a relative or caregiver.

Psychological measures might include those for depression, anxiety, loneliness, positive zest, and sense of mental well-being and perhaps a history of any diagnosable psychiatric disorders, including alcohol or drug dependency. Social functioning might include frequency and nature of contacts with family and friends, presence of a person with whom confidences are exchanged, frequency and nature of social activities, group memberships and church involvement, and receipt of assistance. Some assessment batteries attempt also to measure the adequacy of the environment (the house, the neighborhood, or both), the economic status of the older person, and the extent to which those providing help are themselves burdened. Some attempt to assess perceived social well-being or satisfaction through scales that measure morale, life satisfaction, or a similar construct. Assessments designed for particular settings include a measure of adaptation to that setting; others include a general measure of coping abilities.

Some multidimensional assessments (especially those used to support case management and care planning) also examine the services that the older person is currently receiving from community agencies and from family and friends (Gaugler, Kane, & Langlois, 2000). The latter are often called the "informal caregivers." Less frequently included but sometimes recommended are: measures of spiritual well-being (Olson & Kane, 2000), measures of consumer preference (Kane, 2000), and systematic assessment of the individual's physical environment (Cutler, 2000).

Technical Characteristics

Assessment instruments can be examined for their reliability and validity. Reliability refers to the consistency of the measure in producing the same result in the absence of real change, whereas validity is the property of the instrument actually measuring what is intended. Reliability becomes a factor when many interviewers are involved: Would one case manager get the same result as another? Validity becomes a particular concern because many of the concepts are abstract: Can we be sure when measuring self-esteem or social isolation that we are capturing the aspects of the concept generally defined as relevant?

Combining all the information gathered in a multidimensional assessment is a formidable challenge. Sometimes a single score is produced, which gives weight to each dimension in some predetermined way. More often, separate scores are generated, which gives the assessor a profile of each dimension in the battery. Then, too, the strategies differ regarding how much the answers to the questions are used to calculate scores. In some instances, the interviewer makes general ratings based on his or her own judgment after the questionnaire is completed.

Examples

One of the better-known multidimensional assessment batteries is the OARS methodology (1978). Developed at Duke University's Older Americans Research and Service Center and refined in subsequent years (Fillenbaum, 1988), the OARS instrument takes about an hour to administer and yields a summary rating of Physical Functioning, Psychological Functioning, ADL Functioning, Social Functioning, and Economic Functioning. In a somewhat more psychiatrically focused approach, Gurland, Kuriansky, Sharpe, Simon, Stiller, and Birkett (1977–78) developed the Comprehensive Assessment and Referral Evaluation (CARE). Recently, they have done considerable work with CARE to develop scales directly from the responses to the items. Lawton's Multilevel Assessment Instrument (MAI) (Lawton, Moss, Fulcomer, & Kleban, 1982) assesses behavioral competence in the domains of health, ADL, cognition, time use, and social interaction and in the sectors of psychological well-being and perceived environmental quality. Kane, Bell, Riegler, Wilson, and Kane (1983) developed an instrument particularly designed to measure multiple domains (physical, cognitive, emotional, social, and satisfaction) by getting information directly from nursing home residents; this instrument involved substantial direct demonstration of abilities. Also for nursing homes, the Resident Assessment Instrument (RAI) was developed in the 1980s and has been mandated as a care-planning tool to be used every 6 months for all nursing residents supported by federal funds (Morris, Hawes, Fries, Phillips, Mor, Katz, et al., 1990). This database does not yield a score but rather provides a comprehensive overview of the resident. Finally, virtually every state has one or more assessment tools in use within statewide home- and community-based long-term care programs.

Multidisciplinary Assessment in Practice

Assessment tools are used to establish a baseline understanding of an older person so that change can be monitored and the effects of interventions determined. They are also used to establish benefits according to functional impairment—for that purpose, the information they yield must be defensible as leading to equitable and accurate allocation of resources. In wide-scale demonstration projects that have tested the effectiveness of long-term care services at home, the assessment has provided both clinical information and research data, though there is a tension between these two uses.

By now experts tend to agree that the comprehensive, multidimensional assessment is worthwhile, that some consistency and system should be imposed on information gathering, and that functional status itself must be included. Challenges remain, however. First, the older person's preferences are not yet well incorporated into the comprehensive assessments. Second, case managers are challenged to use the assessment data effectively to make defensible, individualized care plans. Third, assessment data must be available in an accessible form to compare the effectiveness of various programs and to determine how different mixes of services are associated with the older person's changing well-being over time. Thus, in the 1990s the emphasis has been on automation and on using the assessments as the basis for management information systems that permit tracking service clients across a variety of different programs. Fourth, more attention should be devoted to training those who do the assessment, including overcoming resistance on the part of clinicians to using standardized tools in consistent ways. Although much work may have been devoted to creating a reliable and valid instrument, in fact, the ultimate requirements for reliability and validity are that the assessors themselves understand the tools and are committed to using them.

ROSALIE A. KANE

See also
  Geriatric Health
  Minimum Data Set
  Multidimensional Functional Assessment
  OARS Multidimensional Functional Assessment Questionnaire

COMPRESSION OF MORBIDITY/ DISEASE POSTPONEMENT

The health of seniors is both the largest health problem and the largest economic problem in the developed nations. Prevention of illness should play a major role in approaching solutions. Yet *health education*, *disease prevention*, and *health promotion* have been in great need of an underlying theoretical paradigm. Lacking such a paradigm the health promotion community has been subject to criticisms of mistaking association for causality on the one hand or of promoting a world of long-lived disabled and demented individuals on the other.

The *compression of morbidity* paradigm envisions a reduction of overall morbidity and of health care costs, now heavily concentrated in the senior years, by compression of the period of morbidity and high costs between an increasing average age of onset of disability and the age of death, increasing perhaps more slowly (Fries, 1980). The healthy life is seen as potentially a vigorous and vital life until shortly before its natural close. Intuitively, the concept of delaying the onset of disability through reduction in health risks and prevention of diseases seems natural enough. However, in the early and middle years of this century most observers believed that there was movement away from this ideal, with a steady increase in the proportion of a typical life spent ill or infirm. The previously prevalent acute illnesses of 1900 had given way to chronic diseases such as cancer, heart disease, lung disease, and stroke, with longer periods of disability and morbidity. This phenomenon has been termed "the failure of success."

As people took better care of themselves and lived even longer, the pessimists suggested, they would live into those later years in which disability is greatest and would experience an increase in overall lifetime disability. Morbidity would be extended. They assumed that life could be prolonged but that aging and chronic disease could not be postponed (Vita, Terry, Hubert, & Fries, 1998). Such critics feared that good health habits would lead to an epidemic of Alzheimer's disease and a huge population of enfeebled, demented elders who would place an immense strain on medical care resources. The direct test of compression (or extension) of morbidity depends on the effects, studied prospectively and longitudinally, of reduced health risks on cumulative lifetime disability and on mortality. Will age-specific disability decline more rapidly than age-specific mortality, or vice versa?

New and emerging data document that the fears of the pessimists were unfounded. First, life expectancy from advanced ages has plateaued rather than having increased markedly as predicted. In the United States the life expectancy of women from age 65 has increased only 0.6 years over the past 17 years. From age 85, female life expectancy in the United States has been constant at 6.4 years since 1980. There will be a large increase in senior populations in the future, but it will be based on larger birth cohorts and increased survival to age 65 rather than on large longevity increases after age 65 or 85.

Second, recent longitudinal data document the ability to greatly postpone the onset of disability with age. For the past 14 years our research group at Stanford has studied the effects of long-distance running and other vigorous exercise on patient outcomes in 537 members of a runners club, with participants at least 50 years old, compared with 423 age-matched community controls. The study was designed as a test of the compression of morbidity hypothesis. Appropriate controls for self-selection bias included longitudinal study; x-rays of hands, knees, and hips; intention-to-treat analyses; and statistical adjustment for other variables. Disability levels were assessed yearly, allowing the area under the disability curve to be assessed and approximating cumulative lifetime disability. Runners, exercising vigorously for an average of 280 minutes per week, delayed the onset of disability *by about 10 years,* compared with controls. Both male and female runners increased disability at a rate only one-third that of the controls, after adjusting for age, initial disability, educational level, smoking behavior, body mass index, history of arthritis, and the presence of comorbid disease. As these subjects moved from age 58 toward age 70, the differences in physical functional abilities between the exercising and the control population actually showed an increase rather than a decrease. Lifetime disability in exercisers is only one-third to one-half that of sedentary individuals.

In the similarly designed University of Pennsylvania study, we studied 1,741 university attendees in 1939 and 1940, surveyed again in 1962 at an average age of 43, and then annually since 1986. This unique data set contains over 50 years of longitudinal follow-up since the participant's days at the university. Health risk strata were developed for persons at high, moderate, and low risk, based on the three risk factors of smoking, body mass index, and lack of exercise. Cumulative disability from 1986 (at an average age of 67) to 1994 (at an average age of 75) or until death served as a surrogate for lifetime disability. Persons with high health risks in 1962 or in 1986 had approximately twice

the cumulative disability of those with low health risks. Results were consistent across survivors, deceased, males, females, those without disability in 1986, and over the last 1 and 2 years of observation. Deceased low-risk subjects had only one-half the disability of high-risk subjects in their last 1 and 2 years of life. High-risk subjects, despite having increased mortality, had greatly increased lifetime disability. Onset of disability was postponed by approximately 7.75 years in the low-risk stratum as compared with the high-risk stratum. The 100% reduction in disability rates was balanced against only a 50% reduction in mortality rates, documenting compression of morbidity.

Recent major studies by other groups confirm these findings. Daviglus and colleagues showed substantial decreases in Medicare costs for those with few risk factors in mid-life. Freedman and Martin showed significant age-specific functional improvement in seniors over a 7-year period. Reed and colleagues related healthy aging to prospectively determined health risks, with results closely similar to ours. Studies of favored populations such as these provide are an excellent perspective on healthy aging potential, because the confounding effects of education, poverty, and lack of access to medical care are avoided.

Compression of morbidity is readily demonstrable in those who exercise vigorously compared with those who do not, those with low behavioral health risks versus those with high risks, and those with high educational attainment as compared with low attainment, providing proof of concept. Health risk behaviors as determined in midlife and late adulthood strongly predict subsequent lifetime disability. Both cumulative morbidity and morbidity at the end of life are decreased in those with good health habits. Morbidity is postponed and compressed into fewer years in those with fewer health risks.

Third, randomized controlled trials have now proved that health improvement and risk-reduction programs can reduce health risks, improve health status, and reduce the need and demand for medical services in seniors. The Bank of America study of 4,700 retirees reduced costs by 20% and improved health indices by 10% to 20%. The California Public Employees Retirement System study of 57,000 seniors yielded closely similar results. Chronic disease self-management programs in arthritis and in

Parkinson's disease documented the effectiveness of similar interventions in persons with chronic illness. Self-management programs in seniors have improved health and reduced costs (Fries, Koop, Sokolov, Beadle, & Wright, 1998).

There are three stages in developing documentary evidence to support a national health policy to improve senior health. First is the conceptual base, represented by the compression of morbidity paradigm. Second is the epidemiological data associating health risk behaviors with cumulative lifetime health outcomes, comparing effects on morbidity with those on mortality and providing proof of concept. Finally, the randomized controlled trials, now available (Fries, Koop, Sokolov, Beadle, & Wright, 1998), prove that effective behavioral interventions can decrease senior morbidity and medical care costs.

The paradigm of a long, healthy life with a relatively rapid terminal decline represents an attainable ideal. Health policies must be directed at modifying those health risks that precede and cause morbidity if this ideal is to be approached for a population.

Further information can be obtained on the Internet at the website for the Health Project: *http://healthproject.stanford.edu.*

JAMES F. FRIES

See also

Epidemiology of Aging: A New View of Health Status and Risk Factors

Successful Aging

COMPUTED TOMOGRAPHY: COGNITIVE CHANGES

See

Brain Imaging

Central and Peripheral Nervous Systems Morphology

CONGRESSIONAL COMMITTEES

"Fragmented" is the word usually used to describe the U.S. Congress's role in developing elements of a national policy on aging. This judgment persists despite the existence of two fact-finding, advocacy-oriented congressional committees that devote full-time attention to aging.

Legislation of concern to older Americans is channeled through a multitude of committees and subcommittees in both houses of the Congress. In many cases, aging is one of many matters considered by the congressional unit. The House Ways and Means Committee and the Senate Committee on Finance, for example, consider all tax legislation channeled through the Congress. The vast Social Security system comes under the jurisdiction of these committees, therefore, on the basis of the payroll contribution, or tax, that finances the trust funds supporting retirement, disability, survivors' and Medicare Part A hospital health insurance. The same is true of federal tax advantages given to business for private pension plans.

Thus, two vital elements of national aging policy—key sources of retirement income and partial but important protection against hospital costs at age 65 and beyond—are within the domains of these committees. The Ways and Means Committee maintains a Subcommittee on Health, largely concerned with Medicare, and a Subcommittee on Social Security. The Finance Committee has a Health Subcommittee, one on Social Security and Income Maintenance Programs, and another on savings, pensions, and investment policy.

Dominant as these two committees seem to be, their power is not total on health and pension matters. In the House Committee on Energy and Commerce, the Subcommittee on Health and the Environment considers many health issues, including Medicare's Part B (for medical care) on the grounds that it is supported by general revenues and participants' premiums, rather than a trust fund. The Senate Committee on Labor and Human Resources has no health subcommittee but considers a wide range of health matters at the committee level. The same Senate Committee has jurisdiction over pension regulatory issues, other than the tax issues considered by the Finance Committee. Similarly, the Subcommittee on Labor-Management Relations in the House Committee on Education and Labor deals with pension reform and regulatory oversight matters.

To the complexity demonstrated thus far may be added the fact that no single congressional unit has clearcut authority over long-term care, considered by many to be the most pressing issue affecting older Americans. All committees mentioned thus far have jurisdiction over programs involved substantially or tangentially with long-term care, together with other congressional units not yet cited.

Many congressional committees deal with aging as a relatively secondary component of their daily responsibilities. The House Committee on Banking, Finance and Urban Affairs, for example, maintains jurisdiction over the Section 202 direct loan housing program specifically serving older Americans and the handicapped. But aging issues often arise in other programs that come before the Committee that are not specifically concerned with older persons. Approximately 40% of public housing residents, for example, are over age 65. Housing rehabilitation programs also have special meaning for older owners. In the Senate, the Committee on Banking, Housing, and Urban Affairs has similar authority. Here again, however, the authority is not total. Committees on Agriculture in both houses consider housing programs in rural areas, including a demonstration Congregate Housing Services Program to make services more generally available to frail elders living in specially designed quarters.

Other examples, in the House of Representatives alone, include: Committee on the Judiciary (crime prevention), Committee on Public Works and Transportation (categorical transportation services for the elderly), Committee on Education and Labor (employment programs for the elderly and age discrimination), and the Committee on Agriculture (food stamps) (U.S. Congress, 1979). Senate counterparts exist. Appropriations and budget committees in both houses also have considerable influence over programs after authorizing committees have approved them.

Within authorizing committees in both houses are subcommittees dealing with the Older Americans Act: the Subcommittee on Aging of the Senate Committee on Labor and Human Resources, and the Subcommittee on Human Resources in the House Committee on Education and Labor. Related issues may emerge. For example, the House Subcommittee conducted hearings in 1985 on the impact of Medicare's Prospective Payment System (PPS) upon community providers of services needed by elderly patients discharged from hospitals considerably earlier than had been the case

before PPS. Legislative authority to conduct White House Conferences on Aging is also likely to be channeled through these two subcommittees.

The very diversity of congressional concerns related to aging has led to the establishment of two committees mandated to take a comprehensive view of public policy and aging.

In the Senate, a significant step toward comprehensiveness occurred in 1956, when what was then the Committee on Public Welfare (now Labor and Human Resources) compiled 11 volumes of documents summarizing information then available on problems and programs related to aging (U.S. Congress, 1956). Three years later, the same committee established the Subcommittee on Problems of the Aged and Aging to conduct a "full and complete study and investigation on any and all matters pertaining to problems of older people." Special attention was paid to health insurance for hospital treatment since the legislative struggle over what was to become Medicare in 1965 was then entering a crucial phase. But the subcommittee took on a wide range of other subjects including housing, employment opportunities, training of professionals in aging, nursing homes, and social services.

The subcommittee saw a societal, as well as a governmental, challenge in aging. Its first major report declared in 1960:

> The responsibility of seeking solutions to the many problems that are inherent in this population explosion is not one that can handily be assigned. It is no more the sole responsibility of the Federal Government than it is of the town where an aged person happens to reside. Rather the challenging task is a matter of joint responsibility, utilizing all levels of government, private organizations, and individuals. Only through this partnership approach can we hope, in time, to solve the problems of the aging. (U.S. Congress, 1960)

Subcommittee Chairman Pat McNamara of Michigan moved successfully in 1961 to transfer the work of the subcommittee to a new Senate Special Committee on Aging. Prominent among his arguments was the theme that congressional jurisdiction on aging issues was so fragmented that a unified view was needed, together with intense inspection of issues requiring specialized attention. The special committee had only fact-finding and reporting responsibilities; it could not receive bills and report them for senate action. In addition, the Committee was to submit its final report a year later and "cease to exist." In short order, however, the committee issued a number of reports and took other actions causing its members and other senators to see the advantage of continuing the committee. It was extended regularly on a year-to-year basis until 1977, when it was made a permanent unit.

A prominent committee function is to issue reports after hearings or other research. An annual committee report, summarizing policy actions and exploring emerging or continuing issues, has been described as "a major policy document" and a "remarkable storehouse" of information (Rich & Baum, 1984). Individual Committee members—many of them prominent in authorizing, appropriations, or budget committees—often sponsor bills recommended or suggested by Committee on Aging studies. Thus, the committee often serves as a catalyst for legislative action. The committee also provides authoritative statistical information useful to the Congress, specialists, and the general public. For example, in 1985, it issued *Aging America: Trends and Projections, 1985–86 Edition,* in cooperation with the American Association of Retired Persons, the Federal Council on the Aging, and the Administration on Aging.

The House Select Committee on Aging, established in 1974 after years of effort by individual House members to establish a counterpart to the Senate aging unit, performs similar functions. Following the Senate pattern, the House committee has no legislative jurisdiction and cannot report out bills. Its investigative and other oversight functions are often performed through hearings, in Washington, DC, and in the field, through studies by staff or guest experts, and regular communication with federal agencies and informed individuals throughout the field. It "endeavors to be a one-stop information source not only for members of the House but also for private individuals" (Rich & Baum, 1984). It has persistently paid intensive attention to long-term care issues, including development of readily accessible home care services. In 1985, a series of reports drew attention to the fact that health care costs for older Americans were rising rapidly and had already exceeded the proportion of income for health care paid by the elderly before Medicare was enacted. In 1993 the House of Representatives, in reorganizing its committee structure, disbanded its Special Committee on Aging. Subsequently, its Older American Caucus was also disbanded.

In summary, only the Senate Special Committee on Aging remains as a unit of the Congress focused specifically on issues in an aging society. A description of the Special Committee and its functions is available on the Web at: *www.senate.gov/~aging/juris.htm.*

WILLIAM E. ORIOL

See also

    Health Care Policy for the Elderly, History of Older Americans Act

    Policy Analysis: Issues and Practices

    Social Security

    White House Conferences on Aging

CONNECTIVE TISSUES

With increasing biologic age, animal connective tissues undergo a variety of changes. For example, skin becomes thin, rigid, and less elastic. In blood vessels, the walls thicken and the lumen widens (Hall, 1976). In rats, tendon obtained from the tail loses elasticity and tensile strength (Vogel, 1978). Although biochemical events leading to such changes are not completely understood, studies of age-related changes in collagen and elastic fibers have furnished some clues.

Collagen

Collagen is the major structural protein of the body. It is not a single molecule, but consists of at least 20 types, each present in different tissues in different amounts. The basic collagen molecule is long and narrow, measuring 3,000 Å by 15 Å, with an approximate molecular weight of 285,000 daltons. Each molecule consists of three chains, known as alpha chains, which are held together by hydrogen bonds and wound together like the strands of a rope. Except for short segments at each end of the alpha chain, every third amino acid is glycine. Collagen is synthesized in precursor form called procollagen, which undergoes further modifications that result in formation of stabilizing cross-links between individual chains (Pinnell & Murad, 1983).

Aging collagen undergoes a variety of structural alterations. Collagen fibrils from skin, tendon, cornea, sclera, and meninges thicken with age. Wide-angle x-ray diffraction studies of chorda tendinae and Achilles tendon have shown age-related increase in degree of order within the collagen fibril (Gross, 1961). Changes in various physical properties also occur with aging collagen. For example, old tendon fibers show enhanced thermal shrinkage, being able to contract with greater strength upon being heated (Gross, 1961). Collagen from lung (Kohn, 1959), tendon (Kohn & Rollerson, 1958), and myocardium (Kohn & Rollerson, 1959) show an age-dependent decrease in osmotic swelling. In addition, aging collagen becomes stiffer, less soluble in salt solution, more difficult to extract with acetic acid, and more resistant to proteolytic attack by bacterial collagenase (Balazs, 1977).

The resistance of aging collagen to external influences is believed to be a result of formation of cross-links between collagen molecules. In a hypothesis proposed by Cerami (1985), these cross-links result from interaction between glucose and proteins. In a series of reversible, nonenzymatic reactions, the amino group of a protein interacts with the aldehyde function of glucose, forming a Schiff base that undergoes Amadori rearrangement. The Amadori product then undergoes further irreversible rearrangements to result in cross-linking of the involved proteins. One example of such an advanced glycosylation endproduct is 2-furoyl-4(5)-(2-furanyl)-1H-imidazole, a condensation product of two glucose molecules and two lysine-derived amino groups (Cerami, 1985). Such protein cross-links are believed to confer rigidity and stability to aging collagen.

Formation of cross-links may also explain the fluorescent properties of aging collagen. Collagen obtained from human Achilles tendon shows an age-dependent increase in a substance that fluoresces at 406 nm (Labella & Paul, 1965). This is believed to result from progressive cross-linking of peptide chains (Balazs, 1977).

Elastic Fibers

In contrast to collagen, elastic fibers make up only a small proportion of human skin (0.6% of dry weight). They are abundant in ligamentum nuchae, aorta, lung, Achilles tendon, and cardiovascular system. Electron microscopy has shown that elastic fibers consist of an amorphous component called elastin, which is surrounded by microfibrillar protein. Elastin consists of linear polypeptides with a molecular weight of approximately 72,000 daltons. Its content is high in alanine and valine, but it is devoid of hydroxylysine, tryptophan, histidine, and methionine. As in collagen, glycine accounts for one third of the amino acids but is unevenly distributed along the polypeptide chain. A unique feature is the presence of desmosine, a compound formed by covalent linkage of four lysine residues, which serves to connect individual elastin polypeptides. Microfibrillar proteins are thin fibers that surround elastin. Their contents are high in cysteine, methionine, and histidine, but low in alanine, glycine, and valine (Ryhanen & Uitto, 1983). Microfibrillar component proteins consist of fibrillins, latent TGF-beta binding proteins, fibulins, and other microfibril associated proteins.

Although less is known about aging of elastic tissues than about aging of collagen, a variety of age-related changes are well recognized. In the skin, wrinkling and laxity with advancing age are believed to result from loss of the vertical, subepidermal fine skeins of elastic fibers (Kligman, Grove, & Balin, 1985). In contrast, elastic material located deeper in the dermis shows the opposite change. Here, elastic fibers become thicker, more numerous, and more branched and disarrayed (Kligman, Grove, & Balin, 1985). In sun-damaged skin, there is massive accumulation in the dermis of an amorphous material that takes up elastic stains. Although previously thought to result from degenerating collagen, this substance has been shown by electron microscopic studies to represent degenerating elastic fibers (Lavker, 1979). Although it has been shown that concentration of desmosine in sun-exposed skin is four times that of sun-protected skin, this increase is felt to be insufficient to account for the massive deposition of elastotic material in the dermis (Kornberg, Matsouka, & Uitto, 1985).

The composition of elastic fibers changes with age. During embryologic development, newly developed fibers contain microfibrillar protein almost exclusively. With increasing age, an amorphous component (elastin) appears (Ryhanen & Uitto, 1983). The mature elastic fiber consists mainly of elastin surrounded by microfibrillar protein (Ryhanen & Uitto, 1983). Like collagen, elastin exhibits increasing fluorescence with age. In addition, elastin becomes yellow and increasingly calcified (Balazs, 1977). It is possible that like collagen, elastin also undergoes progressive cross-linking with age (Kohn, 1977).

Ground Substance

Although ground substance makes up less than 0.2% of dermal dry weight, it may be important in determining rheologic properties of the skin. Because of its extraordinary capacity to hold water, hyaluronic acid is thought to be responsible for the normal turgor of the dermis (Kligman, Grove, & Balin, 1985). In addition, the ground substance provides a pathway for diffusion of nutrients through the interstices of the dermis and probably functions as a lubricant by allowing collagen fibers to slide past each other (Kligman, Grove, & Balin, 1985).

Between newborn and infancy, a significant reduction in soluble fraction of dermal glycosaminoglycan (GAG) has been noted. Dermal GAG level remains stable through middle age and drops further during old age (Fleischmajer, Perlish, & Bashey, 1972), probably as a result of decreased synthesis (Fleischmajer, Perlish, & Bashey, 1973). It has also been suggested that age-related changes of collagen may result from the interaction of GAG and collagen (Heikkinen, 1973; Jackson & Bentley, 1968). For further study, see Kefalides, 1998.

Matrix Metalloproteinases

Several enzymes are important in the turnover of connective tissue. These are known as matrix metalloproteinases and consist of the interstitial collagenases, the gelatinases, the stromelysins, matrilysin, metalloelastase, and membrane-type matrix metalloproteinases. These enzymes are involved in the turnover of extracellular matrix macromolecules, including collagen, elastin, glucosaminoglycans, and glycoproteins (Seltzer & Eisen, 1999). They are important for wound healing, morphogenesis, angiogenesis, and photoaging.

ARTHUR K. BALIN

See also
  Collagen

CONSUMER ISSUES: THE MATURE MARKET

Market Definition

The mature market is defined as all products and services purchased by or for consumers over the age of 50. The term "mature market" also may refer to the older adults and others who buy and/or consume such products and services.

There are nearly 76 million Americans over the age of 50—about 27% of all adults in the United States. The 50+ age group has a total annual income of more than $2 trillion. Mature Americans control 70% of the total net worth of all U.S. households—more than $7 trillion of wealth (Dychtwald, 1999).

Spending Habits

Mature market consumers are the most affluent group in the United States, and those aged 50–64 are the most affluent of all. Americans aged 50 and over hold 77% of the nation's financial assets and 50% of all discretionary income. Per capita spending is about 2.5 times that of the population. Mature householders also have more discretionary income per capita. The average amount of discretionary dollars in mature households is $13,285, whereas the average amount of discretionary income for all U.S. households is $12,342 (Dychtwald, 1999; "Mature Americans," 1994).

Mature consumers tend to spend more money than do younger consumers on financial services, health, travel, and entertainment. Mature householders aged 55–64 spend more than average on their homes, household furnishings, women's and girls' apparel, vehicle purchases, and entertainment. They also have over $2,000 left annually after major spending to invest, save, or contribute to charitable organizations.

Those aged 55 and over spend more than average on health insurance, medical services, prescription and over-the-counter drugs, and personal care supplies. Thirty percent of all health care dollars are spent by or on the behalf of older consumers. Health care products and services will become a $75 billion industry by the time the baby boomers retire. Americans aged 50 and over spend more in drugstores than do any other age group. They purchase 37% of all over-the-counter medicines, and those aged 65 and over consume 30% of all prescription drugs (Senior Citizens Marketing Group, 1991).

Older consumers buy 41% of all new domestic cars, 48% of all luxury cars, and 51% of all recreational vehicles, and more of them join auto clubs than do those in any other age group. They spend more per capita in grocery stores than any other age group spends on dining out and cultural events (67%); they buy 40% of all live-theater tickets.

Housing and home furnishing purchases are also strong among older consumers. Condos appeal most to older home buyers. Twenty to thirty percent of new home buyers aged 50 and over buy condos, compared to 15% of new home buyers in younger age groups. Of course, this age group is the largest purchaser of retirement housing. Mature adults purchase 37% of all curtains and draperies, 54% of all color TV sets, and 36% of all new furniture.

The 50+ age group spends more money on travel, recreation, and other leisure activities than any other age group does. Mature consumers spend 30% more on travel than do younger travelers. Eighty percent of all commercial vacation travel, especially first-class air travel and luxury sea cruises, is purchased by mature consumers.

One-third of adults aged 45–64 and 25% over 65 exercise regularly and have been doing so for at least 5 years; 52% regularly engage in sports and exercise. Walking is the favorite sport among those aged 55 and over. Older consumers buy 32% of all walking shoes, 45% of treadmills, and 37% of all spa memberships. Fifty-seven percent of older Americans engage in gardening. This group buys one third of the garden tools purchased annually and represents 75% of National Gardening Association membership.

Sixty-six percent of mature consumers read regularly. Seventy-four percent of 55–64-year-olds and 69% of those 66 and over read a daily newspaper. Over 50% of all book and magazine subscriptions are sold to people over 65. The circulation of *Modern Maturity* is bigger than that of *Time*, *Newsweek*, and *U.S. News and World Report* combined. Seventy-six percent watch television; this age group constitutes about half of all heavy viewers in prime time, early, and fringe viewing. Seventy-seven percent visit friends, spending money on home entertainment.

When purchasing products and service, older consumers shop for convenience, comfort, quality, service, luxury items, and brand-name products. Older consumers know what good service is and are willing to pay for it. A positive purchase and ownership experience is valued.

Mature Market Segmentation

Mature consumers display greater heterogeneity and diversity than does any other age group. Following Neugarten's categories of young-old and old-old, the mature market is often divided into four major segments, based on age and life-cycle events (Lazer, 1985; U.S. Bureau of the Census, 1993b).

The young-old are aged 55–64, generally active and healthy. Consisting of about 32.8 million consumers, these individuals are often preparing for retirement. They are "working to live, not living to work." Also called the "sandwich generation," the young-old are prime targets for products and services related to exercise equipment, health programs, and maintaining a youthful appearance. Consumers in this category are increasingly taking early retirement, changing careers (not all willingly), or working part-time.

The middle-old are 65–74 years old. Most of the 16.2 million consumers in this category are generally retired. They are prime targets for health and nutrition products and services, leisure products and activities (eating out, travel), and condos and retirement housing.

The old-old are 75–84 years old. Consisting of about 10.3 million consumers, this group is increasingly frail and displays greater health limitations with increasing age. Individuals in this category more often fit the "senior citizen" stereotype. Most are still healthy, although health may be increasingly problematic. For this reason, financial security is a major concern among the old-old. The most important asset for consumers in this category is their fully paid home.

The oldest old are 85+. This age group is growing in numbers more rapidly than any other age group. With about 3.2 million members, this group is less independent, less mobile, and more in need of support services to accomplish tasks of daily living; they may require acute and chronic medical and hospital care. These consumers are prime targets for home health care products and services, in-home chore services, and assisted living.

Age per se is a poor segmentation device (Morgan & Levy, 1993). A better way to segment older consumers is through milestone events, use of time and money, and health status. Health segments mature Americans into three basic categories: healthy individuals who improve or maintain physical well-being with a wholly independent lifestyle, those who may need some lifestyle accommodations due to limitations posed by health status, and those with major limitations, requiring significant product and service purchases.

Health is a unique segmentation device because it affects who makes the ultimate purchase decision and the purchase itself. Healthy people generally make their own purchase decisions; less-active individuals may send someone else to the store, leaving the purchase decision to a caregiver or other person. Those with major limitations often do not make their own decisions; the product or service is recommended by a professional, and the caregiver makes the purchase.

Time is another segmentation device, categorizing mature consumers into those who are still working versus those who are retired. Purchases of products and services often depend on the activity of work or leisure. Money and attitudes toward money are still another means of segmenting the mature market. Only 13% of older adults fall below the poverty level; about 25% struggle financially.

Segmentation of the mature market as a means to predict purchase behavior is perhaps more difficult than for younger age groups because of the heterogeneity and range of individual differences among older consumers.

Shopping Attitudes and Behaviors

Older consumers tend to be loyal, willing to spend, and extremely quality-conscious, and they demand a hassle-free shopping experience. Older consumers respond to many of the same purchase influences as do younger consumers. However, the older consumers are significantly more likely than younger consumers to be influenced by quality, an unconditional guarantee, and a respected spokesperson.

Mature adults prefer to shop in stores that offer convenience and comfort, everyday discounts (vs. frequent sales), a rest area in the store, proximity to a variety of other stores, convenient parking, a variety of sizes and styles of apparel suited to their age, knowledgeable salespeople, phone-in ordering, and a policy allowing return of unsatisfactory products. Such shopping environment preferences mirror similar desires among younger consumers for convenient parking, a good return policy, and apparel that is right for them.

The Better Business Bureau reports that the number-one complaint against business is unsatisfactory service—38% of complaints among those aged 61 and over, compared to 25% of all age groups. The primary shopping barrier for mature consumers is customer service, followed by complaints related to shopping in general, dissatisfaction with store amenities, and difficulties in finding merchandise.

Perhaps because of these difficulties in shopping and some physiological changes that make shopping harder, mature consumers tend to shop in department and specialty shops more often than in discount stores. According to Management Horizons in Columbus, Ohio, mature consumers are more likely than those in other age groups to shop in department or specialty stores for apparel, domestics, gifts, appliances, home furnishings, and jewelry. These environments, as opposed to discount stores, tend to afford helpful salespeople who can provide the convenience of one-to-one service.

The Department of Commerce reports that 85% of people over the age of 50 make mail order purchases. Simmons Market Research reports that almost 47% of Americans aged 55–64 purchased by mail in 1993. Although the number of all order catalogs aimed at mature adults has increased, Mediamark Research, Inc., reports that catalog purchases by mail or phone have declined among those 65 and over, from 37% in 1986 to 29% in 1993 ("Direct marketers," 1994). Individuals aged 50 and over are among the highest purchasing group for Internet sales.

RONNI S. STERNS
HARVEY L. STERNS

See also
Economics
Images of Aging in the Media
Poverty

CONTINUING CARE RETIREMENT COMMUNITY

Continuing care is not a new concept. In the 19th century some nonprofit church, fraternal, and community groups took responsibility for their older members regardless of their ability to pay for services. These early residences were called old peoples' homes and life care communities. Many of these older facilities are part of the proliferating continuing-care retirement industry. A growing industry requires a useful working definition. The American Association of Homes and Services for Aging (AAHSA, 1997) provides one: a continuing care retirement community (CCRC) is a blend of several things—housing, activities, and health care. A CCRC provides these services by a centrally located administrative structure. The resident and the CCRC have a written agreement that is intended to last for the resident's lifetime. These contractual agreements are of three major types: extensive (full long-term care [LTC]), modified contracts (housing plus partial long-term insurance), and fee for services, where housing is supplemented by access to LTC services that are paid for as used. Depending on the contract, the entrance fees may be nonrefundable, partially refundable, or fully refundable. These various types of CCRCs and their varying contracts numbered over 2,000 facilities in the United States at the end of the century.

A number of for-profit organizations, including hotel chains, have established residences across the country that include the *continuum of care concept* but operate as rental facilities. The resident pays a monthly rental that includes housing, dining services, housekeeping, transportation, and health and wellness services. Residents have priority access to assisted living apartments and a choice for optional LTC insurance. The insurance is a group policy that pays a daily benefit for up to 2 years.

Overview of Industry

The universe of potential CCRCs—entry-fee, rental, and equity-payment plans—is over 2,000 (estimate supplied by American Association of Homes and Services for the aging). Approximately 500,000 residents live in CCRCs, less than 2% of the over-65 population. The average age of existing CCRCs, located in 36 states, is about 25 years.

Pennsylvania, California, Florida, and Virginia are in the lead. The Philadelphia/Delaware Valley area has been called the CCRC capital of the world, with some 45 communities, partly because of Quaker and other religious leadership and partly because of high public acceptance of the concept. CCRCs differ widely with respect to philosophy, costs, fees, services, methods of financing capital costs, and so on. (For brief profiles of over 500 individual CCRCs, see AAHSA [1997]). A major distinction relates to the extent of LTC insurance coverage for residents needing assisted living or skilled nursing care. Although the extensive contracts are more expensive, they appear to be increasing in number relative to fee-for-service plans.

This distinction is important not only to individual residents but to public policy. Under extensive and, to a lesser extent, modified contracts, the potential cost of institutional LTC is shifted from the individual and the public sector to the CCRC. Underwriting the residents' LTC risk most often protects them against the potential of "spending down" their assets to Medicaid eligibility.

The "Seamless Continuum of Health Care"

For most CCRC residents (average age, 81) the assurance of good health care is the major factor in the decision to move to a CCRC. The term "seamless continuum of care" has received considerable publicity from the American Hospital Association (Jack & Paone, 1994) and other professional organizations. This has long been the central feature of CCRC health care philosophy. Moreover, most communities have in place the physical and organizational structure to permit the philosophy to be realized. Almost all provide emergency care, assisted living/personal care, skilled nursing, physical therapy, and social services. Most also provide ambulatory care, and a growing minority add home care for minor conditions, prescription drugs, and hospice-type terminal care. All these elements are usually tied together by a form of managed care facilitated by one master contract. The resident is assured nearly complete coverage for all essential health care needs and costs because most CCRCs require that Medicare parts A and B be supplemented with some form of Medigap insurance. Even in fee-for-service communities, skilled nursing is usually available on the premises under supervision of the same management.

Thus, in contrast to most other retirement arrangements, the CCRC resident can expect to move from independent living to assisted living to whatever form of health care is needed in the final illness without ever having to leave the community, except for temporary hospitalization for acute illness or severe mental illness. Even hospitalization is usually minimized. Residents of many communities have signed living wills requesting no heroic measures.

Costs and Affordability

Fees vary widely—by size of apartment, type of resident contract, age of community, geographic location, and so on. Entry fees have a very wide range, depending on the size of the apartment and the type of health care coverage.

The average monthly cost also depends on the size of the unit and the extent of health care. The largest component of costs in most CCRCs is health care. Taeuber (1992) compared the 1990 CCRC's fees with the average 1989 income and net worth of Americans, who were 65 and over. He concluded that at least 25% of them could have afforded such housing at that time, although less than 1% were actually in residence. This compares with about 2% actually in residence in 1999. Obviously, there are also nonfinancial considerations. Still, it is clear that the majority of older Americans could not afford a CCRC under present conditions.

This is an issue for general public policy. Policy makers should consider whether the CCRC is a desirable model for helping to solve the LTC dilemma in this country, just as it was decided a quarter century ago that the health maintenance organization (HMO) was a desirable model for general acute care. If the answer is positive, ways could and should be found to make the CCRC more widely available. There are several options, such as encouraging or even subsidizing lower-income Americans by partial prepayment of fees through some form of LTC insurance.

Financial Risks

Responsibility for the broad array of CCRC benefits, especially the lifetime guarantee of skilled nursing care if needed, is clearly a weighty one.

Moreover, there is evidence that CCRC residents live significantly longer than other Americans. At Pennswood Village, for example, the average age at death in 1993 was 88.3 years (Spears, 1994). In the past, some communities with more goodwill than actuarial and managerial skill were unable to meet these responsibilities and failed.

In recent years, however, the bankruptcy rate has declined to almost zero—less than 0.5% a year according to one study (Conover & Sloan, 1995/96). This rate may be compared to that of HMOs, reported to vary from 0.3% to 0.1% and is comparable to that for health insurance in general.

This improvement may be attributed to a combination of factors: increasing sophistication on the part of the investment community, better educated and more sophisticated residents (Kytle, 1994), improved actuarial techniques, improved management, the work of the Continuing Care Accreditation Commission, and broader state regulation. Thirty-seven states now regulate the financial aspects of CCRCs; all regulate their health care facilities.

Regulation, however, can be a two-edged sword. The strict financial and other requirements that have contributed to financial stability and consumer protection have also limited investment. The high capital costs and other difficulties associated with starting a new CCRC are limiting the availability of CCRCs in some parts of the country.

Longitudinal Research

A valuable, comprehensive longitudinal study (Sherwood, Ruchlin, Sherwood, & Morris, 1997) provides comparative information about 19 CRCCs, including 5 from the three states with the largest number of CRCCs: California, Florida, and Pennsylvania. Nine CCRCs had extensive contracts, and 10 provided less financial protection against the high cost of LTC. The latter have been designated as limited CCRCs. Interviews were conducted at two points in time. Selected comparative data were also utilized, derived from a Massachusetts study of persons living in the community.

This study of 19 CCRCs was similar to other studies, for it found that CCRCs tend to serve White, well-educated, middle- to upper-middle-class people, the majority of whom are women who are at least 75 years old. One interesting trend reported by the investigators is that more individuals who move into a CCRC with an extended contract had lived previously in an age-dense adult community. The mean age at entrance was 78 years.

Why do elderly persons choose a CCRC living arrangement? The reasons for moving to a CCRC are in agreement with the services that are offered. Access to needed services was the most important reason given by recent entrants and by longer-stay residents. The largest difference between residents who had extensive contracts and those who had limited contracts was noted by those who said the inclusion of nursing home care in the fees was important in the desire to move in a CCRC. About 90% of those with extended contracts offered this opinion, compared to about one third of the residents with limited contracts. Residents in both the extended- and limited-contract CCRCs reported similar use of the amenities and activities and similar perceptions of the living arrangement.

The CCRC residents were compared with their peers in the community. Even though the CCRC residents had as many limiting health conditions as did the community peers, they tended to perceive themselves as being in better health than did the older persons in the traditional community. The researchers attribute this higher perception of perceived health status as due to the fact that the CCRC organization and facilities result in higher levels of interaction with friends and neighbors and participation in the leisure activities provided.

Sherwood and her colleagues (Sherwood, Ruchlin, Sherwood, & Morris, 1997) provide a comprehensive comparative analysis that warrants study by readers interested in many aspects of CCRCs. Policy questions are addressed: concerns about community-based supports, adequate housing for all older Americans, integrating acute and long-term health care services, and the high cost of medical services. The researchers conclude that CCRCs do address the service needs and the quality-of-life issues of residents. But they stress that the residents must be able to afford an entry fee (often substantial) and the monthly fees, which are higher than most older Americans could pay.

What Is the Future for the CCRC?

The number of CCRCs continues to increase to meet the needs of an affluent segment of the aging population. Entry fees are central to the industry; and although for-profit corporations have entered the field, the overwhelming percentage of CCRCs are nonprofit and are likely to remain dominant for the foreseeable future. The for-profit organizations are offering similar services without the requirement of an entry fee. However, it should be noted that the for-profits do not generally *guarantee* access to nursing home care, and they are not committed to allowing residents who are experiencing economic hardship to remain. An important caveat must be noted, namely, that currently organized CCRCs are viable options mainly for the wealthier segments of America's older population and not for vulnerable, low-income seniors.

CCRCs, like other forms of LTC, face a constellation of problems—demographic, economic, political, legal, and ethical, plus the special challenge of administering the complex life-care contracts, especially the health care component.

It is possible, however, that the CCRC is an idea whose time has come. The industry has been involved in an expansion that could continue. The impressive growth over the past 25 years suggests considerable momentum that could continue to reach a growing number of the elderly. The eligible population who may choose CCRCs as the way to meet the final phase of life is increasing. Unless there is a huge economic reversal, there will be a sufficient number of the elderly who will have the net worth, the income, and the buying power to afford living in a CCRC. The mobility and geographic distance that separates older and younger family members will probably not change in the near term. Therefore, CCRCs or similar retirement facilities will supply needed services. An unknown factor in some localities and regions is a labor supply—workers who are necessary to provide the quality of care and services required by CCRCs that emphasize quality of care as a marketing feature. Whether the CCRC industry continues to expand, however, depends not just on projections of elderly income and buying power but on public and private leadership in forging the essential national consensus with respect to LTC financing. It also depends on the industry's ability to function within such a consensus, having effective boards of directors and developing the necessary managerial skills, especially in the health care area. In any case, the experience of the residents of CCRCs, which emphasizes sheltered housing, resident independence, managed health care, and insured LTC, will be a positive yardstick for older Americans.

GORDON F. STREIB

See also
Assisted Living: A New Model of Supportive Housing with Long-Term Care Services

CONTINUITY THEORY

Continuity theory originated from the observation that, despite widespread changes in health, functioning, and social circumstances, a large proportion of older adults show considerable consistency over time in their patterns of thinking, activity profiles, and social relationships. But the long-term consistency that became the foundation of continuity theory was not the homeostatic stability predicted by activity theory. Instead, continuity was conceived of more flexibly, as strong probabilistic relationships between past, present, and anticipated patterns of thought, behavior, and social arrangements. Since the late 1960s the concept of continuity has gone through several stages: empirical description (Maddox, 1968), concept development (Atchley, 1971), theory building (Atchley, 1989), and empirical testing (Atchley, 1999).

Because *continuity* can mean either an absence of change or evolution linked to the individual's past, its use in gerontology has been ambiguous. In some studies, continuity has been equated with absolute stability or lack of change, and in others it has been defined as gradual development and relatedness over time. Perhaps a better word for the evolutionary, developmental concept of continuity would be *consistency*, which does not imply an absence of change, but it is doubtful that the field will switch labels at this point.

In its most elaborated form, continuity theory is a social-psychological theory of continuous adult development (Atchley, 1989, 1999). It uses feedback systems theory imagery to create a view of adults as dynamic, self-aware entities who use patterns of thought created over their lifetimes to describe, analyze, evaluate, decide, act, pursue goals, and interpret input and feedback. Although social processes such as socialization and social control have input to the person's internal system, the conscious being who interprets the input also creates the resulting personal constructs, including personal constructions of the life course, life events, life stages, age norms, and age grading.

Continuity theory makes a number of theoretical assumptions: Individuals invest themselves in the internal and external frameworks of their lives, and these relatively robust frameworks allow individuals to accommodate a considerable amount of evolutionary change without experiencing crisis. Change is assessed in relation to themes of continuity. People are motivated to use continuity of past patterns as their first choice in pursuing goals and adapting to change because the personal systems they have spent their lifetimes developing seem to offer the highest probability for successfully constructing their future. To the extent that a continuity strategy for making plans and coping with change is reinforced by experience, continuity becomes an increasingly strong first choice. Choice of a continuity strategy may be conscious, but it may also be an unconscious path of least resistance.

Elements of Continuity Theory

Continuity theory involves four major constructs: internal structure, external structure, goal setting, and maintaining adaptive capacity. The following sections define these constructs and elaborate their operation in the context of continuity theory.

Internal Structure. The ideas, mental skills, and information stored in the mind are organized into loose structures such as self-concept, personal goals, worldview, philosophy of life, moral framework, attitudes, values, beliefs, knowledge, skills, temperament, preferences, and coping strategies. Note that each of these constructs is a general label under which a large number of specific thoughts and feelings could be subsumed. These general structures represent different dimensions that, when combined, form a unique whole that distinguishes one person from another. In making life choices and in adapting to change, people are motivated to maintain the inner structures that represent a lifetime of selective investment. Ongoing consistency of psychological structures is viewed by individuals as an important prerequisite for psychological security.

External Structure.   Social roles, activities, relationships, living environments, and geographic locations are also organized in a person's mind. As a result of priority setting and selective investment throughout adulthood, by middle age most adults have unique and well-mapped external life structures or lifestyles that differentiate each person from others. Most people attempt to set priorities and make selective investments that will produce the greatest possible satisfaction for them, given their constraints. As a result, they see their evolving life structure as an important source of social security.

Also, continuity of activities and environments concentrates people's energies in familiar domains, where practice can often prevent or minimize the social, psychological, and physical losses that cultural concepts of aging might lead us to expect. Continuity of relationships preserves the network of social support that is important for creating and maintaining solid concepts of self and lifestyle.

Goal Setting.   Continuity theory assumes that adults have goals for developmental direction: ideals about themselves, their activities, their relationships, and their environments toward which they want to evolve. Specific developmental goals, even whether people have such goals, are influenced by both socialization and location in the social structure—family ties, gender, social class, organizational environment, and so forth, but these goals can also be profoundly affected by life experience. Adults use life experiences to make decisions about selective investments: which aspects of themselves to focus their attention on, which activities to engage in, which careers to pursue, which groups to join, what community to be part of, and so on.

Maintaining Adaptive Capacity.   As they continue to evolve, adults also have increasingly clear ideas about what gives them satisfaction in life, and they fashion and refine an external life structure that complements their internal structures and delivers the maximum life satisfaction possible given their circumstances. The ideas aging adults have about adaptation to life are results of a lifetime of learning, adapting, personal evolution, and selective investment, all in interaction or negotiation

with their external social and physical environments. It should not be surprising, then, that in adapting to change, including changes in life stage, adults are motivated to continue to use the internal and external patterns they have spent so much time and energy developing.

Continuity Theory, Positive Outcomes, and Determinism

Continuity theory does not assume that the results of continuity are necessarily positive. The evidence indicates that even those with low self-esteem, abusive relationships, and poor social adaptation resist the idea of abandoning their internal and external frameworks. Apparently, firm ground to stand on, even if it predicts a miserable future, is for some people preferable to an unknown future. Similarly, positive feedback loops may produce positive change, but negative feedback loops can produce disorder.

Continuity theory is not deterministic. It does not predict the content of psychological or social development at any given life stage, during any specific life course transition, or in any particular period of history. Instead, it points to the common social psychological structures and processes that underlie the setting and seeking of goals as well as response to change. It provides a conceptual way of organizing the search for coherence in life stories and of understanding the dynamics that produce basic story lines, but continuity theory has no ideology concerning which stories are "right" or "successful." Through its diagnostic concepts, continuity theory can help us understand why particular people have developed in the way they have. However, similar *types* of social-psychological structures and processes are presumed to be at work even though they produce widely varying individual results. The heart of continuity theory is the presumption that people are motivated to continue to use the adaptive resources they have developed throughout adulthood to diagnose situations, chart future courses, and adapt to change.

Studying Continuity and Change

How can continuity theory be tested? First, continuity is most likely to occur in generalized social-psychological constructs such as the hierarchy of personal goals, general activity preferences, or networks of social relationships rather than in perceptions and memories of very specific ideas, behaviors, or relationships. This conception deals effectively with the apparent paradox that continuity and change usually coexist within individual lives. Continuity is seen by individuals in terms of general themes running through their lives (Fiske & Chiriboga, 1990; Kaufman, 1986), even though there may be substantial changes in the specifics surrounding those themes.

How much relatedness is needed over time in order to qualify as continuity? By tracing measured individual patterns in attitudes, behavior, and relationships over multiple points in time, researchers usually can easily distinguish consistency from sudden change or from chaos. Such objective measures are useful for determining the prevalence of continuity. Here it is important to emphasize substantively meaningful similarities and differences over time rather than simply statistically significant differences, which are often quite small in practical terms.

Ultimately, how much change can occur without triggering perceptions of discontinuity is a judgment that can be made only by the individual experiencing change. Researchers often use definitions of continuity that require more stability than do the definitions used by the research participants. As a result, the findings tend to underestimate the prevalence of perceived continuity.

The difference between objective and subjective assessments of continuity has important implications for research. When it occurs, objective continuity in ideas, behavior, or relationships can be assumed to result from choices on the individual's part. However, it is also important to study subjective continuity, the individual's perceptions of the relative amount of continuity and change over time. Subjective continuity also includes the extent to which individuals express a preference for continuity as a strategy for planning, making decisions, or adapting to change.

Research results generally suggest that subjective continuity is indeed both a goal and an outcome for most aging individuals and that objective continuity of ideas, behavior, and relationships is the most prevalent outcome among aging individuals over time. In a 20-year longitudinal study of adults who were age 70 or older at the conclusion, Atchley (1999) found that two-thirds or more of study participants showed objective continuity in psychological factors such as self-confidence or personal goals and in social factors such as frequency of interaction with family or friends.

Continuity theory seeks to explain why most adults show considerable consistency in their patterns of thought, behavior, and relationship as they move through the later stages of life, often even in the face of substantial external changes such as widowhood or physical disability. Humans create and constantly revise and refine robust patterns of thought and action that become their front-line strategies for planning, making life decisions, and adapting to life changes. By preferring these strategies, adults produce consistencies over time that can provide a sense of security, ease life transitions, and cushion the effects of sudden life changes.

The essence of continuity theory is very straightforward and intuitively appealing. However, to test and refine the theory requires moving from its abstract form toward operational forms that can guide the research process. Continuity theory is currently in this stage of development (Atchley, 1999).

ROBERT C. ATCHLEY

See also
  Activity Theory
  Developmental Psychology
  Disengagement
  Life Course

CONTINUUM OF CARE

A continuum of care refers to the full range of services that might be needed in a community to meet the needs of older citizens. Typically, a continuum of care includes the following: social, nutritional, and recreational services, such as are often associated with senior centers; information and referral services; adult day care; home care (including home health care, personal assistant services, and homemaker service); respite services; family caregiver programs, such as support groups and respite care; home-delivered meals; telephone reassurance services; emergency call systems; home modification and equipment programs; various residential settings, such as adult foster care, group homes, and assisted living; nursing homes; rehabilitation services; hospices; and hospitals. The term is sometimes used to suggest that communities should have many services available for older people with functional impairments. Communities that rely extensively on nursing homes, for example, could be said to lack a full continuum of care.

The concept of a continuum implies a progression. Experts differ, however, in the extent to which they believe that each long-term care service should have a definable target population of users for whom it is deemed appropriate. Those who advocate a continuum in the sense of a progression might, for example, believe that some potential long-term care consumers are appropriately served by home care, that others need a "higher" level of care in a board and care home, whereas still others need a nursing home. According to this view, it is feasible to assess residents of nursing homes to determine whether they are appropriately "placed."

Another view holds that services on the continuum are interchangeable, amenable to being mixed and matched into individualized care plans based on consumer preference and other circumstances (Kane, 1993; Kane, Kane, & Ladd, 1998). In this view, communities should still strive for a wide array of services to enhance the flexibility possible for the consumer. However, professionals are discouraged from trying to determine the correct and appropriate service level for any given individual based on his or her needs and capabilities. Long-term care is viewed as too linked to personal preferences, everyday lifestyles, and idiosyncratic issues to be prescribed solely on the basis of measurable impairment levels.

Some services in a continuum of care are also places where older people reside—for example, nursing homes, assisted living settings, board and care homes, adult foster homes. Current best practice attempts to minimize the requirement that older people physically relocate their residences as their abilities decrease or improve—first, because abilities do fluctuate, such movement is impractical; and second, relocation is disruptive to people's lives. Indeed, some states are scrutinizing the way they regulate various residential settings and are considering dispensing with rules that link licensure of settings to the allowable disability levels of clien-

tele. For instance, they are examining rules that require programs to discharge clients who are bedbound or incontinent or who need nursing assistance for more than a fixed number of days.

Despite these caveats, the continuum idea is a useful planning tool. It can sometimes be tied to efforts to plan the supply of long-term care services through certificate-of-need and licensing programs.

ROSALIE A. KANE

See also

    Assisted Living: A New Model of Supportive Housing with Long-Term Care Services

    Case Management

    Case Mix in Long-Term Care

    Comprehensive Assessment

    Continuing Care Retirement Community

    Home and Community-Based Care

    Long-Term Care Assessment

    Multidimensional Functional Assessment

COPING

Coping refers to those things people do to avoid being harmed by stressful experiences (Pearlin & Schooler, 1978). These coping strategies can include cognitions or behaviors that aim to resolve the problem, as well as to control the impact, either in the way the problem is defined or the emotional response to the *stressor*.

Most of the studies of the relationship between age and coping have been cross-sectional and therefore represent *age differences*, not necessarily developmental changes. Age differences have been found not only in the number of strategies employed but also in the types of strategies used, with older people reporting the use of fewer strategies in general compared to younger people. Among the strategies reported, older people use fewer instrumental, problem-solving, and confrontive strategies to deal with their problems and employ more acceptance, emotion-focused strategies, and positive reappraisal (Aldwin, Sutton, Chiara, & Spiro, 1996; Diehl, Coyle, & Labouvie-Vief, 1996; Folkman, Lazarus, Pimley, & Novacek, 1987).

The assumption that some coping strategies (problem solving) are inherently more efficacious, whereas others (emotion-focused) are more patho-logical could lead one to infer that the coping strategies used by the elderly are inferior. However, research looking at the outcome of coping attempts suggests that the strategies used by the elderly are at least as effective, if not more effective, than those used by younger people (Aldwin, Sutton, Chiara, & Spiro, 1996; Diehl, Coyle, & Labouvie-Vief, 1996).

The point to be emphasized is that those mechanisms that may be effective in solving problems faced by younger people may not work on the less alterable problems faced by older people. Some of the problems with which older people cope tend to be less changeable and therefore less responsive to problem-focused coping. For instance, chronic health problems and "irreversible losses" (Pearlin & Mullan, 1992), such as loss of a lifelong companion or adult child, may not be candidates for active problem solving. Further, when we control for the type of stressor, many age differences disappear (Aldwin, Sutton, Chiara, & Spiro, 1996).

Therefore, it is as important to identify the kinds of problems that confront people of different ages as to identify the ways they cope. One of the most important questions we can ask is "coping with what?" (Kling, Seltzer, & Ryff, 1997). Some of the things that we assume to be stressful or that are found to be stressful to younger people may not have the same meaning in the lives of older people. Murrell, Norris, and Grote (1988) remind us that not all change is stressful for older adults. Put within the perspective of what is normative at that time of life, the older person may respond to our questions on stress with a surprising lack of concern (Aldwin, Sutton, Chiara, & Spiro, 1996). Experience in coping with stressors throughout the life span can affect both the way stressors are appraised and the coping strategies chosen (Aldwin & Brustrom, 1997). Processes such as positive comparisons (compared to other people my age, compared to other problems I have faced in my life) and redefinition of the situation (this experience has presented an opportunity for growth) may affect how experiences are defined.

We need to know more about the kinds of "stressors" that are actually perceived as stressful by the elderly. Older persons may appraise stressors based on their knowledge of those situations that can be changed as well as those that can't and by matching their coping efforts accordingly. Losses or intracta-ble chronic stressors may be compensated for by changing goals, by manipulating the environment, or by developing "management skills" (Aldwin, Sutton, Chiara, & Spiro, 1996) to anticipate or prevent future stressors. Thus, older persons may have developed a mature repertoire of coping responses as well as a sense of their own coping efficacy (Zautra, Hoffman, & Reich, 1997) that can serve as a resource in times of threat.

A more productive perspective on coping in the elderly needs to encompass a life-span view of coping experience, better description of the conditions that older people define as stressful and the meaning of those stressors, consideration of the matching of coping strategy to stressor, and thoughtful consideration of the resources that older people possess, such as self-concept, religiosity, goals and values, and experience. Further, we must recognize the heterogeneity within the older population and avoid attributing coping strategies to age when they may be better explained by such factors as gender, education, income, or ethnicity (Aldwin, Sutton, Chiara, & Spiro, 1996). Finally, we must ask whether the constructs and models of coping and the measures that are used with younger persons are appropriate for understanding how the elderly cope with the problems they face.

MARILYN MCKEAN SKAFF

See also
Adaptation
Social Stress and Life Events

CORESIDENCE

The majority of older adults in the United States who live outside institutionalized settings live with other people, mostly family members. Despite steady increases over the past century in the number of older persons who live alone (Ruggles, 1987), the 1990 census documented that 7 in 10 elders (65+) coreside with another person (U.S. Bureau of the Census, 1992). Moreover, in contrast to popular images of isolated older people living apart from their families, most elders reside in family households (67.8% of all elders or 96.8% of older adults who are not living alone, according to the 1990 census). The household configurations of older adults, however, vary significantly by the age, gender, race, and place of residence of the elder. Nevertheless, most elders who live with someone else and are residing outside group quarters (i.e., do not live in a nursing home, a board-and-care home, or some other type of institution), typically reside in either a two-person, married-couple-only household or in a multigenerational household. Only a very small number of elders live exclusively with nonkin.

Two-Person, Married-Couple-Only Households

The modal living arrangement of all elders is a two-person, married-couple-only household (Coward, Cutler, & Schmidt, 1989). Nearly half (44.4%) of all elders live in this type of situation; indeed, more than half of older men (61.5%) coreside exclusively with their wives, whereas about one-third (32.4%) of older women live exclusively with their husbands. The frequency of this living arrangement declines monotonically with age. Younger elders, aged 65–69, are four times as likely to live with just their spouses than are their counterparts who are age 90 and older (52.6% vs. 13.0%).

There are also racial differences in the frequency of this household type (Coward, Lee, Netzer, Cutler, & Danigelis, 1995). Whites are nearly twice as likely as Blacks (46.6% vs. 24.6%) to live with just their spouses. But whereas most Whites who live with spouses live only with that person (84.8%), this is less likely to be the case among Blacks. More than half (62.2%) of blacks who live with spouses live in two-person, married-couple-only households, and the remainder coreside with both their spouses and other family members (25.5% with spouses in a two-generational household and 8.0% with spouses in a three-or-more-generation household). Finally, the prevalence of two-person, married-couple-only households varies by place of residence. Such living arrangements are more prevalent in rural than in urban places.

Multigenerational Coresidence

Nearly 1 in 5 elders (19.8%) who live outside group quarters resides in a household comprising more

than one generation (Coward & Cutler, 1991). Three-fourths of these elders (75.3%) live in a household where there are only two generations present. In most multigenerational households—84.5% of two-generation households and 96.1% of three-or-more-generation households—the elder represents the oldest generation present. Nearly half (41.6%) of all elders living in multigenerational households have spouses present, although these percentages decline with age. For example, the highest proportion of elders with spouses in the same household are young elders (65–74 years) living in two-generation households (61.6%), whereas the smallest percentage is found among the oldest-old (85+ years) who are living in three-or-more-generation homes (6.2%).

Although rare, there are elders who live with an older parent or parent-in-law in a multigenerational household (they represent, at most, about 6% of elders living in multigenerational households, or approximately 1% of all elders living in noninstitutionalized settings). Mothers (54.3%) and mothers-in-law (28.6%) are the parents who are most likely to be found living with an older adult (Coward & Cutler, 1991). There are large differences in the prevalence of such coresidence, depending on the age of the elder (Coward, Cutler, & Schmidt, 1989). Among younger elders (65–74 years) almost 1 in 10 (9.7%) of those in two-generation households live with an older family member. In contrast, among the oldest-old (85+) only 1 in 100 elders in two-generation households lives with an older family member.

Previous investigators have indicated that living in a multigenerational household varies little by gender or place of residence (Coward, Cutler, & Schmidt, 1989). Older women are only slightly more likely than older men to be living in a multigenerational context (20.8% vs. 18.4%). Although there is more variation by place of residence (from a high of 21.6% among rural farm elders to a low of 15.5% among elders living in places that are not located within the boundaries of an urbanized area but that have a population of more than 2,500 residents), the fluctuations are still rather modest.

In contrast, substantially more variation has been observed by age (Coward, Cutler, & Schmidt, 1989; Coward & Cutler, 1991) and race (Coward, Lee, Netzer, Cutler, & Danigelis, 1995). With respect to the age of the elder, there appears to be a U-shaped association with multigenerational coresidence; that is, more elders report living in multigenerational households at younger ages and at older ages (with the low point of occurrence among older adults aged 70–74 years). Specifically, Coward, Culter, and Schmidt (1989) reported the following percentages of elders living in multigenerational households at different ages: (1) 65–69 years of age: 19.9%; (2) 70–74: 16.6%; (3) 75–79: 17.5%; (4) 80–84: 22.2%; (5) 85–89: 30.0%; and (6) 90+ years of age: 46.6%. Indeed, among the oldest-old (90+) living in a two-generation household is the most prevalent arrangement, characterizing more than 1 in 3 (37.1%) of all elders this age, or more than double the proportion of elders living in such circumstances between the ages of 65 and 69 years.

In a similar manner, Coward, Lee, Netzer, Cutler, and Danigelis (1995) have reported that Blacks are nearly twice as likely to be living in multigenerational households as Whites (34.2% vs. 17.9%). Indeed, these racial differences persist among both two-generation (23.6% vs. 13.8%) and three-or-more-generation households (10.6% vs. 4.1%). Moreover, the racial differences are constant across both males (31.9% Blacks vs. 16.5% Whites) and females (35.8% Blacks vs. 18.9% Whites), and across all age groups—although the gap between the races decreases as age increases to the point that among persons 85 years of age and older the race difference is substantially reduced (to a discrepancy of just 4 percentage points).

The presence of adult children is the most prevalent relationship found in multigenerational households that include an elder, even greater than the availability of spouses. The dominance of close blood relations in these coresidence patterns is evident. Specifically, whereas nearly 9 in 10 elders in a multigenerational household live with a son or a daughter (88.5%), only about 1 in 4 (23.4%) live with a child-in-law.

Given the prominence of daughters in the caregiving networks of older adults, it may surprise some to learn that elders are about equally likely to live with a son (44.2%) as a daughter (44.3%) (Coward & Cutler, 1991). However, there are dramatic coresidence differences when sons and daughters are compared by the type of multigenerational households in which they reside. Whereas more elders in two-generation households live with a son than with a daughter (45.5% vs. 39.3%), in three-or-more-generation households, more elders live with a daughter than with a son (59.6% vs. 40.1%).

Grandchildren also represent an important element in multigenerational living. Approximately 1 in 3 elders (30.7%) who reside in a multigenerational context lives with a grandchild (or about 6% of all elders not living in group quarters) (Coward & Cutler, 1991). This circumstance is nearly universal in three-or-more-generation households (96.3%), whereas it is rarer to find a two-generation household comprising an elder and his or her grandchild (8.9% of two-generation households are of this type). Among two-generation households, the percentage living with a grandchild declines as the age of the elder increases, whereas the presence of grandchildren remains high and relatively stable across age groups in three-or-more-generation households.

Coresiding with Nonkin

Among older adults who do not live in group quarters, only a very small percentage of elders live exclusively with nonkin (less than 3% of all noninstitutionalized elders). Indeed, this is the least prevalent coresident living arrangement of older adults. There is very little variation by age and gender in this type of living arrangement (although the oldest-old are slightly more likely to be found in such circumstances). The largest variation in this household type occurs between elders of different races and between elders living in different residential contexts. Specifically, older Blacks are nearly three times as likely as Whites to reside exclusively with nonkin (5.2% vs. 1.9%). Similarly, central-city residents are more than twice as likely as rural farm elders to live in nonkin-only households (3.0% vs. 1.2%).

Prominence of the Family in Coresidence

Research on the living arrangements of older adults reinforces the importance and preeminence of family ties in the lives of older adults. Although about one third of elders either live alone or with nonkin only, the remaining two thirds reside in some form of family household configuration. The two most prevalent family configurations are the two-person, married-couple-only household and the multigenerational household (with two-generation households being more common than three-or-more-generation households).

Thus, the family remains the principal social context in which most elders live, and research documents the variety, breadth, and richness of the intrahousehold family contacts that exist for elders in the United States. Indeed, older adults can be found living with spouses, parents, siblings, adult children, aunts, uncles, nieces, nephews, grandchildren, and in-laws of all types. Yet the overwhelming majority of elders live with just two types of family members—spouses and adult children. Regardless of the overall configuration of their living arrangements, slightly more than half of older adults (53.3%) coreside with a spouse, whereas about one quarter (22.1%) live with an adult child. The next largest group of family members who coreside with elders is grandchildren, who are present in the homes of less than 1 in 10 elders (7.8%). Thus, although the potential for living with a variety of family members exists (and indeed is the reality for some older adults), there is a high probability that an elder who is coresiding with another person outside an institutionalized setting will be living with spouse and/or with one of the adult children.

RAYMOND T. COWARD
JULIE K. NETZER

See also
   Family
   Housing
   Marriage

CORNELL STUDY OF OCCUPATIONAL RETIREMENT

The Cornell Study of Occupational Retirement, conducted from 1952 to 1962, was the first large-scale longitudinal research to measure the effects of retirement (Streib, 1966). It had previously been postulated that loss of the work role had deleterious effects on the individual, causing mental and physical decline, feelings of uselessness, and so on. In the Cornell research, retirement as both an event

and a process was studied from the perspective of sociology and social psychology. The broad analysis involved determination of the effects of retirement on the individual's health, objective economic condition, and attitude toward income (which was termed subjective economic condition), as well as the person's social-psychological attitudes, particularly with regard to satisfaction in life, adjustment to retirement, feelings of usefulness, and age identity.

Design and Methodology

The longitudinal study design enabled the investigators to study "cause and effect" with somewhat more confidence than in a traditional cross-sectional study at one point in time, in which older persons usually are asked to recollect attitudes, feelings, and behavior that may have occurred some time in the past.

The Cornell study design specified that the same individuals be contacted at age 64 before the standard retirement age and four times subsequently in the next 6 years. A group of participants who remained in the workforce throughout the study served as a control group. This permitted a description of change and process that is essential for an understanding of the dynamics of retirement. Such a comparison is almost impossible in studies that are cross-sectional in design. In this respect, the Cornell Study of Occupational Retirement differs from most of the early studies completed in the field of social gerontology.

Starting with the assumption that arbitrary retirement at a fixed age is characteristic of an urban, industrialized society, the investigators concentrated their attention on employees of urban, industrial, and business organizations and also of government agencies. They included a wide geographical coverage of the United States and limited the study to organizations that employed a substantial number of older workers to make the time and cost of a visit as productive as possible.

The organizations were selected from the census classification of the major businesses and industries. Cooperation of a number of state and civil service systems was obtained, and the cooperation of the trade unions was secured in organizations that were unionized. In one or two large firms, this involved contacting as many as 25 unions. The original participants were employed by 259 organizations.

The first follow-up was made 1 year to 18 months after the initial contact. At that time many participants had retired. The initial contact and subsequent follow-ups were made by mail, with the exception of approximately 100 respondents who were interviewed personally in their homes, most of them after the fourth mail contact.

The original research population of the Cornell Study of Occupational Retirement consisted of a group of 3,793 men and women. Needless to say, as the study continued, persons dropped out of the research project.

The items in the questionnaires can be classified according to content: work, retirement, health, economic factors, general items pertaining to adjustment, specific attitudes and adjustment toward retirement, age identification, leisure activities, stereotypes regarding aging, and demographic characteristics. The analysis focused on the following topics because of their importance: health, general satisfaction with life, age identification, feelings of usefulness, income, economic deprivation, and the retirement situation (particularly as it compared with the former work situation).

Findings

There were two age foci for retirement: age 65 and age 70. The data indicate that both men and women of higher income levels, higher education attainments, and higher levels of the occupational structure tended to work longer than their counterparts with lower socioeconomic status. Women living with a spouse were more likely to retire earlier than those who were widowed, divorced, or separated.

The results showed that there was a moderate decline in subjectively defined health as the respondents aged from 65 to 70. However, this decline in reported health does not seem to be the result of retirement per se since those respondents who continued to work reported about the same degree of decline in the self-assessment of their health as did those who retired. The "myth" that retirement causes a decline in health was not supported.

The respondents in this longitudinal study reported a sharp drop in actual dollar income—an approximately 50% reduction from preretirement levels. However, examination of the data on subjective income, or the way older persons evaluate their incomes, showed that feelings of income inadequacy declined after the first year of retirement. Even after a severe cut in income, approximately two-thirds of the respondents reported that their income was "enough." In fact, approximately one-fourth of the retirees said their standard of living in retirement was better than it had been in earlier periods of their lives.

The social-psychological aspect of retirement—namely, whether persons are "willing" or "reluctant" to retire—indicated, as one might expect, that those persons who were favorably disposed toward retirement were much more likely to retire than those who were psychologically reluctant to do so.

The data suggest that change in psychological health (as measured by a three-item Guttman scale) could not be attributed directly to retirement itself. Although there was a very slight decline reported, retirement did not cause a sudden deterioration in psychological health as had been asserted by other writers. The data tend to support the proposition that one's prior attitude is more important than the mode of retirement (administrative or voluntary) in determining whether a person is "satisfied" with retirement or with life in general.

The researchers concluded that loss of the work role did not result in feelings of uselessness. Before retirement there was a tendency for respondents to exaggerate the possible adverse effects expected. However, the follow-up interviews showed that these negative results generally did not occur, as most people adapted without undue stress. The researchers, in discussing the relation of disengagement theory to retirement, offered the concept of "differential disengagement," which means that disengagement occurs at different rates and in different amounts for the various roles in a person's role set. Cessation of work activity does not signal disengagement in other spheres in one's life involving family, friends, and recreational activities.

An analysis was made to compare those persons who continued to participate to those who dropped out. The data showed that, in general, native-born persons were more likely than the foreign-born to continue to participate in a longitudinal study, and women were more likely than men to do so. Moreover, there seemed to be a slight cumulative relationship in that native-born women were the most likely to continue to participate, and foreign-born men were least likely. Persons of higher socioeconomic status tended to participate. Furthermore, both male and female participants who had more education and higher incomes were more apt to identify with the middle class rather than the working class. Union members were more likely to be dropouts.

This longitudinal study was the first to show with convincing evidence that retirement is not deleterious for the overwhelming majority of workers. This finding has been confirmed by many subsequent studies (Palmore, Burchett, Fillenbaum, George, & Wallman, 1985; Streib, 1984; Streib & Schneider, 1971).

GORDON F. STREIB

See also
Longitudinal Research
Retirement

CORONARY-PRONE BEHAVIOR

The idea that behavior and emotions might contribute to the development of coronary heart disease (CHD) is not a new one, dating back at least to the ancient Egyptians. Yet it has been only in the last 30 years that scientific support for that notion began to emerge. In the mid-1950s, two San Francisco cardiologists, Meyer Friedman and Ray Rosenman, began to observe consistent behavioral characteristics of many of their heart disease patients. These characteristics included excessive time consciousness and competitiveness, hostility, an overwhelming desire for career recognition and advancement, and a rapid pace of speech. Friedman and Rosenman labeled this cluster of behavioral characteristics the Type A or coronary-prone behavior pattern.

Importance of Type A Behavior

To determine whether such behavioral characteristics were, in fact, contributing to the development of heart disease in their patients, Rosenman and Friedman began what is now considered a classic research project, the Western Collaborative Group Study (WCGS) (Rosenman, Brand, Jenkins, Friedman, Strauss, & Wurm, 1975). The project involved the participation of roughly 3,000 healthy middle-aged men from several northern California corporations, who were interviewed and characterized as either Type A or, if they did not exhibit Type A characteristics, Type B. These men were followed for 8.5 years to determine who would develop CHD based on their Type A or Type B classification. Rosenman and Friedman discovered that individuals classified as Type A had twice the prevalence of heart attacks, sudden death, and angina compared with Type B men. The significant differences in rates of CHD between Type A and Type B men remained even after statistical removal of the effects of the traditional risk factors, such as smoking, high blood pressure, and cholesterol. The findings by Rosenman and Friedman in the WCGS have subsequently been replicated in several European countries, and with women subjects as well as men (Belgium-French Pooling Project, 1984; Orth-Gomer & Undén, 1990).

A further testimony to the importance of Type A behavior in the coronary disease process is found in studies involving coronary angiography. Coronary angiography consists of an elaborate series of heart radiographs taken to determine the degree of coronary blockage, technically known as atherosclerosis. Researchers at several institutions including Duke University Medical Center, Boston University School of Medicine, and Columbia College of Physicians and Surgeons, have found that Type A individuals exhibit significantly more blockage of their coronary arteries than do Type B persons. These findings, coupled with the findings of the epidemiological studies, suggested that Type A behavior was not only associated with CHD outcome, such as a heart attack or sudden death, but was associated as well with the underlying pathogenic process of atherosclerosis.

It should be noted that although several studies have, indeed, documented an association between Type A behavior, CHD, and atherosclerosis, several recent studies have failed to find that association. These negative findings have generated considerable controversy in scientific circles as to whether Type A behavior is indeed a risk factor for CHD. At this time, the emerging picture is that some but not all of the characteristics of Type A behavior identified by Rosenman and Friedman are related to the development of heart disease. The situation regarding Type A research today is much like that of cholesterol research several years ago. It was once thought that all types of cholesterol were bad. However, it has since been discovered that although some types of cholesterol are health damaging, other types may even be protective against heart disease. Similarly, researchers have begun to identify those aspects of the Type A behavior pattern that are truly toxic, as opposed to those that are benign. Of the three general aspects of the Type A pattern—speed-impatience, ambition-competitiveness, and hostility-anger—it appears that hostility-anger is the component most likely to be toxic. Those Type A individuals who are relatively high on hostility and anger are much more likely to suffer coronary heart disease, and have more occluded arteries than Type A individuals who are relatively low on hostility-anger. Thus, scientific research on Type A behavior today is experiencing a transition, from an emphasis on the global characteristics of Type A behavior to a focus on the hostility-anger dimension. (See "Hostility," and Rosenman [1991].)

Origin of Type A Behavior

When is Type A behavior first observed and how does it develop? Karen Matthews, a psychologist at the University of Pittsburgh, has been a leading researcher in attempts to answer these questions. Dr. Matthews and other researchers have documented the occurrence of many of the features of the Type A behavior pattern in children enrolled in kindergarten. Many of these children exhibited Type A characteristics of competitiveness, impatience, a high need for achievement, and aggressiveness. Research concerning the origin of these characteristics in children has focused on child-rearing practices of the parents. In summarizing this research, Matthews (1978) concludes that high parental standards of performance may play a role in the etiology of the Type A behavior pattern in children, particularly the achievement-striving component. Children classified as Type A are more likely to have parents who exhibit high expectations and aspirations, provide frequent approval and disapproval concerning their children's performance, have a competitive and involved attitude, and use

authoritarian discipline techniques. The origin of Type A behavior is a relatively new research area, and there remain many unanswered questions concerning the relative contributions of genetic compared with environmental factors in the development of the behavior pattern. Current interest in the correlates and consequences of Type A behavior now range far beyond coronary illness per se to include, for example, gender (Kopper, 1993); retirement (Swan, Dame, & Carmelli, 1991); and ethnicity (Sprafka, Folson, Burke, & Hahn, 1990).

Modification of Type A Behavior

Given that Type A behavior is a risk factor for CHD, many clinicians and researchers have been interested in determining whether the behavior pattern can be changed, and if so, will the changes result in reduced risk for CHD? In general, the most effective approaches for modifying Type A behavior have involved some form of brief behavior therapy as opposed to long-term intensive psychotherapy. Specific approaches have involved progressive muscle relaxation, which provides individuals with specific procedures for reducing muscle tension, or cognitive therapy, which involves teaching individuals to identify and change irrational thought patterns that might increase stress in Type A behavior. Although several studies have demonstrated the effectiveness of these approaches in reducing Type A behavior in healthy individuals as well as cardiac patients, only one large-scale longitudinal study has investigated the efficacy of those techniques in reducing heart disease risk. Meyer Friedman and colleagues treated a group of post–heart-attack patients with either traditional risk-factor-oriented cardiological counseling, a cognitive behavioral treatment program, or not counseling controls. Each group was composed of a high percentage of Type A individuals. Strikingly, the results indicated that the rates of reinfarction (second heart attack), cardiovascular death, and nonfatal heart attacks were lower among the patients who received the cognitive behavioral counseling compared with those who received cardiological counseling alone or the untreated controls. Therefore, based on intervention studies, there is strong indication that behavioral techniques can be used to reduce Type A behavior. There is also some preliminary indication that reducing Type A behavior may in fact reduce risk for heart disease. Further research is clearly needed to identify the specific aspects of the behavior pattern that should be modified in order to effectively reduce risk (Shapiro, Friedman, & Piaget, 1991).

Type A Behavior and Aging

How is age related to the phenomena of Type A behavior and CHD? Although there are few data available to answer this questions definitively, the information we do have suggests that Type A behavior is predictive of CHD during the middle years and becomes less important during the latter years. That is, Type A behavior appears to be predictive of the early onset of CHD, and becomes a less potent risk factor as one ages.

Information is now accumulating, however, concerning changes in Type A behavior as one ages. The basic issue is whether Type A behaviors increase, decrease, or remain stable across the life span. Research suggests that Type A behavior is less prevalent in the elderly as opposed to young and middle-aged groups (Strube, Berry, Goza, & Fennimore, 1985). Of course, such a finding could be interpreted as suggesting that (a) Type A behavior declines with age, or (b) the number of Type A persons in the population has declined because of their increased mortality. Regardless of whether Type A behavior actually changes as one grows older, there is some indication that perceptions of changes in Type A behavior differ across varied age groups. A recent study conducted by researchers at Duke University Medical Center found that although subjects between 30 and 39 years of age perceive themselves as becoming more Type A as they have grown older, subjects older than 60 years of age perceive themselves as becoming less Type A (Blumenthal & Herman, 1985).

To sum up, the coronary-prone or Type A behavior pattern is now considered a significant risk factor for the development of CHD. Research is pointing toward the hostility dimension of Type A behavior as potentially the most toxic dimension of the behavior pattern. The behavior pattern appears to be one that is developed during childhood and may be related to parental child-rearing practices. Behavioral treatment techniques have proved effective in reducing Type A behavior, and there is some preliminary indication that a reduction in Type A behavior may reduce risk for coronary disease, at least in those with a history of heart attack. Information on Type A behavior related to aging has only recently begun to accumulate. At present it appears that Type A behavior is a risk factor for heart disease during the middle years and becomes less toxic in the elderly. There is also some indication that individuals older than the age of 60 years perceive themselves as becoming less Type A as they age. For a review of new perspectives in research on Type A behavior see Thoreson and Powell (1992).

NORMAN B. ANDERSON

See also
Cardiovascular System: Overview
Hostility
Personality

COUNSELING PSYCHOLOGY

Counseling psychology is a branch of professional psychology alongside the other traditional specialties of clinical, school, and industrial/organizational psychology. In the 1940s, after a period in which applied and clinical psychology had a psychodiagnostic and assessment role, counseling psychology now emphasized "the field of counseling as a legitimate applied specialty within the new APA organization" (Darley, 1964) and became a division of the American Psychological Association (APA) in 1946. Counseling psychology has roots in both vocational guidance, with its related psychological and aptitude testing, and in the counseling and psychotherapeutic techniques and research influenced by Carl Roger's (1942) work.

Counseling psychologists work in a variety of settings, including schools, hospitals, social welfare and rehabilitation agencies, and universities, as well as in government, business, industry, and independent practices. They are characterized less by type of problem or population served than by a characteristic philosophy or mind-set that influences their work (Duffy, 1990). Whereas clinical psychology had developed within a medical/illness context focused on psychopathology, counseling psychology concerns itself with the healthy adaptive capacities of both normal and abnormal persons (Gustad, 1953). In common with community and child clinical psychology, counseling psychology espouses a developmental view of psychopathology in which problems are viewed, paradoxically, as frequently serving an adaptive and functional role for the person and even as coping strategies. This view of dysfunction is paralleled by a preference for the use of the term *client* instead of "patient" in the professional practice of counseling and psychotherapy.

A View of Counseling Older Adults

Although counseling as a procedure is not exclusive to counseling psychology, counseling adults in late-life transitions is especially pertinent to its developmental, adaptive focus (Fassinger & Schlossberg, 1992). And even when those transitions in life are traumatic and assume the proportions of crisis, this developmental, adaptive, and normative view of counseling can greatly facilitate crisis resolution (Duffy & Iscoe, 1990). Certainly, aging necessitates coping with change throughout its various stages. This is especially true in those late-life transitions, for example, to long-term nursing home care and in coping with chronic medical problems that significantly challenge mental health (Gibson & Brown, 1992).

Current cohorts of older adults, however, frequently do not readily recognize the internal domain of psychological and emotional well-being and, when distressed, frequently seek out a physician rather than a counselor or psychologist. This frequently results in the medicalization of emotional problems and the loss of opportunity to relieve psychological pain and to teach anticipatory coping strategies. It can also lead to misdiagnosis and subsequent misapplication of psychopharmalogical treatments. Optimally, psychologists and counselors will work collaboratively with physicians in the care of older adults.

Although most techniques developed in counseling psychology apply well to working with older adults, there are critical adaptations to be made by the therapist or counselor (Duffy, 1992). It is important for the therapist to be aware of transferential attitudes toward older adults, which, depending on personal life experience, may tend to infantilize either themselves or their older clients. In fact, clients, despite their age, need the therapist to remain in an adult (vs. childlike or parental) mind-set and to act with both caring and authority. This allows the counseling relationship to remain a powerful force in treatment.

Another important feature in successful counseling with older adults is a disposition to be hopeful about the possibility of change in late life. Although circumscribed by the reality of chronic health problems and the relative consistency of personality over time, the effective therapist knows that change will be unlikely if there is a subtle but pervasive disbelief in the possibility of change in older adults.

Problems Amenable to Late-Life Counseling

Transitions and losses are usually dramatic in late life, so it is not surprising that some older adults will become symptomatic. Indeed, given the acute stresses of losing a spouse or entering a nursing home, for example, it is remarkable that older adults are not more troubled. This is probable testimony to the adaptive resilience acquired over a lifetime. There are several problem areas that are typical in working with older adults.

Anxiety and agitation, or "nerves," are common in late-life stress. Loss of control over daily events, bodily functions, finances, and mobility can engender a pervasive "dis-ease," which can increase just when it seems like should be getting better.

This anxiety can be closely related to a concomitant depression. Very frequently, depression in older adults mimics anxiety, a situation that often leads to misdiagnosis and the application of anti-anxiety medication instead of an antidepressants. When depression is identified, it is frequently useful to explore the experience of loss in the older person's life. This may be as obvious as the loss of a person (a spouse) or as hidden as the many implicit freedoms that are lost in entering a nursing home.

As we reach life's end stage we may become conscious of unfinished business and relationships that are painfully unresolved. Counseling within intergenerational family relationships is immensely effective here, helping both parents and the adult child to "say the unsaid" and find a way to ask for unmet emotional needs.

A final area of great importance for counseling is to assist in the psychological and emotional sequelae of physical and neurological disorders. Coping with the psychological effects of stroke, for example, creates terrible emotional loss for both spouses, often exacerbated by misunderstanding of the nature and extent of physical loss. In a related area, even health professionals assume the absence of emotional and affective needs in older adults with dementia. Counseling family members (and professional staff) can help them recognize that the loss of logic, language, and memory is not loss of the need for love and emotion. Counseling with Alzheimer's disease victims using flexible nonverbal, subverbal and expressive techniques can bring great comfort, help slow cognitive decline, and avoid the onset of depression, which all too frequently accompanies cognitive decline.

MICHAEL DUFFY

See also

Group Psychotherapy
Psychotherapy

CREATIVITY

In investigating the relationship between creativity and aging, most researchers adopt one of two available strategies (Adams-Price, 1998). First, some investigators assume that creativity represents a cognitive skill that can be recorded by a suitable psychometric instrument. Under this assumption, the main task is to show how scores on these tests change over the life span. Second, other researchers focus on creativity as an overt behavior that results in the production of concrete works. From this viewpoint, the aim of research is to show how the output of creative products, whether paintings, poems, compositions, patents, books, or journal articles, changes as a function of a creator's age.

Divergent Thinking Across the Life Span

A large number of psychometric instruments exist that purport to assess creativity. However, most investigators have relied on those creativity tests that evaluate a person's capacity for "divergent thinking." Measures of divergent thinking examine whether a person can produce a large number of alternative and novel responses to test stimuli. There actually exist several such instruments, each concentrating on a particular process (fluency, flexibility, originality, etc.) or medium (verbal vs. visual). Whatever the details, studies using these divergent-thinking tests have often found that creativity tends to exhibit a roughly inverted-U function of age, with a consistent tendency for performance to decline in the latter half of life (Levy & Langer, 1999).

Nevertheless, we cannot infer from these psychometric findings that creativity necessarily declines after an individual reaches middle age. First, many of these studies rely exclusively on cross-sectional data, an approach that confounds age and cohort effects. Thus, we must take special care to estimate the magnitude of the aging effects from genuinely longitudinal data. Second, the form of the age curve depends greatly on the specific tests used. Indeed, divergent-thinking measures represent only one possible psychometric assessment of creativity, and consequently rather different longitudinal trends can obtain when alternative measures are used. For example, tests that evaluate problem-solving skills in more everyday situations can actually produce scores that increase with age (Simonton, 1990). Third, many experts in the area of creativity research seriously question the validity of all so-called creativity tests. Validation studies usually show that such tests display rather modest correlations with direct measures of creative behavior. This suggests that a more optimal strategy might be to use behavioral indicators in the first place.

Creative Productivity as a Function of Age

The scientific study of the relation between age and creative productivity began over 150 years ago, and thus represents one of the oldest topics in life-span developmental psychology (Simonton, 1988). The classic investigations are those conducted by Harvey C. Lehman, especially as summarized in his 1953 book *Age and Achievement*. Although Lehman's work suffered from many methodological deficiencies, research employing more sophisticated techniques has verified the central conclusion:

The output of creative products tends to first increase with age, until a peak is reached, after which productivity declines. In fact, the point of maximum output corresponds fairly closely to the age peak at which scores on divergent-thinking tests tend to be highest.

Nonetheless, this same research also suggests that the prospects for creativity in the later years is not so dismal as might first appear. There are seven relevant findings:

1. The specific shape of the age curve, including the location of the peak and the magnitude of the post-peak drop, varies according to the domain of creative activities (Simonton, 1997). In some disciplines the peak will appear much later in life, and the decline will be very gradual, even imperceptible.

2. The predicted level of creative productivity rarely drops to zero (Simonton, 1997). In most domains of creative activity, individuals in their 70s will be more productive than the same individuals were in their 20s, and they will be producing ideas at a rate only 50% below what they accomplished during their career peaks.

3. Individual differences in creative productivity are so substantial that this cross-sectional variation explains more variance than do the longitudinal fluctuations (Simonton, 1997). Hence, highly prolific contributors in their 70s and 80s can still display more creative productivity than much less prolific contributors who are active at their career peaks.

4. Changes in creative output across the life span are not strictly a function of chronological age but rather of career age (Simonton, 1997). This means that "late bloomers" who launch their careers much later in life will not reach their career optima until much later in life as well.

5. A large proportion of the decline in output in the last half of life is by no means inevitable; much of it can be attributed to extraneous factors (Simonton, 1990). In contrast, certain environments can operate to sustain creativity well into old age. In the sciences, for example, those individuals who are embedded in a rich disciplinary network of colleagues and students tend to display much longer creative careers.

6. If one calculates the "quality ratio" of successful works to total works produced in consecu-

tive age periods, that ratio stays more or less constant across the life span (Simonton, 1997). Thus, the success rate does not decline with age. Creative elders may be generating fewer masterpieces in their last years, but they are also producing fewer neglected pieces besides.

7. Creative output across the life span undergoes qualitative changes that can compensate for quantitative declines. For example, mature creators will more often concentrate on more ambitious works, such as epics, operas, novels, and monographs. More important, creators entering their last years often dramatically alter the approach they take to their creative activities (Lindauer, 1999). In the visual arts this sudden shift has been called the "old-age style"; in music this change has been called the "swan-song phenomenon." The result is frequently a masterwork that serves as a capstone for a creative career.

In combination, these seven considerations indicate that research using psychometric measures may underestimate the creativity of older individuals. The decline may be neither drastic nor inexorable.

DEAN KEITH SIMONTON

See also
Abilities
Cognitive Processes

CRIME (AGAINST AND BY THE ELDERLY)

Crimes Against the Elderly

Victimization Rates. Attention in the media to crimes committed against older persons may leave the impression that the aged are a major target of violent crime in the United States. However, annual (1973–1994) data from the National Crime Victimization Surveys consistently indicated that the violent crime victimization rate (i.e., homicide, rape, robbery, aggravated assault, simple assault) for persons aged 65 years and older was the lowest of any age group (Bureau of Justice Statistics, 1997). The most recent data available, for 1998, showed that this statistic holds true both for violent crimes in general and for personal theft (Bureau of Justice Statistics, 1999). Detailed data from 1995 that examine differences in criminal victimization rates for 18 types of personal crimes showed that no age group had lower rates than persons aged 65 and older (Bureau of Justice Statistics, 1998). Furthermore, the violent crime rate for older persons generally decreased from 1973 to 1994 (Bureau of Justice Statistics, 1997).

Consequences of Victimization.   Although elderly persons are clearly less likely to be victimized by personal crimes, there is evidence that the outcomes may be more serious for them. Data from the 1992, 1993, and 1994 National Crime Victimization Surveys analyzed by Bachman, Dillaway, and Lachs (1998) showed that injuries and the need for medical care resulting from victimization may be more prevalent among older persons than among younger persons. Specifically, for both robbery and assault victimization, women aged 65 and older were more likely to be injured and to require medical care as a result of their injury than those younger than age 65. For men, the pattern differed somewhat: older men were less likely than younger men to be injured when victimized but were more likely to require medical care when injured. Consistent with this evidence, an earlier, detailed analysis of the consequences of victimization indicated that absolute financial losses incurred by older persons were no greater than those incurred by other adults, but relative losses (percentage of monthly income) were the same or higher (Cook, Skogan, Cook, & Antunes, 1978). Although older persons were less likely to be victims, those attacked were more apt to receive internal injuries, lose consciousness, and suffer cuts and bruises. In addition, the costs of medical care associated with injuries constituted a larger proportion of their income.

Fear of Crime

Actual victimization is only one of the ways that crime can touch the lives of older persons. In the 1994 American Association of Retired Persons (AARP) Images of Aging study, 37% of persons aged 65 and older reported that fear of crime was a "serious" problem for them personally (AARP, 1995). Of 13 problem areas about which respondents were asked, fear of crime was by far the most frequently cited concern for persons aged 65 and older, who were two and a half times more likely to identify it as a serious personal problem than to name its nearest successor—poor health (37% vs. 15%). Data from the 1998 National Opinion Research Center's General Social Survey showed that 52% of older Americans lived near an area where they would be afraid to walk alone at night (Davis & Smith, 1999). Data collected in 1992 for the AARP's Annual Survey of Mid-Life and Older Americans showed that 19% of respondents aged 45 years and older reported being very fearful of crime and that approximately a quarter of the respondents had rearranged their activities because of fear (AARP, 1993).

Whether fear of crime is more prevalent among older persons has been the subject of some debate. Although many studies have noted a positive relationship between age and fear of criminal victimization, analyses using a multiple-indicators approach to measure fear of crime and risk of criminal victimization have not found such a relationship (Ferraro & LaGrange, 1992). It also has been alleged that fear confines the elderly to their homes, but most research has failed to support this assumption. One large study of public housing tenants (Lawton & Yaffe, 1980), for example, concluded that there was no evidence to indicate that "elderly tenants respond to victimization, high crime risk, or even fear of crime, by becoming housebound" (p. 778).

Crimes by the Elderly

Few published studies on criminal acts committed by the elderly exist, perhaps because criminal behavior is relatively infrequent in this age group. Though they accounted for 12.7% of the population of the United States in 1997, persons aged 60 and older made up considerably less than 1% of persons arrested, a smaller percentage than any other age group and about a third of the rate for persons aged 12 years and younger (U.S. Department of Justice, 1998). This low rate prevailed for specific types of crimes as well; for no category of crime did the percentage of older persons arrested approximate their distribution in the population. Older persons made up less than 1% of those arrested in 21 of 27 categories of offenses and accounted for as high as 3% of those arrested in only one category (driving under the influence). It is important to note that the vast majority of crimes—over 80%—for which older persons are arrested are minor offenses (i.e., crimes that are not included in the FBI's Crime Index) (U.S. Department of Justice, 1998). When arrested, older offenders (especially males) tend to receive more lenient sentences than their younger counterparts (Steffensmeier & Motivans, 2000).

STEPHEN J. CUTLER

See also
Elder Abuse and Neglect

CRITICAL THEORY AND CRITICAL GERONTOLOGY

The term "critical gerontology" has served to denote a wide range of ideas that seek to challenge or oppose prevailing theories, methods, and orientation of contemporary gerontology. This oppositional stance embodies a feeling that something is wrong with dominant approaches in the study of aging. However, the label "critical gerontology" can mean several distinct things:

• An application of perspectives drawn from the humanities (philosophy, history, literature) in opposition to prevailing scientific approaches to aging (Moody, 1988);
• A version of cultural studies applied to human aging (Laborsky & Sankar, 1993), an outlook increasingly visible in fields such as anthropology, literary theory, ethnic studies, and women's studies;
• A critique of the positivist paradigm (Tornstam, 1992) and, more broadly, a critique of objectivity in favor of interpretation or social construction (Baars, 1991) closely allied with phenomenology and hermeneutics;
• A broader movement of insurgent voices impatient with all forms of hegemony (Cole, Achenbaum, Jakobi, & Kastenbaum, 1993). In this respect, critical gerontology shows an affinity with the left-wing political economy perspective that

has its own body of literature in gerontology (Minkler & Estes, 1991).

Background of Critical Theory

Critical theory in the proper sense refers to a group of thinkers originally associated with the Frankfurt School, above all figures such as T. Adorno, M. Horkheimer, and H. Marcuse, who were inspired by some aspects of Marxism to develop a far-reaching intellectual critique of contemporary society. They took issue with the idea of a "value-free" science or technology and instead sought to expose the dominant ideology behind all forms of cultural organization. More recently, the German philosopher Jürgen Habermas has continued the tradition of critical theory (Turner, 1991). While rejecting any clear demarcation between facts and values, Habermas (1984) favors an approach based on the patterns of communication and social interaction. Habermas calls attention to a variety of human interests, ranging from the instrumental logic of the sciences to the "emancipatory interest" in freedom and equality.

As applied to gerontology, Habermas's (1984) version of critical theory is provocative because he is eager for philosophy and social criticism to incorporate findings from and also influence empirical social science. At the same time, he emphasizes that human beings remain free subjects capable of critical thinking and political action. This openness to both science and human values is congenial to the historical spirit of gerontology, which has elements of both science and advocacy. However, Habermas's writings are abstract and programmatic, containing relatively few examples of how critical theory would actually redirect policy, research, or clinical practice in the field of aging.

Critical Theory and Current Issues in Gerontology

Critical theory has much to offer in stimulating research, education, and social criticism in an aging society. A few topics suggest the possible heuristic impact of critical gerontology in years to come.

Theory and Practice.   Today there is a growing sense of the gap between theory and practice, between social norms and actual behavior at both the policy level and for clinical practice. In the field of geriatric health care, for example, critical theory can help elucidate the reasons for this failure (Moody, 1992). Bridging the gap between theory and practice has far-reaching applications for more realistic education for service providers in health and social welfare systems.

Gerontology and Ideology Critique.   Critical theory can be understood as a form of ideology critique applied to knowledge and professional practice in aging. Ideology critique demands that gerontologists recognize covert interests that shape intellectual traditions and that have influenced the rise of gerontology as a field (Atchley, 1994). Self-reflectiveness and self-criticism are indispensable if gerontology is to contribute to the well-being of older people in the future.

Methodology and Philosophy of Science. Critical gerontology responds to ongoing methodological problems in the scientific study of aging; for example, consider the causes and meaning of retirement, one of the widespread features of later life (Atchley, 1993). Instead of simply measuring labor force participation or examining measures of subjective well-being, a critical perspective would ask deeper questions about the phenomenon of retirement and the social purposes it serves as an institution.

Qualitative Methods in Research.   The ongoing dialogue between Habermas and Gadamer about hermeneutics finds its echo in the recent call for qualitative methods and interpretive social science applied to aging studies (Thomas, 1989). By recovering the human voice, the lived experience of old age, qualitative gerontology can help chart an emancipatory perspective on what it means to grow old.

At bottom, critical gerontology urges us to question and reject what might be called the social engineering approach to gerontology whereby "the elderly" appear as clients, that is, essentially as objects susceptible to instrumental control through social policy or professional practice. Instead, critical gerontology invites us to appreciate the last stage of life as an opportunity for freedom and then to reshape our institutional practices in pursuit of this ideal.

HARRY R. MOODY

See also
Moral Economy Theory

CROSS-CULTURAL RESEARCH

Cross-cultural research designs are among the most powerful available to researchers. By using the comparative method it is possible to increase the range of variation and allow for a full evaluation of theoretical models and potential universality. Intracultural research investigates the variance within a defined context, such as a nation, region, city or other unit. Depending on the problem under study, selected characteristics of individuals and their differing situational circumstances are the study variables. The cultural context is presumed to be a near constant. Cross-cultural research investigates variance across defined contexts, such as cultures, nations, or ethnic and minority groups; the cultural context becomes an important part of the variation.

Cross-cultural research is expensive, especially if it involves a research design calling for the collection of primary data and a staff to collect that data. Thus, the reason for undertaking cross-cultural research must be more than curiosity. Comparative research calls for the examination of an issue in markedly different cultural contexts. The rationale is twofold. First, the effort is to examine the effects of cultural context on the phenomena under investigation. Second, by disentangling the effects of cultural context, it is possible to discover if some aspects of the research question are universal to humans. If we find effects from context, then our investigations turn to an examination of what it is about that cultural context that shapes the relationships among variables. With a comparative design, we also have the potential to determine if the intracultural variation is a spurious product of the culture itself. Cross-cultural research not only increases the generalizability of our findings but also clarifies the relationships between our variables.

Aging is an area in need of cross-cultural research. Aging is a process that is universal to humankind. At the same time, aging is a process that is experienced and interpreted only in diverse cultural contexts of the world. In the past five decades we have revealed much about the aging process in one cultural type, the industrialized nations. We know precious little about the rest of the world and have yet to evaluate our accumulated knowledge by using the comparative perspective.

Cross-Cultural Research Strategies

Research projects using a comparative design have used one of two major strategies. The first is collecting primary data with a particular problem in mind. The second involves employing a reexamination of existing data and analysis of this secondary data.

Primary Research.   Projects calling for the collection of new data from multiple research sites are differentiated by the units selected. This includes projects characterized as follows:

1. *Cross-ethnic:* The research design calls for administration of parallel instruments or data collection techniques within different ethnic groups in order to examine the effects of ethnic identification or membership on the study variables.
2. *Cross-national:* These comparative research designs call for parallel data collection techniques and collaboration between teams of researchers in different nations. The nation-state is the unit selected, and national probability samples are used within that unit to examine the differences and similarities across-nations and the cultural and structural differences involved.
3. *Cross-cultural:* A cross-cultural project takes as its unit a culture that provides us with the most heterogeneous of comparative research designs. This may range from a team of investigators systematically investigating the same question in diverse cultures (Keith, Fry, Glascock, Ikels, Dickerson-Putnam, Harpending, et al., 1994) to several investigators in a geographic region (Counts & Counts, 1985) to a single investigator sequentially examining the same question in different cultures (Guttman, 1987).

Secondary Data.   Some projects call for the reanalysis or secondary analysis of existing data. Differentiating these projects are the research strategies involved. This can range from a reanalysis of primary data collected by experienced fieldworkers to the secondary analysis of a worldwide sample of ethnographic accounts of specific cultures, the Human Relations Area Files (HRAF).

Reexamination of Fieldnotes.   Cowgill and Holmes (1972) used this strategy in their study of aging and modernization. They invited a team of experienced investigators to reexamine data they had collected for other purposes for its relevance to problems of aging and the treatment of the aged. Later, Cowgill (1986) expanded this earlier study with more secondary data from a wide variety of sources.

Analysis of Existing Reports.   Existing case studies and data are selected on either a regional basis or by using some other criterion, such as societal type or topical variables (Foner, 1984).

Holocultural Analysis.   This is a distinctive kind of cross-cultural research based on the HRAF. Holocultural research involves a statistical evaluation of the relationship between two or more variables in a world sample of human societies derived from the HRAF. Simmons's (1945) pioneering work on the aged in primitive society was among the first to use this research design. Glascock's (1997) study of treatment of older people and death-hastening behavior is a more recent example of this research design.

The Comparative Method

For cross-cultural research, two issues are of primary concern for the use and abuse of the comparative method. These are (1) comparability in measurement and (2) sampling and the generalizability of the units selected.

Comparability of Measurement.   All science, from physics to psychology, must come to grips with the issue of comparability of measurement, because all science is based on comparison. The crux of the matter rests in the operational definitions we employ. Are these measuring what we think they are? Is one incident of measurement comparable to another? These issues seem to be more complicated in the social and cultural sciences because the phenomena we are studying are a product of culture and hence are human artifacts subject to interpretation. Thus, our measurement is a human construct measuring another human construction. Also, culture is self-generated as it is learned, leaving communication to be transacted through equivalency structures that may not be equivalent. As we increase differences in language and culture by embarking on cross-cultural research, the difficulties in comparability become more apparent. They are inherent, however, in all research designs. For the cross-cultural researcher, it is imperative that data collection strategies be sensitive to semantic differences across cultures as well as to culturally specific abilities and response patterns. If possible, multiple strategies of measurement are desirable to increase comparability.

Sampling Across Cultures.   With the world as our universe and the 3,000-plus world cultures from which to sample, the issues of site selection should be straightforward. Two issues, however, must be considered. The first is the practical issue that cross-cultural projects are expensive, especially those involving primary data collection. Consequently, a large number of sites is prohibitive. Compromises include (1) restricting the range of variation by selecting a number of sites within a societal type (i.e., cross-national studies of industrialized nations or restricting site selection to a geographic region) and (2) maximizing the variation by using a theoretical rationale to guide the selection of cultures.

Second, if we need a large sample of world cultures, we face the problem that a culture is not an isolated, bounded unit but one that is in continual interaction with other such units. This is known as Galton's problem. To what extent are our results a product of diffusion across cultures? This is a problem that plagues researchers using a research design based on previously collected data and published accounts such as the HRAF. In resolving sample design problems, a standard probability sample has been selected for cross-cultural theory testing that considers both degree of historical relationship and completeness of ethnographic reports.

Questions Asked

Gerontological research was stimulated by an emergent crisis within industrialized nations, which, by the middle of the 20th century, were showing signs of a majority of people living longer and at the same time having fewer children. Old age was increasingly seen as a problematic state for individuals and their societies. Comparative research on aging began with the work of Leo Simmons (1945), who used the HRAF to investigate the status of older people in over 100 nonindustrial societies. Since the early beginning, researchers have used cross-cultural research to investigate successful aging, health, economic security, aging and families, the meaning of age and the life course, and the impacts of societal transformations.

Successful Aging.   Initial speculation that older adults were much better off in smaller, less technological societies, where they do not retire, has not received much empirical support. Each culture has both strengths and weaknesses. In smaller-scale cultures older people continue to work with kin and often increase in importance because of accumulated knowledge or control of resources. On the other hand, the lack of amenities, such as indoor plumbing and medical technology, can make daily living more demanding and illness far more problematic. By comparison, elders in industrialized contexts take for granted the labor-saving devices made possible by electricity, along with medical technology. However, they must have enough accumulated wealth with which to purchase these goods and services on the market. What makes for a good old age? Good and bad are culturally defined, and hence we see much variation. One issue is quite clear: a way to have a bad old age is to have poor health and limited functionality (Fry, Keith, Glascock, Ikels, Dickerson-Putnam, Harpending, et al., 1997).

Health and Functionality.   Human bodies begin to experience difficulties around the 60s—some earlier and some later, but physical problems increase with age. Yet the body is subject to cultural interpretation. For instance, the age-related changes associated with menopause are universal for older women, but the specific symptoms are not (Lock, 1993). Questions of what one must be able to do to function as an adult (activities of daily living) are defined by specific context. What may be problematic in one place, such as lifting water from a well, will not be problematic where there is indoor plumbing. Even difficulties in the ability to see may not hinder people where literacy is not a feature and recreation does not involve watching television or the computer screen.

Economic Security and Political Economies. Wealth is another factor that promotes successful aging. Where material accumulation is possible, this seems to hold true. However, there are economies where wealth is impossible to accumulate, such as foraging societies or those that base their livelihood on herding animals. Here work must be continuous; with physical decline, survival becomes increasingly problematic for an older person. The economic basis for social life is quite variable. One point of variation for industrial societies is a political economy of aging, which, in spite of inequities, has worked to the benefit of older people in these nations through pensions and social security plans.

Aging and Families. With the advent of industry and rising prosperity, the family has been seen as a declining institution. The landmark work of Shanas and her colleagues (Shanas, Townsend, Wedderburn, Friis, Milhoj, & Stehouwer, 1968) decidedly demonstrated that, regardless of change, families were still involved with and supporting their older members. With an expanded comparative view we know that families are universal but highly variable in size, definition of genealogical connections, and in political and economic involvement in people's lives. In spite of diversity, aging takes place in a domestic context among kin who rarely abandon their relatives just because they are old and experiencing disabilities.

Age and the Life Course. Aging is a temporal phenomenon, and age is the time of human lives. On a comparative basis, time is probably experienced much the same, but it certainly is not measured in the same way and does not figure in people's lives in identical fashions (Kertzer & Schaie, 1989). For people in smaller-scale societies, age is reckoned relatively. One is older than or younger than someone else. This is calculated through the temporal aspects of kinship, generations, and birth orders. Only in state-level societies and especially industri-

alized nations do we find age measured absolutely through chronology. Here certificates document birth dates, and age is measured in terms of years lapsed and compared to a timeline starting with a fixed point, the year 1. Age is important the world around, but in industrialized contexts it takes on heightened importance. Age defines thresholds of privilege (e.g., drinking, driving, marriage, voting, and the entitlements to Social Security and Medicare). Here the life course is seen as punctuated by age thresholds and is divisible into stages reflecting responsibilities and involvement. Otherwise, adulthood is seen as a long period of work that is gradually marked by physical decline.

Societal Transformations. One of the best-developed generalizations using cross-cultural analysis is the aging and modernization theory developed by Cowgill and Holmes (1972; Cowgill, 1986). This theory predicts that, as a nation becomes modernized, older people lose status because of health and economic technology, urbanization, and education. Although explicitly formulated, this theory has not received much empirical substantiation. Modernization has largely been abandoned in favor of globalization, which is affecting life all over the world in ways we are just beginning to understand. Comparative research is greatly needed to comprehend what aging in the present has become around the world in all of its diversity.

Comparative research has enriched the development of theory in gerontology. One of the most important benefits of comparative research is that it places our understandings and interpretation of experience in a much broader perspective and range of variation. We can look at what we consider everyday through comparative research to see the ordinary as alien. Our ideas are sharpened and possibly redefined. Of the most recent resources on comparative research in gerontology, the reader is referred to Albert, Cattell, and Cattell's (1994) volume, which synthesizes the comparative, and to a reader by Sokolovsky (1997) that presents original comparative work.

CHRISTINE L. FRY

See also
International Perspectives
Minority Populations: Recruitment and Retention in Aging Research
Modernization Theory

CYTOGERONTOLOGY

See

Cell Aging Relationship Between In Vitro and
In Vivo Models

Telomere Senescence Theory

D

DATABASES

See

Longitudinal Data Sets in Aging
Minimum Data Set

DAY CARE FOR ADULTS

See

Adult Day Care
Home and Community-Based Care

DAY HOSPITALS

In a day hospital the patients spend a working day in the unit but continue to live and sleep at home. The idea originated in Russia as a means of providing care and treatment for psychiatric patients. The first hospital unit built specifically as a geriatric day hospital was opened in Oxford, England, by Dr. Lionel Cosin in 1957. Day hospitals have proved popular in the United Kingdom, where there are now more than 400 geriatric and at least 200 psychogeriatric day hospitals. Day hospitals are one component of adult day care and are characterized by providing nursing, medical, and other health care. This distinguishes them from day centers that offer social support and diversional therapy only.

There are several theoretical advantages of day hospital care over hospital admission or outpatient care for older people. The older person usually prefers to be in the familiar environment of his or her own home at night, and this also reduces the incidence of nocturnal confusion (sundowning), which more commonly afflicts people in unfamiliar surroundings. Some older people become afraid if they are admitted to a hospital that they may not be able to get home again, and may view their doctors and nurses as potential jailers rather than supporters and friends. Not infrequently when dependent older people are admitted to the hospital, their informal support networks break down and may prove to be irretrievably lost. With foresight, networks can be preserved and enhanced during day hospital attendance. The assessment of an older person can be a lengthy and tiring business, and day hospital attendance provides a setting in which it can be carried out in a staged and comparatively leisured way. The extended period of observation of an older person made possible in a day hospital can enable periodic disturbances of function or behavior to be observed. For many aspects of rehabilitation, spaced practice is more effective than longer, less frequent sessions. For example, 12 five-minute sessions of physiotherapy during a working day are likely to be more effective than a single 1-hour session in the outpatient department. Many older people find outpatient clinics rushed and unsettling; the journey into hospital may be taxing, they have no time to get to know the doctors and nurses they meet, and they are in unfamiliar and often frightening surroundings. In a day hospital they will meet the same professional staff each day they attend and are given time to adjust to the environment.

Day hospitals are used in a variety of ways. The most common in the United Kingdom, where most experience in their management has been accumulated, is to use the day hospital as a means of preventing admission to an acute or assessment bed. This requires the day hospital to be able to take a new patient at 24 hours' notice and to have immediate access to a full range of diagnostic facilities. Staffing includes doctors, nurses, physiotherapists, and occupational therapists who are required to be in the day hospital throughout the working day. Social workers need to be immediately accessible and speech therapy readily available for consultation. These requirements call for the day unit to be on an acute hospital site and closely linked with the geriatric service on the site. To maintain availability of places for new patients, there has to be an active turnover and a typical pattern of attendance is for 2 or 3 days a week for 3 to 6 weeks. The days of attendance are chosen to be convenient to the patient and carers, but also with an eye to not disturbing the pattern of social support that the patient may need to return to after discharge.

A day hospital on a main hospital site may also be used to prepare elderly inpatients for discharge and to provide continued rehabilitation after they go home. Familiarizing a patient with the day hospital before discharge helps to ensure compliance with continued treatment. It also reassures anxious relatives that the hospital service is still involved and acknowledging responsibility for the older person.

In addition to assessment, rehabilitation, and investigation, acute day hospitals can provide a range of treatments, including regular blood transfusions, catheter changes, enemata, and other procedures that might be troublesome to carry out in the patient's home. Electroconvulsive therapy can be provided for some patients in psychogeriatric day hospitals.

A second type of day hospital substitutes for admission for long-term care. Ideally this type of hospital should be linked to the long-stay unit the patient may have to be admitted to if care breaks down and that may also provide inpatient respite

care. This will enable an older person to become familiar with staff and ensures that if he or she does have to graduate into permanent inpatient care, the change does not seem so abrupt and final as removal to an entirely unfamiliar setting would be. A day hospital of this type does not require continuous medical staffing or immediate access to investigational facilities. The input of physiotherapy and occupational therapy can be less than in the acute type of day hospital.

To be effective, day hospitals need rigorous management. Each patient must be cared for as an individual, but the unit as a whole has to be subject to continuous audit and control to ensure best use of resources and appropriate turnover. The maximum size for an acute day hospital is typically 25 places a day with two or three always left vacant for potential emergency referrals. The day-to-day management is usually in the hands of a senior nurse, but each patient needs to have a named doctor responsible for his or her care who must review the patient's progress at least once a week. For each patient there has to be an agreed and preferably written care plan for each week's attendances.

Although their popularity testifies to the value geriatricians and psychogeriatricians attribute to day hospitals, particularly in their benefits for the quality of life of the patients attending, their cost-effectiveness has never been adequately assessed. British data show that one of the main costs to be offset against the alternative of inpatient treatment is that of transport. If a patient has to attend an intensive day hospital program more than three times a week, the costs approach those of inpatient care. (Costs per inpatient day are generally lower in the United Kingdom than in the United States.) The relative effectiveness of inpatient and day hospital care has not been adequately assessed, but geriatricians who have worked in services with and without day hospitals are enthusiastic in supporting the value of the day hospital for the quality of life of the patients attending. The lack of conclusive data on cost-effectiveness makes day hospitals vulnerable in a time of retrenchment in health care.

Further information about British geriatric day hospitals can be found in publications by the Research Unit of the Royal College of Physicians (1994) and the National Audit Office (1994). Weissert, Elston, Bolda, Zelman, Mutran, and Mangum

(1990) have reported on a national survey of adult day care in the United States.

J. GRIMLEY EVANS

See also
  Adult Day Care

DEATH

In many ways the meaning of death and the process of dying are the same regardless of age. For everyone, death leads to the cessation of experiencing, abandoning loved ones, leaving unfinished business, and entering the unknown. The dying process varies as a function of the particular cause of death, but frequently involves pain and discomfort, great financial expense, a series of losses that are often cumulative, and the prospect of imminent death. Nevertheless, age has a bearing on the specific ways in which we interpret and cope with our mortality. Young adults facing the prospect of death, for example, may be most concerned with the well-being of their children. Elderly adults may be most alarmed at the prospect of being kept just barely alive in a helpless vegetative state. Often it is not one's age so much as one's experiential world that shapes the response to death.

This entry briefly examines the demography of death, meaning of death, process of dying, and characteristics that differentiate the elderly adult.

Changing Demography of Death

During the present era, and especially in nations that have moderate to high standards of living, most people who die are elderly, and most deaths occur in hospitals. In earlier times, death rates were extremely high for infants and young children as well as for women of childbearing age; further, hospitals were not commonly used, and, when they were, they were as likely to be the cause of death as they were to be a pathway to effective treatment.

The death rate among children and young adults decreased with improvements in public health, housing, and sanitation. Cholera, diphtheria, pneu-

monia, pertussis (whooping cough), scarlet fever, smallpox, tuberculosis, and typhoid are among the acute infectious diseases that were brought under control. As a result, more people survived childhood and survived without the continued effects of a disabling condition. The increasing association between death and advanced age is a natural consequence of the fact that fewer people now die young. Chronic illnesses have now become the major causes of death. Heart disease, stroke, and cancer are the leading causes of death among elders and among the population in general. Females and Whites have derived greater benefits from the overall reduction in the mortality rate compared with males and African Americans. Economic status also continues to be a significant variable in the risk of death at all ages.

Studies suggest that the mortality rate could be further reduced throughout the entire adult age range with modifications in lifestyle. For example, McGinnis and Foege (1993) found that approximately 800,000 American deaths in 1990 could be attributed to tobacco, diet/activity patterns, and alcohol. Another 100,000 deaths were attributed to firearms, sexual behavior, motor vehicles, and illicit use of drugs. The baby-boomer generation, now well along life's journey, has the opportunity to influence its health and survival by lifestyle choices.

The continuing demographic trend affects the expectations of the American public: (1) Dying "ahead of time" may be viewed as unfair and inappropriate, (2) more attention is given to planning for adequate income over a long life, and (3) preparation is needed to use the postretirement years in a fruitful and rewarding manner. New conflicts emerge as well, for example, the issue of whether an elderly couple should pass its estate on to the adult children or use these funds for enjoyment and security in their own "bonus years."

Meanings of Death

It is probable that humans are the only life form that knows well in advance that death will occur. Knowledge of the inevitability of death enables people to establish priorities and structure their time accordingly. When asked how they would spend 6 remaining months of life, younger people describe activities such as traveling and accomplishing things they had not previously done, whereas older people speak in terms of contemplation, meditation, and other inner-focused behavior (Kalish & Reynolds, 1981).

The meaning of death for elderly persons depends much on the perceived quality of their lives. It has often been assumed that with age one becomes weary, detached, and ready to take leave of a life that has lost much of its value. This stereotype tends to be based on errors and fallacies, such as the following:

- *Projection of one's own fears of aging.* Younger adults often fear the terra incognita of the later adult years, apprehensive that they will lose almost everything of value and gain little in return (Kastenbaum, 1995). This dysphoric expectation contributes to a self-perpetuating cycle in which one avoids intimate relationships with elders and, thus, reduces the opportunity for a corrective learning experience.
- *Overgeneralizations from selective observations.* This is the tendency to collect examples that support one's stereotyped view and ignore those that do not.
- *Salve for the social conscience.* If society can convince itself that elderly men and women care little for their own lives and are ready for death, then it is easier to accept age-discriminatory practices in employment, health care, housing, and so forth. There is also less felt need to grieve and mourn. Unfortunately, even such insightful theories as Erikson's (1950) have disseminated the view that the primary "task" of the aged person is to prepare for death.
- *Misreading of the elderly person's behavior.* As the Kalish and Reynolds (1981) study indicated, people may change their priorities in the later adult years. However, this does not necessarily indicate that they no longer find life to be precious. Lifelong learning, involvement in community activities, and the guidance and mentoring of others are among the valuable roles that many elders are creating for themselves (Manheimer, 1994). The fact that elderly men and women often make plans regarding funeral arrangements and disposition of the estate does not necessarily signify that they are preoccupied with death night and day: Usually, they are just taking care of business so they can get on with life.

Process of Dying

The process of dying may be affected in various ways as a function of age. Younger people are more likely to die from violent causes, such as accidents, suicide, and homicide. Older people generally experience a more prolonged trajectory during which there is a gradual decline in health and functional status. There is more time to cope with personal issues and receive support from significant relationships. The management of pain and other symptoms also tends to differ because a longer time span is involved. Choice of treatment and the availability of funds may also differ. It is not unusual for terminally ill elders to express more concern about the symptomatology and the expense than about the prospect of death as such. Manifest death anxiety is usually higher among younger adults (Kastenbaum, 1992). Elderly people often have worked out their basic beliefs and attitudes about death. When intense anxiety or depression is expressed, one looks for situational factors that have undermined the individual's sense of security and value (Gubrium, 1993).

Older dying people often receive less adequate health and personal care than do younger dying persons, primarily because of their lower perceived social value. Fortunately, the increased availability of hospice care organizations has been providing quality care to terminally ill elders and their families. Many of the patients cared for by hospices are senior adults—and senior adults have also proved themselves effective as primary caregivers within the hospice team approach (Mor, Greer, & Kastenbaum, 1988).

Additionally, the family structure of an older person differs from that of a younger person, which influences the possibility of being cared for at home or in the home of a family member. That is a particular concern for older women who, on an actuarial basis, are much more likely to be widowed and living alone than are older men. Another issue that emerges when older people consider their own dying process is having bodily functions continue after meaningful life has ceased. That can occur as the result of significant cognitive loss (e.g., in

Alzheimer's disease) or as the result of being in so much pain and discomfort or so heavily medicated that the quality of life is severely compromised. These increasingly common situations stimulated the development of the living will, an instrument by which a person may instruct health care personnel to refrain from measures that would prolong dying rather than life. Currently, efforts are being made to devise advance directives that are more specific and, therefore, more useful than the original living will (Norrgard & DeMars, 1992). Patients of all adult ages are also discovering that they have a federally mandated opportunity to give instructions on life-and-death matters every time they enter a treatment facility through the new Patients Self-Determination Act.

RICHARD A. KALISH
Updated by
ROBERT KASTENBAUM

See also

Bereavement
End-of-Life Care
Life Expectancy
Physician-Assisted Suicide
Suicide
Thanatology

DEATH ANXIETY IN THE ELDERLY

Philosophers in the modern era have almost unanimously assumed that the human encounter with death is one marked by angst, dread, uncertainty, and fear—in a word, anxiety. At the same time, advances in life-extending technology, diet, and general lifestyle (at least in industrialized countries) have improved the longevity of the majority of people, effectively associating death with old age in the popular imagination. As a result of these two converging trends, one might assume that the elderly, who are statistically "closest" to death, would experience considerable death anxiety. This article summarizes the principal findings in the growing literature on the death attitudes of the elderly, focusing on those factors associated with elevated death concerns among older respondents.

Perhaps paradoxically, the general trend across studies points to a decrease, rather than an increase, in death anxiety with advancing age, at least through the adult years. Moreover, well-designed survey studies have demonstrated that age is a relatively good predictor of fear of death, accounting for more of the variation in death anxiety than other important demographic and social strata variables such as education, income, and ethnicity. However, in later adulthood, death anxiety tends to stabilize. This does not mean that all older people have uniformly low levels of death anxiety, but that as a group they have lower levels of death anxiety than middle-aged people and that death anxiety does not appear to continue decreasing with age in later life. Future researchers need to pay closer attention to factors specific to older adults such as perceived nearness of death, quality of life, subjective passing of time, and achievement of the developmental tasks of late adulthood to gain a clearer picture of psychological transitions in late life that may affect attitudes toward death.

Research has shown that the gender difference in death anxiety evident in younger adults—with women reporting more death fears than men—is not present in older adults. This finding is consistent with research showing that older adults are less differentiated by gender and exhibit a more androgynous gender identity. Ethnicity has been associated with greater death awareness, with African Americans and Hispanics reporting greater familiarity with death and greater exposure to violence than Caucasians. However, results of studies have been mixed regarding whether these ethnic differences are associated with greater anxieties about death among various subgroups.

Because deteriorating health and diminished income necessitates changes in residence for many elderly people, researchers have become interested in whether living arrangements (e.g., in the community vs. in an institution) have an impact on the death attitudes of the elderly. Some evidence suggests that nursing home residents report greater death fears than do those who live more independently, although this may be confounded with the association between death anxiety on the one hand and poor health and diminished life satisfaction on the other. Nonetheless, the findings that the institutionalized elderly are more likely to encounter death, think of it often, experience reduced control over their lives, and suffer deterioration in quality of life make further study of the death concerns of this vulnerable group a continued priority in future research.

Many studies in this area correlate death anxiety with another single variable, such as physical health, psychological status, and religiosity. A systematic review of this literature indicates that greater physical and emotional problems predict higher levels of death anxiety in the older adults although much work is needed to clarify specific medical and psychological characteristics that are responsible for these general trends. In younger age cohorts, people who are more religious generally report lower levels of death anxiety. This relationship is less evident in older adults, although some studies suggest that religious orthodoxy and belief are associated with greater death acceptance, whereas simple church attendance and involvement in religious activities are unrelated to death attitudes.

Perhaps a more enlightened approach in future studies would be to focus on individual personality traits, coping styles, and competencies among older persons and how these interact with environmental conditions to accentuate or ameliorate their specific fears about death and dying. For example, ego integrity or life satisfaction of elderly respondents has been found to interact with their place of residence; institutionalized elderly with low ego integrity are especially vulnerable to heightened concerns about their mortality. Other work has concentrated on the particular coping skills used by older persons (e.g., prayer and reminiscence) to deal with specific aspects of death anxiety of greatest relevance to them (e.g., helplessness, questions about the afterlife, and the pain of dying). Sophisticated studies that examine discrete death fears as a function of styles of coping with developmental transitions would clearly contribute to the information yield of future research.

Unfortunately, our understanding of the nature and predictors of heightened death fear among older individuals has been hampered by several factors, both theoretical and methodological. Theoretically, researchers have concentrated on easily measured demographic characteristics and measures of physical and mental illness, rather than on the potential resources of older adults (e.g., coping and family support) that could yield a more optimistic view of

their ability to face death with equanimity, acceptance, or even affirmation. Methodologically, investigators have also relied too heavily on unvalidated, idiosyncratic death anxiety scales that treat death attitudes as a single, unidimensional trait, rather than a complex construct with many aspects (e.g., fear of pain associated with dying, anxieties about loss of control, and apprehension about punishment in the afterlife). However, valid and reliable multidimensional measures of death anxiety and acceptance are now available that are beginning to add clarity and richness to current studies. Likewise, investigators have only recently begun to ground their studies in more comprehensive psychological, sociological, and developmental theories that could give coherence and direction to future research. As we continue to clarify the environmental and personal determinants of death anxiety, we will be in a better position to design educational, counseling, and policy interventions to promote a more humane encounter with death and loss at all points in the life span.

ROBERT NEIMEYER
BARRY FORTNER

See also
Death

DEHYDROEPIANDROSTERONE

Although the adrenal glands in humans produce large quantities of dehydroepiandrosterone (DHEA) and DHEA-sulfate, and the plasma levels of DHEA-sulfate are the highest of any steroid hormone in the human, the biological role of DHEA remains an enigma. An interesting property of this steroid is the rise and decline of plasma concentrations with age: Plasma concentrations begin to rise around the eighth year, peak during the second decade, and thereafter undergo a continuous, age-related decline to about 20% of their maximal level in the eighth decade. This phenomenon has contributed to the speculation that the decline in DHEA levels with age may contribute to the rate of development of age-related diseases.

The strongest evidence suggesting a role for DHEA in ameliorating the rate of development of age-related diseases is based on experiments in laboratory animals. Numerous studies have demonstrated that DHEA produces an antiobesity effect in various mouse and rat strains and inhibits the development of spontaneous and experimentally induced cancers in many different tissues (Schwartz, Whitcomb, Nyce, Lewbart, & Pashko, 1988; Svec & Porter, 1998). DHEA treatment also inhibits the development of aortic and coronary artery atherosclerosis in rabbits fed a high-cholesterol diet with a balloon catheter-induced aortic injury or with a heterotrophic heart transplant (Svec & Porter, 1998).

In addition to its effects on cancer and atherosclerosis, DHEA produces other important biological actions in laboratory animals, including ameliorating insulin-resistant diabetes (Schwartz, Whitcomb, Nyce, Lewbart, & Pashko, 1988; Svec & Porter, 1998), anti-inflammatory and immunomodulating effects (Svec & Porter, 1998), and neurologic effects (Svec & Porter, 1998).

DHEA is a potent uncompetitive inhibitor of mammalian glucose 6-phosphate dehydrogenase (G6PDH), the rate-controlling enzyme in the pentose phosphate pathway (Schwartz & Pashko, 1993). This pathway is a major source of nicotinamide-adenine dinucleotide phosphate, reduced (NADPH), and ribose-5-phosphate. Inhibition of this pathway very likely accounts for the antiproliferative and antitumor-promoting effects of the steroid (Schwartz & Pashko, 1993). However, other biologic actions of DHEA are likely mediated by specific receptors, which have not been isolated convincingly.

Although DHEA is effective in laboratory animals in ameliorating or retarding the development of many age-related diseases, clinical trials with the steroid have produced limited evidence of efficacy. A case report study found that oral DHEA (300 mg daily) improved insulin resistance in a single diabetic woman (Buffington, Pourmotabbed, & Kitabchi, 1993), and a high oral dose (1,600 mg daily) of DHEA therapy for 10 days significantly lowered fasting plasma glucose levels in a crossover study in seven obese, type 2 diabetic, postmenopausal women (Levy, Burnett, Manley, Taylor, Burke, & Turner, 1991). Other studies have failed to demonstrate any significant antiobesity effect of DHEA (Svec & Porter, 1998). In a phase III, double-blind, placebo-controlled trial in 191 women with steroid-dependent lupus (SLE), women with SLE-disease activity scores >2 who received 200 mg DHEA daily were able to significantly reduce their prednisone dosages (Petri, Lahita, McGuire, van Vollenhoven, Strand, Kunz, et al., 1997). The beneficial effect of DHEA in women with SLE is consistent with animal data demonstrating antiautoimmune, anti-inflammatory, and immunomodulating effects.

Perhaps the greatest obstacle to well-controlled, long-term clinical trials with DHEA are the very large oral dosages likely required to produce efficacy. When administered parenterally, however, much smaller doses of DHEA are required. The poor bioavailability of orally administered DHEA is very likely a result of poor absorption and/or first-passage liver metabolism (Svec & Porter, 1998).

The cancer preventive, antiatherosclerotic, antidiabetic, antiobesity, and anti-inflammatory effects of DHEA in laboratory animals require oral doses on the order of 200 to 400 mg/kg, which, when extrapolated to humans, suggest an oral dose of 1,000 to 2,000 mg daily. Oral dosages of DHEA at 1,600 mg daily for 4 weeks in postmenopausal women raise plasma testosterone and dihydrotestosterone levels 10 to 20-fold; thus, androgenic side effects limit the use of high oral dosages (Schwartz & Pashko, 1993).

Analogs of DHEA with reduced androgenicity and comparable efficacy may enable the clinician to use high oral dosages in clinical trials without untoward androgenicity. One such compound, 16α-fluoro-5-androsten-17-one, is currently in phase I/II trials to assess efficacy in reducing insulin resistance in type 2 diabetes and in ameliorating symptoms in rheumatoid arthritis (Schwartz & Pashko, 1993).

ARTHUR G. SCHWARTZ

See also
   Atherosclerosis
   Diabetes Mellitus
   Immune System

DEINSTITUTIONALIZATION

Deinstitutionalization, as defined by the National Institute of Mental Health (Bachrach, 1977), includes three components: preventing inappropriate hospital admissions through the provision of community alternatives for treatment; releasing to the community all institutional patients who have received adequate preparation for such change; and establishing and maintaining community support systems for noninstitutionalized persons who may be at risk of institutionalization. Most of the literature about deinstitutionalization focuses on the return of patients to the community rather than the other two components. Furthermore, the deinstitutionalization movement as it pertains to the elderly is generally considered in relation to psychiatric patients.

Deinstitutionalization of the mentally ill, begun in the 1950s, has dramatically affected patterns of hospital care, decreasing the number of occupied state hospital beds from 339 to 29 per 100,000 of the population (Lamb, 1998). Deinstitutionalization has also been accompanied by an increase in community-based treatment facilities, such as psychiatric units in general hospitals, treatment programs, and day hospitals (Kelly & McKenna, 1997). Inpatient mental health services have moved from the public sector to private nonprofit agencies and, more recently, even to for-profit corporations.

Issues pertaining to older adults have been addressed only in limited ways in discussions of deinstitutionalization. Yet they are particularly salient to older adults with mental retardation and other developmental disabilities, as well as those with severe mental illness. For aged individuals who encounter episodes of acute illness or major flare-ups of chronic conditions, shorter hospital stays can result in de facto deinstitutionalization.

Furthermore, the impact of the social policy of deinstitutionalization reaches beyond older mental patients, extending to older relatives of chronically mentally ill, mentally retarded, or developmentally disabled persons who have been called upon to become caregivers in late life when their own personal and social resources are diminished. Research indicates that older adult parents of the adult mentally retarded continue to experience caregiving burdens regardless of institutional or community placement of their kin (McDermott, Valentine, Anderson, Gallup, & Thompson, 1997).

Since the early 1960s deinstitutionalization has been embraced as a broad-scale social reform movement. Its intent has been the release of patients from mental hospitals and other institutions back to community-based living arrangements, thereby normalizing their lives and reducing the adverse effects of institutional living. Elderly persons were included in these efforts, especially long-term residents of state mental institutions. The concept has been extended beyond the special populations of the mentally ill to include other groups, such as the mentally retarded, adult criminal offenders, and, to some extent, the elderly in long-term care institutions.

It is difficult to conclude that the intended goal of deinstitutionalization has resulted in returning the mentally ill elderly to independent and satisfactory living situations. Older adults discharged from long-term care institutions back into the community typically encounter insufficient support services and are at high risk for victimization. The majority of elderly patients with psychiatric problems do not get discharged to community living. For them, the nursing home has become a substitute for the mental hospital. Approximately 40% of patients who were deinstitutionalized from public mental hospitals eventually found their way into nursing homes (Johnson & Grant, 1985). The nursing home has thus become an alternative institution for sheltering those older persons who were ostensibly deinstitutionalized.

Despite widespread impressions about the plight of the deinstitutionalized, systematic long-term follow-ups of such populations have only recently begun. Longitudinal research has also underscored major cost savings to the health care system afforded by community rather than institutional care (Rothbard, Schinnar, Hadley, Foley, & Kuno, 1998). At the same time, there is evidence that deinstitutionalization shifts more of the care costs from third-party payers to patients and their families (Deb & Holmes, 1998). Increases in out-of-pocket costs can thus result in more unmet needs, particularly among the most socially disadvantaged groups, such as the elderly and racial minorities.

Data on mortality rates of the deinstitutionalized appear to be mixed. Some researchers report major increases in mortality among the deinstitutionalized mentally retarded (Shavelle & Strauss, 1999), whereas others find decreased mortality rates among the deinstitutionalized relative to expectations had they remained in long-term care institutions (Conroy & Adler, 1998).

Research on deinstitutionalized elderly patients reveals increased mortality rates for the group, particularly during the first 3 months after discharge from a state hospital (Saathoff, Cortina, Jacobson, & Aldrich, 1992). In addition, there is evidence that patients transferred from hospital psychiatric units to nursing homes show greater behavioral deterioration than those transferred to other psychiatric wards (Linn, Gurel, Williford, Overall, Gurland, Laughlin, et al., 1985). Nursing homes lack staff trained to work with the mentally ill and offer few mental health services. An important exception in this area is the increasing attention directed at developing special units offering diverse interventions to care for the growing population of Alzheimer's patients.

The majority of nursing homes admitting deinstitutionalized aged with chronic psychiatric problems report severe problems associated with such admissions generally in the form of crises and disruptive behaviors. Based on their negative experiences, many nursing homes refuse to accept patients with a history of mental illness (Pepper & Ryglewicz, 1985). Medicaid reimbursement policies in many states further limit access. A sizable portion of the deinstitutionalized elderly with chronic forms of mental illness enter unregulated board-and-care homes (Fetterman & Chamberlain, 1994). Inpatient mental health services to the elderly are increasingly provided in the context of the general hospital. Butler and Lewis (1991) summarize the meaning of deinstitutionalization for the aged, noting that "older patients are being increasingly pushed from inadequate custodial facilities known euphemistically as the 'community.' " Without adequate treatment options and community supports, deinstitutionalized mentally ill swell the ranks of the homeless and are often subject to victimization or arrest (Aderibigbe, 1997; Kelly & McKenna, 1997).

The movement of deinstitutionalization has not been followed up with organized community-based support for individuals discharged from large public institutions. It is widely agreed upon and lamented that the deinstitutionalization of the mentally ill has failed to achieve its purported objectives of reintegrating these individuals into meaningful existence in society or transferring their care from state hospitals to community-based programs. These problems have been attributed in large part to the fragmentation of the current mental health system and the political context of health care financing. The rehabilitation potential of seriously mentally ill elderly has been neglected by the deinstitutionalization movement, but directions for addressing their needs have been noted through a continuum of community services (Bernstein & Hensley, 1993).

The deinstitutionalization movement has contributed to examining the appropriateness of placements for elderly individuals in institutions. It also may have sparked the development of alternatives to long-term institutional care for individuals, including the elderly. Where such programs of support and assistance are developed, their efficacy in improving functioning and quality of life for patients living in the community has been demonstrated (Jones, Perry, Lowe, Felce, Toogood, Dunstan, et al., 1999). Older adults with developmental disabilities and other lifelong or chronic impairments have also been moved out of nursing homes into the community. There is evidence that when such moves are planned with adequate supports, improvements can occur for those reentering the community (Heller, Factor, & Hahn, 1999). Success of diverse approaches to community-based treatment of deinstitutionalized mental patients has been reported (Adkins, Safier, & Parker, 1998; Teague, Bond, & Drake, 1998). Yet evaluation of the effectiveness of such programs has posed challenges since conceptual methodological problems in evaluation abound.

An overall review of the sequelae of deinstitutionalization raises many questions about the impact of these policies on society at large. Deinstitutionalization reflects some positive social values that legitimate the autonomy and dignity of individuals and reflect respect for their personal preferences. Yet, in practice, the deinstitutionalization movement has not succeeded in fulfilling its promise. Sparse implementation of systematic treatment programs to care for the deinstitutionalized in the community has thus resulted in only an illusion of policy (Grob, 1996).

Deinstitutionalization may also be considered in a context removed from focus on the mentally ill, and can be applied to older adults who leave long-term care facilities to return to more independent community-based living arrangements. The characteristics of people successfully leaving long-term care institutions have been identified: (1) persons transferred from an acute care facility for specific rehabilitation and recovery (e.g., persons with hip fractures) and (2) persons who have the potential for improving physically or mentally. They are assisted in becoming more independent through treatment and by marshaling available family and community resources. An analysis of the 1995 National Nursing Home Survey data indicates that close to one fourth of institutional admissions are discharged back to the community (National Center for Health Statistics, 1997).

Discharge of individual patients from nursing homes depends on the resident's personal characteristics: marital status, mental health, physical functioning, and social resources. Younger, married, less dependent, non-Medicaid residents are considerably more likely to go home than are those who are very old, unmarried, or dependent on Medicaid. Diagnosis also affects which older persons are discharged into the community. Patients with a fracture are 78% more likely to return to the community than are residents with a primary diagnosis of cancer or stroke. Conversely, mental patients are 70% less likely to be discharged than those persons without psychiatric problems. Absence of a caretaker also reduces the likelihood of return to community living arrangements (George, 1984).

Successful deinstitutionalization is likely to be facilitated by personal characteristics of the patient, environmental factors outside the institutions, and financing, as well as other planning mechanisms that facilitate the transfer and transition of the patient to the community. Innovative residential alternatives that are tailored to the needs of the mentally ill elderly have been successfully developed in some states, such as Massachusetts (Mosher-Ashley & Henrikson, 1993).

Future increases in the number of elderly will continue the pressure to deinstitutionalize them and to develop alternative environments of care. These alternatives assume that the elderly value living at home and remaining independent as long as possible and that independent living arrangements are likely to result in psychosocial well-being. To support independent living and to respond appropriately to mental health problems, development of diverse alternative care environments and financing mechanisms are needed. A spectrum of care that allows individuals to move between long-term institutions and other community-based alternatives is likely to provide the elderly, their caretakers, and society with necessary and desirable options, including that of effective deinstitutionalization (Maddox, Steinhauser, & Bolda, 1996).

EVA KAHANA

See also
Continuum of Care
Home Health Care
Institutionalization
Long-Term Care Assessment

DELIRIUM

Delirium, a syndrome characterized by a transient disturbance of consciousness, cognition, or the development of a perceptual disturbance (American Psychiatric Association [APA], 1994), is a relatively common event for acutely ill older adults that is associated with death, loss of function, falls, and other complications. Patients with delirium are at increased risk for longer lengths of hospital stay, are more likely to be institutionalized posthospital, and require more nursing and home health services. Moreover, agitated behaviors frequently associated with delirium can lead to use of physical and chemical restraints, further compounding the risk of functional loss and serious complications. Cost of delirium has been assessed at $4 billion a year (Inouye, Schlesinger, & Lydon, 1999).

Defining and classifying delirium for clinical and research purposes has been problematic resulting in difficulties with diagnosing delirium and investigating its attributes and treatment. In 1980, delirium was first included in the American Psychiatric Association's (APA) *Diagnostic and Statistical Manual of Mental Disorders* (DSM-III). Revisions in DSM-IV (1994) have simplified and broadened components for diagnosis of delirium. Further work on classification of subtypes of delirium may improve its recognition by clinicians (APA, 1994; Liptzin, 1998).

Wide variations in reported rates of delirium exist due to evolving criteria, variable case-finding methods, and disparate criteria for subject selection by age, type of admitting diagnosis, and severity of illness. Development of reliable, short, clinical questionnaires and instruments that measure observable behavior and cognitive abilities at the bedside with minimal burden for patients, such as the Confusion Assessment Method (CAM), the Clinical Assessment of Confusion-A (CAC-A), and the NEECHAM Confusion Scale, has improved the reliability of rates of delirium among older adults (Foreman, 1993; Inouye, van Dyck, Alessi, Balkin, Siegal, & Horwitz, 1990; Robertsson, 1999).

Studies employing standardized definitions of delirium based on the DSM-III (APA, 1980), Revised DSM-IIIR (APA, 1987), and DSM-IV (APA, 1994) criteria, report prevalence (delirium on admission) rates from 11% to 33% among elderly hospitalized patients, while incidence (delirium developed during hospital stay) rates vary from 3% to 42% (Francis, 1992; Inouye, Rushing, Foreman, Palmer, & Pompei, 1998; Pompei, Foreman, Rudberg, Inouye, Braund, & Cassel, 1994). Medically ill older adults may manifest symptoms of delirium at the time of admission to the hospital or soon thereafter (Johnson, Gottlieb, Sullivan, Wanich, Kinosian, Forciea, et al., 1990). Surgical patients tend to become delirious postoperatively. A rate of 43.9% delirium was reported among adults over age 75 living in nursing homes and county homes in Sweden (Sandberg, Gustafson, Brännström, & Bucht, 1999).

Description

The delirious older adult experiences a new onset of change in cognition and disturbance of consciousness. Disturbance of consciousness is manifested by an impairment in the ability to focus, sustain, or shift attention to the environment. Change in cognition can occur as memory impairment, disorientation, or language disturbance, and may be accompanied by the development of perceptual disturbances. Deficits in short-term memory are more typical than long-term memory impairment. Disorientation to time and place are more common than disorientation to self. Dysnomia and dysgraphia exemplify components of a language disturbance. Perceptual disturbances, most commonly visual, include misinterpretations, illusions, and hallucinations (APA, 1994).

Sleep-wake cycle disturbance manifested by daytime sleepiness or nighttime agitation is a common feature. Disturbed psychomotor behavior can be displayed as either hyperactivity or sluggishness and lethargy. The EEG is abnormal, indicating either generalized slowing or fast activity. An individual in a delirious state often has unpredictable shifts in emotional disturbances including anxiety, fear, depression, irritability, anger, euphoria, and apathy (APA, 1994).

A classic sign of delirium is that it evolves over a short period of time, usually hours to days, and is characterized by fluctuating symptoms over the course of a day. History, physical examination, and laboratory tests verify that the delirium is a direct effect of a general medical condition, substance intoxication or withdrawal, medication use, toxin exposure, or a combination of these conditions (APA, 1994).

The clinician needs to recognize that delirium differs from dementia in several respects. Although cognitive impairment is common to both disorders, symptoms of dementia develop over a longer period of time. An individual with dementia does not display a disturbance of consciousness. Delirium, however, can be and often is superimposed on a preexisting condition of dementia resulting in even more profoundly negative outcomes (Fick & Foreman, 2000). Yet acute changes in cognition and behavior in an elder with dementia is frequently misattributed to a worsening of the dementia, and delirium is infrequently suspected (Fick & Foreman, 2000).

Diagnosis

The cause of delirium is multifactorial. Causal attributes for delirium include most general medical illnesses, particularly infections, metabolic disorders, dehydration, electrolyte disturbances, postsurgical recovery, and head trauma. Conditions associated with delirium are psychosocial distress, sleep deprivation, sensory overload, lack of stimulation, multiple drug regimens, use of physical restraints, use of bladder catheters, visual and hearing impairment, and immobilization. Drugs associated with a high risk for delirium are the anticholinergic drugs, high-dose neuroleptics, and tricyclic antidepressants. Other drugs with risk for delirium include benzodiazepines, sedative-hypnotics, histamine-2 reception blockers, digitalis, and analgesics (Inouye & Charpentier, 1996; Karlsson, 1999; Tune & Egeli, 1999).

Risk factors for delirium include advanced age, dementia, alcoholism, depression, severity of illness, comorbidity of illness, and physical dependence. As risk factors accumulate, the likelihood of developing delirium increases. Contributing factors to the development of new onset of delirium during hospitalization may be iatrogenesis, lack of recognition of delirium by staff, increase in technology of health care interventions, rapid rate of care delivery, and reduction in skilled nursing staff (Eden, Foreman, & Sisk, 1998; George, Bleasdale, & Singleton, 1997; Inouye, Schlesinger, & Lydon, 1999).

Identifying and quantifying risk for delirium has been studied by several investigators (Eden, Foreman, & Sisk, 1998). Predictive models relying on the interaction of predisposing host baseline vulnerability and precipitating factors has proven the most clinically useful in identifying and quantifying risk for delirium, while providing direction for minimizing such risk (Inouye & Charpentier, 1996).

Clinical diagnosis is based on comprehensive history and clinical observation obtained from multiple sources, including families and the health care team. Unfortunately, delirium often is unrecognized and underreported by clinicians. Failure to recognize delirium occurs because of poor assessment and documentation of symptoms, inability to distinguish it from other mental disorders, and an acceptance of the manifestations of delirium as normal for older adults. Multiple causation of delirium and its erratic presentation contribute to the difficulty in recognizing delirium. Nurses and others who provide continuous care and observation of older adults are in a key position to identify delirium and alert the health care team.

Prevention of Delirium

Using an interdisciplinary care intervention from nursing, geriatricians, and physical, occupational, and recreational therapies aimed at patients with risk factors for delirium, Inouye and colleagues lowered incidence of delirium in hospitalized medical patients over age 70 at risk for poor outcomes (Inouye, Bogardius, Charpantier, Leo-Summers, Acampora, Holford, et al., 1999). The intervention consisted of orientation, therapeutic activities, sleep protocol, early mobilization, vision and hearing protocols, and dehydration repletion. Other studies have reported less success in preventing or treating delirium with similar interventions (Cole, Primeau, Bailey, Bonnycastle, Masciarelli, Englesmann, et al., 1994; Wanich, Sullivan-Marx, Gottlieb, & Johnson, 1992).

Management

Management of the patient with delirium consists of identifying the cause of delirium, initiating measures to correct causative factors, and supporting the patient through the course of the delirium. Interdisciplinary collaboration to facilitate care with the patient and family is essential to reverse the delirium and minimize complications.

Nursing interventions, composed of interpersonal interaction and environmental adjustments, have been associated with decreased confusion among elderly hip fracture patients (Cole, Primeau, Bailey, Bonnycastle, Masciarelli, Englesmann, et al., 1994; Simon, Jewell, & Brokel, 1996; Williams, Holloway, Winn, Wolanin, Lawler, Westwick, et al., 1979). Functional outcomes improved, regardless of the presence of delirium or dementia, among hospitalized elderly medical patients who received specialized nursing care consisting of daily supportive contact, staff and family education, mobilization, environmental modifications, and medication management (Wanich, Sullivan-Marx, Gottlieb, & Johnson, 1992). To significantly reduce incidence and overall consequences of delirium, nursing strategies must be coordinated with medical efforts to identify and possibly reverse the delirious process.

Use of physical restraints may result in injury, fear, agitation, and increased confusion for the delirious patient. Physical restraints, therefore, should be avoided or used only briefly. Initially, alternatives to restraint, such as continuous monitoring, or disguising tubes and dressings with reinforced gauze, need to be considered.

Restoring delirious patients to their premorbid level of function can be facilitated by early referral to physical and occupational therapy. Comprehensive discharge planning is imperative to prevent further decline at home and subsequent readmission to the hospital.

Judicious use of pharmacological agents may be useful for patients experiencing psychotic symptoms. Any drug used for symptomatic alleviation potentially can worsen the delirious condition. Because of the acute illness and advanced age of most delirious patients, drugs need to be given in low doses over the shortest possible time. If early and subtle symptoms of delirium are assessed, minimal doses of drugs can be given before exaggerated behaviors occur.

Conclusion

Standardization of criteria for assessment of delirium and identification of risk factors have enhanced our understanding of delirium in older adults. Further research addressing assessment and diagnosis by clinicians is needed. Cost-effective analysis and outcomes of specific interventions aimed at prevention and management of delirium would inform development of policies and guidelines for care of older adults.

EILEEN M. SULLIVAN-MARX
MARQUIS D. FOREMAN

See also
Dementia
Restraints: Physical/Chemical

DELUSIONS

A delusion is a false opinion or belief, contrary to fact, and unaffected by evidence or reason. Because this definition might apply to most religious beliefs, it is necessary to exclude ideas shared by other people of the same culture. The term *illusion* has been used to indicate irrational but culturally "normal" beliefs, such as religious or superstitious ideas, but is more commonly used to refer to a misinterpreted perception as in a visual illusion. A third category of phenomena comprises hallucinations, which may be linked with delusions. These are false sensory perceptions. Usually they involve seeing objects, animals, or people that do not exist, or hearing nonexistent sounds, such as human voices. Tactile, gustatory, or olfactory hallucinations may also occur.

Delusions are a feature of several different types of mental disorder. They are characteristic of schizophrenia, and persecutory delusions are widely known to be a feature of paranoid states. Depressive delusions occur in psychotic depressions and may take the form of false ideas of poverty, guilt about imaginary crimes, or bizarre ideas that one's bowels have set solid or been taken away. Delusions also occur in hypomanic and toxic states (such as delirium) and in dementias, such as Alzheimer's disease. In Alzheimer's disease delusions can be extremely troublesome because they may not be recognized or easily understood by carers. Delusional jealousy, in which the patient believes his or her spouse, who is often the main carer, to be in adulterous liaison with someone else, can be particularly distressing or even dangerous if the idea leads to violence. Various forms of misidentification are related to delusions; one puzzling form is Capgras's syndrome, in which the patient believes that friends or relatives are not themselves but substituted "look-alikes."

Delusions can occur at any stage of Alzheimer's disease, but in the early stages it may be easier to recognize that abnormal behavior is arising from delusional ideas. Such recognition may help in management both of the patient and of distressed relatives. It may be some comfort to a devoted wife to know that a curt rejection by her husband is due to the fact that he thinks she is an overfamiliar stranger. Even in the later stages of a dementia, it can be worthwhile to make efforts to understand why a patient is behaving in a challenging or disruptive way rather than simply containing the behavior with pharmacological agents or physical restraints.

Environmental or physical factors can precipitate or perpetuate delusions. Some medications can foster delusions by impairing brain function, particularly by impairing memory (e.g., as with some anticholinergic drugs) or creating hallucinations (as may occur with dopaminergic drugs). Patients with a memory impairment may have difficulty in maintaining a stable view of where they are. The functional bareness of a hospital room may be interpreted as that of a prison cell, and the sound of a popular singer from a distant television may become the screams of a fellow prisoner being tortured. The doctor or nurse who next comes into the room understandably will be assumed to be a Gestapo interrogator. Nor would it be surprising for a Gestapo interrogator to pretend to be a physician or nurse to gain a prisoner's confidence. Thus, it can be extremely difficult to "break into" a delusional state and bring a patient back to reality. Neuroleptic drugs can sometimes help, possibly by reducing the emotional element (fear or anxiety) of delusions, or by reducing the patient's impetus to act on his or her delusional ideas.

More detailed discussion of delusions occurring in illnesses that afflict people in later life can be found in Jacoby and Oppenheimer (1997) and Swearer, Drachman, and O'Donnell (1988).

J. GRIMLEY EVANS

See also
Delirium
Wandering

DEMENTIA
See
Alzheimer's Disease: Clinical
Alzheimer's Disease: Genetic Factors
Delirium
Dementia with Lewy Bodies
Senile Dementia

DEMENTIA WITH LEWY BODIES

The Lewy body is an intraneuronal, eosinophilic body, 5 to 25 μm in diameter. Lewy body pathology is pathognomic for a spectrum of disorders, the most familiar of which is Parkinson's disease (PD). PD is the prototypic Lewy body disease, characterized by extrapyramidal symptoms and the presence of Lewy bodies in the brainstem. Widespread Lewy bodies in the cerebral cortex of patients with dementia was first noted with significant frequency by Kosaka, Yoshimura, Ikeda, and Budka (1984). Since then, this condition has emerged as the second most common form of degenerative dementia in the elderly after Alzheimer's disease (AD), accounting for 15% to 20% of demented patients. Immunohistochemical visualization of ubiquitin-

positive Lewy bodies played an important part in revealing the extent of the prevalence of this condition. *Dementia with Lewy bodies* (DLB) is the recently recommended term for a syndrome that has been ascribed numerous names during the last two decades, including cortical or diffuse Lewy body disease, senile dementia of Lewy body type, and Lewy body variant of Alzheimer's disease (Perry, McKeith, & Perry, 1996). Pathologically, it is defined by the formation of both brain stem and cortical Lewy bodies in the presence of sparse or absent neurofibrillary pathology. Although there is some overlap between DLB and both AD and PD, a fairly coherent picture of the clinical features of DLB is starting to emerge (McKeith, Galasko, Kosaka, Perry, Dickson, Hansen, et al., 1996; McKeith, Perry, & Perry, 1999; Perry, McKeith, & Perry, 1996).

Clinical Symptoms, Diagnosis, and Management

DLB is a progressive dementia, often accompanied by psychiatric symptoms and occasionally with mild extrapyramidal symptoms. The prevalence increases with advancing age. Most patients are characterized by a syndrome in which there is a fluctuating confusional state, behavioral disturbance, visual or auditory hallucinations, and progressive dementia (McKeith, Galasko, Kosaka, Perry, Dickson, Hansen, et al., 1996; Perry, McKeith, & Perry, 1996). Motor symptoms, characteristic of idiopathic PD, tend to be rare as a presenting feature in DLB. The fluctuating confusional states can lead to a misdiagnosis of vascular dementia. Patients often suffer transient episodes of loss of consciousness, and severe or fatal neuroleptic sensitivity is common. Cognitive decline and mortality tend to be accelerated in DLB when compared with AD. Revised clinical diagnostic criteria (McKeith, Galasko, Kosaka, Perry, Dickson, Hansen, et al., 1996), based on earlier sets of criteria from Nottingham and Newcastle, are being evaluated. Although the specificity of diagnosis remains high (>85%), improvements will be necessary to improve the sensitivity of the current criteria (McKeith, Perry, & Perry, 1999).

DLB causes many problems for disease management largely because of the conflicting requirements of the neuropsychiatric symptoms and parkinsonism (Perry, McKeith, & Perry, 1996). In general, treatments for hallucinations and behavioral disturbance tend to aggravate movement disorder and vice versa. Accurate diagnosis is important to avoid potential neuroleptic sensitivity. Cholinergic drugs, such as tacrine and donepezil, may have benefits on the cognitive impairment of DLB, but prospective trials of these and future novel drugs are still necessary. Collaboration between specialists in dementia and movement disorder will be essential for rapid progress in research and clinical management protocols.

Etiopathogenesis

The etiology of DLB is not understood, and research to date is still aimed at the level of defining changes that are associated with the syndrome. Nevertheless, changes at the neuropathological, neurochemical, genetic, and molecular levels have all been observed in DLB. The extent to which each of these is involved in the pathogenesis of DLB still needs to be ascertained. Likewise, the seminal events that distinguish DLB from AD and PD remain to be elucidated.

DLB is characterized by the presence of a moderate number of neocortical Lewy bodies and sparse or absent neurofibrillary lesions (Dickson, Crystal, Mattiace, Kress, Schwagerl, Ksiezak-Reding, et al., 1989; Perry, Irving, Blessed, Fairbairn, & Perry, 1990). Although lacking the tau pathology characteristic of AD, DLB shares with AD the increased risk that is associated with possession of the apolipoprotein E ε4 allele (Harrington, Louwagie, Rossau, Vanmechelen, Perry, Perry, et al., 1994). Lewy bodies in limbic and neocortical regions are smaller than those found in the brain stem and rarely have the electron dense cores of the latter. The Lewy body is composed of amorphous material and filaments, 10 to 20 nm in diameter, consisting of α-synuclein, that has been identified recently as the major component of this inclusion body (Spillantini, Schmidt, Lee, Trojanowski, Jakes, & Goedert, 1997). Truncated fragments of α-synuclein have been found in isolated Lewy bodies (Baba, Nakajo, Tu, Tomita, Nakaya, Lee, et al., 1998). In addition, neurofilament subunits and ubiquitin and

other related, cell-stress response proteins are present (Perry, McKeith, & Perry, 1996).

Although the quantity of amyloid β-protein deposits is similar to that found in AD, the relative proportion of plaques containing Aβ terminating at residues 40 or 42 distinguish DLB from that in AD. Although Aβ42 plaque numbers are similar in both conditions, the Aβ40 plaques are more frequent in AD than in DLB (Lippa, Ozawa, Mann, Ishii, Smith, Arawaka, et al., 1999). In addition, Lewy-related neurites, absent in AD, are found in the CA2/CA3 region of the hippocampus in DLB (Dickson, Ruan, Crystal, Mark, Davies, Kress, et al., 1991). These neurites contain both α-synuclein and ubiquitin.

Neurochemically, DLB shows features of both PD and AD (Perry, McKeith, & Perry, 1996). Dopamine levels in DLB are decreased in the caudate, and patients are particularly susceptible to typical neuroleptic drugs (dopaminergic D2-receptor antagonists). The cholinergic deficit in DLB generally is more severe than that found in AD, except for the hippocampus, which is usually spared. A correlation, however, between choline acetyltransferase depletion and the prevalence of cortical Lewy bodies in DLB has not been found. This would support the notion that Lewy bodies themselves are not responsible for the clinical phenotype.

DLB may share common disease determinants with both AD and PD. The APOE ε4 allele is a risk factor for both AD and DLB but not PD (Harrington, Louwagie, Rossau, Vanmechelen, Perry, Perry, et al., 1994). Although the cytochrome P-450 gene CYP2D6 was reported to be associated with both DLB and PD (Saitoh, Xia, Chen, Masliah, Galasko, Shults, et al., 1995), this finding has not been substantiated. An elevated frequency of the CYP2D6*4 allele was confirmed in PD, but no such elevations were found in either DLB or AD (Atkinson, Singleton, Steward, Ince, Perry, McKeith, et al., 1999).

Lewy bodies may represent pathological end-products that simply serve as biomarkers for PD and DLB. Almost certainly cortical Lewy bodies themselves do not account for the clinical symptoms of DLB, because the number of affected neurons is approximately one thousandth of the number affected by neurofibrillary pathology in AD. Nevertheless, the process that leads to the formation of Lewy bodies may be central to the pathogenesis of DLB and other "synucleinopathy" disorders. α-Synuclein is a soluble, presynaptic protein that is pathologically redistributed within intracellular lesions characteristic of several neurodegenerative diseases (Goedert, 1999). Insoluble aggregates of α-synuclein in Lewy bodies are found not only in DLB, but also in familial AD patients with mutations in presenilin or amyloid precursor protein genes (Lippa, Fujiwara, Mann, Giasson, Baba, Schmidt, et al., 1998) and in patients with multiple system atrophy. Mutations in α-synuclein have been reported in a few families with PD (Polymeropoulos, Lavedan, Leroy, Ide, Dehejia, Dutra, et al., 1997), and such mutations accelerate α-synuclein aggregation in vitro (Conway, Harper, & Lansbury, 1998) to form filaments that are distinct from those formed from normal α-synuclein (Giasson, Uryu, Trojanowski, & Lee, 1999). Mutations, however, have not been found in sporadic PD or in DLB, and in PD they exhibit incomplete penetrance. Observations of additional axonal pathology and inclusions in DLB indicate that β- and γ-synucleins, in addition to α-synuclein, may be implicated in synaptic dysfunction (Galvin, Uryu, Lee, & Trojanowski, 1999). The identification of a protein, synphilin-1, which interacts with α-synuclein and which produces cytoplasmic eosinophilic inclusions when the two proteins are introduced into mammalian cells, provides a model to study the pathogenesis of α-synuclein aggregation (Engelender, Kaminsky, Guo, Sharp, Amaravi, Kleiderlein, et al., 1999). The possibility that α-synuclein is not necessary for Lewy body formation but is still involved in the neurodegenerative process, is supported by the finding of α-synuclein-negative Lewy bodies in the cortex of a patient lacking the clinical signs of parkinsonism and/or dementia (van Duinen, Lammers, Maat-Schieman, & Roos, 1999).

It will be important to determine whether or not the accumulation of filamentous inclusions is a key pathogenic event in DLB. If not the case, then is synaptic dysfunction a consequence of abnormal α-synuclein processing in these patients? These, and questions regarding the basis of selective neuronal vulnerability in DLB, mean that extensive clinical and biological research is still required in this area.

CHARLES R. HARRINGTON

See also
Parkinson's Disease

DEMOGRAPHY

The demographic facts of aging provide an important key to explaining the emergence of gerontology as a major discipline. Sociology, economics, psychology, and geography are other disciplines in which scholars now devote considerable time to study aspects of aging. The fundamental need to understand the process of population aging and how it affects all segments of a society has led to the development of a specialized field of study termed the *demography of aging*. The demography of aging deals with the dynamic processes of aging, as they are manifested by a population that has a rising proportion of older persons. It also examines the aging of birth cohorts (a group of persons born within a defined time period, e.g., those born in 1960) through their life course. The dynamic process of aging reflects on the ways a total population structure is transformed over time and how cohorts of persons reaching old age may modify the characteristics of the overall aged population. Therefore, the demography of aging draws theoretical insights and methodological approaches from general demography to explain the evidence of populations undergoing aging and to forecast future developments.

The idea of aging as a set of lifelong processes implies that the aging of children or persons of labor force age is as legitimate a focus for the demography of aging as that of older population groups. For example, in demography and other disciplines, aging aspects of the baby-boom generation (cohorts of persons born between 1946 and 1966) have been the subjects of a growing body of literature.

The demography of aging also centrally focuses on the current demographic profile of the older population, as well as changes in its numbers, proportionate size, composition and territorial distribution. Moreover, the disciplinary field addresses the determinants and consequences of changes in attributes of the older population. A substantial body of literature has emerged concerning a wide range of consequences of population aging. Much of this literature is found in disciplines other than demography.

What Is Oldness? A Topic of Growing Controversy

Two decades ago, Siegel (1980) wrote: "The demography of aging brings demographers to focus holistically on a population group, the elderly, and a demographic process, aging" (p. 345). A focus on the "elderly" rests partly on the notion that there is a meaningful concept of oldness and that it is possible to define a useful measure to help the public decide when a person, or a cohort, should be called "old." However, the delineation of a threshold beyond which persons should be considered old, a matter that is central to the theoretical raison d'être of much of the current literature in the demography of aging, is increasingly a matter of controversy (Bourdelais, 1994).

Concurrently, there is growing pressure on government leaders and organizations to find ways of making more effective use of the economic potential of groups of healthy older persons who have passed the age of 65. These developments may help shift the focus of the demography of aging away from the group called "the elderly" and toward aging as a dynamic, lifelong process for cohorts and historically for whole populations.

Key Contributors in the Development of the Demography of Aging

It is worth recounting some key developments in the field of population aging. An initial stimulus came from scholars such as Jean Bourgeois-Pichat at l'Institut National pour l'Etude Démographique (INED) in Paris. Their ideas gained international acclaim through Jean Bourgeois-Pichat's work at the United Nations Population Division starting in the mid-1950s (especially the nonattributed volume; United Nations, 1956). Further impetus came through the work of Coale and his colleagues at Princeton University in the 1950s and 1960s. Aging has now become a prominent focus of work at numerous centers for demographic training and research, with notable sponsorship by the U.S. National Institute on Aging.

United Nations agencies have been key sources of representative literature of current research in the demography of aging (Stolnitz, 1992; United Nations, 1992), along with various journals that publish articles in the field. The Population Activities Unit of the Economic Commission for Europe is leading a new set of national and comparative studies on population aging. In the 1980s, the Committee for International Cooperation in National Research in Demography (CICRED) sponsored the preparation and publication of 19 national studies on aspects of population aging. International reviews of population aging and of the older population have also received important stimulus from the International Programs Center at the U.S. Bureau of the Census, supported in part by the U.S. National Institute on Aging (Kinsella & Taeuber, 1993).

Measurement and Analysis of Population Aging

There is a hierarchical linkage between individual, cohort, and population aging. Although alternative statistical measures of aging are possible, cohort aging is commonly measured in terms of changes in the average age of the members of a cohort. Population aging is usually measured by changes in the proportion of designated "older persons" in a population. The latter measure is not simply the growth rate or changes in the absolute size of the designated older population.

The pace of population aging depends on the aging processes and relative sizes of sequences of cohorts passing from birth to extinction. The impact of population aging on society depends on the pattern of succession among cohorts possessing different characteristics passing through the older ages (Stone, 1999).

A declining birthrate contributes to population aging by creating a faster growth rate among older persons than among youth. Declining death rates at the older ages also contribute significantly to population aging. These facts have supported classification of population aging processes in terms of the extent to which they involve aging at the base of the population age pyramid (associated with current fertility rate changes) or aging at the apex of the pyramid. Aging at the apex gradually develops when large birth cohorts from the past reach older ages and are further swelled by reduced mortality at the older ages. The latter trends have been particularly important in accounting for more recent increases in both the numbers and the proportions of the elderly in developed countries.

Declining birthrates of the depression years of the 1930s in the United States and European countries sparked concern over potential depopulation and population aging. These same concerns are being expressed in current literature concerning a number of countries in Europe. Lestheaghe (1999) recently noted that low fertility due to delayed and completed childbearing appears to show little change in many European countries. Thus, "hyperaging" seems inevitable for many countries, such as Italy, where one third of the population is expected to be 65 and over by 2030.

In the pioneering work of Lotka, a mathematical model of demographic changes was formulated. The stable population model enabled demographers to examine the long-term effects of different levels of fertility and mortality on age structure. Many articles on this topic can be found in the literature (see Stolnitz, 1992, and United Nations, 1992, for examples and for extensive references to other similar articles). In addition to this information, there is a large body of literature concerning consequences of population aging (see Stolnitz, 1992).

Changing Characteristics Among the Older Population

The continuing aging of the population produced by the momentum of growth from previous levels of high fertility, the fall in the birthrate since the early 1960s, and recent marked declines in mortality at the older ages have been accompanied by changes in the characteristics of the aged population. The term *population metabolism* has been used to describe how the aged subpopulation is modified over time by new entrants, selective decrements through differential death rates, and changes in status during the latter stages of life (Myers, 1985). The aged population is subject, therefore, to high levels of turnover. A high percentage of the population 65 years of age and older at any given date will have died within a decade and will be replaced by new entrants to that population. This rapid suc-

cession of cohorts through the older population contributes to a high level of diversity.

The aged population in most developed countries is itself aging through growing numbers of the oldest-old (85 years of age and over), who constitute an increasing proportion of the aged population (Suzman, Willis, & Manton, 1992). This aging trend will continue until the influx of large numbers of persons from the post–World War II baby-boom cohorts reach old age beginning in the second decade of the 21st century.

Another important attribute of the older populations of most countries can be characterized as sex disparity. There are more older women than older men, which results from differential mortality risks that favor women. Along a wide range of social and economic variables, gender disparity is a characteristic feature of the aged population.

Several additional population attributes have been the focus of attention in the demography of the older population. These include family structure among older persons (Myers & Eggers, 1996), living arrangements of older persons, patterns of paid and unpaid work among older persons, the geographic redistribution (migration) of the older population (Bean, Myers, Angel, & Galle, 1994), and disease prevalence, disability, and subjective well-being (Manton, Corder, & Stallard, 1997).

Conclusion

The demography of aging provides theoretical and methodological perspectives on various aspects of population aging. The field has been enriched not only by the contributions from general demography but also by recent developments arising from gerontological research issues and modeling work done by scholars concerned with economic issues. A growing number of countries have research under way and publications in preparation on the demographic aspects of the phenomenon. In particular, one may note the increasing analyses of census sample data, initiation of special surveys dealing with the aged population, and specific projections of disaggregated characteristics of the aged population. Among the important new departures in these efforts is the accumulation of data from longitudinal surveys in the United States, Canada, and other countries (both developed and developing). New efforts are under way to rework historical data to reveal patterns of cohort differentiation along a variety of dimensions of population attributes (Stone, 1999). The knowledge generated by these activities will provide a sounder basis for making policy decisions for increasingly aging societies.

LEROY STONE
GEORGE C. MYERS

See also

Baby Boomers and Their Future
Epidemiology of Aging: A New View of Health Status and Risk Factors
Life Expectancy
Minorities and Aging
Third World Aging
World Assembly on Aging

DEOXYRIBONUCLEIC ACID (DNA) REPAIR PROCESS

DNA in cells is constantly exposed to insults from both endogenous and exogenous factors that may cause a variety of lesions to DNA. In response to DNA damage, multiple repair pathways have evolved in cells (for a review, see Carr & Hoekstra, 1995). In general, these pathways include direct reversal, mismatch, recombinational, base excision, and nucleotide excision repair. The simplest DNA repair pathways involve only single enzymes that catalyze a direct reversal of specific damage (e.g., alkyltransferase, which removes the methyl group from O^6-methylguanine). Mismatch repair corrects mispaired bases, which often occur as a consequence of an error in replication. The importance of this system in mammals is illustrated by the defects in the human homologues of bacterial MutS and MutL, which may be the primary cause of hereditary nonpolyposis colorectal cancer in humans. Recombinational repair occurs when both strands of the DNA helix are damaged and there is no intact template for the DNA polymerase to copy (e.g., double-strand breaks and interstrand cross-links). This pathway has been relatively well characterized in bacteria; however, it is poorly understood in mammalian cells. Base excision and nucleotide excision are involved in repair of much

of the DNA damage that occurs in cells. Through base excision repair, simple base modifications (e.g., oxidation and monofunctional alkylation) are repaired. This pathway is characterized by a series of glycosylases that specifically cleave the glycosylic bond between the damaged bases and the deoxyribose. The resulting apurinic/apyrimidinic site is removed by AP endonuclease and deoxyribophosphodiesterase, and the gap is filled by DNA polymerase β and sealed by DNA ligase. Through nucleotide excision repair, bulky helix-distorting lesions such as cyclobutane primidine dimers and large alkylating adducts are repaired. In addition, some oxidative DNA lesions are corrected by nucleotide excision repair. In mammalian cells, nucleotide excision repair is a complex process involving at least 25 proteins for damage recognition, dual incision, repair synthesis, and ligation. More recently, it has been demonstrated that there are two nucleotide excision repair subpathways, that is, transcription-coupled repair, which preferentially repairs lesions in the transcribed strand of expressed genes, and bulk genome repair, which repairs lesions in the nontranscribed DNA at a relatively slow rate.

The DNA repair theory of aging proposes that DNA repair declines with age and eventually falls below a threshold level necessary to maintain the integrity of the genome. When this occurs, unrepaired damage and mutations accumulate in the genome of cells, resulting in a decrease in cellular function. This theory is supported by the four lines of evidence described below:

1. DNA repair decreases with age (for a review, see Guo & Richardson, 1999). Over the past two decades, a large number of studies have compared the DNA repair capacity of cells/tissues from young and old organisms to determine if DNA repair declines with age. In most of these studies, DNA repair was measured as unscheduled DNA synthesis (UDS) after the cells were exposed to DNA damaging agents, such as ultraviolet (UV) radiation or methyl methanesulfonate; therefore, these studies were measuring primarily nucleotide and base excision repair. UDS has been observed to decrease approximately 30% to 50% in cells from mice, hamsters, rats, rabbits, and humans. However, there are also studies with cells from these animal models

that show no change in UDS with age. It has been proposed that this controversy could be the result of the assay. UDS is a relatively crude assay, which neither directly nor selectively measures the removal of a specific type of damage; it measures the induction of non-replicative DNA synthesis by a damaging agent. Thus, changes in the specific activity of the thymidine precursor pool or replicative DNA synthesis could affect the level of DNA repair measured in the UDS assay. Recently, other techniques have been used to study the effect of age on DNA repair. For example, using a ^{32}P-postlabeling assay, studies have shown a significant decrease in removal of benzo(a)pyrene-DNA adducts from the genome of old mice. Using UV-irradiated plasmids transfected into human lymphocytes, it has been found that the repair of the plasmid declines with age at a rate of 0.6% per year from the first to the tenth decade of life. T4 endonuclease V, which specifically cleaves UV-induced cyclobutane pyrimidine dimers (CPDs), has been used to measure the removal of CPDs from specific genes/DNA regions. An age-related decrease in removal of CPDs has been observed for telomeres of human fibroblasts, as well as transcribed and nontranscribed genes in rat hepatocytes (Guo & Richardson, 1999). However, the age-related decrease in repair appears to be greater in nontranscibed genes/regions of the genome.

2. DNA damage/mutations accumulate with age (for a review, see Walter, Grabowski, Street, Conrad, & Richardson, 1997). For example, one of the most common DNA lesions, DNA strand breaks, has been found to increase with age. In addition, a number of studies have shown an age-related accumulation of oxidative damage (8-hydroxydeoxyquanosine) in nuclear and mitochondrial DNA from cells from humans and animals. An age-related increase in mutations has also been demonstrated. For example, lymphocytes from old individuals have been shown to have higher levels of mutations in the hypoxanthine phosphoribosyl transferase (hprt) gene than those from young individuals. Using the recently developed bacterial LacZ and LacI transgenic

systems, several investigators have shown an increased mutation frequency in the transgene in various tissues of mice.

3. Dietary restriction attenuates age-related changes in DNA repair and DNA damage/mutations (for a review, see Haley-Zitlin & Richardson, 1993). The age-related decrease in DNA repair observed may be physiologically important in aging because studies have shown that the age-related increase in DNA damage/mutations and the age-related decrease in DNA repair can be attenuated by dietary restriction, which has been shown to retard aging and result in increased life span in rodents. For example, studies have shown that the frequency of spontaneous and chemically induced mutations in the hprt gene is significantly reduced in lymphocytes of rats and mice fed a calorie-restricted diet compared with the animals fed ad libitum. In addition, studies have shown that rats and mice fed a calorie-restricted diet exhibited lower levels of oxidative damage in DNA isolated from a variety of tissues than DNA isolated from tissues of rodents fed ad libitum. Studies have also shown that dietary restriction significantly increases the ability of cells from rats and mice to repair DNA damage. For example, the levels of unscheduled DNA synthesis after UV irradiation is higher in the cells obtained from rats and mice fed a calorie-restricted diet than in the cells from animals fed ad libitum. Recent results also show that dietary restriction attenuated the age-related decrease in gene-specific repair in transcriptionally active genes and nontranscribed genes/region in rat hepatocytes.

4. Animal species with a long life span have a higher level of DNA repair. Another approach that has been used to study the relationship of aging and DNA repair is to measure the ability of cells from animals of various life spans to repair DNA damage. The original study by Hart and Setlow showed that UV-induced UDS in fibroblasts from several mammalian species was positively correlated with species life span. Although subsequent studies with additional classes of organisms have shown some limitation in this

correlation, there is reasonable evidence to support the view that cells from a mammalian species with a long life span have a higher level of DNA repair as measured by UDS (Cortopassi & Wang, 1996).

In summary, there are several lines of evidence that support the DNA repair theory of aging; however, it is not clear if there is a causal relationship between DNA repair and aging. In addition, because almost all studies that have measured DNA repair with age have focused on nucleotide excision repair, very little is known on how aging affects the other DNA repair pathways.

ZHONGMAO GUO
ARLAN RICHARDSON

See also

Mitochondrial DNA Abnormalities
Somatic Mutations and Genome Instability

DEPRESSION

Depression is among the most common complaints of older adults and the leading cause of suicide in late life. Depressive disorders should therefore be considered disorders of major concern to all persons caring for older adults. For an overview of research and experience in the management of late-life depression, see Blazer (1993).

Depression, by definition, is so varied in its manifestations and so easily confused with other conditions, such as dementia and hypochondriasis, that clinically depressed older adults are often unidentified. As the term *depression* is ambiguous, many clinicians have reverted to the use of a somewhat archaic term, *dysphoria*, to describe those everyday normal experiences of feeling low, blue or simply down in the dumps. Given the inevitable illnesses experienced by elderly persons, not to mention other stressful life events, symptoms of depression are frequently encountered by those who serve or observe older adults (Blazer, Hughes, & George, 1991). Nevertheless, these dysphoric episodes in late life are usually transient and recovery is spontaneous (Hughes, DeMallie, & Blazer, 1993).

Of greater importance are those "major depressive disorders" that may occur for the first time after the age of 60 or that recur in later life after first occurring earlier in life. Such "clinical depressions" are characterized by severe symptoms and a prolonged duration of a profound depressed mood. Clinicians and other health care providers must learn to recognize these depressive disorders, for they can potentially precipitate a suicide attempt or even a successful suicide (Conwell, 1994). Suicide remains one of the 10 most frequent causes of death in late life and may be preventable if the symptoms of major depression are recognized (Miller, 1979). Unfortunately, severe depressive episodes often remain undetected; therefore, older adults suffer unnecessarily from the burden of depressive illness. Clinical depression is not easily diagnosed in late life because many symptoms are expectations of changes commonly associated with normal aging. For example, older persons have more difficulty sleeping and often complain of a broken sleep pattern and early morning awakening, cardinal symptoms of major depression at any stage of the life cycle. Lethargy, a frequent physical symptom that accompanies depression, can also be overlooked in the elderly for physical illness, and even aging may lead to decreased energy and activity. In hospital and ambulatory settings, depression is frequently associated with physical illness, usually chronic but not life threatening. Other older adults with depressive symptoms complain that they cannot concentrate and notice a problem with their memory. Such persons may be diagnosed as suffering from an irreversible dementing process and be denied appropriate treatment. Yet most cases of depression and memory loss in the elderly reflect a comorbid process of dementia and depression. Nevertheless, the depression may be treatable even though the cognitive impairment does not improve (Reifler, Teri, & Rasking, 1989). The unfortunate circumstance of not treating a depression associated with memory loss may lead to long-term institutionalization for an individual who is suffering from a treatable illness. Persons experiencing depression with cognitive impairment, however, even if the cognitive impairment improves with remission of the depression, are at greater risk in the future for a permanent dementing disorder (Alexopoulos, Meyers, Young, & Mattiss, 1993).

Diagnosis

Recent advances in understanding the psychobiology of depression has assisted clinicians in distinguishing elders experiencing clinical depression from those who report the symptoms of normal aging or other age-related physical and psychiatric disorders. Many depressed elders exhibit subcortical hyperintensities on magnetic resonance imaging (MRI). These hyperintensities probably reflect decreased blood flow to the very areas of the brain that have been associated with mood (i.e., the hypothalamic region) and have been referred to as the syndrome of vascular depression. In addition, approximately one half of those who, throughout the life cycle, develop a major depression with melancholia exhibit an abnormal response to the administration of a synthetic corticosteroid, dexamethasone. The inability of dexamethasone to "turn down" the hypothalamic-pituitary-adrenal (HPA) axis, which regulates the secretion of cortisol, produces an abnormally elevated blood level of cortisol 18 to 24 hours following the dexamethasone challenge. This dexamethasone suppression challenge, although not a diagnostic test, can provide valuable data regarding the behavior of the HPA axis during a late-life depression. Advances in the evaluation of sleep patterns of depressed older adults have enabled researchers to distinguish the depressed elderly from those suffering from dementia and those who are aging normally. The depressed, throughout the life cycle, have a shortened rapid eye movement (REM) latency (i.e., it takes less time to enter first-stage REM, or "dream" sleep, once the individual falls asleep).

Treatment

Severe depression is a treatable illness. When clinical depression of late life is identified, the use of appropriate medications, such as selective serotonin reuptake inhibitors (SSRIs) and tricyclic antidepressants (TCAs), can reverse symptomatology in over 70% of persons so afflicted. However, the physician who prescribes medications to the older adult must always be aware of the potential for adverse side effects from these medications; TCAs are among those medications that in late life produce the most frequent adverse side effects. Be-

cause of the frequency of such effects, medications are often discontinued before an adequate trial is effected, and the depressed older adult is denied effective therapy. Patients who exhibit significant anxiety along with the depression symptoms may be treated with anxiolytic agents such as benzodiazepines without use of an antidepressant. By adjusting the dose of medication downward and monitoring the medications carefully, therapists can assist most depressed older adults to tolerate medications without difficulty. The SSRIs produce fewer side effects, but some of their side effects, such as decreased appetite and agitation, are especially troublesome to the elderly. Today, SSRIs such as fluoxetine, paroxetine, sertraline, and citalopram have become the mainstays of treatment.

When medications fail, electroconvulsive therapy (ECT) often produces dramatic improvement. The negative public image of this therapeutic modality ensures that it is selected only in the most resistant, severe cases of major depression. Its use must be prescribed with special care for older adults, as health problems and difficulties with memory may complicate the therapeutic course. In addition, older adults with recent severe cardiovascular problems must be treated judiciously with ECT because transient increases in blood pressure frequently accompany the treatment process.

The effectiveness of biologic treatments for severe depression in late life has overshadowed the use of psychotherapy in the elderly. Nevertheless, investigators have reported that individuals suffering from major depression with fewer "biological signs" (e.g., sleep problems) can be treated effectively with short-term psychotherapy (Gallagher, Breckenridge, Steinmetz, & Thompson, 1983). These psychotherapies generally have been cognitive and behaviorally oriented and may serve, at the least, as useful adjuncts to biological treatments. Recent studies of the young-old have documented that treatment with a combination of interpersonal therapy (a variant of cognitive behavioral therapy) and antidepressant medications is more effective than either alone both in producing a remission and in preventing a recurrence of an episode of major depression (Reynolds, Frank, Perel, Imber, Cornes, Miller, et al., 1999). When psychotherapeutic medication and/or ECT are not effective, the clinician must rely exclusively on psychotherapy. For severe depression, there is always the hope that remission will occur spontaneously, because depression, by definition, is a self-limiting illness.

DAN G. BLAZER

See also
   Bereavement
   Cognitive Therapy
   Feeding Behavior
   Mental Health and Illness
   Sleep Disorders

DEVELOPMENTAL PSYCHOLOGY

Developmental psychology deals with the description, explanation, and modification of the ontogenesis (intraindividual age-related change) of mind and behavior, from conception to death. Two central goals underlie developmental research: to obtain information about interindividual similarities and differences in ontogenetic development, and to understand the range and conditions of individual plasticity or modifiability of development. The antecedents or causes of development are located in two interacting systems of influences (biological and environmental factors), each associated with specific mechanisms (e.g., maturation and learning). When basic knowledge about psychological development is used for corrective or therapeutic purposes, one speaks of applied developmental psychology. Historically and conceptually, the field of developmental psychology has roots both in psychology and in other disciplines concerned with life (for reviews, see Baltes, Lindenberger, & Staudinger, 1998; Cairns, 1998; Valsiner, 1998).

The degree of specialization reached in developmental psychology, both in North America and in Europe, is such that developmental psychology does not constitute a single coherent field. Numerous specialties have emerged that concentrate on either age-graded periods (infancy, childhood, adolescence, adulthood, old age) or domains of functioning (physical growth, as well as cognitive, social, emotional, and personality development). Many of the subspecialties of psychological development have their own institutional base and peer community (e.g., Society for Research in Child Development, Society for Research in Adoles-

cence, various gerontological societies). One international organization, the Society for the Study of Behavioral Development founded in 1969, is devoted to attracting scholars whose interest is in the entire life course.

Theoretical Frameworks

There is no unified theoretical framework of developmental psychology, although there are numerous scholars working within one or the other of the major approaches, such as social learning theory, cognitive structuralism, biogenetic models, life-span models, and psychoanalysis. Most handbooks are age-specific. For infancy and childhood, summaries of theoretical and empirical work are contained in the four volumes of the *Handbook of Child Development* series (Damon, 1998). For adulthood and old age, the handbooks edited by Birren and Schaie (1996) and Craik and Salthouse (2000) are standard references. Researchers interested in the whole life span find relevant work summarized in the annual series of *Life-Span Development and Behavior*, which was initiated in 1978.

In the present context, it is not possible to review specific substantive theories of development. Instead, we point to work concerned with the definition of development, to major metatheoretical frameworks about the determinants of development, and to a general descriptive framework summarizing factors operative during ontogenesis.

Concept of Development. Not all behavioral change is of the developmental kind. Rather, the long-standing historical influences of developmental biology and Gestalt psychology (reflected in the cognitive structuralism of Piaget and the genetic structuralism of Heinz Werner) have resulted in a family of criteria that are often used as indicators of development. Among these criteria are (1) direction toward a state of maturity, (2) quantitative and qualitative (stagelike) change, (3) relative robustness or irreversibility of change, and (4) movement toward greater complexity and differentiation. An extreme view proposes that all of these criteria need to be fulfilled in order to designate that a behavioral change is of the ontogenetic-developmental kind.

Applying the entire family of criteria to the definition of development results in a precise but possibly too restricted concept. The disadvantages of such a restricted definition are most conspicuous when applied to later periods of the life span. Indeed, there is continued discussion whether processes associated with development differ from those associated with aging (Baltes, Lindenberger, & Staudinger, 1998; Bengtson & Schaie, 1999). Beginning with adolescence, the causes and forms of development are more diverse and open than a universalistic and stagelike definition of development would suggest. The greater regularity of development observed for infancy and childhood than for later age periods may be attributed to the fact that the biological and cultural forces that shape childhood are more programmed (genetically and societally) than is true for later periods of the life span. In old age, the conjoint dynamics of biological and cultural forces are less well orchestrated because the architectural plan of human ontogeny is incomplete (Baltes, 1997).

Metatheoretical Perspectives. Major metatheoretical positions on the descriptive and causal nature of psychological ontogenesis emphasize action-theoretical, transactional, contextualist, dialectical, and dynamic systems perspectives. These models highlight two types of interactions between organisms and their environment. The first is the dynamic interaction in ontogenesis between individuals and their microenvironment; the second is the interactive relationship between individual development and societal change at the level of macrostructure and populations. Organisms do not develop and age only from within, nor do they develop in a stable ecology. Individuals develop and age in a changing society from which they receive and to which they give. Endogenous and exogenous factors not only interact as static elements but are closely intertwined and themselves undergo change.

Descriptive Framework. Traditionally, developmental psychology focused primarily on forms of development that represented positive change in the structure and function of behavior (adaptive capacity or growth). As the study of development was extended to the entire life span and as theories that were less influenced by biological growth conceptions gained in prominence (e.g., social learning theory and social constructivism), it was recognized that ontogenesis is more complex than the concept of growth suggests. Life-span views of development and aging have introduced several additional concepts to reflect this complexity, for example, proposals about multidirectionality, a gain-loss dynamic, and processes of selection, optimization, and compensation (Baltes, Lindenberger, & Staudinger, 1998).

Embedded in the notion of multidirectionality is the idea that categories of behavior show different trajectories of positive and negative change or stability across the life span. A classic example of this concept is research on the trajectories of fluid versus crystallized intelligence during adulthood and into old age. Phenomena of differential aging and subgroup differences in systemic profiles of functioning also illustrate the concept. Expanding the concept of development from a growth model to a multidirectional model led to the insight that development is likely always a combination of gains and losses: that any developmental change entails a dynamic trade-off between features of growth and decline. A gain in one direction, for example, may exclude alternative pathways of development. The search for gains and losses across the life span has been paralleled by the rapid growth of investigations into the range and limits of plasticity of mind and behavior. Research into age-related changes in plasticity (intraindividual variability) is motivated, first, by a search for the latent potential of structure and function and, second, by questions about fundamental component processes of "developmental reserve" or competence. At a more general level, research into the gain-loss dynamic has stimulated various questions about the fundamental role of processes of selection, optimization, and compensation in development (Baltes, 1997). Selection defines the direction, goals, and outcomes of development. Optimization involves the acquisition or application of means to achieve selected goals. Compensation occurs in response to a loss or blockage of previously available goal-relevant means (resources) and involves the acquisition or application of alternative means designed to maintain functioning or reenable goal attainment.

Influences on Development

The methodological requirements of developmental psychologists are complex. In essence, research designs have to take into account the fact that development is determined by multiple factors and mechanisms and that it is a time-related process that occurs within specific sociocultural and historical contexts. Consensus has been reached about the importance of investigating three systems of influence: age-graded, history-graded, and nonnormative. Each of the three influences involves biological and environmental conditions. Age-graded influences include, for example, biological and physical changes (e.g., puberty and menopause), as well as exposure to age-related social factors (e.g., schooling, family life cycle, and retirement). History-graded influences imply changes in societal structure and function (e.g., economic depression, medical and technical modernization, and periods of war or political oppression). Nonnormative influences are conditions that show little correlation with chronological age or historical time, but affect an individual's development in important ways. Most developmental theories can be located with regard to a focus on one or more of these influences.

The age- and history-graded influences produce not only similarities in development but also conditions for individual differentiation during development. On the one hand, there are biogenetic differences that operate throughout life in producing differentiation. On the other hand, there are social-structural differences, such as social class, that are relevant in differentiating individuals in terms of level and directionality of ontogenesis.

The dynamic of influences in development illustrates the multidisciplinary connections of developmental psychology mentioned earlier. The age-graded influences, for example, require an analysis in which biologists, psychologists, and sociologists cooperate. Similarly, the analysis of history-graded influences cannot be accomplished by psychologists alone. In addition to cultural anthropologists and sociologists, social historians have much to offer when the task is one of charting constancy and change in the societal context of human development (Elder, 1998). For developmental psychology to be a fertile specialty, it needs solid ties to its parent discipline. At the same time, it cannot neglect its conceptual and empirical linkages to other specialties forming the larger umbrella of the developmental sciences.

PAUL B. BALTES
JACQUI SMITH

See also
Life Course

DEVELOPMENTAL TASKS

People doing research on the growth and development of children and adults find that the process of successful development depends on the achievement of a number of interrelated tasks so that achievement on a task of one age tends to be associated with other tasks of the same age. Also, achievement on these tasks provides a good base for achievement of the tasks of subsequent age periods.

Consequently, researchers have been able to identify and describe the human life cycle in terms of the following age periods, each with its own developmental tasks: infancy and early childhood, middle childhood, adolescence, early adulthood, middle age, and later maturity (Havighurst, 1972). Here we will concentrate on later maturity. For an illustration of the use of developmental tasks as a concept in the study of human development see Newman and Newman (1984).

Later Maturity

As a general rule, in the later years, defensive strategies of adaptation become relatively more important. Attention shifts to holding on to life and the memory of old achievements rather than reaching out to grasp more of life and undertaking new tasks. The developmental tasks of later maturity include the following:

Adjusting to Decreasing Physical Strength and Health. Even if a person has outlived serious accidents and diseases, biological decline occurs with age. Of all people who live to be more than 50 years old, half die of heart disease or its complications.

A large number of older people must adjust to invalidism related to chronic disease.

Adjustment to Retirement and Reduced Income. In American society a job is the axis of life for most men and many women. A retired individual therefore risks feeling that he or she does not count, feeling unworthy. Yet careers and jobs must be relinquished by the great majority of people, whether professional or manual workers, some time between the ages of 60 and 70. Some people fill up the vacuum created by retirement in their lives with useful and interesting leisure-time activity; others find a part-time job that keeps them busy and happy; some fret and mope over their forced inactivity.

Adjusting to Death of Spouse. After a man and a woman have lived together for 40 years, it is hard for one to get along without the other. Yet death separates nearly every married couple. Women lose their husbands more often than men lose their wives because women are longer lived than men. There are about twice as many widows as widowers in the average community. By the time women are in their late 60s, as many women are widows as are living with their husbands. Among women 85 years of age and over, 85% are widows.

If a woman loses her husband, she may have to move from her house to a smaller place; she may have to learn about business matters; but above all, she has to learn to be alone. A man has the same adjustment to make to loneliness; he may have to learn to cook, clean house, and keep his clothes in order.

Establishing an Explicit Affiliation With One's Age Group. Physiological aging slows down the organism and makes it increasingly difficult for older people to keep up the tempo of life that they followed in middle age. Hence, they tend to drop out of the activities of the middle-age group.

It is useful to look at the rewards and punishments involved in participation by a person turning 65 in (1) the group just younger than he or she (later middle age) and (2) the group just older (early old age).

Rewards in continued participation in the middle-age group: Feeling of achievement— something is going on all the time; satisfaction from the wielding of economic and social power; satisfaction from the repetition of behavior patterns already well learned.

Punishments in continued participation in the middle-age group: Fatigue due to the "rapid" tempo in the group; older persons are increasingly ignored by this group or perhaps unintentionally insulted by references to their age and declining powers.

Rewards in continued participation in the old-age group: Tempo of life is slower and more comfortable; companionship is easily found; people have more leisure time; prestige positions are available in organizations of older people and no longer available in organizations of middle-aged people.

Punishments involved in participation in the old-age group: For 30 or 40 years the individual, now growing old, has participated in occupational, social, and religious groups in which age-grading was at a minimum and status was achieved on the basis of social position, economic power, talent, and other things that were largely independent of age. The aging person must now learn once more to participate in an age-graded group. The ease or difficulty of this task depends on the relative magnitudes of the rewards and punishments that have been suggested above.

Establishing Satisfactory Physical Living Arrangements. The high incidence of heart disease and arthritis in older people makes physical exertion difficult or dangerous for many of them and argues against stair-climbing and heavy housework. There is increasing danger from falls because of the increasing brittleness of bones and their slow mending rates. A decreasing ability to chew foods and an increasing need for a good diet make good food preparation and selection necessary. Decreasing metabolic ability of the body makes it difficult for older people to "keep warm" and requires good heating facilities.

The principal values that older people look for in housing according to studies in this area are as follows: quiet, privacy, independence of action, nearness to relatives and friends, residence among own cultural group, cheapness, and closeness to transportation lines and communal institutions—libraries, shops, movies, churches, and the like.

Newman and Newman (1984) summarize the developmental tasks of later maturity as follows: (1) coping with the physical changes of aging; (2) redirecting energy to new roles and activities such as grandparenting, retirement, and widowhood; (3) accepting one's own life; and (4) developing a point of view about death.

ROBERT J. HAVIGHURST

See also

Adaptation
Geriatric Health
Life Course

DEVIANCE THROUGHOUT THE LIFE COURSE

Whether old, middle-aged, or young, deviants are people who violate group norms defining socially accepted behavior. Although norms vary from society to society and from one era to another, every society has rules that regulate behavior. Rules of acceptable conduct also define deviance. To classify behavior as acceptable automatically creates another category of actions: unacceptable behavior or deviance. At least three decades ago, Doob (1971) commented that when the circus was invented, so also was the sideshow, whose major function is to reassure viewers of their own normality while ridiculing people who differ from the expected. In this way, conformity is bolstered and anxiety over the unusual is abated. Sociologist Emile Durkheim (1893/1984) suggested that deviance is necessary to societal well-being. Behavior that seems unnecessary, irrational, or without purpose indeed has a rationale, for deviance generates social cohesion to oppose the particular act. A second function of deviance is to set boundaries of acceptable behavior, a process reestablishing and affirming shared norms and values within social groups, such as the family, the workplace, the neighborhood, the senior citizen center, the nursing home, and the community. Within these settings, boundaries are placed on the outer limits of acceptable behavior so that conduct is restricted and made relatively predictable.

Deviant behavior thus is not inherent in conduct itself but reflects how the conduct is interpreted within a given culture at a specific point in time. It is not always clear what behavior will be designated as deviant or conforming, for the same act may be viewed differently by various people or social groups. In complex industrialized societies, there are competing norms, based on different value assumptions. The relative power of competing interest groups decides which norms will be most important; the more powerful the group, the more likely its values are to be accepted as the ruling norms. Focus on deviance in any society thus generates information on what is "right" or approved behavior. Much of our knowledge of what is "normal" derives from examining prohibited or disapproved behavior. The script for both is drawn from group experience. A brief review of what is considered deviant behavior in old age thus sheds light on "successful" or "normal" and "unsuccessful" or "abnormal" aging.

What are appropriate norms for behavior in old age? As various authors over the decades (Burgess, 1960; Rosow, 1967; Wood, 1971) have noted, although older people obviously occupy a number of roles, such as parent, grandparent, friend, and retiree, there are almost no role prescriptions or proscriptions defining proper standards (except to avoid bizarre behavior) and little information specifying preferred role behavior. For example, research on the role of grandparent has noted that it is characterized by a multiplicity of behaviors and meanings (Neugarten & Weinstein, 1964; Pruchno, 1999; Robertson, 1977; Troll, 1985; Uhlenberg & Hammill, 1998). Despite the current emphasis on "productive aging," few roles with accompanying well-delineated prescriptions for appropriate behavior exist for the now-old of either gender. Appropriate role behaviors in old age are difficult to identify, for contemporary popular culture is characterized by two contradictory images of aging: the elderly hero (or heroine) who remains youthful and fights old age through lifestyle and plastic surgery, and the dependent, helpless elderly person (Featherstone, 1995).

Almost all forms of deviant behavior in industrialized societies decline with age, from late adolescence and young adulthood on. Elders account for a relatively small proportion of known criminals; people age 60 and over tend to have the lowest arrest and conviction rates for serious crimes. Those 15 to 19 years have the highest arrest rate for property crime, and those 20 to 29 have the highest rates for violent crime (U.S. Department of Commerce, 1998).

Chemical dependency (substance abuse), especially alcohol use, in later life has received increased attention within the past few decades. Defined by the American College of Physicians (1984) as encompassing alcohol and drug addiction, chemical dependence includes addiction to alcohol, legal drugs (both prescription and nonprescription), and illegal drugs. A diagnosis of "psychoactive substance dependence," according to the fourth edition of the *Diagnostic and Statistical Manual of Mental Disorders* (American Psychiatric Association, 1994), includes at least three of the following: (1) substance taken in greater amounts or for longer than intended; (2) persistent desire or inability to control use; (3) considerable time obtaining, taking, or recovering from the drug; (4) frequent intoxication or withdrawal symptoms when expected to fulfill major obligations; (5) reduced social, occupational, or recreational activities; (6) continued use despite persistent problems; (7) marked tolerance; (8) characteristic withdrawal symptoms; (9) substance taken to avoid withdrawal. Several of these criteria have been criticized as inappropriate for the elderly (Atkinson, 1990), and studies of alcoholism in the elder use diverse gauges that make comparisons difficult (Blazer & Pennybacker, 1984; Friedmann, Jin, Karrison, Nerney, Haley, Mulliken, et al., 1999). Not surprisingly, estimates of the percentage of elderly who are alcoholic vary from 1% to 10%. Most studies have found that the prevalence of alcoholism diminishes with age: higher among 60- to 70-year-olds than among those over 70, and higher among men than women (Adams, 1999).

Whether the prevalence of alcoholism decreases with aging is debatable, however, for cohort factors may confound cross-sectional findings. For example, findings from the Normative Aging Study suggest that elderly men neither reduced their alcohol consumption over time nor had fewer problems with drinking (Glynn, Bouchard, LoCastro, & Laird, 1985). But others (Adams, Gerry, Rhyne, Hunt, & Goodwin, 1990) have noted a decline over

7 years in the proportion of elderly drinkers ages 61 to 86 at the outset of the study. What seems likely is that norms about alcohol use—and willingness to admit alcohol use—are affected by birth cohort and gender, as well as changes in public norms and attitudes about drinking. If birth cohort is a decisive factor, future generations who have grown up with more relaxed norms about drinking may show higher incidence and prevalence of alcoholism, receiving more medical and psychological attention (Gurnack & Thomas, 1989). Studies of addiction to illegal drugs among the elderly are few, although there may be far more elderly addicts than commonly realized. Older adults may simply be more adept at concealing their addiction. Whether alcoholism and drug addiction are increasing among the elderly is difficult to detect, as much of what is known has been based on treated or known cases of abuse. Moreover, most studies may tell us far more about age cohort patterns of alcohol and drug use than about old age itself.

Suicide is one form of deviant behavior that does increase with age. Now the eighth leading cause of death in the United States and considered a serious outcome of depression, panic disorder, stress, and other mental conditions, suicide has been identified as a major public health problem, and reduction in late-life suicide was marked as one of the key health status objectives by the U.S. Surgeon General in *Healthy People 2000* (U.S. Department of Health and Human Services, 1990, p. 588). Among Americans, male suicide rates increase in a straight line from age 15 to 85 and, contrary to popular belief, do not peak at retirement. Suicide rates are highest among elderly White men; White men age 85 and over have a suicide rate nearly triple that of African American men in the same birth cohort. In Durkheim's terms, most late-life suicides are egoistic; that is, because of their lack of integration into work, friendship, and family roles, elders lack clear guidelines for behavior and supportive interaction (Durkheim, 1897/1964). Although why suicide peaks among elderly White men remains unclear, it is known that those most at risk are White widowers (Osgood, 1985).

In considering how norms specify social views of deviance, suicide is an interesting example. Rather than aberrant, suicide was a virtuous deed among the ancient Greeks and Romans for many years, and the Greek Stoic philosophers viewed suicide as a rational act: an alternative to life in disharmony with nature. By contemporary standards their definition of rationality might seem excessive, for Zeno, the founder of the Stoic school, apparently hanged himself out of pure exasperation when he stumbled and broke his finger at the age of 98 (Alvarez, 1990). The Romans also advocated planning and executing one's own death as an appropriate, dignified end to life, as "[t]o live nobly also meant to die nobly and at the right moment" (Alvarez, 1990, p. 82). According to Justinian laws, every Roman had a right to kill himself if experiencing "impatience of pain or sickness . . . weariness of life . . . lunacy, or fear of dishonor." Although the early Christians did not stress its rationality, suicide was a legitimate act: a release from a life seen as a vale of tears and sin with the promise of heavenly bliss merely a death away. Martyrdom was popular and offered posthumous glory, for martyrs' names were celebrated and their relics treasured. By the 7th century, however, the cult of martyrdom was no longer relevant to the social situation of the Roman Catholic church. Due largely to the efforts of Augustine, church leaders decreed that to take one's own life defied divine will. Suicide was more serious than other sins or crimes. Those who committed suicide were denied funeral rites and Christian burial, and attempted suicides were excommunicated. In succeeding centuries in Christian societies, suicides were buried, often with a stake driven through the heart, at crossroads to dispel their evil ghosts, their property confiscated, and their families disinherited. Unsuccessful suicides were hanged, burned, or drowned, their corpses mutilated, or, as late as 1961 in England, imprisoned (Alvarez, 1990). Although few if any of us would either espouse suicide or punish those who choose suicide and their families, the ways in which suicide has been viewed makes clear that one era's deviance is another's acceptable behavior.

That so few elderly engage in any of the behaviors delineated as deviant in contemporary Western industrialized society and that these behaviors may be ignored if they do occur remain intriguing. Is a decline in deviant behavior a reflection of waning risk-taking behavior associated with biological changes with aging? Of age-associated increases in wisdom? Or are older deviants more skillful in concealing their behaviors, as they have fewer required secondary group contacts? If their deviance is detected, are elders treated more leniently or tolerated more than younger ones? To what extent does the incidence of deviant behavior mirror birth cohort? As future cohorts age, it will be interesting to learn whether the prevalence of what we now define as deviance in old age changes and the extent to which new definitions of deviance emerge.

ELIZABETH W. MARKSON

See also
    Alcoholism
    Crime (Against and By the Elderly)
    Life Course
    Medication Use and Misuse
    Suicide

DIABETES MELLITUS

Diabetes mellitus is a complex syndrome (or syndromes) of chronic hyperglycemia (high blood glucose levels) in association with vascular, hormonal, and metabolic abnormalities. Because of its high prevalence throughout the world and its association with vascular complications, diabetes gives rise to considerable morbidity, disability, and premature death.

The main classification of diabetes in use is that of the World Health Organization (WHO) Expert Committee on Diabetes (1980) although several modifications have since been made. Two major clinical classes of diabetes exist: Type 1, or insulin-dependent diabetes mellitus (IDDM), tends to occur in young subjects below the age of 40 years and involves an autoimmune destruction of pancreatic beta cells, leading to an absolute insulin-deficient state. Type 1 diabetes often presents with classical symptoms of diabetes (thirst, excessive secretion of urine, weight loss) and in some cases with coma due to the abnormal accumulation of metabolic products known as ketone bodies in the blood. Type 2, or non-insulin-dependent diabetes mellitus (NIDDM), is usually first diagnosed in middle-aged and elderly subjects. Type 2 diabetes is characterized by a combination of impaired insulin secretion from beta cells, decreased hepatic sensitivity to insulin's action in suppressing glucose output, and defective responses of insulin-sensitive tissues such as skeletal muscle and adipose tissue. This results in a state of insulin resistance at both the hepatic and peripheral tissue levels. Symptoms of hyperglycemia may be present at the time of diagnosis of Type 2 diabetes, but in other cases, presentation may be insidious. Type 2 diabetes is a major health problem, with a prevalence of 6.8% in the U.S. population and 16.8% in those aged 65 years and over. In the United States, annual costs of diabetes exceed $20 billion, half of which is spent on diagnosis and treatment and half on management of complications, lost employment, and premature death (300,000 deaths annually).

Two main types of vascular disease are present in diabetes: (1) microangiopathy, such as retinopathy, neuropathy, and nephropathy, characterized by structural changes, including thickening of capillary basement membranes, resulting in increased vascular permeability; and (2) macroangiopathy, such as coronary and peripheral arterial disease, distinguished by extensive atheroma similar to non-diabetic atheroma but often present earlier and more widespread. Diabetes in older subjects, which is predominantly Type 2 diabetes, is not a mild disease by any means and has been shown to have as high a prevalence of microangiopathy as is seen in younger patients, with macroangiopathy (such as ischemic heart disease) being considerably more common.

Whether diabetes in elderly patients is a disease different from that in younger patients is arguable, but some complications, such as diabetic amyotrophy and hyperosmolar nonketotic coma, occur mainly in elderly diabetic patients. Coexisting and often chronic medical problems, such as cerebrovascular disease, arthritis, Parkinson's disease, and dementia, exacerbate the impact of diabetes, increase the level of disability, and hinder management.

The WHO criteria for the diagnosis of diabetes have recently been modified by the American Diabetes Association, and the WHO were ready to make amendments to the scheme in the year 2000. The threshold for diagnosing diabetes has been lowered and the fasting glucose determination has been encouraged. They are identical for young and old. In a symptomatic patient, the diagnosis is established when a random venous plasma glucose level of 11.1 mmol/L or greater is present or when a fasting level of 7.0 mmol/L or greater is present.

A level below 6.1 mmol/L is considered normal and a level between 6.1 and 6.9 is now termed impaired fasting glucose. In the absence of symptoms, at least two elevated venous plasma glucose levels are required to establish the diagnosis. It should be remembered that a sizable proportion of newly diagnosed patients with diabetes have normal fasting glucose levels. If the clinician is uncertain of the diagnosis, a 75-oral glucose tolerance test is required to establish or exclude the diagnosis. A level of 11.1 mmol/L or greater 2 hours after the glucose load is diagnostic of diabetes. The use of glycosylated hemoglobin (HBA1c) and serum fructosamine, which are longer-term measures of glycemic control, should not be relied on in view of the lack of sensitivity. Hyperglycemia may be present in a setting of acute stress such as infection, myocardial infarction, or stroke. Laboratory determinations of plasma glucose should be repeated when the acute illness has subsided in order to establish whether or not diabetes is present.

Vision loss and peripheral vascular disease are major causes of long-term disability in older subjects with diabetes. Good vision is a major prerequisite for maintaining quality of life with increasing age and may threaten independence. It may be affected by cataract, glaucoma, and diabetic retinopathy, especially maculopathy, although age-related macular degeneration is quantitatively a more common cause of visual loss in this age group. Regular screening by funduscopic examination and optometric review are essential. Peripheral vascular disease is a major cause of diabetic foot disease and can lead to leg pain on exercise, ischemia, and even amputation. This inevitably leads to significant personal health burden, an increase in the dependence level, and excessive health service costs. Regular inspection for vascular complications by both the patient and health professionals is essential.

The fundamental aims of care for older patients with diabetes should be essentially similar to those for younger patients. Assessment of coexisting disease, screening for and preventing complications, and maintaining patient well-being and quality of life are of paramount importance, in addition to the traditional aims of avoiding hypoglycemia (low blood glucose) and keeping the patient free of symptoms of hyperglycemia.

The metabolic basis for the treatment of Type 2 diabetes in elderly people includes both pharmacological and nonpharmacological therapies. The majority of patients with Type 2 diabetes can achieve acceptable levels of blood glucose by dietary means alone, in the short term at least, especially if they are at ideal body weight. Noncompliance with dietary instructions is common for many elderly patients, for whom dietary education has not been offered. The diet should include carbohydrates to make up about 50%–55% of the dietary energy intake, the majority of this coming from complex sources, preferably foods naturally high in dietary fiber. A reduction in fat intake to 30%–35% of energy intake remains an important measure that helps to lessen the risk of cardiovascular disease by improving the blood lipid profile and assisting in weight reduction. Of this, about one third should be saturated fat, the remainder being polyunsaturated and monosaturated fat. Cholesterol intake should not exceed 300 mg/day. Protein should provide 10%–15% of the energy intake; this may be of some benefit in slowing down the progression of diabetic neuropathy. Alcohol should be restricted in those with high levels of triglycerides in the blood and those who are overweight.

Physical exercise should be recommended as an adjunct to proper diet and weight control and may even be protective against the development of Type 2 diabetes. It may lead to a fall in blood pressure, a lowering of hyperinsulinemia and an improvement in glucose tolerance, and a less atherogenic lipid profile, with a reduction in total plasma cholesterol and trigylcerides but an increase in high-density lipoprotein (HDL) cholesterol. Elderly patients may be unable to participate in exercise programs because of decreased joint mobility due to diabetes-related joint stiffness and/or osteoarthritis or because of a previous stroke.

If symptoms of hyperglycemia persist and metabolic control remains unsatisfactory after a period of 3–6 months of diet and physical exercise, treatment with oral antidiabetic drugs is usually started. A range of these agents is available: insulin secretagogues (sulfonylureas, rapaglinide), metformin, thiazolidinediones, or alpha-glucosidase inhibitors. Sulfonylureas, which have both pancreatic actions (stimulating insulin secretion from beta cells) and extrapancreatic effects (increasing the response of target tissues to insulin), are often the first choice among oral agents and should lead to a fall in fasting glucose. Failure to respond to sulfonylureas

occurs in about 15% of patients (primary failures), and secondary failure occurs in 3%–5% of treated patients per year. Hypoglycemia is a major worry in treatment with sulfonylureas because it can be fatal if severe and prolonged. For this reason, sulfonylurea drugs with a long biological action (e.g., chlorpropamide) should be avoided for older patients.

Clinical use of a biguanide (metformin) is generally confined to combination therapy with sulfonylureas when the latter have failed to achieve metabolic control or as monotherapy in obese patients (body mass index [BMI] >30) after dietary failure. Several mechanisms of action have been proposed for metformin, including enhancement of insulin-mediated glucose uptake and an inhibitory effect on hepatic glucose production. In the presence of renal or hepatic failure, metformin may precipitate lactic acidosis, although the risk is substantially less than its predecessor, phenformin, which has been withdrawn from use in many countries. Age per se should not be a barrier to the use of metformin as long as proper monitoring of patients takes place. Thiazolidinediones (e.g., rosiglitazone) are relatively new agents that offer glucose-lowering ability either as monotherapy or in combination with sulfonylureas or insulin. They work by lowering insulin resistance and must be avoided in patients with liver disease. Alpha-glucosidase inhibitors, which reduce postprandial glucose levels, have been in use in Europe for several years. They may be used as monotherapy in patients poorly controlled on dietary therapy alone or as an adjunct to treatment with diet and oral agents when metabolic control remains unsatisfactory.

About 50% of patients with Type 2 diabetes require insulin therapy by 10 years after diagnosis, partly because of progressive beta cell dysfunction. Temporary insulin therapy is needed in acute medical and surgical illness, especially if ketosis is present; in hyperosmolar nonketotic coma; in marked weight loss secondary to hyperglycemia; and sometimes in severe complications such as foot ulceration complicated by infection, acute painful neuropathy, and diabetic amyotrophy. Arranging short-term insulin therapy for older patients in the community is often difficult, and hospitalization is usually required. Twice-daily combinations of human short-acting (soluble) and intermediate-acting (e.g., isophane) insulins are popular; patients are now offered pen devices for injection purposes, and the adoption of these devices by elderly patients is increasing. Once-daily insulin schedules are often prescribed for elderly patients, but they may be associated with hypoglycemia during the late afternoon or night and may not give acceptable levels of blood glucose.

In view of the beneficial effects of improved glucose control on microvascular complication rate and of improved blood pressure control in reducing both micro- and macrovascular complications (findings of the recent United Kingdom Prospective Diabetes Group, 1998), clinicians should be more motivated in their therapeutic endeavors to treat elderly patients with Type 2 diabetes. Monitoring of blood glucose levels is an important part of management, and many older patients can manage this, perhaps with help from a spouse or friend. Monitoring diabetes treatment by measurement of urinary glucose is less reliable, particularly in older people.

Along with the above measures, specific attention should be given to the active treatment of coexisting medical disorders, such as hypertension and hyperlipidemia. Large-scale studies such as the Hypertension Optimal Treatment (HOT) randomized trial provide additional support for the efficacy of lowering blood pressure in older subjects with diabetes and hypertension. The potential for health gain in this growing sector of our diabetic population is large and can be achieved at a time of limited health service resources only when patients themselves are motivated enough and encouraged to take personal responsibility for their disorder.

For further information see Ilarde and Tuck (1994), Sinclair (1998), Sinclair and Barnett (1993), and Meneilly (2000).

ALAN J. SINCLAIR

See also
Cardiovascular System: Overview
Eye: Clinical Issues
Hypertension in the Elderly
Kidney and Urinary System

DIAGNOSTIC AND STATISTICAL MANUAL OF MENTAL DISORDERS
See
Psychiatric Diagnosis and DSM-IV
Mental Health and Illness

DIET RESTRICTION

In 1935, McCay and his colleagues (McCay, Crowell, & Maynard, 1935) published a seminal paper in which it was reported that restricting the food intake of a population of rats results in extending the length of life. This finding has been repeated many times in many different strains of mice and rats and also has been observed with hamsters as well as nonmammalian species such as fish, flies, and water fleas.

Studies With Rats and Mice

Most of the research on diet restriction has been done with mice and rats; in these studies, control animals (often allowed to eat ad libitum) are compared with diet restricted animals, usually fed 50% to 70% of food intake of the control animals. That diet restriction slows the rate of aging is supported by a vast amount of evidence (Masoro, 1993). Specifically, diet restriction increases the median and maximum length of life of populations of mice and rats, markedly increases the mortality rate doubling time obtained by Gompertzian analysis, maintains the physiological systems in a youthful state, and delays and in some cases prevents age-associated disease. It has been shown that the antiaging actions are not due to the decreased intake of a specific nutrient or toxic dietary contaminant but rather are due to the reduction in the intake of calories. This phenomenon frequently is called the antiaging action of dietary restriction (DR) or of caloric restriction (CR). DR as used by experimental biological gerontologists involves undernutrition in the absence of malnutrition.

The mechanism by which DR retards the aging of rodents has long been of interest. Several proposed hypotheses have been tested and found wanting. These include the retarded growth and development hypothesis and the reduced body fat hypothesis.

Probably, the hypothesis most favored today is the oxidative damage attenuation hypothesis (Sohal & Weindruch, 1996). Oxidative stress, due to the generation of reactive oxygen molecules, inevitably occurs in aerobic organisms such as mammals. These reactive oxygen molecules oxidatively damage other molecules. DR has been shown to retard the age-associated cellular accumulation of oxidatively damaged molecules. It is often stated that DR causes a state of hypometabolism and thereby decreases the rate of reactive oxygen molecule generation. However, DR can retard aging without causing hypometabolism (McCarter & Palmer, 1992); thus, it is misleading to state that the antiaging action of DR is due to hypometabolism. Nevertheless, the protection from oxidative damage by DR must be due to a reduced rate of reactive oxygen molecule generation, or to increased protection from the damaging action of reactive oxygen molecules, or to better removal and/or repair of oxidatively damaged molecules. There is evidence that all three of these possibilities may be involved. Moreover, there is no need for a decrease in the metabolic rate for a decrease in the rate of generation of reactive oxygen molecules to occur.

Another hypothesis of current interest is the glucose-insulin hypothesis, which states that the reduced glycemia and insulinemia are major factors in the antiaging action of DR. Although it is established that hyperglycemia and hyperinsulinemia cause damage similar to that which occurs during aging, clear evidence is lacking that the reduction in plasma glucose and insulin levels by DR retards aging.

The hormesis hypothesis is attractive because it broadens the scope of protection by DR (Masoro, 1998). Hormesis can be defined as the beneficial action(s) resulting from the response of an organism to a low-level stressor. There is evidence that DR is a low-intensity stressor. Moreover, there is evidence that DR protects mice and rats of any age from the damage of acute, intense stressors, an action fitting the term *hormesis*. If aging is due to long-term stressors of both environmental and intrinsic origin, then hormesis could well be the mechanism that underlies the antiaging action of DR. Genetic modifications that lengthen the life of invertebrate species also protect them from acute stressors; this finding lends credence to the possibility that hormesis may play an important role in the antiaging action of DR.

Studies With Rhesus Monkeys

Does DR retard the aging of humans? This often asked question is not likely to be answered by studies with human subjects because of the length of time required for such studies and the spartan diet that must be consumed for a large part of a subject's lifetime. Thus, studies have been initiated using the rhesus monkey in the belief that if DR retards aging in the rhesus monkey, it is likely that it will also do so in humans. Many of the physiological effects that DR has in rats and mice also occur in the rhesus monkey (Roth, Ingram, & Lane, 1999). Although there has yet to be a systematic appraisal of the effect of DR on age-associated disease of the rhesus monkey, it has been found that DR reduces the risk factors for age-associated diseases. Although the findings are consistent with DR retarding aging in rhesus monkeys, a definitive answer awaits the collection of appropriate mortality data, as well as data from pathohistological analyses. The National Institute on Aging is in the planning stage in regard to initiating such research. However, even if it is undertaken in the near future, 20 years or more will elapse before the study is completed.

Gerontological Significance of DR Research

The interest of biological gerontologists in DR relates to the fact that a manipulation that slows aging provides a powerful tool for the study of aging. Indeed, DR appears to be the only manipulation so far uncovered that reproducibly and robustly slows the aging process in a mammalian species. DR has indeed provided insights into mammalian aging. It provides evidence consistent with oxidative damage playing an important role in aging. DR also has caused gerontologists to focus on the possible role of glycemia and insulinemia in aging. Finally, in accord with the genetic findings in invertebrate species, DR provides evidence that long-term stressors may have a major role in aging.

EDWARD J. MASORO

See also
  Animal and Plant Aging Models
  Life Expectancy
  Life Extension
  Nutrition

DISABILITY

The growing importance worldwide of understanding and responding to the relationship between aging and the need for assistance in maintaining personal independence is illustrated by recent developments in the United States. The National Research Council (1985) in the United States released a landmark report, *Injury in America,* that identified injury as the leading cause of death and disability among children and young adults. In fact, the report surprisingly identified injury as "the principal public health problem facing America" and focused on the number and quality of years lost because of injury. This loss was estimated to be greater than that attributable to cardiovascular disease and cancer combined. In 1991 an inquiry that built on the injury report, *Disability in America* (Pope & Tarlov), was released. This report, which was coincident with the Americans with Disabilities Act of 1990, focused not only on the prevention of disability but also on ways to minimize disability through interventions and, whenever possible, through reversing modifiable disability through rehabilitation.

The *Disability* report made a number of notable contributions to theory and research regarding disability. Conceptually, the report uses the World Health Organization's international classification strategy to clarify important distinctions among three related constructs—impairment, disability, and handicap. Impairment refers to some pathological condition (genetic flaw, a chronic or acute disease, or an injury) that potentially compromises the capacity of an individual to carry out essential physiological, psychological, or social tasks. Disability refers to a process that has as its likely consequence a compromise in capacity to function, that is, the actual inability to carry out essential personally and socially important tasks. Not all impairments are equally consequential in compromising an individual's performance. Clinicians and rehabilitation specialists repeatedly remind us that specific impairments do not necessarily produce the same level of disability, on average, for all individuals. That is why the attention of gerontologists and geriatricians tends to focus on functional disability, not just on impairment.

Handicap adds a distinctly social and environmental component to understanding why the relationship between impairment and disability is complex and variable. Whether and the extent to which an identified impairment is functionally disabling are contingent in part on social or environmental factors. Some disability, for example, is clearly created or exacerbated by social attitudes that stigmatize particular impairments, such as mental illness, retardation, disfigurement, and gross physical limitations. The degree of disability can be exaggerated both by the physical barriers built into everyday environments and by social rejection. Reduce social stigma or physical barriers, and impaired individuals become less handicapped and hence potentially less disabled. Rehabilitation specialists are also well aware of the personal dimensions of handicap and related disability. Individuals with socially reinforced low self-esteem and perceived lack of personal control of their lives are personally handicapped in their capacity to participate in and benefit from rehabilitation and hence in their potential for reducing disability.

The *Disability* report is also distinctive in its emphasis on the life course as well as its emphasis on process. Prevention and minimization of disability in childhood and young adulthood are obviously important. Gerontologists applaud such activities, recognizing that disease and disability prevention early in life benefit adults in their later years. The report, however, is explicit in addressing disability in later adulthood.

In a chapter in the report devoted specifically to exploring the relationship between chronic disease and aging, almost half of all persons of working age are noted to have one or more chronic conditions with the potential to impair functioning. An estimated 80% of older adults report a chronic condition, 40% report some form of activity limitation, and 17% report needing some assistance with basic activities of daily living (ADL), such as eating, dressing, and toileting.

In gerontology and geriatrics, interest in functional disability has competed with and tended to supplement, if not supplant, interest in health status and disease, in part because functional assessment lends itself to investigation by survey methods. But equally important, emphasis on functioning rather than disease is intended to "demedicalize" the disability process by stressing the social components of disability. The most popular and universally recognized standardized procedure for assessing and reporting functional status in later life uses the constructs of ADL and instrumental activities of daily living (IDAL). ADL, in its simplest terms, indexes self-care capacity (e.g., eating, toileting, and dressing). IADL indexes the capacity to deal with basic aspects of one's environment such as shopping, meal preparation, and financial management.

Wiener, Hanley, Clark, and Van Nostrand (1990) documented that, whereas estimates based on sample surveys vary substantially, the probability of having at least one ADL disability among adults in the United States is in the range of 3% to 5%. The observed variability in estimates, which may reflect error in measurement as well as population differences, is significant because it translates into significantly different estimates of compensatory services required. Hence, some concern among policymakers has been expressed about legislation that ties eligibility for services to some characterization of ADL disability, such as "3 or more ADL disabilities." Some suggestions have been made about conceptualizing disabilities among older adults differently, to distinguish basic ADL (self-care) disabilities, household ADL (approximating household management), and advanced ADL (activities requiring cognitive intactness (e.g., Wolinsky & Johnson, 1991). Systematic comparative research that would assess the similarities and differences in the distribution of disability among older adults in various countries remains to be done.

The National Long Term Care Survey (NLTCS) in the United States provides a distinctive and reasonably comprehensive illustration of ways in which large-scale longitudinal survey data can be used to document the extent and variety of functional disability in older populations and estimate how disability as a process is related to community care, institutionalization, and death as outcomes (Manton, 1988). NLTCS data demonstrate that disability is, in fact, a dynamic process that is age related but not simply explained by age. Gender, sex, ethnicity, socioeconomic status, and health status are demonstrably relevant explanatory variables. Manton's findings document that about two or three older persons were not functionally disabled at the first observation in 1982; about 6% were IADL-disabled only, 6% had one or two ADL disabilities, and 5.3% had three or more disabilities. Manton's analysis is distinctive in its inclusion of the differential risk of functional disability by medical conditions. Functional disability among older adults diagnosed with cancer or ischemic heart disease, for example, is relatively low compared with those presenting visual disorders, cognitive decline ("senility"), and arthritis. Manton's research also

documents that functioning is a dynamic process. A significant percentage of moderately and even significantly disabled older adults display an improved status over time when assessed longitudinally.

Experience in the United States indicates that education about disability process and its modifiability is important both for professional providers of preventive and rehabilitative services and for consumers. For a discussion of disability, comorbidity, and frailty in the older adult population, see Fried and Walston (1999).

GEORGE L. MADDOX

See also
  Activities of Daily Living
  Americans with Disabilities Act
  Rehabilitation

DISCOURSE MEMORY

The ability to comprehend and remember discourse is critical for effective functioning throughout the adult life span. Language is the conduit through which we gain information about the world and through which we establish and maintain connections in the social world. Therefore, an understanding of how discourse processing is compromised by age-related processing limitations and, alternatively, maintained through compensation, selection, and strategic self-regulation is an issue of critical importance. Research on discourse memory and aging has focused primarily on three issues:

1. Under what conditions are age differences in memory for discourse apparent?
2. Are there age differences in the quality of what is recalled?
3. What are the processing mechanisms underlying differences in the quantity and/or quality of recall?

Quantitative Age Differences

Although age-related memory declines for word lists and nonverbal material are typical in the literature, deficits in discourse memory are not consistently obtained. Properties of both the discourse and the task demands appear to influence the extent of age differences in discourse memory. First, conditions that optimize the ability to use the inherent structural properties of language mitigate or eliminate age deficits. For example, older adults seem to accrue the same benefit as the young from narrative and thematic schemas. This fact may contribute to the relative resistance of memory for real-world discourse memory to the effects of age-related processing limitations. Second, any factor that increases the processing load of the text is likely to exacerbate age deficits in subsequent memory performance. For example, variables that increase the rate at which idea units must be encoded (e.g., information density or speech rate) can also increase age differences in memory. Finally, the existence and extent of age differences may also depend on the nature of the retrieval task (e.g., free recall, summarization, or comprehension questions), though this latter issue has received little systematic treatment in the literature.

Age differences in discourse memory also appear to depend on verbal ability, with high-verbal individuals showing smaller age differences than their less verbal counterparts. Studies examining longitudinal change in text recall have raised the possibility that cross-sectional and longitudinal age effects may be differentially related to such individual differences.

Thus, although age deficits in the quantity of material remembered from text are often found, there are many exceptions. Existing literature suggests that the magnitude of age deficits may depend on characteristics of the subjects, the discourse, and the task requirements.

Qualitative Age Differences

It is important to know not only *how much* of the content older adults remember from discourse, relative to the young, but also whether they differ in the *kind* of information retained. This is sometimes measured in terms of the "levels effect," a higher level of recall for gist or thematically important information than for detail. The significance of the levels effect is that it suggests that the reader or listener is actively organizing and structuring the content of the discourse. To the extent that this

levels effect obtains for the old, it would suggest an age constancy in the ability to find meaning in discourse. In fact, research findings are mixed, sometimes demonstrating relatively selective recall for gist among older adults and sometimes not. One advantage of this approach is that recall as a function of level is based on a theoretically driven assignment of units to levels of importance, but its inability to yield a consistent phenomenon with respect to aging has weakened its contribution.

An alternative approach to this question is an empirical one in which the unit memorabilities of young and old are directly compared. In this approach, the unit of analysis is the text unit; average recall for each unit by the old (p[Recall/Old]) is plotted as a function of average recall by the young (p[Recall/Young]) to yield a relative memorability function. The correlation between these two variables is typically very high, indicating a large measure of age similarity in the rank ordering of recall probabilities. Furthermore, the slope of the relative memorability function provides an index of the age difference in the relative quality of recall: the higher the slope, the more disproportionate is the number of memorable units in the recall protocol of the old, relative to that of the young. Although the slope is rarely found to be greater than unity (indicating disproportionate recall of more memorable units by the old), the slope is often found to be 1 (indicating age constancy) and has been shown to decrease as a function of propositional density, unfamiliarity, speed of presentation, and length, variables that presumably reflect an increase in processing load. Thus, although there appears to be age preservation in the fundamental mechanisms in the way in which discourse is organized, high demands on memory may compromise the quality of recall just as it does the quantity of recall.

Finally, the quality of discourse memory may be assessed in terms of type and amount of material that is produced in the recall protocol that was not explicitly given in the to-be-remembered text. There are some suggestions in the literature that older adults produce more annotative elaborations that comment on the text rather than regenerate its content, as well as more metaphorical comments about the text's personal significance. Such age differences in quality of recall may reflect the impact of life-span contextualism on the way in which discourse understanding is approached.

Processing Mechanisms

Accounts of age differences in discourse memory have centered on understanding how aging might affect the component processes that translate the acoustic or written signal to rise to the mental representation. Generally speaking, discourse processing is thought to occur in a sequence of cycles. At each step, the phonological or orthographic information of the current language segment is decoded, the decontextualized meanings of individual words are accessed, the relationships among these concepts are coded in the form of idea units (or propositions), idea units are organized so as to achieve coherence, and all of this is integrated with the residual representation from whatever came earlier in the discourse. This integration process involves not only finding interconnections among ideas but also instantiating the meanings of words in context and constructing the appropriate anaphoric inferences (i.e., understanding that a concept is being referenced again even if pronominally or with other lexical items). This processing is attributed to working memory, a limited-capacity buffer that transforms input and stores the products of these transformations across input cycles. The product is a mental representation of the content of the discourse (the "textbase"), as well as of the more general situation described by the discourse (the "situation model"). Although the textbase is generally explicitly contained in the discourse, the situation model is derived from an integration of the textbase with the reader or listener's world knowledge. Presumably good memory performance depends on both facets of this representation being complete and coherent.

There is general consensus that word-level activation of meaning and the instantiation concepts in the context of discourse remain intact into late life. To the extent that it has been assessed, there also appear to be no age differences in situation model construction and updating—for example, in the interpretation of the more subtle nuances of verb aspect and tense, in the repair of spatial and causal coherence breaks, and in the sensitivity to goal structure and emotional tone that contribute to the situation model. Explanations of the nature of age deficits focus on the resource-consuming nature of textbase construction. One hypothesis is that aging brings a reduction in the capacity of working memory. Such a hypothesis can account for the increased age differences in memory performance already described, as well as the difficulty that older adults have in achieving anaphoric inferences when memory load is increased. A derivative of this theoretical account is that older adults are less likely to self-initiate the processing in working memory needed to construct an effective representation under some conditions, particularly in on-line organization. Yet another derivative of the working memory hypothesis is that processing operations within working memory may be slower; such slowing would reduce functional capacity and thus share predictive overlap with the working-memory-capacity account. An additional hypothesis is that aging brings a change in the effectiveness of the inhibitory mechanisms that regulate the contents of working memory. Such changes would also reduce functional capacity because processing capacity is presumed to be devoted to off-target information at a cost to the effective processing of target material. Thus, this hypothesis can account for all the data that other versions of the working-memory hypothesis can, but makes the additional prediction that older adults will have difficulty revising an established text representation in light of new information, a prediction that has garnered some support. The search for a coherent theoretical account for the complex pattern of quantitative and qualitative age differences in discourse memory continues.

Fertile ground for new research includes the extent to which age differences in discourse memory are mitigated by domain knowledge, reliance on the situation model, the selective allocation of processing resources, and metacognitive factors. For more comprehensive reviews of this literature, see Kemper (1992); Radvansky (1999); Stine, Soederberg, and Morrow (1996); and Wingfield and Stine-Morrow (2000).

ELIZABETH A. L. STINE-MORROW
DANIELLE D. GAGNE

See also
Memory and Memory Theory

DISCRIMINATION
See
Age Segregation
Ageism

Attitudes
Equal Employment Opportunity Commission
United States Commission on Civil Rights

DISEASE POSTPONEMENT
See
Compression of Morbidity: Disease Postponement

DISENGAGEMENT

Cumming and Henry (1961) developed the disengagement theory of aging from cross-sectional data gathered for the Kansas City Study of Adult Life. The theory posits withdrawal from social involvement because of the awareness of the shortness of life, a perception of a decreasing life space, and lessening of adaptive energy. Because this withdrawal is intrinsic, in the sense of transcending events external to people, it is inevitable. In turn, because it is a mutual severing of ties between persons and their society, disengagement does not lessen morale.

Some members of the Kansas City team, however, questioned the findings and the theory. Concern about the measure of morale led Neugarten, Havighurst, and Tobin (1961) to develop a morale measure more appropriate to old age. Tobin and Neugarten (1961) found that disengagement was associated with less life satisfaction, a finding supporting the activity theory of aging. Next, adding personality measures revealed diverse patterns of aging that suggested continuity rather than the discontinuity inherent to disengagement theory (Havighurst, Neugarten, & Tobin, 1968). Concurrently, Maddox (1964) argued for longitudinal studies to determine what accounts for lessened disengagement. Possibly social precedes psychological disengagement, and personality influences involvement. Later, Hochschild (1975) questioned whether disengagement was a historical artifact descriptive of aging in the 1950s, when older people were more likely to feel discarded because of public attitudes and policies.

A flurry of research through the 1970s revealed modest associations between greater engagement and morale. Meanwhile, studies of personality traits and the self supported continuity theory. By the 1990s, after nearly 30 years of research, the consensus was that disengagement is neither natural nor inevitable. Lessened involvement may occur from losses of opportunities, of others, and of vigor; and continuity seemed more normative than discontinuity.

C. L. Johnson and Barer (1992), from findings of their 85+ Study, revitalized disengagement. In advanced aging, losses of others and of vitality cause disengaging from previous involvements but with a persistence of a sense of control and the preservation of the self. This formulation makes disengagement salient to only the oldest old, posits a contraction imposed by losses, and assumes the continuity of the self.

SHELDON S. TOBIN

See also
Activity Theory
Continuity Theory
Kansas City Studies of Adult Life

DISPOSABLE SOMA THEORY

The disposable soma theory asks how best an organism should allocate its metabolic resources (primarily energy) between, on the one hand, keeping itself going from one day to the next (maintenance) and, on the other hand, producing progeny to secure the continuance of its genes when it itself has died (reproduction).

No species is immune to sources of extrinsic mortality due to hazards of the environment, such as predation, starvation, and disease. These hazards limit the average survival time, even if aging does not occur. It follows that maintenance is needed only to an extent that ensures that the body (soma) remains intrinsically in sound condition until an age when most individuals will have died from accidental causes. In fact, a greater investment in maintenance is a disadvantage because it consumes resources that in terms of natural selection are better used for reproduction. The theory concludes that the optimum course is to invest fewer resources in the maintenance of somatic tissues than would be necessary for indefinite somatic survival.

The disposable soma theory is named for its analogy with disposable goods, which are manufactured with limited investment in durability, on the principle that they have a short expected duration of use. The theory applies to any species that has a clear distinction between soma and germ line (see Kirkwood & Cremer, 1982).

Central to the disposable soma theory is the idea that maintenance involves energy costs. Although it is not yet possible to detail all of the costs of maintenance, there is evidence that the overall maintenance cost is substantial. Basal metabolism accounts for the major part of the energy budget of a typical organism and is largely concerned with maintenance of one kind or another. In particular, there is an extensive network of intracellular processes (DNA repair, antioxidant defenses, macromolecular synthesis, etc.) whose operation is essential for maintaining homeostasis. Each of these processes requires energy.

In addition to explaining why aging occurs, the disposable soma theory suggests how the genetic control of life span is arranged and how different species have evolved different life spans.

Natural selection operates on the genes that regulate key aspects of somatic cell maintenance in such a way as to secure the optimum balance between surviving long enough and spending too much on survival. The "set point" of a maintenance function determines the average period of longevity assured. As a specific example, consider the protection afforded by antioxidant enzymes. If it is supposed that the exposure of the cell to oxidative damage is constant but the level of production of antioxidant enzymes is increased, then the rate at which oxidative damage accumulates is reduced, whereas the energy cost associated with antioxidant defenses rises. The rate of accumulation of oxidative damage determines the average length of time taken before the damage reaches harmful levels and, hence, longevity.

Now, if it is recalled that it is extrinsic mortality that influences the strategy of limiting the investment in somatic maintenance, it may be seen that it is the level of environmental risk that provides the basis of selection for a longer or shorter intrinsic life span. A species subject to high environmental risk will do better to invest in rapid and prolific

reproduction at the expense of somatic maintenance, whereas a species that has a low level of environmental risk will tend to do the reverse.

Predictions of the disposable soma theory include the following: (1) Longevity should be positively correlated with levels of somatic maintenance, an example of which may be found in a comparative study by Kapahi, Boulton, and Kirkwood (1999); (2) multiple maintenance mechanisms contribute to aging and longevity (this is because the theory applies with equal force to each of the different processes that forms a part of the somatic maintenance network); and (3) the accumulation of somatic defects that lead eventually to aging begins early in life, possibly soon after the differentiation of somatic cell lineages from the germ line. The disposable soma theory also supports the concept that intrinsic chance, acting through a variety of stochastic mechanisms, contributes to the observed variability of the senescent phenotype (Finch & Kirkwood, 2000).

The disposable soma theory complements the mutation accumulation theory of Medawar (1952) and the pleiotropic genes theory of Williams (1957) by making specific predictions about the nature of the mechanisms that cause aging (see also Kirkwood, 1999; Kirkwood & Rose, 1991).

THOMAS B. L. KIRKWOOD

See also
Evolutionary Theory

DISRUPTIVE BEHAVIORS

Disruptive behaviors are observable actions that have the potential for or are perceived by caregivers as (1) endangering the person or others; (2) stressing, frightening, or frustrating the person, the caregiver, or others; and (3) socially unacceptable or isolating (Mace, 1990). Disruptive behaviors represent a broad range of actions including aggression (i.e., indicating some specific verbal or physical action) or agitation (i.e., an interpretation of some behavioral actions).

Disruptive behaviors exhibited by older adults in both long-term care and community settings present a significant problem for both nursing staff and family and informal caregivers (Burgio, Scilley, Hardin, Janosky, Bonino, & Slater, 1994; Chrisman, Tabar, Whall, & Booth, 1991; Cohen-Mansfield, Marx, & Werner, 1992; D. E. Everitt, Fields, Soumerai, & Avorn, 1991). Some of the consequences of these behaviors include (1) stress experienced by both residents and staff (Cohn, Horgas, & Marsiske, 1994); (2) decreased quality of resident care because of the use of physical or pharmacological restraints (Frengley & Mior, 1986; L. J. Robbins, Boyko, Land, Cooper, & Jahnigen, 1987); (3) economic consequences, including injuries, property damage, staff burnout, absenteeism, and turnover (Semala, Palla, Poddig, & Brauner, 1994; W. D. Spector & Jackson, 1994); (4) emotional costs to the disruptive person through social isolation (Ryden, 1988); and (5) increased incidence of falls (Cohen-Mansfield, Werner, Marx, & Freedman, 1991; Gilley, Wilson, Bennett, Bernard, & Fox, 1991).

Estimates suggest approximately 60% to 80% of all nursing home residents are cognitively impaired, and the incidence of disruptive behavior is higher in these residents (Aronson, Post, & Guastadisegni, 1993; Cohen-Mansfield, Billing, Lipson, Rosenthal, & Pawlson, 1990; National Center for Health Statistics, 1985; Reichel, 1989; Teri, Larson, & Reifler, 1988). Consistently, research studies have demonstrated an association between the degree of disruptive behavior and the level of cognitive impairment in older adults with dementia. Mace (1990) and others (Cariaga, Burgio, Flynn, & Martin, 1991; V. K. Lee, 1991; J. M. Richter, Bottenberg, & Roberto, 1993) provide clinical support for these findings by observing that nursing home residents with behavior problems lose insight and self-control but often retain the language and/or motor skills to carry out the behaviors.

The body of research on physical, psychological, and/or social correlates of disruptive behaviors continues to grow. Although some investigators have found no significant relationship between aggression and cognitive status (Bridges-Parlet, Knopman, & Thompson, 1994), most studies have demonstrated that cognitive impairment is associated with some behavior problems (A. Burns, Jacoby, & Levy, 1990; Cooper, Mungas, & Weiler, 1990; M. Jackson, Drugovich, Fretwell, Spector, Sternberg, et al., 1989). Several studies have linked decreased cognitive status to specific behaviors, such as wan-

dering (Algase, 1992), pacing (Cohen-Mansfield, Werner, Marx, & Freedman, 1991), screaming (Cohen-Mansfield, Billing, Lipson, Rosenthal, & Pawlson, 1990), and assaultiveness (Swearer, Drachman, O'Donnell, & Mitchell, 1988). Cohen-Mansfield and colleagues (1990) reported that cognitive impairment was associated with both physically aggressive and nonaggressive behaviors but to a lesser extent with verbally aggressive behaviors. Another investigator found that those who engaged in disruptive vocalizations (including screaming and verbal aggression) were more likely to be diagnosed with dementia than were those who did not but were not significantly more impaired on cognitive testing (Cariaga, Burgio, Flynn, & Martin, 1991). A more recent study revealed that the frequency and duration of disruptive vocalizations was significantly negatively correlated with cognitive deterioration (Burgio, Scilley, Hardin, Janosky, Bonino, & Slater, 1994). Gilley, Wilson, Bennett, Bernard, and Fox (1991) determined that age at onset and extrapyramidal symptoms modified the relationship between cognitive impairment and behavioral disturbance.

An early 1980s study found that psychoactive drugs were used on a regular basis to treat 58% of the subjects with serious behavior problems in a nursing home, although only 14.8% had received a psychiatric consultation (G. Zimmer, Watson, & Treat, 1984). Ryden, Bossenmaier, and McLachlan (1991) reported that psychotropic drugs were given to 68.5% of the observed residents and that those residents had significantly higher aggression scores. Cohen-Mansfield, Billing, Lipson, Rosenthal, and Paulson (1990) observed that residents who received more major tranquilizers screamed more often than those who did not. Cariago and colleagues (Cariago, Burgio, Flynn, & Martin, 1991) noted that nursing home residents who engaged in disruptive vocalizations received significantly more neuroleptics than did those who did not, and Kolanowski and colleagues (Kolanowski, Hurwitz, Taylor, Evans, & Strumpf, 1994) reported a significant correlation between psychotropic drug use and agitated psychomotor behavior.

Kolanowski, Hurwitz, Taylor, Evans, and Strumpf (1994) operationalized communication difficulty as disruptive behavior itself. Other studies have considered communication as a correlate of disruptive behavior, and they have been increasingly linked. Cohen-Mansfield and Marx (1988) used communication as an indicator of social functioning, a dimension of depression. Poor ability to communicate was significantly related to general aggressive behavior and physically nonaggressive behavior. Ability to communicate effectively was positively correlated with verbally agitated behaviors such as complaining and negativism. Meddaugh (1990) found that the aggressive group in her study was generally nonverbal, compared with the nonaggressive group, who retained some verbal skills.

Inconsistent findings on the relationship between the time of day and occurrence of disruptive behaviors point out the need for further research in this area. Cohen-Mansfield and colleagues (Cohen-Mansfield, Billing, Lipson, Rosenthal, & Pawlson, 1990) observed that screaming occurred significantly more often on the evening shift. Burgio, Scilley, Hardin, Janosky, Bonino, and Slater (1994) found an upward trend in the occurrence of disruptive vocalizations across the day shift, but Cariaga, Burgio, Flynn, and Martin (1991) noted that disruptive vocalizations occurred most often upon awakening in the morning, before meals, and before bathing. Malone, Thompson, and Goodwin (1993) concluded that the majority of aggressive behaviors in nursing home residents occurred mainly during the evening and day shifts. These findings were confirmed by C. Beck, Baldwin, Modlin, and Lewis (1990).

Although disruptive behaviors in older adults, regardless of etiology, have received increasing attention in the past decade, from both researchers and clinicians, many contradictory findings remain among the significant correlates, such as the relationship between disruptive behaviors and functional ability, social support, gender, age, sleep patterns, premorbid personality traits, and depression. Greater emphasis is being placed on nonpharmacological approaches to disruptive behavior patterns in the elderly, including positive interaction responses from the caregivers (Burgener & Barton, 1991), the use of touch (C. Beck & Shue, 1994; Cariaga, Burgio, Flynn, & Martin, 1991), positive reinforcement schedules (Brink, 1980; Vaccaro, 1988), exercise (McGrowder-Lin & Bhatt, 1988), environmental changes (Negley & Manley, 1990), and staff training (Mentes & Ferrario, 1989). The impact of these and other behavioral, social, and

environmental interventions on the disruptive behaviors of the elderly is still unclear. Further studies of specific behaviors and the individualization of interventions for older adults in a variety of settings are still needed. The impact on the caregiver, although receiving some research and clinical attention, has not been fully explored.

BEVERLY A. BALDWIN

See also
Delirium
Restraints: Physical/Chemical
Wandering

DIVORCE

The divorce revolution of the past three decades has touched the lives of older adults in a number of ways. First, a small but growing proportion of divorces involve older individuals in long-term marriages. Twelve percent of the half-million divorces granted in the United States in 1988 occurred in marriages lasting 20 or more years. Men age 40 and over were involved in 33% of the divorce cases in 1988, whereas 25% of the cases involved women of the same ages. Later-life divorces, however, are concentrated primarily among persons in their 40s and early 50s, as no more than 6.5% of divorces in 1988 occurred to persons over age 55 (National Center for Health Statistics, 1991). On the basis of age-specific divorce rates for the early 1980s, Uhlenberg, Cooney, and Boyd (1990) estimate that between 11% and 18% of women who reach age 40 in an intact first marriage will eventually divorce.

A second way divorce influences older adults' lives is through its long-term effects. Because the majority of divorces occur during young adulthood and remarriage rates have declined sharply since 1970, an increasing number of individuals are arriving at later life in the divorced status. Consequently, the distribution of marital statuses in later life is likely to shift dramatically in coming decades. Over 20% of women born in the late 1950s are expected to be divorced when they reach ages 65 to 69 in 2025; this compares with only about 5% of that age group in 1975 and 15% in 1985. At the same time, the proportion of women who will be widows at this age is expected to drop substantially, from about 35% in 1975 to less than 20% in 2025 (Uhlenberg, Cooney, & Boyd, 1990). Similar changes are anticipated for men. Uhlenberg (1990) projected that four times as many men ages 55 to 64 would be divorced as widowed by 2000. Such shifts may have severe economic and family life implications for future cohorts.

The effects of divorce in later life, as well as the life-course implications of experiencing divorce in earlier adulthood, have received much recent research attention. One of the most consistent findings in this literature is the severe negative impact of divorce on women's economic well-being. In fact, divorce appears to have stronger socioeconomic effects for women than widowhood has; compared with their widowed peers, divorced women age 65+ are more likely to be employed yet less likely to own a home and be residentially independent. Their incomes also place them closer to the poverty threshold than do those of widows (Cooney, 1989; Uhlenberg, Cooney, & Boyd, 1990). In general, the economic implications of divorce for men are less noticeable and not necessarily negative (G. J. Duncan & Hoffman, 1985). Yet Fethke (1989) argues that both divorced men and divorced women will face economic losses in later life as a result of reduced savings by couples anticipating divorce, shifting assets out of marital property, and the postdivorce division of pensions and loss of insurance benefits.

Later-life family relationships also are altered by divorce, particularly for men. Ever-divorced older men have lower rates of in-person contact with their adult children than do their never-divorced counterparts (Bulcroft & Bulcroft, 1991; Cooney & Uhlenberg, 1990), and they are less likely to view their offspring as potential sources of support in times of need (Cooney & Uhlenberg, 1990). Similar negative influences of divorce on levels of mother-child contact and support are not found consistently (Bulcroft & Bulcroft, 1991).

Finally, divorce influences older adults' lives when their adult offspring divorce. Specific effects largely depend on the gender of the divorced children and their custody status. Maternal grandparents, whose daughters are typically custodial parents, generally have more contact with their grandchildren and provide more support to them than do maternal grandparents whose children are not

divorced. Paternal grandparents, in contrast, tend to report dramatically reduced levels of interaction with their grandchildren following a middle-generation divorce (Cherlin & Furstenberg, 1986). In terms of the support and services older parents receive from children, however, there appear to be few differences based on children's divorce status. Older parents of divorced children do not consistently report noticeably less contact, affective closeness, or assistance from their offspring than do parents whose children have not divorced (Eggebeen & Hogan, 1990; Spitze, Logan, Deane, & Zerger, 1994). What remains to be seen is how divorce will affect older adults when successive generations in the same family have experienced it.

Divorce as an issue in later life largely disappeared as a focus of gerontological research in the 1990s.

TERESA M. COONEY

See also
  Family
  Marital Status
  Women: Changing Status

DNA
See
  Deoxyribonucleic Acid (DNA) Repair Process

DOCTOR-PATIENT RELATIONSHIPS

As older adults represent a larger proportion of our population, and include the largest segment of those seeking health and medical care for chronic and disabling conditions, the relationships between providers and clients in health and medical care settings become more important. Riley and Bond (1983) were among the first to suggest that the apparent increase in demand for chronic care for older adults derives principally from the "unprecedented and rapid extension of life expectancy," not from the natural association of old age with these conditions (p. 243). Rather than viewing this situation as presenting a range of intractable and inevitable problems, Riley and Bond see the situation as presenting a whole new set of challenges to find productive and meaningful roles for older adults in families, in communities, and in the workforce. Moreover, the present era challenges health care provider organizations to find more effective ways of communicating with older adult clients and their families, and to find ways of involving older adults as active participants in their own care and self-management of chronic or disabling conditions.

Communication Versus Therapeutic Effectiveness

One of the most important findings of recent research on the relationships between doctors and their patients is that patient complaints are most often related to problems of communication, not issues related to the technical competency of the service provider (Stewart, Brown, Boon, Galajda, Meredith, & Sangster, 1999). Satisfaction, however, is a measure of outcome from the patient's perspective. If the focus is on adherence to medical recommendations, a measure of outcome of importance to the provider, there is substantial evidence that effective communication between provider and patient enhances the probability of patient adherence. Moreover, adherence can have important effects in terms of patient experiences of pain, symptom occurrence, anxiety, functional status, and physical measures of health outcomes. When communication is effective between providers and patients, patients tend to share similar views of the necessity and feasibility of medication (and other aspects of therapeutic) adherence, and patients have a greater sense of self-efficacy in performing necessary self-management skills. Osman (1997) points out that patients do not always believe their doctors' communications about potential side effects of particular medications, or the likely effects of irregular patterns of medication adherence. Most patients dislike taking any kind of medication on a regular basis. For this reason, evidence suggests that patients who experience difficulty in achieving "control" of such conditions as asthma, diabetes, and hypertension often are the ones with a very chaotic self-management style. If health care providers and patients can communicate more effectively, the

probability increases for both patient satisfaction and therapeutic adherence.

The Current Context of Doctor-Patient Encounters

The present era has brought forth a new dimension of provider-patient relationships in which both health professionals and patients expect a larger and wider scope of involvement of patients (and their families) in making complex diagnostic and therapeutic decisions. Terms such as *therapeutic partnership* have been used to describe the intention of creating a feeling of collaboration between doctors and their patients with regard to clinical decision making and the management of illness and its sequelae. The sharing of responsibility for clinically important decisions necessitates a higher level of communication effectiveness than would otherwise be either feasible or essential. The environment within which health care professionals are encountering their patients is very different than even a decade ago. Laypersons are now widely exposed to all sorts of health and medical information not previously available to nonprofessionals. Television and other media are now marketing prescription drugs directly to patients (direct-to-consumer, or DTC, marketing) with the encouragement to "ask your doctor." Patient questions to providers stimulated by advertising may lead to friction between doctors and patients, possibly as an outgrowth of defensiveness on the part of health care professionals who may not yet have information about the pharmaceuticals or health care products being advertised. One recent study found that a sizeable fraction of patients would react negatively if their physician refused to provide a prescription for a drug advertised in the general media (Bell, Wilkes, & Kravitz, 1999). Added to this are the effects of press coverage of medical and health care events (e.g., malpractice court decisions and disciplinary actions by local boards of medicine, dentistry, and other health professions, and accusations of denial of access to needed services within particular types of managed care plans), all of which heighten the tension of both patients and physicians at the time of a clinical encounter over both the substance and the motivation for communication between them.

Inattention to Patient Preferences and Values

One aspect of doctor-patient relations typically receiving only scant attention by professionals or health care organizations is the matter of patient values. Even when discussing such value-laden issues as end-of-life decisions, a matter requiring older adult or disabled patients to clarify their wishes and values to their family members, close friends, and physicians, recent evidence suggests patient values are essentially not discussed by physicians when covering these topics in their encounters with their patients. Tulsky, Fischer, Rose, and Arnold (1998) audiotaped 56 physician-patient encounters involving the discussion of end-of-life choices that were intended to culminate in the completion of written advance directives for this sample of persons 65 years of age or older. Results indicated that physicians were speaking two thirds of the time in these encounters, which averaged 5.6 minutes in duration. In 91% of cases, physicians used examples of dire circumstances or scenarios in which most patients would not want to be treated. Patients' values were rarely explored in detail. Arrangements for surrogate decision making were part of the discussion in 88% of cases. In most cases, the way these discussions took place ended with patients being informed about the meaning and significance of advance directives, a principal objective of these encounters, but the patients' attitudes and values about the way in which uncertainty might affect their decisions about end-of-life medical care were not explored in a way that would make these discussions helpful for making future decisions in this regard. This study raises the question of how likely it is that the quality of doctor-patient communication could be changed through provider training in communication skills when only 5.6 minutes are set aside in any clinical encounter for discussions of topics of this importance involving deep-seated values and attitudes of patients (Pascoe, 1999). As managed care and other health system changes have so constricted the available time for direct physician encounters with patients, it is probably unreasonable to expect that the dyadic relationship between provider and patient be able to deal with anything other than the most pressing, often acute, illness problem.

The Scope of Doctor-Patient Relationships

One of the more critical areas of research into the dynamics and content of doctor-patient relationships concerns the interest, even the willingness, of patients to have the physicians that are attending to their physical care needs also address other concerns related to their social or mental health. Sherbourne, Sturm, and Wells (1999) report data from 16,689 consecutive adult outpatient visits in 46 primary care clinics operated by managed care plans in five states where patients were asked to complete a 12-item health-related quality-of-life (HRQL) instrument and to express preferences for their current health status based on conventional utility measures. Within the 12-item HRQL instrument, physical health contributes significantly to patient preferences. However, patients also assign high utilities to mental and social health values. Patients with chronic conditions were likely to express strong utility weighting for mental health outcomes. This study reinforces the need to find a way, within the context of doctor-patient relationships, of giving greater attention to the "balance" of concerns of patients for physical, mental, and social health.

In conclusion, although the traditional issues of physician communication skills, patient adherence, and satisfaction remain the dominant themes of the discussion of doctor-patient relationships, there have been several important changes in the context of these relationships in the contemporary period that need to be taken into account. As older adults increase in number and in the proportion of time and resources they will demand from health and medical care providers, these contextual factors will need to be given greater consideration, even as these traditional themes drive the research agenda in this area.

GORDON H. DeFRIESE

See also
Adherence
Geriatric Health

DRUG INTERACTIONS

A drug-drug interaction refers to the modification of the therapeutic or toxic effect of one drug by the prior or concurrent administration of another drug. A drug-nutrient interaction relates to the circumstance in which a food or nutrient alters an individual's response to a drug or in which a drug interferes with an individual's nutrition. Drug-drug or drug-nutrient interactions result from alterations in pharmacokinetic and pharmacodynamic properties of the drug due to the presence of the other drug or nutrient. The pharmacokinetic interactions may be at the level of (1) absorption, (2) distribution, (3) metabolism, or (4) excretion. The pharmacodynamic interactions may occur when drugs with similar pharmacological effects produce an additive or synergistic response, or, conversely, drugs with opposing pharmacological effects may reduce the response to one or both drugs. The drugs may act at the same or different receptor sites located in organs such as the heart, blood vessels, and brain.

Drug interactions are commonly seen in elderly people owing to the large number of prescription and over-the-counter drugs used by this age group. The population age 65 and over consumes 35% of prescription drugs in the United States (Kasper, 1982) but makes up only 12% of the population (Health Care Financing Administration, 1990). Surveys indicate that multiple drug use by elderly people may range from more than four drugs in an ambulatory care setting to eight or more in nursing homes (see review by Tumer, Scarpace, & Lowenthal, 1992). The increased number of medications being consumed by elderly people is closely related to the increased prevalence of disease conditions warranting treatment and hospitalization in this age group (Carbonin, Pahor, Bernabei, & Sgaradari, 1991; Grymonpre, Mitenko, Sitar, Aold, & Montgomery, 1988). Because the occurrence of adverse drug interactions is known to increase with the number of drugs prescribed (Kellay & McCrae, 1973), the three to seven times higher risk for adverse drug reactions in elderly people is not surprising (Goldberg & Roberts, 1983; Gurwitz & Avorn, 1991).

The potential for drug interactions in later life owing to alterations in pharmacokinetics has been reviewed extensively (Block, 1983; Nolan & O'Malley, 1992; Sloan, 1992; Tsujimoto, Hashimoto, & Hoffman, 1989; Vestal, Cusak, Crowley, & Loi, 1993).

Pharmacodynamic changes, although present, are less well studied or described in the elderly.

Homeostatic mechanisms to compensate for adverse drug effects are altered and contribute to the increased potential for drug interaction. The drugs most often involved in drug interactions are diuretics, nonsteroidal anti-inflammatory drugs, benzodiazepines, antiarrhythmics, cardiac glycosides, antihypertensive drugs, oral antidiabetics, and analgesics. These drug interactions may result in malaise, orthostatic hypotension, loss of consciousness, amnesia, confusion, renal insufficiency, and digestive problems (LeJeunne & Hughes, 1995).

Drug use by the aged could result in nutritional deficiencies and may well have serious consequences insofar as drug safety and efficacy for elderly people are concerned (Prendergast, 1989). Undernutrition of elderly people can alter drug pharmacokinetics.

Some examples of drug-drug and drug-nutrition interactions related to pharmacokinetic changes occurring in older people are described below.

Alteration of gastrointestinal absorption of a drug can be influenced by anticholingeric drugs that prolong gastric emptying time and retard movements of certain drugs to their main site of absorption, the small bowel. As a result, concomitantly administered drugs, such as levodopa (used in the treatment of Parkinson's disease), will be slowly absorbed, and this will influence their therapeutic effect. Drug-drug interactions can also take place in the gastrointestinal lumen and interfere with drug absorption, as illustrated by the decreased oral absorption of antibiotics such as ciprofloxacin when taken concurrently with aluminum- or magnesium-containing antacids (Sloan, 1992).

Reduced food intake in the elderly may be further compromised by drugs that impair appetite and absorption. Anticonvulsants and other drugs that induce hepatic microsomal enzymes accelerate vitamin D metabolism and aggravate postmenopausal osteoporosis. Acid-inhibiting agents increase achlorhydria and reduce vitamin B_{12} absorption. Renal clearance of acidic drugs such as acetylsalicylic acid and barbituric acid, which is impaired at old age, is further reduced by high doses of vitamin C. Vitamin B_6 reduces the therapeutic effect of L-dopa (Schumann, 1999).

A drug bound to plasma protein is pharmacologically inactive, whereas unbound drug molecules in plasma are free to equilibrate with the receptor site, storage sites, metabolic processes, and renal excretory mechanisms. Displacement of a highly bound drug from inactivating binding sites can produce a pharmacologically important increase in the unbound active portion. For example, nonsteroidal anti-inflammatory drugs (NSAIDs) are highly bound to serum albumin and are among the most prescribed drugs for elderly patients. Alterations in serum albumin due to aging or poor nutrition may result in higher free NSAID levels in the blood, and NSAIDs have the potential to displace other important drugs commonly given to older people (Girgis & Brooks, 1994).

A drug may stimulate the metabolism of another drug. For example, a larger than usual dose of warfarin is required to produce the desired level of anticoagulant effect when a patient is also given phenobarbital, owing to this drug's capacity to induce warfarin metabolism in the liver.

Several reports of drug interactions induced by clarithromycin (a macrolide antibiotic) with digoxin and with warfarin have been published. Previously, case reports of macrolide-associated interactions mainly involved erythromycin, but more recent ones have implicated clarithromycin. The interaction between clarithromycin and warfarin is thought to occur from an inhibition of the cytochrome P450 drug-metabolizing system. Clarithromycin is thought to cause digoxin toxicity by an alteration of the digoxin-metabolizing gut flora, thereby causing an increase in the digoxin concentration in susceptible individuals (Gooderham, Bolli, & Fernandez, 1999).

Three components of grapefruit juice (naringin/naringenin, scopletin, and umbelliferone) have been shown to increase the oral bioavailability of coumarin (Bourian, Runkel, Krisp, Tegtmeier, Fredudenstine, & Legrum, 1999).

Theophylline is commonly used for the treatment of respiratory disease, but the metabolism of theophylline is reduced in elderly people. Because theophylline has a narrow therapeutic range, the concurrent use of drugs capable of reducing theophylline metabolism might result in serious toxicity (Vestal, Cusack, Crowley, & Loi, 1993). Nonprescription doses of cimetidine have the potential to produce small changes in theophylline concentrations during steady-state dosing with the sustain-release form of the drug (Nix, Di Cicco, Miller, Boyle, Boike, Zariffa, et al., 1999).

Cigarette smoking in elderly people may affect drug therapy by both pharmacokinetic and pharmacodynamic mechanisms. The mechanism involved in most interactions between cigarette smoking and drugs involves the induction of metabolism. Drugs for which induced metabolism because of cigarette smoking may have clinical consequence include theophylline, caffeine, tacrine, imipramine, haloperidol, pentazocine, propranolol, flecainide, and estradiol. Pharmacodynamic interactions also have been described. Cigarette smoking is associated with a lesser magnitude of blood pressure and heart rate lowering during treatment with beta-blockers, less sedation from benzodiazepines, and less analgesia from some opioids, most likely reflecting the effects of the stimulant actions of nicotine (Zevin & Benowitz, 1999).

The nonsedating antihistamines show a diversity of fates in the body and the parent drugs, and metabolites may differ in their biological properties. Clinically significant interactions with inhibitors of cytochrome P450 have been reported primarily for terfenadine, which has the potential for cardiac toxicity and is metabolized to fexofenadine, an antihistamine without cardiac effects. Reduction in cytochrome P450 activity in older people caused by aging or polypharmacy may result in increased amounts of terfenadine and increased potential for drug-induced cardiotoxicity. Astemizole shares many of these characteristics, and important safety-related interactions are likely. Loratadine undergoes extensive metabolism so that pharmacokinetic interactions could occur, but they would be of little clinical importance because of the lack of cardiac activity of the parent drug and its metabolites (Renwick, 1999).

Three selective serotonin reuptake inhibitors (SSRIs)—fluoxetine, fuvoxamine, and sertraline—appear to affect the pharmacokinetics of promazine, a phenothiazine antipsychotic. All three SSRIs administered chronically in pharmacological doses increase the concentrations of promazine in the blood plasma and brain under experimental conditions by inhibiting different metabolic pathways of the neuroleptic. Assuming that similar interactions occur in elderly humans, lower doses of phenotiazines should be considered when one of the above antidepressants is to be given jointly (Daniel, Syrek, & Wojcikowski, 1999).

Midazolam, a hypnotic agent, requires lower doses to produce sedation in the elderly individual. This is due to pharmacodynamic rather than pharmacokinetic changes (Albrecht, Ihmsen, Hering, Geisslinger, Dingemanse, Schwilden, et al., 1999).

Renal function declines from middle to old age. Therefore, drugs that are primarily excreted through the kidneys will be retained longer in elderly patients, and reduced doses or less frequent administration is necessary. Drugs that compete for the reduced numbers of active renal secretion sites in the elderly kidney can produce dramatic elevations in plasma drug concentration. For example, quinidine can produce a 90% increase in digoxin levels by competing for renal secretion and displacing digoxin from binding sites in the tissues (Tsang & Gerson, 1990). Given digoxin's small therapeutic index, elderly patients on digoxin and quindine may be at risk for digoxin toxicity.

Concomitant administration of rifampin (an antibiotic) reduces digoxin plasma concentrations substantially after oral administration. The rifampin-digoxin interaction appears to occur largely at the level of the intestine. The contribution of P-glycoprotein (P-gp) located in the gastrointestinal epithelium to digoxin elimination through the intestine has been suggested. Induction of intestinal P-gp by rifampin could explain this new type of drug-drug interaction (Greiner, Eichelbaum, Fritz, Kreichgauer, von Richter, Zundler, et al., 1999). The importance of this type of interaction in the elderly needs to be determined.

JAY ROBERTS
DAVID L. SNYDER

See also
Drug Reactions
Medication Misuse and Abuse
Pharmacodynamics

DRUG MISUSE AND ABUSE
See
Medication Misuse and Abuse

DRUG REACTIONS

Drug reaction, or adverse drug reaction (ADR), refers to an unintended, untoward, harmful, or noxious response to a drug occurring at dosage levels used in humans for disease prevention, diagnosis, or therapy. There are two classes of drug action: the idiosyncratic and those due to the drug's known actions. ADRs are more common in elderly patients because of polypharmacy (Lamy, 1990; Tumer, Scarpace, & Lowenthal, 1992), inappropriate drug prescribing by physicians (Willcox, Himmelstein, & Woolhandler, 1994), and changes in pharmacokinetics and pharmacodynamics due to declining organ reserve, reduction in homeostatic mechanisms, and multiple pathologies. Other reasons for increased ADRs in elderly patients include failure to test drugs in elderly subjects to determine the proper dosage and side effects in this age group, prescriptions from multiple physicians (leading to polypharmacy and increased drug reactions and interactions), medication errors and noncompliance, and nutritional status (Lamy, 1990). These issues could be minimized by better communications among health care personnel and by developing data for central filing of medications prescribed in the elderly patient.

Cardiovascular psychotropic drugs and nonsteroidal anti-inflammatory drugs (NSAIDs) are most commonly implicated in drug-related illness, probably because they are most commonly prescribed in the elderly. Errors in prescribing account for 19% to 36% of hospital admissions due to drug-related events and up to 72% of drug-related events occurring in the hospital setting (Tamblyn, 1996).

Problems related to prescribing for elderly patients also include the selection of an appropriate dose and failure to look for interactions with nonprescription drugs. In particular, antipsychotic drugs, tranquilizers, sedatives, and antidepressants are overused in nursing facilities, resulting in an increase in falls and hip fractures (Harrington, Tompkins, Curtis, & Grant, 1992). Adverse drug reaction–related hospitalizations may affect as many as one of every seven nursing home residents and appear to be related to polypharmacy, as well as inattention to patient history of contraindications and previous ADRs (Cooper, 1999).

The susceptibility of elderly people to ADRs is underscored by age-associated differences in health and changes in organ function. The pharmacokinetics of many drugs are altered in later life by changes in organ function, which can lead to an increased risk of ADRs if dose adjustments are not made. For example, the distribution of a drug within the body depends on the drug's capacity to bind to serum proteins and the degree to which the drug is fat or water soluble. Because the proportion of lean body mass to total body weight declines with age, drugs such as digoxin that distribute to the lean body mass have a reduced volume of distribution and an increase in blood concentrations. Therefore, the digoxin dosage must be reduced to prevent toxicity (Sloan, 1992). As the liver ages, hepatic blood flow and liver mass decline, usually resulting in a reduction in hepatic extraction of drugs as they are absorbed from the gastrointestinal tract and pass through the liver (first-pass effect). Several drugs, such as propranolol and verapamil, have increased bioavailability in older patients due to a reduction in the first-pass hepatic extraction (Tumer, Scarpace, & Lowenthal, 1992). Drugs requiring substantial biotransformation in the liver (phase I metabolism) are metabolized very slowly. The net effect is that half-life and duration of action are substantially extended. Many classes of drugs are affected by changes in liver function, including antihypertensive and antiarrhythmic agents, tranquilizers, and antipsychotic and antidepressant agents.

Cardiac output and blood flow to the kidney may decline with age; therefore, the amount of blood per hour that can be cleared of a drug may also decline. The drugs that are most affected by diminished clearance are those that are predominantly excreted by kidney filtration. Examples of such drugs include digoxin, the aminoglycoside antibiotics, cimetidine, nitrofurantoin, and procainamide.

Treatment of seizure disorders in older patients is an important problem because of the age-related increase in seizure incidence and the growing size of this segment of the population. The standard antiepileptic drugs (AEDs), for example, phenytoin and carbamazepine, are not ideal for treating older patients because of their complex pharmacokinetics, multiple drug interactions, and possible increased susceptibility to adverse effects.

These examples emphasize the need to match a drug's dosage to the physical condition of the elderly patient. It should also be noted that a frequent cause of acute renal failure in the elderly is drug-induced nephropathy. NSAIDs, antibiotics, and diuretics are most often involved (Muhlberg & Platt, 1999).

The pattern of ADRs experienced by elderly people may differ from that in younger patients. Many reactions manifest in the cerebral, cardiovascular, autonomic, and gastrointestinal systems, where they may exacerbate problems already present. Many of these reactions resemble the common problems and stereotypes of aging and so are more likely to be passed off as age-related rather than as drug-induced (Tumer, Scarpace, & Lowental, 1992). Older patients and individuals with organic brain disorders have an increased propensity for the development of extrapyramidal movement disorders associated with phenothiazine usage.

Older patients appear to be very sensitive to antihypertensive and central nervous system (CNS)–depressant drugs. Thiazide diuretics are often prescribed for elderly hypertensives, but many patients on these drugs lose substantial amounts of potassium and magnesium, which increases the risk of ventricular arrhythmias and digitalis toxicity (Messerli & Losem, 1990). Postural hypotension is common in elderly people, largely because of an impaired baroreceptor response and a reduction in peripheral venous tone. Because postural hypotension is a common side effect of antihypertensive drugs and diuretics, such age-associated changes in control of hemodynamics present additional complications. To avoid severe orthostasis and syncope, an elderly hypertensive patient must be treated with antihypertensive and diuretic drugs even more cautiously than a younger patient (Goldberg & Roberts, 1983).

Depression is common in elderly people, and antidepressants are often prescribed; but dose requirements may be lower, owing to age-associated changes in pharmacokinetics and increased sensitivity (Nolan & O'Malley, 1992). Older people are more sensitive to nitrazepam, diazepam, and chlordiazepoxide than are the young. The sensitivity of the CNS to the depressant effect of flurazepam may also be greater in older than in younger persons (Goldberg & Roberts, 1983).

NSAIDs are commonly used by elderly people for both rheumatic and nonrheumatic conditions, and because of their widespread use they may be responsible for up to 21% of all ADRs (Rossi, Hsu, & Faich, 1987). Elderly patients are more prone to the adverse effects of these drugs, with the gastrointestinal tract being most frequently affected (Girgis & Brooks, 1994). Up to 20% of long-term NSAID users will develop ulcer disease, and in patients over 65 years there is a four times greater chance of developing ulcers, compared with nonusers. NSAIDs inhibit the protective effects of gastrointestinal prostaglandins that normally enhance mucus and bicarbonate secretion in the stomach. Thus, patients over 60 with a history of peptic ulcer disease should be considered for prophylaxis with misoprostol, a synthetic prostaglandin (Gabriel, 1991), or an H_2-antagonist to inhibit gastric acid production. In this regard, with the introduction of cyclooxygenase-2 (COX_2) inhibitors as anti-inflammatory agents, which reportedly inhibit prostaglandin production at the site of inflammation but not at other sites such as the gastrointestinal tract and the kidney, it is possible that the problems with NSAIDs could be circumvented.

The problem of ADRs is compounded when drug interactions occur. In elderly people this relates to the concurrent use of many drugs (polypharmacy), diminution in the function of organs that play a role in drug distribution and elimination, and poor patient compliance. Drugs that most often result in adverse reactions in elderly people have been listed by Lamy (1980) and reviewed by others (Nolan & O'Malley, 1992; Sloan, 1992; Tumer, Scarpace, & Lowenthal, 1992; Vestal, Cusak, Crowley, & Loi, 1993). The list includes many drugs that are obtainable over the counter without prescription, such as aspirin and antacids. Indeed, cimetidine (Zantac), which can be purchased over the counter, administered with topical ocular timolol increases the degree of beta blockage, resulting in a reduction of heart rate, intraocular pressure, and exercise tolerance (Ishii, Nakamura, Tsutsumi, Kotegawa, Nakano, & Nakatsuka, 2000). Examples of drugs and the mechanisms whereby interactions occur, which are of particular significance in geriatric therapeutics, are listed in Goldberg and Roberts, 1983.

JAY ROBERTS
DAVID L. SNYDER

See also
Drug Interactions

DSM-IV
See
Psychiatric Diagnosis and DSM-IV

DUKE LONGITUDINAL STUDIES

Designs

The Duke Longitudinal Studies of Aging, initiated in 1955 (Busse & Maddox, 1985), consist of three separate studies:

First Longitudinal Study. This study began in 1955 with 271 persons age 60 to 90. The subjects were not a probability sample but were selected from a pool of volunteers who lived in the community, so the overall sample reflected the age, sex, and ethnic and socioeconomic characteristics of the older population in Durham, North Carolina. Each panelist was brought to the Duke Medical Center for a 2-day series of medical, psychiatric, psychological, and social examinations. The examinations were repeated every 3 to 4 years until 1965, every 2 years until 1972, and each year between 1972 and 1976. In 1976 the eleventh and final round of examinations of the survivors of this study was completed (Palmore, 1970, 1974, 1981).

Second Longitudinal Study. This study, also known as the "Adaptation Study," began in 1968 with 502 persons age 46 to 70. These panelists were a probability sample of the members of the local health insurance association, stratified by age and sex. The sample and study was designed so that at the end of 5 years there would remain approximately 40 persons in each of 10 five-year, age-sex cohorts. This design makes possible various kinds of cross-sequential types of analyses in order to separate the effects of aging from cohort differences and from changes in the environment over time. Each subject was brought in for a 1-day series of physical, mental, and social examinations. The cohort members were reexamined at 2-year intervals, and in 1976 the fourth and final round of examinations was completed.

Third Longitudinal Study. This study, also known as the "Old-Old Study," began in 1972 with the Older American Resources and Services (OARS) community survey of 1,000 Durham residents age 65 and over. During 1980 to 1983, 300 survivors (then age 75 and over) were brought to the center for 6 hours of comprehensive physical, mental, and social examinations. Each panelist was also given one or two annual follow-up examinations. The focus of this study is on social support and mental health among the very old (Palmore, Nowlin, & Wang, 1985).

Purposes

To Study Normal Aging. The studies dealt with "normal aging" in two senses: healthy aging and typical aging. Those studied were relatively healthy in that most were noninstitutionalized, ambulatory, community residents who were willing and able to come to the Duke Medical Center for tests and examinations. The more common or typical patterns and problems of aging were focused on rather than the abnormalities. The investigators (Palmore, Nowlin, Busse, Siegler, & Maddox, 1985) stated: "Investigations of normal aging are of crucial importance in advancing the science of gerontology and in helping aged persons develop and enjoy a richer and longer life. When we can distinguish normal and inevitable processes of aging from those which may accompany aging simply because of accident, stress, maladjustment, or disuse, we can better focus our attention and efforts on those factors which can be changed and corrected" (p. xvii).

Longitudinal. The investigators believe that the best way to study aging is longitudinally, by repeated observations over time, which can measure changes. Longitudinal studies have unique advantages over cross-sectional studies: Each panel member can be used as his or her own control; consistent trends can be distinguished from temporary fluctuations; errors due to retrospective distortion are minimized; early warning signs of disease or death can be studied; cohort differences can be distinguished from age changes; changes can be precisely measured; and the effects of one kind of change on another kind of change at a later time period can be studied.

Interdisciplinary. The studies were interdisciplinary in two senses: Representatives from the major disciplines dealing with age were on the staff, and insofar as possible, the analyses were interdisciplinary and attempted to take into account all relevant factors. The investigators found that when specialists from different disciplines work together, the mutual stimulation, correction, and combination of perspectives can result in more accurate, thorough, and comprehensive understanding of the aging process.

Themes

The five volumes reporting the results of these studies contain more than 100 specific findings. How-ever, four general themes tie together the findings from several substantive areas.

1. *Declining health and physical function.* The typical pattern of normal aging is one of declining health and physical functions. Ratings of physical function tend to decline, neurological symptoms increase, skin lesions and alterations in blood vessels increase, sexual activity decreases, immune functions decline, vision and hearing decline, cardiovascular diseases increase, cerebral blood flow becomes impaired, and sleep disturbances increase.

2. *Exceptions to physical decline.* Despite the overall declines as measured by averages or group percentages, substantial minorities show no decline and may even have improvement in sexual activity, cardiovascular function, hypertension, brain function, depression, hypochondriasis, vibratory thresholds, serum antigens, skin conditions, vision, hearing, and health ratings. Thus, the process of physical aging is not necessarily an irresistible and irreversible force. Health and function can and do improve for some older persons just as they do for some younger persons.

3. *Little or no decline in social and psychological function.* This theme is in direct contrast to the theme of declining physical functioning. The studies found little or no decline in activities, attitudes, cautiousness, recall, general adjustment, intelligence scores (especially among those free of hypertension and among those under age 75), reaction times, correct signal detection, most measures of mental health, coping with stressful events, personality, internal orientation, self-concept, life satisfaction, voluntary association activity, and religious attitudes. This evidence tends to refute the disengagement theory that social and psychological decline are typical, inevitable, and normal.

4. *Wide variations in aging patterns.* Individual variation tends to persist or increase with aging. There are wide individual and group differences in the aging process: by sex, race, socioeconomic   group,   health   practices,

chronic and acute illness, retirement, stressful events, and coping styles. Thus, these studies document both how multifaceted aging processes are and how much variety there is in the patterns of normal aging.

Availability

The data from the first and second longitudinal studies are available for secondary analysis from Data Archives for Aging and Adult Development, Box 3003, Duke Medical Center, Durham, NC 27710.

ERDMAN B. PALMORE

See also
Longitudinal Studies of Aging

DYSPHAGIA
See
Feeding Behavior
Gastrointestinal Function
Normal Swallow and Dysphagia

E

EARLY RETIREMENT

Retirement is early (or late) only with reference to some normal age or personal timetable for its occurrence. For most of this century, people in the United States regarded age 65 as a typical age for retirement and eventually as *the* normal age for retirement when it was established as the eligibility age for full retirement benefits under the Social Security program. Yet, by the late 1970s, retirement prior to this benchmark had become the norm. Other industrialized nations also saw a trend toward earlier retirement. During the 1980s, early retirement acquired a second connotation as employers offered incentive or "window" programs that allowed workers to begin pension receipt even sooner than foreseen.

For most workers, retirement is not practical without pension income to replace the wages lost from withdrawal from work, and so it is the availability of Social Security and employers' pensions at younger ages that has made early retirement feasible. That expanded availability, which was possible in a nation grown wealthier over the postwar period, has also signaled the social desirability of leisure over work for pension-eligible Americans (Schulz, 1995).

The Means to Retire Early

Congress originally added the early retirement option to Social Security out of concern for vulnerable, older workers whose problems with unemployment or health kept them from working until the eligibility age of 65. Amendments to the program allowed insured workers, women beginning in 1956 and men in 1961, to become eligible for reduced benefits at ages 62 to 64, providing that they met the retirement test of sharply reduced earnings. Under the formula, the monthly retirement benefit to which a worker would normally have been entitled at age 65 was permanently reduced by 5/9% per month for each month that retirement occurred prior to age 65. Thus, retirement at age 62 reduced the monthly benefit by 20%.

As the full-benefit age begins a scheduled rise to 67 over the next two decades, early retirement at age 62 will still be an option, but monthly benefits will be scaled back. By 2022, people with a full-benefit age of 67 will see a 30% benefit reduction if they choose to retire at age 62.

Pension sources other than Social Security likewise have encouraged older workers to contemplate earlier retirement (Turner & Doescher, 1996). In the United States roughly half of private-sector workers and almost all government workers are covered by a pension plan. Employers may originate their plans to serve different objectives: as a reward to long-time employees, as an outcome of collective bargaining, as a device to keep promotion lines open to younger staff, or as a means to shed workforces of older personnel who are believed eventually to become less productive or too costly. The prohibition of mandatory retirement has further enhanced the usefulness of pension incentives to retire.

Employers with defined-benefit plans may schedule normal pension eligibility at ages earlier than 65. Indeed, government and private employees in liberal plans, if they meet a combined age and length-of-service requirement, can achieve retirement with full benefits in their 50s. The great majority of defined-benefit plans also offer workers an early retirement option. Benefits in these arrangements may be reduced actuarially, that is, stretched out to cover a longer lifetime payout. The reduction may be eased by subsidies that enhance the value of pensions taken early. In another design, the early retirement pension can be coordinated with Social Security, providing additional income until the retiree reaches eligibility for the latter. However the plan is structured, workers cannot usually gain an actuarial advantage in working past the normal retirement age, if not the early retirement age; plans, in effect, penalize anything but early retirement (Wise, 1997). Accordingly, retirees commonly report that early retirement was "an offer I couldn't pass up."

Age incentives for retirement are not a feature of defined contribution pensions, yet such savings-style plans increase the financial feasibility of early retirement because distributions can begin at age 59 1/2. The same threshold age applies for withdrawals from individual retirement accounts. Eligibility for employer-provided retiree health insurance can also facilitate job exits in the years before one qualifies for Medicare at age 65.

Social Security and other pension incentives have had a clear effect on the retirement rates and labor force participation of workers in their late 50s and early 60s. One analysis has shown that the average age of final retirement dropped by 2 or 3 years for men and women alike between the early 1960s and early 1990s (Gendell, 1998). By another measure, the proportion of all Social Security worker beneficiaries receiving a reduced (for early retirement) benefit increased between 1970 and 1998, from 36% to 69% for men and from 59% to 75% for women. Among all persons who began receiving Social Security pensions in 1998, 50% of men and 53% of women were awarded benefits at the earliest eligible age of 62 (Social Security Administration, 1999).

Variations

The 1980s saw employers' increasing use of early retirement incentive or "window" programs (also called buyouts, early-outs, or golden handshakes). In contrast to a standing option for early retirement, window programs are temporary, limited offers of special pension incentives to an organization's older employees. Retirement under these programs is "early" in the sense of having been unanticipated under usual plan arrangements. Window programs are commonly designed to cut current labor costs by reducing the size of the higher paid, older workforce. Generous incentives to retire can include a boost in benefit levels, additional years of credited service, lump sum payments, or the provision of employer-provided health insurance (Stein, 1994). Window programs by law must be conducted in ways that do not pressure workers to retire or discriminate on the basis of age.

Window events entail risks for employers and employees both. Employers, for example, risk the departure of certain valued employees whom they would rather retain. Whereas some employees will view special incentives as an unalloyed boon, others can experience the stress of compressing into a hurried timetable all of their decision-making about future lifestyles and finances. They may be anxious as well about the employment consequences of declining the incentive, or feel emotionally unprepared to let go of their jobs (Hardy, Hazelrigg, & Quadagno, 1996).

Early retirement, as indicated by receipt of Social Security or private pensions, is not necessarily final retirement. Indeed, earlier retirement contributes to greater complexity in retirement behavior because it leaves pensioners to face a longer postretirement period. Workers may depart their organizations with a pension and resume employment (or self-employment) elsewhere, later to retire again. Some reenter the labor force after a spell of leisure, or trade full-time jobs for part-time work and partial retirement. Considering these patterns, it may be best to regard retirement behavior as a potential series of transitions rather than a single event (Mutchler, Burr, Pienta, & Massagli, 1997).

Pensions make early retirement possible, but that does not mean that all such exits are voluntary. Workers may depart their jobs for health reasons, or under the pressure of family responsibilities, or because working conditions have become disagreeable. Early retirement also comes about as disabled persons and persons at the margins of the labor market adopt the identity of retiree.

Public Policy and Private Interests

The long-term decline in employment among older workers has been a feature of all developed societies (Gruber & Wise, 1999). The trend toward early retirement, when coupled with increasing life expectancy and, in the United States, large oncoming cohorts of baby boom retirees, has raised apprehension about society's future pension burdens (Burtless & Munnell, 1991). Should—or can—the trend toward early retirement be halted or reversed?

The decline in labor force participation among older U.S. workers appears at present to have leveled off. Recent public policy moves could encourage the extended employment of older workers. These include the prohibition of mandatory retirement, the rise in the full-benefit age for Social Security retirement pensions, an increased Social Security credit for delayed retirement past the normal age, and a liberalized earnings test. These changes, of themselves, are not forecast to reverse substantially the early retirement pattern without analogous changes in the work disincentives now operating in employer pensions (Leonesio, 1996). These pension plan changes, in turn, will depend on personnel objectives and labor market conditions that are not easy to foresee. In addition, decades of pension and Social Security incentives for early

retirement have created social norms about the "right time" for retirement in the reliable course of workers' lives, expectations that workers may not readily relinquish.

DAVID J. EKERDT

See also
   Retirement Communities
   Retirement Planning

ECONOMICS

The economics of aging concerns the economic well-being of older persons; life cycle decisions concerning work, retirement, and savings; national retirement policies including Social Security and Medicare, regulation of employer pensions, and age discrimination; and the macroeconomic implications of aging populations, especially the impact of population aging on the cost of retirement programs.

Economic Well-Being of the Elderly

Economic well-being is determined by an individual's ability to consume goods and services. Consumption possibilities are limited by household wealth and current income. Elderly households face the same choices as other families; however, they may differ in their sources of income, their levels of income, and their ability to continue working. These differences in income are attributable to life cycle patterns of work, changes in health status, and age-based government transfer programs.

Work and Retirement.   Men and increasingly more women spend most of their life from the end of formal schooling until age 60 working outside the home. Earnings are typically the most important source of income during these years. Around age 55, older persons begin to retire and permanently leave the labor force. Retirement decisions are influenced by income, wealth, pension and Social Security characteristics, health, and family considerations (Quinn, Burkhauser, & Myers, 1990). During much of the second half of the twentieth century, two trends dominated changes in the labor force: the increasing proportion of women who were in the labor force and the decline in the labor force participation rate of older men. Interestingly, the trend toward earlier retirement among men stopped during the last decade. In 1950, one half of the men age 65 and older remained in the labor force. By 1985, the proportion of older men in the labor force had fallen to only one sixth. At the end of the twentieth century, the participation rate for men age 65 and older was approximately 16% (Quinn, 1999). Considerable economic research has shown that retirement programs provide strong incentives for workers to retire at particular ages (Kotlikoff & Wise, 1990). Older workers who retire from a career job do not necessarily move directly into complete retirement. Many individuals now choose to enter new jobs and work for several additional years either full or part time.

Sources of Income.   Older families are much less likely to have current earnings than younger households, and they depend more on income from employer pensions and Social Security. Social Security is the primary source of income for many older families, as over 90% of all households age 65 and older receive some income from Social Security. The importance of Social Security as a percentage of family income declines as income rises, whereas pensions and income from assets become more important sources of income (Social Security Administration, 1998). Wealthier families also can use the income from assets to provide additional income in old age; however, wealth among the elderly is very unevenly distributed, and many older households have very few assets.

Real and Relative Economic Status.   The economic status of the elderly has improved significantly since 1970. From 1969 to 1996, the median real income (in 1996 dollars) of couples age 65 and older with no children under age 18 increased from $18,600 to $29,200, an increase of 57%. This increase was much larger than that recorded by younger households. Even larger percentage increases in real income were achieved by older persons living alone (McNeil, 1998).

Cash income is not necessarily a good measure of the relative economic status of the elderly. The elderly receive considerable in-kind transfers from the government. The most prominent in-kind transfer is access to medical services through Medicare.

An alternative measure of economic status is based on cash income plus noncash benefits received, capital gains, and imputed return on home equity minus taxes paid. Using this measure of income, the median income of elderly households rose by 20.2% between 1979 and 1996, compared with an increase of only 4.6% for all households.

Another indicator of the improving economic status of older Americans is the decline in the poverty rate. In 1966, 28.5% of persons age 65 and older had incomes below the official poverty line. This was nearly twice the poverty rate for the entire population and was higher than the poverty rate for children under the age of 18. During the subsequent three decades, the elderly poverty rate declined sharply. In 1996, the poverty rate of older persons had declined to 11%, which was below the poverty rate for the U.S. population. Despite this impressive reduction in elderly poverty rates, certain groups among the elderly, such as widows, minorities, and the very old, continue to have much higher poverty rates, and many older persons have incomes just above the poverty line.

Economic Responses to Population Aging

Population aging refers to an increase in the relative number of older persons in a population and is associated with an increase in the median age of the population. Changes in the population age structure can influence aggregate economic activity due to age-specific differences in employment, productivity, savings, and consumption.

Dependency Ratios.   Dependency ratios are used to measure the relative productive potential of a population. The old-age dependency ratio generally measures the number of elderly persons at or above a certain age divided by the number of persons of working age. This ratio rises with population aging and has been used as an indicator for various population effects on economic activity. There are several problems concerning the economic interpretation of the old-age dependency ratio. First, if population aging follows from reduced fertility, the relative number of youths falls. As a result, the total dependency ratio (youths plus elderly) may fall even as the old-age ratio is rising. Second, age-based dependency ratios are not perfect proxies for the ratio of inactive to active persons. To address this problem, labor force participation rates can be used to determine the dependency ratio. Finally, significant compositional changes may occur within the elderly, youth, and working age populations. These changes have economic effects that may be as important as the effects of changes in the dependency ratio itself.

Social Security. Social Security is very important to the economic well-being of older Americans and is a very large and growing component of the federal budget. The aging of the population has sharply increased the tax rates necessary to finance national retirement benefits. Social Security reform is one of the most import policy debates of the twenty-first century. Restoring the financial integrity of the Social Security systems requires either higher taxes, lower benefits, or higher retirement ages. Alternatively, more fundamental changes, such as providing individual accounts for workers, could be introduced. Economic issues are at the heart of the reform debate. Important concerns include the effect of higher tax rates, the impact of lower benefits, the result of investing national retirement funds in private equity markets, and the effect on national savings (Advisory Council on Social Security, 1997).

Economic Response to Population Aging. The changing age structure of a population may also alter the level of economic activity and productivity. Layoff and quit rates are a decreasing function of age. Because employment stability increases with age, national unemployment rates tend to decline with population aging. Considerable attention has been given to the change in individual productivity with age. As an individual ages, productive capacity generally rises upward to a peak, levels off, and eventually begins to decline. This movement reflects age-specific investment in human capital, changes in physical and mental abilities, and worker expectations concerning future events. The importance of any decrements in job performance in later working years depends on the job requirements and whether the worker or the employer attempts to maintain skills through continued training. The life cycle pattern of job performance differs substantially across workers and jobs.

Any decline in productivity will also be influenced by technological changes that may reduce the value of the existing human capital of older workers. Given the diversity of individuals and job requirements, it is not surprising that research studies have found significant overlap in the age-specific productivity distributions. Older workers may be able to offset productivity declines by having lower absence rates, reduced likelihood of job turnover, and increased accuracy or quality of performance. The macroeconomic significance of population aging on national productivity depends on individual age-specific productivity, and any ensuing changes in investment, consumption, and savings behavior. The net effect of these factors is unclear.

The effect of population aging on national savings and the rate of economic growth depends on age-specific savings rates and the age structure changes that occur as the population ages. The net effect of aging on savings and growth also will depend on the cause of population aging. If population aging results from slowing population growth, then the economic response to population size and the rate of population growth will be observed simultaneously with the aging effect. In general, the independent effect of population aging will not be a major factor influencing future economic growth and development.

ROBERT L. CLARK

See also
Employment
Net Worth
Pensions
Poverty
Productivity
Social Security

EDEN ALTERNATIVE
See
Pets

EEG/ELECTROENCEPHALOGRAM
See
Clinical EEG: Cognitive Changes

EFFECTS OF GOVERNMENT POLICIES ON THE INCOMES OF YOUNGER AND OLDER HOUSEHOLDS

Policies that affect the incomes of older persons have undergone numerous changes since the late

1960s. These changes include alterations to retirement incentives and disincentives in Social Security, the emergence of early retirement incentive programs, the elimination of mandatory retirement in the Age Discrimination in Employment Act, and the maturation of the employer pension system. On balance, the incomes of older persons increased substantially over the past several decades. During the period 1967 to 1996, real median income increased by 76.4% for married couples, by 84.2% for nonmarried persons, by 89.7% for Whites, and by 52.8% for Blacks (Social Security Administration, 1997).

Despite significant improvements in the income of the older population, however, significant pockets of poverty remain among elderly subpopulations (U.S. Bureau of the Census, 1999b). The risk of poverty differs markedly by race, gender, and living arrangements. In 1998, only 8.9% of White older Americans were in poverty, compared with 26.4% of older African Americans and 21% of older Hispanics. The poverty rate among older women was 12.8% compared with 7.2% for older men. It was 20.4% for older persons living alone, but only 6.4% for older persons living in families. The group at greatest risk of poverty was African American women living alone; their poverty rate was 49.3% in 1998.

Unfortunately, concerns about the ability of the economy to support health and retirement benefits for an aging population have dampened the enthusiasm of policy makers to consider income maintenance policies that would improve the economic status of those subgroups of the older population who still suffer from economic deprivation. This lack of political resolve is fueled by the recognition that younger population groups have not experienced income gains comparable to those of the elderly over the past several decades. Particularly alarming is the high rate of poverty among children under age 18, which had risen to 23% in 1991 and remained at 18.9% in 1998.

The divergent trends in the incomes of older and younger persons have led some to conclude that public policy for the elderly has been too generous and has come at the expense of younger population groups (Peterson, 1996). In contrast, others have concluded that the income trends of older and younger persons are largely unrelated (Hurd, 1990); these studies show that the relative economic gains of the elderly have resulted mainly from two sources: (1) the lack of growth in the incomes of working families and (2) Social Security policies directed specifically at older persons.

Effects of Taxes, Government Transfers, and Home Equity Conversion on Income

Given the importance of Social Security policies for the relative economic gains of the elderly, it is useful to examine the effects of government policies on the incomes of households in general, and older households in particular. Table 1 shows how 1998 median incomes for all households and households with members 65+ differ depending on the income definition used. Table 1 also reports the Gini coefficient—a measure of income inequality—for each group. A value of 0 for a Gini coefficient indicates perfect income equality; a value of 1 indicates perfect income inequality.

It is apparent from Table 1 that households in the population at large have higher median incomes than the subpopulation of older households. The Gini coefficients, however, indicate that the inequality of money income is higher among aged households than all households in the population. This result is consistent with other findings that indicate substantial variability in the economic status of the elderly (Radner, 1992).

Government policies can influence income inequality through two basic redistribution mechanisms—taxes and government transfers. The money income figures in column 1 of Table 1 are pretax, but they include the value of cash transfers from the government. To assess the effects of government transfers on income inequality, it is necessary to construct an income figure net of these transfers. Finally, to reflect the full value of pretax money income net of government transfers, it is necessary to add in the value of capital gains and employee health benefits that are not reflected in money income.

The resulting adjusted pretax money income is shown in the second column of Table 1. The median incomes of households in the total population increase after adjusting pretax money income. This indicates that the value of capital gains and employee health insurance is greater than the value of government transfers for the population at large.

TABLE 1   Household Income and Income Inequality by Income Definition

	Income Definition				
Household type	Pretax money income (1)	Adjusted pretax money income[a] (2)	Adjusted after-tax Income[b] (3)	Adjusted after-tax income and transfers (4)	Adjusted after-tax income and transfers plus returns from home equity
All households					
Median income	$38,885	$37,673	$31,816	$37,673	$39,308
Gini coefficient	0.446	0.509	0.484	0.405	0.399
Households with members age 65+					
Median income	$23,369	$10,337	$9,890	$30,314	$33,261
Gini coefficient	0.483	0.675	0.644	0.426	0.411

[a]Money income less government transfers plus capital gains and employee health benefits.
[b]Adjusted pretax money income less Social Security taxes, federal taxes, state taxes, plus income tax credit.
Source: U.S. Bureau of the Census (1999a).

Income inequality increases slightly but not dramatically.

In contrast, median incomes of older households decline significantly when the value of government transfers is subtracted from pretax money income. Moreover, the Gini coefficient measuring income inequality increases from 0.483 for unadjusted money income to 0.675 for the income figure net of government transfers. This, of course, largely reflects the importance of Social Security as an income source for older households.

Columns 3 and 4 of the table show the effects of taxation and government transfers, respectively, on household incomes. Government taxation (at all levels) reduces median incomes of households in the general population more than those of older households. These effects reflect the progressive nature of income taxation because the incomes of nonaged households tend to be higher than those of older households. The Gini coefficients, however, indicate that taxation does not reduce income inequality substantially.

In contrast, government transfers have a major effect in reducing income inequality. The after-tax Gini coefficient for older households declines from 0.644 for pretransfer income to 0.426 after government transfers have been added in. On the other hand, income transfers have less effect in reducing income inequality in all households than in elderly

households, partly because nonelderly households have less income inequality to begin with.

Growing recognition of the greater wealth of older households relative to younger households has led to increased interest in the potential role of asset holdings for meeting public policy objectives. An important example of this growing interest is the concern that some elderly households with low money incomes may have large amounts of assets. Is it right for such older households to receive income transfers from younger households that have higher money incomes but who would not be as well off as older households if one took wealth into account (Venti & Wise, 1990)?

There are numerous dimensions to this question as a public policy issue, but perhaps the most important is the magnitude of the difference that it might make. This is influenced by both recent changes in the net worth of older households and the potential role that assets could play in the generation of an income stream. Wolff (1998) found that real mean net worth of older households declined by 1.5% between 1983 and 1995. Changes in mean net worth among older households varied widely by income, however. Older households at both extremes of the income distribution (i.e., those with incomes under $15,000 or over $50,000) experienced increases in mean net worth, whereas older households between the two extremes experienced declines in net worth. Most importantly, studies have repeatedly found that, except for the most affluent of older households, the majority of net worth is held in the form of home equity (Eller, 1994). The final column of Table 1 indicates that the effects of annuitizing household wealth are fairly similar across age groups, and that such a policy would have almost no effect on reducing household income inequality.

Conclusion

This entry has examined the role of government tax and transfer policies on the incomes of households in the general population and the subset comprised of older households. It was found that older households have lower median incomes than households in the general population and, of course, by extension, that older households have lower median incomes than younger households. Moreover, older households have higher income inequality than the general population, implying that a greater portion of the elderly are clustered at lower income levels while others have extremely high incomes. Government taxation has the effect of lowering median incomes for all households including the elderly, but it has little effect on reducing income inequality in and of itself. Of course, taxation is what enables the government to redistribute income through transfer policies. Income transfers have a major effect on reducing income inequality among the elderly but have less influence on reducing income inequality among households in general.

Not considered here were the many difficulties that arise when making income comparisons across age groups (Crystal, 1996). For example, older households tend to be smaller, so they need less income than larger, younger households. One obvious correction would be to convert household income figures to a per-capita basis. This is too much of a correction, however, because it fails to account for household economies of scale. Careful studies based on the construction of equivalence scales indicate that the incomes of older and younger households are now roughly comparable (Hurd, 1990).

Another difficulty that arises when comparing the incomes of older and younger families is related to their different stages in the life cycle. These different positions in the life cycle imply that older and younger households have different income needs. A comprehensive assessment of income adequacy requires an assessment of consumption needs as well as income levels. To date, however, the literature has focused on the income side of the equation. There have been only a few studies of the relative consumption needs of older and younger households.

WILLIAM H. CROWN

See also
Poverty
Social Security

ELDER ABUSE AND NEGLECT

Violence in the home and abuse of family members who are less capable of defending themselves have always existed, but the problems have been hidden until recent decades. Since the mid-1960s, child abuse and neglect, child sexual assault, woman battering, and marital rape have emerged as private social problems that demand public recognition and action if they are to be solved. In 1978, the issue of elder abuse and neglect started to receive attention due to the increasing awareness of the burgeoning number of older adults in our society ("graying of America") and their unique problems, as a result of the groundwork laid by practitioners who treat children and women suffering from domestic mistreatment, and, finally, due to the evolution of a society that is more compassionate than it once was (Quinn & Tomita, 1986; 1997).

Research

Research into elder abuse and neglect has proceeded in three waves. The first wave included studies that appeared in the late 1970s and early 1980s. These studies were descriptive and exploratory and focused on reports of abuse and neglect by practitioners, as well as definitions of elder abuse and neglect. By the late 1980s, clearer definitions had been developed and were being implemented by reporting agencies and researchers; practitioners had developed detection and intervention techniques, nationwide training and education seminars had been conducted, and mandatory and voluntary reporting laws were passed or updated in nearly every state (Quinn & Tomita, 1986; 1997).

The second wave of research built on the first and confirmed the existence of elder abuse and neglect. It was found that the abusers were frequently dependent on the elders, usually for financial support and for housing, possibly due to their own problems (e.g., substance abuse, poor physical health, or serious psychiatric impairments) (Wolf & Pillemer, 1989).

During the third wave of research, the National Elder Abuse Incidence Study was published (Administration on Aging, 1998). The study estimates that at least one half million older persons in domestic settings were abused and/or neglected, or experienced self-neglect, during 1996. The study also estimates that for every reported incident of elder abuse, neglect, or self-neglect, approximately five went unreported. Types of abuse and neglect explored included physical abuse, sexual abuse, emotional or psychological abuse, financial or material exploitation, abandonment, neglect, and self-neglect. Women were more likely to be the victims, even accounting for their larger proportion in the aging population. The study also found that those 80 years and older were abused and neglected at two to three times their proportion of the elderly population. In almost 90% of the incidents with a known perpetrator, the perpetrator was a family member. Two thirds of the perpetrators were adult children or spouses. Those who are the victims of self-neglect were usually depressed, confused, or extremely frail.

The third wave of research included studies of abuse and neglect in various ethnic groups and of abuse and neglect in nursing homes, as well as the theory of caregiver stress as a causative factor in elder abuse and neglect.

Several studies have focused on caregivers of demented and impaired elderly. Where the abuser is a spouse, the question is raised as to whether there has always been violence in the relationship. In some situations, the mistreatment may come with old age as impairments set in and a caregiver uses violence as a way to control a demented spouse who is combative. The quality of the relationship prior to the caregiving may determine whether abuse or neglect will take place when one spouse becomes dependent on the other. If there has been past abuse in the relationship and the abuser now becomes dependent, the caregiver, formerly the victim, may mistreat the dependent former abuser by way of retaliation.

Elder domestic violence can result in death. A recent study (Nerenberg, 1999) on elderly homicides/suicides found that the relationships were long term and that the men were the perpetrators. The researchers discovered three profiles in these long-standing relationships. About one third were domestic violence cases in which the actual murder event was a surprise attack that was vicious and lethal and resulted in multiple wounds, which were often defensive. The next group, the "dependents protective," accounted for 50% of cases. The man was depressed, and the woman was either asleep during the fatal attack or was shot in the back of the head or torso. The third category involved some evidence that the woman wanted to die, but there is no evidence that these women participated in the acts (e.g., no double-signed suicide notes).

Preliminary studies of elder mistreatment among different ethnic groups are beginning to appear. Acts considered abusive or neglectful in one culture may not be thought abusive in another culture. The intentions of the caregiver may be considered a major factor in some cultures; if the caregiver had good intentions toward the elder, the act might not be considered abusive. Psychological abuse and neglect may be more prevalent in some groups and may constitute the most severe form of mistreatment possible in those groups. The privacy norms of family life may be even stronger than in the dominant culture. In some cultures, it is normal for elders to routinely share financial assets with younger members of the family; it may be difficult to draw the line as to when financial abuse starts (Archstone Foundation, 1998).

Abuse and neglect in nursing homes have received surprisingly little research attention despite the plethora of anecdotal information. A study of 488 incidents of abuse of nursing home residents by Payne and Cikovic (1996) found that the most prevalent abuse acts were physical (84.2%). Sexual abuse (8%) also was present. Male employees were responsible for the majority of incidents. Of the 488 reported incidents, 335 resulted in criminal convictions. Offenders attributed the mistreatment to efforts to control patients whom they judged to be uncooperative or uncontrollable.

Type of Abuse and Neglect

Five types of abuse and neglect have been identified. It is clear that victims may be subjected to more than one type of abuse or neglect at a time and that maltreatment is not limited to a single incident.

Physical abuse and neglect result in such trauma as bruises, cuts, rope burns (from being restrained), broken bones, blood clots beneath the scalp, dehydration and malnutrition, pressure sores, hypothermia, and death. Financial abuse is more common with elders than other forms of domestic abuse, simply because elders are more likely to have assets, such as a home, bank accounts, or other valuables. Deliberate undue influence may play a part in financial abuse. For example, a caregiver may lead the victim from trust to isolation to dependence to manipulation. This may be done subtly over a period of time.

Violation of basic rights is common and includes not being permitted to vote, to practice one's religion, or to open one's own mail. Psychological abuse often accompanies the other types of abuse and can consist of threats to abandon the elderly person or to put him or her into a nursing home. Self-abuse and self-neglect are included in the types of abuse and neglect, although there is substantial disagreement as to whether they should be. However, many states include them as reportable, and they constitute the greatest number of reported cases.

Treatment

Treatment of elder abuse and neglect calls for a variety of approaches because each situation is different. Stopping the abuse and neglect is the first task in a mistreatment situation (Quinn & Tomita, 1986; 1997). The nature of the abuse and neglect will point to the additional interventions. For example, when the abuse and neglect are thought to be due to caregiver stress or ignorance, helping the caregiver is a goal of treatment and prevention. Common interventions involve bringing in supportive services, such as homemaker assistance, home-delivered meals, and personal care. If the abuser is an adult child who is financially and emotionally dependent on the victim, it may be necessary to reduce the dependency with vocational counseling and job placement. There may be need for substance abuse treatment or mental health services. Interventions that can be borrowed from the domestic violence arena include peer support groups, shelters, restraining orders, and prosecution of the abuser. Increasingly, police officers and prosecutors are being trained to recognize and deal with the mistreatment of the elderly.

Self-abuse may include substance abuse or knowingly living in dangerous or unhealthy circumstances. The individual may be mentally capable or competent and refuse all types of intervention. One person's self-abuse may be another's exercise in freedom. Self-neglect, which can include improper nutrition and hygiene, can also be seen as value laden. When is it self-neglect, and when is it the legal right to live as one chooses? The victims of self-neglect are usually depressed, confused, or extremely frail (Administration on Aging, 1998). Again, mental capacity is at issue when considering any intervention. The severity of the situation, as a practical matter, is also a factor. These types of cases are very difficult for practitioners to work with, as they must continually weigh the individual's right to freedom versus the right to be safe.

It is common for several agencies and practitioners to be involved in one case due to the complexities of the issues. Some cities have developed multidisciplinary teams that meet regularly to discuss complex cases or cases that "fall between the cracks." The teams involve a variety of disciplines, including adult protective services, legal services, mental health services, health care, and financial services. This approach has the benefit of sharing information, exploring agency misunderstandings, and promoting mutual problem solving.

Conclusion

Elder abuse and neglect have emerged as significant problems affecting the elderly and their families. There has been a significant response from government at all levels. Active research continues, and interventions are being devised on a daily basis. These activities are sorely needed, not only for current victims but also in view of the prediction of very large numbers of elders in the immediate future due to the graying of America.

MARY JOY QUINN

See also

Crime (Against and By the Elderly)
Nursing Home Reform Law (1987)
Restraints: Physical/Chemical

ELDER HOSTEL

See

Adult Education

EMOTIONS AND AGING

Until recent years, most gerontologists presumed that emotional functioning in old age deteriorated along with functioning in cognitive and physical domains. The presumption that emotional reserves are unduly taxed in later life seemed reasonable in light of the association of old age with internal and external challenges to the self, deaths of friends and loved ones, and pervasive societal discrimination. Emotional discontentment, rigidity, or, alternatively, lability were presumed to characterize old age. One prominent model of social aging—disengagement theory—suggested that emotional quiescence served as a protective strategy that allowed people to adapt psychologically to the approaching end of life. Quite to the contrary, however, research conducted over the last 10 to 15 years suggests that later life is characterized by greater saliency of emotions, improved emotional regulation, more positive and complex emotional experience, and better integration of emotion and cognition. Older people also report the same or even higher levels of global life satisfaction, compared with their younger counterparts. This counterintuitive pattern of findings has come to be called the paradox of aging, and research is under way to identify the mechanisms that underlie the preservation of emotional functioning.

What are emotions? There is reasonable agreement among researchers that emotions are adaptive internal states that come about when particular stimulus events (internal or external) are detected. At this point, an emotion program unfolds. An emotion program involves three component processes: subjective experience, facial expression, and physiological arousal. A related issue is emotion regulation, generally defined as the ability to modulate emotional states, typically by increasing positive experience (but not always, e.g., volitionally going to a sad movie) and decreasing negative experience.

Each of these component processes has been studied under controlled laboratory settings. When emotion-eliciting stimuli are presented to older and younger research participants through viewings of emotionally charged film clips, or when emotions are induced by asking research participants to recollect emotional experiences, virtually no age differences are observed in the subjective intensity of reported emotional experience or concomitant facial displays of emotion. Older and younger people respond very similarly. In contrast, autonomic nervous system activity is somewhat reduced in older as compared with younger adults, a point revisited below (Levenson, Carstensen, Friesen, & Ekman, 1991).

In regard to emotion regulation, older adults appear somewhat more adept at controlling emotional episodes (Gross, Carstensen, Pasupathi, Tsai, Götestam Skorpen, & Hsu, 1997). This is the clear finding in questionnaire studies in which research participants are asked about their ability to control emotion. Arguably more convincing, however, are findings from observational studies. Older, compared with younger, married couples, for example, are likely to interweave displays of affection along with expressions of negative emotions when discussing a conflict in their relationship. This very effective form of social regulation of emotion appears to prevent interactions from becoming overly negative (Carstensen, Levenson, & Gottman, 1995). Also, in an experience sampling study that required research participants to report emotions when signaled at random times throughout the day, not only did older people experience negative emotions less frequently than their younger counterparts, but the negative emotions reported were less likely to persist over multiple sampling occasions, providing additional support for improved emotion regulation in everyday life (Carstensen, Pasupathi, Mayr, & Nesselroade, in press).

A number of studies have supported the notion that emotional processes improve with age. In a study of nursing home residents, Lawton, Parmelee, Katz, and Nesselroade (1996) sampled self-reported negative affect for a 1-month period. Not only did they find that older people report relatively low levels of negative affect, but these states vary little over time. Notably, even in demented populations, the cohesiveness of the emotion system is reasonably well maintained into advanced stages of this organic disease (Magai, Cohen, Gomberg, Malatesta, & Culver, 1996). Using the experience sampling paradigm described above, Carstensen, Pasupathi, Mayr, and Nesselroade (in press) found in a sample ranging in age from 18 to 94 years that older adults experience positive emotional states just as frequently as younger people but negative emotional states less frequently. Moreover, patterns revealed on sampled occasions suggest that emotional experiences may be more complex among older adults. Older people were more likely to report a range of emotions and to include both positive and negative emotions in the same moment of time. This pattern may represent episodes of "poignancy."

There is also evidence that older people are better able to integrate emotions into reasoning and problem solving. Labouvie-Vief and her colleagues (see Labouvie-Vief, 1997) show that, whereas younger people tend to view the world "objectively," namely, independent of feelings and values, older people (peaking in middle age) are more likely to integrate objective knowledge about the world with internal experiences and larger philosophical concerns. This integration of cognition and emotion paves the way for more mature coping and defense mechanisms. In the same vein, Blanchard-Fields and her colleagues (see Blanchard-Fields, 1997) argue that older adults' improved ability to integrate emotion into cognition allows them to reason about emotionally charged social dilemmas more successfully. Asked to respond to social dilemmas that differed in emotional saliency (e.g., conflict over an unwanted pregnancy vs. historical accounts of a fictional war), older and younger people did not differ in solving dilemmas that were unemotional, but older people outperformed younger people when presented with highly emotional problems.

A slight increase in negative emotional experience does appear in very old age. Although more research is needed, this upturn may reflect the "terminal drop" phenomenon associated with the dying process (referring to a precipitous drop in functioning just before death). Nevertheless, compared with research on cognitive and physical functioning, the overall profile of findings about emotion is distinctively positive.

To date, the reasons that emotional functioning is preserved throughout life are not well understood. Speculations rooted in the recent literature suggest that it may be overdetermined. Experience, for example, very likely plays a role. From the earliest days of life people learn to modulate emotional experience and expression, and thus control emotional experience once elicited. One very effective regulation strategy is antecedent emotional control—namely, the seeking out of situations that engender positive reactions and the avoidance of negative ones. Because older people interact with others less and because these reductions are accounted for primarily by reductions in contact with acquaintances and other peripheral social partners, it may be that social selection contributes to well-being. In other words, when interactions are limited primarily to well-known social partners, the predictability and emotional closeness to these social partners may contribute to positive social experiences. However, as noted above, even when negative emotions are activated, they appear to have shorter durations in older as compared with younger people, so antecedent regulation does not account for the full story.

Carstensen and her colleagues (Carstensen, Isaacowitz, & Charles, 1999) argue that the perception of future time as limited contributes paradoxically to positive emotional experience. According to socioemotional selectivity theory, when time is perceived as limited, motivational changes occur such that people pursue emotional goals. In particular, preferences for deepening intimacy in emotionally close social relationships is observed. Evidence for a heightened emphasis on emotional goals is also evident in studies of text memory and mental representations of other people. Both experimental approaches suggest that older people pay more attention to emotional aspects of the world around them.

Another potential contributor to improved emotion regulation is the reduction in the strength of physiological arousal noted above. If older people experience less autonomic arousal during emotion episodes, this reduction renders the task of controlling emotions easier for older people. On the other hand, it remains possible that lower levels of arousal instead reflect emotion control processes. Additional research is needed to reconcile these alternative explanations.

In summary, emotional experience and emotion regulation appear to be relatively unscathed by the aging process. Findings that have accumulated over the past 10 to 15 years suggest that the emotion domain may be characterized by continued growth rather than decline or deterioration. Compared with their younger counterparts, older adults place greater importance on the socioemotional aspects of their lives, regulate their emotions more effectively, report more complex and overall positive emotional experiences, and integrate affect into cognitive processing with greater success. One important caveat remains. Most of the research to date is based on cross-sectional age comparisons. It is quite possible that at least some of this optimistic picture is attributable to cohort differences. Current generations of elderly people lived through military and economic trials that may have rendered them resilient to intransigent negative states. Regardless, research shows that the aging process itself does not hold inevitable negative ramifications for emotional functioning. Even if future generations fare less well, the notable well-being of elderly people today shows that the emotion system does not invariably deteriorate with age.

LAURA L. CARSTENSEN

See also
  Anxiety
  Depression

EMPHYSEMA

Emphysema is an anatomic alteration of the lung characterized by abnormal enlargement of the air spaces distal to the terminal nonrespiratory bronchioles, accompanied by destructive changes in the alveolar walls. As the walls are destroyed the air sacs become larger and fewer in number, reducing the effective respiratory surface of the air sacs of the lung. This process can continue to the point where the calculated 300 million air sacs are reduced by 30 to 45%. While the overall volume of the lungs remains constant, the alveolar capillary surface area involved in oxygen and carbon dioxide gas exchange becomes progressively smaller (Baum & Wilinsky, 1983).

The above description implies that emphysema is more a *condition* rather than a true disease entity. Many clinicians agree with the position of the American Thoracic Society (ATS) which classifies emphysema as one of a group of chronic, usually progressive, respiratory disorders that appear related but have no single cause. The term *chronic obstructive pulmonary disease* (COPD) is applied to patients with chronic bronchitis, asthma, or anatomic emphysema who exhibit persistent obstruction to bronchial air flow. Other names applied to this group of "diseases" are chronic airway obstruction (CAO) and chronic obstructive lung disease (COLD). More and more physicians are using COPD as a reportable cause of death, rather than the more definitive categories of emphysema, bronchitis, or asthma, thus confusing the statistical data on each.

COPD is by far the most common chronic pulmonary disease; its prevalence and death rate have increased greatly in recent years largely because of smoking. The age-adjusted death rate increased by 71% between 1966 and 1986 (Gail & Lenfant, 1992). Death rates are higher in men than in women and increase steeply with age.

Emphysema continues to be a widely used clinical term. The emphysema spectrum ranges from pure obstructive airway disease with bronchitis but no true emphysema, through various combinations to severe emphysema without significant bronchitis. However, "pure" emphysema or "pure" bronchitis is the exception, not the rule; they usually coexist.

Causes of Emphysema

1. Evidence that cigarette smoking is a major cause of emphysema is overwhelming; its severity is roughly dose-related (Jeffrey &

Kunz, 1981). Heavy smokers have more extensive and severe emphysema than do light smokers. However, all studies reflect that even some heavy smokers escape emphysema, indicating that other causes exist or coexist as well.

2. Air pollution. When matched according to age, sex, and smoking history, autopsied lungs from industrial cities showed more emphysema than those from cities with less pollution.

3. Genetic influences. Emphysema is a complication in hereditable diseases of connective tissue, such as cutis laxa, Marfan's syndrome, and Menke's syndrome. There is also a close link to deficiencies of serum protein alpha-1-antitrypsin, an alpha-1-protease inhibitor (alpha-1-PI). The deficiency accounts for 1% of emphysema, specifically of early panacinar types. Evidence is strong that alpha-1-PI is an inhibitor of granulocyte elastase which plays a major role in degradation of pulmonary elastic fibers. Cigarette smoking increases the amount of elastocytic protease brought to the lung and decreases the amount of functioning inhibitor.

Incidence

The incidence of emphysema has been growing in the United States. Mild degrees have been found in 80% of lungs at unselected autopsies. There is a sharp rise in occurrence in the 5th and 6th decades, even though many persons do not show symptoms earlier in life or seek medical attention for the condition. Severe emphysema has been reported in about 7% of the elderly population, usually in men. According to the 1978 Health Interview Study, there were an estimated 2,068,000 cases of emphysema (7,064,000 of chronic bronchitis, 6,035,000 of asthma). Limitation of activity was reported in 45% of persons with emphysema (only 4% limitation for persons with bronchitis). In 1972, emphysema accounted for 17,356 (3.8%) disability allowances under the Social Security Administration (American Lung Association, 1981).

Effects of Aging

While the relative volume of conductive airways remains the same during life, it has been demonstrated that the alveolar duct volume increases with advancing age at the expense of alveolar volume.

The number of alveoli increases from 24 million at birth to approximately 300 million by the eighth year and then remains relatively constant, barring disease. At age 20 they present an internal pulmonary surface area of 20 to 30 m^2. This surface area declines slowly with age, at a rate of 0.27 m^2/year.

"Normal" aging also results in thickened pulmonary arterial walls, hypertrophy and an increase in bronchial mucus glands, calcification of the tracheal and bronchial cartilages with a reduction in their flexibility, and loss of pulmonary surfactant or surface lubricant developed at the air-tissue interface of the alveoli, with loss of lung elasticity.

Whatever the cause, morphological emphysema incidence does increase slowly with age, but the highest incidence, and most severe degrees of change, occur among cigarette smokers.

Due to actual destruction and alteration of pulmonary tissue, emphysema is considered to be irreversible (Kiester, 1982; Rockstein & Sussman, 1979).

Treatment is palliative. Oxygen inhalation, intermittent positive pressure breathing apparatus (IPPB), plus expectorants and cough medicines can be used. Air conditioning can help, as well as deep breathing exercises. Avoidance of smoke and smoking is essential. For additional research and its clinical implications, see Hazzard, Bierman, Blass, Ettinger, and Halter (1994, Ch. 51). For an outline of current approaches to treatment see Keir and Dow (2000).

RUSSELL I. PIERCE
Updated by
J. GRIMLEY EVANS

See also
Respiratory System

EMPLOYEE RETIREMENT INCOME SECURITY ACT

The Employee Retirement Income Security Act (ERISA), signed by President Gerald Ford on Labor Day 1974, was acclaimed as the most important pension legislation since the Social Security Act of 1935. ERISA was enacted to standardize participation and eligibility criteria of all nongovernmental pensions and to secure adequate funding of pension plans by redefining them as corporate liabilities. At its enactment, it covered all plans in existence provided by companies engaged in interstate commerce and set minimum standards for all future plans. It does not apply to government pensions.

The private pension system in the United States had been in existence, and steadily growing, for approximately 100 years by 1974. However, the system was not regulated. Consequently, participation and eligibility standards varied considerably from plan to plan, and corporate fiduciary responsibility for adequate and competent management was not mandated. ERISA and its subsequent amendments have been relatively successful in correcting many earlier abuses (Treynor, Regan, & Priest, 1976).

Major Provisions of ERISA

The major provisions of ERISA, also known as Public Law 93-406, fall under four titles (U.S. General Services Administration, 1976). Title I lays down both general and regulatory provisions for the protection of employee benefit rights. These provisions cover reporting and disclosure, participation and vesting, funding, fiduciary responsibility, and administration and enforcement. Title II amends the Internal Revenue Code of 1954 relating to pension plans to regulate payroll accounting. Title III addresses general jurisdiction, administration, and enforcement of the law, by explicitly coordinating the secretary of the treasury and the Department of Labor by way of the Joint Pension Task Force. Title IV provides for plan termination insurance with the establishment of the Pension Benefit Guaranty Corporation (PBGC) and with the definition of liability criteria in the case of plan termination.

Important among the most recent laws enacting or amending the 1974 provisions of ERISA are the Retirement Equity Act of 1984, the Pension Protection Act of 1987, and the 1990 amendment of Title I of ERISA to require qualifying employer securities to include interest in publicly traded partnerships. Several revisions of Title II have followed tax reform, revenue, and omnibus budget enactments (U.S. House Committee on Education and Labor, 1991).

PBGC, established by Title IV of ERISA, is a self-financing, government-owned corporation, whose purpose is to guarantee basic pension benefits in covered private plans if they terminate with insufficient funds. Two benefit insurance programs are administered for single-employer and multiemployer plans, respectively. All defined benefit plans (i.e., pensions plans with fixed benefits established in advance of retirement) must pay prescribed premiums to PBGC per plan participation. Multiemployer plans can be insured for insolvency instead of termination to assist them when they are unable to pay basic benefits; however, these plans are obligated to repay. Workers whose pensions are guaranteed by the PBGC are protected up to a limit of under $3,000 per month (adjusted annually for inflation). By the mid-1980s, debates developed over the growing deficit of the PBGC. Part of the Omnibus Budget Reconciliation Act of 1987 amended ERISA by requiring tougher minimum funding standards and establishing stricter upper limits on tax-deductible contributions to defined benefit plans.

Other retirement savings strategies, such as individual retirement accounts, defined contribution plans (including 401K), and employment stock ownership plans, are not covered by the PBGC. These alternative savings strategies have grown steadily since the passage of ERISA. Investments in defined contribution plans have more than doubled since 1975. The growth in the ratio of defined contribution to defined benefit plans has occurred across industrial sectors and exceeds 6.0 (seven defined contribution plans for every defined benefit plan) across sectors (O'Rand & Henretta, 1999).

An important implication of these trends is the increased vulnerability of women workers in achieving pension savings. Women participate disproportionately in retirement savings strategies not protected by ERISA (see Employee Benefits Research Institute, 1997). The cash-out and portability features of these new pensions make them attractive and useful in the short term for managing expected and unexpected financial needs (home buying, college tuition, hospitalization costs, etc.). However, these schemes pose higher risks and greater uncertainty for long-term retirement saving.

ANGELA M. O'RAND

See also
Employment
Pensions

EMPLOYMENT

The Older Labor Force

Employment in what is conventionally regarded as old age remains by far the exception among both men and women in the United States. As of 1999, only 4 million of the more than 32 million noninstitutionalized persons 65 and older, or 12.3% of the total, were working or looking for work (U.S. Bureau of Labor Statistics, 2000). Not surprisingly, older men are more likely than older women to be in the labor force—16.9% and 8.9%, respectively, in 1999. Somewhat higher proportions have some paid work experience over the course of any one year, but for the majority of older men and women, participation in the formal labor force is an activity of the past.

Few labor force developments of the postwar era have been as pronounced as the labor force withdrawal of men age 65 and older, 45.8% of whom were in the labor force in 1950. Eligibility for retired worker benefits under Social Security as early as age 62 and, for many, private pension benefits at even younger ages has contributed to a decline in labor force participation rates among younger workers as well. Men between the ages of 55 and 64, for example, had a labor force participation rate of 67.9% in 1999, down from 86.9% in 1950.

The picture is demonstrably different for middle-aged women, millions of whom have accompanied their younger counterparts into the labor force over the past five decades. In 1999, the labor force participation rate of 55- to 64-year-old women stood at 51.5%, up sharply from the 1950s rate of 27%. In contrast, relatively little change has occurred among women age 65 or older, whose attachment to the labor force has historically been weak; their 1999 labor force participation rate of 8.9% was little changed from the 9.7% rate of 1950.

The steady march of middle-aged women into the labor force has not been enough to offset the withdrawal of men, with the result that there are relatively fewer middle-aged and older labor force participants today than in 1950. For example, nearly 43% of the 55+ population were working or looking for work in 1950; by 1999, that was the case for only 31.8%. Nonetheless, the divergent trends have markedly altered the gender composition of the older workforce, which henceforth will refer to persons age 55 and older. Women currently comprise just over 44% of that older labor force, in contrast to about 23% in 1950.

By the mid-1980s, the decline in labor force participation on the part of older men had begun to taper off. Although it is premature to conclude that this development heralds a reversal of early retirement trends—participation rates have both risen and fallen slightly in ensuing years—the trend toward ever earlier retirement does seem to have come to an end.

Unemployment

If they are in the labor force, virtually all older persons have jobs. Unemployment rates tend to fall with age, in part because access to retirement benefits gives many older workers the option of leaving the labor force if they do lose their jobs. Workers who withdraw from the labor force are not counted among the unemployed, even if they would prefer to be working. Persons 55 and older had an unemployment rate of 2.8% in 1999, versus 4.4% for those under the age of 55.

Lower unemployment rates obscure the formidable barriers that older persons face if they decide to undertake a job search. A number of factors, not the least of which is age discrimination, contribute to the difficulties older job seekers experience when looking for work. One consequence is that older job seekers are more likely than younger ones to find themselves among the long-term unemployed. In 1999, one third (34%) of all older unemployed workers were out of work for at least 15 weeks; the comparable figure for the under-55 unemployed was 24%. Nonetheless, this figure represents a decline from earlier in the decade. Older workers, like their younger counterparts, have benefited from the robust job growth of recent years. Even so, average duration of unemployment remains substantially longer for older job losers (18.2 weeks vs. 12.9 weeks in 1999). In addition, older displaced workers who manage to become reemployed are more likely than their younger counterparts to experience a sharp drop in earnings (Couch, 1998; U.S. Congressional Budget Office, 1993).

Older Worker Costs and Benefits

Rare is the survey that fails to reveal exceptionally positive attitudes on the part of employers toward older workers, who time after time receive high marks when it comes to loyalty, dependability, trustworthiness, good work habits, and the like (e.g., American Association of Retired Persons, 1998, 2000; Barth, McNaught, & Rizzi, 1993). Yet, those same employers are notably less effusive when it comes to some very bottom-line attributes, such as flexibility and technological know-how, and it is these attributes that employers apparently want in their workers today.

Concerns about costs also undermine the position of older persons in the workforce. Older workers may be more expensive than younger workers, because, in general, wages rise with tenure, and tenure increases with age; the per-person cost of certain benefits, particularly health insurance and pension contributions, also rises with age (Clark, 1994). According to Clark (1994, p. 1), "[M]any employers seem to believe that older workers are more costly relative to their value than younger workers," but the key words, it should be noted, are "relative to their value." If higher costs are associated with greater productivity or other positive returns to the employer, then those costs may be justified.

Meta-analytic reviews of the literature on the relationship between age and job performance reveal an extremely weak relationship between age and performance. In fact, Sterns and McDaniel (1994) have concluded that, if anything, performance improves slightly with age, regardless of whether supervisory ratings or more objective measures are used to assess performance, but the relationship is tenuous indeed.

Interest in Employment

The extent to which many of the nearly 38 million older persons who are not in the labor force could be enticed back in is by no means certain. Worker surveys and public opinion polls over the years have revealed considerable interest in postretirement employment on the part of preretirees. For example, 80% of baby boomers contend that they expect to work in retirement (American Association

of Retired Persons, 1998). Similar percentages have been reported for other age groups by the National Institute on Aging (1993) and the Employee Benefit Research Institute (Yakoboski & Dickemper, 1997). Yet, although many workers—perhaps one third to one half—retire gradually by moving into what might be called postcareer or bridge employment before full retirement (Quinn, 1999), older nonworkers express little enthusiasm for paid employment. As of 1999, fewer than 800,000 men and women age 55 and older who were not in the labor force—or barely 2%—apparently wished they were working. An even smaller proportion technically qualifies as discouraged workers; that is, they are not bothering to look for work because they do not think they could find it (U.S. Bureau of Labor Statistics, 2000).

One explanation for such disinterest might be the unpleasantness of the job hunt for older seekers; in addition, the paucity of attractive part-time employment options undoubtedly serves as a deterrent. An expansion of employment opportunities for older workers, especially in the form of good part-time jobs, might generate greater enthusiasm for postretirement employment on the part of older men and women who are currently out of the labor force. Formal phased retirement programs that allow workers to ease into retirement by reducing work hours in the jobs they have would seem to hold promise for retaining older workers beyond normal retirement age. To date, however, such programs in the United States are rare outside of higher education.

Job Characteristics

Three fourths of all older workers are employed full time, although interest and involvement in part-time workers increases with age. Regardless of age, the large majority of men and women who work part time do so by choice. By 1999, only 4% of older part-time workers were employed part time because they could not find full-time work.

Older workers can be found in virtually every industry and occupation. Although older men are disproportionately represented in agriculture, the industry and occupational distributions of older and younger workers are, on the whole, quite comparable. The service industries claim the greatest share of older and younger workers—somewhat less than 40% of each age group.

Gender differences in occupation and industry are more pronounced than age differences. Half of older women workers, but less than one third of older men, can be found in service industries, whereas agriculture, construction, and manufacturing claim a greater share of men. Older women also are heavily represented in traditionally female occupations, such as clerical and administrative support.

Again, regardless of age, self-employed workers are in the minority; nonetheless, older workers are substantially more likely than younger ones to work for themselves. As of 1999, some 15% of workers 55 and older and 22% of all 65+ workers were self-employed; this was the case for less than 8% of the under-55 workforce.

Public Policy and Older Workers

Despite the aging of the U.S. labor force, policies to promote older worker employment or to facilitate the transition to retirement are uncommon. The United States lacks a national older worker employment policy or, for that matter, a national retirement policy.

To the extent that older workers have been the focal point of public policy in recent years, it has been in terms of the role a longer worklife might play in alleviating the projected soaring public costs of supporting an aging population. Government efforts are perhaps best reflected in two provisions of the 1983 amendments to the Social Security Act, one of which increases Social Security benefits for each year that workers delay collecting between the ages of 65 and 69, and the other of which gradually increases the eligibility for full Social Security benefits, starting for workers turning 62 in 2000. By 2027, full Social Security benefits will be not be payable until age 67; workers will still be able to collect benefits at 62, but the reduction for early retirement will be greater than it is now. As policy makers begin to grapple with the long-range solvency of the Social Security Trust Funds, proposals to raise the full-benefit eligibility age beyond 67 are being raised. Few workers seem to find appealing the prospect of being required to work longer for full benefits.

In early 2000, Congress voted to eliminate the Social Security earnings cap for beneficiaries between the ages of 65 and 69, who lost $1 in benefits for every $3 in earnings above a limit (set at $17,000 in 2000). Both the House of Representatives and the Senate were unanimous in their vote to repeal, even though the change would benefit relatively few older persons. Most Social Security beneficiaries are out of the labor force and lack any earnings to worry about, and the limit did not apply to beneficiaries age 70 and older. The Congressional Budget Office has estimated that only about 625,000 workers (out of 9.3 million men and women in the affected age group) would see higher Social Security benefits in 2000 as a result of the repeal, which was not extended to younger beneficiaries.

Over the past three decades, the government has taken steps to eliminate discrimination against older workers, thereby making it easier for people who want to remain at work to do so. Although it persists, age-based discrimination against workers and job seekers age 40 and older is illegal under the provisions of the Age Discrimination in Employment Act (ADEA) of 1967 and its subsequent amendments. Most occupations saw the end of mandatory retirement with the ADEA amendments of 1986; however, there is little evidence that mandatory retirement was responsible for much of the labor force withdrawal of the past several decades.

To date, federally funded training programs, in particular those under the Job Training Partnership Act (JTPA) of 1982, that might benefit older workers have for the most part been restricted to the economically disadvantaged. Any JTPA accomplishments aside, the act was not designed to meet the training and retraining needs of the large majority of older workers who are not economically disadvantaged but who might be at risk of obsolescence and vulnerable to unemployment. The job-training system was fundamentally overhauled in 1998 with the passage of the Workforce Investment Act. It remains to be seen how well this legislation serves older workers, who are hardly mentioned in it and are not singled out as an underserved population.

Funded until Title V of the Older Americans Act, the Senior Community Service Employment Program (SCSEP) provides minimum-wage employment to low-income elderly, many of whom are women and/or minorities. This relatively small program ($444 million in fiscal year 1999) assists a group of very disadvantaged job seekers.

Private Sector Policies

Because most workers are employed in the private sector, it makes sense to look there for efforts to hire, train, and retain older workers. Until now, there has been scant evidence that employers are actively responding to the aging of the workforce with programs or policies that might keep older workers employed or employable, despite substantial labor and skills shortages facing many of them (American Association of Retired Persons, 2000; Barth, McNaught, & Rizzi, 1993).

Into the Future

According to the most recent projections by the U.S. Bureau of Labor Statistics (Fullerton, 1999a), by 2008, the labor force participation rate of persons age 55 and older will rise to 36.8%. Projections much further out are speculative at best, especially given rapid technological change, a global economy, and the growth of markets and labor pools in the developing world. Still, projections from the Bureau of Labor Statistics (BLS) point to a participation rate for the 55 and older population of 38.4% in 2015 but falling to 33.6% in 2025, when baby boomers will all be between the ages of 61 and 79 (Fullerton, 1999b).

There is reason to believe that participation rates could well be higher than indicated in these projections. For one thing, boomers themselves, who are marching inexorably toward old age, do say they expect and even want to work in retirement. If they decide to prolong their work lives, boomers may prove a force for employers to reckon with. In some respects, the retirement prospects of the baby boomers appear less promising than those of today's retirees: There is little hope for any significant improvement in Social Security benefits, the growth of defined contribution pension plans at the expense of defined benefit plans has shifted much of the responsibility for retirement income from employers to workers, and many workers are not saving adequately for their retirement years. Employers might well face greater employment demands from middle-aged workers forced to or desirous of postponing retirement beyond what is currently the norm. Furthermore, persistent labor shortages might well cause employers to place greater emphasis on hiring, retaining, and retraining older workers.

Even if the BLS projections prove close to the mark and participation rates rise but modestly, the older workforce will grow more rapidly than that of other age groups, and the number of older persons in the workforce will increase. Looking ahead from 1999, BLS projections point to an additional 7.5 million labor force participants 55 and older in 2008, when older persons will comprise more than 16% of the labor force, up from just 12.7% in 1999. Most of this increase (73%) will be due to the rise in the number of "younger" older workers—ages 55 to 64. Over this period, the median age of the labor force will rise as well, from 38.7 years in 1998 to 40.7 years in 2008, a "record level," according to the BLS (Fullerton, 1999a, p. 19). Employers, policy makers, and others who worry about the impact of an aging workforce on economic growth and competitiveness can take comfort in the fact that the 2008 median age of the labor force is expected to be only slightly above what it was in the early 1960s, when the economy was anything but sluggish.

SARA RIX

See also
    Economics
    Employee Retirement Income Security Act
    Retirement

END-OF-LIFE CARE

Death is not what it used to be (Institute of Medicine, 1997). The typical American's estimated life expectancy reached 75.8 years in 1995 (Cobbs et al., 1999). Women may now expect to live nearly 79 years and men almost 73 years. Those 65 and over constitute an increasingly large number and proportion of the U.S. population.

As the population ages, there is a growing need for end-of-life care, and the costs associated with providing such care are considerable. Data suggest that end-of-life care consumes 10%–12% of all health care expenditures and that 27% of Medicare expenditures are spent for the 5%–6% of Medicare beneficiaries who die in any given year. In 1988 the mean Medicare payment for the final year of life was $13,316, compared with a mean of $1,924 for all other Medicare beneficiaries (Chochinov & Kristjanson, 1998).

Sites of Death

Hospitals. Unfortunately, site-of-death data are incomplete and vary across the country. However, 1980 mortality statistics indicated that 74% of deaths occurred in institutions—60.5% in hospitals and 13.5% in other institutions (Institute of Medicine, 1997). Two important developments contributed to this: coverage for hospice care by Medicare and other private insurance and reduction in the use of inpatient hospital care with the implementation of Medicare's prospective, per case hospital reimbursement. The evolving pattern of care—from institution to institution and from one health care provider to the next—creates fragmented care that is most difficult during the end of life. Hospice and palliative care are responses to perceived inadequacies in the prevention and relief of symptoms and distress in people approaching death.

Hospice Care. Hospices—organizations concerned exclusively with dying patients and those close to them—are intended to provide workable and reliable structures for turning palliative care principles into practice. Hospices are committed to being accessible to patients and families 24 hours a day, 7 days a week; to constructing interdisciplinary teams that provide comprehensive and continuous care; and to developing strategies to guide the provision of services in response to the different dimensions of care (see below) faced by patients and their families.

Today's hospice movement began in Great Britain in the late 1940s with Dame Cicely Saunders's work with dying patients. A physician, social worker, and nurse, Dame Saunders established the St. Christopher's Hospice in London in 1967, a teaching and research facility dedicated to the physical, emotional, and spiritual care of the dying. By 1996, about 1,100 hospices were operating in the

United States (Singh et al., 1996). Approximately 30% were independent organizations, 22% were affiliated with home care agencies, 28% with hospitals, and others with larger integrated health systems (Institute of Medicine, 1997).

Dimensions of End-of-Life Care

The illness experience is characterized by four different dimensions, which vary in importance at different stages of the dying process (Institute of Medicine, 1997).

Physical. In addition to a thorough initial patient evaluation, good end-of-life care requires solid familiarity with the incidence and management of specific symptoms with various illnesses. One should fully understand symptom pathophysiology and complexity, especially the coexistence of multiple symptomatology.

Psychological. This dimension encompasses cognitive and emotional health, as well as patient and family needs. It may include depression, anxiety, and other common psychological issues.

Spiritual. For many, a spiritual approach toward death inspires a search for meaning, peace, or transcendence that may replace fear and despair with hope and serenity. The role of spiritual care is commonly thought to belong to chaplains and religious services, but nurses are often able to identify those patients who might benefit from discussion of spiritual issues.

Practical. Patients and families need assistance in arranging home services, changing the physical features of the home to accommodate the patient's needs, shopping and other errands, and managing schedules. The practical dimension often overlaps with the other three dimensions of care.

Breaking Bad News

One of the most stressful tasks a health care provider faces is informing a patient that he or she has a fatal illness. The manner in which bad news is delivered has a significant impact on the patient's remaining quality of life. Robert Buckman recommends the following six-step protocol for delivering bad news (EPEC, 1999):

• Getting started
• Finding out what the patient knows
• Finding out how much the patient wants to know
• Sharing the information
• Responding to patient and family feelings
• Planning and follow-up

Establishing Goals

Sensitivity to patient and family values is also important in establishing goals and plans for end-of-life care. A fundamental principle of patient-centered care is not to assume what patients want to know but rather to ask them what they want to know and to suggest questions that they may have. One should develop culturally sensitive interview protocols to elicit patient perceptions, expectations, and preferences and goals (Gerteis et al., 1993).

Decisions to Forgo Life-Sustaining Treatment

Forgoing artificial nutrition and hydration at the end of life is fully consistent with the principles of palliative care (Ahronheim, 1996; McCann, 1994). For example, extensive study of parenteral and enteral calorie replacement in patients with the anorexia-cachexia syndrome of AIDS and cancer has failed to show significant improvement of quality of life. Any form of feeding tube, including jejunostomy tubes, has failed to reduce the risk of aspiration and may be associated with serious side effects, such as peritonitis or pain and discomfort.

The practice of hydrating a patient who wishes to forgo life-sustaining treatment is illogical. The palliative effect of hydration is limited. An intravenous line may be intrusive and painful, especially in very ill patients with poor venous access. Sips of water as tolerated, ice chips, and gentle mouth care are likely more palliative than parenteral fluids (Meier, Morrison, & Ahronheim, 1998).

A broad introduction to current issues and practice in palliative and end-of-life care is found in Doyle, Hanks, and MacDonald (1998). Website sources on palliative care and end-of-life care include *www.soros.org/death* and *www.lastacts.org*.

RAINIER SORIANO
DIANE MEIER

See also
    Caregiver Burden
    Hospice
    Living Wills and Durable Power of Attorney
    Pain
    Palliative Care

ENDOCRINE SYSTEM
See
    Dehydroepiandrosterone
    Growth Hormone and Insulin-like Growth Factor-1
    Hormone Replacement Therapy: Estrogen
    Melatonin
    Parathyroid Hormone, Calcitonin, and 1,25 Dihydroxyvitamin D
    Thyroid Gland

ENERGY AND BIOENERGETICS

Limited life span and the occurrence of age-related disease may be viewed as consequences of decreased availability of the energy required for maintenance of cellular integrity. The concept is supported by studies of DNA mutation in the mitochondria of mammalian tissues, yeast, and other fungi (Linnane, 1992). These studies suggest accumulation with time of random mutations of mitochondrial DNA (mtDNA) leading to decreased ability of the organelles to supply energy for maintenance of cellular function. Research linking bioenergetics and aging also suggests that the constant presence of highly reactive metabolic fuels and damaging by-products of oxidative metabolism may be deleterious in the long term (B. Ames, 1992; Masoro & McCarter, 1991).

Metabolic Rate and Body Composition

Twenty-four-hour whole body energy expenditure (24EE) can be measured under free-living conditions in humans, using the "doubly labeled water" (D2180) method, but insufficient data are currently available for definite conclusions (Young, 1992). Studies by McGandy, Barrows, Spania, Meredith, Stone, and Norris (1966) of caloric intake indicate total daily energy expenditure decreases with age in healthy adult men 20 to 99 years of age. Vaughan, Zurlo, and Ravussin (1991) used indirect calorimetry to estimate 24EE in men and women 18 to 85 years old under conditions of restricted physical activity. Their results show significantly lower total energy expenditure in the older versus younger age groups.

These and other studies suggest decreased rates of cellular metabolism or decreased intensity of metabolism with advancing age. Such a conclusion cannot be drawn, however, because of the confounding effects of age-related changes in body mass and composition. A key factor is the almost 100-fold range in metabolic rate (MR) per unit mass of different tissues: Adipose tissue, skeletal muscle, intestines, and bone represent a different class of metabolic activity (30 to 100 times lower activity) in comparison with that of heart, liver, kidney, and brain (Elia, 1991). Current methods of normalizing 24EE to fat-free mass (FFM), lean mass, or an exponential function of body mass ("metabolic mass") assume scaled proportions of vital organs, as well as constancy of tissue composition with age. Both of these are questionable assumptions, indicating the need for more information in this area (Elia, 1991). There is, therefore, no precise basis at present for comparing MRs of individuals of different ages. Strong correlations have been demonstrated between MR and FFM in individuals of different ages (Vaughan, Zurlo, & Ravussin, 1991), possibly because much of the variability of mass with age is due to loss of muscle mass, the major component of FFM (Tzankoff & Norris, 1977). Decreased 24EE with age may be a consequence either of decreased rate of cellular metabolism or of increased proportions of tissues of lower MRs. Major components of 24EE are basal MR (BMR), 60% to 75% of total metabolism; physical activity, 15% to 30%; and diet-induced thermogenesis (DIT) (energy required for processing of ingested nutrients), plus or minus 10% of total metabolism. There is evidence that BMR decreases with age independent of changes in FFM (Fukagawa, Bandani, & Young, 1990) and that physical activity

declines with age. The latter effect also has a positive feedback because decreased activity would lead to loss of FFM and altered body composition. There is little evidence indicating change in DIT with age (Young, 1992). Current information therefore suggests FFM and physical activity, rather than aging processes, are important factors regulating 24EE in humans. Data obtained in rodents by indirect calorimetry do not show decreased 24EE or resting MR with age (McCarter & Palmer, 1992).

Modulators of MR

Many factors influence MR. In the context of aging, those of current interest are mitochondrial content and activity, neuroendocrine systems, and nutrition. A. J. Hulbert, Mantaj, and Janssens (1991) demonstrated differences in rates of energy metabolism of vital organs associated with differences in mean mitochondrial membrane surface area (MMSA). It might be expected, therefore, that during senescence there is loss of capacity for energy metabolism associated with loss of MMSA. The few morphological studies available demonstrate such an effect in liver and heart of aging rodents (Herbener, 1976). In contrast, functional measurements of oxidative capacity in liver of 10- to 30-month-old Fischer 344 rats indicate no loss of capacity with age (Rumsey, Kendrick, & Starnes, 1987). Extensive literature documents age-related changes in mitochondrial structure and function (Gafni, 1987). However, conflicting results have been obtained when studies were conducted in vitro, using homogenates and tissue slices (Peng, Peng, & Chen, 1977). It is not clear how these data relate to MRs in vivo because such results depend greatly on conditions of incubation (Elia, 1991).

Regulation of MR by the nervous and hormonal systems occurs via control of skeletal muscle and fuel mobilization. Activation by the central nervous system of skeletal muscles during physical activity can produce a 10-fold increase in whole-body MR. With advancing age in humans there is decreased intensity and duration of physical activity (Cunningham, Montoye, Metzner, & Keller, 1968). Similarly, with age, laboratory rodents exhibit decreased voluntary wheel running and decreased spontaneous movement in cages (Holloszy, Smith, Vining, & Adams, 1985; Yu, Masoro, & McMahan,

1985). The sympathetic nervous system (SNS) regulates MR directly and also indirectly via effects on DIT. There is evidence of increased sympathetic tone with advancing age, as seen in increased levels of plasma norepinephrine and blunted responsiveness of the SNS in response to a meal (R. S. Schwartz, Jaeger, & Veith, 1990). A direct effect of SNS activity on MR occurs via activation of brown adipose tissue (BAT) in small animals and via skeletal muscle and vital organ metabolism in humans. The extensive studies of Scarpace and colleagues (Scarpace, Mooradian, & Morley, 1988) indicate less capacity for thermogenesis with age in rats, a consequence of decreased mitochondrial content and diminished activation of BAT in older animals. In humans there is little evidence of significant involvement of BAT in facultative thermogenesis. Rather, skeletal muscle metabolism may be modulated by SNS activity (Astrup, Simonsen, Bullow, Madsen, & Christensen, 1989), but variation with age has not been established.

Thyroid hormones (T3 and T4) are known to play a role in regulating MR. There are no consistent data regarding changing levels of plasma T3 and T4 with age, but there is evidence of decreased turnover of T4 with advancing age in humans (Gregerman, 1964). Available literature suggests decreased influence of thyroid hormone on MR, possibly a consequence of peripheral factors rather than decreased output of the thyroid gland with age (Perlmutter & Riggs, 1949).

Nutrition as MR Modulator.   There is overwhelming evidence that restriction of food intake leads to decreased MR per unit mass (Garrow, 1978). The metabolic response appears to vary with age, however. In weanling rats the decrease in MR is transient: Within 6 weeks lean mass adjusts so that MR per unit of lean mass is the same as that of ad libitum–fed rats. When restriction is initiated in older animals (6 months of age), the decrease in MR persists beyond 6 weeks (Gonzales-Pacheco, Buss, Koehler, Woodside, & Alpert, 1993). Indeed, food consumption studies (Yu, Masoro, & McMahan, 1985) suggest that restriction in adulthood would lead to decreased metabolism over several months in rats or several years in the case of longer-lived species such as nonhuman primates (Ramsey, Roecker, Weindruch, & Kemnitz, 1997). The results are of conceptual importance for aging because the life-prolonging action of dietary restriction has been ascribed to decreased MR, in accordance with the "rate of living" theory of aging (Sacher, 1977). Measurements of 24EE following long-term restriction of food intake (initiated at weaning) show that MR per unit of mass is the same in rats fed ad libitum and those fed the restricted diet (P. H. Duffy, Fevers, Leakey, Nakamura, Turturro, & Hart, 1989; McCarter & Palmer, 1992). These measurements demonstrate that decreased MR is not essential for the retardation of aging processes by dietary restriction.

Current Status

The foregoing discussion suggests that age is not a major determinant of MR. It is not clear if the MR of cells of individual tissues declines with age. Altered body and tissue composition with age will change MR via the relative contributions of different tissues to total metabolism. The direct involvement of MR in aging processes is not clear, despite long-standing acceptance of the "rate of living theory" of aging. Support for this theory has come from experiments using poikilotherms, but interpretation of these results has been questioned (Lints, 1989). In addition, Austad and Fischer (1991) reviewed data on lifetime energy expenditures of 164 mammalian species. They concluded that increased body size and behavioral characteristics were more important determinants of life span than MR. Other studies involving increased MR in the absence of decreased survival (Holloszy, 1993) also suggest that aging processes are not directly linked to rate of metabolism. Rather, evidence implicates components of the metabolic system as contributors to aging processes. Components identified by current research include oxidative modification of proteins and nucleic acids (Ames, 1992; Stadtman, 1992), reactive by-products of oxidative metabolism such as free radicals (Sohal, 1993), and metabolic fuels, such as glucose, that undergo nonenzymatic reactions and modify macromolecular structures (Cerami, 1985). It seems likely that the gradual accumulation of modified cellular structures arising from oxidation, glycation, free-radical, and other reactions will in time compromise function and limit survival. This involvement of energy metabolism in aging processes may depend not on the rate of metabolism but rather on the passage of time.

ROGER J. M. McCARTER

See also

Mitochondrial DNA Abnormalities
Musculoskeletal System
Oxidative Stress Theory

ENTITLEMENT

An entitlement is a right that has been granted, and that the individual may exercise. The concept has been associated with policies directed to the redistribution of resources or to the provision of resources that are seen as basic rights of all individuals in society. In the area of welfare, it has come to be contrasted with a notion of "means tests," although the use of the terms are frequently mixed. For a general discussion, for example, of the distinction between age and need as a basis of entitlement, see Neugarten (1982).

A common example of an entitlement as a basic right granted to all individuals in society is embodied in the laws providing for free public education to all. How such a right has varied with changes in values over time can be charted by the changes in the way the right is provided. For example, free public education has been universalized to include all persons, whether citizens or not, excluding no one on the basis of sex, race, nationality, or other characteristics. In recent years, even the handicapped must be provided free public education, no matter how high the unit cost of the provision of this service. Over time free public education has become more broadly based, including younger ages (preschool and kindergarten), older adolescents (since mandatory levels of education increased), and also to some extent even higher and adult education. Additional examples of universal entitlements are incorporated in the public services provided through government, such as the courts, police protection, maintenance of roads, and so forth.

By contrast, many aspects of welfare are drawn from concepts of charity from government, church, and private persons, one characterization of the latter being "Lady Bountiful" giving to the poor. This was articulated in the United States in former President Reagan's emphasis on providing services only for the "truly needy." This notion of provision of services requires "means tests," and these are seen by many analysts of social policy as degrading and inefficient. The degradation is associated with the fact that one has to prove need, and the inefficiency is associated with issues of marginal taxation. In particular, those who do not quite satisfy the cutoff for a means test (i.e., those who are just above the level required to be included for a service), are usually totally excluded from the service, but they may be no better off than others who are provided the service. Phrased another way, for some who are included by a means test, there is no incentive to seek work as a supplement because the additional income might mean loss of services. A broad review of issues associated with social programs covering these issues is found in Garfinkel (1982).

For older persons, issues of entitlement versus means tests have been mixed in considerations of policy. In the United States health services provide coverage through Medicare and Medicaid, but the system does not have the characteristics of the universal health systems of countries like Great Britain or Canada. However, the system does provide coverage for the "truly needy" in a number of ways. For example, there is the observation that once a person enters a nursing home, services there will continue even if the person has no funds.

Social Security was initiated under a concept of insurance. The coverage has been made progressively more universal, and it is clearly recognized now as a tax transfer system providing coverage in one form or another for almost everyone. Further moves in the direction of entitlement for Social Security would involve equalization of payments to all, independent of the amount paid in. Changes in Social Security have not clearly moved in any single direction of entitlement or means tests, although the introduction of taxation of Social Security "benefits" is a clear aspect of adding a means test.

Entitlements specific for older persons have frequently been developed (e.g., lower fares, tax exemptions, property tax reductions). Advancement of policy supporting such entitlements usually is based on notions that older persons are economically deprived. The economics of aging does not provide a clear support for such a position (Schulz, 1980).

In the 1990s the debate over entitlements has become accentuated in the United States for a number of reasons: The increasing national debt has been viewed with alarm; the proportion and amount of federal dollars involved in the fields of health and social security for an aging population has risen substantially; the ratio of employed workers to retired persons is projected to decrease dramatically; and potentially the tax basis for support of entitlements will shrink. Thus, concerns have been expressed about the ability of the economy to support the entitlements when the "baby boom generation" reaches retirement age. The fundamental incompatibility between politically popular values of both maintaining low taxes and providing high support for entitlements will fuel the debate on entitlement in the foreseeable future.

The recent and dramatic improvement in the federal government's budgetary situation—rising surpluses and elimination of the national debt now being projected by as early as 2013—has profound implications for the discussion around entitlements. The issue now becomes less their affordability and more the nation's interest in continuing programs—many of them directed at the old—that confer future benefits independent of annual congressional appropriations decisions. Thus, the entitlement debate is now couched increasingly in political and ideological terms rather than economic or budgetary ones. If entitlements are to be eliminated—as was the case in 1996 with the transition from Aid to Families with Dependent Children to Temporary Aid to Needy Families for low-income families with children—the discussion will now be more about preferred values than about available dollars.

EDGAR F. BORGATTA
Updated by
ROBERT B. HUDSON

See also

Economics
Filial Responsibility
Medicare
Medicaid
Pensions
Social Security

ENVIRONMENTAL PSYCHOLOGY

Individuals and their environments are constantly changing; both must be understood if elderly adults are to function optimally in their environments. Investigation into the relationship between individuals and the environment may focus on the large-scale environment. Rural-urban differences and environmental knowledge, for example, may be studied to determine how older people adapt to their environments or what environmental characteristics contribute to successful negotiation of the old-age process. Studies of smaller-scale environments may focus on nursing homes, retirement communities, or even design features of single-family homes with similar purposes.

Theoretical Conceptions

Behavior may be thought of as a result of the interaction between the individual and the environment, although Altman (1997) and others lament the state of theory in environmental psychology. Several conceptual schemes have been proposed to aid in the understanding of that interaction. Lawton (1982) and colleagues have proposed a model of person-environment fit that takes into account the physical, cognitive, and social characteristics of the individual and the various influences of the environment. Lawton contends that individuals of low competence are especially at risk because they are able to tolerate only small changes in their situation before adverse effects on behavior are evident. More competent individuals, on the other hand, are able to tolerate a wider range of stresses and change before behavioral decrements become evident. Another feature of the model is that the most comfortable situation is not necessarily the best; people function at their maximum level when the influence of the environment is slightly stronger than they can easily manage. A final feature of the model is that if a given individual is showing evidence of inadequate coping, intervention strategies may be applied to increase the capabilities of the individual to cope with the situation, or to modify the environment to make it either easier for the person to manage or to make it more stimulating to provide greater challenge.

Kahana (1982) has proposed an alternate person-environment fit that emphasizes congruence between the needs of the individual and characteristics of the environment. By knowing both the needs of the individual and the features of the setting, an optimal match may be made. Parr (1980) proposed a four-factor model that includes individual characteristics, environmental characteristics, mediators such as expectancies and importance of environmental characteristics, and the resultant behavior. Although none of these models is fully tested, they provide useful frameworks for the understanding of behavior of older adults. In reviews of the diversity of conceptualization in environmental psychology, Stokols (1995) predicts increasing research attention devoted to clarifying transactions between older individuals and their environments.

Large-Scale Environments

Studies of the functioning of older adults in their environments have found that there is a relationship between a range of psychological variables and the environment. Factors such as community involvement and satisfaction with architectural dwelling features may be associated with positive mental health, whereas such factors as environmental barriers and lack of control over the environment can be associated with poorer mental health.

Older adults have shown poorer memory for spatial information compared with young adults, but that difference is diminished when the information to be recalled is taken from a familiar environment. The knowledge elderly adults have of their neighborhoods has been found to be related to several cognitive abilities; neighborhood knowledge also has been found to be related to the use elderly adults actually make of their neighborhoods (Walsh, Krauss, & Regnier, 1981). Nursing home residents with higher spatial skills know their environment better and use a wider range of facilities than less able residents (Norris & Krauss, 1992).

Small-Scale Environments

Characteristics of the living environment have been found to be related to the well-being of older residents. The Multiphasic Environmental Assessment Procedure (Moos & Lemke, 1985) has been used in well over 200 settings to assess physical features, staff characteristics, social climate, and policies and programs. Use of the tool permits patient placement optimizing the person-environment fit. Other efforts in this area have resulted in recommendations for modifications to homes or construction of living environments to facilitate the highest possible functioning of physically impaired older adults (Pirkl, 1994). Recent literature focuses on the functional adaptation of people with varying degrees of dementia to specialized residential units (Kovach, 1998).

Relocation

Large numbers of elderly adults choose, or are forced, to move for a variety of reasons. Although it is exceptionally difficult to carry out controlled studies on the effects of such moves, a considerable body of knowledge on such effects has been accumulating (Kovach, 1998). Positive outcomes in terms of factors such as health, satisfaction with living arrangements, social interaction, and daily functioning are likely to occur if the move was voluntary. Those individuals who move because of necessity are more likely to experience negative outcomes, as are the more elderly and the more frail. Individuals who can predict what their lives will be like in the new locations tend to have more positive experiences following a move than those who move knowing little about their future surroundings or their lives in those surroundings. Individuals moving into housing situations representing significant improvements over previous settings also are likely to experience positive effects from the move. Concern about a possible involuntary move may be associated with increased physical and mental health problems.

People who elect to reside in congregate housing are frequently found to be pleased with the housing arrangements. They avail themselves of a wide range of services, establish social networks, and participate in a variety of activities, especially if they had previously been activity oriented (Moos & Lemke, 1985). At the same time, it is possible to provide so many services that people become less responsible for their own well-being and may develop a dependency that contributes to lowered functional health (Lawton, 1976). In institutional settings, moving groups of people from one setting to another appears to produce fewer negative consequences than moving individuals into new settings where they know neither other residents nor staff members. Although no move should be considered to be problem free, choice, better circumstances, adequate preparation, and availability of support all contribute to positive relocation outcomes.

ISELI K. KRAUSS

See also
    Architecture
    Assisted Living: A New Model of Supportive
        Housing with Long-Term Care Services
    Housing
    Long-Term Care Assessment

EPIDEMIOLOGICAL AND SOCIAL CONTEXT OF AIDS
See
    AIDS/HIV in Older Adults
    AIDS: The Epidemiological and Social Context
        of AIDS

EPIDEMIOLOGY OF AGING: A NEW VIEW OF HEALTH STATUS AND RISK FACTORS

In most developed countries there has been a steady and profound increase in the proportion of older people in the population. In large part, this demographic shift has been due to steep declines in mortality rates and increases in life expectancy at all ages during the past century. In the United States in 1997, men and women surviving to age 65 could expect to live another 15.9 and 19.2 years, respectively (National Center for Health Statistics, 1999). For epidemiology, the expansion of the older population means new challenges to understanding population health.

Traditionally, epidemiologists examine population mortality rates or disease prevalence and incidence rates and try to determine causal factors for each outcome. Aging is associated with higher prevalence and higher incidence of many chronic and acute diseases and with underlying changes in physiological systems. Therefore, aging epidemiology must look at health status and risk factors differently from the traditional epidemiological model. Although mortality and disease are still important, measurement of health status is extended to include functional consequences of diseases and quality-of-life issues (Guralnik, Fried, & Salive, 1996). Focusing on prevention of functional sequelae to disease also requires a more complex approach to risk factors (Kaplan, Haan, & Wallace, 1999), including an interest in health as a dynamic process (Institute of Medicine, 1991; Nagi, 1976). This chapter will give examples of some of the unique aspects of aging epidemiology and outline future challenges for the field.

Health Outcome Measurement

Function and Disability. Although presence of disease remains a cardinal measurement of health at any age, the functional consequences of disease in older people have important effects on health, quality of life, need for medical care, and survival. Aging epidemiology has focused particularly on three domains of function: physical, cognitive, and social. One of the best-researched areas of function is physical disability. Disability was first evaluated in relation to specific diseases, such as stroke, but is now increasingly used to characterize older adults during clinical assessment and epidemiological research. Physical disability is commonly assessed as difficulty with basic self-care tasks, complex tasks considered necessary to live independently in the community, and tasks related to key movements of the body, such as mobility (see Table 1).

Reliable estimates of disability, assessed by using activities of daily living (ADL) and instrumental activities of daily living (IADL), can be made from national surveys, but measurement technique and sampling do affect disability estimates (Jette, 1994). Results from the 1994 National Health Interview Survey (National Center for Health Statistics, 1999) suggest that, among noninstitutionalized people age 70 and above, 32.1% and 36.2% of women reported difficulty with any ADL or IADL task; for men in the same population, prevalence rates of ADL and IADL were 23.7% and 19.7%, respec-

TABLE 1   Examples of Measurement Instruments for Physical Disability

Domain of Physical Disability	Instrument Name	Tasks
Basic self-care tasks	Activities of daily living (ADL)	Bathing, dressing, eating, transferring from a bed to a chair, and using the toilet
Tasks needed for independence in the community	Instrumental activities of daily living (IADL)	Shopping, preparing meals, housework, managing money, writing, using the telephone, and using transportation
Key component tasks	Mobility disability	Walking across a small room, walking 1/4 mile, climbing stairs

Because the activities are complex, disability in ADL and IADL may result from physical dysfunction or from a mixture of physical, cognitive, and social dysfunctions. Other work on physical disability attempts to focus on key physical movements in order to better explore the underlying causal pathway. One such example is mobility disability, a critical constituent of ADL and IADL disability. Like more complex measures of disability, mobility can be measured by using a hierarchical approach: severe mobility disability is assessed as difficulty with basic mobility tasks such as walking across a small room, and more mild mobility disability is assessed as difficulty in walking longer distances and climbing stairs.

Physical Performance.   Disability outcomes such as ADLs frequently rely on self- or proxy report and assess presence of overt disability. In contrast, performance measures are designed to evaluate a specific component of physical function by using direct observation of an individual performing a standardized task. Although strongly associated with self-report measures of disability, per-

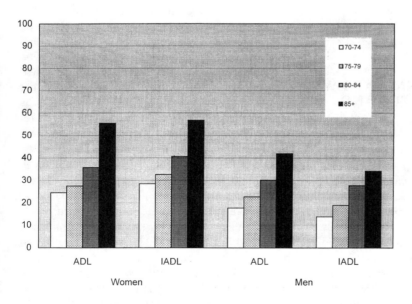

FIGURE 1   Percentage of women and men aged 70 and over with ADL or IADL disability, by 5-year age group, United States, 1997 (National Center for Health Statistics, 1999).

tively (see Figure 1). These estimates, however, do not include nursing home residents; in 1997, 4% of the population over 65 lived in nursing homes, most (96%) of whom needed assistance with ADL tasks.

formance measures add important information to functional assessment that self-report measures cannot: assessment of the full range of functional capacity and identification of functional problems not reported by individuals. Some performance measures gauge ability to perform tasks under standardized conditions, such as turning a key in a lock, and others gauge the speed or accuracy of physical movement, such as walking a timed course. There is a strong association between performance measures and other function and health outcomes, even in the upper range of performance. For example, an objective assessment of lower extremity function administered in the Established Populations for Epidemiologic Studies of the Elderly used a timed 8-foot walk, a timed repeated chair stand, and three hierarchical balance tests to score lower extremity function (Guralnik, Ferrucci, Simonsick, Salive, & Wallace, 1995). Higher scores, indicating better lower extremity function, were associated with lower risk of mobility and ADL disability 1 and 4 years later in persons not reporting disability at baseline.

Cognitive Function. The focus thus far has been on physical disability, but many of the issues relating to the epidemiology of physical disability are paralleled by research in other functional domains. Among the most important for aging research is cognitive function. Like physical function, loss of cognitive function is largely due to underlying disease—most importantly, Alzheimer's disease. Cognitive function is usually assessed by using standardized measures, such as the Mini-Mental State Exam (Folstein, Folstein, & McHugh, 1975), rather than self- and proxy reports of difficulty with cognitive tasks. Standardized cognitive tests rely on simple, structured questions that test different domains of cognitive ability, such as memory, language skills, and executive function, and allow objective documentation of functional declines over time.

Recovery and Healthy Aging. Although the disablement process that proceeds from disease to functional disability receives a lot of attention, physical and cognitive function do not always follow downward trajectories. A substantial amount of recovery is reported in many longitudinal studies, with participants improving in function between baseline and follow-up (Gill, Robinson, & Tinetti, 1997). With more severe disability at baseline or longer duration of disability, the likelihood of recovery decreases. However, the dynamic nature of functional loss points out the possibility of focusing

on what maintains or improves function as well factors that diminish it.

Positively valenced outcomes in aging research are emerging. The most basic approach to healthy aging focuses on the characteristics of people who maintain physical and cognitive abilities or who have high scores on physical performance tests in old age (Schaie, 1993; Seeman, Charpentier, Berkman, Tinetti, Guralnik, Albert, et al., 1994). Another approach augments longevity with information on disability-free survival. Research has examined the prevalence and characteristics of people who survive to very old age and die without disability and the duration of disability-free survival. Based on life-table methods, active life expectancy estimates the number of remaining years of life expected to be free of disability at specific ages. As an outcome measure, active life expectancy is useful in understanding risk factors for population disability and for estimating future burden to the health and assistive care systems (Ferrucci, Izmirlian, Leveille, Phillips, Corti, Brock, et al., 1999; Rogers, Rogers, & Belanger, 1990). Health is, however, more than the absence of negative outcomes. Measures of healthy aging are expanding to measure positive health outcomes or well-being as well as the absence of dysfunction. Emotional vitality has been defined as high levels of personal mastery and happiness as well as absence of depression and anxiety (Penninx, Guralnik, Simonsick, Kasper, Ferrucci, & Fried, 1998). A second measure of healthy aging involves maintenance of socially productive activities (Glass, Mendes de Leon, Marottoli, & Berkman, 1999).

Assessment of Risk Factors

Disease and the Disablement Process. Certain population subgroups experience higher prevalence and incidence rates of disability. Disability, both physical and cognitive, increases substantially with increasing age, is more prevalent in women than men due to higher incidence and longer survival with disability, and is more prevalent in people with lower education and income. Longitudinal epidemiological studies have shown that, after age, disability is the strongest predictor of adverse health outcomes. In part, this is because disability is an excellent measure of burden of disease. Disability

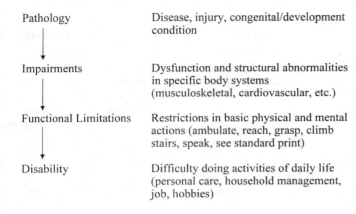

Pathology	Disease, injury, congenital/development condition
↓	
Impairments	Dysfunction and structural abnormalities in specific body systems (musculoskeletal, cardiovascular, etc.)
↓	
Functional Limitations	Restrictions in basic physical and mental actions (ambulate, reach, grasp, climb stairs, speak, see standard print)
↓	
Disability	Difficulty doing activities of daily life (personal care, household management, job, hobbies)

FIGURE 2   A theoretical model of the disablement process (Verbrugge & Jette, 1994).

is associated with mortality, further functional decline, increased risk of acute illness and injuries, and loss of independence. Because of the substantial impact on quality of life and subsequent health of older populations, understanding the risk factors for disability and developing effective prevention strategies might lead to substantial improvement in population health.

With aging, understanding the etiology of functional outcomes means untangling a complex pathway. Most disability in older adults is caused by chronic conditions, injuries, disuse, and altered physiological and metabolic function associated with disease and senescence. A theoretical framework for the pathway from disease to disability, proposed by the Institute of Medicine (1991), progresses from disease to disability through impairments in physiological systems and functional limitations (Figure 2). Much attention has been given to understanding the relationship between disease and disability, but the intricacies of the pathway, including the co-occurrence of multiple diseases and impairments, the timing of exposure to risk factors, and the factors that modify the pathway, all need further study.

Comorbidity and Co-impairments.   A number of chronic conditions common in older populations are consistently and strongly related to disability. These include heart disease, osteoarthritis, diabetes, stroke, hip fracture, visual and hearing impairments, and depression. However, as discussed above, the co-occurrence of multiple chronic conditions, or comorbidity, is common in the older population. Investigation of comorbidity, co-impair-

ments, and competing risks are essential to understanding the health of older populations.

In a nationally representative sample, nearly half of the people aged 60 years and older reported a physician diagnosis of two or more of nine common chronic conditions (Guralnik, LaCroix, Everett, & Kovar, 1989). The most common measure of comorbidity uses a summary of the number of chronic conditions; this measure is consistently associated with overall disability but may obscure an association between specific combinations of diseases and specific components of disability. For example, arthritis was found to cause substantially greater risk of mobility disability when associated with other conditions than when it was found alone (Verbrugge, Lepkowski, & Konkol, 1991). Other research shows that disease combinations can act synergistically to produce much higher risk of specific disabilities than are associated with either disease alone. For example, the risk for ADL and IADL disability associated with the combination of vision impairments and stroke is 5 to 10 times higher than the risk from either disease alone; similarly, the combination of heart disease and cancer is associated with high risk of upper extremity disability (Fried, Bandeen-Roche, Kasper, & Guralnik, 1999). It is not only the interaction of diseases that has an impact on the disablement process. The presence of genetic factors in combination with diseases or conditions also may increase risk of disease and functional impairment. Evidence from national surveys and longitudinal cohort studies suggests that co-occurring physical impairments also may affect disability. Incidence of severe walking disability (measured as walking speed < 0.4

m/s and inability to walk 1/4 mile) was substantially higher among women in the lowest tertiles of both lower extremity strength and balance, compared with incidence among women with the lowest levels of either impairment alone. Consideration of such interactions may be vital to developing effective prevention. In the study discussed above, for example, the interaction of strength and balance revealed that balance may be more essential to mobility than muscle strength and therefore is an important focus for prevention (Rantanen, Guralnik, Ferrucci, & Fried, 1999).

Timing and Heterogeneity of Risk Factor Exposure.   Many conditions and pathophysiological changes associated with aging develop over a long period of time. Risk-factor exposure important to development of these conditions may occur in early, mid-, or later life, or a combination of all three. In addition, the association between the risk factor and health outcome may change across the life span. Evidence from longitudinal epidemiological cohort studies suggests that it is important to know exposure duration, timing, and the point in the life cycle at which the exposure occurred when considering the impact of the risk factor in epidemiological studies.

The association between risk factors and health outcomes is not static across the life span. For example, evidence from longitudinal cohort studies suggests that the strength of the association between some risk factors and outcomes declines with age and in others increases with age; other risk factors associations show mixed patterns across the life span (Kaplan, Haan, & Wallace, 1999). When risk factor and outcome are measured at the same point in time it is difficult to know whether the changing patterns of association are due to actual changes in biological relationships, competing risks from other diseases, or selection of study participants. The time lag between assessment of risk factor and outcome also is important. Many chronic conditions develop over long periods of time, and a risk factor may have its strongest effect during a particular stage in the disease process. For example, among men never treated for hypertension, high blood pressure in midlife had a very strong effect on late-life dementia (Launer, Ross, Petrovitch, Masaki, Foley, White, et al., 2000).

Changes in risk-factor status over time are also important to the health of older populations. Many of the changes in risk factors, such as weight, serum cholesterol, and inflammation, occur because of underlying disease processes. The high prevalence of chronic disease may modify the usual relationship between a risk factor and an outcome. For example, although high body mass index remains a significant predictor of mobility disability among older women, weight *loss* was a significant risk factor for mobility disability among the oldest women. It is probable that the weight loss is due to underlying ill-health (Launer, Harris, Rumpel, & Madans, 1994).

As well as timing of risk-factor measurement and change in risk factors over time, the long exposure to risk factors means that the detrimental or protective effects of exposure may accumulate. Evidence of reserve capacity deteriorating over several decades comes from the Alameda County Study, in which accumulated exposure to economic deprivation over 29 years was strongly associated with physical and cognitive disability and depression at older ages (Lynch, Kaplan, & Shema, 1997). The protective effect of level of education in early life on loss of cognitive function in later life, even among individuals with diagnosed Alzheimer's disease, may also be due to accumulation of reserve functional capacity over the life span (Katzman, 1993; Mortimer, 1988).

Future Challenges to Aging Epidemiology

Studying the trajectory of health and function is a complex undertaking. Frameworks, like that proposed by Nagi (1976) and the Institute of Medicine (1991) for the disablement process, help anchor aging research. The first wave of epidemiological research developed assessment tools for new functional outcomes, described their prevalence and incidence, and examined how factors at each step of the pathway predicted future functional ability. The effects of more global risk factors on the entire pathway from disease to disability also were explored: global risk factors ranged across biological processes such as chronic inflammatory immune response, health behaviors such as exercise, and psychosocial characteristics such as depression and socioeconomic status.

We are now immersed in the second generation of epidemiological studies of aging, and face a new set of challenges. Rather than prevalence or health status change between two time points, newer studies such as the Women's Health and Aging Study and the Health, Aging and Body Composition Study focus on longitudinal change in disease, physiology, and functional status and on the pace of physical change and functional loss (Ferrucci, Guralnik, Simonsick, Salive, Corti, & Langlois, 1996). More complete assessment of disease states, underlying pathophysiology, and impairments allow for better control of confounding and for examination of the effects of interaction and competing risks. New risk factors are being integrated into research on aging and the disablement process. Information on genetic variability, racial and ethnic heterogeneity, and the impact of the physical and social environment on the health of older people may add to our understanding of aging and the disablement process. Examples of such research include the association between genetic traits, cognitive function, and dementia or the association between physical environment, physical activity, and mobility disability. It is important to expand our understanding of why some populations remain healthy with age and others do not and to develop methods of improving the health of older people. Integration of these developments will continue to offer new challenges to aging epidemiology and new potential of improving population health.

JENNIFER L. BALFOUR
JACK M. GURALNIK

See also

Alameda County Study
Demography
Disability
Geriatric Health
Minimum Data Set
Sex Differences in Health

EQUAL EMPLOYMENT OPPORTUNITY COMMISSION

The Equal Employment Opportunity Commission (EEOC) was established under Title VII of the Civil Rights Act of 1964 as amended. The purpose of this federal agency is to eliminate discrimination based on race, color, religion, sex, national origin, disability, or age in hiring, promotions, firing, wages/salaries, testing, training, apprenticeships, and all other conditions of employment. It is responsible for the enforcement of Title VII, the Equal Pay Act (EPA) of 1963, the Age Discrimination in Employment Act (ADEA) of 1967, section 501 of the Rehabilitation Act (RA) of 1973, the Americans with Disabilities Act (ADA) of 1990, and the Civil Rights Act of 1991. Although these laws generally are applicable to employers who have 15 or more employees, employment agencies, and employee (labor) organizations in the public and private sectors, the ADEA covers employers with 20 or more employees.

The EEOC, composed of five commissioners appointed by the president and confirmed by the Senate for 5-year staggered terms, processes complaints of discrimination both informally (through a conciliation process) and formally (with legal action). The commission also develops discrimination law, provides a liaison role across sectors, coordinates joint research and work sharing, and publishes data. The complaint process is initiated at the field office (state) level and consists of (1) the filing of written charges under Title VII, the EPA, the ADEA, the RA, or the ADA, within 180 to 300 days of the alleged violation, depending on specific circumstances and sector location; (2) the investigation of charges; (3) conciliation to encourage settlement before formal charges are brought; and (4) litigation, if appropriate. If the EEOC brings charges, individual suits cannot be presented until the agency's legal action is completed. Attempts at conciliation precede litigation.

Persons who believe they have been discriminated against may file a charge at one of 50 EEOC field offices or with a local or state Fair Employment Practices Agency. Charges must follow strict procedural rules. In recent years individual cases have become more common than class action cases. Timely pursuit of cases has been a problem and led in 1997 to the implementation of new procedures for expediting closure of cases. At the end of fiscal year 1998, the EEOC's pending inventory of charges was just over 52,000, down from a high of over 111,000 in 1995.

A landmark ruling under Title VII was the 1978 Supreme Court ruling in *City of Los Angeles v. Manhart*. The Manhart decision required employers to provide equal monthly benefits to and collect only equal pension plan contributions from men and women employees. This decision prohibited sex discrimination in pension plans based on sex-segregated life expectancy tables (Cain, 1979).

The Age Discrimination in Employment Act was enacted to promote the employment of older workers based on ability and to prohibit arbitrary age requirements leading to discrimination in the workplace. Although legislation against age discrimination originally covered workers age 40 to 65, amendments in 1978 extended the upper age limit to 70. In 1986, age-based mandatory retirement in most occupations was eliminated; workers and job seekers age 40 and older are now protected under the ADEA. A 7-year exemption for tenured faculty and public safety workers expired at the end of 1993. However, 1996 legislation allowed state and local governments once again to set maximum hiring and mandatory retirement ages for public safety employees.

The Americans with Disabilities Act, signed by President George Bush on July 26, 1990, bars discrimination against persons with mental or physical disabilities in their access to government services. Department of Justice regulations in effect in 1992 already require many private sector businesses with 15 or more employees to make "reasonable accommodations" in the workplace for employees and job applicants. These regulations also gave local governments until January 26, 1995, to complete street, walkway, and building improvements required to make employment, programs, and services accessible.

Age discrimination cases have always constituted a minority of total EEOC cases; in fiscal year 1998, they accounted for less than 20% of the total. About 6 out of 10 charges filed tend to be dismissed because the EEOC determines there is no reasonable cause to believe discrimination occurred. Of the age charges resolved in fiscal year 1998, the EEOC found reasonable cause of discrimination in just under 4%, a figure that remained fairly steady throughout the 1990s. Age discrimination lawsuits filed by the EEOC have been relatively rare, though increasing. As a result of EEOC's litigation, victims of discrimination recovered almost $90 million in

fiscal year 1998. An age-bias case resulted in a settlement with Lockheed Martin for $13 million in back pay and 450 jobs for older workers who had been dismissed.

Sara Rix
Angela M. O'Rand

See also
Age Discrimination
Employment

ERIKSON'S THEORY OF GENERATIVITY
See
Generativity

ESTABLISHED POPULATIONS FOR EPIDEMIOLOGICAL STUDIES OF THE ELDERLY

Epidemiological studies completed before 1970 rarely provided age-specific descriptive statistics for persons older than 65 years of age. Usually data for the older age groups were summarized into a single statistic to represent the average or cumulative rate for the entire age span. With the increase in the number of persons surviving for more than 65 years, it became necessary to know the age-specific rates and the patterns of change in these rates. The increase in mortality and morbidity rates could not be assumed to increase linearly. In fact, many rates increased geometrically. The lack of specific descriptive statistics led to the creation of the surveys entitled the Established Populations for Epidemiological Studies of the Elderly (EPESE) (Cornoni-Huntley, Ostfeld, Taylor, Wallace, Blazer, Berkman, et al., 1993).

The Epidemiology, Demography, and Biometry Program of the National Institute on Aging (NIA) initiated studies of representative community populations to provide information on the identification of the leading health problems and the magnitude of these problems for elderly people. Specifically, the goals were to:

1. estimate the prevalence of diseases, health problems, impairments, and disabilities for elderly persons living in communities
2. estimate the incidence of diseases, health problems, impairments, and disabilities for elderly persons living in communities
3. identify and investigate factors that are associated with or predictive of mortality, morbidity, hospitalization, and use of long-term care facilities
4. quantify changes in the physical and social functioning of elderly persons and evaluate how these changes are associated with changes in related health conditions

Sample Populations

In 1980, the NIA initiated contracts to fund three population studies. Five years later, in 1985, a fourth population sample was established to provide the descriptive and comparative data for Black elderly persons. All four locations were selected by the competitive process. The first three locations of the studies are in east Boston, Massachusetts, two rural counties in Iowa, and New Haven, Connecticut. The fourth study location is in segments of five counties in the north-central Piedmont area of North Carolina. Each location has adopted a personalized study name: east Boston, Senior Health Project; Iowa, Iowa 65+ Rural Health Study; New Haven, Yale Health and Aging Project; and North Carolina, Piedmont Health Survey of the Elderly. The sampling methods were different in each location.

The study population of east Boston, Massachusetts, consists of all persons within the community who were 65 years of age and older. Middle- and low-income working-class persons, many of Italian-American background, live in this urban area. Of the 4,562 people eligible to be included, 3,813 (84%) participated in the study.

The Iowa study population consists of all residents of two rural counties in east-central Iowa, namely, Iowa and Washington counties, who were 65 years of age and older. Most of this population is classified as rural. Of approximately 4,600 people eligible to be included, 3,673, or 80%, participated.

The study population of New Haven, Connecticut, is a stratified, representative sample of persons 65 years of age and older living in the area. The sample was stratified for representation of persons living in community and public housing and in community dwellings. Of the 3,337 people in the sample, 82%, or 2,811 people, participated. New Haven is primarily a middle- and low-income urban residential area.

The North Carolina study population is a stratified representative sample of persons residing in five geographically contiguous counties of the north-central part of the state. Franklin, Granville, Vance, and Warren counties are predominantly rural, and Durham is predominantly urban. The area has a wide range of socioeconomic status, but residents are primarily middle- and low-income residents. Of the 5,224 persons sampled, 4,165 participated, for a response rate of 80%. The study population was 51% Black.

Methods

Study Design. The EPESE is a longitudinal study consisting of a baseline survey and six follow-up interviews. During the first years the initial (baseline) survey (1982–1983 for east Boston, Iowa, and New Haven, and 1986–1987 for North Carolina) was a personal interview completed in the residence of the participant to provide estimates of specific health problems and related factors. The second through the seventh years (1983–1989 for east Boston, Iowa, and New Haven, and 1987–1993 for North Carolina) were devoted to continuing surveillance of the population, using annual follow-up contacts, either by a personal or telephone interview, and acquiring data on mortality, hospitalization, and admission to nursing homes. The follow-up date provided the estimates of incidence or onset of health problems and change in physical and social functioning.

The schedule for annual interviews by year and type was the same at all locations, but, chronologically, the interviews for the North Carolina location were completed 5 years after the original three locations. The design included three personal, face-to-face interviews, at baseline, and at the third and sixth follow-up or recontact. The first, second, fourth, and fifth recontacts (follow-up interviews) were by telephone. Attempts were made to complete interim recontacts for both noninstitutionalized and institutionalized participants.

During the course of the study, the investigators developed substudies of problems frequently experienced by elderly persons. The areas of substudies encompassed health and psychosocial problems, such as incontinence, dementia, sleep problems, depression, bereavement, and adjustment to retirement. Some studies required the collection of additional data, whereas others involved an in-depth analysis of the existing data.

Data Collection.   The health problems and related conditions investigated by EPESE reflect the recognition of a need for community estimates of the extent of the problems and that data concerning these problems could be collected by a survey instrument. Published research results and clinical impressions were used in generating the questionnaires.

For all EPESE locations the baseline questionnaire consisted of identical questions on chronic conditions; related health problems and behavior; and physical, social, and cognitive functioning (see Table 1). The baseline questionnaire included additional questions that were not common to all sites and reflect the interest of investigators at different locations.

Identical questions that were common to all EPESE locations were included on personal, face-to-face follow-up interviews (third and sixth recontact). Lifetime history was not repeated, and only current status was obtained. The follow-up telephone interviews were abbreviated. Identical data on the evaluation of outcome (mortality, morbidity, hospitalizations, and admissions to nursing homes) were included on each of the annual recontacts (see Table 2).

During the baseline and third and sixth follow-up interviews the participant's blood pressure was measured. During the sixth follow-up interview, a blood sample was obtained for the analysis of a complete blood count (including hemoglobin, hematocrit, white cell count, differential count, and platelet count), which involved automated chemistry measures of 24 biomedical determinations, low-density lipoprotein cholesterol, and high-density lipoprotein cholesterol. Also, the sixth follow-up included several physical performance measures.

TABLE 1   Items Included on Baseline Questionnaire or EPESE Project

Demographic factors[a]	Ethnic origin, education, occupation and work status, income, residential mobility, marital status, housing type, and recent death of close relatives or friends
Social functioning	Household composition, religion, group membership, and contacts with friends and relatives
Physical functioning	Functional disability,[b] vision,[c] and hearing[c]
Chronic conditions	Cardiac, exertional chest pain, intermittent claudication,[d] stroke, cancer, diabetes, fractures, chronic respiratory symptoms, and hypertension
Related health problems	Cognitive function,[e] depression,[f] bowel habits, weight and weight history, sleep, and self-perceived health status
Health-related behavior	Alcohol, prescription and nonprescription drug use in past 2 weeks, digitalis, and smoking
Use of services	Hospitalizations, nursing home episodes, and dental

[a]All centers obtained Social Security number, Medicare number, name, address, and telephone number of related persons who do not live with them but know where they are for future contacts.
[b]Questions included (1) seven activities of daily living (Katz, Ford, Moskowitz, Jackson, & Jaffe, 1963); (2) an abbreviated measure of functional health (three of the six items reported by Rosow & Breslau, 1969); and (3) four physical activity items (adapted from Nagi, 1976).
[c]Questions from National Health and Nutrition Examination Survey (NHANES) I (National Center for Health Statistics, 1978).
[d]The London School of Hygiene Cardiovascular Questionnaire (NCHS, 1978).
[e]Nine-Item Mental Statics Questionnaire (MSQ) (Pfeiffer, 1975).
[f]Modification of Center for Epidemiology-Depression Modification (CES-D) Scale (Berkman, Berkman, Kasl, Freeman, Leo, Ostfeld et al., 1986).
Note: Adapted from "Established populations for epidemiologic studies of the elderly" by J. Cornoni-Huntley et al., 1993, *Aging/Clinical and Experimental Research, 5,* 27–37. Copyright 1993, Editrice Kurtis s.r.l. Adapted by permission.

TABLE 2 Major Outcomes of EPESE Report

Outcomes	Obtained by
Mortality	Continual surveillance, including local sources, state record, and the National Death Index (death certificates reviewed by single nosologist)
Morbidity	
Chronic conditions and impairments	Annual follow-up interview
Hospitalizations	Annual follow-up interview, continual surveillance, and Medicare Part A files
Nursing home admissions	Annual follow-up interview
Disability in physical functioning	Annual follow-up interview

Note: Reprinted from "Established populations for epidemiologic studies of the elderly" by J. Cornoni-Huntley et al., 1993, *Aging/Clinical and Experimental Research, 5,* 27–37. Copyright 1993, Editrice Kurtis, s.r.l. Reprinted by permission.

Continual surveillance of the study populations occurred during the follow-up period. Data were obtained on the major outcomes, mortality, morbidity (chronic conditions and impairments), hospitalization, and admission to nursing homes. A computer match with the Health Care Financing Administration Medicare records (Medicare Provider and Analysis Review files) has been implemented.

Further details of the methodology can be obtained in previous publications (Cornoni-Huntley, Ostfeld, Taylor, Wallace, Blazer, Berkman, et al., 1993).

Results

Approximately 350 reports have been published based on the EPESE data. Incidence and prevalence rates for hypertension, heart disease, cancer, depression, and loss in physical and cognitive functioning, plus factors related to these conditions among elderly persons, have been published (Berkman, Berkman, Kasl, Freeman, Leo, Ostfeld, et al., 1986; Scherr, Albert, Funkenstein, Cook, Hennek-

ens, Branch, et al., 1988; Seeman, Mendes de Leon, Berkman, & Ostfeld, 1993; Taylor, Cornoni-Huntley, Curb, Manton, Ostfeld, Scherr, et al., 1991). The positive aspect of regular physical activity also has been reported (Mendes de Leon, Beckett, Fillenbaum, Brock, Branch, Evans, et al., 1997). Descriptive and analytical articles have been published from the extensive data on use of medication obtained from the participants (Chrischilles, Foley, Wallace, Lemke, Semla, Hanlon, et al., 1992). Reports on the relationship of social factors, such as social networks and social support, have been published (Seeman & Berkman, 1988).

Investigators have generated in-depth studies of specific diseases, with independent methology but using the EPESE populations. For example, reports have been published on a study of Alzheimer's disease in east Boston presenting the prevalence for a community-living population (Hebert, Scherr, Beckett, Albert, Pilgrim, Chown, et al., 1995). Reports on periodontal and other oral health problems have been published from dental studies completed for the Iowa and North Carolina populations (Beck, Koch, Rozier, & Tudor, 1990).

Although a significant number of studies have been published, there exists a large amount of data that has not been analyzed. Public use tapes are available for the baseline data, and tapes are being completed for the follow-up data. The linkage with hospitalization data from the Medicare Provider Analysis and Review files broadens the opportunity for identifying factors that are related to, or are predictive of, the occurrence of health problems for the elderly.

J. C. CORNONI-HUNTLEY

See also
Longitudinal Studies of Aging

ETHICS

In recent years there has been expanding interest in questions of ethics in the field of aging. This interest has been stimulated by two broad trends: (1) advances in medical technology that have led to dilemmas of clinical bioethics (e.g., decisions surrounding death and dying) and (2) the coming of an aging society with rising numbers of dependent elderly whose care raises far-reaching questions of social policy. The dilemmas of bioethics have principally been of concern to physicians, nurses, social workers, and other professionals; questions of social policy and social ethics in an aging society have become more broadly intertwined with debates about allocation of resources and the role of government. In this article both the clinical and policy issues are examined. For more detailed discussions, see Agich (1993); Collopy, Boyle, and Jennings (1991); Collopy, Dubler, and Zuckerman (1990); Jecker (1991); Moody (1992); and Sachs and Cassel (1994).

Bioethics and Aging

Since the 1960s there has been a revival of analytical work in normative ethics with clear implications for policy and practice. A landmark was John Rawls's (1971) theoretical treatise, *A Theory of Justice,* but major stimulus also came from controversies about war and peace, biomedical technology, and similar public issues. By the early 1980s, ethicists, as well as others, were giving serious attention to ethics and aging. A major achievement of early work in bioethics was a strong emphasis on patients' rights and informed consent. The ideal of autonomy and individual self-determination—so fundamental in American ideology—was readily extended to the elderly. But implementation of the idea in practice quickly encountered obstacles. With advancing age, chronic illness and physical dependency are often accompanied by diminished capacity for decision making. Particularly among the old-old (see "Oldest-Old") and those in nursing homes, there are growing numbers who are unable to make their own decisions. Along with the clinical problem of competency, there is a widespread tendency for both families and professionals to treat older people in the style of paternalism: acting for a person's "best interest," rather than respecting autonomy.

This conflict between paternalism and self-determination is apparent in many arenas of gerontological practice: in the design of social services for individuals and families, in elder abuser and adult protective services, in decisions about involuntary nursing home placement, and, most acutely, in life-

and-death decisions involving termination of treatment or withdrawal of life-support systems. In 1975, the Karen Ann Quinlin case brought these questions to wide public attention, and the courts have repeatedly been involved since. In these cases there have been those with strong opinions—for example, favoring sanctity of life on one side and beneficent euthanasia on the other. But gradually there has grown a strong public consensus in support of the right of a severely ill patient to refuse treatment in order to "die with dignity." To this extent, both law and ethics have worked in favor of expanded autonomy for the severely ill.

But in considering the ethical dilemmas of care for the elderly, other troubling questions remain unanswered. Proponents of patient autonomy have endorsed the concept of advance directives: instruments such as the living will or durable power of attorney that could be invoked when an individual no longer has the capacity to make medical decisions. Yet determination of mental competency is often a matter of drawing borderlines. What about those elderly suffering from dementia or those with fluctuating mental competency? Similar problems arise for diseases that create physical incapacity but are not immediately fatal. What about withholding food and water from those not terminally ill? Far less social consensus has been reached on these controversial matters. Through a series of court decisions, the legal system has moved in contradictory directions: sometime setting clear limits, more often reflecting societal ambivalence about bioethical dilemmas in the last stage of life. For health care professionals and hospitals, another complicating factor has been the fear of malpractice liability, which has promoted a tendency to overtreat patients (Kapp, 1991). Will these practices change under the pressure of cost containment? In the future it seems likely that clinicians will continue to be troubled by decision making for elderly patients of questionable mental competency.

In hospitals and long-term care settings, these familiar dilemmas of clinical practice have been exacerbated by new demands. Placement and discharge planning are becoming major practice problems with unavoidable ethical difficulties. Although ethicists have closely examined problems in hospital settings, until recently, ethical dilemmas in long-term care were relatively neglected. In nursing home settings, for example, many dilemmas are not dramatic life-and-death choices but are likely to involve constraints of institutional living (Kane & Caplan, 1990). Sometimes limits are imposed either for the patient's individual welfare or for the sake of other residents: for example, what to do about residents at risk of falling or wandering and how to secure the tranquility of the healthier residents in an institutional environment where growing numbers of severely demented, sometimes disruptive people are living.

For professionals who are employees of institutions, there can be distinctive dilemmas that arise from the dual roles of professional and employee. For example, when client or patient advocacy is in conflict with rules or policies of an institution, practitioners are caught in the middle. Clearly, new approaches to conflict resolution are needed. In hospitals, one promising innovation has been the introduction of institutional ethics committees, now virtually required by standards of the Joint Commission on Accreditation of Healthcare Organizations, and a number of nursing homes are introducing similar forums to address the ethical issues that arise in practice.

Comparable ethical problems arise outside institutions and within private family life. There are serious ethical dilemmas in cases of elder abuse: for example, when a social service provider has no recourse except to place an abused elder in a nursing home and this outcome is often precisely what the abused elder does not want. Despite the reluctance of some older persons to enter long-term care facilities, there are serious problems that families face in maintaining an elderly relative at home. Often these "tragic choices" involve issues of distributive justice: for example, which family members are to bear the burden of extraordinary day-to-day care for Alzheimer's disease sufferers living at home. Traditional appeals to filial responsibility are sometimes invoked, but distributive justice issues remain unresolved. As ethicists examine the problem of family caregiving in advanced industrialized societies, it becomes evident that traditional forms of filial responsibility were never intended to take into account developments in longevity, family structure, and the changing roles of women. Thus, the balance between family and formal caregiving, a topic of considerable attention among gerontologists, turns out to involve far-reaching ethical questions (Cantor, 1994).

Social Ethics in the Aging Society

This conclusion about family caregiving points to a broader conclusion, namely, that individual ethical dilemmas are fully intelligible only in a wider social and cultural context. Indeed, ethicists have been quick to identify how political and economic policy decisions—for example, reimbursement systems under Medicare and Medicaid—serve to generate many of the dilemmas and contradictions faced in practice (Mehlman & Visocan, 1992). As all public expenditures come under increasing pressure, a major dilemma of social ethics stands out: Will society make use of all of its available, yet expensive, medical technology to prolong life for those at advanced ages (Binstock & Post, 1991; Callahan, 1987)? At the other end of the life cycle, among newborns, decisions are increasingly being made with consideration for a quality-of-life standard. This concept remains controversial, yet many would urge that the same standard be applied to life-and-death decisions in old age. Extension of this idea, for example, could lead to approval of so-called rational suicide on quality-of-life grounds—a concept originally endorsed by the ancient Stoic philosophers.

It is one thing for a person to make an individual judgment about his or her own life, but it becomes a different matter when we make those decisions on a collective basis. The danger is that quality of life becomes equal to worth of life. In an era of cost containment, the dangers of such an ethic are clear. Policy makers in fields such as transportation and occupational health and safety are tempted by the clear economic rationality of cost-benefit calculations. But all such calculations suffer from a classic problem of utilitarianism: above all, the failure of utilitarian ethics to provide a place for ordinary ethical convictions about the value of individual life. In the case of the aged, utilitarian calculations could easily underwrite the prejudices of ageism and negative attitudes toward old age. This is precisely the line of argument offered by those who warn against the dangers of the quality-of-life standard and who reject utilitarian cost-benefit calculations for allocating scarce health care resources to the aged ("Caring for an aging world," 1994; ter Meulen, Topinkova, & Callahan, 1994).

The problem is that if the utilitarian argument is rejected, how are difficult allocation decisions to be made? American public policy for the aging supports a three-level allocation system: an age-based public provision (Medicare), a means-tested public provision (Medicaid), and the option of provision through private payment or health insurance. This arrangement is open to challenge on grounds of distributive justice. But alternatives suffer from serious drawbacks. For example, advocates for the aging are likely to be dismayed by the practice—widespread in the industrialized nations of Europe—of denying some expensive health care on grounds of age alone. In England, older people are routinely denied kidney dialysis.

The current policy debates in health care have a certain parallel in other arenas, such as work and retirement and Social Security. For example, advocates for the aging generally reject mandatory retirement or other limitations based on chronological age, but at the same time they favor other age-based entitlements such as Social Security and Medicare. These contradictions raise interacting questions: Are there principles of distributive justice that could provide a uniform framework for appraising the claims of older people, particularly in a period when governments are faced with difficult allocation decisions? Is there a basis in social ethics for appraising the claims of future generations of older people, an argument on behalf of "intergenerational equity" (Laslett & Fishkin, 1992)? The answers to these questions are not clear. What is clear, however, is that the terms of the new debate on ethics and aging are now very different from what they were as recently as the 1970s. Instead of access, social policy today is dominated by cost containment, and at the clinical level the stubborn problems of autonomy and paternalism, death and life prolongation, the family and social welfare remain vexing for practitioners.

Contemporary debates on clinical and social ethics tend to concentrate on debates about rights and distributive justice. Rarely have they examined deeper issues, such as the nature of the good life, the meaning of the last stage of life, or the ways in which rights and obligations toward the aged might be grounded in some concept of the common good. Yet the meaning of choice in old age is, to some degree, intertwined with the meaning of death. Does death make life meaningful, or does it signify the end of meaning? With biomedical technology and life prolongation, the question no

longer remains speculative. The timing of death becomes increasingly a matter of explicit decision. Therefore, clinical bioethics cannot take either individual or collective meaning for granted in trying to weight competing values such as welfare, justice, and autonomy.

Contemporary ethics has developed a powerful style of conceptual analysis, likely to prove fruitful for gerontologists in the years ahead. Yet the limits of contemporary philosophical ethics should also be noted because those limits are tied to our current cultural environment. By contrast, other cultures have cultivated very different views about the rightness of specific actions, for example, filial responsibility, self-determined death, and the entitlements of different age groups to common resources. Where modern Western culture prizes individualism, rationality, and law, traditional cultures have favored collective decision making, family piety, and religious virtues tied to distinctive life stages. These cultural and historical variations suggest that contemporary debates in bioethics and social policy could benefit from being placed in a wider philosophical context. As current industrial societies seek to cope with the aging of populations and advances in medical technology, concern for ethics and aging is likely to grow in the future.

HARRY R. MOODY
MARSHALL B. KAPP

See also
Ageism
Elder Abuse and Neglect
Euthanasia
Intergenerational Equity
Legal Services
Living Wills and Durable Power of Attorney
Physician-Assisted Suicide
Policy Analysis

ETHNIC ASSOCIATIONS

Ethnicity and the role of race, language, and ethnic status are increasingly recognized as important variables in understanding the relationship of services to diverse elderly, aging within minority groups, and the organizational and public policy response to minority elders. The organization of age-based groups, development of the gerontological discipline, and creation of public benefits and programs for the elderly had been predicated largely on an ethnically homogeneous model—Anglo-Europeans. It has been assumed that other aging groups that differ by race, language, and culture would benefit from general responses to the needs of the Anglo-European elderly. In the 1970s, the government gave increased attention to African American, Hispanic, and Native American elderly who successfully lobbied for increased services and separate programs. White European groups also sought to draw attention to their ethnic traits. However, confusion over what constitutes an ethnic group has affected organizational responses by ethnic associations.

Ethnicity can be defined as a "distinctive sense of peoplehood" (Gelfand, 1982) and may be based on race, religion, or national identity. Included within this broad category are "minority groups—subunits of the society with distinct physical and cultural characteristics" (Gelfand, 1982, p. 14), wherein strong ties exist and lifestyle is distinct from most of the society. This article refers to two groups—minorities and White ethnics—for its purpose. The former includes African Americans, Hispanics (e.g., Mexican Americans, Cubans, Puerto Ricans, and Latin Americans), Asian (e.g., Chinese, Japanese, Korean, and Hmong), Pacific Islanders (e.g., Guamanians, Samoans, and Filipinos), and Native Americans (over 500 different tribes). White ethnics are composed of early immigrant groups (e.g., English, French, German, Irish, Italian, and Polish), more recent arrivals (e.g., Armenian and Russian), and religious groups (e.g., Jews and Mormons).

Understanding organizational responses of these groups to aging requires a dual historical separation: Most White ethnics were early immigrants to the United States and are, therefore, relatively acculturated, whereas minority groups are later arrivals and, therefore, less acculturated (Rivas & Torres-Gil, 1991; Torres-Gil, 1983).

In addition, the minority population has a smaller proportion of elderly than the White population. In 1993, 19.1% of Whites and 9.8% of minority groups were age 65 and older (Hollmann, 1994).

The median ages of White ethnic groups are generally higher than those of minorities. For exam-

ple, the median age for the English is 40.4 years; French, 34.7; German, 33.1; Irish, 34.9; Italian, 33.8; and Polish, 36.1 (U.S. Bureau of the Census, 1993b).

The preceding data are important in understanding why organizational responses of ethnic groups have lagged behind that of the general elderly population. White ethnic groups developed early age-based organizations that were not defined by ethnicity, largely because of the high level of assimilation and the emphasis on income security over ethnic identification. The early age-based organizations included the Townsend movement in 1936, the McLain organizations in the 1940s and 1950s, and groups of the 1960s and 1970s, such as the National Council of Senior Citizens, the American Association of Retired Persons, and the National Council on Aging. With few exceptions, ethnicity has been neither a primary factor in the development of those organizations nor a major policy issue for them. Those groups have been more concerned with advocacy, services to their members, and the provision of public benefits and programs.

The first visible manifestation of ethnicity as an issue in federal policy was influenced by the 1971 White House Conference on Aging, and it stimulated the first organizational response based on minority status. Before that time, there were no nationally based organizations oriented toward minority or ethnic elderly, although some age-based organizations, such as the Gray Panthers and the Urban Elderly Coalition, had interests in issues that affected them. The initial planning of the 1971 White House Conference did not include sessions or workshops on minority or ethnic aging and had few delegates representing ethnic associations. Largely because of that gap, various minority professionals organized a counterconference—the Black House Conference on Aging—to protest their exclusion (Torres-Gil, 1983). Subsequently, the chairman of the White House Conference, Dr. Arthur Fleming, appointed more minority delegates and included sessions on minority issues. That incident led to the formal creation of the National Caucus and Center on the Black Aged and the funding of the National Center on the Black Aging in 1972 by the Administration on Aging. The creation of organizations for other key minority groups followed, including the National Indian Council on Aging in 1976, the Asociación Pro Personas Mayores in

1975, the National Pacific/Asian Resource Center on Aging in 1979, and the National Hispanic Council on Aging in 1978.

All of the preceding organizations received substantial Administration on Aging support. All played significant roles in the advocacy of minority elderly, promoting research and training in minority aging, creating public and scholarly awareness of the diversity of ethnic and minority elderly, and organizing other professionals, service providers, and older persons around issues affecting minority elderly (McNeely & Colen, 1983). Each group was represented in the 1981 White House Conference and held its own mini-White House conference.

Throughout the 1970s and 1980s, those groups represented the principal organizational response to the needs of older minority persons. However, most of the organizational response was at the national level. Few parallel organizations existed at the state level. Increasingly, however, minority elderly are being organized through senior citizen clubs and nutrition centers, silver-haired legislatures, commissions and committees on aging, and advisory boards. Subsequently, we can expect that minority elderly themselves will become more directly involved in organized activities at the state and local levels than at the national level, which traditionally has been dominated by professionals and service providers.

Among nonminority ethnics, religious groups have been likely to form special associations. For example, Amish, Jewish, and Mormon elderly have rich histories of communal organizations at the local level that provide social and health services for their elderly members (Gelfand, 1994; Gelfand & Olsen, 1979). Senior citizen support can also be found among Italians, Irish, and Poles in neighborhoods with common ethnic backgrounds (Gelfand, 1982). However, no visible national or regional organizations had been developed for religious or Euro-American groups, specifically their elderly—at least not on the scale of minority elderly organizations.

That began to change during the planning of the 1981 White House Conference on Aging. A White House conference for Euro-American elderly was held in Baltimore and Cleveland during the fall of 1980. It highlighted the concerns of elderly who identify themselves as members of the many culturally diverse groups that constitute the mosaic of European Americans (from northwestern, eastern, and southern Europe). Their recommendations focused on increasing ethnic and cultural programs, enhancing mediating structures and neighborhoods, and strengthening the family life (White House Conference on Aging, 1981).

In the 1995 White House Conference on Aging, however, ethnic and racial issues were not as prominent nor problematic as at the previous White House Conference on Aging: The national minority organizations and ethnic groups were able to hold "mini–White House Conferences on Aging" focusing on their concerns, thus instilling a greater sense of inclusiveness (White House Conference on Aging, 1996). All groups were more concerned about threats to public benefits and entitlement programs brought on by Republican control of the Congress; thus, advocacy and organizing effort focused on protecting hard-won gains.

Ethnicity and minority status will play an increasing role in public policy debates and political and social participation of the elderly. One reason is that minority populations will be an increasing proportion of the elderly and the nonelderly populations. According to the National Academy on an Aging Society, for example, African American, Asian, and Hispanic populations are all increasing more rapidly than the non-Hispanic White population because of both higher birth rates and higher immigration rates. Non-Hispanic Whites made up 85% of the nonelderly population in 1995, a share that is projected to slip to 67% by 2050. Over the same period, the Hispanic proportion of the elderly population is expected to triple (from 5% to 16%). And the Hispanic proportion of the nonelderly population is projected to more than double over the next 55 years (from 11% to 24%) (National Academy on an Aging Society, 1999).

In addition, as minority and ethnic groups age in the United States, and second- and third-generation minority and ethnic elderly assimilate and acculturate, we can expect to see higher levels of political participation by those elders in the political system (Torres-Gil & Kuo, 1998). In turn, that will elevate their influence and visibility in public policy. Conversely, we will see a continuous influx of immigrants from throughout the world. During the 1990s, increasing numbers of ethnic and minority groups and elders arrived from the Middle East (e.g., Iran), Russia, Armenia, and the Pacific Basin (e.g., Taiwan, Hong Kong, China, and Southeast Asia). Those groups will go through processes of assimilation and acculturation similar to those of earlier ethnic groups. Increasingly, ethnicity—culture, language, and values—is being seen as a positive aspect of aging; with the growing cultural pluralism of the United States, we can expect that more ethnic and minority elderly will organize around aging issues and form ethnic associations (Stanford & Torres-Gil, 1992). Conversely, cultural pluralism raises concerns about the extent to which diversity in American public life is welcomed. The late 1990s witnessed controversies and polarization over the role of ethnicity and immigration. For example, California's passage of initiatives to restrict benefits to legal immigrants, the ending of affirmative action, and restrictions on bilingual education created national debates about the extent to which minority and ethnic groups should receive preferential treatment. The passage of a welfare reform bill in 1996 attempted to restrict Medicaid, Supplemental Security Income, and food stamps to immigrant elderly. These actions caused distress among minority and immigrant elders and their advocacy groups but also led to heightened advocacy by these groups and increases in naturalization and voting participation by minority and immigrant elders. This discomfort over ethnicity is increasingly giving way to concerns by policy elites about the workforce composition of an aging society. Recognition that minorities and immigrants will be an increasing proportion of the labor force upon whose productivity an older population would depend for taxes and economic productivity is shifting attention to how Hispanic, African American, and immigrant groups can support an older, non-English-speaking population of older persons. Social Security reform efforts saw attempts to curry favor with the growing political clout of African American and Hispanic voters and to enlist them in efforts to influence political decisions on Medicare and Social Security. Controversies over unrestricted immigration, providing public benefits to refugees, and the costs of paying for those services, raise questions about the minority and ethnic presence in public life. These shifting politics may signal a growing politics of aging among minority and ethnic groups. Regardless of how these issues are addressed or resolved, ethnic associations will remain an important vehicle for organizing minority and ethnic elders and empowering those groups in American society.

FERNANDO TORRES-GIL

See also
  Ethnicity
  Organizations in Aging
  Religious Organizations

ETHNICITY

Ethnic groups are differentiated by a sense of *peoplehood* that can be based on race, religion, or national origin (M. Gordon, 1964). Social psychologists, such as Shibutani and Kwan (1965), point out that ethnic groups also tend to view themselves as different from other groups. Using either of these definitions, the importance of ethnicity in American life is immediately evident.

Beginning with the immigration of Irish and Germans into this country during the 1840s and culminating in the massive immigrations of the late 19th and early 20th centuries, the United States has remained a country of involuntary and voluntary immigrants. Africans were brought over as slaves, and the immigration of Asians was greatly restricted. The Europeans who formed the bulk of the American population came to establish a life that met their economic and social aspirations. In doing so, these new immigrants did not always exhibit tolerance toward each other or the indigenous Native American population. Interethnic conflicts and racism have been recurring themes in American history.

In the early part of the 20th century, it was often assumed that the United States would witness a "melting pot" phenomenon by which all ethnic groups would lose their individual identity and become "Americans." This change did not occur. Among the factors that have helped to maintain the distinctness and allegiance of individuals to their ethnic background have been (1) residence in an ethnic neighborhood, (2) use of the "mother tongue," (3) common socioeconomic status, and (4) adherence to traditional religious values and customs.

All of these factors were present among first-generation immigrants to the United States. Among their children, the second generation, social mobility increased, and primary reliance on the mother tongue decreased. The roles of family members also shifted among some ethnic groups as they adapted to their new country. Many families moved out of the old ethnic neighborhood into what historians have termed the area of "second settlement." This pattern of economic, social, and geographical mobility has continued among many third-generation individuals, the grandchildren of the original immigrants. Among many immigrant groups, including Irish, Germans, Hispanics, and African Americans, a fourth generation is already in place. Unfortunately, discrimination has retarded the ability of Latinos, African Americans, and Native Americans to achieve the better living conditions found among other ethnic groups.

Socialization of children is a vital mechanism for passing on the ethnic culture. This socialization may be easier among minority groups. Often forced to live together because of discrimination, African Americans and other minority groups frequently find that their physical characteristics make ethnic identity an undeniable part of their daily lives.

A major factor in ethnic change may be the current high intermarriage rates among many ethnic groups. It is not clear what elements of ethnic culture are transmitted to children when each of the parents is from a different ethnic background. This is particularly true of White ethnic groups because research on these groups remains relatively restricted.

Changes within ethnic groups have an important relationship to aging, and these are detailed in several books (Gelfand, 1994; Gelfand & Barresi, 1987; Gelfand & Kutzik, 1979; J. J. Jackson, 1980; Manuel, 1982; Markides & Mindel, 1987; McNeely & Colen, 1983). Changes in ethnic values may affect the way the older individual views the process of aging, as well as the manner in which he or she adapts to growing older. Among some ethnic groups growing older may be viewed as a positive process that allows the individual to move into a role of "elder," exerting authority and power within the family and community. For other ethnic groups being defined as "elderly" may only be seen as a process of losses. Ethnic culture and norms may thus affect psychological adaptation and social adjustment to aging.

Social adjustments include changes in relationships with all elements of the individual's social network, including friends and family. Some of these social adjustments may be defined in the ethnic culture as appropriate or even required because of the person's age. Other adjustments may be required because of migration or deaths of family members and friends.

Among many ethnic cultures close geographical proximity has been maintained between adult children and parents. This proximity has also allowed older persons to take on the role of bearer of the cultural tradition to grandchildren. Failure of children to recognize the traditional role of the older person or provide the assistance expected may lead to great dissatisfaction and loss of morale on the part of the older person.

Ethnic values may also play a major role in determining attitudes toward the use of formal services. Ethnic values may determine whether a condition is defined as serious and the appropriate service provider. Many ethnic groups will often not use a formal service because of an attitude that using formal services represents the group members' failure to "take care of their own." Among some ethnic groups, especially among older individuals, formal services may be seen as akin to charity and may carry a stigma. For some older individuals, the inability of service providers to speak the language of the "old" country may prove a strong barrier to service usage. The cost of services may prove a major deterrent to their extensive use among groups with significant proportions of low-income elderly.

Ethnic values do not develop in a vacuum. Indeed, it has been argued that what are now viewed as traditional ethnic cultures are responses to conditions in the "old" country or the United States. Ethnic culture can thus be regarded as "emergent" rather than as unchanging. In the same manner that ethnic values are changeable within a particular ethnic group, individuals may not be consistent over their lifetime in their commitment to ethnic values. At particular times, an individual may draw on ethnic values and ethnic organizations to provide a sense of identity. Ethnic organizations may also offer an opportunity for association with other people with whom the individual feels comfortable.

Extensive immigration flows during the 1980s, particularly from non-European countries, has produced increased diversity of the ethnic composition of the United States. Many of the new immigrants are younger individuals, but an understanding of a wide variety of ethnic cultures will be crucial as many recent immigrants become part of the older population during the next few decades. Ethnicity thus remains a vital topic for the field of aging.

DONALD E. GELFAND

See also

African American Elderly
American Indian Aged
Asian and Pacific Islander American Elders
Hispanic Elderly
Minorities and Aging
Minority Populations: Recruitment and Retention in Aging Research
Religious Organizations

ETHNOGRAPHIC RESEARCH

Ethnographic research is the primary methodological tool anthropologists have used for exploring the cultural framework and dynamics of contemporary societies. This kind of investigation explores the fabric of values, perceptions, human relationships, and socially engineered behavior that guides people as they pass through the life cycle (Ikels & Beall, 2000). Such varied patterns of created ideology, social organization, and the ways people produce and distribute valued objects constitute the cultural systems into which all humans grow. Ethnographic research has been centered on the community context of how culture dynamically shapes the world people live in. This usually involves long-term residence or extensive contact within a community or in locales where people carry out their everyday lives. The prolonged, very personal encounter with the community under study can provide a special insight into how people experience aging in varied social settings. For example, one of the earliest applications of the ethnographic methods to a specific gerontological issue was the work of medical anthropologist Otto von Mering (1957). In the mid-1950s he conducted fieldwork in the geriatric wards of psychiatric hospitals, illustrating how the cultural devaluing of old age in the United States led to a withdrawal of psychosocial care for older patients.

The "Native" View of Aging

The essential aim of ethnographic research is to understand, as comprehensively as possible, the world through the eyes of the people being studied. This holistic construction of cultural systems is learned through direct observation, participating in daily life, and recording in the native language the meanings of things, persons, and actions. This generalized process of "participant observation" enables researchers to gather data about a culture by living with, or having direct and frequent contact for a prolonged period with, the people they are trying to comprehend (Keith, 1988). The broad connection of ethnographic research techniques to the field of gerontology has been delineated in the volume *New Methods for Old Age Research* (Fry & Keith, 1986). This approach applies as much to studying aging in small villages in the South Pacific as it does to research in nursing homes, in ethnic communities in North America, or among urban Japanese households (Sokolovsky, 1997). For example, anthropologists Dorothy and David Counts (1985, 1996) followed up their long-term ethnographic work on aging in Papua New Guinea with a 2-year study of the communities formed by seniors who travel North America in recreational vehicles (RVs). They undertook this latest project by buying an RV and becoming very active participant observers in the nomadic lifestyle of older adults who travel throughout Canada and the United States.

Global Comparison

To date, the most comprehensive and sophisticated cross-cultural study of aging has been Project AGE (Age, Generation, Experience), codirected by Christine Fry and Jennie Keith. Using a common methodology, complex ethnographies of age and aging were conducted at six sites around the world between 1982 and 1990. The research shows how both "system-wide" community features (e.g., social inequality) and "internal mechanisms" (e.g., values) create distinct contexts for conceptualizing the life cycle, establishing age norms, and influencing the perception of well-being in old age. Key results of this project can be found in *The Aging Experience: Diversity and Commonality Across Cultures* (Keith, Fry, Glascock, Ikels, Dickerson-Putnam, Harpending, et al., 1994).

Over the past 25 years the ethnographic study of aging has produced a large body of work covering most regions of the world. Ethnographic approaches to aging not only have looked at the general influence of cultural differences on aging but also have begun to focus on specific gerontological issues, such as the cultural response to late-life frailty, long-term care environments, senior centers, the impact of community redevelopment, minority/ethnic aging, and gender. Access to this rapidly expanding literature can be found in several texts: *The Cultural Context of Aging* (Sokolovsky, 1997); *Other Cultures, Elder Years* (Rhodes & Holmes, 1995) and *Old Age in Global Perspective* (Albert & Cattell, 1994). Information about new and ongoing ethnographic aging research and related publications can be followed through the Cultural Context of Aging website at: *www.stpt.usf.edu/~jsokolov*.

Ethnographic research in aging studies overlaps with a multidisciplinary movement sometimes referred to as "qualitative gerontology" (Gubrium & Sankar, 1994; Rowles & Schoenberg, 2000). This embraces a wide range of disciplinary practitioners from qualitative sociologists, cultural geographers, and clinical psychologists who rely on case study materials to humanists who use literature, art, and other expressive media to enhance our understanding of aging. It should be emphasized that the ethnographic variant of this qualitative approach to studying aging does not just involve long, complex personal interviews. Rather, it situates culture within a community framework and requires witnessing how meaning is expressed in everyday life.

JAY SOKOLOVSKY

See also
Longitudinal Research

EUTHANASIA

Euthanasia comes from the Greek words meaning "a gentle and easy death" or "the means of bringing about a gentle and easy death." Most ancient Greek and Roman practitioners, Socrates, Plato, and Stoic philosophers from Zeno to Seneca, supported physician-induced death of the sick and suffering to bring about a gentle and easy death (Vanderpool, 1995). In contrast to these dominant Graeco-Roman traditions, the Hippocratic oath required physicians to swear "neither to give a deadly drug to anybody if asked for it, nor . . . [to] make a suggestion to this effect" (Edelstein, 1967, p. 6). The oath, which continues to exert a towering influence in Western medicine, reflects the Pythagorean conviction that human beings are owned by God or gods and should abide by a divine determination of life's completion (Carrick, 1985).

In contemporary usage, discussion of euthanasia has increasingly dealt with the action of inducing a gentle and easy death. Thus, ethical debates about the permissibility of physician involvement in euthanasia concern the question Are physicians ethically permitted to act to end a patient's life? This question should be distinguished from other ethical questions that may arise at the end of life. For example, as the term *euthanasia* is commonly used today, it does not concern questions related to refraining from using or continuing life-sustaining treatments (passive euthanasia), nor does it concern questions related to providing patients with the means necessary to end their own lives (assisted suicide). Many who defend the permissibility of physician-assisted suicide do not support physician-assisted euthanasia. Advocates of physician-assisted suicide approve of letting physicians prescribe medications that patients may use to end their lives; they do not necessarily approve of letting physicians actually administer, for example, lethal injections, for the purpose of terminating patients' lives.

Ethical Perspectives

Contemporary ethical arguments supporting euthanasia often appeal to compassion for the suffering of a terminally ill and imminently dying patient. These arguments purport to show that physician aid in dying is ethically permissible under circumstances in which the patient's condition is associated with severe and unrelenting suffering that is not the result of inadequate pain control or comfort care.

Alternatively, arguments defending the permissibility of euthanasia make reference to the ethical principle of autonomy. The principle of autonomy requires respecting the informed choices of competent patients. Under this approach, physician involvement in euthanasia is ethically limited to situations in which competent patients make repeated informed requests for aid in dying.

Critics of euthanasia charge that both compassion- and autonomy-based ethical arguments are inadequate. Arguments invoking compassion are faulted on the ground that there is no principled basis for limiting euthanasia to competent patients who choose it. After all, many suffering patients are not competent. Therefore, if the ethical basis for providing aid in dying is compassion, then aid in dying should logically be extended to incompetent persons.

Arguments relying on the ethical principle of autonomy are also criticized for failing to offer a principled basis for appropriately limiting euthanasia. Thus, autonomy-based arguments do not require limiting euthanasia to patients who experience severe and unrelenting suffering, but would presumably allow applying euthanasia to healthy people who wished to die. Critics of autonomy-based arguments also doubt that patients' requests to die reflect patients' autonomous choices. Instead, such requests may occur due to inadequate palliative and comfort care, continued use of invasive and futile interventions, and failure to diagnose and treat other underlying causes of the request, such as depression (Emanuel, 1999). In such cases, meeting a patient's request for assistance in dying is not supported by a principle of respect for patient autonomy.

Both autonomy- and compassion-based arguments are vulnerable to the further objection that there is no principled basis for restricting euthanasia to persons who are imminently dying. After all, the prospect of suffering for a long period of time is arguably worse than the prospect of suffering briefly. Likewise, the principle of respect for autonomy presumably applies to all competent individuals, irrespective of whether they are about to die.

Legal Perspectives

Just as the ethical status of euthanasia is controversial, the legal status of both euthanasia and assisted suicide have been the subject of intense debate in the United States. At present, legislative statutes make assisted suicide a criminal act in 29 states; however, the constitutionality of these statutes has been challenged in the states of Michigan and Washington. Defenders of physician-assisted death have placed initiatives on the ballots of several western states to decriminalize euthanasia and/or assisted suicide, but these initiatives have not yet been successful.

Euthanasia is illegal in all other nations, including the Netherlands, although it is a common misconception that euthanasia is legal in the Netherlands. Article 293 of the Dutch penal code clearly states that anyone "who takes another person's life even at his explicit and serious request will be punished by imprisonment of at the most 12 years or a fine of the fifth category." Although assisted death is formally a crime in the Netherlands, the Dutch penal code allows for exceptions. For example, persons who assist with death will not be punished if their act is impelled by an "overwhelming power," or sudden conflict of duties or interests in a situation in which a choice must be made. This exception to punishment has been invoked over the years by Dutch courts and established a legal precedent for excluding certain categories of cases from criminal prosecution.

Euthanasia and the Elderly

Although debates about euthanasia apply to persons of all ages, they may bear special relevance to elderly persons. This is because death is nearer in old age, and therefore aging individuals may be more likely than younger persons to think about death and the dying process. Perhaps the aging of the population that is occurring in most developed nations will lead societies to focus greater attention on how to ensure humane care at the end of life. The question of whether or not euthanasia represents humane medical care for dying patients will continue to be discussed.

NANCY S. JECKER

See also
Death
Ethics

Living Wills and Durable Power of Attorney
Physician-Assisted Suicide

EVERYDAY MEMORY AND AGING

The term *everyday memory* is used to cover a broad range of tasks and procedures in the aging and memory literature. Generally, research on everyday memory includes some features that replicate more aspects of memory function in the real world than occur in standard laboratory experiments on aging and cognition. In some cases, the focus is on using laboratory procedures but with stimuli typical of those in the real world (e.g., memory for news media, names and faces, or the location of landmarks in a macrospatial environment), whereas in other cases the emphasis is on studying memory behaviors as they occur in the actual real-world environment (e.g., telephoning from home at prescribed times as a measure of appointment keeping). Virtually every domain of memory that is of interest to traditional laboratory researchers has an everyday-memory analog. For example, *working memory*, which is of great interest to researchers on cognitive aging, has been the focus in studies of age differences in remembering telephone numbers, quality of speech production, and comprehension of language. Other researchers have focused on *long-term memory* in studies of acquisition of name-face associations, as well as in studies of way finding and spatial cognition. Remembering to perform future actions (*prospective memory*) has been the primary focus of research on appointment keeping and medication adherence. Detailed reviews of the domains of research described above, as well as others, are included in Cohen (1996) and West and Sinnott (1992).

An assumption that is implicit in everyday memory research is that traditional laboratory studies of memory and aging do not accurately characterize differences in memory performance between young and older adults but that studies that are more naturalistic on some dimension will do so. The view typically articulated is that unfamiliar laboratory tasks are biased against older adults due to the enhanced experience younger adults may have with adapting to novel tasks typical of the laboratory. Some believe that laboratory tasks more closely simulate everyday classroom experiences of college students than the daily experiences of older adults. There is considerable evidence, however, for age differences on a variety of everyday memory tasks, despite the enhanced familiarity of the task, including memory for news broadcasts, medication information, and landmarks. Moreover, it is well documented that age differences increase as tasks become more difficult. Thus, one possibility is that, in cases where age differences are not found on everyday memory tasks, the familiarity of the task did indeed mitigate age differences but only because the familiarity made it less demanding of cognitive resources. As a result, age differences did not emerge because adults of both ages possess the requisite cognitive resources to perform the task adequately. Analogous views have been discussed in some detail by Salthouse (1991b) and Park (1999).

The view that everyday memory tasks obscure age-related differences in memory due to familiarity is an important issue if one is attempting to understand differences in fundamental memory processes that occur with age. At the same time, if one wishes to focus on another issue—that of adaptive functioning in an everyday context and compensatory mechanisms that occur in response to declining cognitive resources with age—the study of everyday memory becomes important in its own right. Understanding what variables and strategies permit older adults to perform effectively on everyday cognitive tasks despite diminishing cognitive abilities does require an understanding of basic memory mechanisms but also requires that we understand their interrelationship to contextual and motivational variables that may affect performance. Everyday memory research is well suited to addressing this question, as everyday-memory behaviors are likely more complex than basic laboratory behaviors. Everyday-memory paradigms provide an avenue to address the interaction between basic memory processes and contextual and interpersonal variables. One everyday-memory behavior common to older adults is that of taking medications correctly. An analysis of medication adherence as a prototypical everyday-memory behavior illustrates clearly the complexity of factors that one must consider to understand memory behaviors in the context in which they occur.

Medication adherence refers to taking medication correctly, as prescribed by a physician, in the right amount and at the right time. Medication adherence is a particularly interesting everyday-memory behavior to study because taking a medication correctly involves working memory, long-term memory, and prospective memory. The individual must use working memory to integrate and develop a medication plan for multiple medications; long-term memory is required to remember the plan (unless it is written down); and, finally, actually remembering to take the medication is a prospective memory task. Park, Morrell, Frieske, and Kincaid (1992) reported that very old adults were at greatest risk of taking medications incorrectly, primarily through omission errors, so this is an everyday-memory behavior of particular interest to gerontologists. However, the researchers found that when the oldest-old were provided with memory aids (medications organizers and written plans) that supported both the working memory and long-term memory components of medication adherence, almost no medication errors were made.

Although this finding suggests that medication adherence can best be understood within an exclusively cognitive framework, Park, Morrell, Frieske, and Kincaid (1992) also found that the majority of young-old adults were highly adherent to complex regimens of multiple medications. Thus, we have an example of older adults who likely have declined in component processes of cognition like speed and working memory, evidencing highly adapted and accurate everyday-memory behavior. In fact, Park and colleagues (Park, Hertzog, Leventhal, Morrell, Leventhal, Birchmore, et al., 1999) recently found that medication adherence, as measured by sensitive electronic monitors, was greater in older patients with rheumatoid arthritis than in middle-aged patients with this disease. The researchers attributed this finding to the fact that middle-aged adults reported having busier lifestyles with less of a daily routine than the older adults. In other words, the older adults frequently had taken medications for many years so that the daily environment automatically prompted them to take medications. In contrast, younger adults who led less habitual lives lacked consistent environmental stimuli to serve as cues for taking medications; as a result, this group made more errors. This latter age group could likely benefit from the use of an external reminding device, such as a beeping wristwatch, an intervention that Park, Shifren, Morrell, Watkins, and Stuedemann (1997) found to be effective in nonadherent hypertensive patients.

The above findings suggest the importance of understanding contextual and other noncognitive aspects of an everyday-memory behavior such as medication adherence. For example, Park and Mayhorn (1996) note that internal cues of pain and discomfort could serve as unique and highly personalistic memory aids to take medication. In addition, the presence of a significant other in the home, typically a spouse, may play an important role in cueing the individual to take the medication at the appropriate time. Park and Mayhorn (1996) further suggest that an individual's motivations and beliefs about illnesses and medications may predict his or her adherence. Moreover, there is some evidence that whether or not one remembers to perform a prospective task is related to the perceived consequences of forgetting (Kvavilashvili, 1987). Therefore, to the extent that a patient perceives an illness as trivial, he or she may more likely be nonadherent, whereas adherence rates should be much higher when a patient believes he or she has a serious illness that can be treated effectively with medication. Finally, medication adherence may be affected by individual differences in self-regulatory strategies. For example, Leventhal, Leventhal, Schaefer, and Easterling (1993) reported that older adults monitor their health and seek health care more often than younger adults, with the apparent aim of conserving their more limited physical and emotional resources. Older adults' use of a risk-avoidance strategy helps to explain their high adherence rates in the studies by Park and associates (Park, Hertzog, Leventhal, Morrell, Leventhal, Birchmore, et al., 1999; Park, Morrell, Frieske, & Kincaid, 1992).

It should be noted that memory's role in medication adherence should not be dismissed altogether, as it was found (Park, Hertzog, Leventhal, Morrell, Leventhal, Birchmore, et al., 1999) that individuals of low cognitive status relative to others their own age made more medication errors. In a similar vein, Zwahr, Park, and Shifren (1999) reported that cognitive abilities such as working memory and text memory were the best predictors of age-related variance in medical decision making.

The brief analysis of medication-adherence behavior presented here could be applied in a general fashion to many other everyday-memory behaviors, resulting in a more complete view of the older individual functioning in a complex psychosocial/

cognitive environment, where declining basic resources in cognition may be offset by the use of strategies and environmental supports for everyday cognitive tasks.

It should also be mentioned that an assessment of everyday-memory function has been developed by Crook and Larrabee (1988) for use in the laboratory that includes measures of name-face association, object memory, memory for groceries, telephone numbers, and news. West, Crook, and Barron (1992) found that age mediated substantial amounts of variance on these tasks, even after controlling for education, gender, depression, and vocabulary. This clinical assessment approach to everyday memory is effective for determining the relative status of an aged individual on a range of familiar memory tasks. Such an approach, however, will not provide a window into adaptive strategies the individual may employ to compensate for problems on these tasks, due to the laboratory-based, noncontextual nature of the approach taken by such an assessment battery.

In summary, it would appear that if the study of everyday memory is to offer insight into age-related differences in cognitive function, the everyday-memory behaviors should be studied in the context in which they occur, together with a determination of how contextually based variables affect the memories. The unique contribution of this type of research is likely to be in determining self-regulatory strategies used by individuals to adapt to the declining memories rather than to provide evidence that age-related decline in basic memory function does not occur when more familiar tasks are involved.

DENISE C. PARK
SCOTT C. BROWN

We gratefully acknowledge the support of this work by the National Institute of Aging through projects R01 AG06265, R01 AG09868, and P50 AG11715.

See also
Autobiographical Memory
Memory and Memory Theory

EVOLUTIONARY THEORY

What is the cause of biological aging? This is a question that can be addressed at two different levels, the proximate and the ultimate. The proximate level of explanation addresses mechanistic questions, such as those of physiology, biochemistry, and pathology. It considers the question above as *How* do organisms age? The ultimate level of explanation approaches a question from the perspective of evolutionary theory. It considers the initial question as *Why* do organisms age? Because the two levels of explanation give such different answers to the same question, it might seem that they have little or nothing to offer each other. In tackling the proximate question, researchers have proposed myriad theories involving the immune system, the neuroendocrine system, the reproductive system, free radical accumulation, somatic mutations, and collagen cross-linkage. Each theory can be based on empirical observation, but as the proverbial group of blind men discovered, when each described a different part of an elephant, these proximate theories can fall short of offering a complete answer. The ultimate explanation provided by evolutionary theory of the causes of biological aging has turned out to be an indispensable tool guiding the formulation and interpretation of proximate explanations.

The answer to the proximate question of how we age is complex and far from being known. The answer to the ultimate question, conversely, likely resides in the "evolutionary theory of aging," which considers the inevitability of aging as a simple consequence of the fact that the force of natural selection is lessened at later ages (M. R. Rose, 1991).

According to Darwin's mechanism of evolutionary change via natural selection, when there is heritable variation for a trait within a population, and when certain variants lead their carriers to produce relatively greater numbers of offspring, those beneficial variants of the trait will be present in an increasing proportion of the population over time. Conversely, alleles that reduce the reproductive success of individuals carrying them occur in fewer and fewer individuals with each successive generation. The variation that natural selection acts on is the result of a constant, albeit low, rate of mutation occurring in the germ cells of all individuals. Mutations usually have a relatively specific age-of-action, and generally their effects are slight, but negative (Simmons & Crow, 1977), although their effects occasionally can produce an increase in fitness. Mutations, although making possible all the adaptations we see, also are responsible for many of the decrements in physiological processes that are phenotypically observable as "aging."

Medawar (1946, 1952) first suggested that the declining force of natural selection with advancing age had important ramifications for the problem of human aging. Deleterious alleles for genes with late ages-of-action, he proposed, would accumulate to higher frequencies than deleterious alleles for genes with early ages-of-action. Imagine, to use a simplistic example, two mutations in humans, each of which causes a fatal breakdown in some key biochemical pathway. In one individual the mutation's age-of-action is 13 years. In another, the same deleterious effect is specified, but it does not have this effect until 100 years of age. One generation hence, the mutation with the early age-of-action will not be present because the individual carrying the fatal trait dies before she can pass it on to offspring. The mutation with the late age-of-action, conversely, will be present in all of the offspring of the original carrier because they will be born long before the mutation has its fatal effect. Additionally, environmental sources of mortality, such as predation, starvation, and infectious diseases, will also have greater opportunity to limit the number of individuals in the population whose fitness is reduced by the harmful allele. The later a deleterious trait is expressed, the less likely that it will reduce its carrier's fitness (the less a mutation will have *any* effect on its carrier's fitness). Consequently, harmful alleles with later ages-of-action will accumulate in the genome of each species. This is often referred to as the *mutation-accumulation* mechanism.

A variation of this mechanism, mentioned by Medawar (1946, 1952) and discussed in detail by Williams (1957), is referred to as the *antagonistic pleiotropy* mechanism for the evolution of senescence. G. C. Williams (1957) proposed and Charlesworth (1980) gave a formal mathematical demonstration of the possibility that alleles having favorable early effects on fitness but negative later effects may be selected for and thus increase in frequency in a population. As a possible example of an antagonistic pleiotropy, consider estrogen production in human females. Although estrogen is critical for reproduction, cumulative exposure is linked to increased mortality risk from breast cancer (McManus & Welsch, 1984) and endometrial can-

cer (Henderson, Ross, Pike, & Casagrande, 1982). Additional interesting examples of the antagonistic pleiotropy mechanism include the many semelparous or "big-bang" reproducers, such as several species of Pacific salmon (see Finch, 1990, for review). In these fish, dramatic rapid senescence and death occur as a specific result of reproduction, yet if the fish are prevented from spawning via castration or some other means, senescence is delayed long past the usual age, and life span may be more than doubled (O. H. Robertson, 1961). Analogously, it has been suggested that diet restriction's extending of life span may be brought about in part by delaying maturation and reproduction (Phelan & Austad, 1989).

Together, these two mechanisms, mutation-accumulation and antagonistic pleiotropy, comprise the evolutionary theory of aging. They are not mutually exclusive, and empirical evidence suggests they both are responsible for the evolution of aging, although the relative importance of each is a matter of debate (Rose, 1991; Rose & Charlesworth, 1980). However, each suggests a slightly different role for natural selection in the process. The mutation accumulation mechanism posits a more passive natural selection unable to weed out the deleterious alleles responsible for aging. The antagonistic pleiotropy mechanism suggests active selection for aging when those deleterious alleles responsible for it are simultaneously responsible for positive early traits.

A notable, but often overlooked, aspect of the evolutionary theory of aging is that it defines aging demographically, or as a population process. Different late-acting harmful alleles will accumulate in different lineages of individuals within a population. Consequently, the more closely related any two individuals are, the more likely they will share any of these alleles and in an entire population of organisms, there will be a variety of deleterious late-acting alleles present. This view of the aging process has important ramifications for the experimental designs used by researchers asking both proximate and ultimate questions. Although it is true that individuals age, the specific aging process can differ from individual to individual. Thus, the aging process as a whole must be described as the collective sum of mechanisms of aging in a population, including the full range of different causes that can occur along with the probabilities that each will occur within any individual. In other words, an accurate and complete understanding of aging in a population is only possible by examining many genotypes to observe a representative sampling of the deleterious alleles in the population. Just as close observation of a single human would provide a portrait of aging that is woefully incomplete at best and seriously misleading at worst, observations made on a few inbred strains of animals are inadequate. For example, Phelan (1992) noted the significant differences—including little overlap—in rates of occurrence of common pathological lesions among strains of mice and rats. Animals of different strains seem to experience different patterns of disease and mortality.

Empirical support for the evolutionary theory of aging is found both in the laboratory and the wild. Perhaps the strongest evidence comes from comparisons of populations evolving under conditions of high versus low environmental mortality. Populations living in relatively safe habitats, also known as habitats with a low "hazard factor" (Edney & Gill, 1968), are predicted to have slower rates of senescence than those evolving in habitats with high hazard factors. A high hazard factor quickly reduces the power of natural selection to weed out harmful late-acting alleles, whereas individuals living in an environment with a low hazard factor are more likely to reach the age at which their reproduction will be curtailed by a late-acting harmful allele's expression.

Two examples that support this prediction include comparison between island and mainland populations of opossum, and studies of artificial selection for delayed reproduction in fruit flies. Austad (1993) found that in a genetically isolated, island opossum population with a low hazard factor, senescence (measured as the acceleration of age-specific mortality) was significantly reduced when compared with a nearby mainland opossum population with a high hazard factor. Consistent with the predictions of Edney and Gill (1968), the island opossums, evolving in an environment free from the major opossum predators, exhibited smaller litter sizes and increased longevity relative to opossums from the mainland. In addition, in laboratory selection experiments, the force of natural selection in later ages can be varied. Rose (1984), for example, found that as long as there is sufficient genetic variability present, stocks of fruit flies perpetuated by only permitting individuals to reproduce at later ages showed a postponement of senescent changes when compared with stocks of early reproducing flies. In essence, these late reproducing lines have an experimentally reduced hazard factor: The only flies contributing to the gene pool are those with a genome sufficiently devoid of deleterious alleles to allow the individual to survive to advanced ages.

The evolutionary theory of aging has given us an answer to the question Why do organisms age? This answer, valuable in its own right, is increasingly put to productive use in helping to address the more pragmatic questions How do we age? and Can we postpone it?

JOHN P. PHELAN

See also
Disposable Soma Theory

EXCHANGE THEORY IN AGING

Interpersonal relationships are central to successful aging. Through supportive bonding, people derive many salutatory effects, satisfaction, and sustenance; but personal ties can also be stressful and discomforting. Recognizing the importance of interaction, exchange theorists have spent much of the past two decades identifying positive and negative consequences of one or another type of interaction in both laboratory and field investigations. In that time the focus has moved considerably beyond the neoeconomic origins of exchange theory and its contention that people approach all interaction with an eye to maximizing rewards while minimizing costs of interaction (Cook, 1992). Exchange networks have been recognized as encompassing differential power and influence as well as fixed and variable alternatives to comparable ends (Cook & Yamagishi, 1992; Willer, Lovaglia, & Markovsky, 1997). In gerontology, such an approach looks at the way older people are perceived, how such a view affects their interaction with others, and whether the consequences are positive or negative (Ingersoll-Dayton, Morgan, & Antonucci, 1997; Rook, 1997). Patterns of support, intergenerational interaction, and historical changes in opportunity or network structures and the perceived value of the elderly are frequently analyzed from an exchange theory perspective (Clarke, 1997; Davey & Eggebeen, 1998; Davey & Norris, 1998).

Modern-day exchange theory is foreshadowed in classical economics (Adam Smith, Ricardo, Mill, Bentham); sociology (Weber, Simmel, Durkheim), anthropology (Frazer, Lévi-Strauss, Maus, Malinowski), as well as in generalized principals of behavioral psychology. The seminal contributions of Homans, Blau, Emerson, and Thibaut and Kelley provided the impetus for recent refinements, and within the past decade a new focus has infused exchange theory with a concern for formalized structural considerations of power in exchange networks and applied in a variety of contexts. In the past decade exchange theorists have focused extensively on what have been termed power and resource differentials within networks and on structural bases for positional power within network types. Despite divergence in assumptions and predictions, there is an emerging consensus among exchange proponents that structural placement is as important for manifestations of power within networks as are individual attributes. According to some research, successful negotiations and inclusion in the process raise expectations and demands for valued resources, whereas unsuccessful exchanges or exclusion lowers demands and prompts conciliatory behavior and more modest demands for comparable resources. Furthermore, lower power actors find themselves in competition with one another for inclusion; as a consequence, more powerful actors gain relatively greater benefit from exchanges and greater benefits still when there is an absence of substitutable alternatives (Thye, Lovaglia, & Markovsky, 1997). Notwithstanding the great many definitional and operational disputes, the problem of open versus closed exchange networks, structural power and status, and a conflation of power and influence, network exchange theory offers a number of enticing leads applicable to gerontology. The attention focused on the development of inequalities arising out of structural factors implicit in social networks may be particularly helpful.

Despite considerable variation, most exchange-based explanations found in the gerontological literature are predicated on two neoclassical assumptions. First, the desire for individual gain is basic to all behavior; we all seek rewards. Second, activity that is positively reinforced will endure, that which is not will cease. A corollary of the latter is that the actions of others are a primary source of emotional well-being and morale. A more general principle is that insofar as situations appear similar to situations in which rewards had previously been obtained, they will be reacted to favorably. Another proposition is that the more consequential the result of an action, the more likely it is that action will recur until satiation occurs. Generally, no single transaction is sufficient to affect behavior, because interaction occurs as a part of a network of such interactions. Therefore, patterns of success must be considered, as well as indirect or displaced satisfactions in open and closed networks of exchange. Clearly, the primary theoretical thrust has major implications for ameliorative, as well as disruptive social interaction and the creation of dependencies in the absence of alternatives means to an end.

Buttressing these assumptions are the propositions that actors bring an array of personal resources with them to any exchange, that resources are not distributed equally, and that all interaction involves an interchange of value, material or nonmaterial. Continued participation is predicated on actors maximizing rewards accrued from interaction while minimizing costs. People will persevere in personal exchanges so long as benefits outweigh costs. However, no single interaction occurs in isolation and therefore need not bear the total calculation of cost-benefit reckoning (Cook, 1992). Still, should rewards, tangible or intangible, be devalued relative to what must be undergone or forgone in order to obtain them, social contact will become unstable and eventually cease absent qualifying factors. An assessment of costs also entails an appraisal of status of potential partners and availability of alternatives for reaching the same goal or a viable substitute. According to the logic of the exchange model, relationships involving a unidirectional flow of goods or services are intrinsically imbalanced and may become increasingly precarious (Morgan, Schuster, & Butler, 1991), even potentially exploitative or abusive. Furthermore, to adequately understand the effect diverse types of exchanges have on an actor, the complex of life events characterizing an actor's biography must be part of the estimation (Ingersoll-Dayton, Morgan, & Antonucci, 1997).

Criticisms of exchange theory have concentrated on issues of inference, empirical referents, definitions of rewards, their temporal dimensions plus cost assessments, and the whole question of the relational nature of statuses, role expectations, and benefits derived. Some critics maintain exchange theory has failed to move beyond methodological individualism, simplistic notions of reinforcement, and a tenancy to rely on reductionist logic and problematic assessment of effects. Although the interactive nature of roles, identity, and sense of self is potentially one of the major contributions of exchange theory, few researchers have sought to examine how components of interaction become validating or affirming factors for actors involved or what kinds of time frames are involved (Davey & Eggebeen, 1998). Nor has sufficient attention yet been paid to how normative expectations define roles—their parity and boundaries—or determine behavior. Similarly, network characteristics, in and of themselves, have not received close attention.

In response to these and comparable criticisms, a number of reformulations have appeared. Emphasis has shifted from unilateral maximization of investments to an optimal distribution between costs and benefits to a greater specification of the influence of the norms of distributive justice, relating these to moral economies, and the determination of normative expectations, especially those of reciprocity. In light of the criticisms leveled at too heavy an emphasis on psychologistic explanations, variations known as social-environmental, personal resource, and equity theories have recently addressed issues of transactional definitions of the situation, normative pluralism, and the structural basis of power and influence in decision making. Also, besides positive affect and reinforcement, negative consequences may adhere to exchange-based relationships (Davey & Norris, 1998; Rook, 1997).

Exchange Theory and Aging

Those who adopt an exchange perspective in social gerontology presume there is a rebalancing of exchange relationships as a consequence of the aging process or because of changing statuses. Changes in the social world of the elderly are analyzed in terms of realignments of personal relationships brought on by redefinition of older people's roles, skills, contributions, interpersonal values, or ability to wield power. Since its introduction into gerontol-

ogy in the 1970s, exchange theory has served as a valuable heuristic tool to analyze changes in primary relationships, the strengths and weaknesses of social support networks, family interaction, status decline, and those aspects of interaction built upon the ability of older personas to impose their will and desires on their environment. Exchange theory also has been utilized for analyzing the fluid dimensions of self-concept and a range of other subjective factors crucial to an individual's sense of personal worth. Only recently has it been used as a template for making sense of negative consequences or in the identification of "weak power" as a way to channel interaction.

Particularly important contributions have derived from analyses of the seeming docility, compliance, and deference observed among some elderly as a mediating strategy for bartering with younger interaction partners or bureaucratic organizations. Recent research has concentrated on the structure of opportunity as a key factor in the accrual of power in intergenerational interaction (Ingersoll-Dayton, Morgan, & Antonucci, 1997). In the past decade, exchange models have expanded their focus to examine the buffering effects of network size and affect (Unger, McAvay, Bruce, Berkman, & Seeman, 1999). Investigators are just beginning to consider exogenous determinants of interaction patterns within networks. Cross-linkages with political and moral economic perspectives, shifting away from the early formulation, are leading to macro-levels of analysis that may portend even greater contributions (Hendricks & Leedham, 1992).

JON HENDRICKS

See also
Social Theories in Aging

EXERCISE

Despite the fact that physical activity is recognized as important for health promotion and primary and secondary disease prevention, older persons represent the most sedentary segment of the adult population. Recommendations to increase physical activity recently have received increased attention (American College of Sports Medicine (ACSM),

1998; World Health Organization, 1997), including suggestions for future research in the field (King, Rejeski, & Buchner, 1998). Although the optimal level of exercise for older persons has not been established, it is generally agreed that an exercise program for older adults should include aerobic exercise (e.g., walking, biking, jogging, or swimming), resistance training, and flexibility and balance activities.

Cardiovascular Responses to Exercise

The ability to engage in physical exercise depends on the capacity of the circulatory system to deliver oxygen to exercising muscles, as well as the metabolic characteristics of the exercising skeletal muscle. When exercise is initiated, heart rate increases markedly, first by withdrawal of vagal tone followed by activation of the sympathetic nervous system. Stroke volume, that is, the amount of blood pumped from the heart with each contraction, also increases due to sympathetic activation and especially enhancement of returning venous blood. As a result of the increases in heart rate and stroke volume, cardiac output may increase up to fivefold in highly trained athletes. Heart rate typically doubles, while stroke volume may increase 15% during upright exercise. Systolic blood pressure increases in proportion to exercise intensity, while diastolic blood pressure normally remains unchanged or increases only slightly due to decreases in total peripheral resistance.

The distribution of blood to various organ systems is also altered during exercise. Coronary and skeletal blood flow increases, while renal and mesenteric blood flow is diminished. After the start of exercise, blood flow to the skin is increased to facilitate heat loss. However, at high levels of exercise intensity the skin may vasoconstrict to help redistribute blood to exercising muscles. Cerebral blood flow appears to remain unchanged (Clausen, 1977).

During exercise there is a gradual and systematic increase in oxygen demand by working muscles. As the oxygen supplied in arterial blood is increasingly utilized by the muscle tissue, the oxygen levels in the returning venous blood decrease, resulting in a widening of the arterial-venous oxygen difference. These changes in oxygen demand and utilization are reflected by increased oxygen consumption (VO_2). The more work an individual performs, the higher the energy demand and the greater the amount of oxygen consumed. As the body reaches its maximum ability to consume oxygen (VO_2 max), there is a leveling off of blood pressure and heart rate with increased workload. An individual's state of physical fitness may be inferred from the maximum oxygen consumption.

Effects of Age

Performance of the cardiovascular system declines with advancing age. VO_2 max decreases from 5% to 15% per decade after age 25, along with a progressive decline in cardiac output, heart rate, and stroke volume at maximum workloads. Maximal heart rate decreases 6 to 10 beats per minute per decade, and is largely responsible for the age-related decline in cardiac output and VO_2 max. The VO_2 max achieved by 25- to 30-year-olds is roughly 10 times the basal VO_2; by the age range of 70 to 75, the VO_2 max decreases by 50% over basal. Whereas young adults can achieve maximum values in excess of 200 beats per minute, adults over age 70 may not be able to surpass 125 beats per minute. Age-related changes in cardiac function are thought to be attributable to changes both in peripheral circulation and in intrinsic systolic and diastolic function. Other factors could be responsible for this decline, however, including the presence of occult disease or chronic deconditioning. Older persons are more likely to suffer from comorbid conditions, many of which affect the cardiovascular system, including diabetes, hypertension, coronary artery disease, and obesity. Interestingly, examination of healthy subjects between the ages of 25 and 79, from the Baltimore Longitudinal Study on Aging, who were free from overt or occult coronary disease failed to show a significant age-related decline in cardiac output at rest or exercise (Rodeheffer, Gerstenblith, Becker, Fleg, Weisfeldt, & Lakatta, 1984). However, aging may affect the mechanisms by which cardiac output is maintained during exercise. With advancing age there is a shift from catecholamine-mediated increases in heart rate and reduction in end-systolic volume to a greater reliance on the Frank-Starling mechanism. Older adults also have reduced early diastolic filling at rest and during exercise compared with younger persons, perhaps because of reduced left ventricular compliance. As a result, older adults rely on late atrial diastolic filling to a greater extent than younger persons. End-diastolic volumes are also larger in older adults during exercise, resulting in reduced ejection fractions. Left ventricular contractility may also be reduced during maximal exercise, and maximal blood pressure response may be greater than in younger persons at peak exercise (ACSM, 1998).

In addition, it has been argued that the decline in cardiovascular function observed to accompany advancing age may be a result of deconditioning and inactivity rather than simply the inevitable consequence of the aging process. With the exception of peak exercise heart rate, all of the parameters of cardiovascular function that decline with age have been shown to be improved by exercise training in younger populations (Scheuer & Tipton, 1977). Therefore, there has been a great deal of recent interest in assessing the extent to which cardiovascular function can be modified by physical exercise training among the elderly.

Aerobic Exercise Training

Repeated bouts of physical exercise produce physiological adaptations commonly known as training effects. Training effects refer to a set of cardiovascular, neuroendocrine, and biochemical alterations that can be predictably achieved by engaging in physical exercise at a specified intensity, duration, and frequency.

Exercise training increases the duration of exercise that can be sustained at fixed workloads and reliably increases VO_2 max in both young and older individuals. Saltin and Grimby (1968) reported that former athletes with a mean age of 53 years who had been inactive for at least 10 years still had a 20% higher VO_2 max than age-predicted norms, although their VO_2 max was actually 25% lower than comparable men who had continued their physical training. Although older adults generally achieve 10% to 30% increases in VO_2 max with chronic (e.g., >3 months) aerobic exercise training, which is comparable to younger persons, there appears to be more individual variability in response to standard exercise prescriptions (e.g., 70% of heart rate reserve, 3 times per week for 12 weeks)

among older persons relative to their younger counterparts. When healthy adults undergo an exercise training program, they increase their VO_2 max by augmenting maximal cardiac output and peripheral oxygen extraction (maximal A-VO_2). In contrast, persons with coronary disease typically achieve improvements by increasing peripheral oxygen extraction as evidenced by a greater A-VO_2 difference. The predominant mechanism for this increase in A-VO_2 is an increase in oxygen extraction by the peripheral muscle thought to be due to an increase in mitochondrial number and enzymatic capacity, as well as to alterations in vasomotor regulation of blood flow to working muscle, including an increase in capillary density. The cardiovascular adaptations during submaximal workloads are reduced and stroke volume is increased, although changes tend to be smaller for older persons.

As in cardiac patients, studies have also suggested that older individuals achieve increasing VO_2 max primarily through an increase in maximal A-VO_2 difference, rather than through improvements in central cardiac function. Thus, it has been reported that the elderly experience a fall in left ventricular ejection fraction in response to exercise, which appears unchanged by exercise training. More recently, however, it has been noted that older men (but not necessarily women) undergo central cardiovascular adaptations that increase their VO_2 max with training. Older men rely on the Frank-Starling mechanism to increase their maximal stroke volume, cardiac output, and VO_2 max following chronic aerobic exercise. Similar to younger persons, older men may also achieve exercise-induced increases in VO_2 max as a result of expanded plasma and total blood volumes. Women, on the other hand, may achieve improved VO_2 max as a result of increases in maximal A-VO_2 difference; studies have not observed increases in left ventricular mass, cardiac output, stroke volume, or end-diastolic volume (ACSM, 1998).

Resistance Training

Advancing age is associated with loss of muscle mass (saropenia). The excretion of urinary creatinine, reflecting muscle creatinine content and total muscle mass, decreases by 50% from age 20 to 90 years. There also is a gradual and progressive decline in muscle density and a decline in the number of muscle fibers, especially in Type II muscle fibers. In general, muscle strength is thought to decrease by 15% per decade after age 50 and 30% per decade after age 70, with much of the reduction in strength due to a selective atrophy of Type II muscle fibers. This decline in strength is associated with reduced walking speed and functional capacity (ACSM, 1998).

Resistance (strength) training consists of exercise in which the resistance against which a muscle generates force is systematically increased over time. It has been demonstrated that older persons achieve significant strength gains that may be comparable to younger persons. More intensive resistance training may increase muscle strength two to threefold after 3 to 4 months of training, and may also increase bone density.

Flexibility and Balance

In addition to loss of muscle mass, aging is associated with changes in the structure of connective tissue and in bone density, all three of which influence the range of motion of joints, or flexibility, which peaks in the mid- to late-20s and declines thereafter (ACSM, 1998). Because reduced flexibility impedes mobility and therefore activities of daily living in older adults, exercise programs targeted at improving flexibility appear to have merit. However, research in this area has lagged behind research involving other types of exercise, and results have been somewhat inconsistent. Overall, the evidence suggests that a broad-based training program, including both aerobic exercise and stretching exercises, holds the most promise for improving flexibility and should be included in an exercise prescription.

Aging also brings with it a decline in postural stability, increasing the risk of falling due to loss of balance for older adults. Although the factors responsible for falling are numerous, an individual's postural stability, or balance, is a key factor that is potentially modifiable. Balance itself, however, is influenced by many systems, including motor, sensory, and higher level cognitive functions. Exercise programs have been shown to improve balance, although interventions have included a wide range of activities and quite varied outcome measures,

such as number of falls or tests of balance. Thus, it is not entirely clear what specific exercise-related factors are responsible for improvements in balance. However, as in the case of flexibility, evidence suggests that more inclusive programs, such as those incorporating aerobic activity, resistance training, stretching, and balance practice, are most likely to improve postural stability in older adults and decrease risk of injuries resulting from loss of balance (ACSM, 1998).

Biobehavioral Effects of Exercise

Studies have shown that aerobic exercise has beneficial effects in three biobehavioral domains that may be especially relevant to aging: mood, cognition, and psychophysiologic stress responsivity. Depression is a major health problem, particularly for the elderly, and is associated with significant functional impairment and disability. Cross-sectional studies generally have shown that individuals who are active or physically fit are less likely to be depressed than their unfit counterparts (O'Connor, Aenchbacher, & Dishman, 1993). In one longitudinal study, baseline depressive symptoms were associated with physical inactivity; moreover, subsequent individuals who increased their physical activity reduce their risk of depression to a level comparable to those who had remained active, whereas reductions in activity were associated with increased likelihood of future depression. Interventional studies have demonstrated that aerobic exercise is associated with significant reductions in depressive symptoms in both younger and older individuals. In one recent study, 4 months of supervised aerobic exercise was found to be as effective as antidepressant medication in reducing depressive symptoms in older men and women with major depressive disorder (Blumenthal, Babyak, Moore, Craighead, Herman, Khatri, et al., 1999).

Advancing age is associated with declines in certain cognitive functions, particularly those involving problem-solving skills and the ability to integrate new information (i.e., fluid intelligence). With relatively few exceptions, cross-sectional studies have demonstrated that active or physically fit individuals perform better on cognitive tasks than unfit, sedentary persons. In a classic study, Spirduso (1975) observed that older racquet sportsmen exhibited faster reaction times than older non-exercisers. However, interventional studies are far less consistent. Several randomized controlled studies of healthy older men and women or patients with cardiovascular disease failed to find exercise-related improvements in cognitive performance (Emery & Blumenthal, 1991), although more recent studies have suggested that higher level executive functions including self-control and self-monitoring may show modest improvements with increased aerobic fitness.

Exaggerated cardiovascular and neurohumoral responses to behavioral challenges have been shown to be associated with increased risk of cardiovascular disorders. Cross-sectional studies have demonstrated fairly consistently that high levels of fitness are associated with reduced stress responses. Although interventional studies are generally less consistent, there is evidence that aerobic exercise training results in an attenuation of heart rate and blood pressure levels in response to laboratory challenges such as public speaking, mental arithmetic, and a mirror-tracing task. These reductions appear to be over and above the changes in resting hemodynamic function (Emery & Blumenthal, 1991).

Exercise Safety

The issue of exercise safety has also received much attention, particularly as home-based exercise programs gain more widespread appeal. Generally, exercise is safe for older persons, including patients with cardiovascular disease. Because there are increased comorbidities in older persons that affect cardiovascular functioning, however, exercise testing is an important prerequisite prior to initiation of a new exercise training regimen. The main concern is that sudden death may occur with vigorous exercise, and individuals with occult disease or other unrecognized conditions (e.g., cardiomyopathies, uncontrolled arrhythmias, acute congestive heart failure, and unstable angina) are at increased risk. However, it should be emphasized that the incidence of sudden death is relatively rare, even among the elderly, and that aging should not preclude exercise training. Far more common are musculoskeletal injuries, which may occur in more than 50% of the cases, particularly among older persons. Proper warm-up and cool-down techniques, along

with adherence to appropriate exercise prescriptions with respect to frequency, duration, and intensity, should minimize the risk of serious injury.

JAMES A. BLUMENTHAL
ELIZABETH C. D. GULLETTE

See also
Activities
Cardiovascular System: Overview
Mobility
Musculoskeletal System
Skeletal Muscle Characteristics

EXPERTISE AND AGING
See
Age and Expertise

EYE: CLINICAL ISSUES

The Lens

To see both near and distant objects without optical aid, the lens in the eye must change its shape and thereby its refractive power. Range of accommodative power steadily and linearly decreases from birth onward until all focusing power is lost by age 55. By age 45 or so, so much accommodative power is lost that reading glasses or bifocals become necessary, if one is to see clearly both near and far. This is called presbyopia, from the Greek word *presbys*, meaning "old man" or "elder."

Because so many equate "aging" with processes involving loss, damage, error, or atrophy, it is especially instructive to look at a tissue in which loss of function is the result of perpetually youthful growth. In the embryological development of the eye, a bit of skin is pinched off and incorporated into the eyeball as the primordial lens. This surface ectoderm shares with the skin, the hair, and the nails the property of continued growth throughout life. Although nails, hair, and skin can be cut or sloughed off, the fibers produced by this lens "skin" must continue to accrete within the eye. The result of this progressive accumulation of new lens fibers is a loss of lens flexibility manifesting itself as a loss of focusing power, which we call loss of accommodation.

It is ironic that presbyopia (or elder's eyes) is the result of a continued youthful production of lens fibers by lens epithelium and a preservation of the fibers previously formed. After all lens flexibility is lost, the refractive power of the lens remains reasonably constant for a decade or two. Then the ever-increasing number of fibers causes the lens to become more globular and the light-bending power to increase. A lay term often heard for this myopia or nearsightedness is *second sight*. The elderly can now read again without glasses to the astonishment of their children, who are themselves putting on glasses to read. This near-vision capability (myopia) is, however, accompanied by a progressive increase in the need for distance glasses, and a progressive loss of lens clarity or nuclear cataract. Other lens opacities or cataracts develop as a result of pathological processes, such as chronic ultraviolet light exposure. Twenty-five percent of Americans age 65 and older have cataracts. Removal of this ectodermal excrescence is the most common surgical procedure performed on Americans age 65 or older. An estimated 1.35 million such surgeries are done each year in the United States (U.S. Department of Health and Human Services, 1993). Nevertheless, cataract and its complications remain a major cause of blindness in the elderly.

The Cornea

The cornea is the clear windowlike tissue at the front of the eye. Like the lens, it functions to converge light rays on the retina. Although its curvature is flatter than that of the lens, it is the major refractive surface of the eye because the air-corneal interface is more optically effective than the aqueous-lens-aqueous transitions. Clarity and regularity of the corneal surface are necessary for good visual function.

Corneal clarity is dependent on corneal dehydration. The single layer of endothelial cells lining the posterior surface of the cornea acts as a barrier and also continuously pumps water out of the cornea and back into the eye. There is a decrease with age in the number of these endothelial cells. In the early years of life cell densities of 2,000 to 4,000 cells/mm^2 are found, whereas at age 80 counts as low

as 900 cells/mm^2 may be found. Because of large individual variations, however, it is difficult to predict age accurately from observation of the endothelial cells, although cell size and heterogeneity do increase with age.

A grayish peripheral corneal haze called arcus senilis universally develops in older individuals. This cornea stromal lipid deposition characteristically is seen much earlier in Blacks than in Whites. Although associated with hyperlipidemia in individuals under 40, there is no demonstrable correlation with metabolic abnormalities in older individuals, and the deposits seldom affect visual function.

Complaints of burning, stinging, dry eyes are common in the aged and may be the result of corneal epithelial abnormalities associated with abnormalities of the tear film. Tear production decreases monotonically with age, octogenarians having only 25% of the tear-wetting capacity of teenagers. Corneal function, however, is ordinarily well preserved if the lower lids are not lax and everted.

The Vitreous

At birth the posterior chamber of the eye is packed with a firm gel adherent to the optic nerve, lens, and anterior retinal edge and origin of the ciliary body (ora serrata and pars plana ciliaris). Beginning first in the center of the vitreous body this gel structure gradually breaks down, producing a central liquid pocket surrounded by a cortex of "formed" vitreous gel. In the middle years of life this fluid center will break through the cortex and come to lie against the posterior superior retina. The formed vitreous conversely will peel off the equatorial retina and collapse into the central space vacated by the fluid. This vitreous "detachment" is commonly accompanied by the release of cellular debris and condensation of vitreous fibrils that cast shadows on the retina and result in "vitreous floaters." With the passage of time the vitreous adhesion to the optic nerve may be broken, and the entire posterior globe will then become filled with fluid. Only a shallow layer of vitreous gel persists, extending from side to side across the eye behind the lens.

This more mobile-formed vitreous may mechanically stimulate the retina either by flopping against it or by tugging on it with eye movement. When the eye is dark adapted, bright arcuate flashes of light called Moore's lightning streaks may be noted as a result of this mechanical stimulation. Flashes and floaters may also be associated with a tractional retinal tear, which may lead to retinal detachment.

The Retina

In the absence of trauma or surgery, retinal detachment is a rare but serious condition of the later years. Vitreous detachment is the usual precursor. Peripheral retinal degenerations, particularly lattice degeneration, are also common precursors of retinal detachment. The most common group of age-related degenerations that affect visual function, however, are not the peripheral degenerations, but the central or macular degenerations.

The axial center of the retina is specialized for high resolution and color perception under well-lit conditions. At the center of this macular portion of the retina, cone cells are packed together densely. For reasons that are not clear but may relate to chronic exposure to focused radiant energy, this macular area is particularly subject to age-related loss of function. Indeed, macular degenerations now probably account for most new cases of acquired adult legal blindness in the United States. Fortunately, the various degenerations of this area almost never affect the more peripheral retina. Although legally blind, affected individuals can get about and care for themselves. The inability to read and drive are their major handicaps. Whites are much more susceptible to macular degeneration than Blacks (National Eye Institute, 1969, 1970).

Age-related macular degenerations can be subdivided into two general categories: dry and wet. In the "dry" degenerations no leakage of fluid into or beneath the retina can be demonstrated, but disturbance of the retinal pigment epithelium, with clumping of pigment, loss of pigment, and the formation of drusen deposits is commonly seen. In "wet" degenerations fluorescein angiography reveals pooling of fluid and blood beneath the macular pigment epithelium or sensory retina. In the latter case an abnormal proliferation of blood vessels, a subretinal neovascular membrane, can often be demonstrated angiographically. If this network of vessels is not beneath the fovea, obliteration of the membrane with laser photocoagulation has been shown to be of at least temporary benefit in 70% of treated individuals. Unfortunately, only 5% or less of age-related macular degeneration patients have treatable subretinal neovascular membranes.

Diabetes mellitus is prevalent in the United States, and retinal vascular abnormalities generally can be detected after 16 years of clinically diagnosed diabetes. After 25 years, it is a rare diabetic patient who does not have obvious vasculopathy. Although laser photocoagulation of the retina and vitrectomy surgery are helpful in maintaining visual function, loss of vision from retinal and vitreous hemorrhages and retinal traction are so common that diabetic retinopathy ranks as one of the top three causes of acquired adult blindness in this country. A major underlying process appears to be focal retinal ischemia followed by proliferation of new vessels and membranes on the retina. Such proliferations are often more pronounced in the juvenile-onset diabetic patient than in the adult onset patient, in whom exudative maculopathy and ischemic macular edema may be seen alone.

Glaucoma

Also ranking as a leading cause of acquired adult blindness, glaucoma is a disease rarely seen before age 40 unless associated with congenital ocular anatomical defects (Shields, 1992). Mechanical stability is essential for the function of any optical system, and the eye is not an exception. The problem of combining optical stability with ocular motion is solved by pressurizing the eyeball internally. Maintenance of this pressure depends on a precise balance between the secretion into the eye and the flow of fluid out of the eye. Except for the heart and major vessels, no body organ or tissue maintains a higher pressure. Blood must flow in and out of this pressure chamber, and the function and nutrition of optic nerve axons must be maintained across this high-pressure gradient.

When derangement of this system occurs, usually by loss of outflow facility, but occasionally by mechanical blockage of the filtering meshwork in the anterior chamber angle, the internal pressure of the eye rises to abnormally high levels. Damage to the optic nerve with loss of visual function occurs if the pressure elevation is prolonged. This loss is manifested by cupping of the optic nerve head and progressive loss of peripheral visual field. The insidious nature of this peripheral loss may result in advanced and irreversible damage before the disease is recognized. In its end stages, visual function may be the opposite of that seen in macular degeneration. Although some central vision may be preserved, patients may be unable to walk without bumping into objects because of a peripheral vision so limited that their view is like looking down a gun barrel.

Treatment is directed toward normalizing the intraocular pressure through the use of drugs, such as β-blocker drops, and through surgery, such as laser iridotomy and trabeculoplasty. In severe cases, it may be necessary to make a controlled surgical leak or fistula to vent the fluid from the eye. Despite such measures, blindness may result, and factors other than intraocular pressure are important in some patients with the disease. Unfortunately, the identity of these additional factors remains obscure. The risk of blindness is greater in Blacks affected with the disease than in Whites.

Blindness

The prevalence of blindness defined as best-corrected vision of 20/200 or worse increases almost logarithmically beginning at about age 50. There is no gender difference, but the prevalence in Blacks was twice that in Whites under age 80 in one urban survey (Tielsch et al., 1990). Between the ages of 60 and 69, for example, 2% of Whites and 10% of Blacks were legally blind. The causes of acquired adult blindness are multifactorial.

The major causes of legal blindness in the United States are summarized in Table 1. Although recent data are lacking, demographic changes would indicate that blindness from macular degeneration is now more prevalent than tabulated.

Independent living requires good vision. The greatest threats to the vision of an adult in this country are cataracts, macular degeneration, glaucoma, and diabetes. Patients with the first can usually be completely rehabilitated by cataract surgery with intraocular lens implants. Our success in treating the latter three is limited. Given their high incidence and prevalence, macular degeneration, glaucoma, and diabetic retinopathy rank as major impediments to a satisfactory quality of life for older Americans.

Recent research on clinical issues in aging and visual function is summarized in Kalina (1999).

W. BANKS ANDERSON, JR.

See also
Vision and Visual Perception

TABLE 1   Major Causes of Legal Blindness, United States (1978)

	Existing cases (prevalence)[a]	New cases (incidence)[b]
Glaucoma other than congenital	62,100	5,350
Macular degeneration	58,250	7,850
Senile cataract	41,500	4,550
Optic nerve atrophy	34,500	2,000
Diabetic retinopathy	32,650	4,700
Uveitis including chorioretinitis	30,450	1,650
Retinitis pigmentosa	23,250	1,450
Myopia	19,850	1,250
Retinopathy of prematurity	12,600	150
Detachment of retina	8,300	650

[a]Estimated distribution according to site and type of affection, by National Society to Prevent Blindness, based on unpublished Model Reporting Area register data as of December 31, 1970.
[b]Estimated distribution according to site and type of affection, by National Society to Prevent Blindness, based on unpublished Model Reporting Area data on new additions to the register, 1969–1970 average.

F

FALLS

Falls are a common problem for older persons. Surveys of community-dwelling persons report that about one quarter of individuals age 65 to 74 years and one third of those over 75 fall each year; about 50% of these will experience multiple falling episodes annually. Because older persons underreport falls, the frequency is likely to be underestimated. Within the acute hospital setting, up to 40% of older persons will fall at some time during their stay; as many as 10% of these will fall repeatedly. In the nursing home about 50% of residents fall each year; more than 40% suffer multiple falls. The risk of falls increases dramatically with advancing age; older women are especially vulnerable. Any gender difference in fall rates begins to disappear after age 75; by age 85, the prevalence of falls in men and women is nearly equal.

Consequences

Falls represent a major cause of death and disability in older people, posing a serious threat to their health and well-being. The overall death rate from falls in the United States is estimated at 5.1 per 100,000 persons; in those persons age 65 and older the death rate increases to 31.3 per 100,000. Fall-related mortality increases with age. By age 85, approximately two thirds of all injury-related deaths are due to falls. For individuals who survive, falls are associated with myriad morbid complications. Approximately 24% of those who fall at least once per year sustain a serious injury (i.e., any fracture or soft-tissue injuries requiring medical attention or resulting in activity restriction for more than 48 hours). Between 5% and 10% of falls result in bone fractures. The majority of these are due to distal forearm and hip fractures. Between 1% and 2% of falls result in hip fractures. Most falls, however, do not cause sufficient injury to warrant medical attention.

Hip fracture has the greatest impact. Up to 25% of persons who fracture a hip die within a year of injury, partly because of underlying disease and/or the consequences of immobility. In those who survive, hip fractures are associated with considerable morbidity. Approximately 25% of individuals will lose significant function, and 50% will experience decreased mobility within the first 6 months after fracture. Many of these individuals become functionally dependent, and depend on other people or assistive devices (canes, walkers) for mobility. Subsequent loss of independence and immobility is associated with either temporary or permanent long-term institutionalization.

The risk of fall-related injury increases with age, becoming more common in those persons 75 years and older. Older women are more likely to suffer serious injury than older men, partly because of osteopenia (i.e., increased likelihood of fracture). Even in the absence of physical injury, falls may have serious consequences. Falls are frightening experiences and can cause older persons to lose confidence in their ability to function safely. As a result, many older persons develop a fear of further falls. Up to 56% of older persons restrict or eliminate social and physical activities, because they fear additional falls and injury. The risk of developing fear of falling is increased in those persons with gait and balance disorders, recurrent falls over a short period, and prolonged downtime (i.e., an inability to get up from the floor by oneself). Any restriction of activities that results can lead to periods of immobility and, subsequently, the risk of physical complications (e.g., muscle weakness and osteoporosis) and psychosocial morbidity (e.g., depression and social withdrawal).

Causes of Falls

Normal gait and balance depend on the proper functioning of sensory (visual, proprioceptive, and vestibular systems), central integrative processing (central nervous system), and musculoskeletal effector output (lower extremity muscle strength and joint flexibility). Working together, these mechanisms maintain balance (keep the body's center of gravity within its base of support), detect balance displacements (when the center of gravity moves beyond the base of support), and generate corrective postural control strategies (realign the center of gravity over the base of support). A fall—an event in which the person comes to rest on the ground or another lower level, such as a chair, bed, or stairs—is likely to occur during any activity that results in balance displacement, and the body mechanisms responsible for compensation or stability fail. The risk of balance loss and most falls experienced by older persons occur during common everyday activities, such as walking; descending and climbing stairs; transferring on and off chairs, beds, and toilets; getting in and out of bathtubs and showers; and reaching or bending to retrieve and place objects from shelves and closets.

A fall is symptomatic of an underlying problem indicative of intrinsic factors (age-related physiological changes, acute and chronic diseases, and adverse medication effects) or extrinsic factors (environmental hazards and obstacles interfering with safe mobility). Several intrinsic risk factors have been identified: impaired vision (e.g., decreased visual acuity and depth perception), lower extremity dysfunction (e.g., arthritis, muscle weakness, proprioceptive loss, and foot disorders), gait/balance impairment (e.g., stroke, Parkinson's disease, and peripheral neuropathy), cognitive impairment (e.g., depression and dementia), postural hypotension; bladder dysfunction (e.g., nocturia, incontinence, and urgency), medications (e.g., sedatives, hypnotics, and antidepressants), and mobility impairment (e.g., impaired ambulation and poor seated transfers). The likelihood of falls increases with the number of intrinsic factors a person has.

Extrinsic factors associated with fall risk consist of environmental obstacles and design features that interfere with safe mobility. These include low or elevated bed heights; unstable, low seated chairs; low toilet seats without grab-bar support; poor illumination; elevated ground surfaces (upended carpet edges and door thresholds); slippery ground surfaces (wet or polished floors, sliding rugs, and non-slip-resistant bathtub surfaces); stairways without handrail support and sufficient lighting; and excessively low or high shelf and closet heights. The risk of the environment contributing to falls is greatest in those persons with mobility problems, as the environment and its design interfere with or exceed the competence level of the person. In addition, poorly fitting footwear can lead to gait problems, and ambulation devices, such as canes and walkers that are used improperly and in poor repair (worn tips and structural defects), contribute to instability and fall risk.

Most falls are due to intrinsic and extrinsic factors occurring either in isolation or in combination. For example, a fall may be a nonspecific manifestation of a single underlying acute disease (syncope, arrhythmias, infections, etc.), a chronic disease affecting gait and balance, or a hazardous environmental condition. However, most falls experienced by older persons are multifactorial. The initiating event may involve an extrinsic factor, such as a wet bathtub floor; an intrinsic factor, such as poor vision and lower extremity dysfunction (muscle weakness and unstable joints); and host-related activities engaged in at the time, such as transferring or stepping into the tub. Under these circumstances the fall is probably due to the person's balance-displacing activity, combined with the failure to detect the wet ground surface because of poor vision and because of lower extremity dysfunction, the inability of the body to initiate corrective postural strategies in time to avoid a fall.

Interventions

The overall goal of fall prevention is to minimize fall risk by ameliorating or eliminating contributing factors while maintaining or improving the older person's mobility and autonomy. Potential interventions are based on known risk factors and postulated causes of falls and consist of medical, rehabilitative, behavioral, and environmental strategies. Medical strategies consist of identifying the presence of intrinsic risk factors and attempting to modify each risk factor discovered.

Rehabilitative strategies consist of exercise programs, proper footwear, and appropriate ambulation devices (canes or walkers) to assist with mobility. Exercise regimes aimed at strengthening lower extremity muscles, improving joint flexibility, and balance training designed to enhance sensory interaction, such as tai chi (an ancient form of Chinese exercise), can improve both gait and balance even among frail older persons. In older women with osteoporosis, weight-bearing exercises (walking and stair climbing) can minimize further bone loss and may reduce the risk of bone fracture. Footwear with slip-resistant rubber or crepe soles and low heels can support safe gait patterns. For those older persons with gait and balance disorders, canes and walkers provide an increased standing and walking base of support. To ensure optimum function, ambulation devices need to be "prescribed"—designed for specific gait and balance problems and tailored to fit the person and his or her environmental setting. Behavioral strategies consist of awareness of individual fall risk factors and self-efficacy training directed toward increasing confidence and reducing fear of falls.

Environmental strategies aimed at reducing falls consist of two approaches: (1) to identify and eliminate hazardous conditions that interfere with mobility and increase fall risk, with the help of safety checklists and (2) to simplify or maximize mobility tasks by modifying the environment and existing furnishings and providing durable medical equipment (toilet and bathtub grab bars, bathtub chairs and benches, etc.) (Mann, Ottenbacher, Frass, Tomita, & Granger, 1999). Because falls result from many factors, the best evidence of prevention comes from clinical trials, which have employed a multidisciplinary and multifaceted approach. This includes targeting interventions to individual risk factors (e.g., multiple drug use, use of sedatives/hypnotics, postural hypotension, inability to transfer safely, and environmental hazards), and employing teaching strategies (e.g., exercise, environmental modifications, and assertiveness training) and cognitive-behavioral strategies aimed at reducing falls and their complications (e.g., fear of falling and associated activity restrictions) (Tennstedt, Howland, Lachman, Peterson, Kasten, & Jette, 1998; Tinetti, Baker, McAvay, Claus, Garrett, Grottschalk, et al., 1994).

REIN TIDEIKSAAR

See also
Injury

FAMILY

Traditionally, the family has been the basic social institution of society. The family is a network that typically consists of parents and their children and extended family members (grandparents, aunts, uncles, cousins, nieces, and nephews). Understanding family life requires looking at families over time and within social and historical contexts. As individuals move from childhood to adulthood and into old age, their roles in families change. Similarly, as societies and populations change, the family changes as well.

Social Change and Family Structure

Social and demographic changes of the past century have profoundly affected families. Life expectancy has increased and fertility has decreased around the world. The shape of family structure has changed as people live longer and have fewer children. For most of human history, the structure of families looked like a pyramid, with few older members at the top and many young members at the bottom. Today, families are shaped more vertically, like a bean pole, with a more equal number of members in each generation.

With more generations of family members alive at the same time, people spend more years in family roles and relationships. Today, women at age 70 are twice as likely to have a husband alive than they were 100 years ago. Children and parents may share 50 or more years of life, and grandparents may live to know their grandchildren as adults. Although child rearing remains an important function and focus of families, an increasing proportion of life centers on relations among adult family members. By 2020, most middle-aged adults will have a surviving parent, compared with less than 1 in 5 in the 1960s. This means that adults will spend more years as an adult child of an aging parent than as the parent of children under age 18. As a result, women, the traditional caretakers of children and the elderly, will likely spend more years of life caring for family members than in the past.

Family life depends on who is in the family—the family structure or form. The structure of a person's family might include parents, grandparents, a spouse or partner, siblings, children, grandchildren, other extended kin, step-relatives, and others. Family forms vary by gender, ethnicity, and social class. For example, men typically have a spouse throughout life because of their shorter life expectancy and later age at marriage compared with women. Ethnic differences in death rates and sex ratios (proportion of men to women) make older White men the most likely to be married and older African American women the least likely to be married.

Families exist within societies, so changes in social structures (institutions, organizations, and large-scale patterns of social interaction) and culture (what people believe and value) affect families. Social changes in the second half of the 20th century that have affected families include women's widespread workforce participation, especially among mothers of young children; cohabitation and nonmarital childbearing; increases in divorce, single-parent families, and step-family formation; and grandparents raising grandchildren.

Today, nearly one quarter of American adults have never married, and another one quarter are divorced. Just 25 years ago, only about 15% of adults had never married or ever divorced. Although more than one-quarter of married couples live together before marriage, less than 5% of American households are comprised of cohabiting couples (Smith, 1999). Once rare, divorce and lifelong singlehood are increasingly common among more recent cohorts of Americans. By 2010, 50% of those age 65 and over will have divorced (Quadagno, 1999). An increasing proportion of American households include no children. At the same time, the age that children leave home is increasing, and more young adult children are returning to their parents' homes for a time. The form and patterns of family life are changing, and these changes will affect future cohorts of older adults. Today's elderly, however, typically have married (90%), have children (80%), and have grandchildren (75%).

Social and demographic trends, along with early and late childbearing, affect grandparent-grandchild relations, as well as parents and children. Some individuals may become grandparents at relatively young ages if they or their offspring have children in their teen or early adult years. Other people might become grandparents much later if they or their offspring delay childbearing to complete their education and establish a career. Although divorce and extramarital childbearing were relatively uncommon among today's elderly grandparents, many are affected by their children's divorces and childbearing: Custody arrangements often mean seeing less of the grandchildren or becoming more involved with the grandchildren to assist a custodial parent. Having an adult child with offspring return home also increases grandparent involvement. Step-grandchildren may come into the family through remarriage in the grandparent or parent generation. And, with more individuals choosing not to have children, the minority of people who never become grandparents may grow.

Family Relationships

Marriage. A large body of research consistently indicates that marriage is linked to enhanced well-being, better health, and lower mortality, especially for men. In enduring marriages, marital satisfaction typically waxes and wanes over the life course: Early married life is marked by high levels of satisfaction; then marital satisfaction dips—when children enter the family—before rising again in later life after the children leave home. Couples married for several decades tend to report very high marital satisfaction. Future research may uncover different patterns in marital satisfaction among the growing numbers of older persons who have experienced divorce and remarriage, or those who remarry after being widowed.

Widowhood is a typical life event for women, but not for men. Two of three men age 75 and over are married, whereas only about one in four women is still married at age 75 (U.S. Bureau of the Census, 1998). Widows usually turn to their children for support. Widowhood also alters patterns of social involvement, including increased interaction with other widows. Good health and economic security contribute to widows' ability to maintain social involvement and well-being.

Kinship ties are important among never married older men and women, most of whom never had children. Throughout midlife, unmarried women often have close relationships with their elderly parents, aunts, and uncles, as well as with their nieces and nephews (Bengtson, Rosenthal, & Burton, 1990). In later life, single women's levels of health and economic security are generally akin to their married counterparts. Older single men, however, tend to have poorer health and well-being than married men. Elders without a spouse or children are less likely to receive instrumental help from family and, as a result, are at greater risk of institutionalization. However, they also tend to be self-sufficient and accustomed to living alone. Aging gay men and women may face similar problems. Although some gay men and women are estranged from family members who object to their sexual orientation, most have a support network of created kinship ties among their partner, friends, and selected family members that may provide needed assistance as they age (Cherlin, 1999).

Parents and Children.   Next to the marital relationship, the parent-child relationship tends to be the strongest family bond. Despite some portrayals of the elderly as abandoned by their families, adult children and their parents enjoy considerable solidarity. Intergenerational solidarity encompasses feelings of affection, patterns of interaction and opportunity for contact, shared values and expectations, and the exchange of assistance (Silverstein & Bengtson, 1997). The parent-child family tie may be increasingly important with the growing number of years of life the two generations share, upwards of five decades today. Indeed, parents and their adult children typically feel a great deal of affection for each other. However, parents usually rate the relationship as more warm and close than their children do, suggesting that parents have more at stake in the intergenerational relationship (Bengtson & Kuypers, 1971).

Frequent contact between parents and adult children, in person or by telephone, and more recently by electronic mail, is usual. Reflecting women's traditional kin-keeping role, mothers and daughters typically have more frequent contact than other parent-child pairs. Widowed parents often have more contact with their children than married or divorced parents, and unmarried children tend to have contact with their parents more often than married children. American parents and children usually do not share a household, although after age 75 coresidence with children is common among African Americans and Hispanics.

Parents and adult children exchange various types of assistance. Emotional support is the type of help most frequently exchanged. However, when it comes to other types of assistance, each generation tends to provide the other with different kinds of help (Logan & Spitze, 1996). Parents are more likely to give their adult children help with child care, financial assistance, and advice than they are to receive such help. Adult children are more likely to give their parents instrumental assistance with household chores, repairs, and personal care. Parents in advanced old age tend to receive more help than they give. Expectations about caring for older family members, or norms of filial responsibility, are another aspect of intergenerational solidarity. Although older people generally do not expect their adult children to take care of them, most adult children today feel a high degree of filial responsibility. After spouses, adult children are the primary caregivers to frail elderly family members in the United States.

Grandparents and Grandchildren.   The grandparents-grandchildren relationship is an increasingly important intergenerational bond. The tie between grandparents and grandchildren tends to be meaningful to a majority of those in both generations, representing family continuity and linking the past with the future. Grandparents contribute to their grandchildren's well-being by "being there" as a source of support. The grandparent role may take several forms, depending in part on the age and health of the grandparents, their geographic proximity to the grandchildren, and the grandparents' relationships with the grandchildren's parents. Grandparents may play a significant role in their grandchildren's early years by providing child care and later years by helping with the costs of education. In some cases, grandparents may act as surrogate parents when the grandchildren's own parents are unable to care for them, as in the case of mental illness, drug addiction, incarceration, teen pregnancy, institutionalization, or premature death.

Siblings.   The sibling relationship is unique among family ties. As members of the same generation, siblings typically have a lifelong relationship and share a family history. Brothers and sisters may have infrequent contact—perhaps a few times a year—during early and middle adult life when attention centers on marriage, parenting, and career. As people age, the sibling bond may become closer, especially when siblings face caring for aging parents, reach retirement, or experience widowhood. Siblings generally feel that they can call on one another in times of need, although they do so infrequently. Although siblings typically are not a source of tangible assistance in later life, they often provide emotional support and a sense of security. Women tend to have more contact with their siblings than men do, and sisters tend to be closer than brothers. Sisters also usually facilitate contact among siblings and foster an ethic of care, thereby increasing the amount of assistance siblings provide to elderly parents. The sibling tie is important in later life because it serves as a connection to the past, a source of support and reminiscence, and an anchor for personal identity.

Changing Times, Adapting Families

Although the structure and interactions of families have changed significantly, families remain important to their members and to society. The family continues to serve as the site of socialization and rearing of the young and support and care for the aged. Families provide individuals with a sense of security, continuity, and identity. Family members provide the bulk of older people's close, intimate relationships. Although social changes have greatly affected family life, families appear remarkably adaptive and remain important.

J. BETH MABRY
VERN L. BENGSTON
CAROLYN ROSENTHAL

See also
    Caregivers of Chronically Ill Elders
    Filial Responsibility
    Marital Satisfaction
    Marital Status

FAMILY AND MEDICAL LEAVE ACT

On February 5, 1993, President Bill Clinton signed into law the Family and Medical Leave Act (FMLA) (U.S. Public Law 130-3), the first law passed by the 103rd Congress. The FMLA was, in fact, enacted after a long political campaign. Family and medical leave legislation had been debated in the U.S. Congress since the mid-1980s. The private sector generally opposed the passage of FMLA,

perceiving it as costly and not beneficial to their organizations. The National Federation of Independent Business, for example, argued vigorously that the law would reduce business efficiency and damage the global competitiveness of American businesses. In contrast, women's organizations, such as the Women's Legal Defense and the National Organization for Women, stressed the necessity of a federally mandated leave policy by underscoring the difficulties experienced by American workers in their efforts to strike a balance between the competing demands of workplace and home. They buttressed their argument by citing the dramatic demographic changes that were affecting workers' ability to achieve a healthy balance, including the increasing numbers of working women, particularly those with young children; the rise in single-parent households, many of which are headed by single working parents; and the growth of the elderly population, who often rely on the support of working adult children.

Under this act, which became effective on August 5, 1993, businesses with 50 or more employees are required to grant up to 12 weeks of unpaid leave annually when a child is born or adopted, when an immediate family member with a serious health condition needs care, or when the employee is unable to work because of a serious health condition.

In the event that a collective bargaining agreement was in effect on August 5, 1993, the FMLA became effective when the collective bargaining terminated or on February 5, 1994, whichever was earlier. The FMLA covers employers who have employed 50 or more employees for each working day during 20 or more calendar workweeks in the current or preceding calendar year.

The FMLA defines a serious health condition as an illness, injury, impairment, or physical or mental condition that requires inpatient care in a hospital, hospice, or residential medical facility or continuing treatment by a health care worker. The employee has the right to take the leave intermittently or on a reduced-schedule basis. The employer must maintain any preexisting health coverage during the leave period and, once the leave is completed, must reinstate the employee to the same or an equivalent job. For retirement or pension plans, FMLA leave is counted as continued service for purposes of vesting and eligibility to participate.

To receive an FMLA leave, the employee must fulfill certain responsibilities. First, the employer may require the employee to provide certification from a health care provider confirming the serious health condition. Second, if practical and the employer so requires, the employee should provide 30 days notice for the leave. If, due to circumstances such as a medical emergency, such notification is not possible, the employee must provide notice "as soon as practical." Third, if the employer has a policy requiring all workers taking a medical leave to provide certification of fitness to return to work, the employee may be required to produce this documentation. Finally, if the health insurance premium normally requires an employee copayment, the employee will be required to continue to pay this portion while on leave (Gowan & Zimmerman, 1996).

Because the FMLA applies only to employers who have 50 or more employees, it is estimated that only 10.8% of private-sector work sites are covered under FMLA. This relatively small percentage of U.S. businesses, however, employs 59.5% of American workers. Yet not all workers of covered employers are eligible for benefits under the act. The FMLA provides benefits only to employees who have worked for their employer for at least 12 months (although these need not have been consecutive months) and who, during the 12-month period prior to the leave, worked for the employer for at least 1,250 hours (which reflects an average of 25 hours per week). Because of these criteria it is estimated that only 46.5% of employees working in the private sector are eligible for a leave under FMLA (Commission on Family and Medical Leave, 1996).

The United States was among the last of the industrialized countries to offer a leave policy. Until passage of the FMLA, the United States was the only country out of 118 nations surveyed by the International Labor Organization that had no mandated parental leave policy. A comparison of the American legislation with the leave policies of other countries reveals the limitations of the FMLA. Most other countries' parental leave policies affect all employers, offer a longer leave period, and mandate paid leave. For example, Canada mandates 15 weeks of leave at 60% of normal pay, France has established 16 weeks of leave at 90% of normal pay, and Germany mandates 14 to 19 weeks of leave at 100% of normal pay.

Since passage of the FMLA, usage has been fairly limited. The Employee Survey of the Commission on Family and Medical Leave found that, whereas almost 17% of workers reported taking a leave for reasons covered under the FMLA and another 3% stated that they needed to but did not take leaves, only 7% of this group actually took a leave under the FMLA. The Commission on Family and Medical Leave's Employer Survey, which included only the private sector, found that at covered work sites the ratio of leave taking under the FMLA is 3.6 for every 100 workers.

Given the level of usage, it is not surprising that employers ascribe only modest benefits or costs to the FMLA. The commission's Employer Survey found that the vast majority of respondents felt that the FMLA had "no noticeable effect" on business productivity (86%), business profitability (93%), or business growth (96%). Surveyed employers also overwhelmingly indicated that the FMLA had "no noticeable effect" on employee performance in regard to worker productivity (83%), absences (90%), turnover (95%), or career advancement (91%). When effects of the FMLA on employee performance were noted, employers more often identified positive versus negative outcomes, including productivity (13% reporting positive effect; 5% reporting negative effect), turnover (5% vs. 0%), career advancement (8% vs. 1%), and the ability of employees to care for their families (34% vs. 0%). The commission's survey revealed that, among workers taking a leave under the FMLA, approximately 60% did so because of their own health. About a quarter of FMLA leave is taken by relatively young parents to care for children at birth or adoption or during a serious illness. An additional 10% of FMLA leave is taken by somewhat older employees to care for ill parents or spouses. Waldfogel (1999) notes that although the FMLA is the subject of controversy, there is a little empirical research on the legislation's impacts. In her own research, Waldfogel (1999) found positive, if modest, net employment effects of the FMLA pertaining to maternity leave.

Although the latent demand for leave may be high among employees, relatively high levels of ignorance about the availability of leave and the fact that it is almost always unpaid leave are major barriers to greater utilization. The commission's survey found that of those who were eligible for leave but did not take it the most frequently cited reason (64%) was financial constraints. Those individuals who were unable to take leave because they could not afford the associated loss of wages were more likely to be African American, to be hourly wage earners, and to have low levels of family income.

Proposals to reform the FMLA continue to be debated in the U.S. Congress. On the right, legislators continue to question the basic premises of the law. Republican members of Congress are pressing for clarifying amendments to restore the definition of "serious medical condition" and "intermittent leave" to the original intent of the FMLA. In contrast, Democratic proposals build on the ideology that government has a legitimate role in addressing employment-related tensions between employer and employee. Their most fundamental proposal centers on the importance of wage replacement to leave taking and the need for paid leave. An analysis by the Institute for Women's Policy Research of the use of state temporary disability insurance programs concludes that "for less than the cost of the current Unemployment Insurance program, a new social insurance program could provide paid leave for family care" (Hartmann & Yoon, 1996, p. 3). A recent proposal put forth by the Clinton administration would allow new parents to draw on state unemployment funds for up to 6 months of paid leave.

Democrats have also proposed expanding coverage to employers with at least 25 employees. Analysis of this proposed legislation suggests that it would significantly increase the number and percentages of employees covered without affecting a large number of employers. An additional 13.8% of the private work force would be covered by the FMLA, for a total employee coverage rate of 71.3%. However, only an additional 6.4% of private employers would be newly covered. Other Democratic proposals include extending coverage beyond immediate family members to include a parent-in-law, adult child, sibling, grandchild, grandparent, or domestic partner with a serious health condition; increasing flexibility in use by allowing parents to take up to 4 hours in any 30-day period to go with children to school or extracurricular activities or accompany ill relatives to routine medical appointments; and allowing victims of domestic violence to take an FMLA leave to get shelter, medical help, and legal protection.

In the Democratic and Republican proposals we see a division in fundamental beliefs about personal, private, and public responsibilities for the care of dependent family members. Both political parties, however, are aware that work-family balance is an important issue to American families. A 1998 national survey funded by the National Partnership for Women and Families, for example, revealed that two thirds of Americans say that time pressures on working families are getting worse, not better, and that most want both employers (90%) and government (72%) to do more to help working families.

JUDITH G. GONYEA

See also
Family

FECAL AND URINARY INCONTINENCE

Fecal incontinence is defined as defecation in socially inappropriate situations, occurring at least once a month after the age of 4 years. *Urinary incontinence* is defined as a condition in which involuntary loss of urine is a social or hygienic problem. Incontinence in an older person is a major clinical problem with significant medical and social consequences. It has been estimated that 7.5 per 1,000 community-dwelling persons 65 to 74 years old have problems associated with the control of urination or defecation, and that among persons over the age of 75 the prevalence is 46.7 per 1,000 (Feller, 1983). In a community-based survey of 541 healthy, middle-aged women, 42 to 50 years old, 58% reported urine loss at some time, and 30.7% reported incontinence at least once a month (Burgio, Matthews, & Engel, 1991). Although bladder incontinence is more prevalent than bowel incontinence, the latter is much more disruptive socially and is more likely to lead to institutionalization. The prevalence of incontinence in nursing home residents is much higher than among community-dwelling persons and is frequently associated with increased dependency, such as cognitive impairment or mobility limitation.

Among the elderly, fecal incontinence often is progressive, with an indefinite onset but a worsening course. Incontinence can occur because the patient is unable to retain stool, or it can occur in conjunction with chronic, severe constipation or diarrhea (Whitehead, 1996). The most common mediating conditions for failure to retain stool are postsurgical trauma, neuromuscular deficits associated with progressive diseases such as diabetes mellitus and multiple sclerosis, mobility deficits that prevent the person from toileting appropriately, and cognitive deficits that disrupt usual social inhibitions. Constipation leads to incontinence when there is severe rectal distension (megacolon), followed by loss of stool when the internal anal sphincter is no longer able to provide an adequate barrier against the passage of stool. Treatment for fecal incontinence varies depending on the existence of concomitant disorders; however, many studies have shown that biofeedback can be a highly effective behavioral intervention for reducing the frequency of incontinent episodes (Farrugia, Camilleri, & Whitehead, 1996).

Urinary incontinence can occur as a result of malfunctions in the urethral sphincter or pelvic floor muscles, in the detrusor muscle of the urinary bladder, or in the nervous control of any of these muscles. Among the elderly there are many forms and causes of incontinence; however, there are four distinct kinds of incontinence that probably account for most of the clinically significant instances of the disorder:

1. Stress incontinence, which can be a sign or a symptom reflecting loss of urine during physical activity. It is most common in women, is usually associated with small-volume loss during an activity, and is usually a long-standing problem that may have worsened with age.
2. Urge incontinence, which is loss of urine associated with a strong desire to void. The sense of urgency may be a pure sensory phenomenon, or it may include uncontrollable detrusor contractions. Urge incontinence typically is associated with large-volume losses and can affect men or women.
3. Overflow incontinence, which is an involuntary loss of urine that occurs when pressure in a chronically full bladder exceeds urethral pressure. The rise in bladder pressure is associated with excessive bladder distension attributable to inadequate bladder emptying.

Overflow incontinence also can occur in persons of either sex.
4. "Inappropriate" urination, which can occur in cognitively impaired persons or in persons who have severe motor disabilities that prevent them from toileting themselves. Clearly, in this case the inappropriateness of the urination is defined socially and not physiologically.

The so-called graying of America has caused clinicians and public health officials to recognize the seriousness of incontinence. With this recognition has come the realization that most incontinent patients can be treated successfully, and that proper clinical management of incontinence in an older person calls on the skills of a number of professionals, not only physicians but also nurses, psychologists, and other social service agents. Depending on the underlying disorder, it is possible that proper treatment of an incontinent patient can come from traditional medical procedures, such as drug therapy and surgery; from improved medical management, such as careful supervision of drug regimens (Agency for Health Care Policy and Research, 1996); from improved staff management of the institutionalized patient (Schnelle, Traughber, Morgan, Embry, Binion, & Coleman, 1983); or from a variety of training methods (Burgio, Locher, Goode, & Hardin, 1998; Burgio, Stutzman, & Engel, 1989; Burgio, Whitehead, & Engel, 1985; Whitehead, Burgio, & Engel, 1985). Recently, the United States Public Health Service, Agency for Health Care Policy and Research of the U.S. Department of Health and Human Services, published guidelines for the management of urinary incontinence. The panel of experts responsible for these guidelines concluded that incontinent patients should always have a basic diagnostic evaluation and that behavioral and pharmacological therapies usually are reasonable first steps in management (Agency for Health Care Policy and Research, 1996).

BERNARD T. ENGEL

See also
Behavior Modification
Biofeedback
Gastrointestinal System
Genitourinary System
Kidney and Urinary System

FEDERAL BUDGETING AND EXPENDITURES

Federal expenditures on behalf of older persons have risen dramatically over the past 35 years, and those expenditures have had a notable impact in improving the well-being of today's elders. By various estimates, between 25% and 30% of the federal budget is spent either as direct cash benefits to older persons or as payments to providers for services rendered to older people. Largely as a result of broadened coverage and increased benefits under the Old Age and Survivors Insurance program (OASI) of the Social Security Act, the official poverty rate for older Americans has declined by a factor of 3 over this period, from 35.2% in 1959 to 10.7% in 1997 (Dalaker & Naifeh, 1998). Today, over 93% of older people have Hospital Insurance (Part A) and Supplemental Medical Insurance (Part B) under Medicare, compared with less than one-half of the older population who had any form of health care insurance prior to Medicare's enactment in 1965.

These successes notwithstanding, controversy has surrounded aging-related federal spending over the past two decades. First, growth in these expenditures has been notable in both absolute terms and relative to spending in other areas. Second, because the major budget items are open-ended entitlements (i.e., not subject to annual congressional appropriation decisions), there is a concern in some quarters that growth in these expenditures is relatively uncontrollable. Third, the pending retirement of the baby-boom generation has the most severe critics of current policies alluding to Social Security and Medicare representing a "budgetary black hole" in coming years. Thus, different observers see both "success" and "excess" in aging policy expenditures, and this debate continues to rage (Hudson, 1997).

Major Expenditure Items

Older persons receive cash and in-kind benefits from several major federal programs. Table 1 shows the rising expenditure levels under the two principal programs, OASI and Medicare. The OASI program provided $316.3 billion in 1997, of which $243.6 billion was directed to retired workers and depen-

TABLE 1   OASI and Medicare Expenditures: Selected Years

Year	OASI (billions)	Medicare (billions)
1950	1.0	—
1960	10.7	—
1970	28.8	7.1
1980	105.0	35.7
1990	223.0	107.2
1995	291.6	182.6
1997	316.3	210.6

Source: U.S. Social Security Administration (1998).

dents and $72.5 billion to survivors of covered workers (U.S. Social Security Administration, 1998). Supplemental Security Income (SSI), the principal means-tested income assistance program helping older persons, provided $4.5 billion to 1.4 million individuals for reason of age. The number of older SSI recipients has declined significantly since the early years of the program—there were 2.3 million older SSI recipients in 1975—due largely to the liberalization of OASI benefits instituted beginning in the late 1960s and early 1970s. Expenditures for other major programs exclusively or disproportionately serving the aged include the Railroad Retirement System ($8.1 billion) and the Veterans Administration ($18.2 billion in pension benefits; $16.6 billion for health-related services) (U.S. House of Representatives, 1998).

The two major health-financing programs supported by the federal government—Medicare and Medicaid—provide substantial but not comprehensive health care to older Americans. The elderly constitute 87.4% of Medicare beneficiaries (the remaining beneficiaries being eligible for Social Security disability benefits or suffering from end-stage renal diseases). Expenditures under the Medicare Part A program, primarily funded through the Medicare payroll tax on current workers, totaled $139.5 billion in 1997. Part B expenditures, financed by a combination of general tax revenues and premiums paid by enrollees, totaled $74.1 billion in 1997 (U.S. Social Security Administration, 1998). Medicaid is a federal-state grant-in-aid program for individuals receiving certain public assistance benefits or otherwise deemed "medically indigent." Vendor payments under Medicaid totaled $121.7 billion in 1996, $36.9 billion of which was on behalf of people age 65 and older (U.S. Social Security Administration, 1998).

Although the growth rate in expenditures for both Medicare and Medicaid has declined significantly, there has been notable growth in the area of home health care, a benefit largely directed toward the old. Home health service expenditures under Medicare Part A increased from only $26 million in 1967, to $440 million in 1980, to $3.4 billion in 1990, and to $15.1 billion by 1996 (U.S. Social Security Administration, 1998). Over the 30-year period, the average annual increase for home health services was 24.5%, the largest of any Medicare expenditure category. A major purpose (and success) of the Balanced Budget of 1997 was to rein in these costs. Medicaid increases in home health expenditures have been nearly as great, rising from $3.4 billion in 1990 to $10.9 billion in 1996 (U.S. Social Security Administration, 1998).

The elderly are also beneficiaries of two of the federal government's major social services programs. The Older Americans Act (OAA) is a non-means-tested program providing social, nutritional, employment, and other community-based services to people age 60 and older. After very modest appropriations in its early years, OAA spending increased dramatically in the 1970s. However, it was slightly less than level-funded over the next two decades, with appropriations under the act totaling $1.29 billion in 1997. Service expenditures on behalf of older people are also made through the Social Services Block Grant (Title XX of the Social Security Act), appropriations for which were $2.5 billion in 1997 (U.S. House of Representatives, 1998).

Trends and Issues

From the mid-1970s until the late 1990s, major attention was paid to the rise in age-related public expenditures in the context of escalating budget deficits the federal government was facing. In 1992, the federal deficit (the difference between annual revenues and expenditures) amounted to $290 billion, and, in 1997, the federal debt (the accumulated amount owed by the federal government to the public and other creditors) stood at $3.77 trillion,

or 47.2% of the nation's gross domestic product (Stevenson, 1999; U.S. Congressional Budget Office, 2000). Concern that these numbers would continue to grow was reinforced in 1994 with the secret release of an Office of Management and Budget internal memorandum that projected annual budget deficits would increase to no less than $4.1 trillion if current tax and expenditure policies remained unchanged (Howe, 1997).

However, in a development that has startled all observers, fiscal prospects for the federal government have been radically transformed since the mid-1990s. In 1998, the government balance sheet went into the black for the first time in three decades, running a $68 billion surplus that year. More remarkable yet, the U.S. Congressional Budget Office (2000) now estimates that the entire federal debt, depending on particular spending decisions made by Congress, could be entirely eliminated as early as 2013. Table 2 portrays the stunning shift in federal fiscal fortunes, past and projected, over a 20-year time frame. It is hard to overstate both how unexpected and how enormous these developments are. Most broadly, they have forced a complete restructuring of the revenue/expenditure debate in Washington. Most immediately, the more favorable budgetary picture has taken pressure off

TABLE 2   Federal Budget Balances, 1990–2010

Fiscal year	Actual federal budget deficit (−) or surplus ($ billions)
1990	−221
1992	−290
1994	−203
1996	−108
1998	69
	Estimated federal budget surpluses ($ billions)
2000	176
2002	209
2004	246
2006	325
2008	399
2010	489

Source: U.S. Congressional Budget Office (2000), Table 1-3 and Summary Table 1.

Social Security and Medicare, pushing back the dates of their once-impending "bankruptcy" (more accurately, the point when trust fund expenditures would have exceeded program expenditures).

But the budgetary developments have had effects extending beyond the numbers themselves. First, the improved fiscal situation has at least momentarily served to forestall privatization efforts put forth by congressional Republicans and other conservative interests that had been lent urgency by the perception of the need to save the programs from presumed bankruptcy. Second, and more remarkable, has been the White House's ability to propose that the newly projected surpluses be used to reduce federal debt, thereby helping to preserve Social Security and Medicare as well. Instead of continuing to need to use Social Security surpluses to help cover (or camouflage) annual deficits elsewhere in the federal budget, the improved fiscal situation now allows for all of the Social Security surpluses to be put toward retiring the federal debt. This is the new budgetary reality that undergirds current political promises to "preserve" or not "raid" Social Security. These Social Security surpluses are now projected to total $182 billion in 2002, and $295 billion in 2010 (U.S. Congressional Budget Office, 2000). By using these revenues to draw down the federal debt, the government (1) saves billions of dollars in interest payments (now the second largest item in the budget), thereby freeing up money for the payment of Social Security benefits years hence; and (2) stimulates economic growth, thereby generating additional tax revenues that could also be applied toward Social Security and Medicare expenditures.

In a matter of no more than 3 years, the debate about the respective places of the federal budget and entitlement spending (principally for Social Security and Medicare) has been completely transformed. Not only are entitlement expenditures no longer threatening fiscal mayhem, but governmental revenues (including payroll taxes for Social Security and Medicare) also are now forecast as sufficient to reduce and conceivably eliminate the national debt within 13 years, thereby helping save the entitlement programs themselves.

ROBERT B. HUDSON

See also
Medicaid
Medicare

Older Americans Act
Social Security
Tax Policy

FEDERAL COUNCIL ON THE AGING

The Federal Council on the Aging is the citizen advisory committee within the executive branch of the federal government charged with advising and assisting the president, the secretary of health and human services, and the assistant secretary for aging on the special needs of older Americans.

Created under the 1973 amendments to the Older Americans Act (section 205), the council has 15 members. Five are appointed by each of the two houses of Congress. Council members serve 3-year terms. They are chosen from among individuals with expertise in the field of aging, and they represent a diverse cross section of rural and urban areas, national organizations with an interest in aging, business, labor, Indian tribes, minorities, and the general public. By statute, at least nine members must themselves be age 60 and over.

The president selects the chairperson of the council from the appointed members. The council is mandated to meet at least quarterly at the call of the chair, and the meetings are open to the public.

The council's major functions include serving as spokespersons on behalf of older Americans by making recommendations for federal policies and programs; continually evaluating policies to assess their effectiveness and to promote better coordination between government agencies; informing the public about the problems and needs of the aging by collecting and disseminating information, by conducting or commissioning studies, and by issuing reports; and providing public forums for discussing and publicizing the problems and needs of individuals by holding public hearings and by sponsoring conferences and workshops. The council is also mandated to issue to the president an annual report of its findings and recommendations.

The primary activities of the Federal Council on the Aging have been threefold. First, it has provided leadership in the analysis and evaluation of policy issues affecting the elderly through studies, reports, and hearings. In particular, it has examined the demographic changes affecting an aging society.

Second, it has created a public awareness about those demographic trends affecting society and has highlighted the implications for health, social, income, and public services. Third, it has served as the primary interagency bridge in the federal government for overseeing federal activities for the elderly and has provided input to the president and other public officials on actions affecting older persons.

The council also has focused on providing a voice within the federal government for older persons, who often may not be heard during the shaping of policies. Such older persons include those with mental health needs, those with physical disabilities, those whose families are in need of long-term care—particularly home- and community-based care—victims of elder abuse, and older women living alone. The council's activities also include playing a major role in planning and executing the 1995 White House Conference on Aging, as well as follow-up activities.

Historically, the ability of the Federal Council on Aging to meet its mandated requirements has varied. During the late 1970s and early 1980s, the council played an active and influential role in promoting the concerns of older persons. For example, it issued a report on the need to establish a continuum of long-term care, a concept then only in its infancy. It was instrumental in promoting the concerns of minority elderly. It was responsible for defining the concept of frail elderly and promoting awareness about this rapidly growing segment of the population. And it played a major role in the 1981 White House Conference on Aging. As important, during this time the council had access to the White House and to the secretary of health and human services through the leadership of council members such as Nelson Cruikshank and the Reverend Charles Fahey.

The late 1980s and early 1990s, however, saw a diminution of the council's ability to influence policy. With the exception of a few noteworthy activities (recommendations on the Older Americans Act Reauthorization and the 1995 White House Conference on Aging), it was far less visible during this period. In part, that reflected presidential administrations that gave less priority to domestic affairs and senior citizen issues. Declining funding also hampered the council.

With the advent of an activist administration concerned with domestic matters, such as health care reform, in the 1990s, the potential was good for the council to once again play a major role in policy making. President Bill Clinton had appointed an activist group of individuals with strong ties to the White House and Congress. During the latter half of the 1990s, the council focused particular attention on several critical policy issues of an aging society, including long-term care, mental health, Social Security, the role of the Older Americans Act, planning for a long life across generations, employment opportunities, and the special needs of an increasingly diverse older population. It also played an instrumental role in the planning and implementation of the 1995 White House Conference on Aging. Notwithstanding leadership by the Federal Council on Aging, its funding and authorization were allowed to lapse by 1998. The reasons for this are uncertain, but, paradoxically, the Federal Council's fate might have been due to its success. The efforts by a Democratic White House and a Republican Congress to portray themselves as friends of the elderly, vowing to protect Medicare, Medicaid, and Social Security, the proliferation of advocacy organizations and interest groups across the political spectrum, and the growing awareness by middle-age groups about their retirement needs, all showed that society at large had come to accept aging as a fundamental concern. The Federal Council on Aging's efforts over the years has been to "mainstream" aging issues in the national agenda, and to that extent it was successful. The loss of political and funding support could be seen as a lack of interest in the council's work, or it could be viewed as societal acceptance of aging as a basic issue facing the nation and thus involving a broader cross section of organizations.

FERNANDO TORRES-GIL

See also
Older Americans Act
Organizations in Aging

FEEDING BEHAVIOR

Feeding is the "process of getting food from a plate or its equivalent into the mouth. It is a primitive sense and without concern for social niceties"

(Katz, Downs, Cash, & Grotz, 1970, p. 23). Feeding behavior seeks to explain the influences contributing to the feeding process as an interaction between the person being fed and the caregiver, their separate behaviors, and the environment or context of mealtimes.

Older persons may require partial, intermittent, or total assistance at mealtimes for several reasons: neuromuscular disorders (e.g., parkinsonism or stroke), neurological impairment (e.g., dementia), or psychological issues (e.g., depression or anorexia). In a national survey of 1,509 caregiving households, 320 families were providing care for persons with dementia; of those, 33.1% (n = 106) were feeding family members (Ory, Hoffman, Yee, Tennstedt, & Schulz, 1999). Feeding dependent residents in nursing homes has been noted to require the greatest amount of time compared with other activities of daily living and is performed mostly (92%) by nonlicensed staff (Roddy, Liu, & Meiners, 1987).

Caregivers responsible for feeding older clients with neurological impairments, including dementia, must be vigilant for swallowing problems. Although the progression of dementing illnesses is highly individualized, clinicians have noted predictable stages of decline that culminate with loss of the ability to self-feed (Katz, Downs, Cash, & Grotz, 1970). After the ability to self-feed is lost, a further evolution of behavior is sometimes seen with active and passive styles of resisting food (Watson, 1994), concluding in the inability to ingest any nutrients. Although dementia does not directly cause a decline in the ability to self-feed, various physiologic factors may make ingestion of food difficult. Persons with dementia may misperceive food and develop an apraxia related to the task of eating (LeClerc & Wells, 1998). Even before attempting to swallow food, individuals in the later stage of dementia may not be able to recognize food or eating utensils. Because the first stages of swallowing are under voluntary control (oral prepatory and oral), individuals with Alzheimer's disease may forget the swallow cycle and be unable to initiate movement of the bolus of food. They may be unaware of the need to protect the nasopharynx and oropharynx, placing them at very high risk for aspiration or complete airway blockage (Amella, 1999a). Persons with vascular dementia have swallowing problems similar to stroke victims and are prone to pseudobulbar dysphagia related to a weak and poorly coordinated swallowing mechanism (Miller & Groher, 1997). Dysphagia was noted by researchers but not by providers of care to nursing home residents with severe cognitive impairment (Kayser-Jones & Pengilly, 1999; Volicer & Hurley, 1998). Resistance to taking food may be antecedent to dysphagia or may be a protective mechanism by persons who are choking but who cannot express their dilemma (Fucile, Wright, Chan, Yee, Langlais, & Gisel, 1998; Kayser-Jones & Pengilly, 1999). Resistance to feeding has been operationalized by Watson through development of the EdFED-Q scale that classifies mealtime behavior into obstinacy or passivity (Watson & Dreary, 1997). This tool gives researchers and clinicians a quantifiable measure of resistance to feeding.

Persons who have sustained a stroke may have any or all stages of swallowing affected. Following acute stroke, swallowing problems are very common and may persist, recur, or develop later in the disease process (Smithard, O'Neill, England, Park, Wyatt, Martin, et al., 1997). Thus, clinicians need to be aware of the need for close observation at meals and attend to patient complaints or gestures relating to the inability to swallow despite outward stroke resolution. Referral to a speech-language pathologist for assessment and training is critical. Feeding rehabilitation to promote self-feeding is strongly preferred over passive feeding by caregivers. Occupational therapy and nursing will help to devise strategies that promote independent eating for persons with stroke, dementia, and other disabilities and maximize assisted feeding while the dietitian can suggest alterations in food consistency (Amella, 1998). Strategies for safe feeding include positioning patients in proper alignment, upright with feet on the floor; feeding thickened liquids or changing the consistency of foods; placing food on the unaffected side of the mouth, stimulating the tonsilar area with an iced dental mirror; and performing various oral motor exercises.

Anorexia, or an unwillingness to accept food, has been noted among older persons and may result from a variety of factors. Persons experiencing an undernourished state have extended lengths of hospital stay and have a dramatic rise in complication and premature death in both hospitals and nursing home settings (Morley, 1997). A failure to thrive syndrome identified by unexplained weight loss and loss of function is a dynamic process that occurs on the way from health to frailty among the elderly (Verdery, 1997) and may influence the general health of the individual. Body mass index (BMI) (weight in kilograms/height in meters^2) has been found to be a valid predictor of negative outcomes, such as increased mortality among all adults (Calle, Thun, Petrelli, Rodriguez, & Heath, 1999), particularly older adults (Harris, Cook, & Garrison, 1998). Odds ratios are greatly increased for morbidity, especially for aspiration pneumonia, when an individual needs to be fed and the risk of premature mortality is also increased (Langmore, Terpenning, & Schork, 1998). The loss of the ability to feed oneself is sometimes conceptualized as a terminal or end-of-life phenomenon (Sandman, Norberg, Adolfsson, Eriksson, & Nystrom, 1990). In determining eligibility for hospice care, the following criterion is given for persons with dementia: "[d]ifficulty swallowing food or refusal to eat, sufficiently severe that patient cannot maintain sufficient fluid and calorie intake to sustain life, with patient or surrogate refusing tube feedings or parenteral nutrition" (National Hospice Organization—Minnesota Hospice Organization, 1997, p. 44). Anorexia, increased metabolism, or disturbed functioning of the GI tract can be caused by medications including digoxin, benzodiapezines, opiates, serotonin reuptake inhibitors, laxatives, thyroxine, corticosteroids, chemotherapeutic agents, antihistamines, anticholenergics, and antibiotics (Verdery, 1998).

Unfortunately, many professional and nonprofessional caregivers consider assisting with meals a routine or menial task. Institutions often understaff at mealtimes and assign the least skilled workers to assist with meals or maintain self-feeding with resulting uniformity in approach and lack of individualized care (Kayser-Jones, 1996; Kayser-Jones & Schell, 1997). Although required to report and initiate care planning for persons with low intake, institutional caregivers routinely overestimate the amount of food consumed, resulting in significant weight loss before remedial steps can be taken.

Caregivers need to pay attention to the context as well as the task. Subtle caregiver actions such as gentle touch and verbal encouragement have been found to significantly promote self-feeding and improve nutritional intake for patients with dementia (Eaton, Mitchell-Bonair, & Freidman, 1986). The task and process of feeding a dependent elderly person with dementia can be difficult at times. Society demands that to be socially acceptable, we must be able to "feed ourselves tidily and in a presentable manner" (Jones, 1976, p. 359). Patients may spit, throw food, or, despite the most delicate cajoling, keep their mouths shut. To establish a relationship with these individuals is truly a challenge, yet some caregivers manage to establish such a connection. Amella (1999b) demonstrated that the quality of the exchange between nursing home residents with late-stage dementia and their nurse's aide caregivers ($n = 53$ dyads), positively influenced the amount of food the residents consumed. VanOrt and Phillips (1992, 1995) studied the interaction between nurse's aides and nursing home residents with late-stage dementia, disclosing behaviors by both parties that initiate and support or extinguish feeding. Kayser-Jones and Schell (1997) examined the interaction of a skilled nurse's aide who focused on the process aspects of meals with persons with dementia. The most effective strategies encouraged independence and promoted a more social environment, similar to the home.

Although persons who receive enteral feeding remain a minority in institutions, reimbursement methodologies and time constraints make enteral feeding an accepted alternative for people who do not accept food (patients receiving tube feeds are placed in a higher reimbursement category in some states). However, in an exhaustive review of the literature, Finucane, Christmas, and Travis (1999) found that enteral feeding often leads to aspiration and does not reduce morbidity or mortality in persons with late-stage dementia. They recommend a "comprehensive, motivated, conscientious program of hand feeding" (p. 1369; see also Gillick, 2000). Clearly, hand feeding is a nonintrusive and natural method of providing sustenance.

ELAINE J. AMELLA
ROSE ANN DIMARIA

See also
Depression
Malnutrition
Nutrition
Normal Swallow and Dysphagia

FEMALE REPRODUCTIVE SYSTEM

The *menopause* signals the permanent end of fertility and occurs in women at approximately 51 years of age. Ovarian follicles are depleted in postmenopausal women, resulting in a permanent decrease in ovarian secretion of steroid and peptide hormones. Thus, one consequence of the menopause is a permanent and dramatic decrease in circulating estrogen levels. Until about 1900, most women died before they were 50 years old and therefore never experienced the postmenopausal period of their lives. However, during this century, the average life span of women has increased dramatically, to over 80 years of age. Since the age of the menopause has remained essentially fixed, an increasing number of women will spend a larger fraction of their lives in the postmenopausal state than ever before. Thus, until recently this profound change in the physiology of females never presented the challenge to clinicians, basic scientists, and social and behavioral scientists that it does today.

We are beginning to appreciate that the postmenopausal chronic hypoestrogenic state not only has an impact on the hypothalamic-pituitary-ovarian axis, but also has major effects on bone and mineral metabolism, cardiovascular function, memory and cognition, and the progression of age-related diseases. Thus, it becomes ever more important to understand the mechanisms that regulate this change and the biological, medical, societal, and economic implications of the transition women make from a reproductive to a nonreproductive status. Much progress has been made; however, much needs to be learned before we fully understand the physiology of the menopause or reproductive decline.

It is important to note that only female primates undergo a true menstrual cycle. Therefore, only these species undergo a true menopause (i.e., cessation of the menstrual cycle). Other species exhibit reproductive cycles that are not punctuated by a menstrual bleed, but are nevertheless characterized by a cyclic pattern of hormone release. Many of these species undergo reproductive senescence that is similar in some aspects to menopausal changes. It is important to develop animal models in which we can study the mechanisms of reproductive senescence since humans cannot be used to investigate many of the mechanisms that underlie the menopause.

Maintenance of regular menstrual cyclicity requires a complex interplay of neurochemical and endocrine signals that are precisely timed, occur in a specific order, and are released in the proper amounts (Yen, 1999). The synthesis and release of gonadotropin releasing hormone (GnRH) from neurons in the hypothalamus is regulated by a repertoire of neurotransmitters and neuromodulators. In turn, GnRH stimulates the synthesis and secretion of the gonadotropins, luteinizing hormone (LH) and follicle-stimulating hormone (FSH) from the anterior pituitary gland. These hormones, which are secreted in a pulsatile manner, determine the rate and number of follicles that undergo the final stages of development and differentiation. In addition, they govern the synthesis and secretory patterns of the major ovarian steroids, estradiol and progesterone, and the peptides inhibin and activin. Feedback of ovarian steroids to the level of the anterior pituitary and brain are essential for the menstrual cycle to recur every month. This constellation of endocrine hormones and others that have not been discussed results in a regular and repetitive menstrual cycle of predictable length.

The ovaries play a critical role in the menopause. Females are born with a finite, nonrenewable, postmitotic reserve of follicles. In humans, at birth, this pool consists of approximately 500,000 to 1,000,000 primordial follicles that are made up of a germ cell and surrounding granulosa cells. When mitosis ceases during fetal development, no new germ cells will ever be added to the reserve. Throughout life, germ cells reawaken from a dormant state and begin to grow. The vast majority of follicles die as they grow and develop through a process of programmed cell death. Thus, only a minuscule portion of this pool undergoes full growth, final differentiation, and ovulation. The vast majority of follicles die because they do not receive the trophic and hormonal support required for the final stages of growth and differentiation: They reach a juncture when critical hormonal support is not in synchrony with the stage of follicular development. By the time women are postmenopausal, the ovary no longer contains any follicles and no longer synthesizes ovarian steroids or peptides. The absence of ovarian estrogen and the consequent lack of negative feedback results in hypersecretion of both FSH and LH. For many years, scientists believed that the menopause resulted simply from the exhaustion of ovarian follicles (vom Saal, Finch, & Nelson, 1994). It has been hypothesized that the vast pool of follicles is required to maintain a stream of follicles in the developmental pipeline, and when the number of follicles falls below a critical number, the number that enter the growing pool becomes less well regulated. Subsequently, the patterns of hormone secretion by the larger follicles becomes less dependable, the length of time between cycles becomes more variable, and, consequently, fertility declines.

Changes in the hypothalamus and central nervous system play critical roles during the initial stages of the perimenopausal transition because neuroendocrine changes are already apparent before the final exhaustion of ovarian follicles. As mentioned earlier, the hypothalamus provides precise neurochemical and neuroendocrine signals that determine the patterns of secretion of the gonadotropins, which, in turn, govern the development of follicles and the ovulatory surge of LH. Hypothalamic changes, as measured by several indices, become evident during middle age, at the same time as the diminishing ovary follicular pool reaches the critical size that may no longer be able to support regular reproductive cycles. Therefore, follicular loss may not reflect the need to maintain a threshold number of follicles in the reserve but may be a direct consequence of a change in the pattern of neuroendocrine messages that govern the dynamics of follicular reawakening, recruitment, growth, and differentiation.

Recently, investigators have focused on the period prior to the establishment of permanent acyclicity (the perimenopausal period), that is, the events that occur in women during their early 40s or the equivalent stage in experimental animal models. We now realize that before ovarian follicles are exhausted, fertility and fecundity decrease markedly, reproductive cycles become increasingly irregular in length, and patterns of gonadotropin secretion are altered. One of the first signs that heralds this menopausal transition is an elevation in levels of FSH. Investigators have thought that these alterations indicate simply changes in ovarian estradiol and inhibin feedback. However, alterations in gonadotropin secretion have been reported recently in middle-aged, regularly menstruating women

prior to any change in plasma estradiol. Data from several laboratories suggest that during middle age the precise, synchronized, and interactive patterns of hypothalamic neurotransmitter and neuropeptide activity, which are critical to maintain a specific pattern of GnRH secretion, become less ordered (Wise, Kashon, Krajnak, Rosewell, Cai, Scarbrough, et al., 1999). First, hot flushes, a hallmark of deterioration of the hypothalamic thermoregulatory centers, have been reported in normally cycling women when ovarian follicles may not be limiting. Second, using animal models of the menopause, changes have been observed in several aspects of neurotransmitter activity in middle-aged animals still exhibiting regular reproductive cyclicity. Some researchers propose that this deterioration in the coupling of neurotransmitter signals that regulate GnRH secretion or an uncoupling of the composite of neurochemical signals from GnRH neurons brings about the initial changes in patterns of gonadotropin secretion.

A common feature of these neurochemical changes is that their daily rhythmicity is affected far more frequently than their overall average level of activity or expression, suggesting that deterioration of the "biological clock" underpins the desynchronization of multiple rhythms that may be critical to cyclic GnRH secretion. In mammals, there is a group of neurons in the ventral part of the hypothalamus, which constitutes the suprachiasmatic nucleus, that have the unique property of exhibiting inherent 24-hour rhythmicity in several properties. Even more important, this small region of the brain is considered the master circadian pacemaker because these nuclei not only exhibit 24-hour rhythmicity themselves, but they communicate extensively with many regions of the brain and drive the timing of multiple outputs. The impact of this is so great that virtually all physiological functions show a pervasive daily rhythm. The menstrual cycle is fundamentally grounded upon a circadian foundation. Thus, a fundamental deterioration in this neural pacemaker or the coupling to its outputs may be a component of the gradual disintegration of the temporal organization of neurotransmitter rhythms that are critical for stable, precise, and regular cyclic LH secretion. This may initiate a cascade that leads to the transition to irregular cycles and ultimately contributes to acyclicity.

In summary, the evidence that both the ovary and the brain are key pacemakers in the menopause is compelling. Many more studies will be necessary to understand the precise orchestration of physiological, cellular, and molecular events that weave together and ultimately, lead to reproductive acyclicity. Ultimately, we hope to be able to treat post-menopausal women more effectively during this period in their lives.

PHYLLIS M. WISE
MATTHEW J. SMITH

See also
Hormone Replacement Therapy: Estrogen

FILIAL RESPONSIBILITY

As the population of the United States has moved demographically to larger numbers and proportions of older persons, concern has become focused on issues of who should take care of older persons as they become disabled and unable to care for themselves. If the older person has resources, either through insurance or personal assets, the problem of care may not be a major issue for him or her as long as these resources last. However, when there are no assets, who is to take charge? Pragmatically, either of two sources of support exist, the family or public assistance. Whether the family should take responsibility for care, but particularly for long-term care, or whether this should be something taken over generally by government has been a matter of policy debate for some time.

The actual circumstance of the older person with regard to the structured social situation that exists determines in part what actually happens. For couples, the evidence indicates that the vast majority of wives outlive their husbands, so if there is a terminal-care situation, the task of caregiving falls on the spouse. Either spouse may be a caregiver, obviously, but the model sequence is impressively one of wife as caregiver, and this appears to be a viable situation as long as resources permit. If widows need care, who provides it? Commonly, if a daughter is accessible, she is a likely candidate to be a caregiver. Family ties and histories thus provide avenues of finding willing caregivers. However,

two issues are raised: Is it fair to those who are the caregivers that this activity occupies or displaces significant parts of their time and resources when others do not get so involved? And, more generally, what if persons are unwilling to provide care for their family members?

The question of what responsibility family members should take for one another is not unambiguous in society. Clearly, spouses should take care of one another, but at what point should other family members be held responsible? The focus usually goes promptly to children, who are commonly seen as being obliged to care for their parents. This has been identified as filial responsibility. Schorr (1961) wrote the classic review of the issue of filial responsibility in the United States, and one of the main points he made was that the idea itself is a relatively new one. He noted that there was no such idea in England or the colonial period but that the idea actually came into being when aged parents no longer controlled family property and income. Although filial love existed then, the tie of children to parents was through the control the parents had of resources.

In a review of filial responsibility laws, Garrett (1980) concludes that all attempts to have statutes declared unconstitutional have failed. The laws are variously supported by economic arguments of a liability the children owe parents and by custom and tradition. It may be, therefore, that Supreme Court legal opinions will change as the situation for families change. Somewhat fewer than half the states have filial responsibility laws. The California law reads: "It is the duty of the . . . children of any . . . person in need who is unable to maintain himself by work, to maintain such person to the extent of their ability" (California Civil Code P 206, West Supp. 1974). Idaho attempted to legislate a new filial responsibility law that received national notice in 1984 and 1985, but it did not pass into law. In general, the laws are not well known and are apparently used primarily as last resort threats to persuade unwilling children to take care of their parents. The laws, from the point of view of civil liberties, are suspect because they are not uniformly enforced, and thus are subject to capricious enforcement.

Filial responsibility appears to remain an issue because of the emphases that occur on maintaining family values. However, because there are different rules depending on one's family, realities of providing care universally counter this emphasis. Responsibilities imposed on children who have not had major contact with a parent for some 50 years appear to some to have a dubious basis. The question of extension also provides some perspective. Should a 75-year-old woman be expected to be the caretaker for her 95-year-old mother? And should the 18-year-old great-great-grandchild of the 95-year-old woman be held responsible for her in some way? Such questions, and the changing demographics, which indicate more single and no-child families, further add to the complexity of consideration of policy with regard to filial responsibility.

In the United States since 1985 the law applicable to filial responsibility has changed little. State enforcement of existing laws governing filial responsibility tends to be weak and rather haphazard. States appear to be a bit more interested in the issue of discouraging older adults from divesting themselves of assets (i.e., giving assets to their adult children) in order to qualify for Medicaid when they enter a nursing home. For a general discussion of filial responsibility in its legal and ethical context, see Nelson and Nelson (1992) and Kapp (1991).

EDWARD F. BORGATTA
Updated by
MARSHALL B. KAPP

See also
Caregivers of Chronically Ill Elders
Entitlement
Ethics
Family

FINANCIAL PLANNING: LEGAL ASPECTS

A financial plan for old age is no longer just an issue of concern to the wealthy. It is equally important for middle income persons for whom Social Security, pensions, savings, retirement plans, and equity in home ownership are the primary mainstays of support. Increasingly, financial planning for poor and indigent persons with mental or physical disabilities is becoming a major public policy issue, especially with regard to the management of Supplemental Security Income and other public benefits. The amount of one's resources determines the kinds of planning strategies required, rather than the need for such planning. For example, some persons with considerable assets might choose to purchase an annuity, which can assure a regular income for life, whereas persons who cannot afford traditional annuities, but who own their own home, may be able to achieve a similar result by shopping for a bank that offers home equity annuities. These may provide home upkeep, free housing, and cash payments for life, with the lender taking possession of the home upon death. In addition to the allocation of available resources to meet anticipated needs, financial planning should involve the creation of authority for substitute decision making that would become or remain effective in the event of incapacity. A major reason for early planning is to ensure that any substitute decisions that may be made on one's behalf will accurately reflect one's own standards and values. One can create such mechanisms only so long as one is still competent. At the moment a person becomes incompetent, he or she ceases to have the capacity to give the requisite consent.

Some simple and frequently used financial planning devices for persons of low or moderate income include the following (see also "Legal Counseling for the Elderly," 1983).

Joint Bank Accounts

Two or more persons, whether related or not, may open a bank account together. Either party may draw from the account without the signature of the other. Especially when combined with a system of direct deposits of benefit and entitlement checks, these accounts can ease financial management operations on behalf of an incapacitated person. When opening the account, the parties should specify whether they intend the remainder to be the property of the survivor upon the death of one of them.

Power of Attorney

This is a document by which one individual grants another (not necessarily an attorney) the power to act in his place under certain circumstances. It can be very limited, and grants, for example, the power to convey title to a particular house; or it can be broad, granting the power to conduct all business at the discretion of the holder of the power. The grantor can revoke it at any time. In some states it can be made "durable," that is, be made to remain in effect if the grantor becomes incompetent or incapacitated. If it is not made durable, it becomes void at the moment of incompetence.

Naming of a Guardian

A guardian is appointed by a court to make legally binding decisions, usually including financial decisions, for a person that a court has found to be incapacitated or incompetent. Some states allow competent individuals to name the person they would want to serve as guardian in the event of incompetence.

Representative Payee or Fiduciary

This is a person named by the agency administering certain federal benefits, including Social Security and Supplemental Security Income, to receive and manage the checks of the beneficiary. The beneficiary need not agree, and no court proceeding is necessary. The beneficiary need not be incompetent, but the Social Security Administration must be convinced that the individual would mismanage his or her own check if the payee were not appointed.

Early financial planning is becoming increasingly important for all, and a good plan can greatly enhance the quality of life during old age.

EDMUND DEJOWSKI

See also
   Legal Services
   Retirement Planning

FINANCIAL PLANNING: SOCIAL ASPECTS

There is much more to financial planning than asset allocation, risk management, stocks versus bonds, and mutual funds versus day trading. The social context of these phenomena is also important. In fact, we would argue that it is the pattern of social factors that guides the most important choices that comprise the financial planning process.

For example, we would not think much of a financial planner who gives the same advice to a 30-year-old divorced mother as to grandparents in their mid-60s. Similarly, if general financial rules of thumb are not assessed within a person's unique social context, their application can be dysfunctional. Even accepted rules of asset allocation among stocks, bonds, and cash must be evaluated in the context of such social factors as your (and your spouse's) age, employment, retirement, and pension status; the age and number of your children; the age and number of your parents, as well as their wealth (will you be providing financial assistance or receiving an inheritance?); the nature and size of your pension(s), savings, investments, and real estate; and the amount of uncertainty and risk with which you are willing to live as you get older.

The fundamental proposition is that, although social factors are intertwined with the monetary components of financial planning, they are distinct elements of the overall planning process. This article briefly discusses three sets of social factors: (1) demographic, the impact of increasing life expectancy on financial planning; (2) sociological, how the changing age structure of families expands the need for social context in financial planning; and (3) social-psychological, how the techniques of financial "harvesting"—psychologically as well as financially retaining control over what you have successfully "grown" financially—can be used to manage financial risk and especially the fear that many middle-aged and older people have of "outliving their money."

One especially important introductory observation: Financial planning is not just for rich people. Whether you are a gerontological or a financial professional, or just a friend or relative whose opinion is solicited, the fundamental message is the same: Personal financial profiles—and their demographic, sociological, and social psychological context—are increasingly complex for working- and middle-class people alike. Financial planning, including the critical importance of starting the process early in life, is important for everyone. And understanding the social context of one's financial situation is as much a part of the planning process as are the number and nature of the dollars involved.

Demographics: Increasing Longevity and the Human Wealth Span

Just as the human life span in general includes identifiable stages that are both biological and social (Atchley, 2000a), so too what financial gerontologists refer to as the "wealth span" has identifiable stages that are financial and social (Cutler, 1995). Equally important, evolutionary changes in the wealth span are a critical aspect of the social context of financial planning. The wealth span construct focuses attention on the fact that time is both a resource and a constraint in financial planning. For purposes of discussion, assume that the wealth span has two basic stages: the accumulation stage and the expenditure stage. The problem is that the chronological ages that typically define the beginning and the end of the stages have changed substantially.

Consider the changes that have taken place over the past 70 years or so. In the 1920s–1930s, people entered the accumulation stage earlier, often in their teens, and worked until their 60s. Because life expectancy was shorter, the expenditure stage was a relatively short number of years. Subsequently, both social and biomedical changes have occurred that affect the length of the stages. Nowadays, the accumulation stage starts later because of college (and graduate and professional education) and ends earlier due to early retirement. The expenditure stage now last longer than before because of early retirement and increasing life expectancy. The burden on financial planning is clear: A shorter accumulation stage must now produce sufficient financial resources for a longer expenditure stage.

Of course, as always, the real world is more complex than the model, with partial retirement and bridge jobs increasingly prevalent, making the line between the accumulation and expenditure stages blurry. Nonetheless, the impact of longevity as a social component of the financial planning process will be part of the story for a long time.

The Gerontological Arithmetic of the Aging Family

A basic proposition of financial gerontology is that financial decisions are family decisions. Another

consequence of improving longevity expectancy is its impact on the age structure of families, which offers additional consequences for financial planning. Although longevity is typically discussed in terms of its impact on individuals (e.g., Alzheimer's disease) and society (e.g., Social Security), often overlooked is the substantial impact of increasing longevity on the family as a social and financial entity.

Table 1 identifies the changing age structure of families as abstracted from Uhlenberg's important work in historical demography (Uhlenberg, 1996). In 1900, there was only a 39% chance that a 50-year-old adult child in the United States would have at least one parent alive; today, this is nearly universal. The probability that a 50-year-old will have both parents alive has increased to more than 25% from 4% in 1900. Even more dramatic is the calculation that after 2000 about half of all 60-year-old adult children will have at least one parent still alive.

This research has multiple implications both for intergenerational caregiving within the family and for the financial planning required of such caregiving (Cutler, 1997). The parents of Uhlenberg's 60-year-old adult children are not just 70 years old. That is, almost half of all adult children who are themselves on the cusp of old age have elderly parents in their 80s and 90s who may well require social, personal, and financial assistance. Clearly, intergenerational relationships are undergoing substantial changes as a consequence of increasing longevity. Just as clearly, financial planning is a central part of this new gerontological arithmetic.

TABLE 1 Probability of Middle-Age Adult Children With Surviving Parents

	1900	1940	2000
Adult Child, age 50			
At least one parent alive	39%	52%	80%
Both parents alive	4%	8%	27%
Adult Child, age 60			
At least one parent alive	7%	13%	44%

Source: Adapted from Uhlenberg (1996).

Maximizing Control and Minimizing Anxiety: The "Harvesting" of Financial Resources

Although many financial planners want to give or sell us advice on how to "grow" our retirement money, there is little systematic information on how we can efficiently harvest what has been successfully grown. "Harvesting" is not simply successful investing but, rather, refers to the concepts, strategies, and techniques by which we can retain maximum control and value from the wealth we have grown. Some harvesting choices, such as the size of a first withdrawal from a retirement plan, are made on the eve of retirement. Other choices, such as the number and kind of retirement accounts to have and retain, should be made years before retirement. The timing and nature of some of these choices are procedural and prescribed by law or by pension plan rules. Yet other choices are well within personal decision latitude and are central pieces of the social context of financial planning (Cutler, 1998).

Each of the following questions is directed to a financial component of retirement planning but embodies the nonfinancial context of one's life: Should I consolidate my retirement accounts into one, or can I deal with the complexity and flexibility of multiple accounts? Is it better to annuitize an account so as to guarantee some level of lifetime income, or can/should I take the risk of a higher but not guaranteed return? How should I balance estate planning with retirement planning?

Consider the case study of Mary B., a widowed comfortably employed medical secretary in her late 50s. Should she consolidate her retirement accounts? Central to Mary's choices is current law, which allows withdrawals (without tax penalty) from an individual retirement account or similar retirement fund at age 59, but requires that withdrawals begin by age 70. Within that period, the choices belong to Mary. As with most pre-retirees, an important wealth span objective is to "push" her money as far into the future as possible in response to the fear of outliving her money.

Over the years, Mary has developed three retirement accounts—a "conservative" but low-return bond fund, a somewhat speculative dot.com stock fund, and a balanced asset allocation mutual fund. She just received a persuasive phone call from a nationally known brokerage offering to consolidate her accounts into one easy-to-manage retirement plan. As she enters that period of years when the choices are still hers (age 59 to 70), the following questions become relevant: (1) Should I withdraw money from my retirement resources? (2) When should I withdraw the money? (3) How much should I withdraw—and at what rate of withdrawal? and (4) From which of my three accounts should I make the withdrawals?

In this simplified example, the harvesting strategy is fairly easy: Don't consolidate. Separate accounts mean more decisional degrees of freedom. For example, Mary can take some money out of her dot.com account (before the bubble bursts) and allow the other accounts to continue to grow. Or she can establish a rapid withdrawal rate from the dot.com, supplemented by smaller withdrawals from the balanced fund. Consolidation would shrink her options from three accounts to one. Further, the decision to (not) consolidate affects her annuitization choices: Mary can choose to annuitize only her bond fund in order to get a guaranteed lifetime income from it, while retaining more direct control over the assets in the other two funds.

The discussion comes full circle. Mary's financial choices will reflect not only her fear of outliving her money, but her risk tolerance and her capacity to make wise financial decisions. Her financial planning will also be influenced by several key social factors: Does she have children, grandchildren, or elderly parents? If so, what are their financial, health, and social circumstances? Does Mary have other financial assets aside from these retirement accounts? What is her own health and likely longevity? Will Mary want and be able to work after formal retirement? In summary, surrounding the specific parameters of financial accounts and retirement rules is a much broader set of personal and family, psychological and social characteristics that ultimately guide the dynamics of the overall financial planning process.

NEAL E. CUTLER

See also
Retirement Planning

FLIES

See
Models for the Study of Aging: Flies

FOSTER GRANDPARENT PROGRAM

In the wake of President Lyndon Johnson's promotion of the Great Society, and as a direct result of the 1971 White House Conference on Aging, many new social programs were enacted to benefit aged persons. In 1973 the Domestic Service Act was passed to encourage citizen action and participation in programs expected to enhance the quality of life of older persons and to assist them in achieving good mental health. This was a first step in the utilization of older volunteers in positions of service and leadership. Two results were expected: the volunteer would benefit through participation in a worthwhile service, and clients would be helped by the program. Examples of these kinds of programs are SERVE (Serve and Enrich Retirement by Volunteer Experience), the Foster Grandparent Program, and the Green Thumb Program, which employs poor older men and women in rural areas to work at beautifying parks and roadsides and serve as aides in schools and libraries. The low-income elderly who are employed must be 60 years of age or older. About 35% of participants tend to be from minority groups and to work 30 hours a week. Training and supervision is usually handled by the local agency that receives the grant for specific programs. In addition to the stipend, "Grandparents" receive a daily hot meal, transportation allowance, and an annual physical examination.

The design of the Foster Grandparent Program involves the utilization of older individuals in work with children. Paid a small amount as compensation for their services, foster grandparents work in settings such as schools, homes for retarded or disturbed children, homes for infants, care centers, and convalescent hospitals. A major aspect of their work is that they offer an important service that is not provided by the regular staff of aides, nurses, and doctors. Their goal is to establish a person-to-person relationship with individual children and, ideally, to supply an affectionate concern for the child which is often missing in these settings. Lowy (1980) pointed out that the reward to the caregiver is to feel "the affection and trust of the child."

The demographic context of the Foster Grandparent Program indicated its relevance. Although three-fourths of older persons in the United States have living grandchildren, the age of becoming a grandparent has gradually changed. Today natural grandparenting is an experience of middle age rather than of old age. Over half of these grandparents are employed and not at home to visit or rock their grandchildren. Nor can we forget the extraordinary rate of current family dissolution that complicates relationships with grandchildren when the divorced son, for instance, has remarried and perhaps has a second family. A further fact is that owing to increased longevity grandparents today may have older living parents who must be visited and cared for. Also to be noted is the fact that high geographic mobility often takes children out of range of their grandparents. These are some of the basic reasons why many children in institutions are deprived of older family personal relationships.

Some experienced observers feel that the program has been successful because children who may not be seen frequently by relatives look forward to visits with their foster grandparents. They seem to meet a basic need of institutionalized children. Depression and social immaturity appear to be alleviated by these relationships. The older members of this partnership also report positive reactions to their involvement.

There are, however, problems that prohibit the full utilization of the potential value of such programs as the Foster Grandparent Program, the Green Thumb Program, and the National Nutrition service. The first service has undoubtedly contributed to the good health and spirits of thousands of elderly and deprived children. But unfortunately it is funded to help exactly 1% of the older population when at least 20% are at risk. It is more difficult to calculate the number of children needful of supportive services. The limited amount of funds contributed by the Foster Grandparent Program provides a small model of what the program could be.

In 1981, 18,000 volunteers were employed, serving some 54,000 children. In one recent national study of senior volunteers working in Head Start-preschool programs (Trammel-Seck, 1983) it was found that the average age of volunteers was 69. More than 50% were widowed, and 50% had less than a high school education. The volunteers gave the following reasons for joining the Foster Grandparent Program: (1) to make good use of their time, (2) a need for extra money, (3) to help children and others, (4) death of spouse, and (5) retirement. The study also revealed some problems of the program: (1) the resistance of staff to volunteer support, (2) poor selection of volunteers, such as choosing "troubled persons," and (3) lack of adaptability of the volunteer to learn the philosophy and methods of the setting. Still, the overall conclusion of the study revealed that "it was the prevailing opinion of each of the sites visited that all parties received substantial benefit."

These programs show that older persons "can be reintegrated into society in a useful way and can utilize skills that have been honed during their whole life—to make life richer for others." The program is interesting because it attempts to fill the vacuum left by retirement and family fragmentation and to eliminate the sense of being a "cast-off." All three of the Federal Action Programs—Foster Grandparent as well as Senior Companions and Senior Volunteers—have continued to be funded nationwide.

JAMES PETERSON

See also
  Family
  Generativity
  Grandparents Raising Grandchildren

FOUNDATIONS

Foundation support for the field of aging, after a period of growth in the 1980s, increased less rapidly in the 1990s. At the same time, with the exception of funding for basic research on Alzheimer's disease, federal and state support of research, education, training, and demonstration programs in aging has been reduced. In particular, discretionary funding for education and training under Title IV of the Older Americans Act essentially ceased to exist, and the Geriatric Education Center program was severely cut. Yet some positive patterns and trends have emerged that will serve as the basis for foundation funding in the next few decades.

Early History

No one definitive source exists on foundation support for aging. In the early 20th century, when many foundations were created, there was little funding for aging, reflecting a general lack of concern or awareness about aging as a societal issue. Foundations began to seed small efforts in aging in the 1930s. Among them were the Deutsch Foundation sponsorship of a conference on aging, the Macy Foundation's support of Vincent Cowdry's research on arterioscelorosis and senescence, some aging studies underwritten by the Milbank Memorial Fund, and Rockefeller monies establishing the Committee on Human Development at the University of Chicago (Achenbaum, 1991).

The Macy Foundation continued its earlier efforts in aging well into the 1950s by supporting a series of symposia that identified key research questions in aging, providing some project funding from which Nathan Shock's bibliographical studies emerged, and pledging salary support for a new Public Health Service unit serving as a clearinghouse on aging. Thus, the Macy Foundation laid the basis for creation of the Gerontological Society and the federal Gerontology Research Center. Its efforts were joined by the Ford Foundation in the late 1950s, which funded socioeconomic studies at Duke University and aging-related activities undertaken by the National Welfare Assembly (NWA). The latter, chaired by Ollie Randall, evolved into the National Council on Aging. The Ford Foundation–NWA partnership, in collaboration with the National Institute on Mental Health, also led to the development of curriculum design on aging. Thus, public-private partnerships were an important factor in early support for research and education in aging.

In the 1960s and early 1970s, major foundation funding for aging was still uncommon, with bricks-and-mortar projects rather than programs receiving the lion's share. Notable exceptions were the Russell Sage Foundation's support for the landmark three-volume work *Aging and Society* and the Ford Foundation's 1973 funding of public interest litigation on behalf of the elderly. Small amounts of funding (i.e., less than $5,000) were provided by community or family foundations, but overall little support for aging programs was forthcoming. Some new trends, however, began to develop in the mid-1970s, several of which persisted through the 1990s.

The Filer Commission on Private Giving and Public Needs produced its study of private philanthropy after 2 years (1973–1975) of investigation. A "minority report" filed by the Donee Group criticized the commission for its lack of interest in nonmainstream groups, such as the elderly. Under the leadership of group members, such as Wilbur Cohen, a former secretary of the Department of Health, Education, and Welfare, and Maggie Kuhn of the Gray Panthers, the National Committee on Responsive Philanthropy (NCRP) was created. The NCRP identified older Americans as a group of special concern. During this same period, the National Institute on Aging (NIA) was established and the American Association of Retired Persons (AARP) initiated a special-purpose foundation to fund applied research in aging. The NCRP and the new head of the NIA, Robert Butler, strongly advocated for a more concerted foundation response to aging concerns.

Reports on Foundation Funding in Aging

The first widely disseminated report on foundation support in aging was produced in the late 1970s. Cohen and Oppedisano-Reich (1977) identified 126 foundations in 24 states and the District of Columbia as funders of more than 500 grants exceeding $5,000 during the period January 1972 to August 1976.

A subsequent report listed 177 foundations in 26 states and the District of Columbia, with 855 grants awarded between January 1974 and October 1978. It also enumerated an additional 91 foundations with an identified interest in aging and revealed the emerging interest of several large general-purpose foundations (e.g., Kresge and Kellogg) and of corporate foundations (e.g., General Mills).

During the early to mid-1980s, the activities of foundations were summarized in two reports sponsored by the Florence V. Burden Foundation, covering the early 1970s and the early 1980s. Five years later, a new comprehensive analysis of foundation support was again funded by the Burden Foundation. This study by Greenberg, Gutheil, Parker, and Chernesky (1991) reported on foundation giving in aging from 1983 to 1987. Giving patterns in aging, although inconsistent from year to year, increased from $39 million in 1983 to $68 million in 1987, up by 51% in inflation-adjusted dollars. The number of

grants rose by 44% from 762 in 1983 to 1,096 in 1987. Over the same 5-year period, 415 foundations awarded 4,869 grants in aging, totaling $293.2 million, with aging's share of overall foundation funding ranging from 2% to 3%, in contrast with 1.4% in 1981 (Greenberg et al., 1991).

However, fewer new foundations entered the field of aging, and by the end of the 1980s there was some drop-off in the proportion of foundations providing support for aging. The five largest funders provided nearly 40% of all giving, a pattern still evident in the 1993 Foundation Center's *National Guide to Funding in Aging* on grants for aging in 1991 and 1992 (The Foundation Center, 1993), as well as more recently (The Foundation Center, 1999). In those 2 years, 405 foundations awarded 1,345 grants, totaling $121.5 million in current dollars. In its most recent guide spanning the years 1995 to 1998, The Foundation Center (1999) found that just under 1,400 foundations identified a declared interest in aging and 542 foundations had awarded 2,284 grants, for a total of $152.8 million. In assessing the trends since the early 1980s, the numbers of foundations funding programs in aging have increased overall, with a slight dip in the early 1990s.

More sobering are comparisons of grant activity and average dollar amounts for each of the periods surveyed. The average numbers of grants decreased from a high of 974 in the 5-year period of 1983 to 1987, to 677 in the years 1991 and 1992, to 571 in the most recent 4-year period, 1995 to 1998. The "yield" of those grants shows a mixed trend: a yearly average of $58.64 million for the mid- to late 1980s, with a slight uptick of an annual $60.75 million average for the two earliest years of the 1990s, versus a disheartening slump to a $38.2 average for the late 1990s.

Recent Trends and New Directions

Several trends have emerged over the past two decades in foundation funding for aging, and more generally in the world of philanthropy, with implications for grants in aging in the 21st century. We have seen the creation of new foundations heavily focused on aging, such as the Villers Foundation (now named Families/USA), and a stronger emphasis on aging by existing foundations, most notably the Commonwealth, Pew, Hartford, and Robert Wood Johnson (RWJ) foundations. Conversely, other foundations that were previously active funders in aging, such as the Edna McConnell Clark Foundation, have changed their priorities. And, as noted above, more foundations now list aging as an area of interest. A Grantmaker Search of recent grant awards, however, revealed that many do not actively fund aging programs, despite this declared priority.

Shifts have also occurred in the kinds of grants awarded. More dollars are going to health and biomedical research and fewer to social services and social gerontological research, paralleling similar patterns in federal funding. Between 1983 and 1987 funding for health programs in aging grew by 84%, or 55% of all grant dollars in aging (Greenberg, Gutheil, Parker, & Chernesky, 1991, p. 10). The most recent Foundation Center report corroborates these earlier trends: Nearly two thirds of age-related grants from 1995 to 1998 were awarded for health/biomedical topics, with only 27% for human services.

The priorities of major grantmakers in long-term care and health care access and quality indicate this emphasis is likely to continue. A further indication of this trend is the heavier involvement of foundations in supporting policy research and policy analysis on Medicare, Medicaid, and related topics (see, e.g., Henry J. Kaiser Foundation publications; see also LeRoy & Schwartz, 1999).

Other areas worthy of foundation funding have generally been neglected. During the late 1980s and 1990s, some important but relatively minimal foundation support was awarded for gerontological education and training, such as the AARP–Andrus Foundation Graduate Scholarship and Fellowship Program, and more recently its Undergraduate Scholarship Program for the Study of Aging and Finance. Given the precipitate drop in Title IV and other governmental funding despite the need for more trained personnel in aging, considerably more foundations could play a crucial role in this area. Thus far, however, the majority have not expanded their educational and aging priorities to encompass education and training of future personnel in aging (see Douglass, 1998; Peterson, Douglass, Seymour, & Wendt, 1997).

Other recent trends include joint funding, better access to information about funding, and the "new-philanthropy." A pattern of private-private partnerships has developed in recent years. Foundations are joining together, as well as with corporations, to fund projects. Continuing a much earlier pattern begun in the 1930s and 1940s, public-private partnerships have been developed in such areas as eldercare programs in the workplace (Washington Business Group on Health, 1992). These efforts are being spearheaded in many instances by members of Grantmakers in Aging, an affinity group of the national Council on Foundations.

Information about foundations has been provided by the Foundation Center for several decades, largely in print form and via special searches on demand. Electronic access, however, has been developed via websites that provide detailed financial information about nonprofit groups, including foundations. Assisted by foundation grants totaling nearly $3 million, The Urban Institute and Philanthropic Research, Inc. have introduced scanned images of copies of recent financial filings required by the Internal Revenue Service onto their websites. This will enable those seeking funds to have more timely information.

A final trend in philanthropy reflects a change in foundation funding sources and approaches. Since the early 20th century the biggest foundations were primarily based on the manufacturing might of corporate America. In the next century, people who have made their fortunes in the world of high technology will be the social entrepreneurs of the future. Software developers, such as Bill Gates, are establishing foundations, following in the footsteps of the Packard family and other high-technology firms. Thus far, these new philanthropists have not demonstrated interest in aging; rather, they focus on enhancing technology, the environment, and elementary and secondary education. They represent a new generation of entrepreneurial givers who focus more on measurable results and less on sentiment (Maclean, 1999). This untapped source presents a challenge to those seeking funds for research and education in aging—a challenge that will require new strategies to ensure the growth of foundation funding for aging concerns in the future.

PHOEBE S. LIEBIG

See also
Organizations in Aging

FRAMINGHAM STUDIES OF HEART DISEASE

In 1948, the U.S. Public Health Service set up an epidemiological study of hypertensive or arteriosclerotic cardiovascular diseases (Dawber, 1980). It was assumed from the beginning that these diseases were the result of multiple causes that worked slowly within individuals. The plan was to select a probability sample of persons in the ages at which arteriosclerotic and hypertensive cardiovascular disease were known to develop and determine, by as complete a clinical examination as feasible, the presence or absence of these diseases. Persons free of overt disease would then be observed over a period of years until a sizable number developed the diseases. A search would then be made for the factors that influenced the development of these diseases by classifying the population according to characteristics believed to be related to disease development and looking for associated differences in disease incidence. It was hypothesized that the age of onset of degenerative cardiovascular disease would be a function of three variables: (1) constitutional factors (including hereditary factors), (2) conditioning factors (including external environmental factors), and (3) the time factor or length of time the conditioning factors must act on the constitutionally determined characteristics or interact with them to result in clinical cardiovascular disease.

The town of Framingham, Massachusetts, was selected for the study. In 1948, Framingham, located 21 miles west of Boston, was an industrial and trading center of 28,000 people and included business, residential, and outlying rural areas within the town limits. A total of 5,209 men and women between the ages of 30 through 59 were selected at random from the 10,000 residents of Framingham in that age group. These subjects have been reexamined every 2 years by means of a standardized protocol to determine the onset of the major cardiovascular disease characteristics leading to such endpoints as angina pectoris, coronary insufficiency, myocardial infarction coronary heart disease death, artherothrombotic stroke, embolic stroke, hemorrhagic stroke, congestive heart failure, and peripheral vascular disease. From time to time, new factors were measured. In the late 1960s the Framingham A-B stress scale was created out of a psychoso-

cial interview designed to note such behavioral tendencies as bossiness, dissatisfaction, competitiveness, impatience, and other personality traits. At the same time, lipoproteins, including chylomicron, high-density lipoprotein (HDL), low-density lipoprotein (LDL), very low density lipoprotein (VLDL), and intermediate-density lipoprotein (IDL) were measured.

Throughout the study, multivariate and maximum likelihood ratios were used, in addition to standard statistical tests, to assess the independence and importance of particular risk factors.

Results

The results of the study have identified a number of risk factors that each individually increase the risk of cardiovascular heart disease (Castelli, 1983). Individuals with a combination of two or more of the factors are at even greater risk. The risk factors include the following.

Total Blood Cholesterol.   Early data showed a linear relationship between total blood cholesterol and risk of most cardiovascular disease and coronary heart disease, and it was estimated that for each 1% rise in cholesterol, the incidence of disease increased 2% to 3%. However, as the study population in Framingham aged, the total serum cholesterol level began to lose its significance as a predictor of risk of cardiovascular disease, and beyond the age of 50 years it was no longer a strong predictor. Other correlations were then observed with the measurement of the individual blood lipids: chylomicrons, VLDL, IDL, LDL, and HDL. LDL cholesterol restored the predictive ability of cholesterol. On the other hand, high levels of HDL appeared to have a protective effect; the higher the HDL, the lower the subsequent rate of development of cardiovascular disease, particularly coronary heart disease. Consideration of a combination of lipid measurements showed high total cholesterol/HDL ratios to be predictive and suggested that ratios below 4.5 should be strived for.

Hypertension.   Hypertension (a blood pressure of 160/95 mm Hg or greater) conferred a two- to threefold increased risk on most coronary heart disease indicators. Hypertension increased the risk of stroke sevenfold, and it was the major risk factor in more than 80% of strokes.

Blood Sugar.   Higher blood glucose values were associated with a higher rate of coronary heart disease, and diabetes mellitus conferred a double risk in women, but less in men.

Obesity.   Excess weight was found to be related to cardiovascular disease and angina pectoris.

Cigarette Smoking.   One of the three most significant risk factors in persons under 60 was cigarette smoking. This risk, however, was found to be reversible. In the person who stopped smoking, the cardiovascular heart disease risk declined to the level of a nonsmoker within 1 year, whereas the risk of lung cancer returned to normal only after 10 to 15 years.

Physical Activity.   There was some evidence that increased physical activity protects against coronary heart disease.

Personality Type.   Among women and white-collar working men, type A personalities were at higher risk of developing coronary heart disease than type B personalities. However, the relationship did not hold for blue collar working men.

ECG Abnormalities.   There was a significant relationship between ECG abnormalities and the subsequent risk of heart attack. Left ventricular hypertrophy, bundle-branch block, and nonspecific ST-T wave abnormalities greatly increased the risk of sudden death.

The Framingham Study has provided greater knowledge of the atherosclerotic process. The pessimistic view that atherosclerotic disease is an inevitable result of the aging process has been replaced by the more optimistic concept that atherosclerosis can be prevented or significantly delayed by the identification and management of risk factors.

MARGARET L. HEIDRICK

See also
Cardiovascular System: Overview
Longitudinal Studies of Aging

FRIENDSHIP

Friends are important during adulthood in many ways; by serving as companions, sources of affection, and emotional and instrumental supporters, they contribute to psychological well-being, physical health, and longevity (e.g., Sabin, 1993). Friendship might also have broader social effects, such as maintaining class cultures or creating environments conducive to successful aging.

Compared with other forms of social relationships in our society, friendship is distinctively voluntary. Whereas relatives are specified by blood or legal ties and neighbors by proximity, friends are selected. Furthermore, in Western societies friendship is not institutionalized and thus lacks standard rituals, norms, and nomenclature to guide the partners. Yet friendship choices are not wholly fortuitous, nor is amicable behavior arbitrary. Thus, for example, friends tend to be similar to one another in terms of gender, race, class, and marital status (e.g., Dykstra, 1990).

Researchers who view friendship as voluntary pay special attention to psychological factors in friendship initiation and maintenance. In contrast, those who have a sociological perspective emphasize the effects of social structure and influences mainly beyond individual control. These two traditions are different in another way as well. Psychological theorists tend to focus on the interactive processes that take place in friendship dyads, whereas structuralists tend to study the form of individuals' entire friendship networks (Blieszner & Adams, 1992).

Most of the adult friendship research in both of these traditions has been conducted during the past 30 years, with a notable increase in quantity and quality of studies in the last 20 years. This mature stage of development is marked by the appearance of monographs synthesizing and reviewing extant research, edited collections focused on the friendships of specific adult populations, and volumes reporting primary research results.

Gerontologists have focused more attention on friendship than other researchers have. This is probably due to their preoccupation with factors affecting the psychological well-being of older adults and interest in friends as a source of social support. In contrast to early studies of friendship among older adults, recent ones have focused more on the internal structures and processes of friendship and on predictors of friendship patterns rather than exclusively on the effects of quantity of social contact (e.g., Adams & Torr, 1998; Dugan & Kivett, 1998). Rather than focusing exclusively on the positive aspects of friendships, contemporary researchers also examine their negative qualities (Blieszner & Adams, 1998).

Researchers now more commonly compare the friendships of adults of various ages and sometimes examine changes in friendship patterns longitudinally (e.g., Morgan, Carder, & Neal, 1997; Roberto, 1997). Knowledge of why friendship patterns change over time is still limited, however, because researchers often use the variable age as a proxy measure for both stage of life course and stage of development without distinguishing between these two aspects of aging (Blieszner & Adams, 1992). Furthermore, no longitudinal studies of the friendship patterns of multiple cohorts have been conducted.

Perhaps because of the methodological limitations of existing studies, for many years researchers accepted the common perception that as people age, their friendship circles gradually become smaller. More recent research suggests, however, that the relationship between aging and number of friends varies across types of people and contexts. Rather than viewing the aging process as synonymous with social losses and constraints on friendship activity, researchers now examine the role changes accompanying old age as liberating as well (Johnson & Troll, 1994; Riggs, 1997).

The challenge now facing researchers is to examine the consequences for friendship patterns of the contexts in which they are embedded. Until recently, friendship researchers focused their studies almost exclusively on populations of Caucasian residents of the United States. Although these study populations often included people from a variety of economic backgrounds, researchers rarely treated class as a variable in their analyses of adult friendship patterns. Lately, researchers have examined friendship among various ethnic groups and in various countries (e.g., deVries, Jacoby, & Davis, 1996). Nonetheless, we know little about how ethnicity, race, and national context affect friendship patterns, because researchers almost never compare findings across categories of these variables. More broadly, researchers need to consider the implications for friendship patterns of the characteristics of this period of history, such as the culture of individualism, an emphasis on personal freedom, the privatization of social life, and the development of communications and transportation technologies (Adams & Allan, 1998). In summary, if the literature on adult friendship patterns is to develop further, researchers must conduct longitudinal studies of multiple cohorts; examine variations across classes, ethnic groups, and races; and make comparisons across cultures and historical periods.

REBECCA G. ADAMS

The author would like to thank Samantha Ammons for assistance with library research.

See also
Gender

FRONTAL LOBE DYSFUNCTION

Situated just behind the forehead are the frontal lobes of the brain. Although the frontal lobes are sensitive to the effects of aging, deficits in this area are difficult to measure and report, as well as understand. In the posterior portion lies the motor cortex, mostly responsible for motor functioning. However, impairments to the anterior portion of the frontal lobes (the prefrontal cortex) reflect the executive cognitive deficits, which are most often referred to as "frontal lobe deficits."

Adults have the capacity to engage in higher order cognitive functioning as a result of the development of the prefrontal area of the brain during late childhood and adolescence. These functions include the ability to plan, to possess judgment over one's actions, to think in terms of abstract concepts, to be cognitively flexible, to inhibit inappropriate responses, to delay gratification for extended periods of time, to generate new approaches and ideas to familiar and unfamiliar situations, to control and regulate emotions, and to search memory efficiently and accurately, as well as regulation over internal states of the body. Additionally, the prefrontal lobes are responsible for allowing an individual to monitor his or her own actions, including the development of an internal set of ethics. The prefrontal lobes consists of those abilities that allow one to engage successfully in independent, purposive, self-serving behavior characteristic of adulthood.

Frontal lobe dysfunction reflects deficits in one or more of these skills. These frontal lobe syndromes (groups of symptoms) are not characterized by symptoms such as aphasia, motor deficit, intellectual loss, or other more easily recognized problems. As a result, the individual may appear outwardly to be perfectly normal. However, when frontal lobe functions are impaired, the person may no longer be capable of satisfactory self-care, of performing work independently, or of maintaining normal social relationships. Cases can range from mild (subtle deficits) to severe (more obvious). Milder cases are characterized by patients who are rigid and inflexible in their thinking but otherwise seem normal. Although memory problems exists, they are usually mild and are often dismissed as the effects of normal aging. Change in personality can also occur, with no apparent cognitive problems (intellect, motor).

Moderate cases typically are characterized by difficulty in decision making and poor judgment. Slower thoughts, labile emotions, a deterioration of daily independent living skills, some denial and defensiveness regarding one's problems, impulsivity, and an inability to see the nature of one's problems exist. Noticeable memory changes begin to occur. However, this does not pertain to the actual event, but rather to remembering it at the appropriate time. For example, a patient may be unable to tell you when his or her birthday is when asked but may spontaneously be able to provide such information in the midst of a conversation. The individual begins to have more difficulty taking care of himself or herself. During this stage, financial and personal decisions may become seriously impaired. During this stage and later, it is crucial to monitor such decisions.

In severe cases, patients often become disoriented to time and place. For example, they may not be able to tell you the city and state they live in or what year it is. These are often hallmark signs of severe dysfunction. Symptoms become very exaggerated when they forget personal and family responsibilities. At this stage, it is clear that they are incompetent to handle their own as well as others' affairs and that constant supervision must be employed.

Degenerative diseases, such as dementia of the Alzheimer's type and multi-infarct dementia, are the most common causes of frontal lobe dysfunction. Pick's disease results primarily in atrophy of the frontal and temporal areas of the brain, resulting in marked personality and behavioral changes along with language problems. Other frontal lobe dementias may show symptoms similar to Pick's disease but without the pathological changes seen in that disease. Other causes include head trauma, stroke, demyelinating diseases, tumor, hydrocephalus, and metabolic disorders secondary to problems elsewhere in the body. In almost all cases where brain damage is being considered, an assessment of the frontal lobe dysfunction should be considered mandatory because of the sensitivity of the frontal lobes to many disorders associated with aging.

A variety of measures have been used to assess frontal lobe dysfunction (or the numerous symptoms that accompany it). For example, there are a number of tests that have been devised to assess abstraction capacities and mental flexibility, including tests of concept formation. Such tests include the Similarities subtest of the Wechsler Adult Intelligence Scale (WAIS) (Wecshler, 1981), the Proverb Interpretation Test, the Reasoning subtest of the Primary Mental Abilities Battery (PMA; Thurstone, 1938), and the Category Test of the Halstead–Reitan Battery (Halstead, 1947). Additionally, the Similarities subtest of the WAIS shows the greatest decline with age. Other tests used to assess mental flexibility are the Wisconsin Card Sorting Test (Berg, 1948) and the Visual-Verbal Test (Feldman & Drasgow, 1951), which are tests of sorting and set shifting. In many cases, however, norms for the elderly (especially the very old) are inadequate, and caution should be taken in test interpretation.

Series completion tests also show significant declines with age. These tasks require the patient to examine a series of letters or numbers and determine the rule that governed the sequencing of the items in the series. Such measures that assess this ability include the Abstraction subtest of the Shipley–Hartford Scale and the Reasoning subtests of the PMA (Cornelius, 1984). The Gorham's Proverbs Test is also a measure that can be used to assess abstract formation (Albert, Duffy, & Naeser, 1987). Abstraction tasks that make attentional and memory demands on patients have also produced declines with age. A study by Mack and Carlson (1978) showed that subjects over the age of 60 have been shown to commit significantly more errors on the Halstead–Reitan Category Test than young subjects, even in the absence of obvious pathology. The elderly subjects were most impaired on the subtest that contained the greatest tasks of complexity.

Other measures that have been used to assess frontal lobe dysfunction and executive functions (higher order cognitive processing) include the Trail Making Test (Reitan, 1958); the Modified Card Sorting Test (Nelson, 1976); the Stroop Color and Word Interference Test (Golden, 1978); tests of verbal fluency, such as the Controlled Oral Word Association Test; and tests of visual-motor integration and planning, such as the Rey–Osterrieth Complex Figure Test (Grodzinsky & Diamond, 1992).

CHARLES J. GOLDEN
SAMANTHA DEVARAJU-BACKHAUS

See also
> Alzheimer's Disease: Clinical
> Alzheimer's Disease: Genetic
> Central and Peripheral Nervous Systems Morphology
> Cognitive Processes
> Memory Dysfunction: Drug Treatment
> Memory: Neurochemical Correlates
> Senile Dementia

FUTURE TRENDS

From Nostradamus to modern-day futurists, humans have been trying to predict the future. Futurists tend to interpret the turn of a new century as a significant marker. Gerontologists in the United States view the year 2020 as significant. It is the year that a significant number of the baby-boom generation enter their 60s, at the same time as the oldest baby boomers are in their 70s.

Projections are usually better predictions of future trends than prophecies. The extraordinary 20th-century advances in survivorship and population aging will have major consequences for societies around the world. Before the 20 century, it took 5,000 years of human history to extend average life expectancy by 30 years. In contrast, since the turn of the last century, the average life expectancy from birth in industrialized nations has increased by over 30 years. Between 1982, when the United Nations World Assembly on Aging convened, and 2000, the number of people in the world over age 60 doubled. Sixty percent of this number will be living in the developing world. The age structure of a society depends on birth rates, mortality rates, and net migration.

Aging societies require transformations in existing mind-sets in the areas of cultural attitudes, social practices (e.g., work and retirement patterns), economics, living arrangements and housing, health care and social service delivery, and the general scientific and medical research agenda, among other things. These are beginning to change slowly to adapt to population aging.

The future can be dealt with by actively planning, organizing, and altering the shape of institutions, attitudes, legislation, policies, and practices in response to population projections. Several strategies, then, can be created or adopted by private and public institutions to help respond to future trends, insofar as they can be anticipated. For example, it is prudent to develop specific strategies for scientific research, social and economic progress, and health care and service delivery, as well as cultural and personal development. All of these strategies are interdependent. Following are estimates of what may be expected in each of these areas.

Scientific Strategy

There will be remarkable changes in research on aging, which will further demonstrate the malleability of the aging process. The National Agenda for Research on Aging, developed by the Institute of Medicine of the National Academy of Sciences, will be implemented. The extraordinary contributions of the new biology (e.g., molecular biology, recombinant DNA or gene splicing, immunology, and neurobiology) will help us to better understand the mystery of biological aging.

Aging is subject to intervention to reduce the dysregulation that occurs with age and underlies the many deleterious manifestations of aging processes. Genetic control mechanisms will be introduced; neuroplasticity will be enhanced. The new technologies of positron emission tomography and magnetic resonance imaging will help lead the way to an enhancement of diagnostic power and a better understanding of the body's structure and functioning. This, in turn, will lead to cost-effective applications in the health care industry. The life cycle itself will be increasingly under control, from in vitro fertilization to experimental manipulation of longevity in animals and humans through caloric restriction and free-radical scavenging.

Genetic markers will make early diagnosis, prevention, and treatment of many illnesses possible. For example, if one knows one has the gene for colon cancer, behavior can be changed accordingly (e.g., eating a low-fat diet and having more frequent checkups). Insertion of a normal gene to overcome a defective one will become commonplace. Physicians can now diagnose more than 200 of about 3,000 disorders caused by single-gene defects. The entire map of human genes will be known by 2003, thanks to the Human Genome Project. The National Institutes of Health advisory panel guidelines for somatic genetic therapy will work effectively and reduce fears about "germ-line" transfers and could lead to a "redesign" of the human species.

We will understand better how cholesterol clogs human arteries and causes strokes and heart attacks. Improved cholesterol-lowering drugs will be available. Medications or laser surgery will unclog arteries. Cancer will be treated with monoclonal antibodies, and methods of preventing metastases of cancers will be improved. Medicines closer to naturally occurring body chemicals will replace synthetics, which are more likely to cause adverse side effects.

Immunologic techniques will help restore the vigor of the immune system in old age, thereby mitigating vulnerability to infectious diseases such as flu and pneumonia, as well as reducing the spread of cancer. Cytokines that stimulate T-lymphocyte production will also reduce autoimmune diseases. Human growth factors and hormones will help overcome frailty. In addition to using scalpels, surgeons will perform delicate surgical procedures with beams of light and microscopes. The laser converts electromagnetic energy into light beams, which can be aimed precisely at selected targets.

Universal "presumed consent" organ donation and technological progress in overcoming trans-plant rejection will increase organ availability for the young and the old. Immunosuppressant drugs more potent than cyclosporine will help prevent transplant rejection.

Regenerative medicine, utilizing cell cultivation, will replace diseased tissues and organs. We are moving into increasingly sophisticated bionics with plastics and microprocessors, making, for example, "smart" arms and hands. Artificial hearing will become available, as will sophisticated prosthetic environments to compensate for mobility, communicative, and sensory deficits.

We will see an explosive growth in the field of geriatrics and the utilization of the egalitarian interdisciplinary team (e.g., physician, nurse, and social worker), along with a restructuring of Medicare to cover health promotion, disease prevention, rehabilitation, and long-term care, as well as short-term and acute care. Medicare-supported hospice care will grow. Compassionate care will be developed for persons who are dying. Patient-controlled analgesia, as well as effective confrontation of personal and existential suffering, will be part of end-of-life humanistic therapy.

Neurotransmitters, which are chemicals of the brain, provide neurons with the means to communicate among themselves and produce emotions, thoughts, and behavior. Knowledge about these substances will grow substantially. There will also be considerable progress with regard to Alzheimer's disease and other dementias, especially vascular forms. Increased knowledge about the role of mitochondria, where energy is generated at the cellular level, will be translated into practical measures to enhance the function of the central nervous system.

Health care costs will be reduced through greater efficiency, better training of physicians, the use of paraprofessionals, and direct monitoring of care. The health enterprise will become the nation's leading industry. A national population laboratory will be created to study human change, growth, and performance over time through a variety of comprehensive longitudinal studies, and studies of family life will expand. Most of all, by providing new knowledge and applications to health care, scientific research will prove to be the ultimate cost-containment tool, as well as the ultimate service to humankind.

Social and Economic Strategies

To sustain population aging, continuing national prosperity is critical. There will be major advances in high technology and biotechnology and increasingly stable economic productivity. Sources of energy, such as natural gas, solar power, and nuclear fusion, will be abundant and "clean." To avoid shattering standards of living in the developed and developing countries, international agreements on minimum wages and occupational safety and health in the developing world will be signed. This will also sustain social protection against the unpredictable vicissitudes of human existence, such as unexpected disease and disability, natural disasters, and economic downturns.

Older people will make greater contributions to society. Such human productivity will be included in service corps and service exchanges, involving all the generations collaborating together. We will have a 30-hour work week and expansion of "job-sharing" opportunities.

To maintain human creativity and productivity, continuing education, brief sabbaticals, and other approaches will be instituted to help overcome potential personal obsolescence. As a result, people typically will have four or more careers in a lifetime. The continuing productivity of older persons will reduce the costs of dependency and control Social Security, pension, and health care costs.

One of the great issues in aging is private and public pension liabilities. Private pension funds in 1994 totaled $2.3 trillion. Pension funds will be used for a variety of social purposes and for the financing of late-life support. Pension programs will be portable as people go from job to job.

The "silver industries," or mature markets, will grow remarkably profitable, and businesses in the areas of health, living arrangements, travel, recreation, and leisure, among others, will grow.

Health Care and Service Delivery

A full-scale health care system, including geriatric care, will finally develop. It will meet the needs of people of all ages who suffer from acute to chronic, multiple, complex, interacting psychosocial, and medical conditions, through provision of a contin-uum of care that will meet changing conditions. Thus, people will spend less time in institutions. Instead, they will be cared for at home or in community-based family service centers, which incorporate adult day care services. Hospice-type palliative care will humanize the process of dying by alleviating existential suffering as well as pain and discomfort. Surgical and medical interventions will be conducted increasingly on an outpatient basis.

Cultural Strategy

The great fears of societies over the high cost of old age, such as economic stagnation and intergenerational competition for resources, will be allayed. Intergenerational conflicts will be resolved through the open adoption of intergenerational compacts. As public opinion polls have shown, the generous disposition of the young to the old will continue as the baby-boom generation itself grows older and encourages political activism on behalf of the aged.

We will see new themes in theater, cinema, fiction, visual arts, and music, in keeping with the growing numbers of aged. Novels will have older protagonists. The true beauty of age will be revealed in photography and painting. Ageism will be markedly reduced through antidiscriminatory legislation and growing cultural sensitivity.

Personal Strategy

Personal responsibility for health and aging will be further encouraged and with it effective health promotion and disease prevention programs. There will be successful adoption of national dietary reform. We will eat less animal fat and simple sugars and more complex carbohydrates and fiber. We will continue to learn more about nutrition. The use of tobacco, both smoking and smokeless, will become an anachronism. New discoveries will help prevent addictive tendencies from being realized in highly susceptible individuals. New strategies for preserving intellectual function, beginning in early childhood, will be discovered.

Finally, we will come to better understand ourselves. We will move toward a more balanced life of physical and mental activities, of work and play, of enlightened self-interest and altruism. We will come to conclude that life is of primary value, a common cause to be shared and enhanced, and that longevity is a gift to be prudently and generously used.

ROBERT N. BUTLER

See also
Baby Boomers and Their Future
Health Information Through Telecommunication
Internet and E-mail Resources

G

GASTROINTESTINAL FUNCTION

The main functions of the gastrointestinal system consist of digestion and absorption. Both clinical and basic investigations have demonstrated that there are age-related changes in gastrointestinal functions and that these age-related physiological changes may contribute to the development of various gastrointestinal disorders that are more prevalent among the elderly.

Oropharyngeal Structures and the Esophagus

Age-related changes in oropharyngeal and esophageal structures include subtle structural changes (e.g., thinning of the tongue, weaker oropharyngeal muscles, and altered taste acuity) and functional changes (e.g., prolonged swallowing and altered peristaltic response after deglutition) (Holt, 1995; Tack & Vantrappen, 1997). Salivary output and flow remain normal in the elderly. Corkscrew esophagus (or presbyesophagus), which describes tertiary contractions of the esophagus commonly detected by radiographic evaluation in the elderly, has no known pathophysiologic consequence.

Available data suggest that most swallowing problems in the elderly are due to other medical problems and the intake of numerous drugs. Clinically, esophageal diverticular disease (e.g., Zenker's diverticulum), achalasia (a motility disorder), and esophageal cancer occur more frequently in the elderly (Holt, 1995; Tack & Vantrappen, 1997).

The Stomach

Gastric acid secretion changes little with aging, unless there is concomitant gastric pathology (e.g., atrophic gastritis). Notable age-related physiological changes in the stomach include modest reduction in pepsin output and significantly reduced mucosal prostaglandin biosynthesis. Although gastric emptying rate for solids in healthy volunteers does not change with age, gastric emptying of liquids may be impaired (Holt, 1995; Lee & Feldman, 1997).

Epidemiological studies have demonstrated that peptic ulcer disease and its complications are more common among the elderly. Potential explanations for this observation include a significantly higher prevalence of *Helicobacter pylori* infection among the elderly and increased use of nonsteroidal anti-inflammatory drugs by the elderly; both are known causes of peptic ulcer disease. Data from animal and human studies also suggest that age-related declines in gastric mucosal protective factors (e.g., prostaglandins and bicarbonate secretion) may predispose the elderly to the development of peptic ulcer disease (Holt, 1995).

Although gastric acid secretion remains unchanged in the majority of older, healthy individuals, 25% of the older subjects may develop acid hyposecretion (or hypochlorhydria) secondary to atrophic gastritis. Gastric hypochlorhydria may predispose these older individuals to various enteric infections, because a low intragastric pH is a known defense mechanism against bacterial infections of the gut. Moreover, gastric hypochlorhydria may contribute to the development of malabsorption of iron, folic acid, vitamin B_6, and vitamin B_{12} in the elderly (Holt, 1995).

The Intestines

Although overall intestinal absorption does not change with age, subtle reduction in carbohydrate absorptive capacity and altered calcium absorption can be detected in the elderly (Holt, 1995). There are no significant differences in bowel transit time between healthy younger and older volunteers. Clinically, aging is associated with an increased incidence of diverticular disease, constipation, anorectal dysfunction, and colorectal cancer.

The Liver

Age-related changes in liver functions are not physiologically significant. Modest reductions in liver size, blood flow and perfusion, and dynamic liver functions with aging can be detected in the elderly (James, 1997). Animal studies have shown that, whereas the rate and time course of hepatic regeneration are delayed in senescent animals, complete regeneration of the liver occurs as in young animals. These observations have led to the increased use of livers from older donors for hepatic transplantation (Holt, 1995). Although most liver diseases in the elderly do not differ from those in the young, autoimmune liver diseases (e.g., primary biliary cirrhosis) and hepatocellular carcinoma occur primarily in older individuals.

The Gallbladder and Biliary Tract

Age-related physiological changes in the biliary tree include gradual narrowing of the distal common bile duct, increased incidence of periampullary diverticula, less responsive gallbladder contractions, and more lithogenic bile (due to increased secretion of cholesterol and reduced bile acid synthesis). Consequently, aging is associated with an increased incidence of gallstones, biliary tract disease, and cancer of the bile duct (Siegel & Kasmin, 1997).

The Pancreas

Age-related physiological changes in the pancreas include gradual reduction in pancreatic weight (accompanied by atrophy of the gland and symmetrical ductal dilatation) and an increased frequency of pancreatic duct stones. Subtle declines in exocrine functions with aging are not clinically significant (Cohen, 1996). There is no evidence that these modest changes in pancreatic functions predispose the elderly to the development of malabsorption. Clinically, aging is associated with an increased incidence of pancreatic malignancies.

The Gastrointestinal Epithelium and Carcinogenesis

Finally, the gastrointestinal tract is an epithelial organ with rapid cell turnover and proliferation. Data from animal and human studies have shown increased gastrointestinal mucosal proliferation, as well as impaired proliferative response (to injury or feeding), with aging (Holt, 1995; Lee & Feldman, 1997). This age-associated hyperproliferation in the gastrointestinal tract may contribute to an increase in the risk of tumor formation, as the incidence of various malignancies of the digestive tract increases with age.

Conclusion

Aging is associated with various physiological and structural changes in the digestive system. Due to the enormous reserve capacity that the gastrointestinal tract possesses, digestion and absorption are well preserved in the elderly. Certain gastrointestinal disorders, particularly malignancies, are more common among the elderly.

MAKAU LEE

See also
  Fecal and Urinary Incontinence
  Gastrointestinal System

GASTROINTESTINAL SYSTEM

Gastroenterology deals with disorders of the digestive system. The gastrointestinal tract retains, in general, normal physiological function during the aging process. There are differences, however, in structure and function of organs in the aged compared with younger people, with functioning being particularly affected by stress (for a general overview, see Evans & Williams, 1992, chapter 8; Hazzard, Bierman, Blass, Ettinger, & Halter, 1994, Section D). Also, the frequency of occurrence and manifestation of certain diseases may be different. These generalizations can be illustrated by common problems in the digestive system in late life.

Hiatal Hernia

The diaphragm is the partition between the chest and abdominal cavities. Its hiatus is an opening in it through which the esophagus passes. The esophagus is the tube through which food gets into the stomach. In a sliding hiatal hernia, some of the upper stomach slides through the hiatus into the chest cavity. This type of a hernia may be of no importance as such. It may cause no symptoms; however, it may be associated with reflux (back flow) of digestive juice from the stomach into the esophagus. This may cause esophagitis (inflammation of the esophagus), which may result in a stricture (narrowing of the esophagus), which may require dilatation. Reflux may occur in the absence of a hiatal hernia (Saead & Graham, 1994).

Peptic Ulcers

Ulcers may occur in the stomach (gastric ulcers) or in the duodenum (the first portion of the small intestine). Complications from ulcers, such as perforation or hemorrhage, are more common in older than in young people. Counteracting acid in the stomach is the aim of most medical treatment. Peptic ulcers have the tendency to recur after they have healed. A bacillus, *Helicobacter pylori,* almost always is present in patients with duodenal ulcers. Treating this infection reduces the recurrence rate. There is usually no need for an "ulcer diet" (Peura & Graham, 1994).

Appendicitis

Appendicitis is less common in the aged than in the younger population. The typical findings may not be present, and the condition advances more often to perforation.

Inflammatory Bowel Disease

Crohn's disease and ulcerative colitis are chronic conditions with periodic flare-ups. The onset is usually earlier in life, but they may be found in the aged. Most patients can be treated by medication (Choi & Targan, 1994; Hodgson, 1994), whereas some require surgery.

Colon

Diverticula of the colon are small pockets in the colon. A diverticulum may become inflamed, resulting in diverticulitis. Diverticula can also be the cause of extensive bleeding. In some instances, surgery may be necessary.

Polyps of the colon are growths that may be benign or malignant. Because benign polyps may become malignant, all polyps are typically removed. This can usually be achieved without abdominal operation through the colonoscope. All patients in whom polyps have been removed should be followed regularly.

Cancer of the colon is more common in older than in younger people. Unless cancer has spread or the surgical risk is too great, surgery will usually be attempted. Cure is possible.

Ischemic bowel disease refers to conditions of the intestines or colon brought about by impaired blood supply to these organs. This situation occurs primarily in the older patient. The patient may be suffering from excruciating abdominal pain with few findings on physical examination. Undiagnosed, this condition may be catastrophic.

Irritable Bowel Syndrome

As in the young patient, the irritable bowel syndrome will be encountered in the aged. Onset may occur where there is no evidence of structural change in the organs, but where patients may be uncomfortable (Tolliver, Jorge, Herrera, & DiPulma, 1994). The condition is not "imagined," and statements to the patient, such as "there is nothing wrong with you," will only add insult to injury. The condition is often stress related. Even when this syndrome may be troublesome, it is not usually life threatening. However, when an elderly patient develops the irritable bowel syndrome or sustained constipation, the first step to be taken is exclusion of serious physical disease, particularly cancer. One must remember that the elderly patient may be preoccupied with bowel function. When this is the case, a high-fiber diet, as well as bulk-producing medications, may be useful. Fluid intake may have to be increased.

Liver

Damage to the liver occurs in a variety of ways. Alcohol, drugs, as well as infections may damage the liver, and the list of toxic drugs is ever increasing. Viruses may cause hepatitis A, B, or C. Hepatitis A never develops into chronic hepatitis. Conversely, hepatic B and C are frequently causes of chronic hepatitis. In some of these patients treatment with the drug Interferon is useful (G. Davis, 1994). Chronic hepatitis B and C may go on to cirrhosis of the liver. The most common reason for cirrhosis of the liver, however, is an excessive consumption of alcohol. In the cirrhotic liver there are nodules and scar tissue. Complications of cirrhosis include ascites (fluid in the abdominal cavity), varices in the esophagus resulting from problems of circulation that can cause life-threatening hemorrhages, and encephalopathy in which patients may sink into a coma.

Primary cancer of the liver is not common in the Western world but is more common elsewhere. Cancer that has spread into the liver from other organs, however, is common.

Jaundice is caused by an excessive amount of bile pigment in the blood. This may be due to different mechanisms. Failing liver cells, as in cirrhosis or hepatitis, may cause jaundice. In contrast, "obstructive jaundice" may be due to stones in the common bile duct or pressure on this duct from the outside by a tumor. Obstructive jaundice resulting from malignancy is more common in the aged. Patients with obstructive jaundice frequently require surgery.

Some diseases of the liver may be successfully treated by liver transplant.

Gallbladder

Important problems with the gallbladder are cholelithiasis (gallstones) and inflammation of the gallbladder (cholecystitis). Gallstones may be "silent" (i.e., patients who carry them may have no symptoms). Patients who do not respond to medical treatment may need surgery.

Cholecystectomy (removal of the gallbladder) is the operation of choice that can now be done by laparoscopic techniques, without opening the abdomen. Initial evidence indicates that this results in a faster recovery than conventional surgery.

Pancreas

Among the diseases of the pancreas, pancreatitis and cancer of the pancreas are the most important ones. Pancreatitis occurs in both the aged and in the younger population (Banks, 1994). There are many causes of it, but the most prominent ones are alcohol abuse and gallstones. The presence of gallstones in patients who have pancreatitis is an indication for surgery, and the patient may be cured after cholecystectomy. Patients with pancreatitis caused by alcohol abuse who continue to drink have an elevated risk of chronic problems.

The incidence of cancer of the pancreas increases significantly with advancing age. The most common symptoms are pain and weight loss; at times mental depression is a prominent symptom.

Painless obstructive jaundice may be due to cancer of the pancreas. In the past it was difficult to make a definite objective diagnosis. With newer methods, a precise diagnosis is usually possible. The results of treatment, however, have remained poor even after surgery. Survival beyond 6 months is uncommon.

For further discussion, refer to Holt (1995).

HANS J. BRUNS

See also
Gastrointestinal Function

GENDER

Gender, a cultural construct, refers to the distinction of human characteristics and temperaments as masculine (appropriate to male behavior) or as feminine (appropriate to female behavior). It defines what it means in a particular culture to be and to act as a man or a woman, a boy or a girl. As such, it is perhaps the most central cultural institution in society and the most basic self-definition or identity learned within culture (Bem, 1999; Maccoby, 1990).

The construction of gender is framed by social institutions that allocate individuals from different biological sexes to different social roles that are generally of unequal status. Educational, workplace, and government institutions have conditioned the socialization of boys and girls, women and men, to lifetime role participation that has tended to segregate gender groups. Within the educational institution gender groups persistently differ in the rates at which they follow courses of study in the sciences and the arts, respectively. These differences are maintained in the workplace, where gender groups are occupationally segregated. In old age, differences are maintained by government-based beneficiary categories that are highly associated with gender (i.e., retired worker, dependent spouse, and widow). In effect, succeeding social roles over the life span are highly gendered and reinforce gender identities (O'Rand & Henretta, 1999).

The family institution, which is reinforced by education, workplace, and governmental institu-

tions, is perhaps the most powerful influence on gender identity and gender inequality. The traditional family form in Western societies is the "breadwinner" family predicated on the gender distinction between men as market workers and family heads and women as homeworkers and caregivers (Sainsbury, 1996). This family form is more prevalent in some societies (e.g., Germany) than in others (e.g., United States). Those countries where the breadwinner model persists are characterized by lower labor force participation among women and stronger welfare policies that support women in homemaker and caregiver roles. Countries where welfare policies are weaker are characterized by higher labor force participation among women but also by higher poverty rates among women than men across the life course (O'Rand & Henretta, 1999). The predominance of the market institution in societies like the United States offer women more employment opportunities outside the household, but also segregate women and reward them less for their market work. The consequence for older women in the United States is a higher risk for poverty and poorer health insurance (Smeeding, 1999).

In research on health and illness, a distinction is made between gender and sex in exploring male and female differences in health status. Gender denotes social components of maleness and femaleness that affect health status, such as educational, occupational, and economic opportunity. Sex, in contrast, denotes biological differences that appear to underlie distinctive male/female patterns of morbidity and mortality (Verbrugge & Jette, 1994). However, sex differences in illness and health are only now beginning to be understood in a rigorous sense, because gender biases have permeated health research until recently. These gender biases were reflected best in the exclusion of women as subjects in aging and geriatric research for many years. Not until the 1985 Report of the Public Health Service Task Force on Women's Health Issues was there an official recognition that research on women's health was sorely lacking. Then, it was not until the 1991 Women's Health Initiative that the National Institutes of Health clearly stipulated that women's health should receive equal emphasis.

In summary, gender is a central institution in societies that distinguishes women and men and influences personal development and well-being over the life course. The extent to which gender inequality persists is measurable in workplace wages, government pensions, health research dollars, and old age poverty and health support structures. Although gender is grounded in biological differences, social institutions contribute significantly to the shapes of men's and women's lives.

ANGELA M. O'RAND

See also

Self-Concept
Sex Differences in Health
Social Roles
Women: Changing Status

GENE EXPRESSION

Genes are composed of DNA (deoxyribonucleic acid), the basic hereditary molecule, which is made up of four bases: A, T, G, and C (adenine, thymidine, guanadine, and cytidine). The hereditary information in DNA is encoded in the sequences of DNA bases that code for polypeptides. Each gene generally codes for a single protein or a polypeptide sequence that has a given function. Proteins can function as structural elements of the body, such as collagen molecules, or can function as enzymes. The system of DNA decoding is based on the gene code. The four DNA bases, taken three at a time, code for 20 possible different amino acids. The decoding is accomplished by means of specific types of RNA (ribonucleic acid), known as messenger RNA (mRNA), and transfer RNA (tRNA). A gene sequence of the DNA is first transcribed to make a messenger RNA.

Genes are often broken into pieces of coding information separated by noncoding regions. The coding sequences are known as exons and the noncoding regions as introns. The noncoding introns of the mRNA transcript are removed by splicing. There are fewer bases in the coding sequence of the mRNA than in the original DNA. The encoded information from the mRNA is translated by means of tRNA into amino acid sequences. Each tRNA recognizes a given sequence of three RNA bases in the mRNA, which corresponds to the original DNA sequence of the gene. The tRNAs select spe-

cific amino acids from the 20 possible amino acids. The amino acids encoded by the DNA and attached to the tRNAs are joined together to make a polypeptide. The tRNAs perform this function while attached to the ribosome, essentially a workbench made up of structural ribosomal RNAs (rRNAs) and proteins. The classical rule is that one gene codes for one polypeptide chain. However, there are some exceptions to this rule. Occasionally two different DNA sequences can be joined together to make recombined sequences. This is the case with regard to the generation of antibodies. Likewise, one gene can code for several different proteins, depending on the way it is spliced and decoded.

Gene expression is regulated. The nature of gene regulation is not well understood, but certain conclusions have been deduced. Frequently upstream from the coding DNA sequence in a gene are regions involved in regulation of gene expression. The DNA sequence TAT is one such region, which appears to be essential for the initiation of transcription of DNA to mRNA. Gene regulation is most commonly determined by gene control regions that lie upstream of the gene-coding sequences. This region, commonly referred to as a promotor, has special sequences that bind specific proteins known as transcription factors. Such factors make the gene more accessible to transcription by RNA polymerases. The promotor sequences, which differ from gene to gene, influence or enhance the rate at which transcription occurs. A second level of regulation appears to involve chromatin structure. The genes that are not actively being expressed are often tightly wound around protein complexes called nucleosomes. They are then wound into primary, secondary, and tertiary coils, thus producing a compact structure of inactive genetic material. In humans, the total number of genes has been estimated to be approximately 80,000 (McKusick, 1998). In any specialized tissue, the process of differentiation and the mechanisms regulating gene expression produce a situation where only a few thousand genes are likely to be expressed.

Developments in genetic technology have produced DNA chips that allow for the simultaneous analysis of the level of gene expression for thousands of genes (Gerhold, Rushmore, & Caskey, 1999). These chips hold the promise of being able to analyze gene expression changes during aging for the first time at the whole genome level. For example, a preliminary comparison of the levels of mRNA expression for some 6,000 known genes in actively dividing fibroblast cells from young, middle-aged, old, and progeric individuals revealed that approximately 1% of genes, primarily those involved with mitotic regulation and with extracellular matrix remodeling, show dramatic changes in their levels of expression with aging (Ly, Lockhart, Lerner, & Schultz, 2000). Such investigation should be able to help to elucidate age-related changes in gene regulatory functions of the whole organism.

W. TED BROWN

See also
Genetic Heterogeneity
Genetic Programming Theories
Progeroid Syndromes
Somatic Mutations and Genome Instability

GENERATIONAL EQUITY

The concept of generational equity refers to fairness in the distribution of resources and obligations across age groups and generations. Since the late 1970s, some business leaders, politicians, and activists in the United States have argued that the current public benefit system is too generous to the elderly at the expense of the young and future generations. In the late 1990s, the debate over fairness between the generations narrowly focused on entitlement programs that benefit the old because of the proportion of federal budget outlays that entitlements consume and concerns about the sustainability of future benefit payout obligations the programs require.

The concept of generational equity first came to the attention of policy makers and the public because of the changing demographic profile of our aging population and the consequent catastrophic financial burdens some advocates of generational equity forecast for the future. An increasing aged dependency ratio, reduced national and personal savings, and increasing federal debt and government spending on entitlement programs all helped to bolster the claims that not only was the government spending too much on an aged population, but that this spending was not sustainable and would hurt the ability of the government to assist

other needy and deserving groups in the future. The appeal of this argument has been increased by the proliferation of media images of "greedy geezers" and "golf-cart grannies" enjoying their later years in sun-drenched retirement destinations with plenty of disposable income. The reality of the diversity of economic well-being within the older population was, and has been, largely ignored in the generational equity debate so far. Most recently, the dramatically high returns on Wall Street have led some advocates of generational equity to claim that younger generations will only get their money's worth out of programs such as Social Security if the financing mechanisms of the program are altered to benefit future generations (i.e., privatization of the system). This generational equity concern was discussed in the final report of the 1994–1996 Advisory Council on Social Security (1997).

The generational equity debate has changed since its inception. What was originally viewed as a call for fairness and warnings about generational warfare if policy changes did not occur has largely been discredited as a political tactic of groups such as Americans for Generational Equity (now defunct), the Concord Coalition, and Third Millennium that have the overall goals of reducing the national debt and government spending, rather than increasing spending on children (Marmor, Cook, & Scher, 1997). Third Millennium, in particular, has made moralistic appeals for generational fairness in promoting its policy agenda (Ekerdt, 1998). The larger impact of the generational equity debate, however, has been to change the very standards against which policies are judged (Quadagno, 1996). Moreover, it has been argued that the rhetoric of generational equity, fueled by news media coverage of the "conflict," has undermined public confidence in programs such as Social Security, particularly among the young (Ekerdt, 1998; Marmor et al., 1997).

Although generational equity is largely an American phenomenon and the forecasts of generational warfare have not materialized, there are concerns that such generational conflict is bubbling to the surface at the local level of government and in states with high numbers of retirees who are newly immigrated to the state and feel few connections to the state and their new communities. There is some evidence that in local matters, the elderly have been less likely to support school bond measures and that the elderly prefer municipalities with favorable tax breaks on housing and other amenities (Button, 1992). Older age groups have been shown to be less supportive of government spending on child care, AIDS research, and the environment (Rhodebeck, 1998). Research shows that the elderly are not voting against measures that favor children, but rather support less spending in general, even on themselves (Rhodebeck, 1998). The large (and growing) voting block that the elderly represent makes some advocates of generational equity and children's issues question the future influence that the elderly may have on local and state matters affecting the young.

Advocates for the elderly, gerontologists, and even some children's groups who disapprove of the generational equity movement's tactics, have tried several approaches to combat the claims of generational unfairness in the distribution of public resources. First, they have tried to better define the issues, separating rhetoric from reality in policy and financing discussions. Second, they have critiqued and offered alternative methods of analysis and interpretation of the data used in the political arguments of groups such as Third Millennium. Third, intergenerational coalitions and programs have been promoted, including more focus on the intergenerational aspects of existing programs and policies. For example, the 1995 White House Conference on Aging focused on the intergenerational stake people have in programs such as Social Security and Medicare, the 1999 United Nations' Year of the Older Person had an intergenerational theme, and organizations such as the American Association of Retired Persons have disseminated numerous studies illustrating the groups other than the elderly who benefit from entitlement programs.

It is probable that the future will hold more debate on the generational fairness of existing and proposed policies, but the forecasts of generational combat seem unlikely to be realized. As a political tactic, however, generational equity arguments are here to stay.

TONYA M. PARROTT

See also
    Entitlement
    Family
    Generations

    Generativity
    Grandparent-Grandchild Relationships

GENERATIONS

Generations define a discontinuity of the passage of time in the lives of a social collectivity; discontinuity implies conversely an identity running through the course of generations, within which the discontinuity occurs. Generations have three meanings depending on the meaning of the identity as well as the nature of the discontinuity: (1) Biological generations, which show a sequence of organisms deriving from a common ancestor; the identity here is genetic, and the discontinuity is defined by the genetic change between the succeeding organisms. (2) Macrosocial generations, which show a succession of different individuals in the society. Here the identity is provided by the bounds of the society, while the discontinuity is defined in various ways—either by schematic division of time, which gives generation the same meaning as cohort, by the common experience of some major events, or by the presence of outstanding individuals, which gives a special meaning to a certain cohort. (3) Familial or lineage generations, where the identity is given by the social meaning of lineage and the discontinuities arise through the special relations such as obligations, rights, conflicts, or influence between generations in the sense of biological generations. Studies of generations have differed in the emphasis given to each of these three meanings.

1.   Biological generations form the basic model and remain the underlying metaphor for the other two types of generations. Genetically there is a sense of identity between an organism and its offspring, and this identity is captured by a common term such as strain or lineage. Concurrently one recognizes the stepwise change from generation to generation. This tension of an acknowledged identity with a perceived difference of independent units, occurring through time, forms the model of the sequence, continuity, and conflict of generations.

2.   By contrast, in looking at human societies as large units, one does not assert biological relationships but only the stepwise sequences, roughly

corresponding to length of human biological generations (about 30 years). Traditional mythologies (e.g., Greek or Hebrew) stress this analogy by presenting actual biological generations through personified sequences of heroes or kings. By analogous reasoning, modern writers who reintroduced the concept of generations into the study of social events identify generations with important events or important individuals (Mannheim, 1952; C. W. Roberts & Lang, 1985). In this identification the generation is separated from the continuous process of succession of births and is saved from the arbitrariness of defining cohorts of yearly, 5-yearly, or other divisions. However, in this way generation is tied to age and not genetic relationship.

3. The importance of lineage in generations lies in two facts: One is that here we have a mechanism of transmission within society and the other is that it may account for variation within the larger society, preserving peculiarities in these smaller familial or lineage subsections. Studies of generations in this sense have been able to show relationships of interaction, of responsibility, and of help that have identified the network relations within a family and between generations (Hill, Foote, Aldous, Carlson, & MacDonald, 1970). They also show transmission of values within a family (Bengston, Cutler, Mangen, & Marshall, 1985). The role of generations here shows definite breaks that seem large between two subsequent generations but frequently are small in comparison with the values transmitted in other families. New generations find their own independence in conflict with older generations, but this conflict is still played out within the context of the particular lineage.

Discussion in this field has concentrated on the relations among the three types of generational succession; problems that have come to the fore have included the importance of the genetic succession in human social life. Here most arguments have been on the side of downplaying genetic as against biological factors, partly because of the political implications of a genetic argument. However, the recent rise of sociobiology has encouraged this model. A much-discussed question has been the relation of the familial model to the general macrosocial model. In common with other developments in modern society, the importance of mutual obligations between generations within the lineage weakens, and transfer payment between generational groups in the larger society is substituted for responsibility within the lineage. This development has led to assumptions that the role generations play within the family has become negligible; however, it may be that other functions of transmission within the lineage, such as that of attitudes, values, and traditions have remained. As in other concerns of the family, the decline of economic importance (and its assumption by other social institutions) has been accompanied by an increase in the interpersonal and psychological importance of the lineage and of specific generations within the family.

KURT W. BACK

See also
  Cohorts

GENERATIVITY

In his psychosocial theory of development over the life course, Erikson (1963) described a series of eight crisis stages in personality growth, of which generativity vs. stagnation was the seventh. Although issues pertaining to this stage can arise at any point in the life course, this psychosocial stage most typically arises in the middle adult years and beyond. The polarity implied in this, and all other, stage descriptions reflects Erikson's definition of psychosocial crisis stages in terms of pairs of bipolar opposites. Each pair describes the most favorable and the least favorable resolution of the crisis that can occur after the individual passes through the stage. The individual's ability to achieve a favorable resolution of a stage depends in part on the particular combination of biological, psychological, and social forces that operate at the time of the stage's ascendancy, and in part on how well prior crisis stages have been resolved. The assumption that each psychosocial crisis is associated with a particular point in the life course is based on the likelihood that individuals experience heightened vulnerability to the issues represented by that psychosocial stage due to their maturational levels.

As the favorable end of the continuum proposed by Erikson for the seventh psychosocial stage, generativity represents the component of the individual's personality that develops to incorporate concern beyond the self to the needs, interests, and well-being of future generations. The unfavorable resolution represented by stagnation involves a selfish interest in oneself to the exclusion of others who may follow. Although generativity is most commonly thought of in terms of commitment to parenting and providing for one's own children, there are many ways in which generativity may be expressed in the middle and later years of adulthood. Involvement in occupation is one form of generativity, particularly when this involvement is intended to help future generations through mentoring activities. Efforts to improve the quality of the physical environment, the political climate, or social welfare may be seen as expressions of generativity. Creative endeavors in which the individual leaves something behind for the benefit of future generations may also be seen as forms of generativity.

Erikson regarded the stage of generativity versus stagnation, along with the other adult stages of intimacy versus isolation and ego integrity versus despair, as resulting in the development of new qualities of the ego. In the case of generativity, this quality is care. This view has been challenged in the proposal that it is the self or identity that remains at the core of psychosocial development throughout adulthood. The stage of generativity versus stagnation would be seen, according to this view, as a "developmental task" (Havighurst, 1972). It is theoretically more appropriate to view the adult Eriksonian stages as demands that must be confronted as individuals grow older rather than as stages that present the possibility of fundamental alterations in the ego (Vaillant, 1993; Whitbourne & Connolly, 1999).

The extent to which the concept of generativity has been subjected to empirical test is limited when considered narrowly within the context of Erikson's theory. In part, lack of specific data on generativity is due to the vagueness of Erikson's definition, who gave few operationalizable criteria that could be used to develop methodologically sound indices or scales (Erikson & Erikson, 1981). One generativity scale devised using an extension of a questionnaire format designed to measure the first six Eriksonian stages (Constantinople, 1969) has proved to have a positive relationship to well-being and adjustment in older adults (Walaskay, Whitbourne, & Nehrke,

1983–1984). A large longitudinal sequences study using this measure on a sample ranging from college age to middle adulthood yielded age differences favoring the adult samples (Whitbourne, Zuschlag, Elliot, & Waterman, 1992). Moreover, changes in psychosocial development in related areas of identity and intimacy were found to be related in predicted ways to life events in adulthood in the areas of marital and career involvement (Van Manen & Whitbourne, 1997).

Further support based on empirical measures of generativity comes from a series of longitudinal studies conducted by Vaillant (Vaillant, 1993). Based on this research, Vaillant concluded that the stage of generativity versus stagnation is composed of two substages, one concerned with the individual's own career, labeled "career consolidation versus self-absorption," and one concerned with caring and commitment to one's entire community or culture.

Another line of investigation is based on longitudinal studies of several samples of college-educated women in midlife, including those in Helson's investigation of personality from college through middle adulthood (Helson & Moane, 1987; Helson & Wink, 1992). Although in both studies there was evidence for considerable personality stability, there were longitudinal increases for variables that might be theorized to show increases in adulthood based on Erikson's concept of generativity. These include personality attributes such as assurance, independence, and self-control, which can be regarded as indicative of an overall growth of the ego's ability to control and regulate behavior. Furthermore, certain variables measured in college, such as "psychological mindedness," were predictive of higher ego development at age 43 (Helson & Roberts, 1994). Identity also seems to play a role in influencing personality change in women in midlife. Women higher in identity at age 43 were more likely to have achieved higher levels of generativity at age 48, in part through the influence of identity on involvement in multiple social roles (Vandewater, Ostrove, & Stewart, 1997). Moreover, women who score high on generativity were more likely to be interested in political activities and social movements (Peterson & Stewart, 1996), indicating, as in Vaillant's terms, that they were in some ways carrying out the role of "keepers of the meaning."

If generativity is more broadly conceived in terms of the involvement of adults in occupational pursuits and parenting, the amount of evidence bearing on the concept is far more extensive. Work involvement forms an important route for the expression of generativity in middle-aged adults up through the time of retirement (Parnes & Sommers, 1994). Although not all older workers retain a sense of intrinsic or inner satisfaction with their jobs, they do maintain a high level of commitment to the organization (Mathieu & Dennis, 1990). On the negative side, older workers may begin to disengage mentally when they feel that they are subject to age stereotypes, pressures to retire, and the message that their skills are becoming obsolete (Lease, 1998; Warr, 1994).

In the area of family life, it is well established that by the time individuals reach middle age and beyond, involvement in the parental role is associated with overall feelings of life satisfaction and well-being (Brubaker, 1990). Mothers are especially likely to remain involved with their adult children, but parents of both genders maintain interest and involvement, even after children have left the home. According to the concept of developmental stake, parents maintain a psychological investment in their children, more so than children do in their parents (Bengston & Kuypers, 1971). However, the existence of these strong feelings directed toward children may have unintended negative consequences. A developmental schism may occur, in which an emotional gap is created between parents and their children, due to a discontinuity between generations that reflects their differing emotional concerns (Fingerman, 1996). Tension or divisions between parents and children may also arise from a related phenomenon, the tendency of parents to see their grown children as reflections of the quality of their parenting. According to Ryff and colleagues (Ryff, Lee, Essex, & Schmutte, 1994), parents regard the accomplishments of their children as an indication of the quality of parenting they provided. On the positive side, the ability to have produced a successful child may enhance the parent's feeling of being competent in this very crucial life role and hence become a step toward building a sense of generativity.

These examples from the literature on work and parenting suggest that generativity is an important route toward positive adaptation in the middle years and beyond. Moreover, the development of a sense of generativity may be strongly related to other changes in personality and the self involving altruism (Blanchard-Fields & Irion, 1988; Midlarsky & Hannah, 1989), maturity of defense mechanisms situations (Diehl, Coyle, & Labouvie-Vief, 1996), and the ability to cope flexibly with life stresses (Brandstaedter, Rothermund, & Schmitz, 1997). Constructs such as role involvement and satisfaction, personality, identity, and coping lend themselves more readily to empirical investigation than the more generic and perhaps elusive notion of generativity. Despite these challenges to the study of generativity, the concept remains a useful one for heuristic purposes and as a stimulus to further inquiry regarding the notion of change during the middle and later years of adulthood.

SUSAN KRAUSS WHITBOURNE

See also
Adaptation
Personality

GENETIC HETEROGENEITY

The concept of genetic heterogeneity is of central importance in understanding genetics, genetic differences in aging patterns, and genetic theories of aging. Frequently, mutations in different genes can produce similar appearing conditions, a situation known as *genetic heterogeneity*. When a given genetic disease is investigated, it is common to find that what initially looked like a single disease is in fact two or more slightly different genetic diseases (McKusick, 1998). These may resemble each other in many or most ways but have basic differences at the gene level. Also, similar disorders can he caused by differences that occur within the same gene. They are termed *alleles* and usually have identical modes of inheritance (i.e., dominant, codominant, recessive, or X-linked). Different alleles at a given locus may also produce altered susceptibility to aging-associated diseases. A good example is the increased susceptibility to developing Alzheimer's disease in individuals who carry allele 4 for the apolipoprotein E (McKusick, 1998). Genetic heterogeneity may also be caused by mutations that occur at different genetic loci and that may lead to quite different modes of inheritance. There are a number of methods for demonstrating genetic heterogeneity in humans, including the following.

Differing Inheritance Modes. If it can be shown that a disease may be inherited in two or three different modes, then this is proof that different mutations can cause the same apparent disease. For example, Ehlers-Danlos syndrome is a common connective tissue disorder in which extremely loose joints are present. This syndrome shows different modes of inheritance in different families, including dominant, recessive, and X-linked, which indicates at least three different genetic loci are involved.

Nonallelism of Recessives. In some diseases it is possible to show by mating studies that there are different mutations involved. For example, if two persons with albinism marry, the expected result is for them to have all albino offspring. However, it is commonly observed that none of the children of two albino parents is albino. This implies different genetic mutations underlying the albino locus in both parents.

Linkage Relationships. Another genetic method for demonstrating heterogeneity is with differing linkage relationships. For example, familial Alzheimer's disease has been linked in different families to locations on more than three different chromosomes.

Phenotypic Analysis. Phenotype is the physical expression of a gene. Some diseases, such as the mucopolysaccharidoses, which were previously lumped together and called gargoylism, have now been phenotypically distinguished. Different degrees of corneal cataracts or clouding are found in the different forms.

Biochemical Analysis. Biochemical differences can be used to demonstrate genetic heterogeneity. For example, different types of hereditary hemolytic anemias are due to the deficiencies of different enzymes involved in red blood cell metabolism.

Physiological Analysis. Genetic heterogeneity can sometimes be defined by physiological studies. For example, different types of hemophilia (A and B) can be shown to correct each other when a cross-

transfusion is given, thus indicating that differing clotting deficiencies exist.

Cell Culture Studies. Genetic heterogeneity can sometimes be defined by cell culture mixing studies. For example, genetic diseases in which there is an accumulation of abnormal substances, such as the mucopolysaccharidoses, can sometimes be corrected by coculture of cells from one individual to those of another individual. Thus, each cell supplies a missing enzyme that the other cell is lacking, showing cross-correction and the genetic heterogeneity that exists in this group of conditions.

Somatic Cell Genetics. Cell hybridization studies have allowed recognition that distinct forms of DNA repair exist in the group of conditions known as Xeroderma pigmentosum (XP) and Cockayne syndrome (CS). When cells from two individuals with different types of XP or CS are fused together, defects in DNA repair disappear if genetic heterogeneity is present. This has allowed seven DNA repair complementation groups to be defined in XP and three in CS.

Molecular Genetic Analysis. Defining different alleles at the molecular level is the most basic way to define genetic heterogeneity. For example, the various forms of beta-thalassemia can be shown to result from different specific molecular defects by molecular techniques involving restriction-enzyme mapping or direct sequencing of the underlying mutations.

These various analytic methods may be used to elucidate genetic differences in aging rates of different individuals and species, as well as susceptibility to aging-associated diseases, both at the cellular and the organismic level.

W. TED BROWN

See also
   Gene Expression
   Genetic Programming Theories
   Progeroid Syndromes

GENETIC PROGRAMMING THEORIES

Genetic programming theories of aging emphasize that aging is part of a programmed process that is genetically determined. These theories are in contrast to those that emphasize wear-and-tear mechanisms and environmentally determined mechanisms. Most evolutionary biologists currently believe that senescence is a by-product of natural selection.

It is apparent from looking at the wide range of the maximal potential life spans (MPLs) of various animals that the species MPL is in large part genetically determined (Brown, 1992). Mice have a genetically determined maximum potential life span of no more than about 3 years; for humans it is estimated to be about 120 years. These differences are determined by the hereditary blueprint encoded in DNA.

A number of possible genetic mechanisms have been proposed that might contribute to or account for the underlying genetic component to the aging process. The genetic program that encodes the process of aging may regulate the onset of senescence. Program theories of aging often suggest that the features of senescence are the result of a clock mechanism. For example, with age the brain may regulate the production of certain hormones necessary for the maintenance of the youthful vigor of cells and tissues throughout the body. This may be the case in regard to female reproductive aging, which may be under the control of higher brain centers regulating the release of neuroendocrine factors (Finch, 1976). Individual cells within the brain might thus determine the life span of the entire organism. These individual cells may have a finite life span as well. It has been suggested that cells have an internal clock mechanism, which may be genetically determined and which regulates their individual life spans. The average number of cell divisions of cultured cells is on the order of 50 to 100 generations (Hayflick, 1974).

One theory of aging holds that events occur that are genetically programmed to cause the death of the organism. For example, a death hormone might be released with increasing concentrations during aging and turn off the body's metabolic processes. A decreasing ability to respond to thyroid hormone due to the brain's increasing release of an inhibitor has been postulated (Denckla, 1974). Some animal species, such as the Pacific salmon, do undergo a rapid senescence because of a programmed event. The salmon ages rapidly during the period of time it swims upstream to lay eggs because of a massive release of corticosteroid hormones. Aging in humans could be a reflection of a less drastic and more gradual imbalance of hormones.

A gradual decrease in the release of growth factors needed to maintain full vigor may be due to an underlying genetic program. Programming does occur with maturation in many body systems. In the immune system there are progressive shifts in the activation of genes, which occur with maturation from embryonic to more mature forms. Similar mechanisms occurring at other gene loci could lead to shifts and alterations in gene expression. Gene expression could also be genetically regulated in part by the composition of the extracellular matrix. The makeup of the matrix could be programmed to change significantly during aging.

Martin (1980) suggested that theories of aging that involve an alteration of the genome (i.e., genotropic theories of aging) might be classified into two categories: those that involve modifications in gene structure and those that emphasize modifications in gene expression. In the first class are theories that involve intrinsic mutagenesis, protein error catastrophe, free radical and cross-linking, autoimmunity, and slow viruses causing mutation. In the second category are theories involving neuroendocrine clocks, progressive transcriptional repression, isoenzyme shifts, allelic exclusion, codon restriction, posttranslational protein modifications, altered protein turnover, terminal differentiation, autoimmunity, and depression.

Roses (1991) has pointed out that there are likely to be two different population genetic mechanisms involved with the evolution of aging. The first is antagonistic pleiotrophy, in which alleles (a gene with different genetic varieties) that have beneficial effects at early ages have antagonistic, deleterious effects at later ages. The second is age specificity of gene action, in which alleles with deleterious effects at later ages are essentially neutral at earlier ages and have weak selection at later ages because of the declining force of selection with age.

In summary, genetic programming theories of aging are derived from the observations that species' maximum life span potential appears to be genetically determined. This suggests that development and aging may be under the control of an innate genetic program. However, evolutionary perspectives on aging suggest that constraints may be placed on the programming as the force of natural selection falls off rapidly in the postreproductive age for members of a species. A variety of specific programmed mechanisms have been proposed for consideration, but conclusive proof is lacking for any of them.

W. TED BROWN

See also

Chronobiology: Rhythms, Clocks, Chaos, Aging, and Other Trends
Gene Expression
Genetic Heterogeneity

GENITOURINARY SYSTEM

The medicine of the genitourinary system of old age is dominated by seven problems: renal failure, urinary tract infection, bladder cancer, carcinoma of the prostate, benign prostatic enlargement, bladder storage dysfunction, and urethral sphincter failure.

Renal Failure

There is an age-related reduction of renal function, with a loss of 50% of the glomerular filtration rate between the ages of 30 and 90. Renal blood flow reduces, and the tubules become less effective at handling acid-base balance and in maintaining normal water and electrolyte homeostasis.

Chronic renal failure is most frequently seen in the elderly, and the diseases that lead to renal failure are commoner in the elderly. Financial restraints have prompted the use of age-related criteria for exclusion from dialysis and transplantation. Nowadays the ethics of treatment decisions based on age are being openly discussed, so in the future we are likely to develop a better understanding of the management of renal failure in late life. Not all elderly people in renal failure will prove suitable for dialysis, particularly if affected by serious brain disease. It is our hope that the study of biological aging, ethics, and health economics will lead to better criteria, other than chronological age, for deciding on treatment.

The common causes of renal failure in the elderly include the effects of diabetes, urinary outflow obstruction, atherosclerosis, and the use of nephrotoxic drugs. In each case, the course of these diseases could be altered by early intervention. Proper control of diabetes and the meticulous control of hypertension in diabetics slow the development of diabetic nephropathy. The identification of urinary outflow obstruction and its treatment can relieve the kidneys. Avoidance of smoking and control of hypertension may slow the progress of arterial atheroma. Of the nephrotoxic drugs, nonsteroidal anti-inflammatory drugs (NSAIDs), used to treat the ubiquitous arthritis of late life, are the commonest cause of renal damage, especially when combined with angiotensin converting enzyme (ACE) used to treat hypertension or heart failure.

The effect of age-related decline in renal function is seen most significantly in the failure to excrete drugs effectively, resulting in increased toxicity and poisoning. The drugs causing the most problems to the elderly, because of reduced renal excretion, are digoxin, aminoglycoside antibiotics, NSAIDs, the oral antidiabetic drug chlorpropamide, sedatives, tricyclic antidepressants, and lithium. The other consequences of renal impairment include reduced ability to cope with the physiological stresses associated with intercurrent illness, particularly dehydration (Macias-Nunez & Cameron, 1992).

Urinary Tract Infection

Urinary tract infection is much more common in the elderly. At least 20% of women and 10% of men over age 65 have bacteriuria (bacteria in the urine) (Baldassarre & Kay, 1991). In elderly women reduction in circulating estrogen levels after menopause is associated with a fall in the levels of intravaginal glycogen, on which the normal flora of lactobacilli depend. These bacteria cease to colonize the vagina, which is then occupied by colonic organisms that thrive in the lower pH associated with this change. The atrophy of the urethelium encourages colonization by gram-negative fecal organisms, and the urethelium becomes more adherent for these bacteria. There is some slim evidence that estrogen replacement therapy may reverse this process and give protection to elderly women with recurrent urinary tract infections (van der Linden, Gerretsen, Brandhourst, Ooms, Kremer, & Doesburg, 1993).

In the majority of circumstances, bacteriuria does not cause symptoms, and nothing should be done about it. Higher mortality and morbidity have been associated with bacteriuria in the elderly, but this may be only a reflection of susceptibility because there are no data indicating that treating asymptomatic bacteriuria influences mortality or morbidity.

When assessing a symptomatic urinary tract infection, causing acute dysuria, frequency, and urgency, analysis of the urine should include the use of sticks that test for nitrite and leukocyte esterase because positive responses to these confirm an infection. The test sticks are less expensive than microscopy and are a good means of screening. It is possible to have a urinary infection without proteinuria. Fifteen percent of patients with acute cystitis have hematuria. In the presence of genuine urinary infection, the chances of growing a bacterium are just over 50%, so a urine culture should not be used as a diagnostic test but primarily as a sensitivity test for use on failed therapy (Stamm, 1988).

Bladder Cancer

Bladder cancer has an increased incidence in the elderly, especially men. Other risk factors are smoking and a history of employment in the chemical industry. Nearly 80% of bladder cancers are low-grade and noninvasive, with an 85% 5-year survival following complete transurethral resection. However, it is unfortunate that 80% of invasive cancers are only found at the first cystoscopic examination. Invasive tumors have a very poor prognosis. An effective program of early detection, surgery, and follow-up cystoscopies is therefore essential. The presenting sign of bladder cancer is hematuria, which may be detected by dipstick testing of the urine. A positive test should prompt a microscopic examination of the urinary sediment so as to confirm the presence of significant hematuria. If blood cells are found, then a search for cancer should be instituted, using urine cytology, urinary tract ultrasound, and cystoscopy. All too often hematuria is not properly investigated, with tragic results (R. D. Williams, 1992).

Prostatic Cancer

After cancer of the lung and skin, prostate cancer is the most common and causes cancer death only less often than those of the lung and colon. It is very rarely seen before the age of 50, but then its incidence climbs with age. Between 50% and 60% of men age 85 and older are found to have a prostatic cancer at autopsy, but in most circumstances these have not contributed to death. It has been proposed that radical prostatectomy should be used to treat prostatic cancer. However, there are no data from randomized controlled trials that would support this view. The case has not been proved and should be examined because radical prostatectomy causes impotence in 75% of patients and incontinence in about 10%.

There is considerable interest in screening programs for prostatic cancer. However, there are doubts about the effectiveness of the tools. Digital rectal examination is probably too insensitive. Measurement of the protein prostate-specific antigen (PSA) is difficult to interpret because it may be detected in men with benign prostatic hypertrophy and even in those with normal prostates. The levels of the antigen measured do relate to the evolution of prostatic cancer, but the overlap between different clinical states makes the test difficult to use as a reasonable screening measure. Ultrasound examination of the prostate is more sensitive than digital examination but less sensitive than PSA. It is difficult to see the justification for the widespread use of such fallible screening tools when the results of radical surgery are improperly evaluated (Harwood, 1994).

Benign Prostatic Hypertrophy

Benign prostatic enlargement affects all men, developing after the age of 40. Ten percent of men will require treatment for the symptoms of frequency, nocturia, hesitancy, a reduced stream, terminal dribbling, postmicturition dribbling, straining to void, and incontinence. The most important point is that it can lead to renal failure. Probably the most common treatment used is a transurethral resection of the prostate gland. Various other techniques, such as the use of heating, freezing, and laser, have been found to be inferior to surgical resection. The drugs for the prostate, alpha blockers and the antiandrogenic 5-alpha reductase inhibitors, have been shown to have marginal benefit.

Bladder Storage Dysfunction

In the United Kingdom the prevalence of urinary incontinence increases from 2% in men and 9% in women age 15 to 64 to 7% of men and 12% of women age 65 and older (Thomas, Flymat, Blannin, & Meade, 1980).

Between 75% and 85% of women age 75 and older and 85% and 95% of similarly aged men with lower urinary tract symptoms will be found to have detrusor instability, an overactivity of the bladder muscle, causing frequency, urgency, and urge incontinence. Detrusor instability in both sexes is associated with lower bladder capacities in the elderly. It has also been found that the appreciation of bladder filling is reduced in association with age in women, particularly in those with instability.

Detrusor instability may be treated with antimuscarinic drugs and with a bladder retraining regime. Clinical trials have shown antimuscarinics to be effective in treating detrusor instability in the ambulant elderly but not in the chronically disabled elderly in long-term institutions.

Both sexes void less successfully in late life, and a higher proportion of patients have incomplete bladder emptying. The explanations for this are probably complex. Obstruction will play a part in men. There is evidence of a failure of detrusor function as well as problems in sustaining adequate voiding contractions (Malone-Lee, 1992).

Urethral Sphincter Failure

Elderly women experience a reduction in urethral sphincter function. Multiple childbirth will increase the likelihood of occurrence. Sphincter incompetence leads to stress incontinence, which is experienced on coughing, sneezing, and laughing. Pelvic-floor exercises are a popular means of offering nonsurgical therapy to patients with urethral sphinc-ter incompetence (Fantl, 1989). The evidence for their efficacy is far from established, and they are inferior to surgery. The most widely accepted surgical approach is the colposuspension, which seems to achieve the most consistent successes across a wide variety of centers (Varner & Sparks, 1991).

JAMES MALONE-LEE

See also
  Fecal and Urinary Incontinence
  Female Reproductive System
  Kidney and Urinary System
  Prostatic Hyperplasia
  Sexuality

GEOGRAPHIC MOBILITY

The geographic mobility of retirement-aged people is a rapidly growing topic of research. Demography, geography, and gerontology are the primary disciplines from which this literature has arisen. It is of growing interest because of its relationship to the practical concerns for planning and policy, as well as economic development. Most migration studies use census data; some use local surveys.

Overall residential mobility among older persons is slowing. Evidence from the 1990 census indicates that about three quarters of all persons age 60 and older have not moved recently. This slowdown is accounted for primarily by the decline in local movement within an individual's home county. Longer-distance moves, however, are holding steady. All recent migrants (i.e., within the past 5 years) across county or state lines now make up about 10% of the older population. About half are interstate migrants.

With a few state exceptions, however, the actual geographical distribution of the older population is due more to uneven aging in place than to migration (Bean, Myers, Angel, & Galle, 1994). Areas where baby boomers moved to work, for example, will generate a bumper crop of retirees in the future (Frey, 1995).

Local movers characteristically have become progressively older and more dependent, as a whole, since 1960. Migrants are an advantaged group, by comparison, both economically and socially; and the gap is widening, especially among interstate migrants.

The streams between noncontiguous states went disproportionately to a relatively small number of receiving states: Florida, California, Arizona, Texas, and North Carolina, primarily. The pattern of these streams changed between 1970 and 1990, but Florida has maintained its one-quarter share, within a point or two, of all interstate in-migrants for four census decades. California, however, is declining as a leading destination for older migrants, and Arizona is now competing for the second slot. North Carolina, the fifth-ranked state, is growing rapidly as a migration destination. Texas, an important and growing regional destination, ranks fourth in attracting migrants, whereas other regional destinations, such as sixth-ranked Pennsylvania and seventh-ranked New Jersey, are on the decline (Longino, 1995). A very slight decline in the national share of migrants received by Florida, Arizona, and Texas in 1990 stirred some interest among observers.

The characteristics of migrants in the major state-to-state streams remained highly stable between 1970 and 1980. The small changes included a general upgrading of economic characteristics of migrants into Florida and Arizona and at a somewhat lower level into most of the regional destinations, especially Arkansas. The selectivity patterns were not positive in California and were mixed in New Jersey. The Sunbelt, as a region, therefore, seems to benefit most from these trends. The picture of stability continues in 1990 (Longino, 1995).

Counterstream migration is now clearly documented. Streams from Florida to its major sending states, although small by comparison, contain higher proportions of economically and residentially dependent migrants than the larger streams entering Florida. The reverse is true for California and its exchange partners. Slowly changing cycles of rising and declining attractiveness of particular states may affect the types of older migrants they send and receive (Longino, 1995).

Serow (1978) reported that migration to one's state of birth is not higher among older migrants than others; about one fifth of observed migration is in this direction. Longino (1979) added that one third of older interstate migrants, excluding those

moving out of their home state, were returning home. Rogers (1990) concluded that return migration rates change and differ from place to place because they are so dependent on how many persons were born and moved from their native states many decades earlier. Return migration is strongest in the South (Longino, 1995) because it has experienced the greatest long-term interregional labor force out-migration. Part of the return migration phenomenon derives from the return to racial and ethnic enclaves in retirement (Angel & Angel, 1992).

The dialogue among researchers concerning whether seasonal migration is part of a process leading to permanent migration has concluded that seasonal migration generates its own lifestyle and culture, different from that of permanent migrants but equally valuable in its own right (McHugh & Mings, 1996). Once having adopted the lifestyle, seasonal migration is likely to last for several years, finally interrupted and reluctantly terminated by a fluctuation or decrease in necessary resources. The small minority who settle down and stay tend to have strong person and place ties to the host community.

Interstate migration is expected to increase through the 2030s because of the socioeconomic upgrading of the older population and the retirement of baby boomers (Longino, 1998). World War II veterans, more likely to make long-distance moves than nonveterans, are in their retirement years, and the numbers of retirement-age persons continue to grow. The destinations and characteristics of migrants, however, are expected to gradually change over time (Longino, 1995).

CHARLES F. LONGINO, JR.

See also
Demography

GERIATRIC ASSESSMENT PROGRAMS: THEIR RATIONALE, PROCESS, AND EFFECTIVENESS

Geriatric care programs of several types have been developed over the past two decades for the performance of comprehensive geriatric assessment

(CGA) and associated treatment and follow-up services. CGA is a multidimensional, interdisciplinary, diagnostic procedure intended to determine a frail elderly person's medical, psychosocial, and functional capabilities and problems with the objective of developing an overall plan for treatment and long-term follow-up. CGA includes many components of the standard medical diagnostic evaluation, but it goes well beyond the routine examination in its focus on the frail elderly individual, its emphasis on functional status and quality of life, its comprehensiveness, and its use of standardized measurement instruments and interdisciplinary teams. The rationale underlying CGA is that frail elderly people, with their complex clinical presentations and needs, require a special approach to their evaluation and care not ordinarily supplied by health care providers and that, given this special approach, geriatric patients will have a more accurate and complete diagnosis, will receive more appropriate care, will have better care outcomes, and will ultimately cost less by avoiding unnecessary services.

CGA can be performed in a variety of locations and health care contexts. It is a basic part of care in hospital geriatric units and geriatric consultation teams, it exists in programs within community senior health centers, and it often occurs in primary care settings as a supplement to the standard medical evaluation. In fact, CGA can best be viewed as a continuum, ranging from a limited screening assessment by primary care physicians or community health workers, focused on identifying an older person's functional problems and disabilities, to more thorough evaluation of these problems in specialized geriatric or rehabilitation centers by a geriatrician and/or interdisciplinary team tied to initiation of a therapeutic plan, which often includes long-term case management.

Historical Overview of Geriatric Assessment

The first published reports of programs of geriatric assessment came from the British geriatrician Marjory Warren, who initiated the concept during the 1930s while she was in charge of a large chronic disease hospital. This hospital was filled with bedfast and largely neglected elderly patients who had not received proper medical diagnosis or rehabilitation and who were thought to be in need of lifelong institutionalization. Skilled nursing care kept the patients alive, but lack of diagnostic assessment and rehabilitation kept them disabled. Warren systematically evaluated these patients, initiated active mobilization and selective rehabilitation, and was able to get most of the long-bedfast patients out of bed and often discharged home. As a result of her experiences, Warren advocated that every elderly patient receive what we know today as CGA and an attempt at rehabilitation before being admitted to a long-term care hospital or a nursing home.

The concepts of CGA have evolved in different settings around the world. As geriatric care systems have been initiated in multiple locations, CGA concepts and specific programs have generally been assigned central roles, usually as focal points for entry into the geriatric systems. In the United States, programs incorporating CGA principles began to appear in the 1970s. The first major U.S. health care organization to adopt and adapt CGA in a major way was the Department of Veterans Affairs (VA) health care system, which has in recent years served a disproportionately elderly group of patients—by the year 1998, 37% of the veteran population was over age 65 (vs. 13% of the rest of the U.S. population). Anticipating this challenge, in the mid-1970s the VA developed an innovative network of special demonstration programs focused on aging—Geriatric Research Education and Clinical Centers (GRECCs)—whose role was to devise creative new clinical care models for the special needs of older veterans, as well as to encourage aging-focused research and education. Several of these GRECCs started inpatient CGA units, typically modeled after U.K. programs. As a result of positive program evaluations, CGA units were mandated system-wide, and by 1994, 133 of the 172 VA medical centers had defined CGA programs, usually called geriatric evaluation and management programs (GEMs; Wieland, Rubenstein, Hedrick, Reuben, & Buchner, 1994).

Elsewhere in the United States, CGA concepts also have become increasingly a part of standard geriatric care. CGA has not remained restricted to specific geriatric assessment programs, and its concepts can be found in virtually every program providing geriatric care. For example, in many areas, at least a limited geriatric assessment is required by law prior to a person's admission into a rehabilitation program or a nursing home. In a 1989 survey of U.S. hospitals, 9.7% of responding hospitals ($N = 1,639$) reported having established a GEM unit (Lavizzo-Mourey, Hillman, Diserens, & Schwartz, 1993). Many managed care organizations have introduced systems of screening older enrollees for geriatric care needs and providing CGA and case management services to high-risk patients. In addition, there are growing numbers of programs that provide limited CGA and case management in the home setting.

Comprehensive Geriatric Assessment Process

The basic components of CGA include evaluation of medical problems and relevant comorbidity, functional status, psychological status, social support network and activities, economic needs, and environmental safety. Ideally, each component can be assessed by the most appropriate team member(s) and discussed at an interdisciplinary team conference. In more limited settings, CGA involves fewer specialized disciplines, sometimes the physician or nurse alone. This is much less desirable in terms of both expertise and workload efficiency, because a single person alone cannot ordinarily provide sufficient time or expertise to deal optimally with the complex needs of frail elderly persons.

The process of CGA begins with identifying the patient in need—most commonly, elderly persons who have experienced deteriorations in health status and level of functioning. This can take place in a screening context outside the usual health care system (e.g., screening and referral programs in senior centers) or in a case-finding context within a physician's practice or other medical care setting. Ordinarily, if health status has worsened but functional level is intact, an elderly person can receive adequate care in the usual primary care setting. However, patients who have new or progressive functional deficits or difficult-to-manage geriatric problems (e.g., incontinence, dementia, frequent falls) should ideally receive CGA in a geriatric care context, because geriatric practitioners are generally better prepared than are primary care providers to deal with these kinds of complex problems.

Following review of medical information and performance of a focused physical examination, a typical CGA proceeds to review the major domains of functioning. These are ordinarily captured in measures of basic activities of daily living (ADLs) and instrumental ADLs (IADLs). These scales are used clinically to detect whether the patient has problems performing activities necessary for independent survival in the community. Basic ADLs include self-care activities such as eating, dressing, bathing, transferring, and toileting. Patients unable to perform these activities will generally need 12- to 24-hour support by caregivers at home or in an institutional setting. IADLs include heavier housework, going on errands, managing finances, and telephoning—activities required for the individual to remain fully independent in a house or apartment.

After assessment of function, the CGA gathers information about the patient's environment and social situation. For example, the strength of the patient's social network, presence of environmental challenges, the amount and type of caregiver support available, and the level of social activities in which the patient participates will all influence the clinical approach taken in managing detected deficits. This information is often best obtained by an experienced nurse or social worker. Two other key items of the CGA are screening evaluations for cognitive impairment and depression.

Sometimes a member of the extended assessment team or an outside specialist will need to evaluate the patient prior to the final formulation. For example, a physical or occupational therapist may have to evaluate a complex patient with difficulty dressing, a condition that could be caused by a number of problems, including cognitive impairment, poor finger mobility, or dysfunction of the shoulders, back, or hips.

Once CGA detects and quantifies impairment, disability, and handicap, appropriate treatment and management strategies can be formulated. When a reversible cause is found, a specific treatment may eliminate or ameliorate the disability. When the disability is complex or irreversible, rehabilitative or symptom-relief approaches can often provide substantial relief or improvement in function. Often the involvement and support of community or hospital-based resources are needed to devise an optimal plan for care and long-term follow-up.

Several factors must be considered when deciding where a CGA should take place, including the patient's level of disability and cognition, acuity and complexity of illness, social support strength, and access to transportation. In general, more disabled and complex patients with poorer social supports and transportation access will be more likely to need inpatient CGA services. These patients will be more likely to need prolonged periods of treatment and rehabilitation and less likely to keep outpatient appointments and comply with recommendations on their own. Hospital programs offer greater opportunities for intensive treatment and rehabilitation under the care of interdisciplinary teams. This can occur in designated inpatient geriatric-assessment or special care units or by a careful geriatric team consultation in a nongeriatric hospital service.

Most CGAs do not require the full range of technological capacity nor the intensity of physician and nurse monitoring found in the acute inpatient setting. A specialized geriatric setting outside an acute care hospital ward, such as a day hospital or subacute care inpatient geriatric evaluation unit, will provide the easy availability of an interdisciplinary team with the time and expertise to provide needed services efficiently, an adequate level of monitoring, and beds for patients unable to sit or stand for prolonged periods. Inpatient and day hospital assessment programs have the advantage of intensity, speed, and ability to care for particularly frail or acutely ill patients.

Outpatient and in-home assessment programs are generally cheaper because the need for inpatient stays and institutional resources is avoided. Although nonhospital programs cannot provide the level of technological care possible in the hospital, most elderly persons who are not acutely ill or severely functionally dependent can obtain adequate CGA outside the hospital. Moreover, in-home CGA and management programs can offer the advantages of observational assessment of the home environment and how well the patient actually functions at home.

Effectiveness of Geriatric Assessment Programs

A growing literature supports the effectiveness of CGA programs in a variety of settings. The early descriptive studies of CGA described such benefits as improved diagnostic accuracy, reduced discharges to nursing homes, increased functional status, and reduced medications. Yet, without concurrent control patients, these studies could not distinguish the effects of the programs from the simple effects of improvement over time. Nor was it clear how these apparent benefits, most of which affected process of care, would relate to short- or long-term outcome benefits. Beginning in the 1980s, however, controlled studies began to be published that corroborated some of the earlier studies and documented important additional benefits, such as improved survival, reduced hospital and nursing home utilization, and in some cases reduced costs. However, these studies were by no means uniform in their results. Some showed a whole series of dramatic and interrelated benefits, whereas others showed few if any benefits (Rubenstein, Josephson, Wieland, English, Sayre, & Kane, 1984; Rubenstein, Wieland, & Bernabei, 1997).

A careful meta-analysis of the controlled trials performed through 1993 provided strong confirmation that these programs can improve survival, decrease use of institutional services, and improve levels of both mental and physical functioning (Stuck, Siu, Wieland, Adams, & Rubenstein, 1993). Although not all studies showed equivalent effects, the meta-analysis was able to indicate a number of variables at both the program and patient levels that tended to distinguish trials with large effects from those with more limited ones. On the program level, hospital CGA units and home-visit assessment teams produced the most dramatic benefits, but benefits in office-based programs could not be confirmed. Programs that provided hands-on clinical care and/or long-term follow-up were generally able to produce greater positive effects than did purely consultative programs or ones that lacked follow-up. Among hospital-based programs, careful patient targeting (i.e., selecting patients who were at high risk for deterioration yet who still had "rehabilitation potential") was also associated with larger benefit.

We look to future research to define better the most effective and efficient methods for performing CGA, the best program models, and individuals likely to derive the most benefit. In the meantime, considerable evidence supports the continued growth and expansion of these programs throughout the geriatric care system.

LAURENCE Z. RUBENSTEIN

See also
    Comprehensive Assessment
    Geriatric Research, Education, and Clinical Centers

GERIATRIC/GERONTOLOGICAL NURSING
See
    Nursing

GERIATRIC HEALTH

Geriatrics is a medical discipline concerned with the clinical, preventive, remedial, and social aspects of illness in the older adult. Geriatrics is not a discipline separate from the everyday practice of most clinicians but does require that caregivers keep in mind basic principles of good geriatric care (Warshaw, 1990). First, there is an increasing body of knowledge specific to the medical care of older adults. Second, the success of treatment should be measured with an emphasis on restoration of function. Third, care and rehabilitation must allow sufficient time for healing and repair of older tissues. Fourth, older patients are increasingly at risk of side effects from diagnostic or therapeutic interventions. Avoiding iatrogenic (induced by the clinician) illness is a constant concern of geriatric providers. And fifth, it is impossible to adequately care for older patients without being concerned about their social, family, financial, and psychological support.

In most countries geriatric medicine has developed as a consultative discipline that provides specialized care in support of older adults and their primary care physicians. However, in the United States, geriatric medicine is practiced as a primary care discipline (Burton & Solomon, 1993). Emphasis is placed on accessibility, comprehensiveness and coordination of services, continuity, and accountability for all aspects of the older adults' care. Geriatricians in the United States do provide spe-

cialized consultations, similar to their colleagues in other countries, but for U.S. physicians this amounts to less than 10% of their practice activity.

Clinical Approach to the Older Adult

Older adults are a more heterogeneous group than younger adults. Although many older people are remarkably healthy and functional, many others have chronic illnesses that result in a wide range of functional impairments. This variability is particularly striking in those age 80 and over. At least four major factors interact to determine if an individual will age successfully: (1) normal aging processes, (2) occurrence of diseases, (3) personal health habits and fitness, and (4) social and economic conditions.

The impact of normal aging processes on the health of the older adult is remarkably benign. For example, the resting heart rate and cardiac output do not change with age in older adults who are free of heart disease (Lakatta, 1990). For an individual there may be considerable variation in physiological changes among organ systems.

Chronic health conditions occur commonly in older adults. Arthritis, hypertension, hearing impairment, heart disease, osteoporosis and related fractures, and diabetes are among the most prevalent medical conditions in old age (Fowles, 1998).

Many of the declines in function associated with advancing age may be due to decreases in physical activity. The major physiologic benefits from regular exercise include favorable effects on plasma lipids, better glucose tolerance, improved maximal oxygen capacity, greater strength, stronger bones, improved sleep, and a sense of well-being (Rowe & Kahn, 1998).

The social contexts in which adults develop and age influence the length of their lives, their health, their ability to make decisions, their functional status, and their sense of well-being. Research has demonstrated that public health, nutrition, adequate income, education, and housing have significant effects on life expectancy, health, and function.

Older persons frequently behave differently in response to illness. Critical problems that would in the young produce a great amount of pain and dramatic physical signs might advance quite far in an older person, with only minimal physical signs or symptoms. A painless heart attack is not unusual in an older patient; up to 40% of all infarcts in the old are silent. Poor appetite, nausea, and breathlessness may be the only clues of the recent onset of a heart attack.

Certain "atypical" presentations of disease can occur. For example, hyperthyroidism in the elderly is often unaccompanied by an enlarged gland or eye changes. A rapid, irregular heartbeat and some confusion might be the only clues. Confusion may also be the most evident feature of hypothyroidism.

The older individual may have reduced physiological function in many organ systems, which leads to dramatic, multisystem disease presentation. Common "catastrophic" presentations of disease in previously well older patients include falls, incontinence, and confusion. These nonspecific presentations of illness require alert and careful evaluation. Proper assessment of these presentations rests upon the appreciation of the importance of a good history, particularly with reference to the rate of onset of the symptoms, and the knowledge of the precarious nature of mobility, continence, and orientation in elderly patients. Awareness of these possibilities, together with a broad and searching approach to diagnosis, is essential.

Assessment

The clinical assessment of an older patient includes three core components: correct medical diagnosis, an assessment of the patient's functional status, and an evaluation of the patient's social support system. These three components are the basis of a quality geriatric health assessment (Gallo, Fulmer, Paveza, & Reichel, 2000).

Practical points to consider in geriatric assessment include the following: (1) Adequate assessment requires time. The clinician needs to set aside the necessary time to accomplish the required tasks. (2) Relatives, friends, neighbors, and attending health personnel should be encouraged to contribute and be present with the patient to corroborate or amplify the patient's history. At this time, one can also assess the strain on the caregivers. (3) To ensure an adequate review, all of the patient's medication should be brought to the assessment visit. (4) Assessment at home is valuable. The way a patient functions in the clinician's office may be considerably different from how he or she performs in the home or nursing home environment.

A careful history and physical examination are important parts of any geriatric assessment. When taking a history from an older person, the pace of questioning must be slower, and questions usually need to be more focused and directed. They should be repeated in simple and different ways. A physical exam should include both vision and hearing tests. Blood pressure should always be checked, first with the patient supine, then standing. Significant postural hypotension occurs in as many as 20% of the elderly and may lead to symptoms of lightheadedness and falls.

Of most immediate concern to the individual is often the question of the functional result of disability, which must be as carefully evaluated as the medical diagnosis. Although awareness of functional loss and its reasons are important, emphasis should be toward determining what functional ability remains. With regard to mental functioning, signs of dementia can be masked by patients who retain good social skills despite an existing significant impairment. An objective mental status test should be part of all geriatric assessments.

In assessing physical function, mobility is the cornerstone of physical ability. The assessment should include observation of the elderly patient attempting to rise, stand, and walk, instead of relying on someone's word that walking is impossible. Walking aids should be assessed. Are they appropriate for the disability, and are they in good condition? For example, the hemiplegic infrequently benefits from a walking frame, but the patient with severe arthritis in the knees often finds a frame more useful than one or even two canes. Among the many activities of daily living, the ability to dress and to access the toilet independently is essential. If the patient cannot dress in the morning, why not? Is it because of instability when standing, inability to find clothes because of poor vision, or a more complex difficulty due to dementia? Is the patient incontinent of urine or feces? These are areas of assessment, just as crucial to the older patient as the routine medical examination.

Knowledge of the social support system is also part of the assessment of the older patient. The essential features to review include the following: (1) Who is currently living with the patient, and where are other family and support members living? (2) Does the patient have an opportunity to leave the house for shopping, for church, or for other reasons? (3) Who is currently doing the shopping and cooking, and what, if any, community services are used? (4) Does the patient have financial or legal problems? Finally, housing, whether it be in a group setting or in the patient's own home, should be evaluated for its appropriateness.

Iatrogenic problems are recognized as a significant hazard for older adults. Physiologic declines and multiple medical problems place older adults at risk for adverse effects from diagnostic tests and therapies. There is little room for errors in judgment when caring for frail, older adults. The older person should be assessed on the principle of minimal interference rather than poorly targeted extensive evaluations. There is risk in elective hospitalization, and the laboratory assessment of older patients should be kept to a judicious minimum.

Principles of Management

Basic principles of the management of elderly patients include an understanding of rehabilitation and the appropriate use of medications.

Rehabilitation. One of the great needs of health care for the elderly in the United States is rehabilitation. This need is suggested by the large numbers of disabled older people found in the ambulatory, acute care, or long-term care setting. Three groups of older patients requiring rehabilitation can be identified: (1) those in whom there is some obvious disorder affecting functions, such as stroke or amputation; (2) those in whom there is a general systemic disorder, such as severe cardiovascular or respiratory disease; and (3) those without obvious disorder but suffering from the accumulative effects of frailty in old age.

Principles of successful rehabilitation include (1) a comprehensive approach that incorporates physical, emotional, and social parameters in the care process; (2) a team effort that is multidisciplinary in membership and interdisciplinary in process; (3) a continuous and ongoing intervention that is not time limited; and (4) a focus on function, whether it be lost function that may be restored (restorative therapy) or remaining function that

needs to be modified and strengthened to accommodate other disability (maintenance therapy).

Medication. Older patients take the largest number of medications of any segment of society, and the potential for a greater number of adverse reactions among these patients is documented (Bressler & Katz, 1993). Some general recommendations for prescribing for the elderly can be summarized (Beers, 1997). First, if at all possible, manage medical conditions without medications. Be alert to drug interactions. If there is any doubt, start with the smallest effective doses and increase medications gradually, if necessary. Individualize and simplify the drug regimen. It is usually unnecessary for older patients to be taking medications more than twice daily. Pay attention to impaired mental functioning, poor vision, and poor hearing when instructing patients about their new medications. Finally, it is always necessary to monitor the effectiveness and potential side effects of medications; this should be done on a regular basis, and no medication should be prescribed indefinitely without a regular review.

Conclusion

The geriatrics provider, whether practicing primary or consultative care, has particular contributions to make to the care of older adults: (1) to prevent unnecessary loss of functional ability; (2) to prevent and treat health problems that adversely affect the quality of life in old age; (3) to support the care given by relatives, friends, and professional caregivers that allow older adults to stay in their homes; and (4) to provide appropriate and compassionate care at the end of life.

The more we know about the problems of old age, the more exciting the potential contribution of modern medicine appears. Most important is the knowledge that many of the health problems encountered by the elderly result not from the normal biological aging process but from controllable causes, such as disease, a loss of ability resulting from inactivity, or the poverty and poor housing conditions that characterize the social position of many older people. Assessment and management of problems of the aged require a high standard of clinical skills, as well as an expanded view of health to include functional ability, fitness, socioeconomic status, and psychological functions.

GREGG WARSHAW

See also
Comprehensive Assessment
Drug Reactions
Mental Health and Illness
Multidimensional Functional Assessment
Rehabilitation

GERIATRIC NURSE PRACTITIONER
See
Nursing

GERIATRIC PSYCHIATRY

For over a century psychiatrists in psychiatric facilities have had a major responsibility for the diagnosis and long-term care of persons with organic brain disease. Furthermore, they have had to care for the seriously depressed and for persons with other emotional and behavioral disorders of late life. Unfortunately, this demanding clinical responsibility was not accompanied by adequate education and training in geriatric psychiatry. Until the mid-1960s there was a scarcity of organized educational efforts. The first training program in geriatric psychiatry, supported by the National Institute of Mental Health (NIMH), was established at Duke University Medical Center in 1965 and was the only such program for almost a decade. However, this situation improved when, during the 1970s, federal and state agencies started to provide financial support for training in geriatrics in the medical fields of internal medicine, family practice, psychiatry, and neurology. In 1975, the National Institute of Mental Health established the Center for Studies of the Mental Health of the Aging, which received funds to support and coordinate research, research training, and clinical training projects in geriatric psychiatry. Its efforts have focused on clinical and research training.

The National Institute on Aging (NIA) was established in May 1974 as part of the National Institutes of Health. The NIA's first director was a psychiatrist (Robert N. Butler, M.D.). The establishment of the NIA represented the culmination of 20 years of effort to gain government recognition and support for research in aging. The Administration on Aging (AoA) was created in 1965 to develop and coordinate research and service programs for the elderly. The NIA, NIMH, and AoA continue to have a major impact on gerontology, in particular geriatric psychiatry, in the United States.

Several professional psychiatric societies have given attention to geriatric psychiatry. The Group for the Advancement of Psychiatry (GAP) was organized in 1946. By 1950, its membership was composed of approximately 150 psychiatrists divided into 17 working groups. In 1950, the GAP Committee on Hospitals published *The Problem of the Aged Patients in the Public Psychiatric Hospital*. In 1966, GAP established the Committee on Aging, which has published a number of reports.

In 1970, the American Psychiatric Association (APA) established the APA council on Aging. This council, composed of nine psychiatrists, is responsible for developing and maintaining liaison with other organizations involved in the mental health care of aging Americans, including federal agencies.

Psychiatrists have played a leadership role in the activities of two major U.S. societies concerned with aging, the Gerontological Society of America and the American Geriatrics Society. Psychiatrists have served as presidents of both organizations. The World Psychiatric Association includes a large geriatric section.

Geriatric psychiatry was the first subspecialty area for which the American Board of Psychiatry and Neurology offered an examination for added qualifications. The first examination was administered in 1991 to 661 candidates and in 1992 to 578 candidates. Since the first examination, 2,425 certificates have been issued. The examination was also offered in April 2000, and the first recertification examinations were given in the spring of 2000 (D. Juul, personal communication, September 17, 1999). Recently, there has been a rapid development of professional organizations concerned with geriatric psychiatry. Two of the very active ones are the American Association of Geriatric Psychiatry and the International Association of Geriatric Psychiatry. The American association has made available a geriatric psychiatry self-assessment program. This examination offers more than 400 questions and answers with explanatory critiques to help readers prepare for certification or recertification in geriatric psychiatry.

Three sources reviewing content in this area are the *Handbook of Geriatric Psychiatry* (Busse & Blazer, 1995), *Textbook of Geriatric Neuropsychiatry* (Coffey & Cummings, 1994), and *Geropsychiatric Diagnostics and Treatment* (Bergener, 1983), which provides international perspectives.

EWALD W. BUSSE

See also
   Geriatrics
   International Psychogeriatric Association

GERIATRIC REHABILITATION
See
   Rehabilitation: Evidence of Outcomes
   Rehabilitation: Overview

GERIATRIC RESEARCH, EDUCATION, AND CLINICAL CENTERS

Geriatric research, education, and clinical centers (GRECCs) have become leaders in the integrated research education and clinical systems providing care to older veterans (Goodwin & Morley, 1994; Haber & Moravec, 1982). The Veterans Administration (VA) developed out of the "Old Soldiers Homes" at the end of the 19th century. The VA became a separate entity in 1930, and following World War II it began affiliating with medical schools and emphasizing teaching and research as a way to enhance care of the veteran. In 1964 an executive order by President Kennedy and Public Law 88-450 directed the development of long-term care programs within the VA. Recognition of the rapid growth in the aging veteran population, with the prediction that 37% (9 million) of the veteran population would be over 65 years of age by the year 2000, led to increased enthusiasm for the development of expertise in geriatrics within the VA in the early 1970s. At the instigation of Paul Haber, MD, Congress authorized the establishment of five GRECCs. Congress specifically stated that these GRECCs should not only serve the VA but also provide education for health care professionals caring for the aged in the general population. By 1980 eight GRECCs had been established: in Boston (Bedford and Brockton/West Roxbury); Little Rock, Arkansas; Minneapolis, St. Louis, Seattle (Seattle and American Lake), and Palo Alto, Sepulveda and West Los Angeles, California. In 1984, Durham, North Carolina, and Gainesville, Florida, were added. Since 1987 further GRECCs have been opened: Ann Arbor, Michigan; San Antonio, Texas; Madison, Wisconsin; Miami, Salt Lake City, Baltimore, Cleveland, Pittsburgh, Bronx/New York Harbor and Nashville. Public Law 99-166, passed by Congress in 1985, has authorized an increase in GRECCs to a total of 25. GRECCs are under the direction of the Office of the Assistant Chief Medical Director in the VA central office. Since 1980, GRECCs have also been regularly reviewed by the Geriatrics and Gerontology Advisory Committee (GGAC). All GRECCs are affiliated with a medical school (the Boston GRECC with two schools and Sepulveda and West Los Angeles with UCLA) and have provided a major stimulus in developing geriatric programs at major universities throughout the United States.

The concept behind the GRECCs was that bringing together a cadre of basic and clinical researchers with a focus on aging would stimulate a rapid increase in clinically useful knowledge about older persons. The GRECCs were then required to develop clinical demonstration units to test these concepts. The educational component was responsible for the rapid dissemination of this knowledge throughout the VA and the private sector. Clearly, the most successful example of this strategy was the development of the Geriatric Evaluation and Management Unit (GEMU) at the Sepulveda GRECC, demonstrating its efficacy and its rapid dissemination throughout the VA (133 programs) and the private sector.

GRECCs have proved to be a highly successful research model, with research funding in 1991 averaging over $3 million per GRECC and each GRECC producing over 50 scientific publications in that year. The scientific contributions of the GRECCs have been numerous. They include description of Syndrome X (hypertension, hyperinsulinemia, and hypertriglyceridemia), demonstration (by computer analysis of its receptor structure), that amyloid-beta protein produces amnesia, the finding that 1-alpha-hydroxylase enzyme activity in the kidney is reduced with aging, description of the detrusor hyperactivity and impaired contractility syndrome as a cause of incontinence, pioneering observations on age-related alterations in the immune system, discovery of the key role of protein energy undernutrition in poor outcomes associated with hospitalized older persons, linkage analysis of some familial forms of Alzheimer's disease to chromosome 21, definition of the causes of the anorexia of aging, and the finding that older males develop secondary hypogonadism.

Besides GEMUs, GRECCs have pioneered the development of other clinical demonstration units, including academic nursing home units, special care units, specialized exercise programs, medication reduction clinics, sexual dysfunction clinics, clinics for older persons with spinal cord injuries, a preventive gerontology program for older veterans in the community, and an adapted work therapy program for persons with early dementia. GRECCs, together with other VA sites, have played a leading role in developing interdisciplinary team training.

GRECCs have also played an important role in disseminating geriatric knowledge to health professionals of a variety of disciplines and have played a key part in developing the physician geriatric fellowship. They have developed two novel educational games; Geropady and the Geriatric Challenge Bowl, and were key in introducing the aging game to medical students. GRECCs play a major role in continuing education, with over 5,000 educational activities each year. GRECCs have developed a variety of patient education clinics and a series of videotapes.

GRECCs represent an exciting success story. They have developed key clinical demonstration units and have been leading trainers of health professionals in gerontology. GRECC scientists are among the leaders in geriatric research. The GRECC integration of research, education, and clinical care into "centers of excellence" has played an important role in probing the mysteries of aging

and providing insights into the appropriate care of our graying population.

JOHN E. MORLEY

See also
Geriatric Assessment Units

GERIATRICS

Geriatrics is the study of the medical aspects of old age and the application of knowledge related to the biological, biomedical, behavioral, and social aspects of aging to prevention, diagnosis, treatment, and care of older persons (see, e.g., Butler, 1979; Libow, 1981). The term *geriatrics* was coined by the American physician Ignatz Nascher (1863–1944) in recognition of the similarity to the field of pediatrics. The medical aspects of aging have been studied since early civilization and given various names, such as *gerocomica* and *geronicomia*.

By 1935, Dr. Marjorie Warren had organized the Department for the Aged in London's West Middlesex Hospital. She introduced the concept of rehabilitation, and her work became a primary model for the development of geriatrics in the United Kingdom, as well as in the United States and other countries. The American Geriatrics Society was established in 1942 for physicians. In 1943, Edward J. Steiglitz published a textbook, *Geriatric Medicine*, that further stimulated interest in the field in America (see, e.g., Brocklehurst, 1975).

Geriatrics must be seen from the broadest perspective, encompassing psychosocial, economic, historical, and physiological factors (Butler, 1975). It must be integrated within primary care and specialty branches of medicine, for example, geriatric medicine, geriatric psychiatry, and geriatric neurology. Although 65 years of age is frequently used to indicate the onset of old age, this number is clearly arbitrary and a function of social policy decisions. Indeed, much of geriatric practice is characteristically devoted to the frail elderly, usually 75 years of age and over, with multiple, complex interacting psychosocial and medical conditions. Long-term care needs are critical as individuals move along the continuum of declining functional status and homeostatic integrity.

The presentation and course of an illness in old age differs from that in the rest of the population, in part because of the effects of aging processes upon the host (e.g., the apathetic presentation of hyperthyroidism and the absence of symptoms in appendicitis).

The founding of the National Institute on Aging in 1975 in the United States brought renewed efforts to the field of geriatrics. The Institute of Medicine of the National Academy of Sciences furthered these efforts with publication of the report *Aging and Medical Education* (Kane, Solomon, Beck, Keeler, & Kane, 1981). Leading medical schools that offer programs in geriatrics in the United States include Arkansas, Bowman-Gray, Duke, Harvard, Johns Hopkins, Michigan, Mount Sinai, Oklahoma, UCLA, Pennsylvania, Washington, and Yale. Three full departments of geriatrics exist in the United States: the Mount Sinai Medical Center in New York, the University of Oklahoma College of Medicine, and the University of Arkansas for Medical Sciences. The Brookdale, Hartford, and Reynolds foundations have led the support for geriatric research, as have the American Federation of Aging Research and the Alliance for Aging Research.

Every medical school in Great Britain has a department of geriatrics, as do some Scandinavian medical schools. Japan, too, has been moving in this direction, and currently 12 of its 88 medical schools have departments. The teaching of geriatrics is mandatory in Finland, Ireland, Italy, Norway, and the Netherlands.

Geriatrics is a rapidly growing field. There are now "certificates of added qualification" for competence in geriatrics in the fields of internal medicine, family practice, and psychiatry. Fellowship training and examinations are required. Geriatrics is also a required rotation within internal medicine residency programs. Major textbooks are available in this field (e.g., Abrams & Berkow, 1995; Brocklehurst, Tallis, & Fillit, 1998; Cassel, Cohen, & Larson, 1996; Evans & Williams, 1992; Hazzard, Blass, Ettinger, Halter, & Ouslander, 1999).

ROBERT N. BUTLER

See also
Geriatric Health
Gerontology
Rehabilitation: Overview

GERONTOCRACY

Gerontocracy refers to rule by elders, or dominance by older age groups. The term enjoys informal, normative, as well as more formal, descriptive use.

Informal usage began when an early 19th century pamphleteer coined the word to attack a conservative and aging restoration parliament in France (Eisele, 1979). In the 20th century, journalists and others criticized aging leadership structures in regimes as different as the United States, the former Soviet Union, Israel, and the People's Republic of China, as well as in nongovernmental organizations such as churches, unions, and corporations. In popular usage, the label "gerontocratic" is usually pejorative, implying a causal relationship between advanced age and conservative or unchanging leadership behavior. However, social scientists have shown that this relationship is very difficult to test, and that when testable, it is weak or does not prevail. To assume such a connection without evidence constitutes a form of old-age prejudice.

Popular usage also confounds age with cohort or generational effects on behavior. For example, labeling the aging Soviet and Chinese leadership of the early 1980s as "gerontocratic" overlooks the rival hypothesis that their political behavior may be just as plausibly explained by the collective experience of a particular generation of leaders that seized power decades earlier in youth and held it throughout the life span until old age (Rintala, 1968). Even if leaders' behavior could be analyzed comprehensively and in detail, it would likely be a *mix* of age, cohort, and historical period effects, varying from situation to situation. But to allege that old age is the overriding influence on political behavior—as the popular use of gerontocracy implies—is rarely warranted (Maddox, 1978).

A more formal, scientific use of gerontocracy is confined to old-age dominance, whereby leadership positions are reserved exclusively for elders, historically almost always men. For example, the Greek city-state of Sparta was ruled by a *gerusia,* or council, whose members had to be 60 and served for life. Plato, in *The Laws,* discouraged public office holding before age 50 and limited tenure to 20 years. In the 20th century some primitive societies survived with an age-graded form of social organization, resulting in gerontocratic situations. Anthropologists have described a number of these in East Africa (Gulliver, 1968).

Today, rapid socioeconomic change and the rise of professional leadership careers in almost all societies have made true gerontocracy very rare. Yet increasing longevity, awareness of aging and the aged, acceptance of older leadership, and other trends may well lead to prolonged incumbency and to continued use, and misuse, of the term *gerontocracy*.

FREDERICK EISELE

See also
    Age Conflicts

GERONTOLOGICAL EDUCATION AND TRAINING

The beginning of gerontological (aging) education in the United States can be traced to the early 1950s, although aging research dates from the late 1800s. In 1955, several gerontological researchers came together to form the Inter-University Training Program in Gerontology, housed at the University of Michigan. One of its activities was to survey colleges and universities to determine the extent of aging education being conducted throughout the country. Of the 312 academic institutions responding, only 50 offered credit courses in any aspect of gerontology, and only 72 conducted gerontological research. It was concluded that academic institutions needed to be encouraged to provide additional educational and research opportunities.

The earliest formal gerontology programs were established in 1950 at the University of Michigan, in 1955 at Duke University, in 1957 at the University of Chicago, and in 1964 at the University of Southern California.

In 1965, the U.S. Congress enacted the Older Americans Act, which established the Administration on Aging (AoA) and provided authorization for federal funding of aging research, education, and training activities. The first federal training grants to academic institutions were awarded in 1966, and in those first few years of federal support the University of South Florida and North Texas

State University offered the first gerontology degrees in the United States.

In 1972, there was an expansion of federal support for education and training, and a new wave of colleges and universities received grants from the Administration on Aging to establish gerontology programs. The establishment of the National Institute on Aging (NIA) in 1974 brought an infusion of additional federal support for biomedical, social, and behavioral training and research at the doctoral and postdoctoral levels.

In 1974, on the crest of the expansionist wave of federal support for aging education and research, the Association for Gerontology in Higher Education (AGHE) was founded, because academic researchers and educators saw the need for a national organization that would serve the burgeoning needs of the rapidly growing number of academic institutions becoming involved in the field of aging.

Federal support for gerontological education increased steadily until 1980, the peak year for federal funding. In 1981 and 1982, there were dramatic reductions in federal support for both aging education and research, and this federal support has not returned to the 1980 levels. The early history of gerontological education, training, and research was shaped in large part by federal funding patterns. It was the acquisition of federal grants that enabled dozens of academic institutions to initiate and expand gerontology programs. Likewise, the character of these gerontology programs in the early years paralleled the priorities of federal agencies as academic institutions tried to fashion their gerontology programs after the current AoA and NIA emphases.

Despite the dramatic reduction of federal support, the number of academic institutions offering instruction in gerontology has continued to grow. A survey conducted in 1992 by the AGHE and the University of Southern California determined that 1,639 academic institutions were offering gerontology, geriatrics, or aging-studies instruction, a 23% increase in the number of campuses since the previous survey in 1985. This study focused on describing organized programs of instruction leading to a credential and found that there had been a 69% increase in the number of campuses offering these programs—from 410 in 1985 to 692 schools in 1992.

Many campuses offer more than one aging-related instructional program. In 1992, 920 programs were identified, and since then the number has surpassed 1,000. Information on these programs is maintained by the AGHE in its *Database on Gerontology in Higher Education* and is published periodically in its *Directory of Educational Programs in Gerontology and Geriatrics*. The seventh edition of the directory, published in February 2000, gives up-to-date contact information and current descriptive information on 774 of the gerontology and geriatric programs offered in 354 institutions of higher education in the United States and abroad.

Current data do not exist on the total number of students trained throughout the history of gerontology education. AoA staff estimate that approximately 25,000 students received concentrated training that resulted in the award of a certificate or degree in gerontology during the first 18 years of the career preparation program. The AGHE's 1992 survey indicated that about 20,000 students were enrolled in aging studies programs that year, with over 7,000 students being graduated in 1992 with a formal credential (degree, certificate, or specialization) in aging.

Although aging research historically preceded aging education, the establishment of gerontological education programs generally preceded training programs. Furthermore, education programs differ from training programs in their scope, purpose, and often clientele and sponsorship. Gerontological education programs are most often based in academic institutions. They usually have long-term educational goals and deal with gerontology subject matter in depth. Courses typically are offered for credit.

Currently, the field of gerontological education as a whole has a four-dimensional concern: (1) The education of professionals who will serve the older population is the focus of most programs. Generally, these programs are found at the master's degree level. (2) The education of society about the aging processes—a liberal arts emphasis—is largely found in the proliferation of courses in aging throughout the academic curricula, a "gerontologizing" of the curricula. The concern in these courses is not to educate professionals who will be employed in positions primarily serving the elderly, but rather to educate citizens of our "graying society" about the facts and myths of aging. These programs generally are at the baccalaureate level. (3) Doctoral-level and postdoctoral programs in gerontology are primarily aimed at educating teachers and researchers in the field of gerontology and tend to focus on a scientific approach to studying aging processes. (4) Many academic institutions are actively involved in providing educational opportunities for older persons themselves. Many, though not all, of these programs provide noncredit opportunities for older persons not interested in pursuing a formal degree.

In some schools gerontology is studied as the primary area of concentration, and students graduate from those programs with degrees in gerontology; gerontology degrees are available at all academic levels, from associate through doctoral degrees. The majority of aging-studies programs, however, are adjuncts to more traditional disciplines or professions, and students receive certificates or specializations in gerontology, geriatrics, or aging studies as part of a degree received in another field.

Gerontological training programs, although often offered by institutions of higher education, are increasingly provided by professional associations, employers, direct service providers, community agencies, and state and area agencies on aging. Training programs tend to be directly related to current employment needs, are short-term in duration, are often noncredit, and are practitioner oriented. Examples of such gerontology training are continuing education programs, short-term training conferences and workshops, and on-the-job events.

Training programs have proliferated as a result of several related phenomena: The fields of academic gerontological education and research have produced a gerontologically educated professional labor force, the service delivery network has created a demand for employees to work with older persons, and the "graying" of American society has produced a demand for aging-related programs and services staffed by trained personnel.

The field of gerontological education and training has experienced steady growth and development since the establishment of the Inter-University Training Program at the University of Michigan in 1955. Certainly, in recent years there has been a slowing down of the rapid and frenzied proliferation of programs that occurred in the 1970s when federal grants were prevalent.

Although new programs continue to be established each year, there has been a maturing of the field. Four themes currently characterize academic gerontology:

- *An attention to the quality of programs.* The publication by the AGHE in 1989–1990 of standards and guidelines for gerontology programs reflects a commitment to ensuring that the academic integrity of instructional programs in the field of aging is on a par with other disciplines and professions.

- *The development of instructional outcomes and measures of assessing student competencies.* In response to pressures within higher education to focus on educational outcomes, gerontology educators have begun developing measures of aging-related knowledge, skills, and attitudes against which to evaluate their educational programs.
- *A concern about the "institutionalization" of aging-studies programs.* Studies have shown that the organizational structures, academic authority, and perceived support from upper-level administrators do not typically evidence a secure long-term "entrenchment" of these programs within the academy. Solutions to the vulnerability of gerontology education programs present a serious challenge.
- *A continuing need to "market" gerontology graduates in the wider society.* Although there is evidence of many jobs available for gerontologically trained persons, many of those jobs are filled with persons lacking any aging education. The development of job markets for professional gerontologists is important to the future viability of these education and training programs.

Gerontological education and training opportunities have over the past 50 years expanded in numbers, size, and complexity. With growth and maturity have come many challenges still to be adequately addressed and exciting opportunities inherent in a new field of study.

ELIZABETH B. DOUGLASS
Updated by
CATHERINE J. TOMPKINS

See also
Association for Gerontology in Higher Education

GERONTOLOGICAL SOCIETY OF AMERICA

The Gerontological Society of America (GSA) was founded in 1945, an outgrowth of the Club for Research in Aging, to promote the scientific study of aging and to encourage the exchange of knowledge about aging among scientists, practitioners, and decision makers working in the field. As such, it was the first multidisciplinary organization on aging in the United States. These purposes remain the society's primary missions.

From its inception, the GSA embraced the concept that gerontology is a multidisciplinary field. Its original incorporation papers spoke of the study of aging in terms of public health, mental hygiene, the science and art of medicine, and the cure of diseases and of understanding the nature and problems of aging.

Although membership in its early years leaned toward researchers in the biological, medical, and behavioral sciences, the GSA has expanded to include social scientists, humanists, administrators, policy analysts, and practitioners particularly interested in encouraging the dissemination of research results beyond the research community. Today the society's 6,500 members belong to one of four professional sections: Biological Sciences; Clinical Medicine; Behavioral and Social Sciences; and Social Research, Policy, and Practice. Student members also belong to the society's student organization.

In pursuit of its missions, the GSA publishes five refereed professional journals: *The Journals of Gerontology, Series A: Biological Sciences and Medical Sciences; The Journals of Gerontology, Series B: Psychological Sciences and Social Sciences;* and *The Gerontologist.* The *Journal of Gerontology*—the first journal in the field—began in 1946 as one journal. It was revamped in 1988 to four separate journals under one cover, then further separated to its current format of four journals under two covers in 1995. *Series A* is now produced monthly; *Series B* is issued bimonthly. *The Gerontologist* was first published in 1961 and focuses on applied research and policy. The GSA also conducts the nation's major annual scientific meeting devoted to the full range of disciplines active in gerontology. The meeting, which attracts an average of 3,500 participants, usually includes more than 2,000 symposia, papers, poster sessions, and special presentations. Each section of the society is responsible for developing its portion of the programs and for multi- and interdisciplinary offerings in cooperation with other sections and committees of the society. In addition, the GSA has more than

30 special interest groups that meet at the annual meeting and present programs. Interest group topics include economics of aging, mental retardation and developmental disabilities, technology and aging, nursing care, religion and aging, oral health, nutrition, grandparents as caregivers, researchers based in long-term care, women's issues, HIV/AIDS, and Alzheimer's disease research.

Over the years, the GSA also has promoted the scientific study of aging through the efforts of its individual members and committees. In 1956 and 1957, a special Biology and Medicine subcommittee developed guidelines that were used to shape federal and private policies supporting research in aging. In 1962, the society's representatives were instrumental in securing support of the White House Conference on Aging for six major recommendations to encourage development of urgently needed gerontological research and education programs. These recommendations called for graduate scholarships, postdoctoral fellowships, and training programs; long-term stable programs of research in aging; creation of regional centers of aging research; longitudinal aging studies; establishment of a national institute of gerontology; and demonstration and evaluation projects on the delivery of services to the elderly. Following the conference, the GSA, working with other organizations, continued to press these recommendations, all of which have been implemented in some form through various federal, state, and private programs. The society and its members were particularly involved and instrumental in the establishment of the National Institute on Aging in 1974, as well as the Center on Aging within the National Institute of Mental Health.

The GSA, on its own or in collaboration with other groups, has conducted a number of significant projects over the years, including the development of education and training curricula, identified national training needs, helped design federal research policies, advised key congressional committees and executive branch offices, and published special reports and monographs on key gerontological issues. For example, the society's project from 1971 to 1975 on design and environments for the aged brought together designers, architects, planners, and policy makers and developed some of the baseline data in the area of housing and environments for the elderly. In 1980, with the Association for

Gerontology in Higher Education, the society conducted the first review of components of a basic core of knowledge essential for institutional gerontology programs, as well as for some selected specialties. This was issued in a report titled *Foundations for Gerontological Education*. In response to cutbacks in federal data collection programs, the GSA in 1983 established the Task Force on Data on Aging, which prepared a report on data losses important to aging research and a set of recommendations for the 1990 census. In 1987, the society established the Task Force on Minority Aging. This task force has organized special symposia and conferences and recently issued *Full Color Aging: Facts, Goals, and Recommendations for America's Diverse Elders,* edited by T. P. Miles, the third in a series of publications that examine the information base and policy implications around specific issues of minority aging. The society also contributed to the development of key gerontological faculty through its series of summer research and faculty training institutes conducted from 1970 to 1976.

To help promote the transfer of research results to the media and decision makers, the society initiated its Information Service in 1986. The service includes a computerized database of experts in the field of aging keyworded by area of expertise, a directory of other aging databases, and articles from GSA journals by topic area.

For 22 years, the GSA conducted a program that placed postdoctoral researchers in 3-month fellowships to work on specific problems of serving the elderly. The program offered academic researchers opportunities to work in practice settings and provided service agencies with high-quality technical assistance.

The GSA has also been instrumental in the development of other aging organizations. The society was a founding member of the International Association of Gerontology (IAG) in 1949 and has hosted or helped organize IAG conferences in the United States in 1951, 1960, 1969, and 1985. The society is also a founding member of the Leadership Council of Aging Organizations, a coalition of more than 40 national aging organizations. This organization meets regularly to review the status of aging policies and develop action strategies. The Association for Gerontology in Higher Education (AGHE) was conceived by GSA members and established in 1974.

In 1995, the society celebrated its 50th anniversary and the addition of an independent, nonpartisan public policy institute, the National Academy on an Aging Society (NAAS). The academy serves as a national forum for policy analysis and debate on the major issues of concern to the current and future aging society. The NAAS has assisted media and policy makers through its research materials on current policy issues, producing reports and background papers, fact sheets, and special publications on issues including health care, long-term care, and income security in an intergenerational context. In addition, the NAAS has organized special conferences and seminars for experts and community, business, and political leaders. Recent academy publications include *Demography Is Not Destiny,* a report that uses data from a variety of sources to examine past and anticipated trends in the aging of the population, the impact of those changes on national entitlement programs, and potential policy options for addressing those impacts. The academy is currently releasing a series of data profiles on 16 chronic and disability conditions. The NAAS also issues *The Public Policy and Aging Report*, a quarterly publication that offers a diversity of views on current policy issues.

In January 1999, the Association for Gerontology in Higher Education merged with the GSA. Now a unit of the GSA, the AGHE brings to the society its network of over 300 institutions of higher education and other organizations dedicated to advancing study and scholarship in gerontology. The AGHE sponsors several fellowship and scholarship opportunities, organizes annual meetings that present the latest information on matters of gerontological education and training, maintains a consultation program to assist in developing new gerontology instruction and expanding or evaluating existing gerontology programs, and issues a quarterly newsletter as well as other special publications and reports. Other AGHE resources include a national directory of educational programs in gerontology and geriatrics, a collection of brief bibliographies covering over 30 aging topics, brochures and materials on careers in aging, and special studies and publications on standards and guidelines for gerontology programs.

ROBERT J. HAVIGHURST
Updated by
CAROL A. SCHUTZ

See also
Organizations in Aging

GERONTOLOGY

The study of aging has taken its name from *geront,* the Greek word for "old man." Gerontocracy—government controlled by elders—was a recognized concept long before M. Elie Metchnikoff proposed both a new science and its designation: *gerontology.* Pasteur's successor and himself a distinguished researcher, Metchnikoff allowed himself a visionary statement: "I think it extremely probable that the scientific study of old age and of death, two branches of sciences that may be called *gerontology* and *thanatology,* will bring about great modifications in the course of the last period of life" (Metchnikoff, 1903, pp. 297–298). In this one brief passage, then, Metchnikoff introduced two terms that have since become closely associated with active fields of research that were essentially unknown in his own time.

Although gerontology can be described as either "the study of aging" or "the scientific study of old age," a more complete definition is needed. Contemporary gerontology includes all of the following: (1) scientific studies of processes associated with aging, (2) scientific studies of mature and aged adults, (3) studies from the perspective of the humanities (e.g., history, philosophy, literature), and (4) applications of knowledge for the benefit of mature and aged adults.

The distinction between studies of processes and of populations is not unique to gerontology but is particularly salient in this field. Determining the biological, psychological, and social characteristics of mature adults does not necessarily answer questions about the processes inherent in aging per se. A person who is 80 years of age today has experienced a life course with many distinctive features. This individual was born and reared during a period of sociocultural history whose particular configuration of opportunities, vulnerabilities, and stresses will never again occur. Also unique was the pattern of continuous interaction between individual development and sociocultural circumstances throughout this person's entire life course. For example, the vulnerability to a number of contagious early childhood diseases was greater for today's 80-year-old than that experienced by people born at a later time. Upon reaching early adulthood, this individual was likely to encounter economic difficulties associated with the Great Depression years and also to bring into marriage and parenting a set of values and attitudes that have since been challenged by alternative views of sexuality, sex role, and responsibility. Reaching the later years of life, this person finds himself or herself part of the largest population of elderly people in history, within an ever more mobile society, more likely to receive a pension and other financial benefits, but nevertheless under financial pressure.

In this scenario, or any other, it is obvious that a description and understanding of this individual should encompass genetic endowment, early upbringing, historical experience, health history, cognitive and personality style, and so on. It is much less obvious how these many factors should be weighted or integrated into a coherent view—and even less obvious how a "pure" or "intrinsic" process of aging can be separated from all the particulars of a long and complex human life. Each new generation of older adults represents a unique mixture of its own distinctive characteristics along with those that might be attributed more appropriately to a process or processes of aging. Describing any one generation of elders, then, runs the risk of confounding unique characteristics with whatever is fundamental to "aging" itself.

Gerontologists have responded to this challenge by devising sophisticated research strategies that are sensitive both to the developmental careers of individuals and to the sociohistorical times through which we pass (e.g., Nesselroade & Labouvie, 1985; Schaie & Hertzog, 1985). These research designs typically combine features of cross-sectional and longitudinal studies and employ advanced multivariate statistical techniques. Because such studies are time consuming and require significant funding, relatively few investigations of this kind have been completed. A variety of other methods are employed by gerontologists to estimate the relative contribution of the "aging process" and variables associated with particular adult echelons, a task that continues to demand the most acute and sophisticated research approaches that can be devised. As might be expected, the still young field of gerontology has been more successful thus far

in describing adult populations than in determining precisely the interaction between the "aging process" and specific characteristics of each echelon and subpopulation.

Many gerontologists consider that the time frame of their research efforts must begin at midlife or even earlier. It is not unusual for gerontologists also to study the total life span from birth through advanced age, or at least as much of this span as their resources permit. Often underlying this approach is the belief that processes associated with aging begin long before the individual reaches the advanced years of life.

Most gerontological studies are conducted by researchers trained in one or more well-established fields of science, such as biology, psychology, sociology, and so forth. Attention should be given, however, to the gradually increasing number of contributions from experts in the humanities (e.g., Achenbaum, 1978; Van Tassel, 1979). The methods employed by historians, literary critics, and other humanists sometimes differ from those employed by investigators within the core scientific tradition, but nevertheless represent appropriate and valuable endeavors in their own right. Such questions as What does it *mean* to be old? invite the interest of humanists. Gerontology is widely held to be a field in which contributions from many disciplines are required, and this is proving to include humanists as well as representatives from all the life and social sciences.

The application of knowledge for the benefit of mature and aged adults has also become a goal and, at times, a reality for gerontology. Society's response to the burgeoning number of older adults requires planning and adjustment in many spheres. Some gerontologists have become active in attempting to bring their data into play as policy and program decisions are made.

Areas of ambiguity remain in attempting to determine the boundaries and functions of gerontology. The term *gerontologist* has sometimes been applied not only to those who study aging and the aged, but to those who provide clinical services or are active in public affairs. In the strict sense, this appellation appears to be in error, because *gerontology* strongly implies a scientific or scholarly mission. However, the lack of a more suitable term seems to have created a vacuum filled by *gerontologist*. The term *geriatrics* (analogous to *pediatrics*) is often employed by health care providers to older adults. *Geriatric medicine* is perhaps the most familiar combined term, but other fields such as nursing and dentistry have also adopted this descriptor as more and more practitioners become involved with older clients. From a formalistic standpoint, it would be most straightforward if the term *gerontology* were restricted to the study of aging and the aged, with *geriatrics* reserved for caregivers. It is unlikely, however, that such a simple rule will hold firm as both the scholarly and the applied dimensions of the overall field continue to grow, interact, and change at a rapid rate.

Another area of ambiguity concerns gerontology as a career and as a basis for administrative entities. There are differences of opinion, for example, regarding the viability of awarding degrees in gerontology, as distinguished from degrees within a more established subject area with concentration or specialization in gerontology. Some colleges, universities, and hospitals have established administrative entities under the flag of gerontology. Others have preferred to develop coordinating activities among various disciplines in the name of gerontology but without administrative control by gerontology. Related to this unsettled situation is the fact that some people consider themselves to be primarily gerontologists, whereas others with similar background and activities continue to emphasize their "home discipline" (e.g., psychology, anthropology, or political science). It is reasonable to expect a continued period of variability and ambiguity that will be influenced by the increasing number of people who enter the field with specific training in gerontology, by the nature of employment opportunities, and many other factors.

Despite all ambiguities, however, gerontology has taken its place as an active field of scientific and scholarly endeavor that is just beginning to approach Metchnikoff's prophecy that it "will bring about great modifications in the course of the last period of life."

ROBERT KASTENBAUM

See also
American Geriatrics Society
Geriatrics
Gerontological Society of America

Humanities and the Arts
Organizations in Aging

GÖTEBORG LONGITUDINAL STUDY

Background

The longitudinal gerontological/geriatric study of 70-year-olds in Göteborg, Sweden, started in 1971 after a 2-year planning stage and a pilot study ($n = 50$) (Rinder, Roupe, Steen, & Svanborg, 1975). Through a detailed analysis of morphology, function, metabolism, morbidity, and follow-ups over many years, the goals set were as follows:

1. To differentiate manifestations of aging from symptoms of definable diseases and to improve knowledge of normative values (clinical, psychological, etc., reference values).

2. Through a better understanding of aging, to obtain information on the real incidence/prevalence of abnormal conditions in older persons and to minimize under/overdiagnosis.

3. Through the longitudinal perspective, to identify a subsample of healthy older persons and to study aging per se at the ages at which manifestations of aging become evident but are often mixed with symptoms of morbidity that are similar.

4. Through this combination of detailed evaluations of function and health, to examine the real need for care and other forms of support.

5. To study nongenetical influence on aging per se through the prospective and detailed retrospective information of personal history and main life events. (Historians were at certain times involved to strengthen background data.)

6. To measure age cohort differences for further understanding of the influence of exogenous factors on aging, and through predictions based on ongoing trends in changes of vitality and health to improve prerequisites for societal planning. To what extent would measures not only to prevent disease but to postpone

certain negative consequences of aging be realistic?

When important age cohort differences were observed between the first two age cohorts (born in 1901/1902 and 1906/1907), a medico-social intervention program was added to a third age cohort born in 1911/1912 to test certain hypotheses on relationships between aging/health and lifestyle/environment. Sponsorship was initially obtained from private sources, then from governmental research foundations, mainly the Swedish Medical Research Council and the Delegation for Social Research, and from the Medical and Social Services Administrations in Göteborg.

Methodology

Sweden has a highly reliable population register from which a systematic sampling was performed of 30% ($n = 1,148$, 521 males and 627 females) of 70-year-olds born during the period from July 1, 1901, to June 30, 1902, on dates ending with 2, 5, or 8, and currently living in Göteborg. To minimize nonresponse due to deaths between dates of sampling and of investigation, sampling was performed in four steps during the year; and to compensate for variations over the year, examinations were evenly distributed. A systematic sampling of a control group of people born on dates ending with 0 or 1 ($n = 828$) was performed in September 1972 during the last month of data collection.

Comparison between responders (participation rate of first cohort, 85%; second, 81%; third, 77%) and nonresponders indicated that the responders were generally representative of the total population of 70-year-olds; and longitudinally, up to age 81, mortality in cohort 1 did not differ between nonresponders and responders (Nilsson-Ehle, Jagenburg, Landahl, Svanborg, & Westin, 1988). All participants had a home call for 1 1/2 hours with interview by a registered nurse on social conditions and contacts, drug usage, and housing and home facilities (e.g., illumination) and a full day of detailed examination at the outpatient department of Vasa Hospital. When indicated, further special examinations were given during the following days. Great emphasis was put on diet history, physical activity habits and performance, and cognitive testing. The exami-

nations were generally performed between 1 and 4 weeks after birthdays.

The importance of regular intra/interobserver variation registration is obvious for such detailed studies, involving several examiners and a long time period. The low variations observed were partly due to systematic training before the start of the study (Rinder, Roupe, Steen, & Svanborg, 1975).

Findings

The research has hitherto been documented in more than 250 publications in international journals and books (for reviews, see Berg, Nilsson, & Svanborg, 1988; Svanborg, 1977, 1988, 1993).

The methodology for the identification of "healthy" individuals (persons without symptoms of definable disease) and for the calculation of clinical reference values is complicated, as manifestations of aging can be almost identical with symptoms of morbidity, and interindividual differences for many parameters are greater at age 70 to 80 than in middle-aged people. With increasing age beyond 70 years, the proportion of healthy persons declines; and a greater original sample would have been needed (and followed up) if a substantial group of healthy people had been available for adequate calculations of reference values at ages above 80. For certain calculations such as hematological values (Nilsson-Ehle, Jagenburg, Landahl, & Svanborg, 1986), only persons with conditions known to influence special hematological parameters (e.g., cobalamin [B_{12}]) needed to be excluded, which made for a larger available population.

Both overdiagnosis and underdiagnosis are common in older persons. The studies of normative values and changes caused by aging per se included aging-related changes in blood pressure (Landahl, Bengtsson, Sigurdsson, & Svanborg, 1986), hematological values (Nilsson-Ehle, Jagenburg, Landahl, Svanborg, & Westin, 1988), joint disorders (Bagge, Bjelle, Eden, & Svanborg, 1992), thyroid disorders (Sundbeck, Lundberg, Lindstedt, Jagenburg, & Eden, 1991), and cardiac morphology and function (Lernfelt, Wikstrand, Svanborg, & Landahl, 1991), exemplifying areas where our study has contributed to improved diagnostic criteria. Considerable efforts were made to study aging-related change in cognition, personality traits, and mental health (Berg, Nilsson, & Svanborg, 1988; Persson, Berg, Nilsson, & Svanborg, 1991), including several analyses of prevalence and incidence of different forms of dementia (Persson et al., 1991; Skoog, Nilsson, Palmertz, Andreasson, & Svanborg, 1993). The dementia studies also illustrate estimations of different degrees of severity and needs of care, even in the perspective of time. In general, persons with Alzheimer's disease lived longer and used longer periods of care than did those with vascular forms of dementia. Contrary to the general opinion that Alzheimer's forms of dementia dominate at very old age, detailed examinations showed that vascular dementias were at least as common at age 85 in this Swedish population.

Results proving or indicating an influence of exogenous factors not only on health but on certain functional consequences of aging have been surveyed (Svanborg, 1993). Our longitudinal studies illustrated, for example, the negative influence of tobacco smoking on manifestations of aging such as density of the skeleton, with increased risk for fractures; exacerbated tooth loss; and factors demonstrating accelerated gonadal aging. Also, alcohol abuse, social isolation, and bereavement influenced manifestations of aging (Mellström, Nilsson, Oden, Rundgren, & Svanborg, 1982). Age-cohort differences in, for example, cognitive function (S. Berg, 1980) and blood pressure (Svanborg, 1989) further exemplify major influences of lifestyle and environment. The manifold observations of exogenous influence on aging must result in considerations of possibilities to postpone negative manifestations of aging.

In 1981 an intervention study was added to the third age cohort (Eriksson, Mellström, & Svanborg, 1987). The intervention engaged a team of architects, dentists, dieticians, economists, historians, and a variety of disciplines, such as occupational therapists, physiotherapists, psychologists, sociologists, and statisticians, as well as representatives of local authorities, government agencies, and volunteer organizations. The primary goals were to (1) maintain or improve physical and mental functioning or retard development of disablement, (2) increase the sense of well-being (i.e., improve the subjective quality of life), (3) reduce the need for social services, and (4) offer more appropriate health screening and treatment, thereby reducing the need for medical service.

The intervention program was governed by four main concepts:

1. Adequate medical service, with avoidance of underdiagnosis or overdiagnosis, improves vitality, quality of life, and possibly also slows age-related decline in function.
2. The activity hypothesis: adequate functional loading in areas such as physical and intellectual activity and social integration and engagement decreases the rate of functional decline in the aging person.
3. The lifestyle hypotheses: personal lifestyle has consequences for functional performance and state of health.
4. The resource perspective, focusing on the capacities of the individual and how these capacities can be developed in social interaction and productivity in the widest sense.

The intervention period was 2 years, with a follow-up period of 3 years. The final comparison of three samples at ages 75 to 76 has been finished.

The interest in participation was unexpectedly high. The response rate to the first basic investigations, which included home calls and a 1-day examination at the hospital, was 78% in the intervention sample and 76% in the medical control sample. These samples were shown to be generally representative for the total population in Göteborg, although a difference in income was observed. These first examinations of state of health and functional performance were followed by three group meetings informing participants about the background for the interventions and available intervention programs. The participation in the group meetings was also high, varying from 78% to 67% of those who had agreed to take part in the first basic investigation.

This broad intervention program was generally well accepted. The very fact that our reserve capacity goes down means that the need for preventive/postponing measures becomes more and more obvious. However, we also have to be realistic in the terminal phase of our lives and be aware that reserves available to postpone the negative manifestations of aging and for "reactivation" after events threatening vitality have diminished.

More detailed and active interventions, and possibly also interventions over a longer period of time than 2 years, have to be evaluated until possibilities for positive outcomes of attempts to postpone functional, aging-related decline can be evaluated.

When the survivors of the first age cohort sample (30/70 of the population) reached age 85, all other 85-year-olds in Göteborg were also invited to participate in the further longitudinal follow-ups. Thus, manifestations of aging per se have been studied more in detail at ages when they commonly are obscured by morbidity, sharpening diagnostic and treatment criteria and illustrating that exogenous factors such as personal lifestyle are influencing not only morbidity but also certain aging-related dysfunctions. Measures to postpone functional decline were identified and tested.

The studies at ages above 85 are under the leadership of Dr. Bertil Steen (Steen & Djurfeldt, 1993).

ALVAR SVANBORG

See also
Longitudinal Studies of Aging
Longitudinal Studies: Europe

GRANDPARENT-GRANDCHILD RELATIONSHIPS

Because of recent sociodemographic changes involving greater longevity, decreased fertility, and increased rates of nuclear family disruption through divorce, relationships between grandparents and grandchildren are increasingly important in today's society. A central issue in research concerning grandparent-grandchild relations is the strength of bonds or the solidarity between them. The lives of grandparents and their grandchildren are linked in a number of ways: through roles, through interactions, through sentiments, and through exchanges of support. It is useful to examine grandparent-grandchild relations in terms of six dimensions of intergenerational solidarity (Silverstein, Giarrusso, & Bengtson, 1998): affectual, structural, associational, functional, consensual, and normative family solidarity.

Affectual solidarity involves the degree of closeness that is felt between grandparents and grandchildren. Although both grandparents and grandchildren report feeling close to one another, grandparents report a greater degree of closeness than do grandchildren. Further, the relationship between grandparents and grandchildren is often influenced by the middle generation, because parents provide the opportunities for grandparents and grandchildren to socialize together when the children reside in the parental household. If parents are emotionally close to grandparents, grandparents and grandchildren are more likely to be close as well. As a result of gender differences in the kinkeeper role, there is a tendency for grandchildren to have a closer relationship with their maternal grandparents. Whatever the feelings of closeness between grandparents and grandchildren when they are young, these feelings remain relatively consistent as grandchildren grow up and move away geographically from their grandparents. In a study of adult grandparent-grandchild relationships over 23 years, it was found that, after an initial decline, affective relationships tended to improve very late in the lives of grandparents (Silverstein & Long, 1998).

Structural solidarity is the opportunity for association between grandparents and grandchildren, the foremost being the geographic distance between them. In a nationally representative study of the United States, geographic proximity was found to be the strongest predictor of association between grandparents and grandchildren (Uhlenberg & Hammill, 1998). However, a variety of other factors also influence opportunities for association. Grandparent-grandchild opportunities for association have been found to be influenced by the demographic and personal characteristics of the grandparent and grandchild, such as their age, gender, and health, and by the marital, employment, and socioeconomic status of the parents (Cherlin & Furstenberg, 1986). Divorce, single-parenting, and dual-earner marriages have increased drastically in recent years among the parent generation, which in turn has had a dramatic impact on opportunities for grandparents and grandchildren to associate with one another.

Associational solidarity concerns the frequency of contact between the grandparent and grandchild. Most grandparents and grandchildren do stay in regular contact (Uhlenberg & Hammill, 1998). However, parental divorce has two consequences for association. It can result in greater interaction and solidarity, as is the case when the daughter returns to the parental home temporarily following divorce or when the mother is incapable of caring for the children. On the other hand, parental divorce has a particularly negative effect on the relationship between grandparents and grandchildren whose parents have not been given custody, usually the father. Even though all states now have grandparent's rights legislation, which gives grandparents the power to go to court to secure their right to visit with their grandchildren, associational solidarity will probably become increasingly matrilineal. However, these consequences of divorce do not hold for adult grandchildren whose relationships with grandparents are no longer directly mediated by their parents.

Functional solidarity is the help and assistance that is transferred between grandparents and grandchildren. When grandchildren are young, many if not most American grandparents provide direct help in babysitting them, and an increasing percentage of grandparents assume the role of "surrogate" parent when the middle generation is unable to provide caregiving as a result of problems such as drug and alcohol addiction, AIDS, divorce, incarceration, and unemployment (Giarrusso, Silverstein, & Feng, 2000). Grandparents typically adhere to the "norm of noninterference," which stipulates that grandparents should not interfere with the activities of the nuclear family (Cherlin & Furstenberg, 1986). In most families, the real value of grandparents lies in their simple presence, not their actions.

Consensual solidarity indicates the amount of intergenerational similarity in beliefs and values. Grandparents, as well as parents, are the primary agents of socialization who transmit to their grandchildren the values and norms of social order. Studies of young adult grandchildren indicate that consensual solidarity between grandparents and grandchildren remains high even after grandchildren reach adulthood. The majority of postadolescent grandchildren feel their grandparents influence their values and behaviors. Attitudes toward which grandparents have had the greatest influence include adult grandchildren's beliefs about family, morals, and the work ethic (Brussoni & Boon, 1998). However, both maternal and paternal grandmothers seem to have a stronger sway over their grandchildren; grandsons as well as granddaughters indicate that their values are more greatly influenced by their grandmothers than their grandfathers.

Normative solidarity concerns the perceptions of obligations and expectations about intergenerational connections. Research has identified the many burdens faced by grandparents who assume direct, full-time caregiving responsibilities for their grandchildren, which include economic difficulties; social isolation; grandchildren who have physical and psychological problems; adult children who are dysfunctional, sick, addicted, or incarcerated; and an overall lack of time. However, normative family solidarity tends to mediate the effect of these burdens on the psychological well-being of grandparents. Among caregiving grandparents, stronger normative beliefs about the family are negatively associated with the perception of caregiving as stressful and positively associated with the perception of it as rewarding (Giarrusso, Silverstein, & Feng, 2000).

In conclusion, grandparent-grandchild relations can be evaluated along multiple dimensions of intergenerational solidarity and demonstrate substantial variability along those dimensions. As grandparents and grandchildren spend more and more years of adult life together, due to increases in longevity of older people, such information is increasingly important.

ROSEANN GIARRUSSO
MERRIL SILVERSTEIN

See also
Family
Foster Grandparent Program
Intergenerational Relationships

GRANDPARENTS RAISING GRANDCHILDREN

Although grandparents raising grandchildren is not a new phenomenon, it is a rapidly growing trend. The number of children being raised in a grandparent-headed household increased by 76% between 1970 and 1997, but the greatest increase has been in households where no parent is present. Between 1990 and 1998 alone, the number of these households increased by 53% (Casper & Bryson, 1998).

This surrogate parenting situation usually results from substance abuse, abandonment, child abuse and neglect, teenage pregnancy, death, divorce,

AIDS, or incarceration, as well as mental or physical incapacity of the parent. Research data reveals that 10.9% of all grandparents in the United States will be primary caregivers for one or more grandchildren for a period of at least 6 months during their lives. Nearly half of these will be caregivers for 5 years or more (Fuller-Thompson, Minkler, & Driver, 1997). The scope of the problem was nationally acknowledged when the 1995 White House Conference on Aging made grandparents raising grandchildren one of its top priorities.

This is not just a caregiver's issue, however. Approximately 2.9 million children (4.2% of all American children) currently live in homes with no parent present. Of these, only 500,000 (17.3%) are in the formal foster care system, and they and their foster parents receive significant financial support and services.

The remaining 2.4 million children (82.7%) and the caregivers who are responsible for them receive little assistance and may encounter systems that make it difficult to access even basic services, such as health care and education. Because grandparents are disproportionately represented among the caregivers (two thirds are grandparents), surrogate parenting has now become an aging and intergenerational as well as a family issue, affecting every socioeconomic and ethnic group, as well as both rural and urban communities.

Since 1995 all of the major national conferences in the aging field have offered workshops and symposia approaching the issues of grandparents as parents from a variety of perspectives. There is a growing recognition of the importance of family roles, and publications in the aging field have been giving more attention to intergenerational issues, such as grandparents and relatives as surrogate parents. The Gerontological Society of America has established a Grandparent Caregiver Interest Group, which in turn has encouraged much more extensive research on kincare issues. What is most significant is that, for those caregiving families that are not in the formal system, it has been the aging network that has increasingly responded to meeting their needs.

For grandparents returning to child care responsibilities after many years, the challenges can be daunting. Grandparents are often isolated by their own feelings of failure and guilt in raising their own adult children and do not know where to go

to receive help in dealing with the unexpected new roles they face. In addition, they may find it hard to secure some of the basic services the children need if they are not the legal guardians or custodians.

Nineteen percent of children living in households headed by their parents were in poverty in 1997, compared with 27% of children living in grandparent-headed households. This expands to a staggering 65% in families headed by a grandmother only, with no parents present (Casper & Bryson, 1998). In addition, grandparent caregivers experience other stressors disproportionately.

Generations United indicates that "the stress of caring for young children, accompanied by their own health difficulties, can be overwhelming for many older grandparents, resulting in a variety of stress-related illnesses" (1998). Children may suffer from the health impacts of prenatal drug or alcohol exposure, resulting in special education needs and developmental problems. Studies indicate that grandparent caregivers are inclined to put the children's needs before their own, often compounding the difficulties of their situations. Legal and financial assistance, entitlement information, child care, housing, mental health, and respite services are often cited as unmet needs of caregivers.

A number of state child welfare systems have responded by developing more flexible approaches to financial assistance primarily for those in the formal system. By the end of 1999, 12 states offered some type of "stipended guardianship" (i.e., financial assistance based on a long-term kinship placement that did not require adoption of a child). However, the aging field continues its response to the majority of grandparent caregivers who are unwilling to exacerbate difficult family relationships by taking their adult children to court, and who therefore remain outside the formal system.

A few important national initiatives have been developed over the past number of years, which local communities and states can utilize. One of these is the Grandparent Information Center in Washington, DC, which offers information and referral services to caregivers and those agencies helping them, and has developed relevant studies and publications on kincare issues. Generations United, a national organization focused on promoting intergenerational public policies and programs, has included grandparents and other relatives raising children as a priority area of their intergenerational agenda. It also provides valuable informational material on innovative programs, as well as the status of state and federal policies affecting relatives as surrogate parents.

The Brookdale Foundation Group, as part of its national grant-making activities in the aging field, has enabled the expansion of needed services to relative caregivers through its Relatives as Parents Program, which was initiated in 1996. Since then, it provided seed grants to 75 community-based agencies and 24 public state agencies (18 of which are state offices on aging) across the country. Through the foundation's local initiative, community agencies have developed models of direct, accessible services to caregivers and their families. Through its statewide initiative, state agencies address the broad issues impacting relative caregivers and children, with special emphasis on those outside the system.

Since the White House Conference on Aging in 1995 placed this issue on the national agenda, the aging network has responded. Services, research, and policy development have followed. What is evident is that grandparent caregiving has been a rapidly expanding aging and intergenerational issue.

JANET S. SAINER
KEVIN BRABAZON

GRAY PANTHERS

The Gray Panther Project Fund—better known as The Gray Panthers—is an intergenerational advocacy movement dedicated to promoting a positive attitude toward aging, exposing age-related inequities, influencing social policies, and organizing grass-roots networks to address social issues on the local, state, and national level.

Formed in Philadelphia, Pennsylvania, in 1970, the group was originally named The Consultation of Older and Younger Adults for Social Change. The founder and first convener of the organization was Margaret "Maggie" Kuhn. In recognition of the members' dramatic and sometimes radical tactics, the media dubbed the group The Gray Panthers. That name was officially adopted in 1971. In 1973, The Gray Panthers merged with consumer activist Ralph Nader's Retired Professional Action Group, and The Gray Panther Project Fund was incorporated to receive donations and allocate funds.

In 1999, there were more than 50 local Gray Panther chapters, or networks, in 35 states. Active local chapter membership exceeded 8,000, and 40,000 national members at large represented various age groups and ethnic, social, and economic backgrounds.

During national conventions held every 2 years, delegates representing local networks vote on positions and priorities of the organization's national focus, and verify the national elections of its offices and board of directors, who oversee the organizations national staff. Local networks enjoy a high degree of autonomy in determining local issue focus but collaborate with other networks for unified strategies on national issues.

On national and local levels, The Gray Panthers monitor age-related issues; organize grass-roots actions; form coalitions; attend and present conferences, teach-ins, and seminars; testify before Congress and other governmental bodies; take part in demonstrations, educational activities, and lawsuits in the public interest; conduct research, petition drives, and issue-organizing campaigns; and publish and distribute educational materials. The Gray Panthers are accredited by the United Nations Department of Public Information, have consultative status with the U.N. Economic and Social Council, and are represented on the executive committee of the American Section of the World Assembly on Aging.

National universal health care that is affordable, accessible, and accountable, as a social commitment and public responsibility, has been a primary concern throughout Gray Panther history. Other issues around which The Gray Panthers advocate and organize include age discrimination, Social Security issues, the media's portrayal of stereotypes, nursing home reform, the rights of the disabled, public education, housing, job and labor rights, corporate responsibility, political integrity, and civic participation and responsibility.

Believing that aging is a natural process shared by all living things, The Gray Panthers envision a future in which rigid categories of youth, adulthood, and old age, with their corresponding functions of education, work, and leisure, will be dissolved and people of all ages can enjoy education opportunities, meaningful employment, and social interaction without prejudice.

MARGARET E. KUHN
Updated by
TIMOTHY M. FULLER

See also
    Organizations in Aging

GRAYING OF HAIR
See
    Hair

GRECC
See
    Geriatric Research, Education, and Clinical Centers

GRIEF
See
    Bereavement

GROUP MEMBERSHIP

Extent of Membership

The United States, de Tocqueville noted well over 150 years ago, is a nation of joiners, an observation no less true today and equally applicable to the elderly. Aggregated national data from the 1991, 1992, 1993, and 1994 National Opinion Research Center's General Social Surveys (hereafter, 1990–1994 GSS) showed that 71% of Americans age 65 years and older belonged to one or more different types of voluntary associations, 45% belonged to two or more, and 25% were members of three or more. Although these data did not speak to levels of association participation or involvement, they probably underestimated the extent of membership, because persons were being asked about the *types* of

associations to which they belonged and not the number of individual memberships within each type.

Age Differences and Age Changes in Membership

The typical pattern of cross-sectional age differences in voluntary association membership is curvilinear: increasing affiliation rates through approximately age 35 to 44, roughly stable rates between age 45 and 59, and decreasing rates at some point after age 60. This general curvilinear pattern has persisted at least from the mid-1970s through the mid-1990s. However, studies have also shown that the lower membership rates of older persons compared with middle-aged persons can be accounted for by compositional differences in the characteristics of age groups. For example, on average, older persons are in poorer health; have lower levels of education and higher proportions of women; and are less likely to be married, have young children in the household, and be in the labor force, all of which are characteristics associated with lower membership levels. When such compositional differences are controlled—in effect, equating the characteristics of older and middle-aged persons—the membership levels of the aged are at least as high as, if not higher than, those of middle-aged persons. Longitudinal and retrospective analyses showed that average affiliation and participation levels were unchanged over periods of up to 5 years, and that older persons with stable or increasing levels outnumbered those with declining levels. Thus, among age cohorts, older persons do not seem to be any less likely to belong to associations, especially if compositional differences are taken into account; further, previously established patterns of association participation appear to persist (Cutler & Hendricks, 2000; Moen, Dempster-McClain, & Williams, 1992).

Correlates of Membership

Older persons are not equally likely to belong to voluntary associations. In fact, the 1990–1994 GSS data showed that older men had higher overall membership levels than older women. As was true for the population at large, there was a strong positive relationship between socioeconomic status and association membership and participation. Results have been inconsistent for racial differences, with some studies (Harootyan & Vorek, 1994) showing that older African Americans are more involved than older Whites, whereas the 1990–1994 GSS data indicate no difference by race. Because engagement often requires on-site participation, it is not surprising that healthier elders with transportation available belong to more associations, attend more frequently, and are more involved (Cutler, 1974; Cutler & Hendricks, 2000).

Types of Membership

In the 1990s, older persons most likely belonged, in descending order, to church-affiliated groups, fraternal groups, veterans groups, "other" groups, and hobby or garden clubs. Of these association types, four (church-related, fraternal, veterans, and other) were also in the top five according to GSS data from 1974–1975, and three (fraternal, church-related, and veterans) were in the top five according to 1955 National Opinion Research Center data. Thus, the relative ranking of the types of voluntary associations to which older Americans are most likely to belong has remained more or less constant over more than four decades.

Older persons have the highest membership levels of any age group in fraternal, church-affiliated, farm, political, and veterans groups and the lowest of any age group in sports groups, youth groups, school service groups, and professional or academic societies. Older men are more likely than older women to belong to fraternal groups, veterans groups, labor unions, and sports groups, whereas older women are more likely to belong to church-affiliated groups; other groups; and literary, art, discussion, or study groups. Gender differences in membership are minor for other types of associations.

Consequences of Membership

A variety of theoretical perspectives (e.g., Moen, Dempster-McClain, & Williams, 1992) would suggest that well-being should be related to voluntary association membership and participation. However, the available evidence is mixed. Some studies showed that psychological well-being was unre-

lated to overall membership and participation levels, especially after controlling for health and socioeconomic differences between participants and nonparticipants (Cutler & Danigelis, 1993). On the other hand, membership in church-affiliated groups appeared to be associated with higher levels of psychological well-being, a finding consistent with the growing number of studies documenting a salutary effect of religiosity on the well-being of elders (e.g., Koenig, Hays, Larson, George, Cohen, McCullough, et al., 1999). Other data showed that membership in clubs and organizations during one's adult years has a beneficial effect on health in one's later years (Moen et al., 1992), and that volunteering, at least some of which takes place in formal association contexts, has a protective effect on mortality (Musick, Herzog, & House, 1999).

Research Needs

Much of the research on voluntary association membership has been cross-sectional, descriptive, and quantitative. Longitudinal studies are needed that focus on factors influencing changes, with aging, in membership levels, extent of participation, and types of associations to which older persons belong. Age-specific trend analyses of national data on overall membership levels and participation in specific types of associations would be a valuable addition to the literature. We lack comprehensive, theoretically informed, and methodologically rigorous analyses of the predictors and consequences of membership for the older population as a whole and for major subgroups. Quantitative research on association membership should be supplemented by systematic qualitative analyses of the nature and meaning of participation in such groups. Finally, research on the "volunteer" has emerged as a very important but somewhat distinct focus of inquiry; more studies that examine the conceptual and empirical linkages between group membership in voluntary associations and voluntarism, and that compare their correlates and consequences are also needed.

STEPHEN J. CUTLER

See also
   Activity Theory
   Disengagement
   Volunteerism

GROUP PSYCHOTHERAPY

Psychotherapeutic treatment in groups is intended to ameliorate a wide range of psychological problems through group interaction. Among them are depressions, anxieties, obsessions, and interpersonal conflicts. Group treatments are guided by conceptions regarding the interpersonal causes of these conditions and group techniques for their alleviation. These conceptions may be designated as "dynamic-reconstructive" (derived from psychoanalytic or related ideas), "behavioral" (emphasizing the source of the pathology in faulty learning), and "directive-inspirational" (emotional encouragement for self-management and reorientation toward more positive self-attitudes).

The same problems of mutual avoidance that obstruct useful referrals to individual psychotherapy occur with groups. Butler (1975) has termed "ageism" the tendency among therapists to stereotype older persons as incapable of psychological growth and renewal. Evidence indicates that a wide range of therapeutic techniques with particular old people can be helpful. However, there are important distinctions between individual and group treatment contexts that should be considered in referring elderly clients to either type of therapy.

In recent decades, mainstream "schools" of individual psychotherapy have increasingly coopted group forms, mainly for the purpose of extending treatment to remedy presumed social and interpersonal deficits and disabilities, but also for economic reasons. There is no unequivocal evidence for the superiority of either type of therapy or any reliable distinction among those who should be referred to group as opposed to individual therapies. However, there are bases for inclusion or exclusion based on levels of communicative skills, degrees of emotional vulnerability, and tolerance for interaction with others. Individual treatment may be preferable for those who require a great deal of emotional support, those who are suspicious to the point of paranoia, and for those who cannot communicate with others by reason of excessive anxieties or severity of physiological impairment.

An understanding of comparative processes is essential to effective group treatment of old people. Among the distinctions are the following:

1. Groups are systems of mutual influence in contrast to the sole influence of the individual therapist.

2. In groups other members generate and reinforce a consensual version of emotional "reality."
3. Mood is often "contaged" from member to member in groups.
4. Desirable outcomes are dependent on the development of cohesion among the members of a group.
5. Narratives by clients are multidirectional, directed to group members and not only to the group's therapist.
6. Roles of members are fluid; members exchange roles of helper and helpee in the course of probes, support, and feedback to one another.

The "stuff" of group therapies is less autobiographical narrative, self-exploration, and therapist directive than interactive exchange, self-comparison with other members, and feedback from them (M. Lakin, 1986; M. Lakin, Oppenheimer, & Brewer, 1982). Groups are more "lifelike" in the sense that peers react not as paid and trained professionals but from their own emotional reactions and life experiences. In therapeutic groups the pressures and supports for change are mobilized from peers. However, group reactions are not always necessarily those the therapist might prescribe because they are also influenced by key group members.

Which context, group or individual, is ultimately more beneficial for elderly clients? There is substantial research evidence of the effectiveness of both these therapeutic forms, but no solid basis for saying one is more effective than the other. Groups tend to emphasize the social and the interpersonal more than the intrapersonal. Therefore, groups can provide a supportive social network; they provide a means for learning from the experiences of others who face similar psychological problems. In some cases they provide an opportunity to remedy social skill deficits. They can also reduce painful feelings of negative uniqueness.

Group therapists who treat the elderly must be prepared to modify their techniques of stimulation, probing, and feedback and to substitute techniques aimed at providing collective support if the members are too vulnerable. In groups of old people, the therapist must be prepared to challenge self-held negative stereotypes about being old. Here-and-now analyses of conflicts among the members should be carefully monitored rather than always encouraged; groups of the elderly do not engage in such conflict analysis as productively as younger groups. Gerontologic group therapists should anticipate greater involvement in issues of personal bereavements, financial problems, health concerns, and feelings of being a disadvantaged minority.

Leaders should expect to be more active in initiating, structuring, and mediating discussions. This is especially true of groups that include large discrepancies in participative capacities. It is also more necessary in groups that include high-dominance individuals. Between-session social contacts are often indicated as a means of reinforcing the supportive climate of the group.

There is no justification for concluding that the elderly cannot benefit from group *or* individual psychotherapies. However, cohort and culture are to a considerable extent predictors of characteristics and attitudes among the elderly that do affect their responses to group as well as to individual therapies. Such characteristics and attitudes mandate sensitivity and appropriate modification of traditional group techniques to fit the needs of this subset of the general population.

MARTIN LAKIN

See also
  Counseling Psychology
  Psychotherapy

GROWTH HORMONE AND INSULIN-LIKE GROWTH FACTOR-1

There is abundant empirical and scientific evidence to support the hypothesis that many of the age-related declines in tissue function are closely related to a decrease in hormone concentrations and/or hormone action. A decrease in growth hormone (GH) and insulin-like growth factor-1 (IGF-1) are two potent anabolic hormones that have been hypothesized to contribute to the loss of tissue function with age and the resulting physical disability in the elderly. GH is secreted from the anterior pituitary gland in discrete pulses that occur throughout the day with higher amplitude pulses occurring after

the onset of sleep. The pulsatile nature of GH release has been confirmed in every species examined and is necessary for full biologic actions of the hormone. Activation of the hepatic GH receptor stimulates the synthesis and secretion of IGF-1 into plasma. IGF-1 circulates in the blood at high concentrations and stimulates DNA, RNA, and protein synthesis and is a potent mitogen for many tissues. Because of the wide distribution of the GH receptor, GH may also have a role in regulating the synthesis and secretion of IGF-1 from many tissues, thereby directly influencing the paracrine or local activity of the hormone. Although it was initially proposed that all of the actions of GH were mediated through IGF-1, several studies have provided relatively convincing data that GH has direct effects on specific tissues and/or interacts with IGF-1 in the regulation of tissue function.

In humans, GH is released in pulsatile bursts from the pituitary gland with the majority of secretion occurring at night in association with slow-wave sleep. Similar pulses are observed in rodents, except that high-amplitude secretory pulses occur every 3.5 hours in males and hourly in females. The regulation of these pulses involve at least two hormones released by the hypothalamus: GH-releasing hormone (GHRH), which increases GH release, and somatostatin, which inhibits its release. The dynamic interactions between these hormones regulate high-amplitude, pulsatile GH secretion. GH and IGF-1 suppress GH release from the pituitary in a typical feedback relationship either directly at the level of the pituitary or by stimulating somatostatin and/or inhibiting GHRH release from the hypothalamus.

Early studies in humans reported a substantial decline in the ability to secrete GH with age in response to several stimuli, including insulin-induced hypoglycemia and arginine administration. Subsequent studies revealed a loss of the nocturnal surges of GH and a decrease in plasma IGF-1 that paralleled the decline in GH pulses. These results have been confirmed by numerous investigators, and it is now evident that the decline in high-amplitude GH secretion and plasma IGF-1 concentrations are one of the most robust and well-characterized events that occur with age (Corpas, Harman, & Blackman, 1993). Similarly, decreases in the amplitude of GH pulses are observed in rodent models of aging, and these changes are closely associated with a decline in plasma IGF-1 (Sonntag, Lynch, Cefalu, Ingram, Bennett, Thornton, et al., 1999). Although the specific etiology for the decline in GH pulse amplitude has not been fully detailed, studies in both humans and animals documented a decline in in vivo pituitary response to GHRH with age. However, numerous studies attempting to detail the deficits within the pituitary gland produced controversial results that ultimately were attributed to (1) differential responses of older animals to the pharmacological agents used to suppress endogenous GH pulses during in vivo testing or (2) difficulty in culturing anterior pituitary cells from older animals. Research efforts were eventually directed to an analysis of hypothalamic release and inhibiting hormones after studies revealed that acute administration of somatostatin antiserum in vivo increased GH release identically in young and old animals, passive immunization with somatostatin antiserum restored the in vivo deficiency in pituitary response to GHRH, and stimulation of hypothalamic slices of old animals in a superfusion system released greater quantities of somatostatin than in those of young animals. These results provided compelling evidence that increased somatostatin tone may be a contributing factor in the decline in GH pulses with age. These conclusions were further supported by research in humans, where administration of cholinergic agonists or arginine, considered to preferentially inhibit somatostatin release, increased GH secretion in older individuals. Over the past several years, research has supported these conclusions and demonstrated that translational regulatory factors that normally control the association of somatostatin messenger RNA (mRNA) with the polyribosome are altered in aged animals. In addition, decreases in GHRH mRNA occur with age and the regulation of GHRH mRNA is altered in aged animals. Thus, alterations in both hypothalamic release and inhibiting hormones appear to be a key factor in the decline in GH pulse amplitude with age, although the etiology of these changes remains elusive.

Although an attenuation of growth hormone pulse amplitude is an important contributing factor in the decline in plasma IGF-1, more recent studies demonstrate that, in response to growth hormone administration, IGF-1 secretion is diminished in elderly individuals. These results suggest that resistance to growth hormone action may be an additional contributing factor in the low plasma IGF-1 concentrations. In rodents, a twofold increase in growth hormone receptors has been observed with age that fails to compensate for the reduced levels of growth hormone. More detailed investigations revealed that the K_d and apparent size of the growth hormone receptor were not influenced by age, whereas the capacity of growth hormone to induce IGF-1 gene expression and secretion directly from hepatic slices was 40% to 50% less in old than young animals. Subsequently, deficiencies in the ability of GH to induce JAK, Stat3, and Map kinase were found, suggesting that an impairment in growth hormone receptor signal transduction contributes to the decline in IGF-1 in both animals and man (Xu & Sonntag, 1996).

Even though growth hormone resistance is an important component of the decrease in plasma IGF-1 with age, resistance can be partially overcome by administration of growth hormone. Limited studies in rodents over a decade ago revealed that administration of growth hormone increases IGF-1 and restores cellular protein synthesis in old animals, suggesting that the age-related decline in skeletal muscle mass and function is not solely related to intrinsic deficits within the tissue. Other reports were published demonstrating that growth hormone or IGF-1 administration could partially reverse the decline in immune function, increase the expression of aortic elastin, and increase life span in rodents. These studies were the first indications that the decrease in the concentration of growth hormone has clinical significance and may be responsible for the generalized catabolic state that accompanies normal aging. It has generally been reported that growth hormone increases IGF-1, lean body mass, muscle mass, and skin thickness and reduces total body fat content in the elderly (Rudman, Feller, Nagraj, Gergans, Lalitha, Goldberg, et al., 1990). In addition, there are some reports of elevations in serum osteocalcin (an osteoblast-produced marker of bone formation) and nitrogen retention, raising the possibility that growth hormone treatment may delay osteoporosis. Interestingly, aerobic exercise training for 1 year increases the amount of growth hormone secreted over a 24-hour period, suggesting that the beneficial effects of exercise training may be mediated, at least in part, by increasing growth hormone secretion.

Of recent interest are the effects of growth hormone and IGF-1 on the aging brain. Studies indicate that administration of growth hormone reverses the age-related decline in microvascular density on the surface of the brain and that microvessels produce IGF-1. These results led to the concept that the known deficiencies in brain levels of IGF-1 with age may be the result of low growth hormone levels and the subsequent reduction in plasma and micro-vascular derived IGF-1 (Sonntag, Lynch, Cefalu, Ingram, Bennett, Thornton, et al., 1999). In fact, administration of IGF-1 directly to the brain of aged animals has been shown to improve both reference and working memory (Markowska, Mooney, & Sonntag, 1998), glucose utilization, and function of several neurotransmitter systems. Similar benefits on spatial memory have been noted after twice daily administration of GHRH to increase plasma levels of GH and IGF-1.

Although there are many potential beneficial effects of GH therapy in aged animals and humans, the side effects of therapy include sodium retention, carpal tunnel syndrome, glucose resistance, and hyperinsulinemia. Epidemiological studies also have indicated a significant correlation between levels of IGF-1 and prostate, breast, and lung cancer, raising the concern that administration of these mitogenic hormones may initiate or accelerate pathological changes in the elderly. These issues have not been directly tested to date, but recent studies indicate that moderate caloric restriction (60% of ad libitum fed animals, which decreases pathological risk and increases life span in rodents) decreases levels of IGF-1. Subsequent administration of IGF-1 to these animals appears to remove the protective effects of moderate caloric restriction, providing support for the concept that the beneficial effects of moderate caloric restriction are mediated, in part, by decreasing levels of IGF-1. Thus, the available evidence suggests that a decline in GH and IGF-1 contribute to the aging phenotype but that administration of these hormones has the potential to have both beneficial and deleterious effects.

WILLIAM E. SONNTAG

GUARDIANSHIP/ CONSERVATORSHIP

A major dilemma confronting aging societies is how to provide adequate protection for persons deemed mentally incompetent to manage their affairs. One approach, used in some industrialized societies such as the United States, is to petition the court to grant decision-making power to a surrogate through legal guardianship. In the United States, the authority resides with the state to protect persons who are at risk of physical, emotional, and/or financial harm, and sometimes to protect others from such persons. Although many state statutes are based on the Uniform Probate Code (UPC), procedures and terminology vary substantially from state to state (Hommel, 1996; Kapp, 1999). For example, the majority of states use the term *guardianship* to describe court-appointed surrogate decision making. *Guardian* refers to the legally appointed decision maker, and *ward* indicates the individual judged to lack capacity. Some states, however, use the terms *conservatorship*, *conservator*, and *conservatee*, respectively. A few states use *committee* or *curator*. For purposes of this discussion, the term *guardianship* will be used generically.

Guardianship disproportionately affects older adults because it is designed to serve dependent persons, many of whom suffer from disorders that impair cognitive functioning. It is important to point out, however, that age per se should not be used as an indicator of need for guardianship (Reynolds, 1997). In the United States, less than 2% of persons age 65 and older, or about 500,000 older adults, are under legal guardianship (Schmidt, 1995).

Authority and Powers

Guardianship authority derives from the power of *parens patriae*, which obligates the state to "parent" or protect those who are unable to care for themselves. As such, guardianship is a highly intrusive, protective intervention in which the court appoints a surrogate to make decisions on behalf of an adult. Plenary guardianship is a legal process that grants the guardian authority to make virtually all decisions, including property and assets management, legal transactions, living arrangements, and medical treatment. Advantages of guardianship are that it serves as a vehicle to protect elders and other dependent adults and to conserve their assets by transferring decisional control to a surrogate. A major disadvantage is that granting custodial and economic control of an adult to a proxy rescinds the ward's basic civil rights. Guardianship converts an adult's legal status to that of a minor by court order. Thus, in democratic societies such as the United States, it is at odds with a tradition of civil liberties designed to protect citizens' rights to freedom and self-determination. In addition, guardianship is often costly to initiate and maintain, and may be time-consuming and stressful to the parties involved. Guardianship also is associated with high rates of institutionalization. Studies indicate that over two thirds of adult conservatees reside in institutional settings (Reynolds & Wilber, 1999).

A guardian usually is appointed after the observance of standard legal procedures including the filing of a petition by an "interested person" and a hearing to determine the alleged incompetent's capacity to manage his or her affairs. The hearing may involve evidence by a person of authority, often a physician, to establish that the individual lacks capacity to make reasoned decisions. The hearing also may be used to determine if a responsible party is available to serve as guardian. In the United States, when persons lack qualified and willing family or friends and do not have adequate resources to hire a private professional guardian, most states have provisions for government involvement through various types of public guardian programs. To address both financial and personal risk, states typically separate guardianship into decisional power of the person (e.g., living arrangements, physical well-being, and medical treatment) and the estate (e.g., managing property, assets, and income). A guardian can be appointed for one or both areas. In states that follow the UPC terminology, guardian indicates management of personal decisions and conservator denotes management of the estate.

In addition to plenary guardianship, the majority of states, recognizing that persons may have varying degrees of incapacity, provide limited guardianships. Limited guardianships tailor the guardian's authority to the individual needs of the ward by transferring powers only in areas specifically stipulated by the court (Hommel, 1996; Kapp, 1999; Keith & Wacker, 1994). The advantage of limited guardianship is that the ward is protected without undue restriction. Yet many courts appear reluctant to tailor guardianships because of the potential time

involved and concern that the intervention will be insufficient.

Research

Guardianship research falls into three broad areas: (1) descriptive characteristics of wards and their guardianship; (2) characteristics of guardianship, including judicial processes and procedures; and (3) the use of less restrictive services to avoid or delay guardianship. As reviewed in Reynolds (1997), descriptive studies suggest that conservatees are likely to be females over the age of 65 with relatively low income and some degree of cognitive impairment. Recognizing the need for comparative research across age groups and disability types, a few studies have compared differences among conservatees based on age. For example, Reynolds and Wilber (1997) found that older conservatees are more likely than younger conservatees to be female, divorced or widowed, White, diagnosed with either dementia or developmental disorder, and have higher levels of physical and sensory impairments. In addition, older conservatees are on fewer medications and exhibit fewer dangerous behaviors, but are less likely than younger conservatees to be oriented to time and place.

A number of studies have focused on the process and performance of legal guardianship. Identified problems include lack of due process in court proceedings, poor performance and abuse by guardians, lack of sufficient oversight by the courts, and use of guardianship to serve third-party interests and social control purposes (Hommel, 1996; Keith & Wacker, 1994; Schmidt, 1995). Although reform efforts have been underway during the last decade, implementation has been slow and uneven.

In addition to reform efforts, there has been increasing interest in ensuring that guardianship is used only as a last resort. As a result, a variety of financial and health-related decision-making services have been identified as potential substitutes or preventive interventions for plenary guardianship (Wilber & Reynolds, 1995). These include daily money management (DMM), case management, durable powers of attorney, trusts, and temporary and limited guardianships. Such options hold the promise of safeguarding vulnerable elders without compromising their rights to make personal and financial decisions. To date, studies of case management and DMM interventions have not demonstrated that these less restrictive services replace or delay guardianship (Wilber & Reynolds, 1995).

In recent years, there has been a sharp rise in the number of petitions filed for guardianship (Kapp, 1999). Increases in life expectancy and the concomitant rise in the number of persons with cognitive impairment suggest that the use of guardianship and other forms of surrogate decision making are likely to accelerate in the years to come. Despite guardianship's ancient roots in Roman civil law and medieval English common law, as Schmidt (1995) notes, the concepts underlying guardianship are still evolving. Therefore, continued efforts to systematically describe characteristics of guardianship, wards, and guardians, as well striving to strike the right balance between civil liberties and the need for protective interventions, present important challenges for the 21st century.

KATHLEEN H. WILBER

See also
Living Wills and Durable Power of Attorney
Proxy Decision Making

H

HAIR

Scalp and body hair undergo gradual changes with age, superimposed on the known effects on hair of heredity and ethnic differences, nutrition, drugs, climate, a number of systemic disorders, and the sex of the individual. Asians and Native Americans have less body hair and are less likely to become bald than are Caucasians. Hormones, notably androgens, induce hair growth in sexual areas and lead to selective loss in others; ethnic and racial differences may be a result of different levels of circulating androgens or differential sensitivity of the follicle to androgens. For additional information regarding age-related changes in hair, see Kligman (1961) and Rook and Dawber (1982).

Each hair follicle cycles through a growing phase (anagen), a transitional phase (catagen), and an involutional phase (telogen), with the duration of each phase varying with the region of the body. The average person has approximately 100,000 scalp hairs, of which at least 85% are in the anagen phase. On the scalp, anagen hairs usually grow for 3 to 10 years, then go through the catagen phase for 2 to 3 weeks, and finally the telogen phase for 3 to 4 months, following which the hair is shed and new anagen hair grows from the same follicles. Other body hair follicles have a shorter anagen phase, lasting perhaps months.

This cycling through anagen/catagen/telogen phases partially explains the length of hair of various regions. For example, the long anagen phase of scalp hair helps produce flowing tresses, whereas eyebrow hairs have a short anagen phase. The normal growth rate of scalp hair is 1/2 inch per month, with the rate somewhat faster in women than men; however, the rate of growth of body hair in men is faster than in women.

The two most obvious associations with aging are balding and graying of the hair. Balding is closely associated with changes in the hair cycle as well as the response of the hair follicle to androgens. Scalp balding is androgen dependent; eunuchs castrated before puberty do not become bald. Males appear to develop balding when either homozygous or heterozygous for a "balding" gene, but females do so only when homozygous. In common balding (pattern alopecia) the catagen and telogen cycles appear to remain unchanged, but the anagen phase becomes shorter, increasing the rate of hair loss and decreasing density.

In males, the thinning of pattern balding starts in the frontal hairline and vertex, with the development of sparse fine hairs. The scalp otherwise remains normal in appearance. Female pattern balding tends to be diffuse loss over the top of the scalp, while retaining the frontal hairline. Hair in a male pattern is more common in women whose ancestry goes back to the southern parts of Europe than in those from northern countries.

In addition to balding, graying of scalp and body hair accompanies aging. Graying is an irreversible and progressive process and results from a gradual diminution in melanin production by the melanocytes in the hair bulb matrix. By age 50, approximately half the Caucasian population has at least 50% gray hair. Usually, graying of the beard and body hair begins later than scalp hair, with axillary and pubic hair losing pigmentation last. Dark hair tends to gray earlier than light hair, although persons with light hair are more likely to become completely gray. Graying also is influenced by hereditary and hormonal factors. Graying occurs earlier and more frequently in men than in women, and less often and later in life in Blacks than in Whites.

With aging, the androgen-dependent hair follicles make a gradual transition from producing coarse, long terminal hairs to fine, short, less dense vellus or infantile hairs. The fine vellus hairs in the ears and nose of elderly men change to thick terminal hairs. Some investigators have found that with increasing age past adulthood, groups of three or more hair follicles sprout from existing follicles, although new scalp hair follicles are not believed to develop after birth.

Scalp hair is not necessary for survival, but it is highly valued as a measure of personal attractiveness. However, the timing and extent of balding and graying vary so much from person to person that neither are good measures of the aging process.

ESTHER C. THRASHER
STANFORD I. LAMBERG

See also
  Skin

HEALTH AND RETIREMENT SURVEY

The Health and Retirement Survey (HRS) is a newly developed longitudinal survey focused initially on retirement decisions and eventually on the interconnections between health transitions and economic status in old age. Unique features of the study include the following:

- Lengthy and intensive planning process
- Development of innovative survey techniques designed to reduce measurement error and to provide explicit representation of uncertain future events
- Linkage of household survey data with administrative record data
- Collection of data from both spouses in couple households
- Use of theory and model-based criteria for determining variables or sets of variables to be included on the core database
- Decision to reserve survey content for experimental measures judged to be high risk

The evolution of a new study of retirement and aging is almost certainly attributable to the widespread recognition among economists, demographers, and epidemiologists that the aging of the baby-boom generation will cause an unprecedented shift in the U.S. population toward a greater proportion of dependent to total population, and thus to a greater need to understand the determinants of labor supply, health expenditures, longevity, and transfers.

Planning Process for the Health and Retirement Survey

The need for an extensive deliberative process underpinning the HRS was spelled out in the program announcement by the sponsors of the study, the National Institute on Aging (NIA). It was indicated that planning for a retirement study should last for at least a year and should focus on the following four domains of major concern:

1. Labor force participation and pensions
2. Health conditions and health status, including cognitive health
3. Family structure and transfers
4. Economic status, including income, wealth, housing, and insurance

Although past studies have been concerned with one or more of these domains, none has focused on all four simultaneously. Planning groups involving researchers from academic settings as well as public policy agencies were formed to develop initial content recommendations in each of these areas. Similar planning groups were set up to deal with recommendations about linkages with administrative records, and to be concerned with the details of field activity on the survey. An oversight, or steering, committee responsible to the principal investigator was set up; a second oversight committee, responsible to the NIA, was established, because HRS was specified to be a cooperative agreement rather than a grant. Such agreements provide the NIA with major input into design decisions; each step of the survey must be approved by an NIA-designated data monitoring and design committee. Thus, the decision-making mechanism relating to HRS involved the development of ideas in the planning groups, discussion of these recommendations by the HRS steering committee and the NIA monitoring committee, and ultimately decisions by the principal investigator.

Innovative Survey Content

The unique survey content on HRS consists of two types of measures. The first type, typified by measures of family structure and transfers, has rarely been available in studies of retirement decisions and aging processes, although the measurements themselves are not novel. The basic idea is that certain types of family structures create pressures for people in their 50s to move out of the workforce to provide time-intensive care for family members—typically frail parents. Other family responsibilities create pressures to remain in the labor force and earn income to help family members financially—tuition and living expenses for children would be an example. Without knowing the details of the potential demand for such resources, as well as the details of the potential suppliers of these resources, it is not possible to specify the retirement model adequately. The same is true for health conditions and health status, where the principal HRS innovations were on the side of cognitive measurement, and labor force participation and pension, where the principal innovations were on the side of detailed measurements of the characteristics of pensions.

The second type of innovation consisted of measures that represent technical innovations. The principal ones were designed to reduce measurement error in the income and wealth variables, and to develop measures of subjective preferences and expectations about uncertain future events.

The subjective phenomena measured in HRS include a variety of probabilities associated with uncertain future events—the likelihood of full-time labor force participation in the future, the likelihood of living to ages 75 and 85, the likelihood of major medical events, the likelihood of losing one's job and finding an equivalent new job, and the likelihood of a major depression or of double-digit inflation. Other subjective measures were developed to reflect the rate of time preference among the population, and the degree of risk aversion. All these measures play critical roles in many economic, demographic, and epidemiological models of behavior, although it is rare that direct measurement of such phenomena is attempted in household surveys.

A second technical innovation on HRS is the attempt to reduce measurement errors in income and wealth variables. It is well known that the income and wealth measures obtained on household surveys ordinarily contain substantial amounts of missing data—on the order of 30% for net worth variables and 10% to 20% for income components. The analyst has no choice but to impute the missing data component by making the assumption that households with missing data or particular variables are identical to households who provide exact answers except for measurable differences in characteristics—such as education level, marital status, sex, and age.

HRS adopted the strategy of trying to place households in broad quantitative categories if they were unwilling or unable to provide exact dollar estimates of assets, debts, or income flows. Thus, respondents reporting that they owned an asset but did not know the value were asked whether their asset holdings were greater than x or less than x. If respondents said "greater than," they were asked whether the holdings were greater or less than y $(y > x)$; if they answered "less than," they were asked whether these holdings were greater or less than z $(z < x)$. The specific break points varied with the asset type.

Analysis of these HRS innovations indicates that substantial analytic payoff is likely. The bracketing data on assets and income indicate that respondents unwilling or unable to provide exact answers have substantially higher levels of assets than others, and the differences are large and not related to respondent characteristics. For the subjective probability measures, the evidence is that they clearly have face validity, and those that can be tested against objective data (longevity or probability of full-time work) appear to have little bias.

Administrative Record Linkages

HRS contains three different types of data that come from administrative records rather than from the household survey. First are the details of employer-provided pension plans obtained from firms that employed HRS respondents. Analysts are able to calculate pension rights under various assumptions about future employment. Second, we collected survey data from employers about the characteristics of the health insurance coverage of HRS respondents. Finally, we requested that HRS respondents sign permission forms enabling us to access their Social Security earnings and benefit records, which are lodged at the Social Security Administration. There is a memorandum of understanding between the University of Michigan (which collects and distributes the survey data) and the Social Security Administration regarding the release of a public use tape containing various types of Social Security data. The data have been placed into a protected data category within the Department of Health and Human Services, which prevents federal employees from any attempt to reidentify HRS respondents. Academic users sign an agreement about use restrictions that contains the same prohibitions.

Commitment to Continued Innovations

The HRS not only involves a substantial amount of survey experimentation in the initial wave of data collection, but the project is committed to a continued emphasis on innovative measures in future waves. As an illustration of that proposition, the second wave of HRS contains some measures of hours flexibility that resulted from an experimental module in HRS Wave I, and HRS Wave II also contains some unique measures of medical expenditures.

The general experimental focus of the study is best reflected by the use of experimental modules.

These consist of random subsamples of respondents asked a particular set of experimental questions. The modules run from 2 to 4 minutes in length, and reflect content perceived as too risky for inclusion on the main study but promising enough to warrant some exploration. Many of the modules reflect a methodological focus, in that they will enable analysts to compare HRS results with results of other surveys in which similar questions are asked but where the format of the questions is somewhat different.

Preliminary Results

Data collection on the first wave of HRS began in April 1992 and was completed in March 1993. Some 70,000 households were screened to identify households with one or more persons born between 1931 and 1941 (age 51 to 61 in 1992), with the sample population defined to include age-eligible respondents and their spouses regardless of age. African Americans, Hispanics, and residents of the state of Florida were oversampled at a 2:1 rate. The completed Wave I has approximately 12,600 respondents in roughly 7,600 households, with more than 2,000 African American respondents and more than 1,000 Hispanic respondents. The Wave I response rate was .82.

Of the roughly 7,600 households in the sample, a little over 5,000 are married-couple households where retirement decisions might well be joint between husband and wife, whereas the remaining roughly 2,400 are households in which the age-eligible person is unmarried—either widowed, divorced, or never married. The latter are predominantly women.

HRS Wave II was completed as of January, 1995. Some 11,600 persons were interviewed, with a response rate of approximately .92. The focus of Wave II data collection was on changes since Wave I in variables reflecting discrete states (marital status, employment status, insurance status, housing status, etc.) along with the remeasurement of variables reflecting continuous phenomena (income, wealth, medical expenditures, functional health, cognitive functioning, etc.).

Finally, a spin-off study from HRS was launched in 1993. During the screening activity in which the birth cohorts of 1931 to 1941 were identified for the HRS sample, other households with people in the birth cohorts of 1923 or earlier were also identified. These households, containing someone 70 years or older in 1993, are the subject of the spin-off study titled The Health and Asset Dynamics of the Oldest Old (AHEAD). The first wave of data collection on AHEAD was completed in May 1994.

For additional commentary on the HRS/AHEAD data sets and illustrations of their uses, see Myers (1997).

F. Thomas Juster

See also
Longitudinal Data Sets in Aging
Retirement

HEALTH ASSESSMENT

Health assessment requires a conceptual definition "capable of being translated into suitable operational definitions" (Moriyama, 1968). Health has been characterized as everything from freedom from disease, dysfunction, and disability, to a state of equilibrium, adaptation, harmony, and wholeness. It has ranged from the global World Health Organization (WHO; 1958) definition of health as "a state of complete physical, mental and social well-being and not merely the absence of disease and infirmity," to the most rudimentary definition implicit in mortality measures (Jette, 1980). Furthermore, health has been recognized as a continuum (Atchley, 1980; Bergner, 1985; Moriyama, 1968), but there is no consensus with respect to any of the stages between "health" at one extreme and "death" at the other.

The lack of conceptual clarity is particularly evident in efforts to assess the health of the elderly. This problem can be attributed, in part, to the pathological orientation toward the aging process in which chronological aging is equated with illness and/or degeneration (Arluke & Peterson, 1981). Thus, in this orientation to be old is to be sick and, after a certain age, to be sick is to be old.

Furthermore, the "absence of disease" model that reflects the dominant biomedical paradigm in health research and policy may not be appropriate for older persons. Given the fact that an estimated 86% of those age 65 and over have one or more chronic conditions (Kovar, 1983; Shanas & Maddox, 1976), this biomedical model is a limited conceptual framework for developing meaningful indicators of the health status of the elderly. It has been argued that among elderly persons with multiple chronic conditions, concern is not with cure but rather with maintaining functional independence. Although information on diagnosis is important, "those with the same diagnosis vary with respect to the manifestation of the disease, the course of the illness, the severity of the symptoms, and the resulting disability" (Fillenbaum, 1984, p. 9).

The concern over the limited utility of the "absence of disease" model has led many health researchers (Kane & Kane, 1981; Lawton, 1971; Shanas & Maddox, 1976) to assess the health of the elderly primarily in terms of functional adequacy. This approach is based on a social definition of health, initially proposed by Parsons (1951, 1972), that views health as a state of optimum capacity for performance of the roles and tasks for which a person has been socialized. The functional adequacy model implies that health in the elderly is best defined as "degree of fitness," rather than extent of pathology (WHO, Regional Health Office for Europe, 1959), and acknowledges the relationship between level of expectations and health status. It shifts the focus from an absolute state of health or illness toward a perception of health as a complex process of interaction between individuals and their ecological and cultural contexts. Furthermore, functional adequacy underscores the relative nature of the concept of health and emphasizes the importance of behavioral capability and the personal and social meaning of symptoms.

This model of health has been operationalized in terms of mobility, self-maintenance, role performance, and disability (George & Bearon, 1980). A further conceptual distinction has been drawn between impairment and disability (Office of Technology Assessment, 1983; Shanas & Maddox, 1976). An *impairment* refers to a physiological or psychological abnormality that does not interfere with the "normal" activities of the individual. In contrast, a *disability* refers to a condition that results in partial or total limitation of one's "normal" daily activities. A person may be impaired but not necessarily disabled. Thus, an elderly individual might be partially blind but still be able to work, take care of household needs, and maintain a "functionally adequate" lifestyle.

The Office of Technology Assessment (1983) makes an even finer distinction between disability and handicap, with the former being defined as a generic functional limitation and the latter defined as a socially, environmentally, and/or personally specified limitation. Thus, whereas a disability may involve difficulty in walking, a handicap may involve difficulty in getting to work because of the disability's physical manifestation coupled with inadequate public transportation, lack of accessible doors, or absence of curb cuts.

The consensus among gerontologists involved in the development and testing of health assessment measures (cf. Fillenbaum, 1984; Kane & Kane, 1981; Lawton, Ward, & Yaffe, 1967; Linn, 1976) is that health is a multifaceted concept that encompasses physical, mental, and social dimensions. Although not developed specifically for an elderly population, Ware, Brook, Davies, and Lohr's (1981) multidimensional model of health provides a viable framework for assessing the health of older persons. The elements include *physiological health*, *physical health*, *psychological health*, *social health*, and *health perceptions*.

Bergner (1985, p. 698) has suggested another variant of this comprehensive model that includes the genetic foundations upon which all other aspects of health status are based and the health potential of the individual (i.e., longevity, functional potential, and prognosis of disease and disability). Linn (1976) has added that a way to measure the older subject's reserve capacity for survival as well as reserve capacity for enjoyment of his or her remaining years is needed. He asks, "[F]or certain levels of dysfunction, what is the quality of life that will be produced?" (p. 124).

The health dimensions identified above should not be construed as mutually exclusive, static categories. Rather, they are interrelated and interactive elements of health that are influenced by the sociocultural, political, and economic environment of the individual. Bergner (1985) has identified four groups of factors that may affect health status: social factors, health care system factors, social and familial factors, and personal factors. Some affect individual health status directly, whereas others have a more indirect impact.

Measurement of Health Status

The selection of appropriate health status measures is perhaps the most important step in health assessment. This decision is dictated, in large part, by the purpose for which the measures are to be used. Lawton, Ward, and Yaffe (1967) have noted that for life insurance purposes, the life-threatening aspects of health are the most salient. Retirement policy decisions, on the other hand, are more dependent upon measures of chronic disability. Monitoring of the general health status of the elderly population may require a broader array of indicators including vital statistics, information about the incidence and prevalence of selected diseases, and measures of functional health status and well-being (Bergner, 1985).

The nature of the population to be assessed also is an important factor in selecting appropriate measures. Clinical assessments of individuals tend to employ diagnostic indicators of illness and disease, whereas evaluations of commonality health states may be upon separate or aggregated indices of longevity, presence of disease, function, and other dimensions of health. The choice of health measures also is dependent on such sociodemographic characteristics as age, gender, race, and ethnicity. The distinction between the "young-old" and the "old-old" is particularity important with respect to health assessment in the elderly. For example, the commonly used measures of functional limitation (e.g., eating, bathing, and dressing) are appropriate for evaluating the physical capacity of those 75 years and older but may have little relevance for younger individuals (see Figure 1).

Construction of Health Measures

The method of operationalizing health is a critical issue in assessing health in the elderly. Health can be measured by separate indicators, defined as statistics, which summarize a larger body of data, and indices, which are more complex, multidimensional measures (Murnaghan, 1981). Recent innovations in health status assessment included the construction of standardized health scales from survey measures, a technique that is seen as an improvement over the more common procedure of computing a

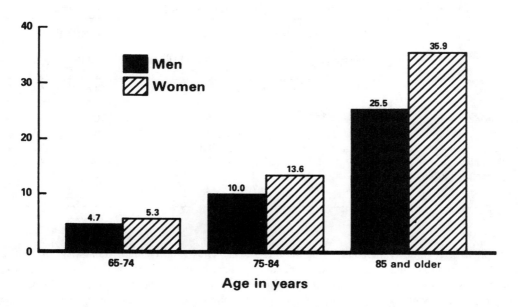

FIGURE 1   Percentage of older people needing help in one or more basic physical activities. *Source:* National Center for Health Statistics, National Health Interview Survey, 1979–1980.

health score from a single survey item (Ware & Karmos, 1976).

A number of scales and multidimensional indices have been developed to assess the health status of elderly persons. One of the more comprehensive is the Older Americans Resources and Services (OARS) Multidimensional Functional Assessment Questionnaire, developed by researchers at the Duke University Center for the Study of Aging and Human Development (1978). This instrument, consisting of a battery of five measurement dimensions (i.e., social resources, economic resources, mental health, physical health, and capacity for self-care), was designed to assess the objective and subjective functioning of an individual.

The Comprehensive Assessment and Referral Evaluation (CARE) is a structured interview guide designed to assess the psychiatric, medical, and social status of older persons (Gurland, Kuriansky, Sharpe, Simon, Stiller, & Birkett, 1977–1978). It originally was developed for the conduct of a cross-national study of older persons residing in New York and London. A SHORT-CARE version also has been developed (Gurland, Golden, Teresi, & Challop, 1984) that focuses on the two main areas of psychiatric impairment (i.e., dementia and de-

pression) and the major area of physical impairment (i.e., disability).

The Activities of Daily Living (ADL) Index (Katz, Ford, Moskowitz, Jackson, & Jaffe, 1963) was developed as a measure of sociobiological function in the chronically ill and aging populations. This observational scale summarizes performance in bathing, dressing, toileting, transfer, continence, and feeding, and provides an order profile of levels of independence among older persons (Katz & Akpom, 1976). Originally developed from observations made on elderly people with hip fractures, the ADL has been used for a variety of purposes ranging from the prediction of the course of specific illnesses to the development of a multidimensional profile measuring the severity of chronic conditions (see Table 1).

The Instrumental Activities of Daily Living (IADL) Index was developed by researchers at the Philadelphia Geriatric Center (Lawton & Brody, 1969) to measure competence in functions that are less bodily oriented than physical self-maintenance. The items include using a telephone, shopping, preparing food, housekeeping, doing laundry, using transportation, taking medication, and handling finances. The IADL focuses on behaviors that are

TABLE 1   Percentage of Older People Living in the Community Who Need Help

	Age of men			Age of women		
	65–74	75–84	85+	65–74	75–84	85+
One or more	4.7	10.0	25.9	5.3	13.6	35.9
Walking	3.5	7.4	18.9	3.9	9.9	26.0
Going outside	2.9	5.5	18.7	3.8	10.0	28.3
Bathing	2.1	4.7	13.2	1.7	5.6	17.0
Dressing	1.5	3.2	8.6	1.3	3.4	10.2
Using the toilet	1.2	2.3	7.2	1.2	3.7	10.7
Moving from bed or chair	1.0	2.0	5.0	1.1	2.8	7.6
Eating	0.5	0.7	2.6	0.3	1.1	3.6

more applicable to elderly persons living in the community than those who are institutionalized. All eight items are used in assessing the functional capacity of women, whereas only a five-item scale is typically used for men.

Subjective Versus Objective Health Assessments

Subjective health rating is the individual's perception and evaluation of his or her overall health status, typically measured by a single item ranging from "poor" to "excellent." The evaluation is often made in reference to the health status of others and/ or one's previous health condition. For the past 20 years, researchers have explored the relationship between self-assessed health and more "objective" indicators of health (e.g., physician ratings, reported symptoms). Some have argued that subjective health measures are convenient but questionable substitutes for objective health status or indicators of well-being (Haberman, 1969). There is, however, a growing body of empirical evidence indicating significant correlations between subjective ratings of health and measures such as physician ratings, disability days, and self-reported illness (Cockerham, Sharp, & Wilcox, 1983; Ferraro, 1980; Linn & Linn, 1980; Maddox & Douglass, 1973; Markides & Martin, 1979). Furthermore, several studies have found that self-assessed health is a strong predictor of mortality among the elderly (Kaplan & Camach, 1983; Mossey & Shapiro, 1982).

The validity and reliability of self-assessed health measures may vary among different subgroups. For example, Ware and Karmos (1976) found that health status perception scores were consistently and notably less reliable for groups of disadvantaged persons than for the nondisadvantaged. Fillenbaum (1979) observed that objective health measures were related to self-assessed health ratings among elderly residents of the community but not among those in institutions. Furthermore, she found gender-related differences among the community residents, with women having a poorer objectively assessed health status than men for a given self-assessment of health.

The rationale and evidence of effectiveness for health assessment in clinical geriatrics has been reviewed by Siu, Reuben, and Moore (1994).

MARY GRACE KOVAR

See also
Comprehensive Assessment
Geriatrics
Multidimensional Functional Assessment

HEALTH BELIEFS

Professionals in practice and research need to understand individuals' health beliefs because what people believe influences how they act. The exact ties between beliefs and behavior have traditionally been difficult to pin down; and one-to-one, cause-

and-effect relationships between a particular belief and a particular behavior almost certainly do not exist. Nonetheless, beliefs about health, treatment, and the health care system are fundamentally associated with health-related practices.

For specific purposes such as studies or presentations of theory, "health beliefs" can take on more detailed definitions and methods of assessment. For example, a single question might be How would you rate your health now? or How much control do you believe you have over your health? or How would you compare your health with people about your age? Of course, such global questions are used to categorize people broadly. If the sample of persons is large and representative (such as the annual National Health Interview Survey), single questions can reveal interesting contrasts among subgroups of the population.

It is quite common in health surveys to include several questions on health beliefs. The challenge becomes how to select a relevant set of questions and how to combine the answers. A theoretical approach usually serves as the guideline. In the Health Belief Model, for example, the four separate dimensions of perceived susceptibility to illness, perceived seriousness of illness, expected benefits of treatment, and expected barriers to treatment could each be assessed by several questions. Then, a "summary score" for each health belief could be computed by averaging. Factor analysis can be used to help identify the questions that best measure each belief (e.g., Jette, Cummings, Brock, Phelps, & Naessens, 1981).

It is possible to become even more focused. In the assessment of health locus of control, for example, multiple questions might be asked about each of several dimensions of one health belief (Wallston & DeVellis, 1978; Winefield, 1982). It is also possible to ask about specific arenas of health beliefs, such as perceived control over heart-related diseases (e.g., O'Connell & Price, 1985).

Self-efficacy is a rapidly emerging topic of interest (Bandura, 1982; Schunk & Carbonari, 1984). Instead of a judgment about one's health, we have a belief about one's behavioral skill to carry out health-related tasks. Questions might be asked about health self-efficacy in general or about perceived skills in specific areas of health (e.g., preventive health practices). In sum, there can be a vast list of health beliefs one might try to assess. The essential point of all inquiries is the element of interpretation, the personal meanings that often redefine "objective" health status. Interpretation is especially important in the period of older adulthood.

Older Adulthood

Later life is characterized by a greater prevalence of chronic illness and by a greater risk of new problems developing. Therefore many older individuals need to assess the significance of their illnesses or impairments. Subjective judgments are clearly necessary to resolve the basic question of, Exactly how healthy or how ill am I really? The older person may simultaneously feel both healthy *and* ill (Rakowski, 1984). This health perception might also occur among others who know the individual and can "see both sides" of how well they carry out daily activities. Working through ambiguous health beliefs/perceptions can, therefore, be an issue for others besides the older person.

Understanding health beliefs in later life has also been important because of the stereotype that aging is inevitably accompanied by illness and marked functional impairment. Health care professionals and gerontologists have waged a continuing fight against automatic acceptance of the "aches and pains" that are supposedly "normal" in older age. From the standpoint of service provision, this has been perhaps the premier undesirable health belief and stereotype of aging against which research data have been marshalled. Actually, surveys reveal a notable percentage of older persons who rate their health as "excellent" or "very good" (e.g., about 35%; Kovar, 1986). Such reports often stand in contrast to the greater prevalence and incidence of illnesses in later life. Limitation of activity also becomes more prevalent, leading to interest in the correspondence between objective and subjective health status. A correlation does exist, but by no means are personal assessments always in agreement with medical judgment or technical data.

Health perceptions are important to understand because older adults often evaluate their health as "good" or "bad" in comparison with their age peers. Given the greater prevalence of illness in later life, the standard of comparison can change in older adulthood. To the extent that age peers encountered in day-to-day settings show a greater number of age-related illnesses or general biological aging, one's own health status can appear adequate by contrast, even if there is some limitation of activity. The macrolevel health status of a particular setting can even change over time (e.g., senior housing, retirement community) as a cohort of residents ages. It will be important for research to determine how people react to this comparison. When does a favorable comparison stimulate someone to continue good health habits? Is an unfavorable assessment an effective motivator to become more proactive toward health, or does it lead to lower motivation due to frustration, disappointment, or pessimism?

Health beliefs influence the decision-making process underlying individual health practices. Reactions to symptoms, for example, often involve choice among numerous options for action, including inaction. Interventions for health promotion aimed at influencing health practices require a corresponding set of beliefs to support the continuity and consistency desired. It is not sufficient to conduct analyses of cross-sectional data to identify and inventory the best set of predictors for health behavior. The chain of decisions also needs to be delineated and represented in models of health behavior. It is here that "health beliefs" will be juxtaposed with other concepts such as health knowledge, symptom perception, symptom labeling, social support, socioeconomic status, personality traits, professional-client interaction, existing habits, and feedback from the actions following one's decision. One conceptual scheme has been outlined pertinent to symptom-related behaviors (Rakowski & Hickey, 1980).

Obviously health beliefs are but one piece of a much larger picture, but in the long run we can expect that across a large range of symptom-related and preventive practices health belief variables will be recognized as important factors, especially when dealing with older adults. Difficulties arise from the multiplicity of health beliefs and from the numerous subgroups of the older population we might study (e.g., old-old, ethnics), and from the problem of linking specific behaviors to specific beliefs. Our current knowledge about health beliefs is at a global level, much of it descriptive. Trained observation by professionals is required to obtain an accurate picture of the salient health beliefs of older persons

for the purpose of maintaining or strengthening their well-being.

WILLIAM RAKOWSKI

See also
  Geriatric Health
  Health Promotion

HEALTH CARE: ORGANIZATION, USE, AND FINANCING

The organization, use, and financing of health care in the United States is undergoing continuous and major revisions. Such changes are largely due to attempts by governmental and corporate entities that pay for an overwhelming proportion of American health care to limit their payments in an era when health care prices are inflating at a high rate. Some changes, however, are also due to efforts by reformers to create new mechanisms for providing more effective care on a cost-efficient basis.

Health care of older persons is a central ingredient in these changes, and will remain so for many years ahead. One reason is that persons age 65 and older account for about one third of annual U.S. health care costs. Per capita expenditures on older persons are four times greater than on younger persons. In addition, a substantial amount of health care for older persons, especially long-term care, is financed through in-kind services from relatives and friends that are not readily quantifiable as expenditures.

A second reason is that the federal Medicare program, which provides a basic package of health insurance for 95% of Americans who are age 65 and over (as well as some 5 million other persons who receive federal disability insurance, or who have end-stage renal disease), is the single biggest source of payment for U.S. health care. Its expenditures are projected to double from $220 billion in 1999 to $444 billion in 2009 (Congressional Budget Office, 1999).

Still another reason is that the economic and political challenges of financing health care for older persons throughout the first half of the 21st century are substantial. The number of older Americans will grow sharply during this period as the baby-boom birth cohort reaches the ranks of old age. Moreover, the number of persons of advanced old age—in their late 70s and older—will increase markedly, and in this older age range the rates of illnesses and disabilities requiring health care are much higher than among the rest of the population. Even if important advances are made in treatments, illness prevention, and health promotion, they are unlikely to have major impact in eliminating the overall extent of illness and disability in old age in the next several decades. Consequently, the aggregate health care needs of the older population will be even greater in the future than they are now. For example, the proportion of national wealth (gross domestic product) spent on Medicare in 1998 was 2.5%; it is projected to more than double, to 5.3%, in 2025, when most baby boomers will be age 65 and older (Moon, 1999).

In the contemporary context of rapid changes in American health care, in which the challenges of providing care for older people are playing a central role, the financing, use, and organization of health care are highly interdependent. Because these elements are inextricably linked and dynamic in their relations, the discussion that follows should be interpreted as artificially compartmentalized, to present a brief overview of a highly complex arena.

Sources of Financing

Governments finance nearly two thirds of health care for older Americans. Medicare accounts for 45% of the total. Medicare (Part A) Hospital Insurance is funded by payroll taxes under the Federal Insurance Contributions Act; 25% of Medicare's Part B (nonhospital) Supplementary Medical Insurance is financed by voluntary premiums paid by program participants and 75% by U.S. general revenues.

Medicaid insurance for poor persons who qualify through income and asset tests, jointly funded by the federal and state governments, provides another 12%, which is principally spent on long-term care. Health care financed through the Department of Veterans Affairs, Department of Defense, Indian Health Services, and a variety of state and local government programs constitutes about 6% of the total. An additional 8% is funded through private

insurance, and less than 1% comes from philanthropy.

Older persons pay 28% of the costs of their care out-of-pocket. Much of this outlay is for skilled nursing, which has only minimal Medicare coverage. About 25% of national health care expenditures on older people is for long-term care in nursing homes, at home, or in other residential settings; nearly half of these costs are paid for out-of-pocket by older persons and their families (Wiener & Illston, 1996). Medicaid pays for most of the rest; only about 1% of nursing home costs is paid for through private long-term care insurance.

About 62% of Medicare beneficiaries have employer-sponsored retiree health insurance and/or "Medigap" private insurance that provides coverage for Medicare deductibles, copayments, partial reimbursement for outpatient prescription drugs, and other gaps in Medicare's coverage. Those who are enrolled in Medicare health maintenance organizations (HMOs) also have supplemental coverage. Yet 36% of prescription drug costs are paid for by older persons out-of-pocket (Poisal, Murray, Chulis, & Cooper, 1999). Poor older persons can have their Medicare Part B premiums, deductibles, and copayments paid for by Medicaid through the Qualified Medicare Beneficiary program and the Specified Low-Income Medicare Beneficiary program, for which they become eligible through low-income "means tests." Nonetheless, out-of-pocket health care spending for a Medicare beneficiary enrolled in the traditional fee-for-service system averages 18.6% of income (Moon, 1999).

Use of Health Care

Physician Services. Older persons contact physicians far more frequently than the rest of the population for examination, diagnosis, treatment, or advice. Persons of all ages average 5.8 contacts per year; but persons age 65 to 74 average 10.2 contacts, and persons age 75 and older average 13.7 contacts (National Center for Health Statistics, 1999). Similarly, the probability of seeing a physician increases by advancing age categories. Among persons 45 to 64 years old, 79.3% see a physician at least once within a 12-month period; 88.3% of persons 65 to 74 years old and 92.4% of people age 75 and older have such a contact in the same time interval.

Hospital Care.   Persons age 65 and older account for 43% of the days of care in short-stay hospitals each year and about 37% of discharged patients (National Center for Health Statistics, 1999). At advanced old ages each of these dimensions of usage increases in rate. The number of days of care for persons age 75 and older is 52% higher than for those age 65 to 74; the hospital discharge rate is 41% higher.

Nursing Home Care.   Nearly 1.5 million older people, or about 4.3% of persons age 65 and older, are in nursing homes (National Center for Health Statistics, 1999). The rate of nursing home use increases sharply at older ages within the elderly population. About 1% of Americans age 65 to 74 years are in nursing homes; this compares with 4.5% of persons age 75 to 84, and 19% of persons age 85 and older. Older nursing home residents are predominantly female, 75% overall, and 82% among residents aged 85 and older.

Home- and Community-Based Long-Term Care.   An additional 7.2 million older people have limitations in activities of daily living or instrumental activities of daily living (Komisar, Lambrew, & Feder, 1996). Most of them receive some form of long-term care—formal, paid services and/or informal, unpaid assistance—in their own homes or some other residential facility, such as an assisted living facility, a congregate living community, an adult foster home, or a board-and-care facility. In 1996, 1.8 million persons age 65 and older received formal home care services (National Center for Health Statistics, 1999). As is the case with nursing home residents, the percentage of older persons residing in the community who need long-term care assistance increases dramatically at advanced old ages. For example, 2% of those age 65 to 74 years need assistance in two or more activities of daily living, as compared with 5% of those age 75 to 84 years and 11% of those age 85 and older (Kassner & Bechtel, 1998).

Other Forms of Health Care.   In general, older persons tend to use the wide range of available health care goods and services at higher rates than younger population groupings. Persons 65 years and older use medical equipment and supplies at twice the rate of younger persons. They also use prescription drugs and vision and hearing aids at higher rates. On the other hand, older persons visit dentists somewhat less than younger persons (National Center for Health Statistics, 1999).

Organization of Primary and Acute Care

Changes in financing, use, and need for care are reflected in and are giving rise to new forms of organization for providing health care to older persons. Traditional institutions and modes of care—acute care and rehabilitation hospitals, outpatient clinics, physician's offices, nursing homes, and home health services—are being complemented and linked with a variety of emergent organizational mechanisms, which are briefly described later.

New Methods for Delivering Acute Care.   Geriatric emergency medicine is developing as a specialty in recognition of the complex challenges frequently involved in treating older patients beset by multiple clinical disorders. Multidisciplinary geriatric assessment teams have been established by hospitals in the belief that they will improve the choice of treatment goals as well as discharge objectives. Special acute care geriatric wards are being developed as environments to facilitate functional recuperation and independence of older patients. Diagnostic and therapeutic interventions traditionally undertaken on an inpatient basis—such as cataract surgery and coronary angiography—are now being done as outpatient procedures.

Hospice Care.   Another relatively new development is hospice care for terminally ill patients, provided by a medically directed team of health care professionals, volunteers, and family members. The goals of hospice are to provide a good quality of life for the dying person (rather than curing the patient's disease or extending life) and to help the patient and family (or caregiver) deal with approaching death. In addition to palliation of pain, hospice programs provide services based on social, spiritual, and emotional needs during the last stages of illness, during the dying process, and during bereavement. About three fourths of hospice patients receive services in their own homes (National Hospice Organization, 1998). From 1986 (when permanent Medicare coverage for hospice care was established) to 1996, Medicare payments for hospice benefits have increased by 2,500%, from $77 million to $2 billion (Health Care Financing Administration, 1998). About 500,000 patients are served annually by 3,100 hospice programs (Mahoney, 1998).

Prepaid Care. From the time that it was established in 1965 until very recently, the Medicare program financed medical care in an open-ended fashion, reimbursing physicians, hospitals, and other health care providers on a fee-for-service (FFS) basis. In the mid-1980s, however, the federal government began efforts to control the growth of Medicare expenditures by launching a prospective payment system through which fixed payments are made to hospitals for a patient's care according to the "diagnosis related group" (DRG) to which the patient is assigned. This measure slowed the growth of payments to hospitals and shortened the average length of hospital stays. A related measure, which began to be implemented in the mid-1990s, was Medicare's attempt to contain its spending for physician services without compromising access to or quality of care. The method combines a resource-based relative value schedule of physician fees, with volume performance standards.

Since the early 1990s, the major strategy for containing Medicare costs has been to shift Medicare's financial risk to private-sector organizations by encouraging the proliferation of Medicare HMOs and other forms of managed care organizations (MCOs). In contrast to the traditional FFS system, managed care limits the federal government's financial risk in that the Health Care Financing Administration (which administers Medicare) makes a prospective per capita payment to MCOs for each Medicare participant who enrolls. In turn, the prepaid MCOs are responsible for providing all needed services that are covered by Medicare. The amount of the per capita payment, termed the average adjusted per capita cost (AAPCC), is approximately 95% of the average fee-for-service reimbursement for Medicare patients in a geographic area. This strategy was accelerated by the Balanced Budget Act of 1997, which established Medicare+Choice, offering Medicare participants a pan-

oply of health plan options that are variations on the basic HMO model (and also made adjustments to increase AAPCCs in some areas of the country and reduce them in others).

The appeal of MCO plans to some Medicare beneficiaries is twofold. First, many plans provide additional services—such as outpatient prescription drugs, routine physical exams, hearing aids, and eyeglasses—that are not covered under traditional Medicare. Second, enrollment in an MCO obviates much of a patient's need to deal with Medicare and Medigap insurance forms. In 1990, 3% of Medicare beneficiaries were enrolled in MCOs (Medicare Payment Advisory Commission, 1998); by mid-1999, the proportion had climbed to 18% (U.S. General Accounting Office, 1999).

So far, however, the federal government's strategy of promoting enrollment in managed care as a means of reducing overall Medicare costs has not succeeded. The reason is that Medicare MCOs have tended to enroll beneficiaries with better-than-average health, who, accordingly, had lower-than-average health care costs (Physician Payment Review Commission, 1996; U.S. General Accounting Office, 1997a). As a result, Medicare has spent more on persons enrolled in MCOs than it would have if the same individuals had been in FFS (U.S. General Accounting Office, 1999).

Moreover, the financial incentives of managed care organizations foster undertreatment of patients (see Mechanic, 1994). Studies have indicated that outcomes for older people who are poor and have chronic diseases and disabilities are worse in HMOs than for those in FFS (Nelson, Brown, Gold, Ciemnecki, & Docteur, 1997; Shaughnessy, 2000; Ware, Bayliss, Rogers, Kosinski, & Tarlove, 1996). Even relatively healthy older persons in MCOs seem to have been underserved in certain respects (Wiener & Skaggs, 1995).

Organization of Long-Term Care

The organization of long-term care for chronically ill and disabled older persons has been undergoing rapid change. Prior to the last two decades, nursing homes and home care (largely provided by family members) were virtually the only modes of care available. The percentage of frail older persons residing in nursing homes has remained relatively stable over the years. But alternative residential settings, services, and programs have developed rapidly in recent years, responsive to the varied needs of frail older persons and their caregivers. And government financing for home care services has increased substantially.

Medicaid Waivers for Home and Community-Based Care. Since its inception, Medicaid has covered skilled nursing care—in nursing homes or at home—for those who are poor or become poor by "spending down" their assets on long-term care. But traditionally, it did not cover the nonmedical services that are essential for functionally disabled persons to reside in their own homes or in other community settings. Since the early 1980s, however, the federal government has allowed states (through special waivers) to provide Medicaid reimbursement for nonmedical home care services, if these home and community-based (HCBS) services are limited to those patients who otherwise would require Medicaid-financed nursing home care at greater cost. In many states that have HCBS waivers, Medicaid funds for this program are supplemented by state revenues and federal monies obtained through the Older Americans Act and Social Security's (Title XX) block grant social services funds. As a consequence, home- and community-based care has become a more viable alternative to nursing homes than it used to be. HCBS spending grew from only $451 million in 1987 to $8.1 billion in 1997 (Burwell, 1998). States vary considerably, however, in their spending on HCBS, with New York spending the most per capita and Mississippi the least (Kane, Kane, & Ladd, 1998).

Medicare-Financed Home Care. Liberalization of Medicare's rules for home health coverage in 1989 (in response to a court order) also made home care a more viable option than in the past. Prior to that time, Medicare only covered skilled nursing care (whether in a nursing home or at home) for short periods of time following an episode of acute illness. The new rules allowed for skilled nursing and home health aide services at home up to 35 hours per week and made somewhat easier medical certification of the need for such care on a long-term basis. Subsequently, there were dramatic growths in the volume of Medicare home care services, users, and expenditures. From 1988 through

1996, the number of service visits per 1,000 Medicare enrollees increased by 587%, the user rate per 1,000 more than doubled, and payments to home health agencies increased by 762% (Health Care Financing Administration, 1998). Provisions in the Balanced Budget Act of 1997, designed to rein in the growth of Medicare home health expenditures, changed this trajectory, at least for the short term. An interim payment system (used until a planned implementation of a prospective payment system for home care) cut reimbursements to Medicare certified home health agencies by 31% in 1998, and more than one tenth of them closed during the year (Flaherty, 1998).

Residential Alternatives. Recent years have also seen the growth of community-based alternatives to home care. State governments have expanded the range of supportive services that it authorizes traditional "board-and-care" facilities to provide, either by facility staff or by home health agencies. A relatively recent and rapidly growing variation of board and care is "assisted living" facilities that combine residential environments with a variety of supportive services (including nursing care, in some instances). Private-pay rates for assisted living range from $1,000 to $3,000 a month (Blanchette, 1997). By 1996, 30 states had created an assisted living licensure category, passed legislation authorizing such a category, or covered assisted living as a Medicaid service (Mollica, 1997). In 1999, the total number of board-and-care and assisted living facilities in the United States was estimated as between 45,000 and 50,000, and the total number of beds in them was estimated as between 900,000 and 1 million (Hawes, Rose, & Phillips, 1999).

Continuing care retirement communities (CCRCs) are a variation on a private insurance approach to financing long-term care, promising comprehensive health care services—including long-term care—to all members. Although there are about 350,000 persons living in CCRCs, only about one third of them provide long-term care for their residents under lifetime contracts in which the CCRC assumes financial risks for a resident's long-term care services, including nursing home care (U.S. General Accounting Office, 1997b). Residents tend to be middle- and upper-income persons who are relatively healthy when they join the community, and they pay a substantial entrance fee and monthly charge in return for a promise of "care for life." It has been estimated that about 10% of older people could afford to join such communities.

Family-Related Care. A number of studies indicate that over 80% of home care services for older persons are provided by their family members on an informal, unpaid basis. In response to this phenomenon, as well as a growing recognition of the stresses experienced by family caregivers, new programs emerged in the 1980s and early 1990s that have now spread to most urban communities. Adult day care programs enable a caregiver to have time for work, to undertake other activities of daily living, and simply to rest from providing care; at the same time, such programs can provide social interaction, supportive services, and rehabilitation activities for older persons who attend them. In addition, "respite" programs provide caregivers with more extended relief for a fixed period of days by temporarily admitting a disabled older person to an institution or by providing substitute caregivers in a home. Similarly, "support" groups comprising family caregivers, particularly those caring for persons with dementia, are a vehicle for moderating the stresses of caregiving and sharing practical information.

Integrating Acute, Chronic, and Long-Term Care. A long-recognized problem in the financing and organization of health care for older people is the fragmentation of the delivery system. Few units of organization integrate acute, chronic, and long-term care in fashions that are optimal either for patient care or cost-efficiency. Separate sources of financing—especially the separate streams of funding through Medicare and Medicaid, and the incentives associated with them—tend to engender this fragmentation and, often, inappropriate care.

Since the early 1980s the federal government has financed innovative managed care demonstration projects, focused on integrating health care services for frail older persons. One of these, the Program of All-Inclusive Care for the Elderly (PACE), is targeted to persons who are sufficiently dependent to be eligible for nursing home placement but still reside in the community; most of them are eligible for Medicaid as well as Medicare. Enrollees are required to attend an adult day health center, where

a wide array of medical, supportive, and social services is provided to them by a multidisciplinary team. Although a primary PACE objective is to delay or prevent use of hospital and nursing home care, the program pays for these services when they become essential. In 1997, after many years of demonstration and replication, PACE was authorized as a permanent program under Medicare and states were granted the option to offer PACE to their Medicaid enrollees. Currently, 25 PACE sites are operational; these programs are typically small, with the largest site enrolling fewer than 1,000 participants (Medicare Payment Advisory Commission, 1999).

Another federal demonstration is the social/health maintenance organization (S/HMO). An initial generation of the S/HMO, launched in the 1980s, tested an integrated model of service delivery (including long-term care) and capitated financing in conventional HMO settings, but did not result in effective coordination of chronic and acute medical benefits (Harrington, Lynch, & Newcomer, 1993). A second generation of S/HMO demonstrations was authorized in the 1990s to test the value of incorporating geriatric practices into the plans—comprehensive geriatric assessment, treatment of functional problems, and a team approach combining nurse practitioners, pharmacists, and other health professionals. So far, however, this demonstration is active at only one site (Medicare Payment Advisory Commission, 1999). EverCare, a demonstration program launched in 1994, enrolls permanent nursing home residents into managed care and endeavors to provide them with more Medicare outpatient services than they would usually receive. The objectives of EverCare are to reduce nursing home residents' use of hospital and emergency room service and to improve the quality of care and health outcomes. In addition to these federal demonstrations, a number of state governments are operating Medicaid managed care programs that provide long-term care.

The various organizational mechanisms and experiments outlined above are evolutionary steps toward the development of a reasonably integrated and wide range of health care services needed by America's older population. Yet the effective integration of acute and long-term care services will be inextricably bound up with the broader challenges of financing American health care in an era in which a predominant concern is to slow inflation of health care costs in general, and the costs of health care for the elderly, in particular.

ROBERT H. BINSTOCK

See also

Continuum of Care
Health Care Policy for the Elderly, History of
Health Maintenance Organizations
Medicare
Medicaid
Nursing Homes
Social Security

HEALTH CARE POLICY FOR THE ELDERLY, HISTORY OF

Health care policy for the elderly has developed incrementally throughout U.S. history following the evolution of the rule of government. Health care policies can be divided into roughly five periods, characterized by different scopes and interests of the federal government in the health and welfare of the population.

Early Years of the Republic (1776–1860)

Government involvement in the health of citizens initially was limited because such activities were seen as the responsibility of individuals and charities. Federal actions were confined to quarantine regulations at ports of entry, merchant seamen's health care, and smallpox vaccination. State and local governments were concerned with sanitation and the quarantine of communicable diseases during this time. Health care for the poor was left principally to private charities. Medical care was rudimentary. The few existing hospitals were intended to isolate people with communicable disease or provide care for the indigent. Different health care philosophies, including allopathy, homeopathy, herbalism, public health, and lay approaches all competed for legitimacy. The health of the population was poor by current standards: communicable diseases were common, infant and maternal mortality was high, and malnutrition was common

among the poor. Life expectancy at birth in Massachusetts in 1798 was estimated to be only 35 years. Health care policy for the elderly was nonexistent as a result of limited life expectancy and the government's narrow focus.

Civil War to the Depression (1861–1931)

The federal government assumed a limited role in promoting the health and welfare of the population. After 20 years of debate, Congress passed the Food and Drug Act in 1906 to prevent the adulteration and misbranding of food and drugs. Although intended to protect consumers' pocketbooks, not their health, the act marked new federal involvement in a health-related area previously left to the states. Public health approaches were embraced at the state and local level. By 1915 public health agencies were established in every state and began to expand beyond infectious disease control to include water pollution, sewage disposal, nutrition, housing, and industrial accidents. The resulting improvements, along with improved social and economic conditions, are commonly credited with decreased morbidity and mortality during this period.

Allopathic medicine gained power as the American Medical Association's (founded 1847) membership and influence grew. Organized medicine and private foundations worked to base all healing on science and to make medical education requirements uniform and high. Often unable to meet the new requirements, 92 medical schools closed their doors or merged between 1902 and 1915, the number of homeopathic and eclectic schools fell by two-thirds, and five of the seven Black medical colleges closed. Hospitals became important sites where health care was provided, growing in number from 178 in 1873 to 4,000 by 1909. Payment for these health services remained the responsibility of individuals and charities. The government took an interest in medical research, and Congress voted to establish the National Institutes of Health (NIH) in 1930.

By 1900, life expectancy had risen to 47.3 years. Acute diseases accounted for the majority of deaths, led by influenza, pneumonia, and tuberculosis. The elderly comprised 4% of the population, and those who lived to the age of 65 had a remaining life expectancy of 11.9 years.

The New Deal to the New Federalism (1933–1981)

This era heralded important political-economic and scientific developments. The Great Depression and the New Deal brought dramatic new government involvement into the health and welfare of the population, while scientific discoveries furthered progress against infectious disease. This period was characterized by an active federal effort to enact policies to improve access, quality, and distribution of health care. The federal government also greatly expanded its involvement in medical research, beginning with the passage of the National Cancer Act in 1937. The National Institutes of Health grew from a small government laboratory to the most significant biomedical research organization in the world.

Probably the most important piece of social legislation enacted in the history of the United States was the Social Security Act of 1935, establishing social insurance to assure a degree of financial security in old age. It also established unemployment insurance and federal aid to states for maternal and child health, public health, and public assistance. Other programs important to the elderly that would be established later, including Medicare, follow the principles laid down in this act.

After World War II, the federal government began to heavily subsidize hospital expansion, providing construction and modernization funds for hospitals, nursing homes, public health clinics, and rehabilitation centers in more than 3,000 communities over a 30-year period. The private, nonprofit institution became the primary type of medical institution because public hospitals, which largely served the poor, were last to receive federal construction funds. New forms of health care financing emerged during this period. Blue Cross and Blue Shield medical insurance was established by hospitals and doctors during the Depression to help ensure payment of their bills. Federal policies encouraged the spread of private health insurance by defining it as nonwage compensation, allowing workers to bargain for increased health benefits during wartime wage freezes and allowing both employers and employees to avoid taxes on premiums paid. The unemployed, poor, and elderly found private insurance difficult to obtain, leaving them dependent on charity and limited public programs. Blacks and other minorities also suffered from overt discrimination in the provision of care until passage of the Civil Rights Act and Medicare in the mid-1960s.

Great Society programs in the 1960s continued New Deal trends. Federal medical insurance was established for the elderly and the poor through Medicare and Medicaid. To overcome organized medical opposition, Medicare incorporated the existing fee-for-service payment method and paid hospitals and doctors retrospectively according to what they charged. With guaranteed funding, hospital and nursing home construction and expansion continued, and new and costly technologies were introduced. By 1980 all public and private expenditures for health care equaled 9.4% of the gross national product (GNP), with 42% coming from public sources.

Infectious disease reduction slowed in the 1950s, as the major cause of death became chronic illnesses such as cancer and cardiovascular disease. The proportion of elderly persons in the population rose from 4.0% in 1900 to 11.3% in 1980, as life expectancy rose 50% to 73.7 years, infant mortality fell, and fertility patterns changed. Remaining life expectancy at age 65 increased to 16.4 years by 1980 (National Center for Health Statistics, 1995).

From 1965 to the mid-1970s the primary policy concern was access to needed health care. As a result, doctor visits per person per year for the poor increased 30% and hospital use (discharges per 100 persons per year) increased between one- and two-thirds for the poor, elderly, and minorities. During this time the debate over national health insurance was seen as key to further health care improvements.

Health Policy Under New Federalism and Fiscal Crisis (1981–1993)

Federalism and devolution denote the relationships among different levels of government and the transfer of responsibility for programs and services from the federal to the state level. Following President Nixon's lead in initiating policies that increased state and local discretion and responsibilities in the 1970s, President Reagan vigorously pursued policies in the 1980s to further limit the federal role in health and welfare through block grants, program cuts, and increased state responsibility.

A surge of "new" federalism initiatives emerged in the mid-1990s including the release of states from the burden of unfunded federal mandates, welfare reform that eradicated entitlement to cash assistance for the poor and imposed restrictions on public benefits for immigrants, and the further devolution of authority and responsibility to states and localities, along with reduced federal funding.

In its most extreme form, new federalism challenges the idea that there is any national responsibility for meeting basic human needs in health, income, housing, or welfare. Serious questions of equity and state and local fiscal capacity are raised by the transfer of federal responsibilities to states. Historically, it has been argued that because state and local governments do not have the revenue capacity of the federal government, national issues and problems necessitate a strong federal financing role. States and localities vary widely in their commitment to health and welfare benefits for the poor, disadvantaged, and elderly (Estes, 1979; Estes & Gerard, 1983).

Deregulation is a hallmark of New Federalism policy and devolution. An important example of the impact of deregulation in health care is the eradication of federal restrictions that precluded the entry of for-profit firms into government-financed programs. There is increased privatization of health care with the growth of for-profits and the conversion of nonprofits to for-profits in managed care. To promote "market competition" and further deregulation, some recent proposals suggest turning Medicare over to private insurers by permitting (or requiring) older persons to buy private insurance using government-supplied vouchers (called "premium support" proposals). Contentious issues are whether the financing of Medicare should be privatized and what the effects of such dramatic policy change might be on the elderly.

Two major forces have shaped health care policy for the elderly during previous periods of health reform: (1) austerity and its political processing and (2) the aging enterprise and the medical-industrial complex.

Austerity has been a force in the politics of aging since the late 1970s as a result of state and local fiscal crises caused by taxpayer revolts, federal budget cuts, economic recession, tax cuts and high defense spending during the Reagan years and afterward. The result was a large federal budget deficit exceeding 3 trillion dollars by the conclusion of President Bush's term in office in 1993.

Social constructions of reality become a force of their own (Estes, 1979). The concepts of austerity and deficit reduction have themselves become the driving ideology behind health and social policy for the elderly since the mid-1990s. Austerity policies result from the socially constructed notions that (1) federal spending on the elderly and poor is a major cause of U.S. economic problems and (2) federal responsibility for health care is neither appropriate nor feasible. Although the U.S. tax burden is lower than virtually all other large industrialized nations, austerity and deficit reduction are represented as the only possible response to declining revenues.

The *aging enterprise and the medical-industrial complex* consist of the growing concentration of private for-profit hospitals, nursing homes, and other medical care organizations, along with businesses related to medical goods and services (Estes, 1979; Relman, 1980; Wohl, 1984). With health care expenditures in the United States exceeding $1 trillion per year (29% spent for the elderly), there are major incentives for corporate involvement in for-profit markets in medical care for the elderly (Estes, Harrington, & Pellow, 2000). The growing role of proprietaries in medicine has intensified a perennial and profound question: should health care be a "market good" that is purchased as a commodity by those who can afford to pay, or should it be provided as a "merit good," or collective good, available as a right regardless of ability to pay (Estes, Gerard, Zones, & Swan, 1984)?

Clinton and Health and Long-Term Care Reform (1993–2000)

As a candidate for president, Clinton campaigned for health care reform that would include cost containment and universal health care coverage. Clinton's health reform proposal would have provided a core benefit package through private and public plans managed by a national health board. Through this board the growth in health care costs would have been brought into line with inflation over a 5-year period. Coverage would have been paid for primarily by employers and partially by employees, depending on income level. When Clinton addressed Congress in September 1993, there was general agreement, both in Congress and in the public, about the general principles of his plan.

A unique component of Clinton's plan was specifically addressing the issue of long-term care. In the final package brought to Congress in 1993 long-term care was presented as a "merit good" that should be available to all. The long-term care portion of the proposal was an advance over earlier proposals because it covered persons in need of such care regardless of age or income. In the end, long-term care was incorporated in the proposed reform. However, there were several key decisions that reduced its political support; for example, not providing fiscal relief to states that were given responsibility for long-term care under the plan. Also, there was no individual federal entitlement and no defined benefit, with the exception of assessment, case management, and personal assistance services (Estes, Wiener, Goldenson, & Goldberg, 2000).

Today, support for universal coverage is still high, and as the population ages it is more concerned with long-term care. Yet the United States is without universal health care coverage or improvements in long-term care. The number of uninsured people has grown by 4 million, to 44 million, since President Clinton took office, and despite a rapidly aging population, the United States still lacks a national strategy for providing long-term care.

Scholars of health policy have attempted to understand the failure of the Clinton proposal. Central to this interpretation are the three incompatible goals of the Clinton plan: to provide universal health insurance, to reduce medical care cost increases, and to reduce the federal deficit (Lee, 2000). Those opposed to him, including new Federalist Republicans in control of Congress, as well as those opposed to universal coverage, particularly the health insurance industry, recognized this inconsistency and utilized it to mobilize against him (Lee, 2000). Although initial support for universal health care coverage was high, President Clinton's complicated and delayed proposal was manipulated and simplified in the media to create fear among the general public.

Even without passage of Clinton's 1993 health care reform, two bills passed during his presidency made significant improvements to health care coverage: the Health Insurance Portability and Accountability Act (Kassabaum-Kennedy Act) of 1996 and the Child Health Insurance Program (CHIP) as a part of the Balanced Budget Act of 1997. The former protects employees from losing health insurance when they change jobs, and the latter expands the number of poor children eligible for Medicaid, increasing the number of insured children by 2 million (Greenberg, 2000).

The failure of Clinton's national health reform and its conversion to market reform has major implications for long-term care policy development. Recently, most of the action relating to long-term care is occurring at the state level. Until Clinton's 1999 proposal for tax credits and limited caregiver support for long-term care, the issue had virtually disappeared from the federal agenda. Although long-term care reform attempted to ride on the big train of health reform in 1993, it was lost in the shuffle. One lesson learned may be that the reform of long-term care must go its own way, although universal health care advocates continue to press for policy that integrates health and long-term care reform.

Future Issues and Trends

In the 2000 presidential election health care was a leading topic. Both candidates, Bush and Gore, advocated incremental changes to the health care system, such as the patient's bill of rights, prescription drug coverage for the elderly, and tax credits to help individuals buy their own health insurance. The president of the United States and Congress will determine the outcomes.

Future health care policy for the elderly will depend on at least two major conditions: (1) aggregate need and (2) the political-economic environment. *Aggregate need* for health and long-term care by the elderly in the 21st century will be determined by their numbers and health status including chronic disease. Demographic projections show the number and proportion of elderly growing in the next century. By 2040, 21% of the population is expected to be 65 or older (vs. 11% in 1980) and to number between 70 million and 90 million (vs. 25 million in 1980). Disability rates during the 1990s have been calculated at 38% for men and 42% for women (Kaye, La Plante, Carlson, & Wenger, 1996). Despite evidence of some declines in the disability rates, increases in the number of elderly in the next century will exacerbate the call for an adequate long-term care policy. In the future there will be an "increasing number of individuals in quite good health nearly up to the point of death and an increasing number with prolonged severe limitation, with a decline in the duration of infirmity" (Rice & Feldman, 1983, p. 391). Chronic care services are particularly important for elderly women and minorities, many of whom are least able pay out of pocket for them. Minority elderly, historically small in number, are increasing faster than White elderly and will need expanded, culturally relevant, affordable health and long-term care.

The manner in which the needs of the elderly will be addressed by health policy and/or long-term care reform also depends on the *political-economic conditions* of the future. The nation's health policy leaders appear divided as to whether access, cost, or quality of care will be the most important issue in the 21st century. Three likely targets of health reform initiatives are coverage for the uninsured, Medicare prescription drug coverage, and long-term care.

If the nation continues to be influenced by the devolution of federal responsibility, deregulation, and austerity and an increasingly powerful medical-industrial complex, health policies will continue the privatization, corporatization, fragmentation, and rationing of health care. Continued federal budget cuts and shifting of responsibility for medical care for the uninsured to states, localities, and individuals could return the nation to an earlier era of health policy when the federal government took little active interest in the health and welfare of the populace and policies were made at the state and local level.

Proposals of Clinton's Medicare Commission to convert Medicare insurance into the market via vouchers for private insurance did not acknowledge the greater medical needs and out-of-pocket expenses of the poor, the disabled, chronically ill, minorities and women. A major question concerns who will pay for the costs of these "unprofitable" patients. Relegating health care distribution to the market and to managed care requires that consumers are sufficiently informed to be able to make the best choice and that access automatically flows from market decisions. However, where public knowledge of costs, quality, and optimal treatments will come from remains problematic. More important, competition is not likely to produce access

without universal coverage (Teisberg, Porter, & Brown, 1994). As such, the health policy debate and reforms for the elderly in the future are indivisible from struggles to achieve universal coverage of health and long-term care in the face of a powerful, well-entrenched, and pluralistically financed medical care system (government, private insurance, and out-of-pocket) and a largely private, profit-driven delivery system. The challenge is to finance, link, and integrate acute care and community-based long-term care services.

A key question concerns the future of federal leadership and the federal role in the face of the current highly charged and divisive partisan political environment and the piecemeal development of policies based on a combination of market reforms and Medicare and Medicaid cost-containment strategies. Such an approach leaves the basic health care financing system intact but augments the power and influence of a highly pluralistic and profitable medical-industrial complex while doing little or nothing about the growing urgency to address the need for long-term care.

If coalitions were to be formed that transcend age and unite groups with common interests (e.g., the elderly and the disabled), they could change the fundamental conditions that presently affect health policy. In the place of austerity and New Federalism they will have to define the right to health care as part of the Constitution's federal mandate to "promote the general welfare." These groups could become successful advocates for the organization, financing, and delivery of health care for the elderly and disabled as a continuum ranging from respite care to the relief of families who provide most of the care to adequate incomes and acute medical services.

CARROLL L. ESTES
DAWN D. OGAWA
TRACY A. WEITZ

See also
Health Care: Organization, Use, and Financing

HEALTH INFORMATION THROUGH TELECOMMUNICATION

Health care and health information have always been of great interest to older adults. Many seniors suffer from a chronic disease, often more than one. Managing these diseases can become overwhelming for both the older adult and the caregiver. Information about the disease, treatment options, drug interactions, prevention, and support groups can make disease management truly manageable. In the past, such information was disseminated through health care professionals, through printed materials, and via television and radio. Collecting the information required a concerted effort on the part of the older adult and caregiver; it was rarely at one's fingertips.

Now, however, with the burgeoning of the Internet and the World Wide Web (Web), health information is, literally, at one's fingertips. A plethora of information is just a couple of mouse clicks away—from government, commercial, educational, and nonprofit health websites. It is interesting to note that the modern collection, acquisition, and dissemination of health information through the Internet results from a confluence of technologies: electricity, electronics, computers, telephone lines, Internet, imaging, health technologies, and laser and fiber optics. This list represents eight of the 20 top engineering marvels of the 20th century, according to the National Academy of Engineering (Martindale, 2000). The time is therefore right for the public to take advantage of the wealth of health information that is so easily accessible through the available technology.

The very accessibility of information on the Internet, however, brings its own set of problems. There is too much information, often of dubious origin and reliability, for a lay person to process effectively and efficiently. Interventions such as training programs and vetted websites are now being tried to help older adults and their caregivers find reliable health information on the Internet. One such training program is a curriculum for older adults developed by the SPRY Foundation in collaboration with the National Library of Medicine. This curriculum teaches computer-literate older adults how to navigate the Web, find information from reliable sites (such as MEDLINEplus), process that information, and put it into printouts from webpages. Thus, the patient has synthesized version of Web-derived information and a list of specific questions for the doctor.

The provision of health information is equally important to the caregivers and health service providers of older adults as their numbers will almost certainly increase in the future. The rapid expansion of medical knowledge makes it imperative that caregivers and practitioners maintain and improve their competence to provide services and also advise those for whom they care (Patel & Arocha, 1999). Traditional methods of print, video, and individual or group health education may not be enough to meet the demand. Most important, the trend within many governmental agencies is to move away from traditional methods and instead present information in electronic formats (i.e., Social Security Administration, Internal Revenue Service). The electronic format allows agencies to update information and reduce printing and distribution costs. Thus, an alternative method of health information delivery must be identified to serve all of those people who will be in need in the future. One of these avenues may be the Web, which is increasingly being used as an invaluable medium for providing information for a global audience. Furthermore, the Web has unlimited potential for supplementing many traditional methods of communication and information exchange.

Health Information on the Web

At present there are several thousand websites, with millions of pages devoted to health information (Post, 1997). Information on these health sites ranges from descriptive and diagnostic material concerning specific conditions and support group linkages to available local health services. Some of this information is already targeted to older adults. By mid-2000 there were two new consumer-based health information websites available that were specifically designed for ease of use by older adults (i.e., the AgePage website sponsored by the National Institute on Aging and the MEDLINEplus website sponsored by the National Library of Medicine). These efforts are part of an initiative by the federal government to provide health information on the Web that is current, reliable, and easily accessible to the older segment of the population.

This direction in health information dissemination is important because older adults have shown significant interest in the direct application of electronic technology for acquiring health care. Effective electronic interfaces have been provided between older patients and clinicians and adherence to prescribed medication regimens has been increased through computerized voice mail. Moreover, results from a recent survey of middle-aged and older adults indicated that about 60% of the sample reported that they would like to learn how to access health information on the Web (Morrell, Mayhorn, & Bennett, in press). With this in mind, SPRY Foundation, together with the National Library of Medicine and the National Institutes of Health, has developed a series of innovative research initiatives that have demonstrated the effectiveness of a curriculum to train older adults to search the Web quickly and efficiently to find reliable health information. This curriculum has also taught older adults how to use information to become better informed about their health condition(s), treatment options, and risks and how to use health information in becoming a consumer-partner with their health care providers.

It has also been demonstrated that users without medical training can use the Web to find answers to medical questions as well as to identify potential sources of information. For example, a site established to provide information on the recognition and treatment of cardiac arrhythmias received 10,732 requests for documents in one month via commercial Internet providers, commercial firms, educational institutions, and other sites (Widman & Tong, 1997). Therefore, the Web is already becoming a part of many people's daily environment. Newly diagnosed patients are usually eager for information about their illnesses. Information, however, may not always be enough (Mizsur, 1997). The Web also has the potential to provide social contact and encouragement, as well as emotional and informational support through chat rooms on specific medical topics (Mallory, 1997).

Health professionals are increasingly using networked, computer-based technologies to share information with one another. Furthermore, the Web may serve as a powerful tool for program development and improvement and for health networking between educational institutions for collaborative research. Use of the Web by clinicians may become an integral part of distance medicine technology, or telemedicine (Balas, Jaffrey, Kuperman, Boren, Brown, Pinciroli, et al., 1997). Thus, the Web is an important potential adjunct to cost-effective health care research and delivery (Doyle, Ruskin, & Engel, 1997).

Can Older Adults Use the Web?

Results from several recent surveys indicate that adults over the age of 65 have less experience with personal computers and the Web than do younger adults (Rogers, Cabrera, Walker, Gilbert, & Fisk, 1996). They also take more time to acquire computer skills and generally make more mistakes than do younger adults when learning how to use computers (Morrell & Echt, 1997). However, other systematic research has shown that older adults can readily learn how to use computers, and they can retain these skills over time (Echt, Morrell, & Park, 1998). Although only a small portion of older computer users rely on their machines for communication or for information gathering at present, they have shown substantial interest in using the Web. Furthermore, older adults currently constitute the fastest growing number of Web users. One reason, among others, that many older adults are not online may be that most websites are complex and difficult to navigate.

The National Institute on Aging has funded a substantial amount of systematic research on the topic of the cognitive aspects of computer use in older adults in the past decade. In March 1999, SPRY Foundation, together with numerous government and private partners, sponsored the first national conference on "Older Adults, Health Information, and the World Wide Web" at the National Institutes of Health in Bethesda, Maryland. This meeting brought together over 300 government and corporate participants and promoted a better understanding of the importance of this topic. A second biennial conference is slated for February 2001.

The findings from basic and applied research on aging and cognition and the use of electronic technology by older adults may well serve as a theoretical framework from which to build a health information website designed for ease of use and comprehension by older adults. A cornerstone of this research is the demonstration that age-related declines in certain underlying cognitive processes might be mediated by the manner in which instructional materials are constructed and subsequently presented in electronic formats. Age-related declines in vision may be addressed by applying specific design directives when constructing a website for use by older adults.

Results have shown that (1) organizing material in a standard format or small discrete segments, (2) writing the text in simple language, (3) avoiding inferences, and (4) phrasing the text in the active, rather than the passive, voice reduces cognitive demands and can increase comprehension of information presented to older adults in print. Medical information, in particular, has been shown to be better understood and remembered by both young and old adults when it was clearly structured and organized, or when cognitive demands were reduced. Similarly, when cognitive demands were reduced through careful organization and presentation of instructional materials, procedural tasks were more easily performed by young and old. Finally, it has been demonstrated that older adults can learn how to perform computer tasks with instructions composed of text and animations as well as instructions presented in the traditional format of text and illustrations. When animations portray the material presented in text, the material is better understood.

Other researchers have offered recommendations for building a website that takes into consideration age-related declines in vision. These include: (1) increasing contrast, especially for detailed stimuli; (2) avoiding subtle discriminations among colors; (3) minimizing the need to discriminate fine detail; (4) omitting the use of distracting visual components such as blinking icons; (5) using at least 14-point type for all text and headers; (6) avoiding the use of the colors in the green-blue-violet range, which are difficult for older adults to see; (7) avoiding the use of novelty typefaces; (8) using Helvetica or a sans serif typeface that is medium or bold weight; (9) presenting the text in caps and lower case and headers in all caps; (10) avoiding single spacing and reducing the number of characters per page; and (11) using nonjustified paragraph formatting (see Echt, in press; Hartley, 1999). SPRY Foundation has published a practical *Guide for Web Site Creators* that explains these recommendations and provides examples. The guide is available on their website: *www.spry.org*.

In brief, these findings, as well as the recommendations just listed, indicate that a website can be constructed that addresses age-related declines in cognition and vision. These innovations might well increase the use of the Web by older adults.

Issues on Web-Based Health Information

Although there are extensive health-related resources currently available on the Web, little systematic research has been conducted on how older adults might use the Web. A literature review located only one systematic study and two surveys on Web use in older adults. Mead, Spaulding, Sit, Meyer, and Walker (1997) examined the effects of age and type of training on efficiency and preferences in a Web search activity. Their results indicated that older adults were able to complete most of the Web search tasks, but they performed more procedures to find the required information than younger adults did. Bow, Williamson, and Wale (1996) surveyed adults over the age of 50 to determine how receptive they were to using the Web. Some of their participants were also observed using the Web. Although their respondents reported in general that they did not think the Web would be useful, their findings suggested that if the individuals in this age group were able to overcome mouse management problems, they became very positive about using the Web. Morrell and his colleagues surveyed young-old and old-old adults on their use of the Web. They found that individuals in these age groups were also enthusiastic about using the Web, and one of their primary goals was to use the Web to seek health information.

In addition, there are other critical issues that must be discussed. Much concern has been expressed about the validity of the information on current health websites. There is no mechanism in place to assure browsers that the information that they are viewing is current and/or reliable. Although health-related telecommunications systems are in use, little research has been conducted on these systems. The few results that have been reported are limited in evaluating the potential benefits and weaknesses of the systems (Scheerhorn, Warisse, & McNeilis, 1995). Finally, research is needed on how to make the Web user-friendly and accessible to older adults who are in low socioeconomic status categories, illiterate, or cognitively impaired. Finally, the issue of confidentiality in using the Web is also of major importance. Some websites currently sell their membership's information.

healthinfo.older adults.web?

In this article, we have described four important issues that concern older adults and their access to health information. First, the need for health information by older individuals, their caregivers, and their health service providers will increase dramatically in the 21st century. Traditional methods of health information delivery may not be enough to meet the demand. Second, the Web may be an additional option for providing health information to older adults, their caregivers, and their health service providers. Third, older adults have shown substantial interest in using the Web, and they *can* learn and retain computer skills. Fourth, websites can be designed that take into consideration age-related declines in cognition and vision, which might ultimately increase the use of the Web for health information for older adults, their caregivers and health service providers, as well as younger individuals. Caution must be taken, however, in the manner in which health information is currently presented on the Web. Clearly, more systematic research is needed on how best to present "new" health information over the Web in ways that facilitate learning, decision making, and maintenance in older adults.

Russell E. Morgan, Jr.
Ann Benbow
Roger W. Morrell

See also
Internet and E-mail Resources

HEALTH MAINTENANCE ORGANIZATIONS

Health maintenance organizations (HMOs) are the fastest growing forms of health insurance in the United States (Tabbush & Swanson, 1999). The term *health maintenance organization* was associated with the Health Maintenance Act of 1973, enacted to stimulate the development of more prepaid practices primarily as a way to control costs. In general, HMOs

- assume a contractual responsibility to provide a specified range of services
- serve a defined population of subscribers who voluntarily enroll in the program

- require a fixed payment in advance, independent of use of the services
- assume part of a financial risk of providing services to subscribers (Luft & Morrison, 1991)

Since their inception, HMOs have grown rapidly in numbers. In 1977, 183 HMOs served approximately 8 million subscribers. In 1997, the number reached 760 HMOs with 78 million enrollees (from Price Waterhouse, 1999, http://www.pwchealth.com/charts/chart49.html).

Although there is constant reorganization within the different types of plans, the following five types of models are commonly described. The *staff model* HMOs employ physicians and other providers directly, *group model HMOs* contract with one or more group practices, *individual independent practice associations (IPAs)* contract with many individual physicians or providers who care for enrollees in their own offices, and *network model HMOs* contract not only with individuals but also with groups of physicians (Retchin, Brown, Yeh, Chu, & Moreno, 1997). In addition, HMOs may frequently combine any of the above models to form *mixed model HMOs*. Whereas staff and group model physicians are often salaried, physicians who are associated with IPAs and network models may receive fee-for-service (FFS) remuneration (Gold, Hurley, & Lake, 1995). Recent literature reviews have shown a reduction in the number of staff/group model HMOs, and an increase in network IPA models or mixed model HMOs. In 1988, group and staff model HMOs constituted about 42% of HMO membership. By the end of 1994, they constituted about 31% (Gabel, 1997). These changes have significantly affected the impact of health maintenance organizations in the delivery of care. It has been shown that the rate of preventive care varies by HMO type. Staff and group model HMOs perform better on prevention programs than the network and IPA models (Retchin & Brown, 1990). Recent evidence using quality criteria (e.g., HEDIS 3.0) shows that for-profit HMOs provide lower quality of care than the not-for-profit HMOs. However, this analysis did not specifically include the elderly population or compare the relative performances of Medicare fee-for-service plans with that of health maintenance organizations (Himmelstein, Woolhandler, Hellander, & Wolfe, 1999). These support the results of an analysis of the current reform of the primary health care system that suggested organizational changes intended to have significant implications for the role of older clients (Counte, 1998).

Effects of HMOs on the Elderly

For the elderly population, Medicare provides nearly universal but limited coverage for health care. Medicare has substantial deductibles and co-payments and does not provide coverage for outpatient pharmaceutical agents. It also requires a monthly subsidized premium for outpatient physician referral services; this may be unaffordable for the poor elderly. Historically, HMOs have resisted enrolling older people primarily because of unfavorable cost-based reimbursement policies. In 1993, only 9% of Medicare beneficiaries were enrolled in Medicare fee-for-service coverage. Seventy-one percent had either employer-based or individually purchased supplemental FFS coverage, 13% were dually enrolled in Medicaid and Medicare programs, and 7% had enrolled in HMOs (Health Care Financing Administration, 1996). Between 1985 and 1996, the rates of Medicare HMO risk-contract enrollments more than doubled (Managed Care Online, 1999). In 1985, 38% of Medicare enrollees were enrolled under risk-contract HMOs. As of March 1996, 84% of Medicare enrollees were with risk-contract HMOs. Under the 1997 Balanced Budget Act, Congress greatly expanded the ability of Medicare enrollees to join health maintenance organizations by creating the Medicare+Choice program.

Medicare contracts with the HMOs in one of the two ways: cost-based contracts and risk-based contracts. In cost-based contracts, HMO bills Medicare based on services rendered. In a risk-based contract, Medicare pays a fixed premium to the plan (approximately 95% of the adjusted average per capita cost), which is equivalent to the expenses for Medicare FFS beneficiaries in the local area (Luft, 1998). In 1996, 95% of the risk-contract HMOs offered coverage for an annual physical examination (this is not covered under Medicare FFS). Immunizations were offered by 86% of the HMOs, and 60% of the HMOs offered outpatient prescription drug coverage. Ninety-four plans offered prescription drug coverage as part of their zero premium plans (Zarabozo, Taylor, & Hicks, 1996). Thus, a majority of elderly HMO enrollees are receiving a much broader range of health care coverage at a lower price than they could receive from Medicare FFS alone or supplemental insurance.

HMOs, operating under the system of capitation, tend to reduce utilization of resources and reward providers for "doing less." Elderly populations, on the other hand, tend to utilize health care services at higher rates than younger and healthier populations. Further, the current Medicare payment structure for HMOs does not take into account the differences in risks for the enrollees. Unlike employer-based enrollments in HMOs, Medicare beneficiaries in HMOs may disenroll within 30 days of enrollment. These policies by Medicare produce adverse risk selection by HMOs by restricting access to sub-specialists for high-risk elderly enrollees, or making use of resources difficult for such enrollees, thus encouraging them to revert to fee-for-service plans (Luft, 1998).

Issues of Quality of Care in HMOs for the Elderly

Evidence from recent literature on quality of care is mixed. In a review of literature based on data collected earlier than 1994, Miller and Luft (1997) failed to find a clear verdict in support of or against the proposition that health maintenance organizations provide inferior quality of care for the elderly compared with fee-for-service plans. In terms of utilization of available health care resources, they found that HMOs use fewer resources than traditional FFS plans. For acute clinical conditions, outcomes for HMO plan enrollees were better than those in the FFS plans, but evidence was equivocal for services for chronic and long-term care for the elderly. Analysis of data from the Medical Outcomes Study has shown that elderly patients with chronic illnesses under managed care tend to fare worse in their physical and health scores (Ware, Bayliss, Rogers, Kosinski, & Tarlov, 1996). An analysis of 4-year data from an HMO census on primary care staffing and access to care has shown that, among the elderly, access to primary care providers is better with the HMOs than with the fee-for-service system. However, neither processes of care nor outcomes of care were found to be different between the two systems (Wholey, Burns, & Lav-izzo-Mourey, 1998).

Several emerging issues in the role of care for the elderly related to HMOs deserve mention. First, the debates on the quality of care will continue despite the studies of HMOs that have failed to show any significant difference in the quality of care for the elderly. Second, at present, Medicare does not cover beneficiaries for prescription drugs. A recent study by the Public Policy Institute of the American Association of Retired Persons found that even private-sector drug coverage is inadequate for the elderly Medicare beneficiary. The study recommended universal coverage of prescription drug benefits for all Medicare beneficiaries (Gibson, Brangan, Gross, & Caplan, 1999). Prescription drug benefits will likely be a major issue for the elderly in the coming years. Third, the trend of increased number of Medicare beneficiaries entering into HMOs will continue and the elderly Medicare beneficiaries will continue to play the role of a wild card in the U.S. health care delivery system. Fourth, liability reform will continue to play a roll in the evolution of services offered by HMOs. Finally, the demand for cost-effective care will not decrease the attractiveness of HMOs for older populations.

JAMES ROMEIS

See also
Managed Care

HEALTH PROMOTION

Although the importance of preventive medicine has been recognized since the 19th century, the term *health promotion* was coined in the 1970s partly in response to the perceived shortcomings of a health care model restricted to the treatment of established disease. Defined as "any combination of health education and related organizational, political, and economic interventions designed to facilitate behavioral and environmental changes conducive to health" (U.S. Department of Health and Human Services [USDHHS], 1980a), health promotion was envisioned as addressing an array of individual lifestyle and broader environmental factors influencing health status.

Although early health promotion efforts frequently overlooked the elderly as a target group (Minkler & Pasick, 1986), the relevance of the concept for older adults had increasingly been recognized. Indeed, with half of all Americans age 65 living to become 80, and one third surviving to age 85 (National Center for Health Statistics [NCHS], 1982), the importance of an approach that seeks to maintain and enhance health status in the later years is underscored. Health promotion for the aged also holds promise from an economic perspective. Thus, although the elderly comprise less than 12% of the U.S. population, they consume 30% of the nation's health care budget and are responsible for 40% of all hospitalizations.

The prevalence of chronic illness among the elderly—80% have at least one chronic disease (NCHS, 1982)—further underscores the wisdom of an approach that stresses improving the functional health and quality of life of older people. Although chronic conditions frequently cannot be prevented, their onset may be delayed, their symptoms diminished, and the overall quality of life enhanced through effective health promotion efforts.

Five behavioral areas—improved nutrition, exercise and fitness, stress control, reduction of drug and alcohol misuse, and smoking cessation—have been identified by the U.S. Department of Health and Human Services as having particular relevance for health promotion in the elderly. Studies thus have suggested that exercise may slow arteriosclerotic development (Fries, 1980) and may increase by 67% the elderly's ability to perform such activities of daily living as cooking, shopping, and climbing stairs (Shepard, 1978). The role of nutrition in the prevention of physical health problems such as osteoporosis and certain forms of dementia (Filner & Williams, 1979) has also been demonstrated. Finally, smoking cessation—even very late in life—has been found to lower heart rate and blood pressure within days and to provide rapid relief from bronchial irritation, coughing, and related symptoms (Fries, 1980).

For the most part, health promotion programs for the elderly, as for other age groups, have tended to stress individual behavior changes in such areas as diet, exercise, and stress management. Although such microlevel foci are important, they must be supplemented with broader macrolevel attempts to address the underlying causes of health problems. Poor nutrition in the elderly may be related to inadequate income, social isolation, or fear of crime on venturing outdoors. Health promotion programs stressing nutrition education without reference to these underlying causes of undernutrition not only may be ineffective but may inadvertently "blame the victim" by suggesting that the onus for improved health rests largely with lifestyles and health practices over which the individual is assumed to have substantial control (Minkler & Pasick, 1986).

In recognition of the fact that a complex of social, cultural, economic, and other factors helps shape and determine health, a "system-centered" approach to health education and health promotion has been advocated. The latter aims at altering the social or cultural structure of a community "in such a way as to provide better conditions, opportunities, supports and incentives for improving the health of individuals in the community" (USDHHS, 1980b). System-centered health promotion for the elderly might include helping to insure a minimum level of "economic health" for elders living in or near poverty, improving access to transportation and to a broad array of health and social services, encouraging positive portrayals of the elderly through the mass media, and creating nursing home environments conducive to greater patient autonomy and decision making. By intervening on the broader systems level, health promotion is more likely to be both ethically sound and effective in improving and maintaining the health and quality of life of the elderly.

MEREDITH MINKLER

See also
Health Information Through Telecommunication

HEARING

Hearing is mediated by the human auditory system and is critical in establishing and maintaining a person's relationship with the sociophysical environment. For the United States, in 1991 the estimated incidence of hearing impairment, a leading

chronic health condition, was 86.1 per 1,000 population, or more than 20 million. The most common auditory disorder in the elderly, affecting 13% of Americans over 65 years, is presbycusis, the bilateral loss of hearing capacity associated with normal physiological aging of the auditory system.

The Stimulus for Hearing

The adequate stimulus for normal human hearing is mechanical energy in the form of acoustic waves generated by a vibrating body and transmitted in a gaseous, liquid, or solid medium with a fundamental frequency between 20 and 20,000 Hz. Auditory stimuli include pure tones, complex tones, speech, and noise.

Schematic Diagram of the Ear

Figure 1 is a schematic representation of the three anatomical divisions of the human ear, with their associated structural and functional characteristics. The vestibular apparatus mediates equilibrium and does not pertain to hearing.

Age-Related Changes in the Human Auditory System

Outer Ear.   With age, hair growth tends to increase within the folds of the pinna. The pinna may increase in length and breadth by several millimeters, and the supporting walls of the external meatus may show atrophic changes.

Cerumen is found normally in the external canal. Approximately one third of the elderly exhibit excessive and impacted cerumen. This common ear problem may appear as a hearing loss.

Middle Ear.   Aging produces a thinning of the tympanic membrane and atrophy of the tensor tympani muscle. Arthritic changes occur in the incudomalleal and incudostapedial joints of the ossicular chain. In otosclerosis, a common condition more prevalent in women than men, new bone forms in the cochlear capsule and tends to immobilize the footplate of the stapes in the oval window.

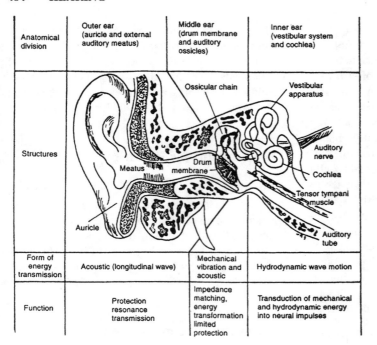

Anatomical division	Outer ear (auricle and external auditory meatus)	Middle ear (drum membrane and auditory ossicles)	Inner ear (vestibular system and cochlea)
Structures			
Form of energy transmission	Acoustic (longitudinal wave)	Mechanical vibration and acoustic	Hydrodynamic wave motion
Function	Protection resonance transmission	Impedance matching, energy transformation limited protection	Transduction of mechanical and hydrodynamic energy into neural impulses

FIGURE 1   A schematic representation of the three anatomical divisions of the human ear, with their associated structural and functional characteristics. *From* Willard R. Zemlin, *Speech and Hearing Science: Anatomy and Physiology* (4th ed.). Copyright © 1998 by Allyn & Bacon. Reprinted with permission.

Stapedial otosclerosis and other conditions in which sound waves are unable to travel properly through the outer and middle ear produce a conductive hearing loss. The progression of this loss, which never exceeds about 60 dB, may be prevented by medical therapy or surgical procedures.

Inner Ear.   Four classes of age-related disorders occur in the inner ear (Schuknecht & Gacek, 1993): (1) sensory presbycusis (atrophy and degeneration of hair cells and supporting cells in the extreme basal coil of the cochlea), (2) neural presbycusis (loss of neurons in the cochlea and the auditory pathways), (3) strial presbycusis (atrophy of the stria vascularis and corresponding deficiencies in the bioelectric and biochemical properties of the endolymphatic fluids), and (4) cochlear conductive presbycusis (atrophic changes in the vibratory structures of the cochlear partition). Each class of presbycusis is characterized by specific audiometric outcomes.

Although the four types of presbycusis often occur in isolation, many hearing losses are evidenced as mixtures of these types. However, about 25% of all cases of presbycusis have indeterminate histologic characteristics.

Auditory Pathways and Brain.   In the retrocochlear region of the auditory system, a loss of neurons appears with age in the ventral cochlear nucleus. Also, the size and shape of the ganglion cells are altered in the medial geniculate body, the superior olivary nucleus, and the inferior colliculus.

Atrophy occurs in the eighth cranial nerve, and the number of neuronal cells in the auditory pathway is reduced. The cortex of the temporal lobes of the brain retains normal stratification, but there is a bilaterally symmetrical loss of ganglion cells. The relationship between decreased auditory processing in presbycusis and the probable reduction in neurochemical/neurotransmitter functions within the auditory system (including brain stem, auditory cortex, and association areas) needs further study.

Basic Psychophysical Functions

Sensitivity for Pure Tones.   The minimal sound pressure required to elicit an auditory response 50% of the time defines the absolute threshold for that particular stimulus under a given set of testing conditions. Reference threshold levels (audiometric zero) have been published by the American National Standards Institute. The relation between age and pure tone thresholds is now well established (Brant & Fozard, 1990). As frequency increases above 1,000 Hz, hearing becomes increasingly poorer as a function of age. Age held constant, men have poorer hearing than women above 1,000 Hz; below 1,000 Hz, women have poorer hearing. Presbycusic changes in auditory thresholds are continual throughout adulthood but are most marked after 60 years. With aging, hearing loss tends to spread from higher to lower frequencies. Frequency discrimination thresholds for pure tones and complex tones are also negatively affected by age. The International Organization for Standardization has specified values of normal hearing by frequency and age.

Speech Sensitivity. The minimal amount of acoustic pressure required for the intelligibility of speech in quiet defines the speech reception threshold. The American National Standards Institute has established 19-dB sound pressure level as the normal speech reception threshold for young adults tested on spondaic words. The speech reception threshold increases markedly with advancing age. This increase has been attributed to elevated frequency thresholds that increase at an accelerating rate between 50 and 90 years.

Speech Discrimination. The intelligibility of words presented at suprathreshold levels in quiet or noise is a measure of speech recognition. When hearing level is controlled across age groups, no differences in speech discrimination occur from 55 to 84 years (Dubno, Lee, Matthews, & Mills, 1997). Under adverse listening conditions (e.g., noise, overlapping words, excessive reverberation, and temporally distorted speech), older persons exhibit disproportionately greater speech discrimination deficits than younger listeners, even when hearing levels are controlled. These findings suggest that neural and cortical processing functions beyond the peripheral level are implicated in age-related deficits in auditory communication. This is of critical importance because central auditory dysfunction has been related to cognitive dysfunction and senile dementia (Gates, Cobb, Linn, Rees, Wolf, & D'Agostino, 1996).

Temporal Discrimination and Summation. The monaural ability to hear the temporal separation between two successive noise segments or tones is a measure of temporal resolution. The minimal gap detection threshold for noise is 2 to 3 msec. Auditory temporal summation involves a reciprocal relationship between stimulus intensity and stimulus duration (up to 200 to 300 msec) to produce a threshold response. Temporal resolution and temporal summation decline with age, even with hearing level controlled. The threshold interaural time difference for clicks at a low sound level is approximately twice as large for elderly than young listeners. Accordingly, older listeners show a decreased ability in sound lateralization and localization. Whether the reduction in temporal processing can account for the speech-understanding problems of the elderly requires further investigation.

Rehabilitation of Impaired Hearing

Conventional Hearing Aids. Deteriorated hearing often may be improved by means of an electronic hearing aid. The optimal interface between hearing aid and hearing loss will depend on the degree and nature of the loss. Hearing aids vary in initial cost, acoustic efficiency, durability, operating expense, service availability, and physical attractiveness. Hearing aid selection will also be influenced by the physical and psychological characteristics of the listener, particularly in the elderly. Whenever feasible, hearing devices should be fitted binaurally for maximal hearing advantage.

Hearing aids provide high-fidelity electronic enhancement of acoustic signals, by analog or digital processing. Types of hearing aids include body-worn, eyeglass, behind the ear, on the ear, and partially or completely in the ear canal. Some hearing aids include a programming function that allows the listener to set the electroacoustic parameters for maximal hearing in particular situations.

Implantable Hearing Aids. For patients with intractable conductive disorders and adequate cochlear reserve, hearing devices are available or under development that circumvent some limitations of conventional hearing aids. The devices stimulate or are attached to one of the following structures: (1) tympanic membrane, (2) temporal bone, (3) ossicular chain, or (4) cochlea. For certain listeners and testing conditions (e.g., speech in noise), an implanted temporal bone device can provide better hearing than a conventional bone-conduction or air-conduction hearing aid.

Cochlear Implants.   In certain kinds of nearly total deafness, the cochlea is nonfunctional, but the auditory nerve remains essentially intact. Thus, implants with 1 to 20 or more electrodes can be inserted into the cochlea of adults and children to provide direct electrical stimulation of functional nerve fibers. The neural patterns generated by the cochlear implant will depend on the encoding strategy designed into the sound processor. In multichannel implants, the encoded information relates to the intensity, temporal characteristics, and frequency of the incoming sound. As the perception of sound through a cochlear implant is markedly different than that in normal hearing, training programs must be provided before the salient features of speech and environmental sounds can be recognized and properly interpreted in their neurally encoded form. Nevertheless, even in cases of prelingual deafness and congenital deafness due to cochlear malformations, multichannel implants can provide substantial improvements in hearing for speech and music. Postsurgical risks of a cochlear implant are always present and include degeneration of surviving auditory nerve fibers, facial nerve damage with paralysis, intracochlear infections, and increased tinnitus.

Education and Training Programs.   Other technological advances are also available to assist hearing-impaired persons. Various kinds of amplifying systems can enhance speech signals, speech-visual interactive systems can improve speechreading, auditory to tactile conversion devices can encode speech information, and radio transmission systems are useful in group situations (Corso, 1985). However, hearing-impaired persons should receive an appropriate educational orientation with counseling for a particular type of aid. Unless there is full participation in a well-developed rehabilitation program, maximal hearing benefits most likely will not be attained from any assistive device.

JOHN F. CORSO

HEARING LOSS
See
   Hearing

HEART
See
   Cardiovascular System: The Heart
   Cardiovascular System: Overview

HEART DISEASE
See
   Cardiovascular System: The Heart

HEMISPHERIC SPECIALIZATION

It has been over 130 years since Paul Broca made his historic announcement in 1865 that "we speak with the left hemisphere." This conclusion was based on postmortem studies of patients with brain lesions in the left hemisphere resulting in language problems. In contrast, lesions in the right hemisphere did not seem to affect speech (Benson & Ardila, 1996).

The *left hemisphere* plays a critical role in language for more than 90% of right-handed individuals and over 70% of left-handed individuals (Rasmussen & Milner, as cited in Kolb & Wishaw, 1990). Although there is functional asymmetry between the two hemispheres in regards to language, the right hemisphere also contributes to certain aspects of language function.

Research indicates that the left hemisphere processes information in a sequential, analytical manner, abstracting out relevant details to which it attaches verbal labels (Kolb & Wishaw, 1990). The left hemisphere is dominant for *language functions* such as lexical retrieval, auditory comprehension, reading, writing, and verbal fluency. Furthermore, abstract thinking and mathematical concepts seem to activate the left hemisphere more than the right hemisphere.

It should be pointed out that languages consist of sets of arbitrary symbols. Although the left hemisphere plays a dominant role in Indo-European languages (like English), the right hemisphere may play a dominant role in language systems such as Braille, which require tactile recognition of patterns.

On the other hand, the *right hemisphere* is an information synthesizer and organizes stimuli in gestalts, or wholes, compared with the analytical roles of the left hemisphere. The right hemisphere controls extralinguistic functions, such as the ability to maintain a conversational topic and also the ability to follow and interpret abstract verbal information such as indirect requests and idioms. The right hemisphere also mediates prosody (e.g., changes in pitch ranges and intonational contours) during conversation.

The right hemisphere is very important in visual-spatial orientation, our sense of direction, and also in visual-spatial memory. In addition, the right hemisphere is important for geometry, mental rotation tasks, visual construction and visual perception as manifested in our ability to copy a design and actually construct a three-dimensional design.

Our ability to remember information is dependent on both hemispheres. The difference may lie in the type of information that we would like to remember. Auditory-verbal information (such as recall of names) seems to be dependent on left-hemisphere functions (Lezak, 1995). In contrast, the right hemisphere mediates memory for nonverbal auditory information (such as environmental sounds or an initial exposure to a musical sequence). Some information to be remembered (such as pictures of people or objects) activates both hemispheres. To recognize a face, the imaginal codes of the right hemisphere and the lexical codes of the left hemisphere are activated in order to retrieve the name of person (Constantinidou, Neils, Bouman, Lee, & Shuren, 1996).

There are anatomical differences between the two hemispheres that could account for some neuropsychological differences. For instance, the planum temporale (the area just posterior to the auditory cortex) in the left hemisphere is larger than the corresponding planum temporale in the right hemisphere. Another reported difference is that the frontal operculum in the right hemisphere is organized differently from the one on the left (Broca's area). Furthermore, the cortical and subcortical distribution of certain neurotransmitters such as GABA, acetylcholine, norepinephrine, and dopamine is asymmetrical (Kolb & Wishaw, 1990).

Prior to the development of sophisticated neurodiagnostic measures, differences between the two hemispheres (in humans) could be observed via the manifestation of symptoms following lesions in specific cortical areas. With the advent of functional techniques, such as positron emission tomography, functional magnetic resonance imaging (MRI), and regional cerebral blood flow studies, it is possible to pinpoint which brain areas are involved or activated during a specific cognitive task. This in vivo information provides an opportunity to determine activity in specific parts of the brain during a given task. Information on how a normal brain functions would enhance our understanding of normal human behavior and also assist in the rehabilitation of patients with brain lesions.

Age Differences

Certain right- and left-hemisphere functions seem to be affected by the aging process. For instance, in a meta-analysis of 32 studies Feyereisen (1997) reported that picture naming (a primarily left-hemisphere language function) declined in subjects aged 70 and older. Younger participants (ages 50–69) performed similarly to those under 50.

Aging also affects visual-perceptual performance. Specifically, older subjects performed similarly to patients with right-hemisphere lesions during visual-perceptual tasks suggestive of right-hemisphere decline associated with aging (Peterson, Gerhardstein, Mennemeier, & Rapcsak, 1998).

The decline in neuropsychological performance can be attributed to *neurophysiological changes* such as neuronal loss and myelin loss (Haug et al., as cited in Lezak, 1995; Terry, as cited in Lezak, 1995; Kemper, as cited in Nicholas, Connor, Obler, & Albert, 1998). These changes begin after age 50 or 60, with an accelerated rate after age 70. Changes in the cellular structure of the brain alter the brain mass, resulting in cortical atrophy. Atrophy is manifested as narrowing of the gyri, widening of the sulci, thinning of the cortical mantle, and increase in ventricular size. The frontal lobes seem to be more susceptible to neuronal cell changes than other parts of the brain. Cowell, Turetsky, Gur, Grossman, Shtasel, and Gur (1994) reported a three-way interaction between age, sex, and hemisphere. There was a greater volume reduction in the frontal lobe versus the temporal lobe with aging. Furthermore, the age-related differences were greater in men than in women.

Changes in the endorhinal cortex and hippocampal areas associated with aging are not a direct result of cell loss but rather due to molecular shifts affecting signal transmission (Morrison & Hof, 1997). Change in signal transmission could be partially responsible for the age-associated memory impairment (AAMI) in normal aging. It should also be pointed out that the above mechanism is separate from actual cell loss observed in Alzheimer's disease; however, estrogen may play an important role in both cases. The multiple roles of estrogen suggest that it may have an impact on hippocampal circuit regulation and also may protect those circuits from degeneration (Morrison & Hof, 1997).

Various neurochemical systems interact with age and could influence cognitive function in the elderly. These include three endocrine systems: the gonoidal systems (estrogen and testosterone), the pancreatic (growth hormone/insulin-like growth factor I axis), and the thyroid (dehydroepiandrosterone and its sulfate) systems (Lamberts, van den Beld, & van der Lely, 1997). Hormones can serve as neurotransmitters, neuromodulators, and neurotrophic substances. In addition to hormonal changes, there are changes in neurotransmitter concentrations in the system. Changes in the dopamine, acetylcholine, and serotonin neurotransmitter systems have been linked to AAMI, as have psychiatric and emotional changes associated with the aging process.

Potential Factors Influencing Differential Impact on the Two Hemispheres

In addition to the above age differences in cognition and neuropsychology, gender differences and environmental factors may affect the two hemispheres differentially. In general, women perform better on verbal fluency and vocabulary tasks and also have better perceptual speed and accuracy, compared with men. On the other hand, men perform superiorly on mental rotation and visual-spatial tasks. These gender differences could be a function of genetic and environmental factors. For instance, brain cells in the basal forebrain and hippocampi have estrogen receptors and are responsive to estrogen. These cholinergic and GABA-ergic neurons

are not related to reproduction but are involved in memory, cognition, and learning. In men there is a gradual decline in testosterone after age 30, but the localization of aromatase (an enzyme that converts testosterone to estradiol) provides the system with a potential source of estrogen. In women the production of estrogen is cyclical up to menopause, and then there is a sudden drop of estrogen supply (Toran-Allerand, Miranda, Bentham, Sohrabji, Brown, Hochberg, et al., 1992). Research on the effects of hormone replacement therapy (HRT) on cognitive abilities in postmenopausal women is needed to determine the exact role of HRT on memory, learning, and other cognitive functions. Furthermore, the effects of decline of gonoidal steroid level and aromatizable testosterone in men should be explored systematically.

Experience also can affect hemispheric specialization. Architects, taxi drivers, design engineers, and those in other professions requiring visual-spatial skills tend to demonstrate superior visual-spatial memory. On the other hand, journalists, English teachers, accountants, and other professionals who deal with analytical, mathematical, and language-based activities perform better on language and abstract verbal tasks (related to left-hemisphere function). It should be mentioned that repeated and intense learning may result in structural changes in the nervous system. An example is the recent research indicating that cab drivers in London have a larger right hippocampus than is found in the general public. This is the result of their daily experiences in driving in a complex city requiring superior visual-spatial memory.

In conclusion, hemispheric specialization and hemispheric differences continue to be present from development and throughout adulthood. Genetic factors as well as gender and environmental factors seem to affect hemispheric specialization and performance in adults throughout their life spans.

FOFI CONSTANTINIDOU

See also
Aphasia
Clinical EEG: Cognitive Changes
Communication Disorders

HIP FRACTURE

Pathogenesis

Hip fracture remains epidemic among the elderly. In the United States, over 250,000 hip fractures occur yearly (Perez, 1994), and hip fracture patients account for one half of all hospital days for all fractures (Griffon, Melton, & Ray, 1990). Hip fracture is significantly related to mortality, with a concentrated effect in the first 6 months postfracture (Wolinsky, Fitzgerald, & Stump, 1997). There is an immediate increase in mortality following hip fracture in medically ill and functionally impaired patients, whereas among those with no comorbidities and few impairments, there is a gradual increase that continues for 5 years postfracture (Magaziner, Lydick, Hawkes, Fox, Zimmerman, Epstein, et al., 1997). Hip fracture also significantly increases the likelihood of subsequent hospitalization, and has been shown to increase the number of subsequent episodes of hip fracture, the number of hospital days by 21%, and total charges by 16% (Wolinsky, Fitzgerald, & Stump, 1997).

Hip fracture results from two important age-related changes. The first is a well-described age-related loss of postural stability, which leads to an increased incidence of *falls* (Alexander, 1996). An equally important factor is the decrease in bone density that results from both a linear decrease in bone mass with age and from trabecular bone loss and diminished bone strength related to postmenopausal *osteoporosis* (Raisz, 1997). The incidence of hip fracture doubles every 5 years after the age of 50 (Lyon & Nevins, 1989). By age 65, it is estimated that 50% of American women have a bone mineral content below the fracture threshold (Perez, 1994). This figure rises to 100% by age 85, as senile osteoporosis causes cortical bone loss, further augmenting menopause-related trabecular bone loss (Black, Browner, & Cauley, 1990). Women have two to four times as many hip fractures as do men (Perez, 1994), and one third of all women who survive to age 90 have suffered a hip fracture.

Prevalence rates may vary with ethnicity, with most studies revealing a higher prevalence of hip fracture among Caucasian females than among African American females (Karagas, Lu-Yao, Barrett, Beach, & Baron, 1996).

Types of Fractures

Hip fractures are generally divided into three types: femoral neck, intertrochanteric, and subtrochanteric (see Figure 1). Femoral neck and intertrochanteric fractures account for 97% of hip fractures in the aged; subtrochanteric fracture constitutes 3% of proximal femoral fractures, and its occurrence often raises the suspicion of pathological fracture due to metastatic disease, as opposed to osteoporotic or traumatic fracture.

Femoral neck fractures are commonly subtyped via the Garden classification system (Stein & Felsenthal, 1994). In the Garden system, a Type I fracture is an incomplete or impacted fracture of the

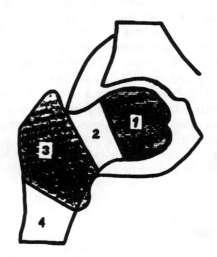

FIGURE 1   Fractures of the hip occurring in region 1 involve the femoral head; in region 2 fractures are located in the femoral neck; in region 3 they are intertrochanteric; and in region 4 they are designated as subtrochanteric. The hip capsule is outlined.

Source: Noble, J. (Ed.), *Textbook of General Medicine and Primary Care.* Boston: Little, Brown and Company, 1987, 245. Reprinted with permission.

femoral neck, with no displacement of the medical trabeculae, whereas a Type II fracture is a complete fracture of the femoral neck, with no displacement of the medical trabeculae. A Type III fracture is a complete fracture of the femoral neck with varus angulation and displacement of the medial trabeculae, and a Type IV fracture is a complete fracture of the femoral neck with total displacement of the fragments. It is important to note that types I and II are nondisplaced fractures, which do well with pinning, and types II and IV are displaced fractures, which are unstable, requiring more extensive open reduction and internal fixation (ORIF) or arthroplasty (Perez, 1994).

Because the femoral neck and head are contained entirely within the joint capsule, they have no periosteum. The arterial supply to the femoral head is disrupted if fracture fragments are displaced, making nonunion and avascular necrosis relatively common complications of ORIF. Many surgeons routinely use arthroplasty for all displaced femoral neck fractures in order to avoid these complications.

Intertrochanteric fractures are usually comminuted and significantly osteoporotic (Raisz, 1997), factors that result in difficulty with good anatomic reduction of fragments and resultant instability of fixation (Ochs, 1990). As the vascular supply to the femoral head and neck is not usually compromised, avascular necrosis and nonunion are uncommon complications. However, patients with intertrochanteric fractures often suffer delayed weight bearing, poorer functional outcomes, and higher mortality than do patients with femoral neck fractures.

Management

Orthopedic management consists largely of evaluating the type of fracture and degree of instability in order to select the most appropriate surgical intervention: pinning, placement of a nail, fixation with a sliding nail or compression screw, hemiarthroplasty, or total hip arthroplasty. However, careful *perioperative medical management* and utilization of an interdisciplinary team is essential to optimize outcome. Common issues in hip fracture management include timing of surgical intervention, use of invasive perioperative hemodynamic monitoring, *anticoagulation* with low-molecular-weight heparin or low-intensity warfarin for prophylaxis against deep venous thrombosis and pulmonary embolus, diagnosis and treatment of perioperative delirium, early mobilization following surgery, and individualized, intensive *rehabilitation* aimed at maximal functional outcome.

Outcomes

A comprehensive rehabilitative approach to older patients with hip fracture has been widely implemented over the past decade. A majority of patients are now discharged within the first week postoperatively to short-term rehabilitation programs that focus on comprehensive rehabilitation, including coordination of medical, nursing, and physical therapy management. Some patients are able to go directly home after orthopedic surgery and continue with therapy at home. Prognosis after a hip fracture is adversely affected by increased age, a high prefracture dependency level, dementia, postsurgical delirium, depression, a poor social network, and any subsequent rehospitalization or major fall (Magaziner, Simonsick, & Kahsner, 1990).

Mortality within 1 year after hip fracture is approximately 20% to 25% (Wood, Ions, & Quinby, 1992). Risk factors for increased mortality include age over 85, dementia, presence of malignancy, and occurrence of postoperative pneumonia or deep wound infection (Wood, Ions, & Quinby, 1992).

Ability to walk is frequently limited after hip fracture. Given the fact that some individuals were not ambulatory prior to the fracture and that 33% to 43% may have required a walking aid prefracture, only 25% to 50% of individuals will recover to the prefracture ambulation status (Stein & Felsenthal, 1994). However, given a longer recovery time, many individuals experience improved function for up to a year (Magaziner, Simonsick, & Kahsner, 1990). Unfortunately, some patients never walk again. The risk of becoming nonambulatory is greatest for the oldest patients, although encouraging results have been reported for use of very aggressive physical therapy programs postfracture (Perez, 1994).

Prevention

Hip fracture prevention has centered around improving gait stability via guided exercise programs

(Gregg, Cauley, Seeley, Ensrud, & Bauer, 1998) and diagnosis and treatment of osteoporosis (Raisz, 1997). Public and physician awareness of osteoporosis has increased sharply in the past decade, resulting in widespread use of dietary calcium supplementation and lifestyle modification to reduce risk factors for osteoporosis. Additional osteoporosis treatment modalities in common use include nasal spray calcitonin, alendronate (an aminobisphosphonate that inhibits osteoclast activity), and estrogen replacement therapy in various forms (most notably, raloxifene, the first available estrogen receptor modulator). Further investigational agents continue to be developed.

LIDIA POUSADA

See also
Falls
Osteoporosis

HISPANIC ELDERLY

In 1990, there were 21 million persons of Hispanic origin living in the United States, or 8% of the total population; it is estimated that this group will increase to 32 million in 2000. The Hispanic population increased 53% between 1980 and 1990. It is expected to increase by an additional 200% between 1990 and 2080, almost five times as fast as non-Hispanics (U.S. General Accounting Office [GAO], 1992). The growth of the Hispanic population in the United States is primarily the result of high fertility and immigration rates. The vast majority of immigrants entering the United States come from Latin America, especially from Mexico. However, increasing numbers are arriving from Central American countries. New immigrants now constitute approximately two thirds of the total Hispanic population in the United States (Cornelius, 1990).

As a result of this immigration wave, the number of Hispanic people who are 65 years and older increased by 75% from 1980 to the early 1990s. Their numbers tripled in the past two decades and are expected to increase from less than 4% of the total elderly population in 1990 to nearly 12% by 2050, a higher rate of growth than that of elderly of other ethnic or racial groups (U.S. GAO, 1992).

About one fifth of elderly Hispanics were 80 years or older in 1990. By 2050, their numbers could well increase by almost one third. The growth in the number of old-old Hispanics has serious implications pertaining to health care, long-term care, and caregiving (Siegel, 1999).

This population shift is the result of complex political, social, and economic forces, many of which are beyond the control of most immigrants. Mexicans seek economic opportunities and family reunification. The long and protracted civil wars in Central America, specifically Guatemala, Nicaragua, and El Salvador, prompted a different migration and therefore different adjustment issues. Although there are significant and visible differences based on class, race/ethnicity, education, and financial and legal supports provided by the U.S. government, there are certain similarities among early Cuban and new Central American political refugees. Leaving the country of origin, with all its familiar places, relationships, culture symbols, and traditions, often results in a deep sense of isolation, even alienation, due to loss of community, economic, and emotional supports.

Adjustment issues related to disruption of the cultural continuum are aggravated when the society the immigrant enters does not value cultural, linguistic, racial, and ethnic diversity. A deep sense of loss is often expressed in depression anxiety, as well as constant longing for the country of origin and familial roots. For Mexican immigrants, both recent ones and those whose families have been here for generations, travel back and forth to Mexico has developed into a "revolving door" and/or cultures of migration that, together with access to the Spanish-speaking media, reinforces culture and language time and time again, passing it from generation to generation. The result is an elderly population of Mexican descent that often functions in this country much as it did back home.

Just as there are marked cultural and socioeconomic differences between elderly people who are direct descendants of 16th-century Spanish settlers, those who came during and immediately after the Mexican Revolution, and Puerto Ricans who came to the mainland after annexation of the island by the United States, there are also marked similarities. The notion of "Hispanidad" and the Spanish language, regardless of speaking proficiency, becomes the glue that binds together the different cultural, racial, and ethnic threads found throughout this hemisphere.

Most recent elderly Central American and Mexican immigrants and those who have been here for decades reside in large urban settings, even though they arrive in the country with a rural orientation, little or no knowledge of the English language, and few marketable work-related skills. Close to two thirds of those who were in the labor force for some time were in unskilled occupations that provided few if any benefits, such as health insurance and pensions (Trevino, 1989). Most Hispanic elderly depend on small Social Security benefits and Supplemental Security Income (SSI) for economic support and on Medicare and Medicaid for health care (Bureau of Data Management and Strategy, 1989).

Because of limited income, poverty rates are high. In 1989, nearly one quarter of all Hispanic households lived in poverty, with a 6.7% increase in a 10-year period. In 1988, their overall unemployment rate was 10.32% higher than that of non-Hispanics (5.8%). When the 1990 average poverty threshold for a family of four was $13,359, 21% of Hispanic households had incomes below $10,000, compared with 15% percent of non-Hispanic households (U.S. GAO, 1992). According to 1990 income figures, almost three times more Hispanic families and individuals fell below the poverty level compared with 9.5% of non-Hispanics. In 1990, Hispanics 65 years of age and older were more likely to live in poverty than were non-Hispanics of comparable age. The Commonwealth Fund Commission on Elderly People Living Alone (1989) reported that Hispanic elderly experienced a poverty rate nearly twice that of all elderly, with 22% living below the federal poverty line (compared with 12% of all elderly).

Most Hispanic elderly receive neither a private pension nor Social Security and are less likely to live alone (Siegel, 1999); nearly one third live with children and other relatives. In 1987, about 42% of all aged Hispanics eligible for SSI reported receiving SSI. This was 6.3% less than in 1976. Presently, the participation rate of Hispanics is lower than that among all elderly (U.S. GAO, 1990). Without eligibility for SSI, access to Medicaid and food stamps decreases; without Social Security, access to Medicare is limited. A significant number of problems faced by Hispanic elderly are derivatives of poverty, such as poor health and nutrition status, lack of access to avenues of information, hunger, and lack of adequate and affordable housing. Because health status is so interrelated to poverty and lack of access to adequate services, health problems are a major concern. Heart disease (38.3%) is the first and cancer (32%) is the second leading cause of death among Hispanics, followed by injuries and stroke. Twice as many Hispanic elderly as non-Hispanics die of diabetes, chronic liver disease, and cirrhosis. As with other groups, cancer affects people 65 years and older more frequently than any other age group (almost 60% of cancer cases). Hispanic women, at any age, are more likely to be unaware or uninformed about breast and cervical cancer risks and what they can do (National Cancer Institute and the Centers for Disease Control, 1994).

Despite the vulnerability of Hispanic elderly, lack of accessibility and underutilization of much-needed services continue to be issues for which effective solutions are yet to be found. No single cause in and of itself appears to be sufficient to account for it; rather, it is the result of several factors that affect different groups at different times under different conditions. Among the factors more often attributed as explanations of low service utilization are discrimination, lack of bilingual and/or bicultural personnel, inadequate outreach agency policies and procedures that discourage use of services, insensitiveness to different cultural and linguistic factors, and issues related to class and education. The complexity of the relationship of all these factors tends to create a situation that is difficult to change, particularly if each is approached separately and individually.

Research could increase understanding of the multiple factors that determine the well-being of the various Hispanic elderly groups. Yet research is inadequate, and most available research reflects limited aspects of the Mexican-American experience that often cannot be generalized to other Hispanic groups (Markides, Rudkin, Angel, & Espino, 1997). Narrow definitions of family, informal networks, community relationships, and perceptions of well-being leave out important configurations that could define the different life experiences of this most varied population group.

Marta Sotomayor
Updated by
Kyriakos S. Markides

See also
    Ethnicity
    Minorities and Aging

HOME AND COMMUNITY-BASED CARE

As complex medical treatment protocols have become more effective, less invasive, and more acceptable to patients, acute health services have continued to shift from inpatient to outpatient. The decrease in the average length of hospital stay for persons 65 years of age continued in the 1990s, with an average length of hospital stay of 6.5 days in 1996, 2 days less than in 1986. Furthermore, 60% of all surgeries are now performed on an outpatient basis (American Hospital Association, 1999). A second trend has been the steady growth in Medicare managed care. Between 1993 and 1998, Medicare enrollment in health maintenance organizations (HMOs) doubled and, as of January 1999, almost 15% of Medicare beneficiaries were part of Medicare managed care plans. Managed care's desire to buy the lowest cost assistance needed coupled with the movement away from the hospital has spurred the growth of in-home care, community-based providers, new medical specialties, and new organizational structures. Hence, patients can now choose among a broad array of medical and social services while continuing to live in the community.

The vast majority of the 35 million persons over 65 years of age in the United States live in the community with no assistance. However, according to the National Center for Health Statistics (NCHS) *Health, United States 1999*, nearly 9% of community-residing persons 70 years of age and older in 1995 were unable to perform one or more activities of daily living (ADLs; defined as needing assistance in one of the following activities: eating, bathing, dressing, transferring, or using the toilet). Furthermore, 23% of the community-living women over 70 years of age and 13% of the men, needed help with instrumental activities of daily living (IADLs; defined as needing assistance in one of the following activities: shopping, using the telephone, cleaning, meal preparation, or paying bills). Need for assistance with ADL and IADL activities increases

with age. Individuals, frequently with the help of family, friends, or paid caregivers, continue to live in the community, accessing a variety of services that constitute the home and community-based system. In 1995, over 12 million paid and unpaid caregivers were providing assistance to elders. Seventy-three percent of caregivers were unpaid or informal helpers (NCHS, 1999). The average amount of care received per week is 27 hours of informal care with no paid assistance. Even for those receiving paid assistance, 16 hours are paid and 31 unpaid. For the one third of Americans who need long-term care at home, the average annual cost is $11,740, paid for entirely out of pocket (Families USA Foundation, 1994).

Rates of elders residing in nursing homes have decreased over the years, with only 4.2% of people over 65 living in nursing homes in 1995, a drop from 4.6% in 1985 (Bishop, 1999). However, there has been a ninefold increase in Medicare-financed postacute care patients in nursing facility beds (Bishop, 1999). These patients generally require a short-term nursing home stay for skilled rehabilitation services after a hospitalization for stroke or hip replacement and do not become permanent nursing home residents. Yet, for unmarried elderly women, the risk of a permanent nursing home placement rises sharply with age. Half of the nursing home residents in 1997 were 85 years of age and over, and three fourths were women (NCHS, 1999).

Older people have a high prevalence of chronic illness, which may lead to functional impairment. The longer one lives, the higher the risk of at least some period of functional dependency. Even though the proportion of noninstitutionalized elders with disability appears to have declined between the mid-1980s and mid-1990s (Crimmons, Saito, & Reynolds, 1997; Manton, Corder, & Stallard, 1997), disability continues to increase with age, and women in 1995 were more likely than men to be disabled and to need assistance. Rising rates of disability increase use of both chronic and acute care (Leutz, Greenlick, & Capitman, 1994). Most interestingly, disability may be a more temporary state than is frequently assumed. In the National Long-Term Care Survey, 23% of the aged with ADL disabilities at baseline had no such disabilities 2 years later (Manton, 1988). The transitory nature of some disabilities suggests that rehabilitation, durable medical equipment, and time create coping mechanisms previously unrecognized.

As the number of elderly with chronic care needs increases and new ways of reversing disabilities are realized, new management care entities and networks of providers are forming with the intent of merging the financial and delivery systems. The federal government has sponsored projects that integrate acute and long-term care in the social health maintenance organizations (SHMOs) and the On Lok/PACE models. These demonstrations target elders with permanent disabilities and pay providers a monthly capitated rate, holding providers at risk for members' acute and long-term care services. The move toward capitated care, with an emphasis on maintenance of function and low-cost providers, is altering what services are available, where they are provided, who delivers the services, and who can obtain the services. President Bill Clinton signed the PACE model into legislation in August 1997 as an option for all 50 states. Currently, 70 organizations in 30 states are in some phase of PACE development.

Both the providers and the payment systems for home and community-based care are evolving in the rapidly changing health care system. New forms of housing, such as assisted living, are creating organizational structures that meld living quarters with a mix of medical and social services, sometimes so quickly that few regulations are in place. Following is an overview of many programs that comprise home and community-based services.

Hospice Services

Hospice services, which administer palliative care to the terminally ill, became a permanent Medicare benefit in 1986. The Balanced Budget Act of 1997 (PL 105-33) created three benefit periods for hospice: (1) an initial 90-day period, (2) a subsequent 90-day period, and (3) an unlimited number of subsequent 60-day benefit periods as long as the patient continues to certified as terminally ill. The growth in Medicare-certified hospice programs and the number of Medicare beneficiaries choosing such services continued in the 1990s. In 1986, 108 hospice programs were certified, and about 11,000 Medicare beneficiaries chose the services. By 1998, over 540,000 terminally ill Medicare patients chose

hospice services from more than 2,287 agencies. Whereas 68% of patients receiving hospice care are age 65 or older, 15% are between the ages of 55 and 64. A recent survey conducted by the National Center for Health Statistics (1999) found 71% of persons discharged from hospice care in 1996 had cancer as their first-listed diagnosis. About 90% of hospices are not-for-profit organizations, and the remaining 10% are split between government agencies and for-profit organizations. In 1998, the National Hospice Organization reported that 39% of all hospices were independent agencies, 25% were hospital programs, 35% were part of a home health agency, and 1% were managed by a skilled nursing facility. If a Medicare patient is enrolled in a Medicare managed care organization (MCO) and meets hospice requirements, the MCO must provide hospice services. The patient does not need a referral from the MCO and maintains his or her membership in the MCO.

Home Care Services

Medicare covers home care visits if the patient is homebound and requires intermittent skilled services from a nurse, physical therapist, or occupational therapist acting on a physician's order. Beneficiaries may also receive assistance with personal care, such as bathing or grooming, but these services are generally limited to fewer than 8 hours per day and for 28 or fewer hours per week. Home care and home health agencies (HHA) grew from $2 billion (3% of the Medicare budget) in 1988 to $20 billion (9% of the Medicare budget) in 1998. As an indication of the widespread acceptance of home-based services beyond the Medicare population, more than 20,000 providers deliver home care services to some 8 billion individuals, with annual expenditures for home care of $40 billion in 1997 (National Association Home Care, 1999). In reaction to the dramatic increases in Medicare home health volume and a tripling of the number of visits per Medicare beneficiary, Congress targeted home health for cuts with the Balanced Budget Act (BBA) of 1997. The BBA limits, combined with Operation Restore Trust, a Medicare fraud and abuse initiative, have resulted in a 4.2% reduction of home health care expenditures in the first year of implementation (HHS Fact Sheet, December 31, 1999).

Respite Care Services

Respite care is a generic term applied to the temporary supportive care of an elder by a substitute caregiver. Respite is offered to relieve the strain of constant caregiving, to prevent burnout, and to assist during a temporary illness of the primary caregiver. Available in most states, respite services are supported through Medicaid funds, private fundraising, and private pay. Respite can be provided in-home through home care agencies, at centers through community programs provided by adult day care programs, or for limited 24-hour stays at hospitals, nursing homes, and other long-term care facilities. Several states have respite associations, and organizations such as the Alzheimer's Association and area Agencies on Aging can act as a referral source for families seeking respite services.

Adult Day Care Services

The adult day care services movement began in the 1970s in the United States. Today, more than 4,000 adult day care centers are operating. Although every state and the District of Columbia now operate programs, the regulations of the industry vary by state and by funding source. Most day care programs operate 5 days a week, but increasingly, centers operate at night and on weekends, although they are not permitted to provide 24-hour care. Services offered by day care centers vary widely, but all provide structured comprehensive programs with social interaction, exercise, transportation services, and meals. Increasingly, adult day care services include nursing treatments, case management, nutrition education, physical or occupational therapy, and counseling services. The adult day care center "average" consumer is a 76-year-old woman who lives with her family, is cognitively impaired, and requires assistance with at least two ADLs. Although most day care participants are functionally dependent elderly and almost half are cognitively impaired, adult day care participants are more likely to be married and less dependent than nursing home residents. Most day care programs averaged 20 participants a day, with a range of 6 to 40. Adult day care services are about half the cost of a nursing home placement.

Continuing Care Retirement Homes

Continuing care retirement homes (also called life care facilities) provide a variety of personal care and medical services. In general, continuing care communities are self-contained facilities that spell out the costs and specify the care available to members (see "Continuing Care Retirement Community"). Although a broad range of social and medical services may be available, continuing care communities are not nursing homes and have no national accreditation services. In fact, a survey of continuing care retirement executives revealed that the industry views their facilities as more akin to the hospitality business than the health care business.

Assisted Living

Assisted-living residences combine housing, hospitality, supportive services, personalized assistance, and health care to respond to the individual needs of those who need help with ADLs or IADLs but do not need the skilled medical care provided in a nursing home. Supportive services are available 24 hours a day to meet consumers' needs, including emergencies. Three meals daily are generally served in congregate dining areas, and transportation, medication management, health promotion programs, social and recreational activities, emergency call systems, housekeeping, personal laundry, and personal care services are usually available. Because consumer choice is an important principle, there is no simple classification of assisted living facilities and the services provided.

KATHRYN HYER

See also
Ambulatory Care
Continuing Care Retirement Community
Health Maintenance Organizations
Home Health Care
Hospice
Medicare
Medicaid
Personal Care/Personal Assistant/Personal Attendant Services

HOME EQUITY CONVERSION

Currently, some 79% of the elderly (age 65 and older) in the United States are homeowners, and about 77% of them own their homes without mortgage debt. Home equity, which is the current market value of the house minus an existing mortgage, if any, represents on average nearly half of the elderly's net worth. A house is an illiquid or a frozen asset, however, because it does not yield cash income to the owner. Furthermore, property taxes and maintenance costs represent demand on cash that the elderly homeowner may not have. Hence, this creates a "house-rich, cash-poor" predicament for some. Converting home equity into cash while still being able to live in the house may resolve the dilemma (Scholen & Chen, 1980).

To alleviate the problem of demand on cash, some state and local governments in the United States offer property tax exemptions for elderly low-income homeowners, or deferred-payment loans for property taxes or for home improvements (which postpone the payment of these loans on owner-occupied houses until the homeowner dies or the house is sold). These tax concessions and deferred-payment home improvement loans may be regarded as one form of home equity conversion. The National Center for Home Equity Conversion (NCHEC) estimates that over 140,000 older homeowners have taken advantage of these public sector plans (see *www.reverse.org*). Information on state and local government measures is available at the website of Commerce Clearing House, a publisher of tax laws, at *tax.cch.com* or through a college library.

Another form of home equity conversion advances cash to the homeowner. It is the *reverse mortgage*, under which the lender pays cash periodically to the borrower (homeowner), while the borrower makes no repayment to the lender until the end of the loan, when a lump sum repayment is due. With this feature, older homeowners (usually the minimum age to qualify is 62) can borrow without fear of involuntary displacement or foreclosure. Upon the borrower's death or a voluntary move-out (e.g., to an assisted living facility or a retirement community), the property is sold to pay off the debt. If the sales proceeds are sufficient to pay the debt, including interest, the remaining cash usually belongs to the borrower or his or her estate. If the sales proceeds are insufficient, the lender absorbs the loss. Some reverse mortgages come with a government guaranty of full repayment, in which case, the lender will be reimbursed for any deficiency.

Dominant in the U.S. market for reverse mortgages in recent years has been a government guaranty program called the Home Equity Conversion Mortgage (HECM), which was introduced by the U.S. Department of Housing and Urban Development (HUD) in 1989. HUD's HECM program, also known as the Federal Housing Administration (FHA) reverse mortgage, has been modestly successful in encouraging private lenders to offer this type of loan. The cost of the government guaranty under the HECM program is borne collectively by borrowers who pay an insurance premium to HUD.

With government backing, lenders could offer more attractive terms than they could without the guaranty. Thus, the HECM program, which historically has received bipartisan support in Congress, has given the United States a new financial instrument that can help alleviate poverty among the house-rich, cash-poor elderly, and help middle-income seniors to liquefy their otherwise-frozen assets, thereby helping to maintain their lifestyle into retirement.

The HECM program allows borrowers to choose among many payment options. Cash may be received as (1) a lump sum received at the time of the loan; (2) monthly payments for as long as the borrower resides in the house (called tenure payments); (3) higher monthly payments for a fixed period of time (called term payments), after which borrowers may continue to reside in the house and defer repayment; (4) a line of credit with which borrowers may vary the amounts and timing of payments up to a maximum; and (5) some combination of all of the above. In addition, borrowers may switch any unused credit from one payment option to another at any time for only a small administrative processing fee. The high degree of flexibility in selecting and modifying payment options may be important to older borrowers, whose life circumstances can change rapidly.

Because older homeowners may be vulnerable to fraudulent practices and costly lending schemes, HUD requires prospective HECM borrowers to receive free (or low-cost) reverse mortgage counseling from a local HUD-approved housing counseling agency.

Nearly 40,000 HECM loans have been made in the 10-year period from 1989 to 1999 (Szymanoski, 1999). Although this number is still small relative to the potential U.S. market for reverse mortgages, which could be up to 7 million households, the market is growing. New lenders are continually joining the ranks of existing reverse mortgage lenders in nearly every state (except Texas, where legal impediments to reverse mortgage lending have existed in the past). A list of active HECM lenders and HUD-approved counselors in any area can be obtained at (888) 466-3487, a toll-free number operated by HUD, from NCHEC (see above), or from the National Reverse Mortgage Lenders' Association (NRMLA) at: *www.reversemortgage.org.*

Fannie Mae, a private company with a public charter, is currently a key player in the reverse mortgage market. Widely known for providing mortgage funds to the traditional home mortgage market, Fannie Mae has a lesser known operation that buys virtually all HECM loans from the original lenders, freeing up their cash to make more HECM loans. Furthermore, Fannie Mae operates a conventional reverse mortgage product, called Home Keeper, which has many features similar to HECM but has no government guaranty. Other purely private lenders offer reverse mortgages without either HUD or Fannie Mae participation. Information on lenders offering these products may be obtained from NCHEC or NRMLA (see above).

Although some forms of home equity conversion involve the government (e.g., property tax concessions), all forms of home equity conversion are voluntary for the elderly homeowner. Home equity conversion may appeal only to those who prefer to receive more current income without relinquishing the house. Home equity conversion could even complement long-term home care (as compared with institutionalization) when home care is feasible and desired (Chen, 1980; Feinstein, Gornick, & Greenberg, 1980; Jacobs, 1985).

The conceptual foundation of home equity conversion should be understood in the context of the retirement income system in the United States, which frequently has been characterized as a three-legged stool: Social Security is designed to provide a basic income protection, with private pensions and individual savings providing supplements to it.

The role of individual savings remains modest, however, because of the typically small or insignificant value of the elderly's financial assets, which are, to varying degrees, liquid. (Voluntary savings, even with tax incentives, do not appear substantial. See "Individual Retirement Accounts.") Another problem is the illiquid nature of home equity. In order to enhance the income status of many elders by means of savings, we need to tap into the income potential of home ownership.

Although home equity conversion could bring current income to many elderly homeowners, this financial option has not met with immense popularity. Several reasons may account for it. Despite its logic, converting one's home equity into cash remains a novel idea for many. Some older people loathe the idea of going into debt in later years. Others are concerned about reducing the size of the estate for their heirs. To an individual, home equity conversion thus may present a difficult choice between (1) resigning to a low-income status in order to ensure a bequest and (2) using home equity to increase retirement income in order to avoid burdening children or society. For future cohorts of homeowners, the choice may not be as difficult, because the current elders are products of the Great Depression, which may have strongly biased their attitudes against incurring debts.

Some public policy actions likewise pose a quandary. For example, if property taxes are excused for some older homeowners, other taxpayers will be paying more taxes (unless government expenditures are reduced commensurately with tax exemptions), thus making it possible for the exempt homeowners to preserve their bequests.

YUNG-PING CHEN

See also
Housing

HOME HEALTH CARE

As the health care paradigm shifts to the community, more individuals will be cared for in the community setting or in their own homes. Home care is becoming the locus of care for many people of all ages. It is believed that home care is less expensive than institutional care, but for those needing extensive, essentially 24-hour care, this may not be so (Maddox & Glass, 1989). It has been estimated that home care will grow 15% to 20% as an industry in the years ahead.

With the increase in the number of older persons in the United States, responding to the need for home care services will be complicated by the fact that adult children in their 60s will be caring for parents in their 80s. Medical home health services, such as nursing, home health aides, and physical, speech, and occupational therapy, will be necessary in combination with in-home support services, such as homemakers, companions, emergency response systems, adult day care, transportation, home-delivered meals, and chore services. All of these services may be and often are prescribed and monitored by a professional nurse or social work care manager. The objective of home care services is to maintain persons in the least restrictive environment for as long as possible. Tailoring care to individual need is easier in an informal home care setting than in formal settings. But such special care also presents challenges to the established care system as it attempts to match the home care workers to the client-family situation.

Home Care Utilization and Demographics

The shift from acute to chronic care, increased life expectancy, and an increasing array of services, including sophisticated medical technology, have resulted in an increase in the Medicare home care benefit from $.02 billion in 1970 to $8.5 billion in 1990. Medicare pays for 42% of all home health care delivered to older adults; Medicaid, a state and federal program, pays for 32% of home health care delivered. The growth in spending for all home care services increased by 53% from 1988 ($4.5 billion) to 1990 (*Health Care Financing [HCF] Review*, 1992).

During 1990, 1.97 million Medicare beneficiaries used home health services, with an annual utilization rate of 57 persons served per 1,000 enrollees. On average, 36 visits per person were delivered at a cost of $2,469 per person served. The use of home care services during the period 1974 to 1983 reflected an increased volume of visits attributable to rising enrollment (8.9%), a 45.4% increase in the average number of visits per person served, and a 35.2% increase in the average cost per visit (*HCF Review*, 1992). In the period from 1987 to 1990, 65.2% of the increase in Medicare payments was for home health care, owing to an increase in the

number of visits per person served, not to increased enrollment or an increase in the cost per visit. Persons 85 years and older were four times more likely to use home care than were persons age 65 to 74. The older enrollees also used more services (5,011 services/1,000 enrollees) compared with those in the 65 to 74 age range (1,098 services/1,000 enrollees). Higher numbers of women were served in both groups (*HCF Review*, 1992). Even though a large amount of care is paid for by public funds, a significant expenditure comes from the consumer's own private resources.

Models of Home Care

In the United States, there are four commonly accepted levels of home care: high-technology home care, hospice care, skilled home health care, and long-term chronic home care (Handy, 1994). Any of these types of care can be provided alternatively by government-sponsored agencies, nonprofit agencies, proprietary agencies, and/or hospital-sponsored home care agencies. As the formal system of care has defined the types of reimbursable care, traditional home care services have tended to be medically related, for example, skilled nursing; home health aid; physical, speech, and occupational therapies; and medical social services. The prescription of a physician has been required after an acute episode of illness, and the care has usually been limited to a brief period. More recently, with the advent of Medicaid waiver programs, most states have added nonmedical services, which include homemakers, companions, chore persons, personal care assistance, adult day care, home-delivered meals, and emergency response systems. Most of the waiver programs include case management services as well. Case management services include comprehensive assessment, care plan implementation, service monitoring, and periodic reassessment when necessary. Finally, private long-term care insurance policies developed in the past 5 years have included a mix of covered medical and nonmedical services for their policyholders. As the home care system continues to refine itself, including its financing, more systems of care will evolve (Quinn, 1992). With the advent of managed care, especially in government-sponsored Medicare and Medicaid risk contracts administered by commercial insurance companies, home care services have become more important as an alternative to more expensive services delivered in hospitals (Naylor, Brooten, Campbell, Jacobsen, Mezey, Pauly, et al., 1999). Home care administrators must respond to a payer (commercial insurer) who has little experience with home care utilization but has demands for standardization of home care services and wants to reimburse home care providers on a per member, per month basis. In addition, outcomes of care for individuals and populations are expected.

Future Challenges in Home Care

There are many challenges facing the development of an adequate system of care in the home. These challenges include development of national uniformity in assessment, in titles of services, in definition of services, and in standards for professionals working in home care, including professional case managers. Quality indicators for every level of care given need to be established and procedures for assessing consumer outcomes developed.

Independent contractors of care must be responsible for oversight of their caregiving, involving assessment by the consumer, the family, or other designated parties. Payment to home care workers must be fair and equitable. Because most paid caregivers are women (90%), less educated, and with few or no health insurance benefits, turnover—which is great—needs to be reduced (Crown, MacAdam, & Sadowsky, 1992).

Finally, the cost of home care has to be considered, particularly as high technology is introduced into caring at home. Home is the place of choice for care expressed by most consumers. The quality of that care is directly related to the knowledge and quality of the workers delivering it. Providing quality care at a cost that is reasonable is a significant challenge for all involved in its delivery.

JOAN L. QUINN

See also

Health Maintenance Organizations
Home and Community-Based Care
Medicare

HOMELESSNESS

Lacking permanent housing of one's own, although not a common condition in Western societies, has achieved a special significance and notoriety, particularly in the United States. The emotional impact of homelessness may be explained, in part, by its connotation of the absence or diminished affiliative bonds with kin, peers, and societal institutions (Lee, 1992).

Homelessness in the United States became recognizable late in the 19th century and in the first half of the 20th century, as displaced and migrant populations congregated in cities and areas within cities known as skid rows or Hoovervilles appeared. Historically, homelessness tended to be linked with individuals afflicted with alcoholism or mental illness. By the 1980s, media coverage of a new homelessness had appeared that focused on particularly vulnerable populations (e.g., the poor, mentally ill, and disorganized families), who were increasingly visible on the streets of American cities. Although old age has not typically been considered a high-risk factor, older adults were put at particular risk in the past decade by the decline of single-room-occupancy (SRO) facilities and the gentrification of previously neglected low-rent urban neighborhoods (Martin, 1990; Ovrebo, Minkler, & Liljestrand, 1991).

The limited data on the number of homeless people in the United States ensure significantly different estimates of the size of the problem. In the 1980s, estimates ranged from 250,000 to 2.2 million. The best estimates surely lie somewhere between these extremes (Lee, 1992). Among the homeless, an estimated 25% are believed to be age 60 and older (Lebowitz, 1991). The problem in estimation stems in large part from lack of consensus about a definition of homelessness but even more so from the difficulty of achieving an unduplicated count of persons who have no fixed residential location (Rossi, 1989). In any case, national estimates may be less important than local ones. The risk of homelessness varies significantly from community to community. This variation stems in part from the differential distribution of high-risk individuals and the affordability of housing options. Ringheim (1990) documented the particular significance of the interaction of income (a personal characteristic) and rent (a housing market characteristic) in explaining the different estimated rates of homelessness in Baltimore, Chicago, Houston, and Seattle. She noted that both the income and rent variables are affected by federal policy.

The effects of aging in the U.S. population on the composition of those at risk for homelessness have been offset, in part, Ringheim (1990) argued, by federal targeting of subsidized housing benefits to older persons and by a declining poverty rate among older adults. Rossi's study of homelessness in Chicago (1989) draws conclusions consistent with this interpretation. The Chicago data identified a disproportionately small number of persons age 55 and older on the street and in shelters for the homeless, but a disproportionately larger representation in the SRO sample. Rossi does not consider SRO persons, for his purposes, to be homeless. Reports on homelessness, when age is mentioned, are more likely to stress the high proportion of younger rather than older persons.

Although elderly persons are not disproportionately vulnerable to homelessness, homeless older adults have the expected array of problems of surviving on the street or in shelters, problems of safety, as well as problems of securing health and welfare services (Cohen, Teresi, Holmes, & Roth, 1988; Elston & Slavin, 1985; Keigher, 1992; Phelan & Link, 1999). Age-associated frailties of old age may add a special poignancy to homelessness. Gerontological research has generated information about elderly survivors on the street and about their needs. A great deal remains to be learned, however, about effective ways of providing emergency aid, as well as continuing health and welfare services and shelter that are both safe and perceived to be safe by older adults. Further, gerontological research on homeless elderly continues to be minimal (Cohen, 1999).

International overviews of homelessness place the experience of the United States in perspective (see Hall, 1994; Huth & Wright, 1997).

GEORGE L. MADDOX

See also
Single Room Occupancy

HOME MODIFICATIONS

The strongest preference of older adults in regard to their housing is to remain in their homes and neighborhoods as long as possible. However, most housing contains barriers that make remaining at home restrictive and even hazardous. Strategic changes to the home can support independent living and facilitate "aging in place." Home modifications are adaptations to the physical environment that can range from inexpensive handheld showers and grab bars, to more costly ramps, powerlifts, and fully remodeled bathrooms and kitchens.

There are several benefits of home modifications. First, a supportive and accessible environment makes it easier to carry out tasks such as cooking and cleaning. Second, adequate space and features facilitate caregiving by relatives and the formal service system (Newman, Struyk, Wright, & Rice, 1990). Third, the addition of supportive features in the home may minimize the need for more costly personal care services, reduce accidents, and delay institutionalization. Fourth, modifications can allow persons to more easily engage in major life activities and tasks.

Incidence and Need for Modifications

According to a survey by the National Center for Health Statistics, approximately 7.1 million persons live in homes that have special features for those with impairments (La Plante, Hendershot, & Moss, 1992). In conventional homes and apartments, grab bars and shower seats are the most common home modification at 23%, followed by wheelchair access inside the home such as wide hallways (9%), special railings (8%), and ramps at street level (5%) (Tabbarah, Silverstein, & Seeman, 2000).

However, a study by the Joint Center for Housing Studies at Harvard University has found that a large number of older people who report problems with physical abilities live in housing without adaptive features. Over 5 million older households have one household member with a functional limitation. Of these households, 2.1 million express the need for home modifications to function independently, but only 1.14 million of these households have the modifications they desire (Joint Center for Housing Studies, 2000).

Injury Prevention

One important goal of home modifications is to reduce injuries such as falls. Although falls are among the leading causes of death for older Americans, with 6 out of 10 falls occurring in the home, older adults may not recognize the importance of home modifications because they have unconsciously altered their behavior over the years to accommodate functional decline.

A study by Gill, Williams, Robinson, and Tinetti (1999) found that the prevalence of environmental hazards in the homes of older adults was high. Overall, almost 60% of bathrooms had two or more hazards. Two or more hazards were found in about one third of other rooms. In particular, the prevalence of the following hazards was particularly high: loose throw rugs (80%), the lack of tub/shower grab bars (61%), and obstructed pathways (50%). Although falls are caused by a combination of personal characteristics, functional limitations, medical conditions, number of medications, and environmental conditions, home modifications can reduce the demand of the environment while making the home safer and more supportive.

Barriers to Home Modifications

Why don't more older persons who need home modifications have them? Several interrelated factors contribute to the problem. First, a lack of awareness of problems in the physical environment and the effectiveness of home modifications reduce the demand for adaptations. Studies suggest that older persons often adapt to their environment rather than change their settings to meet their needs. Even professionals such as doctors or case managers may overlook the role of the environment in supporting frail older persons.

A second barrier is the unattractiveness of some products. Older persons do not want their own homes to look institutional and may, therefore, make adaptations only after having experienced an accident or a disabling condition that threatens their independence.

Third, the service delivery system is a patchwork of providers, few of which are well trained in assessing the environment or in specifying appropriate solutions (Pynoos, Overton, Liebig, & Calvert, 1996). The different providers that potentially play a role in home modifications include case managers, occupational therapists, remodelers, and social service agencies.

Fourth, because there is no entitlement program for home modifications, programs use a variety of sources, such as Community Development Block Grants, Older Americans Act Title III funds, special state and local funds, and increasingly, Medicaid waiver funds. The use of multifunding sources can present problems, as programs differ in terms of eligibility requirements, how much can be spent per client, and the types of repairs and modifications that can be made. Overall, programs operate on relatively small budgets that are insufficient to meet the needs of older persons and generally restrict them to a specific geographic area.

Fifth, some home modifications are costly and may be unaffordable to low- and moderate-income individuals. Over three fourths of home modifications are paid for out of pocket. The cost of home adaptations ranges from less than $100 for the purchase and installation of a simple handrail or grab bar to more than $2,000 for a roll-in shower or a stair lift. A recent study of assistive technology devices found that over half of those persons with unmet needs indicated that the primary reason was the item's unaffordability (Pynoos, Overton, Liebig, & Calvert, 1997). It is likely that the same problem applies to home modifications.

Even though the expense of some adaptations can be a deterrent, home modification may be cost-effective in its ability to reduce health care costs and delay institutionalization. A study by Mann, Ottenbacher, Fraas, Tomita, and Granger (1999) compared the health care costs of a treatment group that received assessment by an occupational therapist, provision of assistive devices and home modifications, and follow-up, with a control group that received the "usual care services" over an 18-month period. The results indicated that the treatment group's expenditures for institutional care, nurse visits, and case manager visits were significantly smaller than the control group. Additional evidence of the cost-effectiveness may attract more third-party payers to reimburse for home modifications, thus lessening the financial burden on individuals and families.

Future Directions

The importance of home modifications can be expected to increase as the elderly population over 75 years of age continues to expand rapidly and as policy emphasizes keeping older persons in their homes for as long as possible. Due to the increasing need and potential benefits of home modifications, further action is needed to promote its availability.

First, efforts should be made to increase awareness through public education programs that inform consumers of the benefits of home modifications. Training programs are also needed for case managers, occupational therapists, and remodelers on assessing the environment and making recommendations. Second, suppliers need to provide more attractive products that blend well into the home setting. Already, some products such as grab bars come in different colors, textures, and finishes. Third, centralized referral systems are needed that furnish provider references and the estimated costs of modifications. In addition, replication is needed of exemplary home modification programs, so new endeavors can avoid pitfalls and develop more rapidly. Fourth, Medicare and Medicaid should continue to pay for equipment and assistive devices and begin to reimburse for home modifications. It would also help if expenditure caps on the Medicaid Waiver programs, which can pay for a broader range of home modifications than traditional Medicaid, were lifted. Managed care, which is based on a philosophy of prevention, could also play a role in home modifications. Health plans could provide its members with educational materials about home modifications and include home assessments as part of treatment plans. Fifth, continuing research should be conducted concerning the need for and impact of home modifications.

Several legislative developments have been pivotal in increasing the prevalence of accessible housing. The most far-reaching legislation related to accessible housing is the Fair Housing Amendments Act of 1988. It establishes the principle of adaptability and basic standards of accessibility in residential buildings of four or more units for entryways, corridors, bathrooms, kitchens, and the heights of switches and electrical outlets. The act states that landlords must make "reasonable accommodations" for persons with disabilities and renters have the right to make changes in their units. The act, however, does not apply to buildings with fewer than four units or to single-family homes.

Recently, a movement to promote "visitability" in all homes has been gaining momentum. Visitability benefits persons with disabilities, especially those in wheelchairs, in gaining entrance and moving around their own home or friends' homes. The first visitability city ordinance was passed in 1992 in Atlanta, which mandated zero-step entrances in certain private, single-family homes. Since then, a city ordinance in Austin, Texas, has been developed that requires basic access in single-family homes, duplexes, and triplexes that have city subsidies. These initiatives at the local levels have been significant victories and should pave the way for future change.

Ideally, the future would bring a housing stock that incorporated the principles of universal design. Instead of modifying existing environments only after the functional abilities of older adults' decline, universal design targets persons of all ages, sizes, and abilities with products and environments that can be used by all people without the need for major adaptation or specialized design. Examples include an accessible and level entrance that makes it easier for baby strollers, bicycles, and wheelchairs; work surfaces of varying heights so the entire family can prepare meals; and easier to access controls for the bath or shower for persons with limited reaching ability. Universally designed homes allow for living on one level and can be easily adapted to the particular needs of residents. The universal design concept, which is gaining acceptance, would make future housing better able to meet the needs of a wide variety of potential residents.

JON PYNOOS

See also
 Housing

HOMEOSTASIS

Informally, *homeostasis* expresses the common belief of biologists that living forms behave in a teleonomic (goal-directed) manner to ensure their continued operation and propagation in variable environments. If challenged, stressed, or perturbed, within limits, organisms have internal resources sufficient to repair damage and to recover their normal operations. Poetically, these resources are thought of as representing the "wisdom of the body."

Homeostasis is a term introduced in 1929 by W. B. Cannon (1929) to specify a stability theory for multicellular organisms, especially mammals. Contrary to common misinterpretations of it, homeostasis did not propose or require constancy of any physiological or biochemical variables. Instead, it argued for a regulation band within which a variable could move, even oscillate, while in its normal operating range, and to which it would return if kicked out of that band by some perturbation—systematic or random. The return path was usually imaged as a first-order, simple, exponential relaxation or decay from the perturbed values back to the regulation band's normal operating domain.

The homeostasis concept (*homeo* = same; *stasis* = condition, not constancy) was based in part on the earlier works of I. Sechenov, and especially of C. Bernard (1878/1927), who wrote what has become the most famous sentence in the history of physiology (translated from the French original): "The constancy (*fixite* in French) of the internal environment is the condition for a free and independent life" (p. viii). It is Bernard's use of *fixite* that has misled generations of biologists to believe that Cannon's homeostasis implies constancy, which error Cannon was careful to warn against. Homeostasis recognizes that organisms are stable in dynamic modes of motion and change. To emphasize that essential characteristic, the terms and theories of homeokinetics (Soodak & Iberall, 1978) or homeodynamics (Yates, 1994) have been offered as a physically based update of homeostasis, and they expand the concept to encompass advances in stability theories for thermodynamically open, nonlinear, complex systems. Other modern approaches include chaos and bifurcation theories (Abraham & Shaw, 1982) and dissipative structure theory (Prigogine, 1978). There is as yet no generally accepted, final, overarching theory for complex systems, and it may be that a complex system can be defined as one for which no such theory or model is possible (Rosen, 1991).

Homeostatic competence of an organism has been quantitatively assessed in terms of gains of linear negative feedback models, as a first approximation (Riggs, 1963), but the deep appreciation of the essential nonlinear nature of life's processes requires a more sophisticated approach, such as those of homeokinetics/dynamics (Iberall & Soodak, 1987; Soodak & Iberall, 1978; Yates, 1982, 1994). These new theories propose that organisms are stabilized by a regularly recurrent trajectory through a small set of nonlinear, near-periodic, thermodynamic action modes, each integrating physical action (energy × time) to achieve a species-scaled value. A universal manifestation of mammalian aging is loss of homeodynamic competence with the inevitable sequelae of fragility, and in the case of human beings, dependency and death.

Homeostasis (or its modern expansion as homeokinetics/homeodynamics) is above all a theory of command and control, through which a marginal stability emerges that can permit (at least partial and transient) adaptations to new environments, such as humans accomplish at altitude, in space, under the seas, in the deserts, and in the Arctic and Antarctic cold. It is the ongoing, core research program of physiology to discover the integrative, hierarchical (i.e.,"vertical") and heterarchical (i.e., same-level, side-by-side, "horizontal") mechanisms by which the marginal stability and the associated adaptational capabilities are achieved, and to incorporate these into a global theory of an organism.

Human Senescence as Loss of Homeostatic Competence

The physiology of a human being is based on structures at many scales. Aging (senescence) causes disintegration both hierarchically and heterarchically. From the *hierarchical perspective*, redundancy in structures on large scales lowers their susceptibility to degradation and allows for some repair by replication of existing structure through lower-level processes. In contrast, the finer scale structures and their operations are more susceptible to degradation through conventional thermodynamic, physicochemical processes. As damage at one scale accumulates over time, the scale of the total damage increases and becomes part of the larger scale behavior. When the scale of the total damage reaches that of the organism as a whole, fragility or death results through loss of homeostatic competence. The extension of degradation at finer scales to larger scales is observed in various multiscale systems, such as vascular and neuronal systems, that are themselves hierarchically organized and therefore most likely to manifest the progression. Parts of the system whose behavior is amplified but are smaller scale structures are likely to fail sooner. Two examples are (1) DNA, whose structure is amplified in process of transcription, and (2) the heart, whose timing mechanism behavior is amplified to create heart dynamics, and whose resultant pumping action is amplified by influence of its persistent activity on the exchange bed that supports metabolism everywhere.

The *heterarchical perspective* can be understood as a network of nodes and connections among them, where a node is a local functional cooperative and its supporting structures, and a connection is an information flow path between nodes. Homeostatic competence requires that both nodes and connections be operable within the normal limits that defined health of the mature organism initially. Senescent damage to homeostatic competence heterarchically can impinge on nodes, on connections, or on both. A universal result is structural and behavioral *simplifications*. These are the essential manifestations of natural aging, and they lead to the inability to respond effectively in controlling aspects of internal or external environments and their fluctuations.

Senescence is a loss of complexity of homeostatic behaviors emerging from a loss of complexity of internal structure. The latter loss occurs inevitably in any complex, self-organizing system whose constructive degrees of freedom have been frozen out by the completion of development. At that point, the energy throughput required for operation (e.g., life) cannot avoid leaving a debilitating thermodynamic residue as weakened nodes and connections (Yates & Benton, 1995).

F. EUGENE YATES

See also
   Acid-Base Balance
   Sodium Balance and Osmolality Regulation

HOMOSEXUALITY

Lesbian, gay, and bisexual older persons are as diverse as any other groups of older persons in terms of education, income, health, race, and other relevant variables. Some have children and grandchildren, some have long-term companions, and some have lived alone for many years. They have, however, often had different life experiences than exclusively heterosexual elders. For example, one gay man of 90 wrote in the University of Chicago alumni magazine: "I'm gay, and I've known since I was 12; I didn't have a steady companion until I was 70, and I didn't come out of the closet until I was 85. I did propose to a woman on New Year's Eve, in 1945. Seven months into our marriage, I realized I had fallen in love with my wife. After suffering terribly from diabetes, she committed suicide about 12 and three-quarters years later. My male companion is now in an Alzheimer's care unit in this building. I visit him every day" (Rusterholtz, 1999, p. 26).

Because one cannot legally marry a person of the same gender in the United States at present, there are structural issues that gay, lesbian, and bisexual elders must recognize. Social Security does not pay spouse benefits or recognize surviving spouses in same-gender relationships. Medical care decisions, hospital and nursing home visitation, inheritance taxes and rights, funeral arrangements, and even the right to continue living in a rental apartment are legally based on family relationships superseding the rights of a companion. Unless the (past) employer had a "domestic partner" policy, long-term same-gender couples may not have health insurance and other benefits of married spouses.

Skilled legal assistance is required to provide appropriate durable powers of attorney, health care directives, wills, and property ownership and division agreements. Tax experts are needed to prevent one's own property and belongings being taxed as inheritance when one's partner (who owned the property in common) dies. Financial consultants are needed to ensure that joint accounts, pensions, and investments are appropriately arranged so that maximum benefits go to the intended person or purpose, as tax laws are written with married spouses, but not friends, exempt from inheritance tax and able to roll over pretax accounts.

Often it is incorrectly assumed that if one is no longer sexually active, or in a committed relationship, sexual orientation does not exist. Organizations such as SAGE (Senior Action in a Gay Environment, Inc.) in New York City offer a wide range of programs for older lesbians, gay men, and bisexuals that are important regardless of the individual's sexual life. Such programs include friendly visiting, dances, support groups for a variety of topics (e.g., bereavement, HIV/AIDS, and women's issues), and many social activities. In general, open lesbians and gay men do not feel welcome in regular senior centers, which assume heterosexuality. Retirement housing is typically designed for married couples and heterosexual widows. Nursing homes typically do not consider the sexual orientation of their residents. In-service training on sexual orientation issues, gay-affirmative services, and lesbian/gay retirement centers are emerging in the United States. Generally, persons working with the elderly should not make any assumptions about a person's sexual orientation, but should inquire about significant persons and relationships; those must be respected as fully as possible, while recognizing that openness may lead to stigmatization (Kimmel, 1995).

Until recent years, lesbians, gay men, and bisexuals have been stigmatized by mental health professions, churches, and the legal system. Many older persons who lived openly with a same-gender companion have experienced and coped with social stigma. For most, it has left some residue of secrecy and fear about being vulnerable; it has often also strengthened their ability to confront oppression and be assertive individuals. The modern gay rights movement has given opportunity for some elders to become spokespersons and to find renewed purpose in life (e.g., Harwood, 1997). Ethnic minorities, however, often see the gay movement as important primarily for White men and may not identify with it (Adams & Kimmel, 1997), despite the presence of towering figures such as James Baldwin, Audre Lorde, Bayard Rustin, and Bessie Smith, whose sexual orientation was well known. Many lesbians and some gay men are unwilling to be open about their sexual orientation until retirement frees them from fears of job-related discrimination or loss of pensions. Bisexuals may progress through alternating periods of same-gender and other-gender relationships, entering late life with a same-gender orientation for the first time since their youth; conversely, some bisexuals find a partner of the other gender after a life of same-gender attractions. Such patterns can be confusing to children and family members.

Health issues reflect past life experiences more than stereotypes about sexual orientation. Lesbians are thought to be at increased risk for breast cancer (Lantz & Booth, 1998; Rankow & Tessaro, 1998). Persons who were infected with HIV are at risk for a range of health complications, but little is currently known about the long-term effects of the disease when it is controlled by medications (Bender, 1997; Siegel, Dean, & Schrimshaw, 1999). An experience of sexual or physical abuse (which some lesbians and gay men experience in their family as youth, or in adolescent or adult relationships) may increase the risk of depression (Roosa, Reinholtz, & Angelini, 1999; Tuel & Russell, 1998). The stress of social oppression may increase the risk of substance abuse, including tobacco use, and suicidal behavior (Fergusson, Horwood, & Beautrais, 1999; Lock & Steiner, 1999); there may be late-life consequences of these risks. In general, education and income can buffer individuals from the health-related impact of life stresses (ethnic minority status, family rejection, and physical disability), but other social stigmas may increase the health-related impact. A careful life history is always important in order to understand the person's particular risks and strengths, especially for individuals outside the mainstream of life.

Counseling and self-help support groups can be important for a variety of these health-related issues. In addition, older lesbians and gay men may appreciate groups or counseling for bereavement support, finding new relationships in late life, relationship issues and changes (perhaps related to health or dementia), and retirement adjustment. Such groups and counselors should be knowledgeable about the gay, lesbian, and bisexual community (and perhaps have single-gender groups) and be gay-affirmative in their personal philosophy and techniques (Fassinger, 1997; Galassi, 1991; Slusher, Mayer, & Dunkle, 1996).

Many educational videotapes and written materials are available in libraries, book stores, and local gay, bisexual, and lesbian centers. The Lesbian and Gay Aging Issues Network (LGAIN) is an interest group within the American Society on Aging (*www.asaging.org*) and can be contacted through that organization. SAGE (*www.sageusa.org*) is located at the Gay and Lesbian Community Services Center in New York City. Both organizations have periodic nationwide conferences that are open to the public.

DOUGLAS C. KIMMEL

See also
    AIDS/HIV in Older Adults
    AIDS: The Epidemiological and Social Context
    Sexuality

HORMONE REPLACEMENT THERAPY: ESTROGEN

At the time of her menopause, a woman's estrogen levels fall rapidly as secretion from the ovaries comes to an end. In the short term, this fall may be associated with several characteristic symptoms, such as hot flashes and sleep disturbance, which usually clear up spontaneously after a time. Longer term consequences of estrogen loss include osteoporosis and atrophy of the lining of the urogenital tract, which may cause dyspareunia (pain or discomfort during sexual intercourse) and a susceptibility to urinary symptoms. Less certainly, lack of estrogen may increase a postmenopausal woman's risk of coronary heart disease and dementia. For these reasons, recent decades have seen an increase in the prescription of estrogen therapy for women at and after their menopause.

Several different methods and patterns of estrogen prescription have come into use. There is a range of different estrogenic drugs that can be given by mouth. Some of these estrogens are artificial, others are naturally occurring forms, either synthesized chemically or derived from animal sources. Estrogens can also be given in the form of skin patches or as subcutaneous implants that release their active hormones over the course of several months. When given by mouth or skin patch to women who have not undergone hysterectomy, it is usual to stop the therapy for a few days each month to produce bleeding of the uterus and so prevent the buildup in the uterine lining (the endometrium) that might otherwise occur. Women who have undergone hysterectomy can usually take continuous therapy. New forms of drug preparations have now been released providing continuous estrogen therapy combined with a progestogen that in-

hibits the growth of the endometrium. For women who have not undergone hysterectomy, this can prevent the inconvenience of monthly bleeding. There has been uncertainty as to whether women who have not had a hysterectomy should normally be treated with estrogen alone or whether in the later part of each cycle progestogens should be given. Progestogens are produced by the body as part of a normal menstrual cycle, and so the use of the dual therapy provides in theory a closer approximation to premenopausal physiology. In the United Kingdom, it has been customary to use estrogen and progestogen for women who have not undergone a hysterectomy, because the combination abolishes the risk of cancer of the endometrium, which is an occasional complication of estrogen therapy alone. Recent studies in the United States have given support to this pattern of therapy (Writing Group for the PEPI Trial, 1996).

Many uncertainties remain about the benefits and possible long-term ill effects of hormone replacement therapy. There is general agreement that women who have undergone early loss of estrogen, for example, following surgical removal of their ovaries, should be given estrogen therapy at least until the age of natural menopause. The problem with postmenopausal therapy is that there have not been any long and large trials in which women have been randomly allocated either to hormone replacement or placebo. In all the observational studies that have been published, the women who have been on estrogen therapy have themselves chosen or sought therapy, and are therefore likely to differ from women who have not opted for therapy. It is likely, for example, that the women who have chosen replacement therapy will be of higher socioeconomic class and more health conscious and so take part in a lot of other health practices, such as high levels of exercise, weight control, and blood pressure management, that will reduce their risk of cardiovascular disease and osteoporosis (Barrett-Connor, 1991). Therefore, although these comparatives suggest that long-term hormone replacement therapy may be associated with a 25%–30% reduction in the incidence of coronary heart disease, this estimate may be seriously biased. Similar types of bias may underlie the suggestion from observational studies that estrogen replacement therapy will reduce the risk of dementia in later life. In regard to osteoporosis, short-term experiments indicate that estrogen will retard the rate of bone loss, but it is not yet known what happens when the hormone is finally withdrawn. One school of thought suggests that the loss of bone that then occurs is equivalent to what would have been lost at the natural menopause. In this model, if a women continues estrogen for 10 years after the menopause, her bones will be for the rest of her life 10 years younger than if she had not taken estrogen. The alternative hypothesis is that following the withdrawal of estrogen, bone density diminishes rapidly to where it would have been if no estrogen at all had been taken (Ettinger & Grady, 1993). The importance of distinguishing between these two hypotheses relates to the benefits of estrogen therapy on fractures of the hip that are an important problem in extreme old age but do not appear until 30 years or more after the time of menopause.

An important concern has been that the use of estrogen might increase the risk of breast cancer. The incidence of breast cancer increases steeply with age up to around 50, when the rate of rise decelerates. There has, therefore, been fear that the use of estrogen after menopause might be associated with a continuation of the more rapid premenopausal rise in incidence. Observational studies suggest that hormone replacement therapy is associated with an increase in risk of cancer of the breast, which rises with duration of use but fades away again over 5 years after cessation (Collaborative Group on Hormone Factors in Breast Cancer, 1997). Again, in the absence of a randomized trial, there is a possibility of bias; women who have opted for hormone replacement therapy may also, for unknown reasons, have been at increased risk of breast cancer. Many doctors will not prescribe estrogen to postmenopausal women they think may be at increased risk of cancer of the breast. It is common to provide for regular breast screening of postmenopausal women taking estrogen so that any possible increase in cancer incidence can be compensated for by more rapid detection and effective treatment.

A new class of drugs, selective estrogen receptor modulators (SERMs), has recently come onto the market. As their name suggests, these have different effects on the various body tissues influenced by estrogens. In particular, they offer the benefits of hormone replacement therapy in preventing osteoporosis and lowering blood lipids but without significant effect on breast or uterine tissue, so obviating the increased risk of cancer in those organs (Agnusdei, 1999). There is still a need for longer-term studies to see if these hopes can be confirmed.

If estimates from the (possibly biased) studies so far published are correct, estrogen therapy could, in the best case, be associated on average with an improvement in both the length and the quality of life for postmenopausal women. However, more accurate estimates of the benefits and side effects need to be available if women are to be able to exercise informed choice about whether they wish to have hormone replacement therapy and if so for how long. Obtaining these estimates will require many women to agree to enter randomized trials with follow-up periods for at least 20 to 25 years. Such trials have now been started. Further discussion of hormone replacement therapy can be found in Greendale, Lee, and Arriola (1999) and Johnson (1998).

J. GRIMLEY EVANS

See also
Female Reproductive System

HOSPICE

Hospice reemerged in the modern era with the establishment of St. Christopher's Hospice outside London in 1967. Its origins are in the Middle Ages, when hospice was a resting place for pilgrims on their way to the Holy Land. However, even in the modern era there were numerous institutions that offered palliative care to the dying before Dame Cicily Saunders opened St. Christopher's. She first learned techniques in pain control in St. Luke's Hospital in London, where she worked as a volunteer after World War II. Founded in 1893 as a home for the dying poor, it specialized in caring for those dying of cancer and tuberculosis. In the United States, similar institutions existed, generally of a secular nature. For example, the Home of the Holy Ghost in Cambridge, Massachusetts, was known as a nursing home "devoted to the care of the incurable patient, particularly those dying of cancer" (Dunphy, 1976).

Thus, by the time Saunders established St. Christopher's Hospice in 1967, a well-formulated philosophy of hospice care existed, emphasizing pain and symptom control and the psychological needs of patients and their families. It was not long before this philosophy found fertile soil in the United States, initially with the establishment of an oncology unit in a Massachusetts chronic disease hospital and subsequently in the founding of Hospice, Inc., in New Haven, Connecticut, in 1974. The first hospice standards of care were formulated in 1974 by a committee of the International Work Group on Death and Dying, led by Saunders, Robert Kastenbaum, and others (Kastenbaum, 1975). Concurrently, hospice was emerging in Canada, with the establishment of the Palliative Care Unit at the Royal Victoria in Montreal under the direction of Dr. Balfour M. Mount. This program consisted of an inpatient unit, a home care service, and a consultation service that served other parts of the hospital.

The hospice movement in the United States grew out of a convergence of two popular trends: disenchantment with the unfulfilled promise of curative medicine and a new sensitivity to death and dying (Kubler-Ross, 1969). These, in turn, were fueled by the demographic transition that began in the late 19th century and the rapid increase in life expectancy, which led to a transformation in who dies from what, from children with infectious disease to the elderly burdened by multiple chronic illnesses. Saunder's original vision of hospice was somewhat transformed in the United States by an emphasis on a "homelike" environment that was consistent with the U.S. perspective on deinstitutionalizing health care. The hospice movement in the United States was founded at a time when deinstitutionalization was prominent and home and community-based care had begun to grow. Strong support for the hospice movement in America led to the formation of the National Hospice Organization (NHO) in 1977, which advocated for the hospice philosophy of care for the dying, educated the public, and provided a resource and structure for information exchange among the burgeoning number of hospices throughout the United States.

The emergence of hospices in the United States was aided by governmental initiatives and not-for-profit foundation funding. In 1978, the National Cancer Institute awarded grants to three hospices, and shortly thereafter, Congress mandated the Health Care Financing Administration to initiate a demonstration project to examine the costs, benefits, and feasibility of having Medicare pay for hospice care (Mor, Greer, & Kastenbaum, 1988; Mor & Masterson-Allen, 1987). Around the same time, the W. K. Kellogg Foundation awarded a grant to the Joint Commission on the Accreditation of Hospitals in 1981 to develop standards that were ultimately transformed into legislation creating a Medicare-funded hospice benefit.

Creating a new covered service under Medicare was a coup for advocates given the cost-cutting orientation of the Reagan administration. However, because a Congressional Budget Office study asserted that hospice would reduce costs relative to conventional care, hospice was introduced as part of cost-saving legislation (Mor & Masterson-Allen, 1987).

The legislation, subsequent regulations, and the reimbursement scheme reinforced the home-based nature of the program. Provisions included requiring a physician-certified survival prognosis of 6 months or less, a cap on the average annual reimbursement per patient, limitation of coverage beyond 210 days, and stipulations that reimbursement for inpatient care be limited to an aggregate of 20% of all hospice patient days and that the hospice maintain financial and clinical control over all care provided to the patient, regardless of setting. Although there have been some modifications of these provisions over the decade, including an increase in the per diem reimbursement rate to hospices, the most important one has been the elimination of the 210-day coverage limit.

Hospice is one of the few innovative health care services introduced in the United States that was extensively evaluated. The largest such study was the National Hospice Study, an evaluation of the impact of the hospice demonstration program introduced by the Health Care Financing Administration. Another study, funded by the Veterans Administration, evaluated the impact of an inpatient hospice program in a single Veterans Administration hospital by using a randomized trial approach (Kane, Wales, Bernstein, Leibowitz, & Kaplan, 1984). Other studies, relying on available data, examined special issues, such as cost differences experienced by hospice and nonhospice patients.

The National Hospice Study found that hospice patients used less hospital care and less costly and intensive diagnostic and therapeutic services in the last weeks of life than did comparable conventional care patients (Mor, Greer, & Kastenbaum, 1988). By and large, there were few differences in the quality-of-life or symptom-control domains of measurement between hospice and nonhospice patients, a National Hospice Study finding that was supported by the randomized study conducted by Kane and his colleagues (1984) in the Veterans Administration (VA) health care system.

Cost savings attributable to hospice were found to occur primarily in the last months of life and were very sensitive to patients' average time under hospice care. In the home care hospice model, savings from avoided inpatient costs were sufficient to offset higher costs incurred by long-staying patients. Patients served in hospital-based hospices incur home care costs in addition to already high levels of inpatient use; however, because they consume relatively low levels of intensive therapy services while in the hospital, they had lower per diem hospitalization costs relative to conventional care, yielding costs that were relatively comparable to those incurred by conventional-care patients in the last year of life (Mor & Kidder, 1985).

The results of the National Hospice Study as well as the VA randomized study found that good hospice programs had outcomes comparable to good conventional-care treatment, suggesting that the individual and his or her family should be able to choose the style of care they preferred. Because the home-care style of hospice relies extensively on the support of family members, providing daily, round-the-clock care of individuals at home, the total societal costs might even be higher for the home-care approach; however, it is clear that this style of care is preferred by a reasonable number of people with terminal disease.

Even before the passage of the hospice legislation in 1982, there were a growing number of agencies claiming to provide hospice care. The U.S. General Accounting Office identified 59 operational hospices in 1978. By 1981, the Joint Commission on the Accreditation of Hospitals received 650 responses to a national survey of hospices, and by 1982, the NHO had 464 provider program members. After a slow start following creation of the Medicare Hospice benefit, growth in the number of certified hospices increased as well. According to the 1994 National Home and Hospice Care Survey,

70.6% of the 1,000 participating hospices were Medicare-certified. In 1996, 349,229 Medicare beneficiaries were enrolled in hospice care; in certain areas upwards of 25% of all cancer decedents were served by hospice (Strahan, 1996). Based on a series of recently completed analyses of Medicare claims data covering hospice stays throughout 1996, 37% of patients have a noncancer diagnosis, over 80% are served for less than the first benefits period of 90 days, and only 8.8% exceed two benefit periods or greater than 180 days (Gage & Dao, 2000). An emerging phenomenon is the expanding role of hospice care delivered to residents of nursing homes. Petrisek and Mor (1999) found that over 30% of all nursing homes in the United States had at least one resident receiving hospice services on any given day, constituting about 6% of all nursing home residents, although this figure varied considerably by state. By matching data on nursing home residents with Medicare hospice data, Miller and her colleagues estimated that approximately 25% of all Medicare hospice beneficiaries in 1996 were cared for in nursing homes, a considerable increase over the estimated 8.4% of hospice admissions preceded by stays in nursing homes that was observed in 1990 (Miller, Gozalo, & Mor, 2000).

The American hospice movement has moved in a different direction from those of Canada, the United Kingdom, and the rest of Europe. The U.S. hospice movement has focused on home care, dehospitalization, and a shift in the care-taking responsibility from the institution to the family. Furthermore, most would agree that since the advent of Medicare/Medicaid coverage, hospice care, which began as a social movement, has evolved into yet another specialty care provider of third-party reimbursable health care services. Although the "hospice industry" is still dominated by not-for-profit providers, increasingly there are inroads made by the proprietary home care sector. How for-profit medicine mixes with the voluntary tradition of hospice remains to be seen.

VINCENT MOR
SUSAN ALLEN

See also
Death
End-of-Life Care
Health Care: Organizations, Use, and Financing

Palliative Care
Respite Care

HOSTILITY

Hostility is a broad complex of characteristics that has cognitive, affective, and behavioral manifestations. The cognitive aspects include cynical and mistrusting beliefs about others. The affective component includes feelings of anger, contempt, and disgust, with their associated autonomic nervous system activity. There is a wide array of possible behavioral expressions of hostility, ranging from overt aggression to subtle changes in facial expression and voice tone. Although the three levels of hostility are part of the same construct, they can be independent and do not necessarily occur together. Therefore, the relationship of each component to aging should be considered separately.

The cognitive component has a curvilinear relationship with age. Self-reports of cynicism and mistrust are highest among young adults and lowest among those in the middle years, with scores among older adults slightly but significantly higher. Men score higher than women do at all ages. These trends have been observed in longitudinal studies as well as cross-sectional analyses (Barefoot, Peterson, Dahlstrom, Siegler, Anderson, & Williams, 1991; Barefoot & Schroll, 1995). Whereas cynicism and mistrust appear to increase in the later years, self-reports of anger and aggressiveness tend to be negatively correlated with age (Barefoot, Beckham, Haney, Siegler, & Lipkus, 1993; Butcher, Aldwin, Levenson, Ben-Porath, Spiro, & Bossé, 1991; Lawton, Kleban, & Dean, 1993). Autonomic nervous system changes during the experience of anger and other emotions do not appear to be as large in the elderly as in young people (Levenson, Carstensen, Friesen, & Ekman, 1991).

Another way to measure hostility that is independent of self-report involves the observation of behavioral indicators of hostility during an interview or other structured interaction. Observers attend to relatively subtle cues such as facial expressions, voice tone, and expressions of irritation. Both longitudinal and cross-sectional studies suggest that these indicators of hostility tend to increase with age (Barefoot, Beckham, Haney, Siegler, & Lipkus,

1993; Carmelli, Dame, & Swan, 1992). Therefore, some behavioral expressions of hostility appear to increase with age, even though overt aggressiveness does not. These trends may be a reflection of an increase of general expressivity with age (Malatesta-Magai, Jonas, Shepard, & Culver, 1992).

Hostility has important ramifications aside from its impact on social and familial relationships. Considerable evidence exists to show that chronic hostility has a variety of deleterious effects on health. Hostility first came to the attention of health researchers from demonstrations that it was a critical component of the Type A behavior pattern, conveying risk for coronary heart disease. It has also been linked to other forms of cardiovascular disease, general functional health, and early mortality from all causes (Siegman & Smith, 1994). It has been suggested that high levels of hostility impair health through associations with higher physiological activity or other biological mediators, higher levels of stress, lower social support, and poorer health habits (T. W. Smith, 1992).

There is some evidence to suggest that the health consequences of hostility may diminish with age. Effect sizes have been larger in studies of young adults, and some studies find effects only in the data of younger people (Barefoot, Beckham, Haney, Siegler, & Lipkus, 1993; Dembroski, MacDougall, Costa, & Grandits, 1989). However, several studies that have used samples of older adults have observed that those who are high in self-reported hostility have poorer functional health, greater risk of coronary heart disease, and earlier mortality (Barefoot, Larsen, Leith, & Schroll, 1994; Barefoot, Siegler, Beckham, & Maynard, 1994; Barefoot, Siegler, Nowlin, Peterson, Haney, & Williams, 1987). Therefore, the various manifestations of hostility are relevant across the life span for their health consequences as well as for psychological and social reasons.

JOHN C. BAREFOOT

See also
Coronary Prone Behavior

HOUSING

Housing is a location where people sleep, a minimalist definition in physical terms. It is more productive to think of housing as a service, embedded among a variety of other services that are instruments for meeting people's needs. For some needs, such as safety, security from intrusion, or protection from the elements, one's residence may be a goal in itself. More often it is a means through which higher-order needs, such as those for autonomy, control of one's life, self-identity, and sources of enjoyment in the aesthetic, activity, and social realms, may be achieved. During the approximate half-century over which the discipline of social gerontology has developed, there have been many changes in the way older people's housing needs have been met and the way housing fits into the larger arena of older people's need satisfaction. This presentation outlines a conceptual basis in which housing and services may be discussed. The bulk of the discussion is devoted to a historical view of national practices and programs, followed by a consideration of the status of housing alternatives and the outlook for the coming decade.

Housing and Services: An Age-Related Ecology?

Where aging was once viewed as a time of personal decline and social withdrawal, these frequent phenomena occurring during old age have come to be understood as health-related rather than intrinsically age-related. In general, good health is likely to be associated with continuity in a person's needs and needs-meeting behaviors, whereas poor health may bring about a rearrangement of such behaviors, in the direction of conserving resources and valuing security more than the person might have in earlier times of better health. This process of attempting to optimize independence and protection has been referred to as "the autonomy-security dialectic" (Parmelee & Lawton, 1990). In this framework, diminishing resources were seen as making the person more susceptible to environmental influences, whether favorable or unfavorable (the "environmental docility hypothesis"). Where personal and social resources remained relatively unaffected by age and pathology, the richness of the environment's resources were seen as increasing the probability that the person would be able to find active stimulation and enjoyment (the "environmental proactivity hypothesis"). Housing occupied a cen-

tral location in the cycle of autonomy and security. In its most functional form, the residential setting offers a means of providing continuity in a person's life, to the extent that the resident is adaptable to the provision of services as function diminishes and to the continuation of levels of engagement with the external world appropriate to diminished function. The concepts that the housing environment served important, but different, functions for both the independent and less-independent provided the motive power for the development of planned housing for the elderly from about 1958 to relatively recently. ("Planned housing" is used to designate multiunit structures whose occupancy is limited to a particular group, in this case people 62 and older.)

Planned Housing in Historical Perspective

Independent Subsidized Housing Programs. In the 1950s, people in the older age range were selectively disadvantaged from an economic perspective (their relative solvency conferred by Social Security was not fully in place and publicly assisted medical care was quite rare). In addition, there had been both a decline in the quality of existing housing and a major lag in the production of new units for aged couples and singles during the post–World War II period. To fill this need, a number of ambitious housing programs were launched, with the express purpose of providing high-quality but low-cost shelter for older people who were otherwise healthy and able to live independently. At the time, housing of this type was marketed aggressively as a model for independent living that contrasted with the institution, or nursing home. The zeal to portray these tenant populations as fully able fit in quite well with the general governmental resistance to housing policies and programs that might include "soft" services such as on-site meals and social services. A major segment of independent housing was subsidized through various federal programs, such as public housing and Section 202 housing loans made to nonprofit corporations. About 1 million such units were produced. Most are still in service, but the flow of new construction has virtually ended.

Private-Sector Housing. Simultaneously with the growth of the federal subsidy programs, the private housing market found a ready constituency of elders to support a range of residential types broader than those that could be found in the subsidized realm. Very large retirement communities were built as fully independent units both for rental and for purchase. Over the past four decades, many variations on the same theme have appeared, offering alternatives such as renting versus purchasing, metropolitan versus nonmetropolitan location, and resort area versus traditional area. One of the major variations available to these private ventures was the ability to fashion a package of other services in addition to housing: meals, medical clinic care, and various social services. One of the first housing types that combined a service package with the housing was the life-care community, now more often referred to as a *continuing care retirement community* (CCRC). In its original form, the CCRC offered the full package of residential and supportive services, whether in an independent dwelling unit or a nursing home, at a monthly price that remained constant except for inflation adjustment. The guarantee for life care was enabled by a large up-front lump sum payment. Over time, many variations in financial arrangements have developed, ranging from nonreturnable to fully returnable initial fees and purely pay-as-you-go.

Most CCRCs serve the top economic segment of older people. Uncoupling economic solvency and service-rich housing has been viewed in the gerontological community as a priority for some time, but the solution has to this date proved resistant. *Congregate housing* involved essentially a grant of minimal services (one or two meals per day, sometimes with formally arranged in-home services) to the independent housing of the Section 202 or occasionally the public housing program. Although congregate housing continues to operate at a lower cost than the CCRC, its cost typically has been great enough to deter new nonprofit, and particularly governmental, sponsors from initiating new sites, and the number of such low-cost units has not grown.

For almost two decades we have seen the heir of congregate housing, *assisted living*, take the foremost position in the age-targeted housing market (Schwarz & Brent, 1999). Although not limited to the private-sector market, the for-profit sector has been the arena for its strongest growth. In fact, with rare exceptions where Medicaid waivers are available for its residents (as in Oregon), assisted living is accessible to and used by only those who can pay full fees (Wilson, 1996). These are less than either CCRC or nursing home fees, but far beyond what the majority of elders can pay. Where congregate housing was a more protected type of independent housing to which people could move in anticipation of future increased dependency, assisted living is an alternative primarily for people who have passed the point when independent living is possible. Assisted living provides private quarters usually with germinal kitchen facilities in a setting with high levels of personal care and behavioral surveillance but without the many physical and staffing requirements of nursing care. As of 2000, assisted living is typically relatively lush in its physical design and decor but with staffing levels considerably below that required in nursing facilities.

Federally subsidized housing and upscale private housing have been important phenomena in contributing to the well-being of older people. These types of housing are natural foci for media attention. Yet the best estimate is that together they account for less than 10% of all people 65 and older. The rest continue to live in ordinary, usually long-occupied homes in the community.

Older People in Ordinary Communities. For decades, surveys result in the same message from older people: Most wish above all to be able to remain where they are. Community homes are familiar to the older occupant; they represent symbolic aspects of the self, such as the family self, the achieving self, and the independent self. Above all, they have been actively chosen by the person and shaped in many ways toward the model of the ideal housing of his or her dreams. As of 1989, 78% of older householders owned their own homes. Both owners and renters were long-term residents (2 or more years). Housing costs for renters and owners were lower for older people (Gaberlavage & Sloan, 1993).

Despite their majority status, this most age-integrated constituent of the older population has been least well served by service programs. National data suggest that well over 5 million elders experience enough health-related limitations on their behavior to bring their sense of security into jeopardy. This is the target population for which a rich mix of services is needed, including those directed toward making the housing itself most functional and those directed toward the person within the dwelling unit. A body of technological expertise has been slow to develop but is becoming available to guide those who wish to help the older householder maintain a safe, accessible, and stimulating living unit. The major barrier is lack of interest shown in one another's turf by the housing services and the social services constituencies, from the federal level to the neighborhood services level. Cross-education of professionals in the two areas (e.g., home modification workers or in-home personal service workers), with the addition of hard-housing expertise to social agencies, is needed to enhance the positive usefulness of the housing unit in maintaining community residences for the vulnerable person.

How Are Housing Needs of Elders To Be Met in the Next Decade?

In attempting to gaze into the future, we have the well-established principle of "aging in place" to help us (Pastalan, 1999; Tillson, 1990). Stability in housing is impossible, because both the person and the environment age in infinite varieties of conjunction and dysfunction. One usually wishes that things would remain the same and that one's present dwelling will be the last. Personal illness, however, and change on the national, community, neighborhood, and housing-unit levels inevitably supervene to alter the best laid plans for aging in place. This conclusion in many ways renders the ideas behind the housing models of the types described earlier dysfunctional from the start. "Person-environment congruence" is a static concept. The autonomy-security dialectic directs us toward assuming change and attempting to optimize the ecology of aging in place as both person and environment change. The three major tasks of the next decade are (1) to optimize the use of the housing already built, (2) to foster the development of new housing forms, and (3) to apportion national resources to minimize disruptive change in people's housing and foster whatever changes enhance the livability and life-enriching potential of their housing.

Use of Existing Housing Stock. Although the worst of the urban renewal policies that uprooted older neighborhoods may be behind us, it still is far too easy to destroy a structure that seems non-contemporary, by whatever meaning, than to exert the energy to reuse it. Thus, a first item on this agenda is renewed effort to help older people maintain, rehabilitate, or upgrade their community housing. The stock of 1 million planned, subsidized housing units is also in jeopardy. These structures are 20 to 40 years old by now. They were underfinanced when new, being built with small units and often pedestrian architecturally. Right now they are full of vulnerable people who have aged in place. One hopes that future planning and, if necessary, additional subsidies can forestall their simply being imploded in the way family public housing has been. Reuse of these structures, with substantial remodeling to accommodate people aging in place, will be considerably less expensive than new construction.

New Housing Forms. It remains to be seen whether the boom in appealing contemporary-design assisted living will still be appealing a decade hence. Time will test the ability of such housing to give appropriate care to the very functionally and cognitively impaired population it now serves. Experiments with waiver use and other service subsidies are needed to test how broad an economic range can be served by assisted living. What else could be new? The "naturally occurring retirement community" (nonpurpose-built residential structures or neighborhoods whose occupants remained in place over time) has been recognized for some time, but the efficiencies of planned services delivered to these concentrations of frail people are just beginning to be recognized. It is likely that there will continue to be an expansion of residential options in geographically and climatically attractive locations (especially outside the United States) for the well-to-do. For low-income elders, however, one cannot help being pessimistic. For the time being, the country does not seem inclined to support new low-cost housing of the public housing or Section 202 type. In compensation, it may be said that the demand for such housing may be lessening as the financial and service options for living in age-mixed normal communities expand.

Optimizing the Effects of Change. As intimated earlier, the major growth in residential care of the future is likely to come in response to the mission to keep frail elders out of the most expensive residence, the nursing home. In-home services of all kinds are likely to be used increasingly to help people off Medicaid nursing home subsidies. Such in-home staff—those who are there for diverse purposes, such as meal assistance, personal care, chores, and home health—need also to be able to recognize safety hazards, barriers to mobility, and sanitation defects. They also need to be trained in how to discuss improvements in the home environment with the occupant so as to be viewed as an ally rather than an interloper. They need to recognize that their ally role may also give them entree to helping improve the aesthetic, individualizing, and stimulating quality of the home. In particular, social-service or medically oriented in-home workers must learn when and how to make referrals to home repair and rehabilitation specialists.

In conclusion, not everyone is emotionally attached to one's home; home may be purely a backdrop for some people's personal and social lives. But everyone requires a home for basic physical needs. The great majority use the home in satisfying their own needs, and for a service-needy minority the home can still be a source of both autonomy and security. There will always be a role for the governmental, nonprofit, and commercial sectors in enhancing the ability of elders to keep up with their own and their housing's aging in place (Pynoos & Liebig, 1995).

M. POWELL LAWTON

See also

Assisted Living: A New Model of Supportive Housing with Long-Term Care Services
Home Equity Conversion
Home Modifications
Retirement Communities

HUMAN AGING STUDY

In 1955, the National Institute of Mental Health (NIMH) undertook collaborative intensive studies of healthy, community-resident men, age 65 to 92 (average age: 71), involving several academic disciplines and medical specialties, to extend over a period of 11 years to 1966 (Birren, Butler, Green-

house, Sokoloff, & Yarrow, 1963; Granick & Patterson, 1971). Most previous studies of older persons were cross-sectional and involved chronic disease samples. The NIMH findings were surprisingly optimistic and, in general, reinforced the hypothesis that much of what had been called aging was really a function of disease, sociocultural effects, and lifelong personality.

Decreased cerebral blood flow and oxygen consumption were found to be the probable results of arteriosclerosis or parenchymal brain disease rather than an inevitable companion of aging. The healthy, community-resident older men presented cerebral physiological and intellectual functions that compared favorably with those in the younger control group with an average age of 21. Some evidence of slowing in speed and responses was found, but this correlated with environmental deprivation, depression, and physical decline, as well as chronological age.

Mentally ill older persons were found to have the same psychiatric disorders as the young, with similar genesis and structure. Adaptation and survival appeared to be associated with the individual's self-view and a sense of ongoing usefulness, as well as continuing good physical health. Current environmental satisfaction and support were found to be of critical importance to psychological stability. Individuals who were "self-starters" and could structure and carry out new contacts, activities, and social involvement were found to have the least disease and the longest survival rates. The interrelationship between sound health and adaptability was validated by the sensitivity of psychometric test results to even minimal disease. The NIMH study also provided evidence of an interrelationship between hearing loss and depression. In general, the healthy age group was characterized by flexibility, resourcefulness, and optimism, whereas manifestations of mental illness were attributed to medical illness, personality factors, and sociocultural effects rather than the aging process. Evidence showed that "senile qualities" were not inevitable with age.

Certain personality disorders adapted differently depending on the stage of the life cycle. This phenomenon of the changing adaptive nature of psychopathology was observed, for example, in the so-called schizoid (introspective) personality, who may function somewhat better in old age when such an individual tends to be insulated against the harsh experiences of life and, therefore, may feel relatively more comfortable with some of the loneliness and difficulties of old age.

Obsessive compulsivity can be constructive in later years if the obsession turns to taking scrupulous care of oneself and keeping busy with many details. In fact, the obsessive-compulsive individual can base a whole life around taking care of possessions, spouse, grandchildren, and so on. On the other hand, a paranoid individual has more problems in later life, when the loss of the few friends and relationships he or she has intensifies the emotional isolation.

The importance of the immediate environment for adaptation was repeatedly observed; for example, education, occupation, and other lifelong social factors were not as decisive to adaptation as was a degree of current environmental deprivation.

Over the 11 years, from 1955 to 1966, the original NIMH sample was followed. The group was readmitted and reevaluated at the end of 5 years. Much of the report of the 5-year follow-up centered on aspects of survival and adaptation. Compared with the survivors, nonsurvivors showed statistically significant differences in the following: a greater incidence of arteriosclerosis and a greater percentage of chronic cigarette smoking. Nonsurvivors also tended toward other statistically significant differences. They had not adapted as well psychologically, had lost a spouse, and were more dissatisfied with their current living conditions. They also had less clearly defined goals. Thus, survival was associated with the individual's self-view and sense of continuing usefulness, in addition to good physical health.

At the end of 11 years, as at the end of 5 years, good physical status and absence of cigarette smoking were related to survival. Varied new contacts and structured, planned, and self-initiated activities and involvement (referred to as "organizations of behavior") were found to be associated with survival. The fact that organization of behavior was so strong a statistical predictor of survival runs counter to the disengagement theory.

ROBERT N. BUTLER

See also
Longitudinal Studies of Aging
Mental Health and Illness

HUMAN FACTORS FOR OLDER ADULTS

The goal of human factors is to optimize the relationship between humans and the environments in which they work and live and the technology they use. Researchers attempt to optimize working and living conditions by designing environments and technology so that they can be used easily and efficiently by humans (Sanders & McCormick, 1987). In general, this goal is achieved by incorporating an awareness of the perceptual, cognitive, and physical capabilities of humans into the design process. The credo of the good designer is "Know the user"; thus, good design does not require people to routinely perform tasks that they are not capable of doing or to function in environments that they are not suited to.

The discipline of human factors can potentially enhance the quality of life for elderly adults. Numerous experimental studies have documented that perceptual, cognitive, and physical capabilities decline with age (for reviews, see Birren & Schaie, 1990; Craik & Salthouse, 1992; Kausler, 1991). Following the human factors goal of designing for the user, the implication is that what represents good design for younger adults may not be adequate for older adults, given the differing capabilities of the two populations. Furthermore, age-related declines frequently reduce the ability of elderly adults to perform many everyday activities such as shopping and driving; that is, functional capacity decreases with age. Thus, human factors has the potential to design environments and technology that are not only adapted to the capabilities of older adults but may also enable them to continue performing many activities despite age-related declines.

To date, comparatively little work has been done in the area of human factors and aging. One of the first attempts to link the results of basic experimental work on aging to practical concerns is represented by Welford's (1958) classic work *Ageing and Human Skill*. In recent years, however, there has been increased interest in human factors and age. For example, special issues devoted to the topic have appeared in the journals *Human Factors* (Czaja, 1990; Fozard, 1981) and *Experimental Aging Research* (Czaja & Glascock, 1994a, 1994b, 1994c). The proceedings of a recent conference devoted to the topic of technology and aging (known as gerontechnology) also have been published (Bouma & Graafmans, 1992). However, despite increased interest, the theoretical and empirical basis of human factors for older adults is in an early state of development. Nonetheless, researchers in the area are beginning to focus on certain areas that have been identified as contributing significantly to the quality of everyday life. For example, there is considerable interest in designing living environments that accommodate age-related changes in sensory functioning and mobility (Regnier & Pynoos, 1987). Another focus of research activities is enhancing computer and technology use by older workers (Charness & Bosman, 1990, 1992). Clearly, a review of these and other human factors applications for older adults is beyond the scope of this article; the interested reader is referred to the sources cited above for reviews. Instead, we will focus on theoretical and empirical issues that we regard as relevant to the emerging field of human factors and aging: defining the older user, sources of information for developing human factors applications for older adults, and sample representativeness.

Defining the Older User

Aging occurs gradually, with some processes beginning to decline in the 30s (e.g., muscular strength) and other processes remaining relatively intact until the late 60s (e.g., measures of intelligence assessing accumulated knowledge). The gradual nature of the aging process means that older adults are a heterogeneous group, with individuals of varying ages exhibiting different patterns of maintained function and disability. Previously, we have suggested that there are three distinct groups of older adults, who vary in the extent to which they exhibit the effects of aging: the middle-aged (45–64 years), the old (65–74 years), and those in late old age (75+ years) (Charness & Bosman, 1992). The middle-aged exhibit the fewest signs of aging, whereas those in late old age exhibit the most pronounced signs of aging. Given such differing capabilities, human factors applications will vary for these groups. Many of the middle-aged will be in the workforce, and the effects of aging coupled with rapid technological change suggest that human factors applications focusing on workplace effi-

ciency and safety will probably be of primary importance. For the old, enhanced product design that promotes safety and ease of use is likely to be important. For those in late old age, human factors interventions that facilitate the maintenance of mobility and independence despite age-related declines will likely be of greatest relevance. Thus, which human factors applications are of greatest potential benefit will depend very much upon the age of the intended user.

Sources of Information for Developing Human Factors Interventions

There are three sources of information about the behavior of older adults that can be used when developing human factors applications for this population: epidemiological studies, experimental laboratory studies, and field studies (Charness & Bosman, 1992). Epidemiological studies provide population statistics such as how age is related to impairments in vision and hearing and what types of injuries older workers or older adults suffer. Such research has the potential to highlight aspects of daily life that can be problematic for older adults and to point toward human factors interventions to facilitate independence and productivity. However, a limitation of such data is that it does not indicate the precise nature of problems that older adults may encounter or solutions to these problems.

Experimental laboratory studies attempt to identify microlevel changes in biological, physiological, cognitive, and social processes as a function of age. The expectation is that identifying such basic processes will provide a framework for predicting how age-related changes can affect more complex activities, such as driving a car. The implication is that it should also be possible to predict areas in which older adults will experience difficulties as a result of age-related changes and to use these predictions to develop human factors interventions. For example, information about typical age-related visual impairments can be used to change the form and size of highway signs (Kline & Fuchs, 1993). Additionally, it is also possible to use laboratory-based studies to investigate the efficacy of human factors interventions in alleviating the negative impact of age on performance. However, a potential limitation of such studies is that laboratory performance may not generalize well to performance of everyday tasks in real-world settings.

Field studies involve observing older adults in real world settings as they attempt to perform various activities (e.g., Clark, Czaja, & Weber, 1990). Such studies can document actual problems that older adults encounter and evaluate the effectiveness of interventions designed to alleviate these problems. It is unlikely that any one type of study will provide sufficient information for developing an effective human factors of aging. We argue that information from all three sources could and should be used when developing human factors interventions for older adults.

Sample Representativeness

The majority of samples used in aging research tend to be positively biased. That is, relative to the general population, the subjects are better educated, healthier, and of higher socioeconomic status. If human factors interventions for older adults are to be effective, research must use samples that are representative.

Concluding Remarks

In this article we argued two main points. First, that human factors has the potential to enhance the quality of life for older adults. Second, that research in this area must consider the following factors: defining the older user, sources of information for designing human factors interventions, and sample representativeness. Research that considers these issues is likely to be highly fruitful.

ELIZABETH A. BOSMAN
NEIL CHARNESS

See also
   Communication Technology and the Older Adult
   Internet and E-mail Resources
   Technology

HUMANITIES AND THE ARTS

Cognitive psychologist Jerome Bruner (1986) asserts that there are two modes of thought by which we make sense of our world: paradigmatic and narrative. The former predominates in the natural sciences and leads to good theory, tight analysis, logical proof, and empirical discovery governed by reasoned hypothesis. The latter is the principal mode of the arts and humanities and, argues Bruner, of the way we experience life itself. Narrative thought deals with the multiple dimensions of reality, the uncertainties of human intention, and contributes to good stories, gripping drama, and believable historical accounts. How does Bruner's distinction apply to the humanities and arts as they add to our understanding of aging and later life?

As both a qualitative method for capturing research data in the form of stories and an expressive/descriptive method for conveying the lived experience of aging and later life, narrative renders life experiences, as John Dewey put it, "more luminous," and our dealing with them "more useful." Narrative makes its primary home in the humanities, the humanistic social sciences, and in the arts, including its history, criticism, production, and performance. Scientific gerontology is heavily influenced by clinical goals in pursuing knowledge leading to instrumental control over the adverse aspect of aging. In contrast, the humanities and arts help us appreciate the meaning and value of aging and later life while questioning the conditions under which a longer life can also be a qualitatively enhanced one.

The appearance of the *Handbook of the Humanities and Aging* (Cole, Van Tassel, & Kastenbaum, 1992), as well as its second edition (Cole, Kastenbaum, & Ray, 1999), bears out Bruner's distinction. These handbooks constitute a historic landmark confirming the rich and varied contributions to gerontology from scholars engaging in humanistic interpretations of aging, those exploring aging through artistic expression, and those developing programs to actively involve older adults in furthering personal growth, social awareness, and possibilities for meaning and belonging in the later years. The second edition of the *Handbook* adds emphasis on interdisciplinary approaches to aging, recognizing that the fast pace of social change around the conditions and perceptions of later life necessitate "crossing academic borders" to achieve a more comprehensive view of later life.

The three major U.S. gerontological handbooks—of biology, psychology, and the social science—have already gone through multiple editions.

How, then, should we assess the role played by the relative latecomers, the humanities and arts, in relation to scientific and human service contributions to aging, as achievements in their own right, and with regard to their capacity to enrich the lives of older adults and members of other generations?

The following discussion will answer these questions by examining (1) the complementary, sometimes critical, role of the humanities and arts in relation to the growth of other professional discourses in gerontology; (2) applications of humanistic and artistic ways of knowing to practice (e.g., older adult education and participation in the arts); (3) connection to the spiritual dimensions of aging and to intergenerational relationships; and (4) prospects for the future.

Humanistic Scholarship

The humanities include the disciplines of language and literature, history, philosophy, religious studies, jurisprudence, and those aspects of the social sciences that emphasize describing, interpreting, explaining, and appreciating the contexts in which, and relationships through which, human beings fashion a world and try to understand it. Humanistic disciplines have subject matters and methods uniquely suited to deepening our knowledge of aging and later life. To the scientist's penchant for causal explanations (e.g., genetic, neurological, and cellular) and verifiable experiments, the humanities add a search for the meaning of aging and later life, values attributed to the experience of growing older, and the shaping influence on later life of historic events, cultural change, ethnic identity, gender, spiritual orientation, and artistic embodiment.

Whereas scientific gerontology and the human services have tended to focus on aging as a set of problems resulting from physical and mental decline and concomitant dependencies (the "failure model of aging"), the orientations of the humanities and arts has been to stress the strengths of aging (attainment of mature insight, practical wisdom, humility, and other virtues) or, at least, to challenge rigidly uniform views whether negative or positive.

An important analytic type of humanistic inquiry into aging, "critical gerontology," has built on the European philosophical schools of existentialism,

phenomenology, hermeneutics, and critical theory to formulate assessments of research findings and policy developments that presume factual, empirical foundations but that, on closer analysis, reveal biases interwoven with social science methodologies or presuppositions based on the narrow view that aging is an irreversible and uniform process of cumulative decline (Cole, Achenbaum, Jakobi, & Kastenbaum, 1993).

Humanities scholars have also examined topics such as representations of old age in literature, the late style of aging artists, the character of wisdom, perspectives on aging in different religious and cultural traditions, values inherent in scientific theories of life course development, ethical issues in health care and end-of-life decisions, and the older person's legacy to the young as reflected in personal narratives, both written and spoken. Some of this work has had direct application to practitioners and policy makers. For example, the significant work on reconceptualizing the function and meaning of reminiscence (Kaminsky, 1984; Sherman, 1991) has led to changes, even reversals, in the way social workers and mental health specialists now regard the life review process as an important adaptive, potentially creative, process among seniors. Research on the history of the Social Security Act of 1935 (Graebner, 1980; Gratton, 1993) has provided policy makers with a better understanding of the multiple motives of the original legislation, and how age-based income supports influence the social construction of retirement, family relationships, and the need for older worker retraining programs. Broadly speaking, the contributions of the humanities also serve as responses to an unprecedented question made possible by a longer and healthier lifetime: Having added years to life, how do we add life to years? The humanities and arts speak to quality-of-life issues in maturity.

Humanistic scholars have helped improve the quality of later life by dispelling negative stereotypes and encouraging older adults to insist on dignified treatment and to project a more audible voice in determining their own destiny. Sometimes this takes the indirect form of interviews with courageous and innovative older people who become role models and mentors. Works of this type range from Berman and Goldman's (1992) interviews with older artists and other creative people, *The Ageless Spirit*, or from anthologies of modern and contemporary literary works that convey enduring passions, paradoxes, and points of view of older characters—for example, Sennett's *Full Measure: Modern Short Stories on Aging* (1988) and Fowler and McCutcheon's *Songs of Experience* (1991). At other times, these contributions take a more direct communicative form, as in Moody's (1988) philosophical critique of policies concerning aging and human development or Cole's (1992) critical analysis of the cultural history of aging in the United States.

Interpretation and practice of the arts play similar indirect and direct roles in helping us appreciate the nuances and textures of later life. This can take the form of examining changes in artists' self-portraits as they reflect theories of life stages. Interpretations may also differ as, for example, scholarly examination of the concept of "late style" has led some to postulate a set of predictable characteristics in artworks such as musical compositions and painting produced in old age—as in the "swan song" motif (Munsterberg, 1983; Simonton, 1998), whereas others have pointed to a multiplicity of counterexamples that defy stylistic classification (Kastenbaum, 1992).

That artistic works might reflect something about how the artist experiences and scrutinizes aging and later life is well documented for painting by McKee and Kauppinen (1987), for poetry by Woodward and Schwartz (1986), and for the novel by Wyatt-Brown and Rossen (1993). In addition, the expressive life of extraordinary ordinary people (i.e., nonartists) has been shown in diaries and journals (Berman, 1994). Creativity has also been linked to successful aging (Adams-Price, 1998).

Older Persons' Involvement in the Humanities and Arts

Not only are older adults the subject matter of humanities and arts discourses, they may become participants and practitioners. Recognizing that seniors would benefit from participation in humanities-focused reading and discussion groups, the National Council on the Aging (NCOA) established its Senior Center Humanities Program (later renamed Discovery Through the Humanities) in 1975 with major funding from the National Endowment for the Humanities (NEH). For 20+ years the program involved tens of thousands of both well and frail elderly in sites such as senior centers, public libraries, and nursing homes utilizing 17 different theme-based large-print anthologies accompanied by audiotapes, leader's guides, and publicity materials. The NCOA humanities program ended operations in 1999, but its resource materials were dispersed to lending centers across the United States.

The same year the NCOA program was established saw the birth of Elderhostel, a college-level educational program for people 60 and older that enables over 300,000 yearly to travel to campuses, conference centers, parks, and even volunteer service sites, where they participate in a wide variety of classes with heavy concentration on the humanities and arts. Again, in 1975, an in-store senior center–type program with emphasis on humanities and arts programming was launched by the May Company department store chain. The Older Adult Services and Information System (OASIS) institutes spread from 1 to, currently, 29 locations.

Another community-based educational program that invites seniors to engage in the study of the humanities and arts are the Shepherd's Centers, sponsored by some 100 coalitions of churches and synagogues, with their Adventures in Learning programs. Shepherd's Centers frequently draw on their members to plan and organize curricula and to teach classes. This peer-learning and -teaching modality represents a major trend in older adult education as seniors themselves take possession of their own learning goals, decision making, curricula, and methods of instruction.

Perhaps the fastest growing informal network of older learner programs is known by the generic term *Institutes for Learning in Retirement* (ILRs). The first ILR-type program, the Institute for Retired Professionals, was established in 1962 at the New School for Social Research in New York. But it was not until the mid-1980s that the ILR movement accelerated with the establishment of ILR programs at colleges and universities across the country. Nationally, over 300 programs provide substantive courses in humanities and arts topics, as well as studio work. A membership organization, the Elderhostel Institute Network (EIN), under the direction of Elderhostel, provides workshops for new ILR programs, convenes regional conferences, and distributes a newsletter among some 300 institute member organizations.

Other organizations promoting networking in older adult education where humanities and arts programming flourish are the Life Enrichment and Renewal Network (LEARN), sponsored by the American Society on Aging; the National University Continuing Education Association (NUCEA); NCOA, with its Humanities and Arts board committee; and the Gerontological Society of America, with its Arts and Humanities Committee—although the latter is primarily devoted to promoting scholarly endeavors among its members, some of whom are teachers of the humanities and arts.

Programs with a strong arts orientation range from Liz Lerman's intergenerational dance troupe, Dancers of the Third Age, to the Senior Neighbors of Chattanooga's drama ensemble, the Ripe and Ready Players. Senior theater, in general, has seen rapid expansion of amateur performance groups and even a yearly conference. Political and cultural challenges to sentimental views of aging and the elderly are emerging in performance art involving older women, individuals suffering from dementia, and mixed gender senior performing groups (Basting, 1998). Some arts programs mix creative dramatics with a therapeutic orientation, such as the New York–based Elders Share the Arts (ESTA) organization, which works with living history theater, or design creative movement programs that are both expressive and therapeutic. A visual arts education program designed specifically for the institutionalized frail elderly, the Washington, DC–based Museum One, has provided art education classes while demonstrating how staff can utilize the arts to promote better communication among residents.

Well-known writers are continuing their careers into later life, often focusing on intergenerational relationships (e.g., Anne Tyler's 1998 novel, *A Patchwork Planet*), whereas other writers are emerging in the later years (e.g., Alison Lurie's 1998 novel, *The Last Resort* and poet Virginia Hamilton Adair's 1996 volume, *Ants on the Melon: A Collection of Poems*). A full discussion of these and other works can be found in Anne Wyatt-Brown's "The Future of Literary Gerontology," found in the second edition of the *Handbook* (Cole, Kastenbaum, & Ray, 1999).

Bringing the humanities and arts to older Americans, especially those in institutions, is the work of the New York City–based Hospital Audiences,

Inc. (HAI), which has enabled over 7 million people to experience first-rate music, theater, and other types of performances.

For surveys of humanities and arts programming, see Mackintosh's *Humanities Programming for Older Adults* (1988) and the annotated bibliography of aging and the humanities, *Where Do We Come From? What Are We? Where Are We Going?* (Polisar, Wygant, Cole, & Perdomo, 1988). For a comprehensive review of research on older adult education, see Manheimer, Snodgrass, and Moskow-McKenzie (1995).

Spirituality and Intergenerational Aspects

Not only do the humanities and arts enrich intellectual and emotional aspects of personal development, they foster growth in spiritual experience and understanding. Contributions to a deeper understanding of how religious traditions help people find meaning and guidance in the face of finitude and frailty come from studies in comparative religion (see the chapters in the first edition of the *Handbook of the Humanities and Aging*, Part II Aging, Spirituality, and World Religion, and Robert Atchley's essay, "Spirituality," in the second edition), philosophy of religion, cultural history of religion (Cole, 1992), and comparative religion (Moody & Caroll, 1997). The role of the arts in enhancing spiritual growth in old age takes the form of guided autobiography groups (Ray, 2000), drawing as a mode of spiritual awareness, writing and performing plays, and scholarly inquiry, such as reflections on spiritual attainment as reflected in the late style of great artists (e.g., Rembrandt and Beethoven).

The humanities and arts have also served as portions of core curricula for dialogue between generations. Works of the humanities, such as anthologies from NCOA's humanities program, have been used in classes bringing older adults together with high school or college students. Intergenerational theater and music groups have been formed around the country. Some of the theater groups focus on relationships between young and old or similarities in the lives of old and young in contemporary society. Intergenerational music groups are an inspiring testimony to the bonds formed through performing together.

Prospects for the Future

Critical issues in gerontology and the trend in the United States, Europe, and parts of Asia of population aging suggest that the humanities and arts will have an increasingly important role in contributing to multifaceted understanding of aging and later life. Empirical studies of aging and the human life course cannot avoid questions about values, meanings, and portrayals of aging—the central preoccupations of the humanities and arts. Increasingly, people want to know not only what to expect from normal aging but what ideals and possibilities are available to them (Manheimer, 1999). The spirit of possibility is captured in the term *Third Age,* which has come to stand for the individual period and outlook of a longer, healthier, and more active later life, as well as a collective phenomenon of societies that have the means to increase the length and quality of longevity. This situation calls for an ongoing, open-ended, interpretive process that can be communicated to a broad public. The humanities and arts, in partnership with the sciences and human services, have the potential to offer holistic views of life course development and possibilities of achieving an age-integrated society.

RONALD J. MANHEIMER

See also
  Adult Education
  Gerontology

HUMOR

Sometimes humor reveals attitudes about the aged that people may not want to admit (McGhee & Goldstein, 1972; Palmore, 1986). It may also be used to reduce anxieties or tensions about an emotional subject. Analysis of humor about the aged can be used to investigate how widespread are negative or ambivalent attitudes toward aging and the aged, what kinds of fears about aging seem to be most prevalent, which aspects of aging produce more negative feelings, and how our attitudes toward aged men differ from those toward aged women. Humor may also be therapeutic.

There have been several analyses of humor about aging: on jokes (Davies, 1977; Palmore, 1986; Richman, 1977), cartoons (Ansello, 1986; Polisar, 1982; Smith, 1979), and greeting cards (Demos & Jache, 1981; Dillon & Jones, 1981; Huyck & Duchon, 1986); one analyzed jokes by the aged (Richman & Tallmer, 1976). Despite the diversity of content and of methods used, the following findings are fairly consistent.

Majority Negative

Most humor reveals definite negative attitudes toward aging or the aged, such as saying, "Old age: The time when the mind forgets and the mirror reminds." But some show positive attitudes, and others are ambivalent. An example of the rare positive joke is the following: An 80-year-old woman gets a physical checkup because she notices she is losing her sexual desire. When asked by her doctor when she first noticed this, she replied, "Last night and then again this morning."

Predominant Themes

The most common themes are longevity (or lack of it), physical ability and appearance, sexual ability (or lack of it), age concealment (for women), retirement, and mental ability. These themes indicate that there is considerable anxiety surrounding the topics of aging and death, illness and disability, sexual decline, age denial, job loss, and loss of mental ability.

Gender

Humor about older women tends to be more negative than humor about older men. This suggests a double standard in our society whereby older women are viewed more negatively than older men. Specifically, there is much negative humor about "old maids" but not about "old bachelors," and much humor about age concealment among women but not among men (Jack Benny is an exception).

Vitulli and Parman (1996) found that both elderly men and women agreed that humor is an important quality for men, but only the women perceived humor as important for women. Solomon (1996) also found that older men used more humor than older women, were quicker to catch on to jokes, and were more likely to see themselves as humorous.

Ageism

Some have suggested that negative humor about the aged should be avoided, just as sexist and racist jokes should be avoided, because a major effect of such jokes is to reinforce negative stereotypes about aging (Davies, 1977). Others (Weber & Cameron, 1978) point out that what seems negative to one observer may not seem so negative to others, and that even negative humor may serve certain desirable functions, such as release of repressed fears, and reinforcement of certain values associated with youth, such as vigor, sexuality, and competence.

A test of whether a joke about aging is ageist or not is to try telling the joke without an age reference. If it is still funny, it would be safest to tell it without the age reference. If it is no longer funny, it probably does depend on some ageist stereotype, and telling it with the age reference will tend to reinforce ageism.

Therapeutic Humor

Some studies have examined the therapeutic effects of humor on elderly patients. Tennant (1986) found that male patients recovering from cataract surgery who scored highest on a "humor survey" had the fastest rate of recovery. In a later study Tennant (1990) found that comedy portrayed in such shows as "I Love Lucy" and "The Honeymooners" enhanced morale and were particularly appealing to a sample of older residents of an apartment complex. She recommended that nurses develop the use of humor as a therapeutic strategy that enhances well-being.

Schultes (1997) described how humor can be used by home health care and hospice nurses to provide more cost-effective and holistic care. Houston, McKee, Carroll, and March (1998) found that nursing home residents who participated in a structured humorous activity (an old-time sing-a-long) had reduced levels of anxiety and depression compared with other residents.

Cousins (1976) claimed that laughing at old comedy movies helped cure him of a degenerative spinal condition. Yoder and Haude (1995) found that 33 older persons rated themselves higher on the Sense of Humor Scale than they rated a deceased sibling. They interpreted this as indicating that humor contributes to longevity. However, Ridley and Harrison (1996) pointed out that this finding is open to several explanations. Clearly, more research is needed to test whether "laughter is the best medicine."

Additional Information

An extensive review of theory and research on humor and aging can be found in Nahemow, McClusky-Fawcett, and McGhee (1986), including analyses of humor across the life span, humor physiology and aging, minority humor and aging, humor and death, humor and aging in children's picture books, and generational differences in humor.

ERDMAN B. PALMORE

See also
   Ageism
   Attitudes
   Person Perception

HYPERTENSION IN THE ELDERLY

Hypertension is the most common treatable cardiovascular disorder of the aged. As the general population increases in age, it is an increasingly important public health concern.

Epidemiology

The prevalence of hypertension is higher in the aged than in the younger population. When defined as a blood pressure reading of greater than 140/90 on a single occasion, hypertension is found in 54% of persons age 65 to 74 in the United States, with a prevalence of 72% in Black Americans in the same age group (Joint National Committee on Detection, Evaluation, and Treatment of High Blood Pressure, 1993). The incidence of complications of hypertension, such as stroke, congestive heart failure, and coronary heart disease (CHD), is also higher in the aged. Most important, treatment has been shown to reduce these complications.

Until 1985, it was not considered appropriate to treat hypertension in the elderly. The concern was that a lower blood pressure would predispose the patient to cardiovascular complications. This concern ignored the findings of the Veterans Administration Cooperative Study Group on Antihypertensive Agents (1972), which had shown a 70% reduction in the incidence of stroke in a small number of treated hypertensives older than 60. In the Australian Therapeutic Trial in Hypertension (1980), a subgroup of treated patients between 60 and 69 had a 33% reduction in stroke and an 18% reduction in coronary artery disease, compared with those taking a placebo. These two trials looked at diastolic hypertension.

The European Working Party on High Blood Pressure in the Elderly trial (EWPHE) included patients in the over-60 age group who had both systolic and diastolic hypertension; it showed a reduction of 32% in stroke deaths and a 38% reduction in cardiac deaths (Amery, Birkenhager, Brixko, Bulpitt, Clement, Deruyttere, et al., 1985). The STOP-Hypertension trial (Dahlof, Lindholm, Hanson, Schersten, Ekbom, & Wester, 1991) studied β-blockers, a diuretic and placebo in systolic and diastolic hypertension in patients age 70 to 84. The incidence of stroke was reduced by 45% in the treatment groups and myocardial infarction by only 12%. The MRC Working Party (1992) trial studied both systolic and diastolic hypertension in patients age 65 to 74, using atenolol, hydrochlorothiazide plus amiloride, or placebo. Stroke events were reduced (31%) but CHD events were only reduced in the diuretic group (44%).

The Systolic Hypertension in the Elderly Program (SHEP Cooperative Research Group, 1991) considered isolated systolic hypertension in the over-60 age group. Treatment was initiated with chlorthalidone and followed, if necessary, by the addition of atenolol or reserpine. Drug treatment reduced the incidence of nonfatal strokes by 37% compared with placebo, and CHD by 25%. The Sys-Eur trial in isolated systolic hypertension in patients over 60 compared nitrendipine, plus enala-

pril and hydrochlorothiazide, if necessary, with the corresponding placebos (Staessen, Fagard, Thijs, Celis, Arabidze, Birkenhager, et al., 1997). The use of calcium channel blockers and angiotensin converting enzyme (ACE) inhibitors reduced stroke events by 42% and cardiac events by 26%.

Several observational studies in the very elderly have suggested poorer survival in subjects with low blood pressure levels, which might argue against the treatment of high blood pressure in the very old (Langer, Ganiats, & Barrett-Connor, 1989; Mattila, Haavisto, Rajala, & Heikinheim, 1988). However, low blood pressure is also a consequence of other diseases and probably reflects poor general health prior to death rather than increased risk per se (Bulpitt & Fletcher, 1992). The pilot Hypertension in the Very Elderly Trial, (HYVET; Bulpitt, Fletcher, Amery, Coope, Evans, Lightowlers, et al., 1994) has been completed. It examined combined systolic and diastolic hypertension in patients over 80 years of age. The main trial is starting with randomization either to placebo or to a low-dose diuretic (Indapamide SR), plus perindopril if necessary. It is hoped that this trial will indicate the risks and benefits of treatment at advanced ages.

Treatment

What antihypertensives should be used in the elderly? Although an individualized approach to therapy is recommended, several points can be made. Lifestyle modification is an important principle of hypertension treatment. This would ideally include weight loss when feasible, reduction in alcohol intake, and salt restriction to less than 2 to 3 g of sodium per day. The elderly are particularly sensitive to salt intake (Weinberger & Fineberg, 1991). Diuretics have done well in the multicenter trials cited above. Concerns regarding their safety have been largely refuted (Freis, 1989) and were probably related to inappropriate dose selection. Prescribing low doses cannot be overemphasized (e.g., 12.5 to 25 mg of hydrochlorothiazide or 2.5 mg of bendrofluazide).

In view of the MRC (1992) results, β-blockers should probably not be first-line therapy. It has been shown that there is a reduced response to monotherapy with β-blockers in the elderly when compared with other antihypertensives (Lewis &

McDevitt, 1986). β-blockers also reduce the capacity for adapting cardiac function in a situation where aging and cardiovascular disease secondary to hypertension already limits such capacity (i.e., cardiac failure is a particular risk). However, in combination with a diuretic, β-blockers give very acceptable results (Dahlof, Lindholm, Hanson, Schersten, Ekbom, & Wester, 1991; SHEP, 1991).

ACE inhibitors should be most effective in the presence of high renin levels. In the elderly, renin levels are usually low. Despite this theoretical limitation, ACE inhibitors have been shown to be effective antihypertensive therapy in the elderly. They are particularly useful in patients with concomitant left ventricular dysfunction and/or diabetes. The combination of an ACE inhibitor and a diuretic is effective, especially as ACE inhibitors lessen diuretic metabolic side effects (Todd & Fitton, 1991). The initial dose of ACE inhibitor should be lower than that used in younger patients because the area under the curve for ACE inhibitors is higher in the elderly (Kelly & O'Malley, 1990). One should also beware of enhanced first-dose hypotension in patients who are already on a diuretic (Di Bianco, 1986), and treatment should then be started under medical supervision. Acute renal failure is a risk in patients with bilateral renal artery stenosis or those with severe renal atheromatous disease. For this reason, renal function should be monitored shortly after commencing ACE inhibitors in the elderly.

There is no reason why β-blockers cannot be used in the elderly, as they are well tolerated and have the added advantage of a beneficial effect in men with concomitant prostatic hypertrophy. The newer agents, such as doxazosin and terazosin, are preferred to prazosin because of the latter's high incidence of orthostatic hypotension (Joint National Committee, 1993). However, these agents have not been studied extensively in the elderly.

The beneficial potential of calcium channel antagonists is now proven (Staessen et al., 1997). Nicardipine has also been shown to be both efficacious and well tolerated (Frampton & Faulds, 1993). Side effects may be somewhat more troublesome than with other antihypertensive agents and include ankle swelling and flushing (Fletcher, Bulpitt, Chase, Collins, Furberg, Goggin, et al., 1992; Palmer, Fletcher, Hamilton, Muriss, & Bulpitt, 1990).

Overall, the phrase "start low and go slow" (Bennet, 1994) is particularly good advice for physicians prescribing antihypertensives for the elderly. In addition, although elderly patients are more prone to side effects, quality of life does not diminish after starting treatment (Beto & Bansal, 1992).

CHRISTOPHER J. BULPITT
ANTHONY A. J. O'BRIEN

See also
Cardiovascular System: Overview

I

IMAGES OF AGING IN THE MEDIA

Since the early 1970s, social scientists have been investigating the power of the media to influence attitudes about aging in America. The overwhelming majority of work in assessing media images of aging has been done in the realm of television. Television wields great power to influence millions of people and therefore commands the greatest amount of attention. In the print medium, those magazines that target the older consumer project an image slanted toward promotion of good health and activity. In other mainline publications, advertising may dictate the predominant image. One might see older people pictured in association with products such as dental and digestive aids and assorted health products. In contrast, upscale business publications might present seniors in positions of implied fiscal power, advertising elegant automobiles, life insurance companies, and financial institutions. Newspaper articles featuring older people tend to focus on extremes: either the severely disadvantaged or the "exotics," those elderly who are interesting because they accomplish feats not thought to be in keeping with their age, such as hang gliding or ski diving.

Television and the Aging

The most common mediated image of aging is projected by television. Often unrealistic expectations about life are encouraged when the world of television is confused with the real world. A major concern is what the absence of material teaches viewers. Elderly people are not seen on television in proportion to their numbers in real life. Moreover, they appear to be marginalized and represented in negative stereotypes. In a review of 28 studies, Vasil and Wass (1993) found that the elderly were underrepresented in both electronic and print media in terms of their presence in the United States population. Robinson and Skill (1995) reported that only 2.8% in their study of the 1,228 adult speaking characters in prime-time television were determined to be 65 years and above. Of those older characters, only 8.8% were in lead roles, a figure that is lower than studies reported in the 1970s.

Although older adults are the group with the greatest exposure time to television, most research describes unfavorable portrayals of older adults on television. Studies of television programs and surveys of older viewers have demonstrated that television caters poorly to the needs of older adults. For example, Powell and Williamson's (1985) review of the mass media revealed stereotypical ageist biases and a trend toward learned helplessness. They emphasize that biased-media portrayals may stifle the "needs of older adults to meet their needs collectively through the political process" (p. 78).

Images of Men Versus Images of Women

Women are far less likely to be seen in programs as they age than are men. Davis and Davis (1985) report that women appear onscreen about one third as often as do men. In fact, men are more likely to be found populating dramas when they are about 30 to 49. Women are likely to be in their 20s and early 30s. They begin to disappear as they approach 40. About 20% of men on television are over 50; however, less than 10% of women are in this age category. This picture is beginning to change, however. Robinson and Skill (1995) reported that the proportion of female characters in prime time, from 50 to 64 years of age, has increased since 1975. They suggest that "this may be one of the reasons the public believes TV portrayals of older Americans have improved in recent years" (p. 117).

Hajjar (1997) found similar effects in her content analysis of television commercials. Over-60 characterizations (8% of the total) were 70% male and 84% White. Positive characterizations tend to be clustered in the categories of food/beverage and financial/insurance; negative ones focus on medical/pharmaceutical products.

Although the predominant image of older women on television has been as a nurturer, followed by those of nags or adoring attendants, that pattern is beginning to change. Thanks to the expansion of cable, shows featuring older women in prominent roles are available in syndication as repeats long after episodes ceased production. In the 1980s, *Golden Girls* presented older women as attractive and sexually active; repeats of that series remain in syndication. With repeat episodes still broadcast via syndication, Jessica Fletcher, a murder mystery writer and amateur detective in *Murder She Wrote*, appears as an attractive older woman who is intelligent, perceptive, courageous, and effective in her investigative skills. Science fiction programs such as *Star Trek: The Next Generation* feature varied images of older women or female aliens such as Guinan, a wise and compassionate bartender and listener, and Luxanna Troi, a sensual, mischievous, mindreading Betazoid. In science fiction series shows, characters are portrayed at ages that would be considered older in human years but are middle-aged in various alien species. Shows in production in 2000 such as *Providence*, *Judging Amy*, and *Ally McBeal* feature older women as wise and wisecracking parents, colleagues, and friends.

Health and the Elderly on Television

The medical show is a popular television staple. Poor health is interesting; it provides more drama than good health. It would be easy to assume that old people are going to be the ill people in the world of television drama. The people in soap operas do not generally have diseases that viewers are likely to have. These characters are usually given health problems that are so exotic that they are not threatening to the average viewer. In many continuing dramas the ill get well. Death is a fate that befalls only those who for some reason must be written out of the story. So older people are not usually, contrary to expectation, victims of ill health on television.

Four shows that focus on medicine and that are in production in the year 2000—*ER*, *Chicago Hope*, *City of Angels*, and *Diagnosis Murder*—portray older adults as patients, concerned family members, and health practitioners. The patients have suffered from various conditions ranging from acute illness and accidents to terminal illness and chronic problems associated with aging. Some have died, just as younger adults and children have on the same shows.

The Consequences of These Images of Age

The images of age presented on television are, by and large, clusters of stereotypes. Such stereotypes are symbolic classifications used to simplify thinking about experiences and people. Unfortunately, such simplistic thinking is often presented on television as though it were truth. Even though there are many statistics that would promote a positive image of age, it seems as though most of the facts are not generally known. At least they are not attended to in the world of television, in fictional portrayals or in new coverage. Stereotyping is convenient shorthand to use for all support characters in television programming. And the elderly are far more likely to be supporting players than central ones. Television educates viewers to see aging as a negative and undesirable experience; it perpetuates a self-fulfilling prophecy. The future often becomes what we are convinced it will be.

Expectations for the Future

The amount of television viewing by adults increases with age (Mundorf & Brownell, 1990). As a result of the rapidly aging American populace and the increasing proportion of disposable income among those over 50 years of age, advertisers and television producers have gradually discovered the "gray market." Networks began to change their programming strategies in the early 1980s in response to these demographic and economic shifts in the population. Extensive programming on cable channels now offers viewers contemporary images of older adults in contrast to what may be contradictory and stereotypical images from rebroadcast shows as far back as the 1950s and movies of the silent era. In a study of viewing preferences, older adults made little reference to cable programming (Mundorf & Brownell, 1990). The potential for influence of cable programming, however, has yet to be fully examined and appears to be increasing as more access and programming options are provided. With the expansion of cable and the increase in programming opportunities, we should expect more targeting of market niches such as older adults, that feature more older adults and especially more in lead characters.

Television is slowly mirroring the changes occurring among American men and women. As adults are living higher quality lives at older ages, what is portrayed as "old" keeps changing. A woman in her 40s, such as Captain Janeway on the series *Star Trek: Voyager*, is portrayed as a dynamic leader and attractive career woman. Women in their 50s and 60s are seen as attractive and sexually active. But the changes are not happening fast enough for many older adults. Chafetz and colleagues (Chafetz, Holmes, Lande, Childress, & Glazer, 1998) reported that many older adults in their research sample expressed serious reservations about the attitudes displayed toward the elderly as shown through lack of or negative news coverage.

Movies made for television frequently present older performers as central characters in both drama and comedy. Age-related issues are often confronted in this day of social problem programming as legitimate subjects for comedy as well as drama. Each season showcases at least one significant film about aging and being old. Series programs have not ignored the story potential of being old in American society. Confronting old age is no longer the taboo it was 15 years ago.

WINIFRED BROWNELL
NORBERT MUNDORF

IMMUNE SYSTEM

The immune system comprises a complex mixture of cells that are distributed throughout the body and that function coordinately in defense against infectious agents. Because of a generalized decrease in immune function, the elderly have an increased susceptibility to infectious diseases and a decreased ability to develop protective immunity upon vaccination. There are two general types of immune responses: humoral immunity, wherein pathogen-specific antibodies are secreted into the serum and body fluids, and cellular immunity, wherein activated lymphocytes foster inflammatory reactions and kill infected cells. Both types of immunity are markedly diminished with aging.

Humoral Immunity

Humoral immune responses are the consequence of the stimulation of B cells that specifically recognize components (antigenic determinants) of an infectious organism and, as a result of this stimulation, proliferate and differentiate into antibody-forming cells (AFC). Throughout adulthood, B cells are generated in the bone marrow from multipotential stem cells by a complex differentiative and maturational pathway. Through a series of rearrangements of the genes that encode the specificity region of the two polypeptides (heavy [H] and light [L] chains) that comprise antibody molecules and the combinatory association of diverse H and L chains, each B cell acquires a unique antibody specificity and expresses cell surface immunoglobulin molecules (sIg) that display this specificity. Newly generated B cells whose sIg receptors recognize self-antigen in their environment are eliminated (tolerance), or forced to express a new L chain and thus a new receptor (receptor editing) (see Klinman, 1996, for review). When pathogens are presented to the resultant population of B cells, those B cells whose sIg recognizes an antigenic determinant on that pathogen can be induced to proliferate and generate a clone of AFC-producing soluble antibody identical in specificity to the receptor of the founder B cell. By this means, numerous antibody populations recognizing each of the variety of antigenic determinants on the pathogen are secreted into the serum and bind the pathogen. These antibodies can lead directly to the inactivation (viruses or toxins) or, in concert with a set of other serum proteins (complement), to the lysis of the pathogen (bacteria). Alternatively, antibodies can adhere the pathogens to cells (opsonization) that subsequently engulf and catabolize the pathogen. Some pathogens can stimulate B cells directly by being bound not only by the sIg but also by other cell surface molecules that nonspecifically facilitate B cell stimulation (mitogenic stimulation). However, B cell stimulation by most antigens requires a complex set of cellular interactions that involve both T cells and cells such as macrophages and dendritic cells that process and present antigens to specific T cells.

Cellular Immunity

Cellular immunity represents the second major arm of the immune response. Whereas T cells participate in humoral immune responses by facilitating B cell responses, the T cells represent the primary effector cells in cellular immune responses. In the adult, T cells, like B cells, emanate from multipotential cells in the bone marrow and, through a series of receptor gene rearrangements and cellular differentiative events, emerge as a vast repertoire of cells, each with a unique receptor. However, rather than undergoing diversification and maturation in the bone marrow, precursor cells that are destined to become T cells leave the bone marrow for the thymus, where T cell development takes place. As with B cells, newly generated T cells with high affinity for self-antigens are eliminated (tolerance); however, low affinity for self-antigens appears necessary for T-cell survival (positive selection) (von Boehmer, 1992). Unlike B cells, whose secreted antibodies can recognize antigenic determinants directly, recognition by T-cell receptors is dependent on the presentation of peptides derived from degraded antigens presented in the context of cell surface molecules called major histocompatibility complex (MHC) antigens (Zinkernagel & Doherty, 1979).

There are two general types of T cells, cytolytic T cells (CTL) and helper T cells (T_H). CTL generally recognize peptides of antigens such as viral antigens that are synthesized within a cell. Such peptides are presented in the context of a type of MHC molecules (Class I) that are expressed on almost all cells of the body. CTL that recognize a cell whose MHC presents a non-self peptide are stimulated to proliferate; they become activated and acquire the ability to lyse the infected cells that express those antigens. In contrast, T_H generally recognize peptides from foreign antigens that are ingested and degraded, yielding peptides that are presented in the context of a second category of MHC molecules (Class II), which are primarily expressed on specialized antigen-presenting cells such as macrophages, dendritic cells, and also B cells. Upon stimulation, T_H proliferate and release a variety of lymphokines that engender inflammatory responses and facilitate responses of both CTL and B cells. In addition, the direct interaction of T_H with a B cell that has processed an antigen and presented its peptides complexed to its cell surface, Class II MHC molecules can be an essential step to the response of that B cell. Such T_H-dependent B cell responses generate large AFC clones, and the antibodies produced by such clones can be of multiple molecular forms wherein the specificity region can be attached to any of several constant regions (isotypes) with distinct functional capabilities (e.g., secretion into the gut or across the placental barrier, mediating complement fixation and bacterial lysis, or mediating opsonization). In addition, the antigen-driven interaction of T_H with certain B cells in the follicles of reticular endothelial organs (e.g., spleen, lymph nodes) can lead to the generation of memory B cells specific for the stimulating antigen. Memory B cells can be far more numerous and more responsive than the B cells that exist before immunization (naïve or primary B cells), and their sIg receptors can display a much higher affinity for antigens. This increased affinity is achieved by both selection and the induction of somatic mutations in the genes that encode the specificity region of the antibody molecule. Some of these mutations can increase the antibody's affinity

for antigen, and B cells expressing such antibodies are strongly selected.

T_H cells can be stratified by their expression of various cell surface molecules and their functionality. Upon stimulation, resting T cells proliferate under the influence of various lymphokines, IL-2 in particular; up-regulate their expression of IL-2 receptor (IL-2R); and express higher levels of the surface antigen CD44 and decreased levels of CD45RB. This surface phenotype is also characteristic of memory T cells. In young adults, most T cells are naïve (CD44^{lo}, CD45RB^{hi}), and in addition, most T cells express low levels of the plasma membrane pump p-glycoprotein (p-Gp). As animals age, the population of memory phenotype cells increases, as does the percentage of both naïve and memory T cells that express high p-Gp levels (Miller, Garcia, Kirk, & Witkowski, 1997).

Aging and the Immune System

Aging is accompanied by dramatic decreases in the capacity to mount both humoral and cellular immune responses. Most dramatic is the hyporesponsiveness of T_H. However, because T_H play an important role in CTL and B cell stimulation, all aspects of immunity are impaired. Although aging is accompanied by an apparent increase in the onset of certain autoimmune states, no aging-associated alterations in the tolerance susceptibility of newly generated T or B cells has yet been identified. There is some evidence that antigen-presenting cell function is partially decreased with aging; however, the most dramatic affect of aging on antigen presentation is found among a highly specialized set of dendritic-type cells that are found in follicles (follicular dendritic cells [FDC]) and that play an important role in capturing and maintaining antigen in the milieu of newly generating memory B cells. Both the frequency and antigen-capturing capacity of FDC decrease with aging, a phenomenon that may contribute to the poor capacity of aged individuals to generate memory B cells (Kosco, Burton, Kapasi, Szakal, & Tew, 1989).

There is no measurable decrease with age in the number of naïve B cells nor, when given adequate T cell help, in either their capacity to generate AFC clones producing multiple immunoglobulin isotypes or their capacity to generate memory B cells. However, there are alterations in the repertoire of available antibody specificities and the distribution of B cells is greatly altered in that the proportion of mature B cells is decreased in the spleen and greatly increased in the bone marrow (Klinman & Kline, 1997). Most dramatic is an alteration in the homeostasis of the B cell population with age. For example, in mice the generation of B cells from the bone marrow is decreased four- to sixfold in aged (20–24 months) versus young adult (4–8 months) animals. This decrease is the result of blocks both in B cell development and maturation. This is compensated for by a marked increase in the average half-life of mature B cells, from 6–10 weeks in young adults to more than 8 months in aged mice (Klinman & Kline, 1997). Nonetheless, there appears to be no intrinsic functional deficit that correlates to the increased longevity of B cells in aged mice.

In spite of the maintenance of the intrinsic functionality of B cells and most antigen-presenting cells with aging, humoral immune responses and the generation of memory B cells is greatly compromised. This is due, in part, to an accumulated recognition by the immune system of its own antibodies (antiidiotypic suppression) (Klinman, 1981), as well as a decrease in T_H function, which also affects the responsiveness of CTL. T cells are generated in the thymus, and at sexual maturity the thymus begins to involute. Because of this, with age, thymic function and T cell neogenesis are greatly reduced. Additionally, unlike B cells, with time the T cell population of both humans and rodents shifts toward memory phenotype cells (Miller, 1996). Recent evidence suggests that this shift is probably the result of a lifetime of antigenic contact (Linton, Haynes, Tsui, Zhang, & Swain, 1997). With time these memory phenotype cells appear to become less and less responsive. Interestingly, naïve cells of aged mice appear hyporesponsive as well (Linton, Haynes, Tsui, Zhang, & Swain, 1997). In both cases, poor responsiveness appears to correlate with a low expression of IL-2R and an increase in the proportion of p-Gp^{hi} cells (Miller, Garcia, Kirk, & Witkowski, 1997). Importantly, T_H in aged individuals produce low levels of IL-2, and there are low levels of IL-2 in the environment. Taken together, these alterations in T_H function compromise both

CTL and B cell responses in the elderly and by so doing diminish their ability to contend with infectious agents.

NORMAN R. KLINMAN

See also
Immunizations

IMMUNIZATIONS

Although there are 27 vaccines and toxoids licensed for use in the United States (Advisory Committee on Immunization Practices, 1994a), primary prevention of infections in the elderly through vaccination has been an elusive goal. This failure stems from: (1) lack of vaccines for many of the most common pathogens; (2) less effective immunological responses in the elderly to vaccination, and (3) underutilization of existing vaccines (Powers, 1992). Despite these barriers, certain vaccinations are recommended for use in the elderly, and experimental and epidemiological data support these recommendations.

Influenza Vaccination

Influenza vaccination is clearly effective. A serial cohort study of community-dwelling elderly (Nichol, Margolis, Wuorenma, & Von Sternberg, 1994) documented that vaccination was associated with cost savings and reductions in rates of mortality and hospitalization for pneumonia, influenza, and chronic respiratory conditions. Vaccination in long-term care facilities is also effective, both for those vaccinated and for others, by inducing herd immunity (Advisory Committee, 1994b), but protection is incomplete.

Both the Centers for Disease Control and Prevention (CDC) and the American College of Physicians (ACP) Task Force on Adult Immunization recommend yearly influenza vaccination for all individuals 65 and over (Advisory Committee on Immunization Practices 1994a; ACP, 1994). In addition, the CDC recommends vaccination of all long-term care facility residents (Advisory Committee,

1994a). When outbreaks of influenza A occur in nursing homes despite vaccination, prophylaxis with amantidine (or rimantidine) is a cost-effective strategy (Advisory Committee, 1994c; Patriarca, Arden, Koplan, & Goodman, 1987).

Because they can infect high-risk persons, health care personnel in a number of settings should also be immunized yearly. These include, but are not limited to, hospital and outpatient health care personnel, employees of long-term care facilities who come in contact with residents, and those who come in contact with high-risk individuals in the home, whether as household members or home care providers.

The effectiveness of pneumococcal vaccine has been controversial, and there are many contradictory studies in the literature. A recent meta-analysis (Hutchison, Oxman, Shannon, Lloyd, Altmayer, & Thomas, 1999) concluded that the vaccine reduced systemic infection significantly and found no evidence that effectiveness was lower in older people. Other studies (Sisk, Moskowitz, Whang, Lin, Fedson, McBean, et al., 1997; Nichol, Baken, Wuorenma, & Nelson, 1999) have concluded that pneumococcal vaccination is cost-effective and considerably underused in the older population. In contrast, a randomized trial in Sweden found no benefit in terms of preventing pneumonia in an elderly population (Ortqvist, Hedlund, Burman, Elbel, Hofer, Leinonen, et al., 1998). The general view is that the vaccine reduces the severity and health care costs associated with pneumococcal infection but may not have a perceptible effect on the incidence of pneumonia in the general community.

Currently, immunization with pneumococcal vaccination is recommended for all individuals 65 years of age and older and those placed at high risk because of chronic illness (Advisory Committee, 1994a). The current vaccine, which consists of antigens from 23 serotypes, has been available since 1983; the first vaccine, which was introduced in 1977, had only 14 serotypes (ACP, 1994). Because antibody levels decline more quickly in the elderly than in younger patients and may be undetectable after 6 years (ACP, 1994), the ACP Task Force on Adult Immunization recommends that older adults with high-risk conditions (such as functional asplenia) be revaccinated after 6 years (ACP, 1994).

They do not recommend revaccination for healthy elderly.

Tetanus

Currently, revaccination with a combined tetanus diphtheria (Td) booster is recommended every 10 years after the initial immunization series (ACIP, 1994a). The ACP Task Force on Adult Immunization (1994) recommends an alterative strategy, that of a single booster at age 50 for those who completed the primary series of three in childhood followed by boosters in their teens and early 20s. A cost-effectiveness analysis examining a single immunization at age 65 for those who had previously received the primary immunization before age 6 (Balestra & Littenberg, 1993) lends support to the utilization of this simpler, single booster strategy. None of the proposed strategies changes the recommendations regarding wound prophylaxis.

Other Immunizations

The recommendations regarding immunization of older adults are based on the research and experience in the United States. Other countries have developed policies based on their own experience.

EUGENIA L. SIEGLER
Updated by J. GRIMLEY EVANS

See also
Immune System

IMPLICIT MEMORY AND LEARNING

Implicit memory occurs when performance reveals the effects of prior experiences (usually individual items or events), even in the absence of conscious recollection of those experiences. *Implicit learning* refers to acquiring information about the structural properties of relations among objects or events in the absence of either the intent to learn or the awareness of what has been learned. Implicit forms of learning and memory differ from their explicit counterparts in that they obey different principles of operation, rely on distinct brain areas, are differentially sensitive to brain injury, and serve different functions (for reviews, see Stadler & Frensch, 1997). For example, although being distracted during an initial encounter with an event usually hurts explicit memory for that event, it often does not hurt implicit memory. And although patients suffering from amnesia have profound impairments of explicit memory and learning, their performance on implicit tests is often indistinguishable from that of normal controls. Because implicit memory and learning differ from each other in important ways, implicit memory is considered first, followed by implicit learning.

Explicit tests of memory require *conscious recollection. Explicit memory* is called on when people attempt to recall an event from their childhood, to recall which words occurred on a list encountered in the laboratory, or to decide whether or not a particular stimulus, such as a word or face, occurred in a list they encountered earlier. In all these cases, memory requires that the person be aware that some event occurred in the past. In contrast, implicit tests do not require such conscious recollection, such awareness of remembering. For example, implicit memory for a word is demonstrated if that word is read more rapidly on its second presentation than its first, even in the absence of explicit memory for the earlier encounter; such facilitation is called *priming.*

Dissociations between implicit and explicit memory occur in the course of normal aging (for reviews, see Fleischman & Gabrieli, 1998; LaVoie & Light, 1994). Although substantial age-related deficits occur on almost all explicit tests of memory, age differences are usually smaller or absent on implicit tests. Whether the small age-related deficits seen on implicit tests are due to true age-related changes in implicit memory processes occurring for most individuals, to a decline in a small proportion of older people who are in the early stages of as yet undiagnosed dementia, or to the undetected influence of conscious recollection is as yet unknown. One observation favoring the latter interpretation is that the small number of studies using the process-dissociation procedure have consistently yielded age differences on the estimates of recollection but not on the automatic components of memory (e.g., Hay & Jacoby, 1999). However, these data too must be interpreted with caution, because this procedure also requires assumptions that are subject to debate.

The reliability of the finding of no or minimal age difference in implicit memory is as yet unclear. There are many different implicit tests, and although there is as yet no agreed on taxonomy nor an adequate theoretical account, it is clear that these different implicit memory tasks do not all tap the same underlying cognitive processes. Some implicit tests of memory require that new associations be formed, whereas others do not. Some implicit tests seem to reflect the continuing activation of perceptual processes, whereas others appear to be more conceptually based, reflecting the activation of a conceptually or semantically organized memory. So far, there is no consistent evidence that any of these categories of implicit memory is more likely than others to be impaired by normal aging (e.g., Fleischman & Gabrieli, 1998; LaVoie & Light, 1994).

Implicit forms of learning are at least as diverse as their implicit memory counterparts. Implicit learning, which is often called *procedural learning,* includes classical conditioning, skill learning (of both cognitive and motor skills), learning of stimulus covariations, sequence learning, learning of artificial grammars, and learning in control of complex systems. Here too, as in the case of memory, it is difficult to separate implicit from explicit learning, because both often occur simultaneously. To make generalizations yet more difficult, the aging of implicit learning has been studied even less than that of implicit memory. So far, all of the types of implicit learning that have been studied have revealed age-related deficits, at least under certain conditions. For example, classical conditioning is reduced in older people compared to younger ones (e.g., Woodruff-Pak & Jaeger, 1998), and implicit learning of sequential patterns shows age-related deficits at least when the patterns are complex and subtle (e.g., Howard & Howard, 1997). But even though implicit forms of learning are not completely spared the ravages of age, they do seem to be less severely impaired than most forms of explicit learning.

The demonstration of the relative age-constancy of implicit memory and learning has presented new challenges for theories of cognitive aging and has encouraged researchers to compare the patterns of savings and loss seen in amnesia, normal aging, and dementia, such as Alzheimer's disease. The relative age-constancy of implicit memory and learning also is important for everyday life, because implicit processes exert subtle, usually unnoticed, influences on common activities. For example, implicit memory affects the likelihood that particular ideas will come to mind. It also affects the meaning people assign to stimuli they encounter. Implicit learning and memory influence the ease and accuracy with which people perceive external stimuli, and they influence the preferences, impressions, and stereotypes they form. Implicit learning is involved in adapting to new environments, in learning the syntax of unfamiliar languages, and in learning to use new technologies, such as computers. In addition, the fact that implicit memory and learning are relatively age-constant suggests that they take on an even more central role, compared to explicit forms, as people get older. This relative age-constancy also implies that the effectiveness of cognitive interventions might be improved if memory remediation programs for normal elderly and for amnesia and dementia patients attempted to build on implicit memory and if rehabilitation programs for stroke victims took advantage of relatively preserved implicit learning abilities.

DARLENE V. HOWARD

See also
Memory and Memory Theory

INCARCERATION
See
Crime (Against and By the Elderly)

INCONTINENCE
See
Fecal and Urinary Incontinence

INDIVIDUAL DIFFERENCES

The term *individual differences* has served social, behavioral, and biological science for decades. It identifies differences among individuals—variation—in each given attribute or characteristic. Individual differences can refer to biological, behavioral, or social-contextual attributes. The attributes can be either qualitative or quantitative in character; as simple as single observables or as complex as patterns of age-related changes defined on multiple variables; as concrete as physical height or as abstract as spatial intelligence. Individual differences of this kind are sometimes referred to specifically as *interindividual differences*. In contrast, the term *intraindividual differences* identifies variation or differences manifested over different attributes within the same individual unit, and the term *intraindividual change* signifies variation or change over the same attribute within the same individual unit (Buss, 1979). The present discussion will attend only to interindividual differences.

Beginning in a major way with the investigations of Francis Galton, although the roots can be traced much farther back in history (Boring, 1950), many of the specialty areas of behavioral and social science have leaned heavily on the examination of individual differences. Included are human abilities, personality, developmental, and social psychology, status attainment deviance, social mobility, fertility, and behavior genetics, to name but a few. Work on individual differences has contributed substantially to the current status of empirical science and helped bring to the fore the names of Binet, Burt, Cattell, Spearman, Thorndike, Thurstone, and many others.

An Approach to the Study of Phenomena

Individual differences characterize a paradigmatic approach to the description, explanation, and prediction of behavior, broadly defined (Anastasi, 1958). Cronbach (1957) identified differential psychology—the study of behavior by focusing on individual differences—as one of two disciplines of scientific psychology. For the differential psychologist, the variation that can be measured among units is the source of data to be studied and analyzed. For example, relationships among the variations in different attributes (covariation) can be used to predict the individual's status on one attribute from his/her status on another attribute. Systematic analysis of covariation patterns can illustrate explanatory representations of the nature of behavior and behavioral changes, including those associated with age. In contrast to differential psychology, Cronbach identified experimental psychology as involving the attempt to understand behavior by creating variation among units under controlled conditions that are explicitly designed to permit the unambiguous evaluation of the nature of the variation created.

Both differential and experimental work focus on the production of statements of lawful relationships. Controls of various kinds are needed to make causal interpretations of the relationships among variables. Within the experimental orientation, the desired control conditions are accomplished prior to data collection by design arrangements. Because of the focus on existing rather than experimentally created variation, the study of individual differences does not ordinarily permit the introduction of suitable controls by manipulation of conditions. Rather, controls are imposed at the time of data analysis by statistical procedures. Thus, there is a flavor of historical analysis to the study of individual differences but with the possibility of replications across the units of analysis.

In part because of the different kinds of controls used, the primary analysis methods of the two traditions show considerable divergence. Whereas the *experimental* perspective has favored comparisons among means by the methods of analysis of variance, the *differential* perspective has led to various measurement and data analysis techniques that permit one to establish, and then systematically dissect, the relationships among the individual differences manifested by two or more variables. These are generally referred to as correlational methods. For example, some correlational methods are aimed at identifying the extent to which one set of variables can be used to predict status on other variables while controlling for variation on still other variables. Structural (causal) modeling is a statistical method that formally and systematically partitions existing variations among individuals in relation to hypothesized causal relationships. The techniques permit the modeling of causal relationships in terms of unobserved as well as manifest variables.

Individual Differences and Aging

Adult development and aging research has been conducted within both the differential and experi-

mental traditions. Many pertinent phenomena involve variables that are not manipulable, and thus there is a need in aging research for alternatives to classical experimentation in the pursuit of descriptive and explanatory goals.

Within the life-span orientation to the study of adult development and aging, especially, there has been heavy reliance on studying individual differences. The emphasis has been on identifying individual differences in developmental trajectories or change patterns as well as on comparing level or status across different age groups. Two important general questions (Hertzog, 1985) are: How do individuals' developmental trajectories differ from each other? and What are the correlates of these differences in developmental trajectories?

The question concerning differences in trajectories has led to several important findings concerning the richness of possibilities during adulthood. Included are the multidirectionality and multidimensionality of age-related changes in adulthood and the increasing variability that one sees in certain attributes in cross-sections of older and older individuals (Baltes, Reese, & Nesselroade, 1977). The question concerning correlates of differences in change patterns sets the stage for developing predictors of, and eventually explanations for, the individual differences in the changes in attributes manifested through old age. The systematic application of individual differences and methods to broad arrays of variables constitutes a major avenue that leads toward that goal; one on which a great deal of progress has already occurred and which promises still more as sophistication in the use of its techniques and procedures continues to grow.

JOHN R. NESSELROADE

See also
Cohorts
Longitudinal Research

INDIVIDUAL RETIREMENT ARRANGEMENTS

Overview

An individual retirement arrangement (or account) (IRA) is a tax-favored savings investment mechanism for individuals. IRAs were established in the Employee Retirement Income Security Act of 1974 (ERISA), beginning in 1975, intended as a vehicle for individual retirement savings in order to supplement Social Security and employment-based pensions. Under current law (as of January 1, 2000), there are three types of IRAs: (1) deductible IRAs, (2) nondeductible IRAs, and (3) Roth IRAs (named after Senator Bill Roth, chairman of the Senate Committee on Finance when enacted in 1997). A maximum of $2,000 per year (or up to the person's earned income) may be contributed to all of a person's IRAs (plus up to an additional $2,000 for a nonworking spouse's IRAs if the combined earned income is $4,000 or more).

For deductible IRAs, a maximum of $2,000 of earned income per year may be deducted by each person if neither the person nor the spouse actively participates in an employer-sponsored retirement plan (employer plan). A nonworking spouse may also contribute up to $2,000 to a deductible IRA if the couple has earned income of at least the contributed amount. If the person is a participant in an employer plan, the maximum deductible amount is phased out (for the year 2000) between adjusted gross income (AGI) of $52,000 to $62,000 for married couples filing a joint return and between $32,000 to $42,000 for single taxpayers. (These AGI phase-out limits are scheduled to gradually increase over the years 2001–2007.) Amounts in a deductible IRA, including earnings, are not taxable until withdrawn.

For nondeductible IRAs, there are no income limits. However, the $2,000 maximum limit on annual contributions (of earned income) applies to a person's combined IRAs. Earnings on a nondeductible IRA are not taxable until withdrawn.

For Roth IRAs, contributions are not deductible and earnings are not currently taxable. Withdrawals from Roth IRAs are tax-free if the amounts remain in the account for at least 5 years. The maximum annual amount for a Roth IRA is phased out for married couples filing a joint return with AGI between $150,000 and $160,000 and for single taxpayers with AGI between $95,000 and $110,000.

All taxable withdrawals from an IRA are taxed as ordinary income in the year withdrawn. Taxable withdrawals from an IRA prior to age 59 1/2 (except for death or disability) are generally subject to an additional 10% early-withdrawal tax. However, certain withdrawals are not subject to the additional tax: periodic payments (e.g., an annuity), for medical expenses of the person or spouse or dependents in excess of 7.5% of AGI, for medical insurance of certain unemployed persons (and spouse and dependents), for education expenses, and for certain first-time home-buyer expenditures.

IRA assets are similar to defined contribution pension plan assets. Thus, the individual is subject to the risk of gains and losses on the IRA investments. IRA amounts generally may be invested as individuals decide, except that IRAs may not be invested in life insurance or collectibles (other than certain coins). Also, IRAs generally may not be invested in assets in which the IRA owner has an interest. IRAs cannot accept amounts in excess of $2,000 per year, except for amounts "rolled over" from another IRA or pension plan.

When the IRA holder reaches age 70 1/2, a minimum percentage of the amount in the IRA (other than for a Roth IRA) must be withdrawn each year, based on the life expectancy of the IRA holder or the joint life expectancy of the IRA holder and spouse. IRA holders may recalculate their life expectancies annually and adjust withdrawals accordingly.

Participation in IRAs

Taxpayer participation in IRAs increased dramatically in 1982–1986 after the 1981 legislation which permitted persons in employer plans to also have deductible IRAs (see Table 1). The percentage of tax returns claiming IRA deductions increased from 2.6% in 1979 to a peak of 15.9% in 1985. After 1986 legislation limited IRA eligibility rules, participation in IRAs declined to 6.8% in 1987 and to 3.6% in 1996.

Participation in IRAs tends to increase as taxpayers' income rises. Tables 2 and 3 show the relative participation in IRAs by AGI class for 1985 and 1996, respectively. In 1985 the percentage of tax returns reporting IRA contributions was 2.3% for AGI under $10,000, rising to 76.1% for AGI over $100,000. Data for 1996 tax returns showed a marked difference in relative participation in IRAs by AGI class. The percentage of tax returns with earned income reporting IRA contributions was 1.1% for AGI under $10,000. It rose to 6.9% for

TABLE 1   Participation in IRAs, 1979–1996

Year	Returns claiming IRA deduction (millions)	Percentage of all returns	Deductions claimed ($ billions)
1979	2.5	2.6%	3.2
1980	2.6	2.7	3.4
1981	3.4	3.6	4.8
1982	12.0	12.6	28.3
1983	13.6	14.1	32.1
1984	15.2	15.3	35.4
1985	16.2	15.9	37.8
1986	15.5	15.1	38.2
1987	7.3	6.8	14.1
1988	6.4	5.8	11.9
1989	5.8	5.2	10.8
1990	5.2	4.6	9.9
1991	4.7	4.1	9.0
1992	4.5	3.9	8.7
1993	4.4	3.8	8.5
1994	4.3	3.7	8.4
1995	4.3	3.6	8.3
1996	4.4	3.6	8.6

Source: Internal Revenue Service, *Statistics of Income* (various years) and Joint Committee on Taxation, U.S. Congress, *Present Law and Background Relating to Tax Incentives for Savings* (JCX-7-99), February 23, 1999.

TABLE 2   IRA Participation by AGI Class, 1985

AGI class	Number (millions)	Percent of eligible returns	Amount of contributions ($ billions)
Under $10,000	0.6	2.3%	1.1
$10,000 to $30,000	5.1	13.6	9.7
$30,000 to $50,000	5.7	32.9	13.5
$50,000 to $75,000	3.0	56.5	8.7
$75,000 to $100,000	0.9	74.1	2.7
Over $100,000	0.8	76.1	2.6
All AGI classes	16.2	17.8	38.2

Returns reporting IRA contributions

Source: Internal Revenue Service, *1985 Statistics of Income,* and Joint Committee on Taxation, Ibid.

AGI between $30,000 and $50,000, dropped to 3.5% for AGI between $50,000 and $75,000, and then increased to 6.6% for AGI over $100,000.

We should note that the AGI classes for these two years are in current dollar terms and therefore are not comparable in purchasing power. However, differences in the degree or incidence of participa-tion are readily apparent between the two years—doubles-digits in all AGI classes but one in 1985 and single-digits in all AGI classes in 1996. Obvious differences between these two years may also be observed from either the number of returns (with IRA participation) or the total dollar amount of IRA contributions.

TABLE 3   IRA Participation by AGI Class, 1996

AGI Class	Returns reporting IRA contributions		
	Number (millions)	Percent of returns with earned income	Contributions ($ billions)
Under $10,000	0.3	1.1%	0.4
$10,000 to $30,000	1.6	4.3	2.8
$30,000 to $50,000	1.4	6.9	2.4
$50,000 to $75,000	0.5	3.5	1.1
$75,000 to $100,000	0.2	4.5	0.7
Over $100,000	0.4	6.6	1.1
All AGI classes	4.4	4.1	8.6

Source: Internal Revenue Service, *1996 Statistics of Income,* and Joint Committee on Taxation, Ibid.

Under a graduated income tax, the amount of taxes saved (resulting from tax deduction for IRA contributions and tax deferral for IRA earnings) increases as the income tax rate bracket increases. For example, a taxpayer in the 15% tax bracket will save $300 in tax on a $2,000 IRA deduction, and a taxpayer in the 28% tax bracket will save $560 in tax. The effects of 1997 legislation establishing the Roth IRAs and gradually increasing the income phase-outs for IRA deductibility are yet to be adequately measured.

Other Related Legislative Provisions and Proposals

Legislation enacted in 1997 established Education IRAs (education savings accounts) whereby taxpayers may deduct up to $500 per year for contributions to such savings accounts for college education expenses and may withdraw such savings tax-free for qualified college expenses. The deduction is phased out for taxpayers with AGI above $150,000 for married couples filing joint returns and above $95,000 for single taxpayers.

Medical savings accounts (MSAs) were established under Health Insurance Portability and Accountability Act of 1996 to provide tax deduction and deferral benefits to eligible persons not participating in employer-provided medical insurance. Effective January 1, 1997, MSAs were enacted as a pilot program for 1997–2000, with the number of allowed participants limited to no more than 750,000 taxpayers. After 2000, no new contributions may be made to MSAs except by or on behalf of individuals who previously had MSA contributions, and employees of a "participating" employer. Self-employed individuals who made contributions to an MSA during 1997–2000 also may continue to make contributions after 2000.

In addition, the president's fiscal year 2001 budget included a proposal for retirement savings accounts to assist lower- and middle-income people to save for retirement. Under the proposal the federal government would provide matching funds for couples with incomes up to $25,000, with a phase-out of matching for incomes between $25,000 and $80,000 (one-half of these amounts for individuals). Contributions to the accounts would accumulate tax-free. Withdrawals would be allowed after 5 years for certain qualified purposes (medical care, purchase of a house, or college expenses).

The budget proposal is similar in concept to a demonstration program under the 1996 Work Opportunity Reconciliation Act that allows states to use their welfare block grants to set up individual development accounts (IDAs). Under the IDA's 5-year demonstration program, the state administering agency provides a match of between $1 and $8 for each $1 that an eligible low-income family deposits into an IDA.

YUNG-PING CHEN
LEON W. KLUD

See also
Retirement

INDUSTRIAL GERONTOLOGY

Industrial gerontology is the study of aging and work and focuses on employment and retirement issues of middle-aged and older workers. Major areas include social policy and law, stereotypes of the older worker, selection, job performance and appraisal, training and retraining, career progressions and development, motivational factors and organizational design, job design and redesign, obsolescence, reentry workers, alternative work patterns, plant designs and layoffs, and retirement decisions. Over four decades ago industrial gerontology in Great Britain began to address issues in aging and work. Research was motivated by concern regarding technological change and automation and the effects on the older worker ("New opportunities," 1999; Sterns & Gray, 1999).

A common theme for several decades and still a major concern is the negative stereotype of the older worker. The social impact of this stereotype is substantial when held by an employer and creates even greater problems when held by older persons themselves. A major finding in industrial settings is that employers encourage older workers to take early retirement buy-outs and remain reluctant to hire or offer training to persons over 40 or to train or retrain those already employed. Many middle-aged and older workers have been affected by layoffs, downsizing, and plant closings; however, many of these same companies are hiring individuals in new positions. Career patterns are now more likely to be interrupted and may involve dramatic changes in job skills. More frequent and intensive periods of education will be required to remain effective in the work force (Schaie & Schooler, 1998).

In response to changing social and organizational environments, self-management has emerged as a theme permeating the 1990s: self-management of career, leisure activities, and retirement. With workers changing occupations, employers, or jobs within their own company, greater individual responsibilities are required for maintaining and updating knowledge, skills, and abilities (Sterns & Sterns, 1995).

Characteristics of Older Workers

Older workers have developed fine work records, indicating that they are healthy, dependable, and productive and have low accident rates. Performance of older workers is not necessarily different from that of younger workers and often depends on level of motivation, self-reliance, recognition, workplace climate, experience, and job demands (Sterns & Gray, 1999).

Age Discrimination in Employment Act

The Age Discrimination in Employment Act (ADEA) of 1967, revised in 1978 and 1986, defines older workers as individuals in the age range of 40 and older. By law, workers aged 40 and older, working in businesses with more than 20 employees, cannot be limited, segregated, or classified in any way that would restrict their employment opportunities or otherwise adversely affect their status as employees.

The law recognizes that age may sometimes be a BFOQ, "a bona fide occupational qualification," reasonably necessary for the normal operations of a particular business. Currently, occupations such as commercial airline pilot and actor are covered by such an exception. Also, businesses are allowed to follow the terms of a bona fide seniority system or any bona fide benefit plan, such as a retirement, pension, or insurance plan. Executives in major leadership positions or high policy-making employees with sizable pension benefits can be required to retire at age 65 (Crown, 1996).

Performance Appraisal

Performance appraisals are used by supervisors to determine which individuals will be selected for promotion, training, transfer, demotion, or layoff. Such judgments are often made by a supervisor and based on formal subjective ratings. Major issues in such ratings are rater error and rater bias; but training of raters is necessary to minimize bias against the older worker. Stereotypes about aging may influence the subjective appraisal of an older worker and not accurately reflect that worker's actual job performance. Studies comparing older and younger workers, using performance appraisal techniques based on job-relevant behaviors, have shown that many older workers perform as well as or better than younger workers (Schaie & Schooler, 1998).

Selection

Older workers may find themselves competing with younger individuals for job placement by participating in extensive selection and assessment procedures. There is some evidence justifying a concern about age discrimination in testing. It has been found that although older subjects had significantly lower scores on a predictor battery, their performance on the job was equal to that of a younger group. The adverse impact of selection batteries on capable older workers is, therefore, a matter of some concern (Sterns & Gray, 1999).

Training and Retraining

A major issue in the training of older workers is assuring equitable access to training opportunities. Training policies and practices may reflect informal age restrictions, standards, and assumptions that may exclude older employees. In an era of extended work life, training and retraining provide older workers with opportunities to strengthen their knowledge and skills (Sterns & Sterns, 1995).

Highly productive older workers run the risk of not being included in training opportunities. Their involvement in important ongoing projects makes supervisors reluctant to spare them. The problem faced by workers of any age is that, if they do not engage in retraining, they grow further and further out of touch with new information, technology, and processes. Rapid technological changes create obsolescence of knowledge among all age groups. The need for retraining is shared by people in their 20s to their 70s and beyond. Special training techniques have been developed to meet the special needs of the older worker Older workers often take longer than younger workers to learn a new task; however, with sufficient time, older people perform as well as younger workers after training (Sterns & Sterns, 1995; Sterns & Gray, 1999).

Demographic Changes and the Workplace

The U.S. Bureau of Labor Statistics (BLS) projects that the U.S. labor force will grow from 127 million workers in 1992 to 151 million in 2005, an increase of approximately 19%. Workers 55 and older represented 12.2% of the entire labor force in 1992 and will represent 14.2% in 2005.

Over the 1998–2008 period, total employment is projected to increase by 14%. The labor force aged 45–64 will grow faster than the labor force of any other age group as the baby boom generation (born 1946–64) continues to age. The participation rate of workers aged 55 and older is expected to increase 47.8% between 1998 and 2008, from 17 million to 25 million workers.

Recent research indicates that as many as 5.4 million Americans 55 and over report that they are willing and able to work but do not have jobs, 14.3 million are working, 26.4 million are retired and prefer not to work, and 6.3 million prefer to work but are unable to (Sterns & Sterns, 1995).

Once older workers lose their jobs, they stay unemployed longer than younger workers do, suffer a greater earnings loss in subsequent jobs than do younger workers, and are more likely to give up looking for another job ("New opportunities," 1999; Crown, 1996).

HARVEY L. STERNS
ANTHONY A. STERNS

See also
Ageism
Retirement

INFLATION IMPACT AND MEASUREMENT

The impact of inflation relative to aging over the past several decades can be viewed from two perspectives: its effects on individuals and especially its differential impact on subgroups of the elderly and, more broadly, on society. Its impact also differs depending on whether its levels are high (e.g., in the upper single digits and above) or low (2%–3%) and on the type of inflation (e.g., general, medical, or housing). During the 1960s and especially the 1970s and early 1980s, with their unprecedented and sustained double-digit inflation, aging advocates decried the disproportionately adverse impact of inflation on the elderly, the largest population group with fixed incomes. Thanks to arguments presented at the 1961 and 1971 White House

Conferences on Aging, special programs (e.g., Medicare, Supplemental Security Income [SSI], Section 202 housing) were enacted or expanded to assist poor elders and all aged to cope with inflation more effectively. More important, Social Security benefits were increased and then indexed (adjusted upward) through automatic cost-of-living adjustments (COLAs) to compensate for the negative effects of high inflation.

Differential Impacts of Inflation on the Aged

Although this public policy response to inflation is generally credited with raising more of the elderly above the poverty line (Kingson & Berkowitz, 1993; Moon & Mulvey, 1996), high rates of inflation have had varying effects on different groups of retirees. Recipients of employer-provided pensions, which generally are not indexed for inflation (except in the public sector) or only minimally so, were disadvantaged, especially if they were not eligible for Social Security as, for example, has often been true of many teachers (Liebig, 1986). Only 5% inflation erodes the value of unindexed pensions by 22% in 5 years.

At the lower end of the economic scale, inflated rents consumed greater proportions of older renters' incomes, with many paying considerably in excess of the standard 30% of income. Especially in areas with a shortage of affordable rental housing, this pattern persisted during the 1990s. Similarly, although SSI payments were, like Social Security, pegged to the Consumer Price Index (CPI), the asset tests was not similarly indexed for inflation, resulting in fewer aged poor being eligible for that program. Conversely, those elders with substantial assets benefitted from or at least kept pace with inflation and the prevailing standard of living, as the value of their homes rose and their savings earned high rates of interest. The somewhat regressive nature of the payroll tax during the 1970s and early 1980s, high rates of inflation, and high rates of unemployment experienced by the nonretired population led to a drop in the purchasing power of some younger age groups. Thus, both the young and the aged poor (and particularly the near poor, or "tweeners" [Smeeding, 1986]), were especially hard hit.

By contrast, since the mid-1980s, the U.S. economy has enjoyed 15 years of disinflation (Steindel, 1997). As measured by the CPI, inflation in the 1990s has ranged from a high of 6.1% in 1990 to a low of 1.6% in 1998, exhibiting a steadily downward path, except for 1996. These swings in the rate of inflation over the past two decades have led to proposals for different remedies.

Societal Effects of Compensating for Inflation Impacts

In the late 1970s and early 1980s, the longer range effects of policies designed to cushion the elderly against inflation were examined in depth. Leading economists, such as Alicia Munnell and Martin Feldstein, focused on the overindexation of Social Security benefits and its negative effects on financing of the system and on capital formation and savings behavior. Others, such as Robert Samuelson, emphasized the cost burdens of an aging population, especially for retirement benefits and medical care, and a growing intergenerational equity gap, a view that they continued to espouse throughout the 1990s. These perceptions were heightened by contrasting the poverty rates of the elderly with those of children (Preston, 1984) and by widespread recognition that all elders were indeed not poor. As a result of this controversy, aging advocates found themselves in a more defensive posture. Calls for reducing or freezing Social Security benefits or COLAs were countered by facts about the high poverty rates of subgroups of the elderly: women, the "old old," and minorities.

Over time, broader proposals were generated to reform Social Security, Medicare, and other programs to reduce overall costs. Among the proposed remedies was a revision of the CPI itself. This index affects COLAs for Social Security, military and government employee pensions, and veterans' benefits. Rental rate increases, federal and state income tax brackets and deductions, and eligibility standards also are tied to this measure, thereby affecting old and young alike. Under the 1987 amendments to the Older Americans Act, the Bureau of Labor Statistics (BLS) was instructed to compile an experimental index (the CPI-E) for persons aged 62 and over. Although flawed, this 6-year study showed consistently that elders experience higher inflation, with expenditures for medical care accounting almost entirely for this difference (Amble & Stewart, 1994).

A more concerted approach was undertaken by the Advisory Commission to Study the CPI, a blue-ribbon panel chaired by Michael Boskin. The commission's basic purpose was to determine if the CPI overstated the rate of inflation, a position held by many leading economists, including Alan Greenspan, the head of the Federal Reserve. Its report, issued in 1996, determined that the CPI overstates the rate of inflation by an average of 1.1% annually and therefore should be changed. If enacted, this adjustment would result in lower government outlays, of interest to Washington policy makers eager to balance the federal budget and to cut taxes. Recipients of Social Security, veterans' benefits, and government pensions would receive less because of the CPI's effects on the calculation of initial benefit amounts and annual COLAs. Similarly, Medicare reimbursement rates to doctors and hospitals, also calibrated to the CPI, would drop, thereby reducing general revenue outlays for medical care for retirees and the disabled.

Medical Inflation

Another advocacy battleground has centered on the escalating rates of inflation for medical services—higher than general inflation and one of the factors leading to continued demands for cost controls in Medicare, Medicaid, and employer-provided retiree health benefits. Although general inflation dropped to 4% in the early 1980s, medical inflation was more than double that rate, at 11%. This pattern of medical inflation, twice that of general inflation, persisted through 1993; since then it has continued to rise but is more in line with general inflation (except in 1998, when it again was double that rate). But overall, medical inflation characteristically has outpaced overall inflation, measured by the CPI, over the past 20 years ("By the numbers," 1999).

Combined with the knowledge that the elderly are far more likely than younger persons to require medical interventions, increased attention has been paid to the effects of medical inflation on the aged, especially on out-of-pocket costs. Much of this increase has been attributed to the costs of prescription drugs, especially problematic for elders with

incomes under the poverty level who are without Medicaid protection (Gibson, Brangan, Gross, & Caplan, 1999). Despite Social Security COLAs, benefits have not increased to compensate for the higher costs of medical care for the elderly. Those retirees without employer-provided postretirement health benefits—usually women, minorities, and low-income elders—have been particularly disadvantaged, although somewhat less so if they are covered by Medicaid or by the special low-income Medicare programs or are able to afford "Medigap" insurance, an out-of-pocket outlay in addition to the costs of Medicare Part B premiums.

More recently, as general inflation has abated, the earlier rationale for compensating the elderly for its adverse effects has become less germane. However, low inflation rates have had negative effects on some elderly, especially those who are risk-aversive relative to the stock market. Interest rates on certificates of deposit and other short-term savings vehicles have fallen, leaving many lower- and middle-income elders less able to meet expenses, especially for out-of-pocket health and long-term care costs and/or higher rents. However, in contrast to the early 1990s, when deflation in the housing sector led to smaller retirement nest eggs for many elders, at the end of the 1990s home prices climbed in 95% of zip codes nationally and were beating inflation. Recent double-digit increases in home values should allow elders to capitalize on this asset and should provide a larger base for executing home equity conversion mortgages to cover health and other expenditures.

Thus, the impact of inflation on aging has continued to be a two-edged sword. On the one hand, unprecedented high inflation in the 1960s, 1970s, and early 1980s, coupled with the generally low income levels of the aged, led to policy changes and compensatory mechanisms that raised the overall economic well-being of the elderly. Conversely, when inflation abated and the costs of these antiinflationary measures were perceived as burdensome and unfair, the elderly experienced cutbacks in income maintenance, health care, housing, and many social services. Should the CPI be changed in accordance with the recommendations of the advisory commission, cutbacks will continue. Thus, the relative levels of inflation, whether high or low, can be viewed as having played a role in changing the philosophy and substance of elderly entitlements.

Perhaps more important, our greater awareness of the economic diversity of the elderly requires us to focus more on how different rates and types of inflation will affect different groups of the aged. Constructing politically and economically feasible policies that consider this diversity will require extraordinary skill.

PHOEBE S. LIEBIG

See also
   Economics
   Pensions
   Poverty
   Social Security

INFORMAL CAREGIVING

Informal care for chronically ill and disabled older persons is generally defined as unpaid assistance from family members, friends, and neighbors with one or more personal care tasks (e.g., bathing, dressing) or instrumental activities of daily living (e.g., transportation, housekeeping). Research on informal caregiving burgeoned following two landmark studies, one refuting the myth that families abandon their elderly members (Shanas & Streib, 1968) and the other showing that informal caregivers supply 80% of the long-term care received by noninstitutionalized elderly (Comptroller General, 1977). Over subsequent decades, widespread attention has been given to caregiving's prevalence, nature, and outcomes as well as to its negative effects, and services and interventions that alleviate these effects (see cross-referenced entries). This section focuses on informal caregivers, their prevalence and characteristics and their caregiving patterns and transitions.

Prevalence of Informal Caregiving

Prevalence estimates indicate there are 2.6 to 22 million active caregivers assisting noninstitutionalized disabled older persons (Stone, Cafferata, & Sangl, 1987; National Alliance for Caregiving [NAC] and American Association of Retired Persons [AARP], 1997). These estimates vary in relation to the criteria used to define *caregiver*. Narrower definitions emphasize primary caregivers, namely, spouses or adult children who have major responsibility for caregiving, caregivers living with disabled persons, and those providing help with personal care activities. More inclusive criteria give consideration to a broader range of caregiving tasks (e.g., managing money, arranging services), to extended kin and non-kin caregivers, caregivers in separate households, and caregivers of middle-aged and elderly persons (e.g., 50 and over).

This enormous unpaid labor pool of informal caregivers bears the burden of long-term care. If these or future cohorts decide to diminish or relinquish the caregiving role, there is the potential to add billions to U.S. health care costs.

Estimates of caregiving's prevalence increase when the informal caregivers of 1.69 million institutionalized elderly are included (Manton, Corder, & Stallard, 1993a). Although these caregivers typically are omitted from estimates, research indicates that most institutionalized elderly have regular contact with family and friends. These caregivers often continue to provide direct care, such as help with eating and transporting, and they exhibit stress effects similar to the caregivers of disabled elderly in the community.

Characteristics of Informal Caregivers

The number of informal caregivers has increased dramatically over the past decade and will continue to grow as population ages. In 1987 an estimated 7 million households were involved in caring for a frail elder, compared to 22 million in 1997 (U.S. Department of Health and Human Services, 1998). By the year 2007 the number of caregiver households in the United States could reach 39 million (Wagner, 1997). Research findings on the characteristics of informal caregivers underscore the central role of immediate family in the elderly's care. Over 70% of caregivers are women, mainly wives and daughters (in-law) (Stone, Cafferata, & Sangl, 1987). Caregiver characteristics differ by ethnic group, the extent to which the care receiver is functionally impaired, and the extent of help provided (NAC & AARP, 1997). Asian and Hispanic caregivers are younger than Whites, African American caregivers are predominantly women, and employed caregivers are less likely than those not employed to help with activities of daily living (ADL) tasks. Reports on the average age of caregivers range from 46 to 55, and about half live with the care receiver, especially when the care receiver is seriously impaired. About two-thirds are employed full- or part-time, and estimates indicate another 10% to 30% who were employed stopped working because of care-related responsibilities (Neal, Chapman, Ingersoll-Dayton, & Emlen, 1993).

Greater research attention is now being given to minority caregivers, specifically, to the 20% to 25% of U.S. caregivers who are of African American, Hispanic, Native American, or Asian descent (Dilworth-Anderson & Burton, 1999; NAC & AARP, 1997). Comparisons of minority and nonminority caregivers indicate minority caregivers report less burden and provide more care to more disabled elderly (NAC & AARP, 1997). Findings are inconsistent regarding the effects of ethnicity on the use of informal and formal assistance. Research findings indicate no differences in formal service use by ethnicity, more reliance on informal care among minorities (Dilworth-Anderson & Burton, 1999; Tennstedt & Chang, 1998), as well as less reliance on informal care among minorities (Norgard & Rogers, 1997). Comparisons of Asian, African American, Hispanic, and White caregivers and care receivers show differences in their sociodemographic characteristics, living arrangements, and type of assistance given (NAC & AARP, 1997). African American caregivers are less likely to be married than are Asian, Hispanic, and White caregivers, and Asian caregivers are more highly educated and have considerably higher annual household incomes in contrast to caregivers in the other groups. Others have asserted that too little is known about social support in general and caregiving for elders in minority families to draw meaningful conclusions (Dilworth-Anderson & Burton, 1999). Future studies, using appropriate conceptual approaches and a variety of research methods, are needed to address the ways in which the history, culture, and social conditions of ethnic groups affect the social support they provide to their oldest members. Some of these conceptual approaches include the application of a life-course perspective, social support, and systems theories to family care-giving, and greater use of qualitative methods and data gathering from multiple family members.

Caregiving Structures and Patterns

Considerable attention has been given to the type and amount of assistance from informal caregivers. Most caregivers have been providing assistance from 1 to 4 years, about 80% are involved in caregiving on a daily basis, and the average number of hours spent per day ranges from 2 to 8 (NAC & AARP, 1997; Stone, Cafferata, & Sangl, 1987). Socioemotional support is the most commonly cited type of assistance, followed by help with transportation, shopping, and household tasks and help with mobility, bathing, and dressing in the area of personal care.

Although the focus of earlier research was on primary caregivers or those providing all or most help, subsequent studies have examined caregiving networks or systems. Evidence suggests that about 20% to 30% of primary caregivers, typically spouses, receive little or no help from others. Secondary informal caregivers tend to be involved when the care receiver is of more advanced age, unmarried, living with others, and more functionally impaired.

Formal helpers often are not included in the caregiving networks of frail and impaired elderly. Estimates of community-based health and social service use range from 25% to 36%, and only about 5% to 10% of noninstitutionalized elderly rely exclusively on formal service providers (NAC & AARP, 1997). Assistance from formal providers is more likely to be enlisted when the older person is in poorer health, or more disabled, has dementia, is female, is unmarried, and has a higher income and more assets. Explanations for why community-based services are used so sparingly include the caregiver's lack of perceived need for and awareness of available services. Caregiver services, mainly respite care, are more likely to be used when the care receiver is more impaired and thus requires more care, has dementia, lives with the caregiver, and receives formal services.

Divergent models have been proposed to explain the interface between the elderly's informal and formal caregivers and how various types of helpers provide assistance with similar or different caregiving tasks. One model posits a division of labor between informal and formal helpers by type of task (Litwak, 1985); others view formal helpers as supplementing or substituting for the help provided by informal caregivers (Noelker & Bass, 1994). Little information currently exists about the ways in which the structure of caregiving networks and activities changes over time and the factors underlying these changes. Only recently has attention turned from the more instrumental aspects of caregiving (care-related tasks and the relationship of helpers) to more subjective aspects, such as caregiving's meaning to helpers and their appraisals of its experience, resulting in a broader understanding of caregiving consequences (both positive and negative).

Transitions in Informal Caregiving

At least three stages of caregiving have been identified, including the onset of providing informal assistance in either a shared or a separate household, placement in a residential care facility, and bereavement (Aneshensal, Pearlin, Mullan, Zarit, & Whitlatch, 1995). The transitions into these stages, as well as each stage itself, involve a host of changing stresses and demands that have led researchers to view caregiving as a career (Aneshensel et al., 1995). Indeed, efforts have been made in recent years to gain a clearer understanding of how the dynamic process of caregiving is related to a variety of short- and long-term outcomes.

Among those who become caregivers, 23% can expect to place the care receiver in a nursing home (Stone, Cafferata, & Sangl, 1987). Only about 5% of informal caregivers relinquish their role despite the care receiver's continuing needs for assistance. When caregivers relinquish their role, it is often because of both objective and subjective factors, such as care receivers' extensive personal care needs and caregivers' negative appraisals of their role (Boaz & Muller, 1991; Kasper, Steinbach, & Andrews, 1994). Research on caregivers following the care receiver's nursing home placement suggest that some relief is gained from the responsibilities of constant care, with diminished feelings of tension and overload; however, general well-being, as assessed by depression and other psychological measures, is generally unchanged. In essence, care-

related responsibilities and associated stress change in nature but the caregiver role continues (Aneshensel, Pearlin, Mullan, Zarit, & Whitlatch, 1995). Commonly reported sources of stress associated with placement include finding an acceptable facility, concern about the quality of care, the care receiver's mental state and inability to accept the need for placement, and problems with staff.

Existing evidence about the adjustment of former caregivers to the care receiver's death is inconsistent. Some studies indicate improved physical health; others note increased psychological distress (Aneshensel, Pearlin, Mullan, Zarit, & Whitlatch, 1995). Spouse caregivers appear most at risk of adverse health consequences during the bereavement process. Other research suggests that caregiving and bereavement have a long-lasting impact on the employment status of adult daughters and daughters-in-law (Pohl, Collins, & Given, 1998). Those employed part-time were more likely to quit their jobs early in the caregiving process, care for a dying parent (in-law) who lived with them, spend more time caregiving, rate themselves in poorer health, and not return to work following the parent's death.

Conclusions

After nearly three decades of research on family caregiving, recent studies are beginning to underscore the diversity among caregivers and in caregiving patterns. Awareness of this diversity comes from recent research on caregiving in different ethnic groups (Dilworth-Anderson & Burton, 1999) and cross-cultural differences in caregiving (Keith, Fry, Glascock, Ikels, Dickerson-Putman, Harpending, et al., 1994). Additionally, greater attention is being given to elderly persons who are caring for HIV/AIDS patients and grandchildren.

Although informal caregivers currently assume major responsibility for the long-term care of noninstitutionalized elderly, concerns have been raised about their ability and willingness to continue in this role. Sociodemographic changes resulting in growing numbers of the oldest old, smaller families, working women, and blended families pose obstacles to family care that can increase the stress of caregiving. As a result, future research should focus on a neglected area: the quality and impact of informal care on all persons involved, including the care receiver, and services and interventions that alleviate the burden on informal caregivers. Implicit in the existing literature is the assumption that family members, as the preferred source for care, provide the most appropriate care. This assumption is unwarranted until outcome indicators related to the care receiver's quality of informal care are widely used (e.g., nutritional status, emotional well-being) and their relationships to various caregiving structures and processes are established and empirically tested.

LINDA S. NOELKER
CAROL J. WHITLATCH

See also
Caregiver Burden
Caregiving of Chronically Ill Elderly
Social Supports

INFORMATION-PROCESSING THEORY

The information-processing approach is not a single coherent theory but rather is a general framework in which the focus is on the examination of the processes responsible for a given type of behavior. Concepts borrowed from the field of computer science and developments in the information theory of communication were very influential in the early years, but an enduring characteristic of this approach has been an emphasis on analysis of intervening processes. (See Lachman, Lachman, and Butterfield [1979] for a further discussion of the historical background of the information-processing perspective in psychology and Salthouse [1991a] for a more recent description and critical appraisal in the context of research on aging.)

The concept of *information* is considered very abstractly in the information-processing approach; in fact, in formal information theory, information was defined as anything that reduced uncertainty. More precisely, one bit of information was equivalent to a reduction of the total uncertainty by exactly 50%. Some early research in psychology relied upon this definition of information, but because of the variety of ways in which stimulus material could

be coded and organized, most subsequent researchers have favored a more vague measurement unit, termed the *chunk*. In one of the classic articles in the information-processing tradition, Miller (1956) proposed that the information-processing capacity of normal human adults was "seven-plus-or-minus-two" chunks.

Two monographs that stimulated much interest in the information-processing approach and ultimately served to define the initial perspective were Broadbent's (1958) *Perception and Communication* and Neisser's (1967) *Cognitive Psychology.* Both books incorporated a process-oriented approach to the topics of human thinking and cognition and proposed specific theoretical hypotheses that inspired considerable empirical research. However, in subsequent years the information-processing perspective has pervaded nearly all fields of psychology, and it is no longer possible to identify a single source containing all relevant information.

One of the most successful applications of the information-processing approach in cognitive psychology is the memory-scanning model proposed by Sternberg (e.g., 1969, 1975). Sternberg's theorizing was motivated by an attempt to explain a phenomenon in which the reaction time to classify a stimulus was found to be linearly dependent upon the number of previously presented target stimuli. Following a tradition dating back to Donders, a mid-19th-century Dutch scientist, Sternberg proposed that this reaction time included several discrete stages, each responsible for a different type of processing. In particular, he suggested (1) that the probe stimulus is initially registered and encoded, (2) that the stimulus is compared in a serial (i.e., item-by-item) fashion against the target stimuli in memory, (3) that a decision is reached concerning a match or mismatch of the probe to the target stimuli, and (4) that this decision is communicated by executing the appropriate response as rapidly as possible.

The Sternberg model (Sternberg, 1969, 1975) epitomizes the information-processing approach because a series of detailed processes is postulated to account for the observable behavior. This particular model also elicited considerable interest because it provided very specific interpretations of several aspects of the reaction time data. For example, the slope of the function relating reaction time to the number of target stimuli is typically quite linear and often with the same slope for both positive (i.e., probe stimulus matching an item in the target set) and negative (i.e., probe stimulus not matching an item in the target set) trials. Sternberg's interpretation of these results was that the memory comparison, or scanning operation, was serial and exhaustive, involving a sequential examination of each and every item in the target set, continuing even after a match was found.

Another much admired characteristic of Sternberg's model (Sternberg, 1969, 1975) was that one or more independent manipulations were identified that were thought to selectively influence each of the postulated processing stages. This feature has proved useful in attempting to specify the origins in the sequence of information-processing operations of performance variations associated with individual differences, such as disease status, neurological impairment, or chronological age.

The strategy of relying upon an information-processing model and then utilizing clever experimental manipulations to isolate the contribution of specific processing components has been termed the "localizing the loss" approach in gerontological cognitive psychology. A great many studies involving a variety of different tasks have now been reported in which adults of a range of ages have been compared with one another, and in the majority of the cases older adults have been found slower than young adults in each of the processing components investigated. For example, older adults have been reported to be slower than young adults in the encoding, scanning, and response selection/execution components in Sternberg's model (e.g., Salthouse & Somberg, 1982), in the mental rotation component in Shepard's model of decisions involving internal transformations (e.g., Berg, Hertzog, & Hunt, 1982), and in the long-term memory access component in Posner's model of letter comparison decisions (e.g., Lindholm & Parkinson, 1983).

Among the challenges faced by information-processing researchers in aging are to explain why so many different components appear to be sensitive to the effects of aging (i.e., the losses seem not be easily localizable) and to document and account for the relation between efficiency (i.e., time) of these molecular processes and effectiveness (i.e., quality) of the overall behavior. Regardless of the resolution of these issues, it is indisputable that the information-processing approach has been very popular in research on the psychology of aging. Because of its focus on detailed mechanisms and intervening processes, many researchers believe that the information-processing approach will continue to be very useful in helping to understand the exact nature of and reasons for adult age differences in cognitive functioning.

TIMOTHY A. SALTHOUSE

See also
Learning
Memory and Memory Theory

INJURY

Injury is a leading cause of disability in the elderly. The most common types of injury are those that result from falls, from motor vehicle crashes, and from fires and burns.

Injury is caused by acute exposure to energy, such as heat or electricity, or the kinetic energy of a crash or fall. Injuries that occur from falls, crashes, and burns are not random events or accidents. They are predictable in their association with well-studied risk factors. Disability and death from falls, crashes, and burns increase with age in late life.

Injuries among older persons result from a combination of circumstances in which the demands of task exceed the combined resources of individual abilities and environmental support (Hogue, 1982). Frailty, especially mobility impairment and inactivity, clearly places older persons at greater risk for injury from falls (Bohannon, Hanlon, Landerman, & Gold, 1999; Tromp, Smit, Deeg, Bouter, & Lips, 1998). Older drivers with cataracts restrict their driving, report more difficulty with challenging driving situations, and are 2.5 times more likely to have at-fault crash involvement even when driving exposure is controlled (Owsley, Stalvey, Wells, & Sloane, 1999). Recent research on fire fatalities (McGwin, Chapman, Curtis, & Rousculp, 1999) has confirmed earlier studies showing that older persons have the highest case-fatality rates following fire injury.

As a cause of death, the type of injury varies by age group. For persons 65 to 74 years old, slightly more than one third of deaths due to injury are related to motor vehicles and one fourth to falls. In those 75 and older, more than one half of deaths due to injury are related to falls and less than one fifth to motor vehicles.

Strategies to reduce death and disability from injury can be grouped: changing the environment, decreasing task demand, and strengthening individuals. All strategies must support autonomy, independence, and mobility as much as possible.

To prevent injuries among older people, health care providers should suggest modifications to home environments (Rubenstein, 1999), test their visual acuity periodically, monitor their use of drugs, counsel them on medical conditions affecting mobility, and recommend physical exercise to maintain and improve flexibility and mobility (Close, 1999; Gill, 1999; Hogue, 1991, 1992; Ory, Schectman, Miller, Hadley, Fiatarone, Province, et al., 1993; Tinetti, Baker, McAvay, Claus, Garrett, Gottschalk, et al., 1994).

CAROL C. HOGUE

See also
   Falls

INSTITUTES FOR LEARNING IN RETIREMENT

Past and Present

The first officially designated Institute for Learning in Retirement (ILR) was initiated at the New School for Social Research, New York, in 1962. Since that singular creation, the concept of an ILR has been disseminated and interpreted, with different degrees of emphasis, over 250 times throughout the United States, Canada, and Bermuda. In 1989 the Elderhostel Institute Network was established to serve as a clearinghouse and liaison for individuals and institutions interested in developing their own retirement programs and Institutes for Learning in Retirement was adopted as a generic title. Although the network was motivated and funded by Elderhostel, Inc., the ILR concept represents a very different form of lifelong learning for older adult learners

from that implemented by Elderhostel. The ILR momentum, especially in terms of program growth in the past decade, suggests that the concept is uniquely responsive to fundamental shifts in the geography of older adult education.

The population demographics of the United States alone speak to the magnitude of change that is occurring—by 2030, the population of adults over the age of 65 will be twice what it was in 1984, or approximately 21% of the U.S. population (Beatty & Wolf, 1996). With every generation that reaches retirement age, individuals will be better educated, in better health, and more interested in maintaining options and choices regarding lifestyles and continuing education interests and goals.

The ILR learning and teaching model offers a new and creative format for the self-directed and choice-conscious older adult learner interested in exploring new relationships with higher education resources in the community. The typical ILR program components of academic study, travel/study, membership activities, financial accountability, community outreach, and public relations are all developed and expanded by the members themselves and sponsored by a higher education institution. These unique program elements suggest that ILRs will have a continued viability into the future of older adult programming, and ILRs are, by their very nature, receptive to the characteristics of both today's and tomorrow's older adult learners. By so doing, however, ILR programs challenge more traditional older adult programming to become responsive to the themes of the ILR concept: (a) the desire for leadership and personal autonomy in both developing program content and in program operations, (b) learner characteristics requiring new and different forms of client service, and (c) a deepening appreciation for the need to nurture mutually satisfying and beneficial relationships between communities of older learners and the educational resources existing in their communities (Fischer, 1991).

In 1977, ILRs began to be developed within a variety of sponsor institution settings, and a growth spurt begun in 1988 accounts for the fact that well over half of the ILRs now in existence have been developed since the late 1980s. Many varieties of formal model and concept implementation now exist, and some of these differences in program operations and expectations are explained by documented differences in the relationships between ILRs and their sponsor institutions. The results of the first comprehensive ILR survey suggested that the sponsoring higher education institution can have an impact on several program elements, including style of governance, faculty collaboration, resources, benefits, funding, and sponsor commitment (DeJoy, 1997). These impacts were associated with differences in institution type; for example, ILR programs at private sponsor institutions enjoyed choices of governance, a home base in academic affairs units, ready access to resources and student benefits, and startup funding. These programs often enjoyed less faculty collaboration, however, and academic content was often decided with institutional staff input. On the other hand, the sponsorship offered at public land-grant institutions differed in that some ILRs did not enjoy access to resources or benefits, almost all were based in continuing education/extension units, and some did not receive startup funding; however, many did control their own academic content and had the use of classroom space. The data support the conclusion that future ILR development will continue to be prescribed by the specific educational environments involved. This conclusion offers both guidance for current program development and a challenge to the unique characteristics of the ILR model.

Educational Implications

The growth of the ILR concept within higher education environments has been impressive in the past 10 years, from fewer than 75 such programs in 1989 to over 260 in 1999 and with over 66,000 ILR members involved. These numbers provide evidence of the viability of such older adult programs in partnership with higher education institutions and serve to document the emphasis on and interest in liberal arts programming as a vital component of quality of life for older adults. The earlier and sustained success of Elderhostel programming helped awaken this awareness on the part of higher education, and ILR programming has served to deepen that awareness and translate it into the sustained year-round educational activities of ILRs. This is a programming model that clearly supports

the lifelong learning tempo of the learning society—the continued, lifelong needs of individuals to expand their knowledge/skills in order to survive and prosper, at *all* ages. The ILR model speaks to the growing demographic cohort of older adults and the expansion of life expectancy for future generations and provides a way of looking at and thinking about several issues and trends that are part of understanding what "retirement" will be in the 21st century. The concept of "healthy aging" embraces a range of factors, such as enhancing one's physical and mental functioning, being productive and involved, maintaining one's independence, and maintaining meaningful personal relationships (American Association for World Health, 1999); and the ILR model speaks to each of these factors in a creative way. ILR programs contain the potential to serve as vehicles for changing conditioned stereotypes and behavioral patterns about the "required" dependency of older adults (Bates, 1996). The current trend, on higher education campuses, to create retirement living/learning communities also appears conducive to the ILR programming concept (Sack, 1999).

Challenges

The fundamentals are in place for an enlarged model of lifelong learning programming for older adults, one that provides a vehicle for higher education outreach involving adult learners who are both self-directed and focused on problem solving in this phase of their lives. To drive this expansion and reinterpretation of the original concepts, however, several challenges must be successfully met.

In order to expand and deepen the educational impact, the ILR programming model must seriously address ways to reach a larger, more heterogeneous population of older adults—those adults whose educational attainment, discretionary income, health status, and/or support system stands in the way of their participation. As a corollary to this challenge, ILR programs have to move from the fringes of their higher education environments into the mainstream of academic life on their campuses, in a new spirit of partnership and collaboration framed by the lifelong learning needs of the 21st century's largest student cohort.

With these challenges successfully met, the ILR model and translations of the model will offer a responsive template for the full participation of older adult learners in the "learning society."

JUDITH K. DEJOY

See also
Adult Education

INSTITUTIONALIZATION

Characteristics of Institutionalized Aged

Institutionalization of older persons represents a central concern of gerontological researchers and service professionals alike. Processes and consequences of institutionalization will therefore comprise the focus of this discussion. Long-term care facilities represent extensive financial investments by our society toward care of the frail. There is also concern about the potentially high human costs of institutionalization. It has been argued that vulnerable elderly persons entering institutions are particularly susceptible to adverse environmental conditions (Lawton, 1980). Institutionalization is often used not as a treatment of choice but rather as a comprehensive approach to deal with multiple frailties and lack of personal and social resources of the aged. Older persons entering institutions have typically experienced declining physical and/or psychological resources, along with deficits in areas of social support. Accordingly, it must be recognized that even where competent and state-of-the-art care is provided, therapeutic effects are likely to be limited (Kahana, Kahana, & Chirayath, 1999).

About 5% of the total U.S. population over age 65 lives in long-term care institutions at any given time, and 75% of those institutionalized are women (National Center for Health Statistics, 1997). It is estimated that over 40% of the elderly will spend time in a nursing home at some point in their lives (Murtaugh, Kemper, & Spillman, 1990). After age 85, an individual can expect to live in a nursing home for close to half of her remaining life span (Liang, Liu, Tu, & Witelaw, 1996). Accordingly, the problem of institutionalization for older persons

is likely to grow in importance as more and more Americans live to be very old.

The overriding cause of placement in a long-term care institution remains poor health and frailty. Other factors that can lead to institutionalization include widowhood, solitary living, economic deprivation, and interpersonal conflicts (Bauer, 1996). Lack of community alternatives, concern about adverse effects on caretakers, and advice of health care professionals also have been found to contribute to entry decisions (Dwyer, Barton, & Vogel, 1994). Institutional placement of an elder involves complex family processes of planning and decision making and is typically accompanied by urgency and a sense of turmoil for family members. Institutionalization of a spouse often results in complex role changes and new role demands for the community-residing spouse. Although caregiving hours provided by families diminish after institutionalization of a parent, frequent visitation and attachments remain the norm (Pruchno, Peters, Kleban, & Burant, 1994). The majority of elderly persons move to long-term care facilities from acute care hospitals or other institutional settings. Most suffer from multiple impairments and have significant functional limitations (National Center for Health Statistics, 1997). Nevertheless, many elderly persons who have functional impairments as severe as those who are institutionalized continue to function in the community (Morris, Sherwood, & Mor, 1984). Although there are generally recognized placement criteria, there is evidence that many elderly persons placed in long-term care facilities could appropriately be treated at lower levels of care (Spector, Reschovsky, & Cohen, 1996). Furthermore, close to one fourth of institutional admissions are discharged back to the community (National Center for Health Statistics, 1997). Ultimately, it is the interaction between personal vulnerability and loss or inadequacy of social supports that is most likely to bring about institutional placements.

Elderly persons with mental illness and those suffering from Alzheimer's disease increasingly comprise a major subgroup of nursing home dwellers. During the 1985 National Nursing Home Survey, 66% of residents were found to have mental disorders, but only 4.5% of these aged received any mental health services (Burns, Wagner, Taube, Magiziner, Permutt, & Launderman, 1993). Special care units represent one service trend that is aimed at enhancing quality of life for patients with Alzheimer's disease and other forms of dementia.

During the era of managed care it has been recognized that both patient preferences and staff characteristics (such as workload of case managers) impact on likelihood of institutionalization (Degenholtz, Kane, Kane, & Finch, 1999). It is also increasingly evident that specific nursing home placements are often affected by cost and personal resource factors and facility availability, as well as organizational characteristics ranging from reputation of the facility to resident selection criteria used by the facility (McAuley & Usita, 1998). Macro-level variables related to characteristics of the state health care system, such as Medicaid spending on home- and community-based services, and the number of home health agencies in a given state also exert a significant impact on the likelihood of institutionalization of frail elders (Miller, Prohaska, Runer, Freels, Brody, & Levy, 1998).

Nursing homes now collect Minimum Data Sets on all patients (Hawes, Mor, Phillips, Fries-Brant, Morris, Steel-Friedlob, et al., 1997). Because many Western countries use Minimum Data Sets, it is now possible to make cross-national comparisons concerning transitions between home, hospital, and long-term care settings. Patterns of admission and likelihood of discharge back into the community appear to vary widely among countries. In comparison to the United States, elderly persons living in Japan are far more likely to be admitted to nursing homes from other long-term care settings; however, elderly in Denmark are more likely to be admitted from their homes. Return of nursing home residents to the community is far more likely in the Netherlands (27%) than in the United States (10%) (Frijters, Mor, DuPaquier, Berg, Carpenter, & Ribbe, 1997).

Demographic trends shape the characteristics of nursing home populations, resulting in marked changes in the racial and ethnic composition of nursing homes over time. Accordingly, the ratio of institutionalized Blacks relative to Whites has grown from .65 in 1982 to .85 in 1989 (Clark, 1997). Nevertheless, it is important to recognize that, among older Blacks, relatively lower rates of institutionalization still exist and are complemented by higher use of paid home care, informal care, and no care (Wallace, Levy-Storms, Kington, & Andersen, 1998).

In recent years there have also been important changes in the types of services offered by nursing homes. These changes reflect both the increasing diversity of institutionalized persons and the changing characteristics of the health care system. Nursing homes have expanded the spectrum of services they offer to include hospice care, postacute or rehabilitation services, and specialized care for chronic illness such as Alzheimer's disease.

The Impact of Institutionalization

The methodological challenges of determining the effects of institutionalization are considerable. The problems of attributing postinstitutional changes in residents to the impact of institutional environments have been noted by Lieberman and Kramer (1991). Even when longitudinal data are available, the effects of relocation, environmental change, and illness-related changes are often difficult to distinguish from those of institutionalization. Furthermore, there are few populations that can serve as true control groups in studies that consider the impact of institutionalization. Nevertheless, valuable information may be gleaned by considering evidence from diverse studies, even with their methodological limitations, regarding the experiences of institutionalized older persons and the impact of institutionalization on those individuals.

Institutionalization poses many discontinuities in relation to customary lifestyles in a community setting. Even when institutions provide high-quality health care, residents are likely to experience changes in their customary ways of living and their patterns of social interaction. Patients typically experience a loss of independence, privacy, and familiarity upon entry into an institution (Savishinsky, 1991). Interaction with old friends and family members may be minimized, organizational involvements are curtailed, and customary social activities are altered. Institutionalized elderly persons have been found to show loss of self-esteem, withdrawal, and depressive symptoms (Kane, 1995–96). Evidence also has been found for a "failure to thrive" syndrome, akin to that manifested by institutionalized children, among elderly nursing home residents (Braun, Wykle, & Cowling, 1988).

The negative and dehumanizing effects of institutional living have generally been documented in qualitative studies of single institutions, using participant observation and field study approaches (Diamond, 1992; Gubrium, 1993). Goffman's (1961) classic study of the career of the institutionalized mental patient presents a prototype for accounts by anthropologists (Henry, 1963; Shavishinsky, 1991) and gerontologists (Gubrium, 1993; Vladeck, 1980). These accounts depict the "stripping," humiliation, loss of freedom, dignity, and deprivation of choice that are experienced by "obsolescent" human beings (Henry, 1963) who have been placed in institutional settings. However, they also document valiant and often creative efforts of institutionalized aged to adapt to their environment and create meaning in their lives.

Some confirmation of negative effects of institutionalization also has come from research using more quantitative approaches. Such research has indicated that isolation and loss of personal control (which may result from dependency-inducing behavior of staff) lead to learned helplessness among institutionalized aged (Baltes, 1996). Resident inactivity and neglect by staff have been observed in institutional facilities (Gottesman & Bourstom, 1974).

Counterbalancing reports of negative influences of institutional living is a smaller body of research, which has failed to confirm the negative impact of institutional living (Patchner & Balgopal, 1993). An early study by Morris (1974) documents improved morale over a 1-year period among residents of nursing homes. High levels of satisfaction and positive adaptations to life in long-term care settings have been observed by researchers (Joiner & Freudiger, 1993; Kahana, Kahana, & Young, 1984). Improved family relations have also been reported subsequent to institutionalization (Smith & Bengston, 1979). There is evidence that, for some people at least, institutionalization may present positive alterations in lifestyle. Improved nutrition and medical care, availability of activities, and opportunities to be exposed to social interaction, as well as cognitive stimulation, have been cited as enhancing lives of the institutionalized aged (DePaola & Ebersole, 1995).

Special initiatives to enhance quality of life in nursing homes have been reported to yield success (Kahana, Kahana, & Chirayath, 1999). Those include widely used restraint reduction programs (Kane, 1993), as well as interventions to improve nutritional status among residents (Johnson, Dooley, & Gleick, 1993). Programs reflecting psychosocial orientations include intergenerational programs, which introduce contacts with children and young adults (Gaston, 1994), as well as interventions aimed at enhancing environmental control and autonomy (Wagner, Wahlberg, & Worning, 1994). Recent therapeutic efforts have targeted the large and growing number of cognitively impaired residents in institutions (Camp & Mattern, 1999).

The Americans With Disabilities Act also opened up far-reaching potentials for protection of elderly in nursing homes (Gottlich, 1995). Alternative dispute resolution techniques, including mediation and nursing home ombudsman programs (J. S. Kahana, 1995), also have contributed to advocacy for the institutionalized elderly. With increasing numbers of cognitively impaired residents in institutions, growing attention has been directed toward decision making in long-term care (Schimer & Kahana, 1992). Questions have been raised about the impact of the widespread use of cognitive testing as a means of relocating residents to special care units within long-term care facilities and determining their competency for medical decision making (Kane, 1993). It may be argued that apparently contradictory data about the impact of institutionalization on older clients may be better understood when the complexities of the phenomena under study are considered. Changes in well-being of the elderly are a function of environmental influences, on the one hand, and individual differences in human adaptations on the other. Much of the research focusing on negative aspects of institutional life has concentrated on adverse environmental influences. In contrast, the focus of studies documenting positive postinstitutional outcomes has often been on human resiliency and adaptability (Kahana, Kahana, & Young, 1984). Whereas earlier research tended to treat institutions as if they had a global or unitary effect on residents, more recent efforts have been directed at identifying conditions of both the person and the environment that maximize well-being (Soth, 1997).

Congruence between personal preferences and environmental characteristics has been found to influence resident morale and satisfaction, in addition to effects attributable to personal or environmental characteristics alone (Kahana, Liang, & Felton, 1980). Research has called attention to personal coping strategies as important mediators of the stress of institutionalization (Kahana, Kahana, & Young, 1984).

Research findings have also shed new light on long-held assumptions about the functioning of institutions. Staff members have been observed to portray positive attitudes toward patients and to treat patients as equals (Kahana & Kiyak, 1984). The expectation of long-term institutionalization for all those entering such facilities has been found to be incorrect, with significant numbers now returning to community living. Patients without diagnoses of dementia and with first-time nursing home admissions are most likely to be discharged into the community (Engle & Graney, 1993). After entry into institutions, levels of health among residents appear to hold up. Major shifts in health status among nursing home residents occur only during their last 4 to 6 weeks of life (Kiely, Morris, & Morris, 1997).

As research and conceptual approaches to institutionalization become more sophisticated, there have been calls to focus research on processes that occur in the course of institutionalization and on the dimension of time that is implicit in studies of change (George, 1984). An important challenge for future research in this area is the simultaneous consideration and linking of institutional input variables to patient outcomes and satisfaction. It is now also recognized that the institutional setting must be considered as embedded in a community and social context. Experts suggest developing incentives for care that improve provision and outcomes of institutional services (Kane, Bell, Riegler, Wilson, & Keeler, 1983). Changing characteristics of the elderly, in the direction of more native-born, more educated, and more sophisticated consumers, are likely to lead to changing expectations of future consumers of institutional care and even demands for greater options and more self-determination. At the same time, unique needs of minority populations requiring long-term care must also be recognized as we note greater diversity among the aged. There are indications of impending major changes in financing, organization, and delivery of long-term care in the near future, with growing trends toward community-based care (Rowland, Burns, Schafft, & Randolff, 1997). These changes are likely to result in more diversified services provided in alternative settings, altering the meaning of insti-

tutionalization and requiring multidimensional approaches to assessing its role and impact in the spectrum of services that comprise long-term care.

EVA KAHANA

See also
Deinstitutionalization
Long-Term Care Assessment
Nursing Homes

INTELLIGENCE

Maintaining the quality of intellectual competence assumes major importance in the lives of many older persons. The assessment of intellectual competence is often required to provide information relevant to questions of retirement for cause (in the absence of mandatory retirement at an early age) and of sufficient competence remaining for independent living and/or the control and disposition of property,

Changes in competence that represent the actual decrement that individuals experience should be differentiated from performance below that of younger persons that is not due to a person's decline but instead reflects the obsolescent functioning of older cohorts when compared to younger peers. We want to know at what age developmental peaks occur in order to assess generational differences as well as within-generation age changes. We also want to know why some individuals show intellectual decrement in early adulthood whereas others maintain or increase their level of functioning on some ability variables well into old age.

The intellectual processes required for the acquisition of cognitive structures and functions in childhood are not necessarily relevant to the maintenance of functions and the reorganization of structures needed to meet the demands of later life. Whether during earlier development or in old age, it is nevertheless certain that basic concepts relevant to the understanding of intelligence in childhood continue to remain relevant at adult levels. It is therefore of considerable interest to examine age changes on basic ability measures over much of the life course, although the manner in which observable behaviors (phenotypes) express the basic constructs (genotypes) may change with age in pattern and organization.

Intellectual Development in Old Age

Most data on adult intellectual development are based on work with the Wechsler Adult Intelligence Scale (WAIS) (Matarazzo, 1972) or with Thurstone's Primary Mental Abilities test (PMA) (Schaie, 1985). Studies with the WAIS have focused on a so-called classical pattern that shows a plateau reached in the 20s, maintenance of performance on verbal subtests, such as Vocabulary and Comprehension, until the 60s, but early adult decline on performance tests such as Block Design or Object Assembly. More recent studies, however, suggest that, in healthy individuals, WAIS performance may hold up well into old age (cf. Busse, 1993). Age comparisons on the WAIS are compromised by the finding that the factorial structure of that battery changes from early adulthood to old age. By contrast, it has been established that the structure of the primary mental abilities remains rather stable across adulthood (Schaie, Maitland, Willis, & Intrieri, 1998). Data for the PMA indicate continued gains for most abilities until the late 30s or early 40s. Thereafter a plateau is maintained until the early 60s are reached, with the exception of the highly speeded measure of Word Fluency (vocabulary recall) that shows significant decline in the 50s. Gender differences have been reported that suggest earlier decline for spatial ability in men and word fluency in women. The average magnitude of intellectual decline, however, is quite small during the 60s and early 70s and is probably of little significance for the competent behavior of the young-old. However, substantial average decline for most abilities are observed once the 80s are reached (Schaie, 1996).

Individual Differences in Adult Intellectual Development

The data on average age changes tend to conceal a most important item of information. That is, they might indicate to the casual observer that intellectual decrement in old age is universal and unavoidable. Data from the Seattle Longitudinal Study (Schaie, 1996) argue to the contrary. Only about one third of the individuals studied declined reliably over a 7-year period from age 60 to 67, and about 40% declined from age 67 to 74. Even by age 81, about 50% of the members of our longitudinal panels maintained their functional level over a 7-year period.

What accounts for these individual differences in intellectual change over time? In addition to factors that might be genetic in nature, other attributes characterize individuals who do not decline in old age: (1) they are free of cardiovascular disease, (2) their perceptual speed has declined less than average, (3) they have at least average socioeconomic status, (4) they exhibit a stimulating and engaged lifestyle, and (5) they describe themselves as having flexible attitudes and behaviors at midlife (see Schaie, 1996).

Can Intellectual Decrement Be Reversed?

In studies related to optimal or adaptive intellectual functioning, it has been recognized that older adults can be disadvantaged in at least two different ways. First, some age-related decline may occur through disuse, whether by personal choice or environmental restrictions. Second, some people may be disadvantaged because of rapid sociocultural and technological change. Cross-sectional cognitive training research has strongly suggested the modifiability of older adults' performance on a number of intelligence dimensions. However, the cross-sectional nature of this research made it impossible to examine one of the most fundamental questions: To what extent did training procedures result in remediation of age-related decline versus the acquisition of new performance levels in subjects experiencing no decline? Within the context of a longitudinal study it has been found that reliably documented 14-year decrement could be reversed in approximately 40% of subjects undergoing a cognitive training program and significantly reduced in an additional 25% of participants. Performance levels were enhanced also in substantial numbers of persons whose performance had remained stable. Effects of training were maintained over as long as 7 years (Willis & Schaie, 1994). These data suggest that for many older persons intellectual decline or cohort-related disadvantage (compared to younger peers) may be largely experiential in nature and can be modified by modest intervention efforts.

Intelligence in the Everyday World

Attention has turned to the question of how traditional measures of intelligence relate to performance in real-life circumstances. Measures of so-called practical intelligence often appear to assess situation-specific competence rather than basic components of intelligence that would be widely generalizable. For an examination of practical intelligence from various points of view, see Schaie and Willis (1999).

K. WARNER SCHAIE

See also
  Abilities
  Competence

INTERFERENCE

Interference is a generic term used to describe the disruptive effects of three sources of irrelevant information: concurrent distractors, currently irrelevant memories, and strong but situationally inappropriate responses. All three sources tend to slow correct responding and reduce accuracy. In general, older adults are more susceptible than young adults to each source of interference (Hasher, Zacks, & May, 1999; McDowd, Oseas-Kreger, & Filion, 1995).

Older adults' vulnerability to interference from environmental *distraction* can be seen in visual search, categorization, problem-solving, and reading tasks. When searching for a target in a visual display, the presence of distractors impairs older adults more than it does young adults (e.g., LePage, Stuss, & Richer, 1999). Age differences in errors or slowing will increase with the number of distractors (e.g., Scialfa, Esau, & Joffe, 1998), unless targets and distractors are easily distinguished (e.g., Zeef, Sonke, Kok, Buiten, & Kenemans, 1996) or occur in predictable locations (see Madden & Plude, 1993, for sparing factors).

Age differences in distractor interference are particularly large if the distractors are related to the targets. For example, older adults' reading times are slowed more than those of young adults by distracting words scattered throughout a passage of text (Dywan & Murphy, 1996), and older but not younger adults are further slowed if distractors have meanings related to the passage. In some cases, distractors strongly related to the target can lead to age differences even if they appear in predictable locations. For example, older adults are more affected than younger adults by the nature of distractors in the Remote Associations Test, which asks participants to find the connection between three words (e.g., ship, outer, crawl: SPACE). Distractor words congruent with the solution (e.g., rocket, atmosphere, attic) result in greater benefits for older adults than for young adults, and incongruent distractors (e.g., ocean, inner, floor) result in greater costs (May, 1999). Both younger and older adults are slower to identify the category a word belongs to if that word is flanked by distractors from a different category than if it is flanked by distractors from the same category, but this difference is especially large for older adults (Shaw, 1991). In short, interference from distractors will have a greater impact on older adults' ability to identify and use target information than on that of younger adults. Exceptions occur only when distractors are very distinct from targets.

Interference from distractors (here, irrelevant material that is similar to the target) will also differentially impair the ability of older adults to retrieve a target memory. The irrelevant information may have been learned before (*proactive interference* [PI]) or after (*retroactive interference* [RI]) the targeted information. For example, if a friend moves and changes phone numbers, it may be difficult at first to remember the correct phone number because the memory for the old number gets in the way. Conversely, after the new phone number is well learned, it may be more difficult to remember the previous number.

Interference in *memory* is traditionally studied by using lists of unrelated word pairs in which one element arbitrarily serves as the cue (stimulus) for recall of the other (response). At test, participants are given one of these words (the stimulus word) and asked to remember the other (the response word). Interference can be created by pairing the stimulus word with additional response words in a list presented either before (PI) or after (RI) the to-be-remembered list.

A review of earlier work using this methodology confirms that older adults are more susceptible than young adults to both PI and RI (see Kane & Hasher, 1995). The few exceptions can generally be explained by differences in materials or methodology. These differences include floor effects and the use of list lengths, numbers of lists, or memory measures insensitive to age differences or "young" samples that were actually middle-aged. Proactive interference has also been studied by using other procedures (e.g., Brown-Peterson, release from PI). Here the findings are more mixed, with some investigations finding greater decrements for older adults, and others finding no age differences. Again, the lack of age differences in some studies may be due to methodology: Kane and Hasher (1995) found that those studies that did not show age differences used, on average, many more lists (25.1 lists) than studies that did (7.0 lists). They suggest that the use of many lists may have caused PI to build up for both young and older adults, making age differences difficult to discern.

Although few recent studies have directly addressed the issue of age differences in either PI or RI, they generally support the idea that older adults are more susceptible to both (e.g., LePage, Stuss, & Richer, 1999; May, Hasher, & Kane, 1999). Other studies have found age differences in the major mechanism underlying interference, competition between to-be-remembered information and similar but incorrect information. This type of competition can be investigated by varying the number of items associated with a memory cue. Increasing the number of items associated with a cue makes retrieval of any one of those items slower and more error-prone (Anderson, 1983). For example, learning three facts about an object (e.g., "The potted palm is in the lobby," "The potted palm is in the laundromat," "The potted palm is in the stairwell") makes retrieval of any one fact about that object more difficult than if only one fact is learned about an object (e.g., "The pay phone is in the hall"). The increase in difficulty as more facts "fan off" a single cue and compete with each other at retrieval is referred to as the fan effect. Older adults show larger fan effects than do young adults (Radvansky, Zacks, & Hasher, 1996). However, presenting mul-

tiple pieces of information in a way that allows their integration into a single scene (e.g., "The potted palm is in the hotel lobby," "The pay phone is in the hotel lobby," "The wastebasket is in the hotel lobby") eliminates competition and thus fan effects for both younger and older adults.

Older adults show greater competition from irrelevant information even when explicitly instructed to forget such information, as in directed forgetting studies. Successful directed forgetting is demonstrated by lower memory for "forget" items and greater memory for "remember" items, compared to conditions in which all studied items are to be remembered. Relative to younger adults, older adults remember more "forget" items as a proportion of the total number of items recalled and are more likely to intrude "forget" items when trying to recall "remember" words (Zacks, Radvansky, & Hasher, 1996).

Older adults are also more vulnerable to interference from previously learned behaviors. Interference of this sort is often assessed by the Stroop Test or the Wisconsin Card Sort Test (WCST). Interference in Stroop is measured by comparing the time needed to name the ink color of incompatible color words (e.g., green ink used to spell the word *red*) to that needed to name the ink color of simple stimuli (e.g., colored blocks). Participants must overcome a strong word-reading tendency in order to name the color; interference from the word information results in slower and more inaccurate naming than in the simple condition. Stroop interference is typically greater for older adults than for young adults (e.g., Comalli, Wapner, & Werner, 1962). In the WCST, participants match response cards to key cards on the basis of one of three dimensions (color, shape, or number); the dimension to be sorted on changes without warning after 10 correct trials. Older adults are more likely than young adults to persist in a previously correct but now incorrect response rule (e.g., Kramer, Humphrey, Larish, Logan, & Strayer, 1994). Similarly, older adults have difficulty withholding a category decision when, on rare occasion, a signal sounds to do so (May & Hasher, 1998).

In general, then, older adults are more vulnerable than young adults to interference from concurrent distractors, from currently irrelevant memories, and from strong but inappropriate habitual responses. Age differences in interference proneness may contribute to age differences on many tasks, including those measuring working memory (May, Hasher, & Kane, 1999; McDowd, Oseas-Kreger, & Filion, 1995). In some cases, reducing the role of interference in a task can reduce or even eliminate age differences in performance (e.g., May et al., 1999; Radvansky, Zacks, & Hasher, 1996). Finally, recent work has shown that some age differences in interference can be exaggerated when participants are tested in the afternoon, rather than the morning, a finding tied to age differences in circadian arousal (May, 1999).

CINDY LUSTIG
LYNN HASHER

See also

Cognitive Processes
Learning
Memory and Memory Theory

INTERGENERATIONAL RELATIONSHIPS

Much research in aging focuses on the relationships and interactions among people of different ages or in different age groups. *Intergenerational* relationships are between family members in a lineage—parents and children, grandparents and grandchildren—interacting at the microsocial level. Intergenerational family relations typically reflect varying degrees of solidarity, conflict, ambivalence, and ambiguity.

Solidarity refers to the positive dimensions of sentiment, interaction, and cohesion in intergenerational relations between parents and children or grandparents and grandchildren (Bengtson & Schrader, 1982). Solidarity encompasses six components: (1) *affectual solidarity*, the sentiments and emotional evaluations of a relationship with a parent, child, or grandparent; (2) *associational solidarity*, the type and frequency of interaction between two family members of different generations; (3) *consensual solidarity*, how closely the generations within a family agree on values, opinions, and orientations; (4) *functional solidarity*, the exchange of material and instrumental support and assistance between generations; (5) *normative solidarity*, the

shared expectations about intergenerational support and filial obligations; and (6) *structural solidarity*, the opportunities the generations have for interaction based on the number, gender, and geographic proximity of intergenerational family members.

Research on solidarity indicates that strong emotional and instrumental bonds connect the generations of contemporary American families. Rather than either being very close or distant, families vary considerably. Silverstein and Bengtson (1997) find five general types of relationships between adult children and their parents: (1) tight-knit, where children engage with parents on all six dimensions of solidarity; (2) sociable, with interaction, proximity, shared values, and closeness but not exchange and support; (3) obligatory, including frequent contact, proximity, and exchange of assistance, but relations lack closeness and shared values; (4) intimate but distant, characterized by closeness and shared vales but without proximity, frequent contact, or exchange of assistance; and (5) detached, as children and parents are not engaged on any dimension of solidarity.

Intergenerational solidarity has positive consequences for both younger and older generations. Positive memories of early-childhood relationships with their parents are associated with greater concern and support for aging parents by adult children (Silverstein, Parrott, & Bengtson, 1995). Aging parents' solidarity with adult children also enhances well-being and decreases their mortality risks (Wang, Silverstein, & Bengtson, 1999). In addition, the greater economic security of today's aging cohorts makes it possible for older family members to provide instrumental support to younger family members in need. These new links may strengthen older adults' roles within the family while bolstering the younger generation and family cohesion (Kohli, 1999).

Because conflict is a common element of human interaction, conflict is often a part of family life. Disagreement, competition, and conflict can coexist with order, stability, and cooperation within the family and between generations (Bengtson, Rosenthal, & Burton, 1996). *Conflict* encompasses: (1) the collision of individuals' agendas and interests, (2) tactics or responses to the clash of interests, or (3) hostility toward others (Straus, 1979). The frequency and degree of intergenerational disagreements, arguments, tension, criticism, and/or violence represent conflict. Families typically embody elements of both solidarity and conflict, rather than extremes representing either harmony and refuge or anger and abuse.

Research on intergenerational conflict shows that adult children and their parents tend to disagree on a variety of issues. Clarke, Preston, Raskin, and Bengtson (1999) identified six general sources of intergenerational conflict between aging parents and adult children in open-ended responses to the Longitudinal Study of Generations surveys: (1) communication and interaction style; (2) habits and lifestyles; (3) child-rearing practices and values; (4) politics, religion, and ideology; (5) work orientation; and (6) household maintenance. These findings suggest that conflict is an integral part of ongoing intergenerational relations, and further exploration in this area is warranted.

Family relationships typically produce both positive and negative sentiments, such as affection and resentment, as well as conflicting roles, such as mother of children and caregiver of aged parents. Luescher and Pillemer (1998) propose ambivalence as a new perspective on the study of intergenerational relationships. Intergenerational *ambivalence* connotes contradictions in relationships both at the psychological level, where people experience contradictory feelings, motivations, and cognitions, and at the sociological level, where social norms, roles, and statuses come into conflict in intergenerational relations. Ambivalence stems from tensions between autonomy and dependence; conflicting norms and values about family, mutual dependency, and obligations; status transitions and their inherent gains and losses; and ambiguous expectations accompanying changes in family structures and roles. Because ambivalence is difficult to operationalize and measure, research in this area is scant. As a result, little is known about the extent of ambivalence in intergenerational relations or its causes and consequences.

Changes in family structures and cultural norms surrounding family life contribute to greater *ambiguity* in intergenerational relations. Ambiguity is reflected in undefined roles and uncertainty over expectations for relationships, such as contemporary stepparent/stepchildren relations. Given the incredible structural diversity of families today, new conceptual approaches to understanding intergenerational relations are needed. Pauline Boss (1999) explores the concept of boundary ambiguity in in-

tergenerational relations. Boundary ambiguity in intergenerational relations can occur when family members are physically present but psychologically absent (as in the case of family members with severe Alzheimer's disease) or when family members are physically absent but psychologically present (as in the case of some noncustodial divorced fathers with minor-age children). The body of evidence built by Boss and her colleagues exploring boundary ambiguity in families and its consequences suggests that ambiguity offers new ways of thinking about intergenerational relationships as they are affected by trends in nonmarital childbearing, divorce, cohabitation, and remarriage.

Intergenerational relationships involve solidarity and conflict, positive and negative feelings, tensions and uncertainties. Some past research and popular portrayals tend to characterize the family either as harmonious and idyllic or as dysfunctional and abusive. Such extremes are inaccurate representations that ignore the complexities of the American family both past and present. Future research on aging should take into account the multiple facets of family life, their transformations over time, and their effects on intergenerational relationships.

J. Beth Mabry
Maria Schmeeckle
Vern L. Bengtson

See also
  Cohorts
  Family
  Generational Equity
  Generations
  Grandparent/Grandchild Relationships
  Grandparents Raising Grandchildren

INTERGENERATIONAL STAKE HYPOTHESIS

Two decades ago, Bengtson and Kuypers (1971) proposed the "developmental stake hypothesis" to explain the generational bias they found in perceptions of parent-child relationships: middle-age parents consistently reported higher levels of closeness and consensus in the parent-child relationship, relative to the reports of their postadolescent children. They hypothesized that such systematic contrasts emerge because each generation has different developmental concerns, and in consequence each has a different "stake" in their common intergenerational relationship. Parents, they suggested, are more concerned with the continuity of values they have found important over the course of their lives and with the closeness of relationships in the family they have founded, so they tend to minimize conflict and overstate solidarity with their offspring. Adolescent and young adult children, by contrast, are more motivated to establish autonomy from their parents in values and social relationships and have less commitment to the parent-child bond, so they tend to understate intergenerational solidarity and overstate intergenerational contrasts. Thus, according to Bengtson and Kuypers's original hypothesis, contrasts in life-course developmental needs explain differences in the stake each generation has in intergenerational cohesion, continuity, and conflict; and these contrasts in turn lead to generational biases in the perception of parent-child relationships.

Since 1971 the developmental stake hypothesis has been referred to as the generational stake or, most recently, the intergenerational stake, to acknowledge that social-structural factors, based on generational location itself, may be as inconsistent as contrasts in life-course individual development levels in accounting for cross-generational differences in perception. By virtue of their greater resources and lineage position in the family, parents invest more in their children than their children invest in them. The greater input of parents relative to their children motivates them to perceive a closer parent-child bond than their children find necessary.

Intergenerational stake is an inclusive term that refers to both the developmental stake (individual-level) and the generational stake (sociostructural-level) hypotheses. This term better connotes the cross-generational nature of the phenomenon, and it reflects the fact that the intergenerational stake hypothesis incorporates two predictions: (1) parent's descriptions of parent-child relationships will generally be more positive than children's descriptions, and (2) differential investment as well as differential development may account for cross-generational biases in perception.

The intergenerational stake hypothesis has become a useful explanatory framework, as indicated by the number of studies using it to explain empiri-

cal findings (it has been cited in over 100 articles to date). Other studies have replicated much of the original formulation of the hypothesis and have refined or extended it. For example, Giarrusso, Stallings, and Bengtson (1995) documented that the generational bias between middle-aged parents and postadolescent children was maintained across 20 years of adult life. Marshall (1995) found evidence of the generational bias at even later stages of the life course; elder parent's ratings of affectual and consensual solidarity were higher than their middle-aged child's. Fingerman's (1995, 1996) research on White mother-daughter dyads suggested that the generational bias includes descriptions of conflict as well as solidarity: mothers were more likely than daughters to downplay the conflict in their relationship. Caldwell, Antonucci, and Jackson (1998) extended this finding on conflict to African American mothers and their teenage daughters. Finally, Lynott and Roberts (1997) revealed differences in the magnitude of intergenerational stake phenomenon by gender and political ideology: women and political conservatives perceived less of a gap between the generations than men or political liberals did. However, not every study has found support for the intergenerational stake phenomenon. Munro, Keating, and Zhang (1995), using a sample of farming families, did not find a difference in the stake parents and children had in their family or farm. Munro et al. attributed this null finding to the greater interdependence of generations jointly engaged in the business of farming.

The intergenerational stake phenomenon suggests a caution for research based on individual-level, self-report data on parent-child relationships, because each generation views their joint relationship differently.

ROSEANN GIARRUSSO

See also
Social Theories of Aging

INTERNATIONAL ASSOCIATION OF GERONTOLOGY

The International Association of Gerontology (IAG) was founded early in 1950. The primary purpose of the IAG is to improve the communication within and across disciplines and between scholars and scientists of all nations (Thomae & Maddox, 1982). The IAG strives to maintain a close working relationship with such organizations as the United Nations, the World Health Organization, and the Pan American Organization. A definitive history of IAG has been written by Shock (1988).

The IAG is primarily composed of member societies representing many nations throughout the world. Individual memberships can be granted to persons who reside in nations that do not have a member society. The IAG is governed by a council representing the various member nations. The executive committee is composed of a president, a secretary, a treasurer, an immediate past president, and a president-elect. The officers of the IAG, past and present, represent a diversity of scientific disciplines, including biological, behavioral, social, and clinical sciences concerned with aging and the health and well-being of the elderly.

The international congresses of the IAG are scientific meetings, and the programs are composed of sections that include medicine (geriatric), biology, behavioral and social sciences, and social research and planning, as well as interdisciplinary symposia. The First International Congress was held in Liege, Belgium, July 9–12, 1950; the second was held in St. Louis, Missouri, USA, in 1951. Since that date, an international congress sponsored by IAG has been held every 3 to 4 years. The duration of each congress has been 5 to 6 days. The places and the years of the congresses are as follows: England (1954); Merano, Italy (1957); San Francisco (1960); Copenhagen (1963); Vienna (1966); Washington, DC (1969); Kiev (1972); Jerusalem (1975); Tokyo (1978); Hamburg (1981); and New York (1985). The 1985 international congress, held in New York City, was attended by more than 3,000 registrants representing 52 nations. The 14th International Congress, held in Acapulco, Mexico in 1989, reported 2,577 registrants. In 1993 the 15th congress, in Budapest, Hungary, registered 2,973 registrants and 258 accompanying persons representing 52 nations. In 1997 the congress was held in Australia and in 2001 in Canada.

In the 4 years between international congresses, regional meetings are held. They are set up by the regional committees in the four regions of the world established by the IAG: Asia/Oceania, Europe, Latin America, and North America. Regional meet-ings have been held in Budapest; Singapore; Brighton, England (1987); and Bangkok (1987).

The Sandoz Prize is awarded by the IAG every 2 years. This prize, which includes a substantial monetary award, is for outstanding contributions to gerontology, with an emphasis upon interdisciplinary research.

EWALD W. BUSSE
Updated by
EDIT BEREGI

See also
Organizations in Aging

INTERNATIONAL FEDERATION ON AGEING

The International Federation on Ageing (IFA) is a private, nonprofit organization, founded in 1973, linking approximately 151 associations that represent or serve older persons at the grass-roots level in some 54 nations around the world. IFA is committed to the dignity, independence, and empowerment of older persons. Through IFA, individuals and organizations that work with older persons or on their behalf can exchange information and ideas, communicate common concerns, share practical applications, and learn from each other's experience. IFA strives for a future where everyone is working together to advance the well-being and active involvement of all persons in an aging world population.

Through the service of committed older volunteers, IFA serves as an advocate for the well-being of older persons around the world with the following organizations with which it has consultative status:

- Economic and Social Council of the United Nations (ECOSOC)
- International Labor Organization (ILO)
- World Health Organization (WHO)
- United Nations Educational, Scientific and Cultural Organization (UNESCO)
- Council for Europe
- South Asian Association for Regional Cooperation

IFA also has established an informal network of Ministers of Aging around the world with which it shares information and holds periodic meetings.

IFA's *Declaration of Rights and Responsibilities of Older Persons* became the model for the *UN Principles for Older Persons*, adopted by the UN General Assembly in 1991. And the *Montreal Declaration*, launched at IFA's Global Conference on Ageing in 1999, put forth some forceful recommendations for strengthening activities on behalf of aging within the UN and among member states.

IFA promotes the international exchange of information through its quarterly journal, *Ageing International,* which carries accounts of innovative programs for older persons from all over the world. These accounts are edited to be practical and to encourage cross-cultural and cross-national adaptation. In addition, *Ageing International* features articles on cross-national trends and gives special attention to selected country developments and policy issues. IFA also publishes a monthly newsletter for its members, *Intercom.*

Other publications include titles such as *Empowering Older People, Rethinking Worklife Options for Older Persons, Shared Living: A Viable Alternative, Toward Planning for Aging in Local Communities,* and *Older Persons and Their Families in a Changing Village Society.*

IFA is committed to providing a worldwide forum on issues and concerns of aging and to fostering the development of associations and agencies that serve or represent older persons. Information exchanges are promoted through the organization of biennial Global Conferences on Ageing. Conferences have been held in India, Israel, South Africa, and Quebec, Canada. A global conference is planned in Argentina in 2000 and in Australia in 2002. Seminars and training programs are also available.

Full IFA membership is reserved for nongovernmental, national, voluntary organizations that represent or serve older persons. Governmental and corporate support is extended through associate membership. The number of individual memberships is also growing.

IFA is headquartered in Canada (425 rue Viger Ouest, Bureau 520, Montreal, PQ, Canada H2Z 1X2. Tel.: 514/396-3358; fax: 514/396-3378; E-mail: *ifa@citenet.net*). Visit IFA's website at: *http://www.ifa-fiv.org.*

DANIEL THURSZ

See also
International Association of Gerontology
International Perspectives
Organizations in Aging
World Assembly on Aging

INTERNATIONAL GERONTOLOGY
See
International Association of Gerontology
International Longevity Center
International Perspectives
Longitudinal Studies: Europe
Longitudinal Studies of Aging
Modernization Theory
Third World Aging
World Assembly on Aging
World Health Organization

INTERNATIONAL LONGEVITY CENTER

The International Longevity Center (ILC) is a non-profit, nonpartisan, independent organization (with 501C3 status) devoted to the study of population aging and longevity and their impact on society. The ILC is international, interdisciplinary, and intergenerational. Its mission is to help societies prepare for aging in positive and productive ways. ILC priorities are the promotion of a productive work life and an active (healthy) life expectancy through education, research, and policy initiatives.

The ILC was co-founded in 1990 by Robert N. Butler in the United States (ILC-USA) and Shigeo Morioka in Japan (ILC-Japan). It now includes sister organizations in France, the United Kingdom, and the Dominican Republic. Future plans include the development of centers around the world, with an emphasis on the developing nations.

The ILC-USA research program involves such studies as an analysis of housing arrangements of older persons in selected developed countries (Muller, Gnanasekaran, & Knapp, 1998), the disparities in retirement wealth between White and minority households (Honig, 2000), and the transmission of values across generations in the United States and Japan (Muller & Silver, 1995).

The Cities Project studies health care and social services delivery to children and older persons in Tokyo, London, Paris, New York, and Santo Domingo.

Communication and education programs encompass a variety of areas. Publications include the following:

> *Life in an Older America* (Butler, Grossman, & Oberlink, 1999) assembles insights from many of the nation's leading analysts on population aging. A wide range of issues, including Social Security, Medicare, pensions, family savings, and productivity are explored.
>
> *Cognitive Decline: Strategies for Prevention* (Fillit & Butler, 1997) examines the problems associated with understanding the aging brain: whether decline is inevitable and if there are practical steps that can be taken to prevent or minimize cognitive decline in late life.
>
> *The International Longevity Review 2000* (ILC, 2000) presents annual trends in population aging.
>
> *Longevity and Quality of Life* is the proceedings of the UNESCO Congress on the "Worldwide Revolution in Longevity and Quality of Life," held in Paris in May 1998 (Butler & Jasmin, 2000).

The Visiting Scholars Program will be drawn from diverse academic disciplines of labor and health economics, epidemiology, the humanities, and ethics, among others. The scholars will spend a sabbatical period at the center, conducting research on population aging.

The Partnerships Program includes Harris Interactive (which polls in 82 countries), Canyon Ranch, and the American Museum of Natural History.

ROBERT N. BUTLER

INTERNATIONAL PERSPECTIVES

Until recent decades, gerontology and geriatrics were professional and academic interests primarily in the United States and some Western European countries. Consequently, some early observers re-marked that the "problems of aging" appear to be really the problems of capitalistic sociopolitical systems. This conclusion is increasingly less appropriate, because aging populations are observed worldwide, and aging in less-developed nations is occurring at a very rapid rate (see "Demography"). By the year 2025, less-developed nations worldwide are expected to have twice as many older adults as the total older populations in more-developed nations.

Cross-national comparative research on aging and on aging problems has developed significantly since the pioneering work of Leo Simmons (1960), Shanas, Townsend, Wedderburn, Friis, Milhoj, and Stehouwer (1968), and Cowgill and Holmes (1972). An international handbook of aging (Palmore, 1980; 1993) was published over a decade ago, and comparative anthropological and sociological monographs and collections have appeared (see, e.g., Keith, 1990; Maddox & Lawton, 1993). Palmore specifically characterized the experience of aging in Japan in the 1970s, in contrast to the United States, and was joined by a Japanese colleague a decade later (Palmore & Maeda, 1985) in revisiting and reaffirming much of their earlier characterization of older Japanese as "honorable elders." Maddox and Lawton (1993) have edited a volume whose chapters explore the differential responses of aging individuals and societies to the prevalent forces of social change in the United States, Canada, Mexico, Spain, and Pacific Rim countries. This volume provides extensive coverage of publications on aging in Canada.

As the differential experience of aging individuals and societies around the world has been explored, the capacity and willingness of modern societies to provide for the well-being of older adults has been established. Societies differ widely in their capacity to ensure income and health in the later years. Average life expectancy at birth is increasing everywhere, ensuring an increasingly large population of elders worldwide. Although some societies do not have an established and reliable social security system, many do, and the historic development and current status of such programs internationally are increasingly well documented (Tracy & Pampel, 1991; Williamson & Pampel, 1993).

The International Association of Gerontology (IAG; see entry) involves professional associations of gerontologists from over 50 countries. Its periodic international scientific meetings have had a large attendance over the years when held in the United States, Israel, the Soviet Union, Japan, West Germany, Mexico, Australia, and Hungary. The 1997 meeting took place in Australia and the 2001 meeting is scheduled in Canada. The IAG has periodically cooperated with the United Nations and the World Health Organization in the implementation of initiatives in aging. The International Federation of Aging (see entry) is a nonprofit, nongovernmental worldwide federation of organizations serving older adults.

Professional publications in gerontology and geriatrics are numerous in the United States and are also found in Canada and in various European and Asian countries. The English journals *Ageing* and *Ageing and Society* are widely read in Europe. Major journals on aging in the United States publish research and scholarship from throughout the world

Gerontological and geriatric research in Europe and the United States has produced some notable longitudinal evidence about aging populations illustrated by a number of accessible data sets described in this volume (see "Longitudinal Data Sets in Aging").

ERDMAN B. PALMORE
GEORGE MADDOX

INTERNATIONAL PSYCHOGERIATRIC ASSOCIATION

Founded in 1980, the International Psychogeriatric Association (IPA) is dedicated to providing health care professionals throughout the world with the most up-to-date information concerning the behavioral and biological aspects of mental health of the elderly. IPA encourages a broad, comprehensive, and interdisciplinary approach, encompassing psychiatry, neurology, general medicine, pharmacology, nursing, psychology, social work, and the behavioral and biological sciences.

Because of the continued and unprecedented aging of the world population, the need for improved understanding of the problems of the elderly has grown substantially. IPA strives to promote

understanding and consensus about psychogeriatric issues on an international and cross-cultural basis.

By emphasizing multidisciplinary and interdisciplinary services, education, and research, IPA promotes integration of multiple perspectives of individuals in a biopsychosocial context, with consideration of biological, psychological, environmental, socioeconomic, and spiritual factors. By combining the efforts and skills of its professionals, IPA attempts to promote a field that has a synergistic effect, in which the total exceeds the sum of the parts. By providing multiple perspectives, we discover a greater whole.

Membership in the IPA is open to all health care professionals from various disciplines, including physicians, psychologists, nurses, and social workers, who are interested in the behavioral and biological aspects of mental health of the aged. In 1995, IPA had more than 1,000 members from 49 countries.

IPA meetings are held twice a year. Every 2 years one meeting is an international congress that covers a broad spectrum of important issues in the field of psychogeriatrics. IPA Research Awards in Psychogeriatrics are given to the three best original research papers in psychogeriatrics submitted to the IPA congresses.

IPA publishes a peer-reviewed journal, *International Psychogeriatrics,* featuring articles on research, clinical practice, and international developments, and a quarterly newsletter. The headquarters of IPA are at 5700 Old Orchard Road, First Floor, Skokie, IL 60077-1057.

MANFRED BERGENER

See also
Geriatric Psychiatry
International Association of Gerontology
Organizations in Aging

INTERNET AND E-MAIL RESOURCES

The explosion of Web-based sites on aging has mirrored the overall growth of the World Wide Web. It began in 1994. Early guides to this growth were published (Post, 1996–1997), and on-line subject directories of sites on aging were developed. As the number of sites approached 1,500 the directories became too time-consuming for their human creators to maintain, and at this writing the only major one remaining is the U.S. Administration on Aging home page at *http://www.aoa.gov*.

This is the most comprehensive site for professionals, students, and caregivers. It includes information about government legislation, policy, and funding; an Eldercare Locator that can be searched by zip code for such specific local community resources, such as state and local Area Agencies on Aging; a Resource Directory for Older People, with the home pages of many organizations; a "Web Sites on Aging" section at *http://www.aoa.gov/ agingsites/default.htm* with links to nongovernmental resources in 50 different topics, ranging from Alzheimer's disease, caregiving, disability, diversity, and falls, to intergenerational programs, international aging, mental health, rural aging, and women; and a section of links to on-line sources of statistical information about older persons.

There are so many sites on the different topics of aging that it is safe to assume there is at least one home page for every interest and organization. If you don't know where to begin, start with the list of Web sites at the AoA page mentioned above or use a search engine like Metacrawler at *http:// www.Go2Net.com*. Look for sites that are sponsored by authoritative sources, that give the date when they were last updated and it is recent, and that include links to similar resources and these are currently maintained. If a site does not have what you expect to find there, look for another one; there probably is one.

SeniorNet at *http://www.seniornet.com* and Third Age Media at *http://www.thirdage.com*, a major Internet portal for seniors, were both started by Mary Furlong (1997), the first person to promote the use of computers by older persons. Another major site for this group is the American Association of Retired Persons, with a home page at *http://www.aarp.org*.

In-depth studies of the patterns and effects of computer, Internet, and E-mail use by older persons are becoming available. These include the impact of technology on older persons (Finn, 1997), studies of the use of E-mail by residents of retirement communities and nursing homes (White, McConnell, Clipp, Bynum, Teague, Navas, et al., 1999),

and analyses of E-mail requests and discussion group threads on on-line sites (Ellis, 1999; Mahoney, 1998). Statistics on the number of seniors who own computers and are on-line range from 14% to 22%. One authoritative source for use statistics is the age charts in the Appendix of the U.S. Census Bureau's 1999 report, *Falling Through the Net: Defining the Digital Divide*, at *http://www.ntia.doc. gov/ntiahome/fttn99/*.

The home pages of the American Association of Homes and Services for the Aging at *http:// www.aahsa.org* and its affiliated state associations and member facilities and Nursing Home Compare at *http://www.medicare.gov/nursing/home.asp*, a Health Care Financing Administration on-line database of information about every Medicare- and Medicaid-certified nursing home in the United States, are useful for long-term care administrators.

Advice on creating home pages for professionals is available at *http://www.aoa.gov/webresources/ default.htm* and for older people at *http:// www.spry.org/WebGuide/webguideform.htm*.

Most professional associations have home pages. Some of the major ones are the Gerontological Society of America at *http://www.geron.org*, the American Society on Aging at *http://www.asaging.org*, the American Geriatrics Society at *http:// www.americangeriatrics.org*, and the International Federation on Ageing at *http://www.ifs-fiv.org*.

Almost all gerontology and geriatrics departments at institutions of higher learning have one or more home pages for their academic, research, or clinical activities. These home pages are often difficult to find and there is no single comprehensive current on-line source for them. In the meantime use the links in the "Educational Programs" and "Medical Facilities/Programs" sections under each individual state and country at "Internet and E-Mail Resources on Aging" at *http://www.aoa.gov/ aoa/PAGES/jpostlst.html*. Research links will also be found at this site in both the "Aging in General" and "Alzheimer's Disease" sections under "General Resources."

The home pages of the National Institute on Aging at *http://www.nih.gov/nia* and the Alzheimer Web at *http://www.alzweb.org* specialize in biomedical research. Two other useful sites for researchers are the National Archive of Computerized Data on Aging at *http://www.icpsr.umich.edu/ nacda/* and Internet Resources for Grant Seekers

in Aging at *http://www.aoa.gov/aoa/PAGES/
grants.html*.

At last check, the *Alzheimer's Disease Review*
at *http://www.coa.uky.edu/ADReview/* is the one
journal in aging available only in electronic format.
As the thorny issues of peer review and copyright
are resolved, more journals and publications will
become available in full text electronically. A challenge will be to stay abreast of expanding sources
of information available in an increasing variety
of formats.

JOYCE A. POST

See also

Communication Technologies and Older Adults
Health Information Through Telecommunica-
tion
Organizations in Aging

INTERVIEWING

Interviewing is a special kind of conversation in
which the only purpose is the transmission of information and not interpersonal relationships. This action results in an unequal relation between the participants, with one giving the information, and the
other eliciting it. The interviewer defines the situation and sets the agenda; even the different names
given to the interviewee reflect the control exerted
by the interviewer.

In an interview, observations may be sought that
cannot be obtained through other means; in this
case the interviewee is an informant or source. Information about an interviewee as representative of
a group may be sought, as in the survey interview; in
this case, the interviewee is a respondent. Finally,
an interview may seek understanding about the interviewee for a particular personal purpose, as in
a clinical or psychotherapeutic interview; in this
case, the interviewee is a client or patient. Although
basic abilities of the interviewer can be standardized
across all situations, the stances of the interviewee
can differ according to the situation. The survey
interview is a practice peculiar to present-day society, and the theory and practice of interviewing in
itself have been worked out primarily by practitioners in this field. Most practitioner applications,

for instance oral history (informant interviewing)
or clinical work (patient interviewing), assume that
there are facts to be discovered, and they are little
concerned with the interviewing process as a special
issue. Thus, analysis and research has been conducted mainly in survey research, but the main
results are applicable to the other situations, especially in relation to older interviewees (Back, 1993).

An advantage of this viewpoint is that accuracy
can be employed as criterion, as the answers can
be checked by other interviews and outside facts.
Two aspects of the respondent become relevant in
the performance in the interview: cognition and
motivation. Motivation becomes conspicuous as a
barrier in the process, especially for the professionals using a psychodynamic approach, where such
concepts as resistance become important.

In general, systematic research on the validity
of interviews has found the effect of age on the
accuracy of survey interviews to be small. Three
exhaustive studies of respondent effects (Gove,
1982; Herzog & Dielman, 1985; Sudman & Bradburn, 1974) found age to be an unimportant variable
regarding biasing responses. In a study designed
for determining the accuracy of factual information
in interviewing the aged, Rodgers and Herzog
(1987) found no difference in many measures of
accuracy; in the remaining measures no consistent
trend for difference in accuracy could be discovered.

Extreme conditions produce cognitive constraints: sensory deficiencies in hearing and vision,
disabilities in speech and writing, mental disturbances, and general weakness make interviews difficult, if not impossible. Such conditions lengthen
the process, tax the patience of the interviewer, and
lead to the exclusion of older respondents from
many surveys.

Subtler than these major constraints but of equal
importance are general cognitive habits that interfere with the interviewing process. In cognitive
organization, we may distinguish between storage
and retrieval as aspects of memory. Both aspects
of memory can be affected by aging.

Age seems to be important in interviews when
recall of past events and the time of their occurrence
is desired. Sudman and Bradburn (1974) found that
older people will recall fewer past events and are
more likely to "telescope" them, that is put them
within a shorter period, usually within the period

for which the information is desired. However, this is true for only respondents older than 55 years. In a survey, these tendencies may compensate for each other—older respondents may remember fewer incidents overall but bunch them into the required period. However, in a medical interview, telescoping alone would lead to overstating of symptoms within, say, the last month without any compensation by smaller overall recall.

In interviews covering the whole life course, older respondents tend to recall more earlier events than later ones. This may be due to the influence of the interviewer, when personal history is elicited, especially if the interviewer has psychoanalytic leanings. However, in questions about national and world events experiences in adolescence and early adulthood are more often mentioned than later ones (Schuman, Rieger, & Gaidys, 1994; Schuman & Scott, 1989). Stress on events during the early periods of life would lead to preference in recall of earlier over recent events in older people.

Retrieval of information in interviews can be related to age because of ways in which surveys are typically conducted. Social survey managers have trained younger cohorts to respond to interviews with short, codable answers and also to believe interviewees have opinions about practically everything; this represents a part of the general culture of the mass media in which collecting over a short interval disconnected simultaneous events in the newspapers and newscasts by individuals is expected and accepted (Anderson, 1991). In contrast, the culture of earlier generations emphasized storytelling and embedding of events into connected sequences; this difference reinforces with age the general tendency of relying more on reminiscence and less on categorization. Both trends lead to sequences of events being connected as units and may make it difficult to extract the units of information requested in a survey. Conversely, the tendency to give long, connected stories makes elderly persons good subjects for oral histories where they typically are informants about events of personal importance. The aged may have been good witnesses to events about which only they still have knowledge (Riesman & Benney, 1956).

The findings of a negative effect of aging in interviewing may be surprising but may be explained by the way the issue has been studied. Survey interviewing is a relatively recent technique in social research, and efforts have been made to justify this approach as equally applicable to all population groups, including the aged. The application of cognitive theory to survey interviewing is more recent (Jobe & Loftus, 1991; Schwartz & Sudman, 1992). Here the response in the interview is seen as a cognitive task, influenced by the whole setting of a particular question. The answer of an interviewer is expected and depends on the structure of the whole situation that can influence the performance in this task; the form of the questionnaire, the experience and current interests of the respondent, the ease in using such easy escapes from making any effort (such as agreement, nondifferentiation, acceptance of the status quo, or "don't know" response) can influence answers (Krosnick, 1991; Schwarz & Scheuring, 1988). But the influence of age on these maneuvers in interviewing mediated by such variables as restriction of interest, difference in standard of comparison to aging, although plausible, has been little explored. One study has indicated that older respondents are more influenced by the method of inquiry than younger ones (Rodgers, Herzog, & Andrews, 1988); this may be a promising direction of research.

KURT W. BACK

See also
   Cohort Analysis
   Multidimensional Functional Assessment
   Research Methods

INTROVERSION

In Jungian (1923) psychology, as in some dictionary definitions, *introversion* is used to mean an inward, subjective orientation, a concern for and interest in the self rather than the environment. In this sense, the introvert is absorbed in his or her own thoughts, feelings, and values, and may be described as reflective or meditative. The term *introversion* also is used by many psychologists to refer not to thoughtfulness, but to the low end of a broad dimension of personality traits that include sociability, adventurousness, assertiveness, activity, and cheerfulness. In this sense, the introvert is reserved, cautious, unassertive, low-keyed, and sober. These two meanings are entirely distinct, for the reflective person is as likely to be sociable as reserved, and the individual who is oriented to the environment is as likely to be cautious as adventurous in his or her approach to it. Psychologists dispute the proper use of the term (Guilford, 1977), but it appears that the second definition corresponds more closely to the organization of traits actually found in most individuals.

It is widely believed that introversion increases with age; an evaluation of that claim requires attention to the two different meanings of introversion. Inner orientation in the Jungian sense is not easily measured. Using the Thematic Apperception Test, a projective instrument in which individuals are asked to create a story to fit a picture presented to them, Neugarten (1964) reported that older respondents evidenced a greater preoccupation with inner life, less emotional attachment to the world, and a movement from active to passive mastery. Interviewers also inferred "a lessened sense of relatedness to others" (p. 189) among older subjects. However, when more objective measures of social functioning were employed, there were no apparent age differences.

Introversion as the opposite of social extraversion can be more easily studied using standard personality inventories. Longitudinal studies show more evidence of stability than change. Douglas and Arenberg (1978) reported small maturational declines in Activity level on the Guilford-Zimmerman Temperament Survey (GZTS; Guilford, Zimmerman, & Guilford, 1976) but no changes in Ascendance or Sociability in a sample of 336 men retested after 7 years. Costa and McCrae (1992) examined peer ratings of personality for a sample of adults aged 31 to 81; over a 7-year interval there was no evidence of change in introversion-extraversion for either men or women. However, cross-sectional studies, which can cover a larger portion of the adult life span, often detect small increases in social introversion (McCrae, Costa, de Lima, Simões, Ostendorf, Angleitner, et al., 1999).

Individual differences in introversion-extraversion are highly stable in adulthood. Leon, Gillum, Gillum, and Gouze (1979), for example, found a stability coefficient of .74 for the MMPI Social Introversion scale over a period of 30 years in a group of 71 men initially middle-aged. Peer ratings of extraversion over a 7-year interval showed retest

correlations of .78 for men and .81 for women (Costa & McCrae, 1992). Introverts remain introverts, and extraverts remain extraverts across the adult life span. Intervention programs aimed at providing social opportunities for the elderly should recognize that there are stable individual differences in the desire for social contact. Not all older men and women enjoy socializing, nor should they be expected to.

ROBERT R. MCCRAE

See also
Locus of Control
Personality

INVERTEBRATE MODELS
See
Models for the Study of Aging: Flies
Models for the Study of Aging: Nematodes

ISOLATION

Social isolation is generally used to denote an absence of social interaction, contacts, and relationships with family, neighbors, and society at large. The term *isolation* has diverse meanings in the gerontological literature. Thus, Weiss (1973) refers to social isolation (i.e., without a social network) and to emotional isolation (i.e., absence of an attachment figure). Issues of isolation are generally considered in the literature dealing with social supports and networks but have also been included in research on health risk variables (Strawbridge & Wallhagen, 1999). Isolation should be distinguished from loneliness, the latter reflecting the subjective state of negative feelings that may be associated with isolation (Wenger, Davies, Shahtahmasebi, & Scott, 1996). Isolation is sometimes defined as living alone. However, although most isolated persons live alone, only a fraction of those living alone are isolated.

Extreme social isolation, as reflected in total absence of meaningful relationships or absence of daily social contacts, is rather infrequent among the elderly. In an early large-scale study of aging in three industrial societies, only about 4% of elderly in the United States, Denmark, and Britain were found to be extremely isolated (Townsend, 1968). These findings were confirmed in later studies, over the next 30 years. Thus, only 4% of the elderly were found to have no companion (Atchley, 1994a). Similarly, 4.3% of African American older women were found to be isolated, in a rural community study (LaVeist, Sellers, Brown, Elliott, & Nickerson, 1997). Even among disabled older women, complete social isolation appeared low (3%), although relative social isolation appeared much more common (i.e., 23%) (Sinosick, Kasper, & Phillips, 1998).

Social isolation does not generally emerge as a phenomenon in late life. Most elderly isolates have a lifelong history of withdrawal and may have long-term personality traits that foster a solitary existence. Accordingly, social isolation is significantly higher among elderly persons with paranoid symptoms than among those without such symptoms (Forsell & Henderson, 1998). At the same time, experiences of trauma earlier in people's lives may predispose them to later-life isolation (Kahana, Kahana, Harel, Kelly, Monaghan, & Holland, 1998). In a national probability sample of persons aged 65 and over, the probability of isolation was strongly determined by the childless status of the older persons, but this effect is tempered by the person's health status and occupational class (Bachrach, 1980). However, elderly people who are spouseless or have no children often find support from others and do not experience isolation (Marcil-Gratton & Legare, 1992). Among the aged, isolation from relatives and friends was also found to be related to poor functional health (Thompson & Heller, 1990), incontinence, and disability (Sinosick, Kasper, & Phillips, 1998). Other physical limitations contributing to isolation include a decline in hearing and vision (Dugan & Kivett, 1994; Sinosick et al., 1998). Stigmatizing illness, such as HIV infection, also increases the risk of isolation (Rickard, 1995). Dementia patients and their caregivers represent other groups at high risk of isolation (Parsons, 1999).

Although social isolation is involuntary for most older persons, in some instances it may be the result of increasing introversion or disengagement from society on the part of the individual (Cumming & Henry, 1961). However, research has not generally supported the notions of personality changes in late life that could bring about such isolation (Costa & McCrae, 1980).

An "autonomy model" of aging also has been suggested (Cohler, 1983), in which elderly persons want to minimize dependency and, in so doing, may limit their involvement with others in order to emphasize their self reliance and to avoid being a burden to others.

Involuntary late-life isolation has been attributed to mental illness, environmental circumstance, and social role losses (Bennett, 1980). Bereavement in general and widowhood in particular are seen as resulting in social isolation. Widowhood is often accompanied by loneliness (Atchley, 1994a). Physical impairments, loss of mobility, and relocation of older persons, and/or friends also may contribute to late-life social isolation (Eckert, 1990; Sinosick, Kasper, & Phillips, 1998). Furthermore, it appears that a combination of role losses, infirmity, and distance from kin interacts to place the elderly at far greater risk of social isolation (Rubinstein, Lubben, & Mintzer, 1994).

For special populations of high-risk elderly, social isolation has been brought about by an interaction of personal characteristics, life events, and societal influences. The deinstitutionalized mentally ill aged, elderly urban dwellers living in inner city neighborhoods, and residents of single room occupancy (SRO) hotels comprise such subgroups.

Social isolation and withdrawal have been found to be associated with negative psychosocial outcomes (LaRue, Dessonville, & Jarvik, 1985; Wenger, Davies, Shahtahmasebi, & Scott, 1996). Thus, both physical and social isolation from family and friends were found to be related to feelings of loneliness among a group of hospitalized elderly (Proffitt & Byrne, 1993). Chappell and Badger (1989) found that several facets of social isolation (absence of companions and confidantes) are associated with low levels of psychological well-being. Similarly, Thompson and Heller (1990) found that elderly women who were isolated had poorer psychological well-being than did their nonisolated counterparts. It has also been contended that social isolation imposed on elderly is a form of elder abuse (Wolf, 1997). Social isolation causes a reduction in the supports available to older persons and hence renders them less capable of coping with late-life losses. Social isolation also has been found to be an important stressor that has an impact on psychological well-being in late life (Kahana, Redmond, Hill, Kercher, & Kahana, 1995). Social isolation may increase the likelihood of experiencing other major stressors, such as fraud, criminal victimization, and exposure to elder abuse and mistreatment. Where elder abuse exists, social isolation can impede the detection of such abuse (Penhale & Kingston, 1995).

Some studies have found an association between absence of close social ties and mental illnesses, including depression in late life (LaRue, Dessonville, & Jarvik, 1985). Social isolation also appears to be a risk factor for late-life suicide (Nowers, 1998). A history of social isolation seems to be predictive of poor adjustment to institutional living, a phenomenon that Bennett (1980) attributes to desocialization, or an unlearning of interactive behaviors. In prospective studies, extreme social isolation has been found to predict greater likelihood of mortality, even when age, education, income, and health status are controlled (LaVeist, Sellers, Brown, Elliott, & Nickerson, 1997).

In recognition of the deleterious effects of extreme social isolation in late life, various intervention programs have been initiated to reduce social isolation. Among the most innovative is the use of the Internet with isolated elderly (Redford & Parkins, 1997). Information technology provides a strong potential for fostering intergenerational connectedness, which, in turn, can reduce social isolation of the elderly and foster a sense of community through the electronic media (Ward & Smith, 1997). Although the promise of electronic technology is strong, it should not be overrated, because isolated elderly who have not come to the attention of social service networks may very well not have the financial resources or the initiative to utilize the Internet. Alternative approaches to reducing isolation can range from traditional social work intervention to community-responsive transportation systems and friendly visitor programs. Discussion of emotional isolation of the elderly in the context of theatrical dialogue groups also appears to be beneficial (Worley & Henderson, 1995). Day care programs have been found to reduce isolation among dementia patients and their caregivers (Parson, 1999).

It is important to note that the directionality of causation remains an open question in research considering the antecedents of negative outcomes of isolation. Thus, Krause (1993) found that older persons who were mistrustful of others tended to be more socially isolated. In the absence of longitudinal data, it is entirely possible that isolation and emotional disorders promote each other.

The above literature portrays an impressive array of negative outcomes associated with the absence of close social ties. The emergence of intervention techniques to reduce late-life isolation represents, therefore, an encouraging development.

BOAZ KAHANA

See also
Disengagement
Langley Porter Studies of Aging
Loneliness

ISOMERIZATION

Ribosomal protein synthesis links aspartic acid (Asp) to other amino acid residues only through its alpha-carboxyl group. This places the side-chain beta-carboxyl group in the precise orientation needed for the proper structure and function of the protein. As a protein ages, however, it can undergo a spontaneous chemical reaction involving the nucleophilic attack of the adjacent backbone nitrogen on the side-chain carbonyl carbon of both Asp and asparaginyl (Asn) residues, forming a five-membered cyclic succinimide (Fig. 1). This succinimide ring is spontaneously opened by the attack of water on either of the carbonyl carbons, resulting in the formation of a normal Asp residue or an isomerized "isoaspartyl" (isoAsp) or "beta-aspartyl" linkage, in which the peptide backbone goes through the beta-carboxyl group (Fig. 1).

The kinetics of these reactions have been extensively studied in vitro. The half-life ($t_{1/2}$) of succinimide formation in synthetic peptides under physiological conditions (37°C, pH, 7.3–7.5) ranges from as little as 0.24–1.4 days for Asn-Gly and 41 days for Asp-Gly sequences to more than 200 days when the Asn/Asp (Asx) residue is adjacent to bulky hydrophobic residues (reviewed by Brennan & Clarke, 1995). In proteins, however, constraints imposed by secondary or tertiary structure can stabi-

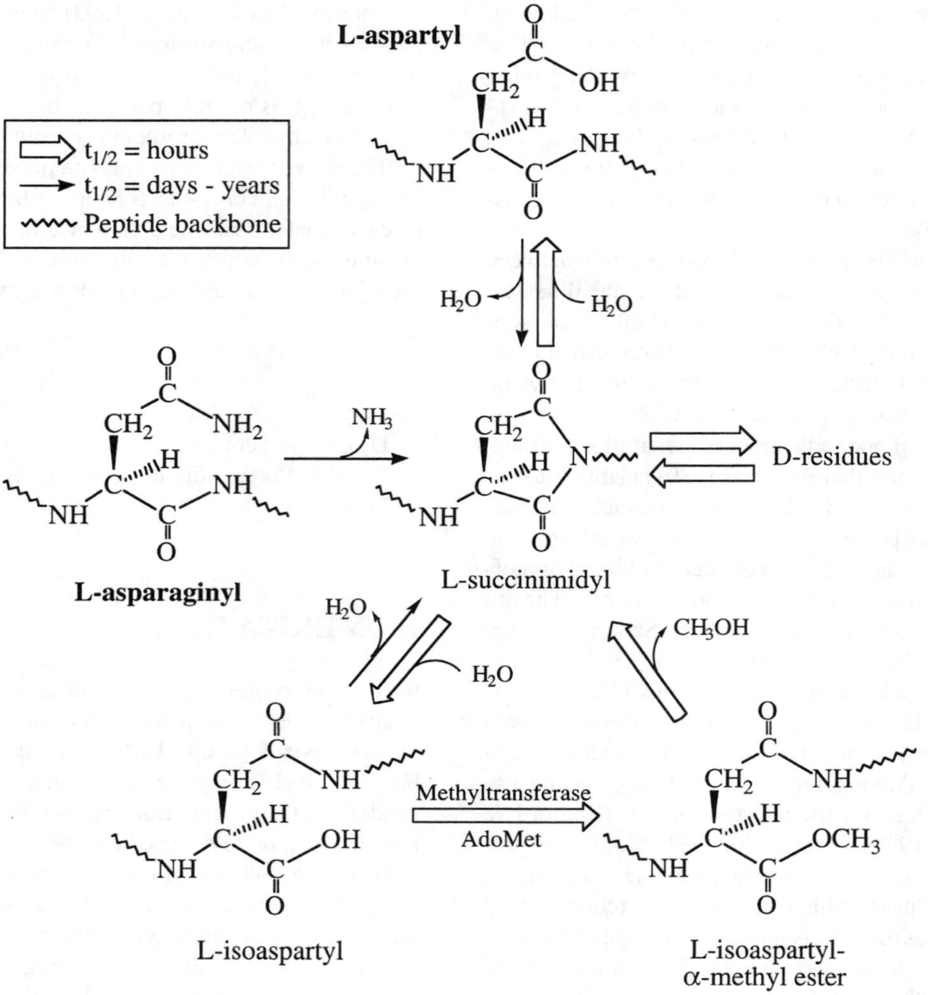

FIGURE 1   Mechanisms of degradation and methyltransferase-linked repair of protein L-aspartic acid and L-asparagine residues.

lize some Asx residues so that no degradation at all is seen at those sites (Clarke, 1987). Local flexibility, the presence of small or hydrophilic adjacent residues, and increases in temperature or pH all promote succinimide formation. The succinimide itself is quite unstable, hydrolyzing with a $t_{1/2}$ of only 2.4 hours under physiological conditions (Geiger & Clarke, 1987). Interestingly, this hydrolysis generates the isoAsp product three to four times more often than the Asp product under a variety of conditions.

Two other reactions are associated with succinimide formation. First, the succinimide is prone to racemization (inversion of the chiral alpha-carbon); the L-succinimide in one hexapeptide was found to racemize to the D-succinimide with a $t_{1/2}$ of 19.5 hours, much faster than occurs in the open-chain Asp and isoAsp forms (Geiger & Clarke, 1987). D-Asp and D-isoAsp residues are therefore likely to be found whenever a succinimide-linked mechanism is involved. Second, Asn-containing peptides can undergo a reaction in which the side-chain nitrogen attacks the backbone carbonyl carbon and cleaves the peptide bond, leaving a C-terminal succinimide on one of the peptide fragments. This reaction is significant in synthetic peptides when the residue to the carboxyl side of the Asn is bulky and hydrophobic and is predominant in Asn-Pro sequences (Geiger & Clarke, 1987; Tyler-Cross & Schirch, 1991). These succinimide-linked reactions have also been observed in in vivo–aged proteins in eye lens and brain (Fujii, Ishibashi, Satoh, Fujino, & Harada, 1994; Roher, Lowenson, Clarke, Wolkow, Wang, Cotter, et al., 1993; Voorter, deHaard-Hoekman, van den Oetelaar, Bloemendal, & de Jong, 1988).

Given these in vitro reaction rates, it seems likely that isoAsp formation would be a significant problem within physiological systems. Spontaneous deamidation of proteins in vivo is widely recognized and easily detected by the increase in negative charge that accompanies the conversion of Asn to Asp or isoAsp residues (reviewed by Wright, 1991). The $t_{1/2}$ of deamidation of an Asn-His sequence in the rabbit muscle aldolase is just 8 days in vivo, indicating that, at least in this case, the reaction rate is similar to those measured with small peptides in vitro. It must be noted, however, that Asn deamidation in some proteins may proceed through succinimide-independent mechanisms and thus not form isoAsp residues (Wright, 1991). The conversion of Asp to isoAsp residues in proteins slightly alters their net charge but is more easily detected by using the enzymatic methylation assay described below. Asp residues in human erythrocyte calmodulin (Ota & Clarke, 1990) and brain beta-amyloid (Roher, Lowenson, Clarke, Wolkow, Wang, Cotter, et al., 1993) are known to undergo succinimide formation in vivo, and similar results have been seen in a variety of native and recombinant proteins in vitro.

What are the effects of isoAsp residues on protein function? The transfer of a methylene group from a side-chain to the peptide backbone is a significant change, but except for the fact that all isoAsp bonds are resistant to digestion by proteases, their effects should vary with the importance of that residue in maintaining the structure and function of the protein. The presence of just one or two isoAsp residues, for example, can decrease by 80% the biological activity of recombinant human epidermal growth factor (George-Nascimento, Lowenson, Bo-

rissenko, Calderon, Medina-Selby, Kuo, et al., 1990) and the ability of bovine calmodulin to activate calmodulin-dependent protein kinase (Johnson, Langmack, & Aswad, 1987), can limit the affinity of chicken egg lysozyme for its chitin substrate (Yamada, Ueda, Kuroki, Fukumura, Yasukochi, Hirabayashi, et al., 1985), can alter the affinity of calbindin D9k for calcium (Chazin, Kördel, Thulin, Hofman, Drakenberg, & Forsen, 1989), and can alter the angiogenic properties of human angiogenin (Hallahan, Shapiro, Strydom, & Vallee, 1992).

The detrimental nature of these residues within living cells is supported by the existence of an L-isoaspartate (D-aspartate) o-methyltransferase that specifically catalyzes the transfer of a methyl group from s-adenosylmethionine (AdoMet) to damaged Asp residues, initiating their 'repair' back to the normal L-Asp form. This enzyme is present in bacteria, fungi, plants, and all human tissues thus far examined (Johnson, Ngo, & Aswad, 1991). Methylation of the alpha-carboxyl group of an L-isoAsp residue can increase the rate at which it forms a succinimide 10^3- to 10^4-fold; the net result of methylation, succinimide formation, and succinimide hydrolysis is the conversion of L-isoAsp to L-Asp residues, with the slow accumulation of racemized residues (Fig. 1). Mammalian methyltransferases also recognize D-Asp residues, but with lower affinity than for L-isoAsp residues (Lowenson & Clarke, 1992). L-IsoAsp residues in many peptides and proteins are methylated by the human enzyme with high affinity (K_m values of 0.5–20 µM) and comparable velocities; only constrained higher order structure and a few sequence elements can inhibit the reaction (Lowenson & Clarke, 1991). With radiolabeled AdoMet, the methyltransferase can be used in an assay sensitive enough to detect less than 200 fmol of L-isoAsp residues. It cannot, however, restore deamidated Asn to its original form.

The repair pathway described above has been demonstrated in vitro with the up to 80% conversion of L-isoAsp-containing synthetic peptides to their L-Asp-containing forms (Johnson, Murray, Clarke, Glass, & Aswad, 1987). Furthermore, the activities of L-isoAsp-containing deamidated bovine calmodulin (Johnson, Langmack, & Aswad, 1987) and deamidated E. coli phosphocarrier protein HPr (Brennan, Anderson, Jia, Waygood, & Clarke, 1994) are partially restored upon incubation in vitro with the methyltransferase and AdoMet. Mice lacking the methyltransferase have recently been developed, and cytosolic proteins in these animals accumulate two- to six-fold more L-isoAsps than do normal mice, establishing that repair of these residues has physiological importance (Kim, Lowenson, MacLaren, Clarke, & Young, 1997). Although born and weaned at the expected frequency, these mice have abnormal cortical activity about 50% of the time and suffer fatal seizures at an average age of 42 days (Kim, Lowenson, Clarke, & Young, 1999). The role of L-isoAsp accumulation in the seizure activity is as yet undetermined.

Although the methyltransferase remains fully active in aging healthy eye lens and brain, it cannot completely prevent isoAsp accumulation as these tissues age (McFadden & Clarke, 1986; Man, Fisher, Payan, Cadilla-Perezrios, Garcia, Chemburker, et al., 1987; Johnson, Shirokawa, Geddes, Choi, Kim, & Aswad, 1991), perhaps because of limited protein turnover or because succinimide formation is increased in denatured proteins. Expression of the enzyme appears to be lower in human cataractous eye lens, which contains abundant L-isoAsp residues in aggregated crystallins (Kodama, Mizobuchi, Takeda, Torikai, Shinomiya, & Ohashi, 1995), but higher in Alzheimer's disease (AD) brain (Kondo, Shirasawa, Itoyama, & Mori, 1996). Furthermore, the methyltransferase activity can be significantly inhibited in diseases like uremia, in which

the s-adenosylhomocysteine level is elevated (Perna, Ingrosso, De Santo, Galletti, & Zappia, 1995). The accumulation of isoAsp residues in cellular proteins with age may also contribute to the loss of self-tolerance in autoimmune diseases such as systemic lupus erythematosus (Mamula, Gee, Elliott, Sette, Southwood, Jones, et al., 1999).

Extracellular proteins are not subject to the repair pathway. In fact, about 75% of the beta-amyloid peptides found in dense extracellular plaques (Roher, Lowenson, Clarke, Wolkow, Wang, Cotter, et al., 1993) and much of the tau protein from paired helical filaments (Watanabe, Takio, & Ihara, 1999) in AD brains contain one or more isoAsp residues. Immunohistochemistry using antibodies specific for L-isoAsp-containing beta-amyloid have identified older plaques that are correlated with dementia severity (Fonseca, Head, Velazquez, Cottman, & Tenner, 1999). In addition, antibodies against an L-isoAsp-containing fragment of aged collagen are being used to diagnose certain bone diseases (Fledelius, Johnsen, Cloos, Bonde, & Qvist, 1997). Whether damaged Asp residues contribute to the pathology of these diseases or are simply a consequence of the long-term stability of selected proteins is as yet unknown.

JONATHAN D. LOWENSON

See also
  Racemization

J

JOINTS

There are many types of joints in the human body, but this article will concentrate on the synovial joints. Age-related degenerative joint disease, such as osteoarthritis, will increase over the next decade with the growth of the elderly population. This

will impose an increasing socioeconomic burden, resulting in higher costs for medical care, disability, and lost workdays. Current therapies are inadequate, owing to insufficient knowledge about the molecular mechanisms governing aging of joint tissues, particularly the articular cartilage and how this becomes increasingly susceptible to degenerative changes. At advanced age, most individuals have one or several joints with osteoarthritis and ensuing destruction of the articular cartilage.

Most studies of aging have concentrated on articular cartilage, simply because it is perceived as the tissue that changes most in composition and structure in age-related, degenerative lesions such as osteoarthritis. However, the articulating joint should be thought of as an organ. It is made up of a number of structural components in addition to the articular cartilage, for example, subchondral bone, menisci (in the knee joint), anterior and posterior cruciate ligaments (knee joint), ligamentum teres (hip joint), synovium, capsule, tendon, and muscle. Consequently, a change in the structural organization of any one of these is going to upset the homeostatic balance of the whole joint. This will lead to changes in the composition and structure of the other tissues and can have two possible consequences. First, the biochemistry of the other tissues compensate for the changing environment that they find themselves in and halt the process of degeneration of the joint (organ), that is, they would stabilize the joint. Second, they may not be able to make an adjustment in time, or any adjustment they do make may not last and the joint will ultimately fail. This scenario would account for the multifactorial nature of age-related, degenerative joint disease and for the lack of a universal pathway to explain joint degeneration in all cases. Normal joint function depends on the mechanical properties of the articular cartilage, which has a role in providing low-friction movement and in resisting and distributing load. The collagen network is considered crucial for maintenance of cartilage function. However, because of inadequate technology, it has not been possible to corroborate that failure of the collagen network is a point of no return in cartilage pathology.

The space between the opposing joint surfaces should also be considered as a tissue, because the composition of this milieu (synovial fluid) can tell us a lot about the turnover of the macromolecules that make up the various tissues of the joint. Surrogate markers of tissue turnover are being actively pursued, and many have been used to verify changes in joint structure visualized by radiography. For example, antisera recognizing various fragments of collagen types I (bone) and II (cartilage) and the cross-links associated with these molecules have been used very effectively. Similarly, antisera raised against macromolecules such as cartilage oligomeric matrix protein (COMP) and bone sialo protein (BSP) have been used to determine the temporal changes that take place in bone and cartilage in specific populations of patients suffering from joint degeneration. It is highly unlikely that a single marker of osteoarthritis will be discovered; it is more likely that a profile of the state of the patient's joint can be obtained by using this technology. For these methods to be effective it is vital that the process(es) that the surrogate marker is measuring is understood as fully as possible (i.e., is the fragment a measure of an anabolic or catabolic event?). To date it has been assumed that most markers of joint tissue turnover reflect changes in the articular cartilage, but it has not been shown conclusively that the other tissues do not also contribute to the pool of turnover products in the synovial fluid. Surrogate markers of bone turnover and the involvement of this tissue in age-related degeneration of the joint have also been investigated. These markers have proved to be very useful in studying the bony changes occurring during the development of osteoporosis, the most prevalent metabolic disease of bone in the aged.

No specific treatment of degenerative joint disease has been developed by the pharmaceutical industry, and the clinician has usually treated the symptoms of the disease, rather than the process(es) involved, with nonsteroidal antiinflammatory drugs (NSAIDs). However, it should be appreciated that many forms of therapy are used, depending on the stage of the disease in an individual and the rate at which it is progressing. By understanding the process(es) that are induced in the joint at different stages of the disease and by devising better means of monitoring them, it should be possible to make rapid advances in understanding this debilitating age-related condition.

A number of biological events should therefore be investigated: (1) the mechanisms that lead to the alterations in the aging joint predisposing it to loss of function and failure; (2) the mechanisms that bring about fragmentation of structural molecules and altered protein substituents, with the ensuing functional impairment that leads to the irreversible destruction of the articular surface; and (3) failure of repair by unbalanced synthesis of matrix constituents and the potential correction of this by growth factors. New tools should be developed that allow monitoring of early processes in the joint that lead to cartilage destruction.

MICHAEL T. BAYLISS

See also
Musculoskeletal System

JOURNALISM AND AGING

"One of the biggest and most important stories of our time—indeed one of the miracles of the twentieth century—has been mostly ignored so far by the nation's mainstream media. It is a little-known fact that the equivalent of an *entire generation* has been added to the average person's life [expectancy]," writes Lawrence K. Grossman in his chapter on the media's role in *Life in Older America* (Butler, Grossman, & Oberlink, 1999, pp. 231–238). Grossman's active interest in the modest but emerging age beat is one sign of the growing stature of the journalism on aging during the late 1990s. Septuagenarian Grossman, a former president of both the Public Broadcasting Service and NBC News, is columnist for the *Columbia Journalism Review*.

Grossman goes on to state: "Journalistically, the most interesting aspect of the 'grown-ups' movement is that it represents not a special interest beat or, what in current media jargon is called a 'niche' beat, but one of the most important general interest beats of the coming century." One such reporter he mentions is Michael M. Vitez, who began covering aging for the *Philadelphia Inquirer* in 1995. Two years later he was awarded a Pulitzer Prize for his five-part series, "Final Choices: Seeking the Good Death," later released as a book by the same title (1997). According to Vitez, the key factor in his ability to devote 6 months to his investigation was the carte blanche he was given by the newspaper's former executive editor, Max King, who had observed the peaceful, well-supported passing of a favorite aunt and knew that too few Americans die with such dignity.

Vitez is one of about 600 reporters listed by the Journalists Exchange on Aging (JEoA) who expressed interest in following issues in aging, approximately 200 of whom cover stories in aging on an ongoing basis. According to the JEoA's "1997 Second National Survey of Journalists on Aging," these reporters are "seasoned and sensitized." The 129 respondents to the survey (a 23.9% response rate) are seasoned journalists, averaging 21.1 years in their professions. They are sensitized to concerns of an older population because 95.3% said they had experienced aspects of issues in aging themselves or through their families. Furthermore, 89.6% of those participants said the experience had "affected their journalistic perspective." The survey report concluded, "Clearly, this group did not feel that their objectivity was in any way compromised. Instead, they perceived that their personal experience gave depth to their understanding of these issues."

The JEoA, an unincorporated professional group provided in-kind organizational support by the American Society on Aging, was founded in 1993 by journalists who found themselves covering the complications of an aging society and in need of sources, education, and mutual networking to understand the complexities of aging. For example, Wendy Schmelzer, who covers aging full-time for National Public Radio's Science Unit and who won the American Society on Aging Media Award for national coverage in 1996 and 2000, acknowledges that the media often equated stories in aging with medical or health coverage. Defining her beat as combining social and health issues, Schmelzer states, "I think the disease of the week approach happily is disappearing" (Kleyman, 1999).

Grossman (Butler et al., 1999) notes that although "relatively few reporters" are assigned to the age beat, the personal commitment that has caused so many of them to establish the assignment at their news organizations suggests that the coverage of issues in aging is likely to increase in size and prominence with the aging of the boomer generation. He stresses that "the commitment to the age beat did not come from the top down but from the bottom up" in news organizations. This often intense personal devotion to the age beat has meant that reporters, especially those in midlife who have dealt with aging parents or younger journalists who, having had strong relationships with a family elder, continue to emerge. In daily journalism, for example, fewer than 35 newspapers in the United States have a reporter who works at least 50% of the time on aging. Among major newspapers assigning reporters to the age beat are the *Arizona Republic, New York Times, Newark Star-Ledger, Orange County Regis-*

ter, *Richmond (Virginia) Times Dispatch, St. Petersburg Times, San Diego Union-Tribune, Minneapolis Star-Tribune,* and *St. Paul Pioneer Press.*

Because of the personal commitment rather than management interest that generated so many age beats at new organizations, when a reporter on aging is reassigned or leaves, the beat is often not restaffed. The pattern throughout the 1990s, however, was that when a reporter left or reduced his or her coverage of aging, another would appear elsewhere. Two important recent additions with full-time age-beat assignments were at the *Seattle Times* in 1999 and the *Newark Star-Ledger* at the beginning of 2000. That the age beat is journalist-driven was underscored by those like Rebecca Goldsmith, at the *Star-Ledger*, who covered aging at another newspaper and worked 6 months to persuade editors to allow her to initiate the age beat in Newark.

A further instance of a journalist's devotion to issues in aging was the decision of CNN executive producer Bailey Barash to resign her position in early 1999, after working at the network for 18 years. Although she was an executive producer of science and technology news and features, she resigned "in order to change my beat to aging."

Although she has continued producing freelance pieces for CNN's science unit after leaving her staff job, Barash, who had been a family caregiver, obtained a journalism fellowship at the University of Hawaii for the 1999–2000 academic year to study aging. She also established an independent documentary production company to focus primarily on this subject area, and she plans to continue producing for CNN and other television outlets. Although quitting one's job to pursue or deepen one's coverage of aging is rare, Barash's example is not unique.

"After almost 10 years we now have an experienced journalism faculty," said John A. Cutter, a founder of the JEoA. Cutter won numerous awards for his coverage of aging at the *St. Petersburg Times* before leaving in 1998 to write about aging at greater length and depth than is permitted by even the best newspapers and to complete a master's degree in gerontology. He noted that age-beat veterans will be needed as more news outlets assign reporters to cover aging, especially as the middle of the boomer generation approaches age 50. By the beginning of 2000 the JEoA had cosponsored

or assisted with educational programs for journalists with such organizations as the Freedom Forum; the University of Minnesota's School of Journalism and Mass Communication and Minnesota Journalism Center; the Knight Center for Specialized Journalism, University of Maryland; the International Longevity Center; Journalists of Color, Inc.'s Unity '99 conference in Seattle; the American Society on Aging; the AARP Andrus Foundation, and others.

Another important organizational development was the founding in 1995 of the North American Mature Publisher's Association (NAMPA), the first national trade group, bringing together owners of many of the nation's approximately 200 local and regional senior newspapers and magazines. As the odd name, which has inspired quips about the whether there might be an "immature publishers" association, suggests, the group consists of business people focused on the "mature market." An important long-term goal of the group, however, is to raise the now uneven journalistic quality of these mostly free-distribution papers. In 2000 there continued to be only three general interest magazines addressed to older people, the AARP's *Modern Maturity*, *New Choices* (owned by *Reader's Digest*), and *Mature Outlook*, which is produced by Meredith Publishing for Sears. The AARP announced in early 2000 that it searching for a new name for *Modern Maturity* that would be more appealing to aging baby boomers. Early 2000 also saw the launching of numerous websites devoted to aging boomers, aimed at competing with the established *thirdage.com*. Among the new entries attracting venture capital were *seniors.com* and *inyourprime.com*, along with other sites dealing specifically with family caregiving issues, such as *CaregiverZone.com*. All of these commercial developments are creating opportunities for qualified writers and editors to focus on concerns of aging, but their long-range influence remains to be seen.

Lawrence K. Grossman's recognition of the emerging importance of journalism on aging is tempered by his knowledge that most mainstream media outlets continue to give short shrift to the information and entertainment needs and interests of older viewers because of the long-held desire to reach the 18–49-year-old market and the even narrower 18–34 group, regarded as the most lucrative. He reports that a radio talk-show host admitted that his station's telephone operators "filter out older people just in case any advertisers happen to be listening. We don't want them coming away with the impression that our show appeals to old folks. It's bad for sales."

The media's ageist neglect, causing elders to be invisible and sometimes misrepresented in reports, was shown to be an international phenomenon during an October 13–15, 1999, conference at the United Nations headquarters in New York City, titled, "The Impact of Globalization on the Image of Older Women." *Aging Today*, newspaper of the American Society on Aging, reported on results of a 1997–98 study ("U.N. conference," 1999) of gender portrayals by six public broadcasters in Northern Europe (the Netherlands, Norway, Sweden, Finland, Denmark, and Germany). The research found that women and men age 65 or more accounted for merely 2% of the television populations, and older women, represented by less than 1%, "were mainly invisible," according to Bernadette van Dijck, who heads the Gender Portrayal Department, Netherlands Broadcasting Organization, Utrecht. Furthermore, in news and informational programming, although one third of interviewed experts were aged 50–64, only one in nine among them was a woman, and no female expert past age 65 appeared.

Since early 1998, veteran news anchor Nigel Kay has chaired a group of BBC producers charged with examining "how we could be more responsive to the needs and the aspirations" of diverse population segments. Working with the nongovernmental organizations Age Concern and researchers at Worcester College of Higher Education, Worcester, they began an annual survey of BBC programs to gauge how well the network is meeting goals regarding older people set by the "BBC Producers' Guidelines."

"The rather depressing news," Kay said, is that the group's 1999 survey revealed that, compared to the 20% proportion of British people age 60 or more, "only 7% of the people seen on TV during the snapshot period were aged 60-plus." Kay was optimistic and reported that the survey process was already leading to improvements.

A conference cosponsor, the AARP, hosted a "networking session" for representatives of the media and nongovernmental organizations (NGOs) in aging. The session resulted in formation of an international committee to pursue such goals as stimulating research on the media's representation of older women, to sensitize the media to inequalities in the depiction of older women, and to encourage the media "to take responsibility for dispelling destructive stereotypes," according to a summary memo to participants.

The third sponsor of the conference, held as part of the U.N.'s International Year of Older Persons, was Netherlands Platform Ouderen en Europa (NPOE), which oversees *Media Age*, an on-line news service. This research and information entity was created in 1998 by a consortium of NGOs serving elders throughout the European Union. According to NPOE director Ger Tielen, one of the group's primary efforts was to create a "modest" news service on issues and developments in aging. The on-line service *www.mediaage.net* issues several news dispatches in English to subscribers at no charge per week, via an E-mail service to which anyone can subscribe. The larger purpose of *Media Age*, Tielen explained, "was to bring NGOs and the media together in the debate on the aging of society, and for the NGOs to understand the workings of the media and the working of changes in the media landscape" ("JEOA goes global," 2000). *Media Age* also has issued several impressive reports both on older people's representation in the media and on elders' inclusion in government policies and industrial planning for the new communications technologies. Examined are efforts (or lack of them) in European countries and the United States.

Generally, the spread of news and information in specialized fields like aging is greatly facilitated by the Internet. Even though most of the commercial services being created for the Web carry little more than consumer-service articles or sales opportunities, outlets like *mediaage.net* will be increasingly important as consolidators of news reporting from multiple sources. The emerging role of nontraditional gatherers and disseminators of news and information, including commercial entities and nonprofit groups or NGOs, is already gaining notice. For example, the Online News Association, founded by Internet editors of major U.S. news organizations in 1999, held a presentation in San Francisco, August 30, 1999, at which leaders of the group stated that some nontraditional information disseminators, such as nonprofits in the science and health communities, had already emerged as more current and reliable sources than major media outlets. The journalism community will continue to raise legitimate concerns about the blurring of lines between news emanating from disinterested journalistic sources and those with inherent conflicts. However, the low cost and far reach of new electronic media is also likely to test the world of journalism, which has poorly served specialized areas like aging by ignoring certain populations and often being open to misrepresentation of difficult public issues.

Despite gains in knowledgeable coverage made by the increasing numbers of reporters on the age beat, the public can expect to see at least some continuation of the biased reporting that has dogged issues in aging in press reports, especially since the mid-1980s. For example, the antientitlement tenor of the infamous "Greedy Geezers" cover story in the *New Republic* (Fairlie, 1988) was echoed by *U.S. News & World Report* in its March 1, 1999, cover article, "The Global Aging Crisis" (Longman, 1999). This heading was followed by the cover line, "With the elderly population exploding, the social and economic costs could be staggering—for all of us." The article was written by one of the magazine's deputy editors, Phillip J. Longman, an author associated since the middle 1980s with books and organizations taking issue with social insurance programs for elders. Perhaps a more egregious example of an established news organization aligning itself with a slanted point of view on aging was documented by University of Kansas gerontologist, David J. Ekerdt, Ph.D. (1998) in *The Gerontologist*. His article shows how the *Kansas City Star* (Kansas City, MO) shamelessly formed a year-long partnership with an ideologically and economically biased organization, the Concord Coalition, to undermine public confidence in Social Security, Medicare, and related public entitlement programs. This was done throughout 1996, in the high-minded name of civic journalism, through newspaper articles, public forums, on-line discussions, and other means. The newspaper's editors identified the organization as "nonpartisan," because of its inclusion of people from both parties but never exposed its widely documented ties to Wall Street interests or its leadership on one side of a national debate, such as favoring means-testing of Medicare, according to Ekerdt.

Slanted reporting misguided by ideological commitment of news owners and managers will always exist, of course, but if these instances are to be minimized, perhaps the best remedy is a growing force of reporters who are well versed in the complexities of issues in aging. Prejudicial reporting can certainly happen when, as in the case of *U.S. News & World Report*, the news organization takes a position in its news pages without consulting a staff reporter who actually is well versed in the area. Even in these cases, though, the best defense is a well-informed public.

How will this come about in the United States? One clue may be found in Japan. That nation's public-policy commitment to aging through its 1989 Gold Plan for old-age health and security (enhanced in 1994) and later adoption of the Public Long-Term Care Insurance Act, which became effective in April 2000, led to widespread media assignments to cover aging.

A conference of Japanese and American reporters covering the age beat was held in New York by the International Longevity Center's U.S.A. and Japan affiliates at the Freedom Forum's Media Studies Center in September 1997. Later, Ritsuko Inokuma, age-beat reporter for one of Japan's largest national dailies, *Yoriumi Shimbun* (circulation, 10 million), spent the 1998–99 academic year at Stanford University on a Fulbright Fellowship and a Knight Journalism Fellowship to study aging in the United States.

She explained for this article:

> For a long time, the coverage of aging was minor in Japanese newspapers. It was often covered in a feature section. But recently, after about 1996, almost all newspapers are covering these issues because the aging or social security (health insurance, public pension, the number of adult children) issues are very crucial and political problems in Japan. Now, articles about aging are done by many staff writers on political, economic, city and regional affairs desks, besides lifestyle affairs (Ritsuko Inokuma, personal communication, November, 1999).

Perhaps, as has happened in Japan, greater media attention to the issues of aging will necessarily follow the demographic shift and the increased public-policy interest that is likely to accompany the aging of the boomer generation.

PAUL KLEYMAN

See also
Images of Aging in the Media

K

KANSAS CITY STUDIES OF ADULT LIFE

In the early 1940s, members of the Committee on Human Development at the University of Chicago began large-scale investigations of social and psychological aging that became the forerunners of the Kansas City Studies of Adult Life. The Kansas City project, begun in 1952, was carried out over a 10-year period under the direction of Robert J. Havighurst, William E. Henry, and Bernice L. Neugarten. It was the first community-based research to focus attention on middle age and the changes that occur as persons move from middle to old age. The project was funded first by the Carnegie Corporation, then by the (U.S.) National Institute of Mental Health, and involved a large number of anthropologists, sociologists, and psychologists, including Ernest W. Burgess, Elaine Cumming, Eugene Friedman, David L. Gutmann, Everett C. Hughes, Martin B. Loeb, Warren A. Peterson, Sheldon S. Tobin, W. Lloyd Warner, and many others.

Two sets of studies were completed. The first was based on a stratified, systematic probability sample of 750 persons aged 40 to 70 interviewed at one point in time, and dealt with a broad range of topics: social role performance, age differences in family, work, and leisure patterns, social mobility, age-grading, personality processes, psychological adjustment, and life satisfaction. The second set of studies was based on a group of 280 persons aged 50 to 90 who were interviewed multiple times over a 6-year period and focused primarily on social-psychological changes of aging.

The Kansas City project had several notable characteristics:

1. The research team was multidisciplinary, and the lines of inquiry were multiple, as reported not only in the major books cited below, but also in scores of monographs, book chapters, and journal articles.
2. The respondents lived in an urban metropolitan area—a more representative American community than any previously used as the context for studies of normal aging. The community itself was part of the investigation, the first time Lloyd Warner's methods of studying social status were applied to a large community. The social class structure of Kansas City in the 1950s was described by Coleman and Neugarten in *Social Status in the City* (1971).
3. The studies were based on relatively large samples of persons from whom complex social and psychological data were gathered. When multiple measures of personality and social behaviors were combined for individuals, a wide diversity of patterns of aging emerged. Age changes in personality and a set of personality types were described by Neugarten and Associates in *Personality in Middle and Late Life* (1964); and various life patterns were described by Williams and Wirth in *Lives Through the Years* (1965).
4. Attention to social-psychological changes led to the question of optimum patterns of aging and gave rise to the disengagement theory as set forth in the book by Cumming and Henry, *Growing Old* (1961) and to later modifications of that theory reported in separate papers by those authors. Because the disengagement theory set off a great wave of controversy among both American and European gerontologists, a brief elaboration is appropriate.

In the 1950s the widely held view, although not formally stated as a theory, was the activity theory of optimum aging. That theory implied that, except for the inevitable changes in biology and health, older people are the same as middle-aged people and have essentially the same psychological and social needs. Based on the observed facts that as people grow old their social interaction decreases, it was postulated that the decrease is the result of society's "withdrawing"; that this withdrawal proceeds against the desires of the aging person; and that those persons who age optimally are those who manage to resist the shrinkage of their social worlds by finding substitutes for the interactions they are forced to relinquish, such as those that come with retirement or the deaths of significant others.

The disengagement theory offered a different interpretation of the observed facts, namely, that the decreased social interaction occurs because of a mutual withdrawal by society and the aging person; that the individual's withdrawal has intrinsic as well as responsive qualities and is a natural rather than an imposed process; and that the old person who has disengaged is the one who has a sense of psychological well-being and who will enjoy a high level of life satisfaction.

The disengagement theory has been both supported and rebutted by other investigators, often on the basis of empirical evidence, often, not.

The Kansas City data were reanalyzed by Havighurst, Neugarten, and Tobin who, using different measures than those used by Cumming and Henry, found a moderate positive correlation between activity and life satisfaction—in short, moderate support for the activity theory. More important, they found a diversity of patterns of aging based on combinations of personality type, role activity, and life satisfaction. These findings are reported in two chapters in the book edited by Neugarten, *Middle Age and Aging* (1968). These authors concluded that, because neither the activity nor the disengagement theory can account for the diversity, both theories are reductionist. Further, when the Kansas City measures were used on datasets from several European countries, it was shown that, as might well have been anticipated, differences in sociocultural settings produce major variations in patterns of aging (Havighurst, Munnichs, Neugarten, & Thomae, 1969).

Overall, then, a major contribution of the Kansas City Studies has been to demonstrate not only that there is no single direction or pattern of social-psychological aging but also no single pattern of optimum aging. The significance of the Kansas City Studies for gerontological theory and research has been reviewed in *The Gerontologist* (see Symposium, 1994).

BERNICE L. NEUGARTEN
Updated by GEORGE MADDOX

See also
Activity Theory
Disengagement
Longitudinal Studies of Aging

KIDNEY AND URINARY SYSTEM

Normal Anatomy and Function

The two kidneys normally are located in the back just below the rib cage; however, anatomic variations in number and location are common. The kidneys function by filtering through the glomeruli large quantities of blood, allowing fluid and small molecules but not large molecules (e.g., protein) and cellular structures (e.g., red and white blood cells and platelets) to enter a tubular system. In these tubules, molecules (e.g., glucose, sodium, and potassium) that the body needs to conserve are reabsorbed back into the bloodstream, and waste products of body metabolism (e.g., creatinine) can further be excreted. This way fluid and electrolyte content of the body can be carefully regulated, varying the rates of reabsorption or secretion as necessary.

Ureters connect the two kidneys to a bladder (detrusor) made up of smooth muscle, which serves as a reservoir for urine until the time is convenient for emptying, when urine leaves the bladder through the urethra. Filling and emptying of the bladder are under control of the autonomic (sympathetic, parasympathetic) nervous system and voluntary (cortical) controls. Between the bladder and urethra there are two sphincters (valves) that control urination (internal and external sphincters). Sympathetic stimulation allows filling of the bladder by relaxing bladder musculature and closing the internal sphincter. Parasympathetic stimulation promotes opening of this sphincter and contraction of bladder musculature, initiating urination (micturation). When the bladder fills to a certain pressure, the micturation reflex alerts the individual of the need to urinate. This reflex can be inhibited or facilitated by centers in the brain stem and cerebral cortex (brain stem micturation center) controlling the external sphincter. This sphincter is under voluntary control and can initiate, prevent, or interrupt urination. Whereas interruption of the sympathetic nervous system has no effect on micturation, interruption of the parasympathetic nervous system results in complete bladder dysfunction. In males, the prostate gland, normally walnut size, encircles the start of the urethra. With age this tends to increase in size, so it may cause difficulty in the passage of urine or even obstruction of urine flow.

Aging and the Kidney

Although kidney function declines substantially with age, it usually remains sufficient to remove all waste products of metabolism (e.g., urea, creatinine, phosphorus) and to regulate volume and composition (e.g., sodium and potassium) of bodily fluids. A decrease in capacity for filtering the plasma or serum component of blood (glomerular filtration rate [GFR]) is the most important functional defect caused by age-related anatomic and physiological changes. The GFR can be measured by performing a creatinine clearance, using a timed urine sample and serum sample. This measure is stable in the normal young adult at 100–120 ml/min until age 30–40 years, after which it decreases at a mean rate approaching 1 ml/min/yr. Kidney function also can be estimated for clinical purposes with a serum creatinine determination (normally, 0.6–1.2 mg/dl) or serum urea nitrogen (normally, 6–22 mg/dl). These values become elevated only after some pathological process affects the kidneys to reduce their function below one third of normal. Because the creatinine in serum comes from muscle metabolism and because muscle mass decreases with age, the creatinine clearance may decrease substantially with age without any appreciable increase in serum creatinine concentrations. This is important to recognize when using serum creatinines to estimate ability to clear drugs such as digoxin and some antibiotics that are excreted by the kidneys (estimates of kidney function and clearance may be inappropriately high, leading to overdosage).

Longitudinal studies show that aging's effect on the kidney (creatinine clearance) varies substantially with age. In a study of healthy, upper-middle-class male volunteers (Baltimore Longitudinal Study of Aging), one third of older individuals showed no decrease in clearances over periods up to 20 years or more (Lindeman, Tobin, & Shock, 1985). This variability suggests that other factors (i.e., pathology) than aging (senescence) are responsible for the mean decrease in renal function observed with age.

Other functions of the kidney (ability to concentrate and dilute urine, ability to reabsorb sugar, ability to excrete acid) closely parallel changes in GFR. Leakage of protein (proteinuria) does not increase with age, and its appearance in the urine generally is due to a disease process.

Common Disorders of the Kidney

The most common kidney problems seen in the elderly are (1) nephrotic syndrome, (2) glomerulonephritis, (3) partial or complete blockage of the renal artery or arteries (stenosis, thrombosis, embolism), and (4) acute and chronic renal failure (insufficiency).

The nephrotic syndrome is characterized by a loss of protein in the urine (>3 gm/day) with generalized edema and susceptibility to infections. Diabetes mellitus is the most common cause, but a variety of immunological and systemic processes can be factors.

Glomerulonephritis (diffuse inflammatory changes in the glomeruli) can be acute in onset, following a variety of infections (postinfectious glomerulonephritis), or more chronic, often associated with systemic immunological diseases such as lupus erythematosis. Symptoms and findings include blood and protein in the urine, fluid retention (edema), and high blood pressure.

Partial (renal artery stenosis) and total occlusion (thrombosis, embolism) are generally atherosclerotic in origin and cause loss of renal function and hypertension. Cholesterol emboli are unique to the elderly.

Acute renal failure (ARF), characterized by rapidly rising serum urea nitrogen and creatinine levels, can be ischemic or toxic in origin. Ischemic ARF results from poor perfusion of the kidneys due to dehydration, heart failure, or low blood pressure (hypertension). Prolonged periods of poor perfusion, especially during surgery, may result in injury to the renal tubules (acute tubular necrosis). Toxic ARF results from administration of certain antibiotics and other medications, anaesthetics, or diagnostic agents or from release of hemoglobin or myoglobin (rhabdomyolysis) into the blood. It is important to rule out urinary tract obstruction (e.g., prostatic hypertrophy, stricture) as a cause as this is readily reversible.

Chronic renal failure (CRF) is the end result of a wide array of pathological processes that reduce kidney function to the point where dialysis or transplantation is necessary for survival. Heavy usage of analgesics (e.g., phenacetin and nonsteroidal anti-inflammatory drugs such as ibuprofen [Motrin]) are important causes not previously mentioned. Chronic maintenance dialysis (hemodialysis or chronic ambulatory peritoneal dialysis) are the mainstays of treatment for over half of all patients more than 60 years of age on chronic dialysis. Most elderly patients do well on dialysis, and complications are due to comorbidity (e.g., atherosclerotic heart disease) rather than to age alone. Renal transplantation is increasingly being utilized in persons over 60 years, but there remains a reluctance to allocate a scarce resource (the donor kidney) to those with a limited life expectancy. Nevertheless, elderly transplant patients matched with dialysis patients by age, underlying diagnosis, and comorbidities have 5-year survival rates of 81% versus 51% (Schaubel, Desmeules, Mao, Jeffrey, & Fenton, 1995). Further descriptions of these conditions are reported elsewhere (Lindeman, 1998).

Urinary Incontinence, Infections, Tumors, and Stones

Urinary incontinence can result from inadequate closure of the sphincter between the bladder and urethra (stress incontinence), from hyperactive bladder musculature (urge incontinence), or a combination of both (mixed incontinence). It also can result from excessive filling of the bladder resulting from obstruction (prostatic hypertrophy, stricture) or loss of bladder stimulation (diabetic neuropathy, spinal cord disruption), resulting in overflow incontinence.

Another common problem affecting the bladder is recurrent infection. Females are particularly prone presumably because their short urethra facilitates bacterial access. Males with obstruction due to large prostates (hypertrophy or cancer) also may develop infections. Symptoms include a need to urinate frequently, pain on urination (dysuria), and/or blood in the urine. Fever is generally low grade or absent. High fevers and back (flank) pain generally indicate that the infection has involved the kidneys (pyelonephritis). Short courses of antibiotics control symptoms in bladder infections, but recurrence is common. More aggressive antibiotic therapy is needed for kidney infections. Elderly persons may have permanent bacterial colonization without

symptoms. Treatment of this asymptomatic bacteriuria is generally unnecessary.

Kidney cancers (hypernephromas) often are widely disseminated before detection. Blood in the urine is the most common first symptom, but unexplained fever, and low (anemia) or high (polycythemia) hemoglobins also may be clues. Bladder cancers are common in the elderly and also usually present with blood in the urine. The diagnosis can be made by viewing the inside of the bladder with a cystoscope inserted through the urethra. Treatment with radiation therapy and/or surgical removal usually controls the cancer.

Kidney stones occur at any age. Stone collection and analysis helps to determine the type of stone and aid medical management. Many stones pass spontaneously, with intense pain and blood in the urine the primary manifestations. When associated with recurrent infections or blockage of urine flow, stones become larger, requiring surgical removal or destruction with ultrasound (lithotripsy).

ROBERT D. LINDEMAN

See also
Acid-Base Balance
Fecal and Urinary Incontinence
Genitourinary System
Sodium Balance and Osmolality Regulation

KNOWLEDGE UTILIZATION

Research on knowledge utilization suggests that cognitive performance in the later years of life depends on the interactions between what the person knows and the computational processes or mechanics of intelligence. To a large extent, the age-related deficits that are reported in many laboratory research studies of the mechanics of intelligence are or appear unrelated to everyday cognitive functioning because of knowledge utilization. In cognitive tasks outside the laboratory, individuals use their acquired knowledge and familiarity with situations as a way of compensating for normally occurring losses in the speed and efficiency of memory and other cognitive functions. Compensatory reliance on prior knowledge can be either deliberate or nondeliberate (nonconscious) in producing effective cognitive performance (Bäckman & Dixon, 1992).

The use of accumulated knowledge within particular substantive domains plays an especially important role in understanding cognitive functioning in the later years. In research exploring the interactive effects of age and knowledge use in selected cognitive domains (e.g., Clancy & Hoyer, 1994; Salthouse, 1984), it has been reported that the efficiency of cognitive performance depends on what knowledge or information is being processed. That is, age-related deficits are found for general cognitive tasks that do not tap the individual's knowledge, but smaller or no age differences are found for cognitive tasks relevant to the individual's acquired knowledge. These findings help us to understand how older adults perform competently in demanding cognitive situations despite age-related deficits in the speed and efficiency of general cognitive abilities.

WILLIAM J. HOYER

See also
 Cognitive Processes
 Memory and Memory Theory
 Wisdom

L

LANGLEY PORTER STUDIES OF AGING

The two Langley Porter interdisciplinary longitudinal studies of aging cover 27 years. The first, known as Studies in Normal and Abnormal Aging, started in 1958 and continued for 10 years. The second, The Longitudinal Study of Transitions, started in the fall of 1967, and the fifth and last round in interviewing was completed in mid-1980. Staff for the first study included psychiatrists, sociologists, psychologists, and anthropologists. Four books provide an overview of a broad range of publications based on these studies (Clark & Andersen, 1967; Lowenthal, Berkman, Pierce, Buehler, Brissette, & Robinson, 1967; Lowenthal, Thurnher, Chiriboga, Spence, Lurie, Weiss, et al., 1975; Simon, Lowenthal, & Epstein, 1970).

Among the objectives of the studies of normal and abnormal aging were, for the hospital sample (534 first admissions age 60 or over to a psychiatric screening ward), to identify characteristics of the patients' behavioral and interpersonal circum-

stances that precipitated hospitalization; to identify factors associated with these patients' social disorganization culminating in a petition for commitment to a state hospital; to identify circumstances associated with release from the screening ward or from the hospital; and to compare these patients and ex-patients with a sample of 600 community-resident persons aged 60 or over. A major goal of this section of the research was to test the then very prevalent hypothesis that old people were being shunted off to state hospitals because their families (or community agencies) wanted to get rid of them. Findings did *not* support the hypothesis (Lowenthal, Berkman, Pierce, et al., 1967; Simon, Lowenthal, & Epstein, 1970).

The community sample of 600 people 60 and over, like the hospital sample, was followed up twice at approximately annual intervals. Among the conclusions of this part of the study is the finding that the majority of the psychiatrically impaired in the community, like those who were hospitalized, also suffer from acute or chronic physical illness. In families and the community in general there is strong evidence of tolerance for eccentric or even overt pathological behavior among older people as long as those persons can take care of themselves physically. At the two follow-up assessments as many psychiatrically disturbed subjects had improved as had deteriorated in all domains of the study. The great majority of these community residents had no serious psychological symptoms, and from the residents we learned that intellectual deterioration is not an inevitable accompaniment of growing older (Lowenthal, Berkman, Pierce, et al., 1967).

A different perspective on the hospitalized and community-resident groups was supplied by the work of anthropologists Margaret Clark and Barbara Anderson (1967) and from Lowenthal's summary of social factors and mental health. Pertinent conclusions from these studies include the finding that among community-resident elderly there is a relatively modest association between socioeconomic status and psychiatric impairment, more so for men than women. This association decreases with age; among the hospitalized there is a strong association with low socioeconomic status and mental illness and no correlation with social supports. Although the capacity for intimacy is a major resource for community-resident aged, social isolation or withdrawal is not necessarily a handicap, and there is little evidence that widowhood or retirement triggers mental illness. As to conceptions of the self, community-resident elderly women have a more positive self-image than men; among the hospitalized there are no sex differences. Loss of independence is by far the most demoralizing factor for hospitalized and community-resident elderly alike, far more so than pain or social isolation. Being married is *the* major resource for the elderly, while having grandchildren has primarily symbolic significance.

The Longitudinal Study of Transitions started with a planning year in the fall of 1967; by the summer of 1972 two rounds of interviewing had been completed, and by 1978 two additional follow-up studies had been completed. The fifth and last interview round was completed in 1980. Two books were based on the study: Lowenthal and associates (1975) and Fiske and Chiriboga (1986). The study sample was purposely chosen to represent middle-class and blue-collar workers to balance longitudinal studies whose subjects were drawn from more elitist groups, giving rise to findings and theories

not necessarily typical of mainstream Americans. Study participants were drawn from four stages: high school seniors, newlyweds without children, people whose youngest child was a high school senior, and a group planning to retire in two or three years—216 in all.

Objectives of the study were to assess processes of psychosocial change across the adult life course and the comparative influence of sociocultural, situational, and personal factors at successive life stages. The major focus has been on the two older groups (preempty nest and preretirement at baseline); the two younger groups were introduced for generational comparisons. By the last follow-up, cross-cohort analyses became feasible, providing for analysis of the interaction between personal and social change. One of the more surprising findings is that in all of the major transitions there are greater differences between the sexes than between the life-stage groups. For example, at the second (5 years) follow-up more older women than men reported changes in self-concept, and at the last (11 years) contact, this gap between the sexes had become even greater. At this point, too, an interesting relationship emerged between change in self-image and social changes affecting them: the two younger groups reported far more personal than perceived social change, supporting prevalent theories about increasing narcissism among the young of our time. Women in the two older groups ranked highest on both personal and social change. These women had been more concerned with social issues than their male life-stage peers all along, but only at the last contact were their (increasing) concerns significantly associated with a decline in their sense of well-being. Juxtaposing these findings with a notable increase in self-concerns (including hedonism) among older men conveys an important message: among these mainstream Americans, it is the women's lives that become more complex, reflecting continued growth rarely found among older men.

Self-concerns are part of a paradigm of change developed for this research. The three other components are Altruistic, Interpersonal, and Autonomous commitments. In general, change is more common than consistency, and there is a reciprocal relationship among the four categories. In the two older groups, those who became *less* self-preoccupied also *increased* in one or more of the other three commitments. Cross-cohort analyses compared change among the original preretirees, between the first and third contact, with that of the "empty-nest" group, between the third and fifth. One hypothesis for which we found support is that empty-nest subjects at the last contact would rank higher on self-concern than did the preretirees at the third, because the accelerated pace of social change tends to overwhelm them. Once more, however, there is a crucial difference between the sexes: within the empty-nest group at the fifth contact many women whose level of concern with the self *increased* also became *more* committed to one or more of the other three components, whereas most men who became more self-preoccupied manifested significant decreases.

Another finding could only have been traced through a longitudinal study including several age ranges, namely, change in the consequences of childhood deprivation on adaptive levels in adulthood. At the baseline, both men and women in the two younger groups, as well as women in the two older groups, who had experienced such deprivation were less well adapted than their stage peers who had not. Five years later these differences disappeared among men but not women. At the last contact the oldest (originally preretirement) group had criss-crossing trajectories: women were no longer influenced by the circumstances of their childhood, but the oldest men were.

In sum, there is evidence of growth among older women and of stagnation or regression among older men.

MARJORIE FISKE

See also

Baltimore Longitudinal Study of Aging
Duke Longitudinal Studies
Longitudinal Research
Longitudinal Studies of Aging

LANGUAGE COMPREHENSION

Language comprehension in healthy aging reflects a balance between declining function on the one hand and compensatory processes on the other. On the negative side, normal aging is often accompanied by factors that can affect language comprehension. These factors include changes in auditory acu-

ity, declines in working memory capacity, and declines in processing speed. On the positive side, older adults make good use of linguistic and real-world knowledge to aid in effective comprehension.

The effect of working memory limitations on language comprehension has received considerable attention in the aging literature. This attention has been motivated by the concern that age-related limitations in working memory can put older adults at a disadvantage in comprehending spoken or written language, especially when the text contains difficult linguistic structures whose processing places an especially heavy drain on working memory. Such examples include sentences with complex syntax, such as sentences with embedded clauses; very long sentences containing many propositions (units of information) that must be held in memory for full comprehension; and cases where inferences must be developed on the basis of elements separated by large distances in the text. "Working memory limitations also come into play in comprehending sentences that contain temporary syntactic ambiguities where the correct meaning becomes apparent only after hearing the linguistic context that follows the ambiguous region, or when a listener retrospectively realizes the identity of a poorly articulated word based on the linguistic context that follows it" (Wingfield, 1996). Although age-related declines in working memory capacity are thought to limit language comprehension, an unresolved theoretical question is where in the processing stream these limitations come into play (Caplan & Waters, 1999).

Rapid speech also puts older adults at a special disadvantage. Typical speech rates in ordinary conversations average between 140 and 180 words per minute—slower when engaged in thoughtful conversation and faster if working from a prepared script, as in the case of, for example, a television newsreader. Both young and older adults show systematic declines in comprehension and memory as speech rates are progressively increased. However, the rate of decline with increasing speech rate is significantly steeper for older than for younger adults. This age difference in rate of decline with increasing speech rates occurs independently of the changes in auditory acuity that often accompany older adulthood (presbycusis). The detrimental effect of rapid speech on comprehension can be ameliorated to a significant degree by allowing older (and younger) adults more processing time through the addition of especially long pauses to the speech signal at important linguistic boundaries, such as at the ends of sentences and clauses (Wingfield, Tun, Koh, & Rosen, 1999). Giving older adults additional processing time becomes less effective when speech rates exceed 300 words per minute. In addition to rapid speech, speech heard in a noisy background of other speakers also can impose a special problem for older adults (Tun, 1998).

By contrast to these processing deficits, linguistic knowledge is ordinarily well preserved in normal aging (Light, 1990), and older adults have been shown to make effective use of linguistic structure and other context to aid in recognition and recall of spoken language (Wingfield, 1996). This ability to use context, or "top-down" information, in rapid language processing is an inherent part of the perceptual process for listeners. This is necessary because of the rapid rate of ordinary speech and because words in fluent discourse are often poorly articulated. The latter effect is the result of a functional adaptation in which speakers unconsciously reduce their speech-motor effort by adjusting the clarity of their articulation according to the linguistic context in which the words are embedded. This can be revealed in laboratory experiments but is ordinarily unnoticed in everyday speech comprehension because of the perceptual systems' use of linguistic context to automatically compensate for impoverished input.

In addition to effective use of linguistic and real-world context to aid comprehension and memory for language, comprehension is also facilitated by older adults' effective use the intonation, stress, and timing patterns that normally accompany natural speech (speech prosody). Older adults are as adept as young adults in using speech prosody to aid in syntactic resolution as a necessary step to language comprehension (Kjelgaard, Titone, & Wingfield, 1999).

In large part because of these compensatory mechanisms, everyday language comprehension remains among the most stable of cognitive skills in normal aging.

ARTHUR WINGFIELD

See also

Aphasia

Communication Disorders

Hearing

Perception

Senile Dementia

LANGUAGE PRODUCTION

Language production begins with the formulation of a message and includes steps of lexical selection, grammatical encoding, and articulation. Errors, reflecting attentional lapses, processing limitations, and execution problems, can arise at any stage of production. Research on aging and language production has, like the study of production processes in general, lagged behind studies of language comprehension and memory because of the difficulties inherent in experimentally manipulating production processes.

Articulation and Phonology

Apart from motor speech disorders associated with neurological diseases such as apraxia and dysarthria, aging does not seem to be associated with significant changes to articulation and phonology. Paradoxically, the judgment of age on the basis of voice cues is highly accurate. Some researchers have noted age-related increases in disfluencies such as increased hesitations and pauses, increased vocal jitter and voice hoarseness, as well as a slower speaking rate and lower fundamental frequency or pitch. Phonological substitutions and errors, which are common in children's speech, have not been noted in the speech of older adults.

Syntax

The syntax of the speech of older adults appears simplified in comparison to that of young adults (Kemper, 1992). Although sentence length in words remains constant, older adults show a reduction in their use of complex syntactic constructions such as those involving subordinate and embedded clauses. Subordinate and embedded clauses appear to tax older adults' working memories, often analogized as a pool of processing resources that must be shared with different tasks. During undemanding interpersonal conversation or simple picture-description tasks, older adults may be able to use complex syntactic constructions with some ease. But as task demands increase, complex syntax may be sacrificed to free working memory for other uses, such as constructing elaborate narrative plots.

Semantics

Word-finding problems are among the most frequent complaints of older adults. Pauses, circumlocutions, "empty speech" (such as pronouns lacking clear referents), and substitution errors during spontaneous speech may all reflect an age-related impairment in accessing and retrieving lexical information. Studies using word recognition and naming tasks have generally failed to find evidence for a decline in the content or organization of semantic memory; rather it appears that older adults have more difficulty in accessing lexical information, especially the phonological form of words (Burke, MacKay, Worthley, & Wade, 1991). Consequently, tip-of-the-tongue experiences, in which familiar words are temporarily unretrievable, are more common for older adults than for young adults.

Discourse Pragmatics

Pragmatics encompasses a variety of discourse skills, ranging from opening and closing conversations, maintaining and shifting topics, and telling stories to establishing and modifying personal relationships, conveying individual and group identity, gaining and avoiding compliance, and being polite, saving face, or giving offense.

Some discourse skills increase with age: elderly adults create elaborate narrative structures that include hierarchically elaborated episodes with beginnings describing initiating events and motivating states, developments detailing the protagonists' goals and actions, and endings summarizing the outcomes of the protagonists' efforts; evaluative codas are often attached to older adults' narratives, assessing the contemporary significance of these stories. Narrative stories told by older adults' are evaluated more positively, are preferred by listeners, and are more memorable than those told by young adults (Kemper, 1992).

Dyads of older adults mix talk about the past with talk about the present to achieve a shared sense of meaning and personal worth that is lacking in the discourse of young adults. However, intergeneration conversation is often marked by painful self-disclosures by older adults of bereavement, ill-health, immobility, and assorted personal and family events (Coupland, Coupland, Giles, & Wiemann, 1988). Painful self-disclosures may maintain face by contrasting personal strengths and competencies with past problems and limitations. Yet self-disclosures also maintain negative age stereotypes and reinforce age stereotypes about the elderly as weak and disabled. Consequently, self-disclosures can suppress conversational interactions and limit intergenerational talk.

Disorders of Language Production

Language production is disrupted by a number of age-related diseases and disorders: discourse impairments are observed in adults with sensorineural hearing loss (presbycusis); apraxia and aphasia often result from stroke and other neurological trauma; dysarthria is associated with Parkinson's disease and other neurodegenerative diseases; and progressive impairments to semantic and pragmatic aspects of language are common consequences to senile dementia of the Alzheimer's type as well as other forms of dementia. Often language impairments are secondary to motoric or mnemonic impairments but may constitute early markers of undiagnosed conditions.

Considerable interest has focused on disorders of language production with regard to the modularity of language. For example, there is some evidence (Kempler, Curtiss, & Jackson, 1987) that syntactic knowledge is buffered from the effects of Alzheimer's disease, although Alzheimer's disease is associated with severe impairments of semantic and pragmatic aspects of language. Thus, older adults with presumed Alzheimer's dementia exhibit significant word-finding problems as well as disruptions of discourse coherence yet are capable of producing complex grammatical constructions. Some simplifications of syntax may result, but their speech does not appear to become agrammatic. This is taken as evidence for the modularity of syntax as an autonomous or encapsulated system.

A breakdown of inhibition has been attributed to older adults by Hasher and Zacks (1988). As a result, irrelevant information is not suppressed; it intrudes into working memory. According to this view, language production by older adults should be disrupted by the intrusion of irrelevant thoughts and habitual preoccupations. According to this view, verbosity, or repetitious, prolonged, off-target speech, may result (Arbuckle & Gold, 1993), although recent research has suggested that verbosity is not a general characteristic of older adults but is an extreme form of talkativeness that results from intellectual decline associated with frontal lobe impairments. James, Burke, Austin, and Hulme (1998) argue that older adults adopt communicative goals that emphasize conveying meaningful life experiences at the expense of conciseness.

Because fluent language is central to the establishment and maintenance of social relations, language disorders can severely limit older adults' quality of life (Ryan, Giles, Bartolucci, & Henwood, 1986). A negative spiral can result, such that age-related language impairments plus negative stereotyping of older adults lead to the ascription of incompetence and dependency to older adults, patronizing speech, and limited opportunities for social interaction; as a result, older adults may become socially withdrawn or depressed and suffer a further erosion of language skills.

SUSAN KEMPER

See also

Aphasia
Communication Disorders
Memory Dysfunction: Drug Treatment
Memory and Memory Theory
Senile Dementia

LAW
See

Living Wills and Durable Power of Attorney
Legal Services
Older Americans Act
Proxy Decision Making

LEARNED HELPLESSNESS

Learned helplessness, a term coined by Seligman and his coworkers, refers to a syndrome of behavioral deficits resulting from exposure to noncontingent aversive events. Reformulations have expanded the model to include concepts of explanatory style and attribution so that the model is embedded in the larger framework of the psychology of control and motivation (Peterson, 2000; Peterson, Maier, & Seligman, 1993; Skinner, 1995).

The original concept of learned helplessness was based on animal research and leaned heavily on behaviorist conceptions of classical and operant conditioning. In this context, the antecedent-causal factor of learned helplessness was conceived as a condition of noncontingency between the behaviors in an organism's response repertoire and an outcome. This antecedent condition in turn produced in an organism the behavioral consequences of lack of response initiation and reduced performance. The relationship between lack of objective contingency and subsequent behavioral deficit was called learned helplessness. Seligman and his coworkers expanded their original definition in terms of both its antecedents and consequences for two reasons: (1) to accommodate theory-discrepant findings, and (2) to generalize the theory to human behavior.

The reformulated model posited cognitive mediators (expectancies and attributions) as links between "objective" contingency and behavioral deficits. It was argued that individuals interpret the relationships between their behavior or action and particular outcomes and attribute causes to their actions. Seligman and his coworkers distinguished three key bipolar dimensions that are involved when individuals interpret the causes of their action: internal-external, global-specific, and stable-labile. Using these dimensions, several types of attributional or explanatory style can be distinguished that differ in the probability of generating the syndrome of learned helplessness. For example, attributing an outcome of failure in the classroom to lack of ability would imply a cause for failure that is internal, global, and stable. For situations of failure, such an attributional style is considered helplessness-prone (for an outcome of success the opposite conclusion applies).

The syndrome of the behavioral indicators for learned helplessness was also expanded in the reformulated model. Beyond lack of response initiation and difficulty in learning, the syndrome was seen as including general motivational and cognitive deficits, biochemical and physiological correlates, and clinical depression (Peterson, Maier, & Seligman, 1993).

As the original theory gained in scope, it may have lost in precision (Peterson, 2000). The temporal course and causal linkages of the factors and mechanisms involved have become more complex and less explicit. For example, it is no longer clear whether objective conditions of existing noncontingency are necessary for the onset of learned helplessness or if subjective experiences and interpretations of lack of contingency are sufficient. Further, in the case of depression, it is an open empirical question whether attributional styles putatively generative of learned helplessness are antecedents, correlates, or consequences of the depression.

In gerontology, the theory of learned helplessness offers much promise and is often invoked, although it has rarely been employed with adequate rigor and understanding. The attractiveness of the theory of learned helplessness for gerontologists is based on the phenotypic similarity between the learned helplessness behavioral syndrome (e.g., lack of response initiation) and proposals that old age is a time of increased vulnerability and passivity. Passivity in elderly persons, however, is not necessarily due to learned helplessness. According to the original theory of learned helplessness, an outcome of passivity would result because the contingency between the behavior of older individuals and outcomes is reduced.

Observational work by M. M. Baltes and her colleagues in nursing homes offered evidence to the contrary, at least where dependency is concerned (Baltes, 1996). Passive, dependent behavior of elderly persons in nursing homes was found to be connected with a highly systematic contingency provided by the behavior of social partners. Social partners (e.g., caregivers) responded to dependent behavior displayed by older individuals not with noncontingency but with complementary behavior, that served to support the dependency. Thus, with regard to the contingency of dependency, the world of the aged is frequently one of systematic reinforcement of dependent behavior. This example illustrates the pitfalls one encounters if learned helplessness is invoked without demonstration of lack of contingency.

If the evidence on the nature of objective contingency in the world of the aged is not available or is equivocal, what about evidence relevant for the reformulated model involving attributional style and sense of personal control? Is there evidence for changes in attribution of causality with aging? It is tempting to assume that aging brings with it a greater tendency toward dysfunctional attributions and beliefs favoring lack of control. Relevant research is contradictory, in part, because existing work has not attended sufficiently to the complexity of the theory of learned helplessness and instead has used simple bipolar dimensions such as internal versus external locus of control. The absence of relevant work does not detract from the usefulness of the learned helplessness theory as a framework for examining phenomena in old age. What seems most important is to use the theory appropriately and to study in situ whether the factors postulated by the theory are operative.

PAUL B. BALTES
JACQUI SMITH

See also
Learning
Locus of Control

LEARNING

Learning pertains to the acquisition of new information or adaptation of acquired knowledge to new situations. Strictly speaking, learning, or acquisition, cannot be separated from the storage and retrieval, as they are part and parcel of the same process.

Extant literature has documented age-related differences and changes in memory processes, and the findings on learning are similar. Based on periodic reviews of findings on learning and memory (e.g., Poon, 1985; Smith, 1996), the following are four generalizations about older adults' ability to acquire new information:

1. Older adults, as a group, tend to be slower or have more problems learning new informa-

tion, compared with their own performances when they were younger or with performances of a younger cohort.

2. Some of the decline can be explained by learning-related or individual difference–related factors other than chronological age.
3. Older adults' learning performances can be improved with instructions and practice. It is noted that younger adults can improve more than older adults can, given the same instructions or practice.
4. Older adults tend to perform well when they learn new information that is related to their areas of expertise, and they tend to do worse when they acquire information unfamiliar to them.

The extant literature also shows that learning and memory of older adults can be influenced by environmental, biomedical, cognitive, and psychological factors (see Poon, 1985, 1997; Poon, Gurland, Eisdorfer, Crook, Thompson, Kaszniak, et al., 1986, for reviews). Learning efficiency can be influenced by the learner's intelligence and education level, motivation, familiarity with the material, and cognitive and learning styles, as well as by the demands of the learning task, rate of information processing, the amount and type of inter- and intra-task interference, and the amount of familiarity or practice.

Aside from learning deficits that are the direct results of irreversible pathological causes (such as dementia), learning rates and skills can be improved regardless of age. It can be said that being old is not a tenable excuse for being a poor learner.

The question of how to improve learning in older adults is controversial. Biomedical intervention, such as anticholinergic drugs, may have a biological basis for improving memory; their impact has shown to be minimal so far. In contrast, psychological intervention focusing on learning techniques was able to improve learning several-fold and could make noticeable improvement (see Poon & Siegler, 1991). Environmental, cognitive, and biomedical factors are all determinants of the observed performance. To produce meaningful and lasting improvements in learning among older adults, a systems approach has shown to be beneficial for diagnosis and intervention on learning and memory difficulties (See Poon, Gurland, Eisendorfer,

Crook, Thompson, & Kaszniak, 1986; Poon & Siegler, 1991).

LEONARD W. POON

See also
Memory and Memory Theory

LEGAL SERVICES

Besides those provided by privately practicing attorneys retained directly by older persons or persons acting on their behalf, legal services for the elderly are available from a variety of other sources. These sources include pro bono (donated) services by the private bar; legal aid offices funded through the federal Legal Services Corporation, Title 3 of the Older Americans Act, local charitable contributions, and frequently, law school clinical programs. Information on reduced or nonfee legal services for the elderly generally may be obtained from a local bar association, long-term care ombudsman's office, legal aid office, or Area Agency on Aging.

The federal Administration on Aging funds several legal support resource centers to assist attorneys serving older clients. These currently are the American Bar Association Commission on Legal Problems of the Elderly (Washington, DC), National Clearinghouse for Legal Services (Chicago), Legal Counsel for the Elderly of AARP (Washington, DC), National Bar Association (Washington, DC), National Senior Citizens Law Center (Los Angeles), and the Center for Social Gerontology (Ann Arbor, MI).

The field of elder law as a specialty of attorney practice has burgeoned recently. Educational institutions offer specialized courses and other learning experiences in this area, focused textbooks (Frolik & Barnes, 1998; Gallanis, Dayton, & Wood, 2000) and practice handbooks (Krauskopf, Brown, Tokarz, & Bogutz, 1993; Barnes, Frolik, & Whitman, 1997) have proliferated, journals have arisen (e.g., University of Illinois College of Law's *Elder Law Journal*), and national and state organizations (e.g., National Academy of Elder Law Attorneys) devoted to the field have developed and grown.

There are several explanations for this development (Frolik, 1993). The rapid growth in the older population makes it increasingly likely that any legal transaction or dispute will in some way involve older persons, their families, or vendors of goods or services to the elderly and their families. A substantial body of federal and state statutory and regulatory law has been enacted to target older persons particularly, either for special protection against improper discrimination or for the receipt of cash or in-kind benefits. Even generic laws usually take on unique twists and nuances when applied to situations involving older persons.

The content of elder law is broad. Matters falling within this ambit include (but are not limited to) counsel to and representation of older persons, their families, and service providers, regarding Social Security retirement and disability benefits, other federal and state benefits, private pensions and other retirement issues, Medicare and Medicaid (including asset sheltering and divestiture for eligibility purposes), housing issues, financial management (e.g., trusts) and estate planning, medical treatment decision making and advance planning, judicial and nonjudicial forms of substitute decision making, elder abuse and neglect, employment discrimination, and tax counseling. Elder law practice is necessarily interdisciplinary and interprofessional in nature, entailing cooperation among the attorney, other human service providers, governmental agencies, and nonlegal advocacy and support organizations.

According to the National Academy of Elder Law Attorneys (NAELA),

> "Rather than being defined by technical legal distinctions, elder law is defined by the client to be served. In other words, the lawyer who practices elder law may handle a range of issues but has a specific type of clients—seniors. Elder law attorneys focus on the legal needs of the elderly, and work with a variety of legal tools and techniques to meet the goals and objectives of the older client" (quotation from website: *www.naela.org*).

The implications of elder law as a recognized specialty area of legal practice are profound for older persons and society. Older individuals are now firmly entrenched as distinct legal service consumers and beneficiaries of the law, as are agencies that serve the elderly. Laws and practices that target the elderly for particular protections or entitlements are tools that both reflect and help to shape heightened social attitudes toward and respectful treatment of the nation's older citizens.

For further information, visit the National Academy of Elder Law Attorneys (NAELA) website: *www.naela.org*.

MARSHALL B. KAPP

See also
Ethics
Liability and Risk
Living Wills and Durable Power of Attorney
Proxy Decision Making

LEISURE

Definitions of leisure are many and diverse but can be subsumed under four categories: time, activity, state of mind or experience, and action. Aristotle defined leisure as time free from the necessity of labor (*Politics,* Book 1), emphasized the idea of freedom, and conceived of leisure as "available time" in which people do as they want to. Leisure is defined as free time or unobligated time when one is not at work or as discretionary time. Dumazedier defined leisure as "activity—apart from the obligation of work, family, and society—to which the individual turns at will, for either relaxation, diversion, or broadening his knowledge and his spontaneous social participation, the free exercise of his creative capacity" (quoted in Kelly & Godbey, 1992, p. 15). Leisure is defined as a state of mind or being, a condition of the mind and spirit, and as action. Kelly (1987b) suggests that leisure encompasses the existential thrust of "becoming" and offers a social space in which the individual can explore aspects of identity and create personal meaning. Kelly identifies four functions that leisure serves for older adults. It is a source of identity, interaction, intimacy, and personal and social integration. Most definitions of leisure stress the element of relative freedom of choice and intrinsic motivation.

A major question addressed in the literature on leisure and aging is, how does participation in leisure activities change as one ages? On the basis of telephone interviews with 400 people aged 40 and older in Peoria, Illinois, Kelly (1987a) identified a "core" of leisure activities that persist throughout the life course, including informal interaction with household companions, media use and reading, conversation, and play, and found the balance of involvement in other leisure activities shifts throughout the life cycle as roles, self-definitions, and opportunities for involvement change. Kelly found a constriction in activities among the oldest group, who engaged in home-based leisure with family and friends and who decreased their participation in exercise and sports, outdoor recreation, travel, and other activities outside of the home.

The Ohio Longitudinal Study of Aging and Adaptation (OLSAA), a longitudinal study of age-related changes over a 20-year period begun in 1975, surveyed individuals 50 years of age and older in one small town in America and followed these individuals over a 20-year period. Individuals were surveyed in 1975, 1977, 1979, 1981, 1991, and 1995. Approximately 3,000 individuals were surveyed. Atchley (1999) reported the following findings: There is considerable continuity over time in activity level. Age was a significant predictor of activity level, with older age being associated with a lower activity level for women. Participation in senior citizens organizations increased significantly as respondents passed age 65. Socializing with family and friends, reading, and church participation remained stable over time. Activity level in younger years was a major predictor of activity level later in life.

The Baltimore Longitudinal Study of Aging (BLSA) surveyed a large sample of men and women between 1958 and 1992. One questionnaire asked questions about the amount of time spent in 108 activities. Younger, middle-aged, and older adults were included. Verbrugge and associates (Verbrugge, Gruber-Baldini, & Fozard, 1996) reported the following findings about age-related participation in activities: The data suggest a narrower repertoire (less diversity) of activities for older people than for younger or middle-aged adults. Continuity in choice of activities over the life cycle is the rule. Time spent on personal care, sleep and rest, hobbies, and leisure is greater for older people than for young and middle-aged adults. The most physically demanding leisure activities are given less time by older people than by other age groups. Many studies have shown that, compared to younger individuals, older adults watch much more television. Chafetz and colleagues (Chafetz, Holmes, Lande, Childress, & Glazer, 1998) found a high level of media usage in a sample of 868 community-dwelling older adults. All reported watching TV news more frequently than reading the paper, but 61% also read newspapers frequently, and 40% listened to news on the radio.

Another important question addressed in the literature on leisure and aging is, what is the relationship between leisure participation and life satisfaction in late life? Several studies have documented a strong positive relationship between participation in leisure activities and higher life satisfaction in late life (Kelly, 1987a; Patterson & Carpenter, 1994). Leisure is an arena in which to develop a valued identity and achieve competence and recognition and a social space in which to develop and nurture important social relationships with family and friends. Leisure may help to integrate elders into the community by placing them in times and places for exploring relationships that may lead to friendship, intimacy, bonding, and commitment. Leisure participation also provides a source of status and prestige and contributes to feelings of self-worth and self-respect.

In one study, comparing 618 retired White women and retired Black women, Riddick and Stewart (1994) found that the strongest predictor of life satisfaction for Blacks was perceived health, followed by leisure repertoire planning; and the strongest predictor of life satisfaction for older White retired women was perceived health, followed by leisure activity participation and leisure repertoire planning.

Stebbins (1992) suggests that "serious leisure" makes the most important contribution to life satisfaction. Serious leisure is defined as "the systematic pursuit of an amateur, hobbyist, or volunteer activity that is sufficiently substantial and interesting for the participant to find a career there in the acquisition and expression of its special skills, and knowledge" (p. 3). Serious leisure demands perseverance, personal effort to develop a special skill and acquire knowledge, and strong attachment to or commitment to the career of leisure. Csikszentmihalyi (1990), emphasizes the importance of "flow" in leisure. Flow is the "fit" between the demands of an activity and the participants' skill level to meet those demands. According to Csikszentmihalyi, "When a person is able to express his or her consciousness so as to experience flow as often as possible, the quality of life is going to improve" (p. 52). The flow experience involves centering or focusing intently on the task at hand, loss of self-consciousness, and enjoyment. It includes a high level of involvement and mental investment in and commitment to the leisure activity. Kelly and colleagues (Kelly, Steinkamp, & Kelly, 1987) found that older adults who were the happiest engaged in what they termed "high-investment" leisure activities, which were those that were developed over time and required a great deal of effort and resources and acquisition of a skill. Leisure activities that require a high degree of personal effort and intense involvement and commitment, as well as the development of skills and acquisition of knowledge, are the ones most likely to provide for achievement of personal competence and feelings of personal control and mastery, achievement, and recognition and to contribute to life satisfaction and enhance self-concept in later life.

Many new directions in the use of leisure time by older adults are beginning to appear as concomitants of age-congregated living, where not only recreational facilities but also organized activities are part of the expected lifestyle package. Age-related organizations such as the American Association of Retired Persons, National Association of Retired Federal Employees, National Council of Senior Citizens, Elderhostels, and other voluntary associations are influencing the use of leisure. They provide opportunities and training for various types of activities, promote travel and tourism through reduced room rates and other travel specials, and encourage creative expression through education, craft fairs, contests, and other such activities. Senior citizens' clubs, senior centers, day care centers for the elderly, leisure counseling programs, and adult leisure education services are also opening up new opportunities for older adults. Outdoor recreational facilities of all types are increasingly available to older people today. Many older adults are using the computer and the Internet to obtain information, interact electronically with others, and find enjoyment and entertainment.

The trend we can anticipate will be for people to continue the types of leisure activities in old age that they had been involved in as younger adults, with a widening range of specific options from which they will be able to choose, as well as a liberalized view of leisure as a legitimate way to spend the later years.

NANCY J. OSGOOD

See also
Activity Theory
Leisure Programs

LEISURE PROGRAMS

Today, most Americans can expect to spend approximately one third of their lives in leisure, free of the responsibilities of raising a family and working full-time. Michelon (1954), who refers to the elderly in our society as the "new leisure class," suggests that the major dilemma facing retired older people is essentially "how to substitute a new set of personal values and new kinds of activities for the lifelong job of earning a living, raising a family, and overcoming the day-to-day obstacles which affect income, status, and career" (p. 371). Participation in various leisure experiences and programs could be the answer for many older adults.

Maintenance of independence and self-direction are central tasks of late life. Three significant adjustive tasks in later life are adaptation to loss, the life review process, and remaining active to retain function (Kaluger & Kaluger, 1979). Late life is a time in which the social-role changes, such as retirement and widowhood, become obvious. Most leisure choices are motivated by the need to perceive oneself as a valuable, functioning, and contributing member of society, as the older person reappraises and redefines his or her personal worth (Peck, 1968). Another motivation may be the need for affiliation and social integration. Much leisure is focused on establishing or maintaining active involvements with family and friends, or in the church or community (Kelly Steinkamp, & Kelly, 1986; Kelly & Westcott, 1991).

Leisure programmers can help to minimize the severity of late-life adjustments and facilitate accomplishment of developmental tasks through the creative application of leisure programs that address these issues. For older persons, organized leisure experiences may be central to expressive identities, feelings of competence, and social integration. Leisure programs for seniors can help fill the void left by lost work and family roles; contribute to better physical and mental health and functioning; enhance feelings of self worth, self-esteem, mastery, and competence; contribute to human growth and development and personal fulfillment; provide rest, relaxation, and diversion; and help older adults achieve a sense of ego integrity and personal and social integration (Allen & Chin-Sang, 1990; Kelly, 1992).

Leisure programs for older adults should encourage social interaction, belonging, and relatedness, as well as creative expression. Perceived personal control, which is vital to the physical and psychological well-being of older adults, should be the cornerstone of leisure programs that challenge older people through choice and responsibility. Several writers in the field emphasize the importance of programs that provide for exercise and physical activity (Cowper, Morey, Bearon, Sullivan, DiPasquale, Crowley, et al., 1991; O'Brien & Vertinsky, 1991). In developing leisure programs that aim to meet the needs of older adults, we must consider the different needs and interests of participants as well as their levels of physical and cognitive functioning. Consideration also should be given to factors such as cost, timing, accessibility, and transportation.

Leisure programs for seniors abound in this country. Some programs emphasize exercise and physical fitness, whereas others stress social skills and activities. Creative arts and culture programs are available, as are programs that offer educational experiences, travel, and outdoor camping. Intergenerational programs, which provide an opportunity for older people to interact with children and younger people, are becoming popular. Numerous volunteer opportunities and organized volunteer programs also appeal to seniors.

Physical exercise improves cardiovascular functioning, strengthens muscles and bones, and relieves stress and tension. Physical activities, such as walking, cycling, swimming, and aerobics, are popular with seniors and are available through senior centers, departments of parks and recreation, and other commercial avenues. One of the most organized and well-known leisure programs, which emphasizes exercise and physical fitness, is the golden olympics, or senior olympics/senior games

program. These programs, which began in 1970 and are now available in many states, provide opportunities for older individuals to compete for medals in a variety of events, such as basketball, bowling, cycling, fishing, golf, racquetball, softball, and swimming. These programs help older individuals keep in shape and compete physically with others their own age while at the same time providing for social interaction among competitors.

Outdoor programs for seniors offer activities such as nature walks, hiking, fishing and hunting, shelling, picnics, and overnight camping. Most outdoor activities encourage physical fitness. Nature offers a learning laboratory and provides space and freedom not available indoors. After being outdoors, older individuals are usually mildly fatigued, which allows for relaxation and a more restful sleep.

Programs in the creative arts include creative writing and poetry, art, drama, dance, and music. The arts allow for creativity, individuality, and expression of feelings and emotions. The arts provide a means to achieve a personal identity and enhance personal growth. The arts are inspirational and fun. Creative writing includes letter writing, essay writing, journal writing, poetry writing, group poetry, and production of short stories, plays, and novels. Art programs encompass painting, drawing, sculpting, ceramics, woodcrafting, clay modeling, and other plastic art. Music programs include all forms of creating, listening, or participating in music. Drama programs range from puppet shows and organized performances to spontaneous creation. Dance programs use gliding, sliding, hopping, jumping, bending, and stretching. Folk dancing, tap dancing, square dancing, and ballroom dancing may all be used. Many arts programs are intergenerational programs in which older adults participate with children and young people (Clark & Osgood, 1985; Clements, 1994; Vorenberg, 1999).

Recently, intergenerational programs have become popular (Kaplan, 1991). One good example of an intergenerational program is Model Neighborhoods 2000, developed in 1987 by the Center for Human Environments (Kaplan, 1993) at the City University of New York. Projects have been implemented in Honolulu; Mount Vernon, New York; East Harlem, New York; and Long Island, New York. School- and community-based activities, such as reminiscence interviews with elders, autobiographical city walking tours, and community improvement campaigns bring senior adult volunteers and elementary school children (fourth, fifth, and sixth grades) together in a meaningful way.

In the past 20 years many intergenerational programs have brought older adults and children together (Lowenthal & Egan, 1991; Lyons, Onawala, & Newman, 1985). These programs have had positive effects on older adults and children. One intergenerational program, Computer Ease, successfully placed elementary school students as teachers for retired older people who wanted to become computer literate (Drenning & Getz, 1992). Southern Illinois University implemented a successful intergenerational program using retired faculty members as mentors for college students needing special help (Bedient, Synder, & Simon, 1992).

Education programs are another valuable type of leisure program available to older individuals. Many universities, colleges, and community colleges offer courses to older adults. Special-interest courses such as photography are popular. Other courses focus on special needs and problems of late life. Many states waive tuition for students aged 60 and older. Learning can be a rewarding and enriching experience at any age. Through educational programs, older adults learn new knowledge and skills, thereby increasing their functional competence; they meet new friends who share similar interests and a love of learning; and they discover more about how to cope with retirement, widowhood, depression, and other problems associated with aging.

One of the best-attended and best-known organized educational leisure programs is Elderhostel. First offered in 1975 in five New Hampshire colleges, Elderhostel is an education program for older adults patterned after the tradition of hostelling among European youth. Older individuals live cheaply in college dormitories and eat in college cafeterias while attending short-term educational programs that offer subjects as varied as computer science and medieval literature. Today, more than 1,500 educational institutions in every continent of the world offer the Elderhostel program to approximately 200,000 older participants. This program, which has grown from 200 to 200,000 in the past 20 years, demonstrates the high level of interest in learning and leisure among the older population.

In 1976 the National Council on Aging (NCOA) received the first of many demonstration grants from the National Endowment for the Humanities (NEH) to deliver free reading and discussion programs to senior center participants. NEH funded many programs for seniors across the country in the 1970s and 1980s.

Other Education Programs

- Shepherd's Center Movement. Founded in Kansas City, Missouri, in 1972 the Shepherd's Center offers the Adventures in Learning Program. This educational program used older adults as teachers and students through religious congregations.
- Older Adult Service and Information System (OASIS). The OASIS program provides courses for older adults in the arts and humanities, as well as health and wellness education.
- Senior Net. In 1986, Senior Net, a nonprofit learning organization for older computer users, opened the first computer center where older adults taught other older adults how to use computers and do on-line networking.
- Learning-in-retirement programs (LIRs). LIRs are educational programs offered on college campuses in which older adults "determine their own curricula, teach their own courses and engage in self-governance" (Fischer, 1992).
- TraveLearn. This program combines travel to exotic places with learning. In the past 22 years since its inception, TraveLearn has provided learning vacations for older people through more than 300 colleges and universities nationwide. TraveLearn provides on-site lectures, seminars, and field experiences conducted by local resource specialists.

Volunteer opportunities and programs offer older adults a work substitute and a meaningful way to remain active and spend time socializing with and helping others. Several studies have found a strong association between being a volunteer and having higher life satisfaction (Chambré, 1987; Farkas, 1991). Thousands of older people participate in the four volunteer programs initiated by the federal government in the 1960s: The Service Corps of Retired Executives, started in 1964 by the Small Business Administration, coordinates opportunities for 13,000 members to provide management expertise to prospective or current small businesses (Chambré, 1993); Foster Grandparent Program, an intergenerational program begun in 1965, provides situations to 27,000 volunteers, who are low-income elders, to give social and emotional support to developmentally disabled, autistic, physically handicapped, abused and neglected children and receive a small stipend (Action, 1990); Retired Senior Volunteer Program (RSVP), established in 1969, provides 410,000 retired people age 60 and older opportunities to volunteer in many different types of RSVP-sponsored community organizations (Action, 1990); and the Senior Companion Program, established in 1974, offers a stipend to 10,000 volunteers who visit frail elders in their homes (Action, 1990).

Vista and the Peace Corps also offer many opportunities for seniors to volunteer. The American Association of Retired Persons offers many volunteer opportunities through the Widowed Persons Service, the Volunteer in Tax Assistance Program, and other programs. There are many volunteer opportunities for older adults in the Boy Scouts, Girl Scouts, and Campfire Girls. At the local level in communities across the country, there are many opportunities for seniors to spend their leisure time volunteering in hospitals, nursing homes, jails, schools, mental health and substance abuse facilities, day care centers, and voter registration programs.

Leisure programs are as varied as the background and interests of the older individuals they serve. Today's older population is the healthiest, best educated, and most affluent population of seniors in our nation's history. Leisure programs of all types, offered through senior centers, colleges and universities, departments of parks and recreation, local museums and libraries, community service agencies, churches, and other organizations can help fill the ever-increasing hours of leisure and make life in the later years more exciting and meaningful.

NANCY J. OSGOOD

See also
   Adult Education
   Leisure
   Volunteerism

LIABILITY AND RISK
See
   Legal Services
   Living Wills and Durable Power of Attorney
   Provider Liability and Risk
   Proxy Decision Making

LICENSED NURSING
See
   Nursing

LIFE COURSE

The human life course represents an expanding field of inquiry within the social and behavioral sciences. This expansion owes much to the increasing salience of aging as a domain of research since World War II. Pioneering longitudinal studies of children with birth dates before 1930 became studies of adult development in the postwar era. Demographic changes assigned greater priority to the study of adults and aging. The scientific challenge presented by these new priorities focused attention on the social pathways of life and their relation to aging and changes in society.

Elementary Concepts

As concept, the life course refers to a sequence of age-graded events and social roles that are embedded in social structure, culture, and historical change (Elder & O'Rand, 1995). The life course is composed of multiple interlocking trajectories with sequences of this kind in family, work, and health. Social transitions, like changes in status, make up each trajectory and derive particular meaning from them. Thus, the loss of employment derives meaning from its timing within the adult life course, whether early or late in life. A work transition at midlife may entail little change or actually produce a change in course, a turning point that redirects the life course down a different path.

Change in the social life course increases the potential for change in the trajectory of individual aging. Birth cohorts presumably age in different ways when they follow different pathways. This interaction constitutes a meeting ground for life course theory and the developmental science of aging. Building on advances since the 1960s, life course theory has forged a conceptual bridge between aging processes, the life course, and ongoing changes in society, one based on the premise that age places people in the social order and in particular birth cohorts.

References to the life course frequently make use of such terms as *approach*, or *paradigm, perspective, model*, and *framework*. These terms generally belong to the category of a theoretical orientation. Life course theory resembles in function a theoretical orientation. In its most general expression, it defines a common domain of life course inquiry with a framework that guides research in terms of problem identification and formulation, variable selection, and strategies of design and explanatory analysis.

Investigations of the life course and aging may follow one level of analysis or link different levels. At the macroscopic level, social pathways are established by rules, regulations, and social policies of the state and firm (Kohli, 1986). Within a context of late-life pathways, individuals make choices and work out their life course in terms of the constraints and options. This individual life course represents a context for processes of biobehavioral aging. Only cross-level analyses take full advantage of life course theory for knowledge of patterns of aging.

The life course has become increasingly institutionalized over time. According to Kohli (1986), this historical transition features (1) the evolution of "lifetime" as a core dimension of social structure (temporalization); (2) the emergence of age and age-grading as basic elements of life structure (chronologization), with greater standardization in terms of age norms; and (3) greater "individualization," as freedom from local mechanisms of social control. Kohli also depicts a shift toward a life course structured by work. There are both some consensus and some debate on this characterization of life course change.

Three concepts have been used interchangeably with the life course—life cycle, life history, and life span. The term *life cycle* generally describes a sequence of life events and behaviors from birth to death, especially in relation to stages of parenthood over the life course. This sequence is repeated from one generation to the next but only within the framework of a population. Some people do not have children and consequently are not part of an intergenerational life cycle.

Life history refers to a lifetime chronology of events and activities that variably combine data records on life events. These records may be obtained from interviews with a respondent or from archival materials. Some life history interviews are prospective and focus on the present and future, whereas others are retrospective. Life calendars for retrospective data (Giele & Elder, 1998) record the age (year and month) at which transitions occur in each activity domain and thus depict an unfolding life course.

Life span specifies the temporal scope of inquiry and specialization, as in life-span developmental psychology or life-span sociology. A life-span study generally links behavior in two or more life stages. It refers to investigations of antecedents and consequences that extend beyond a single life stage. Each concept—life cycle, life history, and life span—has an important place in studies of the life course.

The Emergence of Life Course Theory

Life course ideas began to form a theoretical orientation on aging during the 1960s and 1970s. The crystallizing forces included the pioneering longitudinal studies that followed children into their adult years from the 1920s; examples include the Oakland Growth Study and the Berkeley Guidance Study at the University of California, Berkeley (Elder, 1999). These studies posed three challenges for a life-course account of aging: (1) to move from child-based concepts of human development to concepts that apply across the life course, (2) to think about how human lives are socially organized and evolve over time, and (3) to relate lives to an ever-changing society.

The first challenge led to the formulation of life-span concepts of human development and aging (see "Life Span" and "Theories of Aging"). Distinctive concepts include the lifelong interaction between changing social contexts and the individual and the cumulation of advantages and disadvantages as people age. The differentiating and cumulating experiences of individuals across the life span fuel a process of complementary aging dynamics: (1) the increasing heterogeneity of individuals over time and (2) the enhanced continuity within individuals.

The second challenge revealed the temporal limitations of a "role theoretical perspective on aging." Role sequences provide information on the order of social roles and transitions, but they do not indicate their precise timing. Social roles also fail to locate people in historical time and thus according to social change. New studies of age in lives brought social and historical time to accounts of the life course.

Neugarten (1968) documented substantial variations in social roles by age, and the pioneering work of Matilda Riley (with Johnson & Foner, 1972) viewed aging in terms of the interplay of age groups and cohort differentiation. Year of birth specifies entry into a particular birth cohort. Trajectories of aging reflect the life stage at which birth cohorts encounter a historical change—some people come of age in a time of prosperity, others in a time of retrenchment.

By the year 2000 the life course had become one of the leading theoretical frameworks in studies of aging (Binstock & George, 1996). This advance was made possible by the remarkable growth of longitudinal studies and the emergence of new methodologies for the collection and analysis of life history data (Giele & Elder, 1998). In addition, a set of theoretical principles gave definition to the life course as a theoretical orientation.

At the most general level, the principle of *lifespan development and aging* states that human development and aging are lifelong processes. The origins of late-life behavior generally lead back to the dependency years and childhood discipline and nurturance. Preventive measures for health in the later years require knowledge that can come only from programmatic life-course studies of early influences and behavior.

The principle of *timing* addresses temporal variations across the life course: The developmental antecedents and consequences of life transitions, events, and behavior patterns vary for the trajectory of aging according to their timing in a person's life. The meaning and personal consequences of life transitions frequently vary across the life course, such as the loss of a child and spouse versus the more expectable event of death in old age. Histori-

cally, the timing of events has changed in ways that have important social consequences. Thus, age at retirement has declined in Western societies along with norms concerning the duration of work.

The principle of *linked lives* states that the individual life course is embedded in relationships with others: Lives are lived interdependently, and social-historical influences are expressed through this network of relationships. From this perspective, the synchronization of life transitions and events entails the coordination of related lives, as expressed in the retirement of a couple and caregiving by the partner. It is also expressed in modes of solidarity and conflict across the generations and the lives of aging individuals (Bengtson, 1996). Certain events in the younger generation have immediate consequences for parents, as when young daughters become pregnant and give birth to a child during the adolescent years. The mother becomes a grandmother.

The principle of *lives in time and place* views the life course and aging in historical context: The life course of individuals is embedded in and shaped by the historical times and places they experience over their lifetime. Particularly in societies undergoing rapid change, historical effects generally take the form of a cohort effect when social change differentiates the life experience of successive cohorts, such as younger and older men in the Great Depression and World War II (Elder, 1999). History also takes the form of a period effect when the influence of a social change is relatively uniform across successive birth cohorts. A third type of effect occurs through maturation or aging. The diversity of historical experience within birth cohorts favors investigation of the change process itself, such as income loss during depressions and recessions.

The fifth principle recognizes that the life course is not simply influenced by social structure and historical circumstance. It is also shaped by the choices or decisions that people make—the decision to change residence, to take a different job, to continue with advanced education, and to live alone, with family, or in a retirement community. The principle of *human agency* asserts that individuals construct their own life course through the choices and actions they have taken within the constraints and opportunities of history and social conditions. Individual competencies make a difference in the quality of these choices.

The evolving life course generally indicates a loose connection between social stages and transitions. Age grades and this loose coupling (Elder & O'Rand, 1995) represent opposite sides of the adult life course—its social patterning and regulation, on the one hand, and the individual's initiative on the other, with elements of disorder.

Conclusion

The life course of aging has become a vigorous field of cross-disciplinary inquiry over the past 40 years, drawing upon fundamental sociological contributions to an understanding of how lives are socially patterned and altered under conditions of historical change.

The life course has achieved prominence as a theoretical orientation for the study of aging in the 21st century. This achievement reflects theoretical advances, the dramatic growth of longitudinal samples, and statistical innovations for the study of change and multilevel contexts. Studies are centering on the social pathways of human lives and adaptations, with increasing emphasis on the imprint of historical change for trajectories of human development and aging. An understanding of mechanisms of behavioral continuity and change in aging requires panel studies that link the early years of life with subsequent patterns of aging.

GLEN H. ELDER, JR.

See also
Age Stratification
Life Events
Longitudinal Research

LIFE CYCLE
See
Life Course

LIFE EVENTS

Occasionally, a concept or theory is so irresistible that it takes the scientific community by storm.

Introduction of the concept of life events to the social and biomedical sciences had precisely that effect. And life events remain a major topic in aging research today. Life events are identifiable, discrete changes in life patterns that create stress and can lead to illness onset or the exacerbation of preexisting illness. Life events research traces its roots to the pioneering biomedical research of Holmes and Rahe (1967) and the classic sociological study of stress known as the Midtown Manhattan Study (Langner & Michael, 1963). Subsequently, literally thousands of studies examined the impact of life events on physical and mental health and the factors that mediate and moderate the effects of life events on health outcomes.

Why was the concept of life events so compelling? Numerous other variables are equally powerful predictors of physical and mental illness. Primarily, life events offered a potential social risk factor compatible with epidemiologic theories of illness onset, theories that emphasize the role of environmental agents on the health of human organisms. Although there is virtual consensus that social environments play a powerful role in health and illness, isolating relevant parameters of social environments and documenting their effects has been a difficult challenge. Life events are especially attractive because they represent a social risk factor rivaling physical risk factors in terms of being objective (i.e., occurrence of the event can be verified), potentially quantifiable, and occurring prior to illness onset (thus clarifying causal order).

Interest in life events research did not originate in aging research, but many gerontologists have examined the effects of life events on health in later life. The life events perspective is compatible with the crisis orientation that characterized early research on aging—an orientation that focused on the losses that are common in later life. Many of those losses (e.g., widowhood, economic problems) can be viewed as life events. Research has shown that older adults actually experience fewer life events than do young adults. Interest in the impact of life events on late life health continues because of evidence that (a) the life events experienced by older adults are more likely than those that happen to younger adults to involve major losses, especially bereavement, and (b) resources for coping with stress typically decrease in later life. Thus, older adults may be more vulnerable than younger adults to the adaptive challenges posed by life events.

Evolution of the Life Events Perspective

Initially, research emphasized only one element of life events: the degree to which they disrupt established behavior patterns. Early research explicitly stated that subjective perceptions of stress are unimportant; it is the degree of change that calibrates the stressfulness of life events. Investigators using a more interactionist perspective demonstrated convincingly, however, that change itself is not the "active ingredient" in the link between life events and illness. Rather, perceptions of stress are crucial for understanding the effects of life events on health. Consequently, measures of life events now are routinely restricted to events that are perceived as negative or stressful by the individuals who experience them. The importance of experiential measures of life events is further documented by evidence that there is no life event that is uniformly described as positive or negative—stress is indeed in the eye of the beholder.

In early research, life events were considered synonymous with social stress. It is now clear, however, that they are but one category of stressful experiences. Also important are chronic stressors, which are ongoing stressful experiences that do not represent sudden changes in behavior patterns, but persist over long periods of time (e.g., chronic poverty, chronic marital conflict, long-term commitments to providing care for an impaired relative). Thus, social stress is a broad concept with, with life events representing only one important area of inquiry.

Major Issues in Life Events Research

Research on life events covers a broad range of issues. For purposes of convenience, three major research areas of special relevance to late life are briefly reviewed.

Mediators and Moderators. Without question, the major focus of life events research has been understanding the effects of life events on health outcomes. It was observed early on that life events have variable outcomes; although they are statistically significant predictors of illness, most individuals who experience life events do not become ill. The central research question then became: Under what conditions do life events lead to negative health outcomes? More than two decades of sophisticated research has focused on the causal pathways between stress and illness and, more recently, the antecedents of social stress.

It is now clearly documented that whether or not stressful life events harm health is a function of both the strength of the life event (e.g., death of a loved one poses a greater threat than retirement) and the resources available to the individual for responding to the stress. Two major types of social resources are especially powerful in offsetting the effects of stress: economic resources and social support. The value of economic resources is straightforward: many stressful situations can be remedied or at least diminished by adequate financial resources (e.g., one can live comfortably through involuntary job loss, the economic consequences of widowhood are minimized). Social support, which refers to the tangible and intangible forms of assistance provided by family and friends, is a broader resource. A number of typologies have been suggested for understanding the multiple functions of social support. One useful typology consists of three types of social support: (1) instrumental support, which refers to the provision of tangible assistance (e.g., provision of transportation or personal care); (2) informational support, which refers to the provision of essential information about relevant resources external to the support system (e.g., information about relevant community services); and (3) emotional support, which refers to the comfort, self-validation, and companionship offered by intimate others. (See Krause, 1999, for a recent review.)

Although both economic resources and social support have been shown to mediate the effects of stress on health outcomes, other research suggests that the relationship is statistically interactive rather than mediating. This issue is commonly referred to as the stress-buffering hypothesis (e.g., Lin, Woelfel, & Light, 1985). Its proponents suggest that social support protects health only under conditions of stress, rather than having a more general protective effect that exists independent of stress. Research provides empirical confirmation for both the stress-buffering hypothesis and the alternate main effects hypothesis. Either way, however, social support plays a vital role in reducing the likelihood that stress will have negative effects on health.

There also is convincing evidence that psychosocial resources such as self-esteem and a sense of mastery mediate some of the effects of life events on health (e.g., Pearlin, 1989). These relationships are complex. On the one hand, high levels of self-esteem and mastery offset some of the potentially harmful effects of life events on health outcomes. On the other hand, stressful life events can erode self-esteem and mastery, increasing the individual's vulnerability to stress-related health problems. One of the important functions of effective social support is bolstering individuals' psychosocial resources so that they can better meet the challenges of stressful life events.

Life events (and stressors more generally) also have been investigated as mediators of the effects of causally prior risk factors on health. A number of investigators, especially Aneshensel (1992) and Pearlin (1989), have suggested that the different roles and locations in social structures that individuals occupy may affect their amounts of exposure to life events and, thus, ultimately affect health. The primary factors examined as potential antecedents of exposure to life events have been standard demographic variables (age, sex, race) and socioeconomic status (SES). This is a complex research literature; nonetheless, the general pattern of findings suggests that life events mediate some, but not all of the effects of demographic characteristics and SES on health. The unmediated effects of these variables has served as the foundation for theoretical speculation that specific subgroups of the population may be differentially vulnerable to life events and other stressors.

Developmental Perspectives on Life Events. Although the volume of research is small, psychologists have begun to articulate the links between psychological development and life events. Efforts to understand psychological growth, subjective well-being, and positive mental health have spurred attention to the developmental consequences of life events. The major foci of this research is the ways in which life events often trigger developmental changes (e.g., in personality and self-concept) and how the effects of life events can differ depending upon the age or developmental stage of the individuals who experience them. Ryff's work in this area has been especially impressive (e.g., Ryff & Dunn,

1985; Showers & Ryff, 1997). In addition, a variety of other research ranging from investigation of the differential effects of parental divorce, depending on the age of the child; the benefits and rewards of caring for an impaired older adult, and the rewards of late life marriage all speak to the issue of changes in personality that can result from life events. Unlike research from the stress and illness perspective, this research suggests that life events can have positive, as well as negative effects.

Life Events in Life Course Perspective. Sociological studies of the life course also pay substantial attention to life events, although the term "life course transitions" is used more frequently in that research tradition. One important element of life course perspectives is emphasis upon the sequences of transitions that create long-term trajectories or pathways. Life course studies have focused primary attention on the timing and sequencing of events/transitions, and the broad range of outcomes related to them (e.g., socioeconomic achievement, marital stability) (see George, 1993 for a review of research in this tradition). Most life course studies have focused on sequences of transitions in early adulthood. An important contribution to aging research, however, is the body of work by O'Rand and Henretta (1999), demonstrating that economic status in late life is, to a substantial degree, a result of work and family decisions made earlier in the life course.

After more than 30 years, the antecedents and consequences of life events continue to engage the energies of social, behavioral, and biomedical scientists. The core of this research has been the links between stress and illness. More recently, life events have proven to be important for understanding psychological development across adulthood and the ways that status and well-being in late life are, in large part, a result of events experienced decades earlier.

LINDA K. GEORGE

See also
Epidemiology of Aging: A New View of Health Status and Risk Factors

LIFE EXPECTANCY

Life expectancy, also known as the expectation of life at birth, is a measure of current mortality conditions in a population. It is calculated by imposing a set of age-specific death rates on a hypothetical cohort of newborns. In computing the life expectancy for U.S. females in 1995, for instance, it would be assumed that when the hypothetical cohort reached age 80, the proportion of survivors who die would be the same as the proportion of 80-year-old U.S. women who died in 1995 (Shryock & Siegel, 1976). The life expectancy of the hypothetical cohort is the mean age at death of the members of the cohort.

Life expectancy can also be calculated starting at an age other than birth. To calculate remaining life expectancy at age 65, for instance, a hypothetical cohort of 65-year-olds would be subjected to the observed age-specific death rates prevailing among individuals age 65, 66, and so on up to the highest age attained.

Actual cohorts live over time: a newborn will not reach age 80 for 80 years. Death rates for 80-year-olds may change considerably in that period. In most populations in recent decades death rates have declined at most ages, but there are also many instances of rising mortality and considerable uncertainty exists about future health conditions. It is, therefore, crucial to emphasize that life expectancy is a measure of current mortality and not a forecast about how long individuals will actually live.

Over the course of human history, up until about 1800 or so, life expectancy was low, between 20 and 30 years for most populations, largely because a third to a half of newborns typically died before reaching age 5. Even at age 5, however, remaining life expectancy was generally only 30 to 40 years, and for the minority who survived to age 50, remaining life expectancy was probably only 10 to 15 years. In contrast, in most developed countries today, life expectancy at birth is around 75 years for men and 80 years for women, and remaining life expectancy at age 50 exceeds 25 years for men and 30 years for women. Japan has overtaken Sweden, Norway, and Iceland as the world's leader: life expectancy at birth in Japan is currently 79 years for men and 84 years for women, and life expectancy at age 50 is more than 30 years for men and 35 years for women.

Up until 1950, most of the increase in life expectancy at birth was attributable to reductions in death rates at younger ages and especially infant mortality. Today the probability of surviving from birth to age 60 is around 90% in most developed countries. Consequently, increases in life expectancy now hinge on improvements in mortality at older ages. In most developed countries, death rates at all ages above 60 have declined substantially since 1950, with improvements even among nonagenarians and centenarians (Kannisto, 1995a). The rate of reduction has accelerated since 1950: Over the last decade, mortality has declined among octogenarians and nonagenarians at an average rate of about 2% per year in most developed countries and at a rate of almost 3% per year in Japan (Kannisto, Lauritsen, Thatcher, & Vaupel, 1994).

If mortality at younger ages can be kept at low levels, average annual reductions in mortality at older ages of 2% per year would increase life expectancy by about 2 years per decade. A newborn girl in developed countries has a life expectancy of about 80 years, but if such improvements could be sustained for a century, the average newborn girl would actually live about a century (Vaupel, 1997; Vaupel & Gowan, 1986). Whether mortality can continue to be reduced—and if so, whether the pace of reduction will slow or continue to accelerate—is a hotly disputed matter of speculation (Vaupel, 1998; Wilmoth, 1998). The difference between a life expectancy of 80 and an average length of life of 100 does, however, illustrate the fact that life expectancy is a measure of current mortality conditions and not a forecast.

JAMES W. VAUPEL

See also
Compression of Morbidity: Disease Postponement
Demography
Epidemiology: A New View of Health Status and Risk Factors
Life Extension
Life Span

LIFE EXTENSION

Life extension can be evaluated only by statistical analyses of populations. Although life expectancy from birth (estimated average length of life) is widely employed in such evaluations of human populations, median length of life is commonly used in experimental studies with animal models, wherein life extension is inferred if a manipulation increases the median length of life. However, many investigators use the term *life extension* only for manipulations that increase the maximum length of life (the length of life of the last member of a birth cohort to die). Indeed, maximum length of life was long considered a reliable index of the rate of aging. Based on this belief, when a manipulation increased maximum length of life, it was felt to do so by slowing the rate of aging. In recent years this concept has been challenged by the recognition that the maximum length of life is influenced by population size, tending to increase as the population size increases (Gavrilov & Gavrilova, 1990). Moreover, even when comparing populations of similar sizes, factors other than the rate of aging have been shown to influence the maximum length of life (Promislow, 1993). In studies with animal models, these problems can be partially overcome by utilizing the age of the long-lived survivors of a cohort (e.g., age of the hundredth percentile survivors) to provide an index of maximum length of life (Yu, 1995). In the total human population, the oldest age reached by only one in 100 million people is felt to be a reasonable index of maximum length of human life.

Experimental Findings with Model Organisms

The first study to show that maximum length of life can be extended was that of Loeb and Northrop (1917), who found that in populations of fruit flies (*Drosophila melanogaster*) living in the temperature range of 10°C to 30°C those in lower temperatures have a longer maximum length of life than those in higher temperatures. This finding also has been obtained with other poikilothermic species, such as nematodes and fish but not with homeothermic species (i.e., mammals and birds). This increase in maximum length of life has been thought to be due to the fact that lowering the environmental temperature of a poikilotherm decreases its metabolic rate (McCarter, 1995). However, there is disagreement as to whether reduction in metabolic rate plays an important role in such life extension.

Decreasing the dietary energy intake, a manipulation called caloric restriction or dietary restriction, is the only experimental manipulation that has been consistently found to extend the maximum length of life of a mammalian species. Since first described in a study on rats by McCay, Crowell, and Maynard (1935), caloric restriction has been found to extend life in a variety of rat and mouse strains as well as in hamsters (Masoro, 1996). It is not known if caloric restriction causes life extension in other mammalian species because the relevant research has not been done; compared to rodent species, the larger size and longer life spans of mammals make such research extremely costly. However, such studies are now underway on nonhuman primates, although it will be many years before the results will be available (Roth, Ingram, & Lane, 1999). In addition to increasing the maximum length of life of rodent species, caloric restriction has had this action in a variety of poikilothermic species, including fish (Finch, 1990).

Studies on the effect of exercise on life extension in rats have had a long and controversial history. It now appears that there are two reasons for the conflicting findings: the use of rats suffering chronic infections and the stressful procedures used to make the rats exercise. In studies free of these problems, exercise programs were found to extend the median length of life but not the maximum length of life of rat populations (Holloszy & Kohrt, 1995).

Genetic manipulations have extended length of life in both mammalian and invertebrate species. Selective breeding has resulted in long-lived strains of fruit flies (Arking, Buck, Berrios, Dwyer, & Baker, 1991) and nematodes (Johnson, 1990). Single-gene mutations have been found to increase the length of life of nematodes (Lithgow & Kirkwood, 1996) and yeast (Kennedy, Austriaco, Zhang, & Guarente, 1995). In addition, single-gene mutations have extended the length of life of mice (Miller, 1999). Transgenic fruit flies that overexpress both superoxide dismutase and catalase also have an extended length of life (Orr & Sohal, 1994).

Many pharmacological agents have been used in attempts to extend length of life in animal models. Because oxidative stress is felt to be, at least in part, a cause of aging, antioxidants have been much studied in this regard. Naturally occurring antioxidants, such as vitamin E, vitamin C, and beta-carotene, as well as synthetic antioxidants, such as butylated hydroxytoluene, have been administered either singly or in mixtures to rats and mice. None of these has had a significant effect on either the median or the maximum length of life in rat and mice populations (Yu, 1995). The pharmacological agent that has shown the most promise as a life-extending agent is deprenyl. Knoll (1988) reported that deprenyl markedly increased the length of life when administered to old rats. Since then, other investigators have found that deprenyl extends the life of rats, mice, and hamsters, but the magnitude of this effect was much less in the more recent studies than that reported by Knoll. The administration of dehydroepiandrosterone (DHEA) has been claimed to extend the life of rodents and to have other antiaging actions (Bellino, Daynes, Hornsby, Lavrin, & Nestler, 1995). However, it is unclear if these actions are merely due to the fact that DHEA reduces food intake; that is, it may be causing caloric restriction rather than having a direct life-prolonging action. It has been claimed that melatonin added to the drinking water extends the life of rats and mice, but these findings must be viewed with caution because only small numbers of animals were studied and food intake was not carefully monitored (Reiter, 1995).

Information on Humans

Probably the most remarkable biological phenomenon of the 20th century is the marked increase in human life expectancy from birth, increasing in the United States from about 47 years for both sexes in 1890 to 73 years for men and 78 years for women in 1990. Public health measures, such as sanitary engineering, have certainly played a major role in this increase. Other factors include medical advances, nutrition, and protection from damaging environments (e.g., air conditioning, central heating), and there are possibly others yet to be identified. Much of the increase relates to the prevention of premature death at young ages. However, in the last half of the century, significant increases in life expectancy from age 60 also have occurred (Vaupel, 1997). It is difficult to know with certainty whether the maximum length of human life has been extended during the 20th century, but the increasing fraction of centenarians in the world population makes it likely that there has been such an extension.

Health food stores and pharmacies sell many food additives and other agents that purportedly extend life. None of these has been proven to do so. However, there is one intervention that does increase life expectancy in humans, and that is habitual exercise (Lee, Paffenbarger, & Hennekens, 1997). Whether the maximum length of life is also affected by such exercise has yet to be addressed.

EDWARD J. MASORO

See also
    Centenarians
    Diet Restriction
    Exercise
    Life Expectancy
    Life Span
    Long-Lived Human Populations
    Oldest Old

LIFE REVIEW

The tendency of older persons toward self-reflection and reminiscence used to be considered a sign of loss of recent memory and therefore of aging-related pathology. However, in 1961 Butler (1963) postulated that reminiscence in the aged was part of a normal life-review process brought about by realization of approaching dissolution and death. It is characterized by the progressive return to consciousness of past experiences and particularly the resurgence of unresolved conflicts for reexamination and reintegration. If the reintegration is successful, such reminiscence can give new significance and meaning to life and prepare the person for death by mitigating fear and anxiety.

This evaluative process is believed to occur universally in all persons in the final years of their lives, although they may not be totally aware of it and may in part defend themselves against realizing its presence. It is spontaneous and unselective and is seen in other age groups as well (adolescence, middle age), especially when confronted by death or a major crisis; but the intensity and emphasis on putting one's life in order are most striking in old age. In late life, people have a particularly vivid imagination and memory for the past and can recall with sudden and remarkable clarity early life events. They often experience a renewed ability to free-associate and to bring up material from the unconscious. Individuals realize that their own personal myth of invulnerability and immortality can no longer be maintained. All of this results in reassessment of life, which, depending on the individual, may bring depression, acceptance, or satisfaction.

The life review can occur in a mild form through mild nostalgia, mild regret, a tendency to reminisce, tell stories, and the like. Often the life story will be told to anyone who will listen. At other times it is conducted in monologue in private and is not meant to be overheard. It is in many ways similar to the psychotherapeutic situation in which a person is reviewing his or her life in order to understand present circumstances (Haight & Webster, 1995).

As part of the life review one may experience a sense of regret that is increasingly painful. In severe forms it can lead to anxiety, guilt, despair, and depression. And in extreme cases, if a person is unable to resolve problems or accept them, terror, panic, and suicide can result. The most tragic life review is one in which a person decides that his/her life was a total waste.

Some of the positive results of a life review can be the righting of old wrongs, making up with enemies, coming to accept one's mortality, and gaining a sense of serenity, pride in accomplishment, and a feeling of having done one's best. Life review gives people an opportunity to decide what to do with the time left to them and to work out emotional and material legacies. People become ready to die, although they are in no hurry. Possibly, the qualities of serenity, philosophical development, and wisdom observable in some older people reflect a state of resolution of their life conflicts. This is usually accompanied by a lively capacity to live in the present, including the direct enjoyment of elemental pleasures such as nature, children, forms, colors, warmth, love, and humor. Some become more capable of mutuality, with a comfortable acceptance of the life cycle, the universe, and the generations. Creative works may result, such as memoirs, art, and music. People may put together family albums and scrapbooks and study their genealogies.

One of the great difficulties for younger persons (including mental health personnel) is to listen thoughtfully to the reminiscences of older people. Nostalgia is viewed as dysfunctional behavior, representative of living in the past, and a preoccupation with self, as well as boring, meaningless and time-consuming. Yet, as a natural healing process, it represents one of the underlying human capacities on which all psychotherapy depends. The life review is a necessary and healthy process and should be recognized in daily life as well as used in the mental health care of older people (Lewis & Butler, 1974). Life review therapy and reminiscence therapy are employed, for example, in nursing homes (Burnside, 1988). Many people are taping their lives for their families.

There have been a number of studies related to life review and life review therapy, and there has been growing interest in related topics, such as storytelling, oral history, guided autobiography (Birren & Deutchman, 1991), and narrative or experiential gerontology (Haight & Webster, 1995). The International Society of Reminiscence and Life Review was established in 1995.

ROBERT N. BUTLER

See also
Autobiographical Memory
Biography
Life Review: Reminiscence

LIFE REVIEW: REMINISCENCE

When discussing the issue of life review, it seems useful to distinguish between three terms of have been variously applied to the phenomenon of individuals reflecting about their lives: life review, reminiscence, and autobiographical memory. These terms stem mostly from different research traditions, which have had little exchange with each other. Research on autobiographical memory emerged out of classical memory research and is concerned with the episodic memories about our past (see e.g., Rubin, 1995). Reminiscence, in the sense of remembering episodes of one's life, probably comes closest to that notion. In aging research, starting with Butler's work on life review, the empirical interest in the concepts of reminiscence and life review flourished in the 60s and 70s (for review see Webster & Cappeliez, 1993). Most of this literature was not very precise, however, neither in terms of conceptual usage nor in terms of methodology. A strong emphasis was put on clinical applications in gerontological settings. Research in the late 80s and 90s started to remedy such shortcomings.

There is agreement now that reminiscence is part of life review but not synonymous with it. Reminiscence refers to the (re-)construction of past events, life review in addition includes the attempt to explain and interpret these reconstructed events. From a social-cognitive perspective, life review is the more complex process. Life review can be considered a product as well as a process. When distinguishing these two terms, it is important to keep process functions and process components separate.

A number of traditional developmental theorists have assigned a particular timing and function to life review. Erikson, for instance, assigned life review exclusively and normatively to old age. Life review should support the solution of the final psychosocial crisis, the one between integrity and despair. C. G. Jung, Charlotte Bühler, and Bernice Neugarten extended the time window for life review to occur from old age to the second half of life. In their views, life review helps to restore psychic balance after realizing that time until death may be shorter than time since birth. Finally, Levinson linked life review to life transitions in general, irrespective of age. He has argued that life review supports adaptation during life transitions. It helps to prepare for new demands and a change in life structure. More recently, Webster (1993) has distinguished the following functions of reminiscence: boredom reduction, death preparation, identity formation/problem solving, conversation, intimacy maintenance, bitterness revival, teaching/informing. Pillemer (1993) offered a more highly aggregated tripartite distinction; however, it seems compatible with the Webster categorization. He differentiates directive, psychodynamic, and communicative functions of reminiscence.

Empirical research has demonstrated that life review and reminiscence not only occur in old age but indeed serve important functions throughout life. Certainly, given the differences in the amount of life to be reminisced or reviewed, the styles may vary. Also given that different life tasks are at stake at different periods in the adult life span, the primary function of life review and reminiscence may change as we move through life but it is wrong to

assume that these processes only start to occur in old age. It also seems wrong to assume that they occur normatively in old age. Not all older adults—at least according to self report—review their lives (Fitzgerald, 1995). It has been suggested that life review is an important social-cognitive process that helps to gain insight into life in general and into one's own life in particular (e.g., Staudinger, 1989). Furthermore, life review has been considered as a coping mechanism. Whether this coping mechanism turns out to be functional or dysfunctional depends on a number of circumstances that as a whole have not yet been systematically investigated. By comparing our current status to that in the past or by selectively remembering good times and successes of the past, we may gain strength for dealing with the present (e.g., Aldwin, Sutton, & Lachman, 1996). Thinking back over one's life may also help to find meaning in losses and failures, accept mistakes and weaknesses, and actually mature by doing so. However, life review may also be romanticizing, self-pitying or self-aggrandizing. It seems obvious that the kind of self-reflection that leads to maturation is not always comforting but rather challenging and taxing. Thus, recently it has been suggested that doing life review together with someone else may support the emancipatory and maturing function of life review (Staudinger, 1996).

Finally, it is important to acknowledge the diachronic function of life review. It is by thinking back over our past that we extend our existence into the past; and certainly by thinking into the future, as it is the case when doing life planning, we extend ourselves beyond the present into the future. With increasing age, it seems that the evaluation of our present state is more and more closely linked to that of the past and the future. Whereas in young adulthood, the past is evaluated as much worse and the future as much more positive than the present, such big evaluative differences disappear in old age (Ryff, 1991).

In sum, research on reminiscence and life review has made progress over the last decade. It seems that people reminisce and review their lives throughout the life span but they do so in different ways and for different reasons. Many questions are still to be explored: we are only beginning to understand how we construct our identity by creating our life story (McAdams, 1998), or how it works on a microanalytic level that we gain insight about ourselves and life in general from reviewing our lives and the lives of others (Staudinger, 1999).

URSULA M. STAUDINGER

See also
Autobiographical Memory
Biography
Life Review

LIFE SATISFACTION
See
Subjective Well-Being

LIFE SPAN

Life span is a traditional but confusing phrase with several meanings, including mean, median, or modal age of adult death; the age that only a small fraction of a cohort attain; and the maximum observed age for a species. Life span is widely misused in gerontology to refer to the maximum age to which any individual in a species can possibly live. This hypothesized species-specific life span is assumed to be determined by intrinsic forces, independent of the environment. There is no empirical evidence supporting this concept, and there appears to be no theoretical reason for such an intrinsic limit to life to have evolved: The notion is apparently sustained by a process of mutual citation (Gavrilov & Gavrilova, 1990).

An individual who attains some exceptional age may survive yet another day. Hence, as the human population grows and if health conditions improve, the maximum attained human life span will increase. The high death rates suffered by the extremely old impose, however, a practical, probabilistic limit to the maximum life span achieved by a population of a certain size in a particular environment.

By the year 2000 there may be 100,000 centenarians alive around the world, but at the turn of the 20th century there were probably well under 1,000.

In most years before 1800 there may have been no genuine centenarian alive anywhere in the world. The first plausible supercentenarian, Katherine Plunkett, died in 1931 in Northern Ireland, probably at age 111. Jeanne Calment in France celebrated her 120th birthday on February 21, 1995: Her age has been carefully verified. If life span is defined either as the maximum reliably reported age or as the age that only one person in 100 million can be expected to reach, then the human life span may have increased by about two decades since the industrial revolution (Jeune & Vaupel, 1995).

For medflies (Carey, Liedo, Orozco, & Vaupel, 1992), and probably various other species of animals and plants (Finch, 1990), death rates decline to low levels at advanced ages. Even for these species, however, the relentless risk of mortality eventually fells even the longest-lived survivor of any cohort, albeit at an age that is highly variable from cohort to cohort.

JAMES W. VAUPEL

See also
Centenarians
Compression of Morbidity: Disease Postponement
Demography
Life Expectancy
Oldest Old

LIPOFUSCIN

First identified in 1911 by Stubel, lipofuscin is a golden-brown, partly insoluble pigment composed of polymers of lipids and phospholipids complexed with protein. The formation and accumulation of this autoflorescent intracellular pigment is among the most constant morphological changes occurring with increasing age. It is often referred to as "wear and tear" or aging pigment (Sohal, 1981) and is found in the cells of myocardium, spleen, liver, prostate, interstitium of the testes, and the nervous system. Although lipofuscin is not injurious to the cell or its function, its importance lies in its being the telltale sign of free radical injury and lipid peroxidation (Costran, Kumar, & Robbins, 1994) and when present is associated with the age of the cell.

The protein oxidation by free radicals and/or peroxidases may play an important role in lipofuscin accumulation (Kato, Maruyama, Naoi, Hashizuma, & Osawa, 1998). Lipofuscin has a heterogeneous chemical composition, including lipid, carbohydrate, and protein, which may be examined by several histochemical methods. Although arguments abound as to the origin of lipofuscin, there appear to be more adherents to the belief that lipofuscin originates from lysosomes. These latter structures are cytoplasmic particles 50–80 Å in diameter and bound by a unit membrane. The lipofuscin particles may be insoluble residues remaining from lysosomal activity. This origin is strongly supported by the high degree of acid phosphate activity present in both lysosomes and lipofuscin. Examination by electron microscopy reveals electron-dense osmiophilic particles, bound by a single membrane, with polymorphic internal structures ranging from fine particles in early stages to aggregates of coarse laminated bodies composed of dense bands or dense granular material (Brody & Vijayashankar, 1977). Fat globules are an integral part of lipofuscin. The most intriguing questions regarding lipofuscin are its function and the effect it may have on cellular activity.

Lipofuscin granules may have a variable distribution within a cell, evidently dependent on the cell type. Strehler, Mark, Midvan, and Gee (1959) found that the amount of pigment occupying a cell and its rate of accumulation increased linearly with age, so that by 90 years, up to 7% of the intracellular volume of a myocardial cell may be occupied by these pigment granules. The volume occupied by lipofuscin in neurons is even more striking. These granules may be scattered in the cytoplasm or clumped together at one pole of the cell, or they may, as in certain brain stem nuclei, occupy 85% of the intracellular volume of the cell, pushing the nucleus into an eccentric position within the nerve cell. It might be assumed that this should interfere with the cell's metabolism or function, but this has not been substantiated experimentally. In fact, an important physiological study by Rogers, Silver, Shoemaker, and Bloom (1980) shows that the accumulation of lipofuscin in cerebellar Purkinje neurons and in the inferior olive is not the primary cause of electrophysiological dysfunction in the cerebellum, even though the number of aberrant, very slow firing cells increased in the older animals.

Although nearly all the Purkinje cells contained considerable amounts of lipofuscin, half of those cells from older animals demonstrated normal firing patterns and rates. It is just as doubtful that the accumulation of lipofuscin plays a role in the loss of cells that occurs in certain areas of the central nervous system with increasing age. The inferior olive, as an example, maintains a constant and stable number of cells from birth through the 10th decade (a fact recently verified by Sjobeck, Dahlen, and Englund [1999]), whereas 85% of the cells are completely filled with lipofuscin by 38 years of age, and all the inferior olivary cells are filled by age 70 (Monagle & Brody, 1974).

If the accumulation of this material can be considered to be a cause of cell death, as has been maintained by some investigators, it cannot be demonstrated in a group of cells that contain more lipofuscin than any other region of the nervous system. We are then faced with a contradiction in that the one element that is a principal marker for the age of the cell (at least for most mammals, including the human) does not appear to have a specific effect on that cell's activity. In fact, in Alzheimer's disease there appears to be no relationship between the presence of this pigment and the level of dementia (Mann, 1988). The presence of lipofuscin may only provide evidence that an aging-related mechanism, whose function remains to be discovered, is occurring.

HAROLD BRODY

See also
    Central and Peripheral Nervous Systems Morphology
    Oxidative Stress Theory

LIPOPROTEINS, SERUM

Age-associated increases in serum lipid and lipoprotein levels are readily apparent in the U.S. population. Estimates of high blood cholesterol in adults in the United States indicate that approximately 24 million men and women older than 60 years of age are potential candidates for medical counsel and treatment for high blood cholesterol concentrations (Sempos, Fulwood, Haines, Carroll, Anda,

Williamson, et al., 1989). The elevation of total cholesterol (TC) and low-density lipoprotein cholesterol (LDL-C), as well as reductions in high-density lipoprotein cholesterol (HDL-C), are risk factors for cardiovascular disease. Moreover, mortality rates rise as cholesterol levels increase, which emphasizes the need for appropriate and successful strategies to lower blood cholesterol levels. Furthermore, certain populations, including diabetic patients, often have an accelerated development of atherosclerosis. The initiative to adequately detect, prevent, and treat adverse lipid profiles is considered a significant health concern.

Current Recommendations

The National Cholesterol Education Program (NCEP) guidelines include recommendations to lower high blood cholesterol and LDL-C by dietary therapy, an increase in energy expenditure through physical activity, and some degree of caloric restriction. The Step I Diet of the NCEP is similar to the nutrient composition suggested to the general population of $\leq 30\%$ of total calories from total fat, 8%–10% of total calories from saturated fat, < 300 mg/dl of cholesterol, $\geq 55\%$ of total calories from carbohydrates, and ~15% of total calories from protein. Some patients may need to follow the Step II Diet of the NCEP to achieve cholesterol goals, which requires a further reduction in saturated fat to < 7% and cholesterol to < 200 mg/dl. The NCEP recommends that total cholesterol (TC) be measured at least once every 5 years in adults ≥ 20 years of age. TC levels of < 200 mg/dl are desirable, whereas ≥ 200–239 mg/dl is considered borderline high, and > 240 mg/dl is classified as high blood cholesterol. The addition of a lipoprotein analysis is suggested for individuals with borderline high TC and low HDL-C.

The lipoprotein analysis would include the measurement of lipoproteins, which are lipid-protein complexes that transport water-insoluble lipid in the plasma. These lipoproteins consists of a hydrophobic core of cholesterol ester, or triglyceride (TG), and a surface coat of phospholipids, free cholesterol, and proteins called apolipoproteins. High-density lipoproteins transport surplus cholesterol away from peripheral tissues to the liver, where it is catabolized. The NCEP regards low

HDL-C as < 35 mg/dl and classifies this as a risk factor for coronary artery disease. There are five HDL subclasses, which increase in particle size and include HDL_{3c}, HDL_{3b}, HDL_{3a}, HDL_{2a}, and HDL_{2b}. HDL_3 may more effectively inhibit oxidation of LDL than HDL_2, thereby offering a greater protective effect against atherosclerosis. These different subclasses of HDL exhibit specific relationships with age, menopause, adiposity, weight loss, exercise, and certain disease states. HDL-C levels are higher in women than in men and higher in African Americans than in White individuals. Similar observations are reported for apolipoprotein A-I, the major protein constituent of HDL-C. Low levels of apo A-I appear to reflect a reduced number of HDL particles and thus may increase one's predisposition to atherosclerosis. However, plasma apo A-I levels may not be associated with the metabolic abnormalities associated with insulin resistance.

Low-density lipoproteins carry cholesterol to cells that can use this lipid. LDL-C contains the protein, apolipoprotein B (apo B), which is located on the surface coat and functions in the removal of LDL-C from the plasma by binding to LDL receptors on cells. LDL-C levels are classified as follows: < 130 mg/dL desirable; between 130 and 159 mg/dl, borderline high risk; and ≥ 160 mg/dl, high risk. The goals and approaches to treatment change with the addition of coronary heart disease (CHD) risk factors or evidence of CHD. Eight LDL subfractions have been identified. Individuals can be classified as having the subclass pattern A (predominance of larger LDLs with diameter greater than 255 Å) or pattern B (predominance of smaller LDLs with diameters ≤ 255 Å). Those individuals exhibiting pattern B have higher TG and lower HDL-C levels, are more insulin resistant, and are at an increased risk for the development of coronary artery disease. Low-fat and high-carbohydrate diets are associated with the presence of small LDL particles. Identification of individuals at high risk for cardiovascular disease may be improved by measurement of apolipoprotein B levels and of small, dense LDL particles, in addition to the determination of conventional lipid variables (Lamarche, Tchernof, Mauriege, Cantin, Dagenais, Lupien, et al., 1998).

Triglyceride levels are classified as normal (< 200 mg/dl), borderline–high (200–400 mg/dl), high (400–1000 mg/dl), and very high (> 1000 mg/dl).

A high TG level is an independent risk factor for cardiovascular disease, even after adjustment for HDL-C. The major carrier of plasma TGs during fasting are very low density lipoproteins (VLDLs). The particle size and TG content of VLDLs determines whether they are taken up by the liver, (larger, TG-rich VLDLs) or converted to LDL (small, TG-poor VLDLs).

Lipids and Aging

Plasma cholesterol, TGs, and LDL-C increase with age up to age 70 years, whereas HDL-C changes little with age. TC, LDL-C and TG levels decline after age 70 years in men and later in women. The decrease in TC, LDL, and TGs can be in part attributed to selected mortality of CHD individuals with elevated cholesterol levels and in larger part to decreased food intake with advancing age. Women have higher HDL-C levels throughout their entire adult age span (20–100 years) than men (~1.4 vs. 1.2 mmol/L, or ~56 vs. 46 mg/dl). In men, TC increases from the third decade of life by 8%, 6%, and 4% in the fourth, fifth, and sixth decades, respectively. In the eighth decade, TC has declined by 12% from the third decade. In women, the largest increase in TC compared to the third decade, occurs in the sixth decade of life (14%). It drops by 6% in the ninth decade. Essentially similar patterns are observed for LDL-C (Lamon-Favas, Jenner, Jacques, & Schaefer, 1994). TC, LDL-C, and TGs increase following menopause which may be partly dependent on changes in fat distribution and increases in visceral fat.

Evidence suggests that the age-associated changes in serum lipids are mediated by alterations in body composition. Body composition and lipid and lipoprotein level changes over a time period of 4 to 20 years of 423 adult participants of the Fels Longitudinal Study (Siervogel, Wisemandel, Maynard, Guo, Roche, Chumlea, et al., 1998) were analyzed by sex and age group (18–44 and 45–65 years). In men, mean rates of change in TC levels increased to middle age, after which a decreased rate of change occurred. In women, the rate of increase was much slower and continued after age 45 years. Moreover, the annual changes in adiposity, independent of lean tissue mass changes were significantly correlated with corresponding annual changes in cholesterol and LDL-C in men and women. In the 12-year prospective Quebec family Study, increases in subcutaneous trunk fat were associated with adverse changes in plasma HDL-C levels in men and in TC and TG levels in women.

Increases in adiposity are associated with changes in lipid and lipoprotein levels in the direction of increased risk for cardiovascular disease. Obese subjects have higher TC, LDL-C, and TG levels and lower HDL-C concentrations. Regional adiposity of the upper body is also associated with high TG and low HDL-C levels. Abnormal postprandial lipid and lipoprotein responses are observed in those with visceral obesity. The significantly elevated chylomicron TGs are even more exacerbated in patients with android obesity and fasting hypertriglyceridemia. Additional factors— genetic, environmental, dietary intake, and others— must contribute to the variability in lipids and lipoproteins, as certain populations, such as the Pima Indians, exhibit a low prevalence of dyslipidemia but a high prevalence of obesity.

Several lipoprotein metabolizing enzymes play important roles in arteriosclerosis and the relationships between obesity and adverse changes in lipoproteins. Lipoprotein lipase (LPL) is the enzyme responsible for the hydrolysis of TG molecules in circulating lipoproteins to produce free fatty acids. LPL is important in the conversion of VLDL to LDL and also regulates HDL-C. A review of LPL, its actions, and relation to atherogenesis is available (Goldberg, 1996). Either high or normal levels of adipose tissue LPL, which promotes adipose tissue storage, may explain differences in lipids among individuals. Some studies have found that levels of adipose tissue LPL are increased in obesity, whereas other studies report no correlations between adipose tissue LPL and body fat. Skeletal muscle LPL is inversely related to total triglyceride and VLDL triglyceride concentrations. An increase in hepatic lipase activity may lead to smaller and denser LDL and HDL particles. Other studies report that postheparin plasma lipoprotein lipase, when released into the circulation from adipose and muscle tissue, is either reduced or normal in obese individuals. High, normal, or low lecithin cholesterol acyltransferase (LCAT) activity, which converts HDL_3 to HDL_2 particles, and high cholesterol ester transfer protein (CETP) activity may be associated with altered TG levels and HDL-C. CETP catalyses the transfer of cholesteryl esters, TG, and phospholipids between HDL and VLDL. Phospholipid transfer protein (PLTP) also functions in HDL metabolism as it facilitates the transfer of phospholipids between lipoproteins and can convert HDL_3 into other HDL particles. Higher levels of PLTP are observed in obese individuals and type 2 diabetics and are associated with plasma TG levels. Thus, various enzymes are associated with the regulation of lipoprotein metabolism and, as such, are critical in the concentrations of serum lipids.

Lipids and Genetics

Familial combined hyperlipidemia is present in ~1% of the Western population and results in approximately 10% of premature cardiovascular disease. Affected family members have hypercholesterolemia and/or hypertriglyceridemia, which may result from an overproduction of VLDL and apo B. Various polymorphisms associated with dyslipidemia have been discovered. This can be easily observed in children with the rare homozygous familial hypercholesterolemia resulting from the absence of cell-surface receptors, which remove LDL-C from the circulatory system, and to a lesser extent in patients with the more common heterozygous form of hypercholesterolemia (Ross, 1993). The apo E-4 phenotype is associated with increased risk for hypertriglyceridemia, especially in those with central or visceral obesity.

It is difficult to distinguish the independent effects of obesity and genetic influences on lipoprotein levels. Yet studies in twins lend credence to the associations between obesity and lipid and lipoprotein disorders. Higher total cholesterol, LDL-C levels and apo B concentrations, as well as lower HDL-C levels, are reported in the obese compared to the lean twin. Some of these differences may be explained by visceral fat accumulation.

Lipids and Weight Loss/Exercise

Low-fat, high-carbohydrate diets reduce LDL-C and increase TG and VLDL particle size. A low-fat intake can decrease HDL-C and apo A-1 levels but may not change HDL particle size. It may be necessary to combine weight loss with a low-fat diet to offset the decline in HDL-C. The benefits of weight loss on lipoprotein lipid levels include reductions in total cholesterol, TG, and LDL-C and increases in HDL-C. The changes in TG and HDL-C may be dependent on their initial concentrations so that higher initial concentrations are associated with greater changes after weight loss.

Endurance athletes have higher HDL-C levels and lower TG concentrations than do sedentary individuals. Trained men have less small, dense LDL and more large LDL subfraction particles than do sedentary men. Yet TC and LDL-C increase with age even in healthy, lean, trained women athletes (Nicklas, Ryan, & Katzel, 1999). However, in contrast to what is typically observed in the general population, LDL size and LDL1-C, a subfraction of LDL, do not increase in women with high levels of aerobic fitness. This suggests that physical activity has a protective cardiovascular effect mediated through alterations in lipoprotein subfraction distribution. Likewise, aerobic exercise training reduces TC and LDL-C and increases HDL-C in obese premenopausal women. Endurance training also lowers TC and TG in older men and women. Exercise training reduces the concentration of small, dense LDL particles, increases LDL particle diameter, increases HDL_2 mass, and decreases VLDL mass (Williams, Krauss, Vranizan, & Wood, 1990). Physical activity also prevents the reduction of HDL-C normally observed when overweight men and women undergo a low-fat diet. Even an aerobic exercise program as short as 3 months can decrease TG and increase HDL-C but may not change TC in patients with type 2 diabetes. Although some studies indicate that exercise training alone does not increase HDL-C in men with low initial HDL-C, a meta-analysis of 66 studies reported otherwise; those with the lowest initial HDL-C levels had the greatest improvements in HDL-C with exercise training (Tran, Weltman, Glass, & Mood, 1983).

In a controlled comparison of the effects of weight loss and aerobic exercise training in obese older men, weight loss increased HDL-C levels more than exercise did. The reductions in TG (18% vs. 9%) and LDL-C (7% vs. no change) were significantly greater with weight loss than with exercise (Katzel, Bleecker, Colman, Rogus, Sorkin, & Goldberg, 1995). However, in a randomized controlled trial in men and women with low HDL-C and elevated LDL-C, the addition of aerobic exercise to the NCEP Step 2 diet was necessary in order for reductions of LDL-C to occur (Stefanick, Mackey, Sheehan, Ellsworth, Haskell, & Wood, 1998). In conclusion, the NCEP advocates both weight loss and an increase in physical activity to protect against arteriosclerosis and reduce future risk of a coronary event.

Pharmacological Treatment

Drug therapy is indicated only if at least 6 months of diet therapy, regular exercise program, and control of other risk factors have been unsuccessful in lowering elevated LDL-C ($\geq$ 190 mg/dl). Effective therapy that reduces LDL-C by $\geq$ 15% includes anion-exchange resins (e.g., cholestyramine), niacin and 3-hydroxy-β-methyl-glutaryl coenzyme A (HMGCoA) reductase inhibitors (e.g., pravastatin). The latter are the drugs of choice in middle-aged and older patients because of their efficacy ($\geq$ 30% lowering of LDL-C) and tolerability. Several other agents that lower triglyceride levels are available; these can also lower LDL-C and raise HDL-C levels (e.g., gemfibrozil). Estrogen replacement therapy is also recommended in postmenopausal women who are hypercholesterolemic if they do not have high levels of TGs. Finally, a recent meta-analysis of all experimental studies (42 studies providing 67 separate data records) has established the effects of moderate alcohol intake. This analysis has shown that 30 g of alcohol per day increases HDL-C levels (Rimm, William, Fosher, Criqui, & Stamfer, 1999).

ALICE S. RYAN
DARIUSH ELAHI

See also
Apolipoprotein E

LIVING ARRANGEMENTS

The term *living arrangements*, when used in connection with the older population, distinguishes among residential types—mainly, the distinction between institutional and private dwellings—and household composition, that is, the presence or absence of others and the types of kin relationships among coresident individuals. Nursing homes are the most prominent type of institutional housing occupied by the elderly. With respect to household composition, most researchers distinguish among living alone, living with a spouse, living with other relatives (especially children), and a residual "other" category.

Population censuses, which in most countries are taken infrequently, tend to be the most comprehensive source of information that includes both the institutionalized and noninstitutionalized populations. Surveys containing information on living arrangements, even those using large, nationally representative samples, are usually limited to the noninstitutionalized population. Thus, available data limit researchers' ability to investigate changes in living arrangements over time, as well as to compare the living arrangements of the elderly across nations.

Patterns and Trends

When considering the distribution of the older population across living arrangement types, differences by sex are so pronounced that men and women should be discussed separately. For example, in the United States in 1998, 30.9% of the noninstitutionalized 65-and-older population lived alone; however, among men in this group only 17.3% lived alone, whereas 40.8% of women lived alone. The majority of noninstitutionalized older men but only a minority of older women live with spouses. The remainder live with others, in nearly all cases relatives. The institutionalized population is a small percentage of the total (4.2% in 1995), but here as well sex differences are substantial: the older noninstitutionalized population is 58% female; the older institutionalized population is 75% female (Bishop, 1999; Lugaila, 1998).

The countries for which living arrangements of the elderly have been most extensively studied are found in Europe, North America, and Asia, that is, in the regions for which population aging is most developed or is proceeding most rapidly. There is considerable diversity among the countries of the world in living arrangements of the elderly, but two generalizations are supported by available evidence: first, older women are substantially more likely than older men to live alone; second, only a small percentage of the older population lives in institutions.

One of the most distinctive demographic trends of the post–World War II era, exhibited throughout much of the world, is the trend toward smaller households, accompanied by a rising percentage of people living alone. The upward trend in solitary living arrangements has been particularly evident among older women. Wolf (1995), using data from 21 European and North American countries for the period 1960–1992, found that on average there was a 0.83 percentage-point increase per year in older women living alone. This rise in solitary living has been accompanied by a drop in the percentage of elderly living with relatives other than their spouses.

The upward trend in one-person households among older women has been shown to be associated with underlying demographic and economic forces. The demographic forces include falling male-female ratios among the elderly, which translates into a relative shortage of spouses with whom to coreside, and falling ratios of surviving children relative to surviving elderly parents, a consequence of reduced fertility, which also translates into a relative shortage of kin—in this case, children—with whom to coreside. Economic forces promoting solitary living include rising real incomes, particularly income provided to the elderly through private and public pension schemes and governmental housing subsidy programs.

Recent data from the United States reveals a decline in the prevalence of older persons living in nursing homes from 1985 to 1995 (Bishop, 1999). This trend is due in part to a decrease in the prevalence of disabling conditions, but it also reflects a growth in alternative housing, such as assisted-living facilities, independent units in continuing-care retirement communities, and supportive elderly housing. Another development that may be related to recent trends in living arrangements is the increased utilization of assistive technology devices (LaPlante, Hendershot, & Moss, 1992). These technological and housing-sector trends suggest that more complex typologies of household and living arrangements should be adopted in future research.

The Significance of Living Arrangements

Living arrangements reflect the extent to which individuals and family members achieve some degree of independence and, as well, reflect the sharing of resources within families and in society as a whole. It is widely acknowledged that older people prefer to live independently as long as possible. The elderly seek "intimacy at a distance" (Rosenmayr & Köckeis, 1963), that is, to have family members living in close proximity but not under the same roof. Living alone (or with spouse only) and living in a nursing home can be taken to represent the polar cases of independent and dependent living arrangements, respectively. Shared living arrangements are often adopted in response to an older person's needs for personal care, but children who care for an elderly parent do not necessarily live with that parent. Furthermore, coresidence of an elderly parent and an adult child often serves the needs of the child.

Research on living arrangements often adopts a conceptual framework whereby decisions about living arrangements take into account opportunities for shared living (represented by an array of available kin, such as spouse, siblings, children, and other kin); preferences (assumed, for the typical individual, to favor independent over shared living arrangements); and constraints on one's ability to attain the most preferred type of living arrangement. The most prominent constraints are those of income and functional capacity (e.g., the ability to attend to one's own needs with respect to activities of daily living [ADLs], such as eating, dressing, bathing, and using the toilet). Deciding among the set of potential living arrangements considered by an older individual or couple requires that trade-offs be made among "component" household goods such as privacy, autonomy, domestic services, and sources of personal care (Burch & Matthews, 1987).

Correlates of Living Arrangements

Not only are there differences in living arrangements across countries and within countries over time, but there exists substantial heterogeneity in living arrangements patterns within countries at any given time as well. Numerous demographic, socioeconomic and other factors have been identified as correlates of living arrangement outcomes (Wolf, 1994). For example, within the 65-plus population there are striking differences by age. The "old old" are more likely to live alone than the "young old," in part because of the increasing prevalence of widowhood with advanced age. Rates of institutionalization also rise sharply with age. Marital status is also a strong predictor of living arrangements: nearly all married elderly live with their spouses and, if unable to care for themselves, are cared for by the spouse; the unmarried elderly tend to live alone or with a child.

Elderly with many living kin have greater opportunities for coresidence, compared to those with few or no living kin. Available evidence shows that those with more living children and with more living siblings are correspondingly more likely to coreside with kin. Furthermore, just as rising real per capita income over time increases the prevalence of solitary living arrangements, income differences at a point in time influence living arrangements, with higher income elderly more likely to live alone.

Elderly in better health and those with the greatest capacity to provide for their own personal care, are more likely to live alone or with a spouse only; declines in health and in functional status are associated with increased chances of living with children or others and at the greatest levels of need for care, with transitions into nursing homes.

Many other factors influencing living patterns have been studied, of which only a few can be mentioned. Differentials associated with ethnicity and with population movement are particularly interesting. Given the differences across countries in living arrangements, due in part to cultural forces, it is not surprising to find differences by ethnicity and nativity. Differences in the propensity to live alone and to live in institutions have been found between the Hispanic and non-Hispanic populations of the United States and within the Hispanic population by country of origin. Among older foreign-born women there are differences in the propensity to live with others by age at immigration, not of differences due to country of origin. Emigration also can be linked to living arrangements: it has been suggested that the strikingly high percentages of Caribbean island older women living alone (relative to older women in other developing countries) is partly attributable to migration patterns. Local-area conditions have been shown to be associated with living arrangements; for example, the availability of some in-home care services and out-of-home services is positively correlated with the percentage of elderly living alone.

DOUGLAS A. WOLF

See also
> Assisted Living: A New Model of Supportive
>   Housing with Long-Term Care Services
> Family
> Housing
> Nursing Homes
> Senior Companion Program

LIVING WILLS AND DURABLE POWER OF ATTORNEY

Two kinds of legal documents provide adults of all ages with the opportunity to plan for the possibility that, sometime in the future, an individual may lack the decision-making capacity to make known his or her wishes about medical treatment. All states have legislation authorizing the use of legal documents such as living wills and durable powers of attorney for health care (sometimes referred to as health care proxy, surrogate, agent, or attorney-in-factor), that together are known as advance directives. Fifty states plus the District of Columbia recognize durable power of attorney, 48 states recognize living wills, and 39 states have statutes that grant to family and others close to them the right to make decisions for patients without capacity (American Bar Association, Commission on Legal Problems of the Elderly, 2000). It is thought that between 12% and 20% of the population have completed a living will or durable power of attorney for health care.

The impetus for encouraging the use of advance directives, which was evident in the 1980s (President's Commission for the Study of Ethical Problems in Medicine and Biomedical and Behavioral Research, 1982), culminated in the Patient Self Determination Act (PSDA). The PSDA, which went into effect in 1991, mandates that all health care institutions receiving Medicare or Medicaid funds inform individuals, in writing, of their right under state law to refuse medical and surgical care and the right to prepare written advance directives. Hospitals and nursing homes must make this information available on admission; health maintenance organizations (HMOs), on enrollment; hospices, on first receipt of care; and home care agencies, before the patient comes under an agency's care. The

Health Care Financing Administration (HCFA) estimated that in 1992 approximately 15 million people would use the services of providers and institutions covered by the PSDA (Cate, 1993).

The PSDA statute specifically prohibits institutions from making care conditional on whether patients have directives or otherwise discriminate against them based on whether the patients have executed a directive. The intent of the PSDA is to enhance people's participation in health care decisions by educating them about their options of executing a living will or a durable power of attorney for health care.

Issues that call into question the utility of advance directives should not detract from the fact that advance directives remain the clearest way for adults to state their treatment preferences. Although the number of adults overall who have advance directives remains small, in nursing homes, where directives are invoked frequently, more than 50% of residents have a directive. Despite the fact that decisions made by health care proxies are not always congruent with those of the patient and that directives are overridden approximately 20% of the time, directives generally provide a close approximation of adults' treatment preferences. Finally, while most (48) states give family members legal authority to make health care decisions for an incapacitated adult, the algorithm for determining which family member has authority to make decisions may not match the preference of the patients themselves as to whom they would have chosen to make decisions on their behalf.

Living Wills

Instructions About Treatment. Living wills are documents in which people specify their preferences to consent to or to forgo specific treatments in the event of future incompetence. By enacting laws called Natural Death Acts, the legislatures of all states recognize the right of competent persons to refuse life-sustaining treatment and may do so through written directives or declarations (Meisel, 2000). Jurisdictions that recognize living wills note that refusal of life-prolonging treatment through such declarations does not constitute suicide for insurance (or any other) purposes. This position is consistent with the teachings of the major religions

in the United States (President's Commission, 1982).

Living wills instruct physicians and family members regarding the application of medical treatments that will prolong life, once it is clear that the patient lacks decision-making capacity. Caregivers may be asked to administer only treatments that are necessary to relieve pain and to maintain dignity and personal hygiene; or on the other hand, living wills may request application of all life-prolonging treatments. Living wills have limitations because no one can precisely foresee the future, and because lack of specificity and ambiguity in the use of terms can interfere with the interpretation of the person's true intent.

Protection for Physicians and Other Health Care Practitioners. Laws that give legal force to living wills protect physicians and other health practitioners from civil or criminal liability for withholding or withdrawing treatment as directed by a living will (President's Commission, 1982). Most living-will laws recognize that, occasionally, a physician or other health practitioner may find it difficult to follow the instructions in a living will because of personal or religious beliefs. When that occurs, the practitioner is directed to transfer the care of the patient to someone else, who will comply with the patient's wishes.

The formalities for creating a legally valid living will vary in the United States from state to state. Individuals who wish to make a living will must therefore determine what the laws of a particular state require in the way of special forms, witnesses, notary, and the like ("You and your choice," 2000).

Durable Power of Attorney for Health Care

A durable power of attorney for health care (health care proxy) is a document appointing a proxy decision maker to make decisions on the behalf of the patient in the event of future incapacity. Durable power of attorney remains in force, or takes effect, when the person delegating the power becomes unable to make decisions. Durable power of attorney for health care applies specifically to health care decisions.

Appointment of Decision Makers. Historically, powers of attorney were designed to delegate authority for business matters. Durable powers of attorney for health care permit the appointment of a trusted friend or relative to make health care decisions on behalf of an individual if he or she should become unable, because of an accident or serious illness, to make or express a choice at the time a treatment decision must be made.

Even in states where relatives have clear authority to make health care decisions, a durable power of attorney is useful for indicating which of several family members should be the decision maker. This can be important if several relatives disagree about the decision to be made.

Advantages of Powers of Attorney. Durable powers of attorney for health care can be used in a number of situations in which living wills cannot (Cate, 1993). For example, living wills may apply only to patients who are terminally ill, whereas powers of attorney can be used on behalf of patients who are not terminally ill but who are unable to make their own health care decisions due to serious injury or mental impairment, for example, following a stroke or as a result of Alzheimer's disease or similar disorders.

It is not always clear from a living will whether a particular medical intervention should or should not be administered. A durable power of attorney for health care may resolve some of the uncertainty by appointing someone who can make health care decisions in light of the patient's condition at the time the decision must be made, taking into account the probable effects of the proposed treatment and any available alternative treatments. As a result, there is greater likelihood that the decision will reflect what the patient's choice would be under the given circumstances (President's Commission, 1982).

Finally, the threshold of decisional capacity necessary to appoint a health care proxy is thought to be lower than that necessary to execute a living will. Some people who evidence cognitive impairment can demonstrate sufficient decisional capacity to execute a durable power of attorney (Mezey, Teresi, Ramsey, Mitty, & Bobrowitz, 2000).

Using Advance Directives

Copies of living wills and durable powers of attorney for health care should be given to relatives; to health care providers, such as physicians, nurses, and social workers; and to appropriate personnel in hospitals, nursing homes, and home care agencies. Additional copies should be kept for later use. Wallet-size cards indicating that an individual has signed a living will or durable power of attorney for health care can be very useful, especially for individuals who travel frequently ("You and your choice," 2000). In the case of durable powers of attorney for health care, proxies should be educated as to their roles and responsibilities in making health care decisions (Dubler, Farber Post, & Barnes, 1999).

Additional information about living wills and durable powers of attorney in the United States may be obtained from the American Association of Retired Persons, Washington, DC; American Bar Association, Commission on Legal Problems of the Elderly, Washington, DC; and Partnership for Caring, Inc., 1035 30th Street, NW, Washington, DC 20007.

MATHY D. MEZEY
GLORIA RAMSEY

See also
Legal Services
Proxy Decision Making

LOCUS OF CONTROL

Perceived control refers to beliefs about the extent to which one can bring about or influence outcomes in one's life. Locus of control refers to the sources of this control, which are usually characterized as internal or external. Rotter (1966) developed an instrument to assess the internal-external locus of control construct. However, there has been some criticism of this bipolar dichotomy because not all internal sources are within one's control (e.g., genetic influences) and not all outside forces are outside one's control (e.g., influences over other people). Internal sources of control include one's ability, personality characteristics, behaviors, and efforts. External control refers to random factors such as chance, luck, or fate as well as to more ordered or predictable occurrences such as the influences of powerful other people. Although much of the work on locus of control has utilized this conception, there has been movement toward more differentiated views of control.

A related construct is attributions, in which the focus is on explaining outcomes in terms of the source (internal or external), chronicity (stable or unstable), and controllability (within control or not) (Skinner, 1996). Attributions deal with how people appraise the cause of a positive or negative event after it happens. In contrast, the sense of control is the expectation people have about the extent to which their own efforts will bring about desired outcomes.

Another distinction involves objective versus subjective control. On the one hand, there is the actual amount of control that an individual has in a given situation. In some cases this can be measured and known, but in other cases it is more ambiguous. What is most often studied is the sense of control (i.e., the perception of one's control), without concern for veridicality. Of particular interest are the individual differences in these beliefs, given the same objective circumstances. These differences have important implications for behavior and performance.

A general definition of control beliefs is the extent to which an individual believes that he or she can bring about desired outcomes. There have been at least two key developments in terms of the assessment of control beliefs: multidimensionality and domain specificity.

Multidimensionality

Although Rotter (1996) proposed a dichotomous scoring system, with scores that varied along a continuum from internal to external, more recent conceptions (see Lefcourt, 1981) present these on separate dimensions. This allows for the possibility that both internal and external forces contribute to a given outcome. Correlations between internal and external dimensions are usually low, suggesting that those high in internal beliefs may vary from high to low on external beliefs.

Other twofold conceptualizations have been developed. Bandura (1977) refers to self-efficacy and outcome expectations, and Skinner (1996) refers to perceived competence and contingency. One may believe that one has the requisite skills but that environmental contingencies are such that one can-

not accomplish one's goals. By the same token, one may believe that even though there are no external constraints, one is not competent to bring about the outcome. These would lead to very different affective outcomes as well as different levels of effort expenditure.

Domain Specificity

Although Rotter (1966) initially conceptualized control as a generalized expectancy, control beliefs may vary across different situations. Individuals may feel they are responsible for outcomes in some areas of their lives but are less so in others. A number of instruments have been developed to assess control in specific areas such as health or interpersonal relationships (Lefcourt, 1981; Wallston & Wallston, 1981).

Age and Gender Differences

The nature of age differences in control varies as a function of the dimension. Thus, different trajectories are found for internal and external dimensions and across different domains. In both cross-sectional and longitudinal studies there is evidence that internal beliefs remain relatively stable, whereas external beliefs increase more dramatically with age. In some domains, control shows a decline with age, and in others control is expected to increase (Lachman & Weaver, 1998).

Gender differences in control are sometimes found, but the differences are usually small. The tendency is for men to have a greater sense of control than women have (Lachman & Weaver, 1998).

Other Variations

Social class and education are also related to control beliefs. The higher the social class and educational level, the greater the sense of control. This may be due to differences in actual control over the environment. It remains to be seen to what extent fostering a sense of control among more disadvantaged groups can lead to positive outcomes.

There are also cultural differences in control beliefs. In some societies there is a strong belief in fatalism, and this is reflected in higher external beliefs. The distinction between primary and secondary control beliefs has been examined and compared in Eastern and Western cultures (Skinner, 1996). Both primary and secondary control strategies are means to taking control, but they vary in their focus. Primary control aims to change the situation to fit one's own needs and desires. In contrast, secondary control is concerned with changing the way one thinks about a situation or changing goals. Both are means to achieving control, and it has been suggested that they may be used at different points in the process of coping or managing goals.

The evidence suggests that those in Western cultures prefer to use primary modes of control, whereas those in Eastern cultures are more likely to use secondary control. There is also the suggestion that secondary modes of control increase in prevalence in later life (Skinner, 1996).

Correlates

Much research has uncovered significant correlations with control beliefs in later life (Rodin, Timko, & Harris, 1985). Having strong internal control beliefs is associated with greater happiness, better memory, higher cognitive functioning, better health, and more health-promoting behaviors. Although there is evidence for the adaptive value of control, there are also indications that in some circumstances, where the environmental constraints are high or where control is not possible (e.g., a nursing home), that a strong internal sense of control may be less adaptive than more realistic views (Rodin et al., 1985).

Interventions

There have been some effective intervention studies aimed at enhancing the sense of control over memory and physical activity in older adults (Lachman, Ziff, & Spiro, 1994; Rodin, Timko, & Harris, 1985). Further work is needed to examine the mechanisms that link control beliefs and adaptive outcomes.

M. LACHMAN

See also
 Adaptive Capacity
 Coping

Learned Helplessness
Social Stress and Life Events

LONELINESS

Loneliness is a sentiment experienced by a person defining his/her form or level of relationships as inadequate (Lopata, 1969; Weiss, 1973). The sentiment is one of relative deprivation, seeing one's own lifestyle, situation, or relationships as emotionally or socially inadequate in comparison to the past, to the anticipated future, or to other people who are assumed to be satisfactorily engaged. Older persons, who are a high risk for experience of change and loss, are consequently at high risk for experiencing loneliness.

A study of older widows identified and illustrated numerous forms and components of loneliness (Lopata, 1969). The widowed can feel lonely for a specific other, having a love object, being a love object, being an important person to another who is even willing to argue and fight; being a sexual partner, a companion, a confidant, a "best friend," an escort in public places, part of a team, a couple's compassionate interaction; having someone to share work and responsibility and around whom work and time can be organized or simply another presence in the home. Widows and others for whom life is changed dramatically and involuntarily may yearn for the whole previous lifestyle, which is perceived as lost. Old friends may no longer be available, as relations with them become strained under the new circumstances. Activities previously enjoyed or hoped for may not be possible. Kin and friends may find it difficult to remain emotionally involved with persons who experience painful events such as illness, divorce, deviant behavior, or death in the family and may withdraw in discomfort. The person going through all this may experience the double loss from both the event and the perceived abandonment of others.

Many people find it difficult to enter new social roles or relations in mid- or later life because they were socialized to depend on the family or long-known school chums and neighbors for support. The Kansas City elderly studied by Cumming and Henry (1961) described in this way their disengaged subjects who lacked the social skills and self-confidence necessary for reengagement once prior relations and roles were dissolved or became unavailable due to death, immobility, change of circumstances, or financial and health problems. Waiting for someone to knock on the door or to telephone an invitation can be a very lonely experience at any age.

Modern urban life, with its mobility, density, and heterogeneity of people, many of whom have been socialized into a different world, makes creating and maintaining a satisfactory social and emotional support network difficult, and the possibility of loneliness likely. This is particularly true of certain categories of people who are most mobile or who live in high turnover urban areas; such individuals cling to their independence and privacy to the point of creating a wall around themselves. All urbanites are not lonely, but situations creating at least temporary loneliness are more likely to happen in modern urban areas than in more stabilized small communities with ascribed social relationships. Recent publications focusing on loneliness point out repeatedly the impermanence of social relationships due to the social structure of American society. For example, mass media constantly idealize popularity and suggest steps for avoiding social isolation (Peplau & Perlman, 1981).

Research by Lopata (1969, 1973a, 1979, 1996a) suggest that education is the most important factor influencing the kinds of social engagement likely to reduce loneliness, enabling individuals to engage in emerging social roles in modernized societies. When traditional support systems change as social structure changes, members of a society must develop new methods for social involvement.

Central to the feeling of loneliness is the way people construct the reality in which they live and their ability to change that reality if they feel dissatisfied. Loneliness involves the feeling of relative deprivation—that one has been, is, or will be lonely in comparison to others. The solution to loneliness is therefore either a redefinition of the situation or modification of the forms or levels of social relationships. If loneliness is accompanied by depression, passivity rather than voluntaristic action can prevent both solutions. Certain forms of loneliness may be accepted as inevitable, as is true of people who have lost an irreplaceable, loved companion.

HELENA Z. LOPATA

See also
Loss
Widowhood

LONGEVITY: SOCIETAL IMPACT

Increased longevity (i.e., life expectancy) in this century has been unprecedented. Since 1900 in the industrialized world, we have gained nearly 30 years in average life expectancy from birth. Previously, it took 5,000 years of human history to achieve a similar increase in longevity.

A significant percentage of added years of life have resulted from reductions in maternal, childhood, and infant mortality rates. But in the past 30 years, reductions in mortality from heart disease and stroke have increased the life expectancy of people aged 65 and older. This longevity revolution has not been limited to the industrialized world. We are seeing dramatic increases in the absolute number and, to a lesser degree, the proportion of older people in developing countries as well. Indeed, 60% of all people over age 60 reside in developing nations. By 2025 that number will rise to about 80%.

The social, economic, political, medical, and cultural impact of societal longevity has been striking. For example, social and medical protections, such as Social Security and Medicare in the United States, have helped to support the greater number of older people in the population. At the same time, rising costs have increased the pressure to fund more cost-effective ways of providing such social support.

The political impact has been considerable, too. Older persons have formed organizations dedicated to providing and sustaining a variety of social protections, as well as other systems of support for the aging. Increased longevity also has encouraged the development of the fields of geriatrics and gerontology, which have sought to understand better the nature of the later years from social, behavioral, and medical perspectives (Butler & Jasmin, 2000).

Because 80% of all deaths occur after age 60, attention is being increasingly drawn to end-of-life decision making and care. Family life also has been touched by increased longevity. The 20th century was the first in which three- and even four-generation families became common.

The very idea that people can survive and live out a natural life span has had cultural implications as well, especially in the arts, where we are seeing more attention being paid to older protagonists. Increased longevity has made an impact on individuals, too. With greater expectations for a long life, people have become increasingly attentive to health habits and financial planning that will sustain them over a longer period of time. Finally, at all levels, increased longevity is inspiring consideration of such philosophical questions as, to what end and purpose is longevity, and what are the responsibilities that go along with old age?

ROBERT N. BUTLER

See also
    Centenarians
    Compression of Morbidity: Disease Postponement
    Life Expectancy
    Life Extension
    Life Span
    Long-Lived Human Populations
    Oldest Old

LONGITUDINAL DATA SETS IN AGING

Understanding the Database for the Study of Aging

The study of aging, like most sciences, depends on data. What is somewhat unique to aging, however, is that it requires a constant flow of *new* data—there are very few if any findings that can be taken as constant. Humans age in environments characterized by changing biological, social, economic, and technological conditions. As cohorts flow through this matrix, they age in different ways and at different rates. Not only do age-specific averages change, so also does variation about them. The probability that any given data set on aging, however complete or sophisticated, will be the last word is zero. This is as true for the biological aspects of aging as

it is for the social, as the current debate about compression of morbidity makes clear. Eventually, a mature science of aging will seek to model changes in the aging process as a function of the changing environment and seek to model changes in the environment as a function of changes in aging.

Early attempts at data collection on aging recognized from the start that longitudinal data were a necessity. Pioneering efforts, such as the Baltimore and Duke longitudinal studies, begun in the 1950s, were for many years the best data sources available, although only the second Duke Longitudinal Study (Busse & Maddox, 1985) is routinely available for secondary analysis. During the 1960s and 1970s more data slowly became available, and since the 1980s there has been a virtual flood. In addition to specialized studies of aging, many of which are described in this book, several general population surveys such as the Panel Study of Income Dynamics (Hill, 1992) and the National Medical Care Expenditure Survey (Corder & Manton, 1991) now obtain over-samples of the elderly.

One can think about data needs for aging in terms of a row-by-column table, with cohorts on the rows and topics on the columns. Examples of major topic headings might be "Income and Wealth," "Cognitive Capacity," and "Health." Although researchers will disagree about the specifics of the topic list, its broad outlines are generally agreed upon. Thus, any study will cover some range of cohorts on some set of topics. As longitudinal studies of aging become more commonplace throughout the world, several fundamental design issues have become clear.

The first is *breadth* versus *focus*. Should a study attempt to cover a very wide range of topics, obtaining information of interest for virtually all students of aging, or should it focus on a few specific topics like health and income? For example, in the United States the Longitudinal Study of Aging has focused on a very wide range of topics, whereas the Health and Retirement Survey has a somewhat narrower focus.

Second is *replication and comparison.* How much attention should be paid to exact replication of sampling and measurement protocols so as to permit exact comparison, both temporally and cross-culturally? Here the issue often is the trade-off between the use of measures that are now understood to be flawed but do permit replication and new measures that do not link to previous studies.

Third is the issue of *cohort coverage*. Because one cannot assume that any result will hold forever in the face of cohort replacement, how often should studies be replicated? For example, the Longitudinal Retirement History Survey, carried out in the United States from 1969 to 1979, was a major source of policy on the economics of aging. But by the early 1990s its youngest subjects were in their 80s, and more recent cohorts of persons in their 60s had very different characteristics (e.g., they had not been in the labor force during the Great Depression). The issue is, how does one decide that data are out of date and replication is necessary? Should new studies be launched every N years?

Finally, there is the issue of *rare events and specialized populations*. Some events, like widowhood or nursing home entry, are rare in the sense that in a general population sample they occur for only a small proportion of subjects in any one year. Thus, it is tempting to sample directly on the event of interest at the cost of losing important pre-event data.

It is difficult to resolve these issues without some rigorously defined national policy on data collection, an unlikely outcome in most countries and one that would have many undesirable consequences in any case. As a result, researchers will continue to be faced with a mélange of unrelated and uncoordinated studies, and the task will be to draw the results together in some meaningful way. Corder and Manton (1991) discuss these issues in some detail, but much remains to be done. In particular, even if studies are only loosely coordinated, there is room for greater cooperation and agreement on measurement protocols. With regard to a basic measure such as activities of daily living (ADL), for example, it makes little sense to have as many as five or six different approaches to measurement (Wiener, Hanley, Clark, & van Nostrand 1990).

Access to Data

Increasingly, studies of aging are becoming available for secondary analysis by other investigators. Governments are beginning to insist that studies funded with tax revenues be made generally avail-

able. Fienberg (1994) lays out the arguments for data sharing in some detail. A new standard for this process was recently set by AHEAD (Assets and Health Dynamics of the Oldest Old) at the University of Michigan. Fully documented data from that survey were available to investigators throughout the world, via the Internet, less than a year after the baseline survey was completed. Although it will be difficult for most studies to reach that standard, most major surveys now find their way into the public domain eventually. For a variety of reasons, this has been less true of medically-based studies than of others. For example, information from the famed Framingham Heart Study is still sharply restricted, as are many other similar studies.

The National Archive of Computerized Data on Aging (NACDA) at the University of Michigan is a major source of secondary data. It lists literally hundreds of surveys that are available free to its member institutions and its catalog (NACDA, 1994) lists more than two dozen other archives, half of which are outside the United States. NACDA distributes data in many forms, including tape, disk, CD, and direct electronic transfer.

With technological developments in networking, there is some question as to the future of data archives such as NACDA. The AHEAD survey already referred to, for example, was made available via a file server using file transfer protocol. With this technology, anyone with access to the Internet and knowledge of AHEAD's address could obtain the data directly in a manner of minutes without having to deal with an intermediary. This process transfers many responsibilities to the end user of the data, including printing of the documentation and management of fairly large data sets on desktop equipment, but it appears to be the wave of the future.

Issues in Data Access

As more and more data sets become available for analysis, several issues have come to light. Perhaps the most important is how one finds out about data. Although organizations such as NACDA maintain detailed lists of available data sets, a mere list is not enough information on which to base a judgment as to whether a given data set meets one's needs. Although there have been various proposals for sophisticated keyword searching, researchers usually need to see complete documentation. For example, it is difficult to judge the meaning of a given item without seeing the context in which it is asked. Much of this information is available only in hardcopy form, which is expensive to ship and store. Modern scanning technologies make much of this information potentially available in electronic form although not necessarily searchable. Standardized ways of coding and describing data would be of great help.

A second issue, already alluded to, is comparability. If one takes a cohort-based view of the study of aging, then comparable measures over time and space are crucial. The issue is not so much that investigators do not want to maintain comparability as it is that there are few institutional mechanisms to bring it about. Because innovation tends to be rewarded in science, it often wins over replication. The latter needs more support.

Finally, because of rapid developments in computing, surveys are becoming more and more complex. Computer-assisted interviewing permits extremely complex surveys that are not easily stored in traditional rectangular form. New mechanisms of data management and retrieval (e.g., CD-ROMs) are emerging, but much remains to be done.

Into the New Millennium

The National Archive of Computerized Data on Aging (whose information and data sets are available at *www.icpsr.umich.edu/NACDA*), remains a major international resource for scholars and investigators in gerontology. A number of countries have begun longitudinal research on aging (e.g., Australia, England, Germany, Mexico, the Netherlands, and Japan). As international data resources proliferate, specialized data archives will become increasingly necessary to index resources, develop computer-driven interview sequencing, and provide access to electronically accessible codebooks. As publicly available data resources and related technology also proliferate, issues of data confidentiality and of intellectual property will increase (for a

discussion of issues, see Fienberg, Makov, & Steele, 1998; Maddox, 1997).

RICHARD T. CAMPBELL

See also
Longitudinal Studies of Aging

LONGITUDINAL RESEARCH

Developmental scientists often argue that lawful relationships in human development can be understood only if the *same* organism is observed over the time frame during which the developmental phenomena of interest is thought to occur. This article identifies those aspects of aging research that require longitudinal inquiry; it also calls attention to some methodological pitfalls that limit longitudinal work from being the design of choice in all circumstances. More detailed discussions of longitudinal research methods may be found in Baltes and Nesselroade (1979) and in Schaie (1983, 1996). Extensive recent presentations of major longitudinal studies of adult development may be found in Busse (1993), Schaie (1996), and Shock and colleagues (Shock, Greulich, Costa, Andres, Lakatta, Arenberg, et al., 1984).

Advantages of Longitudinal Studies

The primary advantage of the longitudinal approach is that it offers information on intraindividual change (IAC). Cross-sectional studies, by contrast, allow inferences only about interindividual differences (IED). Five distinct rationales can be attributed to the longitudinal study of aging organisms:

Direct Identification of Intraindividual Change. Intraindividual change may be quantitative and continuous or may involve qualitative change, such as the transformation of one behavior into another. In either case, determination of change requires observation of behaviors over more than one occasion. When cross-sectional data are used to estimate IAC, it must be assumed that (1) subjects of different ages come from the same parent population at birth, (2) subjects have been matched across age levels for all characteristics other than age and the dependent variable, and (3) different-aged subjects have experienced identical life histories. Such assumptions are quite unreasonable in studies with human subjects.

Identification of Interindividual Variability in Intraindividual Change. Determination of different patterns of growth and decline requires the examination of similarities and differences in developmental trajectories. Data from longitudinal studies provide information on the degree of variability displayed by different individuals in their behavioral course over time that is needed for the construction of growth or decline typologies. Only longitudinal data allow the determination of whether group parameters accurately describe changes in any particular individual. The valuable hypothesis-generating method of single-subject research, therefore, depends on longitudinal observations.

Interrelationships Among Intraindividual Changes. Modern aging research operates within a multivariate context. Following individuals over time allows the discovery of constancies and changes, not only in individual variables but also in structural patterns that describe the relationship among these variables. The multivariate longitudinal approach is essential for the identification of progressive differentiation and dedifferentiation processes.

Analysis of Determinants of Intraindividual Change. Longitudinal studies identify time-ordered, antecedent-consequent relationships. It is the longitudinal approach alone that can uncover causal processes that involve discontinuities, such as the so-called sleeper effects.

Analysis of Interindividual Variability in the Determinants of Intraindividual Change. Longitudinal data, finally, allow inferences concerning the problem that many individuals show similar patterns in IAC that are determined by different change processes. For example, different change processes may occur at different levels in the range of talent, or different permutations of causal sequences may lead to similar outcomes in groups having different demographic attributes.

Pitfalls of Longitudinal Studies

Longitudinal studies do not conform to the rules for true experiments because age is a subject attribute that is not randomly assignable. Such studies are subject, therefore, to all the problems common to quasi-experimental research designs (Schaie, 1988, 1996). A threat to the internal validity of longitudinal studies that is of particular concern is the confounding of age and historical effects (what may appear to be maturational normative change may be the consequence of time-limited secular trends). Because the traditional longitudinal design is a special case of the pretest-posttest design, other validity threats include the effects of testing, instrumentation, statistical regression, experimental mortality, and selection (Schaie, 1988, 1996). Longitudinal studies also share certain limitations with respect to generalizability. Concerns here involve *experimental units*, the extent to which data collected on one sample can be generalized to another; *experimental settings*, the extent to which findings have cross-sectional validity; *treatment variables*, limitations imposed by measurement-implicit reinforcement schedules; and *measurement variables*, the appropriateness of task characteristics at different developmental stages as a longitudinal study progresses. In spite of these concerns, most of which are shared by age-comparative (cross-sectional) research, longitudinal data remain essential for the purposes described above. Some of the enumerated design problems can be handled by the use of suitable control groups and/or use of sequential strategies involving multiple cohorts (see Schaie, 1988).

K. Warner Schaie

See also
> Longitudinal Data Sets in Aging
> Longitudinal Studies: Europe
> Models for the Study of Aging

LONGITUDINAL RESEARCH: STATISTICAL ANALYSIS

Utility of Longitudinal Designs

Longitudinal research designs make use of information collected at two or more points of time. These designs are important to gerontology because they permit one to observe age- or cohort-related changes. Designs with three or more occasions of measurement are even more useful because they permit assessment of the pace of change. The public archiving of data sets has made more multiwave longitudinal data sets available, and use of these data has increased appreciably during the past decade. Although longitudinal data are not the panacea for gerontology, most scholars conclude that they offer greater potential for advancing the science of aging. Unlike cross-sectional data, there is the potential to distinguish age differences from age changes with data from multiple points in time.

Although there are many types of longitudinal data, it may be useful to distinguish two general groups. First, a *longitudinal panel design* refers to a study in which information from the same subjects is collected over time. These designs measure intraindividual change and are often referred to as panel designs because a panel of subjects is followed over time. Second, a *repeated cross-sectional design* refers to a study with the same measurements at different times on different subjects. The same subjects are not studied over time, but representative subjects are drawn from the same population over time. Although one cannot observe individual age-related changes, these designs are suitable for examining how age groups compare at different times or how these groups change. The age groups are usually referred to as cohorts, and analyses of repeated cross-sectional designs are often described as cohort analyses (Ferraro, 1990).

Each of these designs offers special opportunities for gerontological research, and each has its limitations. Panel designs are ideal for measuring individual-level changes, but they face the problem of attrition—not all subjects who begin a study will finish it. Attrition is not an issue for cohort analyses, but individual-level change cannot be determined. The universe of publicly archived data sets for cohort analysis is much larger, but most longitudinal research projects on aging rely on panel designs. Therefore, the remainder of this essay focuses on panel designs.

Statistical Analysis of Repeated Measures

In most panel designs, researchers have repeated measures on selected variables—identical measurements of selected information on subjects followed over time. With such information the investigator can identify change in the repeated measure(s) to be considered as a dependent variable, an independent variable, or both. The statistical analysis of panel data is distinct for quantitative (interval or ratio scale) and qualitative (nominal scale) variables. The former is often referred to as linear panel analysis and uses either difference scores or residualized regression scores (Menard, 1991). Analyses for qualitative variables may take many forms including logit, probit, Markov chain, and Poisson models (Hamerle & Ronning, 1995).

Preferred methods of statistical analysis have evolved in recent years to account for the longer observation periods of panel studies as well as the number of follow-ups. The longer observation periods hold great promise for scientific advances but require special consideration regarding nonresponse and selection effects. Regardless of whether quantitative or qualitative variables are studied, researchers are increasingly taking steps to assure that attrition is accounted for in statistical estimation. For example, if a researcher uses a 20-year panel study to examine changes in physical disability, it is possible that some of the most disabled persons will either die or be so incapacitated that they are not available for reinterview. Failure to consider how the sample changes in a nonrandom way may result in *selection bias*. This can be a problem if nonrandom attrition is associated with the independent variables, but it is more likely to be a concern if it is related to the dependent variable (as in the case of studying disability). In this example, selection bias would likely lead to an underestimate of disability in the sample.

Most scholars agree that nonrandom selection must be accounted for in generating meaningful estimates of age-related changes in longitudinal data, but the specific procedures to be used remain a matter of debate. Selection bias models developed by Heckman are among the most widely used (Stolzenberg & Relles, 1997), but other promising approaches include structural equation models (McArdle & Hamagami, 1991), hierarchical linear models (Campbell, 1999), and multiple imputation (Lavori, Dawson, & Shera, 1995). Although these and other approaches differ in how to account for the attrition, each incorporates some modeling of the attrition process and adjusts parameter estimates of change to account for the possibility of nonrandom selection.

Statistical Analysis of Event Data

Gerontologists are often interested in events experienced by subjects over the course of longitudinal panel designs. Such events include retirement, hospitalization, nursing home admission, or death. When information about the timing of these events is known, we may refer to it as event data. Event data may be of two basic types. First, one may know that an event was experienced between waves of a study but not know precisely when; these are typically referred to as *discrete-time data*. Second, one may know the precise date at which an event occurred; these are referred to as *continuous-time data*.

For years, many investigators applied logistic regression methods to study an event experienced between waves. This may be appropriate in some circumstances, but it may not be optimal if the event experienced is time-dependent. For example, imagine a panel study that has two data collection points—baseline and a 10-year follow-up. If one has continuous-time data on mortality during the study period, logistic regression procedures would treat deaths occurring 1 year after the baseline as no different from deaths occurring 9 years after the baseline. With continuous-time event data, however, a more efficient statistical analysis would simultaneously identify the subjects who died as well as when they died (thereby differentiating subjects by time of death). Such an analysis is referred to as *event history analysis,* survival analysis, or hazard rate modeling. This analytic approach has become quite popular in gerontology in the past decade.

There are two basic types of statistical models for event history analyses (Allison, 1995). *Parametric methods* of analysis require specifying a model to fit the observed event histories so that the estimates are asymptotically unbiased and efficient. There are many different parametric models to use for event history analysis of nonrepeated events (e.g., Weibull, Gompertz). *Semiparametric methods* based on proportional hazards, often referred to as Cox models, have achieved widespread popularity in recent years for several reasons. First, these

proportional hazards models do not require one to determine the shape of the survival curve because the method relies on the *order* of the event times, not their exact times of occurrence. Second, proportional hazards modeling offers the flexibility of incorporating time-dependent covariates into the model. For instance, if the independent variables are observed more than once, even for just some cases, the transitions in them can be used in model estimation. These models also can handle repeated events (e.g., hospitalization), multiple types of events (e.g., acute care hospitalization vs. nursing home admission), and events indexed by discrete-time data if arrayed across three or more survey waves (e.g., relocation). These advantages make these semiparametric models quite popular, but they are not as statistically efficient as the parametric methods. Nevertheless, this is viewed as a minor limitation for many researchers. In addition, as more multiwave panel studies on aging become available, the ability to include time-dependent covariates will likely increase the application of the semiparametric methods.

KENNETH F. FERRARO

LONGITUDINAL RETIREMENT HISTORY SURVEY

The Social Security Administration's Longitudinal Retirement History Survey (LRHS; 1969–1979) is a model national study designed to examine the complex process and broad effect of retirement. Its value was such that, within less than a decade of its termination, plans were underway for a new survey, using more recently developed approaches to the same basic issues (see "Health and Retirement Survey").

LRHS built on the findings of several excellent smaller studies. It chose its sample (a nationally representative group of 58–63-year-olds: 8,132 men and 3,021 women with no husband in the household), its biennial interviewing interval, and finite duration (10 years) to maximize the possibility of examining its focal interest within fiscal constraints.

The study and the potentially unique characteristics of the population it represented, were carefully introduced to the relevant research and policy communities (Irelan, 1972). The developers were responsive to the needs of investigators. Intramural findings from the study were published rapidly and in convenient formats (Irelan, Motley, Schwab, Sherman, & Murray, 1976). Data were released to the public at reasonable speed, and after the first wave they were clean and included many derived variables. A guide to using the first wave, which identifies problems and suggests solutions has been developed (*User's Guide,* 1977). The codebooks are fully descriptive but lack frequencies. Data tapes for the LRHS are available from the National Archives and Records Service, Washington, DC 20408, and ICPSR, P.O. Box 1248, Ann Arbor, MI 48106-1248. Based on experience with this survey, a guide to avoiding problems in studies of this type also has been published (Fox & Irelan, 1989).

Data gathering was by means of structured in-person interviews with information obtained biennially (1969, 1971, 1973, 1975, 1977, 1979). During this 10-year period the percentage of persons reporting that they were completely retired increased from 16% (1969) to 76% (1979); those in the labor force declined from 73% (1969) to 18% (1979).

Although the specific information gathered varied from wave to wave, focus was on labor force history; expectations and plans for retirement; health; family, social activities, living arrangements; financial resources and assets, debts, and expenditures. For those who were married, information was also obtained on the labor force history of the spouse (typically the wife), her attitude to work and retirement, and in the later waves (1975, 1977, 1979), her health. Certain information was gathered on only a single wave. For example, information on work commitment and on the father's occupational history and retirement was obtained in 1971, spouse's marital history in 1973, early unemployment history in 1975, future work plans in 1977, and accurate relocation history for the previous decade in 1979. An item continuity log covering all waves has been developed (Institute on Aging, 1984).

When a married respondent died, the surviving spouse (typically the wife) was retained in the study because her life was viewed as an extension of her spouse's work life and preparation for retirement. She was asked those questions normally reserved for the primary respondent. Extensive information on widowhood was gathered during the last three waves (1975, 1977, 1979). The number of persons widowed during the study increased from 245 in 1971 to 1,082 in 1979. The LRHS thus affords a unique opportunity to examine the impact of widowhood on a substantial group of persons whose prewidowhood status is known.

Table 1 indicates how sample size changed over time. In 1969, 73% of the sample was male (70% in 1979); 89% were White, 10% Black, and 1% other race; 8% had never married, 64% were married, and 29% were widowed, divorced, or separated (6%, 51%, and 43% in 1979); 41% had no more than elementary school education, 42% had high school only, and 17% had gone beyond high school.

Three data sets can be linked to the LRHS: (1) Social Security earnings record (for 11,085 of the 11,153 respondents), which provides information on date of birth, sex, race, earnings subject to Social Security (1937–1975), and quarters of earned eligibility; (2) master beneficiary record that includes details of benefit history and date of death; (3) nonresponse tape, which provides reason for nonresponse on a particular wave.

An annotated listing of the majority of published studies based on the LRHS through mid-1984 is given in Fillenbaum, Abolafia, Maddox, and Manton (1984). Issues examined using LRHS data include, but are not limited to, the determinants, timing and impact of retirement on individuals and/or married couples, the economics of retirement and dissaving, women's income history, pension effects, and work after retirement. Studies have been published on health economics (the cost of dying, health-related expenses) and on determinants of change in and the cost and impact of services on functional status as well as on social issues (e.g., family and friend relationships, relocation and how it is influenced by retirement, change in household composition, and widowhood). Some studies have focused on special groups, primarily women but occasionally Blacks. Such studies are somewhat hampered because the women present are not nationally representative, and the Blacks constitute a small group.

The data are appropriate for examination of theory (particularly within a life-course framework) and important for policy. They merit further analy-

TABLE 1   Sample Size Changes

	1969	1971	1973	1975	1977	1979
Sample size	11,153	10,169	9,423	8,716	7,993	7,352
Widowed into the study	—	245	495	727	914	1,082

sis, both in their own right and, increasingly, for historical comparison.

GERDA G. FILLENBAUM

See also

OARS Multidimensional Functional Assessment Questionnaire

LONGITUDINAL STUDIES: EUROPE

The seven longitudinal studies that were started in Europe in the mid-1950s and early 1960s were mostly initiated by physicians and focused on biological and physiological data (e.g., the Switzerland, Hungary, and Kiev studies). Some studies have included psychosocial variables (the Netherlands and the Göteborg studies); others focused on psychological data (personality variables, cognitive functioning, and psychomotor performance), as did the Jerusalem study; and yet others emphasized psychological research and also included medical data (the Bonn Longitudinal Study on Aging).

For the early 1990s, 70 longitudinal studies on adult development are documented for European countries (Deeg, 1989; Schneider & Edelstein, 1990). In a 1994 survey, 17 additional projects were reported. Like most of the studies included in the 1990 report, they were initiated in the late 1980s and after 1990. There was a considerable degree of variation in the design, methods, and time spent at each measurement point for the assessment of each subject. In one of the studies the subjects stayed for 9 days in a hospital; within some of the longitudinal health or social surveys, the sample was interviewed 1 to 3 hours at each measurement point.

Paul Verzàr, one of the pioneers of biology of aging in Switzerland, initiated in 1955 a longitudi-

nal study on a sample of 100 employees of a pharmaceutical company at Basel; they belonged to three age groups: 13 to 22, 31 to 39, and 45 to 59 years. This sample was followed for 10 years.

Although most of the subjects belonged to younger and middle-aged groups, the author concluded that variables, such as the decrease of the amplitude of blood pressure, vital capability, and increase of systolic and diastolic blood pressure, pulse rate, and girth were identified as predictors of premature aging.

A health survey undertaken by van Zonneveld in 1954 in the Netherlands, with the help of many medical practitioners, was continued to 1974, with six measurement points. At the beginning of the study, the subjects were between the ages of 65 and 100. Data analysis was related mainly to psychosocial variables. Continued work, interest in newspapers, and higher scores in a memory test were predictors of longevity, whereas none of the physical characteristics investigated showed a clear connection with the longevity quotient.

Other earlier projects include the Swedish Göteborg Longitudinal Study (Steen & Djurfeldt, 1993), begun in 1969, and a Hungarian study. The latter was started in 1965 at the Gerontology Center at Budapest. The sample decreased to 73 persons after 7 to 8 years and to 25 persons after 10 years because of lack of motivation. Data contained in the study are related to stability and changes in certain disorders, such as cardiovascular or cerebral malfunctioning.

A large longitudinal study of human aging was started in 1973 at the Institute of Gerontology at Kiev, using inpatient and ambulatory examinations of various physiological functions. The longitudinal data from the first stages of the study point to a great degree of interindividual differences in the onset of changes of the functions measured. A nonuniform rate of onset of age-related changes in various functions of the same individual also was observed.

Genetic influences on aging were studied in two twin studies. The Swedish Twin Registry is following 10.9–15 pairs of twins by using questionnaires on health status, health, history, food habits and food intake, smoking habits, alcohol intake, social background, and other data.

Another twin study was started by Pedersen and associates in 1991 covering a core sample of 1,637 twins in the age range of 26–93 years (Pedersen, McClearn, Plomin, Nesselroade, Berg, & deFaire, 1991). It stresses the role of genetic factors for the aging process. A different view of this role was suggested by Weinert and Geppert (1998) from an analysis of the data of the Gottschaldt Twin Study. The subjects of this study were tested for the first time in 1937 and followed into old age. An analysis of the monozygotic (MZ) differences in cognitive measures showed that environmental and genetic influences became increasingly identical with increasing age. From this point of view a balance between genes and environment is achieved in old age.

The differential aspect of the aging process was the focus of the Bonn Longitudinal Study of Aging, started in 1965 with men and women of two cohorts: those born between 1890 and 1895 and those born between 1900 and 1905 (Thomae, 1993). Seven observations had been completed by 1980, and visits to the homes of the survivors were made in 1984. The study program focused, through lengthy semistructured interviews, on present and past social, psychological, and physical situations; measurement of cognitive functioning; psychomotor performance; personality tests; and medical examinations by a specialist in internal medicine. The data confirmed findings related to (a) the impact of health, social status, and activity on cognitive functioning and overall adjustment to aging and (b) the greater interindividual variability with increasing age. From the data of 81 survivors of the first 12 years of observation, Thomae derived 12 "patterns of aging," defined by longitudinal scores for activity, life satisfaction, perceived life stress, and social competence.

The data of the Bonn study that were related to prediction of longevity confirmed previous analyses of the problem by pointing to the positive role of intelligence, activity, responsiveness, health, and socioeconomic status in distinguishing between long- and short-lived persons. Additional factors in predicting longevity proved to be perceived health, life satisfaction, extrafamilial orientation, and identification with children and grandchildren (Thomae, 1993). Furthermore, gender and cohort appeared as variables in the prediction of survivorship.

The Jerusalem Study of Middle Age and Aging involves an urban sample of 134 persons (birth cohorts 1902–1927) who were available for two measurement points separated by 7 to 8 years. The main variable investigated was coping behavior, which was classified in the groups as active versus passive coping. Coping was assessed by sentence completion and Thematic Apperception Test techniques. Using Q-sort techniques and cluster analysis, Shanan found different types of coping at the first and the second measurement points (e.g., an "active integrated coper," a "dependent passive coper," a "failing overcoper," and a "self-negating undercoper" at measurement point 1; and an "aging active coper," an "aging passive coper," a "tired hero," and a "disenchanted moralist" at measurement point 2. Shanan (1985) stresses the importance of interindividual variation and suggests the necessity for approaches to the study of human development and aging.

Examples of longitudinal studies on aging started after 1980 are the North-East Age Research Longitudinal Programme at the University of Manchester (UK) Age and Cognitive Performance Research Centre and the TURVA project of the Department of Psychiatry of the University of Turku (Finland). Both projects were started in 1982. The Manchester study is focusing on cognitive changes in old age, with a sample of 6,000 volunteers (aged 50–96 years). First findings point to slight changes in average levels of cognitive ability with increasing age and to massive increases in variability between individuals within the cohorts tested. Relationships between health and cognitive competence are approached in several subsidiary studies.

The TURVA project is related to the issue of retirement. Preliminary findings point to the role of the previous life in the adaptation to retirement, which was not experienced as a crisis by most of the study participants.

A follow-up is planned for the Berlin Aging Study (Baltes & Mayer, 1999). The Amsterdam Longitudinal Study (Beurs & Deeg, 1999) showed that older persons' subjective experience of health is more important for later anxiety than objective indices of health. Of these indices, cancer and cardiovascular diseases had, together with age, income, education, and gender, significant effects on mortality. In the Lund 80+ Study, survival in a period of 7 years was predicted by a combination of type of change experienced, personality, coping strategy, and locus of control. Neuroticism and avoidance coping were found to increase survival (Hagberg, Dehlin, Samuelsson, & Svensson, 1999). The same longitudinal study also confirmed the terminal decline hypothesis: the closer to death, the lower the scores for cognitive tests.

The impact of social and political change on human development is to be studied in the Interdisciplinary Longitudinal Study on Aging (ILSE) at the German Centre for Research on Ageing at the Universities of Heidelberg and Leipzig (Lehr, Jüchtern, Schmitt, Sperling, Fischer, Grünendahl, et al., 1998). Samples of men and women born 1930–1932 and 1950–1952 from the "old" states of West Germany and the "new" ones of East Germany (living formerly under a Communist regime) have been followed since 1993 regarding health, cognitive development, psychological well-being, ways of coping, and personality.

Longitudinal research became very popular in Europe after the 1970s. The quality of this research, however, differs considerably.

URSULA LEHR

See also
    Canadian Research
    International Perspectives
    Longitudinal Data Sets in Aging
    Longitudinal Research

LONGITUDINAL STUDIES OF AGING

For illustrative data sets See
    Australian Longitudinal Study of Aging
    Baltimore Longitudinal Study of Aging
    Berlin Aging Study
    Cornell Study of Occupational Retirement
    Duke Longitudinal Studies
    Established Populations for Epidemiological Studies of the Elderly
    Framingham Studies of Heart Disease
    Göteborg Longitudinal Studies
    Health and Retirement Survey
    Human Aging Study
    Kansas City Studies of Adult Life
    Longitudinal Retirement History Survey
    Longitudinal Study of Aging
    Longitudinal Study of Generations
    Longitudinal Studies: Europe
    National Institute of Mental Health Epidemiologic Catchment Area Project
    National Long-Term Care Survey
    MacArthur Community Study of Successful Aging
    Normative Aging Study
    Tampere Longitudinal Study on Aging

See also
    Cohorts
    Compression of Morbidity: Disease Postponement
    Cross-Cultural Research
    Longitudinal Data Sets in Aging
    Longitudinal Research
    Longitudinal Research: Statistical Analysis
    Nutrition
    OARS Multidimensional Functional Assessment Questionnaire

LONGITUDINAL STUDY OF AGING

Purpose

The Longitudinal Study of Aging (LSOA) was designed to measure transitions in functional status and living arrangements for a nationally representative cohort of Americans aged 70 and older. It was a collaborative project of the National Center for Health Statistics and the National Institute on Aging. The LSOA was based on a sample of older persons who originally were interviewed in the 1984 National Health Interview Survey (NHIS). An important feature of the LSOA is the availability of edited data files for use by the research community.

Methodology

Methodology for the LSOA consisted of several types of data collection: (1) a personal interview for the 1984 baseline; (2) primarily telephone interviews for recontacts in 1986, 1988, and 1990; and (3) linkage to death records and Medicare claims data.

The 1984 baseline interview for the LSOA was the Supplement on Aging (SOA) of the 1984 NHIS. The NHIS consists of personal interviews of a nationally representative sample of the civilian noninstitutionalized population. Major design characteristics of the NHIS are its complex, multistage sampling of about 40,000 households and its continuous interviewing throughout the year. Immediately after the NHIS interview, the SOA interview was conducted. The SOA sample consisted of all persons in the household who were aged 65 and over and half of those aged 55 to 64. Persons living in nursing homes were out of the scope of the NHIS and hence of the SOA.

The sampling frame for the LSOA was based on persons who in 1984 were age 70 or over and had participated in the SOA. Because of resource constraints, only a subsample of the SOA respondents was included in the 1986 LSOA recontact. The subsample was selected on the basis of race-ethnic categories and age at the time of the 1984 SOA. It consisted of all persons aged 80 or over, all Hispanic or Black persons aged 70 to 79, and one half of all White, non-Hispanic persons aged 70 to 79. Relatives aged 70 to 79 living in the same households were also in the 1986 sample. In the 1988 and 1990 LSOA recontacts the entire 1984 SOA sample was included. Although the number of older persons eligible for the LSOAs changes, the analytic sample remains constant. If three points in time are used (1984, 1988, 1990), the sample is 7,527 people aged 70 and over who participated in the 1984 SOA. If all four points are used (1984, 1986, 1988, 1990), the sample is 5,151 people eligible for the 1986 recontact. Different weights are available on the public-use tapes to calculate the national estimates from these two samples.

The LSOA interviews were conducted primarily by telephone. Mail questionnaires were used for persons who could not be reached by phone or did not respond to telephone calls. The intent was to interview the sampled persons unless they were incapacitated or temporarily absent (usually in a hospital). About 65% of the LSOA interviews were with self-respondents.

Data collected in the LSOA interviews were augmented with data from record matches conducted for 1984 to 1991. Permission to make these matches and the information necessary to do so were obtained from the respondents during the 1984 SOA. The matches were (1) to the National Death Index (NDI) and the multiple cause-of-death file to obtain information about decedents and causes of death, and (2) to the Medicare Automated Data Retrieval System (MADRS) to obtain data about hospital visits and "other" health care covered by Medicare.

Content and Uses of the Data

The LSOA was designed to measure changes since the 1984 baseline in the following areas:

- Functioning, including activities for daily living (ADLs), instrumental ADLs, and physical movements such as walking long distances, lifting heavy items, stooping, and manipulating fingers.
- Family structure, including changes in marital status and contacts with children.
- Housing and living arrangements, including housing characteristics and intercounty/interstate migration.
- Health care, including nursing home stays in the past year, physician contacts, and health insurance.
- Economic and retirement indicators, including sources of retirement income and family income.

Information from record matches includes:

- Identification of decedents, dates and causes of death, occupation and industry recodes.
- All hospitalizations covered by Medicare, including length of stay, diagnoses, and procedures for each stay.
- Receipt of home health care, hospice, or outpatient care covered by Medicare.

Baseline data from the SOA also permit analyses of selected risk factors: chronic conditions, household composition, family structure, and social activities.

The strengths of the LSOA include data to analyze "healthy aging" as well as transitions from functional independence, to disability, to institutionalization, to death. See, for example, Crimmins, Hayward, and Saito (1994) on transitions in functioning and chapters 2 and 3 in Van Nostrand, Furner, and Suzman (1993) on outcomes of institutionalization and death.

Data Availability

Public use tapes and diskettes are available from several sources: the National Center for Health Statistics, National Technical Information Service (NTIS), and the Inter-University Consortium for Political and Social Research. A CD-ROM is available from NTIS. The tapes of the 1984 NHIS, the 1984 SOA, and the LSOA (version 4) can be linked by a common ID number; so can the diskettes of data from the matches to the NDI, cause-of-death file, and MADRS.

JOAN F. VAN NOSTRAND

See also
Longitudinal Studies of Aging

LONGITUDINAL STUDY OF GENERATIONS

Have the structures, functions, or consequences of intergenerational relationships changed or stayed the same across recent decades? How do intergenerational relationships influence the well-being of family members as they undergo various life-course transitions? These questions form the core of the Longitudinal Study of Generations (LSOG). The focus of the LSOG is on intergenerational dynamics in changing times, as well as implications of increasing years of joint survivorship and shared lifetimes for individuals in multigenerational families.

Initiated at the University of Southern California in 1971, the LSOG is a study of linked members from over 300 three- and four-generation families as they have grown up and grown old over more than a quarter century. The specific aims reflect four major goals:

1. To chart effects of sociohistorical change on families, intergenerational relationships, and aging since the 1960s.

2. To track life-course trajectories of family intergenerational solidarity over several decades, and across successive generations of family members.
3. To identify how intergenerational solidarity influences the well-being of family members through the adult life course and across successive generations.
4. To examine women's roles and relationships in multigenerational families across 32 years of aging and social change.

The study began in 1971 with 2,044 respondents, aged 16–91, representing 328 three-generation families. Eligible sample members were recruited from the families of potential grandparents randomly selected from the membership of a large (840,000-member) prepaid health maintenance organization in the Southern California area. The sample pool is generally representative of White, economically stable working- and middle-class families. Self-administered questionnaires were mailed to the grandparents and their spouses, their adult children and their spouses, and their adolescent or young adult grandchildren aged 16–26. Overall, a response rate of 70% was attained across the generations (for details, see Bengtson, 1975).

At Time 1 (1971) the baseline sample included 516 grandparents (G1, average age 67), 701 parents (G2, 44 years), and 827 grandchildren (G3, 19 years). The study became longitudinal in 1985 with a follow-up survey to the original respondents. Since then surveys have been repeated every 3 years, in 1988, 1991, 1994, 1997, 2000, and 2003 (projected). Thus, the study will follow the same family members for 32 years of time and over eight waves of measurement.

The LSOG has had high longitudinal participation rates since 1971, considering the age of the original respondents, the duration of the study, the use of self-administered surveys, and the gap between Time 1 and Time 2. The longitudinal response rate between Time 1 and Time 2 was 67% (after 14 years of no contact with respondents), but it has averaged 85% between waves since 1985. Attrition analyses comparing those who remained in the study to those who dropped out revealed few systematic biases over the two decades of time elapsed.

Since 1991 the sample has been augmented by the addition of new spouses and the young adult great-grandchildren (G4s, or fourth generation) of the G1s, as they became 16 years of age. The average age of the 196 G4s added in 1991 was 20 years, about the same age as their parents were when they first became part of the study in 1971. In the 1994 and 1997 surveys, an additional 804 G4s were added. Newly eligible G4s will again be added in 2000 and 2003.

The key constructs measured in the surveys include (1) six dimensions of family intergenerational solidarity, (2) sociopolitical attitudes, (3) value orientations, (4) psychological well-being, (5) physical health, (6) life events, (7) family caregiving, and (8) intergenerational transmission. The reliability and validity of the construct measures and scales have been extensively examined in numerous publications. The most comprehensive analyses have been conducted on the six dimensions of intergenerational solidarity, comprising affect, association, consensus, function, norms, and structure (see Mangen, Bengtson, & Landry, 1988).

Research findings over the course of the study have contributed to knowledge about the structure, function, and consequences of intergenerational family relations. For example, the six dimensions of intergenerational solidarity, while initially thought to be components of one theoretical construct, have been found to be statistically independent. Further, these dimensions can be used to construct five theoretically and empirically derived "types" of parent-child relationships: tight-knit, sociable, intimate but distant, obligatory, and detached (Silverstein & Bengtson, 1997). Such a typology is important because it shows the inherently multidimensional nature of parent-child relationships.

Findings from the LSOG have also shown that intergenerational relations are relatively stable over two decades. For example, levels of affection remain high for both parents and children across many years, although parents consistently report closer relationships than children do (a phenomenon referred to as the "intergenerational stake"). Moreover, earlier intergenerational relations have been found to play a strong role in structuring contemporary relationships. For example, early parental affection provides long-term psychological benefits for both sons and daughters in adulthood (Roberts & Bengtson, 1996), and improvements in the quality of parent-child relationships are associated with an increase in self-esteem across 20 years (Giarrusso, Feng, Silverstein, & Bengtson, 2000). Other findings reveal that social support received from adult children positively influences parents' psychological well-being. However, there are limits to the benefits of social support: "oversupport" sometimes magnifies the psychological distress of older parents.

Finally, the LSOG research program has shed light on the extent to which values, status, and behaviors are transmitted from one generation to the next. For example, transmission of occupational status is superseded by historical changes in the societal opportunity structure. Each successive LSOG generation of offspring (adult grandchildren, parents, and grandparents) has been found to have a higher occupational attainment than that of the generation before it (although the rate of upward mobility slowed across generations). Further, sometimes transmission effects are gendered. In an investigation of the intergenerational transmission of divorce, it was found that parental divorce increased daughters' likelihood of divorce but not that of sons (Feng, Giarrusso, Bengtson, & Frye, 1999).

LSOG data gathering continues to examine issues related to continuity, change, and transmission within intergenerational families over time. Future analyses will focus on (1) identifying the diversity of types of intergenerational relationships among and within families in bonding and conflict over time; (2) examining the relative influences of familial, sociostructural, and historical period factors on intergenerational transmission involving generational-sequential analyses of the family data; and (3) assessing consequences of developmental life events for family relationships. Data from early waves of the study are archived with the Henry A. Murray Research Center of Radcliffe College and are available for public use.

VERN L. BENGSTON
MORRIS SILVERSTEIN
ROSEANN GIARRUSSO
MARIA SCHMEECKLE

See also
Longitudinal Studies of Aging

LONG-LIVED HUMAN POPULATIONS

Throughout history and around the world, claims of extreme longevity and long-lived populations have been common. For example, almost 5,000 years ago Huang Ti wrote that "in ancient times the people lived to be over a hundred years, and yet they remained active and did not become decrepit in their activities" (Veith, 1966). According to the Bible, Adam lived 930 years; Noah, 950 years; and Methuselah, 969 years. Benjamin Franklin informed the readers of *Poor Richard's Almanac* that Thomas Parr, a Shropshire farmer, lived to be "something above 150" and that Henry Jenkins of Bolton, Yorkshire, lived to be 169 years (Franklin, 1976). However, in 1879, Thoms exposed the complete lack of documentation of Parr's claims for longevity (Pieroni, 1984).

The *Guinness Book of World Records* states that "no single subject is more obscured by vanity, deceit, falsehood, and deliberate fraud than the extremes of human longevity" (Young, 1997). After an examination of the claims and the records, the *Guinness Book* concludes that the greatest authenticated age was achieved by Jeanne Louise Calment, who died at the age of 122 in 1997. She was well educated and physically active, but she also smoked cigarettes until she was 117.

In the mid-1970s there were many widely publicized reports of long-lived populations in Hunza, Pakistan; Vilcabamba, Ecuador; and Abkhazia, USSR. These reports all claimed that large numbers of centenarians were surviving in these regions and that several had reached the age of 150 or more (Davies, 1975; Kyuchayants, 1974; Leaf, 1975). No one has yet investigated the claims for longevity in Hunza because the Hunzukuts have no written language and no birth records (Medvedev, 1974). However, a careful census made in Vilcabamba found no evidence of increased longevity and determined that all claims of ages over 100 were either incorrect or unsubstantiated (Mazes & Forman, 1979). An intensive study in the Soviet Union (Bolshakov, Brook, & Kozlov, 1982) of a sample of Abkhazians thought to be over 90 years of age concluded that less than 40% were actually over 90. Furthermore, none was found to be actually over 110. Using these percentages to correct the USSR census figures for Abkhazia, Palmore (1984b) concluded that there is no more longevity in Abkhazia than in the United States. Kozlov attacked Palmore's conclusions, primarily on the grounds that there is age exaggeration in the U.S. census also (Kozlov, 1984). However, Palmore responded that there is much less age exaggeration in the U.S. census because ages can be corrected by comparison to Social Security records, which require documentation of claimed ages (Palmore, 1984c).

Beller and Palmore (1974) compared 50 Turks with probable ages of 90 or more with a control group of 110 Turks, ranging in age from 11 to 80, to find what physical and behavioral factors were associated with longevity. The physical factors were blood types P2 and Le(a-b-), relatively good health throughout life, being male, and having normal height and weight. The behavioral factors associated with longevity were simple diets with little meat or animal fat, no cigarette smoking, vigorous physical activity, marriage and sexual activity, social activity, and a positive view of life.

Apparently, there are no human populations with authenticated unusual longevity. However, there is general agreement from the studies of those few individuals who do have unusual longevity that contributing factors appear to include simple diets with little animal fats, abstinence in use of tobacco and alcohol, vigorous physical activity, and a positive mental attitude.

Authentication of age has continued to be a major problem in research on long-lived populations (Perls, Bochen, Freeman, Alpert, & Silver, 1999). For this reason, attention has shifted to the study of centenarians with authenticated ages (Martin, Poon, Kim, & Johnson, 1996; Samuelsson, Alfredson, Hagberg, Samuelsson, Nordbeck, Brun, et al., 1997; Smith, 1997).

ERDMAN B. PALMORE

See also
Centenarians
Life Expectancy
Life Extension
Oldest Old

LONG-TERM CARE
See
Continuum of Care
Long-Term Care Policy

LONG-TERM CARE ASSESSMENT

Common reasons for assessment in long-term care are to determine eligibility for services, to make decisions concerning the content and intensity of interventions, and to monitor patients' status over time and their responses to treatment. Long-term care assessments are relevant to a variety of non-acute services such as specialized rehabilitation, nursing homes, and home health. Services provided may be of relatively short duration, as in the case of postacute care or require longer supportive services and permanent placement. As need cannot be predicted in advance and because many older adults use combinations of services, assessments in these settings should address similar dimensions and share components.

When choosing instruments, potential users should know for which populations they have been tested and under what conditions. Assessment instruments should demonstrate the essential characteristics of reliability and validity. Validity expresses the degree to which an instrument measures what it intends to measure. Test-retest reliability refers to the reproducibility of scores or laboratory equipment with repeated testing. When raters administer the tests, the consistency of scores should be assessed among two or more raters (interrater reliability) and within one rater at two points in time (intrarater reliability). In addition, when multiple items are scored and summed, it is advisable to see how individual items relate to each other and to the total score. This type of reliability is termed *internal consistency*. To maximize generalizability, psychometric testing should be examined in different groups and in situations that reflect real-life circumstances in which the instruments might be used.

Beyond evidence of reliability and validity, the desired characteristics of an instrument may vary relative to the demands of the situation, but the same instruments may serve multiple purposes. At the individual level, assessments can be used for screening, care plan development, monitoring, and prediction. Screening may involve decisions about performing more thorough evaluation in specific areas, referring to specialized services, or determining eligibility for services. Efficient screening instruments are brief and easy to administer but have appropriate sensitivity and specificity for the purpose at hand. They do not have to distinguish small differences among individuals.

To develop a care plan, it is necessary to evaluate multiple areas and make reasonably fine distinctions between patients. Selecting the domains of the assessment and the depth required within areas depends on the level of ability of the patient, the situation, and the goals as prioritized by the patient and family. When evaluating the effects of the intervention and monitoring the status of patients over time, instruments should demonstrate an additional property: responsiveness, or the ability to detect clinically meaningful change even if it is small. Making decisions about individuals on the basis of repeated measurements demands high standards of reliability (above .94) because errors can occur at each testing (Helmstadter, 1964). Lastly, instruments used to make clinical decisions require predictive validity concerning the outcome of the decision. For example, is it safe for the patient to return home alone?

At a health service level, measures may be used to monitor quality of care, allocate resources based on case mix, or plan for the development of appropriate resources. Assessments based on group scores do not, in general, require as high reliability and precision as those used to make decisions about individuals, but the same measures may be used to accomplish multiple purposes.

Comprehensive assessment should address different domains of impairment, disability, and health-related quality of life. As classified by the World Health Organization (WHO), impairments refer to a loss or abnormality of psychological, physiological, or anatomical structure or function. Tests of cognitive status, mood, affect, cardiovascular fitness, strength, motor performance, and sensory and perceptual deficits are considered impairment-level assessments. Disability reflects the consequences of impairments in terms of functional performance and is assessed by using measures of basic and instrumental activities of daily living. Health-related quality of life encompasses physical and cognitive functioning, mental health, well-being, and social interactions. Impairment and disability are related to quality-of-life domains, and improvements in physical function or symptoms can have a positive impact on quality of life. Patients with similar levels of disability may, however, differ in their of quality of life because they may have different expectations of their role, or they may have adequate material and social resources to compensate for the disability. Similarly, patients with similar impairments may vary in functional ability because they learn to compensate and adapt to the existing constraints. It is therefore important to choose measures that represent different levels as well as different domains.

For each domain or attribute, we cannot recommend any one best measure, and it is beyond the scope of this article to describe and review all possible measures. Separate measures are available to assess strength, mobility, cognitive status, self-confidence, and endurance (6-minute walk). Existing instruments may address different aspects of the attribute. For example, strength may be assessed with a dynamometer in a laboratory or indirectly, using functional tasks such as stair climbing. Physical performance measures have been developed for multiple purposes, including indications of functional limitations that precede disability, identification of those at risk of falling, and outcome measures to monitor the effects of interventions targeting specific areas, such as balance or gait (Berg & Norman, 1996).

Basic activities of daily living (ADLs) are a fundamental part of an assessment. They are often the focal point of the patient's concerns and thus, goals targeting function encourage greater motivation. Knowledge of functional status also helps guide professionals in determining the immediate needs of the patient. The two oldest and best-known ADL scales were developed by Katz, Ford, Moskowitz, Jackson, and Jaffe (1963) and by Mahoney and Barthel (1965). Each is considered to address basic ADLs, such as bathing, dressing, and toileting. These tasks are also included as part of comprehensive measuring instruments, as mentioned below, and by national surveys such as the Longitudinal Study of Aging and the National Health and Disability Survey. Although they may contain the same items, each instrument addresses somewhat different aspects of physical function. Community-based surveys commonly ask subjects to rate their level of difficulty when performing the tasks, whereas patient populations are more likely to be asked to demonstrate each ADL task. The other dimension of performance is consistency over a period of time. For example, the MDS-ADL scale rates actual performance and consistency of performance over the past 7 days (Morris, Fries, & Morris, 1999).

Instrumental activities of daily living (IADLs), such as shopping and housecleaning represent a bridge between basic ADLs and measures of social functioning. As such, IADL measures should be included when evaluating a patient's ability to live independently. As with ADL measures, subjects may be asked to self-rate difficulty or demonstrate performance of IADL tasks. Disability, however, is also a function of social role and expectations. Instruments such as the SF-36 (Ware & Sherbourne, 1993) and the Reintegration to Normal Living Index (Wood-Dauphinee, Opzoomer, Williams, Marchand, & Spitzer, 1988) are being used to address health-related quality of life and adjustment to chronic disease for individuals living in the community. More work is needed to develop measures that identify facilities that excel in improving residents' quality of life, beyond providing very good physical care.

Three instruments deserve special mention when discussing long-term care. The Functional Independence Measure (FIM) is the principal component of the Uniform Dataset (UDSmr); the Minimum Dataset (MDS), a component of the Resident Assessment Instrument (RAI); and the OASIS (Outcomes Assessment and Information Set). The FIM is used mainly in rehabilitation settings; the MDS v2 is used in nursing homes for assessment, reimbursement, and quality monitoring; and the OASIS is a condition of participation for Medicare home health agencies and will also be used for per episode reimbursement. The large data sets have tremendous potential for describing outcomes of care in postacute care settings and their subsequent impact on the long-term care careers of older adults.

The FIM is based on the Barthel Index but was adapted for use as an outcome measure in rehabilitation settings. It consists of 18 items, each of which is scored on a 7-point scale, from completely independent to completely dependent. Total scores range from 18 (lowest) to 126 (highest). The FIM may be separated into two subscales: cognitive (5 items) and motor (13 items). Interrater reliability was reported as adequate (Heinemann, Linacre, Wright, Hamilton, & Granger, 1993), but relatively little is known about intrarater agreement or if reliability varies by profession of the rater or characteristics of the patients. Nonetheless, more institutions across the United States and internationally are voluntarily submitting information to the UDSmr on FIM scores, as well as patient demographics, diagnosis, rehabilitation hospital length of stay, and inpatient charges. The FIM has demonstrated validity relative to burden of care. The information is used for monitoring outcomes, quality assurance, and program planning.

Use of the MDS is yet more widespread. In the United States, it is mandated as a uniform resident assessment system and basis for Medicare reimbursement for all nursing homes, whereas internationally it is being used on a voluntary basis (see also "Minimum Data Set"). Items of the MDS examine impairments such as weakness, sensory deficits, and cognitive status. They also ask about functional performance in bathing, dressing, and eating. In addition, there are items that more directly address issues of quality of life such as well-being, activity, mood, and social interactions. Subscales based on MDS items have been developed to assess certain areas, for example, the MDS Cognitive Performance Scale and the social engagement measure. Intraclass correlation coefficients for individual MDS items have been .7 or higher in areas such as cognition, ADL, and continence.

The OASIS was designed to collect the information needed to measure changes in health status, labeled end-result outcome measures (Shaughnessy, Schlenker, Crisler, Powell, Hittle, Kramer, et al., 1994). The OASIS is divided into 11 subsections: demographics and patient history, living arrangements, supportive assistance, sensory status, integumentary status, respiratory status, elimination status, neurobehavioral status, IADL/ADL (covering both current ability and premorbid physical functioning), medications, and equipment management. In addition, the OASIS contains provisions for questions specific to emergent care and/or discharge. To date there is little published information on the reliability of the OASIS.

The availability of instruments with good measurement properties has encouraged the use of the same measures in clinical practice and research. Additional work is needed to assure that information can be transferred across the continuum of care: hospitals, rehabilitation, skilled nursing homes, and home care. This sharing of information is important to expand existing knowledge of the long-term care careers of older adults and to evaluate the outcomes of long-term care interventions. We need a greater depth of knowledge to plan more effective intervention strategies, efficiently allocate services, and set appropriate policies to meet the health and social needs of older Americans.

K. BERG
VINCENT MOR

See also
  Case Management
  Case Mix in Long-Term Care
  Comprehensive Assessment
  Minimum Data Set
  Multidimensional Functional Assessment

LONG-TERM CARE INSURANCE
See
  Medicare
  Medicaid
  Private Long-Term Care Insurance

LONG-TERM CARE POLICY

Public policy on long-term care is extremely important to people with disabilities and to providers of nursing home care and home and community-based services. First, long-term care is heavily dependent on public financing from Medicaid, Medicare, the Department of Veterans Affairs, and state-funded programs (Braden, Cowan, Lazenby, Martin, McDonnell, Sensenig, et al., 1998). Small policy changes may have a big impact on providers and consumers. Second, although it should not be overstated, some people with disabilities are vulnerable to exploitation and poor care. As a result, the federal and state governments bear a special responsibility to assure adequate quality of care, especially from publicly-funded providers.

Public Versus Private Financing

A key public policy issue is the extent to which long-term care ought to be financed through the private or the public sectors. During the late 1980s and early 1990s, there were numerous proposals for new social insurance programs (Rivlin & Wiener, 1988; Wiener, Illston, & Hanley, 1994). However, after the collapse of the Clinton health plan in 1994, most financing proposals have promoted private long-term care insurance rather than public programs.

Perhaps the most important barrier to the expansion of private long-term care insurance is that premiums are expensive. Most studies estimate that only 10% to 20% of the older population can afford good quality private long-term care insurance policies (Crown, Capitman, & Leutz, 1992; Rivlin & Wiener, 1988; Wiener, Illston, & Hanley, 1994).

Given the limitations of the current market, public subsidies to promote purchase are frequently proposed and some have been enacted (Wiener, 2000). One approach is to allow employers to deduct their contributions for group private long-term care insurance as a business expense. A second strategy is to provide tax deductions or credits to individuals who purchase private insurance. Tax incentives for employers and individuals were part of the Health Insurance Portability and Accountability Act of 1996, and additional incentives have been actively debated in Congress in recent years. A final strategy is to allow purchasers of state-approved private long-term care insurance to be eligible for Medicaid while retaining more in assets than is normally allowed, an approach being tried in New York, Connecticut, Indiana, and California (Meiners, 1998).

Opponents of public subsidies for private long-term care insurance emphasize that the initiatives tend to benefit upper- and upper-middle-income older people (Wiener, Illston, & Hanley, 1994). Even with subsidies, most people will not have private coverage (Rivlin & Wiener, 1988; Wiener, Illston, & Hanley, 1994). Moreover, these initiatives will mostly help people who have already purchased insurance, making the cost per additional person insured very large. Finally, the high overhead costs of private long-term care insurance means that it is an inefficient source of funding.

Balance Between Institutional and Home and Community-Based Care

A second key public policy issue concerns the balance between nursing home care and home and community-based services. Many policymakers would like to spend more on home care and less on institutional care (Wiener & Stevenson, 1998). First, most disabled older people live in the community but receive only unpaid, informal care from family and friends, often imposing a great burden on these caregivers (Liu, Manton, & Aragon, 1998). Second, most public long-term care expenditures are for institutional rather than noninstitutional services. Only 14% of Medicaid long-term care expenditures for the older people in 1997 were for home and community-based services (Urban Institute, 2000).

Third, policymakers believe that expansion of home care will result in a less expensive long-term care system and reduce the growth in public expenditures. However, a large, rigorous (although rather old) research literature strongly suggests that expanding home care is more likely to increase rather than decrease total long-term care costs (Weissert & Hedrick, 1994; Wiener & Hanley, 1992). Expenditures rise because large increases in home care use more than offsets relatively small reductions in nursing home use. More recent research is more optimistic about the possibility of cost savings, but these studies have less rigorous research designs (Greene, Ondrich, & Laditka, 1998; Alecxih, Lutzky, & Corea, 1996).

One of the main barriers to expanding coverage of home and community-based services, especially in the context of open-ended entitlement programs such as Medicare and Medicaid, is the fear that utilization will increase uncontrollably. This potential increase in use is called the "woodwork effect," referring to the notion that people would "come out of the woodwork" to obtain services.

Quality of Care in Nursing Homes

A third policy issue concerns poor quality of care and ineffective regulation of nursing homes, an issue that dates back to the mid-1970s (New York State Moreland Act Commission, 1975; U.S. Special Committee on Aging, 1974; Wiener, 1981). The Omnibus Budget Reconciliation Act of 1987 (OBRA 87) raised quality-of-care standards for facilities that participate in Medicare and Medicaid and strengthened federal and state oversight. Following the implementation of OBRA 87, several studies found an improvement in quality of care in nursing facilities, especially related to the use of physical and chemical restraints, prevalence of dehydration and stasis ulcers, and use of catheters (Hawes, Mor, Phillips, Fries, Morris, Steel-Friedlob, et al., 1997; Phillips, Hawes, Mor, Fries, Morris, & Nennestiel, 1996; Fries, Hawes, Morris, Phillips, Mor, & Park, 1997; Phillips, Morris, Hawes, Fries, Mor, Nennestiel, 1997; Moseley, 1996).

Despite these improvements, there is substantial evidence of continuing poor-quality care in nursing facilities and problematic oversight. In a series of studies, the U.S. General Accounting Office found serious problems (U.S. General Accounting Office, 1998, 1999b, 1999c). One fourth of nursing facilities nationwide had serious deficiencies that caused actual harm to residents or placed them at risk of death or serious injury, with about 40% of these homes having repeated serious deficiencies. In addition, even when serious deficiencies are identified, enforcement policies were not effective in ensuring that deficiencies were corrected.

In recent years, federal and state regulators have stepped up their inspection and enforcement of nursing home quality standards, which has been applauded by consumer groups. On the other hand, many nursing home providers believe that the federal standards do not adequately measure quality and that nursing facility staff are demoralized as a result of the negative approach of regulators.

Role of Medicare in Long-Term Care

A fourth issue is the extent to which Medicare should finance long-term care services. Medicare covers services provided by skilled nursing facilities, home health agencies, rehabilitation hospitals, hospice agencies, various therapy services, and durable medical equipment. Historically, however, Medicare covered only very narrow, medically oriented postacute care, mostly as an alternative to hospital care, and policy emphasized that Medicare did not cover long-term care. In 1986 skilled nursing facility expenditures and home health expenditures accounted for only 3% of Medicare spending, but rose to 15% by 1996 (Liu, Manton, & Aragon, 2000).

Medicare spending for postacute care services began to increase rapidly in 1989, when the Health Care Financing Administration made what were thought to be slight liberalizations of the coverage rules for home health and skilled nursing facility care in response to lawsuits challenging the agency's restrictive coverage interpretations. Expenditure growth was partly the result of providing services to more people and a greater supply of providers. Home health expenditures increased largely because beneficiaries received many more visits. As a result of the coverage change, Medicare began providing home health services to medically fragile and long-term care populations that it previously did not serve (Leon, Neuman, & Parente, 1997). In addition, there have been reports of fraud and abuse in Medicare home health which may have increased expenditures (U.S. General Accounting Office, 1997).

In order to curb the rate of expenditure growth, the Balanced Budget Act (BBA) of 1997 made major changes to Medicare skilled nursing facility and home health reimbursement methods that are highly controversial and that have resulted in very large savings. The BBA established a case-mix-adjusted prospective payment for nursing facilities that bundles nursing, therapy, and capital payments into a single per diem amount. This change has strongly constrained the use of therapies, which was a major cause of the expenditure increases. Some observers argue that the methodology does not adequately account for the costs of nontherapy ancillaries, such as prescription drugs (Medicare Payment Advisory Commission, 1998a). Several large nursing facility chains have experienced severe financial problems in the wake of BBA, and some have filed for bankruptcy protection, although it is not clear how much of their financial problems are attributable to the Medicare payment methodology (U.S. General Accounting Office, 1999d).

The BBA has also dramatically changed reimbursement for home health agencies. Ultimately, home health agencies will be reimbursed by using a case-mix-adjusted prospective payment system basis, but until then, agency reimbursement is set through an "interim payment system." This methodology has many cost constraints, the most important being a per-beneficiary ceiling on payments, which makes long-stay patients less financially attractive. Thus, the reimbursement changes will likely result in a reduction in the use of Medicare home health by beneficiaries needing long-term care. Although the impact on access is unclear, these changes have had a major impact on the home health industry, causing many agencies to close or reduce services (U.S. General Accounting Office, 1999a).

Conclusion

Long-term care is an important policy issue that affects billions of dollars in public expenditures and millions of people with disabilities. Over the next 30 years, long-term care will rise on the national political agenda as the baby boomers become elderly. However, the near-term aging of the parents of the baby boomers and their need for nursing home and home care may raise the policy profile of this issue sooner rather than later.

JOSHUA M. WIENER

LONG-TERM MEMORY
See
Remote Memory

LOSS

Late-life losses encompass a broad spectrum of events and domains in the lives of the elderly. Losses may range from decrements in personal abilities and function to the loss of social roles and life events, which involve losses in social resources, attachments, and contacts of the older person (Kahana & Kahana, 1996). This discussion will focus on social losses and will only briefly deal with decrements in personal abilities.

Significant persons and significant social roles may be seen as comprising the social resources of an individual. Hence, losses in both of these areas may adversely influence well-being and even personal functioning (Arbuckle & de Vries, 1995). Losses threaten well-being because they often involve permanent and uncontrollable change, which disrupts plans and hopes for the future and challenges assumptions about the self. Social losses, particularly bereavement, are also accompanied by changes in social position, social networks, and social lifestyles. These represent stressors to which the aged may be particularly vulnerable. Social losses have been studied as stressful life events that directly affect outcomes (Kahana & Kahana, 1996) or as losses in resources that mediate the impact of stress on the older person (Elwell & Maltbie-Crannell, 1981). Most of life's transitions involve some role loss, yet what is unique about late-life role losses is that highly valued roles are typically exchanged for ones yielding less gratification and meaning. Giving up the role of spouse and assuming the role of widow or widower illustrates such unwelcome role changes, wherein loss is the major component of the role change (Lopata & Brehm, 1986). Loss of status and self-esteem frequently accompanies loss of roles in later life. A major negative aspect of the role loss may be the stress posed by stigma and the sense of feeling devalued by others. The study of role loss assumes special importance because the frequently observed negative relationships between age and subjective well-being (Larson, 1978) may reflect an interaction between age and social losses (Troll, 1994).

Although diverse social losses have been documented among elderly persons, there have been only a few attempts to develop conceptual frameworks that would unify and integrate the meaning of loss in late life (Baltes, Lindenberger, & Staudinger, 1998; Uttal & Perlmutter, 1989).

It is notable that theoretical work relevant to loss tends to focus on personal rather than social loss and on adaptation to personal loss. A systematic examination of developmental gains and losses throughout the life course has been undertaken primarily within psychological frameworks focusing on intrapersonal change (Baltes, Lindenberger, & Staudinger, 1998; Kruger & Heckhausen, 1993). Theorists consider the developmental tasks of minimizing or managing internal losses to be central to notions of successful aging. Social definitions of loss are also seen as key normative stressors of aging in the context of Kahana (2000) and Kahana and Kahana's (1996) successful aging model. Determining developmental relationships between personal and social losses and gains remains an important challenge to researchers in the field of life course development (Settersten, 1999; Uttal &

Perlmutter, 1989). In addition, postmodernist sociologists have challenged notions about the finality of losses and bereavement by focusing on the continuing salience and meaning of significant others, such as a deceased spouse, in the lives of those left behind and experiencing the loss (Hallam, Hockey, & Howarth, 1999). Recent orientations to loss among sociologists call attention to the gendered nature of bereavement, which is seen as the prototype of social losses (Field, Hockey, & Small, 1997).

Conceptual developments in formulations about social losses of bereavement include psychological perspectives, such as Stroebe and Stroebe's (1992) deficit models of partner loss, and sociological perspectives on devalued roles of widows (Lopata & Brehm, 1986). Older persons confront a disproportionate number of losses or "exit" events in relation to the gains or entrance events of younger persons. Nevertheless, it is important to note that role losses in late life may be counterbalanced by smaller but potentially important role gains, such as grandparenthood and volunteer or helping roles. Such roles may play a compensatory function relative to losses. Remarriage after widowhood also represents an important potential for reversing role loss, particularly for older men (Moss & Moss, 1996). Recent longitudinal research on major losses (Wortman & Silver, 1990) has documented striking variability in response to loss and suggests that losses that shatter a person's worldview are most likely to result in long-term adverse effects. Existential resources, such as personal meaning, choice, and optimism, have been found to buffer adverse effects of losses for both community living and institutionalized elderly (Reker, 1997).

Consideration of major social losses among the elderly has generally focused on bereavement, particularly widowhood. Other losses include retirement, divorce, and environmental losses, such as loss of the family home. Following widowhood there appears to be a general disruption of the survivor's life, with concomitant reorganization of remaining roles (Lopata, 1993). Widowhood has been found to bring negative changes in physical and mental health, along with increased mortality rates (Wisocki, 1998). Longitudinal research found that although older widows initially showed fewer intrusive symptoms of grief than did their younger counterparts, they also showed slower recovery in the grieving process (Sanders, 1981). Divergent findings are also reported in the literature, suggesting that bereavement does not result in long-term adverse physical health or mental health effects among the aged (Wolinsky & Johnson, 1992).

Mediators of the stressful impact of widowhood and bereavement include income status (Lopata, 1993), social supports (Wisocki, 1998), and religious commitment (Siegel & Kuykendall, 1990). Anticipation of death has not been found to buffer the adverse impact of widowhood (DeVries, 1997). In comparing reactions of the elderly to loss of parents, spouses, and adult children, grief reactions were found to be most severe in relation to spouses and children (Fulton, Gottesman, & Owen, 1982).

There is evidence that older adult widows and widowers adjust better to their loss and show the most consistent improvements in levels of distress over time (Zisook, Schuchter, Sledge, & Mulvihil, 1993). Significant gender differences in responses to widowhood have been observed, documenting more detrimental consequences among widowers than among widows (Stroebe, 1998).

Although the above review substantiated negative influences of late-life social role losses, it is important to recognize that losses do not have a uniform impact on all elderly, and research support has not consistently been found for adverse loss effects. Thus, for example, financial problems were not found to be associated with adverse outcomes (Keith & Lorenz, 1989). Diverse coping strategies and social supports are likely to mediate the impact of losses (Bar-tur, Levy-Shiff, & Burns, 1998; Kahana, Kahana, & Young, 1987). There is also growing recognition of proactive adaptations, such as migration to sunbelt retirement communities, which older adults may undertake to compensate for role losses (Kahana, 2000; Kahana & Kahana, 1996). Furthermore, subjective appraisals of events as losses appear to play an important role in affecting both coping and outcomes subsequent to loss. Cumulative stresses and losses throughout life have been alternatively viewed as leading to negative mental health sequalae or to strengthened coping abilities. Research has documented the resilience and adaptability of older persons in the face of diverse losses (Bradstadter & Renner, 1990). There is a potentially useful new direction for gerontological research in considering growth opportunities that exist throughout life and that may be embedded even in losses or after adverse circumstances (Tarackova, 1996).

Recent work has begun to recognize the potential importance of the timing, sequencing, and accumulation of losses. Multiple losses over a short period have been noted as prevalent and challenging to the aged (Ingebretsen & Solem, 1998). The impact of being exposed to repeated losses over a 4-year period has been explored in work by Kahana and associates (Kahana, Kahana, Chirayath, Kercher, & Brown, 1999). The stresses of anticipated loss also have been documented and been found to surpass even those experienced subsequent to loss among older adults (Norris & Stanley, 1987). A fuller understanding of late-life losses must be based on considering both the context and nature of loss and must place outcomes in the framework of personal characteristics and prior experiences of the aging person.

EVA KAHANA

See also
Bereavement
Multidimensional Functional Assessment
Retirement
Widowhood

LOW VISION

Vision impairment refers to altered ability to see normally due to an anatomical or physiological change in the visual system. Examples of vision impairments include decreased central vision, loss of detail, or color blindness. Low vision refers to vision loss that cannot be corrected medically, surgically, or with conventional lenses and that causes difficulty in carrying out daily tasks. Symptoms of low vision may include decreased visual acuity, cloudy vision, constricted visual fields, sensitivity to glare, abnormal color perception, and difficulty seeing in low-contrast conditions. Individuals with low vision are not legally blind; although they may experience substantial visual loss, they have some useful vision.

Leading causes of low vision among the elderly include macular degeneration, diabetic retinopathy, complicated cataracts, glaucoma, optic atrophy, ret-

initis pigmentosa, and corneal dystrophy. Low vision is increasingly prevalent because eye disorders appear with advanced age and with conditions associated with aging. Over 75% of visually impaired individuals in the United States are 65 years or older (Faye, 1999).

Individuals with low vision cannot see their world in the same way they previously did. Although a change in vision can radically alter one's ability to care for oneself and navigate the environment, the disability is not readily apparent to others: The person looks and feels the same, but his or her functioning has decreased.

Social isolation may ensue when individuals cannot see facial details to identify people or pursue usual pleasurable activities that require eyesight (e.g., playing cards, attending theater, or viewing movies). Additionally, inability to drive due to visual loss may further compound social isolation and reduce social support.

Frustration, depression, grief, fear of blindness, concerns about driving, losing access to former pleasures, loss of independence, and/or loss of self-esteem are commonly experienced by those with low vision. Clinically, depending on severity, these reactions may lead to diagnoses of adjustment disorder or major depression. Individuals who demonstrate apathy, extreme withdrawal, or unwillingness to engage in activities may need treatment for depression. Also, particular care must be paid to those individuals with low vision who already have some degree of cognitive or hearing impairment.

When speaking with a low-vision individual, the speaker should introduce him/herself and stand close to the person. Instructions should be explained verbally, rather than with hand gestures. If the environment has little contrast, the person should be oriented to the room and objects within it (Seidman, 1995). If written instructions are provided, print should be large and in high contrast. The height of the print depends on the individual; the letters must be large enough to meet the person's needs. When low vision has been affirmed, a hearing assessment should be performed to rule out (or treat) a dual sensory loss.

Vision rehabilitation is the logical but frequently overlooked referral that should follow a determination that low vision exists. A vision rehabilitation program will address visual function impairments by assessing visual loss, prescribing and educating the person in use of low-vision aids, and teaching about vision enhancing and vision substituting skills and potential changes in the environment. Although adaptive devices cannot make the vision normal, they may improve the ability to conduct activities of daily living by making it easier to see objects.

Low-vision aids include convex lens aids, such as spectacles and magnifiers (from 1× to 60×); telescopic systems; adaptive devices that can assist in everyday activities that require reading or close work (e.g., large-print watches, clocks, timers, and telephones and magnifiers for insulin syringes); tints and coatings (e.g., use of light or medium gray lenses to reduce light intensity or amber or yellow lenses to improve contrast); and electronic reading systems that use a closed-circuit television reading machine (Faye, 1999).

Patient support groups are helpful in the adjustment to low vision. Suggestions may be offered by professional caregivers, but recommendations originating from others with low vision are more readily accepted. Creative strategies reported by low-vision individuals include greater reliance on hearing to recognize others, reliance on memory for telephone numbers, ordering foods in public that do not require cutting, and recording recipes and other instructions on audiocassette tapes (Moore, 1999). Unfortunately, dependence on others to provide transportation may be a barrier for some who wish to attend support groups.

Principles of environmental modification applicable to low vision include simplifying the layout to promote order and predictability, increasing contrast sensitivity as needed, and attending to lighting levels. Passageways should be free of both large and small obstacles, and everyday items should be stored in their designated places to aid future retrieval. Contrasting colors for walls, floor, and furniture promote visual orientation. Keys can be marked with large letters to indicate their use; house or apartment entrances should be adequately lit. Edges of steps should be clearly marked with high contrast strips (Seidman, 1995). Directional or instructional signs should contain large, high-contrast letters and receive adequate lighting. Many people with low vision see better in sunlight. Good lighting improves the contrast of written materials. A sheet of yellow acetate may be used to increase contrast of written materials, if necessary. For reading, a 60-watt bulb in a lamp with a shade that focuses the light on the page is recommended. The page may have to be held close to the eyes, but this is not harmful (Brown, 1997).

In summary, individuals with low vision face challenges in learning to live with an irreversible process that poses challenges in conducting daily activities. Once the determination is made that no additional treatment will improve vision, the ophthalmologist should ensure that a referral is made for visual rehabilitation. Caregivers and family members can modify the environment to increase contrast and support the person in the adjustment to visual limitations.

World Wide Web Sites

American Foundation for the Blind
http://www.afb.org

The Lighthouse
http://www.lighthouse.org

Macular Degeneration Foundation Education, Inc.
http://www.eyesight.org

National Eye Institute
http://www.nei.nih.gov

American Academy of Ophthalmology
http://www.eyenet.org

American Optometric Association
http://www.aoanet.org

ELAINE SOUDER

See also
   Vision and Visual Perception

Entries M–Z continue in Volume II.

SUBJECT INDEX

CONTRIBUTOR INDEX

NOTE TO THE READER

References to citations in Volumes I and II begin on page 1070 of Volume II.